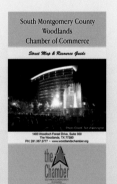
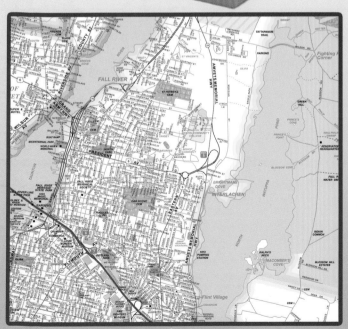

**Do you need a new marketing plan?**

# Increase your revenue with targeted direct mail!

## All lists in the directory are available for mailings.

Mailing lists are available as labels or electronic files.

Please contact us by phone or e-mail to order your list.

**888-883-3231**

**info@worldchamberlist.com**

**World Chamber of Commerce Directory**

# World Chamber of Commerce Directory

## 2009

### Published Annually in June

If you have any changes to your listing, please contact us at any time:

(888) 883-3231

info@worldchamberlist.com

# World Chamber of Commerce Directory

2009 edition

P.O. Box 1029 Loveland, CO 80539 U.S.A. (970) 663-3231 Fax (970) 663-6187 Email info@worldchamberlist.com

ISBN-13: 978-0-943581-22-4

ISBN-10: 0-943581-22-2

ISSN: 1048-2849

VDMTY

# WORLD
## Chamber of Commerce
# DIRECTORY

# 2009

## Published Annually in June

Loveland, Colorado • www.worldchamberlist.com

# Contents

## World Chamber of Commerce Directory

## U.S. Government Information

## Legend

C/C    Chamber of Commerce

P      Population of the Area Served

M      Membership

## Sample Listing

1      Name of City

2      Name of Organization

3      Population of the Area Served

4      Membership of Organization

**Loveland** • *Loveland C/C* • Brian Willms, Pres./CEO, 5400 Stone Creek Circle, Ste. 200, 80538, P 65,000, M 820, (970) 667-6311, Fax (970) 667-5211, info@loveland.org, www.loveland.org

**LOVELAND VALENTINE RE-MAILING PROGRAM AND SWEETHEART CITY ACTIVITIES, FEBRUARY 1-14; BUSINESS EXPO & TRADE SHOW, MARCH; OLD FASHIONED CORN ROAST FESTIVAL, AUGUST; SCULPTURE IN THE PARK, 2ND WEEKEND IN AUGUST–LARGEST SCULPTURE SHOW WEST OF THE MISSISSIPPI**

Note: Every effort has been made to enter the e-mail and internet addresses as they were provided to us. There is an assumed "http://" at the beginning of each internet (web site) address. If you have problems with a particular e-mail or internet address, please contact the appropriate chamber. Also note that many area codes are changing. If you experience difficulty reaching a number, please check with Directory Assistance.

# U.S. C/C
# United States Chamber of Commerce

1615 H Street, N.W. • Washington, D.C. • 20062-2000 • (202) 659-6000 • www.uschamber.com

| | | |
|---|---|---|
| **Chairman of the Board** | | **Vice Chairman of the Board** |
| Donald J. Shepard | (202) 955-1157 | Robert Milligan | (202) 955-1157 |

## Executive Staff

| | | |
|---|---|---|
| **President & CEO** | | **Membership Development** |
| Thomas J. Donohue | (202) 463-5300 | Dr. Carl Grant | (202) 463-5425 |
| **Exec. V.P. & COO** | | **CFO & CIO** |
| David Chavern | (202) 463-5363 | Stan Harrell | (202) 463-5590 |
| **Exec. V.P. Government Affairs** | | |
| R. Bruce Josten | (202) 463-5310 | |

## Department Heads

| | | |
|---|---|---|
| **Communications & Strategy** | | **Human Resources** |
| Thomas Collamore | (202) 463-5939 | Shannon DiBari | (202) 463-5391 |
| **Center for Capital Markets** | | **Institute for 21st Energy** |
| David Hirschmann | (202) 463-5430 | Karen Harbert | (202) 463-5558 |
| **Congressional & Public Affairs** | | **Institute for Legal Reform** |
| Rolf Lundberg | (202) 463-5600 | Lisa Rickard | (202) 463-5819 |
| **Economic Policy** | | **International Policy** |
| Dr. Martin A. Regalia | (202) 463-5620 | Myron Brilliant | (202) 463-5514 |
| **Environment, Energy & Food Policy** | | **Labor Policy** |
| William L. Kovacs | (202) 463-5457 | Randel Johnson | (202) 463-5448 |
| **General Counsel** | | **Political Affairs & Federation Relations** |
| Steven J. Law | (202) 463-3124 | William C. Miller Jr. | (202) 463-5532 |

# State Chambers of Commerce

**Alabama** · *Bus. Cncl. of Alabama* · William J. Canary, Pres./CEO, 2 N. Jackson, P.O. Box 76, Montgomery, 36101, M 4,500, (334) 834-6000, Fax (334) 262-7371, www.bcatoday.org

**Alaska** · *Alaska State C of C* · Wayne A. Stevens, Pres., 217 2nd St., Ste. 201, Juneau, 99801, P 650,000, M 550, (907) 586-2323, Fax (907) 463-5515, info@alaskachamber.com, www.alaska chamber.com

**Arizona** · *Arizona C of C & Ind.* · Glenn Hamer, Pres./CEO, Public Policy & Legislative Issues Only, 1850 N. Central Ave., Ste.1433, Phoenix, 85004, P 5,900,000, M 500, (602) 248-9172, Fax (602) 265-1262, info@azchamber.com, www.azchamber.com

**Arkansas** · *Arkansas State C of C* · Randy Zook, Pres./CEO, 1200 W. Capitol, P.O. Box 3645, Little Rock, 72203, P 2,400,000, M 1,200, (501) 372-2222, Fax (501) 372-2722, www.arkansas statechamber.com

**California** · *California C of C* · Allan Zaremberg, Pres., 1215 K St., Ste. 1400, P.O. Box 1736, Sacramento, 95812, P 34,000,000, M 16,000, (916) 444-6670, Fax (916) 325-1272, information@ calchamber.com, www.calchamber.com

**Colorado** · *Colorado Assn. of Comm. & Ind.* · Chuck Berry, Pres., 1600 Broadway, Ste. 1000, Denver, 80202, M 500, (303) 831-7411, Fax (303) 860-1439, info@cochamber.com, www. cochamber.com

**Connecticut** · *Connecticut Bus. & Ind. Assn.* · John Rathgeber, Pres./CEO, 350 Church St., Hartford, 06103, P 3,295,669, M 10,000, (860) 244-1900, Fax (860) 278-8562, www.cbia.com

**Delaware** · *Delaware State C of C* · James A. Wolfe, Pres./CEO, 1201 N. Orange St., Ste. 200, P.O. Box 671, Wilmington, 19899, P 750,000, M 2,800, (302) 655-7221, Fax (302) 654-0691, info@ dscc.com, www.dscc.com

**District of Columbia** · *No State Chamber*

**Florida** · *Florida C of C* · Mark Wilson, Pres., 136 S. Bronough St., P.O. Box 11309, Tallahassee, 32302, P 16,000,000, M 7,000, (850) 521-1200, Fax (850) 521-1219, policy@flchamber.com, www.flchamber.com

**Georgia** · *Georgia C of C* · George M. Israel III, Pres./CEO, 233 Peachtree St. N.E., Ste. 2000, Atlanta, 30303, M 4,000, (404) 223-2264, (800) 241-2286, Fax (404) 223-2290, www.gachamber.com

**Hawaii** · *C of C of Hawaii* · James Tollefson, Pres./CEO, 1132 Bishop St. #402, Honolulu, 96813, P 1,400,000, M 1,100, (808) 545-4300, Fax (808) 545-4369, info@cochawaii.org, www. cochawaii.org

**Idaho** · *Idaho Chamber Alliance* · Kent Just, Dir., P.O. Box 2368, Attn: Kent Just, Boise, 83701, (208) 284-2988, chambers@idaho chamberalliance.com, www.idahochamberalliance.com

**Illinois** · *Illinois C of C* · Douglas L. Whitley, Pres./CEO, 300 S. Wacker Dr., Ste. 1600, Chicago, 60606, P 11,430,602, M 4,000, (312) 983-7100, Fax (312) 983-7101, info@ilchamber.org, www. ilchamber.org

**Indiana** · *Indiana C of C* · Kevin Brinegar, Pres., 115 W. Washington St. #850S, Indianapolis, 46204, P 6,000,000, M 4,750, (317) 264-3110, Fax (317) 264-6855, kbrinegar@ indianachamber.com, www.indianachamber.com

**Iowa** · *Iowa Assn. of Bus. and Ind.* · Michael Ralston, Pres., 904 Walnut St., Ste. 100, Des Moines, 50309, P 2,988,046, M 1,200, (515) 280-8000, (800) 383-4224, Fax (515) 282-8085, abi@iowaabi.org, www.iowaabi.org

**Kansas** · *Kansas C of C* · 835 S.W. Topeka Blvd., Topeka, 66612, P 2,500,000, M 10,000, (785) 357-6321, Fax (785) 357-4732, info@kansaschamber.org, www.kansaschamber.org

**Kentucky** · *Kentucky C of C* · David Adkisson, Pres./CEO, 464 Chenault Rd., Frankfort, 40601, M 2,400, (502) 695-4700, Fax (502) 695-5051, kcc@kychamber.com, www.kychamber.com

**Louisiana** · *Louisiana Assn. of Bus. & Ind.* · Daniel Juneau, Pres., 3113 Valley Creek Dr., P.O. Box 80258, Baton Rouge, 70898, P 4,000,000, M 3,000, (225) 928-5388, Fax (225) 929-6054, labi@labi.org, www.labi.org

**Maine** · *Maine State C of C* · Dana F. Connors, Pres., 7 University Dr., Augusta, 04330, P 1,300,000, M 1,200, (207) 623-4568, Fax (207) 622-7723, rstoddard@mainechamber.org, www.maine chamber.org.

**Maryland** · *Maryland C of C* · Kathleen T. Snyder CCE, Pres./ CEO, 60 West St., Ste. 100, Annapolis, 21401, P 5,300,000, M 800, (410) 269-0642, (301) 261-2858, Fax (410) 269-5247, mcc@ mdchamber.org, www.mdchamber.org

**Massachusetts** · *Mass. Chamber of Bus. & Ind.* · Debra A. Boronski-Burack, Pres./CEO, 143 Shaker Rd., P.O. Box 414, East Longmeadow, 01028, (617) 512-9667, Fax (413) 525-1184, president@masscbi.com, www.masscbi.com.

**Michigan** · *Michigan C of C* · Rich Studley, Pres./CEO, 600 S. Walnut St., Lansing, 48933, P 9,200,000, M 7,000, (517) 371-2100, (800) 748-0266, Fax (517) 371-7224, info@michamber. com, www.michamber.com

**Minnesota** · *Minnesota C of C* · David Olson, Pres., 400 Roberts St. N., Ste. 1500, Saint Paul, 55101, P 4,500,000, M 2,600, (651) 292-4650, (800) 821-2230, Fax (651) 292-4656, www.mnchamber.com

**Mississippi** · *Mississippi Eco.Cncl.* · Blake Wilson, Pres., P.O. Box 23276, Jackson, 39225, M 8,000, (601) 969-0022, Fax (601) 353-0247, www.mec.ms

**Missouri** · *Missouri C of C & Ind.* · Daniel P. Mehan, Pres./ CEO, 428 E. Capitol Ave., P.O. Box 149, Jefferson City, 65102, P 4,500,000, M 2,864, (573) 634-3511, Fax (573) 634-8855, dmehan@mochamber.com, www.mochamber.com

**Montana** · *Montana C of C* · Webb Brown, Pres./CEO, P.O. Box 1730, Helena, 59624, P 800,000, M 1,500, (406) 442-2405, Fax (406) 442-2409, leah@montanachamber.com, www.montana chamber.com

**Nebraska** • *Nebraska C of C & Ind.* • Barry L. Kennedy CAE IOM, Pres., P.O. Box 95128, Lincoln, 68509, P 1,800,000, M 1,300, (402) 474-4422, Fax (402) 474-5681, nechamber@nechamber. com, www.nechamber.com.

**Nevada** • *Nevada State C of C* • One E. First St. #1600, P.O. Box 3499, Reno, 89505, P 1,781,750, M 1,500, (775) 337-3030, Fax (775) 337-3038, info@renosparkschamber.org, www.renosparks chamber.org

**New Hampshire** • *Bus. & Ind. Assn. of N.H.* • Jim Roche, Pres., 122 N. Main, Concord, 03301, P 1,200,000, M 400, (603) 224-5388, Fax (603) 224-2872, www.nhbia.org

**New Jersey** • *New Jersey C of C* • Joan Verplanck, Pres., 216 W. State St., Trenton, 08608, P 8,500,000, M 1,600, (609) 989-7888, Fax (609) 989-9696, linda@njchamber.com, www.njchamber.com.

**New Mexico** • *Assn. Of Commerce & Ind. Of New Mexico* • Dr. Beverlee McClure, Pres., P.O. Box 9706, Albuquerque, 87119, P 1,800,000, M 1,300, (505) 842-0644, Fax (505) 842-0734, info@aci-nm.org, www.aci-nm.org

**New York** • *No State Chamber*

**North Carolina** • *North Carolina Chamber* • S. Lewis Ebert, Pres./CEO, 701 Corporate Center Dr., Ste. 400, Raleigh, 27607, P 9,222,414, M 1,900, (919) 836-1400, Fax (919) 836-1425, info@nccbi.org, www.ncchamber.net

**North Dakota** • *North Dakota C of C* • Dave Maciver, Pres., 2000 Schafer St., P.O. Box 2639, Bismarck, 58502, P 639,715, M 1,100, (701) 222-0929, (800) 382-1405, Fax (701) 222-1611, ndchamber@ndchamber.com, www.ndchamber.com

**Ohio** • *Ohio C of C* • Andrew E. Doehrel, Pres., 230 E. Town, P.O. Box 15159, Columbus, 43215, P 11,000,000, M 4,000, (614) 228-4201, (800) 622-1893, Fax (614) 228-6403, www.ohiochamber. com

**Oklahoma** • *The State Chamber of Oklahoma* • Richard P. Rush CCE, Pres./CEO, 330 N.E. 10th St., Oklahoma City, 73104, P 3,600,000, M 3,000, (405) 235-3669, Fax (405) 235-3670, drush@okstatechamber.com, www.okstatechamber.com.

**Oregon** • *Oregon State C of C* • Dave Hauser, Admin., P.O. Box 1107, Eugene, 97440, M 33,000, (541) 484-1314, Fax (541) 484-4942, www.oregonstatechamber.org.

**Pennsylvania** • *Harrisburg Reg. C/C* • David E. Black, Pres./ CEO, 3211 N. Front St., Ste. 201, Harrisburg, 17110, P 550,000, M 1,700, (717) 232-4099, (877) 883-8339, Fax (717) 232-5184, frontdesk@hbgrc.org, www.HarrisburgRegionalChamber.org

**Puerto Rico** • *Puerto Rico C of C* • Edgardo Bigas, Exec. V.P., P.O. Box 9024033, San Juan, 00902, P 3,850,000, M 2,000, (787) 721-6060, Fax (787) 723-1891, camarapr@camarapr.org, www. camarapr.org.

**Rhode Island** • *No State Chamber*

**South Carolina** • *South Carolina C of C* • Otis Rawl, Pres./CEO, 1201 Main St., Ste. 1700, Columbia, 29201, P 3,700,000, M 2,300, (803) 799-4601, Fax (803) 779-6043, chamber@scchamber.net, www.scchamber.net.

**South Dakota** • *South Dakota C of C & Ind.* • David Owen, Pres., P.O. Box 190, Pierre, 57501, P 765,000, M 450, (605) 224-6161, (800) 742-8112, Fax (605) 224-7198, contactus@sdchamber.biz, www. sdchamber.biz

**Tennessee** • *Tennessee C of C & Ind.* • Deb Woolley, Pres., 611 Commerce St. #3030, Nashville, 37203, M 600, (615) 256-5141, Fax (615) 256-6726, www.tnchamber.org

**Texas** • *Texas Assn. of Bus.* • Bill Hammond, Pres., 1209 Nueces St., Austin, 78701, P 20,851,820, M 5,000, (512) 477-6721, Fax (512) 477-0836, info@txbiz.org, www.txbiz.org

**Utah** • *Utah State C of C* • Donna Brown, Chair, 175 E. 400 S. #600, Salt Lake City, 84111, P 2,758,000, M 15,500, (801) 328-5090, Fax (801) 328-5093, www.utahstatechamber.org

**Vermont** • *Vermont C of C* • Christopher Barbieri, Interim Pres., P.O. Box 37, Montpelier, 05601, P 639,000, M 1,500, (802) 223-3443, Fax (802) 223-4257, info@vtchamber.com, www. vtchamber.com.

**Virginia** • *Virginia C of C* • Hugh D. Keogh, Pres./CEO, 9 S. Fifth St., Richmond, 23219, M 1,000, (804) 644-1607, Fax (804) 783-6112, m.crowder@vachamber.com, www.vachamber.com

**Washington** • *Assn. Of Washington Business* • Don Brunell, Pres., 1414 Cherry St. S.E., P.O. Box 658, Olympia, 98507, P 5,400,000, M 6,200, (360) 943-1600, (800) 521-9325, Fax (360) 943-5811, members@awb.org, www.awb.org

**West Virginia** • *West Virginia C of C* • Stephen Roberts, Pres., 1624 Kanawha Blvd. E., P.O. Box 2789, Charleston, 25330, P 1,818,470, M 1,800, (304) 342-1115, Fax (304) 342-1130, forjobs@wvchamber.com, www.wvchamber.com.

**Wisconsin** • *Wisconsin Manufacturers & Commerce* • James S. Haney, Pres., 501 E. Washington Ave., P.O. Box 352, Madison, 53701, P 4,900,000, M 4,000, (608) 258-3400, Fax (608) 258-3413, wmc@wmc.org, www.wmc.org

**Wyoming** • *No State Chamber*

# Notes

# United States Chambers of Commerce

## Alabama

**Bus. Cncl. of Alabama** • William J. Canary, Pres./CEO, 2 N. Jackson, P.O. Box 76, Montgomery, 36101, M 4,500, (334) 834-6000, Fax (334) 262-7371, www.bcatoday.org

**Chamber of Commerce Assn. of Alabama** • L. Ralph Stacy CAE, Pres./CEO, 2 N. Jackson St., Montgomery, 36104, P 4,500,000, M 60,000, (334) 264-2112, Fax (334) 264-2113, lrstacy@alaweb.com, www.alabamachambers.org

**Abbeville** • *Abbeville C/C* • Ronnie Marshall, Pres., 300 Kirkland St., P.O. Box 202, 36310, P 3,000, M 119, (334) 585-2273, Fax (334) 585-2273, abbevillechamber@centurytel.net, www.abbevillecoc.com

**Alabaster** • *see Pelham*

**Albertville** • *Albertville C/C* • Jennifer Palmer, Pres., 316 E. Sand Mountain Dr., P.O. Box 1457, 35950, P 24,156, M 538, (256) 878-3821, (800) 878-3821, Fax (256) 878-3822, albertvillechamber@charter.net, www.albertvillechamberofcommerce.com

**Alexander City** • *Alexander City C/C* • Marvin Wagoner, Pres./CEO, 120 Tallapoosa St., P.O. Box 926, 35011, P 16,000, M 400, (256) 234-3461, Fax (256) 234-0094, mwagoner@charterinternet.com, www.alexandercity.org

**Aliceville** • *Aliceville Area C/C* • Debbie Fason, Mgr., 419 Memorial Pkwy. N.E. #A, P.O. Drawer A, 35442, P 3,009, M 200, (205) 373-2820, Fax (205) 373-8692, acc@nctv.com, www.cityofaliceville.com

**Andalusia** • *Andalusia Area C/C* • Joey Langley, Pres., 1208 W. Bypass, P.O. Box 667, 36420, P 10,000, M 387, (334) 222-2030, Fax (334) 222-7844, ashley@andalusiachamber.com, www.andalusiachamber.com

**Anniston** • *Calhoun County C/C* • Sherri Sumners CCE, Pres., 1330 Quintard Ave., P.O. Box 1087, 36202, P 112,000, M 1,200, (256) 237-3536, (800) 487-1087, Fax (256) 237-0126, info@calhounchamber.com, www.calhounchamber.com.

**Arab** • *Arab C/C* • Deneille Dunn, Pres., P.O. Box 626, 35016, P 7,600, M 478, (256) 586-3138, (888) 403-2722, Fax (256) 586-0233, info@arab-chamber.org, www.arab-chamber.org.

**Ardmore** • *see Ardmore, TN*

**Ashford** • *Ashford Area C/C* • James Ethridge, Pres., P.O. Box 463, 36312, P 2,700, M 75, (334) 899-4769, Fax (334) 899-3033

**Athens** • *Greater Limestone County C/C* • Hugh Ball, Pres., 101 S. Beaty St., P.O. Box 150, 35612, P 70,757, M 511, (256) 232-2600, Fax (256) 232-2609, info@tourathens.com, www.tourathens.com.

**Atmore** • *Atmore Area C/C* • Sheryl Vickery, Exec. Dir., 501 S. Pensacola Ave., 36502, P 8,800, M 295, (251) 368-3305, Fax (251) 368-0800, atmoreal@frontiernet.net, www.atmorechamber.com

**Auburn** • *Auburn C/C* • Lolly Steiner, Pres., 714 E. Glenn Ave., P.O. Box 1370, 36831, P 51,906, M 850, (334) 887-7011, Fax (334) 821-5500, lolly@auburnchamber.com, www.auburnchamber.com

**Bay Minette** • *North Baldwin C/C* • Margo Allen, Exec. Dir., 301 McMeans Ave., P.O. Box 310, 36507, P 30,000, M 300, (251) 937-5665, Fax (251) 937-2300, assist@northbaldwinchamber.com, www.northbaldwinchamber.com.

**Bayou La Batre** • *Bayou La Batre Area C/C* • Harold Hodges, Pres., P.O. Box 486, 36509, P 6,000, M 88, (251) 824-4088, Fax (251) 824-4088, www.bayoulabatrechamber.com

**Bessemer** • *Bessemer Area C/C* • Ronnie Acker, Pres., 321 N. 18th St., P.O. Box 648, 35021, P 29,500, M 450, (205) 425-3253, (888) 4-BESSEMER, Fax (205) 425-4979, ronacker@bellsouth.net, www.bessemerchamber.com

**Birmingham** • *Birmingham Reg. C/C* • Russell Cunningham, Pres./CEO, 505 20th St. N. #200, Financial Center, 35203, P 1,100,000, M 4,200, (205) 324-2100, Fax (205) 324-2560, president@birminghamchamber.com, www.birminghamchamber.com

**Boaz** • *Boaz Area C/C* • Keyesta Sherman, Pres., 100 E. Bartlett Ave., 35957, P 10,000, M 400, (256) 593-8154, Fax (256) 593-1233, boazchamber@charter.net, www.boazchamberofcommerce.com

**Brewton** • *Greater Brewton Area C/C* • Judy Crane, Exec. Dir., 1010-B Douglas Ave., 36426, P 10,000, M 220, (251) 867-3224, Fax (251) 809-1793, jcrane@brewtonchamber.com, www.brewtonchamber.com.

**Butler** • *Choctaw County C/C & Comm. Dev. Found.* • Virginia Loftis, Exec. Dir., P.O. Box 180, 36904, P 16,000, M 170, (205) 459-3459, (205) 459-3795

**Camden** • *Wilcox Area C/C* • William Malone, Chrmn., 110 Court St., 36726, P 3,500, M 100, (334) 682-4929, Fax (334) 682-5304, wilcoxdev@pinebelt.net, www.wilcoxareachamber.org

**Centre** • *Cherokee County C/C* • Thereasa Hulgan, Exec. Dir., 801 Cedar Bluff Rd., Bldg. A, 35960, P 25,000, M 350, (256) 927-8455, Fax (256) 927-2768, cccoc@tds.net, www.cherokee-chamber.org

**Centreville** • *Bibb County C/C* • Tracey Mitchell, Exec. Dir., P.O. Box 25, 35042, P 20,000, M 95, (205) 926-5222, www.bibbchamber.org

**Chickasaw** • *Chickasaw C/C* • Dr. Ervin Dailey, Pres., P.O. Box 11307, 36671, P 6,364, M 78, (251) 452-6450, www.chickasawchamber.com

**Childersburg** • *Childersburg C/C* • Peter Storey, Pres./CEO, 805 Third St. S.W., P.O. Box 527, 35044, P 5,000, M 287, (256) 378-5482, Fax (256) 378-5833, pbstorey@childersburg.com, www.childersburg.com

**Citronelle** • *Citronelle Area C/C* • Danyelle Portis, Pres., 8175 State St., P.O. Box 394, 36522, P 5,000, M 200, (251) 866-7733, Fax (251) 866-7767, citronellechamber@yahoo.com, www.citronellechamber.com

**Clanton** • *Chilton County C/C* • Pennie Broussard, Exec. Dir., P.O. Box 66, 35046, P 42,000, M 350, (205) 755-2400, (800) 553-0493, Fax (205) 755-8444, chiltonchamber@bellsouth.net, www.chiltoncountychamber.com

**Cullman** • *Cullman Area C/C* • Kirk Mancer IOM CCE, Pres., 301 2nd Ave. S.W., P.O. Box 1104, 35056, P 81,000, M 1,200, (256) 734-0454, Fax (256) 737-7443, info@cullmanchamber.org, www.cullmanchamber.org

**Dadeville** • *Dadeville Area C/C* • Carla Berry, Exec. Secy., 185 S. Tallassee St., Ste. 103, 36853, P 4,000, M 230, (256) 825-4019, Fax (256) 825-0547, chamber@dadeville.com, www.dadeville.com

**Daleville** • *Daleville C/C* • Pam Souders, Exec. Dir., 750 S. Daleville Ave., P.O. Box 688, 36322, P 5,000, M 125, (334) 598-6331, Fax (334) 598-2333, chamber@dalevilleal.com, www.dalevilleal.com

**Daphne** • *Eastern Shore C/C* • Darrelyn J. Bender, Pres., 29750 Larry Dee Cawyer Dr., P.O. Drawer 310, 36526, P 65,000, M 900, (251) 621-8222, Fax (251) 621-8001, office@eschamber.com, www.eschamber.com.

**Dauphin Island** • *Dauphin Island C/C* • Mary Scarchiff, Pres., P.O. Box 5, 36528, P 1,200, M 70, (251) 861-5524, Fax (251) 861-0055, www.gulfinfo.com, www.dauphinislandcoc.com

**Decatur** • *Decatur-Morgan County C/C* • John Seymour, Pres./CEO, 515 Sixth Ave. N.E., P.O. Box 2003, 35602, P 56,000, M 1,000, (256) 353-5312, Fax (256) 353-2384, chamber@dcc.org, www.dcc.org.

**Demopolis** • *Demopolis Area C/C* • Kelley Smith, Pres., 102 E. Washington, P.O. Box 667, 36732, P 8,000, M 250, (334) 289-0270, Fax (334) 289-1382, dacc@westal.net, www.demopolischamber.com

**Dora** • *see Sumiton*

**Dothan** • *Dothan Area C/C* • Matt Parker, Exec. Dir., 102 Jamestown Blvd., P.O. Box 638, 36302, P 92,000, M 1,000, (334) 792-5138, (800) 221-1027, Fax (334) 794-4796, chamber@dothan.com, www.dothan.com.

**Elba** • *Elba C/C* • Kaye Whitworth, Exec. Dir., 329 Putnam St., 36323, P 4,185, M 130, (334) 897-3125, Fax (334) 897-1762, echamber329@troycable.net, www.elbaalabama.net

**Enterprise** • *Enterprise C/C Inc.* • Phil Thomas, Pres., 553 Glover Ave., P.O. Box 310577, 36331, P 29,903, M 640, (334) 347-0581, (800) 235-4730, Fax (334) 393-8204, chamberpresident@century-tel.net, www.enterprisealabama.com, www.buyenterprise.com.

**Eufaula** • *Eufaula-Barbour County C/C* • 333 E. Broad St., 36027, P 29,000, M 400, (334) 687-6664, (800) 524-7529, Fax (334) 687-5240, info@eufaulachamber.com, www.eufaula chamber.com

**Eutaw** • *Eutaw Area C/C* • Gavin Edgar, Pres., 111 Main St., P.O. Box 31, 35462, P 11,000, M 40, (205) 372-9002, Fax (205) 372-1393, eutawchamber@bellsouth.net, www.eutawchamber.com

**Evergreen** • *Evergreen/Conecuh County Area C/C* • Clinton Hyde, Pres., 100 Depot Sq., 36401, P 14,000, M 300, (251) 578-1707, Fax (251) 578-5660

**Fairfield** • *Fairfield C/C* • Betty Smith, Pres., P.O. Box 528, 35064, P 13,000, M 65, (205) 788-2492

**Fairhope** • *see Daphne*

**Fayette** • *Fayette Area C/C* • Anne Hamner, Exec. Dir., 203 Temple Ave., P.O. Box 247, 35555, P 4,600, M 165, (205) 932-4587, Fax (205) 932-8788, info@fayetteareachamber.org, www.fayetteareachamber.org

**Flomaton** • *Flomaton C/C* • Wanda Vanlandingham, Pres., P.O. Box 636, 36441, P 2,000, M 60, (251) 296-1110

**Florala** • *Tri-Cities C/C* • Jimmy Waldrop, Pres., 1099 5th St., 36442, P 2,000, M 70, (334) 858-6252, tricity@fairpoint.net, www.tricitieschamberofcommerce.com

**Florence** • *Shoals C/C* • Stephen B. Holt, Pres., 20 Hightower Pl., P.O. Box 1331, 35631, P 142,950, M 890, (256) 764-4661, (877) 764-4661, Fax (256) 766-9017, shoals@shoalschamber.com, www.shoalschamber.com.

**Foley** • *South Baldwin C/C* • Donna Watts, Pres., 104 N. McKenzie St., P.O. Box 1117, 36536, P 45,000, M 830, (251) 943-3291, Fax (251) 943-6810, info@southbaldwinchamber.com, www.southbaldwinchamber.com

**Fort Deposit** • *Fort Deposit C/C* • Barbara Payne, Pres., P.O. Box 162, 36032, P 1,519, M 30, (334) 227-4411

**Fort Payne** • *Fort Payne C/C* • Carol Beddingfield, Exec. Dir., 300 Gault Ave. N., P.O. Box 680125, 35968, P 12,938, M 310, (256) 845-2741, Fax (256) 845-5849, info@fortpaynechamber.com, www.fortpaynechamber.com.

**Gadsden** • *The Chamber, Gadsden/Etowah County* • Tom Quinn, Pres., One Commerce Sq., P.O. Box 185, 35902, P 103,000, M 1,200, (256) 543-3472, Fax (256) 543-9887, info@gadsden chamber.com, www.gadsdenchamber.com

**Gardendale** • *Gardendale C/C* • Joy Clayton, Pres./CEO, 2109 Moncrief Rd., Ste. 115, 35071, P 13,000, M 280, (205) 631-9195, (888) 631-4422, Fax (205) 631-9034, joy@gardendalechamber ofcommerce.com, www.gardendalechamberofcommerce.com

**Geneva** • *Greater Geneva Area C/C* • Olivia McCray, Exec. Dir., 406 S. Commerce St., P.O. Box 477, 36340, P 5,000, M 96, (334) 684-6582, Fax (334) 684-6582, chamber@genevaareachamber. com, genevaareachamber.com.

**Gordo** • *Gordo Area C/C* • Robin Patterson, Pres., P.O. Box 33, 35466, P 4,537, M 75, (205) 364-7870, Fax (205) 364-7870

**Greenville** • *Greenville Area C/C* • Francine Wasden, Exec. Dir., One Depot Sq., 36037, P 25,000, M 300, (334) 382-3251, (800) 959-0717, Fax (334) 382-3181, chamber@greenville-alabama. com, www.greenville-alabama.com.

**Grove Hill** • *Grove Hill Area C/C* • Cheryl Horton, Exec. Dir., 104 N. Jackson St., P.O. Box 567, 36451, P 1,438, M 70, (251) 275-4188, Fax (251) 275-2278, grovehillcoc@tds.net, www.grovehillal.com

**Gulf Shores** • *Alabama Gulf Coast C/C* • Mark Berson, Pres., 3150 Gulf Shores Pkwy., P.O. Drawer 3869, 36547, P 10,000, M 1,000, (251) 968-6904, Fax (251) 968-5332, info@alagulfcoast chamber.com, www.alagulfcoastchamber.com

**Guntersville** • *Lake Guntersville C/C* • Morri Yancy, Pres., 200 Gunter Ave., P.O. Box 577, 35976, P 8,700, M 600, (256) 582-3612, (800) 869-LAKE, Fax (256) 582-3682, gcc@lakeguntersville.org, www.lakeguntersville.org

**Haleyville** • *Haleyville C/C* • 1200 21st St., P.O. Box 634, 35565, P 4,200, M 75, (205) 486-4611, www.haleyvillechamber.org

**Hamilton** • *Hamilton Area C/C* • Tanya Tilberg, Dir., 422 2nd St. S.W., P.O. Box 1168, 35570, P 7,000, M 175, (205) 921-7786, Fax (205) 921-2220, chamber@cityofhamilton.org, www.city ofhamilton.org

**Hartselle** • *Hartselle Area C/C* • Susan Hines, Pres., 110 Railroad St. S.W., P.O. Box 817, 35640, P 13,500, M 400, (256) 773-4370, (800) 294-0692, Fax (256) 773-4379, hartsell@hiwaay.net, www. hartsellechamber.com.

**Headland** • *Headland C/C* • Charles A. Lueck, Pres., P.O. Box 236, 36345, P 5,000, M 125, (334) 693-3303, Fax (334) 693-3303, headlandchamber@centurytel.net, www.headlandal.com

**Heflin** • *Cleburne County C/C* • Beverly Casey, Dir., P.O. Box 413, 36264, P 15,000, M 100, (256) 463-2222, Fax (256) 463-4668, cleburnecoc@aol.com

**Homewood** • *Homewood C/C* • Tricia Ford, Exec. Dir., 1721 Oxmoor Rd., P.O. Box 59494, 35259, P 24,000, M 460, (205) 871-5631, Fax (205) 871-5632, director@homewoodchamber.com, www.homewoodchamber.org

**Hoover** • *Hoover Area C/C* • Bill Powell, Exec. Dir., 1694 Montgomery Hwy. #108, P.O. Box 36005, 35236, P 70,000, M 1,200, (205) 988-5672, Fax (205) 988-8383, bill@hooverchamber.org, www.hooverchamber.org

**Hueytown** • *Hueytown Area C/C* • Rebecca Williams, Exec. Secy., P.O. Box 3356, 35023, P 15,000, M 237, (205) 491-8039, Fax (205) 491-7961, www.hueytownchamber.com

**Huntsville** • *C of C of Huntsville/Madison County* • Brian Hilson, Pres./CEO, 225 Church St., P.O. Box 408, 35804, P 168,000, M 2,000, (256) 535-2000, Fax (256) 535-2015, hcc@hsvchamber. org, www.huntsvillealabamausa.com

**Irondale** • *Greater Irondale C/C* • Joyce Franklin, Exec. Dir., 1912 1st Ave. S., 35210, P 11,000, M 100, (205) 956-3104, Fax (205) 956-5964, caboose500@aol.com, www.greaterirondalechamber.com

**Jackson** • *Jackson C/C* • LaShaunda Holly, Exec. Dir., 500 Commerce St., 36545, P 5,600, M 150, (251) 246-3251, Fax (251) 246-3213, jacksonchamber@bellsouth.net, www.jacksonalabama.org

**Jasper** • *C/C of Walker County* • Linda Lewis, Pres., 204 19th St. E. #101, P.O. Box 972, 35502, P 70,000, M 400, (205) 384-4571, Fax (205) 384-4901, linda@walkerchamber.us, www.walkerchamber.us.

**Lafayette** • *see Lanett*

**Lanett** • *Greater Valley Area C/C* • Elinor Crowder, Exec. Dir., 2102 S. Broad Ave., P.O. Box 205, 36863, P 40,000, M 300, (334) 642-1411, Fax (334) 642-1410, gvacc@knology.net, www.greatervalleyarea.com.

**Leeds** • *Leeds Area C/C* • Sandra McGuire, Exec. Dir., 7901 Parkway Dr., P.O. Box 900, 35094, P 12,000, M 250, (205) 699-5001, Fax (205) 699-5001, leedschamber@windstream.net, www.leedsareachamber.com

**Lincoln** • *Greater Talladega Area C/C* • Mack Ferguson, Exec. Dir., 176 Magnolia St., 35096, P 5,000, M , (205) 763-1535, lincoln.chamber@yahoo.com, www.talladegachamber.com

**Lineville** • *Clay County C/C* • Mary Patchunka-Smith, Exec. Dir., 86838 Hwy. 9, P.O. Box 85, 36266, P 13,000, M 130, (256) 396-2828, Fax (256) 396-5532, claychamber@centurytel.net, www.claycochamber.com

**Lockhart** • *see Florala*

**Luverne** • *Crenshaw County C/C* • Martha Dickey, P.O. Box 4, 36049, P 13,000, M 100, (334) 335-4468, Fax (334) 335-3820, www.luverne.org

**Marion** • *Perry County C/C* • John Martin, Dir., 1200 S. Washington St., 36756, P 11,135, M 75, (334) 683-9622, Fax (334) 683-4561, perrycountychamb@bellsouth.net, www.perrycountyalabamachamber.com

**Millbrook** • *Millbrook Area C/C* • Stephanie Godwin, Exec. Dir., 3540 Main St., P.O. Box 353, 36054, P 18,000, M 305, (334) 285-0085, Fax (334) 285-9854, info@millbrookareachamber.com, www.millbrookareachamber.com

**Millport** • *South Lamar Area C/C* • Melissa Swanson, Pres., P.O. Box 205, 35576, P 1,600, M 25, (205) 662-5784

**Mobile** • *Mobile Area C/C* • Winthrop M. Hallett III, Pres., 451 Government St., P.O. Box 2187, 36652, P 404,111, M 2,400, (251) 433-6951, Fax (251) 432-1143, info@mobilechamber.com, www.mobilechamber.com.

**Monroeville** • *Monroeville/Monroe County C/C* • Sandy C. Smith, Exec. Dir., 63 N. Mt. Pleasant Ave., P.O. Box 214, 36461, P 25,000, M 195, (251) 743-2879, (251) 743-2880, Fax (251) 743-2189, info@monroecountyal.com, www.monroecountyal.com

**Montevallo** • *Montevallo C/C* • Mary Lou Williams, Pres., 720 Oak St., 35115, P 6,000, M 120, (205) 665-1519, montevallocc@bellsouth.net, www.montevallocc.org

**Montgomery** • *Montgomery Area C/C* • Randall L. George, Pres., 41 Commerce St., P.O. Box 79, 36101, P 335,000, M 2,100, (334) 834-5200, Fax (334) 265-4745, www.montgomerychamber.com

**Montrose** • *see Daphne*

**Moody** • *Moody Area C/C* • Andrea Machen, Exec. Dir., 670 Park Ave., 35004, P 12,000, M 160, (205) 640-6262, Fax (205) 640-2996, chamber@moodyalabama.gov, www.moodyalchamber.com

**Moulton** • *Lawrence County C/C* • Kim Hood, Pres., 12467 Alabama Hwy. 157, 35650, P 35,000, M 320, (256) 974-1658, Fax (256) 974-2400, www.lawrencealabama.com

**Munford** • *see Talladega*

**Oneonta** • *Blount County-Oneonta C/C* • Charles Carr, Pres., 227 2nd Ave. E., P.O. Box 1487, 35121, P 58,000, M 375, (205) 274-2153, Fax (205) 274-2099, cvbridge@otelco.net, www.blountoneontachamber.org.

**Opelika** • *Opelika C/C* • Wendi Routhier, Pres., 601 Ave. A, P.O. Box 2366, 36803, P 26,000, M 750, (334) 745-4861, Fax (334) 749-4740, coc@opelika.com, www.opelika.com.

**Opp** • *Opp & Covington County Area C/C* • Tonitta Sauls, Exec. Dir., 101 E. Ida Ave., P.O. Box 148, 36467, P 7,000, M 250, (334) 493-3070, (800) 239-8054, Fax (334) 493-1060, chamber@oppcatv.com, www.oppchamber.com.

**Oxford** • *see Anniston*

**Ozark** • *Ozark Area C/C* • Jeanette Reeves, Exec. Dir., 294 Painter Ave., 36360, P 15,119, M 400, (334) 774-9321, (800) 582-8497, Fax (334) 774-8736, ozarkcc@snowhill.com, www.ozarkalchamber.com.

**Pelham** • *Greater Shelby County C/C* • Jennifer Trammell, Pres., 1301 County Services Dr., 35124, P 143,000, M 1,650, (205) 663-4542, Fax (205) 663-4524, info@shelbychamber.org, www.shelbychamber.org

**Pell City** • *Greater Pell City C/C* • Lynn Batemon, Exec. Dir., 1618 Cogswell Ave., 35125, P 12,000, M 375, (205) 338-3377, Fax (205) 338-1913, pellcitychamber@centurytel.net, www.cityofpellcity.com.

**Phenix City** • *Phenix City-Russell County C/C* • Victor W. Cross, Pres., 1107 Broad St., P.O. Box 1326, 36868, P 53,000, M 470, (334) 298-3639, (800) 892-2248, Fax (334) 298-3846, pcrccham@ldl.net, pc-rcchamber.com.

**Point Clear** • *see Daphne*

**Prattville** • *Prattville Area C/C* • Jeremy Arthur, Exec. V.P., 131 N. Court St., 36067, P 34,000, M 850, (334) 365-7392, Fax (334) 361-1314, jarthur@prattvillechamber.com, www.prattvillechamber.com.

**Prichard** • *Prichard Area C/C* • Cederick McMillan, Pres., 117 E. Clark St., P.O. Box 10266, 36610, P 28,000, M 40, (251) 452-2760, www.prichardchamber.com

**Rainsville** • *Rainsville C/C* • P.O. Box 396, 35986, P 5,000, M 110, (256) 638-7800

**Reform** • *Reform Area C/C* • Jenny Fields, Mgr., City Hall, P.O. Box 891, 35481, P 1,979, M 48, (205) 375-6363

**Roanoke** • *Randolph County C/C* • Dorothy B. Tidwell, Exec. Dir., 3355 Hwy. 431 #11, P.O. Box 431, 36274, P 23,253, M 175, (334) 863-6612, (800) 863-6612, Fax (334) 863-7280, rancococ@teleclipse.net, www.randolphcountyal.com

**Robertsdale** • *Central Baldwin C/C* • Marian Mason, Exec. Dir., 23150 Hwy. 59, P.O. Box 587, 36567, P 8,000, M 300, (251) 947-5932, (251) 947-2626, marian@cbchamber.org, www.centralbaldwin.com

**Russellville** • *Franklin County C/C* • Cheryl Bradford, Exec. Dir., 103 N. Jackson Ave., P.O. Box 44, 35653, P 32,000, M 200, (256) 332-1760, Fax (256) 332-1740, franklincounty@charter.net, www.franklincountychamber.org

**Saraland** • *Saraland Area C/C* • Pamela Burnham, Exec. Dir., 939 Hwy. 43 S., 36571, P 13,000, M 210, (251) 675-4444, Fax (251) 675-2307, info@saralandcoc.com, www.saralandcoc.com

**Scottsboro** · *Greater Jackson County C/C* · Rick Roden, Pres./CEO, 407 E. Willow St., P.O. Box 973, 35768, P 55,000, M 650, (256) 259-5500, (800) 259-5508, Fax (256) 259-4447, chamber@scottsboro.org, www.jacksoncountychamber.com.

**Selma** · *Selma-Dallas County C/C* · 912 Selma Ave., 36701, P 46,365, M 500, (334) 875-7241, Fax (334) 875-7142, info@SelmaAlabama.com, www.SelmaAlabama.com.

**Spanish Fort** · *see Daphne*

**Springville** · *Springville Area C/C* · Misty Fowler, Pres., 6496 U.S. Hwy. 11, 35146, P 5,000, M 60, (205) 467-2339, info@springvillealabama.org, www.springvillealabama.org

**Sumiton** · *East Walker County C/C* · Chee-vee Whitfield, Dir., P.O. Box 188, 35148, P 12,000, M 60, (205) 255-0202, Fax (205) 255-0202, chee-vee@eastwalkerchamber.com, www.eastwalkerchamber.com

**Sylacauga** · *Sylacauga C/C* · Joe Richardson, Exec. Dir., 17 W. Fort Williams St., P.O. Box 185, 35150, P 13,000, M 550, (256) 249-0308, Fax (256) 249-0315, chamber@sylacauga.net, www.sylacauga.net/chamber

**Talladega** · *Greater Talladega Area C/C* · Mack Ferguson, Exec. Dir., 210 East St. S., P.O. Drawer A, 35161, P 31,000, M 200, (256) 362-9075, Fax (256) 362-9093, talladegachamber@yahoo.com, www.talladegachamber.com.

**Tallassee** · *Tallassee C/C* · Mickey Shaw, Exec. Dir., 650 Gilmer Ave., 36078, P 5,000, M 220, (334) 283-5151, Fax (334) 252-0774, chamber@elmore.rr.com, www.tallassee.al.us

**Thomasville** · *Southwest Alabama C/C* · Marlo Anderson, Dir., 138 Wilson Ave., P.O. Box 44, 36784, P 5,000, M 180, (334) 636-1542, Fax (334) 636-1543, southwestchamber@bellsouth.net, www.southwestalabamachamber.com

**Tillman's Corner** · *Tillman's Corner C/C* · Lois Rockhold, Pres., 5055 Carol Plantation Rd., 36619, P 17,000, M 200, (251) 666-2846, Fax (251) 666-2813, tillmanscornerco@bellsouth.net, www.tillmanscornerchamber.com

**Troy** · *Pike County C/C* · Jenniffer Barner, Pres., 100 Industrial Blvd., P.O. Box 249, 36081, P 29,605, M 500, (334) 566-2294, Fax (334) 566-2298, pikecoc@troycable.net, www.pikecountychamber.net

**Trussville** · *Trussville Area C/C* · Diane Poole, Exec. Dir., 225 Parkway Dr., 35173, P 19,000, M 350, (205) 655-7535, (800) 494-8222, Fax (205) 655-3705, diane.poole@trussvillechamber.com, www.trussvillechamber.com

**Tuscaloosa** · *C/C of West Alabama* · Johnnie R. Aycock, Pres., 2200 University Blvd., P.O. Box 020410, 35402, P 177,906, M 2,700, (205) 758-7588, Fax (205) 391-0565, chamber@dbtech.net, www.tuscaloosachamber.com

**Tuskegee** · *Tuskegee Area C/C* · 121 S. Main St., 36083, P 24,000, M 225, (334) 727-6619, Fax (334) 725-1801, www.tuskegeechamber.org

**Union Springs** · *Union Springs-Bullock County C/C* · Joyce Perrin, Pres., 126 N. Prairie St., P.O. Box 5006, 36089, P 11,714, M 58, (334) 738-2424, Fax (334) 738-5000, www.usacoc.com

**Valley** · *see Lanett*

**Vernon** · *Vernon C/C* · Glen Bardon, Pres., P.O. Box 336, 35592, P 3,000, M 65, (205) 695-7029, Fax (205) 695-9501

**Vestavia Hills** · *Vestavia Hills C/C* · Karen Odle, Exec. Dir., 1975 Merryvale Rd., 35216, P 32,000, M 850, (205) 823-5011, Fax (205) 823-8974, chamber@vestaviahills.org, www.vestaviahills.org

**Wetumpka** · *Wetumpka Area C/C* · Jan Wood, Exec. Dir., 110 E. Bridge St., P.O. Box 785, 36092, P 7,000, M 300, (334) 567-4811, Fax (334) 567-1811, wacc@bellsouth.net, www.wetumpkachamber.com.

**Winfield** · *Winfield C/C* · Chele Bussey, Pres., P.O. Box 916, 35594, P 5,000, M 85, (205) 487-8841, www.winfieldcity.org

# Alaska

**Alaska State C of C** · Wayne A. Stevens, Pres., 217 2nd St., Ste. 201, Juneau, 99801, P 650,000, M 550, (907) 586-2323, Fax (907) 463-5515, info@alaskachamber.com, www.alaskachamber.com

**Anchor Point** · *Anchor Point C/C* · P.O. Box 610, 99556, P 2,500, M 150, (907) 235-2600, Fax (907) 235-2600, info@anchorpointchamber.org, www.anchorpointchamber.org

**Anchorage** · *Anchorage C/C* · Sami Glascott, Pres., 1016 W. 6th Ave. #303, 99501, P 277,000, M 1,289, (907) 272-2401, Fax (907) 272-4117, info@anchoragechamber.org, www.anchoragechamber.org

**Barrow** · *City of Barrow* · Jane Nelson, City Clerk, P.O. Box 629, 99723, P 4,600, (907) 852-5211, Fax (907) 852-5871, jane.nelson@cityofbarrow.org, cityofbarrow.org

**Bethel** · *Bethel C/C* · Bonnie Bradbury, Admin. Asst., P.O. Box 329, 99559, P 6,000, M 80, (907) 543-2911, Fax (907) 543-2255, bethelchamber1@alaska.com, www.bethelakchamber.org

**Big Lake** · *Big Lake C/C* · Donna Love, Treas., P.O. Box 520067, 99652, P 3,500, M 115, (907) 892-6109, Fax (907) 892-6189, info@biglakechamber.org, www.biglakechamber.org

**Chugiak** · *see Eagle River*

**Cooper Landing** · *Cooper Landing C/C* · Cheryle James, Pres., P.O. Box 809, 99572, P 300, M 60, (907) 595-8888, info@cooperlandingchamber.com, www.cooperlandingchamber.com

**Cordova** · *Cordova C/C* · Jennifer Gibbins, Pres., 404 1st St., P.O. Box 99, 99574, P 2,000, M 150, (907) 424-7260, Fax (907) 424-7259, visitcordova@ak.net, www.cordovachamber.com

**Delta Junction** · *Delta C/C & Visitor Center* · Brenda Peterson, Exec. Dir., 2855 Alaska Hwy., Ste. 1B, P.O. Box 987, 99737, P 5,700, M 200, (907) 895-5068, (907) 895-5069 Summer, Fax (907) 895-5141, deltacc@deltachamber.org, www.deltachamber.org

**Dillingham** · *Dillingham C/C* · Tammy Conahan, Exec. Dir., P.O. Box 348, 99576, P 2,400, M 70, (907) 842-5115, Fax (907) 842-4097, dlgchmbr@nushtel.com, www.dillinghamak.com

**Eagle River** · *Chugiak-Eagle River C/C* · Susan Gorski, Exec. Dir., 11401 Old Glenn Hwy. #105, P.O. Box 770353, 99577, P 35,000, M 400, (907) 694-4702, Fax (907) 694-1205, info@cer.org, www.cer.org.

**Fairbanks** · *Greater Fairbanks C/C* · 100 Cushman St., Ste. 102, 99701, P 97,000, M 750, (907) 452-1105, Fax (907) 456-6968, info@fairbankschamber.org, www.fairbankschamber.org

**Glennallen** · *Copper Valley C/C* · Warren Ulrich, Pres., P.O. Box 469, 99588, P 3,500, M 175, (907) 822-5555, chamber@cvinternet.net, www.traveltoalaska.com

**Haines** · *Haines C/C* · Joan Carlson, Ofc. Mgr., P.O. Box 1449, 99827, P 2,400, M 150, (907) 766-2202, Fax (907) 766-2271, chamber@haineschamber.org, www.haineschamber.org

**Healy** · *Greater Healy-Denali C/C & Visitors Center* · Healy Spur Rd., P.O. Box 437, 99743, P 1,848, M 85, (907) 683-4636, info@denalichamber.com, www.denalichamber.com

**Homer** · *Homer C/C* · Tina Day, Exec. Dir., 201 Sterling Hwy., 99603, P 12,000, M 565, (907) 235-7740, Fax (907) 235-8766, info@homeralaska.org, www.homeralaska.org

**Houston** • *Houston C/C* • Nancy Sult, Pres., P.O. Box 940356, 99694, P 1,500, M 50, (907) 232-1387, (907) 892-6812, Fax (907) 892-6813, houstonakchamber@hotmail.com, www.houstonak chamber.com

**Hyder** • *Stewart-Hyder Intl. C/C* • Gwen McKay, Mgr., P.O. Box 149, 99923, P 100, M 85, (250) 636-9224, (888) 366-5999, Fax (250) 636-9224, info@stewart-hyder.com, www.stewart-hyder.com

**Juneau** • *Juneau C/C* • Cathie Roemmich, CEO, 3100 Channel Dr., Ste. 300, 99801, P 32,000, M 450, (907) 463-3488, Fax (907) 463-3489, juneauchamber@gci.net, www.juneauchamber.com

**Kenai** • *Kenai C/C* • Tina Baldridge, Exec. Dir., 402 Overland, 99611, P 8,000, M 371, (907) 283-7989, Fax (907) 283-7183, info@kenaichamber.org, www.kenaichamber.org

**Ketchikan** • *Greater Ketchikan C/C* • Blaine Ashcraft, Exec. Dir., P.O. Box 5957, 99901, P 14,000, M 400, (907) 225-3184, Fax (907) 225-3187, info@ketchikanchamber.com, www.ketchikanchamber.com

**Klawock** • *Prince of Wales C/C* • Jan Bush, Pres., 6488 Klawock Hollis Hwy #7, P.O. Box 490, 99925, P 4,000, M 180, (907) 755-2626, Fax (907) 755-2627, info@princeofwalescoc.org, www.princeofwalescoc.org

**Kodiak** • *Kodiak C/C* • Debora King, Exec. Dir., 100 E. Marine Way, Ste. 300, 99615, P 14,000, M 350, (907) 486-5557, Fax (907) 486-7605, chamber@kodiak.org, www.kodiak.org

**Kotzebue** • *City of Kotzebue* • D. Eugene Smith, Mayor, 258A 3rd Ave., P.O. Box 46, 99752, P 3,104, (907) 442-3401, Fax (907) 442-3742, esmith@maniilaq.org, www.cityofkotzebue.com

**Nenana** • *Nenana Valley C/C* • Miles Martin, Chrmn., P.O. Box 00070, 99760, P 460, M 30, (907) 832-5442, miles@mtaonline.net, www.nenanahomepage.com

**Ninilchik** • *Ninilchik C/C* • Jodi Evers, P.O. Box 39164, 99639, P 1,000, M 50, (907) 567-3571, info@ninilchikchamber.com, www.ninilchikchamber.com

**Nome** • *Nome C/C* • Mitch Erickson, 110 W. Front St., Ste. 211, P.O. Box 250, 99762, P 3,500, M 60, (907) 443-3879, Fax (907) 443-3892, nomechamber@gci.net, www.nomechamber.org

**North Pole** • *North Pole Comm. C/C & Visitor Center* • Betsy Bear, Pres., 2550 Mistletoe Dr., P.O. Box 55071, 99705, P 35,000, M 100, (907) 488-2242, Fax (907) 488-3002, info@northpole chamber.com, www.northpolechamber.org

**Palmer** • *Greater Palmer C/C* • Jillyan Webb, Exec. Dir., 550 S. Alaska St., Ste. 101, P.O. Box 45, 99645, P 4,800, M 320, (907) 745-2880, Fax (907) 746-4164, info@palmerchamber.org, www.palmerchamber.org

**Petersburg** • *Petersburg C/C* • Sally Dwyer, Mgr., P.O. Box 649, 99833, P 3,200, M 140, (907) 772-3646, Fax (907) 772-2453, pcoc@alaska.com, www.petersburg.org

**Seldovia** • *Seldovia C/C* • Peggy Keesecker, Pres., P.O. Drawer F, 99663, P 300, M 60, (907) 234-7612, www.seldovia.com

**Seward** • *Seward C of C, Conf. & Visitors Bur.* • Laura Cloward, Exec. Dir., 2001 Seward Hwy., P.O. Box 749, 99664, P 3,200, M 400, (907) 224-8051, Fax (907) 224-5353, chamber@seward.net, www.seward.com

**Sitka** • *Greater Sitka C/C* • Sheila Finkenbinder, Exec. Dir., 329 Harbor Dr., Ste. 212, P.O. Box 638, 99835, P 8,800, M 180, (907) 747-8604, (907) 738-3098, Fax (907) 747-7413, chamber@ptialaska.net, www.sitkacoc.com

**Skagway** • *Skagway C/C* • Karla Ray, Dir., 701 State St., P.O. Box 194, 99840, P 800, M 160, (907) 983-1898, Fax (907) 983-2031, chamber@aptalaska.net, www.skagwaychamber.org

**Soldotna** • *Funny River C/C* • 35850 Pioneer Rd., 99669, P 1,000, M 100, (907) 262-0879, (907) 262-6161

**Soldotna** • *Greater Soldotna C/C & Visitors Info. Center* • Michelle Glaves, Exec. Dir., 44790 Sterling Hwy., 99669, P 5,000, M 650, (907) 262-9814, (907) 262-1337, Fax (907) 262-3566, director@soldotnachamber.com, www.soldotnachamber.com, www.visitsoldotna.com

**Talkeetna** • *Talkeetna C/C* • Trisha Costello, Pres., P.O. Box 334, 99676, P 850, M 80, (907) 733-2330, info@talkeetnachamber.org, www.talkeetnachamber.org

**Tok** • *Tok C/C* • P.O. Box 389, 99780, P 1,400, M 43, (907) 883-5775, info@tokalaskainfo.com, www.tokalaskainfo.com

**Wasilla** • *Greater Wasilla C/C* • Cheryl Metiva, Exec. Dir., 415 E. Railroad Ave., 99654, P 7,100, M 702, (907) 376-1299, Fax (907) 373-2560, contact@wasillachamber.org, www.wasillachamber.org

**Whittier** • *Greater Whittier C/C* • Pete Heddell, Pres., P.O. Box 607, 99693, P 175, M 65, (907) 472-2493, (907) 677-WHIT, www.whittieralaskachamber.org

**Willow** • *Willow C/C* • Jim Houston, Pres., P.O. Box 183, 99688, P 3,000, M 50, (907) 495-6800, mail@willowchamber.org, www.willowchamber.org

**Wrangell** • *Wrangell C/C* • Janell Privett, Pres., 224 Front St., P.O. Box 49, 99929, P 1,200, M 100, (907) 874-3901, Fax (907) 874-3905, wchamber@gci.net, www.wrangellchamber.org

# Arizona

**Arizona C of C & Ind.** • Glenn Hamer, Pres./CEO, Public Policy & Legislative Issues Only, 1850 N. Central Ave., Ste.1433, Phoenix, 85004, P 5,900,000, M 500, (602) 248-9172, Fax (602) 265-1262, info@azchamber.com, www.azchamber.com

**Ajo** • *Ajo Dist. C/C* • Silvia Howard, Exec. Dir., 400 Taladro St., 85321, P 4,000, M 94, (520) 387-7742, Fax (520) 387-3641, ajocofc@tabletoptelephone.com, www.ajochamber.com

**Alpine** • *Alpine Area C/C* • Paul Reitz, Pres., P.O. Box 410, 85920, P 600, M 55, (928) 339-4330, thechamber@alpinearizona.com, www.alpinearizona.com

**Apache Junction** • *Apache Junction C/C* • Rayna Palmer, Pres./CEO, 567 W. Apache Trail, P.O. Box 1747, 85217, P 42,000, M 480, (480) 982-3141, (800) 252-3141, Fax (480) 982-3234, ajchamber@qwest.net, www.apachejunctioncoc.com.

**Arizona City** • *Arizona City C/C* • Linda Borozinski, Exec. Dir., P.O. Box 5, 85223, P 5,500, M 250, (520) 466-5141, Fax (520) 466-8204, azchamber@cgmailbox.com, www.azcchamber.com

**Avondale** • *see Goodyear*

**Benson** • *Benson-San Pedro Valley C/C* • Robert Mucci, Exec. Dir., 249 E. 4th St., P.O. Box 2255, 85602, P 4,700, M 160, (520) 586-2842, Fax (520) 586-1972, info@bensonchamberaz.com, www.bensonchamberaz.com

**Bisbee** • *Bisbee C/C* • Nancy Jacobsen, Dir., 1 Main St., P.O. Box BA, 85603, P 6,000, M 223, (520) 432-5421, chamber@bisbee arizona.com, www.bisbeearizona.com

**Black Canyon City** • *Black Canyon City C/C* • Lori Martinez, Pres., P.O. Box 1919, 85324, P 4,000, M 64, (623) 374-9797, Fax (623) 374-0182, bccadmin@blackcanyoncity.org, www.black canyoncity.org

**Bouse** • *Bouse C/C* • Norm Simpson, Pres., P.O. Box 817, 85325, P 850, M 45, (928) 851-2509, bousechamber@rraz.net, www.bousechamberofcommerce.com

**Bowie** · *Bowie C/C* · Nancy-Jean Welker, Pres., P.O. Box 287, 85605, P 700, M 12, (520) 253-0930, b2caz@vtc.net, www.bowiechamber.com

**Buckeye** · *Buckeye Valley C/C* · Deanna Kupcik, Pres./CEO, 508 E. Monroe Ave., 85326, P 40,000, M 350, (623) 386-2727, Fax (623) 386-7527, deanna@buckeyevalleychamber.org, www.buckeye valleychamber.org.

**Bullhead City** · *Bullhead Area C/C* · Michael Conner, Pres., 1251 Hwy. 95, 86429, P 45,000, M 730, (928) 754-4121, Fax (928) 754-5514, info@bullheadchamber.com, www.bullheadchamber.com, www.visitbullheadcity.com

**Camp Verde** · *Camp Verde C/C* · Tracie Schimikowsky, Dir. of Op., 385 S. Main St., 86322, P 12,000, M 175, (928) 567-9294, Fax (928) 567-4793, info@campverde.org, www.visitcampverde.com.

**Carefree** · *Carefree-Cave Creek C/C* · Ian Ellison, Exec. Dir., 748 Easy St., P.O. Box 734, 85377, P 7,200, M 340, (480) 488-3381, Fax (480) 488-0328, chamber@carefreecavecreek.org, www.carefreecavecreek.org

**Casa Grande** · *Greater Casa Grande C/C* · Helen Neuharth, Pres./CEO, 575 N. Marshall St., 85222, P 45,000, M 620, (520) 836-2125, (800) 916-1515, Fax (520) 836-6233, chamber@cgmailbox.com, www.casagrandechamber.org

**Chandler** · *Chandler C/C* · Jerry Bustamante, Pres./CEO, 25 S. Arizona Pl., Ste. 201, 85225, P 259,936, M 1,400, (480) 963-4571, (800) 963-4571, Fax (480) 963-0188, www.chandlerchamber.com

**Chino Valley** · *Chino Valley Area C/C* · Ab Jackson, CEO, 448 N. Hwy. 89, P.O. Box 419, 86323, P 19,000, M 400, (928) 636-2493, chamber@chinovalley.org, www.chinovalley.org

**Chloride** · *Chloride C/C* · Donna Meyer, P.O. Box 268, 86431, P 450, M 22, (928) 565-2204, chloride_az@yahoo.com, www.chloridearizona.com

**Clarkdale** · *Clarkdale C/C* · Katy Cannon, Pres., P.O. Box 161, 86324, P 3,600, M 100, (928) 634-8700, www.clarkdalechamber.com

**Coolidge** · *Coolidge C/C* · Jerri Koehn, Dir., 320 W. Central Ave., 85228, P 12,000, M 200, (520) 723-3009, Fax (520) 723-9410, coolidgechamber@qwestoffice.net, www.coolidgechamber.org

**Cottonwood** · *Cottonwood C/C* · Lana Tolleson, Pres./CEO, 1010 S. Main St., 86326, P 23,000, M 400, (928) 634-7593, Fax (928) 634-7594, info@cottonwoodchamberaz.org, www.cottonwoodchamberaz.org

**Dolan Springs** · *Dolan Springs C/C* · John Dahlberg, Pres., 16154 N. Pierce Ferry Rd., P.O. Box 274, 86441, P 1,500, M 170, (928) 767-4473, Fax (928) 767-4473, johndahlberg@yahoo.com, www.dolanspringschamber.org

**Douglas** · *Douglas C/C* · Evelyn Arvizu, Treas., 345 16th St., 85607, P 18,000, M 50, (520) 364-2477, Fax (520) 364-6304, douglaschamber@gmail.com, www.douglasaz.gov

**Eagar** · *see Springerville*

**El Mirage** · *see Surprise*

**Eloy** · *Eloy C/C* · Belinda Akes, Exec. Dir., 305 Stuart Blvd., 85231, P 11,000, M 164, (520) 466-3411, Fax (520) 466-4698, info@eloychamber.com, www.eloychamber.com

**Flagstaff** · *Flagstaff C/C* · Julie Pastrick, Pres./CEO, 101 W. Rte. 66, 86001, P 62,000, M 1,200, (928) 774-4505, Fax (928) 779-1209, info@flagstaffchamber.com, www.flagstaffchamber.com

**Florence** · *Greater Florence C/C* · Lina Austin, Exec. Dir., 234 N. Main St., P.O. Box 929, 85232, P 6,200, M 200, (520) 868-9433, (800) 437-9433, Fax (520) 868-5797, info@florenceaz.org, www.florenceaz.org

**Fort Mohave** · *see Mohave Valley*

**Fountain Hills** · *Fountain Hills C/C* · Frank S. Ferrara, Pres./CEO, 16837 E. Palisades Blvd., P.O. Box 17598, 85269, P 23,115, M 580, (480) 837-1654, Fax (480) 837-3077, www.fountainhills chamber.com

**Fredonia** · *Fredonia C/C* · Jan Judd, Pres., P.O. Box 1162, 86022, P 1,050, M 20, (928) 643-7241

**Gila Bend** · *Gila Bend C/C* · Melissa Kantor, Exec. Dir., P.O. Box CC, 85337, P 1,900, M 38, (928) 683-2002, Fax (928) 683-6430, www.gilabendaz.org

**Gilbert** · *Gilbert C/C* · Kathy Langdon, Pres./CEO, 119 N. Gilbert Rd., Ste. 101, P.O. Box 527, 85299, P 250,000, M 650, (480) 892-0056, Fax (480) 892-1980, info@gilbertchamber.com, www.gilbertaz.com

**Glendale** · *Glendale C/C* · Don Rinehart, Pres., 7501 N. 59th Ave., P.O. Box 249, 85311, P 250,000, M 900, (623) 937-4754, (800) ID-SUNNY, Fax (623) 937-3333, info@glendaleazchamber.org, www.glendaleazchamber.org.

**Globe** · *Globe-Miami Reg. C/C & Eco. Dev. Corp.* · Ellen Kretsch, Dir., 1360 N. Broad St., 85501, P 23,000, M 400, (928) 425-4495, (800) 804-5623, Fax (928) 425-3410, visitorinfo@globemiami chamber.com, www.globemiamichamber.com

**Golden Valley** · *Golden Valley C/C* · Patricia J. Randolph, Pres., 3395 N. Verde Rd., 86413, P 17,000, M 200, (928) 565-3311, Fax (928) 565-3133, info@goldenvalleychamber.com, www.golden valleychamber.com

**Goodyear** · *Southwest Valley C/C* · Sharolyn Hohman, Pres./CEO, 289 N. Litchfield Rd., 85338, P 110,000, M 1,000, (623) 932-2260, Fax (623) 932-9057, info@southwestvalleychamber.org, www.southwestvalleychamber.org.

**Grand Canyon** · *Grand Canyon C/C & Visitors Bur.* · Craig Andresen, Exec. Dir., P.O. Box 3007, 86023, P 1,500, M 85, (928) 638-2901, (888) 472-2696, Fax (928) 638-4095, info@grand canyonvisitorbureau.com, www.grandcanyonchamber.com

**Green Valley** · *Green Valley Sahuarita C/C & Visitor Center* · Jim DiGiacomo, Exec. Dir., 270 W. Continental Rd., Ste. 100, P.O. Box 566, 85622, P 33,000, M 600, (520) 625-7575, (800) 858-5872, Fax (520) 648-6154, gvchamber@qwest.net, www.greenvalleychamber.com.

**Hayden** · *see Kearny*

**Heber** · *see Overgaard*

**Holbrook** · *Holbrook C/C* · Joshua Wenger, Exec. Dir., 100 E. Arizona St., 86025, P 5,544, M 130, (928) 524-6558, (800) 524-2459, Fax (928) 524-1719, holbrook@gotouraz.com, www.gotouraz.com.

**Jerome** · *Jerome C/C* · P.O. Box K, 86331, P 450, M 125, (928) 634-2900, staff@jeromechamber.com, www.jeromechamber.com

**Joseph City** · *Joseph City C/C* · Derron Hansen, Pres., P.O. Box 36, 86032, P 1,500, M 30, (928) 288-3475

**Kayenta** · *Kayenta Chamber & Film Office* · Bill Crawley, P.O. Box 187, 86033, P 12,000, (928) 697-3463

**Kearny** · *Copper Basin C/C* · Myra Warren, Dir., 355 Alden Rd., P.O. Box 206, 85237, P 5,000, M 65, (520) 363-7607, myra@copper basinaz.com, www.copperbasinaz.com

**Kingman** · *Kingman Area C/C* · Beverly J. Liles, Pres./CEO, 120 W. Rte. 66, P.O. Box 1150, 86402, P 60,000, M 722, (928) 753-6253, Fax (928) 753-1049, kgmncofc@ctaz.com, www.kingmanchamber.org.

**Lake Havasu City** · *Lake Havasu Area C/C* · Lisa Krueger, Pres./CEO, 314 London Bridge Rd., 86403, P 57,000, M 800, (928) 855-4115, Fax (928) 680-0010, lisak@havasuchamber.com, www.havasuchamber.com

**Lakeside** · *see Pinetop*

**Litchfield Park** · *see Goodyear*

**Mammoth** · *see San Manuel-SMOR C/C*

**Marana** · *Marana C/C* · Ed Stolmaker, Pres., 13881 N. Casa Grande Hwy., 85653, P 35,000, M 525, (520) 682-4314, Fax (520) 682-2303, info@maranachamber.com, www.marana chamber.com

**Maricopa** · *Maricopa Community C/C* · Terri Kingery, Exec. Dir., P.O. Box 1203, 85239, P 35,000, M 300, (520) 568-9573, info@maricopachamber.com, www.maricopachamber.com

**Mayer** · *Arizona Highway 69 C/C* · Providence Ponomaroff, Ofc. Mgr., P.O. Box 248, 86333, P 6,700, M 50, (928) 632-4355, Fax (928) 632-4355, Hwy69chamber@commspeed.net, www.arizona highway69chamber.org

**Meadview** · *Meadview Area C/C* · Lucy Vaillancourt, Pres., P.O. Box 26, 86444, P 3,000, M 20, (928) 564-2425, www.meadview azchamber.org

**Mesa** · *Mesa C/C* · Charles Deaton, Pres./CEO, 120 N. Center St., 85201, P 453,000, M 1,500, (480) 969-1307, Fax (480) 827-0727, info@mesachamber.org, www.mesachamber.org

**Miami** · *see Globe*

**Mohave Valley** · *Mohave Valley C/C* · Judy Gaston, Admin., 8045 Hwy. 95, Ste. C, P.O. Box 5439, 86446, P 16,000, M 230, (928) 768-2777, Fax (928) 768-6610, info@mohavevalleychamber.com, www.mohavevalleychamber.com

**Nogales** · *Nogales-Santa Cruz County C/C* · Olivia Ainza-Kramer, Chrmn., 123 W. Kino Park Pl., 85621, P 32,000, M 200, (520) 287-3685, Fax (520) 287-3687, info@thenogaleschamber. com, www.thenogaleschamber.com

**Oatman** · *Oatman-Goldroad C/C* · Linda Woodard, Pres., P.O. Box 423, 86433, P 150, M 38, (928) 768-6222, www.oatman goldroad.com

**Oracle** · *see San Manuel-SMOR C/C*

**Overgaard** · *Heber-Overgaard C/C* · Jerry Call, Pres., P.O. Box 1926, 85933, P 4,800, M 160, (928) 535-5777, Fax (928) 535-3254, coc@heberovergaard.org, www.heberovergaard.org

**Page** · *Page-Lake Powell C/C* · Vin Paitoon, Exec. Dir., 608 Elm St. #C, P.O. Box 727, 86040, P 7,100, M 250, (928) 645-2741, Fax (928) 645-3181, chamber@pagechamber.com, www.page chamber.com

**Parker** · *Parker Area C/C* · Randy Hartless, Exec. Dir., 1217 California Ave., 85344, P 21,529, M 375, (928) 669-2174, Fax (928) 669-6304, parker.chamber@redrivernet.com, www. parkeraz.org

**Payson** · *Rim Country Reg. C/C* · John P. Stanton, Mgr., 100 W. Main St., P.O. Box 1380, 85547, P 15,000, M 500, (928) 474-4515, (800) 672-9766, Fax (928) 474-8812, info@rimcountrychamber. com, www.rimcountrychamber.com.

**Pearce** · *Pearce-Sunsites C/C* · Murray McClelland, Pres., 225 N. Frontage Rd., P.O. Box 536, 85625, P 2,200, M 75, (520) 826-3535, info@pearcesunsiteschamber.org, www.pearce sunsiteschamber.org

**Peoria** · *Peoria C/C* · Diana Bedient, Exec. Dir., 8765 W. Kelton Ln., Bldg. C1, 85382, P 140,000, M 729, (623) 979-3601, (800) 580-2645, Fax (623) 486-4729, info1@peoriachamber.com, www. peoriachamber.com

## Phoenix Area

**Greater Phoenix C/C** · Todd Sanders, Pres./CEO, 201 N. Central Ave., Ste. 2700, 85004, P 3,907,492, M 3,400, (602) 254-5521, Fax (602) 495-8913, info@phoenixchamber.com, www.phoenix chamber.com

**Ahwatukee Foothills C/C** · 10235 S. 51st St., Ste. 185, 85044, P 90,000, M 550, (480) 753-7676, Fax (480) 753-3898, info@ ahwatukeechamber.com, www.ahwatukeechamber.com

**Arizona Asian C/C** · Madeline Ong-Sakata, Exec. Dir., 7217 N. 6 Way, 85020, M 410, (602) 222-2009, Fax (602) 870-7562, www. asianchamber.org

**Arizona Hispanic C/C** · P.J. Passo, Interim Pres./CEO, 255 E. Osborn Rd., Ste. 201, 85012, M 425, (602) 279-1800, Fax (602) 279-8900, info@azhcc.net, www.azhcc.net

**Greater Phoenix Black C/C** · Ron Busby, Pres./CEO, 201 E. Washington St., Ste. 350, 85004, M 350, (602) 307-5200, Fax (602) 307-5204, heather@phoenixblackchamber.com, www. phoenix blackchamber.com

**North Phoenix C/C** · Jean Lukens, Exec. Dir., P.O. Box 72265, 85050, P 500,000, M 400, (602) 482-3344, Fax (602) 482-3344, jean@north phoenixchamber.com, www.northphoenixchamber.com

**Paradise Valley C/C** · Natalie McAvoy, Pres., 85016, (602) 490-0134, info@paradisevalleychamber.com, www.paradise valleychamber.com

**Pine** · *see Payson*

**Pinetop** · *Pinetop-Lakeside C/C* · Beverly Stepp, Dir., P.O. Box 4220, 85935, P 4,700, M 488, (928) 367-4290, (800) 573-4031, Fax (928) 367-1247, info@pinetoplakesidechamber.com, www. pinetoplakesidechamber.com

**Prescott** · *Prescott C/C & Visitors Info. Center* · David Maurer, CEO, 117 W. Goodwin, P.O. Box 1147, 86302, P 43,280, M 1,150, (928) 445-2000, (800) 266-7534, Fax (928) 445-0068, dmaurer@ prescott.org, www.prescott.org

**Prescott Valley** · *Prescott Valley C/C* · Marnie Uhl, Pres./CEO, 3001 N. Main St., Ste. 2A, 86314, P 38,000, M 750, (928) 772-8857, Fax (928) 772-4267, info@pvchamber.org, www.pvchamber.org.

**Quartzsite** · *Quartzsite C/C* · Carlos Castros, Pres., P.O. Box 85, 85346, P 4,000, M 250, (928) 927-5600, Fax (928) 927-7438, frontdesk@quartzsitetourism.com, www.quartzsitechamber.org

**Queen Creek** · *Queen Creek C/C* · Rustyn Sherer, Pres., P.O. Box 505, 85242, P 25,000, M 233, (480) 888-1709, info@queencreek chamber.org, www.queencreekchamber.org

**Safford** · *Graham County C/C* · Sheldon Miller, Pres./CEO, 1111 W. Thatcher Blvd., 85546, P 37,000, M 403, (928) 428-2511, (888) 837-1841, Fax (928) 428-0744, info@graham-chamber.com, www.graham-chamber.com

**Saint Johns** · *Saint Johns Reg. C/C* · Kelly Waite, Exec. Dir., 180 W. Cleveland, P.O. Box 929, 85936, P 3,900, M 135, (928) 337-2000, Fax (928) 337-2020, office@stjohnschamber.com, www. stjohnschamber.com

**Salome** · *McMullen Valley C/C* · P.O. Box 700, 85348, P 3,000, M 200, (928) 859-3846, Fax (928) 859-4399, mcmullencoc@tds. net, www.azoutback.com

**U.S. Chambers of Commerce**

**San Manuel** • *SMOR C/C* • Genevieve Schwandt, Dir., 330 McNab Pkwy., P.O. Box 416, 85631, P 4,500, M 60, (520) 385-9322, Fax (520) 385-9322, smor_1992@netzero.net, www.smorchamber.org

**Scottsdale** • *Pinnacle Peak C/C* • Richard Marquez, Pres., 8707 E. Vista Bonita Dr., Ste. 240, 85255, (602) 490-0045, info@pinnacle peakchamber.com, www.pinnaclepeakchamber.com

**Scottsdale** • *Scottsdale Area C/C* • Rick Kidder, Pres./CEO, 4725 N. Scottsdale Rd., Ste. 210, 85251, P 225,000, M 1,500, (480) 355-2700, Fax (480) 355-2710, www.scottsdalechamber.com.

**Sedona** • *Sedona C/C* • Jennifer Wesselhoff, Pres./CEO, 331 Forest Rd., P.O. Box 478, 86339, P 18,000, M 1,020, (928) 204-1123, (928) 282-7722, Fax (928) 204-1064, info@sedonachamber.com, www.visitsedona.com.

**Seligman** • *Seligman C/C* • Violet Searles, Pres., P.O. Box 65, 86337, P 1,500, M 40, (928) 308-8210, www.seligmanarizona.org

**Show Low** • *Show Low C/C & Tourist Info. Center* • Gordon Kearl, Exec. Dir., 81 E. Deuce of Clubs, 85901, P 12,500, M 500, (928) 537-2326, (888) SHOWLOW, Fax (928) 532-7610, info@ showlowchamberofcommerce.com, www.showlowchamber ofcommerce.com

**Sierra Vista** • *Greater Sierra Vista Area C/C* • Susan Tegmeyer, Pres./CEO, 21 E. Wilcox Dr., 85635, P 43,000, M 771, (520) 458-6940, Fax (520) 452-0878, info@sierravistachamber.org, www.sierravistachamber.org

**Snowflake** • *Snowflake-Taylor C/C* • Greg Hudson, Exec. Dir., 113 N. Main St., Ste. A, 85937, P 10,000, M 350, (928) 536-4331, Fax (928) 536-5656, snowcham1@frontiernet.net, www.snow flaketaylorchamber.org.

**Sonoita** • *Sonoita-Elgin C/C* • Doug Sposito, Pres., P.O. Box 607, 85637, P 3,000, M 100, (520) 455-5498, www.sonoitaelgin chamber.org

**Springerville** • *Springerville-Eagar Reg. C/C* • Jennifer Prochnow, Dir., 418 E. Main St., P.O. Box 31, 85938, P 8,000, M 275, (928) 333-2123, (866) 733-2123, Fax (928) 333-5690, info@ springerville-eager.com, www.springerville-eagarchamber.com

**Strawberry** • *see Payson*

**Sun City** • *see Surprise*

**Sun City West** • *see Surprise*

**Superior** • *Superior C/C* • Hank Gutierrez, Pres., 230 Main St., P.O. Box 95, 85273, P 3,200, M 59, (520) 689-0200, Fax (520) 689-0200, www.superiorarizonachamber.org

**Surprise** • *Surprise Reg. C/C* • David Lewis, Pres./CEO, 12801 W. Bell Rd., Ste. 14, 85374, P 105,000, M 750, (623) 583-0692, Fax (623) 583-0694, chamber@surpriseregionalchamber.com, www.surpriseregionalchamber.com

**Taylor** • *see Snowflake*

**Tempe** • *Tempe C/C* • Mary Ann Miller, Pres./CEO, 909 E. Apache Blvd., P.O. Box 28500, 85285, P 165,000, M 1,000, (480) 967-7891, Fax (480) 966-5365, info@tempechamber.org, www.tempe chamber.org

**Tolleson** • *see Goodyear*

**Tombstone** • *Tombstone C/C* • Elizabeth Ingalls, Exec. Dir., P.O. Box 995, 85638, P 1,700, M 100, (520) 457-9317, (888) 457-3929, Fax (520) 457-2458, info@tombstonechamber.com, www.tomb stonechamber.com

**Tonto Basin** • *Tonto Basin C/C* • Alan Carpenter, Pres., Hwy. 188 & Rattlesnake Ln., P.O. Box 687, 85553, P 2,000, M 54, (928) 479-2839, www.tontobasinchamber.com

**Topock** • *Topock-Golden Shores C/C* • Adam Leahy, Pres., P.O. Box 663, 86436, P 2,500, M 40, (928) 768-7744, www.golden shoreschamber.com

**Tubac** • *Tubac C/C* • Carol Cullen, Exec. Dir., P.O. Box 1866, 85646, P 1,100, M 100, (520) 398-2704, Fax (520) 398-1704, assistance@ tubacaz.com, www.tubacaz.com

## Tuscon Area

**Tucson Metropolitan C/C** • John Camper CCE, Pres./CEO, 465 W. St. Mary's Rd., P.O. Box 991, 85702, P 1,000,000, M 2,000, (520) 792-1212, (520) 792-2250, Fax (520) 882-5704, jcamper@ tucsonchamber.org, www.tucsonchamber.org.

**Northern Pima County C/C** • Ramon Gaanderse, Pres./CEO, 200 W. Magee Rd., Ste. 120, 85704, P 210,000, M 620, (520) 297-2191, Fax (520) 742-7960, admin@the-chamber.com, www.the-chamber.com

**Tucson Hispanic C/C** • Maricela Solis DeKester, Pres., 120 N. Stone Ave., Ste. 200, 85701, P 1,000,000, M 650, (520) 620-0005, Fax (520) 620-9685, office @tucsonhispanicchamber.org, www. tucsonhispanicchamber.org

**Wickenburg** • *Wickenburg C/C* • Julia Brooks, Exec. Dir., 216 N. Frontier St., 85390, P 10,000, M 700, (928) 684-5479, (928) 684-0977, Fax (928) 684-5470, info@wickenburgchamber.com, www. wickenburgchamber.com.

**Willcox** • *Willcox C/C & Ag.* • Kathy Smith, Exec. Dir., 1500 N. Circle I Rd., 85643, P 4,000, M 135, (520) 384-2272, (800) 200-2272, Fax (520) 384-0293, willcoxchamber@vtc.net, www. willcoxchamber.com.

**Williams** • *Williams-Grand Canyon C/C* • 200 W. Railroad Ave., 86046, P 3,150, M 250, (928) 635-0273, Fax (928) 635-1417, info@williamschamber.com, www.williamschamber.com

**Winkelman** • *see Kearny*

**Winslow** • *Winslow C/C & Visitors Center* • Bob Hall, Exec. Dir., 523 W. 2nd St., P.O. Box 460, 86047, P 9,520, M 200, (928) 289-2434, Fax (928) 289-5660, winslowchamber@cableone.net, www. winslowarizona.org.

**Yarnell** • *Yarnell-Peeples Valley C/C* • Vicki Velasquez, Pres., P.O. Box 275, 85362, P 2,000, M 100, (928) 427-6582, visitus@ y-pvchamber.com, www.y-pvchamber.com

**Youngtown** • *see Surprise*

**Yuma** • *Yuma County C/C* • Ken Rosevear, Exec. Dir., 180 W. First St., Ste. A, 85364, P 200,000, M 1,000, (928) 782-2567, Fax (928) 343-0038, info@yumachamber.org, www.yumachamber.org.

# Arkansas

**Arkansas State C of C** • Randy Zook, Pres./CEO, 1200 W. Capitol, P.O. Box 3645, Little Rock, 72203, P 2,400,000, M 1,200, (501) 372-2222, Fax (501) 372-2722, www.arkansasstatechamber.com

**Altus** • *Altus C/C* • 125 W. Main, P.O. Box 404, 72821, P 817, M 20, (479) 468-4684, Fax (479) 468-4684

**Arkadelphia** • *Arkadelphia Area C/C* • Connie D. Nelson, Exec. Dir., 700 Clay St., P.O. Box 38, 71923, P 10,912, M 330, (870) 246-5542, Fax (870) 246-5543, chamber@cityofarkadelphia.com, www.arkadelphia.org

**Arkansas City** • *Arkansas City C/C* • Steve Morley, Pres., P.O. Box 369, 71630, P 560, M 40, (870) 877-2306, Fax (870) 877-2306

**Ash Flat** • *see Highland*

**Ashdown** • *Little River C/C* • P.O. Box 160, 71822, P 14,000, M 130, (870) 898-2758, Fax (870) 898-6699, lrcoc0436@sbcglobal. net, www.littlerivercounty.org

**Augusta** · *Augusta Area C/C* · Regina Burkett, Pres., 115 S. 2nd St., 72006, P 2,700, M 22, (870) 347-1802

**Bald Knob** · *Bald Knob Area C/C* · P.O. Box 338, 72010, P 3,600, M 130, (501) 724-3140, Fax (501) 724-3140, baldknobchamber@centurytel.net, www.baldknobchamber.com

**Batesville** · *Batesville Area C/C* · 409 Vine St., 72501, P 10,000, M 635, (870) 793-2378, Fax (870) 793-3061, info@mybatesville.org, www.mybatesville.org.

**Beebe** · *Beebe C/C* · Dr. Ruth Couch, Dir., 321 N. Elm, 72012, P 4,930, M 70, (501) 882-8135, Fax (501) 882-8140, chamber@beebeark.org, www.beebeark.org

**Benton** · *Benton Area C/C* · Eddie Black, Exec. Dir., 607 N. Market St., 72015, P 27,712, M 625, (501) 315-8272, Fax (501) 315-8290, bentonchamber@bentonchamber.com, www.bentonchamber.com.

**Bentonville** · *Bentonville/Bella Vista C/C* · Ed Clifford, Pres./CEO, 200 E. Central, P.O. Box 330, 72712, P 30,000, M 1,200, (479) 273-2841, Fax (479) 273-2180, info@bbvchamber.com, www.bbvchamber.com.

**Berryville** · *Berryville C/C* · Ginger Oaks, Dir., P.O. Box 402, 72616, P 4,600, M 160, (870) 423-3704, chamber@hbeark.com, www.berryvillear.com

**Blytheville** · *Blytheville/Gosnell Area C/C* · Elizabeth Smith, Exec. Dir., 300 W. Walnut, P.O. Box 485, 72316, P 22,000, M 300, (870) 762-2012, Fax (870) 762-0551, info@blythevillegosnell.com, www.blythevillegosnell.com

**Booneville** · *South Logan County C/C* · Vanessa Wyrick, Exec. Dir., 210 E. Main St., P.O. Box 55, 72927, P 4,300, M 135, (479) 675-2666, Fax (479) 675-5158, information@booneville.com, www.booneville.com.

**Bradley** · *Bradley C/C* · Joe Middlebrooks, Pres., P.O. Box 662, 71826, P 600, M 100, (870) 894-3554, Fax (870) 894-3554

**Brinkley** · *Brinkley C/C* · Lynda Roche, Exec. Asst., 217 W. Cypress, 72021, P 3,940, M 102, (870) 734-2262, Fax (870) 589-2020, brinkleychamber@sbcglobal.net, www.brinkleychamber.com

**Bryant** · *Bryant C/C* · Rae Ann Fields, Exec. Dir., P.O. Box 261, 72089, P 17,146, M 386, (501) 847-4702, Fax (501) 847-7576, bryantcofc@aristotle.net, www.bryant-ar.com

**Bull Shoals** · *Bull Shoals Lake-White River C/C* · Norm Allen, Exec. Dir., P.O. Box 354, 72619, P 2,000, M 150, (870) 445-4443, (800) 447-1290, havefun@bullshoals.org, www.bullshoals.org

**Cabot** · *Cabot C/C* · Billye Everett, Exec. Dir., P.O. Box 631, 72023, P 22,000, M 368, (501) 843-2136, Fax (501) 843-1861, chamber@cabotcc.org, www.cabotcc.org

**Calico Rock** · *Calico Rock-Pineville Trade Area C/C* · 102 Main St., 72519, P 992, M 50, (870) 297-4129, calicorock@yahoo.com, www.calicorock.us

**Camden** · *Camden Area C/C* · Beth Osteen, Exec. Dir., 314 Adams S.W., P.O. Box 99, 71711, P 13,154, M 300, (870) 836-6426, Fax (870) 836-6400, info@camdenareachamberofcommerce.org

**Cave City** · *Cave City C/C* · Ed Kegley, Pres., P.O. Box 274, 72521, P 1,900, M 40, (870) 283-7040, www.cavecityarkansas.info

**Charleston** · *Charleston C/C* · Alice Wood, Pres., P.O. Box 456, 72933, P 2,965, M 55, (479) 965-2201, Fax (479) 965-2205, www.aboutcharleston.com

**Cherokee Village** · *see Highland*

**Clarendon** · *Clarendon C/C* · Susan Caplener, Secy., P.O. Box 153, 72029, P 1,960, M 38, (870) 747-5414, (870) 747-3802, www.clarendon-ar.com

**Clarksville** · *Clarksville-Johnson County C/C* · Vicki Lyons, Exec. Dir., 101 N. Johnson, 72830, P 8,000, M 200, (479) 754-2340, Fax (479) 754-4923, cjccofc@centurytel.net, www.clarksvillearchamber.com.

**Clinton** · *Clinton Area C/C* · Cindy Herring, Exec. Dir., 214 Griggs St., P.O. Box 52, 72031, P 19,000, M 244, (501) 745-6500, Fax (501) 745-6500, cltchamber@artelco.com, www.clintonchamber.com

**Conway** · *Conway Area C/C* · Brad Lacy, Pres./CEO, 900 Oak St., 72032, P 120,000, M 1,500, (501) 329-7788, Fax (501) 327-7790, getsmart@conwayarkansas.org, www.conwayarkansas.org.

**Corning** · *Corning Area C/C* · Barry Sellers , Dir., 1621 W. Main St., P.O. Box 93, 72422, P 3,600, M 100, (870) 857-3874, Fax (870) 857-3874, corning72422@hotmail.com, www.corningarchamber.org

**Cotter** · *Cotter C/C* · P.O. Box 489, 72626, P 1,000, M 120, (870) 321-1243, chamber@cotterarkansas.com, www.cotterarkansas.com

**Crossett** · *Crossett Area C/C* · Pam Ferguson, 101 W. First Ave., 71635, P 13,500, M 220, (870) 364-6591, Fax (870) 364-7488, pam_ferguson@windstream.net, www.gocrossett.com

**Danville** · *Danville Area C/C* · Sheila Thomas, Pres./CEO, P.O. Box 1140, 72833, P 2,500, M 70, (479) 495-3419, Fax (479) 495-3347, danark@danark.com, www.danark.com

**Dardanelle** · *Dardanelle C/C* · Vicki Sutton, Exec. Dir., 2011 State Hwy. 22 W., P.O. Box 208, 72834, P 4,228, M 125, (479) 229-3328, Fax (479) 229-5086, vsdardchamber@hotmail.com, www.dardanellechamber.com

**Decatur** · *Decatur C/C* · Royce Johnson, Pres., 18032 Bethlehem Rd., 72722, P 1,350, M 30, (479) 752-3248, www.decaturar.com

**DeQueen** · *DeQueen/Sevier County C/C* · Bonita Smith, Pres., 315 W. Stillwell, P.O. Box 67, 71832, P 18,000, M 155, (870) 584-3225, Fax (870) 642-5533, dqscoc@ipa.net, www.dequeenchamberofcommerce.com

**Dermott** · *Dermott Area C/C* · Frank Henry Jr., Exec. Dir., 106 E. Peddicord, P.O. Box 147, 71638, P 4,000, M 100, (870) 538-5656, Fax (870) 538-5493, email@dermottchamber.com, www.dermottchamber.com

**Des Arc** · *Des Arc C/C* · P.O. Box 845, 72040, P 2,000, M 30, (870) 256-3600, www.desarcchamber.org

**DeWitt** · *DeWitt C/C* · David Horton, Pres., P.O. Box 366, 72042, P 3,500, M 125, (870) 946-4666, david.horton.b2wn@statefarm.com, www.dewittchamberofcommerce.com

**Diamond City** · *Diamond City Area C/C* · Mike Kansier, Pres., P.O. Box 1161, 72630, P 730, M 54, (870) 422-7575, dcchamber@diamondcity.net, www.diamondcity.org

**Dierks** · *Dierks C/C* · Misty Eudy, Pres., P.O. Box 292, 71833, P 1,263, M 40, dierkschamberofcommerce.com

**Dover** · *Dover C/C* · Sandra Drittler, Bd. Member, P.O. Box 731, 72837, P 1,500, M 130, (479) 967-2838, Fax (479) 331-4151, drittler3@hotmail.com

**Dumas** · *Dumas C/C* · Sammye Owen, Exec. Dir., P.O. Box 431, 71639, P 5,280, M 202, (870) 382-5447, Fax (870) 382-3031, dumaschamber@centurytel.net, www.dumasar.net

**Earle** · *Earle Area C/C* · Linda McCain, Pres., P.O. Box 652, 72331, P 3,038, M 55, (870) 792-8500

**El Dorado** · *El Dorado C/C* · Don Wales, Pres./CEO, 111 W. Main, 71730, P 21,530, M 850, (870) 863-6113, Fax (870) 863-6115, info@goeldorado.com, www.goeldorado.com

**Eudora** · *Eudora C/C* · Mack Ball Jr., 185 S. Main, P.O. Box 325, 71640, P 2,900, M 40, (870) 355-8443, Fax (870) 355-8443, eudoracofc@sbcglobal.net

**Eureka Springs** · *Greater Eureka Springs C/C* · Jess Feldman, Pres., 516 Village Cir., P.O. Box 551, 72632, P 2,278, M 500, (479) 253-8737, (800) 6-EUREKA, Fax (479) 253-5037, info@eureka springschamber.com, www.eurekaspringschamber.com

**Fairfield Bay** · *Fairfield Bay Area C/C* · Robbie Ingle, Exec. Dir., 383 Dave Creek Pkwy., Ste. C, P.O. Box 1159, 72088, P 2,600, M 255, (501) 884-3324, Fax (501) 884-6250, director@ffbchamber. org, www.ffbchamber.org.

**Farmington** · *Farmington C/C* · Joe Bailey, Pres., P.O. Box 1152, 72730, P 3,650, M 100, (479) 267-2368, www.cityoffarmington.com

**Fayetteville** · *Fayetteville C/C* · Steve Clark, Pres./CEO, 123 W. Mountain St., P.O. Box 4216, 72702, P 60,018, M 1,500, (479) 521-1710, Fax (479) 521-1791, sclark@fayettevillear.com, www. fayettevillear.com.

**Flippin** · *Flippin C/C* · Claudia Hicks, Pres., P.O. Box 118, 72634, P 1,400, M 75, (870) 453-8480, www.flippinchamber.com

**Fordyce** · *Fordyce C/C* · 119 W. 3rd St., P.O. Box 588, 71742, P 4,799, M 150, (870) 352-3520, Fax (870) 352-8090

**Forrest City** · *Forrest City Area C/C* · David Dunn, Exec. Dir., 203 N. Izard, 72335, P 14,700, M 200, (870) 633-1651, Fax (870) 633-9500, info@forrestcitychamber.com, www.forrestcity chamber.com.

**Fort Smith** · *Fort Smith Reg. C/C* · Paul Harvel, Pres./CEO, 612 Garrison Ave., P.O. Box 1668, 72902, P 200,000, M 1,500, (479) 783-6118, Fax (479) 783-6110, info@fortsmithchamber.com, www.fortsmithchamber.com

**Gentry** · *Main Street Gentry/Chamber of Commerce* · Bev Saunders, Dir., P.O. Box 642, 72734, P 2,200, M 70, (479) 736-2358, Fax (479) 736-2877, info@gentrychamber.com, www.gentry chamber.com

**Glenwood** · *Glenwood Reg. C/C* · Joe Mays, Pres., P.O. Box 2006, 71943, P 2,000, M 45, (870) 356-5266, glenwoodregional@yahoo. com, www.glenwood-ar.com

**Gravette** · *Greater Gravette C/C* · Patrick Hall, Exec. Dir., P.O. Box 112, 72736, P 2,500, M 68, (479) 790-7296, www.gravette arkansas.com

**Green Forest** · *Green Forest C/C* · 909 Enterprise Ave., 72638, P 2,600, M 65, (870) 438-6641

**Greenbrier** · *Greenbrier C/C* · Jon Patrom, Pres., P.O. Box 418, 72058, P 3,200, M 120, (501) 679-4009, info@greenbrierchamber. org, www.greenbrierchamber.org

**Greenwood** · *Greenwood C/C* · P.O. Box 511, 72936, P 7,000, M 200, (479) 996-6357, Fax (479) 996-1162, info@greenwood chamber.net, www.greenwoodarkansas.com

**Greers Ferry** · *Greers Ferry Area C/C* · Gene Eddleman, Pres., P.O. Box 1354, 72067, P 2,000, M 145, (501) 825-7188, (888) 825-7199, Fax (501) 825-6782, info@greersferry.com, www. greersferry.com

**Gurdon** · *Gurdon C/C* · Steven Orsburn, Pres., P.O. Box 187, 71743, P 2,300, M 45, (870) 353-2661, www.gurdonchamber ofcommerce.com

**Hamburg** · *Hamburg Area C/C* · Jennifer Foote, Exec. Dir., 200 E. Lincoln St., P.O. Box 460, 71646, P 3,098, M 100, (870) 853-8345, Fax (870) 853-8134, info@hamburgareachamber.org, www. hamburgareachamber.org

**Hardy** · *see Highland*

**Harrisburg** · *Harrisburg Area C/C* · Mildred Traynom, Secy./ Treas., P.O. Box 265, 72432, P 5,500, M 60, (870) 578-5461, Fax (870) 578-4113, www.harrisburgchamber.com

**Harrison** · *Harrison C/C* · Patti Methvin, Pres./CEO, 621 E. Rush Ave., 72601, P 37,000, M 500, (870) 741-2659, (800) 880-6265, Fax (870) 741-9059, cocinfo@harrison-chamber.com, www. harrison-chamber.com.

**Hazen** · *Hazen C/C* · Bob Juola, P.O. Box 907, 72064, P 1,800, M 35, (870) 255-3352

**Heber Springs** · *Heber Springs Area C/C* · Marilyn Wright, Exec. Dir., 1001 W. Main, 72543, P 6,862, M 430, (501) 362-2444, (800) 774-3237, Fax (501) 362-9953, chamber@heber-springs.com, www.heber-springs.com

**Helena** · *Phillips County C/C* · Billy Ray, Dir., 111 Hickory Hill Dr., P.O. Box 447, 72342, P 24,309, M 210, (870) 338-8327, Fax (870) 338-8882, info@phillipscountychamber.org, www.phillipscounty chamber.org.

**Highland** · *Spring River Area C/C* · Charlotte Goodwin, Pres., 2852D Hwy. 62/412, 72542, P 6,000, M 130, (870) 856-3210, (870) 994-7324, Fax (870) 856-3320, sracc@centurytel.net, www.sracc.com

**Hope** · *Hope-Hempstead County C/C* · Mark Keith, Dir., 101 W. 2nd, P.O. Box 250, 71802, P 23,000, M 325, (870) 777-3640, Fax (870) 722-6154, hopeark@arkansas.net, www.hopemelonfest.com

**Horseshoe Bend** · *Horseshoe Bend Area C/C* · 811 2nd St., Ste. 18, P.O. Box 4083, 72512, P 2,278, M 110, (870) 670-5433, info@ horseshoebendar.info, www.horseshoebendarcc.com

**Hot Springs** · *Greater Hot Springs C/C* · Dave Byerly, Pres., 659 Ouachita, P.O. Box 6090, 71902, P 88,000, M 1,122, (501) 321-1700, Fax (501) 321-3551, info@hotspringschamber.com, www.hotspringschamber.com

**Hot Springs Village** · *Hot Springs Village Area C/C* · Lee Ann Branch, Exec. Dir., 4585 Hwy. 7 N., Ste. 9, P.O. Box 8575, 71910, P 15,000, M 247, (501) 915-9940, (877) 915-9940, Fax (501) 984-9961, hsvchamber@suddenlinkmail.com, www.hotsprings villagechamber.com.

**Huntsville** · *Huntsville Area C/C* · David Pemberton, Exec. Dir., 104 E. Main, P.O. Box 950, 72740, P 2,000, M 60, (479) 738-6000, Fax (479) 738-6000, chamber@madisoncounty.net, www.hunts villearchamber.com

**Jacksonville** · *Jacksonville C/C* · Amy Mattison, CEO, 200 Dupree Dr., 72076, P 30,900, M 400, (501) 982-1511, Fax (501) 982-1464, events@jacksonville-arkansas.com, www.jacksonville-arkansas.com

**Jasper** · *Jasper/Newton County C/C* · 204 N. Spring St., P.O. Box 250, 72641, P 8,800, M 141, (870) 446-2455, (800) 670-7792, Fax (870) 446-2477, chamber@ritternet.com, www.theozark mountains.com

**Jonesboro** · *Jonesboro Reg. C/C* · Mark Young, Pres., P.O. Box 789, 72403, P 82,148, M 1,433, (870) 932-6691, Fax (870) 933-5758, jonesboroinfo@jonesborochamber.com, www.jonesboro chamber.com.

**Lake Village** · *Lake Village C/C* · 111 Main St., P.O. Box 752, 71653, P 2,823, M 100, (870) 265-5997, Fax (870) 265-5254, request@lakevillagechamber.com, www.lakevillagechamber.com

**Lewisville** · *Lewisville C/C* · Peggy Pulliam, Treas., P.O. Box 506, 71845, P 1,245, M 65, (870) 921-5668

**Lincoln** · *Lincoln Area C/C* · Earl Hunton, Pres., P.O. Box 942, 72744, P 1,860, M 52, (479) 824-5100, lincolnareacofc.com

**Little Rock** · *Little Rock Reg. C/C* · Jay Chesshir, Pres., 1 Chamber Plaza, 72201, P 652,834, M 1,710, (501) 374-2001, Fax (501) 374-6018, chamber@littlerockchamber.com, www. littlerockchamber.com

**Lonoke** • *Lonoke Area C/C* • John Garner, Mgr., 102 1/2 N.W. Front St., P.O. Box 294, 72086, P 4,800, M 151, (501) 676-4399, Fax (501) 676-4399, uni1mac55@sbcglobal.net, www.lonoke.com

**Lowell** • *see Rogers*

**Magnolia** • *Magnolia-Columbia County C/C* • Cammie Hambrice, Dir., 529 E. Main, P.O. Box 866, 71754, P 30,000, M 350, (870) 234-4352, Fax (870) 234-9291, ea@ccalliance.us, www.magnoliachamber.com

**Malvern** • *Malvern & Hot Spring County C/C* • Nikki Cranford Thornton, Exec. Dir., 213 W. 3rd St., P.O. Box 266, 72104, P 30,000, M 300, (501) 332-2721, Fax (501) 332-8558, president@malvern chamber.com, www.malvernchamber.com

**Mammoth Spring** • *Mammoth Spring C/C* • Glynda Pryor, Pres., P.O. Box 185, 72554, P 1,147, M 43, (870) 625-3518, mammoth spring@arkansas.gov, www.mammothspringar.com

**Marianna** • *Marianna-Lee County C/C* • 67 W. Main St., P.O. Box 584, 72360, P 5,181, M 150, (870) 295-2469, Fax (870) 295-6207, www.mariannaarkansas.org

**Marion** • *Marion C/C* • Paul Brewster, Pres., 13 Military Rd., P.O. Box 652, 72364, P 10,500, M 300, (870) 739-6041, Fax (870) 739-5448, chamber@marionarkansas.org, www.marionarkansas.org

**Marked Tree** • *Marked Tree C/C* • 1 Elm St., 72365, P 2,800, M 75, (870) 358-3000, Fax (870) 358-7867, www.markedtree arkansas.org

**Marshall** • *Greater Searcy County C/C* • Jack Treat, Dir., P.O. Box 1385, 72650, P 7,800, M 130, (870) 448-2557, Fax (870) 448-4858, webmaster@searcycountyarkansas.org, www.searcy countyarkansas.org

**Maumelle** • *Maumelle Area C/C* • Pam Rantisi, Exec. Dir., 115 Audubon Dr., Ste. 14, P.O. Box 13099, 72113, P 15,200, M 356, (501) 851-9700, Fax (501) 851-6690, execdir@maumellechamber. com, www.maumellechamber.com.

**McGehee** • *McGehee C/C* • Paula Mote, Secy., 901 Holly St., P.O. Box 521, 71654, P 4,750, M 130, (870) 222-4451, Fax (870) 222-5729, admin@mcgeheechamber.com, www.mcgeheechamber.com

**Mena** • *Mena/Polk County C/C* • Greg Goss, Pres., 524 Sherwood Ave., 71953, P 22,000, M 260, (479) 394-2912, Fax (479) 394-1267, chamberofcommerce2@sbcglobal.net, menapolkchamber.com

**Monticello** • *Monticello/Drew County C/C* • Glenda Nichols, Exec. Dir., 335 E. Gaines, 71655, P 18,723, M 200, (870) 367-6741, Fax (870) 367-0050, monticellochamber@sbcglobal.net, www.montdrewchamber.com.

**Morrilton** • *Morrilton Area C/C* • John Gibson, Pres., 120 N. Division St., P.O. Box 589, 72110, P 6,550, M 343, (501) 354-2393, Fax (501) 354-8642, macc_ccedc@suddenlinkmail.com, www.morrilton.com.

**Mount Ida** • *Mount Ida Area C/C* • Maureen Walther, Dir., 111 S. West St., P.O. Box 6, 71957, P 9,240, M 170, (870) 867-2723, Fax (870) 867-2723, director@mtidachamber.com, www.mtida chamber.com

**Mountain Home** • *Mountain Home Area C/C* • Eddie Majeste, Exec. Dir., 1023 Hwy. 62 E., P.O. Box 488, 72654, P 38,000, M 600, (870) 425-5111, (800) 822-3536, Fax (870) 425-4446, salms@ EnjoyMountainHome.com, www.EnjoyMountainHome.com.

**Mountain View** • *Mountain View Area C/C* • Michalle Coon, Exec. Dir., 107 N. Peabody Ave., P.O. Box 133, 72560, P 2,900, M 190, (870) 269-8068, (888) 679-2859, Fax (870) 269-8748, mvchamber@mvtel.net, www.yourplaceinthemountains.com

**Murfreesboro** • *Murfreesboro C/C* • Debbie Shuckers, Pres., P.O. Box 166, 71958, P 2,000, M 80, (870) 285-3131, Fax (870) 285-3131, murfreesboro.chamber@yahoo.com, www.murfreesboroark.com

**Nashville** • *Nashville C/C* • Tammy Smith, Exec. Dir., 107 S. Main St., P.O. Box 1506, 71852, P 5,000, M 140, (870) 845-1262, Fax (870) 845-1262, nashvillecc@sbcglobal.net, www.nashvillear.com

**Newark** • *Newark Area C/C* • 560 S. Main St., P.O. Box 222, 72562, P 1,250, M 50, (870) 799-8888, Fax (870) 799-8493

**Newport** • *Newport Area C/C* • Julie Allen, Exec. Dir., 201 Hazel St., 72112, P 7,811, M 280, (870) 523-3618, Fax (870) 523-2528, director@newportarchamber.org, www.newportarchamber.org

**North Little Rock** • *North Little Rock C/C* • Terry Hartwick, Pres./CEO, 100 Main St., P.O. Box 5288, 72119, P 61,329, M 986, (501) 372-5959, Fax (501) 372-5955, nlrchamber@nlrchamber.org, www.nlrchamber.org.

**Osceola** • *Osceola-South Mississippi County C/C* • Eric Golde, Exec. Dir., 116 N. Maple, P.O. Box 174, 72370, P 9,000, M 200, (870) 563-2281, Fax (870) 563-5385, osceolachamber@sbcglobal. net, www.osceolachamber.net

**Ozark** • *Ozark Area C/C* • Susan Mcilroy, Dir., 300 W. Commercial, 72949, P 3,700, M 200, (479) 667-2525, (800) 951-2525, Fax (479) 667-5750, ozarkareacoc@centurytel.net, www.ozarkareacoc.org

**Paragould** • *Paragould Reg. C/C* • Sue McGowan, CEO, 300 W. Court St., P.O. Box 124, 72450, P 24,000, M 778, (870) 236-7684, Fax (870) 236-7142, smcgowan@paragould.org, www.paragould.org.

**Paris** • *Paris Area C/C* • Linda Hixson, Exec. Dir., 301 W. Walnut, 72855, P 3,700, M 175, (479) 963-2244, Fax (479) 963-8321, pariscoc@gmail.com, www.parisaronline.com

**Piggott** • *Piggott C/C* • Sharon Bellers, Secy., 100 W. Main, P.O. Box 96, 72454, P 3,980, M 80, (870) 598-3167, Fax (870) 598-3955, pchamber@piggott.net, www.piggottchamber.org

**Pine Bluff** • *Greater Pine Bluff C/C* • Ann Green & Michelle Rocha, Co-Dirs., 510 Main St., P.O. Box 5069, 71611, P 55,085, M 950, (870) 535-0110, Fax (870) 535-1643, info@pinebluff chamber.com, www.pinebluffchamber.com.

**Pocahontas** • *Randolph County C/C* • Tim Scott, Exec. Dir., 107 E. Everett, P.O. Box 466, 72455, P 18,195, M 200, (870) 892-3956, Fax (870) 892-5399, chamber010@centurytel.net, www.randolph chamber.com

**Prairie Grove** • *Prairie Grove C/C* • Casey Copeland, Pres., P.O. Box 23, 72753, P 2,800, M 40, (479) 846-2197, info@pgchamber. com, www.pgchamber.com

**Prescott** • *Prescott-Nevada County C/C* • Brandy Jones, Dir., 116 E. 2nd S., P.O. Box 307, 71857, P 9,986, M 120, (870) 887-2101, Fax (870) 887-5317, bjones@pnpartnership.org , www.pnpartnership.org

**Rector** • *Rector Area C/C* • Ron Kemp, Pres., P.O. Box 307, 72461, P 2,107, M 60, (870) 595-3035, Fax (870) 595-3611, rector communitydevelopment@centurytel.net, www.rectorarkansas.com

**Rogers** • *Rogers-Lowell Area C/C* • Raymond M. Burns CCE, Pres./CEO, 317 W. Walnut, 72756, P 55,000, M 2,100, (479) 636-1240, Fax (479) 636-5485, beth@rogerslowell.com, www.rogerslowell.com

**Russellville** • *Russellville C/C* • Jeff Pipkin, Pres./CEO, 708 W. Main, 72801, P 26,000, M 850, (479) 968-2530, Fax (479) 968-5894, chamber@russellville.org, www.russellvillechamber.org

**Salem** • *Salem C/C* • Holly Pate, Pres., P.O. Box 649, 72576, P 1,574, M 90, (870) 895-5565, chamber@salemar.com, www.salemar.com

**Searcy** · *Searcy Reg. C/C* · Buck C. Layne Jr. CEcD, Pres., 2323 S. Main, 72143, P 20,000, M 700, (501) 268-2458, Fax (501) 268-9530, scc@searcychamber.com, www.searcyarkansas.org

**Sheridan** · *Grant County C/C* · Leann Williams, Exec. Secy., 202 N. Oak St., 72150, P 16,000, M 151, (870) 942-3021, Fax (870) 942-3378, gccc@windstream.net, www.grantcountychamber.com

**Sherwood** · *Sherwood C/C* · Patricia Layton, Exec. Dir., 2303 E. Lee Ave., P.O. Box 6082, 72124, P 21,500, M 260, (501) 835-7600, Fax (501) 835-2326, shwdchamber@att.net, www.sherwood chamber.net

**Siloam Springs** · *Siloam Springs C/C* · Wayne Mays, Pres./CEO, 108 E. University, P.O. Box 476, 72761, P 14,000, M 375, (479) 524-6466, Fax (479) 549-3032, info@siloamchamber.com, www.siloamchamber.com

**Smackover** · *Smackover C/C* · Tommie Fleming, Mgr., 710 Pershing Hwy., P.O. Box 275, 71762, P 2,005, M 130, (870) 725-3521, Fax (870) 725-3521, chamber@smackoverar.com, www.smackoverar.com

**Springdale** · *Springdale C/C* · Perry Webb, Pres./CEO, 202 W. Emma St., P.O. Box 166, 72765, P 65,000, M 955, (479) 872-2222, (800) 972-7261, Fax (479) 751-4699, info@chamber.springdale.com, www.springdale.com

**Stamps** · *Stamps C/C* · Rose Wiegand, Secy., P.O. Box 274, 71860, P 2,200, M 40, (870) 533-4771, Fax (870) 533-4788

**Star City** · *Star City C/C* · Mark Owen, Pres., P.O. Box 88, 71667, P 2,500, M 100, (870) 628-3100, Fax (870) 628-9943, scacc@netstorm.net, stardazefestival.com

**Stephens** · *Stephens C/C* · Margie L. Wagnon, Secy./Mgr., 105 N. First St., P.O. Box 572, 71764, P 1,300, M 34, (870) 786-5221, Fax (870) 786-5749

**Stuttgart** · *Stuttgart C/C* · Stephen R. Bell, Exec. V.P., 507 S. Main, P.O. Box 1500, 72160, P 9,800, M 400, (870) 673-1602, Fax (870) 673-1604, stuttgartchamber@centurytel.net, www.stuttgartarkansas.com

**Sulphur Springs** · *Sulphur Springs Comm. C/C* · P.O. Box 115, 72768, P 670, M 15, (479) 298-3218

**Texarkana** · *see Texarkana, TX*

**Trumann** · *Trumann Area C/C* · Jackie Ross, Exec. Dir., 225 Hwy. 463, P.O. Box 215, 72472, P 7,600, M 125, (870) 483-5424, Fax (870) 483-6660, tchamber@centurytel.net, www.trumannchamber.com

**Tuckerman** · *Tuckerman C/C* · Jarrod Bowen, Main St., City Hall, P.O. Box 287, 72473, P 1,800, M 40, (870) 523-2465, (870) 349-5313, cityoftuckerman@yahoo.com

**Van Buren** · *Van Buren C/C* · Jackie Krutsch, Exec. Dir., 510 Main St., 72956, P 18,986, M 320, (479) 474-2761, Fax (479) 474-6259, www.vanburenchamber.org.

**Waldron** · *Waldron Area C/C* · Jeff Brewer, Pres., 323 Washington St., P.O. Box 1985, 72958, P 10,628, M 125, (479) 637-2775, www.waldronchamberofcommerce.com

**Walnut Ridge** · *Lawrence County C/C* · Kathy Bradley, Exec. Secy., 109 S.W. Front, P.O. Box 842, 72476, P 17,587, M 207, (870) 886-3232, Fax (870) 886-1736, lawrencecofc@suddenlinkmail.com, www.lawcochamber.org

**Ward** · *Ward C/C* · 80 S. 2nd St., P.O. Box 106, 72176, P 2,500, M 90, (501) 843-6533, (501) 843-8348, www.bestofward.com

**Warren** · *Bradley County C/C* · 104 N. Myrtle St., 71671, P 12,600, M 200, (870) 226-5225, Fax (870) 226-6285, info@bradleychamber.com, www.bradleychamber.com

**Watson** · *Watson C/C* · Kalvin Fuller, P.O. Box 16, 71674, P 288, M 48, (870) 866-7666

**West Memphis** · *West Memphis Area C/C* · Holmes Hammett, Exec. Dir., 108 W. Broadway, P.O. Box 594, 72303, P 30,000, M 520, (870) 735-1134, Fax (870) 735-6283, wmcoc@wmcoc.com, www.wmcoc.com.

**White Hall** · *White Hall C/C* · Dane Reed, Pres., 102 Anderson Ave., 71602, P 5,114, M 185, (870) 247-5502, whitehallarchamber.com

**Wynne** · *Cross County C/C* · Aaron Stewart, Exec. Dir., 1790 N. Falls Blvd., Ste. 2, P.O. Box 234, 72396, P 20,000, M 220, (870) 238-2601, Fax (870) 238-7844, info@crosscountrychamber.com, www.crosscountychamber.com

**Yellville** · *Yellville C/C* · Lyn Baker, Pres., 204 Hwy. 62 E., P.O. Box 369, 72687, P 2,000, M 125, (870) 449-4676, chamber@yellville.com, www.yellville.com.

# California

**California C of C** · Allan Zaremberg, Pres., 1215 K St., Ste. 1400, P.O. Box 1736, Sacramento, 95812, P 34,000,000, M 16,000, (916) 444-6670, Fax (916) 325-1272, information@calchamber.com, www.calchamber.com

**Acton** · *Acton C/C* · Jim Schutte, Pres., P.O. Box 81, 93510, P 10,000, M 200, (661) 269-5785, Fax (661) 269-4121, www.actoncoc.org

**Adelanto** · *Adelanto C/C* · Stephanie Casteel, Ofc. Mgr., 12012 Air Expressway, P.O. Box 712, 92301, P 24,880, M 200, (760) 246-5711, Fax (760) 246-4019, office@adelantochamber.com, www.adelantochamber.com

**Agoura Hills** · *Agoura-Oak Park-Conejo Valley C/C* · Mr. Alex Coteras, Exec. Dir., 30101 Agoura Court, Ste. 207, 91301, P 23,000, M 1,500, (818) 876-9913, Fax (818) 889-3366, info@agoura chamber.org acoteras@yahoo.com, www.agourachamber.org

**Agua Dulce** · *see Santa Clarita*

**Alameda** · *Alameda C/C* · Melody Marr, CEO, 1416 Park Ave., 94501, P 78,000, M 700, (510) 522-0414, Fax (510) 522-7677, connect@alamedachamber.com, www.alamedachamber.com

**Alamo** · *see Danville*

**Albany** · *Albany C/C* · Tod Abbott, Pres., 1108 Solano Ave., 94706, P 17,311, M 270, (510) 525-1771, Fax (510) 525-6068, albany chamber@albanychamber.org, www.albanychamber.org

**Alhambra** · *Alhambra C/C* · Owen Guenthard, Exec. Dir., 104 S. First St., 91801, P 90,000, M 500, (626) 282-8481, Fax (626) 282-5596, alhambrachamber@yahoo.com, alhambrachamber.org.

**Aliso Viejo** · *see South Orange County*

**Alpine** · *Alpine & Mountain Empire C/C* · Patricia Cannon, Pres./CEO, 2707 Alpine Blvd., P.O. Box 69, 91903, P 18,000, M 400, (619) 445-2722, Fax (619) 445-2871, info@alpinechamber.com, www.alpinechamber.com

**Altadena** · *Altadena C/C* · 730 E. Altadena Dr., 91001, P 42,000, M 225, (626) 794-3988, Fax (626) 794-6015, altadenachamber@yahoo.com, abacus-es.com/altadena

**Alturas** · *Alturas C/C* · Jennifer Barcia, Pres., 522 S. Main St., 96101, P 3,000, M 150, (530) 233-4434, Fax (530) 233-4434, contactus@alturaschamber.org, www.alturaschamber.org

**Amador County** · *see Jackson*

**American Canyon** · *American Canyon C/C* · Pam Wilkinson, Pres./CEO, 3419 Broadway, Ste. H11, P.O. Box 10114, 94503, P 16,000, M 350, (707) 552-3650, Fax (707) 552-9724, chamber@amcanchamber.org, www.amcanchamber.org

**Anaheim** · *Anaheim C/C* · Todd Ament, Pres./CEO, 201 E. Center St., 92805, P 350,000, M 800, (714) 758-0222, Fax (714) 758-0468, info@anaheimchamber.org, www.anaheimchamber.org

**Anaheim** · *La Palma C/C* · Esther Deleon-Hernandez, Exec. Dir., P.O. Box 3014, 92803, P 15,400, M 120, (714) 931-8166, Fax (714) 209-4071, staff@lapalmachamber.com, www.lapalmachamber.com

**Anderson** · *Anderson C/C* · Irish Robertson, Exec. Dir., 2375 North St., P.O. Box 1144, 96007, P 13,000, M 350, (530) 365-8095, Fax (530) 365-4561, info@andersonchamber.info, www.andersonchamber.info

**Angels Camp** · *Calaveras County C/C* · Diane Gray, Exec. Dir., 52 S. Main St., P.O. Box 1145, 95222, P 41,000, M 486, (209) 736-1111, Fax (209) 736-1105, chamber@calaveras.org, www.calaveras.org

**Angwin** · *Angwin Comm. Cncl.* · Barbara Spelletich, Pres., P.O. Box 747, 94508, P 3,000, M 400, (707) 965-2867, www.angwincouncil.org

**Antelope** · *see North Highlands*

**Antioch** · *Antioch C/C* · Devi Lanphere, Pres./CEO, 324 G St., 94509, P 100,000, M 550, (925) 757-1800, Fax (925) 757-5286, info@antiochchamber.com, www.antiochchamber.com

**Anza** · *Anza Valley C/C* · Robyn Garrison, Pres., P.O. Box 391460, 92539, P 8,500, M 119, (951) 763-0141, www.anzavalleychamber.com

**Apple Valley** · *Apple Valley C/C* · Janice Moore, Pres./CEO, 16010 Apple Valley Rd., 92307, P 75,000, M 450, (760) 242-2753, Fax (760) 242-0303, info@avchamber.org, www.avchamber.org

**Aptos** · *Aptos C/C* · Karen Hibble, Dir., 7605-A Old Dominion Ct., 95003, P 32,000, M 675, (831) 688-1467, Fax (831) 688-6961, info@aptoschamber.com, www.aptoschamber.com

**Arcadia** · *Arcadia C/C* · Beth Costanza, Exec. Dir., 388 W. Huntington Dr., 91007, P 56,000, M 700, (626) 447-2159, Fax (626) 445-0273, arcadiac@pacbell.net, www.arcadiachamber.com

**Arcata** · *Arcata C/C* · Brenda Bishop, Exec. Dir./CEO, 1635 Heindon Rd., 95521, P 18,000, M 400, (707) 822-3619, Fax (707) 822-3515, arcata@arcatachamber.com, www.arcatachamber.com

**Arroyo Grande** · *Arroyo Grande Valley C/C* · Judith Bean, Pres./CEO, 800-A W. Branch St., 93420, P 17,000, M 400, (805) 489-1488, Fax (805) 489-2239, info@agchamber.com, www.agchamber.com

**Arvin** · *Arvin C/C* · P.O. Box 645, 93203, P 16,000, M 60, (661) 854-2265, Fax same, arvinchamberofcommerce@yahoo.com, www.arvinchamberofcommerce.com

**Atascadero** · *Atascadero C/C* · Joanne Main, Pres./CEO, 6904 El Camino Real, 93422, P 28,000, M 600, (805) 466-2044, Fax (805) 466-9218, jmain@atascaderochamber.org, atascaderochamber.org.

**Atwater** · *also see Los Angeles-Atwater/Griffith Park C/C*

**Atwater** · *Atwater C/C* · Sarah Sanders, Admin. Asst., 1181 Third St., 95301, P 30,000, M 200, (209) 358-4251, Fax (209) 358-0934, chamber@atwaterchamberofcommerce.org, www.atwaterchamberofcommerce.org

**Auburn** · *Auburn C/C* · Bruce L. Cosgrove, CEO, 601 Lincoln Way, 95603, P 65,000, M 700, (530) 885-5616, (800) 971-1888 CA only, Fax (530) 885-5854, info@auburnchamber.net, www.auburnchamber.net.

**Avalon** · *Catalina Island C/C & Visitors Bur.* · Wayne Griffin, Pres./CEO, #1 Green Pier, P.O. Box 217, 90704, P 3,500, M 261, (310) 510-1520, Fax (310) 510-7606, info@catalinachamber.com, www.catalinachamber.com

**Azusa** · *Azusa C/C* · Irene Villapania, CEO, 240 W. Foothill Blvd., 91702, P 45,200, M 225, (626) 334-1507, Fax (626) 334-5217, info@azusachamber.org, www.azusachamber.org.

**Badger** · *see Miramonte*

## Bakersfield Area

**Greater Bakersfield C/C** · Debra Moreno, Pres./CEO, 1725 Eye St., P.O. Box 1947, 93303, P 301,000, M 1,600, (661) 327-4421, Fax (661) 327-8751, info@bakersfieldchamber.org, www.bakersfieldchamber.org.

**Kern County Bd. of Trade** · Rick Davis, Exec. Dir., 2101 Oak St., 93301, P 661,000, (661) 868-5376, Fax (661) 861-2017, kerninfo@co.kern.ca.us, www.visitkern.com

**North of the River C/C** · Stan Shires, Exec. Dir., P.O. Box 5551, 93388, P 100,000, M 95, (661) 871-4555, norchamber@bak.rr.com

**Baldwin Park** · *Baldwin Park C/C* · David Luevano, Exec. Dir., 3942 Main Ave., 91706, P 75,837, M 300, (626) 960-4848, Fax (626) 960-2990, info@bpchamber.com, www.bpchamber.com

**Banning** · *Banning C/C* · Jack Holden, Exec. Dir., 60 E. Ramsey, P.O. Box 665, 92220, P 28,000, M 400, (951) 849-4695, Fax (951) 849-9395, info@banningchamber.org, www.banningchamber.org.

**Barstow** · *Barstow Area C/C* · Jeri Justus, Exec. Dir., 681 N. First Ave., P.O. Box 698, 92312, P 23,056, M 411, (760) 256-8617, Fax (760) 256-7675, bacc@barstowchamber.com, www.barstowchamber.com

**Bass Lake** · *Bass Lake C/C* · P.O. Box 126, 93604, P 2,500, M 27, (559) 642-3676, www.basslakechamber.com

**Bay Point** · *see California Delta*

**Baywood Park** · *see Los Osos*

**Beaumont** · *Beaumont C/C* · Kathy Munyas, Exec. Dir., 726 Beaumont Ave., 92223, P 35,000, M 422, (951) 845-9541, Fax (951) 769-9080, info@beaumontcachamber.com, www.beaumontcachamber.com.

**Bell** · *Bell C/C* · Julie Gonzalez, Gen. Mgr., 4401 E. Gage Ave., P.O. Box 294, 90201-0294, P 42,600, M 125, (323) 560-8755, Fax (323) 560-2060, bellchamber@sbcglobal.net

**Bell Gardens** · *Bell Gardens C/C* · Dennis Grizzle, Exec. Dir., 7535 Perry Rd., 90201, P 45,000, M 150, (562) 806-2355, Fax (562) 806-1585, bellgardens1@earthlink.net, www.bellgardenschamber.org

**Bellflower** · *Bellflower C/C* · Michele Moore, Chamber Mgr., 16730 Bellflower Blvd., Ste. A, 90706, P 75,000, M 275, (562) 867-1744, Fax (562) 866-7545, bellflowercoc@juno.com, www.bellflowerchamber.com

**Belmont** · *Belmont C/C* · Michael Kazarian, Pres., 1059A Alameda de las Pulgas, 94002, P 27,000, M 220, (650) 595-8696, Fax (650) 595-8731, execdirector@belmontchamber.org, www.belmontchamber.org

**Benicia** · *Benicia C/C & Visitors Center* · Stephanie Christiansen, Pres./CEO, 601 First St., Ste. 100, 94510, P 28,000, M 650, (707) 745-2120, Fax (707) 745-2275, beniciachamber@aol.com, www.beniciachamber.com

**Berkeley** · *Berkeley C/C* · Jonathan DeYoe, 1834 University Ave., 94703, P 103,000, M 375, (510) 549-7000, Fax (510) 549-1789, info@berkeleychamber.com, www.berkeleychamber.com

**Bethel Island** · *Bethel Island C/C* · Linda Nowak, Mgr., P.O. Box 263, 94511, P 2,300, M 150, (925) 684-3220, Fax (925) 684-9025, bicc@cctrap.com, www.bethelisland-chamber.com

**Beverly Hills** · *Beverly Hills C of C & Civic Assoc.* · Dan Walsh, CEO, 239 S. Beverly Dr., 90212, P 36,000, M 800, (310) 248-1000, Fax (310) 248-1020, info@beverlyhillschamber.com, www.beverlyhillschamber.com

**Big Bear Lake** · *Big Bear C/C* · Sara Russ, Exec. Dir., 630 Bartlett Rd., P.O. Box 2860, 92315, P 21,000, M 550, (909) 866-4607, (877) 866-5253, Fax (909) 866-5412, www.bigbearchamber.com

**Big Bend** · *see Burney*

**Bird's Landing** · *see California Delta*

**Bishop** · *Bishop Area C/C & Visitors Bureau* · Tawni Tomson, Exec. Dir., 690 N. Main St., 93514, P 14,000, M 320, (760) 873-8405, Fax (760) 873-6999, info@bishopvisitor.com, www.bishopvisitor.com

**Black Hawk** · *see Danville*

**Blue Lake** · *Blue Lake C/C* · Saremy Duffy, Pres., P.O. Box 476, 95525, P 1,200, M 50, (707) 668-5655, www.bluelakechamber.org

**Blythe** · *Blythe Area C/C* · Jim Shipley, COO, 201 S. Broadway, 92225, P 13,500, M 350, (760) 922-8166, Fax (760) 922-4010, blythecoc@yahoo.com, www.blytheareachamberofcommerce.com

**Bolinas** · *see Stinson Beach*

**Boonville** · *Anderson Valley C/C* · Glad Donahue, P.O. Box 275, 95415, P 2,000, M 50, (707) 895-2379, info@andersonvalley-chamber.com, www.andersonvalleychamber.com

**Boron** · *Boron C/C* · Randy Smith, Pres., 26962-20 Mule Team Rd., 93516, P 3,500, M 50, (760) 762-5810, Fax (760) 762-0012, chamber@boronchamber.org, www.boronchamber.org

**Borrego Springs** · *Borrego Springs C/C* · Kimberly Williamson, Admin. Dir., 786 Palm Canyon Dr., P.O. Box 420, 92004, P 3,500, M 200, (760) 767-5555, (800) 559-5524, Fax (760) 767-5976, info@borregospringschamber.com, www.borregospringschamber.com

**Brawley** · *Brawley C/C* · Nicole Nicholas Gilles, CEO, 204 S. Imperial Ave., P.O. Box 218, 92227, P 25,000, M 405, (760) 344-3160, Fax (760) 344-7611, chamber@brawleychamber.com, www.brawleychamber.com.

**Brea** · *Brea C/C* · Sharon Wegner, Exec. Dir., One Civic Center Cir., 92821, P 38,000, M 950, (714) 529-4938, Fax (714) 529-6103, breachamber@breachamber.com, www.breachamber.com

**Brentwood** · *Brentwood C/C* · Harry York, CEO, 8440 Brentwood Blvd., Ste. C, 94513, P 50,000, M 847, (925) 634-3344, Fax (925) 634-3731, info@brentwoodchamber.com, www.brentwoodchamber.com

**Bridgeport** · *Bridgeport C/C* · P.O. Box 541, 93517, P 800, M 42, (760) 932-7500, Fax same, bridgeportcalifornia@bridgeportcalifornia.com, www.bridgeportcalifornia.com

**Brisbane** · *Brisbane C/C* · Mitch Bull, Exec. Dir., 50 Park Place, 94005, P 3,700, M 211, (415) 467-7283, Fax (415) 467-5421, mitch.bull@brisbanechamber.com, www.brisbanechamber.com

**Buellton** · *Buellton C/C* · Kathy Vreeland, Exec. Dir., 597 Ave. of Flags, Ste. 101, P.O. Box 231, 93427, P 4,500, M 160, (805) 688-7829, (800) 324-3800, Fax (805) 688-5399, info@buellton.org, www.buellton.org.

**Buena Park** · *Buena Park Area C/C* · Gail S. Dixon, Pres./CEO, 6601 Beach Blvd., 90621, P 82,000, M 300, (714) 521-0261, Fax (714) 521-1851, info@buenaparkchamber.org, www.buenapark chamber.org

**Burbank** · *Burbank C/C* · Gary Olson, Pres./CEO, 200 W. Magnolia Blvd., 91502, P 105,000, M 1,000, (818) 846-3111, Fax (818) 846-0109, info@burbankchamber.org, www.burbankchamber.org

**Burlingame** · *Burlingame C/C* · Georgette Naylor, Pres./CEO, 290 California Dr., 94010, P 29,000, M 460, (650) 344-1735, Fax (650) 344-1763, info@burlingamechamber.org, www.burlingamechamber.org

**Burney** · *Burney C/C* · Sherri Quinlan, Exec. Dir., 37028 Main St., P.O. Box 36, 96013, P 4,500, M 120, (530) 335-2111, Fax (530) 335-2111, burneycc@c-zone.net, www.burneychamber.com

**Buttonwillow** · *Buttonwillow C/C* · 104 W. 2nd St., P.O. Box 251, 93206, P 1,266, M 112, (661) 764-5406, Fax (661) 764-5406, buttonwillowchamber@bak.rr.com, www.buttonwillowchamber.com

**Byron** · *see California Delta*

**Calabasas** · *Calabasas C/C* · Carol Washburn, CEO, 23564 Calabasas Rd., Ste. 101, 91302, P 25,000, M 522, (818) 222-5680, Fax (818) 222-5690, info@calabasaschamber.com, www.calabasaschamber.com

**Calaveras County** · *see Angels Camp*

**Calexico** · *Calexico C/C* · Hildy Carrillo-Rivera, Exec. Dir., 1100 Imperial Ave., P.O. Box 948, 92231, P 37,000, M 400, (760) 357-1166, Fax (760) 357-9043, calexicochamber@hotmail.com, www.calexicochamber.net

**California City** · *California City C/C* · Alverdia McMillian, Pres., 8001 California City Blvd., P.O. Box 2008, 93504, P 13,500, M 150, (760) 373-8676, Fax (760) 373-1414, californiacitychamber@verizon.net, www.californiacitychamber.com

**California Delta** · *California Delta C of C & Visitors Bur.* · Bill Wells, Exec. Dir., 169 W. Brannan Island Rd., Isleton, 95641, P 500,000, M 300, (916) 777-4041, Fax (916) 777-4042, info@californiadelta.org, www.californiadelta.org

**Calimesa** · *Calimesa C/C* · Nanette Peykani, Exec. Dir., 1007 Calimesa Blvd., Ste. D, 92320, P 8,200, M 125, (909) 795-7612, Fax (909) 795-2822, calimesachamber@cybertime.net, www.calimesachamber.org

**Calistoga** · *Calistoga C/C* · Rex Albright, Exec. Dir./CEO, 1506 Lincoln Ave., 94515, P 5,200, M 330, (707) 942-6333, (866) 306-5588, Fax (707) 942-9287, www.calistogavisitors.com, office@calistogachamber.com, www.calistogachamber.com

**Camarillo** · *Camarillo C/C* · Thomas P. Kelley, Pres./CEO, 2400 E. Ventura Blvd., 93010, P 66,000, M 800, (805) 484-4383, Fax (805) 484-1395, info@camarillochamber.org, www.camarillochamber.org

**Cambria** · *Cambria C/C* · Mary Ann Carson, Exec. Dir., 767 Main St., 93428, P 6,624, M 385, (805) 927-3624, Fax (805) 927-9426, info@cambriachamber.org, www.cambriachamber.org

**Cameron Park** · *see Shingle Springs*

**Campbell** · *Campbell C/C* · Betty Deal,.Exec. Dir., 1628 W. Campbell Ave., 95008, P 42,000, M 700, (408) 378-6252, Fax (408) 378-0192, ccoc@pacbell.net, www.campbellchamber.com.

**Canoga Park** · *Canoga Park/West Hills C/C* · Nora Ross, Exec. Dir., 7248 Owensmouth Ave., 91303, P 75,000, M 275, (818) 884-4222, Fax (818) 884-4604, info@cpwhchamber.org, www.cpwhchamber.org

**Canyon Country** · *see Santa Clarita*

**Canyon Lake** · *Canyon Lake C/C* · Lee Clark, Exec. Dir., 31640 Railroad Canyon Rd., 92587, P 13,356, M 194, (951) 244-6124, Fax (951) 244-0831, www.canyonlakechamber.net

**Capitola** • *Capitola-Soquel C/C* • Ms. Toni Castro, CEO, 716-G Capitola Ave., 95010, P 9,500, M 450, (831) 475-6522, (800) 474-6522, Fax (831) 475-6530, capcham@capitolachamber.com, www.capitolasoquelchamber.com

**Cardiff-By-The-Sea** • *Cardiff 101 C/C* • Brad Maassen, Pres., P.O. Box 552, 92007, P 18,000, M 100, (760) 436-0431, Fax (760) 753-0144, cardiff101chamber@gmail.com, www.cardiffbythesea.org

**Carlsbad** • *Carlsbad C/C* • Ted Owen, Pres./CEO, 5934 Priestly Dr., 92008, P 95,146, M 1,600, (760) 931-8400, Fax (760) 931-9153, carlsbadchamber@carlsbad.org, www.carlsbad.org

**Carmel** • *Carmel C/C* • Monta Potter, CEO, P.O. Box 4444, 93921, P 4,400, M 500, (831) 624-2522, (800) 550-4333, Fax (831) 624-1329, info@carmelcalifornia.org, www.carmelcalifornia.org

**Carmel Mountain Ranch** • *see San Diego North C/C*

**Carmel Valley** • *Carmel Valley C/C* • Elizabeth Suro, Managing Dir., 13 W. Carmel Valley Rd., Ste. 3, P.O. Box 288, 93924, P 15,000, M 250, (831) 644-9476, Fax (831) 659-8415, info@carmelvalleychamber.com, www.carmelvalleychamber.com

**Carmichael** • *Carmichael C/C* • Kris Kingdom, Exec. Dir., 6825 Fair Oaks Blvd., Ste. 100, 95608, P 72,000, M 325, (916) 481-1002, Fax (916) 481-1003, carmichaelchamber@sbcglobal.net, www.carmichaelchamber.com

**Carpinteria** • *Carpinteria Valley C/C* • Lynda Lang, CEO, 1056B Eugenia Pl., P.O. Box 956, 93014, P 14,600, M 400, (805) 684-5479, Fax (805) 684-3477, info@carpinteriachamber.org, www.carpinteriachamber.org

**Carson** • *Carson C/C* • John Wogan, Exec. Dir., 530 E. Del Amo Blvd., 90746, P 100,000, M 600, (310) 217-4590, Fax (310) 217-4591, wogan@carsonchamber.com, www.carsonchamber.com

**Cassel** • *see Burney*

**Castaic** • *see Santa Clarita*

**Castro Valley** • *Castro Valley/Eden Area C/C* • Roberta Rivet, Exec. Dir., 3467 Castro Valley Blvd., 94546, P 60,000, M 500, (510) 537-5300, Fax (510) 537-5335, info@castrovalleychamber.com, www.castrovalleychamber.com

**Castroville** • *North Monterey County C/C* • Gary DeAmaral, Pres, 10683 Merritt St., P.O. Box 744, 95012, P 13,000, M 200, (831) 633-2465, Fax (831) 633-0485, info@northmonterey countychamber.org, www.northmontereycountychamber.org

**Catalina Island** • *see Avalon*

**Cathedral City** • *Cathedral City C/C* • Steven Morris, Pres./CEO, 68-950 Hwy. 111, Ste. 106, 92234, P 57,000, M 400, (760) 328-1213, Fax (760) 321-0659, info@cathedralcitycc.com, www.cathedralcitycc.com

**Cayucos** • *Cayucos C/C* • Bill Shea, Pres., P.O. Box 346, 93430, P 3,500, M 90, (805) 995-1200, Fax (805) 995-1200, cayucoschamber@charter.net, www.cayucoschamber.com

**Cedarville** • *Surprise Valley C/C* • Nicole Munholand, Pres., P.O. Box 518, 96104, P 1,500, M 60, (530) 279-2001, Fax (530) 279-2012, contactsvc@surprisevalleychamber.com, www.surprise valleychamber.com

**Century City** • *see Los Angeles Area*

**Ceres** • *Ceres C/C* • Bertie Plante, Pres., 2491 Lawrence St., 95307, P 40,000, M 235, (209) 537-2601, Fax (209) 537-2699, chamber@cereschamber.org, www.cereschamber.org

**Cerritos** • *Cerritos Reg. C/C* • Catherine Gaughen, Exec. Dir., 13259 E. South St., 90703, P 51,488, M 475, (562) 467-0800, Fax (562) 467-0840, chamber@cerritos.org, www.cerritos.org

**Chatsworth** • *Chatsworth/Porter Ranch C/C* • Athena Boren, Exec. Dir., 10038 Old Depot Plaza Rd., 91311, P 90,000, M 300, (818) 341-2428, Fax (818) 341-4930, info@chatsworthchamber.com, www.chatsworthchamber.com

**Chester** • *Chester-Lake Almanor C/C* • Susan Bryner, Exec. Dir., 529 Main St., P.O. Box 1198, 96020, P 5,000, M 224, (530) 258-2426, (800) 350-4838, Fax (530) 258-2760, info@lakealmanor area.com, www.lakealmanorarea.com

**Chico** • *Chico C/C* • Jolene Francis, Pres./CEO, 300 Salem St., 95928, P 105,000, M 1,100, (530) 891-5556, (800) 852-8570, Fax (530) 891-3613, info@chicochamber.com, www.chicochamber.com

**Chino** • *Chino Valley C/C* • Andy Ronquillo, Pres./CEO, 13150 Seventh St., 91710, P 150,000, M 650, (909) 627-6177, Fax (909) 627-4180, info@chinovalleychamber.com, www.chinovalley chamber.com.

**Chowchilla** • *Chowchilla Dist. C/C* • Jacki Flanagan, Mgr., 228 Trinity Ave., Civic Center Plaza, 93610, P 18,780, M 200, (559) 665-5603, Fax (559) 665-0896, chamberofcommerce@ci.chowchilla.ca.us, www.ci.chowchilla.ca.us

**Chula Vista** • *Chula Vista C/C* • Lisa Cohen, CEO, 233 Fourth Ave., 91910, P 225,000, M 950, (619) 420-6602, Fax (619) 420-1269, lisa@chulavistachamber.org, www.chulavistachamber.org

**Citrus Heights** • *Citrus Heights Reg. C/C* • Bettie Cosby, CEO, 7115A Greenback Ln., P.O. Box 191, 95611, P 87,000, M 525, (916) 722-4545, Fax (916) 722-4543, chamber@chchamber.com, www.chchamber.com

**City of Industry** • *Industry Mfg. Cncl.* • Donald Sachs, Exec. Dir., 15651 Stafford St., 91744, P 800, M 2,500, (626) 968-3737, Fax (626) 330-5060, dsachs@cityofindustry.org, www.cityofindustry.org

**Claremont** • *Claremont C/C* • Maureen Aldridge, CEO, 205 Yale Ave., 91711, P 35,500, M 520, (909) 624-1681, Fax (909) 624-6629, contact@claremontchamber.org, www.claremontchamber.org.

**Clarksburg** • *see California Delta*

**Clearlake** • *Clearlake C/C* • Lori Peters, Exec. Dir., 3245 Bowers Rd., P.O. Box 5330, 95422, P 14,000, M 250, (707) 994-3600, Fax (707) 994-3603, clearlakechamber@yahoo.com, www.clearlake chamber.com

**Cloverdale** • *Cloverdale C/C* • Carla Howell, CEO, 105 N. Cloverdale Blvd., 95425, P 8,500, M 264, (707) 894-4470, Fax (707) 894-9568, chamberinfo@cloverdale.com, www.cloverdale.net

**Clovis** • *Clovis C/C* • Mark Blackney, Pres., 325 Pollasky Ave., 93612, P 100,000, M 1,150, (559) 299-7363, Fax (559) 299-2969, mark@clovischamber.com, www.clovischamber.com

**Coachella** • *Coachella C/C* • Cynthia J Tinoco, Exec. Dir., 1258 Sixth St., 92236, P 35,000, M 200, (760) 398-8089, Fax (760) 398-8589, contact@coachellachamber.com, www.coachellachamber.com

**Coalinga** • *Coalinga Area C/C* • Marilyn Gabriel, CEO, 380 Coalinga Plaza, 93210, P 18,061, M 125, (559) 935-2948, (800) 854-3885, Fax (559) 935-9044, exec@coalingachamber.com, www.coalingachamber.com

**Coleville** • *see Topaz*

**Colfax** • *Colfax Area C/C* • Dorothy Elliot, Exec. Dir., P.O. Box 86, 95713, P 100,000, M 173, (530) 346-8888, Fax (530) 346-8888, railcar@colfaxarea.com, www.colfaxarea.com

**Collinsville** • *see California Delta*

**Colma** • *see Daly City*

**Colton** · *Colton C/C* · 655 N. La Cadena Dr., 92324, P 52,400, M 275, (909) 825-2222, Fax (909) 824-1650, colton.chamber@ sbcglobal.net, www.coltonchamber.org

**Columbia** · *Columbia C/C* · Mike Keene, Pres., P.O. Box 1824, 95310, P 5,000, M 30, (209) 536-1672, info@columbiacalifornia. com, www.columbiacalifornia.com

**Colusa** · *Colusa County C/C* · Lloyd Green Jr., Pres., 2963 Davison Ct., 95932, P 22,000, M 240, (530) 458-5525, Fax (530) 458-8180, www.colusacountychamber.com

**Commerce** · *Commerce Ind. Cncl.-Chamber of Commerce* · Eddie Tafoya, Exec. Dir., 6055 E. Washington Blvd., Ste. 120, 90091, P 13,400, M 340, (323) 728-7222, Fax (323) 728-7565, eddie@ industrialcouncil.org, www.industrialcouncil.org

**Compton** · *Compton C/C* · Lestean Johnson, Pres., 700 N. Bullis Rd., Ste. 6A, 90221, P 130,000, M 300, (310) 631-8611, Fax (310) 631-2066, CptChamber@aol.com, www.comptonchamberof commerce.com

**Compton** · *Latino C/C* · 208 N. Long Beach Blvd, P.O. Box 449, 90221, P 130,000, (310) 639-4455

**Concord** · *Greater Concord C/C* · 2280 Diamond Blvd., Ste. 200, 94520, P 127,600, M 700, (925) 685-1181, Fax (925) 685-5623, info@concordchamber.com, www.concordchamber.com

**Corcoran** · *Corcoran C/C* · Darrell Frey, Exec. Dir., 1099 Otis Ave., P.O. Box 459, 93212, P 14,000, M 160, (559) 992-4514, Fax (559) 992-2341, darrell@corcoranchamber.com, www.corcoran chamber.com

**Corning** · *Corning Dist. C/C* · Valanne Cardenas, Mgr., 1110 Solano St., P.O. Box 871, 96021, P 7,200, M 290, (530) 824-5550, Fax (530) 824-9499, corningchamber@sbcglobal.net, corning chamber.org.

**Corona** · *Corona C/C* · Bobby Spiegel, Pres./CEO, 904 E. Sixth St., 92879, P 146,000, M 1,400, (951) 737-3350, Fax (951) 737-3531, info@coronachamber.org, www.coronachamber.org

**Corona del Mar** · *Corona del Mar C/C* · Linda Leonhard, Pres./ CEO, 2855 E. Coast Hwy., Ste. 101, 92625, P 14,500, M 400, (949) 673-4050, Fax (949) 673-3940, info@cdmchamber.com, www. cdmchamber.com

**Coronado** · *Coronado C/C* · Karen Finch, CEO, 875 Orange Ave., Ste. 102, 92118, P 26,000, M 400, (619) 435-9260, Fax (619) 522-6577, info@coronadochamber.com, www.coronadochamber.com.

**Corte Madera** · *Corte Madera C/C* · Julie Kritzberger, Exec. Dir., 129 Corte Madera Town Center, 94925, P 9,700, M 214, (415) 924-0441, Fax (415) 924-1839, chamber@cortemadera.org, www. cortemadera.org

**Costa Mesa** · *Costa Mesa C/C* · Ed Fawcett, Pres./CEO, 1700 Adams Ave., Ste. 101, 92626, P 113,440, M 720, (714) 885-9090, Fax (714) 885-9094, efawcett@costamesachamber.com, www. costamesachamber.com

**Cotati** · *Cotati C/C* · Suzanne Whipple, Exec. Dir., 216 E. School St., P.O. Box 592, 94931, P 7,200, M 180, (707) 795-5508, Fax (707) 795-5868, chamber@cotati.org, www.cotati.org

**Cottonwood** · *Cottonwood C/C* · Cheri Skudlarek, Pres., P.O. Box 584, 96022, P 13,000, M 90, (530) 347-6800, Fax (530) 347-6800, cskudlarek@novb.com, www.cottonwoodcofc.org

**Coulterville** · *Mariposa County C/C & Coulterville Visitor Center* · Nina Coleman, Ofc. Mgr., 5007 Main St., P.O. Box 333, 95311, P 115, M 25, (209) 878-3074, coultervillevc@sti.net

**Courtland** · *see California Delta*

**Covelo** · *Round Valley C/C* · Greg Braden, Pres., P.O. Box 458, 95428, P 3,000, M 150, (707) 983-6413, info@roundvalley.org, www.roundvalley.org

**Covina** · *Covina C/C* · Dawn Nelson, Pres./CEO, 935 W. Badillo, Ste. 100, 91722, P 48,000, M 630, (626) 967-4191, Fax (626) 966-9660, chamber@covina.org, www.covina.org

**Crenshaw** · *see Los Angeles Area C/C*

**Crescent City** · *Crescent City-Del Norte County C/C* · Gina Zottola, Exec. Dir., 1001 Front St., 95531, P 28,000, M 445, (707) 464-3174, (800) 343-8300, Fax (707) 464-9676, ccchamber@ charterinternet.com, www.delnorte.org

**Crestline** · *Crestline C/C* · Dave Lanham, Pres., 24385 Lake Dr., P.O. Box 926, 92325, P 16,000, M 115, (909) 338-2706, info@ crestlinechamber.net, www.crestlinechamber.net

**Crockett** · *Crockett C/C* · Aimee Lohr, Pres., 1214 Pomona St., P.O. Box 191, 94525, P 3,300, M 110, (510) 787-1155, Fax (510) 787-1155, crockettchamber@aol.com, www.crockettca-chamber.org

**Cuddy Valley** · *see Frazier Park*

**Culver City** · *Culver City C/C* · Steven J. Rose, Pres., 4249 Overland Ave., 90230, P 40,000, M 775, (310) 287-3850, Fax (310) 287-1350, steve@culvercitychamber.com, www.culvercity chamber.com

**Cupertino** · *Cupertino C/C* · Suzi Blackman, CEO, 20455 Silverado Ave., 95014, P 55,000, M 400, (408) 252-7054, Fax (408) 252-0638, info@cupertino-chamber.org, www.cupertino-chamber.org

**Cypress** · *Cypress C/C* · Ed Munson, Exec. Dir., 5550 Cerritos Ave. #D, 90630, P 48,000, M 260, (714) 827-2430, Fax (714) 827-1229, ed.munson@cypresschamber.org, www.cypresschamber.org

**Daggett** · *Daggett C/C* · Velma Stark, Treas., P.O. Box 327, 92327, P 1,000, M 18, (760) 254-2594

**Daly City** · *Daly City-Colma C/C* · Georgette Sarles, Pres./ CEO, 355 Gellert Blvd., Ste. 138, 94015, P 101,000, M 535, (650) 755-3900, Fax (650) 755-5160, staff@dalycity-colmachamber.org, www.dalycity-colmachamber.org

**Dana Point** · *Dana Point C/C* · Nichole Chambers, Pres./CEO, 24681 La Plaza, Ste. 115, 92629, P 38,000, M 350, (949) 496-1555, (800) 290-DANA, Fax (949) 496-5321, chamber@danapoint chamber.com, www.danapointchamber.com

**Danville** · *Danville Area C/C* · Melony Newman, Pres./CEO, 117-E Town & Country Dr., 94526, P 65,000, M 600, (925) 837-4400, Fax (925) 837-5709, office@danvilleareachamber.com, www.danvilleareachamber.com

**Davis** · *Davis C/C* · Christi Skibbins, Exec. Dir., 130 G St., Ste. B, 95616, P 64,000, M 700, (530) 756-5160, Fax (530) 756-5190, askus@davischamber.com, www.davischamber.com

**Death Valley** · *see Shoshone*

**Del Mar** · *Del Mar Reg. C/C* · Nancy Wasko, CEO, 1104 Camino Del Mar, Ste. 1, 92014, P 43,500, M 425, (858) 755-4844, Fax (858) 793-5293, info@delmarchamber.org, www.delmarchamber.org

**Delano** · *Delano C/C* · Carla Lapadula, Exec. Dir., 931 High St., 93215, P 50,000, M 216, (661) 725-2518, Fax (661) 725-4743, chamberofdelano@sbcglobal.net, www.chamberofdelano.com

**Desert Hot Springs** · *Desert Hot Springs C/C* · Eric Pontius, Pres.carole@deserthotsprings.com, 11-711 West Dr., 92240, P 22,000, M 300, (760) 329-6403, (800) 346-3347, Fax (760) 329-2833, info2@deserthotsprings.com, www.deserthotsprings.com

**Diablo** · *see Danville*

**Diamond Bar** • *Reg. Chamber of Commerce-San Gabriel Valley* • Heidi Gallegos, Exec. Dir./CEO, 21845 E. Copley Dr., Ste. 1170, 91765, P 65,000, M 370, (909) 860-1904, Fax (909) 860-6064, info@regionalchambersgv.com, www.regionalchambersgv.org.

**Dinuba** • *Dinuba C/C* • Exec. Dir., 210 North L St., 93618, P 20,007, M 162, (559) 591-2707, (559) 591-7000, Fax (559) 591-2712, dinubachamber@sbcglobal.net, www.dinubacommerce.org.

**Discovery Bay** • *Discovery Bay C/C* • 2465 Discovery Bay Blvd., Ste. 200, 94505, P 16,000, M 140, (925) 240-6600, (888) 832-3291, info@discoverybaychamber.com, www.discovery baychamber.com

**Dixon** • *Dixon Dist. C/C* • Tiffany Wing, Exec. Dir., 220 N. Jefferson St., P.O. Box 159, 95620, P 18,000, M 278, (707) 678-2650, Fax (707) 678-3654, info@dixonchamber.org, www.dixonchamber.org.

**Dorris** • *Butte Valley C/C* • Gene Lane, Pres., P.O. Box 541, 96023, P 2,500, M 40, (530) 397-3711, Fax (530) 397-3711, contact@ buttevalleychamber.com, www.buttevalleychamber.com

**Downey** • *Downey C/C* • Susan Nordin, Exec. Dir., 11131 Brookshire Ave., 90241, P 110,000, M 500, (562) 923-2191, Fax (562) 869-0461, downeychamber@aol.com, www.downey chamber.com

**Duarte** • *Duarte C/C* • Jim Kirchner, Pres./CEO, 1105 Oak Ave., P.O. Box 1438, 91009, P 22,000, M 300, (626) 357-3333, Fax (626) 357-3645, diana@duartechamber.com, www.duartechamber.com

**Dublin** • *Dublin C/C* • Nancy Feeley, Pres./CEO, 7080 Donlon Way, Ste. 110, 94568, P 48,000, M 400, (925) 828-6200, Fax (925) 828-4247, info@dublinchamberofcommerce.org, www.dublin chamberofcommerce.org

**Dunlap** • *see Miramonte*

**Dunsmuir** • *Dunsmuir C of C & Visitors Center* • Denise Bailey, Ofc. Mgr., 5915 Dunsmuir Ave., Ste. 100, 96025, P 1,800, M 100, (530) 235-2177, (800) DUNSMUIR, Fax (530) 235-0911, chamber@ dunsmuir.com, www.dunsmuir.com

**Eagle Rock** • *Eagle Rock C/C* • Michael A. Nogueira, Pres., P.O. Box 41354, 90041, P 39,000, M 120, (323) 257-2197, erccwebguy@aol.com, www.eaglerockchamberofcommerce.com

**Eagleville** • *see Cedarville*

**East Los Angeles** • *see Los Angeles-East Los Angeles C/C*

**El Cajon** • *San Diego East County C/C* • Mike Cully, Pres./CEO, 201 S. Magnolia Ave., 92020, P 151,000, M 800, (619) 440-6161, Fax (619) 440-6164, eccham@eastcountychamber.org, www.eastcountychamber.org

**El Centro** • *El Centro C/C & Visitors Bur.* • Cathy Kennerson, CEO, 1095 S. 4th St., P.O. Box 3006, 92244, P 42,000, M 800, (760) 352-3681, Fax (760) 352-3246, info@elcentrochamber.com, www.elcentrochamber.com.

**El Cerrito** • *El Cerrito C/C* • Mark L. Scott, Mgr., 406 Colusa Ave., P.O. Box 538, 94530, P 23,200, M 220, (510) 705-1202, info@ elcerritochamber.org, www.elcerritochamber.org

**El Dorado Hills** • *El Dorado Hills C/C* • Debbie Manning, Pres./ CEO, 981 Governors Dr., Ste. 103, P.O. Box 5055, 95762, P 32,000, M 600, (916) 933-1335, Fax (916) 933-5908, chamber@eldorado-hillschamber.org, www.eldoradohillschamber.org

**El Monte** • *El Monte/South El Monte C/C* • Richard Nichols, Exec. Dir., 10505 Valley Blvd., Ste. 312, P.O. Box 5866, 91734, P 135,000, M 500, (626) 443-0180, Fax (626) 443-0463, chamber@emsem. com, www.emsem.com.

**El Segundo** • *El Segundo C/C* • Marsha Hansen, Exec. Dir., 427 Main St., 90245, P 16,000, M 380, (310) 322-1220, Fax (310) 322-6880, info@elsegundochamber.org, www.elsegundochamber.org

**El Sobrante** • *El Sobrante C/C* • Janice Harmon, Secy., 3769 San Pablo Dam Rd., Ste. B, 94803, P 40,000, M 100, (510) 223-0757

**Elk Grove** • *Elk Grove C/C* • Janet Toppenberg, Pres./CEO, 9370 Studio Ct., Ste. 110, 95758, P 131,000, M 700, (916) 691-3760, Fax (916) 691-3810, chamber@elkgroveca.com, www.elkgroveca.com

**Emeryville** • *Emeryville C/C* • Bob Canter, Pres./CEO, 3980 Harlan St., 94608, P 9,500, M 150, (510) 652-5223, Fax (510) 652-4223, info@emeryvillechamber.com, www.emeryville chamber.com

**Encinitas** • *Encinitas Chamber & Visitors Center* • 1106 Second St., Ste. 112, 92024, P 62,000, M 600, (760) 753-6041, Fax (760) 753-6270, info@encinitaschamber.com, www. encinitaschamber.com

**Encino** • *Encino C/C* • Diana Donovan, CEO, 4933 Balboa Blvd., 91316, P 44,000, M 530, (818) 789-4711, Fax (818) 789-2485, info@encinochamber.org, www.encinochamber.org

**Escalon** • *Escalon C/C* • Pat Brown, Pres., 1111 First St. , PMB 1356, 95320, P 8,000, M 75, (209) 838-2793, escalonba@yahoo. com, www.escalonchambersite.org

**Escondido** • *Escondido C/C* • Harvey Mitchell, CEO, 720 N. Broadway, 92025, P 141,000, M 845, (760) 745-2125, Fax (760) 745-1183, info@ escondidochamber.org, www.escondidochamber.org

**Esparto** • *Esparto Dist. C/C* • Tom Frederick, Pres., P.O. Box 194, 95627, P 3,500, M 87, (530) 787-3242, espartochamber@mac. com, www.espartoregionalchamber.org

**Etna** • *Scott Valley C/C* • Marilyn Seward, Secy./Treas., P.O. Box 374, 96027, P 8,000, M 25, (530) 467-3355, www.scottvalley.org

**Eureka** • *Greater Eureka C/C* • J Warren Hockaday, Pres./CEO, 2112 Broadway, 95501, P 45,000, M 650, (707) 442-3738, (800) 356-6381, Fax (707) 442-0079, chamber@eurekachamber.com, www.eurekachamber.com

**Exeter** • *Exeter C/C* • Sandy Blankenship, Exec. Dir., 101 W. Pine St., 93221, P 10,700, M 335, (559) 592-2919, Fax (559) 592-3720, chamber@exeterchamber.com, www.exeterchamber.com.

**Fair Oaks** • *Fair Oaks C/C* • Jan Bass Otto, Exec. Dir., 10224 Fair Oaks Blvd., P.O. Box 352, 95628, P 50,000, M 350, (916) 967-2903, Fax (916) 967-8536, info@fairoakschamber.com, www.fairoaks chamber.com.

**Fairfax** • *Fairfax C/C* • Ingrid Weiss, Exec. Dir., P.O. Box 1111, 94978, P 7,500, M 80, (415) 453-5928, www.fairfaxcoc.com

**Fairfield** • *Fairfield-Suisun C/C* • G. Leslie Fay, Pres./CEO, 1111 Webster St., 94533, P 120,000, M 700, (707) 425-4625, Fax (707) 425-0826, reception@ffsc-chamber.com, www.ffsc-chamber.com

**Fall River Mills** • *Fall River Valley C/C* • Ed Siegal, Pres., P.O. Box 475, 96028, P 4,000, M 70, (530) 336-5840, gemsjaz@gmail.com, www.fallrivervalleycc.org

**Fallbrook** • *Fallbrook C/C* • Robert K. Leonard, CEO, 233 E. Mission Rd., 92028, P 41,000, M 525, (760) 728-5845, Fax (760) 728-4031, bob@fallbrookchamber.com, www.fallbrookchamber.com.

**Ferndale** • *Ferndale C/C* • P.O. Box 325, 95536, P 1,400, M 132, (707) 786-4477, Fax (707) 786-4477, ferndale@humboldt1.com, www.victorianferndale.org/chamber

**Fillmore** • *Fillmore C/C* • Mike McMahan, Pres., 557 Ventura St., P.O. Box 815, 93016, P 15,000, M 75, (805) 524-0351, Fax (805) 524-2551, info@fillmorechamber.com, www.fillmorechamber.com

**Folsom** • *Folsom C/C* • Joseph P. Gagliardi, CEO, 200 Wool St., 95630, P 73,000, M 1,050, (916) 985-2698, (916) 985-5555 or (800) 377-1414 Events, Fax (916) 985-4117, reception@folsom chamber.com, www.folsomchamber.com, www.visitfolsom.com

**Fontana** · *Fontana C/C* · David Pulido, Pres./CEO, 8491 Sierra Ave., 92335, P 190,000, M 440, (909) 822-4433, Fax (909) 822-6238, david@fontanachamber.com, www.fontanachamber.com

**Foothill Farms** · *see North Highlands*

**Foresthill** · *Foresthill-Divide C/C* · Sean Salveson, Pres., 24600 Main St., Ste. A, P.O. Box 346, 95631, P 6,000, M 150, (530) 367-2474, Fax (530) 367-2474, foresthillchamber@ftcnet.net, www.foresthillchamber.org

**Forestville** · *Forestville C/C* · Leslie Zumwalt, P.O. Box 546, 95436, P 8,000, M 75, (707) 887-1111, Fax (707) 887-0106, www.forestvillechamber.org

**Fort Bidwell** · *see Cedarville*

**Fort Bragg** · *Mendocino Coast C/C* · Debra DeGraw, CEO, 217 S. Main St., P.O. Box 1141, 95437, P 20,000, M 546, (707) 961-6300, Fax (707) 964-2056, chamber@mcn.org, www.mendocinocoast.com.

**Fortuna** · *Fortuna C/C* · Erin Dunn, Exec. Dir., 735 14th St., P.O. Box 797, 95540, P 11,350, M 455, (707) 725-3959, (800) 426-8166, Fax (707) 725-4766, chamber@sunnyfortuna.com, www.discovertheredwoods.com.

**Foster City** · *Foster City C/C* · Mae Heagerty-Matos, Pres./CEO, 1031 E. Hillsdale Blvd., Ste. F, 94404, P 30,359, M 290, (650) 573-7600, Fax (650) 573-5201, info@fostercitychamber.com, www.fostercitychamber.com

**Fountain Valley** · *Fountain Valley C/C* · Beverly White, Exec. Dir., 8840 Warner Ave., Ste. 207, 92708, P 58,000, M 300, (714) 841-3822, Fax (714) 841-3877, bwhite@fvchamber.com, www.fvchamber.com

**Fowler** · *Fowler C/C* · Craig J. Mellon, Pres., 420 E. Merced St., Ste. 100, 93625, P 5,500, M 105, (559) 834-3869, Fax (559) 834-5318, fowlerchamber@yahoo.com, www.fowlerchamber.com

**Frazier Park** · *Mountain Comm. C/C* · Pamela Low, Pres., P.O. Box 552, 93225, P 10,000, M 80, (661) 245-1212, 1mccoc@gmail.com, www.frazierparkinfo.com

**Freeport** · *see California Delta*

**Fremont** · *Fremont C/C* · Cindy Bonior, Pres./CEO, 39488 Stevenson Pl., Ste. 100, 94539, P 213,000, M 1,200, (510) 795-2244, Fax (510) 795-2240, fmtcc@fremontbusiness.com, www.fremontbusiness.com

**French Camp** · *see California Delta*

**Fresno** · *Central Calif. Hispanic C/C* · John Hernandez, Exec. Dir, 2331 Fresno St., 93721, P 1,200,000, M 621, (559) 495-4817, Fax (559) 495-4811, info@cchcc.net, www.cchcc.net

**Fresno** · *Greater Fresno Area C/C* · Al Smith, Pres./CEO, 2331 Fresno St., 93721, P 862,600, M 2,000, (559) 495-4800, Fax (559) 495-4811, info@fresnochamber.com, www.fresnochamber.com

**Friant** · *Millerton Lake Area C/C* · P.O. Box 430, 93626, P 520, (559) 822-7450

**Fruitvale** · *see Bakersfield-North of the River C/C*

**Fullerton** · *Fullerton C/C* · Theresa Harvey, Exec. Dir., 444 N. Harbor Blvd., Ste. 200, P.O. Box 529, 92836-0529, P 132,721, M 700, (714) 871-3100, Fax (714) 871-2871, questions@fullertonchamber.com, www.fullertonchamber.com

**Galt** · *Galt Dist. C/C* · 431 S. Lincoln Way, P.O. Box 1446, 95632, P 22,000, M 300, (209) 745-2529, info@galtchamber.com, www.galtchamber.com

**Garberville** · *Garberville-Redway Area C/C* · Dee Dower, Exec. Dir., 782 Redwood Dr., P.O. Box 445, 95542, P 15,000, M 220, (707) 923-2613, (800) 923-2613, Fax (707) 923-4789, chamber@garberville.org, www.garberville.org

**Garden Grove** · *Garden Grove C/C* · Connie Margolin, Pres./CEO, 12866 Main St., Ste. 102, 92840, P 172,000, M 360, (714) 638-7950, (800) 959-5560, Fax (714) 636-6672, connie.margolin@gardengrovechamber.org, www.gardengrovechamber.org

**Gardena** · *Gardena Valley C/C* · Wanda Love, Pres., 1204 W. Gardena Blvd. #E, 90247, P 69,000, M 435, (310) 532-9905, Fax (310) 329-7307, gardenacc@sbcglobal.net, www.gardenachamber.com

**Geyserville** · *Geyserville C/C* · Harry Bosworth, Pres., P.O. Box 276, 95441, P 1,650, M 272, (707) 857-3745, moreinfo@geyservillecc.com, www.geyservillecc.com

**Gilroy** · *Gilroy C/C* · Susan Valenta, Pres./CEO, 7471 Monterey St., 95020, P 51,000, M 740, (408) 842-6437, Fax (408) 842-6010, chamber@gilroy.org, www.gilroy.org

**Glendale** · *Glendale C/C* · Judee Kendall, Exec. V.P., 200 S. Louise St., 91205, P 207,000, M 1,100, (818) 240-7870, Fax (818) 240-2872, info@glendalechamber.com, www.glendalechamber.com

**Glendale** · *Montrose-Verdugo City C/C* · Marian Jocz, Exec. Dir., 3516 N. Verdugo Rd., 91208, P 6,528, M 350, (818) 249-7171, Fax (818) 249-8919, mvcc@montrosechamber.org, www.montrosechamber.org

**Glendora** · *Glendora C/C* · Kathy Hodge, Dir. of Op., 131 E. Foothill Blvd., 91741, P 52,770, M 450, (626) 963-4128, Fax (626) 914-4822, info@glendora-chamber.org, www.glendora-chamber.org

**Goleta** · *Goleta Valley C/C* · Kristen Amyx, Pres./CEO, 271 N. Fairview, Ste. 104, P.O. Box 781, 93116, P 86,000, M 550, (805) 967-2500, Fax (805) 967-4615, info@goletavalley.com, www.goletavalleychamber.com

**Gonzales** · *Gonzales C/C* · Julia Rocha, Pres., P.O. Box 216, 93926, P 7,800, M 55, (831) 675-9019, gonzaleschamber@sbcglobal.net, www.gonzaleschamber.org

**Gorman** · *see Frazier Park*

**Graeagle** · *Eastern Plumas C/C* · Betty Heck, Mgr., 8989 Hwy. 89, P.O. Box 1043, 96103, P 8,000, M 235, (530) 836-6811, (800) 995-6057, Fax (530) 836-6809, epluchmb@psln.com, www.easternplumaschamber.com

**Granada Hills** · *Granada Hills C/C* · Irv Selman, Pres., 17723 Chatsworth St., 91344, P 57,000, M 300, (818) 368-3235, Fax (818) 366-7425, email@granadachamber.com, www.granadachamber.com

**Grand Terrace** · *Grand Terrace Area C/C* · Jessica Borzilleri, Pres., 21900 Barton Rd., Ste. 102, 92313, P 15,600, M 150, (909) 783-3581, Fax (909) 370-2906, office@gtchamber.com, www.gtchamber.com

**Granite Bay** · *see Roseville*

**Grass Valley** · *Grass Valley/Nevada County C/C* · Mary Ann Mueller, Pres./CEO, 248 Mill St., 95945, P 12,000, M 600, (530) 273-4667, (800) 655-4667, Fax (530) 272-5440, info@grassvalleychamber.com, www.grassvalleychamber.com

**Greenville** · *Indian Valley C/C* · Mr. Huddleston, Pres., 408 Main St., P.O. Box 516, 95947, P 2,750, M 90, (530) 284-6633, Fax (530) 284-6907, indianvalleychamber@frontiernet.net, www.indianvalley.net

**Gridley** · *Gridley Area C/C* · 613 Kentucky St., 95948, P 5,650, M 151, (530) 846-3142, Fax (530) 846-7165, gridleychamber@hotmail.com, gridleyareachamber.com

**Griffith Park** · *see Los Angeles-Atwater Village C/C*

**Groveland** · *Yosemite C/C* · Jackie Sample, Admin. Asst., P.O. Box 1263, 95321, P 5,000, M 140, (209) 962-0429, (800) 449-9120, info@groveland.org, www.groveland.org

**Grover Beach** · *Grover Beach C/C* · Margo Mason, Exec. Dir., 180 Hwy. 1, 93433, P 13,130, M 200, (805) 489-9091, Fax (805) 489-4147, info@groverbeachchamber.com, www.groverbeach chamber.com

**Gualala** · *Redwood Coast C/C* · Marla Skibbins, Pres., P.O. Box 199, 95445, P 6,000, M 160, (707) 884-1080, (800) 778-5252, Fax (707) 884-1620, info@redwoodcoastchamber.com, www. redwoodcoastchamber.com

**Guerneville** · *Russian River C/C & Visitor Center* · Margaret Kennett, Pres., 16209 First St., P.O. Box 331, 95446, P 7,000, M 250, (707) 869-9000, Fax (707) 869-9009, info@russianriver. com, www.russianriver.com

**Gustine** · *Gustine C/C* · Glen Beard, Pres., 375 5th St., P.O. Box 306, 95322, P 5,200, M 150, (209) 854-6975, Fax (209) 854-3511, gustinechamber@inreach.com, www.gustinechamberof commerce.com

**Half Moon Bay** · *Half Moon Bay Coastside C/C & Visitors Bur.* · Charise McHugh, Pres./CEO, 235 Main St., 94019, P 28,000, M 720, (650) 726-8380, Fax (650) 726-8389, info@hmbchamber. com, www.hmbchamber.com

**Hanford** · *Hanford C/C* · Hope Morikawa, CEO, 200 Santa Fe Ave., Ste. D, 93230, P 50,000, M 750, (559) 582-0483, Fax (559) 582-0960, hope@hanfordchamber.com, www.hanfordchamber.com

**Happy Camp** · *Happy Camp C/C* · Chris Sorensen, Pres., P.O. Box 1188, 96039, P 1,277, M 50, (530) 493-2900, info@happycamp-chamber.com, www.happycampchamber.com

**Harbor Gateway-Torrance** · *Harbor City-Harbor Gateway C/C* · Joeann Valle, Exec. Dir., 19401 S. Vermont Ave., Ste. I102, 90502, P 50,000, M 300, (310) 516-7933, Fax (310) 516-7734, hchgchamber@sbcglobal.net, www.hchgchamber.com

**Hat Creek** · *see Burney*

**Hawthorne** · *Hawthorne C/C* · Sherice Fernandez, Ofc. Mgr., 4444 El Segundo Blvd., 90250, P 87,000, M 230, (310) 676-1163, Fax (310) 676-7661, info@hawthorne-chamber.com, www. hawthorne-chamber.com

**Hayfork** · *see Trinity County*

**Hayward** · *Hayward C/C* · Jim Wieder, Pres./CEO, 22561 Main St., 94541, P 149,800, M 750, (510) 537-2424, Fax (510) 537-2730, info@hayward.org, www.hayward.org

**Healdsburg** · *Healdsburg C/C* · Craig Schmidt, Pres., 217 Healdsburg Ave., 95448, P 13,000, M 750, (707) 433-6935, Fax (707) 433-7562, info@healdsburg.com, www.healdsburg.com

**Helendale** · *Helendale C/C* · Kristi Rossman, Pres., P.O. Box 1449, 92342, P 7,000, M 150, (760) 952-2231, Fax (760) 952-2231, www.helendalechamberofcommerce.org

**Hemet** · *Hemet/San Jacinto Valley C/C* · Patti Drusky, Pres./CEO, 615 N. San Jacinto, 92543, P 150,000, M 1,000, (951) 658-3211, Fax (951) 766-5013, info@hemetsanjacintochamber.com, www. hemetsanjacintochamber.com

**Hercules** · *Hercules C/C* · Shirley Gotelli, Exec. Dir., 500 Alfred Nobel Dr., Ste. 195, P.O. Box 5283, 94547, P 25,000, M 120, (510) 741-7945, Fax (510) 741-8965, office@herculeschamber.com, www.herculeschamber.com

**Hermosa Beach** · *Hermosa Beach C/C* · Carla Merrimen, Exec. Dir., 1007 Hermosa Ave., 90254, P 18,585, M 350, (310) 376-0951, Fax (310) 798-2594, info@hbchamber.net, www.hbchamber.net

**Hesperia** · *Hesperia C/C* · Yvonne Woytovich, Pres./CEO, 16816 Main St., Ste. D, 92345, P 91,000, M 500, (760) 244-2135, Fax (760) 244-1333, info@hesperiachamber.org, www.hesperia chamber.org

**Highland** · *Highland C/C* · Lindsay Mingee, Exec. Dir., 7750 Palm Ave., Ste. N, P.O. Box 455, 92346, P 53,000, M 368, (909) 864-4073, Fax (909) 864-4583, hcoc@highlandchamber.org, www.highlandchamber.org

**Hilmar** · *Hilmar C/C* · Carlos Rocha, Pres., P.O. Box 385, 95324, P 5,000, M 110, (209) 632-2028

**Hollister** · *San Benito County C/C* · Jessica French, Exec. Dir., 650 San Benito St., Ste. 130, 95023, P 57,000, M 540, (831) 637-5315, Fax (831) 637-1008, info1@sanbenitocountychamber.com, www.sanbenitocountychamber.com

**Hollywood** · *Hollywood C/C* · Leron Gubler, Pres./CEO, 7018 Hollywood Blvd., 90028, P 300,000, M 1,075, (323) 469-8311, Fax (323) 469-2805, leron@hollywoodchamber.net, www.hollywood chamber.net

**Holtville** · *Holtville C/C* · Matt Hester, Pres., 101 W. 5th St., 92250, P 6,000, M 180, (760) 356-2923, Fax (760) 356-2925, holtvillechamber@yahoo.com, www.holtvillechamber.com

**Hood** · *see California Delta*

**Hopland** · *see Ukiah*

**Huntington Beach** · *Huntington Beach C/C* · Joyce Riddell, Pres., 19891 Beach Blvd., Ste. 140, 92648, P 200,000, M 1,030, (714) 536-8888, Fax (714) 960-7654, hbchamber@hbcoc.com, www.hbchamber.org.

**Huntington Park** · *Greater Huntington Park Area C/C* · Dante D'Eramo, Exec. Dir./CEO, 6330 Pacific Blvd., Ste. 208, 90255, P 60,000, M 550, (323) 585-1155, Fax (323) 585-2176, info@ hpchamber1.com, www.hpchamber1.com.

**Idyllwild** · *Idyllwild C/C* · P.O. Box 304, 92549, P 3,000, M 132, (951) 659-3259, (888) 659-3259, Fax (951) 659-6216, info@ idyllwildchamber.com, www.idyllwildchamber.com

**Imperial** · *Imperial C/C* · Meredith Jones, Exec. Dir., 101 E. Fourth St., 92251, P 15,000, M 300, (760) 355-1609, Fax (760) 355-3920, info@imperialchamber.org, www.imperialchamber.org.

**Imperial Beach** · *Imperial Beach C/C & Visitors Bur.* · Cynthia Melcher, Pres., 702 Seacoast Dr., 91932, P 27,800, M 207, (619) 424-3151, Fax (619) 424-3008, ibchamber@yahoo.com, www. ib-chamber.com

**Independence** · *Independence C/C* · Beth White, Pres., 139 N. Edwards St., P.O. Box 397, 93526, P 600, M 70, (760) 878-0084, info@independence-ca.com, www.independence-ca.com

**Indian Wells** · *Indian Wells C/C* · Ruth Finholt, Exec. Dir./CEO, 74-980 Hwy. 111, Ste. 101, 92210, P 4,800, M 300, (760) 346-7095, Fax (760) 346-7605, info@indianwellschamber.com, www. indianwellschamber.com

**Indio** · *Indio C/C* · 82-921 Indio Blvd., 92201, P 83,000, M 650, (760) 347-0676, (800) 775-8440, Fax (760) 347-6069, info@ indiochamber.org, www.indiochamber.org

**Inglewood** · *Inglewood/Airport Area C/C* · Shannon R. Howe, Exec. V.P., 330 E. Queen St., 90301, P 149,000, M 700, (310) 677-1121, Fax (310) 677-1001, inglewoodchamber@sbcglobal.net, www.inglewoodchamber.org.

**Irvine** · *Irvine C/C* · Jacquie Warren, Pres./CEO, 2485 McCabe Way, Ste. 150, 92614, P 202,000, M 1,000, (949) 660-9112, Fax (949) 660-0829, icc@irvinechamber.com, www.irvinechamber.com

**Irvine** · *Orange County Bus. Cncl.* · Lucy Dunn, Pres./CEO, 2 Park Plaza, Ste. 100, 92614, P 3,000,000, M 250, (949) 476-2242, Fax (949) 476-9240, www.ocbc.org

**Irwindale** · *Irwindale C/C* · Lisa Bailey, Pres./CEO, 16102 Arrow Highway, P.O. Box 2307, 91706, P 1,446, M 306, (626) 960-6606, Fax (626) 960-3868, info@irwindalechamber.org, www.irwindalechamber.org

**Isleton** · *Isleton C/C* · Charline Hand, Pres., P.O. Box 758, 95641, P 838, M 70, (916) 777-5880, Fax (916) 777-4330, isletoncoc@citilink.net, www.isletoncoc.org

**Jackson** · *Amador County C/C & Visitors Bur.* · Jacqueline Lucido, Exec. Dir., 571 S. Hwy. 49, P.O. Box 596, 95642, P 37,000, M 653, (209) 223-0350, (800) 649-4988, Fax (209) 223-4425, info@amadorcountychamber.com, www.amadorcountychamber.com

**Johnson Park** · *see Burney*

**Joshua Tree** · *Joshua Tree C/C* · Barbara Waddle, Exec. Dir., 6470 Veterans Way, P.O. Box 600, 92252, P 10,000, M 205, (760) 366-3723, Fax (760) 366-2573, info@joshuatreechamber.org, joshuatreechamber.org

**Julian** · *Julian C/C* · Michael Menghini, Pres., 2129 Main St., P.O. Box 1866, 92036, P 4,000, M 280, (760) 765-1857, Fax (760) 765-2544, chamber@julianca.com, www.julianca.com

**June Lake** · *June Lake C/C* · P.O. Box 2, 93529, P 630, M 48, www.junelakechamber.org

**Kerman** · *Kerman C/C* · Linda Geringer, Exec. Dir., 783 S. Madera Ave., 93630, P 13,250, M 120, (559) 846-6343, Fax (559) 846-6344, krmchmbr@kermantel.net, www.kermanchamber.org

**Kernville** · *Kernville C/C* · Cheryl Borthick, Pres., 11447 Kernville Rd., P.O. Box 397, 93238, P 16,000, M 200, (760) 376-2629, (866) KERNVILLE, Fax (760) 376-4371, office@kernville chamber.org, www.kernvillechamber.org

**King City** · *King City & Southern Monterey County C/C & Ag.* · Brigid Aguirre, Ofc. Mgr., 200 Broadway, Ste. 40, 93930, P 16,000, M 200, (831) 385-3814, Fax (831) 386-9462, kingcitychamber@sbcglobal.net, www.kingcitychamber.com

**Kingsburg** · *Kingsburg Dist. C/C* · Jess Chambers, Exec. Dir., 1475 Draper St., 93631, P 11,000, M 230, (559) 897-1111, Fax (559) 897-4621, jessatkingsburg@aol.com, www.kingsburg chamberofcommerce.com

**Klamath** · *Klamath C/C* · Jan Crandall, Treas., P.O. Box 476, 95548, P 1,200, M 70, (707) 482-7165, (800) 200-2335, info@klamathcc.org, www.klamathcc.org

**Knightsen** · *see California Delta*

**La Canada Flintridge** · *La Canada Flintridge C/C* · Patricia A. Anderson, Pres./CEO, 4529 Angeles Crest Hwy. #102, 91011, P 20,000, M 680, (818) 790-4289, Fax (818) 790-8930, exec@lacanadaflintridge.com, www.lacanadaflintridge.com

**La Crescenta** · *Crescenta Valley C/C* · Julia Rabago, Exec. Dir., 3131 Foothill Blvd., Ste. D, 91214, P 30,000, M 350, (818) 248-4957, Fax (818) 248-9625, crescentachamber@aol.com, www.lacrescenta.org

**La Habra** · *La Habra Area C/C* · Mark Sturdevant, Exec. Dir., 321 E. La Habra Blvd., 90631, P 60,000, M 400, (562) 697-1704, Fax (562) 697-8359, mark@lahabrachamber.com, www.lahabra chamber.com

**La Jolla** · *La Jolla Town Cncl.* · Cindy Hoge, Ofc. Mgr., 7734 Herschel Ave., Ste. F, P.O. Box 1101, 92038, P 42,000, M 1,000, (858) 454-1444, Fax (858) 454-1848, lajollatowncncl@san.rr.com, www.lajollatowncouncil.org

**La Mesa** · *see El Cajon*

**La Mirada** · *La Mirada C/C* · Demian Ross, Exec. Dir., 11900 La Mirada Blvd. #9, 90638, P 50,000, M 250, (562) 902-1970, Fax (562) 902-1218, info@lmchamber.org, www.lmchamber.org

**La Quinta** · *La Quinta C/C* · David Archer, Pres./CEO, 78-275 Calle Tampico, Ste. B, 92253, P 41,000, M 700, (760) 564-3199, Fax (760) 564-3111, contactus@lqchamber.com, www.lqchamber.com

**La Verne** · *La Verne C/C* · Brian McNerney, Pres./CEO, 2078 Bonita Ave., 91750, P 32,000, M 340, (909) 593-5265, Fax (909) 596-0579, ceo@lavernechamber.org, www.lavernechamber.org.

**Ladera Ranch** · *see South Orange County*

**Lafayette** · *Lafayette C/C* · Jay Lifson, CEO, 100 Lafayette Cir., Ste. 103, 94549, P 24,000, M 625, (925) 284-7404, Fax (925) 284-3109, info@lafayettechamber.org, www.lafayettechamber.org

**Laguna Beach** · *Laguna Beach C/C* · Rose Hancock, Exec. Dir., 357 Glenneyre, 92651, P 25,000, M 650, (949) 494-1018, Fax (949) 376-8916, info@lagunabeachchamber.org, www.laguna beachchamber.org

**Laguna Hills** · *see South Orange County*

**Laguna Niguel** · *Laguna Niguel C/C* · Debbie Newman, Pres./CEO, 28062 Forbes Rd., Ste. C, 92677, P 66,000, M 525, (949) 363-0136, Fax (949) 363-9026, info@lagunaniguelchamber.net, www.lagunanigelchamber.net

**Laguna Woods** · *see South Orange County*

**Lake Almanor** · *see Chester*

**Lake Arrowhead** · *Lake Arrowhead Comm. C/C* · Lewis Murray, Pres./CEO, P.O. Box 219, 92352, P 14,900, M 550, (909) 337-3715, Fax (909) 336-1548, info@lakearrowhead.net, www.lakearrowhead.net

**Lake City** · *see Cedarville*

**Lake County** · *see Lakeport*

**Lake Elsinore** · *Lake Elsinore Valley C/C* · Mr. Kim Cousins, Pres./CEO, 132 W. Graham Ave., 92530, P 42,000, M 600, (951) 245-8848, Fax (951) 245-9127, www.visitlakeelsinore.com, info@lakeelsinorechamber.com, www.lakeelsinorechamber.com

**Lake Forest** · *see South Orange County*

**Lake Isabella** · *Kern River Valley C/C* · Linda Mann, Ofc. Coord., 6904 Lake Isabella Blvd., Ste. B, P.O. Box 567, 93240, P 18,000, M 180, (760) 379-5236, (866) KRV-4-FUN, Fax (760) 379-5457, office@kernrivervalley.com, www.kernrivervalley.com

**Lake Los Angeles** · *Lake Los Angeles C/C* · Mari Larocco, Pres., P.O. Box 500071, 93591, P 13,500, M 40, (661) 264-2786, www.lakelachamber.org

**Lake Tahoe** · *North Lake Tahoe C/C* · Steve Teshara, Dir., 380 N. Lake Blvd., P.O. Box 884, Tahoe City, 96145, P 10,000, M 650, (530) 581-6900, Fax (530) 581-6904, stevet@puretahoenorth.com, www.northlaketahoechamber.com

**Lakeport** · *Lakeport Reg. C/C* · Melissa Fulton, CEO, 875 Lakeport Blvd., P.O. Box 295, 95453, P 60,000, M 600, (707) 263-5092, (866) 525-3767, Fax (707) 263-5104, info@lakeportchamber.com, www.lakeportchamber.com

**Lakeside** · *Lakeside C/C* · Kathy Kassel, Exec. Dir., 9924 Vine St., 92040, P 57,000, M 170, (619) 561-1031, Fax (619) 561-7951, chamber@lakesideca.com, www.lakesideca.com

**Lakewood** · *Greater Lakewood C/C* · John Kelsall, Pres./CEO, 24 Lakewood Center Mall, P.O. Box 160, 90714, P 80,000, M 265, (564) 531-9733, Fax (564) 531-9737, info@lakewoodchamber.com, www.lakewoodchamber.com

**Lamont** · *Greater Lamont C/C* · Jim Bates, Pres., P.O. Box 593, 93241, P 15,500, M 40, (661) 845-1992

**Lancaster • *Antelope Valley Bd. of Trade* •** Josh Mann, Exec. Dir., 548 W. Lancaster Blvd., Ste. 103, 93534, P 400,000, M 185, (661) 942-9581, Fax (661) 723-9279, josh@avbot.org, www.avbot.org

**Lancaster • *Antelope Valley Chambers of Commerce-Lancaster* •** Ramon Ortega, Pres./CEO, 554 W. Lancaster Blvd., 93534, P 135,000, M 705, (661) 948-4518, Fax (661) 949-1212, avcoc@avchambers.com, www.avchambers.com

**Larkspur • *see Corte Madera***

**Lathrop • *Lathrop C/C* •** Mary Kennedy-Bracken, Pres., 16976 S. Harlan Rd., P.O. Box 313, 95330, P 17,886, M 134, (209) 858-4486, lathropchamber@hotmail.com, www.lathropchamber.org

**Lawndale • *Lawndale C/C* •** Dyan Davis, Exec. Dir., 14717 S. Hawthorne Blvd., Ste. A, 90260, P 33,000, M 125, (310) 679-3306, Fax (310) 679-3306, lawndalechamber@sbcglobal.net, lawndale chamber.org

**Lebec • *see Frazier Park***

**Lee Vining • *Lee Vining C/C* •** P.O. Box 130, 93541, P 398, M 23, (760) 647-6629, Fax (760) 647-6377, info@leevining.com, www.leevining.com

**Leggett • *Leggett Valley C/C* •** Helen Ochoa, Pres., P.O. Box 105, 95585, P 380, M 15, (707) 925-6385

**Lemon Grove • *Lemon Grove C/C* •** P.O. Box 1076, 91946, P 25,000, M 200, (619) 469-9621, info@lemongrovechamber.com, www.lemongrovechamber.com

**Lemoore • *Lemoore Dist. C/C* •** Lynda Lahodny, CEO, 300 E St., 93245, P 21,900, M 270, (559) 924-6401, Fax (559) 924-4520, ceo@lemoorechamberofcommerce.com, www.lemoorechamberofcommerce.com

**Leucadia • *see Encinitas***

**Lewiston • *see Trinity County***

**Lincoln • *Lincoln Area C/C* •** Bob Romness, CEO, 540 F St., P.O. Box 608, 95648, P 40,000, M 500, (916) 645-2035, Fax (916) 645-9455, info@lincolnchamber.com, www.lincolnchamber.com

**Linda • *see Marysville***

**Linden • *Linden-Peters C/C* •** P.O. Box 557, 95236, P 2,000, M 145, (209) 547-3046, www.lindenchamber.net

**Lindsay • *Lindsay C/C* •** Juanita Hernandez, Exec. Dir., 133 W. Honolulu, Ste. E, P.O. Box 989, 93247, P 10,000, M 300, (559) 562-4929, Fax (559) 562-5219, lindsaychamber@lindsay.ca.us, www.chamber.lindsay.ca.us

**Littlerock • *Littlerock C/C* •** Ronni Di Giovanni, Pres., P.O. Box 326, 93543, P 15,000, M 40, (661) 944-6990, s8f230@gmail.com, www.littlerock-ca.us

**Live Oak • *Live Oak Dist. C/C* •** Annette Bertolini, Pres., P.O. Box 391, 95953, P 6,200, M 85, (530) 695-1519, liveoakchamber@syix.com, www.liveoakchamber.org

**Livermore • *Livermore C/C* •** Ms. Dale Kaye, Pres./CEO, 2157 First St., 94550, P 83,000, M 850, (925) 447-1606, Fax (925) 447-1641, lccinfo@livermorechamber.org, www.livermorechamber.org

**Lockeford • *Clements-Lockeford C/C* •** Cynthia Haynes, Pres./CEO, 19000 N. Hwy. 88, Ste. B, 95237, P 3,000, M 90, (209) 727-3142, Fax (209) 727-3365, clchamber@sbcglobal.net, www.clementslockefordchamber.com

**Lodi • *Lodi Dist. C/C* •** Pat Patrick, CEO, 35 S. School St., 95240, P 60,000, M 750, (209) 367-7840, Fax (209) 369-9344, info@lodichamber.com, www.lodichamber.com

**Loleta • •** Barbara Petersen, P.O. Box 327, 95551, P 800, M 50, loletachamber@yahoo.com

**Loma Linda • *Loma Linda C/C* •** Dina Weiss, CEO, 25541 Barton Rd., Ste. 4, P.O. Box 343, 92354, P 20,000, M 280, (909) 799-2828, Fax (909) 799-2825, info@lomalindachamber.com, www.lomalindachamber.com

**Lomita • *Lomita C/C* •** Chuck Taylor, Exec. Dir., 25332 Narbonne Ave., Ste. 250, P.O. Box 425, 90717, P 20,065, M 250, (310) 326-6378, Fax (310) 326-2904, info@lomitacoc.com, www.lomitacoc.com

**Lompoc • *Lompoc Valley C/C & Visitor Bur.* •** C. Dennis Anderson, Pres./CEO, 111 S. I St., P.O. Box 626, 93438, P 58,301, M 500, (805) 736-4567, (800) 240-0999, Fax (805) 737-0453, chamber@lompoc.com, www.lompoc.com

**Lone Pine • *Lone Pine C/C* •** Kathleen New, Pres./CEO, 120 S. Main St., P.O. Box 749, 93545, P 1,665, M 257, (760) 876-4444, Fax (760) 876-0076, info@lonepinechamber.org, www.lonepine chamber.org

**Long Beach • *Long Beach Area C/C* •** Randy Gordon, Pres./CEO, One World Trade Center, Ste. 206, 90831-0206, P 490,166, M 1,500, (562) 436-1251, Fax (562) 436-7099, info@lbchamber.com, www.lbchamber.com.

**Long Beach • *Reg. Hispanic C/C* •** Sandy Cajas, CEO, 555 E. Ocean Blvd., Ste. 101, 90802, P 490,166, M 350, (562) 590-7302, Fax (562) 685-0542, info@regionalhispaniccc.org, www.regional hispaniccc.org

**Loomis • *Loomis Basin C/C* •** Carol Voyiatzes, Exec. Dir., 6090 Horseshoe Bar Rd., 95650, P 6,300, M 310, (916) 652-7252, Fax (916) 652-7211, manager@loomischamber.com, www.loomis chamber.com

**Los Alamitos • *Los Alamitos Area C/C* •** Chris Barnes, CEO, 3231 Katella Ave., P.O. Box 111, 90720, P 30,000, M 300, (562) 598-6659, Fax (562) 598-7035, info@losalchamber.org, www.losalchamber.org

**Los Altos • *Los Altos C/C* •** Julie Rose, Pres., 321 University Ave., 94022, P 36,000, M 525, (650) 948-1455, Fax (650) 948-6238, info@losaltoschamber.org, www.losaltoschamber.org

## Los Angeles Area

**Atwater Village C/C •** Mark Newman-Kuzel, Pres./CEO, P.O. Box 39754, 90039, P 39,000, M 70, (323) 634-2535, webmail@atwaterchamber.org, www.atwaterchamber.org

**Black Business Assn •** Earl Skip Cooper II, Pres./CEO, P.O. Box 43159, 90043, M 1,200, (323) 291-9334, Fax (323) 291-9234, mail@bbala.org, www.bbala.org

**Boyle Heights C/C •** Ralph Carmona, Coord., 5271 E. Beverly Blvd., P.O. Box 33167, 90033, P 93,000, M 100, (323) 888-2685, Fax (323) 721-9794, info@boyleheightschamber.com, www.boyleheightschamber.com

**Century City C/C •** Susan Bursk, Pres./CEO, 2029 Century Park East, Concourse Level, 90067, P 50,000, M 300, (310) 553-2222, Fax (310) 553-4623, contact@centurycitycc.com, www.century citycc.com

**East Los Angeles C/C •** Blanca Espinoza, Pres., P.O. Box 63220, 90063, P 128,000, M 121, (323) 722-2005, Fax (323) 722-2405, elacoc@pacbell.net, www.elacoc.com

**Japanese C/C of Southern Calif. •** Toshio Handa, Pres., 244 S. San Pedro, Ste. 504, 90012, M 250, (213) 626-3067, Fax (213) 626-3070, office@jccsc.com, www.jccsc.com

**Lincoln Heights C/C •** Richard Macias, Pres., 2716 N. Broadway, Ste. 210, 90031, P 50,000, M 142, (323) 221-6571, Fax (323) 221-1513, lhchamber@earthlink.net

## Los Angeles Area, *continued*

**Los Angeles Area C/C** · Gary Toebben, Pres./CEO, 350 S. Bixel St., Ste. 201, 90017, P 9,128,200, M 1,600, (213) 580-7500, Fax (213) 580-7510, info@lachamber.com, www.lachamber.com

**Silverlake C/C** · Dyan Collings Ralph, Pres., 2814 Rowena Ave., Ste. 3, 90039, M 300, (323) 908-4086, Fax (323) 908-4086, info@silverlakechamber.com, www.silverlakechamber.com

**West Los Angeles C/C** · Paul Reznik, Pres., P.O. Box 64512, 90064, P 282,000, M 1,000, (310) 481-0600, Fax (310) 478-2068, info@westlachamber.org, www.westlachamber.org

**Los Banos** · *Los Banos C/C* · Keith Groninga, CEO, 503 J St., 93635, P 34,200, M 347, (209) 826-2495, (800) 336-6354, Fax (209) 826-9689, lbcofc@pacbell.net, www.losbanos.com

**Los Gatos** · *Town of Los Gatos C/C* · Ronee Nassi, Exec. Dir., 349 N. Santa Cruz Ave., 95030, P 29,000, M 440, (408) 354-9300, Fax (408) 399-1594, chamber@losgatoschamber.com, www.losgatoschamber.com

**Los Molinos** · *Los Molinos C/C* · Betty Joe Morales, Pres., P.O. Box 334, 96055, P 3,000, M 75, (530) 384-2251, Fax (530) 384-2251, lmchamber@att.net, www.losmochamber.com

**Los Osos** · *Los Osos/Baywood Park C/C* · Julie Downey, Exec. Dir., 781 Los Osos Valley Rd., P.O. Box 6282, 93412, P 15,000, M 240, (805) 528-4884, Fax (805) 528-8401, info@lobpchamber.org, www.lobpchamber.org

**Lucerne Valley** · *Lucerne Valley C/C* · Lorane Abercrombie, Pres., 32750 Old Woman Springs Rd., P.O. Box 491, 92356, P 8,500, M 100, (760) 248-7215, Fax (760) 248-2024, chamber@lucernevalley.net, www.lvcal.org/chamber

**Lynwood** · *Lynwood C/C* · Maria Garcia, CEO, 3651 E. Imperial Hwy., 90262, P 85,000, M 350, (310) 527-1431, lynwoodchamber@gmail.com, www.lynwoodchamber.org

**Madera** · *Golden Valley C/C* · Randy Bailey, Pres., 37167 Ave. 12, Ste. 5C, 93636, P 12,000, M 115, (559) 645-4001, goldenvalleychamber@theranchos.com

**Madera** · *Madera C/C* · Debi Bray, Pres./CEO, 120 North E St., 93638, P 56,710, M 400, (559) 673-3563, Fax (559) 673-5009, dbray@maderachamber.com, www.maderachamber.com

**Malibu** · *Malibu C/C* · Rebekah Evans, CEO, 23805 Stuart Ranch Rd., Ste. 210, 90265, P 15,000, M 600, (310) 456-9025, Fax (310) 456-0195, info@malibu.org, www.malibu.org

**Mammoth Lakes** · *Mammoth Lakes C/C* · Annette Scholl, Admin., P.O. Box 3268, 93546, P 8,000, M 200, (760) 934-6717, info@mammothlakeschamber.org, www.mammothlakeschamber.org

**Manhattan Beach** · *Manhattan Beach C/C* · Helen Duncan, Pres./CEO, 425 15th St., P.O. Box 3007, 90266, P 34,000, M 750, (310) 545-5313, Fax (310) 545-7203, info@manhattanbeachchamber.net, www.manhattanbeachchamber.net

**Manteca** · *Manteca C/C* · Debby Moorehead, Exec. Dir., 821 W. Yosemite, 95336, P 64,000, M 380, (209) 823-6121, Fax (209) 239-6131, chamber@manteca.org, www.manteca.org

**Marina** · *Marina C/C* · 3170 Vista Del Camino, Ste. C, 93933, P 25,000, M 200, (831) 384-9155, Fax (831) 883-9077, marinacc@sbcglobal.net, www.marinachamber.com

**Marina del Rey** · *see Westchester*

**Mariposa** · *Mariposa County C/C* · Peter Schimmelfennig, Exec. Dir., 5158 Hwy. 140, P.O. Box 425, 95338, P 18,000, M 354, (209) 966-2456, Fax (209) 966-4193, mariposachamber@sti.net, www.mariposachamber.org

**Mark West** · *see Santa Rosa-Mark West Area C/C*

**Markleeville** · *Alpine County C/C* · Teresa Burkhauser, Exec. Dir., P.O. Box 265, 96120, P 1,208, M 93, (530) 694-2475, Fax (530) 694-2478, info@alpinecounty.com, www.alpinecounty.com

**Martinez** · *Martinez Area C/C* · Cynthia Murdough, Exec. Dir., 603 Marina Vista, 94553, P 39,000, M 300, (925) 228-2345, Fax (925) 228-2356, info@martinezchamber.com, www.martinezchamber.com

**Marysville** · *Yuba-Sutter C/C* · Laura Nicholson, Exec. Dir./CEO, 429 10th St., P.O. Box 1429, 95901, P 154,000, M 650, (530) 743-6501, Fax (530) 741-8645, chamber@yubasutterchamber.com, www.yubasutterchamber.com.

**McClellan Park** · *see North Highlands*

**McCloud** · *McCloud C/C* · P.O. Box 372, 96057, P 1,600, M 70, (530) 964-3113, contact@mccloudchamber.com, www.mccloudchamber.com

**McKinleyville** · *McKinleyville C/C* · Shonnie Bradbury, Pres., 1640 Central Ave., P.O. Box 2144, 95519, P 14,000, M 250, (707) 839-2449, Fax (707) 839-1205, www.mckinleyvillechamber.com

**Menlo Park** · *Menlo Park C/C* · Fran Dehn, Pres./CEO, 1100 Merrill St., 94025, P 30,648, M 360, (650) 325-2818, Fax (650) 325-0920, info@menloparkchamber.com, www.menloparkchamber.com

**Merced** · *Greater Merced C/C* · Jennifer Krumm, COO, 360 E. Yosemite Ave., Ste. 100, 95340, P 85,000, M 800, (209) 384-7092, Fax (209) 384-8472, info@merced-chamber.com, www.merced-chamber.com

**Merced** · *Merced County C/C* · Julius Pekar, CEO, P.O. Box 1112, 95341, P 275,000, M 700, (209) 722-3864, Fax (209) 722-2406, info@mercedcountychamber.com, www.mercedcountychamber.com.

**Mill Valley** · *Mill Valley C/C* · Elaine Cramer, Pres., 85 Throckmorton Ave., 94941, P 13,000, M 400, (415) 388-9700, Fax (415) 388-9770, info@millvalley.org, www.millvalley.org

**Millbrae** · *Millbrae C/C* · John Ford, Pres./CEO, 50 Victoria Ave., Ste. 103, 94030, P 22,000, M 200, (650) 697-7324, Fax (650) 259-7918, info@millbrae.com, www.millbrae.com

**Milpitas** · *Milpitas C/C* · Gaye S. Morando, Exec. Dir., 828 N. Hillview Dr., 95035, P 69,000, M 700, (408) 262-2613, Fax (408) 262-2823, info@milpitaschamber.com, www.milpitaschamber.com.

**Mira Mesa** · *see San Diego North C/C*

**Miramar** · *see San Diego North C/C*

**Miramonte** · *Central Sierra C/C* · P.O. Box 65, 93641, P 2,500, M 100, (559) 336-9076, www.centralsierrachamber.org

**Mission Hills** · *see San Fernando*

**Mission Viejo** · *see South Orange County*

**Modesto** · *Modesto C/C* · Joy Madison, Pres./CEO, 1114 J St., P.O. Box 844, 95353, P 209,000, M 1,300, (209) 577-5757, Fax (209) 577-2673, info@modchamber.org, www.modchamber.org.

**Modesto** · *The Hispanic C/C of Stanislaus County* · 1314 H St., 95354, M 290, caro@thehccsc.org, www.thehccsc.org

**Monrovia** · *Monrovia C/C* · Karin Crehan, Exec. Dir., 620 S. Myrtle Ave., 91016, P 40,000, M 450, (626) 358-1159, Fax (626) 357-6036, chamber@monroviacc.com, www.monroviacc.com

**Montclair** · *Montclair C/C* · Kelly Johnson, Exec. Dir., 5220 Benito St., 91763, P 38,000, M 200, (909) 624-4569, Fax (909) 625-2009, info@montclairchamber.com, www.montclairchamber.com

**Montebello** · *Montebello C/C* · Andrea Wagg, Pres., 817 W. Whittier Blvd., Ste. 200, 90640, P 75,000, M 500, (323) 721-1153, Fax (323) 721-7946, andrea@montebellochamber.org, www.montebellochamber.org

**Monterey** · *Monterey Peninsula C/C* · Astrid Coleman, Pres./CEO, 380 Alvarado St., 93940, P 150,000, M 1,000, (831) 648-5360, Fax (831) 649-3502, info@mpcc.com, www.mpcc.com

**Monterey Park** · *Monterey Park C/C* · Mr. Ronald Lee, Pres., 700 El Mercado Ave., P.O. Box 387, 91754, P 70,000, M 200, (626) 570-9429, Fax (626) 570-9491, mpccusa@yahoo.com, .

**Montgomery Creek** · *see Burney*

**Montrose** · *see Glendale--Montrose-Verdugo City C/C*

**Moorpark** · *Moorpark C/C* · Patrick Ellis, Pres./CEO, 18 E. High St., 93021, P 36,000, M 275, (805) 529-0322, Fax (805) 529-5304, patrick@moorparkchamber.com, www.moorparkchamber.com

**Moraga** · *Moraga C/C* · Edy Schwartz, Pres., 1480 Moraga Rd., Ste. I, Box 254, 94556, P 17,000, M 135, information@moraga chamber.org, www.moragachamber.org

**Moreno Valley** · *Moreno Valley C/C* · Oscar Valdepena, Exec. Dir., 22500 Town Circle, Ste. 2090, 92553, P 180,000, M 300, (951) 697-4404, Fax (951) 697-0995, office@movalchamber.org, www.movalchamber.org

**Morgan Hill** · *Morgan Hill C/C* · Christine Giusiana, Pres./CEO, 90 E. Second St., P.O. Box 786, 95037, P 37,000, M 680, (408) 779-9444, Fax (408) 779-5405, mhcc@morganhill.org, www.morganhill.org

**Morro Bay** · *Morro Bay C/C* · Peter Candela, CEO, 845 Embarcadero, Ste. D, 93442, P 10,500, M 600, (805) 772-4467, (800) 231-0592, Fax (805) 772-6038, brownpelican@morrobay.org, www.morrobay.org

**Moss Landing** · *Moss Landing C/C* · P.O. Box 41, 95039, P 1,000, M 85, (831) 633-4501, Fax same, www.mosslandingchamber.com

**Mount Shasta** · *Mount Shasta C/C* · Marie Wells, Exec. Dir., 300 Pine St., 96067, P 3,700, M 370, (530) 926-3696, (800) 926-4865, Fax (530) 926-0976, info@mtshastachamber.com, www.mtshastachamber.com

**Mountain View** · *Mountain View C/C* · Oscar Garcia, Pres./CEO, 580 Castro St., 94041, P 75,000, M 600, (650) 968-8378, Fax (650) 968-5668, info@chambermv.org, www.chambermv.org

**Muir Beach** · *see Stinson Beach*

**Murrieta** · *Murrieta C/C* · Rex Oliver IOM ACE, Pres./CEO, 41870 Kalmia St., Ste. 155, 92562, P 101,000, M 880, (951) 677-7916, Fax (951) 677-9976, roliver@murrietachamber.org, www.murrietachamber.org.

**Napa** · *Napa C/C* · Kate King, Pres./CEO, 1556 First St., P.O. Box 636, 94559, P 74,000, M 1,280, (707) 226-7455, Fax (707) 226-1171, kate@napachamber.com, www.napachamber.com

**National City** · *National City C/C* · Jacqueline L. Reynoso, Pres./CEO, 901 National City Blvd., 91950, P 57,000, M 600, (619) 477-9339, Fax (619) 477-5018, thechamber@nationalcitychamber.org, www.nationalcitychamber.org.

**Needles** · *Needles Area C/C* · Sue Godnick, Exec. Dir., 100 G St., P.O. Box 705, 92363, P 4,830, M 185, (760) 326-2050, Fax (760) 326-2194, needlescofc@rraz.net, www.needleschamber.com

**Nevada City** · *Nevada City C/C* · Cathy Whittlesey, Exec. Mgr., 132 Main St., 95959, P 2,850, M 375, (530) 265-2692, (800) 655-NJOY, Fax (530) 265-3892, info@nevadacitychamber.com, www.nevadacitychamber.com.

**Newark** · *Newark C/C* · Linda Ashley, Pres./CEO, 6066 Civic Terrace Ave., Ste. 8, 94560, P 44,000, M 335, (510) 744-1000, Fax (510) 744-1003, info@newark-chamber.com, www.newark-chamber.com

**Newberry Springs** · *Newberry Springs C/C* · Sandra Brittian, Pres., P.O. Box 116, 92365, P 4,000, M 30, (760) 257-1072, Fax same, nschamber@newberrysprings.com, www.newberrysprings chamber.org

**Newbury Park** · *see Westlake Village*

**Newhall** · *see Santa Clarita*

**Newman** · *Newman C/C* · Phyllis Peavler, Pres., P.O. Box 753, 95360, P 10,400, M 80, (209) 862-1000, Fax (209) 862-4133, www.cityofnewman.com

**Newport Beach** · *Newport Beach C/C* · Richard Luehrs, Pres., 1470 Jamboree Rd., 92660, P 86,000, M 1,000, (949) 729-4400, Fax (949) 729-4417, info@newportbeach.com, www.newport beach.com

**Niland** · *Niland C/C* · John Almueti, Pres., P.O. Box 97, 92257, P 1,200, M 150, (760) 359-0870

**Nipomo** · *Nipomo C/C* · Cees Dobbe, Pres., 671 W. Tefft St., Ste. 2, 93444, P 14,000, M 220, (805) 929-1583, Fax (805) 929-5835, nipomochamber@yahoo.com, www.nipomochamber.org

**Norco** · *Norco C/C* · Kevin Russell, Pres., 2816 Hamner Ave., 92860, P 24,182, M 400, (951) 737-2531, Fax (951) 737-2574, staff@norcochamber.com, www.norcochamber.com

**North Fork** · *North Fork C/C* · Steve Cook, Pres., P.O. Box 426, 93643, P 3,500, M 100, (559) 877-2410, Fax (559) 877-2332, info@north-fork-chamber.com, www.north-fork-chamber.com

**North Highlands** · *Antelope Highlands C/C* · P.O. Box 20, 95660, P 47,000, M 150, (916) 725-5652, www.antelopehigh landschamber.com

**North Hollywood** · *Universal City North Hollywood C/C* · Patti Lippel, Admin. Dir., 6369 Bellingham Ave., 91606, P 144,188, M 250, (818) 508-5155, Fax (818) 508-5156, info@noho.org, www.noho.org

**North Sacramento** · *see Sacramento-North Sacramento C/C*

**Northridge** · *North Valley Reg. C/C* · Joyce Sipes, Pres./CEO, 9401 Reseda Blvd., Ste. 100, 91324, P 90,000, M 500, (818) 349-5676, Fax (818) 349-4343, info@nvrcc.com, www.nvrcc.com

**Norwalk** · *Norwalk C/C* · Vivian Hansen, Exec. Dir., 12040 Foster Rd., 90650, P 105,000, M 260, (562) 864-7785, Fax (562) 864-8539, ceo@norwalkchamber.com, www.norwalkchamber.com

**Novato** · *Novato C/C* · Coy Smith, CEO, 807 DeLong Ave., 94945, P 52,000, M 600, (415) 897-1164, Fax (415) 898-9097, info@novatochamber.com, www.novatochamber.com

**Oakdale** · *Oakdale Dist. C/C & Visitors Bur.* · Mary Guardiola, CEO, 590 N. Yosemite Ave., 95361, P 17,119, M 450, (209) 847-2244, Fax (209) 847-0826, info@oakdalechamber.com, www.oakdalechamber.com

**Oakhurst** · *Oakhurst Area C/C* · Kathy McCorry, Exec. Dir., 49074 Civic Circle Dr., 93644, P 32,000, M 454, (559) 683-7766, Fax (559) 658-2942, chamber@oakhurstchamber.com, www.oakhurstchamber.com.

## Oakland Area

**Calif. Asia Business Cncl.** · Jeremy Potash, Exec. Dir., c/o APL 1111 Broadway, 94607, M 100, (510) 272-7331, Fax (510) 272-7339, info@calasia.org, www.calasia.org

**Oakland African-American C/C** · Robert Bobb, Founding Pres., 449 15th St., Ste. 410, 94612, P 500,000, M 390, (510) 268-1600, Fax (510) 268-1602, info@oaacc.org, www.oaacc.org

## Oakland Area, *continued*

**Oakland Chinatown C/C** · Jenny Ong, Exec. Dir., Pacific Renaissance Plaza, 388 9th St., Ste. 258, 94607, M 425, (510) 893-8979, Fax (510) 893-8988, oaklandctchamber@aol.com, www.oaklandchinatownchamber.org

**Oakland Metro C/C** · Joseph Haraburda, Pres./CEO, 475 14th St., 94612, P 400,000, M 1,600, (510) 874-4800, Fax (510) 839-8817, jharaburda@oaklandchamber.com, www.oaklandchamber.com

**Oakley** · *Oakley C/C* · Steve Nosanchuk, Pres., 3510 Main St., P.O. Box 1340, 94561, P 26,000, M 125, (925) 625-1035, Fax (925) 625-4051, oakleychamber@sbcglobal.net, www.oakleychamber.com

**Occidental** · *Occidental C/C* · P.O. Box 159, 95465, P 5,000, M 50, (707) 874-3279

**Oceanside** · *Oceanside C/C* · David L. Nydegger, CEO, 928 N. Coast Hwy., 92054, P 180,000, M 950, (760) 722-1534, Fax (760) 722-8336, info@oceansidechamber.com, www.oceansidechamber.com

**Oildale** · *see Bakersfield-North of the River C/C*

**Ojai** · *Ojai Valley C/C* · Scott Eicher, CEO, 201 S. Signal St., P.O. Box 1134, 93024, P 28,000, M 300, (805) 646-8126, Fax (805) 646-9762, info@ojaichamber.org, www.ojaichamber.org.

**Old Station** · *see Burney*

**Olive Drive** · *see Bakersfield-North of the River C/C*

**Ontario** · *Ontario C/C* · Stephanie Palomar, Interim Dir., 500 E. E St., Ste. 200, 91764, P 175,000, M 715, (909) 984-2458, Fax (909) 984-6439, info@ontario.org, www.ontario.org

**Orange** · *Orange C/C* · Heidi Larkin-Reed, Pres./CEO, 439 E. Chapman Ave., 92866, P 136,000, M 650, (714) 538-3581, Fax (714) 532-1675, info@orangechamber.com, www.orangechamber.com

**Orangevale** · *Orangevale C/C* · Cindysue Jones, Ofc. Mgr., 9267 Greenback Lane #B91, 95662, P 36,000, M 220, (916) 988-0175, Fax (916) 988-1049, ovchamber@sbcglobal.net, www.orangevalechamber.com

**Orick** · *Orick C/C* · John Sutter, Pres., P.O. Box 234, 95555, P 400, M 40, (707) 488-2885, (707) 488-2602, Fax (707) 488-5295, www.orick.net

**Orinda** · *Orinda C/C* · Candy Kattenburg, Exec. Dir., 26 Orinda Way, P.O. Box 2271, 94563, P 17,500, M 200, (925) 254-3909, Fax (925) 254-8312, info@orindachamber.org, www.orindachamber.org

**Orland** · *Orland Area C/C* · Candice Anderson, Mgr., 401 Walker St., 95963, P 7,200, M 200, (530) 865-2311, Fax (530) 865-8171, orlandchamber@sbcglobal.net, www.orland-ca.com

**Oroville** · *Oroville Area C/C* · Claudia Knaus, Exec. Dir., 1789 Montgomery St., 95965, P 55,000, M 450, (530) 538-2542, (800) 655-GOLD, Fax (530) 538-2546, info@orovillechamber.net, www.orovillechamber.net

**Otay Mesa** · *Otay Mesa C/C* · Alejandra Mier y Teran, Exec. Dir., 9163 Siempre Viva Rd., Ste. I-2, San Diego, 92154, P 14,000, M 370, (619) 661-6111, Fax (619) 661-6178, amieryteran@otaymesa.org, www.otaymesa.org

**Oxnard** · *Oxnard C/C* · Nancy Lindholm, Pres./CEO, 400 Esplanade Dr., Ste. 302, 93036, P 190,000, M 750, (805) 983-6118, Fax (805) 604-7331, n.lindholm@oxnardchamber.org, www.oxnardchamber.org

**Pacific Grove** · *Pacific Grove C/C* · Mr. Moe Ammar, Pres., 584 Central Ave., P.O. Box 167, 93950, P 15,500, M 575, (831) 373-3304, Fax (831) 373-3317, chamber@pacificgrove.org, www.pacificgrove.org

**Pacific Palisades** · *Pacific Palisades C/C* · Arnie Wishnick, Exec. Dir., 15330 Antioch St., 90272, P 27,000, M 450, (310) 459-7963, Fax (310) 459-9534, info@palisadeschamber.com, www.palisadeschamber.com.

**Pacifica** · *Pacifica C/C* · Don Eagleston, CEO, 225 Rockaway Beach, Ste. 1, 94044, P 39,000, M 250, (650) 355-4122, Fax (650) 355-6949, don@pacificachamber.org, www.pacificachamber.com

**Pacoima** · *see San Fernando*

**Palm Desert** · *Palm Desert C/C* · Barbara deBoom, Pres./CEO, 72559 Hwy. 111, 92260, P 49,000, M 1,400, (760) 346-6111, Fax (760) 346-3263, info@pdcc.org, www.palmdesert.org

**Palm Springs** · *Palm Springs C/C* · John Pivinski, CEO, 190 W. Amado Rd., 92262, P 45,737, M 950, (760) 325-1577, Fax (760) 325-8549, info@pschamber.org, www.pschamber.org

**Palmdale** · *Palmdale C/C* · Bill Hogrefe, CAO, 817 E. Ave. Q-9, 93550, P 148,000, M 800, (661) 273-3232, Fax (661) 273-8508, bhogrefe@palmdalechamber.org, www.palmdalechamber.org

**Palo Alto** · *Palo Alto C/C* · Paula Sandas, Pres./CEO, 122 Hamilton Ave., 94301, P 61,200, M 675, (650) 324-3121, Fax (650) 324-1215, info@paloaltochamber.com, www.paloaltochamber.com

**Panorama City** · *see Van Nuys*

**Paradise** · *Paradise Ridge C/C* · Katie Simmons, Exec. Dir., 5550 Skyway, Ste. 1, 95969, P 26,300, M 400, (530) 877-9356, (888) 845-2769, Fax (530) 877-1865, info@paradisechamber.com, www.paradisechamber.com.

**Paramount** · *Paramount C/C* · Peggy Lemons, Exec. Dir., 15357 Paramount Blvd., 90723, P 53,000, M 400, (562) 634-3980, Fax (562) 634-0891, plemons@paramountchamber.com, www.paramountchamber.com

**Parlier** · *Parlier C/C* · Francine Vindiola, Secy., 580 Tulare St., P.O. Box 453, 93648, P 12,000, M 25, (559) 646-9628, www.cityofparlier.com

**Pasadena** · *Pasadena C/C & Civic Assn.* · Paul Little, Pres./CEO, 865 E. Del Mar Blvd., 91101, P 135,000, M 1,400, (626) 795-3355, Fax (626) 795-5603, paul@pasadena-chamber.org, www.pasadena-chamber.org

**Paso Robles** · *Paso Robles C/C* · Mike Gibson, Pres./CEO, 1225 Park St., 93446, P 30,000, M 1,100, (805) 238-0506, Fax (805) 238-0527, info@pasorobleschamber.com, www.pasorobleschamber.com.

**Patterson** · *Patterson-Westley C/C* · Ellen Calmettes, Pres., #2 Plaza Cir., P.O. Box 365, 95363, P 11,000, M 154, (209) 892-2821, chamberofcommerce@gvni.com, www.patterson-westleychamber.com

**Pearblossom** · *Pearblossom C/C* · Duane Carles, Pres., P.O. Box 591, 93553, P 3,000, M 75, (661) 944-2564

**Penn Valley** · *Penn Valley Area C/C* · Julie Frenzel & Susan George, Co-Chrmn., 17500-B Penn Valley Dr., P.O. Box 202, 95946, P 14,000, M 140, (530) 432-1802, Fax (530) 432-7762, info@pennvalleycoc.org, www.pennvalleycoc.org

**Perris** · *Perris Valley C/C* · Bob Turner, Pres., 227 N. D St., Ste. A, 92570, P 47,139, M 136, (951) 657-3555, Fax (951) 657-3085, perrischamber@puhsd.org, www.perrischamber.org

**Petaluma** · *Petaluma Area C/C* · Onita Pellegrini, CEO, 6 Petaluma Blvd. N., Ste. A-2, 94952, P 59,000, M 900, (707) 762-2785, Fax (707) 762-4721, pacc@petalumachamber.com, www.petalumachamber.com

**Phelan** · *Phelan C/C* · Rosella Bernal, Pres., P.O. Box 290010, 92329, P 17,000, M 90, (760) 868-3291, Fax (760) 868-3291, phelanchamber@verizon.net, phelanchamber.org

**Pico Rivera** · *Pico Rivera C/C* · 5016 Passons Blvd., 90660, P 62,600, M 300, (562) 949-2473, Fax (562) 949-8320, info@picoriverachamber.org, www.picoriverachamber.org

**Pine Mountain Club** · *see Frazier Park*

**Pinehurst** · *see Miramonte*

**Pinion Pines** · *see Frazier Park*

**Pinole** · *Pinole C/C* · Deanna Million, Exec. Dir., P.O. Box 1, 94564, P 20,000, M 150, (510) 724-4484, Fax (510) 724-4408, pinolechamber@yahoo.com, www.pinolechamber.org

**Pinon Hills** · *Pinon Hills C/C* · Jane Rowan, Pres., P.O. Box 720095, 92372, P 7,000, M 75, (760) 868-5801, Fax (760) 868-5801, pinonhillschamber@verizon.net, www.pinonhillschamber.com

**Pismo Beach** · *Pismo Beach C of C & Visitors Info Center* · Rebecca McMurry, Exec. Dir., 581 Dolliver St., 93449, P 9,000, M 466, (805) 773-4382, (800) 443-7778, Fax (805) 773-6772, pbcoc@charter.net, www.pismochamber.com

**Pittsburg** · *Pittsburg C/C* · Mary Coniglio, CEO, 485 Railroad Ave., 94565, P 78,800, M 500, (925) 432-7301, Fax (925) 427-5555, chamber@pittsburgchamber.org, www.pittsburgchamber.org

**Placentia** · *Placentia C/C* · Crystal Gates, Exec. Dir., 201 E. Yorba Linda Blvd., Ste. C, 92870, P 52,000, M 255, (714) 528-1873, Fax (714) 528-1879, info@placentiachamber.com, www.placentiachamber.com.

**Placerville** · *El Dorado County C/C* · Laurel Brent-Bumb, CEO, 542 Main St., 95667, P 166,000, M 900, (530) 621-5885, (800) 457-6279, Fax (530) 642-1624, psi@eldoradocounty.org, www.eldoradocounty.org

**Pleasant Hill** · *Pleasant Hill C/C* · Charley Daley, Exec. Dir., 91 Gregory Ln., Ste. 11, 94523, P 32,500, M 400, (925) 687-0700, Fax (925) 676-7422, info@pleasanthillchamber.com, www.pleasanthillchamber.com

**Pleasanton** · *Pleasanton C/C* · Scott Raty, Pres./CEO, 777 Peters Ave., 94566, P 67,000, M 800, (925) 846-5858, Fax (925) 846-9697, scott@pleasanton.org, www.pleasanton.org

**Plumas Lake** · *see Marysville*

**Point Reyes Station** · *West Marin C/C* · Frank Borodic, P.O. Box 1045, 94956, P 8,000, M 100, (415) 663-9232, info@pointreyes.org, www.pointreyes.org

**Pomona** · *Pomona C/C* · Frank Garcia, Exec. Dir., 101 W. Mission Blvd., Ste 222A, P.O. Box 1457, 91769, P 175,000, M 480, (909) 622-1256, Fax (909) 620-5986, info@pomonachamber.org, www.pomonachamber.org

**Port Hueneme** · *Port Hueneme C/C* · Kathleen Misewitch, Pres./CEO, 220 N. Market St., 93041, P 22,621, M 175, (805) 488-2023, Fax (805) 488-6993, phc@huenemechamber.com, www.huenemechamber.com

**Porterville** · *Porterville C/C* · Donnette Silva Carter IOM, Pres./CEO, 93 N. Main St., Ste. A, 93257, P 55,000, M 785, (559) 784-7502, Fax (559) 784-0770, chamber@portervillechamber.org, portervillechamber.org.

**Portola** · *see Graeagle*

**Poway** · *Poway C/C* · Luanne Hulsizer, Pres./CEO, 13381 Poway Rd., P.O. Box 868, 92074, P 90,000, M 780, (858) 748-0016, Fax (858) 748-1710, chamber@poway.com, www.poway.com

**Prunedale** · *see Castroville*

**Quartz Hill** · *Quartz Hill C/C* · Lee Barron, Pres., 42043 50th St. W., 93536, P 18,000, M 200, (661) 722-4811, Fax (661) 722-3235, quartzhillchamber@yahoo.com, www.quartzhillchamber.org

**Quincy** · *Plumas County Visitor Bur.* · Suzi Brakken, Dir., 550 Crescent St., 95971, P 22,000, (530) 283-6345, (800) 326-2247, Fax (530) 283-5465, info@plumascounty.org, www.plumascounty.org

**Quincy** · *Quincy C/C* · Sarah Metzler, Exec. Dir., 464 Main St., 95971, P 6,849, M 187, (530) 283-0188, (877) 283-0188, Fax (530) 283-5864, office@quincychamber.com, www.quincychamber.com

**Ramona** · *Ramona C/C* · Thad Clendenen, Pres., 960 Main St., 92065, P 48,000, M 418, (760) 789-1311, Fax (760) 789-1317, info@ramonachamber.com, www.ramonachamber.com

**Rancho Bernardo** · *see San Diego North C/C*

**Rancho Cordova** · *Rancho Cordova C/C* · Jane Daly, CEO, 2729 Prospect Dr., Ste. 117, 95670, P 58,000, M 750, (916) 273-5688, Fax (916) 273-5727, www.ranchocordova.org

**Rancho Cucamonga** · *Rancho Cucamonga C/C* · Michelle Alonzo, V.P., 7945 Vineyard Ave., Ste. D-5, 91730, P 172,000, M 1,200, (909) 987-1012, Fax (909) 987-5917, info@ranchochamber.org, www.ranchochamber.org

**Rancho Mirage** · *Rancho Mirage C/C* · Stuart W. Ackley, Pres./CEO, 42-520 Bob Hope Dr., Ste. B, 92270, P 17,410, M 500, (760) 568-9351, Fax (760) 779-9684, info@ranchomirage.org, www.ranchomirage.org

**Rancho Penasquitos** · *see San Diego North C/C*

**Rancho Santa Margarita** · *see South Orange County*

**Red Bluff** · *Red Bluff-Tehama County C/C* · John Yingling, Exec. V.P., 100 S. Main St., P.O. Box 850, 96080, P 14,000, M 400, (530) 527-6220, (800) 655-6225, Fax (530) 527-2908, rbchamber@att.net, www.redbluffchamberofcommerce.com.

**Redding** · *Greater Redding C/C* · Frank Strazzarino Jr., Pres./CEO, 747 Auditorium Dr., 96001, P 90,000, M 1,100, (530) 225-4433, Fax (530) 225-4398, info@reddingchamber.com, www.reddingchamber.com.

**Redlands** · *Redlands C/C* · Kathie Thurston, Exec. Dir., 1 E. Redlands Blvd., 92373, P 68,000, M 810, (909) 793-2546, Fax (909) 335-6388, info@redlandschamber.org, www.redlandschamber.org

**Redondo Beach** · *Redondo Beach C/C & Visitors Bur.* · Marna Smeltzer, Pres./CEO, 200 N. Pacific Coast Hwy., 90277, P 65,000, M 630, (310) 376-6911, Fax (310) 374-7373, info@redondochamber.org, www.redondochamber.org

**Redwood City** · *Redwood City-San Mateo County C/C* · Laurence Buckmaster, Pres./CEO, 1450 Veterans Blvd., Ste. 125, 94063, P 76,000, M 1,400, (650) 364-1722, Fax (650) 364-1729, rwcchamber@redwoodcitychamber.com, www.redwoodcitychamber.com

**Reedley** · *Greater Reedley C/C* · 1717 9th St., 93654, P 25,723, M 325, (559) 637-4200, www.reedleychamber.com

**Reseda** · *Reseda C/C* · Ann Kinzle, Exec. Dir., 18210 Sherman Way, Ste. 107, 91335, P 62,113, M 200, (818) 345-1920, Fax (818) 345-1925, akr1920@aol.com

**Rialto** · *Rialto C/C* · Roslyn Garner, Exec. Dir., 120 N. Riverside Ave., 92376, P 97,400, M 300, (909) 875-5364, Fax (909) 875-6790, info@rialtochamber.com, www.rialtochamber.com

**Richmond** · *Richmond C/C* · Judith Morgan, Pres./CEO, 3925 Macdonald Ave., 94805, P 103,000, M 500, (510) 234-3512, Fax (510) 234-3540, staff@rcoc.com, www.rcoc.com.

**Ridgecrest** · *Ridgecrest C/C* · Jan Bennett, CEO, 128 E. California St., Ste. B, 93555, P 28,000, M 390, (760) 375-8331, Fax (760) 375-0365, chamber@ridgenet.net, www.ridgecrestchamber.com.

**Rio Dell** · *Rio Dell-Scotia C/C* · Susan Davis, Pres., 715B Wildwood Ave., 95562, P 3,250, M 80, (707) 764-3436, rdscoc@aol.com, www.riodellcity.com

U.S. Chambers of Commerce

**Rio Linda** · *Rio Linda-Elverta C/C* · P.O. Box 75, 95673, P 30,000, M 100, (916) 991-9344, info@rlechamber.com, www.rlechamber.com

**Rio Vista** · *Rio Vista C/C* · Mary Peinado, Exec. Dir., 6 N. Front St., 94571, P 10,000, M 150, (707) 374-2700, Fax (707) 374-2424, mary.peinado@riovista.org, www.riovista.org

**Ripon** · *Ripon C/C* · Dorothy Booth, Dir., 929 W. Main St., P.O. Box 327, 95366, P 13,700, M 219, (209) 599-7519, Fax (209) 599-2286, info@riponchamber.org, www.riponchamber.org

**Riverbank** · *Riverbank C/C* · P.O. Box 340, 95367, P 15,000, M 250, (209) 869-4541, info@riverbankchamber.org, www.riverbankchamber.org

**Riverside** · *Greater Riverside Chambers of Commerce* · Cindy Roth, Pres./CEO, 3985 University Ave., 92501, P 291,398, M 1,608, (951) 683-7100, Fax (951) 683-2670, rchamber@riverside-chamber.com, www.riverside-chamber.com

**Riverside** · *Jurupa Valley C/C* · Bobby Hernandez, Pres., 8175 Limonite, Ste. A, PMB V13, 92509, P 92,000, M 250, (951) 727-4359, jurupachamber@aol.com

**Rocklin** · *Rocklin Area C/C* · Robin Trimble, CEO, 3700 Rocklin Rd., 95677, P 50,000, M 650, (916) 624-2548, Fax (916) 624-5743, info@rocklinchamber.com, www.rocklinchamber.com

**Rodeo** · *Rodeo C/C* · Mark Hughes , Pres., P.O. Box 548, 94572, P 12,000, M 60, (510) 799-7351, Fax (510) 741-4945, rcoc@rodeoca.org, www.rodeoca.org

**Rohnert Park** · *Rohnert Park C/C* · Roy Gugliotta, Pres./CEO, 101 Golf Course Dr., Ste. C-7, 94928, P 42,550, M 400, (707) 584-1415, Fax (707) 584-2945, info@rohnertparkchamber.org, www.rohnertparkchamber.org

**Rolling Hills Estate** · *Palos Verdes Peninsula C/C* · Kay Finer, Pres./CEO, 707 Silver Spur Rd., Ste. 100, 90274, P 75,000, M 500, (310) 377-8111, Fax (310) 377-0614, office@palosverdeschamber.com, www.palosverdeschamber.com

**Rosamond** · *Antelope Valley Chambers of Commerce-Rosamond* · Ramon Ortega, Pres./CEO, 2861 Diamond St., P.O. Box 365, 93560, P 20,000, M 750, (661) 256-3248, Fax (661) 256-3249, www.avchambers.com

**Rosedale** · *see Bakersfield-North of the River C/C*

**Rosemead** · *Rosemead C/C* · 3953 Muscatel Ave., 91770, P 60,000, M 220, (626) 288-0811, Fax (626) 288-2514, rosemeadcc@aol.com, www.rosemeadchamber.org

**Roseville** · *Roseville C/C* · Wendy Gerig, CEO, 650 Douglas Blvd., 95678, P 130,000, M 1,700, (916) 783-8136, Fax (916) 783-5261, admin@rosevillechamber.com, www.rosevillechamber.com.

**Rough and Ready** · *Rough and Ready C/C* · Charles Creciluis, Pres., P.O. Box 801, 95975, P 2,500, M 135, (530) 272-4320, www.roughandreadychamber.com

**Round Mountain** · *see Burney*

**Rubidoux** · *see Riverside-Jurupa Valley C/C*

**Running Springs** · *Running Springs Area C/C* · Kevin Somes, Pres., P.O. Box 96, 92382, P 6,000, M 155, (909) 867-2411, Fax (909) 867-2411, info@runningspringschamber.com, www.runningspringschamber.com

**Sabre Springs** · *see San Diego North C/C*

## Sacramento Area

**Sacramento Metro Chamber** · Matt Mahood, Pres./CEO, One Capitol Mall, Ste. 300, 95814, P 2,000,000, M 2,200, (916) 552-6800, Fax (916) 443-2672, chamber@metrochamber.org, www.metrochamber.org

**Sacramento Area,** *continued*

**North Sacramento C/C** · P.O. Box 15468, 95815, P 50,000, M 102, (916) 925-6773, www.northsacramentochamber.org

**Sacramento Hispanic C/C** · Steve Gandola, CEO, 1491 River Park Dr., Ste. 101, 95815, P 2,000,000, M 800, (916) 486-7700, Fax (916) 486-7728, info@sachcc.org, www.sachcc.org

**Saint Helena** · *Saint Helena C/C* · Nancy Levenberg, Pres./CEO, 1010 Main St., Ste. A, 94574, P 6,100, M 550, (707) 963-4456, (800) 799-6456, Fax (707) 963-5396, nancy@sthelena.com, www.sthelena.com

**Salinas** · *Salinas Valley C/C* · Tiffany M. DiTullio, Pres./CEO, 119 E. Alisal St., 93901, P 151,000, M 1,000, (831) 751-7725, Fax (831) 424-8639, info@salinaschamber.com, www.salinaschamber.com.

**Salton City** · *West Shores C/C of the Salton Sea* · Carlene Ness, Secy., 4112 Haven Dr., P.O. Box 5185, 92275, P 4,500, M 215, (760) 394-4112, wschamber@saltonseas.com, www.westshoreschamber.org

**San Andreas** · *see Angels Camp*

**San Anselmo** · *San Anselmo C/C* · Connie Rodgers, Pres./CEO, P.O. Box 2844, 94979, P 13,000, M 250, (415) 454-2510, Fax (415) 258-9458, info@sananselmochamber.org, www.sananselmochamber.org

**San Bernardino** · *San Bernardino Area C/C* · Judi Penman, Pres./CEO, 546 W. Sixth St., P.O. Box 658, 92402, P 202,000, M 1,000, (909) 885-7515, Fax (909) 384-9979, sba.chamber@verizon.net, www.sbachamber.com

**San Bruno** · *San Bruno C/C* · Laura Baughman, Exec. Dir., 618 San Mateo Ave., 94066, P 41,000, M 200, (650) 588-0180, Fax (650) 588-6473, office@sanbrunochamber.com, www.sanbrunochamber.com

**San Carlos** · *San Carlos C/C* · Sheryl Pomerenk, CEO, 1500 Laurel St., Ste. B, 94070, P 28,500, M 745, (650) 593-1068, Fax (650) 593-9108, staff@sancarloschamber.org, www.sancarloschamber.org

**San Clemente** · *San Clemente C/C* · Lynn Wood, Pres./CEO, 1100 N. El Camino Real, 92672, P 66,000, M 500, (949) 492-1131, Fax (949) 492-3764, info@scchamber.com, www.scchamber.com

## San Diego Area

**San Diego Reg. C/C** · Ruben Barrales, Pres./CEO, 402 W. Broadway, Ste. 1000, 92101, P 2,900,000, M 2,800, (619) 544-1300, webinfo@sdchamber.org, www.sdchamber.org.

**Golden Triangle C/C** · George Schmall, Pres., 1011 Camino Del Mar, Ste. 256 , P.O. Box 927729, 92192, P 300,000, M 310, (858) 350-1253, www.goldentrianglechamber.com.

**Old Town San Diego C/C** · Richard Stegner, Exec. Dir., 2383 San Diego Ave., 92110, P 1,200,000, M 485, (619) 291-4903, Fax (619) 291-9383, otsd@aol.com, www.oldtownsandiego.org

**San Diego County Hispanic C/C** · Nicholas Inzunza, Chrmn., P.O. Box 131548, 92113, M 1,000, (619) 702-0790, Fax (619) 521-6722, sdhcc@sdchcc.com, www.sdhcc.com

**San Diego North C/C** · Debra Rosen, Pres./CEO, 11650 Iberia Pl., Ste. 220, 92128, P 240,000, M 850, (858) 487-1767, Fax (858) 487-8051, infodesk@sdncc.com, www.sdncc.com

**San Dimas** · *San Dimas C/C* · Ted Powl, Pres./CEO, 246 E. Bonita Ave., P.O. Box 175, 91773, P 35,756, M 410, (909) 592-3818, Fax (909) 592-8178, info@sandimaschamber.com, sandimaschamber.com.

**San Fernando** · *San Fernando C/C* · David Hernandez, Dir., P.O. Box 990, 91341, P 30,000, M 300, (818) 448-3403, drhassoc@earthlink.net, www.sanfernando.com

**San Francisco** · *Chinese C/C* · Sidney Chan, Pres., 730 Sacramento St., 94108, M 400, (415) 982-3000, Fax (415) 982-4720

**San Francisco** · *San Francisco C/C* · Steven Falk, Pres./CEO, 235 Montgomery St., 12th Floor, 94104, P 789,000, M 1,900, (415) 392-4520, Fax (415) 392-0485, info@sfchamber.com, www.sfchamber.com.

**San Gabriel** · *San Gabriel C/C* · 620 W. Santa Anita St., 91776, P 49,000, M 200, (626) 576-2525, Fax (626) 289-2901, rosco_sandy@yahoo.com, www.sangabrielchamber.com

**San Jacinto** · *see Hemet*

**San Jose** · *San Jose Silicon Valley C/C* · Pat Dando, Pres./CEO, 101 W. Santa Clara St., 95113, P 945,000, M 2,200, (408) 291-5250, Fax (408) 286-5019, info@sjchamber.com, www.sjchamber.com

**San Juan Bautista** · *San Juan Bautista C/C* · 209 3rd St., P.O. Box 1037, 95045, P 1,650, M 160, (831) 623-2454, Fax (831) 623-0674, sjbcc@sbcglobal.net, www.sjbchamber.com

**San Juan Capistrano** · *San Juan Capistrano C/C* · Karen Richesin, Dir., 31421 La Matanza St., P.O. Box 1878, 92693, P 35,000, M 350, (949) 493-4700, Fax (949) 489-2695, info@sanjuanchamber.com, www.sanjuanchamber.com

**San Leandro** · *San Leandro C/C* · Dave Johnson, CEO, 15555 E. 14th St., Ste. 100, 94578, P 80,000, M 550, (510) 317-1400, Fax (510) 317-1404, ceo@sanleandrochamber.com, www.sanleandrochamber.com

**San Luis Obispo** · *San Luis Obispo C/C* · David E. Garth, Pres./CEO, 1039 Chorro St., 93401, P 44,000, M 1,488, (805) 781-2777, Fax (805) 543-1255, www.VisitSLO.com, slochamber@slochamber.org, www.slochamber.org

**San Marcos** · *San Marcos C/C* · Joan Priest, Exec. Admin., 939 Grand Ave., 92078, P 77,000, M 625, (760) 744-1270, Fax (760) 744-5230, info@sanmarcoschamber.com, www.sanmarcoschamber.com

**San Marino** · *San Marino C/C* · Chris Carlos, Pres., 2304 Huntington Dr., Ste. 202, 91108, P 14,000, M 300, (626) 286-1022, Fax (626) 286-7765, snmarinocofc@earthlink.net, www.sanmarinochamber.com

**San Mateo** · *San Mateo Area C/C* · Linda Asbury, Pres., 385 First Ave., 94401, P 93,600, M 1,000, (650) 401-2440, Fax (650) 401-2446, linda@sanmateochamber.org, www.sanmateochamber.org

**San Mateo County** · *see Redwood City*

**San Pablo** · *San Pablo C/C* · Jerry Sattler, Pres., P.O. Box 6204, 94806, P 32,000, M 125, (510) 234-2067, Fax (510) 234-0604, spchamber39@yahoo.com , www.ci.san-pablo.ca.us

**San Pedro** · *San Pedro C/C* · Camilla Townsend, Pres./CEO, 390 W. 7th St., 90731, P 81,000, M 600, (310) 832-7272, Fax (310) 832-0685, info@sanpedrochamber.com, www.sanpedrochamber.com

**San Rafael** · *Hispanic C/C of Marin* · Cecilia Zamora, Pres., P.O. Box 4423, 94913, P 265,000, M 185, (415) 721-9686, Fax (415) 454-0102, www.hccmarin.com

**San Rafael** · *San Rafael C/C* · Tallia Hart, Pres./CEO, 817 Mission Ave., 94901, P 56,000, M 950, (415) 454-4163, (800) 454-4163, Fax (415) 454-7039, srcc@sanrafaelchamber.com, www.sanrafaelchamber.com

**San Ramon** · *San Ramon C/C Inc.* · Carolyn Degnan, Pres./CEO, 12667 Alcosta Blvd., Ste. 160, 94583, P 60,000, M 540, (925) 242-0600, Fax (925) 242-0603, info@sanramon.org, www.sanramon.org

**San Simeon** · *San Simeon C/C* · Michael Hanchett, Pres., 250 San Simeon Ave., Ste. 3A, 93452, P 6,000, M 50, (805) 927-3500, Fax (805) 927-6453, sansimeonchamber@yahoo.com, www.sansimeonchamber.com

**San Ysidro** · *San Ysidro C of C & Visitor Info. Ctr.* · Jason M-B Wells, Exec. Dir., 663 E. San Ysidro Blvd., 92173, P 40,000, M 200, (619) 428-1281, Fax (619) 428-1294, info@sanysidrochamber.org, www.sanysidrochamber.org

**Sanger** · *Sanger Dist. C/C & Visitors Ctr.* · Jeanette Inouye, Pres./CEO, 1789 Jensen Ave., Ste. B, 93657, P 25,385, M 275, (559) 875-4575, Fax (559) 875-0745, sanger@psnw.com, www.sanger.org.

**Santa Ana** · *Hispanic C/C of Orange County* · Priscilla Lopez, Pres./CEO, 2130 E. 4th St., Ste. 160, 92705, M 450, (714) 953-4289, Fax (714) 953-0273, mmonter@hcoc.org, www.hcoc.org

**Santa Ana** · *Santa Ana C/C* · Michael Metzler, Pres./CEO, 2020 N. Broadway, 2nd Flr., 92706, P 351,000, M 1,090, (714) 541-5353, Fax (714) 541-2238, info@santaanachamber.com, www.santaanachamber.com

**Santa Barbara** · *Hispanic C/C of Santa Barbara* · Sergio Villa, Chair, P.O. Box 6592, 93160, M 350, (805) 637-3680, Fax (805) 681-1260, info@sbhispanicchamber.org, www.sbhispanicchamber.org

**Santa Barbara** · *Santa Barbara Region C/C* · Steve Cushman, Exec. Dir., 924 Anacapa St., Ste. 1, P.O. Box 299, 93101, P 407,310, M 2,000, (805) 965-3023, Fax (805) 966-5954, info@sbchamber.org, www.sbchamber.org

**Santa Clara** · *Santa Clara C of C & CVB* · Steve VanDorn, Pres./CEO, 1850 Warburton Ave., 95050, P 105,830, M 625, (408) 244-8244, (800) 272-6822, Fax (408) 244-7830, steve.vandorn@santaclara.org, www.santaclarachamber.org

**Santa Clarita** · *Santa Clarita Valley C/C* · Larry Mankin, CEO, 28460 Ave. Stanford, Ste. 100, 91355, P 213,178, M 1,600, (661) 702-6977, Fax (661) 702-6980, info@scvchamber.com, www.scvchamber.com

**Santa Cruz** · *Santa Cruz C/C* · William Tysseling, Exec. Dir., 611 Ocean St., Ste. 1, 95060, P 55,000, M 800, (831) 457-3713, Fax (831) 423-1847, info@santacruzchamber.org, www.santacruzchamber.org

**Santa Fe Springs** · *Santa Fe Springs C/C* · Kathie Fink, CEO, 12016 E. Telegraph Rd., Ste. 100, 90670, P 17,500, M 790, (562) 944-1616, Fax (562) 946-3976, mail@sfschamber.com, www.sfschamber.com

**Santa Maria** · *Santa Maria Valley C/C* · Robert Hatch, Pres./CEO, 614 S. Broadway, 93454, P 137,000, M 1,100, (805) 925-2403, (800) 331-3779, Fax (805) 928-7559, info@santamaria.com, www.santamaria.com

**Santa Monica** · *Santa Monica C/C* · Laurel Rosen, Pres./CEO, 1234 6th St., Ste. 100, 90401, P 94,000, M 900, (310) 393-9825, Fax (310) 394-1868, info@smchamber.com, www.smchamber.com

**Santa Paula** · *Santa Paula C/C* · Sam Hishmeh, Chair, 200 N. Tenth St., P.O. Box 1, 93061, P 29,000, M 300, (805) 525-5561, Fax (805) 525-8950, info@santapaulachamber.com, www.santapaulachamber.com

## Santa Rosa Area

**Santa Rosa C/C** · 637 First St., 95404, P 154,000, M 1,000, (707) 545-1414, Fax (707) 545-6914, chamber@santarosachamber.com, www.santarosachamber.com

**Hispanic C/C of Sonoma County** · Juan M. Hernandez, Pres., 3033 Cleveland Ave., Ste. 306, P.O. Box 11392, 95406, P 490,000, M 260, (707) 575-3648, Fax (707) 575-3693, hccadmin@hcc-sc.org, www.hcc-sc.org

**Mark West Area C/C** · Patricia Morelli, Ofc. Mgr., 4787 Old Redwood Hwy., Ste. 101, 95403, P 25,000, M 175, (707) 578-7975, Fax (707) 578-0397, markwest@markwest.org, www.markwest.org

**Santee** · *Santee C/C* · Warren H. Savage Jr., Exec. Dir., 10315 Mission Gorge Rd., 92071, P 56,000, M 312, (619) 449-6572, Fax (619) 562-7906, info@santee-chamber.org, www.santee-chamber.org.

**Saratoga** · *Saratoga C/C* · Emily Lo, Pres., 14485 Big Basin Way, 95070, P 31,000, M 325, (408) 867-0753, Fax (408) 867-5213, info@saratogachamber.org, www.saratogachamber.org

**Saugus** · *see Santa Clarita*

**Sausalito** · *Sausalito C/C* · Oonagh Kavanagh, CEO, 10 Liberty Ship Way, Bay 2,, Ste. 250, 94965, P 7,500, M 375, (415) 331-7262, Fax (415) 332-0323, chamber@sausalito.org, www.sausalito.org

**Scotts Valley** · *Scotts Valley C/C* · Sharollynn Ullestad, Exec. Dir., 360 Kings Village Rd., 95066, P 12,000, M 300, (831) 438-1010, Fax (831) 438-6544, info@scottsvalleychamber.com, www.scottsvalleychamber.com

**Scripps Ranch** · *see San Diego North C/C*

**Seal Beach** · *Seal Beach C/C* · 201 8th St., Ste. 120, 90740, P 28,000, M 398, (562) 799-0179, Fax (562) 795-5637, info@sealbeachchamber.org, www.sealbeachchamber.org

**Seaside** · *Seaside-Sand City C/C* · 505 Broadway Ave., 93955, P 36,000, M 400, (831) 394-6501, sschambr@embay.net

**Sebastopol** · *Sebastopol Area C/C* · Teresa Ramondo, Exec. Dir., 265 S. Main St., P.O. Box 178, 95473, P 35,000, M 400, (707) 823-3032, (877) 828-4748, Fax (707) 823-8439, chamber@sebastopol.org, www.sebastopol.org

**Selma** · *Selma District C/C* · Cindy L. Howell, Exec. Dir., 1821 Tucker St., 93662, P 24,000, M 350, (559) 891-2235, Fax (559) 896-7075, cindyh@cityofselma.com, www.cityofselma.com/chamber.

**Sepulveda** · *see Van Nuys*

**Shafter** · *Shafter C/C* · Debbe Haley, Pres., 336 Pacific Ave., 93263, P 15,609, M 100, (661) 746-2600, Fax (661) 746-0607, shafterchamber@shafter.com, www.shafter.com

**Shasta Dam** · *see Redding*

**Shaver Lake** · *Shaver Lake C/C* · 41777 Tollhouse Rd., P.O. Box 58, 93664, P 1,850, M 300, (559) 841-3350, (866) 500-3350, Fax (559) 841-8645, shaverchamber@psnw.com, www.shaverlakechamber.com

**Sherman Oaks** · *Greater Sherman Oaks C/C* · Lisa Clayden, Exec. Dir., 14827 Ventura Blvd., Ste. 207, 91403, P 57,000, M 250, (818) 906-1951, Fax (818) 783-3100, chamber@shermanoakschamber.org, www.shermanoakschamber.org

**Shingle Springs** · *Shingle Springs/Cameron Park C/C* · Al Carrier, Pres., 3300 Coach Lane, Ste. B7, P.O. Box 341, 95682, P 18,000, M 315, (530) 677-8000, Fax (530) 676-8313, info@sscpchamber.org, www.sscpchamber.org

**Shoshone** · *Death Valley C/C* · Jennifer Viereck, Admin. Asst., 118 Hwy. 127, P.O. Box 157, 92384, P 800, M 120, (760) 852-4524, deathvalleych@veawb.coop, www.deathvalleychamber.org

**Sierra City** · *Sierra County C/C* · P.O. Box 436, 96125, P 3,557, M 71, (530) 862-1275, (800) 200-4949, Fax (530) 862-1275, scchamber@nccn.net, www.sierracountychamber.net

**Sierra Madre** · *Sierra Madre C/C* · Bill Coburn, Pres., 37 Auburn Ave. #1, 91024, P 10,700, M 200, (626) 355-5111, Fax (626) 306-1150, info@sierramadrechamber.com, www.sierramadrechamber.com

**Signal Hill** · *Signal Hill C/C* · Bart De Lio, Pres., 2201 E. Willow, Ste.#D, P.O. Box 138, 90755, P 11,089, M 175, (562) 424-6489, Fax (562) 989-0833, admin@signalhillchamber.com, www.signalhillchamber.com

**Simi Valley** · *Simi Valley C/C* · Leigh Nixon, Pres./CEO, 40 W. Cochran St., Ste. 100, 93065, P 126,166, M 850, (805) 526-3900, Fax (805) 526-6234, info@simichamber.org, www.simivalleychamber.org.

**Slide Ranch** · *see Stinson Beach*

**Solana Beach** · *Solana Beach C/C* · Frieda Silveira, Dir., 210 W. Plaza St., P.O. Box 623, 92075, P 14,000, M 325, (858) 755-4775, Fax (858) 755-4889, info@solanabeachchamber.com, www.solanabeachchamber.com

**Soledad** · *Soledad Mission C/C* · Lucy Jensen, Pres., 641 Front St., 93960, P 23,200, M 100, (831) 678-3941, Fax (831) 678-3941, soledadmissionchamber@yahoo.com, www.soledadmissionchamber.com

**Solvang** · *Solvang C/C* · Linda Jackson, Exec. Dir., 1693 Mission Dr., Ste. 201C, P.O. Box 465, 93464, P 5,400, M 300, (805) 688-0701, linda@solvangcc.org, www.solvangcc.com

**Sonoma** · *Sonoma Valley C/C* · Jennifer Yankovich, Exec. Dir., 651-A Broadway, 95476, P 10,000, M 720, (707) 996-1033, Fax (707) 996-9402, info@sonomachamber.com, www.sonomachamber.com

**Sonora** · *Tuolumne County C/C* · George Segarini, Pres./CEO, 222 S. Shepherd St., 95370, P 59,380, M 500, (209) 532-4212, (877) 532-4212, Fax (209) 532-8068, info@tcchamber.com, www.tcchamber.com

**Soquel** · *see Capitola*

**Sorrento Mesa** · *see San Diego North C/C*

**South Gate** · *South Gate C/C* · Jaime Garcia, Exec. Dir., 3350 Tweedy Blvd., 90280, P 98,000, M 182, (323) 567-1203, Fax (323) 567-1204, sgchamber@sbcglobal.net, www.sgchamber.org

**South Lake Tahoe** · *see Stateline, NV*

**South Orange County** · *South Orange County Reg. Chambers of Commerce* · 26111 Antonio Pkwy., Ste. 400, Las Flores, 92688, P 305,000, M 1,000, (949) 635-5800, Fax (949) 635-1635, info@socchambers.com, www.socchambers.com

**South San Francisco** · *South San Francisco C/C* · Maria Martinucci, CEO, 213 Linden Ave., 94080, P 68,500, M 600, (650) 588-1911, Fax (650) 588-2534, info@ssfchamber.com, www.ssfchamber.com

**Spring Valley** · *Spring Valley C/C* · Tina Carlson, Exec. Dir., 3322 Sweetwater Springs Blvd., Ste. 202, P.O. Box 1211, 91979, P 80,000, M 300, (619) 670-9902, Fax (619) 670-9924, info@springvalleychamber.org, www.springvalleychamber.org

**Springville** · *Springville C/C* · Rick Mitchell, Pres., P.O. Box 104, 93265, P 5,000, M 90, (559) 539-0100, chamber@springville.ca.us, www.springville.ca.us

**Squaw Valley** · *see Miramonte*

**Stanton** · *Stanton C/C* · Billie Turner, Exec. Dir., 8381 Katella Ave., Ste.#H, P.O. Box 353, 90680, P 39,000, M 140, (714) 995-1485, Fax (714) 995-1184, service@stantonchamber.org, www.stantonchamber.org

**Stinson Beach** · *Stinson Beach C/C* · John Posadas, Pres., P.O. Box 404, 94970, P 500, M 1, (415) 868-1034, beach@stinson-beach.net, www.stinson-beach.net

**Stockton** · *Greater Stockton C/C* · Douglass W. Wilhoit Jr., CEO, 445 W. Weber Ave., Ste. 220, 95203, P 263,000, M 1,600, (209) 547-2770, Fax (209) 466-5271, schamber@stocktonchamber.org, www.stocktonchamber.org

**Studio City** · *Studio City C/C* · Esther Walker, Exec. Dir., 4024 Radford Ave., Ed. 2, Ste. F, 91604, P 42,000, M 300, (818) 655-5916, Fax (818) 655-8392, admin@studiocitychamber.com, www.studiocitychamber.com

**Suisun** · *see Fairfield*

**Sun City** · *Menifee Valley C/C* · Dorothy Wolons, Pres./CEO, 27070 Sun City Blvd., 92586, P 66,000, M 400, (951) 672-1991, Fax (951) 672-4022, info@menifeevalleychamber.com, www.menifeevalleychamber.com

**Sun Valley** · *Sun Valley Area C/C* · Dennis O'Sullivan, Pres., P.O. Box 308, 91353, P 73,000, M 200, (818) 768-2014, Fax (818) 767-1947, info@svacc.com, www.svacc.com

**Sunland** · *see Tujunga*

**Sunnyvale** · *Sunnyvale C/C* · Paul Stewart, Pres./CEO, 260 S. Sunnyvale Ave., Ste. 4, 94086, P 140,000, M 700, (408) 736-4971, Fax (408) 736-1919, info@svcoc.org, www.svcoc.org

**Susanville** · *Lassen County C/C* · Patricia Hagata, Exec. Dir., 75 N. Weatherlow St., P.O. Box 338, 96130, P 34,109, M 400, (530) 257-4323, Fax (530) 251-2561, director@lassencountychamber.org, www.lassencountychamber.org.

**Sutter County** · *see Marysville*

**Sylmar** · *see San Fernando*

**Taft** · *Taft District C/C* · Randy Miller, Exec. Dir., 400 Kern St., 93268, P 22,000, M 250, (661) 765-2165, Fax (661) 765-6639, taftchamber@bak.rr.com, www.taftchamber.com

**Tahoe City** · *see Lake Tahoe*

**Tarzana** · *see Woodland Hills*

**Tehachapi** · *Greater Tehachapi C/C* · Ida Perkins, Pres., 209 E. Tehachapi Blvd., P.O. Box 401, 93581, P 38,000, M 500, (661) 822-4180, Fax (661) 822-9036, chamber@tehachapi.com, www.tehachapi.com

**Temecula** · *Temecula Valley C/C* · Alice Sullivan, Pres./CEO, 26790 Ynez Ct., Ste. A, 92591, P 94,000, M 1,400, (951) 676-5090, Fax (951) 694-0201, info@temecula.org, www.temecula.org

**Temple City** · *Temple City C/C* · Linda Payne, Pres./CEO, 9050 Las Tunas Dr., 91780, P 36,000, M 420, (626) 286-3101, Fax (626) 286-2590, info@templecitychamber.org, www.templecitychamber.org

**Templeton** · *Templeton C/C* · Robert Rosales, Pres., P.O. Box 701, 93465, P 7,000, M 185, (805) 434-1789, info@templetonchamber.com, www.templetonchamber.com

**Terminous** · *see California Delta*

**Thornton** · *Thornton C/C* · Marlene Corbitt, Secy., P.O. Box 138, 95686, P 2,000, M 31, (209) 794-2255, Fax (209) 794-2355, mlcorbitt@att.net

**Thousand Oaks** · *see Westlake Village*

**Thousand Palms** · *Thousand Palms C/C* · 72-715 La Canada Way, P.O. Box 365, 92276, P 5,000, M 150, (760) 343-1988, Fax (760) 343-1988, tp4business@yahoo.com, www.thousandpalmscc.com

**Tiburon** · *Tiburon Peninsula C/C* · Georgia Kirchmaier, Exec. Dir., 96-B Main St., P.O. Box 563, 94920, P 11,000, M 300, (415) 435-5633, Fax (415) 435-1132, tibcc@sbcglobal.net, www.tiburonchamber.org

**Toluca Lake** · *Toluca Lake C/C* · Roy Disney, Pres., P.O. Box 2312, 91610, P 15,000, M 125, (818) 761-6594, info@tolucalakechamber.com, www.tolucalakechamber.com

**Topanga** · *Topanga C/C* · Kamakshi Hart, P.O. Box 185, 90290, P 14,500, M 200, (310) 455-0790, info@topangachamber.org, www.topangachamber.org

**Topaz** · *Northern Mono C/C* · 115281 U.S. Hwy. 395, 96133, P 1,000, M 65, (530) 208-6078, info@northernmonochamber.com, www.northernmonochamber.com

**Torrance** · *Torrance Area C/C* · Barbara Glennie, Pres./CEO, 3400 Torrance Blvd., Ste. 100, 90503, P 147,400, M 1,000, (310) 540-5858, Fax (310) 540-7662, barbara@torrancechamber.com, www.torrancechamber.com

**Torrey Highlands** · *see San Diego North C/C*

**Tracy** · *Tracy C/C* · Sofia Valenzuela, Op. Mgr., 223 E. 10th St., 95376, P 78,000, M 710, (209) 835-2131, Fax (209) 833-9526, info@tracychamber.org, www.tracychamber.org

**Trinidad** · *Greater Trinidad C/C* · Richard Johnson, Pres., P.O. Box 356, 95570, P 311, M 125, (707) 677-1610, dori@discover trinidadca.com, www.discovertrinidadca.com

**Trinity County** · *Trinity County C/C* · Patricia Zugg, Exec. Dir., 215 Main St., P.O. Box 517, Weaverville, 96093, P 13,050, M 200, (530) 623-6101, (800) 4-TRINITY, Fax (530) 623-3753, trinitycoc@yahoo.com, www.trinitycounty.com

**Truckee** · *Truckee/Donner C/C* · Lynn Saunders, Pres./CEO, 10065 Donner Pass Rd., 96161, P 15,800, M 665, (530) 587-2757, Fax (530) 587-2439, info@truckee.com, www.truckee.com

**Tujunga** · *Sunland-Tujunga C/C* · Nancy Raper, Exec. Dir., P.O. Box 571, 91043, P 55,000, M 200, (818) 352-4433, www.stchamber.com

**Tulare** · *Tulare C/C* · Marc Limas, Interim Pres./CEO, 220 E. Tulare Ave., P.O. Box 1435, 93275, P 57,000, M 800, (559) 686-1547, Fax (559) 686-4915, info@tularechamber.org, www.tularechamber.org.

**Tulelake** · *Tulelake C/C* · Dave Misso, Pres., P.O. Box 1152, 96134, P 1,000, M 30, (530) 667-5522, (530) 664-3918, Fax (530) 667-5351, cityoftulelake@cot.net, www.visittulelakecalifornia.com

**Tuolumne County** · *see Sonora*

**Turlock** · *Turlock Chamber/CVB* · Sharon Silva, Pres./CEO, 115 S. Golden State Blvd., 95380, P 70,000, M 500, (209) 632-2221, Fax (209) 632-5289, sharonsilva@turlockchamber.com, www.turlockchamber.com

**Tustin** · *Tustin C/C* · Marisa Charette, Pres., 399 El Camino Real, 92780, P 70,000, M 500, (714) 544-5341, Fax (714) 544-2083, info@tustinchamber.org, www.tustinchamber.org

**Twain Harte** · *Twain Harte Area C/C* · Rebecca Halvorsen, Pres., 23000 Meadow Ln., P.O. Box 404, 95383, P 2,500, M 200, (209) 586-4482, Fax (209) 586-0360, info@twainhartecc.com, www.twainhartecc.com

**Twentynine Palms** · *Twentynine Palms C/C* · Jessica Wagner-Schultz, Exec. Dir., 73660 Civic Center Dr., Ste. D, 92277, P 28,000, M 255, (760) 367-3445, Fax (760) 367-3366, 29coc@29chamber.com, www.29chamber.com

**Ukiah** · *Greater Ukiah C/C* · Bert Mosier, Pres./CEO, 200 S. School St., 95482, P 36,000, M 500, (707) 462-4705, Fax (707) 462-2088, info@ukiahchamber.com, www.ukiahchamber.com

**Union City** · *Union City C/C* · 3939 Smith St., 94587, P 62,000, M 283, (510) 952-9637, Fax (510) 952-9647, info@unioncitychamber.com, www.unioncitychamber.com

**Universal City** · *see North Hollywood*

**Upland** · *Upland C/C* · Sonnie Faires, Pres./CEO, 215 N. 2nd Ave., Ste. D, 91786, P 74,000, M 700, (909) 204-4465, Fax (909) 204-4464, realpeople@uplandchamber.org, www.uplandchamber.org

**Vacaville** · *Vacaville C/C* · Gary H. Tatum, Pres./CEO, 300 Main St. #A, 95688, P 98,000, M 700, (707) 448-6424, Fax (707) 448-0424, alex@vacavillechamber.com, www.vacavillechamber.com

**Val Verde** · *see Santa Clarita*

**Valencia** · *see Santa Clarita*

U.S. Chambers of Commerce

**Vallejo** · *Vallejo C/C* · Rick Wells, Pres./CEO, 427 York St., 94590, P 119,000, M 600, (707) 644-5551, Fax (707) 644-5590, info@vallejochamber.com, www.vallejochamber.com

**Valley Center** · *Valley Center C/C* · Shawneen Burdick, Pres., 27301 Valley Center Rd. , P.O. Box 8, 92082, P 19,000, M 150, (760) 749-8472, Fax (760) 749-8483, info@vcchamber.com, www.vcchamber.com

**Van Nuys** · *Greater San Fernando Valley C/C* · Nancy Hoffman Vanyek, CEO, 7120 Hayvenhurst, Ste. 114, 91406, P 213,000, M 400, (818) 989-0300, Fax (818) 989-3836, info@sanfernandovalleychamber.com, www.sanfernandovalleychamber.com

**Venice** · *Venice C/C* · Andy Layman, Pres., P.O. Box 202, 90294, P 52,000, M 170, (310) 822-5425, Fax (310) 664-7938, info@venicechamber.net, www.venicechamber.net

**Ventura** · *Ventura C/C* · Zoe J. Taylor, Pres./CEO, 801 S. Victoria Ave., Ste. 200, 93003, P 105,800, M 985, (805) 676-7500, Fax (805) 650-1414, info@ventura-chamber.org, www.venturachamber.com

**Verdugo City** · *see Glendale--Montrose-Verdugo City C/C*

**Vernon** · *Vernon C/C* · Marisa Olguin, Pres./CEO, 3801 Santa Fe Ave., 90058, P 80, M 300, (323) 583-3313, Fax (323) 583-0704, molguin@vernonchamber.org, www.vernonchamber.org

**Victorville** · *Victorville C/C* · Michele Spears, Pres./CEO, 14174 Greentree Blvd., P.O. Box 997, 92395, P 104,000, M 780, (760) 245-6506, Fax (760) 245-6505, vvchamber@vvchamber.com, vvchamber.com

**Visalia** · *Visalia C/C* · Glenn Morris, Pres./CEO, 220 N. Santa Fe Ave., 93291, P 128,000, M 1,200, (559) 734-5876, Fax (559) 734-7479, info@visaliachamber.org, www.visaliachamber.org

**Vista** · *Vista C/C* · Paul O'Neal, Pres./CEO, 201 Washington St., 92084, P 94,500, M 550, (760) 726-1122, Fax (760) 726-8654, info@vistachamber.org, www.vistachamber.org

**Walnut** · *see Diamond Bar*

**Walnut Creek** · *Walnut Creek C/C* · Jay Hoyer, Pres./CEO, 1777 Botelho Dr., Ste. 103, 94596, P 66,000, M 800, (925) 934-2007, Fax (925) 934-2404, chamber@walnut-creek.com, www.walnut-creek.com

**Wasco** · *Wasco C of C & Ag.* · Vickie Hight, Ofc. Mgr., 700 G St., P.O. Box 783, 93280, P 21,000, M 130, (661) 758-2746, Fax (661) 758-2900, vhight@ci.wasco.ca.us, www.ci.wasco.ca.us

**Watsonville** · *Pajaro Valley C/C & Ag.* · Jerry Beyersdorff, CEO, 449 Union St., P.O. Box 1748, 95077, P 49,601, M 450, (831) 724-3900, Fax (831) 728-5300, info@pajarovalleychamber.com, www.pajarovalleychamber.com

**Weaverville** · *see Trinity County*

**Weed** · *Weed C/C & Visitor Center* · Brenda Woods, Pres., 34 Main St., 96094, P 3,000, M 160, (530) 938-4624, (877) 938-4624, Fax (530) 938-1658, weedchamber@ncen.org, www.weedchamber.com

**West Covina** · *West Covina C/C* · 811 S. Sunset Ave., 91790, P 110,000, M 400, (626) 338-8496, Fax (626) 960-0511, gcarlson@westcovinachamber.com, www.westcovinachamber.com

**West Hollywood** · *West Hollywood C/C* · Sharon Sandow, Pres./CEO, 8272 Santa Monica Blvd., 90046, P 39,500, M 530, (323) 650-2688, Fax (323) 650-2689, info@wehochamber.com, www.wehochamber.com

**West Sacramento** · *West Sacramento C/C* · Denice Seals, CEO, 1414 Merkley Ave. #1, 95691, P 42,000, M 450, (916) 371-7042, Fax (916) 371-7007, info@westsacramentochamber.com, www.westsacramentochamber.com

**Westchester** · *LAX Coastal Area C/C* · Christina Davis, Pres./CEO, 9100 S. Sepulveda, Ste. 210, 90045, P 50,000, M 650, (310) 645-5151, Fax (310) 645-0130, christina@laxcoastal.com, www.laxcoastal.com

**Westlake Village** · *Thousand Oaks-Westlake Village Regional C/C* · Jill Lederer, Pres./CEO, 600 Hampshire Rd., Ste. 200, 91361, P 135,905, M 1,500, (805) 370-0035, Fax (805) 370-1083, jlederer@towlvchamber.org, www.towlvchamber.org

**Westley** · *see Patterson*

**Westminster** · *Vietnamese American C/C* · 9121 Bolsa Ave., Ste. 203, 92683, M 800, (714) 892-6928, Fax (714) 892-6938, info@vacoc.com, www.vacoc.com

**Westminster** · *Westminster C/C* · Crystal Wadsworth, Exec. Dir., 14491 Beach Blvd., 92683, P 89,683, M 200, (714) 898-9648, Fax (714) 373-1499, biz@westminsterchamber.org, www.westminsterchamber.org

**Westwood** · *Westwood Area C/C* · Regina Dickson, Exec. Secy., 462-885 Third St., P.O. Box 1247, 96137, P 2,200, M 50, (530) 256-2456, wacc1@citlink.net, www.westwoodchamber.org

**Wheatland** · *see Marysville*

**Whittier** · *Whittier Area C/C* · Mary Ann Bakotich, Exec Dir., 8158 Painter Ave., 90602, P 89,000, M 800, (562) 698-9554, Fax (562) 693-2700, maryann@whittierchamber.com, www.whittierchamber.com

**Wildomar** · *Wildomar C/C* · Michele Thomas, Exec. Dir., 33751 Mission Tr., P.O. Box 885, 92595, P 15,000, M 220, (951) 245-0437, Fax (951) 245-0437, info@wildomarchamber.org, www.wildomarchamber.org

**Willits** · *Willits C/C* · Lynn R. Kennelly, Exec. Dir., 299 E. Commercial St., 95490, P 15,000, M 200, (707) 459-7910, Fax (707) 459-7914, info@willits.org, www.willits.org.

**Willow Creek** · *Willow Creek C/C* · Tangie Markle, Pres., 38973 Hwy. 299, P.O. Box 704, 95573, P 1,500, M 85, (530) 629-2693, (800) 628-5156, Fax (530) 629-4051, info@willowcreekchamber.com, www.willowcreekchamber.com.

**Willows** · *Willows C/C* · Kathy Araiza, Ofc. Mgr., 118 W. Sycamore, 95988, P 6,700, M 173, (530) 934-8150, Fax (530) 934-8710, willowschamber@sbcglobal.net, www.willowschamber.com

**Wilmington** · *Wilmington C/C* · Daniel Hoffman, Exec. Dir., 544 N. Avalon Blvd., Ste. 104, P.O. Box 90, 90748, P 65,000, M 260, (310) 834-8586, Fax (310) 834-8887, info@wilmington-chamber.com, www.wilmington-chamber.com

**Windsor** · *Windsor C of C & Visitors Center* · Christine Tevini, Pres., 9001 Windsor Rd., P.O. Box 367, 95492, P 25,500, M 380, (707) 838-7285, Fax (707) 838-2778, info@windsorchamber.com, www.windsorchamber.com

**Winnetka** · *Winnetka C/C* · Diana Holly, Secy., 20122 Dan Owen St., P.O. Box 2051, 91306, P 19,200, M 100, (818) 998-3833, Fax (818) 998-4056, secretary@winnetkacachamber.com, www.winnetkacachamber.com

**Winters** · *Winters Dist. C/C* · Tom Stone, Exec. Dir., P.O. Box 423, 95694, P 6,900, M 120, (530) 795-2329, Fax (530) 795-3202, chamberwinters@yahoo.com, www.winterschamber.com

**Woodland** · *Woodland Area C/C* · Kristy Wright, CEO, 307 1st St., 95695, P 53,000, M 680, (530) 662-7327, Fax (530) 662-4086, kristy@woodlandchamber.org, www.woodlandchamber.org

**Woodland Hills** · *Woodland Hills-Tarzana C/C* · Diana Williams, Exec. Dir., 20121 Ventura Blvd., Ste. 309, 91364, P 75,000, M 720, (818) 347-4737, Fax (818) 347-3321, diana@woodlandhillscc.net, www.woodlandhillscc.net

**Wrightwood** · *Wrightwood C/C* · Loretta Thompson, Pres., P.O. Box 416, 92397, P 4,100, M 93, (760) 249-4320, Fax (760) 249-6822, wwchamber@dslextreme.com, www.wrightwoodchamber.org

**Yorba Linda** · *Yorba Linda C/C* · Phyllis Coleman, Exec. Dir., 17670 Yorba Linda Blvd., 92886, P 69,000, M 380, (714) 993-9537, Fax (714) 993-7764, yorbalindachamber@sbcglobal.net, www.yorbalindachamber.org

**Yountville** · *Yountville C/C* · Cindy Sauserman, Exec. Dir., P.O. Box 2064, 94599, P 3,200, M 270, (707) 944-0904, Fax (707) 944-4465, info@yountville.com, www.yountville.com

**Yreka** · *Yreka C/C* · Pete Lafortune, Exec. Dir., 117 W. Miner St., 96097, P 7,300, M 350, (530) 842-1649, Fax (530) 842-2670, yrekachamber@nctv.com, www.yrekachamber.com

**Yuba City** · *see Marysville*

**Yucaipa** · *Yucaipa Valley C/C* · Pamela Emenger, Exec. Dir., 35139 Yucaipa Blvd., P.O. Box 45, 92399, P 52,000, M 350, (909) 790-1841, Fax (909) 363-7373, info@yucaipachamber.org, www.yucaipachamber.org

**Yucca Valley** · *Yucca Valley C/C* · Cheryl Nankervis, Exec. Dir., 56711 29 Palms Hwy., 92284, P 20,000, M 460, (760) 365-6323, Fax (760) 365-0763, chamber@yuccavalley.org, www.yuccavalley.org

# Colorado

**Colorado Assn. of Comm. & Ind.** · Chuck Berry, Pres., 1600 Broadway, Ste. 1000, Denver, 80202, M 500, (303) 831-7411, Fax (303) 860-1439, info@cochamber.com, www.cochamber.com

**Akron** · *Akron C/C* · Janet Starlin, Pres., P.O. Box 233, 80720, P 1,800, M 50, (970) 345-2624, www.washingtoncountychamber.com

**Alamosa** · *Alamosa County C/C* · 300 Chamber Dr., 81101, P 8,500, M 243, (719) 589-3681, Fax (719) 589-1773, office@alamosachamber.com, www.alamosa.org

**Alma** · *see Fairplay*

**Antonito** · *Antonito C/C* · Bill Laurell, Pres., 220 Main St., P.O. Box 427, 81120, P 1,200, M 65, (719) 376-2277, Fax (719) 376-2277

**Arrowhead** · *see Avon*

**Arvada** · *Arvada C/C* · Dot Wright, Pres., 7305 Grandview Ave., 80002, P 104,000, M 600, (303) 424-0313, Fax (303) 424-5370, dot@arvadachamber.org, www.arvadachamber.org

**Aspen** · *Aspen Chamber Resort Assn.* · Debbie Braun, Pres./CEO, 425 Rio Grande Pl., 81611, P 6,000, M 860, (970) 925-1940, (800) 670-0792, Fax (970) 920-1173, info@aspenchamber.org, www.aspenchamber.org

**Aurora** · *Aurora C/C* · Kevin Hougen, Pres./CEO, 14305 E. Alameda Ave., Ste. 300, 80012, P 308,000, M 1,500, (303) 344-1500, Fax (303) 344-1564, info@aurorachamber.org, www.aurorachamber.org.

**Avon** · *Vail Valley Partnership* · Michael Kurz, Pres./CEO, 101 Fawcett Rd., Ste. 240, P.O. Box 1130, 81620, P 48,000, M 1,000, (970) 476-1000, (800) 525-3875, Fax (970) 476-6008, info@visitvailvalley.com, www.visitvailvalley.com

**Bailey** · *Platte Canyon Area C/C* · Mary Sasser, Pres., P.O. Box 477, 80421, P 10,000, M 150, (303) 838-9080, baileycountrystore@hotmail.com, www.baileycolorado.org

**Basalt** · *Basalt C/C* · Heather Smith, Exec. Dir., Two Rivers Rd. & Midland Ave., P.O. Box 514, 81621, P 4,000, M 450, (970) 927-4031, Fax (970) 927-2833, info@basaltchamber.com, www.basaltchamber.com

**Bayfield** · *Bayfield Area C/C & Visitor Info. Center* · Roadside Park, P.O. Box 7, 81122, P 1,800, M 100, (970) 884-7372, (866) 984-7372, Fax (970) 884-7372, info@bayfieldchamber.org, www.bayfieldchamber.org

**Bayfield** · *Vallecito Lake C/C* · P.O. Box 804, 81122, P 300, M 45, (970) 247-1573, www.vallecitolakechamber.com

**Beaver Creek** · *see Avon*

**Bennett** · *I-70 Corridor C/C* · Gary Duke, Pres., 401 S. First St., 80102, P 8,296, M 131, (303) 644-4607, Fax (303) 644-6271, admin@i70ccoc.com, www.i70ccoc.com

**Berthoud** · *Berthoud Area C/C* · Don Dana, Exec. Dir., 345 Mountain Ave., P.O. Box 1709, 80513, P 4,975, M 150, (970) 532-4200, Fax (970) 532-7690, bcc@berthoudcolorado.com, www.berthoudcolorado.com

**Boulder** · *Boulder C/C* · Susan Graf, Pres., 2440 Pearl St., P.O. Box 73, 80306, P 101,000, M 1,600, (303) 442-1044, Fax (303) 938-8837, info@boulderchamber.com, www.boulderchamber.com.

**Breckenridge** · *also see Summit County*

**Breckenridge** · *Breckenridge Resort C/C* · John McMahon, Exec. Dir., 311 S. Ridge, P.O. Box 1909, 80424, P 3,406, M 500, (970) 453-2913, (970) 453-6018, Fax (970) 453-7238, gobreck@gobreck.com, www.gobreck.com

**Brighton** · *Greater Brighton Area C/C* · Karen Crawford, Exec. Dir., 36 S. Main St., 80601, P 35,000, M 330, (303) 659-0223, Fax (303) 659-5115, info@brightonchamber.com, www.brighton-chamber.com

**Broomfield** · *Broomfield C/C* · Jennifer Kerr, Pres./CEO, 350 Interlocken Blvd., Ste. 250, 80021, P 50,000, M 550, (303) 466-1775, Fax (303) 466-4481, info@broomfieldchamber.com, www.broomfieldchamber.com

**Brush** · *Brush Area C/C* · Dr. Ronald Prascher, Exec. Dir., 218 Clayton St., 80723, P 5,300, M 160, (970) 842-2666, (800) 354-8659, Fax (970) 842-3828, brush@brushchamber.org, www.brushchamber.org.

**Buena Vista** · *Buena Vista Area C/C* · Judy Hassell, Exec. Dir., 343 S. U.S. Hwy. 24, P.O. Box 2021, 81211, P 5,000, M 350, (719) 395-6612, Fax (719) 395-8035, chamber@buenavistacolorado.org, www.buenavistacolorado.org

**Burlington** · *Burlington C/C* · Dayla Hertneky, Pres., 420 S. 14th St., 80807, P 3,500, M 100, (719) 346-8070, www.burlingtoncolo.com

**Byers** · *see Bennett*

**Canon City** · *Canon City C/C* · Doug Shane, Exec. Dir., 403 Royal Gorge Blvd., 81212, P 29,000, M 375, (719) 275-2331, (800) 876-7922, Fax (719) 275-2332, chamber@canoncity.com, www.canoncitychamber.com

**Carbondale** · *Carbondale C/C* · Sherri Harrison, Exec. Dir., 981 Cowen Dr., Ste. C, P.O. Box 1645, 81623, P 5,900, M 585, (970) 963-1890, Fax (970) 963-4719, chamber@carbondale.com, www.carbondale.com

**Castle Rock** · *Castle Rock C/C* · Pam Ridler, Pres., 420 Jerry St., P.O. Box 282, 80104, P 46,000, M 667, (303) 688-4597, Fax (303) 688-2688, info@castlerock.org, www.castlerock.org.

**Cedaredge** · *Cedaredge Area C/C* · Carol Ferner, 245 W. Main St., P.O. Box 278, 81413, P 6,000, M 150, (970) 856-6961, Fax (970) 856-7292, info@cedaredgechamber.com, www.cedaredgechamber.com

**Centennial** · *South Metro Denver C/C* · John Brackney, Pres., 6840 S. University Blvd., 80122, P 630,000, M 1,600, (303) 795-0142, Fax (303) 795-7520, jbrackney@bestchamber.com, www.bestchamber.com.

**Cherry Creek** · *Cherry Creek C/C* · Christine Des Enfants, Exec. Dir., P.O. Box 6449, Denver, 80206, P 156,378, M 200, (303) 388-6022, Fax (303) 957-2327, staff@cherrycreekchamber.org, www.cherrycreekchamber.org

**Collbran** · *Plateau Valley C/C* · P.O. Box 143, 81624, P 3,500, M 40, (970) 487-3180, www.plateauvalley.com

**Colorado City** · *Greenhorn Valley C/C* · Sara Blackhurst, Dir., P.O. Box 19429, 81019, P 5,000, M 90, (719) 676-3000, slblackhurst@greenhornchamber.org, www.greenhornchamber.org

**Colorado Springs** · *Greater Colorado Springs C/C* · Dave Csintyan, CEO, 6 S. Tejon St., Ste. 700, 80903, P 578,151, M 1,800, (719) 635-1551, Fax (719) 635-1571, info@cscc.org, www.coloradospringschamber.org.

**Colorado Springs** · *Southern Colorado Women's C/C* · Leslie Eldridge, Pres., P.O. Box 49218, 80949, P 400,000, M 120, (719) 442-2007, sec@scwcc.com, www.scwcc.com

**Commerce City** · *see Westminster*

**Como** · *see Fairplay*

**Conifer** · *Conifer Area C/C* · Cathy Davis , Exec. Dir., P.O. Box 127, 80433, P 22,000, M 280, (303) 838-5711, Fax (303) 838-5712, info@goconifer.com, www.goconifer.com

**Copper Mountain** · *see Summit County*

**Cordillera** · *see Avon*

**Cortez** · *Cortez Area C/C* · Marcy Cummings, Exec. Dir., 928 E. Main St., P.O. Box 968, 81321, P 9,000, M 475, (970) 565-3414, Fax (970) 565-8373, cortezchamber@cityofcortez.com, www.cortezchamber.com

**Cowdrey** · *see Walden*

**Craig** · *Craig C/C* · Christina Currie, Exec. Dir., 360 E. Victory Way, 81625, P 11,900, M 375, (970) 824-5689, (800) 864-4405, Fax (970) 824-0231, info@craig-chamber.com, www.craig-chamber.com

**Crawford** · *Crawford Area C/C* · Mike Hart, Pres., P.O. Box 22, 81415, P 1,500, M 75, (970) 921-4000, info@crawfordcountry.org, www.crawfordcountry.org

**Creede** · *Creede-Mineral County C/C* · 904 S. Main St., P.O. Box 580, 81130, P 850, M 100, (719) 658-2374, (800) 327-2102, Fax (719) 658-2717, office@creede.com, www.creede.com

**Crested Butte** · *Crested Butte/Mt. Crested Butte C/C* · Christi Matthews, Dir., 601 Elk Ave., P.O. Box 1288, 81224, P 4,500, M 350, (970) 349-6438, (800) 545-4505, Fax (970) 349-1023, cbinfo@cbchamber.com, www.cbchamber.com

**Cripple Creek** · *Cripple Creek C/C* · P.O. Box 430, 80813, P 1,500, (719) 689-2502, info@cripple-creek.co.us, /www.cripplecreek gov.com

**Dacono** · *see Westminster*

**Deer Trail** · *see Bennett*

**Delta** · *Delta Area C/C* · TJ Davis, Exec. Dir., 301 Main St., 81416, P 8,500, M 275, (970) 874-8616, Fax (970) 874-8618, chamber@deltacolorado.org, www.deltacolorado.org.

## Denver Area

**Denver Metro C/C** · Joe Blake, Pres./CEO, 1445 Market St., 80202, P 2,800,000, M 3,000, (303) 534-8500, Fax (303) 534-3200, membership@denverchamber.org, www.denverchamber.org.

**Colorado Black C/C** · 410 17th St., Ste. 220, 80202, M 800, (303) 831-0720, Fax (303) 831-0755, staff@coloradoblack chamber.org, www.coloradoblackchamber.org

**Denver Area,** *continued*

**Denver Hispanic C/C** · Jeffrey Campos, Pres./CEO, 924 W. Colfax Ave., Ste. 201, 80204, M 1,800, (303) 534-7783, Fax (303) 595-8977, jcampos@dhcc.com, www.dhcc.com

**Dillon** · *see Summit County*

**Divide** · *Divide C/C* · P.O. Box 101, 80814, P 5,000, M 50, (719) 686-7605, info@dividechamber.org, www.dividechamber.org

**Dolores** · *Dolores C/C* · Stewart Hanold, 201 Railroad Ave., P.O. Box 602, 81323, P 1,000, M 160, (970) 882-4018, doloreschamber@centurytel.net, www.doloreschamber.com

**Downieville** · *see Idaho Springs*

**Dumont** · *see Idaho Springs*

**Durango** · *Durango Area C/C* · Jack Llewellyn, Exec. Dir., 111 S. Camino del Rio, P.O. Box 2587, 81302, P 45,000, M 800, (970) 247-0312, Fax (970) 385-7884, chamber@durangobusiness.org, www.durangobusiness.org

**Eads** · *Eads C/C* · Dennis Pearson, Pres., P.O. Box 163, 81036, P 747, M 30, (719) 438-5590, www.kiowacountycolo.com

**Eagle** · *Eagle Valley C/C* · 100 Fairgrounds Rd., P.O. Box 964, 81631, P 5,000, M 435, (970) 328-5220, Fax (970) 328-1120, evcc@centurytel.net, www.eaglevalley.org

**Eagle-Vail** · *see Avon*

**Edwards** · *see Avon*

**Elizabeth** · *Elizabeth Area C/C* · 166 Main St., P.O. Box 595, 80107, P 5,000, M 150, (303) 646-4287, Fax (303) 646-2509, director@elizabethchamber.org, www.elizabethchamber.org

**Empire** · *see Idaho Springs*

**Englewood** · *also see Centennial*

**Englewood** · *Greater Englewood C/C* · Randy Penn, Exec. Dir., 3501 S. Broadway, 2nd Flr., 80113, P 33,000, M 200, (303) 789-4473, Fax (303) 789-0098, info@myenglewoodchamber.com, www.myenglewoodchamber.com.

**Erie** · *Erie C/C* · Elle Cabbage, Exec. Dir., 235 Wells St., P.O. Box 97, 80516, P 18,000, M 250, (303) 828-3440, Fax (303) 828-3330, erie@eriechamber.org, www.eriechamber.org.

**Estes Park** · *Estes Park C/C* · P.O. Box 1818, 80517, P 8,000, M 60, (970) 586-4431, (800) 378-3708, cs2@estesparkchamber.org, www.estesparkchamber.com

**Evans** · *Evans Area C/C* · Michele Jones, Exec. Dir., 3700 Golden St., 80620, P 18,500, M 320, (970) 330-4204, Fax (970) 506-2726, ecc@evanschamber.org, www.evanschamber.org

**Evergreen** · *Evergreen Area C/C* · Melanie Nuchols, Pres., 28065 Hwy. 74 #201, 80439, P 44,000, M 710, (303) 674-3412, Fax (303) 674-8463, info@evergreenchamber.org, www.evergreenchamber.org

**Fairplay** · *South Park C/C* · P.O. Box 312, 80440, P 4,000, M 95, (719) 836-3410, info@southparkchamber.com, southpark chamber.com

**Federal Heights** · *see Westminster*

**Firestone** · *see Frederick*

**Firestone** · *see Westminster*

**Florence** · *Florence C/C* · Linda Smith, Exec. Dir., 117 S. Pikes Peak Ave., P.O. Box 145, 81226, P 5,000, M 130, (719) 784-3544, flochamber@coshi.net, www.florencecolorado.net

**Fort Collins** · *Fort Collins Area C/C* · David May, Pres./CEO, 225 S. Meldrum St., P.O. Drawer D, 80521, P 127,000, M 1,236, (970) 482-3746, Fax (970) 482-3774, general@fcchamber.org, www.fcchamber.org.

**Fort Lupton** · *Fort Lupton C/C* · Sheryl Johnke, Exec. Dir., 321 Denver Ave., 80621, P 7,300, M 95, (303) 857-4474, flchamber@frii.com, www.fortluptonchamber.org

**Fort Morgan** · *Fort Morgan Area C/C* · Trish Moreno, Exec. Dir., 300 Main St., P.O. Box 971, 80701, P 27,000, M 280, (970) 867-6702, (800) 354-8660, Fax (970) 867-6121, fortmorganchamber@flci.net, www.fortmorganchamber.org.

**Fountain** · *Fountain Valley C/C* · Scott Turner, Pres., P.O. Box 201, 80817, P 25,000, M 140, (719) 382-3190, Fax (719) 322-9395, fvcc@qwest.net, www.fountaincolorado.org

**Fowler** · *Fowler C/C* · Shawn Tagnotta, Dir., P.O. Box 172, 81039, P 1,200, M 45, (719) 263-4461

**Fraser Valley** · *see Winter Park*

**Frederick** · *also see Westminster*

**Frederick** · *Carbon Valley C/C* · Stephanie Martin, Exec. Dir., P.O. Box 800, 80530, P 18,270, M 270, (303) 833-5933, stephanie@carbonvalleychamber.com, www.carbonvalleychamber.com

**Frisco** · *see Summit County*

**Fruita** · *Fruita Area C/C* · Mary Lou Wilson, Dir., 432 E. Aspen Ave., 81521, P 11,000, M 430, (970) 858-3894, Fax (970) 858-3121, info@fruitachamber.org, www.fruitachamber.org

**Georgetown** · *see Idaho Springs*

**Gilcrest** · *see Platteville*

**Glendale** · *Greater Glendale C/C* · Larry Harte, Exec. Dir., 950 S. Birch St., 80246, P 5,000, M 180, (303) 584-4180, www.ggchamber.com

**Glenwood Springs** · *Glenwood Springs Chamber Resort Assn.* · Marianne Virgili CCE, Exec. Dir., 1102 Grand Ave., 81601, P 8,500, M 650, (970) 945-6589, Fax (970) 945-1531, info@glenwoodchamber.com, www.glenwoodchamber.com

**Golden** · *Greater Golden C/C & Visitors Center* · Gary L. Wink, Pres./CEO, 1010 Washington Ave., 80401, P 18,000, M 520, (303) 279-3113, (800) 590-3113, Fax (303) 279-0332, info@goldencochamber.org, www.goldencochamber.org.

**Gould** · *see Walden*

**Granby** · *Greater Granby Area C/C* · Sharon Brenner, Exec. Dir., 365 E. Agate Ave., Ste. B, P.O. Box 35, 80446, P 1,525, M 180, (970) 887-2311, (800) 325-1661, Fax (970) 887-3895, grcoc@rkymtnhi.com, www.granbychamber.com

**Grand Junction** · *Grand Junction Area C/C* · Diane Schwenke, Pres., 360 Grand Ave., 81501, P 130,000, M 1,400, (970) 242-3214, Fax (970) 242-3694, info@gjchamber.org, www.gjchamber.org.

**Grand Lake** · *Grand Lake Area C/C* · Brad Taylor, Exec. Dir., P.O. Box 429, 80447, P 550, M 212, (970) 627-3372, (970) 627-3402, (800) 531-1019, Fax (970) 627-8007, glinfo@grandlakechamber.com, www.grandlakechamber.com

**Greeley** · *Greeley C/C* · Sarah MacQuiddy, Pres., 902 7th Ave., 80631, P 100,000, M 740, (970) 352-3566, Fax (970) 352-3572, info@greeleychamber.com, www.greeleychamber.com

**Greenwood Village** · *see Centennial*

**Guffey** · *see Fairplay*

**Gunnison** · *Gunnison Country C/C* · Tammy Scott, Exec. Dir., 500 E. Tomichi, P.O. Box 36, 81230, P 10,000, M 368, (970) 641-1501, (800) 274-7580, info@gunnisonchamber.com, www.gunnisonchamber.com.

**Hartsel** · *see Fairplay*

**Haxtun** · *Haxtun C/C* · Barb Shafer, P.O. Box 535, 80731, P 971, M 48, (970) 774-6104, Fax (970) 774-5875, www.haxtunchamber.com

**Heeny** · *see Summit County*

**Highlands Ranch** · *C/C of Highlands Ranch* · Steve Dyer, Pres., 300 W. Plaza Dr., Ste. 225, 80129, P 90,000, M 250, (303) 791-3500, Fax (303) 791-3522, steve@highlandsranchchamber.org, www.highlandsranchchamber.org.

**Holyoke** · *Holyoke C/C* · Mary Tomky, Dir., 212 S. Interocean, P.O. Box 134, 80734, P 2,200, M 100, (970) 854-3517, Fax (970) 854-3514, holyokec@pctelcom.coop, www.holyokechamber.org

**Hotchkiss** · *Hotchkiss Comm. C/C* · Kathy Shiles, Secy., P.O. Box 158, 81419, P 1,000, M 80, (970) 872-3226, Fax (970) 872-4050, www.hotchkisschamber.com

**Idaho Springs** · *Greater Idaho Springs C/C* · Skipper Gorman, Pres., PO Box 1774, 80452, P 9,000, M 33, (303) 567-4382, info@idahospringschamber.org, www.idahospringschamber.org

**Jefferson County** · *see Lakewood*

**Johnstown** · *Johnstown-Milliken C/C* · Jim and Pam Lutey, Co-Dirs., P.O. Box 501, 80534, P 11,500, M 170, (970) 587-7042, Fax (970) 587-8703, info@johnstownmillikenchamber.com, www.johnstownmillikenchamber.com

**Julesburg** · *Sedgwick County C/C* · Patricia Stever, Exec. Dir., 100 W. 2nd St., 80737, P 2,700, M 50, (970) 474-3504, Fax (970) 474-4008, sced@kci.net, www.sedgwickcountyco.com

**Keenesburg** · *Keenesburg C/C* · Ken Gfeller, Pres., P.O. Box 44, 80643, P 1,100, M 40, (303) 732-9257, www.keenesburgco.org

**Kersey** · *Kersey Area C/C* · Steve Kramer, Pres., P.O. Box 397, 80644, P 1,200, M 35, (970) 356-8669, www.kerseycolorado.com

**Keystone** · *see Summit County*

**Kremmling** · *Kremmling Area C/C* · Kacey Beres, Exec. Dir., P.O. Box 471, 80459, P 3,000, M 200, (970) 724-3472, (877) 573-6654, Fax (970) 724-0397, kacey@kremmlingchamber.com, www.kremmlingchamber.com

**La Junta** · *La Junta C/C* · 110 Santa Fe Ave., 81050, P 8,500, M 128, (719) 384-7411, Fax (719) 384-2217, ljcc@centurytel.net, www.lajuntachamber.com

**La Veta** · *La Veta/Cuchara C/C* · Steve Perkins, Pres., P.O. Box 32, 81055, P 1,024, M 115, (719) 742-3676, (866) 615-3676, www.lavetacucharachamber.com

**Lafayette** · *Lafayette C/C* · Vicki Trumbo, Exec. Dir., P.O. Box 1018, 80026, P 27,000, M 370, (303) 666-9555, Fax (303) 666-4392, info@lafayettecolorado.com, www.lafayettecolorado.com.

**Lake City** · *Lake City/Hinsdale County C/C* · Ms. Lynn McNitt, Pres., 800 N. Gunnison Ave., P.O. Box 430, 81235, P 730, M 150, (970) 944-2527, (800) 569-1874, Fax (970) 944-2720, chamber@lakecity.com, www.lakecity.com

**Lake County** · *see Leadville*

**Lakewood** · *West C/C Serving Jefferson County* · Amy Sherman, Pres./CEO, 1667 Cole Blvd., Ste. 400, 80401, P 530,000, M 900, (303) 233-5555, Fax (303) 237-7633, info@westchamber.org, www.westchamber.org

**Lamar** · *Lamar C/C* · Chana Reed, Ofc. Mgr., 109A E. Beech, 81052, P 13,347, M 220, (719) 336-4379, Fax (719) 336-4370, lamarchamber@bresnan.net, www.lamarchamber.com

**Las Animas** · *Las Animas-Bent County C/C* · Russell Smith, Exec. V.P., 332 Amb. Thompson Blvd., 81054, P 6,500, M 135, (719) 456-0453, Fax (719) 456-0455, russellatchamber@lycos.com, www.bentcounty.org

**LaSalle** · *see Platteville*

**Lawson** · *see Idaho Springs*

**Leadville** · *Leadville/Lake County C/C* · 809 Harrison Ave., P.O. Box 861, 80461, P 7,800, M 134, (719) 486-3900, (888) 532-3845, Fax (719) 486-8478, leadville@leadvilleusa.com, www.leadvilleusa.com

**Limon** · *Limon C/C* · Tim Andersen, Chair, P.O. Box 101, 80828, P 2,315, M 90, (719) 775-9418, www.limonchamber.com.

**Littleton** · *see Centennial*

**Logan County** · *see Sterling*

**Longmont** · *Longmont Area C/C* · Kathy Weber-Harding, Pres./CEO, 528 Main St., 80501, P 85,000, M 700, (303) 776-5295, Fax (303) 776-5657, staff@longmontchamber.org, www.longmont chamber.org.

**Louisville** · *Louisville C/C* · Shelley Angell, Exec. Dir., 901 Main St., 80027, P 19,500, M 385, (303) 666-5747, Fax (303) 666-4285, info@louisvillechamber.com, www.louisvillechamber.com.

**Loveland** · *Loveland C/C* · Brian Willms, Pres./CEO, 5400 Stone Creek Circle, Ste. 200, 80538, P 65,000, M 820, (970) 667-6311, Fax (970) 667-5211, info@loveland.org, www.loveland.org

**LOVELAND VALENTINE RE-MAILING PROGRAM AND SWEETHEART CITY ACTIVITIES, FEBRUARY 1-14; BUSINESS EXPO & TRADE SHOW, MARCH; OLD FASHIONED CORN ROAST FESTIVAL, AUGUST; SCULPTURE IN THE PARK, 2ND WEEKEND IN AUGUST—LARGEST SCULPTURE SHOW WEST OF THE MISSISSIPPI**

**Loveland** · *Loveland Info C/C* · Dave Elbert, Exec. Dir., 2296 Glen Haven Dr., 80538, (970) 667-6311, Fax (970) 667-5211, delbert38@yahoo.com

**Lyons** · *Lyons Area C/C* · P.O. Box 426, 80540, P 1,600, M 165, (303) 823-5215, (877) LYONS-CO, admin@lyons-colorado.com, www.lyons-colorado.com

**Mancos** · *Mancos Valley C/C* · Betsy Harrison, P.O. Box 494, 81328, P 1,100, M 85, (970) 533-7434, chamber@mancosvalley.com, www.mancosvalley.com

**Manitou Springs** · *Manitou Springs C/C* · Leslie Lewis, Exec. Dir., 354 Manitou Ave., 80829, P 5,000, M 280, (719) 685-5089, (800) 642-2567, Fax (719) 685-0355, manitou@pikes-peak.com, www.manitousprings.org.

**Meeker** · *Meeker C/C* · David Cole, Exec. Dir., P.O. Box 869, 81641, P 2,200, M 220, (970) 878-5510, Fax (970) 878-0271, info@meekerchamber.com, www.meekerchamber.com

**Minturn** · *see Avon*

**Monte Vista** · *Monte Vista C/C* · 947 1st Ave., 81144, P 5,700, M 200, (719) 852-2731, (800) 562-7085, Fax (719) 852-9382, chamber@monte-vista.org, www.monte-vista.org

**Montezuma** · *see Summit County*

**Montrose** · *Montrose C/C* · Terri Leben, Exec. Dir., 1519 E. Main St., 81401, P 41,000, M 625, (970) 249-5515, (970) 249-5000, (800) 923-5515, Fax (970) 249-2907, information@montrose chamber.com, www.montrosechamber.com

**Monument** · *Tri-Lakes C/C & Visitor Center* · David Van Ness, Exec. Dir., 300 Hwy. 105, P.O. Box 147, 80132, P 35,000, M 315, (719) 481-3282, Fax (719) 481-1638, info@trilakeschamber.com, www.trilakeschamber.com

**Naturita** · *Nucla-Naturita Area C/C* · Terri Tooker, Pres., P.O. Box 425, 81422, P 1,400, M 50, (970) 865-2350, csbterri@fone.net, www.nucla.org

**Nederland** · *Nederland Area C/C* · Lindy Bolt, Admin., P.O. Box 85, 80466, P 1,500, M 130, (303) 258-3936, info@nederland chamber.org, www.nederlandchamber.org

**New Castle** · *New Castle Area C/C* · Clinton Carroll, Pres., 240 W. Main St., Ste. 1-E, P.O. Box 983, 81647, P 3,500, M 72, (970) 984-2897, info@newcastlechamber.org, www.newcastlechamber.org

**Northglenn** · *see Westminster*

**Norwood** · *Norwood C/C* · Terry Esch, Pres., P.O. Box 116, 81423, P 1,300, M 96, (970) 327-4288, (800) 282-5988, info@norwood colorado.com, www.norwoodcolorado.com

**Nucla** · *see Naturita*

**Ordway** · *Crowley County C/C* · Betty Bruch, Pres., 301 Main St., P.O. Box 332, 81063, P 4,300, M 65, (719) 267-3134, Fax (719) 267-3192

**Ouray** · *Ouray Chamber Resort Assn.* · Jennifer Loshaw, Exec. Dir., 1230 Main St., P.O. Box 145, 81427, P 812, M 230, (970) 325-4746, (800) 228-1876, Fax (970) 325-4868, ouray@ouraycolorado.com, www.ouraycolorado.com

**Pagosa Springs** · *Pagosa Springs Area C/C* · Mary Jo Coulehan, Exec. Dir., 402 San Juan St., P.O. Box 787, 81147, P 12,000, M 750, (970) 264-2360, (800) 252-2204, Fax (970) 264-4625, info@pagosachamber.com, www.pagosaspringschamber.com.

**Palisade** · *Palisade C/C* · Leif Johnson, Exec. Dir., P.O. Box 729, 81526, P 2,579, M 225, (970) 464-7458, Fax (970) 464-4757, info@palisadecoc.com, palisadecoc.com, palisadepeachfest.com

**Paonia** · *Paonia C/C* · Regna Jones, Pres., P.O. Box 366, 81428, P 1,500, M 70, (970) 527-3886, naturally@paoniachamber.com, www.paoniachamber.com

**Parker** · *Parker C/C* · JoAnn Dedmon, Chrmn. of the Bd. , 19751 E. Mainstreet, Ste. R12, 80138, P 50,000, M 650, (303) 841-4268, Fax (303) 841-8061, reception@parkerchamber.com, www.parkerchamber.com.

**Penrose** · *Penrose C/C* · Bill McGuire, Exec. Dir., P.O. Box 379, 81240, P 6,500, M 100, (719) 372-3994, Fax (719) 372-3994, www.penrosechamber.com

**Platteville** · *South Central Weld C/C* · Kay Masselink, Coord., P.O. Box 606, 80651, P 3,500, M 45, (970) 324-3111, info@south-centralweldchamber.com, www.southcentralweldchamber.com

**Pueblo** · *Greater Pueblo C/C* · Rod Slyhoff, Pres./CEO, 302 N. Santa Fe Ave., 81003, P 160,000, M 1,200, (719) 542-1704, (800) 233-3446, Fax (719) 542-1624, mail@pueblochamber.net, www.pueblochamber.org.

**Rand** · *see Walden*

**Rangely** · *Rangely Area C/C* · Vanessa Popham, Chamber Asst., 209 E. Main St., 81648, P 2,500, M 150, (970) 675-5290, info@rangelychamber.com, www.rangelychamber.com

**Ridgway** · *Ridgway Area C/C* · Linda Lysaght, Dir., 150 Racecourse Rd., 81432, P 1,000, M 150, (970) 626-5181, (800) 220-4959, Fax (970) 626-9708, racc@ridgwaycolorado.com, www.ridgwaycolorado.com

**Rifle** · *Rifle Area C/C* · Annick Pruett, Exec. Dir., 200 Lions Park Cir., 81650, P 7,800, M 330, (970) 625-2085, (800) 842-2085, Fax (970) 625-4757, mail@riflechamber.com, www.riflechamber.com

**Rocky Ford** · *Rocky Ford C/C* · Susan Bumstead-Smith, Pres., 105 N. Main St., 81067, P 4,300, M 126, (719) 254-7483, Fax (719) 254-7483, info@rockyfordchamber.org, www.rockyfordchamber.net

**Salida** · *Heart of the Rockies C/C* · Lori Roberts, Admin., 406 W. Hwy. 50, 81201, P 5,800, M 460, (719) 539-2068, (877) 772-5432, Fax (719) 539-7844, info@salidachamber.org, salidachamber.org.

**Sheridan** · *see Centennial*

**Silt** · *Silt Area C/C* · Carole Chandler, Pres., P.O. Box 921, 81652, P 2,200, M 75, (970) 876-9922, sacc@siltchamber.org, www.siltchamber.org

**Silver Plume** · *see Idaho Springs*

**Silverthorne** · *see Summit County*

**Silverton** · *Silverton C/C* · P.O. Box 565, 81433, P 560, M 176, (970) 387-5654, (800) 752-4494, Fax (970) 387-0282, chamber@silvertoncolorado.com, www.silvertoncolorado.com

**South Fork** · *South Fork C/C* · Traci Gillespie, Ofc. Mgr., 30359 Hwy. 160, 81154, P 750, M 80, (719) 873-5512, (800) 571-0881, Fax (719) 873-5693, southfrk@amigo.net, www.southforkcolorado.org

**South Jeffco** · *see Lakewood*

**Springfield** · *Springfield C/C* · Jodi Ricker, Pres., P.O. Box 12, 81073, P 1,500, M 55, (719) 523-4061, springfieldcolorado chamber@springfieldco.info, www.springfieldco.info

**Steamboat Springs** · *Steamboat Springs Chamber Resort Assn.* · Sandy Evans Hall, Exec. V.P., 125 Anglers Dr. , P.O. Box 774408, 80477, P 10,000, M 902, (970) 879-0882, Fax (970) 879-2543, sevans@steamboatchamber.com, www.steamboatchamber.com.

**Sterling** · *Logan County C/C* · Kimberly Sellers, Exec. Dir., 109 N. Front St., P.O. Box 1683, 80751, P 21,000, M 300, (970) 522-5070, (866) 522-5070, Fax (970) 522-4082, execdir@logancountychamber.com, www.logancountychamber.com

**Strasburg** · *see Bennett*

**Summit County** · *Summit C/C* · Sharon Russell, Exec. Dir., 101 W. Main St., Ste. 107, P.O. Box 5451, Frisco, 80443, P 25,000, M 600, (970) 668-2051, Fax (970) 668-1515, srussell@summit-chamber.org, www.summitchamber.org

**Superior** · *Superior C/C* · Heather Cracraft, Exec. Dir., 122 William St., 80027, P 12,000, M 150, (303) 554-0789, Fax (303) 499-1340, info@superiorchamber.com, www.superiorchamber.com

**Trinidad** · *Trinidad & Las Animas County C/C* · Kimberly Pacheco, Exec. Dir./CEO, 136 W. Main St., 81082, P 15,000, M 450, (719) 846-9285, (866) 480-4750, Fax (719) 846-3545, kimberly pacheco@comcast.net, www.trinidadchamber.com.

**Trinidad** · *Trinidad-Las Animas County Hispanic C/C* · Jennie Garduno, Pres., P.O. Box 17, 81082, P 175,000, M 150, (719) 846-8234, (719) 846-6678

**Vail** · *Vail Chamber & Bus. Assn.* · Rich Tenbraak, Exec. Dir., 241 S. Frontage Rd. E., Ste. 2, 81657, P 4,531, M 350, (970) 477-0075, (877) 477-0075, Fax (970) 477-0079, info@vailchamber.org, www.vailchamber.org

**Walden** · *North Park C/C* · 416 4th St., P.O. Box 68, 80480, P 1,300, M 45, (970) 723-4600, northparkchamber@centurytel.net, www.northparkchamber.homestead.com

**Walsenburg** · *Huerfano County C/C* · Mike Hurley, Pres., 400 Main St., 81089, P 8,100, M 56, (719) 738-1065, Fax (719) 738-1065, www.hcchamber.org

**Watkins** · *see Bennett*

**Wellington** · *Wellington Area C/C* · Tom Gillespie, Chrmn., P.O. Box 1500, 80549, P 4,800, M 90, (970) 568-4133, info@wellington coloradochamber.com, www.wellingtoncoloradochamber.net

**Westcliffe** · *Custer County C/C* · Claire McCutcheon, 502 Main St., P.O. Box 81, 81252, P 3,800, M 220, (719) 783-9163, (877) 793-3170, Fax (719) 783-2724, info@custercountyco.com, www.custercountyco.com

**Westminster** · *Metro North Reg. C/C* · Deborah Obermeyer, Pres./CEO, 2921 W. 120th Ave., Ste. 210, 80234, P 1,209,000, M 1,100, (303) 288-1000, Fax (303) 227-1050, info@metronorth-chamber.com, www.metronorthchamber.com

**Wheat Ridge** · *see Lakewood*

**Windsor** · *Windsor C/C* · Michal Connors, Ofc. Mgr., 421 Main St., 80550, P 19,001, M 420, (970) 686-7189, Fax (970) 686-0352, information@windsorchamber.net, www.windsorchamber.net.

**Winter Park** · *Winter Park-Fraser Valley C/C* · Catherine Ross, Exec. Dir., 78841 U.S. Hwy. 40, P.O. Box 3236, 80482, P 1,500, M 400, (970) 726-4118, (800) 903-7275, Fax (970) 726-9449, visitorcenter@playwinterpark.com, www.playwinterpark.com

**Wolcott** · *see Avon*

**Woodland Park** · *Greater Woodland Park C/C* · Debbie Miller, Pres., Ute Pass Cultural Center, 210 E. Midland, P.O. Box 9022, 80866, P 7,500, M 450, (719) 687-9885, (800) 551-7886, Fax (719) 687-8216, info@gwpcc.biz, debmiller@gwpcc.biz, www.woodlandparkchamber.com.

**Wray** · *Wray C/C* · Steve Orender, Dir., 110 E. 3rd St., P.O. Box 101, 80758, P 2,200, M 100, (970) 332-3484, Fax (970) 332-3486, wraychambercomm@centurytel.net, www.wraychamber.net

**Yuma** · *West Yuma County C/C* · Darlene Carpio, Exec. Dir., 14 W. Second Ave., 80759, P 3,362, M 135, (970) 848-2704, Fax (970) 848-5700, chamber@seeyuma.com, www.seeyuma.com

# Connecticut

**Connecticut Bus. & Ind. Assn.** · John Rathgeber, Pres./CEO, 350 Church St., Hartford, 06103, P 3,295,669, M 10,000, (860) 244-1900, Fax (860) 278-8562, www.cbia.com

**Amesville** · *see Lakeville*

**Andover** · *see Vernon*

**Ansonia** · *see Shelton*

**Avon** · *Avon C/C* · Lisa Bohman, Exec. Dir., 412 W. Avon Rd., 06001, P 17,000, M 310, (860) 675-4832, Fax (860) 675-0469, www.avonchamber.com

**Barkhamsted** · *see Torrington*

**Beacon Falls** · *see Shelton*

**Berlin** · *Berlin C/C* · Katherine Fuechsel, Exec. Dir., 40 Chamberlin Hwy., 06037, P 18,831, M 230, (860) 829-1033, Fax (860) 829-1243, director@berlinctchamber.org, www.berlinctchamber.org

**Bethel** · *Bethel C/C* · Violet Mattone, Exec. Dir., 16 P.T. Barnum Sq., 06801, P 18,000, M 400, (203) 743-6500, Fax (203) 744-5265, info@bethelchamber.com, www.bethelchamber.com

**Bloomfield** · *Bloomfield C/C* · Vera Smith-Winfree, Exec. Dir., 330 Park Ave., 2nd Flr., P.O. Box 938, 06002, P 8,000, M 200, (860) 242-3710, Fax (860) 242-6129, director@bloomfieldchamber.org, www.bloomfieldchamber.org

**Bolton** · *see Vernon*

**Branford** · *Branford C/C* · Edward Lazarus, Pres., 239 N. Main St., 06405, P 30,000, M 340, (203) 488-5500, Fax (203) 488-5046, info@branfordct.com, www.branfordct.com

**Bridgeport** · *Bridgeport Reg. Bus. Cncl.* · Paul S. Timpanelli, Pres./CEO, 10 Middle St., P.O. Box 999, 06601, P 250,000, M 1,000, (203) 335-3800, Fax (203) 366-0105, info@brbc.org, www.brbc.org

**Bristol** · *Greater Bristol C/C* · Michael Nicastro, Pres./CEO, 200 Main St., 06010, P 150,000, M 1,800, (860) 584-4718, Fax (860) 584-4722, info@bristol-chamber.org, www.bristol-chamber.org.

**Brooklyn** · *see Danielson*

**Burlington** · *see Bristol*

**Canaan** · *see Torrington*

**Canton** · *Canton C/C* · Phil Worley, Exec. Dir., 220 Albany Tpk. (Rte. 44), Bldg. 5, P.O. Box 704, 06019, P 8,500, M 284, (860) 693-0405, Fax (860) 693-9105, info@cantonchamberofcommerce.com, www.cantonchamberofcommerce.com

**Cheshire** · *Cheshire C/C* · Sheldon Dill, Exec. Dir., 195 S. Main St., 06410, P 28,000, M 325, (203) 272-2345, Fax (203) 271-3044, info@cheshirechamber.com, www.cheshirechamber.com

**Clinton** · *Clinton C/C* · Ellen Cavanagh, Exec. Dir., 50 E. Main St., P.O. Box 334, 06413, P 13,000, M 350, (860) 669-3889, Fax Fax same, chamber@ClintonCt.com, ClintonCt.com

**Colebrook** · *see Torrington*

**Columbia** · *see Vernon*

**Cornwall** · *see Torrington*

**Coventry** · *see Vernon*

**Danbury** · *Greater Danbury C/C* · Stephen Bull, Pres., 39 West St., 06810, P 190,000, M 1,000, (203) 743-5565, Fax (203) 794-1439, info@danburychamber.com, www.danburychamber.com

**Danielson** · *Northeastern Connecticut C/C* · Elizabeth Kuszaj, Exec. Dir., 3 Central St. #3, 06239, P 78,000, M 600, (860) 774-8001, Fax (860) 774-4299, info@nectchamber.com, www.nectchamber.com

**Darien** · *Darien C/C* · Carol Wilder-Tamme, Pres./CEO, 10 Corbin Drive, 06820, P 20,000, M 325, (203) 655-3600, Fax (203) 655-2074, darienchamber@optonline.net, www.dcc.darien.org

**Derby** · *see Shelton*

**East Berlin** · *see Berlin*

**East Granby** · *East Granby C/C* · Tami Zawistowski, Pres., P.O. Box 1335, 06026, P 5,000, M 110, (860) 653-3833, Fax (860) 653-3855, admin@eastgranbycoc.org, www.eastgranbycoc.org

**East Hartford** · *East Hartford C/C* · Mary Beth Reid, Exec. Dir., 1137 Main St., 06108, P 50,000, M 400, (860) 289-0239, Fax (860) 289-0230, ehchamber@sbcglobal.net, www.ehcoc.com

**East Haven** · *East Haven C/C* · Mary W. Cacace, Exec. Dir., 200 Kimberly Ave., P.O. Box 120055, 06512, P 28,000, M 165, (203) 467-4305, Fax (203) 469-2299, generalinfo@easthavenchamber.com, www.easthavenchamber.com

**East Windsor** · *see Enfield*

**Ellington** · *see Tolland County*

**Enfield** · *North Central Connecticut C/C* · Larry Tracey, Exec. Dir., 73 Hazard Ave., P.O. Box 294, 06083, P 75,726, M 400, (860) 741-3838, Fax (860) 741-3512, chamber@ncccc.org, www.ncccc.org.

**Fairfield** · *Fairfield C/C* · Patricia L. Ritchie, Pres./CEO, 1597 Post Rd., 06824, P 57,000, M 500, (203) 255-1011, Fax (203) 256-9990, info@fairfieldctchamber.com, www.fairfieldctchamber.com.

**Falls Village** · *see Torrington*

**Farmington** · *Farmington C/C* · Carol Presutti, Pres., 827 Farmington Ave., 06032, P 24,658, M 310, (860) 676-8490, Fax (860) 677-8332, www.farmingtonchamber.com

**Gales Ferry** · *C/C of Eastern Connecticut* · Tony Sheridan, Pres., 39 Kings Hwy., P.O. Box 726, 06335, P 293,000, M 1,700, (860) 464-7373, Fax (860) 464-7374, info@chamberect.com, www.chamberect.com

**Glastonbury** · *Glastonbury C/C* · Mary Ellen Dombrowski, Pres., 2400 Main St., Ste. 2, 06033, P 33,000, M 550, (860) 659-3587, Fax (860) 659-0102, maryellen@glastonburychamber.com, www.glastonburychamber.com

**Goshen** · *see Torrington*

**Granby** · *Granby C/C* · Roger Voyer, Admin., P.O. Box 211, 06035, P 14,000, M 250, (860) 653-5085, Fax (860) 844-8692, gcoc@granbycoc.org, www.granbycoc.org

**Greenwich** · *Greenwich C/C* · Mary Ann Morrison, Pres./CEO, 45 E. Putnam Ave., Ste. 121, 06830, P 65,000, M 700, (203) 869-3500, Fax (203) 869-3502, info@greenwichchamber.com, www.greenwichchamber.com

**Guilford** · *Guilford C/C* · Dale Lehman, Exec. Dir., 51 Whitfield St., 06437, P 20,000, M 300, (203) 453-9677, Fax (203) 453-6022, chamber@guilfordct.com, www.guilfordct.com

**Hamden** · *Hamden C/C* · Nancy Dudchik, Pres., 2969 Whitney Ave., 06518, P 58,000, M 400, (203) 288-6431, Fax (203) 288-4499, hcc@hamdenchamber.com, www.hamdenchamber.com

**Hartford** · *Metro Hartford Alliance* · Oz Griebel, Pres., 31 Pratt St., 5th Flr., 06103, P 910,000, M 1,000, (860) 525-4451, Fax (860) 293-2592, info@metrohartford.com, www.metrohartford.com

**Harwinton** · *see Torrington*

**Hebron** · *see Vernon*

**Kensington** · *see Berlin*

**Kent** · *also see Torrington*

**Kent** · *Kent C/C* · Elissa Potts, Pres., P.O. Box 124, 06757, P 3,000, M 150, (860) 927-1463, president@kentct.com, www.kentct.com

**Killingly** · *see Danielson*

**Lakeville** · *Tri-State C/C* · Rachel Call, Exec. Dir., 326 Main St., P.O. Box 386, 06039, P 4,500, M 180, (860) 435-0740, info@tristatechamber.com, www.tristatechamber.com

**Lime Rock** · *see Lakeville*

**Litchfield** · *see Torrington*

**Lyme** · *see Old Lyme*

**Madison** · *Madison C/C* · Eileen Banisch, Exec. Dir., P.O. Box 706, 06443, P 18,000, M 350, (203) 245-7394, Fax (203) 245-4279, chamber@madisonct.com, www.madisonct.com

**Manchester** · *Greater Manchester C/C* · Sue O'Connor, Pres., 20 Hartford Rd., 06040, P 55,000, M 550, (860) 646-2223, Fax (860) 646-5871, staffgmcc@manchesterchamber.com, www.manchesterchamber.com

**Mansfield** · *see Vernon*

**Meriden** · *Greater Meriden C/C* · Sean W. Moore, Pres., 3 Colony St. #301, 06451, P 59,000, M 670, (203) 235-7901, Fax (203) 686-0172, info@meridenchamber.com, www.meridenchamber.com

**Middlebury** · *see Southbury*

**Middletown** · *Middlesex County C/C* · Larry McHugh, Pres., 393 Main St., 06457, P 154,241, M 2,400, (860) 347-6924, Fax (860) 346-1043, info@middlesexchamber.com, www.middlesexchamber.com

**Milford** · *Milford C/C* · Kathleen Alagno, Pres./CEO, 5 Broad St., P.O. Box 389, 06460, P 54,000, M 775, (203) 878-0681, Fax (203) 876-8517, chamber@milfordct.com, www.milfordct.com

**Monroe** · *Monroe C/C* · Jo-Ellen Stipak, Exec. Dir., 641 Main St., 06468, P 20,000, M 225, (203) 268-6518, Fax (203) 268-3337, info@monroe-chamber.com, www.monroe-chamber.com

**Morris** · *see Torrington*

**Mystic** · *Greater Mystic C/C* · Tricia Cunningham, Pres., 14 Holmes St., P.O. Box 143, 06355, P 12,000, M 750, (860) 572-9578, (866) 572-9578, Fax (860) 572-9273, info@mysticchamber.org, www.mysticchamber.org

**Naugatuck** · *Naugatuck C/C* · Lynn Ward, Dir., 195 Water St., 06770, P 30,860, M 200, (203) 729-4511, Fax (203) 729-4512, cligi@waterburychamber.com, www.naugatuckchamber.com

**New Britain** · *New Britain C/C* · William Millerick, Pres., One Court St., 06051, P 69,000, M 450, (860) 229-1665, Fax (860) 223-8341, bill@newbritainchamber.com, www.newbritainchamber.com

**New Canaan** · *New Canaan C/C* · Pamela B. Ogilvie, Exec. Dir., 111 Elm St., 06840, P 19,612, M 400, (203) 966-2004, Fax (203) 966-3810, pogilvie@newcanaanchamber.com, www.newcanaan chamber.com

**New Haven** · *Greater New Haven C/C* · Anthony P. Rescigno, Pres., 900 Chapel St., 10th Flr., 06510, P 500,000, M 1,400, (203) 787-6735, Fax (203) 782-4329, info@gnhcc.com, www. newhavenchamber.com.

**New London** · *see Gales Ferry*

**New Milford** · *Greater New Milford C/C & Visitor Center* · Denise Del Mastro, Exec. Dir., 11 Railroad St., 06776, P 29,090, M 360, (860) 354-6080, Fax (860) 354-8526, nmcc@newmilford-chamber.com, www.newmilford-chamber.com

**Newington** · *Newington C/C* · Gail Whitney, Exec. Dir., 1046 Main St., 06111, P 30,000, M 320, (860) 666-2089, Fax (860) 665-7551, office@newingtonchamber.com, www.newingtonchamber.com

**Newtown** · *Newtown Area C/C* · Alice Baye, Admin. Secy., P.O. Box 314, 06470, P 26,000, M 220, (203) 426-2695, Fax Fax same, chamber@newtown-ct.com, www.newtown-ct.com

**Norfolk** · *see Torrington*

**North Branford** · *North Branford C/C* · 1599 Foxon Rd., P.O. Box 229, 06471, P 13,000, M 110, (203) 483-6803, www.town ofnorthbranfordct.com

**North Canaan** · *see Torrington*

**North Haven** · *see Wallingford*

**Norwalk** · *Greater Norwalk C/C* · Edward Musante, Pres., 101 East Ave., P.O. Box 668, 06852, P 80,000, M 1,000, (203) 866-2521, Fax (203) 852-0583, info@norwalkchamberofcommerce.com, www.norwalkchamberofcommerce.com.

**Norwich** · *see Gales Ferry*

**Oakville** · *see Waterbury*

**Old Lyme** · *Lyme & Old Lyme C/C* · Steven Ross, Treas., P.O. Box 4152, 06371, P 7,000, M 190, (860) 434-3647, email@lolcc.com, www.lolcc.com

**Old Saybrook** · *Old Saybrook C/C* · Judy Sullivan, Exec. Dir., One Main St., P.O. Box 625, 06475, P 25,000, M 400, (860) 388-3266, Fax (860) 388-9433, info@oldsaybrookchamber.com, www. oldsaybrookchamber.com

**Orange** · *Orange C/C* · Carol Smullen, Exec. Dir., 605A Orange Center Rd., 06477, P 13,500, M 270, (203) 795-3328, Fax (203) 795-5926, info@orangectchamber.com, www.orangectchamber. com

**Oxford** · *see Shelton*

**Plainfield** · *see Danielson*

**Plainville** · *Plainville C/C* · Maureen Saverick, Ofc. Mgr., 58 W. Main St., P.O. Box C, 06062, P 17,000, M 275, (860) 747-6867, Fax (860) 793-1832, plvchamber@snet.net, www.plainvillechamber.com

**Plymouth** · *see Bristol*

**Portland** · *see Middletown*

**Prospect** · *see Naugatuck*

**Putnam** · *see Danielson*

**Ridgefield** · *Ridgefield C/C* · Marion Roth, Pres./CEO, 9 Bailey Ave., 06877, P 24,000, M 380, (203) 438-5992, Fax (203) 438-9175, mroth@ridgefieldchamber.org, www.ridgefieldchamber.org

**Rockville** · *see Vernon*

**Rocky Hill** · *Rocky Hill C/C* · Claudia Baio, Pres., 2264 Silas Deane Hwy., 06067, P 16,700, M 181, (860) 258-7633, Fax (860) 258-7637, info@rockyhillchamberofcommerce.com, www.rocky hillchamberofcommerce.com

**Salisbury** · *see Lakeville*

**Seymour** · *see Shelton*

**Sharon** · *see Torrington*

**Shelton** · *Greater Valley C/C* · William Purcell CAE CCE, Pres., 900 Bridgeport Ave., 2nd Flr., 06484, P 100,000, M 650, (203) 925-4981, Fax (203) 925-4984, info@greatervalleychamber.com, www.greatervalleychamber.com

**Simsbury** · *Simsbury C/C* · Charity P. Folk, Exec. Dir., 749 Hopmeadow St., P.O. Box 224, 06070, P 23,000, M 500, (860) 651-7307, Fax (860) 651-1933, info@simsburycoc.org, www. simsburycoc.org

**Somers** · *see Enfield*

**Somers** · *see Vernon*

**South Windsor** · *South Windsor C/C* · Cate Evans, Exec. Dir., 22 Morgan Farms Dr., 06074, P 24,000, M 500, (860) 644-9442, Fax (860) 648-1911, info@southwindsorchamber.org, www. southwindsorchamber.org

**Southbury** · *Tribury C/C* · Margot Melaas, P.O. Box 807, 06488, P 35,000, M 160, (203) 267-4466, info@triburychamber.org, www.triburychamber.org

**Southington** · *Greater Southington C/C* · Art Secondo, Pres./ CEO, 1 Factory Sq., Ste. 201, 06489, P 42,000, M 550, (860) 628-8036, Fax (860) 276-9696, info@southingtoncoc.com, www. southingtoncoc.com

**Stafford** · *see Vernon*

**Stamford** · *Bus. Cncl. Of Fairfield County* · Christopher Bruhl, Pres./CEO, One Landmark Sq., Ste. 300, 06901, P 900,440, M 400, (203) 359-3220, Fax (203) 967-8294, info@businessfairfield.com, www.businessfairfield.com

**Stamford** · *Stamford C/C* · John P. Condlin, Pres./CEO, 733 Summer St., Ste. 104, 06901, P 121,073, M 2,600, (203) 359-4761, Fax (203) 363-5069, stamfordchamber@stamfordchamber.com, www.stamfordchamber.com

**Stratford** · *see Bridgeport*

**Suffield** · *Suffield C/C* · Greg Heineman, Pres., P.O. Box 741, 06078, P 11,370, M 200, (860) 668-4848, Fax same, info@suffield chamber.com, www.suffieldchamber.com

**Suthington** · *see Bristol*

**Taconic** · *see Lakeville*

**Tolland** · *see Vernon*

**Torrington** · *C/C of Northwest Connecticut* · JoAnn Ryan, Pres./ CEO, 333 Kennedy Dr., Ste. R101, P.O. Box 59, 06790, P 190,000, M 750, (860) 482-6586, Fax (860) 489-8851, joann@nwctchamber ofcommerce.org, www.nwctchamberofcommerce.org

**Trumbull** · *see Bridgeport*

**Union** · *see Vernon*

**Vernon** · *Tolland County C/C* · Candice Corcione, Exec. Dir., 30 Lafayette Sq., 06066, P 130,705, M 500, (860) 872-0587, Fax (860) 872-0588, tccc@tollandcountychamber.org, www.tolland countychamber.org

**Wallingford** · *Quinnipiac C/C* · Robin Wilson, Pres., 100 S. Turnpike Rd., 06492, P 61,000, M 850, (203) 269-9891, (203) 234-0332, Fax (203) 269-1358, qcc@quinncham.com, www. quinncham.com

**Warren** · *see Torrington*

**Washington** · *see Torrington*

**Waterbury** · *Waterbury Reg. C/C* · Lynn Ward, Interim Pres./ CEO, 83 Bank St., P.O. Box 1469, 06721, P 261,031, M 1,000, (203) 757-0701, Fax (203) 756-3507, info@waterburychamber.com, www.waterburychamber.com.

**Watertown** · *see Waterbury*

**West Hartford** · *West Hartford C/C* · Marjorie Luke, Dir., 948 Farmington Ave., 06107, P 61,045, M 700, (860) 521-2300, Fax (860) 521-1996, info@WHChamber.com, www.WHChamber.com

**West Haven** · *West Haven C/C* · Robert Rosenberg, Pres., 263 Center St., 06516, P 55,000, M 350, (203) 933-1500, Fax (203) 931-1940, info@westhavenchamber.com, www.westhaven chamber.com

**Weston** · *see Westport*

**Westport** · *Westport/Weston C/C* · Kevin Lally, Exec. Dir., 215 Main St., 06880, P 33,000, M 400, (203) 227-9234, Fax (203) 454-4019, info@westportchamber.com, www.westportchamber.com

**Wethersfield** · *Wethersfield C/C* · Jeanne Kelly, Pres./CEO, 860B Silas Deane Hwy., 06109, P 27,000, M 205, (860) 721-6200, Fax (860) 721-8703, wethersfield@sbcglobal.net, www.wethers fieldchamber.com

**Willimantic** · *The Chamber of Commerce Inc. [Windham Region]* · Roger A. Adams, Exec. Dir., 1010 Main St., P.O. Box 43, 06226, P 78,000, M 375, (860) 423-6389, (860) 423-6380, Fax (860) 423-8235, info@windhamchamber.com, www.windham chamber.com.

**Willington** · *see Vernon*

**Wilton** · *Wilton C/C* · Stephanie Barksdale, Exec. Dir., P.O. Box 7094, 06897, P 17,000, M 350, (203) 762-0567, Fax (203) 762-9096, wiltoncoc@snet.net, www.wiltonchamber.com

**Winchester** · *see Torrington*

**Windsor** · *Windsor C/C* · Jane Garibay, Exec. Dir., 261 Broad St., P.O. Box 9, 06095, P 28,400, M 325, (860) 688-5165, Fax (860) 688-0809, jane@windsorcc.org, www.windsorcc.org.

**Windsor Locks** · *Windsor Locks C/C* · Jared Carillo, Pres., P.O. Box 257, 06096, P 12,190, M 100, (860) 623-9319, Fax (860) 831-1036, info@windsorlockschamber.org, www.windsorlocks chamber.org

**Winsted** · *see Torrington*

**Wolcott** · *see Bristol*

**Woodbury** · *see Southbury*

# Delaware

**Delaware State C of C** · James A. Wolfe, Pres./CEO, 1201 N. Orange St., Ste. 200, P.O. Box 671, Wilmington, 19899, P 750,000, M 2,800, (302) 655-7221, Fax (302) 654-0691, info@dscc.com, www.dscc.com

**Bethany Beach** · *see Fenwick Island*

**Delmar** · *Greater Delmar C/C* · John Johnson, Pres., P.O. Box 416, 19940, P 3,500, M 84, (302) 846-3336, www.townofdelmar.us

**Dewey Beach** · *see Rehoboth Beach*

**Dover** · *Central Delaware C/C* · Judith Diogo, Pres., 435 N. DuPont Hwy., 19901, P 127,000, M 870, (302) 734-7513, Fax (302) 678-0189, info@cdcc.net, www.cdcc.net.

**Fenwick Island** · *Bethany-Fenwick Area C/C* · Andrew Cripps, Exec. Dir., 36913 Coastal Hwy., 19944, P 20,000, M 800, (302) 539-2100, (800) 962-SURF, Fax (302) 539-9434, info@bethany-fenwick.org, www.thequietresorts.com

**Georgetown** · *Greater Georgetown C/C* · Debbie Hartstein, Pres., 140 Layton Ave., P.O. Box 1, 19947, P 10,555, M 455, (302) 856-1544, Fax (302) 856-1577, info@georgetowncoc.com, www. georgetowncoc.com

**Laurel** · *Laurel C/C* · Donald Dykes, Pres., P.O. Box 696, 19956, P 17,000, M 126, (302) 875-9319, Fax (302) 875-4660, info@ laurelchamber.com, www.laurelchamber.com

**Lewes** · *Lewes C/C* · Betsy Reamer, Exec. Dir., 120 Kings Hwy., P.O. Box 1, 19958, P 3,100, M 450, (302) 645-8073, (877) 465-3937, Fax (302) 645-8412, inquiry@leweschamber.com, www. leweschamber.com

**Middletown** · *Middletown Area C/C* · Margaret Ryan, Admin. Asst., 216 N. Broad St., P.O. Box 1, 19709, P 10,000, M 320, (302) 378-7545, Fax (302) 378-6260, info@middletownareachamber. com, www.middletownareachamber.com

**Milford** · *C/C for Greater Milford Inc.* · Jo Schmeiser, Exec. Dir., 5 S. Washington St., P.O. Box 805, 19963, P 16,000, M 300, (302) 422-3344, Fax (302) 422-7503, milford@milfordchamber.com, www.milfordchamber.com

**Millsboro** · *Millsboro C/C* · Fran Bruce, Exec. Dir., 322 Wilson Hwy., P.O. Box 187, 19966, P 4,000, M 290, (302) 934-6777, Fax (302) 934-6065, millsboro@intercom.net, www.millsborocham ber.com

**Milton** · *Milton C/C* · Georgia Dalzell, Exec. Dir., 707 Chestnut St., P.O. Box 61, 19968, P 3,000, M 100, (302) 684-1101, chamber@ historicmilton.com, www.historicmilton.com

**Newark** · *see Wilmington*

**Rehoboth Beach** · *Rehoboth Beach-Dewey Beach C/C* · Carol Everhart, Pres./CEO, 501 Rehoboth Ave., P.O. Box 216, 19971, P 168,000, M 1,304, (302) 227-2233, (800) 441-1329, Fax (302) 227-8351, rehoboth@beach-fun.com, www.beach-fun.com

**Seaford** · *Greater Seaford C/C* · Paula K. Gunson, Exec. Dir., P.O. Box 26, 19973, P 24,000, M 350, (302) 629-9690, Fax (302) 629-0281, admin@seafordchamber.com, www.seafordchamber.com.

**Wilmington** · *New Castle County C/C* · Mark Kleinschmidt, Pres., 12 Penns Way, 19720, P 500,000, M 1,700, (302) 737-4343, Fax (302) 322-3593, info@ncccc.com, www.ncccc.com

# District of Columbia

**Washington** · *Dist. of Columbia C of C* · Barbara Lang, Pres./ CEO, 1213 K St. N.W., 20005, P 550,000, M 2,057, (202) 347-7201, Fax (202) 638-6762, blang@dcchamber.org, www.dcchamber.org

**Washington** · *United States C/C* · Thomas J. Donohue, Pres./ CEO, 1615 H St. N.W., 20062, (202) 659-6000, (800) 638-6582, custsvc@uschamber.com, www.uschamber.com

**Washington** · *United States Hispanic C/C* · Augustine Martinez, Pres./CEO, 2175 K St. N.W., Ste. 100, 20037, M 200, (202) 842-1212, Fax (202) 842-3221, ushcc@ushcc.com, www.ushcc.com

# Florida

**Florida C of C** • Mark Wilson, Pres., 136 S. Bronough St., P.O. Box 11309, Tallahassee, 32302, P 16,000,000, M 7,000, (850) 521-1200, Fax (850) 521-1219, policy@flchamber.com, www. flchamber.com

**Alachua** • *Alachua C/C* • Jay Murray, Pres., P.O. Box 387, 32616, P 8,000, M 151, (386) 462-3333, info@alachua.com, www. alachua.com

**Altamonte Springs** • *see Heathrow*

**Amelia Island** • *Amelia Island-Fernandina Beach-Yulee C/C* • Regina Duncan, Pres., 961687 Gateway Blvd., Ste. 101G, 32034, P 60,000, M 850, (904) 261-3248, Fax (904) 261-6997, regina@ aifby.com, www.islandchamber.com

**Anna Maria Island** • *see Holmes Beach*

**Apalachicola** • *Apalachicola Bay C/C* • Anita Gregory Grove, Exec. Dir., 122 Commerce St., 32320, P 3,000, M 450, (850) 653-9419, Fax (850) 653-8219, info@apalachicolabay.org, www.apalachicolabay.org

**Apollo Beach** • *Apollo Beach C/C* • Joanne Gadek, Exec. Dir., 137 Harbor Village Ln., P.O. Box 3686, 33572, P 10,000, M 275, (813) 645-1366, Fax (813) 641-2612, abeachcham@verizon.net, www. apollobeachchamber.com

**Apopka** • *Apopka Area C/C* • Paul Seago, Pres., 180 E. Main St., 32703, P 40,000, M 650, (407) 886-1441, Fax (407) 886-1131, pauls@apopkachamber.org, www.apopkachamber.org.

**Arcadia** • *DeSoto County C/C* • Linda Williams, 16 S. Volusia Ave., 34266, P 33,000, M 300, (863) 494-4033, Fax (863) 494-3312, desotochamber@embarqmail.com, www.desotochamber.net

**Astor** • *Astor Area C/C* • P.O. Box 329, 32102, P 1,500, M 65, (352) 759-2679, info@astorchamber.com, www.astorchamber.com

**Auburndale** • *Auburndale C/C* • Joy Pruitt, Exec. Dir., 109 Main St., 33823, P 26,000, M 300, (863) 967-3400, Fax (863) 967-0880, information@auburndalechamber.com, myauburn dalechamber.com

**Aventura** • *Aventura-Sunny Isles Beach C/C* • David Sheinheit, Pres., 20533 Biscayne Blvd., Ste. 536, 33180, P 26,000, M 275, (305) 935-2131, Fax (305) 690-9124, info@aventura.org, www. aventura.org

**Avon Park** • *Avon Park C/C* • David Greenslade, Exec. Dir., 28 E. Main St., 33825, P 19,500, M 350, (863) 453-3350, Fax (863) 453-0973, apcc@apfla.com, www.apfla.com

**Bartow** • *Greater Bartow C/C* • Jeff Clark, Exec. Dir., 510 N. Broadway Ave., 33830, P 16,043, M 740, (863) 533-7125, Fax (863) 533-3793, discoverbartow@bartowchamber.com, www. bartowchamber.com

**Bay Harbor** • *Florida Gold Coast C/C* • Peter Cohn, Pres., 1100 Kane Concourse, Ste. 210, 33154, P 45,000, M 200, (305) 866-6020, Fax (305) 866-0635

**Bayonet Point** • *see New Port Richey*

**Belle Glade** • *Belle Glade C/C* • Brenda Bunting, Exec. Dir., 540 S. Main St., 33430, P 14,906, M 300, (561) 996-2745, Fax (561) 996-2252, bgchamber@aol.com, www.belleglChamber.com

**Belleair Beach** • *see Saint Pete Beach*

**Belleair Bluffs** • *see Saint Pete Beach*

**Belleair Shores** • *see Saint Pete Beach*

**Belleview** • *Belleview-South Marion C/C* • Debbie Hendrix, Ofc. Mgr., 5301 S.E. Abshier Blvd., 34420, P 4,000, M 300, (352) 245-2178, Fax (352) 245-7673, belleviewsmcc@aol.com, www. bsmcc.org

**Beverly Beach** • *see Palm Coast*

**Big Pine Key** • *Lower Keys C/C* • Carole Stevens, Exec. Dir., 31020 Overseas Hwy., P.O. Box 430511, 33043, P 16,000, M 225, (305) 872-2411, (800) 872-3722, Fax (305) 872-0752, lkchamber@aol. com, www.lowerkeyschamber.com

**Blountstown** • *Calhoun County C/C* • Kristy Halley Speers, Exec. Dir., 20816 Central Ave. E., Ste. 2, 32424, P 13,500, M 175, (850) 674-4519, Fax (850) 674-4962, chamber@calhounco.org, www. calhounco.org

**Boca Grande** • *Boca Grande Area C/C* • Lynda Landcaster, Exec. Dir., 5800 Gasparilla Rd., Ste. A1, P.O. Box 704, 33921, P 1,000, M 275, (941) 964-0568, Fax (941) 964-0620, info@bocagrande chamber.com, www.bocagrandechamber.com

**Boca Raton** • *Greater Boca Raton C/C* • Troy M. McLellan, Pres./ CEO, 1800 N. Dixie Hwy., 33432, P 200,000, M 1,700, (561) 395-4433, Fax (561) 392-3780, info@bocaratonchamber.com, www. bocaratonchamber.com.

**Bonifay** • *Holmes County C/C* • Jim Brook, Exec. Dir., 106 E. Byrd Ave., 32425, P 19,000, M 190, (850) 547-4682, Fax (850) 547-4206, hcflcofc@gmail.com, www.holmescountyonline.com

**Bonita Springs** • *Bonita Springs Area C/C* • Christine A. Ross, Pres./CEO, 25071 Chamber of Commerce Dr., 34135, P 47,000, M 1,300, (239) 992-2943, Fax (239) 992-5011, info@bonita springschamber.com, www.bonitaspringschamber.com

**Boynton Beach** • *Greater Boynton Beach C/C* • Glenn P. Jergensen, Pres./CEO, 1880 N. Congress Ave., Ste. 106, 33426, P 155,000, M 750, (561) 732-9501, Fax (561) 734-4304, chamber@ boyntonbeach.org, www.boyntonbeach.org.

**Bradenton** • *Manatee C/C* • Robert P. Bartz, Pres., 222 10th St. W., P.O. Box 321, 34206, P 324,000, M 2,540, (941) 748-3411, Fax (941) 745-1877, info@manateechamber.com, www.manatee chamber.com

**Brandon** • *Greater Brandon C/C* • Tammy C. Bracewell, Pres./ CEO, 330 Pauls Dr., Ste. 100, 33511, P 255,000, M 1,800, (813) 689-1221, Fax (813) 689-9440, info@brandonchamber.com, www. brandonchamber.com, www.brandondirectory.com.

**Bristol** • *Liberty County C/C* • Johnny Eubanks, Dir., P.O. Box 523, 32321, P 8,500, M 50, (850) 643-2359, Fax (850) 643-3334

**Brooksville** • *Greater Hernando County C/C* • Patricia Crowley, Pres./CEO, 101 E. Fort Dade Ave., 34601, P 165,464, M 1,100, (352) 796-0697, Fax (352) 796-3704, pat@hernandochamber.com, www.hernandochamber.com.

**Bunnell** • *see Palm Coast*

**Bushnell** • *see Sumterville*

**Callahan** • *Greater Nassau County C/C* • Ms. Chris Goodell, Pres., P.O. Box 98, 32011, P 56,843, M 240, (904) 879-1441, Fax (904) 879-4033, info@greaternassaucounty.com, www.greaternassau county.com

**Cape Canaveral** • *see Cocoa Beach*

**Cape Coral** • *Cape Coral C/C* • Michael Quaintance, Pres., 2051 Cape Coral Pkwy. E., P.O. Box 100747, 33910, P 169,000, M 1,000, (239) 549-6900, (800) 226-9609, Fax (239) 549-9609, info@ capecoralchamber.com, www.capecoralchamber.com.

**Cape Coral** · *Cape Coral C/C* · Michael Quaintance, Pres., 2051 Cape Coral Pkwy. E., 33904, P 150,000, M 1,000, (239) 549-6900, (800) 226-9609, Fax (239) 549-9609, info@capecoralchamber. com, www.capecoralchamber.com

**Cape Haze** · *see Englewood*

**Captiva Islands** · *see Sanibel*

**Carrabelle** · *Carrabelle Area C/C* · P.O. Drawer DD, 32322, P 1,300, M 150, (850) 697-2585, chamber@nettally.com, www. carrabellechamber.org

**Casselberry** · *see Heathrow*

**Cedar Key** · *Cedar Key Area C/C* · 618 2nd St., P.O. Box 610, 32625, P 900, M 130, (352) 543-5600, Fax (352) 543-5600, info@ cedarkey.org, www.cedarkey.org

**Center Hill** · *see Sumterville*

**Century** · *Century C/C* · Freddie McCall, Pres./CEO, 7811 N. Century Blvd., P.O. Box 857, 32535, P 1,800, M 54, (850) 256-3155, Fax (850) 256-3155

**Chiefland** · *Greater Chiefland Area C/C* · Janet Minor, Exec. Dir., 23 S.E. 2nd Ave., P.O. Box 1397, 32644, P 32,500, M 172, (352) 493-1849, Fax (352) 493-0282, chieflandchamber@bellsouth.net, www.chieflandchamber.com

**Chipley** · *Washington County C/C* · Ted Everett, Exec. Dir., 672 5th St., P.O. Box 457, 32428, P 22,155, M 382, (850) 638-4157, Fax (850) 638-8770, wcchamber@wfeca.net, www.washcomall.com.

**Chokoloskee** · *see Everglades City*

**Clay County** · *see Orange Park*

**Clearwater** · *Clearwater Reg. C/C* · Bob Clifford, Pres./CEO, 1130 Cleveland St., 33755, P 108,000, M 1,100, (727) 461-0011, Fax (727) 449-2889, info@clearwaterflorida.org, www.clear waterflorida.org

**Clearwater Beach** · *Clearwater Beach C/C* · Sheila Cole, Exec. Dir., 333C S. Gulfview Blvd., P.O. Box 3573, 33767, P 117,000, M 265, (727) 447-7600, (888) 799-3199, Fax (727) 443-7812, office@beachchamber.com, www.beachchamber.com

**Clermont** · *South Lake C/C* · Ray San Fratello, Pres., 691 W. Montrose St., 34712, P 100,000, M 820, (352) 394-4191, Fax (352) 394-5799, rays@southlakechamber-fl.com, www.southlake chamber-fl.com

**Clewiston** · *Clewiston C/C* · 109 Central Ave., P.O. Box 275, 33440, P 32,000, M 410, (863) 983-7979, Fax (863) 983-7108, clewistonchamber@embarqmail.com, www.clewiston.org

**Cocoa Beach** · *Cocoa Beach Area C/C* · Randy Harris, Pres./CEO, 400 Fortenberry Rd., Merritt Island, 32952, P 250,000, M 1,890, (321) 459-2200, Fax (321) 459-2232, info@cocoabeachchamber. com, www.cocoabeachchamber.com

**Coconut Grove** · *Coconut Grove C/C* · David Guzikowski, Chief Admin. Officer, 2820 McFarlane Rd., 33133, P 27,000, M 300, (305) 444-7270, Fax (305) 444-2498, info@coconutgrove.com, www.coconutgrovechamber.com

**Coleman** · *see Sumterville*

**Cooper City** · *see Davie*

**Coral Gables** · *Coral Gables C/C* · Mark Trowbridge, Pres./CEO, 224 Catalonia Ave., 33134, P 43,000, M 1,800, (305) 446-1657, Fax (305) 446-9900, info@coralgableschamber.org, www.coral gableschamber.org

**Coral Springs** · *Coral Springs C/C* · Cindy Brief, Pres., 11805 Heron Bay Blvd., 33076, P 126,500, M 550, (954) 752-4242, Fax (954) 827-0543, info@cschamber.com, www.cschamber.com

**Crawfordville** · *Wakulla County C/C* · Petra Shuff, Ofc. Admin., P.O. Box 598, 32326, P 26,000, M 347, (850) 926-1848, Fax (850) 926-2050, wakullacochamber@embarqmail.com, www.wakulla countychamber.com

**Crescent City** · *Putnam County C/C-South Putnam Branch* · 115 N. Summit St., 32112, P 1,843, M 125, (386) 698-1657, Fax (386) 698-3484, info@southputnamcountychamber.org, www. putnamcountychamber.org

**Crestview** · *Crestview Area C/C* · Wayne Harris, Exec. Dir., 1447 Commerce Dr., 32539, P 75,000, M 680, (850) 682-3212, Fax (850) 682-7413, info@crestviewchamber.com, www.crestviewchamber. com

**Cross City** · *Dixie County C/C* · P.O. Box 547, 32628, P 18,000, M 108, (352) 498-5454, Fax (352) 498-7549, dixiechamber@usa. net, www.dixiecounty.org

**Crystal River** · *Citrus County C/C* · Kitty L. Barnes, Exec. Dir., 28 N.W. US Hwy. 19, 34428, P 130,000, M 1,040, (352) 795-3149, Fax (352) 795-1921, ccommerce2@tampabay.rr.com, www. citruscountychamber.com.

**Dade City** · *Greater Dade City C/C* · Nita H. Beckwith, Exec. Dir., 14112 8th St., 33525, P 17,500, M 450, (352) 567-3769, Fax (352) 567-3770, info@dadecitychamber.org, www.dadecitychamber.org.

**Dania Beach** · *Greater Dania Beach C/C* · Victoria Payne, Exec. Dir., 102 W. Dania Beach Blvd., P.O. Box 1017, 33004, P 28,000, M 325, (954) 926-2323, Fax (954) 926-2384, info@greaterdania. org, www.greaterdania.org

**Davenport** · *City of Davenport C/C* · Cheryl Burgess, Pres., P.O. Box 125, 33836, P 2,000, M 41, (863) 419-3300

**Davie** · *Davie-Cooper City C/C* · Alice Harrington, Pres., 4185 Davie Rd., 33314, P 90,000, M 500, (954) 581-0790, Fax (954) 581-9684, dcch@davie-coopercity.org, www.davie-coopercity.org

**Daytona Beach** · *Daytona Beach-Halifax Area C/C* · Larry McKinney, Pres./CEO, 126 E. Orange Ave., P.O. Box 2475, 32115, P 68,000, M 1,200, (386) 255-0981, (800) 854-1234, Fax (386) 258-5104, info@daytonachamber.com, www.daytonachamber.com

**Daytona Beach Shores** · *see Port Orange*

**DeBary** · *see Orange City*

**Deerfield Beach** · *Greater Deerfield Beach C/C* · Janyce Becker, Exec. Dir., 1601 E. Hillsboro Blvd., 33441, P 78,000, M 650, (954) 427-1050, Fax (954) 427-1056, info@deerfieldchamber.com, www.deerfieldchamber.com.

**DeFuniak Springs** · *Walton County C/C* · Dawn A. Moliterno, Pres./CEO, 95 Circle Dr., 32435, P 46,000, M 1,251, (850) 892-3191, Fax (850) 892-9688, info@waltoncountychamber.com, www. waltoncountychamber.com

**DeLand** · *DeLand Area C/C* · Jenny Stumbras, Exec. Dir., 336 N. Woodland Blvd., 32720, P 60,000, M 650, (386) 734-4331, Fax (386) 734-4333, office@delandchamber.org, www.deland chamber.org

**Delray Beach** · *Greater Delray Beach C/C* · William Wood, Pres., 64-A S.E. 5th Ave., 33483, P 120,000, M 1,200, (561) 278-0424, Fax (561) 278-0555, webmaster@delraybeach.com, www. delraybeach.com.

**Deltona** · *see Orange City*

**Destin** · *Destin Area C/C* · Shane Moody, Pres./CEO, 4484 Legendary Dr., Ste. A, 32541, P 12,350, M 1,100, (850) 837-6241, Fax (850) 654-5612, mail@destinchamber.com, www.destin chamber.com

**Dover** · *see Seffner*

**Dundee** · *Dundee Area C/C* · 310 Main St., P.O. Box 241, 33838, P 3,300, M 120, (863) 439-3261, dundeechamber@hotmail.com, www.dundeechamber.com

**Dunedin** · *Dunedin C/C* · Lynn Wargo, Pres./CEO, 301 Main St., 34698, P 37,000, M 450, (727) 733-3197, Fax (727) 734-8942, chamber@dunedin-fl.com, www.dunedin-fl.com.

**Dunnellon** · *Dunnellon Area C/C* · Beverly Leisure, Exec. Dir., 20500 E. Pennsylvania Ave., P.O. Box 868, 34430, P 60,000, M 350, (352) 489-2320, (800) 830-2087, Fax (352) 489-6846, dunnellonchamber@bellsouth.net, www.dunnellonchamber.org

**Edgewater** · *see New Smyrna Beach*

**Englewood** · *Englewood-Cape Haze Area C/C* · Jon Bednerik CAE, Exec. Dir., 601 S. Indiana Ave., 34223, P 47,000, M 550, (941) 474-5511, (800) 603-7198, Fax (941) 475-9257, business@englewoodchamber.com, www.englewoodchamber.com

**Estero** · *Estero C/C* · Grace Fortuna, Exec. Dir., P.O. Box 588, 33928, P 30,000, M 250, (239) 948-7990, Fax (239) 948-5072, www.estero.org, info@esterochamber.com, www.esterochamber.com

**Eustis** · *Lake Eustis Area C/C* · Sharron Semento, Exec. Dir., #1 W. Orange Ave., P.O. Box 1210, 32727, P 18,401, M 500, (352) 357-3434, Fax (352) 357-1392, info@eustischamber.org, www.eustischamber.org

**Everglades City** · *Everglades Area C/C* · P.O. Box 130, 34139, P 525, M 147, (239) 695-3172, (800) 914-6355, Fax (239) 695-3171, info@evergladeschamber.com, www.evergladeschamber.com

**Fernandina Beach** · *see Amelia Island*

**Flagler Beach** · *see Palm Coast*

**Florida City** · *see Homestead*

**Fort Lauderdale** · *America C/C* · Jack Miller, Pres./CEO, 1290 Weston Rd., Ste. 312, 33326, P 1,900,000, M 870, (702) 260-9425, jack@americachamber.com, www.americachamber.com.

**THE CHAMBER OF COMMERCE WAS CREATED TO PROMOTE AND SERVE THE LOCAL, REGIONAL, NATIONAL & INTERNATIONAL NEEDS OF ITS MEMBERS–FOR BUSINESS & BUSINESS TO CONSUMER.**

**Fort Lauderdale** · *Greater Fort Lauderdale C/C* · Dan Lindblade CAE, Pres./CEO, 512 N.E. Third Ave., 33301, P 173,000, M 1,600, (954) 462-6000, Fax (954) 527-8766, info@ftlchamber.com, www.ftlchamber.com

**Fort Meade** · *Fort Meade C/C* · Regina Cino, Exec. Dir., 214 W. Broadway, Ste. B, P.O. Box 91, 33841, P 5,800, M 140, (863) 285-8253, Fax (863) 285-6968, ftmeadechamber@aol.com, www.fortmeadechamber.com

## Fort Myers Area

**Greater Fort Myers C/C** · Marietta B. Mudgett, Exec. Dir., 2310 Edwards Dr., P.O. Box 9289, 33902, P 550,000, M 1,500, (239) 332-3624, (800) 366-3622, Fax (239) 332-7276, fortmyers@fortmyers.org, www.fortmyers.org

**Chamber of Southwest Florida** · Stephen Tirey, Pres., 5237 Summerlin Commons Blvd., Ste. 114, 33919, P 500,000, M 200, (239) 278-4001, Fax (239) 275-2103, chamberswf@gmail.com, www.chamber-swflorida.com

**Southwest Florida Hispanic C/C** · Veronica Culbertson, Pres., 10051 McGregor Blvd., Ste. 204, 33919, M 250, (239) 418-1441, Fax (239) 418-1475, www.hispanicchamberflorida.org

**Fort Myers Beach** · *Fort Myers Beach C/C* · John E. Albion, Pres., 17200 San Carlos Blvd., 33931, P 523,121, M 656, (239) 454-7500, Fax (239) 454-7910, info@fmbchamber.com, www.fortmyersbeach.org

**Fort Walton Beach** · *Greater Fort Walton Beach C/C* · Ted Corcoran, Pres./CEO, 34 Miracle Strip Pkwy. S.E., P.O. Box 640, 32549, P 125,000, M 1,400, (850) 244-8191, Fax (850) 244-1935, info@fwbchamber.org, www.fwbchamber.org.

**Frostproof** · *Frostproof Area C/C* · 118 E. Wall St., P.O. Box 968, 33843, P 3,000, M 160, (863) 635-9112, Fax (863) 635-6582, info@frostproofchamber.com, www.frostproofchamber.com

**Gainesville** · *Gainesville Area C/C* · Brent Christensen, Pres./CEO, 300 E. University Ave., Ste. 100, P.O. Box 1187, 32602, P 240,000, M 1,400, (352) 334-7100, Fax (352) 334-7141, info@gainesvillechamber.com, www.gainesvillechamber.com

**Goldenrod** · *Goldenrod Area C/C* · Darlene Dangel, Exec. Dir., 4755 Palmetto, P.O. Box 61, 32733, P 100,000, M 250, (407) 677-5980, Fax (407) 677-4928, director@goldenrodchamber.com, www.goldenrodchamber.com

**Green Cove Springs** · *see Orange Park*

**Groveland** · *see Clermont*

**Gulf Breeze** · *Gulf Breeze Area C/C* · Meg Peltier, Pres./CEO, 409 Gulf Breeze Pkwy., 32561, P 30,000, M 485, (850) 932-7888, Fax (850) 934-4601, info@gulfbreezechamber.com, www.gulfbreezechamber.com

**Haines City** · *Haines City-NE Polk County Reg. C/C* · Jane Patton, Pres., 35610 Hwy. 27, P.O. Box 986, 33845, P 18,000, M 450, (863) 422-3751, Fax (863) 422-4704, info@hainescity.com, www.hainescity.com

**Hallandale Beach** · *Hallandale Beach C/C* · Patricia Genetti, Exec. Dir., 1117 E. Hallandale Beach Blvd., Ste. 5, 33009, P 38,000, M 250, (954) 454-0541, Fax (954) 454-0930, info@hallandalebeachchamber.com, www.hallandalebeachchamber.com.

**Harmony** · *see Saint Cloud*

**Hawthorne** · *Hawthorne Area C/C* · Stan Kitching, Pres., P.O. Box 125, 32640, P 2,500, M 55, (352) 481-4818, chamber@hawthorneflorida.org, www.hawthorneflorida.org

**Heathrow** · *Seminole County Reg. C/C* · 1055 AAA Dr., Ste. 153, 32746, P 375,000, M 3,000, (407) 333-4748, Fax (407) 708-4615, www.seminolebusiness.org

**Hernando County** · *see Brooksville*

**Hialeah** · *Camara de Comercio Hispana de Hialeah* · Vicente Rodriguez, Pres., 4410 W. 16th Ave., Ste. 62, P.O. Box 133187, 33013, P 265,000, M 1,696, (305) 557-5060, Fax (305) 556-7333

**Hialeah** · *Hialeah C of C & Ind. [Latin C/C]* · Daniel Hernandez, Pres., 240 E. 1st Ave., Ste. 217, 33010, P 300,000, M 450, (305) 888-7780, Fax (305) 888-7804, edelcastillo@hialeahchamber.org, www.hialeahchamber.org

**High Springs** · *High Springs C/C* · Wanda Kemp, Ofc. Coord., P.O. Box 863, 32655, P 4,300, M 130, (386) 454-3120, Fax (386) 454-5848, chamber@highsprings.com, www.highsprings.com

**Hobe Sound** · *Hobe Sound C/C* · Jennifer Ferrari, Exec. Dir., 11954 Dixie Hwy., P.O. Box 1507, 33475, P 18,000, M 500, (772) 546-4724, Fax (772) 546-9969, info@hobesound.org, www.hobesound.org.

**Holiday** · *see New Port Richey*

**Holly Hill** · *Holly Hill C/C* · 1056 Ridgewood Ave., P.O. Box 250615, 32125, P 15,000, M 300, (386) 255-7311, Fax (386) 267-0485, office@hollyhillchamber.com, www.hollyhillchamber.com

**Hollywood** · *Greater Hollywood C/C* · Laura Gambino, Exec. Dir., 330 N. Federal Hwy., 33020, P 139,357, M 1,100, (954) 923-4000, (800) 231-5562, Fax (954) 923-8737, information@hollywood chamber.org, www.hollywoodchamber.org.

**Holmes Beach** · *Anna Maria Island C/C* · Mary Ann Brockman, Pres., 5313 Gulf Dr. N., 34217, P 8,500, M 508, (941) 778-1541, (800) 392-9975, Fax (941) 778-9679, info@annamariaisland chamber.org, www.amichamber.org

**Homestead** · *Greater Homestead-Florida City C/C* · Mary Finlan, Exec. Dir., Historic Old Town Hall, 43 N. Krome Ave., 33030, P 37,000, M 700, (305) 247-2332, (888) 352-4891, Fax (305) 246-1100, info@chamberinaction.com, www.chamberinaction.com

**Homosassa Springs** · *Citrus County C/C* · Kitty L. Barnes, Exec. Dir., 3495 S. Suncoast Blvd., P.O. Box 709, 34447, P 130,000, M 1,040, (352) 628-2666, Fax (352) 621-0920, ccommerce@ tampabay.rr.com, www.citruscountychamber.com.

**Hudson** · *see New Port Richey*

**Immokalee** · *Eastern Collier C/C* · Richard Rice, Exec. Dir., 1300 N. 15th St.. Ste. 2, 34143, P 28,000, M 250, (239) 657-3237, Fax (239) 657-5450, ecoc@comcast.net, www.easterncollierchamber.com

**Indialantic** · *see Melbourne*

**Indian Harbour Beach** · *see Melbourne*

**Indian Rocks Beach** · *see Saint Pete Beach*

**Indian Shores** · *see Saint Pete Beach*

**Indiantown** · *Indiantown Western Martin County C/C* · Allon R. Fish, Pres./CEO, 15935 S.W. Warfield Blvd., P.O. Box 602, 34956, P 10,000, M 185, (772) 597-2184, Fax (772) 597-6063, itowncc@ onearrow.net, www.indiantownfl.org.

**Inglis** · *Withlacoochee Gulf Area C/C* · Edwin Day, Pres., 167 Hwy. 40 W., P.O. Box 427, 34449, P 2,100, M 45, (352) 447-3383, www.inglisyankeetown.org

**Inverness** · *Citrus County C/C* · Kitty L. Barnes, Exec. Dir., 401 Tompkins St., 34450, P 130,000, M 1,040, (352) 726-2801, Fax (352) 637-6498, ccommerce1@tampabay.rr.com, www. citruscountychamber.com.

**Islamorada** · *Islamorada C/C* · Judy Hull, Exec. Dir., 83224 Overseas Hwy., P.O. Box 915, 33036, P 8,000, M 350, (305) 664-4503, (800) FAB-KEYS, Fax (305) 664-4289, director@islamorada chamber.com, www.islamoradachamber.com

**Jacksonville** · *Jacksonville Reg. C/C* · Walter M. Lee III, Pres., 3 Independent Dr., 32202, P 1,321,013, M 4,000, (904) 366-6600, Fax (904) 632-0617, www.myjaxchamber.com

**Jacksonville Beach** · *Jacksonville Reg. C/C-Beaches Div.* · Jill Sprowell, Exec. Dir., 1300 Marsh Landing Pkwy., Ste. 108, 32250, P 71,000, M 448, (904) 273-5366, Fax (904) 273-5266, beaches@ myjaxchamber.com, www.myjaxchamber.com

**Jasper** · *Hamilton County C/C* · Regina Hester, Pres., 1153 US Hwy 41 N.W., Ste. 9, P.O. Box 366, 32052, P 14,800, M 107, (386) 792-1300, (866) 341-2492, Fax (386) 792-0559, hamcoc@ windstream.net, www.hamiltoncountyflorida.com

**Jensen Beach** · *Jensen Beach C/C* · Ronald Rose, Exec. Dir., 1900 Ricou Terrace, P.O. Box 1536, 34958, P 15,000, M 460, (772) 334-3444, Fax (772) 334-0817, info@jensenbeachchamber.biz, www.jensenbeachchamber.biz

**Juno Beach** · *see Jupiter*

**Jupiter** · *Florida State Hispanic C/C* · Albert Collazo , 800 N. U.S. Hwy. 1, 33477, (561) 748-3951, Fax (561) 748-3951, www. fshcc.com

**Jupiter** · *Northern Palm Beach County C/C* · Nicole Christian CCE, Pres./CEO, 800 N. U.S. Hwy. 1, 33477, P 140,000, M 1,500, (561) 746-7111, Fax (561) 745-7519, info@npbchamber.com, www.npbchamber.com.

**Kendall** · *see South Miami*

**Kennedy Space Center** · *see Cocoa Beach*

**Key Biscayne** · *Key Biscayne C of C & Visitors Center* · Kathye Susnjer, Exec. Dir., 88 W. McIntyre St., Ste. 100, 33149, P 13,000, M 410, (305) 361-5207, Fax (305) 361-9411, info@keybiscayne chamber.org, www.keybiscaynechamber.org

**Key Colony Beach** · *Key Colony Beach Comm. Assn.* · Ms. Lyn Paterson, Pres., P.O. Box 510884, 33051, P 2,500, M 800, (305) 289-1212, lynkcb@yahoo.com

**Key Largo** · *Key Largo C/C* · Jackie Harder, Pres., 106000 Overseas Hwy., 33037, P 12,000, M 390, (305) 451-1414, (800) 822-1088, Fax (305) 451-4726, info@keylargochamber.org, www.keylargochamber.org

**Key West** · *Key West C/C* · Virginia A. Panico, Exec. V.P., 402 Wall St., 33040, P 28,000, M 677, (305) 294-2587, (800) LAST-KEY, Fax (305) 294-7806, info@keywestchamber.org, www.keywestchamber.org

**Keystone Heights** · *see Starke*

**Kissimmee** · *Kissimmee/Osceola County C/C* · Michael Horner, Pres., 1425 E. Vine St., 34744, P 255,000, M 1,400, (407) 847-3174, Fax (407) 870-8607, info@kissimmeechamber.com, www. kissimmeechamber.com.

**LaBelle** · *Greater LaBelle C/C* · Sara Townsend, Exec. Secy., 125 E. Hickpochee Ave., P.O. Box 456, 33975, P 12,000, M 316, (863) 675-0125, Fax (863) 675-6160, lchamberofcomm@embarqmail. com, www.labellechamber.com.

**Lady Lake** · *Lady Lake Area C/C* · Betty Bernard, Exec. Dir., 106 S. U.S. Hwy. 441/27, P.O. Box 1430, 32158, P 15,000, M 258, (352) 753-6029, Fax (352) 753-8029, www.ladylakechamber.com

**Lake Alfred** · *Lake Alfred C/C* · Jennifer Cone, Pres., 210 N. Seminole Ave., P.O. Box 956, 33850, P 4,000, M 181, (863) 291-5380, Fax (863) 291-5380, lachamber@lake-alfred.com, www. mylake-alfred.com

**Lake Butler** · *see Starke*

**Lake City** · *Lake City-Columbia County C/C* · Jim Poole, Exec. Dir., 162 S. Marion Ave., 32025, P 68,682, M 650, (386) 752-3690, Fax (386) 755-7744, jim@lakecitychamber.com, www.lakecity chamber.com.

**Lake Mary** · *see Heathrow*

**Lake Panasoffkee** · *see Sumterville*

**Lake Park** · *see Jupiter*

**Lake Placid** · *Greater Lake Placid C/C* · Eileen May, CEO/Pres. of Op., 18 N. Oak Ave., 33852, P 25,000, M 550, (863) 465-4331, Fax (863) 465-2588, chamber@lpfla.com, www.visitlakeplacidflorida.com

**Lake Wales** · *Lake Wales Area C/C* · Betty Wojcik, Exec. Dir., 340 W. Central Ave., P.O. Box 191, 33859, P 40,000, M 400, (863) 676-3445, Fax (863) 676-3446, info@lakewaleschamber.com, www. lakewaleschamber.com.

**Lake Worth** · *Greater Lake Worth C/C* · Thomas Ramiccio, Pres./ CEO, 501 Lake Ave., 33460, P 41,000, M 700, (561) 582-4401, Fax (561) 547-8300, lwchamber@lwchamber.com, www.lwchamber.com

**Lakeland** · *Lakeland Area C/C* · Kathleen L. Munson, Pres., 35 Lake Morton Dr., P.O. Box 3607, 33802, P 237,000, M 2,100, (863) 688-8551, Fax (863) 683-7454, info@lakelandchamber.com, www. lakelandchamber.com.

**Land O'Lakes** · *Central Pasco C/C* · Kathy Dunkley, Exec. Dir., 2810 Land O'Lakes Blvd. (US 41), P.O. Box 98, 34639, P 40,000, M 620, (813) 909-2722, Fax (813) 909-0827, office@centralpasco chamber.com, www.centralpascochamber.com.

**Lantana** · *Greater Lantana C/C* · Ron Washam, Pres., 212 Iris Ave., 33462, P 9,500, M 200, (561) 585-8664, Fax (561) 585-0644, lantanachamber@bellsouth.net, www.lantanachamber.com

**Largo** · *Largo/Mid-Pinellas C/C* · Tom Morrissette, Pres., 151 3rd St. N.W., 33770, P 75,000, M 600, (727) 584-2321, Fax (727) 586-3112, info@largochamber.org, www.largochamber.org

**Lauderdale By The Sea** · *Lauderdale By The Sea C/C* · Judy Swaggerty, Exec. Dir., 4201 Ocean Dr., 33308, P 7,000, M 295, (954) 776-1000, Fax (954) 776-6203, lbts@bellsouth.net, www. lbts.com.

**Leesburg** · *Leesburg Area C/C* · Jan Zacharchuk, Exec. Dir., 103 S. 6th St., P.O. Box 490309, 34749, P 20,000, M 720, (352) 787-2131, Fax (352) 787-3985, admin@leesburgchamber.com, www.leesburgchamber.com

**Lehigh Acres** · *Lehigh Acres C/C* · Joseph Whalen, Pres./CEO, P.O. Box 757, 33970, P 85,000, M 500, (239) 369-3322, Fax (239) 368-0500, www.lehighacreschamber.org

**Live Oak** · *Suwannee County C/C* · Dennis Cason, Pres., 816 S. Ohio Ave., P.O. Drawer C, 32064, P 35,000, M 400, (386) 362-3071, Fax (386) 362-4758, staff@suwanneechamber.com, www. suwanneechamber.com

**Longboat Key** · *Longboat Key C/C* · 5570 Gulf of Mexico Dr., 34228, P 8,000, M 425, (941) 383-2466, Fax (941) 383-8217, info@longboatkeychamber.com, www.longboatkeychamber.com

**Loxahatchee** · *Palms West C/C* · Jaene Miranda, Exec. Dir., 13901 Southern Blvd., P.O. Box 1062, 33470, P 175,000, M 800, (561) 790-6200, Fax (561) 791-2069, info@palmswest.com, www.palmswest.com

**Macclenny** · *Baker County C/C* · Darryl Register, Exec. Dir., 20 E. Macclenny Ave., 32063, P 25,000, M 250, (904) 259-6433, Fax (904) 259-2737, dregister@bakerchamberfl.com, www.baker chamberfl.com.

**Madeira Beach** · *see Saint Pete Beach*

**Madison** · *Madison County C/C* · 177 S.W. Horry Ave., 32340, P 19,850, M 204, (850) 973-2788, Fax (850) 973-8864, chamber@ madisonfl.org, www.madisonfl.org

**Maitland** · *Maitland Area C/C* · Mary Hodge, Exec. Dir., 110 N. Maitland Ave., 32751, P 17,600, M 300, (407) 644-0741, Fax (407) 539-2529, info@maitlandchamber.com, www.maitlandchamber.com.

**Malabar** · *see Palm Bay*

**Mango** · *see Seffner*

**Mangonia Park** · *see Jupiter*

**Marathon** · *Greater Marathon C/C* · Daniel Famess, Exec. Dir., 12222 Overseas Hwy., 33050, P 10,000, M 400, (305) 743-5417, (800) 262-7284, Fax (305) 289-0183, visitus@floridakeys marathon.com, www.floridakeysmarathon.com

**Marco Island** · *Marco Island Area C/C* · Sandi Riedemann, Exec. Dir., 1102 N. Collier Blvd., 34145, P 16,000, M 700, (239) 394-7549, (800) 788-6272, Fax (239) 394-3061, info@marcoisland chamber.org, www.marcoislandchamber.org

**Marianna** · *Jackson County C/C* · Art Kimbrough, Pres./CEO, 4318 Lafayette St., P.O. Box 130, 32447, P 50,000, M 400, (850) 482-8060, Fax (850) 482-8002, info@jacksoncounty.com, www. jacksoncounty.com

**Marineland** · *see Palm Coast*

**Marion Oaks** · *see Belleview*

**Mascotte** · *see Clermont*

**Matlacha** · *Greater Pine Island C/C* · Lisa Benton, Exec. Dir., 3640 Pine Island Rd., P.O. Box 525, 33993, P 11,000, M 275, (239) 283-0888, Fax (239) 283-0336, info@pineislandchamber.org, www.pineislandchamber.org

**Mayo** · *Lafayette County C/C* · 116 S.W. Monroe, P..O. Box 416, 32066, P 7,000, M 50, (386) 294-2705, Fax (386) 294-3073, lafayettecnty@aol.com, www.lafayettecountychamber.com

**Melbourne** · *Melbourne-Palm Bay Area C/C* · Chuck Galy, Exec. V.P., 1005 E. Strawbridge Ave., 32901, P 500,000, M 1,300, (321) 724-5400, Fax (321) 725-2093, chuck@melpb-chamber.org, www. melpb-chamber.org.

**Melbourne Beach** · *see Melbourne*

**Melbourne Village** · *see Melbourne*

**Merritt Island** · *see Cocoa Beach*

**Miami** · *Greater Miami C/C* · Barry E. Johnson, Pres./CEO, Ballroom Level, 1601 Biscayne Blvd., 33132, P 2,600,000, M 5,500, (305) 350-7700, Fax (305) 374-6902, info@miamichamber.com, www.miamichamber.com

**Miami** · *Miami-Dade C/C* · Bill Diggs, Pres./CEO, 11380 N.W. 27th Ave., Bldg. I, Ste. 1328, 33167, P 2,000,000, M 500, (305) 751-8648, Fax (305) 758-3839, m-dcc@m-dcc.org, www.m-dcc.org

**Miami Beach** · *Miami Beach C/C* · Wendy Kallergis, Pres./CEO, 1920 Meridian Ave., 33139, P 95,000, M 1,700, (305) 674-1300, Fax (305) 538-4336, visitorinfo@miamibeachchamber.com, www. miamibeachchamber.com

**Miami Gardens** · *North Dade Reg. C/C* · Jaap Donath, Chrmn., 1300 N.W. 167th St., Ste. 2, 33169, P 2,300,000, M 2,223, (305) 690-9123, Fax (305) 690-9124, thechamber@thechamber.cc, www.thechamber.cc

**Miami Shores** · *Greater Miami Shores C/C* · Lew Soli, Exec. Dir., 9701 N.E. 2nd Ave., 33138, P 10,000, M 320, (305) 754-5466, Fax (305) 759-8872, www.miamishores.com

**Middleburg** · *see Orange Park*

**Milton** · *Santa Rosa County C/C* · Donna Tucker, Exec. Dir., 5247 Stewart St., 32570, P 148,000, M 589, (850) 623-2339, Fax (850) 623-4413, membership@srcchamber.com, www.srcchamber.com

**Minneola** · *see Clermont*

**Miramar** · *see Pembroke Pines*

**Monticello** · *Monticello-Jefferson County C/C* · Mary Frances Gramling, Dir., 420 W. Washington St., 32344, P 14,500, M 260, (850) 997-5552, Fax (850) 997-1020, info@monticellojeffersonfl. com, www.monticellojeffersonfl.com

**Montverde** · *see Clermont*

**Mount Dora** · *Mount Dora Area C/C* · Cathy Hoechst, Pres., 341 Alexander St., P.O. Box 196, 32756, P 11,000, M 600, (352) 383-2165, Fax (352) 383-1668, chamber@mountdora.com, www.mountdora.com

**Mulberry** · *Greater Mulberry C/C* · Sharron Jones, Exec. Dir., 400 N. Church Ave., P.O. Box 254, 33860, P 3,500, M 180, (863) 425-4414, Fax (863) 425-3837, sharron@mulberrychamber.org, www.mulberrychamber.org

**Naples** · *Greater Naples C/C* · Michael Reagen, Pres./CEO, 2390 Tamiami Trl. N., Ste. 210, 34103, P 341,000, M 2,178, (239) 262-6376, Fax (239) 262-8374, info@napleschamber.org, www. napleschamber.org

U.S. Chambers of Commerce

**Navarre** · *Navarre Beach Area C/C* · Tracey Terry, Exec. Dir., P.O. Drawer 5430, 32566, P 29,997, M 634, (850) 939-3267, Fax (850) 939-0085, exec@navarrechamber.com, www.navarrechamber.com

**New Port Richey** · *West Pasco C/C* · Joe Alpine, Pres., 5443 Main St., 34652, P 424,355, M 1,050, (727) 842-7651, Fax (727) 848-0202, chamber@westpasco.com, www.westpasco.com.

**New Smyrna Beach** · *Southeast Volusia C/C* · Steve Dennis, Exec. V.P., 115 Canal St., 32168, P 35,000, M 700, (386) 428-2449, Fax (386) 423-3512, lsdennis@sevchamber.com, www.sevchamber.com

**Newberry** · *Newberry-Jonesville C/C* · Anne Maria Alfano, Pres., P.O. Box 495, 32669, P 5,000, M 110, (352) 472-6611, info@newberrychamber.com, www.newberrychamber.com

**Niceville** · *Niceville Valparaiso C/C* · Tricia Brunson, Pres./CEO, 1055 E. John Sims Pkwy., 32578, P 35,000, M 650, (850) 678-2323, Fax (850) 678-2602, info@nicevillechamber.com, www.nicevillechamber.com

**North Fort Myers** · *North Fort Myers C/C* · 2787 N. Tamiami Trl., Ste. 10, 33903, P 65,000, M 244, (239) 997-9111, Fax (239) 997-4026, info@nfmchamber.org, www.nfmchamber.org

**North Miami** · *Greater North Miami C/C* · Penny Valentine, Exec. Dir., 13100 W. Dixie Hwy., 33161, P 50,000, M 550, (305) 891-7811, Fax (305) 893-8522, info@northmiamichamber.com, www.northmiamichamber.com

**North Miami Beach** · *Greater North Miami Beach C/C* · Paul Lemay, Pres., 1870 N.E. 171st St., 33162, P 35,000, M 400, (305) 944-8500, Fax (305) 944-8191, chamber@nmbchamber.com, www.nmbchamber.com

**North Palm Beach County** · *see Jupiter*

**North Port** · *North Port Area C/C* · Mindy Tew, Exec. Dir., 15141 Tamiami Trl., 34287, P 52,000, M 520, (941) 423-5040, Fax (941) 423-5042, info@northportareachamber.com, www.northportareachamber.com

**North Redington Beach** · *see Saint Pete Beach*

**Oak Hill** · *see New Smyrna Beach*

**Oakland** · *see Winter Garden*

**Ocala** · *Ocala-Marion County C/C* · Ms. Jaye Baillie, Pres./CEO, 110 E. Silver Springs Blvd., 34470, P 275,000, M 1,700, (352) 629-8051, Fax (352) 629-7651, ourguest@ocalacc.com, www.ocalacc.com

**Ochopee** · *see Everglades City*

**Ocoee** · *see Winter Garden*

**Okeechobee** · *Okeechobee County C/C* · Candace Burke, Exec. Dir., 55 S. Parrott Ave., 34972, P 37,481, M 350, (863) 763-6464, Fax (863) 763-3467, candace7@gmail.com, www.okeechobeechamberofcommerce.com.

**Oklawaha** · *Lake Weir C/C* · Richard Lillie, Pres., 13125 S.E. Hwy. C-25, 32179, P 13,000, M 130, (352) 288-3751, Fax (352) 288-3980, lakeweirchamcom@juno.com, www.searchmelakeweir.com

**Oldsmar** · *Upper Tampa Bay Reg. C/C* · Jerry Custin, Pres./CEO, 163 State Rd. 580 W., 34677, P 14,000, M 700, (813) 855-4233, Fax (813) 854-1237, jcustin@utbchamber.com, www.utbchamber.com

**Opa Locka** · *see Miami Gardens*

**Orange City** · *C/C of West Volusia* · Linda White, Pres., 1656 S. Volusia Ave., 32763, P 117,000, M 520, (386) 775-2793, Fax (386) 775-4575, info@gwvcc.org, www.gwvcc.org

**Orange Park** · *Clay County C/C* · Kellie Jo Kilberg, Pres./CEO, 1734 Kingsley Ave., 32073, P 170,000, M 800, (904) 264-2651, Fax (904) 264-0070, newinfo@claychamber.com, www.claychamber.org

**Orlando** · *East Orlando C/C* · Crockett Bohannon, Chrmn., 2860 S. Alafaya Trail, Ste. 130, 32828, P 230,000, M 900, (407) 277-5951, Fax (407) 381-1720, info@eocc.org, www.eocc.org

**Orlando** · *Orlando Reg. C/C* · Leslie J. Hielema, Pres., 75 S. Ivanhoe Blvd., P.O. Box 1234, 32802, P 1,851,872, M 6,000, (407) 425-1234, Fax (407) 835-2500, www.orlando.org.

**Ormond Beach** · *Ormond Beach C/C* · Mary Rhodes, Exec. Dir., 165 W. Granada Blvd., 32174, P 38,000, M 900, (386) 677-3454, Fax (386) 677-4363, obccinfo@ormondchamber.com, www.ormondchamber.com

**Oviedo** · *Oviedo-Winter Springs Reg. C/C* · Cory Skeates, Exec. Dir., 1511 E. State Rd. 434, Ste. 2001, P.O. Box 621236, 32762, P 75,000, M 625, (407) 365-6500, Fax (407) 365-6587, staff@oviedowintersprings.org, www.oviedowintersprings.org

**Pahokee** · *Pahokee C/C* · Lewis Pope III, Pres., 115 E. Main St., 33476, P 7,000, M 200, (561) 924-5579, Fax (561) 924-8116, pahokeechamber@aol.com, www.pahokee.com

**Palatka** · *Putnam County C/C* · Wes Larson, Pres., 1100 Reid St., P.O. Box 550, 32178, P 72,000, M 700, (386) 328-1503, Fax (386) 328-7076, wes@pcccfl.org, www.putnamcountychamber.org.

**Palm Bay** · *Greater Palm Bay C/C* · Kathleen Bishop IOM, Pres./CEO, 4100 Dixie Hwy. N.E., 32905, P 100,000, M 800, (321) 951-9998, (800) 276-9130, Fax (321) 951-0012, info@palmbaychamber.com, www.palmbaychamber.com

**Palm Beach** · *Palm Beach C/C* · Laurel Baker, Exec. Dir., 400 Royal Palm Way, Ste. 106, 33480, P 10,500, M 615, (561) 655-3282, Fax (561) 655-7191, info@palmbeachchamber.com, www.palmbeachchamber.com.

**Palm Beach Gardens** · *see Jupiter*

**Palm Beach Shores** · *see Jupiter*

**Palm City** · *Palm City C/C* · Carolyn Davi, Exec. Dir., 880 S.W. Martin Downs Blvd., 34990, P 24,000, M 435, (772) 286-8121, Fax (772) 286-3331, info@palmcitychamber.com, www.palmcitychamber.com

**Palm Coast** · *Flagler County C/C* · Doug Baxter, Pres., 20 Airport Rd., 32164, P 70,000, M 875, (386) 437-0106, (800) 881-1022, Fax (386) 437-5700, info@flaglerchamber.org, www.flaglerchamber.org.

**Palm Harbor** · *Greater Palm Harbor Area C/C* · Connie Davis, Pres./CEO, 1151 Nebraska Ave., 34683, P 70,000, M 550, (727) 784-4287, Fax (727) 786-2336, phcc@palmharborcc.org, www.palmharborcc.org

**Palm Shores** · *see Melbourne*

**Panama City** · *Panama City-Bay County C/C* · Carol Roberts, Pres./CEO, 235 W. 5th St., P.O. Box 1850, 32402, P 167,600, M 975, (850) 785-5206, Fax (850) 763-6229, carol@baychamberfl.com, www.panamacity.org.

**Panama City Beach** · *Panama City Beach C/C* · Beth Oltman, Pres./CEO, 309 Richard Jackson Blvd., 32407, P 40,000, M 1,000, (850) 234-3193, (850) 235-1159, Fax (850) 235-2301, chamber@pcbeach.org, www.pcbeach.org.

**Patrick Air Force Base** · *see Melbourne and Cocoa Beach*

**Paxton** · *see Florala, AL*

**Pembroke Pines** · *Miramar-Pembroke Pines Reg. C/C* · Stella Tokar, Pres., 10100 Pines Blvd., 4th Flr., 33026, P 247,000, M 500, (954) 432-9808, Fax (954) 432-9193, info@miramarpembroke-pines.org, www.miramarpembrokepines.org

**Pensacola** · *Pensacola Bay Area C/C* · Ms. Evon Emerson, Pres./CEO, 117 W. Garden St., P.O. Box 550, 32591, P 305,000, M 1,470, (850) 438-4081, Fax (850) 438-6369, www.pensacolachamber.com

**Pensacola Beach** · *Pensacola Beach C of C & Visitor Info. Center* · Maureen Lamar, Exec. Dir., 735 Pensacola Beach Blvd., 32561, P 3,500, M 121, (850) 932-1500, (800) 635-4803, Fax (850) 932-1551, beachchamber@visitpensacolabeach.com, www.visitpensacolabeach.com

**Perdido Key** · *Perdido Key Area C/C* · Bill Stromquist, Chair, 15500 Perdido Key Dr., Pensacola, 32507, P 2,000, M 300, (850) 492-4660, (800) 328-0107, Fax (850) 492-2932, chamber@perdidochamber.com, www.perdidochamber.com

**Perrine** · *Perrine Office of the Chamber South* · Mary Scott Russell, Pres., 900 Perrine Ave., Miami, 33157, P 300,000, M 1,500, (305) 238-7192, Fax (305) 254-0805, msrussell@chambersouth.com, www.chambersouth.com

**Perry** · *Perry-Taylor County C/C* · Dawn Taylor, Pres./Exec. Dir., 428 N. Jefferson St., P.O. Box 892, 32348, P 19,422, M 365, (850) 584-5366, (800) 257-8881, Fax (850) 584-8030, taylorchamber@gtcom.net, www.taylorcountychamber.com.

**CHAMBER SERVING THE TAYLOR COUNTY AREA WHICH INCLUDES STEINHATCHEE, KEATON BEACH, SALEM AND SHADY GROVE.**

**Pinellas Park** · *Pinellas Park/Gateway C/C* · Kenn Brown, Pres./CEO, 5851 Park Blvd., 33781, P 62,000, M 600, (727) 544-4777, Fax (727) 209-0837, info@pinellasparkchamber.com, www.pinellasparkchamber.com

**Plant City** · *Greater Plant City C/C* · Marion Smith, Pres., 106 N. Evers St., P.O. Box CC, 33564, P 37,000, M 761, (813) 754-3707, (800) 760-2315, Fax (813) 752-8793, info@plantcity.org, www.plantcitychamber.com.

**Plantation** · *Greater Plantation C/C* · Siobhan Edwards, Pres., 7401 N.W. 4th St., 33317, P 89,000, M 500, (954) 587-1410, Fax (954) 587-1886, info@plantationchamber.org, www.plantationchamber.org

**Pompano Beach** · *Greater Pompano Beach C/C* · Ric Green, Pres./CEO, 2200 E. Atlantic Blvd., 33062, P 101,457, M 650, (954) 941-2940, Fax (954) 785-8358, info@pompanobeachchamber.com, www.pompanobeachchamber.com.

**Ponte Vedra Beach** · *Ponte Vedra Beach C/C* · Ginger Peace, Exec. Dir., 50 A1A N., Ste. 102, 32082, P 33,000, M 300, (904) 285-2004, Fax (904) 285-8488, ginger@pontevedrachamber.org, www.pontevedrachamber.org

**Port Charlotte** · *Charlotte County C/C* · Julie Mathis, Exec. Dir., 2702 Tamiami Trl., 33952, P 154,438, M 1,300, (941) 627-2222, Fax (941) 627-9730, askus@charlottecountychamber.org, www.charlottecountychamber.org

**Port Orange** · *Port Orange-South Daytona C/C* · Debbie Connors, Exec. Dir., 3431 Ridgewood Ave., 32129, P 62,000, M 650, (386) 761-1601, Fax (386) 788-9165, info@pschamber.com, www.pschamber.com

**Port Richey** · *see New Port Richey*

**Port Saint Joe** · *Gulf County C/C* · Sandra Chafin, Exec. Dir., 101 Reid Ave., Ste. 101, P.O. Box 964, 32456, P 15,500, M 410, (850) 227-1223, (800) 239-9553, Fax (850) 227-9684, info@gulfchamber.org, www.gulfchamber.org

**Port St. Lucie** · *St. Lucie County C/C* · Linda Cox, Pres., 1850 S.W. Fountainview Blvd., Ste. 201, 34986, P 202,000, M 1,400, (772) 340-1333, Fax (772) 785-7021, info@stluciechamber.org, www.stluciechamber.org.

**Punta Gorda** · *Charlotte County C/C* · Julie Mathis, Exec. Dir., 311 W. Retta Esplanade, 33950, P 154,438, M 1,400, (941) 639-2222, Fax (941) 639-6330, askus@charlottecountychamber.org, www.charlottecountychamber.org

**Quincy** · *Gadsden County C/C* · David Gardner, Exec. Dir., 208 N. Adams St., P.O. Box 389, 32353, P 50,000, M 400, (850) 627-9231, Fax (850) 875-3299, gadsdencc@tds.net, www.gadsdenfla.com

**Redington Beach** · *see Saint Pete Beach*

**Redington Shores** · *see Saint Pete Beach*

**Ridge Manor** · *see Brooksville*

**Riverview** · *Greater Riverview C/C* · Tanya Doran, Exec. Dir., 10520 Riverview Dr., P.O. Box 128, 33568, P 45,000, M 380, (813) 234-5944, Fax (813) 234-5945, riverviewchamber@verizon.net, www.riverviewchamber.com

**Riviera Beach** · *see Jupiter*

**Rockledge** · *see Cocoa Beach*

**Royal Palm Beach** · *see Loxahatchee*

**Ruskin** · *Ruskin C/C* · Melanie Morrison, Exec. Dir., 315 S. Tamiami Trl., 33570, P 83,000, M 326, (813) 645-3808, Fax (813) 645-2099, ruskinchamber@earthlink.net, www.ruskinchamber.org.

**Safety Harbor** · *Safety Harbor C/C* · Betsy Byrd, Chrmn., 200 Main St., 34695, P 18,000, M 250, (727) 726-2890, Fax (727) 726-2733, info@safetyharborchamber.com, www.safetyharborchamber.com

**Saint Augustine** · *St. Johns County C/C* · Robin Burchfield, Pres., One Riberia St., 32084, P 155,000, M 1,100, (904) 829-5681, Fax (904) 829-6477, robin.burchfield@sjcchamber.com, www.stjohnscountychamber.com.

**Saint Cloud** · *St. Cloud/Greater Osceola C/C* · David Lane, Pres./CEO, 1200 New York Ave., 34769, P 193,000, M 615, (407) 892-3671, Fax (407) 892-5289, info@stcloudflchamber.com, www.stcloudflchamber.com

**Saint Pete Beach** · *Tampa Bay Beaches C/C* · Robin Grabowski, Pres., 6990 Gulf Blvd., 33706, P 40,000, M 500, (727) 360-6957, Fax (727) 360-2233, info@tampabaybeaches.com, www.tampabaybeaches.com

**Saint Petersburg** · *St. Petersburg Area C/C* · John T. Long, Pres./CEO, 100 Second Ave. N., Ste. 150, P.O. Box 1371, 33731, P 250,000, M 2,700, (727) 821-4069, Fax (727) 895-6326, info@stpete.com, www.stpete.com.

**Sand Key** · *see Saint Pete Beach*

**Sanford** · *Sanford C/C* · Pam Czopp, Exec. Dir., 400 E. First St., 32771, P 51,000, M 450, (407) 322-2212, Fax (407) 322-8160, info@sanfordchamber.com, www.sanfordchamber.com

**Sanibel** · *Sanibel-Captiva Islands C/C* · Ric Base, Exec. Dir., 1159 Causeway Rd., 33957, P 6,500, M 608, (239) 472-1080, Fax (239) 472-1070, island@sanibel-captiva.org, www.sanibel-captiva.org

**Santa Rosa Beach** · *Walton County C/C* · Dawn A. Moliterno, Pres./CEO, 63 S. Centre Tr., 32459, P 46,000, M 1,251, (850) 267-0683, Fax (850) 267-0603, info@waltoncountychamber.com, www.waltoncountychamber.com

**Santa Rosa County** · *see Milton*

**Sarasota** · *Greater Sarasota C/C* · Stephen Queior, Pres., 1945 Fruitville Rd., 34236, P 393,000, M 2,000, (941) 955-8187, Fax (941) 366-5621, info@sarasotachamber.com, www.sarasotachamber.com.

**Satellite Beach** · *see Melbourne*

**Sebastian** · *Sebastian River Area C/C* · Beth Mitchell, Exec. Dir., 700 Main St., 32958, P 20,000, M 600, (772) 589-5969, Fax (772) 589-5993, info@sebastianchamber.com, www.sebastianchamber.com

**Sebring** · *Greater Sebring C/C* · Sarah Pallone, Pres./CEO, 227 U.S. 27 N., 33870, P 100,000, M 675, (863) 385-8448, Fax (863) 385-8810, information@sebring.org, www.sebring.org.

**Seffner** · *Greater Seffner Area C/C* · P.O. Box 1920, 33583, P 75,000, M 158, (813) 627-8686, info@seffnerchamber.com, www.seffnerchamber.com

**Seminole** · *Greater Seminole Area C/C* · Jimmy Johnson, Dir., 8400 113th St. N., 33772, P 20,000, M 450, (727) 392-3245, Fax (727) 397-7753, www.seminolechamber.net

**Seminole County** · *see Heathrow*

**Siesta Key** · *Siesta Key C/C* · Jim Haberman, Exec. Dir., 5118 Ocean Blvd., 34242, P 25,000, M 570, (941) 349-3800, Fax (941) 349-9699, info@siestakeychamber.com, www.siestakeychamber.com

**Sorrento** · *East Lake County C/C* · Pam Jennelle, Exec. Dir., P.O. Box 774, 32776, P 19,000, M 187, (352) 383-8801, Fax (352) 383-9343, chamber@elcchamber.com, www.elcchamber.com

**South Daytona** · *see Port Orange*

**South Miami** · *Chamber South* · Mary Scott Russell, Pres., 6410 S.W. 80th St., 33143, P 300,000, M 1,500, (305) 661-1621, (305) CHAMBER, Fax (305) 666-0508, msrussell@chambersouth.com, www.chambersouth.com

**Spring Hill** · *see Brooksville*

**Starke** · *North Florida Reg. C/C* · Pam Whittle, Pres./CEO, 100 E. Call St., 32091, P 28,000, M 400, (904) 964-5278, Fax (904) 964-2863, pam@northfloridachamber.com, www.northflorida chamber.com.

**Stuart** · *Stuart-Martin County C/C* · Joseph A. Catrambone, Pres., 1650 S. Kanner Hwy., 34994, P 163,503, M 1,500, (772) 287-1088, Fax (772) 220-3437, info@goodnature.org, www.goodnature.org.

**Sumterville** · *Sumter County C/C* · Lee Ann Carr, Exec. Dir., 102 N. Hwy. 470 Lake Panasoffkee, P.O. Box 100, 33585, P 92,000, M 325, (352) 793-3099, Fax (352) 793-2120, sumter-coc@sumter chamber.org, www.sumterchamber.org.

**Sun City Center** · *Sun City Center Area C/C* · Elaine Brad, Pres., 1651 Sun City Center Plaza, P.O. Box 5623, 33573, P 25,000, M 520, (813) 634-5111, Fax (813) 634-8438, sccchamber@aol.com, www.suncitycenterchamber.org.

**Sunrise** · *Greater Sunrise C/C* · Kitty McGowan, Exec. Dir., 12717 W. Sunrise Blvd., Ste. 318, 33323, P 90,000, M 300, (954) 835-2428, Fax (954) 523-0607, suncc@sunrisechamber.org, www.sunrisechamber.org

**Suntree** · *see Melbourne and Cocoa Beach*

**Tallahassee** · *Tallahassee C/C* · Sue Dick, Pres., 100 N. Duval St., P.O. Box 1639, 32302, P 276,000, M 1,800, (850) 224-8116, Fax (850) 561-3860, info@talchamber.com, www.talchamber.com

**Tamarac** · *Tamarac C/C* · Vicki Reid, Exec. Dir., 7525 Pine Island Rd., 33321, P 60,000, M 200, (954) 722-1520, Fax (954) 721-2725, info@tamaracchamber.org, www.tamaracchamber.org

## Tampa Area

**Greater Tampa C/C** · Joe House, Interim Pres./CEO, 615 Channelside Dr., Ste. 108, P.O. Box 420, 33601, P 1,118,988, M 2,000, (813) 228-7777, (800) 298-2672, Fax (813) 223-7899, info@tampachamber.com, www.tampachamber.com

**Tampa Area,** *continued*

**North Tampa C/C** · Carol Rehfelt, Exec. Dir., P.O. Box 82043, 33682, P 450,000, M 150, (813) 961-2420, Fax (813) 961-2903, info@northtampachamber.com, www.northtampachamber.com

**South Tampa C/C** · Judy Gay, Exec. Dir., 3715 W. Horatio St, 33609, P 900,000, M 500, (813) 637-0156, Fax (813) 514-1885, executivedirector@southtampachamber.org, www.southtampa chamber.org

**Ybor City C/C** · Tom Keating, Pres./CEO, 1800 E. 9th Ave., 33605, P 3,600, M 409, (813) 248-3712, Fax (813) 247-1764, info@ybor.org, www.ybor.org

**Tarpon Springs** · *Tarpon Springs C/C* · Sue Thomas, Pres., 11 E. Orange St., 34689, P 22,000, M 380, (727) 937-6109, Fax (727) 937-2879, chamber@tarponspringschamber.org, www.tarpon springschamber.com

**Tavares** · *Tavares C/C* · Colleen McGinley, Exec. Dir., 912 N. Sinclair Ave., 32778, P 10,755, M 253, (352) 343-2531, Fax (352) 343-7565, shannon@tavareschamber.com, www.tavareschamber.com

**Temple Terrace** · *Greater Temple Terrace C/C* · Cheri Donohue, Exec. Dir., 9385 N. 56th St., 33617, P 28,000, M 650, (813) 989-7004, Fax (813) 989-7005, cdonohue@templeterracechamber.com, www.templeterracechamber.com.

**Tequesta** · *see Jupiter*

**Titusville** · *Titusville Area C/C* · Marcia Gaedcke, Pres., 2000 S. Washington Ave., 32780, P 44,000, M 800, (321) 267-3036, Fax (321) 264-0127, gaedcke@titusville.org, www.titusville.org

**Treasure Island** · *see Saint Pete Beach*

**Trenton** · *Gilchrist County C/C* · Kyle Stone, Exec. Dir., 220 S. Main St., 32693, P 21,000, M 279, (352) 463-3467, Fax (352) 463-3469, chamber@GilchristCounty.com, www.GilchristCounty.com

**Umatilla** · *Umatilla C/C* · Susan Martin, Exec. Dir., 23 S. Central Ave., P.O. Box 300, 32784, P 2,800, M 200, (352) 669-3511, Fax (352) 669-8900, umatilla@umatillachamber.org, www.umatillac hamber.org

**Valparaiso** · *see Niceville*

**Valrico** · *see Seffner*

**Venice** · *Venice Area C/C* · John G. Ryan, Pres./CEO, 597 Tamiami Trl. S., 34285, P 99,000, M 1,300, (941) 488-2236, Fax (941) 484-5903, vchamber@venicechamber.com, www.venicechamber.com

**Vero Beach** · *Indian River County C/C* · Penny S. Chandler, Exec. Dir., 1146 21st St., Ste. B, P.O. Box 2947, 32961, P 130,000, M 1,160, (772) 567-3491, Fax (772) 778-3181, info@indianriver chamber.com, www.indianriverchamber.com

**Viera** · *see Melbourne*

**Village of North Palm** · *see Jupiter*

**Wakulla County** · *see Crawfordville*

**Wauchula** · *Hardee County C/C* · Casey Dickson, Exec. Dir., 107 E. Main St., P.O. Box 683, 33873, P 28,000, M 150, (863) 773-6967, Fax (863) 773-0229, casey@hardeecc.com, www.hardeecc.com

**Webster** · *see Sumterville*

**Weeki Wachee** · *see Brooksville*

**Wellington** · *Wellington C/C* · Michela Perillo-Green, Exec. Dir., 12230 Forest Hill Blvd., Ste. 183, 33414, P 60,000, M 468, (561) 792-6525, Fax (561) 792-6200, info@wellingtonchamber.com, www.wellingtonchamber.com

**Wesley Chapel** · *Greater Wesley Chapel C/C* · Sheri Goldberg, Exec. Dir., 29142 Chapel Park Dr., 33543, P 100,000, M 505, (813) 994-8534, Fax (813) 994-8154, office@wesleychapelchamber.com, www.wesleychapelchamber.com

**West Melbourne** · *see Melbourne*

**West Palm Beach** · *C/C of the Palm Beaches* · Dennis Grady, CEO, 401 N. Flagler Dr., 33401, P 1,200,000, M 1,800, (561) 833-3711, Fax (561) 833-5582, chamber@palmbeaches.org, www.palmbeaches.org.

**Weston** · *Weston Area C/C* · Jack Miller, Pres./CEO, 1290 Weston Rd., Ste. 312, Fort Lauderdale, 33326, P 1,900,000, M 870, (954) 389-0600, Fax (954) 384-6133, jack@westonchamber.com, www.westonchamber.com.

**THE CHAMBER OF COMMERCE WAS CREATED TO PROMOTE AND SERVE THE LOCAL, REGIONAL, NATIONAL & INTERNATIONAL ECONOMICAL NEEDS OF ITS MEMBERS– FOR BUSINESS & BUSINESS TO CONSUMER.**

**Wildwood** · *see Sumterville*

**Williston** · *Williston Area C/C* · Mary Kline, Exec. Dir., P.O. Box 369, 32696, P 2,400, M 160, (352) 528-5552, Fax (352) 528-4342, wcoc@willistonfl.com, www.willistonfl.com

**Windermere** · *see Winter Garden*

**Winter Garden** · *West Orange C/C* · Stina D'Uva, Pres., 12184 W. Colonial Dr., 34787, P 240,000, M 1,050, (407) 656-1304, Fax (407) 656-0221, info@wochamber.com, www.wochamber.com

**Winter Haven** · *Greater Winter Haven C/C* · Bob Gernert Jr., Exec. Dir., 401 Ave. B N.W., P.O. Box 1420, 33882, P 35,000, M 800, (863) 293-2138, Fax (863) 297-5818, bobg@winterhavenfl.com, www.winterhavenfl.com

**Winter Park** · *Winter Park C/C* · Patrick Chapin, Pres./CEO, 151 W. Lyman Ave., P.O. Box 280, 32790, P 28,000, M 1,800, (407) 644-8281, Fax (407) 644-7826, wpcc@winterpark.org, www.winterpark.org

**Winter Springs** · *see Oviedo*

**Ybor City** · *see Tampa-Ybor City C/C*

**Yulee** · *see Amelia Island*

**Zephyrhills** · *Zephyrhills C/C* · Jan Slater, Exec. Dir., 38550 Fifth Ave., 33542, P 53,000, M 471, (813) 782-1913, Fax (813) 783-6060, info@zephyrhillschamber.org, www.zephyrhillschamber.org

# Georgia

**Georgia C of C** · George M. Israel III, Pres./CEO, 233 Peachtree St. N.E., Ste. 2000, Atlanta, 30303, M 4,000, (404) 223-2264, (800) 241-2286, Fax (404) 223-2290, www.gachamber.com

**Adel** · *Adel-Cook County C/C* · Jennifer Schneider, Pres., 100 S. Hutchinson Ave., 31620, P 16,000, M 200, (229) 896-2281, Fax (229) 896-8201, cookcochamber@windstream.net, .

**Alamo** · *Wheeler County C/C & Dev. Auth.* · P.O. Box 654, 30411, P 6,179, M 143, (912) 568-7808, Fax same, wchamber1@windstream.net, www.wheelercounty.org

**Albany** · *Albany Area C/C* · Catherine Glover, Pres./CEO, 225 W. Broad Ave., 31701, P 170,000, M 1,200, (229) 434-8700, Fax (229) 434-8716, chamber@albanyga.com, www.albanyga.com

**Alma** · *Alma-Bacon County C/C* · Cherry Rewis, Exec. Asst., 1120 W. 12th St., P.O. Box 450, 31510, P 10,000, M 40, (912) 632-5859, Fax (912) 632-7710, abcchamber@accessatc.net, www.alma chamberdevelopment.com

**Alpharetta** · *Greater North Fulton C/C* · Brandon Beach, Pres./CEO, 11605 Haynes Bridge Rd., Ste. 100, 30009, P 500,000, M 1,800, (770) 993-8806, Fax (770) 594-1059, info@gnfcc.com, www.gnfcc.com

**Americus** · *Americus-Sumter County C/C* · Alice Bolstridge, Pres., 409 Elm Ave., Ste. A, P.O. Box 724, 31709, P 33,000, M 400, (229) 924-2646, Fax (229) 924-8784, americus-sumterchamber.com.

**Ashburn** · *Ashburn-Turner County C/C* · Shelley Zorn, Pres./Eco. Dev., 238 E. College Ave., 31714, P 10,000, M 238, (229) 567-9696, (800) 471-9696, Fax (229) 567-2541, szorn@windstream.net, www.turnerchamber.com.

**Athens** · *Athens Area C/C* · Doc Eldridge, Pres., 246 W. Hancock Ave., 30601, P 103,691, M 1,100, (706) 549-6800, Fax (706) 549-5636, info@athensga.com, www.athensga.com

**Atlanta** · *Airport Area C/C* · Neil Harris, Exec. Dir., Regions Bank Bldg., Ste. 100, 600 S. Central Ave., 30354, P 30,000, M 250, (404) 209-0910, Fax (404) 389-0271, info@airportchamber.com, www.airportchamber.com

**Atlanta** · *Metro Atlanta C/C* · Sam A. Williams, Pres., 235 Andrew Young Intl. Blvd. N.W., 30303, P 5,300,000, M 4,000, (404) 880-9000, Fax (404) 586-8416, www.metroatlantachamber.com

**Augusta** · *Augusta Metro C/C* · Sue Parr, Pres., 600 Broad St. Plz., P.O. Box 1837, 30903, P 500,000, M 995, (706) 821-1300, (888) 639-8188, Fax (706) 821-1330, info@augustagausa.com, www.augustagausa.com

**Bainbridge** · *Bainbridge-Decatur County C/C* · Evelyn Clay, Pres., 100 Basin Cir., P.O. Box 755, 39818, P 28,700, M 455, (229) 246-4774, Fax (229) 243-7633, info@bainbridgegachamber.com, www.bainbridgegachamber.com

**Barnesville** · *Barnesville-Lamar County C/C* · Amanda Rose, Pres./CEO, 100 Commerce Pl., P.O. Box 506, 30204, P 16,000, M 250, (770) 358-5884, Fax (770) 358-5886, lchamber5884@charterinternet.com, www.barnesville.org

**Baxley** · *Baxley-Appling County C/C* · Karen Glenn, Exec. V.P., 305 W. Parker St., P.O. Box 413, 31515, P 17,000, M 275, (912) 367-7731, Fax (912) 367-2073, glennkk@bellsouth.net, www.baxley.org.

**Blackshear** · *Pierce County C/C* · Debra Lee, Exec. Dir., 200 S. Central Ave., P.O. Box 47, 31516, P 17,000, M 275, (912) 449-7044, Fax (912) 449-7045, pierceco@accessatc.net, www.pierceco.org

**Blairsville** · *Blairsville-Union County C/C* · Cindy Williams, Pres., 385 Welcome Center Ln., P.O. Box 789, 30514, P 22,000, M 550, (706) 745-5789, (877) 745-5789, Fax (706) 745-1382, admin@blairsvillechamber.com, www.blairsvillechamber.com

**Blakely** · *Blakely-Early County C/C* · Hillary Hallford, Pres., 214 Court Sq., P.O. Box 189, 39823, P 12,000, M 179, (229) 723-3741, Fax (229) 723-6876, earlycoc@windstream.net, www.blakely earlycountychamber.com

**Blue Ridge** · *Fannin County C/C* · Jan Hackett, Pres., 152 Orvin Lance Dr., P.O. Box 1689, 30513, P 22,000, M 800, (706) 632-5680, (800) 899-MTNS, Fax (706) 632-2241, chamber@blueridge mountains.com, www.blueridgemountains.com.

**Brunswick** · *Brunswick-Golden Isles C/C* · M.H. 'Woody' Woodside, Pres., 4 Glynn Ave., 31520, P 75,000, M 1,350, (912) 265-0620, Fax (912) 265-0629, www.brunswick-georgia.com.

**Buena Vista** · *Buena Vista-Marion County C/C* · Libby Wells, P.O. Box 471, 31803, P 5,500, M 40, (229) 649-2842, (800) 647-2842, Fax (229) 649-2429, bvmccoc@windstream.net, www.bvmccoc.com

**Bulloch County** · *see Statesboro*

**Byromville** · *see Vienna*

**Cairo** · *Cairo-Grady County C/C* · Brian Marlowe, Exec. Dir., 961 N. Broad St., P.O. Box 387, 39828, P 21,300, M 300, (229) 377-3663, Fax (229) 377-3901, cairochamber@syrupcity.net, www.cairogachamber.com

**Calhoun** · *Gordon County C/C* · Jimmy Phillips, Pres., 300 S. Wall St., 30701, P 51,500, M 458, (706) 625-3200, (800) 887-3811, Fax (706) 625-5062, jp@gordonchamber.org, www.gordonchamber.org.

**Camden County** · *Camden County C/C* · Christine M. Daniel, Pres./CEO, 2603 Osborne Rd., Ste. R, St. Marys, 31558, P 48,000, M 520, (912) 729-5840, Fax (912) 576-7924, cdaniel@camden chamber.com, www.camdenchamber.com.

**Camilla** · *Camilla C/C* · 212 E. Broad St., P.O. Box 226, 31730, P 6,200, M 300, (229) 336-5255, Fax (229) 336-5256, info@ camillageorgia.com, www.camillageorgia.com

**Canton** · *Cherokee County C/C* · Pamela W. Carnes, Pres./CEO, 3605 Marietta Hwy., P.O. Box 4998, 30114, P 215,000, M 1,100, (770) 345-0400, Fax (770) 345-0030, info@CherokeeChamber.com, www.CherokeeChamber.com.

**Carnesville** · *Franklin County C/C* · Michelle Doster, Exec. Secy., 165 Athens St., P.O. Box 151, 30521, P 24,000, M 200, (706) 384-4659, Fax (706) 384-3204, chamber@franklin-county.com, www.franklin-county.com

**Carrollton** · *Carroll County C/C* · Daniel Jackson, Pres./CEO, 200 Northside Dr., 30117, P 115,143, M 700, (770) 832-2446, Fax (770) 832-1300, daniel@carroll-ga.org, www.carroll-ga.org.

**Cartersville** · *Cartersville-Bartow County C/C* · Kay Read, Pres./CEO, 122 W. Main St., P.O. Box 307, 30120, P 95,000, M 1,225, (770) 382-1466, Fax (770) 382-2704, reception@cartersville chamber.com, www.cartersvillechamber.com

**Cedartown** · *Polk County C/C in Cedartown* · Eric McDonald, Pres., 609 S. Main St., 30125, P 40,000, M 270, (770) 749-1652, Fax (770) 684-9155, emcdonald@polkgeorgia.com, www.polkgeorgia.com

**Chatsworth** · *Chatsworth-Murray County C/C* · Dinah Rowe, Pres., 126 N. 3rd Ave., 30705, P 42,000, M 300, (706) 695-6060, (800) 969-9490, Fax (706) 517-0198, murraychamber@wind stream.net, www.murraycountychamber.org

**Clarkesville** · *see Cornelia*

**Claxton** · *Claxton-Evans County C/C* · Tammi Hall, Exec. Dir., 4 N. Duval St., 30417, P 11,000, M 225, (912) 739-1391, Fax (912) 739-3827, info@claxtonevanschamber.com, www.claxtonevans chamber.com.

**Clayton** · *Rabun County C/C* · Sean Brady, Exec. Dir., 232 Hwy. 441 N., P.O. Box 750, 30525, P 17,500, M 480, (706) 782-4812, Fax (706) 782-4810, rabunchamber@gamountains.com, www.gamountains.com

**Cleveland** · *White County C/C* · Judy Walker, Pres., 122 N. Main St., 30528, P 26,432, M 561, (706) 865-5356, (800) 392-8279, Fax (706) 865-0758, whitecountychamber@whitecountychamber.org, www.whitecountychamber.org.

**Cochran** · *Cochran-Bleckley C/C* · Kathrine Fisher, Pres./CEO, 102 N. Second St., P.O. Box 305, 31014, P 11,735, M 100, (478) 934-2965, Fax (478) 934-0353, cbchamber@comsouth.net, www.cochran-bleckleychamber.org

**College Park** · *see Jonesboro*

**Colquitt** · *Colquitt-Miller County C/C* · Veryl Garland-Cockey, Pres., 302 E. College St., 39837, P 7,000, M 210, (229) 758-2400, Fax (229) 758-8140, cmccoc@bellsouth.net, www.colquitt-georgia.com

**Columbus** · *Greater Columbus C/C* · F. Michael Gaymon, Pres., P.O. Box 1200, 31902, P 190,000, M 1,800, (706) 327-1566, Fax (706) 327-7512, mgaymon@columbusgachamber.com, www.columbusgachamber.com

**Commerce** · *see Jefferson*

**Concord** · *see Zebulon*

**Conyers** · *Conyers-Rockdale C/C* · Fred Boscarino, Pres., 1186 Scott St., P.O. Box 483, 30012, P 78,000, M 700, (770) 483-7049, Fax (770) 922-8415, katy@conyers-rockdale.com, www.conyers-rockdale.com.

**Cordele** · *Cordele-Crisp C/C* · Monica G. Simmons, Pres., 302 E. 16th Ave., P.O. Box 158, 31010, P 21,000, M 518, (229) 273-1668, Fax (229) 273-5132, msimmons@cordele-crisp-chamber.com, www.cordele-crisp-chamber.com

**Cornelia** · *Habersham County C/C* · Judy Taylor, PhD, Exec. Dir., 668 Hwy. 441, P.O. Box 366, 30531, P 43,000, M 670, (706) 778-4654, (800) 835-2559, Fax (706) 776-1416, taylorjudy@ windstream.net, www.habershamchamber.com

**Covington** · *Covington/Newton County C/C* · John Boothsby, Pres., 2100 Washington St., P.O. Box 168, 30015, P 86,000, M 610, (770) 786-7510, Fax (770) 786-1294, info@newtonchamber.com, www.newtonchamber.com

**Crawford** · *Oglethorpe County C/C* · 1158 Athens Rd., P.O. Box 56, 30630, P 14,000, M 140, (706) 743-3113, office@oglethorpe cofc.org, www.countycommerce.org

**Cumming** · *Cumming-Forsyth County C/C* · James McCoy, Pres./CEO, 212 Kelly Mill Rd., 30040, P 160,000, M 1,200, (770) 887-6461, Fax (770) 781-8800, cfccoc@cummingforsythchamber. org, www.cummingforsythchamber.org

**Cuthbert** · *Randolph County C/C* · Patricia Goodman, Exec. Dir., P.O. Box 31, 39840, P 10,000, M 150, (229) 732-2683, Fax (229) 732-6590, ppgoodman@hotmail.com

**Dahlonega** · *Dahlonega-Lumpkin County C/C & CVB* · Gary L. Powers, Pres./CEO, 13 Park St. S., 30533, P 27,019, M 580, (706) 864-3711, (800) 231-5543, Fax (706) 864-0139, info@dahlonega. org, www.dahlonega.org

**Dallas** · *Paulding County C/C* · Carolyn S. Delamont, Pres./CEO, 455 Jimmy Campbell Pkwy., 30132, P 127,000, M 800, (770) 445-6016, Fax (770) 445-3050, sbohannon@pauldingcountychamber. org, www.pauldingcountychamber.org

**Dalton** · *Dalton-Whitfield C/C* · Brian Anderson, Pres./CEO, 890 College Dr., 30720, P 83,500, M 950, (706) 278-7373, Fax (706) 226-8739, info@daltonchamber.org, www.daltonchamber.org.

**Danielsville** · *Madison County C/C & Ind. Auth.* · Barry Hardeman, Chair, 101 Courthouse Sq., Ste. 1, P.O. Box 381, 30633, P 26,000, M 300, (706) 795-3473, Fax (706) 795-3262, mccc@ madisoncountyga.org, www.madisoncountyga.org

**Darien** · *Darien-McIntosh County C/C & Visitor Center* · Wally Orrel, Pres., 1111 Magnolia Bluff Way S.W., Ste. 255, 31305, P 13,000, M 260, (912) 437-6684, Fax (912) 437-5251, info@ visitdarien.com, www.visitdarien.com

**Dawson** · *Terrell County C/C* · Gina Webb, Exec. Dir., 211 W. Lee St., P.O. Box 405, 39842, P 11,000, M 110, (229) 995-2011, Fax (229) 995-3971, tccc@windstream.net, www.terrellcountygeorgia.org

**Dawsonville** · *Dawson County C/C* · Linda Williams, Pres., Old Jail on the Square, 54 Hwy. 53 W., P.O. Box 299, 30534, P 20,000, M 500, (706) 265-6278, Fax (706) 265-6279, info@dawson.org, www.dawson.org

**Decatur** · *see Tucker*

**Dillard** · *see Clayton*

**Donalsonville** • *Donalsonville-Seminole County C/C* • Brenda Broome, Pres., 122 E. Second St., P.O. Box 713, 39845, P 9,000, M 150, (229) 524-2588, Fax (229) 524-8406, dosemcc@windstream.net.

**Douglas** • *Douglas-Coffee County C/C* • JoAnne Lewis, Pres., 211 S. Gaskin Ave., 31533, P 41,000, M 500, (912) 384-1873, Fax (912) 383-6304, jlewis@douglasga.org, www.douglasga.org

**Douglasville** • *Douglas County C/C* • Kali Boatright, Pres., 6658 Church St., 30134, P 113,000, M 800, (770) 942-5022, Fax (770) 942-5876, info@douglascountygeorgia.com, www.douglas countygeorgia.com

**Dublin** • *Dublin-Laurens County C/C* • Ms. Willie Paulk, Pres., 1200 Bellevue Ave., P.O. Box 818, 31040, P 47,000, M 682, (478) 272-5546, Fax (478) 275-0811, chamber@dublin-georgia.com, www.dublin-georgia.com.

**Duluth** • *Gwinnett C/C* • James Maran, Pres./CEO, 6500 Sugarloaf Pkwy., 30097, P 726,500, M 3,000, (770) 232-3000, Fax (770) 232-8807, info@gwinnettchamber.org, www.gwinnettchamber.org.

**Dunwoody** • *see Alpharetta*

**Eastman** • *Eastman/Dodge County C/C* • 116 9th Ave., P.O. Box 550, 31023, P 19,501, M 250, (478) 374-4723, Fax (478) 374-4626, chamberofcommerce@eastman-georgia.com, www.eastman-georgia.com

**Eatonton** • *Eatonton-Putnam C/C* • Roddie-Anne Blackwell, Pres., 305 N. Madison Ave., P.O. Box 4088, 31024, P 22,000, M 450, (706) 485-7701, Fax (706) 485-3277, epchamber@eatonton.com, www.eatonton.com

**Elberton** • *Elbert County C/C* • Phyllis Brooks, Pres., 104 Heard St., P.O. Box 537, 30635, P 22,000, M 300, (706) 283-5651, Fax (706) 283-5722, chamber@elbertga.com, elbertga.com.

**Ellaville** • *Ellaville-Schley County C/C* • Deborah Poole, Pres., P.O. Box 4, 31806, P 4,200, M 131, (229) 937-2262, Fax (229) 937-2262, www.ellavillega.com/chamber_of_commerce

**Ellijay** • *Gilmer County C/C* • Paige Green, Pres., 368 Craig St., P.O. Box 505, 30540, P 35,000, M 600, (706) 635-7400, Fax (706) 635-7410, chamber@ellijay.com, www.gilmerchamber.com.

**Evans** • *Columbia County C/C* • Jim Tingen, Exec. Dir., 4424 Evans to Locks Rd., 30809, P 102,278, M 700, (706) 651-0018, Fax (706) 651-0023, info@columbiacountychamber.com, www.columbiacountychamber.com

**Fannin County** • *see Blue Ridge*

**Fayetteville** • *Fayette County C/C* • Virginia Gibbs, Pres., 200 Courthouse Sq., 30214, P 103,000, M 800, (770) 461-9983, Fax (770) 461-9622, info@FayetteChamber.org, www.FayetteChamber.org.

**Fitzgerald** • *Fitzgerald-Ben Hill County C/C* • Betsy Giddens, Pres., P.O. Box 218, 31750, P 20,000, M 325, (229) 423-9357, (800) 225-7899, Fax (229) 423-1052, bgiddens@mchsi.com, www.fitzgeraldchamber.org.

**Folkston** • *Okefenokee C/C & Folkston/Charlton Co. Dev. Auth.* • Rhonda Del Boccio, Exec. Dir., 3795 Main St., P.O. Box 756, 31537, P 11,000, M 115, (912) 496-2536, Fax (912) 496-4601, okechamber@windstream.net, www.folkston.com.

**Forsyth** • *Forsyth-Monroe County C/C* • Tiffany Andrews, Pres./CEO, 68 N. Lee St., 31029, P 25,145, M 350, (478) 994-9239, (888) 642-4628, Fax (478) 994-9240, tiffany@forsyth-monroechamber.com, www.forsyth-monroechamber.com

**Fort Gaines** • *see Cuthbert*

**Fort Oglethorpe** • *see Ringgold*

**Fort Valley** • *Peach County C/C* • Perry Swanson, Pres., 201 Oakland Hts. Pkwy., P.O. Box 1238, 31030, P 25,000, M 267, (478) 825-3733, Fax (478) 825-2501, chamber@peachchamber.com, www.peachchamber.com

**Franklin Springs** • *see Carnesville*

**Gainesville** • *Greater Hall C/C* • Kit Dunlap, Pres./CEO, 230 E.E. Butler Pkwy., P.O. Box 374, 30503, P 175,000, M 2,800, (770) 532-6206, Fax (770) 535-8419, kit@ghcc.com, www.greaterhall chamber.com

**Gray** • *Jones County/Gray C/C* • Carmen Copeland, Exec. Dir., 161 W. Clinton St., P.O. Box 686, 31032, P 27,000, M 250, (478) 986-1123, Fax (478) 986-1022, info@jonescounty.org, www.jonescounty.org

**Greensboro** • *Greene County C/C* • Becky Cronic, Dir., 111 N. Main St., P.O. Box 741, 30642, P 16,396, M 400, (706) 453-7592, (800) 886-LAKE, Fax (706) 453-1430, chamber@greeneccoc.org, www.greeneccoc.org.

**Griffin** • *Griffin-Spalding C/C* • Bonnie Pfrogner, Exec. Dir., 143 N. Hill St., P.O. Box 73, 30224, P 59,410, M 900, (770) 228-8200, Fax (770) 228-8031, griffinchamber@cityofgriffin.com, www.griffinchamber.com.

**Gwinnett** • *see Duluth*

**Habersham County** • *see Cornelia*

**Hamilton** • *Harris County C/C* • Lynda Dawson, Pres., 143 S. College St., P.O. Box 426, 31811, P 30,000, M 324, (706) 628-0010, (888) 478-0010, Fax (706) 628-4429, info@harriscountychamber.org, www.harriscountychamber.org

**Hartwell** • *Hart County C/C* • Michele Dipert, Pres., 31 E. Howell St., P.O. Box 793, 30643, P 23,000, M 275, (706) 376-8590, hartchamber@hartcom.net, www.hart-chamber.org

**Hawkinsville** • *Hawkinsville-Pulaski County C/C* • Kim Brown, Exec. Dir., 108 Lumpkin St., P.O. Box 300, 31036, P 10,000, M 140, (478) 783-1717, Fax (478) 783-1700, hawkinsville@cstel.net, www.hawkinsville.org

**Hazlehurst** • *Hazlehurst-Jeff Davis County C/C* • Rebecca Burnette, Exec. Dir., 95 E. Jarman St., P.O. Box 546, 31539, P 12,684, M 150, (912) 375-4543, Fax (912) 375-7948, hazjdcoc@jeffdavisga.com, www.hazlehurst-jeffdavis.com

**Helen** • *Greater Helen Area C/C* • P.O. Box 192, 30545, P 420, M 130, (706) 878-1908, Fax (706) 878-3064, director@helenchamber.com, www.helenchamber.com

**Hiawassee** • *Towns County C/C & Tourism Assn.* • 1411 Jack Dayton Cir., Young Harris, 30582, P 10,203, M 375, (706) 896-4966, (800) 984-1543, Fax (706) 896-5441, info@mountaintopga.com, www.mountaintopga.com

**Hinesville** • *Liberty County C/C* • Kenny Smiley, Exec. Dir., 425 W. Oglethorpe Hwy., 31313, P 64,000, M 400, (912) 368-4445, Fax (912) 368-4677, kenny@libertycounty.org, www.libertycounty.org

**Hogansville** • *see La Grange*

**Homer** • *Banks County C/C* • Tara Fulcher, Exec. Dir., P.O. Box 57, 30547, P 16,000, M 150, (706) 677-2108, (800) 638-5004, Fax (706) 677-2109, bankscountychamber@windstream.net, www.bankscochamber.org

**Homerville** • *Homerville-Clinch County C/C* • Phil Martin, Exec. V.P., 23 W. Plant Ave., 31634, P 6,900, M 120, (912) 487-2360, Fax (912) 487-2384, clinchcountychamberofcommerce@windstream.net, www.clinchcountychamber.org.

**Jackson** • *Butts County C/C* • Melinda Atha, Exec. Dir., P.O. Box 147, 30233, P 22,000, M 350, (770) 775-4839, Fax (770) 775-4868, matha2@bellsouth.net, www.chamberbuttscounty.com.

**Jasper** · *Pickens County C/C* · Denise M. Duncan, Pres., 500 Stegall Dr., 30143, P 30,000, M 600, (706) 692-5600, Fax (706) 692-9453, info@pickenschamber.com, www.pickenschamber.com

**Jefferson** · *Jackson County Area C/C* · Shane Short, Pres./CEO, 270 Athens St., P.O. Box 629, 30549, P 60,000, M 560, (706) 387-0300, Fax (706) 387-0304, info@jacksoncountyga.com, www.jacksoncountyga.com

**Jesup** · *Jesup/Wayne County C/C* · John Riddle, Pres./CEO, 124 N.W. Broad St., 31545, P 29,000, M 430, (912) 427-2028, (888) 224-5983, Fax (912) 427-2778, web@waynechamber.com, www.waynechamber.com

**Jonesboro** · *Clayton County C/C* · Yulonda Beauford, Pres./CEO, 2270 Mt. Zion Rd., 30236, P 236,517, M 675, (678) 610-4021, Fax (678) 610-4025, info@claytonchamber.org, www.claytonchamber.org

**Kingsland** · *see Camden County*

**La Grange** · *LaGrange-Troup County C/C* · Page Estes, Pres., 111 Bull St., P.O. Box 636, 30241, P 60,000, M 850, (706) 884-8671, Fax (706) 884-6388, pestes@lagrangechamber.com, www.lagrangechamber.com.

**LaFayette** · *see Rock Spring*

**Lake City** · *see Jonesboro*

**Lake Park** · *Lake Park Area C/C & Visitors Center* · Michele Mullins, Exec. Dir., 5227 Millstore Rd., P.O. Box 278, 31636, P 18,000, M 160, (229) 559-5302, Fax (229) 559-0828, lpacocv@bellsouth.net, www.lakeparkga.com

**Lakeland** · *Lakeland-Lanier County C/C* · Ruth May, Exec. Dir., P.O. Box 215, 31635, P 8,000, M 125, (229) 482-9755, Fax (229) 482-9501, llcoc@windstream.net, www.lakelandlanierchamber.com

**Lavonia** · *Lavonia C/C* · Vivian Young, Secy., 1269 E. Main, 30553, P 2,200, M 250, (706) 356-8202, lavoniacofc@alltel.net, www.lavonia-ga.com

**Lawrenceville** · *see Duluth*

**Leesburg** · *Lee County C/C* · Winston Oxford, Exec. Dir., 100B Starksville Ave. N., 31763, P 33,000, M 525, (229) 759-2422, Fax (229) 759-9224, winstono@lee.ga.us, www.leechamber.net

**Lilly** · *see Vienna*

**Lincolnton** · *Lincolnton-Lincoln County C/C* · Al Danner, Pres., 112 N. Washington St., P.O. Box 810, 30817, P 10,000, M 175, (706) 359-7970, Fax (706) 359-5477, lincolncham@nu-z.net, www.lincolncountyga.com

**Lithonia** · *Greater Lithonia C/C* · P.O. Box 57, 30058, P 3,000, M 50, (770) 482-1808, info@lithoniachamber.com, www.lithonia-chamber.com

**Loganville** · *Loganville C/C* · Betty McCullers, Pres., 254 Main St., Ste. 200, P.O. Box 2390, 30052, P 9,800, M 300, (770) 466-1601, Fax (770) 466-1668, info@loganvillechamber.com, www.loganvillechamber.com.

**Louisville** · *Jefferson County C/C* · Lillian Easterlin, Exec. Dir., 302 E. Broad St., P.O. Box 630, 30434, P 17,266, M 100, (478) 625-8134, (866) 527-2642, Fax (478) 625-9060, leasterlin@jeffersoncounty.org, jeffersoncounty.org

**Lovejoy** · *see Jonesboro*

**Ludowici** · *Long County C/C* · Terri Hrisak Godding, Dir., P.O. Box 400, 31316, P 11,452, M 75, (912) 545-2367, Fax (912) 545-2380, thrisak@longcountychamber.com, www.longcountychamber.com

**Lyons** · *see Vidalia*

**Macon** · *Greater Macon C/C* · Chip Cherry, Pres., 305 Coliseum Dr., P.O. Box 169, 31202, P 160,000, M 1,200, (478) 621-2000, Fax (478) 621-2021, info@maconchamber.com, www.maconchamber.com.

**Madison** · *Madison-Morgan County C/C & CVB* · Marguerite Copeland, Pres., 115 E. Jefferson St., P.O. Box 826, 30650, P 17,000, M 370, (706) 342-4454, (800) 709-7406, Fax (706) 342-4455, margueritec@madisonga.org, www.madisonga.org

**Marietta** · *Cobb C/C* · Bill Cooper, Pres./CEO, P.O. Box 671868, 30006, P 671,868, M 2,500, (770) 980-2000, Fax (770) 980-9510, info@cobbchamber.org, www.cobbchamber.org.

**McDonough** · *Henry County C/C* · Kay Pippin, Pres., 1709 Highway 20 W., Westridge Business Center, 30253, P 198,000, M 800, (770) 957-5786, Fax (770) 957-8030, kpippin@henry county.com, www.henrycounty.com.

**McRae** · *Telfair County C/C* · Paula Rogers, Pres., 120 E. Oak St., 31055, P 13,205, M 130, (229) 868-6365, Fax (229) 868-7970, info@telfairco.com, www.telfairco.com

**Meansville** · *see Zebulon*

**Metter** · *Metter-Candler C/C* · Eddy Jones, Chrmn., 1210 S. Lewis St., P.O. Box 497, 30439, P 10,000, M 159, (912) 685-2159, Fax (912) 685-2108, ebim@pineland.net, www.metter-candler.com

**Milledgeville** · *Milledgeville-Baldwin County C/C* · Tara Peters, Pres./CEO, 130 S. Jefferson St., P.O. Box 751, 31059, P 44,750, M 600, (478) 453-9311, Fax (478) 453-0051, mbcchamber@windstream.net, www.milledgevillega.com.

**Millen** · *Jenkins County C/C & Dev. Auth.* · Paula Herrington, Exec. Dir., 548 Cotton Ave., 30442, P 8,700, M 135, (478) 982-5595, Fax (478) 982-5512, pauladepot@bellsouth.net, www.jenkinscountyga.com

**Molena** · *see Zebulon*

**Monroe** · *Walton County C/C* · Teri H. Wommack, Pres., 132 E. Spring St., P.O. Box 89, 30655, P 85,000, M 906, (770) 267-6594, Fax (770) 267-0961, staff@waltonchamber.org, www.walton chamber.org

**Monroe County** · *see Forsyth*

**Montezuma** · *Macon County C/C & Dev. Auth.* · Jimmy Davis, Pres., 109 N. Dooly St., 31063, P 14,594, M 125, (478) 472-2391, Fax (478) 472-5186, jcdavisjr@windstream.net, maconcountyga.org

**Monticello** · *Monticello-Jasper County C/C* · Nancy Arnold-Wood, Pres., 119 W. Washington St., P.O. Box 133, 31064, P 15,000, M 150, (706) 468-8994, Fax (706) 468-8043, www.monticelloga.org, jasperchamber@historicmonticello.com, www.historic monticello.com

**Morrow** · *see Jonesboro*

**Moultrie** · *Moultrie-Colquitt County C/C* · Amanda Holt Statom, Exec. Dir., 116 First Ave. S.E., P.O. Box 487, 31776, P 46,000, M 560, (229) 985-2131, (888) 40-VISIT, Fax (229) 890-2638, moultrie@windstream.net, www.moultriechamber.com

**Mountain City** · *see Clayton*

**Mountain Park** · *see Alpharetta*

**Nahunta** · *Brantley County C/C* · P.O. Drawer B, 31553, (912) 462-6282, bchamber@btconline.net, www.brantleycounty chamber.org

**Nashville** · *Nashville-Berrien C/C* · Chrissy Staley, Exec. Dir., 201 N. Jefferson St., P.O. Box 217, 31639, P 16,235, M 300, (229) 686-5123, Fax (229) 686-1905, berrienchamber@windstream.net, www.berrienchamber.com

**Newnan** · *Newnan-Coweta C/C* · Candace LaForge, Pres., 23 Bullsboro Dr., 30263, P 123,000, M 650, (770) 253-2270, Fax (770) 253-2271, info@newnancowetachamber.org, www.newnan cowetachamber.org

**Ocilla** • *Ocilla-Irwin C/C* • Hazel McCranie, Pres., P.O. Box 104, 31774, P 11,000, M 165, (229) 468-9114, Fax (229) 468-4452, irwinchamber@windstream.net, www.ocillachamber.net

**Peach County** • *see Fort Valley*

**Peachtree City** • *see Fayetteville*

**Pelham** • *Pelham C/C* • Deborah Laufenburger, Exec. Dir., 128 W. Railroad St., P.O. Box 151, 31779, P 5,200, M 220, (229) 294-4924, Fax (229) 294-1583, pelhamchamber@pelhamga.org, www.pelhamchamber.org.

**Pembroke** • *North Bryan County C/C* • Mary Warnell, Pres., 18 E. Bacon St., P.O. Box 916, 31321, P 3,000, M 65, (912) 653-2244, (912) 653-4040, www.bryancounty.org

**Perry** • *Perry Area C/C* • Megan Smith, Pres./CEO, 101 General Courtney Hodges Blvd., Ste. B, 31069, P 11,000, M 400, (478) 987-1234, Fax (478) 988-1234, mail@perrygachamber.com, perrygachamber.com.

**Pine Mountain** • *Pine Mountain C/C* • Lee Hale, Pres., P.O. Box 483, 31822, P 1,100, M 65, (706) 663-8850, www.pinemountainchamber.com

**Pinehurst** • *see Vienna*

**Port Wentworth** • *Port Wentworth C/C* • P.O. Box 4186, 31407, P 4,000, M 100, (912) 965-1999, Fax (912) 965-1199, ptwchamcom@aol.com, www.visitportwentworth.com

**Quitman** • *Quitman-Brooks County C/C* • John Cox, Pres., 900 E. Screven St., 31643, P 16,800, M 190, (229) 263-4841, Fax (229) 263-4822, chamber@quitmangeorgia.org, www.quitmangeorgia.org.

**Rabun County** • *see Clayton*

**Reidsville** • *Greater Tattnall C/C* • David Avery, Exec. Dir., P.O. Box 759, 30453, P 21,000, M 170, (912) 557-6323, Fax (912) 557-3046, avery582@hotmail.com, www.tattnall.com

**Richmond Hill** • *Richmond Hill-Bryan County C/C* • Kittie Franklin, Exec. Dir., 2591 Hwy. 17, Ste. 100, 31324, P 28,000, M 375, (912) 756-3444, (800) 834-3960, Fax (912) 756-4236, kfranklin@coastalnow.net, www.rhbcchamber.org

**Ringgold** • *Catoosa County C/C* • Martha Eaker, Pres., 264 Catoosa Cir., 30736, P 65,000, M 400, (706) 965-5201, (877) 965-5201, Fax (706) 965-8224, meaker@catoosachamberofcommerce.com, www.catoosachamberofcommerce.com

**Riverdale** • *see Jonesboro*

**Roberta** • *Roberta-Crawford County C/C* • 38 Wright Ave., P.O. Box 417, 31078, P 14,000, M 78, (478) 836-3825, Fax (478) 836-4509, rcccoc@pstel.net, www.robertacrawfordchamber.org

**Rochelle** • *Wilcox County C/C* • P.O. Box 839, 31079, P 8,600, M 50, (229) 365-2509

**Rock Spring** • *Walker County C/C* • Stacey Mauer, Pres., 10052 Hwy. 27 N., P.O. Box 430, 30739, P 61,000, M 340, (706) 375-7702, Fax (706) 375-7797, info@walkercochamber.com, www.walker-cochamber.com

**Rockmart** • *Polk County C/C-Dev. Auth. of Polk County* • Eric McDonald, Pres., 604 Goodyear St., 30153, P 40,000, M 270, (770) 684-8760, Fax (770) 684-9155, emcdonald@polkgeorgia.com, www.polkgeorgia.com

**Rome** • *Greater Rome C/C* • Al Hodge, Pres./CEO, 1 Riverside Pkwy., 30161, P 95,000, M 1,000, (706) 291-ROME, Fax (706) 232-5755, grcc@romega.com, www.romega.com.

**Roswell** • *see Alpharetta*

**Royston** • *see Carnesville*

**Saint Simons Island** • *see Brunswick*

**Sandersville** • *Washington County C/C* • Theo McDonald, Pres., 131 W. Haynes St., Ste. B, P.O. Box 582, 31082, P 21,119, M 375, (478) 552-3288, Fax (478) 552-1449, tmcdonald@sandersville.net, www.washingtoncounty-ga.com

**Sandy Springs** • *see Alpharetta*

**Savannah** • *Savannah Area C/C* • William W. Hubbard, Pres./CEO, 101 E. Bay St., P.O. Box 1628, 31402, P 304,000, M 2,300, (912) 644-6400, Fax (912) 644-6499, info@savannahchamber.com, www.savannahchamber.com.

**Sky Valley** • *see Clayton*

**Smyrna** • *see Marietta*

**Soperton** • *Soperton-Treutlen C/C* • Tammi Walraven, Secy., 488 Second St., P.O. Box 296, 30457, P 6,000, M 56, (912) 529-6868, Fax (912) 529-4385, agt_soperton@hotmail.com, www.soperton.org.

**Springfield** • *Effingham County C/C* • John A. Henry, Exec. Dir., 520 W. Third St., P.O. Box 1078, 31329, P 56,000, M 408, (912) 754-3301, (866) 754-3301, Fax (912) 754-1236, effingham@windstream.net, www.effinghamcounty.com.

**St. Marys** • *see Camden County* • St Marys

**Statesboro** • *Statesboro-Bulloch C/C* • Peggy Chapman, Pres., 102 S. Main St., P.O. Box 303, 30459, P 68,521, M 800, (912) 764-6111, Fax (912) 489-3108, peggy@statesboro-chamber.org, www.statesboro-chamber.org.

**Summerville** • *Chattooga County C/C* • David Tidmore, Pres., #44 Hwy. 48, P.O. Box 217, 30747, P 25,474, M 156, (706) 857-4033, Fax (706) 857-6963, chattooga_chamber@windstream.net, www.chattooga-chamber.org.

**Swainsboro** • *Swainsboro-Emanuel County C/C* • Bill Rogers Jr., Exec. Dir., 102 S. Main St., 30401, P 22,600, M 294, (478) 237-6426, Fax (478) 237-7460, swainsborochambr@bellsouth.net, www.emanuelchamber.org

**Sylvania** • *Screven County C/C* • Heidi Jeffers, Exec. Dir., 101 S. Main St., 30467, P 15,374, M 350, (912) 564-7878, Fax (912) 564-7245, hjeffersplanters@planters.net, www.screvencounty.com

**Sylvester** • *Sylvester-Worth County C/C* • Hollie Jones, Pres., 301 E. Franklin St., P.O. Box 768, 31791, P 20,000, M 250, (229) 776-7718, Fax (229) 776-7719, www.sylvesterworthcochamber.com.

**Talbotton** • *Talbot County C/C* • Pam Jordon, Exec. Dir., P.O. Box 98, 31827, P 6,500, M 100, (706) 665-8079, Fax (706) 665-8660, info@talbotcountychamber.org, www.talbotcountychamber.org

**Tallulah Falls** • *see Clayton*

**Thomaston** • *Thomaston-Upson C/C* • Lori Showalter-Smith, Pres., P.O. Box 827, 30286, P 27,000, M 320, (706) 647-9686, Fax (706) 647-1703, lorishowalter@windstream.net, www.thomastonchamber.com

**Thomasville** • *Thomasville-Thomas County C/C* • Donald P. Sims, Pres., 401 S. Broad St., P.O. Box 560, 31799, P 45,000, M 750, (229) 226-9600, (229) 225-1422, Fax (229) 226-9603, thomasvillechamber@rose.net, www.thomasvillechamber.com

**Thomson** • *Thomson-McDuffie C/C* • Carolyn Gilbert, Dir., 111 Railroad St., 30824, P 22,000, M 275, (706) 597-1000, Fax (706) 595-2143, cgilbert@thomson-mcduffie.com, www.thomson-mcduffie.com.

**Tifton** • *Tifton-Tift County C/C* • Brad Day, Pres./CEO, 100 Central Ave., P.O. Box 165, 31793, P 40,000, M 600, (229) 382-6200, (800) 550-TIFT, Fax (229) 386-2232, www.tiftonchamber.org

**Tiger** • *see Clayton*

U.S. Chambers of Commerce

**Toccoa** · *Toccoa-Stephens County C/C* · Wendi Bailey, Pres., 160 N. Alexander St., P.O. Box 577, 30577, P 28,000, M 370, (706) 886-2132, Fax (706) 886-2133, wbaileytoccoaga@windstram.net, www.toccoagachamber.com.

**Towns County** · *see Hiawassee*

**Trenton** · *Dade County C/C & Welcome Center* · Debbie Tinker, Exec. Dir., 111 Railway Ln., P.O. Box 1014, 30752, P 16,500, M 130, (706) 657-4488, Fax (706) 657-7513, dcoc@tvn.net, www.dadechamber.com

**Tucker** · *DeKalb C/C* · Leonardo McClarty, Pres., 100 Crescent Centre Pkwy., Ste. 680, 30084, P 700,000, M 600, (404) 378-8000, Fax (404) 378-3397, info@dekalbchamber.org, www.dekalbchamber.org

**Tyrone** · *see Fayetteville*

**Unadilla** · *see Vienna*

**Union City** · *South Fulton C/C* · LaVonne Deavers, Chrmn. of Bd., 6400 Shannon Pkwy., 30291, P 158,000, M 404, (770) 964-1984, Fax (770) 969-1969, ldeavers@sfcoc.org, www.sfcoc.org

**Valdosta** · *Valdosta-Lowndes County C/C* · Myrna Ballard, Pres., 416 N. Ashley St., P.O. Box 790, 31603, P 106,000, M 1,525, (229) 247-8100, Fax (229) 245-0071, chamber@valdostachamber.com, www.valdostachamber.com.

**Vidalia** · *Toombs-Montgomery C/C* · Bill Mitchell, Pres., 2805 E. First St., 30474, P 34,337, M 550, (912) 537-4466, Fax (912) 537-1805, information@toombschamber.com, www.toombs montgomerychamber.com

**Vienna** · *Dooly County C/C* · Rhonda Lamb-Heath, Exec. Dir., 117 E. Union St., P.O. Box 308, 31092, P 11,525, M 150, (229) 268-8275, Fax (229) 268-8200, bigpigjig@sowega.net, www.doolychamber.com

**Waco** · *Haralson County C/C* · Jennie English, Pres., 70 Murphy Campus Blvd., 30182, P 29,000, M 375, (770) 537-5594, Fax (770) 537-5873, hccoc@haralson.org, www.haralson.org

**Wadley** · *see Louisville*

**Ware County** · *see Waycross*

**Warm Springs** · *Meriwether County C/C* · Carolyn McKinley, Exec. Dir., 91 Broad St., P.O. Box 9, 31830, P 22,534, M 183, (706) 655-2558, Fax (706) 655-2812, meriwetherchamber@windstream. net, www.meriwethercountychamberofcommerce.com

**Warner Robins** · *Warner Robins Area C/C* · Ed Rodriguez, Pres./CEO, 1228 Watson Blvd., 31093, P 125,000, M 1,291, (478) 922-8585, Fax (478) 328-7745, info@warner-robins.com, www. warner-robins.com.

**Warrenton** · *Warren County C/C* · O.B. McCorkle, Exec. Dir., P.O. Box 27, 30828, P 6,200, M 120, (706) 465-9604, Fax (706) 465-1789, chamber@warrencountyga.com, www.warrencountyga.com

**Washington** · *Washington-Wilkes C/C* · 29 West Sq., P.O. Box 661, 30673, P 10,671, M 200, (706) 678-2013, (706) 678-5111, Fax (706) 678-3033, tourism@washingtonwilkes.org, www.washingtonwilkes.org

**Watkinsville** · *Oconee County C/C* · JR Whitfield, Pres., 55 Nancy Dr., P.O. Box 348, 30677, P 30,000, M 346, (706) 769-7947, Fax (706) 769-7948, jrwhitfield@occoc.org, www.occoc.org

**Waycross** · *Waycross-Ware County C/C* · Robin Blackard, Dir., 315 Plant Ave., Ste. B, 31501, P 35,503, M 400, (912) 283-3742, Fax (912) 283-0121, wwcocrobin@atc.cc, www.waycrosschamber.org

**Waynesboro** · *Burke County C/C* · Ashley Roberts, Exec. Dir., 241 E. Sixth St., 30830, P 20,579, M 200, (706) 554-5451, Fax (706) 554-7091, www.burkecounty-ga.gov

**West Point** · *see Lanett, AL*

**Williamson** · *see Zebulon*

**Winder** · *Barrow County C/C* · Thomas Jennings, Pres., #6 Porter St., P.O. Box 456, 30680, P 60,000, M 600, (770) 867-9444, Fax (770) 867-6366, mmilner@barrowchamber.com, www. barrowchamber.com

**Woodbine** · *see Camden County*

**Wrens** · *see Louisville*

**Wrightsville** · *Wrightsville-Johnson County C/C* · Charlene Milligan, Admin., 6745 E. College St., P.O. Box 94, 31096, P 8,600, M 95, (478) 864-7200, Fax (478) 864-7200, commerce@ wrightsville-johnsoncounty.com, www.wrightsville-johnson county.com

**Young Harris** · *see Hiawassee*

**Zebulon** · *Pike County C/C & Dev. Auth.* · Karen Brown, Pres., 416 Thomaston St., P.O. Box 1147, 30295, P 17,500, M 280, (770) 567-2029, (770) 567-7291, Fax (770) 567-7290, pikeida@pike countygachamber.com, www.pikecountygachamber.com.

# Guam

**Hagatna** · *Guam C of C* · Reina A. Leddy, Pres., 173 Aspinall Ave., Ste. 101, Ada Plaza Center Bldg., 96910, P 170,000, M 350, (671) 472-6311, (671) 472-8001, Fax (671) 472-6202, gchamber@ guamchamber.com.gu, www.guamchamber.com.gu.

# Hawaii

**C of C of Hawaii** · James Tollefson, Pres./CEO, 1132 Bishop St. #402, Honolulu, 96813, P 1,400,000, M 1,100, (808) 545-4300, Fax (808) 545-4369, info@cochawaii.org, www.cochawaii.org

**Haleiwa** · *North Shore C/C* · 66-434 Kamehameha Hwy., P.O. Box 878, 96712, P 18,300, M 160, (808) 637-4558, Fax (808) 637-4556, info@gonorthshore.org, www.gonorthshore.org

**Hilo** · *Hawaii Island C/C* · Judi Steinman, Exec. Officer, 106 Kamehameha Ave., 96720, P 138,000, M 700, (808) 935-7178, Fax (808) 961-4435, exec@hicc.biz, www.hicc.biz

## Honolulu Area

**Chinese C/C of Hawaii** · Wen Chung Lin, Exec. V.P., 76 N. King St. #202, 96817, M 350, (808) 533-3181, info@chinesechamber.com, www.chinesechamber.com

**Filipino C/C** · Jason Pascua, Pres., 1136 Union Mall, Ste. 804, 96813, P 800,000, M 400, (808) 386-3823, info@filipinochamber. org, www.filipinochamber.org

**Native Hawaiian C/C** · Robson Hind, P.O. Box 597, 96809, M 250, (808) 531-3744, www.nativehawaiian.cc

**Kahului** · *Maui C/C* · Pamela Tumpap, Pres., 313 Ano St., 96732, P 144,000, M 920, (808) 871-7711, Fax (808) 871-0706, pamela@ mauichamber.com, www.mauichamber.com

**Kailua, Oahu** · *Kailua-Oahu C/C* · Evan Scherman, Pres., 600 Kailua Rd., Ste. 107, P.O. Box 1496, 96734, P 50,000, M 200, (808) 261-7997, (888) 261-7997, kcoc@kailuachamber.com, www. kailuachamber.com

**Kailua-Kona** · *Kona-Kohala C/C* · Vivian Landrum, Exec. Dir., 75-5737 Kuakini Hwy., Ste. 208, 96740, P 50,000, M 675, (808) 329-1758, Fax (808) 329-8564, info@kona-kohala.com, www. kona-kohala.com

**Kaunakakai** · *Moloka'i C/C* · Barbara Haliniak, Pres., P.O. Box 515, 96748, P 7,000, M 108, (808) 553-4482, Fax (808) 553-4482, molokaichamber@hawaiiantel.biz, www.molokaichamber.org

**Lihu'e** • *Kauai C/C* • Randall Francisco, Pres., 4268 Rice St., Ste. H, P.O. Box 1969, 96766, P 58,303, M 450, (808) 245-7363, Fax (808) 245-8815, info@kauaichamber.org, www.kauaichamber.org

**Ocean View** • *Ka'u C/C* • Starina Leilani, Secy., P.O. Box 6710, 96737, P 6,000, M 160, (808) 939-8449, (808) 937-2750, starina@alohabroadband.com, www.kauchamber.com

# Idaho

**Idaho Chamber Alliance** • Kent Just, Dir., P.O. Box 2368, Attn: Kent Just, Boise, 83701, (208) 284-2988, chambers@idahochamberalliance.com, www.idahochamberalliance.com

**American Falls** • *American Falls C/C* • P.O. Box 207, 83211, P 4,100, M 50, (208) 226-7214, info@americanfallschamber.org, www.americanfallschamber.org

**Arco** • *Butte County C/C* • Janet Thornock, Pres., P.O. Box 837, 83213, P 3,000, M 48, (208) 527-8977, Fax (208) 527-3036, buttechamber@atcnet.net, www.cityarco.com

**Ashton** • *Ashton C/C* • 714 Main St., P.O. Box 351, 83420, P 2,000, M 75, (208) 652-3355, info@ashtonidaho.com, www.ashtonidaho.com

**Bayview** • *Bayview C/C* • P.O. Box 121, 83803, P 400, M 80, (208) 683-2963, bviewchmbr@hotmail.com, www.bayview-idaho.org

**Bellevue** • *Bellevue C/C* • Stefany Mahoney, Pres., P.O. Box 406, 83313, P 1,900, M 75, (208) 720-8227, bellevueidahochamber@yahoo.com, www.bellevueidaho.us

**Blackfoot** • *Greater Blackfoot Area C/C* • Stephanie Govatos, Exec. Dir., P.O. Box 801, 83221, P 11,000, M 225, (208) 785-0510, Fax (208) 785-7974, chamber@blackfootchamber.org, www.blackfootchamber.org

**Boise** • *Boise Metro C/C* • Tami Brandstetter, Chrmn., 250 S. 5th St., Ste. 300, P.O. Box 2368, 83701, P 615,000, M 2,000, (208) 472-5200, Fax (208) 472-5201, info@boisechamber.org, www.boisechamber.org

**Bonners Ferry** • *Greater Bonners Ferry C/C* • Brett Brown, Pres., P.O. Box X, 83805, P 10,000, M 72, (208) 267-5922, Fax (208) 267-5922, info@bonnersferrychamber.com, www.bonnersferrychamber.com

**Buhl** • *Buhl C/C* • Michelle Olsen, Admin., 716 U.S. Hwy. 30 E., 83316, P 4,200, M 180, (208) 543-6682, Fax (208) 543-2185, michelle@buhlchamber.org, buhlchamber.org

**Burley** • *see Mini-Cassia*

**Caldwell** • *Caldwell C/C* • Diana L. Brown, Pres./CEO, 704 Blaine, P.O. Box 819, 83606, P 43,000, M 426, (208) 459-7493, (866) 206-6944, Fax (208) 454-1284, chamber@ci.caldwell.id.us, www.caldwellidaho.org.

**Cascade** • *Cascade C/C* • Mike Crevelt, Pres., P.O. Box 571, 83611, P 1,000, M 100, (208) 382-3833, info@cascadechamber.com, www.cascadechamber.com

**Clark Fork** • *Hope-Clark Fork C/C* • Terry Stevens, Secy./Treas., P.O. Box 159, 83811, P 1,500, M 25, (208) 266-1101, info@poby.org, www.poby.org

**Coeur d'Alene** • *Coeur d'Alene Area C/C* • Jonathan Coe, Pres./Gen. Mgr., 105 N. 1st St., Ste. 100, 83814, P 130,000, M 2,000, (208) 664-3194, Fax (208) 667-9338, info@cdachamber.com, www.cdachamber.com

**Coolin** • *Priest Lake C/C* • P.O. Box 174, 83821, P 3,000, M 120, (208) 443-3191, (888) 774-3785, Fax (208) 443-3191, info@priestlake.org, www.priestlake.org

**Cottonwood** • *Cottonwood C/C* • Cheri Holthaus, Pres., P.O. Box 15, 83522, P 944, M , (208) 962-3231, www.cottonwoodidaho.org

**Council** • *Council C/C* • Ken Bell, Pres., P.O. Box 527, 83612, P 815, M 100, (208) 253-6830, Fax (208) 253-6830, councilchamber@ctcweb.net, www.councilchamberofcommerce.com

**Craigmont** • *Greater Craigmont C/C* • P.O. Box 365, 83523, P 562, M 25, (208) 924-5432, (208) 924-0050, ednac@camasnet.com, www.craigmontareachamber.com

**Darlington** • *see Arco*

**Dixie** • *see Elk City*

**Donnelly** • *Donnelly Area C/C* • Monty Ivey, Exec. Dir., P.O. Box 83, 83615, P 140, M 58, (208) 325-3545, (208) 315-3231, info@donnellychamber.org, www.donnellychamber.org

**Downey** • *Downey C/C* • Rex Anderson, Pres., P.O. Box 353, 83234, P 650, M 28, (208) 897-5342, Fax (208) 897-5677, www.downeyidaho.com

**Driggs** • *Teton Valley C/C* • Reid Rogers, Pres./Exec. Dir., P.O. Box 250, 83422, P 7,500, M 260, (208) 354-2500, Fax (208) 354-2517, tvcc@tetonvalleychamber.com, www.tetonvalleychamber.com

**Eagle** • *Eagle C/C* • Teri Bath, Pres., 597 E. State St., P.O. Box 1300, 83616, P 20,000, M 500, (208) 939-4222, Fax (208) 939-4234, teri@eaglechamber.com, www.eaglechamber.com

**Elk City** • *Elk City Area Alliance* • Earl Sherrer, Pres., P.O. Box 402, 83525, P 275, M 60, (208) 842-2597, Fax (208) 842-2597, elkcity@camasnet.com, www.elkcityidaho.com

**Emmett** • *Gem County C/C* • Wisti Rosenthal, Exec. Dir., 127 E. Main, P.O. Box 592, 83617, P 17,000, M 280, (208) 365-3485, Fax (208) 365-3220, chamber@emmettidaho.com, www.emmettidaho.com

**Fruitland** • *Fruitland C/C* • P.O. Box 408, 83619, P 4,505, M 140, (208) 452-4350, Fax (208) 452-5028, chamber@fmtc.com, www.fruitlandidaho.org

**Garden Valley** • *Greater Garden Valley Area C/C* • Greg Simione, Pres., P.O. Box 10, 83622, P 3,000, M 85, (208) 462-5003, gvchamber@gardenvalleyidaho.net, www.gvchamber.org

**Glenns Ferry** • *Glenns Ferry C/C & Visitors Center* • P.O. Box 317, 83623, P 1,500, M 90, (208) 366-7345, Fax (208) 366-2238, www.glennsferryidaho.org

**Grace** • *Grace C/C* • P.O. Box 214, 83241, P 1,000, M 150, (208) 425-3912, info@graceidaho.com, www.graceidaho.com

**Grangeville** • *Grangeville C/C* • Melinda Hall, Pres., Pine & Hwy. 95 N., P.O. Box 212, 83530, P 3,300, M 135, (208) 983-0460, www.grangevilleidaho.com

**Hagerman** • *Hagerman Valley C/C* • P.O. Box 599, 83332, P 850, M 50, (208) 837-9131, www.hagermanchamber.com

**Hailey** • *Hailey C/C* • Jim Spinelli, Exec. Dir., 309 S. Main, P.O. Box 100, 83333, P 9,500, M 300, (208) 788-3484, Fax (208) 578-1595, info@haileyidaho.com, www.haileyidaho.com

**Hayden** • *Hayden C/C* • P.O. Box 1210, 83835, P 14,000, M 184, (208) 762-1185, join@haydenchamber.org, www.haydenchamber.org

**Heyburn** • *see Mini-Cassia*

**Homedale** • *Homedale C/C* • Gavin Parker, Pres., P.O. Box 845, 83628, P 2,500, M 30, (208) 337-3271, Fax (208) 337-3272

**Hope** • *see Clark Fork*

**Horseshoe Bend** • *Horseshoe Bend Area C/C* • P.O. Box 216, 83629, P 770, M 50, www.horseshoebendchamber.com

**Howe** • *see Arco*

**Idaho City** • *Idaho City C/C* • Bill Stirling, Pres., P.O. Box 507, 83631, P 458, M 40, (208) 392-4159, www.idahocitychamber.com

**Idaho Falls** • *Greater Idaho Falls C/C* • Robb Chiles, CEO, 630 W. Broadway, P.O. Box 50498, 83405, P 52,000, M 830, (208) 523-1010, Fax (208) 523-2255, info@idahofallschamber.com, www. idahofallschamber.com.

**Island Park** • *Island Park C/C* • Connie Funkhouser, Pres., P.O. Box 83, 83429, P 1,500, M 150, (208) 558-7755, ipchamber@ yahoo.com, www.islandparkchamber.org

**Jerome** • *Jerome C/C* • 104 W. Main St., Ste. 101, 83338, P 18,342, M 323, (208) 324-2711, Fax (208) 324-6881, chamber@ visitjerome.com, www.visitjerome.com

**Kamiah** • *Kamiah C/C* • Robert Simmons, Pres., 518 Main St., P.O. Box 1124, 83536, P 1,200, M 80, (208) 935-2290, info@ kamiahchamber.com, www.kamiahchamber.com

**Kellogg** • *Historic Silver Valley C/C* • Norma Douglas, Coord., 10 Station Ave., 83837, P 2,500, M 280, (208) 784-0821, Fax (208) 783-4343, svchamber@usamedia.tv, www.historicsilvervalley chamberofcommerce.com

**Ketchum** • *see Sun Valley*

**Kooskia** • *Kooskia C/C* • Lara Smith, Pres., P.O. Box 310, 83539, P 652, M 30, (208) 926-4362, (208) 926-4109, Fax (208) 926-4362, kooskiachamber@groidaho.net, www.kooskia.com

**Kuna** • *Kuna C/C* • 123 Swan Falls Rd., 83634, P 14,000, M 223, (208) 922-9254, information@kunachamber.com, www.kunach amber.com

**Lava Hot Springs** • *Greater Lava Hot Springs C/C* • P.O. Box 238, 83246, P 527, M 56, (208) 776-5500, findout@lavahotsprings. org, www.lavahotsprings.org

**Leslie** • *see Arco*

**Lewiston** • *Lewiston C/C* • Keith Havens, Pres./CEO, 111 Main St. #120, 83501, P 32,000, M 750, (208) 743-3531, (800) 473-3543, Fax (208) 743-2176, info@lewistonchamber.org, www.lewiston chamber.org

**Mackay** • *see Arco*

**McCall** • *McCall Area C/C* • Tim Cockrane, Dir., 102 N. 3rd St., P.O. Box 350, 83638, P 3,000, M 260, (208) 634-7631, Fax (208) 634-7752, info@mccallchamber.org, www.mccallchamber.org

**Meridian** • *Meridian C/C* • Teri Sackman, Exec. Dir., 215 E. Franklin Rd., P.O. Box 7, 83680, P 70,000, M 650, (208) 888-2817, Fax (208) 888-2682, info@meridianchamber.org, www.meridian chamber.org

**Middleton** • *Middleton C/C* • Rick Fried, Pres., P.O. Box 434, 83644, P 5,000, (208) 713-5662, info@middletonchamber.org, www.middletonchamber.org

**Mini-Cassia** • *Mini-Cassia C/C* • Kae D. Cameron, Exec. Dir., P.O. Box 640, Heyburn, 83336, P 40,000, M 500, (208) 679-4793, Fax (208) 679-4794, director@pmt.org, www.minicassiachamber.com.

**Montpelier** • *Greater Bear Lake Valley C/C* • Lori Bowers, Exec. Dir., 915 Washington St., P.O. Box 265, 83254, P 6,000, M 82, (208) 847-0067, (800) 448-2327, Fax (208) 847-0067, info@bearlake chamber.org, www.bearlakechamber.org

**Moore** • *see Arco*

**Moscow** • *Moscow C/C* • Steven Hacker, Exec. Dir., 411 S. Main St., P.O. Box 8936, 83843, P 21,000, M 650, (208) 882-1800, (800) 380-1801, Fax (208) 882-6186, info@moscowchamber.com, www. moscowchamber.com

**Mountain Home** • *Mountain Home C/C* • Debra Shoemaker, Exec. Dir, 205 N. 3rd E., 83647, P 14,000, M 250, (208) 587-4334, Fax (208) 587-0042, chamber@mountainhomechamber.com, www.mountainhomechamber.com

**Nampa** • *Nampa C/C* • Georgia Bowman-Gunstream, Pres./CEO, 312 13th Ave. S., 83651, P 81,000, M 580, (208) 466-4641, (877) 20-NAMPA, Fax (208) 466-4677, info@nampa.com, www.nampa.com

**New Meadows** • *Meadows Valley C/C* • P.O. Box 170, 83654, P 800, M 70, (208) 347-2171, (208) 347-4636, Fax (208) 347-2384, new_meadows@frontiernet.net, www.newmeadowsidaho.org

**New Plymouth** • *New Plymouth C/C* • Janet Warnke, Bd. Member, P.O. Box 26, 83655, P 1,500, M 100, (208) 278-3696

**Orofino** • *Orofino C/C* • Phillip Shriver, Exec. Dir., P.O. Box 2346, 83544, P 3,500, M 100, (208) 476-4335, director@orofino.com, www.orofino.com

**Orogrande** • *see Elk City*

**Payette** • *Payette C/C* • Jody Clements, Pres., 695 2nd Ave. S., 83661, P 7,400, M 250, (208) 642-2362, info@payettechamber. com, www.payettechamber.com

**Pierce** • *see Weippe*

**Pocatello** • *Greater Pocatello C/C* • Matthew J. Hunter, Exec. Dir., 324 S. Main, P.O. Box 626, 83204, P 62,000, M 831, (208) 233-1525, Fax (208) 233-1527, amiles@pocatelloidaho.com, www. pocatelloidaho.com.

**Post Falls** • *Post Falls C/C* • Pam Houser, Pres./CEO, 510 E. 6th Ave., P.O. Box 908, 83877, P 25,000, M 500, (208) 773-5016, (800) 292-2553, Fax (208) 773-3843, info@postfallschamber.com, www. postfallschamber.com

**Preston** • *Preston Area C/C* • Pennie Christensen, Exec. Dir., 49 N. State, Ste. A, 83263, P 14,000, M 200, (208) 852-2703, Fax (208) 852-1475, pacc@ida.net, www.prestonidaho.org

**Priest River** • *Priest River C/C* • Ray Roberts, Pres., P.O. Box 929, 83856, P 1,800, M 160, (208) 448-2721, Fax (208) 448-2721, prchamber@conceptcable.com, www.priestriver.org

**Rathdrum** • *Rathdrum Area C/C* • Marge Huddlestone, Gen. Mgr., 8184 W. Main St., 83858, P 6,000, M 130, (208) 687-2866, office@rathdrumchamberofcommerce.com, www.rathdrum chamberofcommerce.com

**Red River** • *see Elk City*

**Reubens** • *see Craigmont*

**Rexburg** • *Rexburg Area C/C* • Donna Benfield, Exec. Dir., 420 West 4th South, 83440, P 27,000, M 440, (208) 356-5700, (888) 463-6880, Fax (208) 356-5799, info@rexcc.com, www.rexcc.com.

**Riggins** • *Salmon River C/C* • Carolyn Friend, Treas., P.O. Box 289, 83549, P 438, M 100, (866) 221-3901, cfriend@frontiernet.net, www.rigginsidaho.com

**Rupert** • *see Mini-Cassia*

**Saint Anthony** • *Greater Saint Anthony C/C* • Sherri Jackson, Pres., 420 N. Bridge St., Ste. C, 83445, P 3,400, M 100, (208) 624-4870, sachamber@fretel.com, www.stanthonychamber.com

**Saint Maries** • *Saint Maries C/C* • Shirley Ackerman, Pres., 906 Main Ave., P.O. Box 162, 83861, P 2,900, M 150, (208) 245-3563, manager@stmarieschamber.org, www.stmarieschamber.org

**Salmon** • *Salmon Valley C/C* • Debbie Ellis, Admin., 200 Main St., 83467, P 5,702, M 190, (208) 756-2100, (800) 727-2540, Fax (208) 756-4935, info@salmonchamber.com, www.salmon chamber.com

**Sandpoint** • *Greater Sandpoint C/C* • Amy Little, Exec. Dir., 1202 Hwy. 95, P.O. Box 928, 83864, P 41,000, M 620, (208) 263-0887, (800) 800-2106, Fax (208) 265-5289, info@sandpoint chamber.com, www.sandpointchamber.com

**Soda Springs** • *Soda Springs C/C* • Bob Ward, Pres., 9 W. 2nd S., P.O. Box 697, 83276, P 3,000, M 130, (208) 547-4964, (888) 399-0888, Fax (208) 547-2601, sodacoc@sodachamber.com, www.sodachamber.com

**Spirit Lake** • *Spirit Lake C/C* • Roxanne Kusler, Pres., 32173 N. 5th, P.O. Box 772, 83869, P 1,600, M 94, (208) 623-3411, rkusler@inb.com, www.spiritlakechamber.com

**Stanley** • *Stanley-Sawtooth C/C* • Greg Edson, Exec. Dir., Hwy. 21, Community Bldg., P.O. Box 8, 83278, P 100, M 110, (208) 774-3411, (800) 878-7950, info@stanleycc.org, www.stanleycc.org

**Sun Valley** • *Sun Valley-Ketchum C/C & CVB* • Carol Waller, Exec. Dir., P.O. Box 2420, 83353, P 4,547, M 550, (208) 726-3423, (866) 226-8817, Fax (208) 726-4533, info@visitsunvalley.com, www.visitsunvalley.com

**Tetonia** • *see Driggs*

**Trestle Creek** • *see Clark Fork*

**Twin Falls** • *Twin Falls Area C/C* • Shawn Barigar, Pres./CEO, 858 Blue Lakes Blvd. N., 83301, P 67,000, M 750, (208) 733-3974, Fax (208) 733-9216, info@twinfallschamber.com, www.twinfalls chamber.com.

**Victor** • *see Driggs*

**Wallace** • *Historical Wallace C/C* • Debbie Mikesell, Pres., 10 River St., Exit 61, 83873, P 1,000, M 185, (208) 753-7151, (800) 434-4204, Fax (208) 753-7151, director@wallaceidahochamber.com, www.wallaceidahochamber.com

**Weippe** • *Pierce-Weippe C/C* • Colleen Nelson, Secy., P.O. Box 378, 83553, P 1,000, M 42, (208) 435-4406, info@pierce-weippechamber.com, www.pierce-weippechamber.com

**Weiser** • *Greater Weiser Area C/C* • Laurel Adams, Exec. Dir., 309 State St., 83672, P 5,374, M 200, (208) 414-0452, Fax (208) 414-0451, info@weiserchamber.com, www.weiserchamber.com

**Wilder** • *Wilder C/C* • Tamara Patrick, Pres., P.O. Box 265, 83676, P 1,700, M 20, (208) 697-3571, tap@speedyquick.net

**Winchester** • *see Craigmont*

# Illinois

**Illinois C of C** • Douglas L. Whitley, Pres./CEO, 300 S. Wacker Dr., Ste. 1600, Chicago, 60606, P 11,430,602, M 4,000, (312) 983-7100, Fax (312) 983-7101, info@ilchamber.org, www.ilchamber.org

**Abingdon** • *Abingdon C/C* • Bunny Dalton, Pres., 106 N. Monroe, 61410, P 3,600, M 54, (309) 462-2629, (309) 462-3182, www.abingdonillinois.com

**Addison** • *Addison C/C & Ind.* • Bernadette LaRocca, Exec. Dir., 777 W. Army Tr, Ste. D, 60101, P 33,175, M 300, (630) 543-4300, Fax (630) 543-4355, addisonchamber@sbcglobal.net, www.addisonchamber.org

**Albion** • *Albion Area C/C* • Reece Copeland, Pres., P.O. Box 82, 62806, P 2,000, M 80, (618) 445-2303, Fax (618) 445-2911, www.albionchamber.com

**Aledo** • *Aledo Area C/C* • Diane Sharp, Exec. Asst., 201 W. Main St., P.O. Box 261, 61231, P 3,600, M 100, (309) 582-5373, Fax (309) 582-5373, aledochamber@frontiernet.net, www.aledo chamber.org

**Algonquin** • *Algonquin-Lake in the Hills C/C* • Sandy Oslance, Exec. Dir., 2114 W. Algonquin Rd., 60156, P 61,000, M 400, (847) 658-5300, Fax (847) 658-6546, info@algonquin-lith-chamber.com, www.algonquin-lith-chamber.com

**Alsip** • *Alsip C/C* • Mary Schmidt, Exec. Dir., 12159 S. Pulaski Rd., 60803, P 20,000, M 300, (708) 597-2668, (800) IN-ALSIP, Fax (708) 597-5962, alsipccedc@aol.com, www.alsipchamber.org

**Altamont** • *Altamont C/C* • Terri Beal, Pres., P.O. Box 141, 62411, P 2,283, M 70, (618) 483-5714, info@altamontchamber.com, www.altamontchamber.com

**Alton** • *see Godfrey*

**Amboy** • *Amboy Area C/C* • Glenda Fleming, Pres., P.O. Box 163, 61310, P 2,561, M 100, (815) 857-3625, (815) 857-3814, www.amboychamber.com

**Anna** • *Union County C/C* • Jeannie Landis, Exec. Secy., 330 S. Main St., 62906, P 18,000, M 185, (618) 833-6311, Fax (618) 833-1903, uccc@ajinternet.net, www.shawneeheartland.com

**Antioch** • *Antioch C/C & Ind.* • Barbara Porch, Exec. Dir., 882 Main St., 60002, P 13,750, M 350, (847) 395-2233, Fax (847) 395-8954, info@antiochchamber.org, www.antiochchamber.org

**Aptakisic** • *see Lincolnshire*

**Arcola** • *Arcola C/C* • Rachael Crane, Exec. Dir., P.O. Box 274, 61910, P 2,700, M 90, (217) 268-4530, (800) 336-5456, Fax (217) 268-3690, staff@arcolachamber.com, www.arcolachamber.com

**Arlington Heights** • *Arlington Heights C/C* • Jon S. Ridler, Exec. Dir., 311 S. Arlington Heights Rd., Ste. 20, 60005, P 80,000, M 530, (847) 253-1703, Fax (847) 253-9133, info@arlingtonhtschamber.com, www.arlingtonhtschamber.com

**Arthur** • *Arthur Area Assn. of Commerce* • Rod Randall, Pres., P.O. Box 42, 61911, P 2,300, M 100, (217) 543-2999, www.arthurchamber.com

**Aurora** • *Greater Aurora C/C* • Joseph Henning, Pres./CEO, 43 W. Galena Blvd., 60506, P 182,000, M 1,290, (630) 897-9214, Fax (630) 897-7002, jhenning@aurora-il.org, www.aurorachamber.com

**Bannockburn** • *see Deerfield*

**Barrington** • *Barrington Area C/C* • Janet Meyer, Pres., 325 N. Hough St., 60010, P 44,000, M 775, (847) 381-2525, Fax (847) 381-2540, email@barringtonchamber.com, www.barrington chamber.com

**Bartlett** • *Bartlett C/C* • Diane Hubberts, Exec. Dir., 138 S. Oak Ave., 60103, P 41,000, M 350, (630) 830-0324, Fax (630) 830-9724, info@BartlettChamber.com, www.BartlettChamber.com

**Bartonville** • *Limestone Area C/C* • Diana Kelly, Pres., P.O. Box 4043, 61607, P 20,000, M 110, email@limestonechamber.com, www.limestonechamber.com

**Batavia** • *Batavia C/C* • Roger Breisch, Exec. Dir., 106 W. Wilson St., 60510, P 27,000, M 340, (630) 879-7134, Fax (630) 879-7215, info@bataviachamber.org, www.bataviachamber.org.

**Beach Park** • *see Gurnee*

**Beardstown** • *Beardstown C/C* • Donna Strieker, Exec. Dir., 101 W. 3rd St., 62618, P 6,000, M 100, (217) 323-3271, Fax (217) 323-3271, info@beardstownil.org, www.beardstownil.org

**Beecher** • *Beecher C/C* • Chuck Hoehn, Pres., P.O. Box 292, 60401, P 3,000, M 100, (708) 946-6803, bchamber@villageofbeecher.org

**Belleville** • *Greater Belleville C/C* • Kathleen Kaiser, Exec. Dir., 216 E. A St., 62220, P 41,000, M 750, (618) 233-2015, Fax (618) 233-2077, info@bellevillechamber.org, www.bellevillechamber.org

**Bellwood** · *Bellwood C/C & Ind.* · P.O. Box 86, 60104, P 20,241, M 100, (708) 547-5030, Fax (708) 547-5030, www.villageof bellwood.com

**Belvidere** · *Belvidere Area C/C* · Thomas Lassandro, Exec. Dir., 130 S. State St., Ste. 300, 61008, P 50,000, M 475, (815) 544-4357, Fax (815) 547-7654, tlassandro@belviderechamber.com, www. belviderechamber.com

**Benld** · *see Gillespie*

**Bensenville** · *Bensenville C/C* · 117 W. Main St., P.O. Box 905, 60106, P 20,500, M 60, (630) 860-3800, www.bensenville.il.us

**Benton** · *Benton-West City Area C/C* · Gloria Atchison, Exec. Dir., 211 N. Main St., P.O. Box 574, 62812, P 10,000, M 250, (618) 438-2121, (866) 536-8423, Fax (618) 438-8011, chamber@ bentonwestcity.com, www.bentonwestcity.com

**Bethalto** · *see Godfrey*

**Bloomingdale** · *Bloomingdale C/C* · Jane Hove, Exec. Dir., 108 W. Lake St., 60108, P 24,000, M 270, (630) 980-9082, Fax (630) 980-9092, bloomcham@sbcglobal.net, www.bloomingdale chamber.com

**Bloomington** · *McLean County C/C* · Charlie Moore, Exec. Dir., 210 S. East St., P.O. Box 1586, 61702, P 130,000, M 1,200, (309) 829-6344, Fax (309) 827-3940, info@mcleancochamber.org, www.mcleancochamber.org

**Blue Island** · *Blue Island Area C/C & Ind.* · Ruth Sheahan, Exec. Dir., 2434 Vermont St., 60406, P 22,298, M 200, (708) 388-1000, Fax (708) 388-1062, blueislandchamber@sbcglobal.net, www. blueislandchamber.org

**Bolingbrook** · *Bolingbrook Area C/C* · Michael Evans, Exec. Dir., 201-B Canterbury Ln., 60440, P 70,000, M 590, (630) 226-8420, Fax (630) 226-8426, executivedirector@bolingbrookchamber.org, www.bolingbrookchamber.org

**Bourbonnais** · *Bradley-Bourbonnais C/C* · Jaclyn Dugan-Roof, CEO, 1690 Newtowne Dr., 60914, P 35,000, M 500, (815) 932-2222, Fax (815) 932-3294, bbcc@bbchamber.com, www. bbchamber.com

**Bourbonnais** · *Kankakee Reg. C/C* · David Hinderliter, Pres./ CEO, 1137 E. 5000 N. Rd., P.O. Box 395, 60901, P 109,000, M 600, (815) 933-7721, Fax (815) 933-7675, david@kankakee.org, www. kankakee.org

**Breese** · *Breese C/C* · Brandon Wade, Pres., P.O. Box 132, 62230, P 4,000, M 100, (618) 526-7731, www.breesechamber.org

**Bridgeview** · *Bridgeview C/C & Ind.* · Dr. Bruce Milkint, Pres., 7300 W. 87th, Bridgeview Bank Bldg., 60455, P 15,200, M 280, (708) 598-1700, Fax (708) 598-1709, info@bridgeviewchamber. com, www.bridgeviewchamber.com

**Bridgeview** · *Hills C/C* · Phyllis Majka, Pres., P.O. Box 1164, 60455, P 25,000, M 230, (708) 364-7739, Fax (708) 364-7735, thehillschamber@yahoo.com, www.thehillschamber.com

**Brookfield** · *Brookfield C/C* · Betty LeClere, Pres., 9138 Broadway, 60513, P 19,323, M 90, (708) 485-3893

**Bucktown** · *see Chicago-Wicker Park and Bucktown C/C*

**Buffalo Grove** · *Buffalo Grove Area C/C* · Lynne Schneider, Exec. Dir., 50 1/2 Raupp Blvd., P.O. Box 7124, 60089, P 44,000, M 425, (847) 541-7799, Fax (847) 541-7819, info@bgacc.org, buffalogrovechamber.org

**Bunker Hill** · *Bunker Hill Area C/C* · Robert F. Johnessee, Pres., 200 S. Brighton St., 62014, P 4,000, M 56, (618) 585-3890, (618) 585-6676, rjohnessee@yahoo.com, www.bunkerhill-il.com

**Burbank** · *Burbank C/C* · Sandra Coleman, Exec. Dir., 5501 W. 79th St., 60459, P 27,500, M 140, (708) 425-4668, Fax (708) 424-9492, burilcc@wmconnect.com

**Burr Ridge** · *Willowbrook/Burr Ridge C/C & Ind.* · Cheryl Collins, Exec. Dir., 8300 S. Madison, 60527, P 7,000, M 250, (630) 654-0909, Fax (630) 654-0922, info@wbbrchamber.org, www. wbbrchamber.org

**Bushnell** · *Bushnell C/C* · Don Swartzbaugh, Pres., P.O. Box 111, 61422, P 3,400, M 50, (309) 772-2171, www.bushnell.illinois.gov/ chamber

**Byron** · *Byron Area C/C* · Caryn Huber, Exec. Dir., 418 W. Blackhawk Dr., Ste. 101, P.O. Box 405, 61010, P 12,000, M 178, (815) 234-5500, Fax (815) 234-7114, byronchamber@byronil.net, www.byronchamber.org

**Cahokia** · *Cahokia Area C/C* · Debbie Craig, Pres., 103 Main St., 62206, P 19,000, M 65, (618) 332-4258, Fax (618) 332-6690, www.cahokiachamber.com

**Cairo** · *Cairo C/C* · Monica Smith, Pres., 220 8th St., 62914, P 3,500, M 60, (618) 734-2737, cairochamber@lazernetwireless.net

**Calumet City** · *Calumet City C/C* · 80 River Oaks Center, 60409, P 40,000, M 100, (708) 891-5888, Fax (708) 891-8877, info@ calumetcitychamber.com, www.calumetcity.org

**Canton** · *Canton Area C/C* · Missy Towery, Dir., 45 Eastside Sq., Ste. 303, 61520, P 15,000, M 247, (309) 647-2677, Fax (309) 647-2712, mtowery@cantonillinois.org, www.cantonillinois.org

**Carbondale** · *Carbondale C/C* · Kristin Gregory, Exec. Dir., 131 S. Illinois Ave., P.O. Box 877, 62903, P 30,000, M 450, (618) 549-2146, Fax (618) 529-5063, carbondalechamberofcommerce@ gmail.com, www.carbondalechamber.com

**Carlinville** · *Carlinville Comm. C/C* · 112 North Side Sq., 62626, P 5,685, M 150, (217) 854-2141, Fax (217) 854-8548, info@ carlinvillechamber.com

**Carlyle** · *Carlyle Lake C/C* · Lori Jansen, Pres., P.O. Box 246, 62231, P 3,500, M 80, (618) 594-2468, admin@playandstaycarlyle. com, www.playandstaycarlyle.com

**Carmi** · *Carmi C/C* · David Port, Exec. Dir., 225 E. Main St., 62821, P 5,400, M 140, (618) 382-7606, Fax (618) 382-3458, ccc@cityof-carmi.com, www.cityofcarmi.com

**Carol Stream** · *Carol Stream C/C* · Luanne Triolo, Exec. Dir., 150 S. Gary Ave., 60188, P 42,000, M 375, (630) 665-3325, info@ carolstreamchamber.com, carolstreamchamber.com

**Carpentersville** · *Northern Kane County C/C* · Melissa Hernandez, Exec. Dir., 2429 Randall Rd., Ste. B, 60110, P 70,000, M 260, (847) 426-8565, Fax (847) 426-1098, nkcchamber@ ameritech.net, www.nkcchamber.com

**Carriers Mills** · *see Harrisburg*

**Carrollton** · *Carrollton C/C* · Debbie Field , V.P., P.O. Box 69, 62016, P 2,500, M 35, (217) 942-3187, fieldsteve@hotmail.com

**Carterville** · *Carterville C/C* · Mike Williams, Exec. Dir., 120 N. Greenbriar, P.O. Box 262, 62918, P 4,600, M 160, (618) 985-6942, Fax (618) 985-6942, chamber@midamer.net, www.cartervil-lechamber.com

**Carthage** · *Carthage Area C/C* · Carol Post, Secy./Treas., 8 S. Madison St., P.O. Box 247, 62321, P 3,000, M 120, (217) 357-3024, Fax (217) 357-3024, chamber@carthage-il.com, www.carthage-il.com

**Cary** · *Cary Grove Area C/C* · Suzanne Corr, Exec. Dir., 27 E. Main St., 60013, P 27,000, M 480, (847) 639-2800, Fax (847) 639-2168, info@carygrovechamber.com, www.carygrovechamber.com

**Casey** • *Casey C/C* • Mary Gard, P.O. Box 343, 62420, P 3,000, M 50, (217) 232-3430

**Caseyville** • *Caseyville C/C* • P.O. Box 470, 62232, P 4,500, M 60, (618) 345-4690, www.caseyville.org

**Centralia** • *Greater Centralia C/C & Tourism Ofc.* • Bob Kelsheimer, Exec. Dir., 130 S. Locust St., 62801, P 20,000, M 375, (618) 532-6789, (888) 533-2600, Fax (618) 533-7305, gccoc@centraliail.com, www.centraliail.com

**Champaign** • *Champaign County C/C* • Laura Weis IOM ACE, Pres./CEO, 1817 S. Neil St., Ste. 201, 61820, P 180,000, M 1,300, (217) 359-1791, Fax (217) 359-1809, info@champaigncounty.org, www.ccchamber.org

**Channahon** • *see Minooka*

**Charleston** • *Charleston Area C/C* • Cynthia Titus, Exec. Dir., 501 Jackson Ave., P.O. Box 77, 61920, P 31,528, M 315, (217) 345-7041, Fax (217) 345-7042, cacc@charlestonchamber.com, www.charlestonchamber.com

**Chatham** • *Chatham Area C/C* • Kim DuVall, Pres., 320 N. Main, 62629, P 10,200, M 120, (217) 483-6450, Fax (217) 483-6450, info@chatham-il-chamber.com, www.chatham-il-chamber.com

**Chester** • *Chester C/C* • Linda Sympson, Exec. Dir., P.O. Box 585, 62233, P 8,400, M 135, (618) 826-2732, (618) 826-2721, chesterc@egyptian.net, www.chesterill.com

## Chicago area

**Chicagoland C/C** • Gerald Roper, Pres./CEO, 200 E. Randolph, Ste. 2200, 60601, P 8,065,633, M 2,600, (312) 494-6700, Fax (312) 861-0660, staff@chicagolandchamber.org, www.chicagolandchamber.org

**Albany Park C/C** • Liz Griffiths, Exec. Dir., 3403 W. Lawrence Ave., Ste. 201, 60625, P 100,000, M 150, (773) 478-0202, Fax (773) 478-0282, www.albanyparkchamber.org

**Bronzeville C/C** • Johnnie Blair, Pres., 4650 S. King Dr., P.O. Box 53-634, 60653, P 125,000, M 225, (773) 268-1800, Fax (773) 442-0852, brvlchamber@aol.com, www.bronzevillechamber.com

**Chicago Southland C/C** • Patrice Brooks, Exec. V.P., 1916 W. 174th St., East Hazel Crest, 60429, P 1,300,000, M 900, (708) 957-6950, Fax (708) 957-6968, info@chicagosouthland.com, www.chicagosouthland.com

**Cosmopolitan C/C** • Carnice Cary, Exec. Dir., 203 N. Wabash, Ste. 518, 60601, P 3,000,000, M 300, (312) 499-0611, Fax (312) 701-0095, info@cosmococ.org, www.cosmococ.org

**East Side C/C** • Jackie Herod, Exec. Dir., 3501 E. 106th, Ste. 200, 60617, P 26,000, M 100, (773) 721-7948, Fax (773) 721-7446, eastsidechamber@sbcglobal.net

**Edgebrook-Sauganash C/C** • Bob Madiar, Exec. Dir., 6440 N. Central Ave., 60646, P 17,000, M 140, (773) 775-0378, Fax (773) 775-0371, edgebrookchamber@sbcglobal.net, www.edgebrookchamber.com

**Hyde Park C/C** • Lenora Austin, Exec. Dir., 5211D S. Harper Ave., 60615, P 50,000, M 200, (773) 288-0124, Fax (773) 288-0464, contact@hydeparkchamberchicago.org, www.hydeparkchamberchicago.org

**Chicago** • *Jefferson Park C/C* • Carol Gawron, Exec. Dir., 4849 N. Milwaukee Ave., Ste. 305, 60630, P 153,000, M 135, (773) 736-6697, Fax (773) 736-3508, info@jeffersonpark.net, www.jeffersonpark.net

**Lake View East C/C** • Maureen Martino, Exec. Dir., 3138 N. Broadway, 60657, P 81,000, M 335, (773) 348-8608, Fax (773) 348-7409, info@lakevieweast.com, www.lakevieweast.com

**Chicago area,** *continued*

**Lincoln Park C/C** • Kim Schilf, Pres./CEO, 1925 N. Clybourn, Ste. 301, 60614, P 64,000, M 620, (773) 880-5200, Fax (773) 880-0266, info@lincolnparkchamber.com, www.lincolnparkchamber.com

**Mount Greenwood C/C** • Darlene Larsen, Exec. Dir., 3052 W. 111 St., 60655, P 12,000, M 260, (773) 238-6103, Fax (773) 238-6103, dtmyers@ameritech.net, www.mgcofc.org

**Portage Park C/C** • 4849-A W. Irving Park Rd., 60641, P 200,000, M 150, (773) 777-2020, Fax (773) 777-0202, info@portageparkchamber.org, www.portageparkchamber.org

**Uptown C/C** • Mr. Paul Collurafici, Pres., 4753 N. Broadway, Ste. 822, 60640, P 64,000, M 150, (773) 878-1184, Fax (773) 878-3678, info@uptownbusinesspartners.com, www.uptownbusinesspartners.com

**Wicker Park and Bucktown C/C** • Paula Barrington, Exec. Dir., 1414 N. Milwaukee Ave., 60622, P 53,000, M 275, (773) 384-2672, Fax (773) 384-7525, paula@wickerparkbucktown.com, www.wickerparkbucktown.com

**Chicago Ridge** • *see Worth*

**Chillicothe** • *Chillicothe C/C* • Irvin Latta, Pres., 1028 N. 2nd St., 61523, P 6,000, M 120, (309) 274-4556, info@chillicothechamber.com, www.chillicothechamber.com

**Christopher** • *Christopher Area C/C* • Susan Williams, V.P., P.O. Box 111, 62822, P 2,900, M 29, (618) 724-9416

**Cicero** • *Cicero C/C & Ind.* • Mary Esther Hernandez, Exec. Dir., 5801 W. Cermak Rd., 2nd Flr., 60804, P 95,000, M 230, (708) 863-6000, Fax (708) 863-8981, cicerochamber@ameritech.net, www.cicerochamber.org

**Clinton** • *Clinton Area C/C* • Marian Brisard, Exec. Dir., 100 S. Center St., Ste. 101, 61727, P 7,485, M 185, (217) 935-3364, Fax (217) 935-0064, info@clintonilchamber.com, www.clintonilchamber.com

**Coal City** • *see Morris*

**Collinsville** • *Collinsville C/C* • Wendi Valenti, Exec. Dir., 221 W. Main St., 62234, P 25,200, M 376, (618) 344-2884, Fax (618) 344-7499, info@discovercollinsville.com, www.discovercollinsville.com

**Cook County** • *Cook County C/C* • Gerald L. Murphy, Pres., One Westbrook Corporate Center, Ste. 300, Westchester, 60154, P 5,200,000, M 25, (708) 531-1117, Fax (708) 449-7701, cookbusiness@comcast.net

**Countryside** • *see LaGrange*

**Crete** • *Crete Area C/C* • Patricia Catherine Herbert, Exec. Dir., 1182 N. Main, P.O. Box 263, 60417, P 32,000, M 110, (708) 672-9216, Fax (708) 672-7640, cretechamber@sbcglobal.net, www.cretechamber.com

**Crystal Lake** • *Crystal Lake C/C* • Gary Reece, Pres., 427 Virginia St., 60014, P 50,793, M 925, (815) 459-1300, Fax (815) 459-0243, info@clchamber.com, www.clchamber.com.

**Danville** • *Vermilion Advantage-Chamber of Commerce Div.* • Vicki Haugen, Pres./CEO, 28 W. North St., 61832, P 85,000, M 415, (217) 442-6201, Fax (217) 442-6228, vhaugen@vermilionadvantage.com, www.vermilionadvantage.com

**Darien** • *Darien C/C* • Bill Carpenter, Pres., 1702 Plainfield Rd., 60561, P 23,000, M 180, (630) 968-0004, Fax (630) 968-2474, www.darienchamber.com

**Decatur** • *Greater Decatur C/C* • Randy Prince, Pres., 111 E. Main St., Ste. 110, 62523, P 118,000, M 875, (217) 422-2200, Fax (217) 422-4576, chamber@decaturchamber.com, www.decaturchamber.com

**Deerfield** · *Deerfield-Bannockburn-Riverwoods C/C* · Victoria Case, Exec. Dir., 601 Deerfield Rd., Ste. 200, 60015, P 24,000, M 460, (847) 945-4660, Fax (847) 940-0381, info@dbrchamber. com, www.dbrchamber.com

**DeKalb** · *DeKalb C/C* · James E. Allen, Exec. Dir., 164 E. Lincoln Hwy., 60115, P 45,000, M 500, (815) 756-6306, Fax (815) 756-5164, chamber@dekalb.org, www.dekalb.org

**Des Plaines** · *Des Plaines C/C & Ind.* · James Macchiaroli, Pres., 1401 E. Oakton St., 60018, P 58,700, M 592, (847) 824-4200, Fax (847) 824-7932, info@dpchamber.com, www.dpchamber.com

**Dixon** · *Dixon Area C/C & Ind.* · John R. Thompson, Pres./ CEO, 101 W. Second St., Ste. 301, 61021, P 16,000, M 400, (815) 284-3361, Fax (815) 284-3675, dchamber@essex1.com, www. dixonillinoischamber.com.

**Dolton** · *Dolton C/C* · Larceeda Jefferson, Admin. Asst., P.O. Box 823, 60419, P 25,000, M 60, (708) 841-4810, Fax (708) 841-4833, www.villageofdolton.com

**Dorchester** · *see Gillespie*

**Downers Grove** · *Downers Grove Area C/C* · Laura Crawford, Pres./CEO, 2001 Butterfield Rd., Ste. 105, 60515, P 50,000, M 700, (630) 968-4050, Fax (630) 968-8368, chamber@downersgrove.org, www.downersgrove.org

**Du Quoin** · *Du Quoin C/C* · Chuck Novak, Pres., 20 N. Chestnut, P.O. Box 57, 62832, P 6,448, M 145, (618) 542-9570, Fax (618) 542-8778, dqchamber@comcast.net, www.duquoin.org

**Dwight** · *Dwight Area C/C* · Shirley Seabert, Admin., 119 W. Main St., 60420, P 4,800, M 143, (815) 584-2091, Fax (815) 584-2091, admin@dwightchamber.net, www.dwightchamber.net

**Eagarville** · *see Gillespie*

**East Alton** · *see Godfrey*

**East Dundee** · *see Carpentersville*

**East Gillespie** · *see Gillespie*

**East Moline** · *see Moline*

**East Peoria** · *East Peoria C/C* · Rick Swan, Exec. Dir., 111 W. Washington St., Ste. 290, 61611, P 23,000, M 475, (309) 699-6212, Fax (309) 699-6220, epcc@epcc.org, www.epcc.org

**East Saint Louis** · *Greater East Saint Louis C/C* · Norman Ross, Exec. Dir., 327 Missouri Ave., Ste. 602, 62201, P 31,524, M 130, (618) 271-2855, Fax (618) 271-4622, eslchamber@sbcglobal.net, www.eslcoc.org

**Edwardsville** · *Edwardsville/Glen Carbon C/C* · Carol Foreman, Exec. Dir., 200 University Park Dr., Ste. 260, 62025, P 34,000, M 530, (618) 656-7600, Fax (618) 656-7611, cforeman@edglen chamber.com, www.edglenchamber.com

**Effingham** · *Greater Effingham C/C & Ind.* · Norma Lansing, Pres., 903 N. Keller Dr., P.O. Box 643, 62401, P 34,000, M 500, (217) 342-4147, Fax (217) 342-4228, nlansing@effingham chamber.org, www.effinghamchamber.org

**El Paso** · *El Paso C/C* · Lisa Barhum, Secy., P.O. Box 196, 61738, P 2,700, M 80, (309) 527-4400, lbarhum@hbtbank.com, www. elpasoil.org/chamber/

**Eldorado** · *see Harrisburg*

**Elgin** · *Elgin Area C/C* · Leo Nelson, Pres., 31 S. Grove Ave., P.O. Box 648, 60121, P 100,000, M 900, (847) 741-5660, Fax (847) 741-5677, info@elginchamber.com, www.elginchamber.com

**Elizabeth** · *Elizabeth C/C* · Joe Orourke, Pres., P.O. Box 371, 61028, P 700, M 85, (815) 858-2221, info@elizabeth-il.com, www.elizabeth-il.com

**Elk Grove Village** · *Greater O`Hare Assn. of Ind. & Comm.* · Shirlanne Lemm, Pres., P.O. Box 1516, 60009, P 4,000,000, M 800, (630) 732-9444, Fax (630) 350-2979, info@greater-ohare.com, www.greater-ohare.com

**Elmhurst** · *Elmhurst C of C & Ind.* · John Quigley, Pres./CEO, 113 Adell Pl., P.O. Box 752, 60126, P 42,762, M 660, (630) 834-6060, Fax (630) 834-6002, info@elmhurstchamber.org, www.elmhurst chamber.org

**Elmwood Park** · *Mont Clare-Elmwood Park C/C* · Barbara Melnyk, Exec. Dir., 11 Conti Pkwy., 60707, P 28,000, M 253, (708) 456-8000, Fax (708) 456-8680, mcepcoc@aol.com, www. mcepchamber.org

**Elsah** · *see Godfrey*

**Evanston** · *Evanston C/C* · Jonathan D. Perman, Exec. Dir., One Rotary Center, 1560 Sherman Ave., Ste. 860, 60201, P 76,000, M 650, (847) 328-1500, Fax (847) 328-1510, info@evchamber. com, www.evchamber.com.

**Evergreen Park** · *Evergreen Park C/C* · Glenn Pniewski, Exec. Dir., 3960 W. 95th St., 3rd Flr., 60805, P 23,000, M 150, (708) 423-1118, Fax (708) 423-1859, epchamber@sbcglobal.net, www. evergreenparkchamber.org

**Fairbury** · *Fairbury C/C* · Holly Rogers, Exec. Secy., 101 E. Locust, P.O. Box 86, 61739, P 3,900, M 130, (815) 692-3899, Fax (815) 692-4273, fcc@fairburyil.org, www.fairburyil.org

**Fairfield** · *Greater Fairfield Area C/C* · Ann Ayers, Exec. Secy., 121 E. Main St., 62837, P 5,421, M 130, (618) 842-6116, Fax (618) 842-5654, chamber@fairfieldwireless.net, www.fairfieldillinois chamber.com

**Fairview Heights** · *Fairview Heights C/C* · Scott Leas, Exec. Dir., 10003 Bunkum Rd., 62208, P 15,745, M 220, (618) 397-3127, Fax (618) 397-5563, office@fairviewheightschamber.org, www. fairviewheightschamber.org

**Flora** · *Flora C/C* · Heather Lucas, Exec. Asst., 122 N. Main St., 62839, P 5,100, M 101, (618) 662-5646, Fax (618) 662-5646, commerce@wabash.net, www.florachamber.com, www.florail.us

**Forest Park** · *Forest Park C/C & Dev.* · Laurie Kokenes, Exec. Dir., 7344 W. Madison, P.O. Box 617, 60130, P 16,000, M 210, (708) 366-2543, Fax (708) 366-3373, laurie@exploreforestpark.com, www.exploreforestpark.com

**Fox Lake** · *Fox Lake Area C/C & Ind.* · Linnea Pioro, Ofc. Mgr., 71 N. Nippersink Blvd., P.O. Box 203, 60020, P 10,000, M 230, (847) 587-7474, Fax (847) 587-1725, foxlakechamber@yahoo.com, www.discoverfoxlake.com

**Fox River Grove** · *see Cary*

**Frankfort** · *Frankfort C/C* · Lynne Doogan, Exec. Dir., 123 Kansas St., 60423, P 16,000, M 620, (815) 469-3356, (877) 469-3356, Fax (815) 469-4352, lynne@frankfortchamber.com, www. frankfortchamber.com

**Franklin Park** · *Franklin Park/Schiller Park C/C* · Kenneth Kollar, Pres., P.O. Box 186, 60131, P 32,000, M 100, (708) 865-9510, info@chamberbyohare.com, www.chamberbyohare.org

**Freeburg** · *Freeburg C/C* · Peter Vogel, Pres., P.O. Box 179, 62243, P 4,000, M 165, (618) 539-6075, (618) 539-5613, Fax (618) 539-6077, www.freeburgchamberofcommerce.com

**Freeport** · *Freeport Area C/C* · Mr. Kim Grimes, Pres./CEO, 27 W. Stephenson St., 61032, P 26,000, M 500, (815) 233-1350, Fax (815) 235-4038, kim.grimes@aeroinc.net, www.freeportilchamber.com

**Fulton** · *Fulton C/C* · Heather Bennett, Exec. Dir., P.O. Box 253, 61252, P 3,900, M 115, (815) 589-4545, Fax (815) 589-4421, chamber@cityoffulton.us, www.cityoffulton.us

**Galatia** • see Harrisburg

**Galena** • *Galena Area C/C* • Ed Schmit, Exec. Dir., 101 Bouthillier St., 61036, P 3,600, M 325, (815) 777-9050, Fax (815) 777-8465, office@galenachamber.com, www.galenachamber.com

**Galesburg** • *Galesburg Area C/C* • Robert C. Maus, Pres., 185 S. Kellogg St., P.O. Box 749, 61401, P 35,000, M 448, (309) 343-1194, Fax (309) 343-1195, chamber@galesburg.org, www.galesburg.org

**Galva** • *Galva C/C* • Mechelle Dyer, Pres., P.O. Box 112, 61434, P 2,700, M 65, (309) 932-2131, (309) 932-2555, www.galva.com

**Geneseo** • *Geneseo C/C* • Rhonda Ludwig, Exec. Dir., 100 W. Main, 61254, P 6,500, M 180, (309) 944-2686, Fax (309) 944-2647, geneseo@geneseo.net, www.geneseo.org

**Geneva** • *Geneva C/C* • Jean Gaines, Pres., 8 S. Third St. 2nd Flr., P.O. Box 481, 60134, P 22,000, M 580, (630) 232-6060, (866) 4-GENEVA, Fax (630) 232-6083, chamberinfo@genevachamber. com, www.genevachamber.com

**Genoa** • *Genoa C/C* • Bonnie Hanson, Exec. Dir., 327 W. Main St. Upper Level, 60135, P 3,890, M 100, (815) 784-2212, Fax (815) 784-2212, genoacham@tbcnet.com, www.genoa-il-chamberof commerce.com

**Gibson City** • *Gibson Area C/C* • Pam Bradbury, Secy., 126 N. Sangamon Ave., P.O. Box 294, 60936, P 3,600, M 140, (217) 784-5217, (217) 784-4636, Fax (217) 784-4119, chamber@ gibsoncityillinois.com, www.gibsoncityillinois.com

**Gilberts** • see Carpentersville

**Gillespie** • *Coal Country C/C* • Mickey Robinson, Exec. Dir., 213 S. Macoupin, P.O. Box 57, 62033, P 10,000, M 110, (217) 839-4888, www.coalcountrychamber.com

**Gilman** • *Gilman C/C* • Rita Silles, Secy./Treas., P.O. Box 13, 60938, P 1,800, M 62, (815) 265-4818, Fax (815) 265-4961, www.gilmanil.com

**Girard** • *Girard C/C* • Debra Burnett, Secy., P.O. Box 92, 62640, P 2,300, M 52, (217) 627-3512, Fax (217) 627-3528, www.girardilusa.com

**Glen Carbon** • see Edwardsville

**Glen Ellyn** • *Glen Ellyn C/C* • Georgia Koch & Mike Formento, Exec. Dir., 800 Roosevelt Rd., Ste. D108, 60137, P 28,000, M 400, (630) 469-0907, Fax (630) 469-0426, director@glenellynchamber. com, www.glenellynchamber.com

**Glencoe** • *Glencoe C/C* • Sally Kelly, Exec. Dir., P.O. Box 575, 60022, P 8,762, M 90, (847) 835-3333, glencoechamber@yahoo. com, www.glencoechamber.org

**Glendale Heights** • *Glendale Heights C/C* • Sharon Mennemeier, Prog. Coord., P.O. Box 5054, 60139, P 39,000, M 120, (630) 545-1099, Fax (630) 858-4418, www.glendaleheightschamber.com

**Glenview** • *Glenview C/C* • Kathleen Miles, Pres., 2320 Glenview Rd., 60025, P 45,000, M 490, (847) 724-0900, Fax (847) 724-0202, gcstaff@glenviewchamber.com, www.glenviewchamber.com

**Godfrey** • *River Bend Growth Assn.* • Monica Bristow, Pres., 5800 Godfrey Rd., Alden Hall, 62035, P 100,000, M 650, (618) 467-2280, Fax (618) 466-8289, info@growthassociation.com, www.growthassociation.com.

**Golconda** • *Golconda/Pope County C/C* • William Altman, Pres., P.O. Box 688, 62938, P 4,500, M 25, (618) 683-9702

**Grafton** • see Godfrey

**Granite City** • *Chamber of Commerce of Southwestern Madison County* • Rosemarie Brown, Exec. Dir., 3600 Nameoki Rd., Ste. 202, P.O. Box 370, 62040, P 88,000, M 300, (618) 876-6400, Fax (618) 876-6448, chamber@chamberswmadisoncounty. com, www.chamberswmadisoncounty.com

**Grant Park** • *Grant Park C/C* • P.O. Box 446, 60940, P 1,500, (815) 466-0604

**Grayslake** • *Grayslake Area C/C & Ind.* • Karen Christian-Smith, Exec. Dir., 10 S. Seymour St., P.O. Box 167, 60030, P 25,000, M 250, (847) 223-6888, Fax (847) 223-6895, business@grayslakechamber. com, www.grayslakechamber.com.

**Grayville** • *Grayville C/C* • Dana Schroeder, Pres., P.O. Box 117, 62844, P 1,800, M 50, (618) 375-7518, www.cityofgrayville.com

**Greenville** • *Greenville C/C* • Julia Jenner, Exec. Dir., P.O. Box 283, 62246, P 6,300, M 180, (618) 664-9272, (888) 862-8201, greenville@newwavecomm.net , www.Greenvilleusa.org

**Grundy County** • see Morris

**Gurnee** • *Lake County C/C* • Lou Molitor, Pres., 5221 W. Grand Ave., 60031, P 582,983, M 450, (847) 249-3800, Fax (847) 249-3892, info@lakecountychamber.com, www.lakecountychamber.com

**Half Day** • see Lincolnshire

**Hampshire** • *Hampshire Area C/C* • Art Zwemke, Pres., 153 South State St., P.O. Box 157, 60140, P 4,000, M 175, (847) 683-1122, Fax (847) 683-1146, 153 South State Street , www. hampshirechamber.org

**Hanover Park** • *Hanover Park C/C & Ind.* • Patricia Langenstrass, 1945 Ontarioville Rd., 60133, P 40,000, M 25, (630) 372-2009, Fax (630) 372-2052, plang@hanoverparkchamber.com, www.hanover parkchamber.com

**Harrisburg** • *Saline County C/C* • Lori Cox, Exec. Dir., 2 E. Locust, Ste. 200, 62946, P 27,000, M 150, (618) 252-4192, Fax (618) 252-0210, chamber@salinecountychamber.org, www.saline countychamber.org

**Hartford** • see Godfrey

**Harvard** • *Harvard C/C & Ind.* • Crystal Musgrove, Exec. Dir., 62 N. Ayer, Ste. B, 60033, P 9,000, M 200, (815) 943-4404, Fax (815) 943-4410, info@harvcc.net, www.harvcc.net

**Havana** • *Havana Area C/C* • Wendy Martin, P.O. Box 116, 62644, P 3,600, M 115, (309) 543-3528, (888) 236-8406, havana@ scenichavana.com, www.scenichavana.com

**Henry** • *Henry Area C/C* • Sandy Turpen, Pres., P.O. Box 211, 61537, P 3,000, M 90, (309) 364-3261, Fax (309) 364-3261, henrychamber@henrychamber.org, www.henrychamber.org

**Herrin** • *Herrin C/C* • Sue Douglas, Exec. Dir., Three S. Park Ave., 62948, P 11,000, M 390, (618) 942-5163, (888) 942-5163, Fax (618) 942-3301, herrincc@herrinillinois.com, www.herrinillinois.com

**Herscher** • *Herscher C/C* • Adam Wagner, Pres., P.O. Box 437, 60941, P 1,600, M 100, (815) 426-2348, www.herscher.net

**Hickory Hills** • see Bridgeview-Hills C/C

**Highland** • *Highland C/C* • Jami Jansen, Exec. Dir., 907 Main St., 62249, P 10,000, M 300, (618) 654-3721, Fax (618) 654-8966, info@highlandillinois.com, www.highlandillinois.com

**Highland Park** • *Highland Park C/C* • Virginia Glasner, Exec. Dir., 508 Central Ave., Ste. 206, 60035, P 32,000, M 425, (847) 432-0284, Fax (847) 432-2802, chamber@ehighlandpark.com, www. ehighlandpark.com

**Highwood** • *Highwood C/C* • P.O. Box 305, 60040, P 5,500, M 100, (847) 433-2100, Fax (847) 433-7959, info@highwoodchamber ofcommerce.com, www.highwoodchamberofcommerce.com

**Hillsboro** • *Hillsboro Area C/C* • Megan Beeler, Exec. Dir., 447 S. Main St., P.O. Box 6, 62049, P 7,000, M 80, (217) 532-3711, Fax (217) 532-5567, info@hillsborochamber.net, www.hillsborochamber.net

U.S. Chambers of Commerce

**Hillside** · *Hillside C/C* · Rick Smolke , Pres., P.O. Box 601, 60162, P 8,000, M 98, (708) 449-2449, Fax (708) 449-2442, hcochq@ sbcglobal.net, www.hillsidechamberofcommerce.com

**Hinsdale** · *Hinsdale C/C* · Janet Anderson, Exec. Dir., 22 E. First St., 60521, P 18,000, M 310, (630) 323-3952, Fax (630) 323-3953, staff@hinsdalechamber.com, www.hinsdalechamber.com

**Hodgkins** · *see LaGrange*

**Hoffman Estates** · *Hoffman Estates C/C* · Cheri Sisson, Pres., 2200 W. Higgins Rd., Ste. 201, 60195, P 50,500, M 350, (847) 781-9100, Fax (847) 781-9172, info@hechamber.com, www. hechamber.com

**Homer Glen** · *Homer Twp. C/C* · 15801 S. Bell Rd., 60491, P 25,000, M 300, (708) 301-8111, Fax (708) 301-2751, office@ homerchamber.com, www.homerchamber.com

**Homewood** · *Homewood Area C/C* · Kathy Nussbaum, Dir., 2023 Ridge Rd., Ste. 2NE-B, 60430, P 20,000, M 200, (708) 206-3384, Fax (708) 206-3605, kathy@homewoodareachamber.com, www.homewoodareachamber.com

**Hoopeston** · *Hoopeston C/C* · Tami Goin, Ofc. Mgr., 301 W. Main, P.O. Box 346, 60942, P 5,800, M 100, (217) 283-7873, Fax (217) 283-7873, hoopestonchamber@yahoo.com, www.hoopeston chamber.com

**Huntley** · *Huntley Area C/C & Ind.* · Rita Slawek, Pres./CEO, 11419 S. Rte. 47, 60142, P 15,000, M 372, (847) 669-0166, Fax (847) 669-0170, rita@huntleychamber.org, www.huntleychamber.org

**Indian Creek** · *see Lincolnshire*

**Indian Head Park** · *see LaGrange*

**Jacksonville** · *Jacksonville Area C/C* · Ginny Fanning, Pres., 155 W. Morton, 62650, P 33,000, M 600, (217) 245-2174, Fax (217) 245-0661, chamber@jacksonvilleareachamber.org, www. jacksonvilleareachamber.org

**Jerseyville** · *Jersey County Bus. Assn.* · Brent Thompson, Pres., 209 N. State St., 62052, P 23,000, M 260, (618) 639-5222, Fax (618) 498-3871, brent@jcba-il.us, www.jcba.us

**Johnsburg** · *see McHenry*

**Joliet** · *Joliet Region C/C & Ind.* · Russ Slinkard, Pres./CEO, 63 N. Chicago St., P.O. Box 752, 60434, P 150,000, M 1,500, (815) 727-5371, Fax (815) 727-5374, info@jolietchamber.com, www. jolietchamber.

**Kewanee** · *Kewanee C/C* · Mark Mikenas, Exec. V.P., 113 E. Second, 61443, P 13,000, M 225, (309) 852-2175, Fax (309) 852-2176, chamber@kewanee-il.com, kewanee-il.com.

**La Salle** · *Illinois Valley Area C/C & Eco. Dev.* · Barb Koch, Exec. Dir./ CEO, 300 Bucklin St., P.O. Box 446, 61301, P 40,550, M 400, (815) 223-0227, Fax (815) 223-4827, ivaced@ivaced.org, www.ivaced.org

**LaGrange** · *West Suburban C/C* · Robert E. Ware, Exec. Dir., P.O. Box 187, 60525, P 55,000, M 400, (708) 387-7550, Fax (708) 387-7556, info@westsuburbanchamber.org, www.westsuburban chamber.org

**LaGrange Park** · *see LaGrange*

**Lake Bluff** · *see Lake Forest*

**Lake Forest** · *Lake Forest/Lake Bluff C/C* · Joanna Rolek, Exec. Dir., 695 N. Western Ave., 60045, P 25,000, M 460, (847) 234-4282, Fax (847) 234-4297, info@LFLBchamber.com, www. LakeForestOnline.com

**Lake in the Hills** · *see Algonquin and Carpentersville*

**Lake Zurich** · *Lake Zurich Area C/C* · Dale Perrin, Exec. Dir., 1st Bank Plaza, Ste. 308, 60047, P 33,000, M 500, (847) 438-5572, Fax (847) 438-5574, info@lzacc.com, www.lzacc.com

**Lansing** · *Lansing C/C* · Vivian Payne, Exec. Dir., 3404 Lake St., 60438, P 30,000, M 300, (708) 474-4170, www.chamberof lansing.com

**Lawrenceville** · *Lawrence County C/C* · Delilah Gray, Exec. Dir., 619 12th St., 62439, P 15,929, M 160, (618) 943-3516, Fax (618) 943-4748, lccc@midwest.net, lawrencecountyillinois.com/ chamber.html

**Lebanon** · *Lebanon C/C* · 221 W. St. Louis St., 62254, P 4,000, M 93, (618) 537-8420, Fax (618) 537-8420, lebanonchamber@ gmail.com, www.lebanonil.org

**Lemont** · *Lemont Area C/C* · Ryan Sullivan, Pres., 101 Main St., 60439, P 14,000, M 250, (630) 257-5997, Fax (630) 257-3238, info@lemontchamber.com, www.lemontchamber.com

**Lewistown** · *Lewistown C/C* · Becky Humphrey, 119 S. Adams St., 61542, P 2,531, M 40, (309) 547-2501, (309) 547-4300

**Libertyville** · *Green Oaks/Libertyville/Mundelein/Vernon Hills C/C* · Mark Foley, Exec. Dir., 1123 S. Milwaukee Ave., 60048, P 83,000, M 700, (847) 680-0750, Fax (847) 680-0760, info@ glmvchamber.org, www.glmvchamber.org

**Lincoln** · *Lincoln/Logan County C/C* · Andi Hake, Exec. Dir., 1555 5th St., 62656, P 31,183, M 345, (217) 735-2385, Fax (217) 735-9205, chamber@lincolnillinois.com, www.lincolnillinois.com

**Lincoln Park** · *see Chicago-Lincoln Park C/C*

**Lincolnshire** · *Greater Lincolnshire C/C* · Lenna Scott, Exec. Dir., 175 Olde Half Day Rd., 60069, P 6,500, M 250, (847) 793-2409, Fax (847) 793-2405, glcc@lincolnshirechamber.org, www.lincolnshire chamber.org

**Lincolnwood** · *Lincolnwood C/C & Ind.* · Diana Lass, Exec. Dir., 7001 N. Lawndale Ave., 60712, P 12,280, M 172, (847) 679-5760, Fax (847) 679-5790, dlass@lincolnwoodchamber.org, www. lincolnwoodchamber.org

**Lindenhurst** · *Lindenhurst-Lake Villa C/C* · Connie Meadie, Exec. Dir., 500 Grand Ave., P.O. Box 6075, 60046, P 20,000, M 340, (847) 356-8446, Fax (847) 356-8561, llvchamber@llvchamber. com, www.llvchamber.com

**Lisle** · *Lisle Area C/C* · Tom Althoff, Pres./CEO, 4733 Main St., 60532, P 21,200, M 400, (630) 964-0052, Fax (630) 964-2726, info@lislechamber.com, www.lislechamber.com

**Litchfield** · *Litchfield C/C* · Nikki Bishop, Exec. Dir., 311 N. Madison, P.O. Box 334, 62056, P 9,000, M 170, (217) 324-2533, Fax (217) 324-3559, chamber@litchfieldil.com, www.litchfield chamber.com

**Lockport** · *Lockport C/C* · Michele Bogdan, Exec. Dir., 921 S. State St., 60441, P 19,000, M 270, (815) 838-3357, Fax (815) 838-2653, office@lockportchamber.com, www.lockportchamber.com

**Lombard** · *Lombard Area C/C & Ind.* · Yvonne Invergo, Exec. Dir., 10 Lilac Ln., 60148, P 42,322, M 325, (630) 627-5040, Fax (630) 627-5519, info@lombardchamber.com, www.lombardchamber.com

**Long Grove** · *see Lincolnshire*

**Loves Park** · *Parks C/C* · Diana Johnson, Exec. Dir., 100 Heart Blvd., 61111, P 45,000, M 225, (815) 633-3999, Fax (815) 633-4057, info@parkschamber.com, www.parkschamber.com

**Lynwood** · *Lynwood C/C* · Joseph Levy, Pres., 21460 Lincoln Hwy., 60411, P 9,000, M 65, (708) 474-2272, Fax (708) 474-2207, /www.lynwoodchamber-lcc.com

**Lyons** · *Lyons C/C* · 4121 Joliet Ave., 60534, P 10,500, M 40, (708) 447-5565

**Machesney Park** · *see Loves Park*

**Macomb** • *Macomb Area C/C & Downtown Dev. Corp.* • Penny Lawyer, Pres., 214 N. Lafayette St., P.O. Box 274, 61455, P 33,000, M 368, (309) 837-4855, Fax (309) 837-4857, chamber@macomb.com, www.macombareachamber.com

**Madison** • *see Granite City*

**Mahomet** • *Mahomet C/C* • Lee Jessup, P.O. Box 1031, 61853, P 5,000, M 85, (217) 586-3165, Fax (217) 586-3165, office@mahometchamberofcommerce.com, www.mahometchamberofcommerce.com

**Manhattan** • *Manhattan C/C* • Glenna Johnston, Exec. Dir., P.O. Box 357, 60442, P 3,700, M 120, (815) 478-3811, Fax (815) 478-7761, chamber@manhattan-il.com, www.manhattan-il.com

**Manito** • *Manito Area C/C* • Curt Jibben, Pres., P.O. Box 143, 61546, P 1,800, M 62, (309) 968-7200, www.manitoil.com

**Manteno** • *Manteno C/C* • Lisa Price, P.O. Box 574, 60950, P 8,000, M 175, (815) 468-6226, Fax (815) 534-5333, lisarprice@comcast.net, www.mantenochamber.com

**Marengo** • *Marengo-Union C/C* • Marlene Slavin, Pres./CEO, 116 S. State St., 60152, P 7,200, M 200, (815) 568-6680, Fax (815) 568-6879, info@marengo-union.com, www.marengo-union.com

**Marion** • *Marion Area C/C* • George R. Trammell, Pres./CEO, 2305 W. Main St., P.O. Box 307, 62959, P 61,296, M 650, (618) 997-6311, Fax (618) 997-4665, marionchamber@marionillinois.com, www.marionillinois.com.

**Marseilles** • *Illinois River Area C/C* • Patricia Smith, Exec. Dir., 135 Washington St., 61341, P 5,000, M 225, (815) 795-2323, Fax (815) 795-4546, iracc@mtco.com, www.marseillesil.org, www.senecail.org

**Marshall** • *Marshall Area C/C* • George Dalmier, Pres., 708 Archer Ave., 62441, P 3,900, M 60, (217) 826-2034, Fax (217) 826-2034, marshall.chamber@abcs.com, www.marshall-il.com

**Martinsville** • *Martinsville C/C* • Gary Heningman, P.O. Box 429, 62442, P 1,300, M 50, (217) 382-4323, www.martinsvilleilcity.com

**Maryville** • *see Troy*

**Mascoutah** • *Mascoutah C/C* • Spring Ramsey, Admin., 200 E. Main St., Ste. 101, 62258, P 7,500, M 129, (618) 566-7355, Fax (618) 566-7355, chamber@mascoutahchamber.com, www.mascoutah.com

**Matteson** • *see Park Forest*

**Mattoon** • *Mattoon C/C* • Mary E. Wetzel, Exec. Dir., 500 Broadway Ave., 61938, P 23,000, M 385, (217) 235-5661, Fax (217) 234-6544, matchamber@consolidated.net, mattoonchamber.com

**Maywood** • *Maywood C/C* • Edwin H. Walker IV, Pres./CEO, P.O. Box 172, 60153, P 28,000, M 150, (708) 345-7077, Fax (708) 345-9455, info@maywoodchamber.org, www.maywood.org

**McHenry** • *McHenry Area C/C* • Kay Rial-Bates, Pres., 1257 N. Green St., 60050, P 34,000, M 720, (815) 385-4300, Fax (815) 385-9142, info@mchenrychamber.com, www.mchenrychamber.com

**McLeansboro** • *Hamilton County C/C & EDC* • Bradley Futrell, Pres., P.O. Box 456, 62859, P 9,000, M 65, (618) 643-3531, Fax (618) 643-2292, www.mcleansboro.com

**Melrose Park** • *Melrose Park C/C* • Cathy Stenberg, Exec. Dir., 1718 W. Lake St., 60160, P 21,000, M 300, (708) 338-1007, Fax (708) 338-9924, info@melroseparkchamber.org, www.melroseparkchamber.org

**Mendota** • *Mendota Area C/C* • Alison Wasmer, Exec. Dir., 800 Washington St., P.O. Box 620, 61342, P 7,272, M 240, (815) 539-6507, Fax (815) 539-6025, mendotachamber@yahoo.com, www.mendotachamber.com

**Metropolis** • *Metropolis Area C/C, Tourism & Eco. Dev.* • Karla Ogle, Pres., 607 Market St., P.O. Box 188, 62960, P 7,200, M 225, (618) 524-2714, (800) 949-5740, Fax (618) 524-4780, metrochamber@hcis.net, www.metropolischamber.com

**Mettawa** • *see Lincolnshire*

**Midlothian** • *Midlothian Area C/C* • P.O. Box 909, 60445, P 15,000, M 160, (708) 389-0020, Fax (708) 389-0020, www.villageofmidlothian.net

**Milan** • *see Moline*

**Minooka** • *Greater Channahon-Minooka Area C/C* • Gloria Tasharski, Exec. Dir., 408 Mondamin St., P.O. Box 444, 60447, P 22,000, M 200, (815) 521-9999, Fax (815) 521-0903, cmchamber@att.net, www.cmchamber.org

**Mitchell** • *see Granite City*

**Mokena** • *Mokena C/C* • Sharon Filkins Jenrich, Pres., 19820A Wolf Rd., 60448, P 16,000, M 275, (708) 479-2468, Fax (708) 479-7144, mokena@mokena.com, www.mokena.com

**Moline** • *Illinois Quad City C/C* • Rick L. Baker, Pres./CEO, 622 19th St., 61265, P 165,000, M 961, (309) 757-5416, Fax (309) 757-5435, info@quadcitychamber.com, www.quadcitychamber.com

**Momence** • *Momence C/C* • Rick Seemann, Admin. Asst., P.O. Box 34, 60954, P 7,800, M 100, (815) 472-4620, Fax (815) 472-6453, momencechamber@sbcglobal.net, www.momence.net

**Monee** • *Monee Area C/C* • Mike Haller, Pres., P.O. Box 177, 60449, P 3,500, M 75, (708) 212-4133, Fax (708) 534-5320, info@moneechamber.org, www.moneechamber.org

**Monmouth** • *Monmouth Area C/C* • Angie McElwee, Exec. Dir., 90 Public Sq., P.O. Box 857, 61462, P 9,800, M 230, (309) 734-3181, Fax (309) 734-6595, macc@maplecity.com, www.monmouthilchamber.com

**Mont Clare** • *see Elmwood Park*

**Montgomery** • *Greater Montgomery Area C/C* • Alice Sutcliff, Pres., 200 Webster, 60538, P 14,500, M 144, (630) 897-8137, Fax (630) 897-6747, gmacc@montgomery-illinois.org, www.chamberofmontgomeryil.org

**Monticello** • *Monticello C/C* • Sue Gortner, Exec. Dir., P.O. Box 313, 61856, P 5,150, M 180, (217) 762-7921, (800) 952-3396, Fax (217) 762-2711, info@monticellochamber.org, www.monticelloillinois.net

**Morris** • *Grundy County C/C & Ind.* • Caroline Portlock, Exec. Dir., 909 N. Liberty St., 60450, P 40,000, M 400, (815) 942-0113, Fax (815) 942-0117, info@grundychamber.com, www.grundychamber.com

**Morrison** • *Morrison C/C* • Corinne Bender, Secy., 221 W. Main St., P.O. Box 8, 61270, P 4,500, M 70, (815) 772-3757, Fax (815) 772-3757, morrisonchamber@frontiernet.net, www.morrisonchamber.com

**Morton** • *Morton C/C* • Jennifer Daly, Exec. Dir., 415 W. Jefferson St., 61550, P 16,000, M 320, (309) 263-2491, (888) 765-6588, Fax (309) 263-2401, chamber@mtco.com, www.mortonchamber.org

**Morton Grove** • *Morton Grove C/C & Ind.* • Mark Pendergrass, Exec. Dir., 6101 Capulina Ave., 60053, P 23,000, M 255, (847) 965-0330, Fax (847) 965-0349, director@mgcci.org, www.mgcci.org

**Mount Carmel** • *Wabash County C/C* • Tanja Bingham, Exec. Dir., 219 Market St., Ste. 1A, 62863, P 12,570, M 150, (618) 262-5116, Fax (618) 262-2424, info@wabashcountychamber.com, www.wabashcountychamber.com.

**Mount Carroll** • *Mount Carroll C/C* • Nancy Tobin, P.O. Box 94, 61053, P 1,800, M 90, (815) 244-2255, info@mtcarrollil.org, www.mtcarrollil.org

**Mount Clare** · *see Gillespie*

**Mount Prospect** · *Mount Prospect C/C* · James Uszler, Exec. Dir., 107 S. Main St., 60056, P 56,285, M 345, (847) 398-6616, Fax (847) 398-6780, staff@mountprospect.com, www.mount prospectchamber.org

**Mount Vernon** · *Jefferson County C/C* · Brandon Bullard, Exec. Dir., 200 Potomac Blvd., P.O. Box 1047, 62864, P 40,000, M 650, (618) 242-5725, Fax (618) 242-5130, chambermarketing@mvn. net, www.southernillinois.com.

**Mount Zion** · *Mount Zion C/C* · Judy Kaiser, Admin., P.O. Box 84, 62549, P 8,000, M 225, (217) 864-2526, Fax (217) 864-6115, AskJudy4@aol.com, www.mtzionchamber.com

**Mundelein** · *see Libertyville*

**Murphysboro** · *Murphysboro C/C* · Kaye Carr, Exec. Dir., 203 S. 13th St., P.O. Box 606, 62966, P 10,000, M 170, (618) 684-6421, Fax (618) 684-2010, executive4@verizon.net, www.murphysboro.com

**Naperville** · *Naperville Area C/C* · Richard Greene, Pres./ CEO, 55 S. Main St., Ste. 351, 60540, P 150,000, M 2,000, (630) 355-4141, Fax (630) 355-8335, chamber@naperville.net, www. naperville.net

**Nashville** · *Nashville C/C* · Cheryl Zapp, Exec. Dir., 163 E. St. Louis St., 62263, P 3,147, M 112, (618) 327-3700, Fax (618) 327-9757, nashvillechamber@sbcglobal.net, www.nashville-il.cc

**Nauvoo** · *Nauvoo C/C* · Vern Kaaiakamanu, Pres., P.O. Box 41, 62354, P 1,071, M 75, (217) 453-2587, info@nauvoochamber.com, www.nauvoochamber.com

**New Baden** · *New Baden C/C* · Larry Wankel, Pres., P.O. Box 22, 62265, P 3,000, M 60, (618) 588-3813, www.newbadenchamber. com

**New Lenox** · *New Lenox C/C* · Debbera Hypke, CEO, 1 Veterans Pkwy., Ste. 104, P.O. Box 42, 60451, P 38,000, M 475, (815) 485-4241, Fax (815) 485-5001, deb@newlenoxchamber.com, www. newlenoxchamber.com

**Newton** · *Jasper County C/C* · 207 1/2 Jourdan, P.O. Box 21, 62448, P 10,000, M 200, (618) 783-3399, Fax (618) 783-4556, jasperchamber@psbnewton.com, www.newtonillinois.com.

**Niles** · *Niles C of C & Ind.* · Katie Schneider, Exec. Dir., 8060 W. Oakton, 60714, P 30,000, M 478, (847) 268-8180, Fax (847) 268-8186, katie@nileschamber.com, www.nileschamber.com

**Normal** · *see Bloomington*

**North Aurora** · *see Aurora*

**North Chicago** · *North Chicago C/C* · Marvin Bembry, Pres., P.O. Box 554, 60064, P 40,000, M 70, (847) 785-1912, Fax (847) 785-0109, northchicagochamber@yahoo.com, www.north chicagochamber.org

**Northbrook** · *Northbrook C/C & Ind.* · Tensley Garris, Pres., 2002 Walters Ave., 60062, P 34,400, M 675, (847) 498-5555, Fax (847) 498-5510, info@northbrookchamber.org, www.northbrook chamber.org

**Northlake** · *Northlake C/C* · Eileen Alexanderson, Pres., P.O. Box 2067, 60164, P 17,000, M 80, (708) 562-3110

**Oak Brook** · *Greater Oak Brook C/C* · Tracy Mulqueen, Pres./ CEO, 619 Enterprise Dr., Ste. 100, 60523, P 8,700, M 400, (630) 472-9377, Fax (630) 954-1327, info@obchamber.com, www. obchamber.com

**Oak Forest** · *Oak Forest C/C* · Tamara Kostecki, Exec. Dir., 15440 S. Central Ave., 60452, P 31,000, M 200, (708) 687-4600, Fax (708) 687-7878, info@oakforestchamber.org, www.oakforestchamber.org

**Oak Lawn** · *Oak Lawn C/C* · Glen Kato, Pres., 5314 W. 95th St., 60453, P 56,000, M 350, (708) 424-8300, Fax (708) 229-2236, office@oaklawnchamber.com, www.oaklawnchamber.com

**Oak Park** · *Oak Park-River Forest C/C* · Jim Doss, Exec. Dir., 1110 North Blvd., 60301, P 52,500, M 500, (708) 848-8151, Fax (708) 848-8182, info@oprfchamber.org, www.oprfchamber.org

**Oakland** · *Oakland C/C* · Kyley Willison, Pres., P.O. Box 283, 61943, P 1,000, M 40, (217) 346-2229, willison@consolidated.net

**Oblong** · *Oblong C/C* · P.O. Box 122, 62449, P 1,600, M 100, (618) 592-4355, Fax (618) 592-4224, info@theonlyoblong.com, www. theonlyoblong.com

**O'Fallon** · *O'Fallon C/C* · 116 E. First St., P.O. Box 371, 62269, P 27,000, M 380, (618) 632-3377, Fax (618) 632-8162, chamber@ ofallonchamber.com, www.ofallonchamber.com

**Okawville** · *Okawville C/C* · P.O. Box 345, 62271, P 1,300, M 50, (618) 243-5694, tourokaw@htc.net, www.okawvillecc.com

**Olney** · *Olney and the Greater Richland County C/C* · Jessica Akes, Exec. Dir., 201 E. Chestnut, P.O. Box 575, 62450, P 9,500, M 190, (618) 392-2241, (888) 393-2241, Fax (618) 392-4179, olneychamber@otbnet.com, www.olneychamber.com

**Olympia Fields** · *see Park Forest*

**Oregon** · *Oregon Area C/C* · Marcia Heuer, Exec. Dir., 303 W. Washington, P.O. Box 69, 61061, P 4,100, M 380, (815) 732-2100, Fax (815) 732-2177, ococ@oregonil.com, www.oregonil.com.

**Orland Park** · *Orland Park Area C/C* · Keloryn Putnam IOM, Exec. Dir., 8799 W. 151st St., 60462, P 60,000, M 625, (708) 349-2972, Fax (708) 349-7454, info@orlandparkchamber.org, www. orlandparkchamber.org

**Oswego** · *Oswego C/C* · Steve Hatcher, Exec. Dir., 22 W. Van Buren, 60543, P 24,000, M 367, (630) 554-3505, Fax (630) 554-0050, info@oswegochamber.org, www.oswegochamber.org

**Ottawa** · *Ottawa Area C/C & Ind.* · Boyd Palmer, Exec. Dir., 633 E. LaSalle St., Ste. 401, 61350, P 24,000, M 391, (815) 433-0084, Fax (815) 433-2405, info@ottawachamberillinois.com, www. ottawachamberillinois.com

**Palatine** · *Palatine Area C/C & Ind.* · Mindy Phillips, Dir., 625 N. North Ct., Ste. 320, 60067, P 70,000, M 450, (847) 359-7200, Fax (847) 359-7246, info@palatinechamber.com, www.palatine chamber.com

**Palestine** · *Palestine C/C* · Dee Fulling, Admin., 103 S. Main St., P.O. Box 155, 62451, P 1,400, M 80, (618) 586-2222, Fax (618) 586-9477, palestinecofc@verizon.net, www.pioneercity.com

**Palos Heights** · *Palos Heights C/C* · Dan Harris, Pres., P.O. Box 138, 60463, P 21,000, M 200, (708) 923-2300, Fax (708) 361-9711, www.paloschamber.org

**Palos Hills** · *see Bridgeview-Hills C/C*

**Pana** · *Pana C/C* · Jim Deere, Secy./Treas., 120 E. 3rd St., City Hall, 62557, P 7,100, M 130, (217) 562-4240, Fax (217) 562-3823, panail@consolidated.net, www.panaillinois.com

**Paris** · *Paris Area C/C & Tourism* · Brenda Buckley, Exec. Dir., 105 N. Central Ave., 61944, P 20,000, M 370, (217) 465-4179, Fax (217) 465-4170, info@parisilchamber.com, www.parisilchamber.com

**Park Forest** · *Matteson Area C/C* · Lauren Alspaugh, Exec. Dir., 298 Main St., 60466, P 60,000, M 240, (708) 747-6000, Fax (708) 747-6054, www.macclink.com

**Park Ridge** · *Park Ridge C/C* · Chelle O'Connell, Exec. Dir., 32 Main St., Ste. F, 60068, P 38,000, M 400, (847) 825-3121, Fax (847) 825-3122, info@parkridgechamber.org, www.parkridge chamber.org

**Pawnee** • *Pawnee Area C/C* • Patty Williams, Secy, 704 7th St., P.O. Box 1096, 62558, P 2,700, M 40, (217) 625-8270, pawnee chamber@yahoo.com, www.pawneechamber.org.

**Paxton** • *Paxton Area C/C* • P.O. Box 75, 60957, P 4,600, M 145, (217) 379-4655

**Pekin** • *Pekin Area C/C* • Bill Fleming, Exec. Dir., 402 Court St., P.O. Box 636, 61555, P 35,000, M 400, (309) 346-2106, Fax (309) 346-2104, chamber@pekin.net, www.pekin.net

**Peoria** • *Peoria Area C/C* • Roberta M. Parks, Sr. V.P./COO, 100 S.W. Water St., 61602, P 110,000, M 1,280, (309) 676-0755, Fax (309) 676-7534, chamber@mail.h-p.org, www.peoriachamber.org

**Peoria Heights** • *Peoria Heights C/C* • 1203 E. Kingman Ave., P.O. Box 9783, 61612, P 6,700, M 82, (309) 685-4812, Fax (309) 685-4812, info@itshappeninginthehaights.com, www.peoria heightschamber.com

**Peotone** • *Peotone C/C* • Marty Schmidt, P.O. Box 877, 60468, P 3,500, M 60, (708) 258-9450, peotonechamber@hotmail.com, www.peotonechamber.com

**Petersburg** • *Petersburg C/C* • Judy Loving, Pres., 125 S. 7th St., P.O. Box 452, 62675, P 2,300, M 80, (217) 632-7363, Fax (217) 632-7363, information@petersburg-illinois-chamber-of-commerce.com, www.petersburgilchamber.com

**Pinckneyville** • *Pinckneyville C/C* • Joan Smith, Exec. Coord., 4 S. Walnut St., P.O. Box 183, 62274, P 5,500, M 90, (618) 357-3243, Fax (618) 357-2688, pinckneyvillechamber@verizon.net, www. pinckneyville.com

**Pittsfield** • *Pike County C/C* • Karen Griggs, Exec. Dir., 224 W. Washington, P.O. Box 283, 62363, P 18,000, M 200, (217) 285-2971, Fax (217) 285-5251, info@pikeil.org, www.pikeil.org

**Plainfield** • *Plainfield Area C/C* • Liz Collins, Pres./CEO, 24047 W. Lockport St., Ste. 109, 60544, P 50,000, M 594, (815) 436-4431, Fax (815) 436-0520, pacc@plainfieldchamber.com, www. plainfieldchamber.com

**Plano** • *Plano Area C/C* • 101 W. Main St., 60545, P 10,000, M 160, (630) 552-7272, www.planocommerce.org

**Polo** • *Polo C/C* • Jo Bittinger, Pres., 115 S. Franklin Ave., 61064, P 2,477, M 126, (815) 946-3131, Fax (815) 946-2004, estes secretarialservice@yahoo.com, www.poloil.org

**Pontiac** • *Pontiac Area C/C* • Cheri Lambert, Pres./CEO, 210 N. Plum St., P.O. Box 534, 61764, P 12,000, M 300, (815) 844-5131, Fax (815) 844-2600, clambert@pontiacchamber.org, www. pontiacchamber.org.

**Pontoon Beach** • *see Granite City*

**Prairie View** • *see Lincolnshire*

**Princeton** • *Princeton Area C/C & Main Street* • Erika Robbins, Exec. Dir., 435 S. Main St., 61356, P 8,000, M 260, (815) 875-2616, (877) 730-4306, Fax (815) 875-1156, erobbins@princeton-il.com, www.visitprinceton-il.com

**Quincy** • *Quincy Area C/C* • Amy Looten, Exec. Dir., 300 Civic Center Plaza, Ste. 245, 62301, P 40,366, M 565, (217) 222-7980, Fax (217) 222-3033, qacc@quincychamber.org, www.quincy chamber.org

**Rantoul** • *Rantoul Area C/C* • Joe Bolser, Exec. Dir., 100 W. Sangamon Ave., Ste. 101, 61866, P 15,000, M 360, (217) 893-3323, Fax (217) 893-3325, dir@mchsi.com, www.rantoulchamber.com

**Red Bud** • *Red Bud C/C* • Rodney Nevois, Pres., P.O. Box 66, 62278, P 3,500, M 218, (618) 282-3505, redbudchamber@gmail. com, www.redbudchamber.com

**Richmond** • *Richmond/Spring Grove C/C* • Loretta Podeszwa IOM, Exec. Dir., 10906 Main St., P.O. Box 475, 60071, P 6,000, M 260, (815) 678-7742, Fax (815) 678-2070, info@rsgchamber. com, www.rsgchamber.com.

**Richton Park** • *see Park Forest*

**River Forest** • *see Oak Park*

**Riverdale** • *Riverdale C/C* • Adelle Swanson, Secy., 208 W. 144th St., 60827, P 15,055, M 85, (708) 841-3311, Fax (708) 841-1805, rdpl2@earthlink.net, www.district148.net/rcoc

**Riverside** • *Riverside C/C* • David Moravecek, Pres., P.O. Box 7, 60546, P 15,000, M 75, (708) 447-8510, business@riversidechamberof commerce.com, www.riversidechamberofcommerce.com

**Riverwoods** • *see Deerfield*

**Robinson** • *Robinson C/C* • Mary Kindt, Admin., 113 S. Court St., 62454, P 7,500, M 150, (618) 546-1557, Fax (618) 546-0182, robinsonchamber@hotmail.com, www.robinsonchamber.org

**Rochelle** • *Rochelle Area C/C* • Jeana Abbott, Exec. Dir., 350 May Mart Dr., P.O. Box 220, 61068, P 17,000, M 250, (815) 562-4189, Fax (815) 562-4180, chamber@rochelle.net, www.rochellechamber.org

**Rock Falls** • *Rock Falls C/C* • Doug Wiersema, Pres./CEO, 601 W. 10th St., 61071, P 9,600, M 370, (815) 625-4500, Fax (815) 625-4558, doug@rockfallschamber.com, www.rockfallschamber.com

**Rock Island** • *see Moline*

**Rockford** • *Rockford C/C* • Einar K. Forsman, Pres./CEO, 308 W. State St., Ste. 190, 61101, P 371,236, M 1,500, (815) 987-8100, Fax (815) 987-8122, info@rockfordchamber.com, www.rockford chamber.com

**Rockton** • *Rockton C/C* • Carol Lamb, Exec. Dir., 330 E. Main St., Ste. 700, P.O. Box 237, 61072, P 7,440, M 170, (815) 624-7625, Fax (815) 624-7385, info@rocktonchamber.com, www.rockton chamber.com

**Rolling Meadows** • *Rolling Meadows C/C* • Linda Liles Ballantine, Exec. Dir., 2775 Algonquin Rd., Ste. 310, 60008, P 26,000, M 220, (847) 398-3730, Fax (847) 398-3745, office@ rmchamber.org, rmchamber.org

**Romeoville** • *Romeoville Area C/C* • Sharon Eck, Exec. Dir., 27 Montrose Dr., 60446, P 34,000, M 217, (815) 886-2076, Fax (815) 886-2096, info@romeovillechamber.org, www.romeovillechamber.org

**Roscoe** • *Roscoe Area C/C* • Cindy Ogden, Exec. Dir., 5310 Williams Dr., 61073, P 17,000, M 350, (815) 623-9065, Fax (815) 623-1755, info@roscoechamber.com, roscoechamber.com

**Roselle** • *Roselle C /C & Ind.* • Gail Croson, Exec. Dir., 81 E. Devon Ave., 60172, P 23,000, M 200, (630) 894-3010, Fax (630) 894-3042, executivedirector@rosellechamber.com, www.roselle chamber.com

**Rosemont** • *Rosemont C/C* • Pam Hogan, Exec. Dir., 9501 W. Devon Ave., Ste. 700, 60018, P 4,224, M 250, (847) 698-1190, Fax (847) 698-1195, info@rosemontchamber.com, www.rose montchamber.com

**Roseville** • *Roseville Area C/C* • Bob Pritchett, Pres., P.O. Box 54, 61473, P 1,100, M 60, (309) 426-2351

**Round Lake Beach** • *Round Lake Area C/C & Ind.* • Shanna Coakley , Exec. Dir., 2007 Civic Center Way, 60073, P 42,000, M 200, (847) 546-2002, Fax (847) 546-2254, info@rlchamber.org, www. rlchamber.org

**Roxanna** • *see Godfrey*

**Rushville** • *Rushville Area C/C* • Becky Briney, Pres., P.O. Box 171, 62681, P 3,300, M 70, (217) 322-3689, www.schuyler countyillinois.com

**U.S. Chambers of Commerce**

**Saint Charles** · *St. Charles C/C* · Lori Hewitt, Pres./CEO, 3755 E. Main St., Ste. 140, 60174, P 45,000, M 800, (630) 584-8384, Fax (630) 584-6065, info@stcharleschamber.com, www.stcharleschamber.com

**Salem** · *Greater Salem C/C* · Art Carnahan, Exec. Dir., 615 W. Main St., 62881, P 7,800, M 280, (618) 548-3010, Fax (618) 548-3014, visitus@salemilchamber.com, www.salemilchamber.com

**Sandwich** · *Sandwich C/C* · Vicki A. Schuler, Exec. Dir., 128 E. Railroad St., P.O. Box 214, 60548, P 6,600, M 172, (815) 786-9075, Fax (815) 786-2505, info@sandwich-il.org, www.sandwich-il.org

**Savanna** · *Savanna C/C* · Pam Brown, Exec. Dir., 312 Main St., P.O. Box 315, 61074, P 3,300, M 100, (815) 273-2722, Fax (815) 273-2754, savchamber@grics.net, www.savanna-il.com

**Sawyerville** · *see Gillespie*

**Schiller Park** · *see Franklin Park*

**Seneca** · *see Marseilles*

**Sesser** · *Sesser Area C/C* · P.O. Box 367, 62884, P 2,400, M 35, (618) 625-5566, Fax (618) 625-6291, sesser@dtnspeed.net, www.sesser.org

**Shelbyville** · *Greater Shelbyville C/C* · Dena Bolin, Ofc. Mgr., 124 N. Morgan, 62565, P 5,000, M 150, (217) 774-2221, Fax (217) 774-2243, chamber01@consolidated.net, www.shelbyvillechamberofcommerce.com

**Silvis** · *see Moline*

**Skokie** · *Skokie C/C* · Howard Meyer, Exec. Dir., 5002 Oakton St., P.O. Box 106, 60077, P 63,500, M 550, (847) 673-0240, Fax (847) 673-0249, info@skokiechamber.org, www.skokiechamber.org

**Sleepy Hollow** · *see Carpentersville*

**South Elgin** · *South Elgin C/C* · Ann Dondelinger-Migatz, Exec. Dir., 888 N. LaFox St., Ste. 2C, 60177, P 20,188, M 300, (847) 888-2287, Fax (847) 429-6849, ann@southelginchamber.com, www.southelginchamber.com

**South Holland** · *South Holland Business Assn.* · Blevian Moore, P.O. Box 334, 60473, P 24,000, M 320, (708) 596-0065, Fax (708) 596-6696, info@shba.org, www.shba.org

**South Roxanna** · *see Godfrey*

**Sparta** · *Sparta Area C/C* · Ron Stork, Pres., 1805 N. Market, P.O. Box 93, 62286, P 5,000, M 145, (618) 317-7222, spartacc@spartaillinois.us, www.spartailchamber.com

**Spring Grove** · *see Richmond*

**Springfield** · *Greater Springfield C/C* · Gary Plummer, Pres./CEO, 3 S. Old State Capitol Plaza, 62701, P 192,745, M 1,500, (217) 525-1173, Fax (217) 525-8768, info@gscc.org, www.gscc.org

**Springfield** · *Illinois Assn. of C/C Execs.* · Elizabeth Kerns, Pres., 215 E. Adams St., 62701, P 11,500,000, M 200, (217) 522-5512, Fax (217) 522-5518, www.ilchamber.org, lkerns@ilchamber.org, www.iacce.org

**Staunton** · *Staunton C/C* · P.O. Box 248, 62088, P 5,100, M 55, (618) 635-8356, Fax (618) 635-3644, info@stauntonil.com, www.stauntonil.com

**Steeleville** · *Steeleville C/C* · P.O. Box 177, 62288, P 2,077, M 50, (618) 965-3134, www.steeleville.org

**Sterling** · *Sauk Valley Area C/C* · Kimberly Janssen, Exec. Dir., 211 Locust St., 61081, P 16,000, M 400, (815) 625-2400, Fax (815) 625-9361, chamber@essex1.com, www.saukvalleyareachamber.com

**Stockton** · *Stockton C/C* · Amy Laskye, Dir., P.O. Box 3, 61085, P 2,000, M 145, (815) 947-2878, Fax (815) 947-2878, info@stocktonil.com, www.stocktonil.com

**Streamwood** · *Streamwood C/C* · Susan Berg, Exec. Dir., 22 W. Streamwood Blvd., P.O. Box 545, 60107, P 39,500, M 215, (630) 837-5200, Fax (630) 837-5251, staff@streamwoodchamber.com, www.streamwoodchamber.com

**Streator** · *Streator Area C/C* · Jack Dzuris, Exec. Dir., 320 E. Main, P.O. Box 360, 61364, P 25,000, M 250, (815) 672-2921, Fax (815) 672-1768, sacci@mchsi.com, www.streatorchamber.com

**Sullivan** · *Sullivan Area C/C & EDC* · Stepheny McMahon, Exec. Dir., 112 W. Harrison St., 61951, P 4,600, M 188, (217) 728-4223, Fax (217) 728-4064, info@sullivanchamber.com, www.sullivanchamber.com

**Swansea** · *Swansea C/C* · Colleen Newlin, Exec. Dir., 1501 Caseyville Ave., 62226, P 11,341, M 175, (618) 233-3938, Fax (618) 233-3936, swansea@swanseachamber.org, www.swanseachamber.org

**Sycamore** · *Sycamore C/C* · Rosemarie M. Treml, Exec. Dir., 407 W. State St., Ste. 10, 60178, P 14,000, M 450, (815) 895-3456, Fax (815) 895-0125, info@sycamorechamber.com, www.sycamorechamber.com

**Taylorville** · *Greater Taylorville C/C* · Fred Ronnow, Pres./CEO, 108 W. Market St., 2nd Flr., 62568, P 11,500, M 350, (217) 824-4919, Fax (217) 824-6689, fredgtcc@consolidated.net, www.taylorvillechamber.com.

**Tinley Park** · *Tinley Park C/C* · Bernadette Shanahan-Haas, Pres./CEO, 17316 S. Oak Park Ave., 60477, P 56,000, M 500, (708) 532-5700, Fax (708) 532-1475, info@tinleychamber.org, www.tinleychamber.org

**Trenton** · *Trenton C/C* · James Rakers, Pres., P.O. Box 37, 62293, P 2,610, M 86, (618) 224-9329, www.trenton-ilchamber.com

**Troy** · *Troy/Maryville Area C/C* · Dawn Mushill, Exec. Dir., 647 E. U.S. Hwy. 40, 62294, P 10,000, M 350, (618) 667-8769, Fax (618) 667-8759, dawn@troycoc.com, www.troycoc.com

**Tuscola** · *Tuscola C/C* · Lyn Selen, Pres., P.O. Box 434, 61953, P 6,000, M 150, (217) 253-5013, www.tuscola.org

**University Park** · *see Park Forest*

**Vandalia** · *Vandalia C/C* · Kay Wasser, Admin. Secy., 1408 N. 5th St., P.O. Box 238, 62471, P 6,975, M 140, (618) 283-2728, Fax (618) 283-4439, www.vandaliaillinois.com

**Venice** · *see Granite City*

**Vernon Hills** · *see Libertyville*

**Vienna** · *Johnson County C/C* · Kelly Harper, Pres., 298 E. Vine St., 62995, P 17,000, M 130, (618) 658-2063, jo.co.chamber@juno.com

**Villa Park** · *Villa Park C/C* · Alesia Bailey, Exec. Dir., 10 W. Park Blvd., 60181, P 22,500, M 205, (630) 941-9133, Fax (630) 941-9134, info@villaparkchamber.org, www.villaparkchamber.org

**Viola** · *Viola C/C* · Jim Morrison, Pres., P.O. Box 403, 61486, P 1,000, M 21, (309) 596-2620, www.villageofviola.org

**Virden** · *Virden Area Assn. of Comm.* · P.O. Box 252, 62690, P 3,400, M 45, (217) 965-5805

**Walnut** · *Walnut C/C* · Nicole Blessing, Exec. Dir., 105 N. Main St., P.O. Box 56, 61376, P 1,500, M 105, (815) 379-2141, Fax (815) 379-9375, director@villageofwalnut.com, www.villageofwalnut.com

**Warrenville** · *Warrenville C/C* · Patricia Haskins, Pres./CEO, 29 W. 522 Batavia Rd., P.O. Box 432, 60555, P 13,450, M 225, (630) 393-9080, Fax (630) 393-9171, info@warrenvillechamber.com, www.warrenvillechamber.com

**Warsaw** · *Warsaw C/C* · Jim Scott, Dir., 415 LeClaire, 62379, P 1,810, M 25, (217) 256-4478, (217) 256-3214

**Washington** • *Washington C/C* • Carol Hamilton, Dir., 114 Washington Sq., 61571, P 13,500, M 270, (309) 444-9921, Fax (309) 444-9225, wcoc@mtco.com, www.washingtoncoc.com

**Waterloo** • *Waterloo C/C* • Debbie Ruggeri, Exec. Dir., 118 E. 3rd St., P.O. Box 1, 62298, P 13,000, M 250, (618) 939-5300, Fax (618) 939-1805, chamber@htc.net, www.enjoywaterloo.com

**Watseka** • *Watseka Area C/C* • Carrie Yana, Exec. Dir., 110 S. 3rd St., 60970, P 5,500, M 200, (815) 432-2416, Fax (815) 432-2762, www.watsekachamber.org

**Wauconda** • *Wauconda C/C* • Debra Ogorzaly, Exec. Dir., 100 N. Main St., 60084, P 13,000, M 330, (847) 526-5580, Fax (847) 526-3059, info@waucondachamber.org, www.waucondachamber.org

**Waukegan** • *see Gurnee*

**West Chicago** • *West Chicago C/C & Ind.* • David Sabathne, Pres./CEO, 306 Main St., 60185, P 25,000, M 300, (630) 231-3003, Fax (630) 231-3009, info@westchicagochamber.com, www.westchicagochamber.com.

**West Dundee** • *see Carpentersville*

**West Frankfort** • *West Frankfort C/C* • Steve Cook, Pres., 201 E. Nolen, 62896, P 8,526, M 150, (618) 932-2181, Fax (618) 932-6330, wfchamber@verizon.net, www.westfrankfort-il.com

**Westchester** • *Westchester C/C* • Bill Ernst , Pres., P.O. Box 7309, 60154, P 17,301, M 150, (708) 240-8400, Fax (708) 240-8400, www.westchesterchamber.org

**Western Springs** • *see LaGrange*

**Westmont** • *Westmont C/C & Tourism Bur.* • Larry Forssberg, Exec. Dir., 1 S. Cass Ave., Ste. 101, 60559, P 25,000, M 300, (630) 960-5553, Fax (630) 960-5554, wcctb@westmontchamber.com, www.westmontchamber.com

**Wheaton** • *Wheaton C/C* • Lisa Bock, Pres., 108 E. Wesley St., 60187, P 57,000, M 600, (630) 668-6464, Fax (630) 668-2744, wccinfo@ewheaton.com, www.ewheaton.com

**Wheeling** • *Wheeling-Prospect Heights Area C/C & Ind.* • Catherine Powers, Exec. Dir., 395 E. Dundee Rd., Ste. 450, 60090, P 45,000, M 300, (847) 541-0170, Fax (847) 541-0296, info@wphchamber.com, wphchamber.com

**Wicker Park** • *see Chicago-Wicker Park and Bucktown C/C*

**Willow Springs** • *see LaGrange*

**Willowbrook** • *see Burr Ridge*

**Wilmette** • *Wilmette C/C* • Julie Yusim, Exec. Dir., 1150 Wilmette Ave., 60091, P 28,000, M 430, (847) 251-3800, Fax (847) 251-6321, info@wilmettechamber.org, www.wilmettechamber.org

**Wilmington** • *Wilmington C/C* • Eric Fisher, Pres., 111 S. Water St., P.O. Box 724, 60481, P 5,100, M 80, (815) 476-5991, (815) 476-7966, Fax (815) 476-7002, www.wilmingtonchamberof commerce.org

**Wilsonville** • *see Gillespie*

**Winchester** • *Winchester C/C* • Andy Moss, Pres., P.O. Box 201, 62694, P 1,700, M 83, (217) 742-3219

**Winfield** • *Winfield C/C* • Rich Bysina, Exec. Dir., 125 S. Church St., P.O. Box 209, 60190, P 9,500, M 200, (630) 682-3712, Fax (630) 682-3726, winfieldchamber@sbcglobal.net, www.winfieldchamber.biz

**Winnetka** • *Winnetka C/C* • Cicely Clarke Michalak, Exec. Dir., 841 Spruce St., Ste. 204, 60093, P 12,500, M 250, (847) 446-4451, Fax (847) 446-4452, wcc@winnetkachamber.com, www.winnetka chamber.com

**Winthrop Harbor** • *Winthrop Harbor C/C* • 830 Sheridan Rd., P.O. Box 347, 60096, P 10,000, M 37, www.cocwh.com

**Wonder Lake** • *Wonder Lake C/C* • Donna Sullivan, Dir., 7602 Hancock Dr., 60097, P 15,000, M 120, (815) 728-0682, Fax (815) 653-6762, chamber@wonderlake.org, www.wonderlake.org

**Wood Dale** • *also see Elk Grove Village*

**Wood Dale** • *Wood Dale C/C* • Lorrie Heggaton, Pres., P.O. Box 353, 60191, P 14,000, M 150, (630) 595-0505, Fax (630) 595-0677, info@wooddalechamber.com, www.wooddalechamber.com

**Wood River** • *see Godfrey*

**Woodridge** • *Woodridge Area C/C* • Amy Melinder, Pres./CEO, 5 Plaza Dr., Ste. 212, 60517, P 35,000, M 300, (630) 960-7080, Fax (630) 852-2316, chamber@woodridgechamber.org, www.woodridgechamber.org

**Woodstock** • *Woodstock C/C & Ind.* • Quinn Keefe, Dir., 136 Cass St., 60098, P 23,500, M 340, (815) 338-2436, Fax (815) 338-2927, chamber@woodstockilchamber.com, www.woodstockilchamber.com

**Worth** • *Chicago Ridge-Worth C/C* • Bonnie Price, V.P., P.O. Box 356, 60482, P 25,000, M 50, (708) 923-2050, (708) 448-1181, crwc@crwchamber.com, www.crwchamber.com

**Wyanet** • *Wyanet C/C* • John Gordon, Pres., P.O. Box 373, 61379, P 1,100, M 30, (815) 699-2631, Fax (815) 699-2631, villageof wyanet@comcast.net

**Wyoming** • *Wyoming C/C* • Rich St. John, Pres., P.O. Box 157, 61491, P 1,424, M 40, (309) 286-4444, Fax (309) 286-5555

**Yorkville** • *Yorkville Area C/C* • Sherri Farley, Exec. Dir., 26 W. Countryside Pkwy., 60560, P 11,600, M 300, (630) 553-6853, Fax (630) 553-0702, sherri@yorkvillechamber.org, www.york villechamber.org

**Zion** • *Zion C/C* • Diana Gornik, Exec. Dir., 2730 Sheridan Rd., Ste. 1, 60099, P 22,000, M 160, (847) 872-5405, Fax (847) 872-9309, info@zionchamber.com, www.zionchamber.com

# Indiana

**Indiana C of C** • Kevin Brinegar, Pres., 115 W. Washington St. #850S, Indianapolis, 46204, P 6,000,000, M 4,750, (317) 264-3110, Fax (317) 264-6855, kbrinegar@indianachamber.com, www.indianachamber.com

**Akron** • *Akron C/C* • Royce Wright, Pres., P.O. Box 248, 46910, P 1,100, M 35, (574) 505-0881, Fax (574) 893-7339, www.akronin.com

**Albion** • *Albion C/C* • Phyllis Herendeen, Pres., P.O. Box 63, 46701, P 2,284, M 120, (260) 636-2748, chamber@albionin.org, www.albionin.org

**Alexandria** • *Alexandria-Monroe C/C* • John Dockrey, Exec. Dir., 125 N. Wayne St., 46001, P 6,000, M 130, (765) 724-3144, Fax (765) 683-3504, info@alexandriachamber.com, www.alexandria chamber.com

**Anderson** • *C of C for Anderson & Madison County* • Keith J. Pitcher, Pres., 2701 Enterprise Dr., Ste. 109, 46013, P 60,000, M 550, (765) 642-0264, Fax (765) 642-0266, andersonchamber@ameritech.net, www.andersoninchamber.com

**Angola** • *Angola Area C/C* • Jack Bercaw, Exec. Dir., 211 E. Maumee, Ste. B, 46703, P 7,500, M 430, (260) 665-3512, Fax (260) 665-7418, info@angolachamber.org, www.angolachamber.org

**Arcadia** • *see Cicero*

**Ashley** • *Ashley-Hudson Area C/C* • Sherri Hoffman, Pres., P.O. Box 99, 46705, P 1,500, M 60, (260) 587-3300

**Atlanta** · *see Cicero*

**Auburn** · *Auburn-Butler C/C* · Kelly Knox, Exec. Dir., 208 S. Jackson, P.O. Box 168, 46706, P 46,000, M 320, (260) 925-2100, Fax (260) 925-2199, kelly@chamberinauburn.com, www.chamberinauburn.com.

**HOME TO SEVEN HISTORIC MUSEUMS–AUBURN CORD DUSENBERG AUTOMOBILE MUSEUM & ACD FESTIVAL, HOOSIER AIR MUSEUM, KRUSE AUTOMOTIVE & CARRIAGE MUSEUM, NATMUS MUSEUM, WWII VICTORY MUSEUM, AMERICAN HERITAGE VILLAGE**

**Aurora** · *see Lawrenceburg*

**Avilla** · *Avilla C/C* · Julie Scher, P.O. Box 313, 46710, P 2,049, M 60, (260) 897-2674, www.avilla.org

**Avon** · *Greater Avon C/C* · Tom Downard, Exec. Dir., 8244 E. Hwy. 36, Ste. 140, 46123, P 9,500, M 240, (317) 272-4333, Fax (317) 272-7217, info@avonchamber.org, www.avonchamber.org

**Batesville** · *Batesville Area C/C* · Melissa Tucker, Exec. Dir., 132 S. Main St., 47006, P 7,000, M 300, (812) 934-3101, Fax (812) 932-0202, chamber@batesvillein.com, www.batesvillein.com

**Bedford** · *Bedford Area C/C* · Adele Bowden-Purlee, Pres., 1116 16th St., 47421, P 13,800, M 500, (812) 275-4493, Fax (812) 279-5998, bedford@bedfordchamber.com, www.bedfordchamber.com.

**Berne** · *Berne C/C* · Connie Potter, Exec. Dir., 205 E. Main St., 46711, P 4,500, M 210, (260) 589-8080, Fax (260) 589-8384, tourism@bernein.com, chamber@bernein.com, www.bernein.com, www.berneswissdays.com

**Beverly Shores** · *see Chesterton*

**Bloomington** · *Greater Bloomington C/C* · Christy Gillenwater, Pres./CEO, 400 W. 7th St., Ste. 102, P.O. Box 1302, 47402, P 183,000, M 1,000, (812) 336-6381, Fax (812) 336-0651, info@chamberbloomington.org, www.chamberbloomington.org

**Bluffton** · *Wells County C/C* · Suzanne Huffman, Dir., 211 W. Water St., 46714, P 26,800, M 251, (260) 824-0510, Fax (260) 824-5871, shuffman@wellscoc.com, www.wellscoc.com

**Boonville** · *Warrick County C/C* · Tracy Holder, Exec. Dir., 224 W. Main, P.O. Box 377, 47601, P 55,465, M 245, (812) 897-2340, Fax (812) 897-2360, warco@sigecom.net, www.warrickcounty.us

**Brazil** · *Clay County C/C* · Dalene Nelson, Ofc. Mgr., 535 E. National Ave., P.O. Box 23, 47834, P 26,492, M 125, (812) 448-8457, Fax (812) 448-9957, dalene@claycountychamber.org, www.claycountychamber.org

**Bremen** · *Bremen C/C* · Trent Mile, Coord., 111 S. Center, P.O. Box 125, 46506, P 4,500, M 100, (574) 546-2044, Fax (574) 546-5487, townbremenin@mchsi.com, www.bremenin.org

**Brookville** · *Brookville/Franklin County C/C* · Lois Clark, Exec. Dir., 444 Main, P.O. Box 211, 47012, P 20,000, M 250, (765) 647-3177, Fax (765) 647-4150, lois@fcchamber.net, www.fcchamber.net

**Brownsburg** · *Greater Brownsburg C/C* · Walter Duncan, Exec. Dir., 61 N. Green, P.O. Box 82, 46112, P 20,000, M 310, (317) 852-7885, Fax (317) 852-8688, chamber@brownsburg.com, www.brownsburg.com

**Brownstown** · *Brownstown C/C* · Janet Peters, Ofc. Mgr., 119 W. Walnut St., P.O. Box 334, 47220, P 4,200, M 112, (812) 358-2930, Fax (812) 358-9321, secretary@brownstownchamber.org, www.brownstownchamber.org

**Burns Harbor** · *see Chesterton*

**Butler** · *see Auburn*

**Carmel** · *Carmel C/C* · Maureen Merhoff, Pres., 37 E. Main #300, 46032, P 68,000, M 700, (317) 846-1049, Fax (317) 844-6843, chamberinfo@carmelchamber.com, www.carmelchamber.com

**Cedar Lake** · *Cedar Lake C/C* · Charles Kaper, Pres., 7925 Lake Shore Dr., P.O. Box 101, 46303, P 12,000, M 150, (219) 374-6157, Fax same, cl-chamber@sbcglobal.net, www.cedarlakechamber.com

**Chesterton** · *Chesterton/Duneland C/C* · Heather Ennis, Managing Dir., 220 Broadway, 46304, P 11,300, M 450, (219) 926-5513, Fax (219) 926-7593, info@chestertonchamber.org, www.chestertonchamber.org.

**Chrisney** · *see Rockport*

**Churubusco** · *Churubusco C/C* · Dee Dee McCoy, Dir., P.O. Box 83, 46723, P 2,700, M 70, (260) 693-9810, Fax (260) 693-9428, www.churubuscochamber.org

**Cicero** · *Hamilton North C/C* · Jane Hunter, Exec. Dir., 70 N. Byron St., P.O. Box 466, 46034, P 4,700, M 160, (317) 984-4079, Fax (317) 984-4079, jane@hamiltonnorthchamber.com, www.hamiltonnorthchamber.com

**Clay County** · *see Brazil*

**Clinton** · *Greater Clinton C/C* · P.O. Box 7, 47842, P 16,893, M 131, (765) 832-3844, Fax (765) 832-3525, vermillionchamber@sbcglobal.net, www.greaterclintonchamber.org

**Columbia City** · *Columbia City Area C/C* · Patricia Hatcher, Exec. Dir., 201 N. Line St., P.O. Box 166, 46725, P 8,024, M 250, (260) 248-8131, Fax (260) 248-8162, chamber@columbiacity.org, www.columbiacity.org.

**Columbus** · *Columbus Area C/C* · Jack Hess, Pres., 500 Franklin St., 47201, P 69,000, M 700, (812) 379-4457, Fax (812) 378-7308, info@columbusareachamber.com, www.columbusareachamber.com

**Connersville** · *Connersville/Fayette County C/C* · Katrina Griffin, Exec. Dir., 504 N. Central Ave., 47331, P 24,000, M 220, (765) 825-2561, Fax (765) 825-4613, chamber@ydial.net, www.connersvillechamber.com

**Corydon** · *C/C of Harrison County* · Lisa M. Long, Pres., 310 N. Elm St., 47112, P 36,827, M 400, (812) 738-2137, Fax (812) 738-6438, llong@harrisonchamber.org, www.harrisonchamber.org.

**Crawfordsville** · *Crawfordsville-Montgomery County C/C* · S. David Long, Exec. V.P., 309 N. Green St., 47933, P 37,000, M 300, (765) 362-6800, Fax (765) 362-6900, candy.hodges@sbcglobal.net, www.crawfordsvillechamber.com

**Crown Point** · *Greater Crown Point C/C* · Gayle Van Sessen, Exec. Dir., Court House Sq., Ste. 206, P.O. Box 343, 46308, P 24,000, M 350, (219) 663-1800, (866) 663-1905, Fax (219) 663-1989, gayle@crownpointguide.com, www.crownpointguide.com

**Culver** · *Culver C/C* · Bobbie Ruhnow, Exec. Secy., P.O. Box 129, 46511, P 1,583, M 91, (574) 842-5253, (888) 252-5253, Fax (574) 842-5253, www.culverchamber.com

**Dale** · *see Rockport*

**Danville** · *Greater Danville C/C* · Amanda Jensen, Exec. Dir., 17 W. Marion, P.O. Box 273, 46122, P 7,500, M 150, (317) 745-0670, Fax (317) 745-0682, amanda@danville-chamber.org, danville-chamber.org

**Decatur** · *Decatur C/C* · 125 E. Monroe St., 46733, P 10,000, M 240, (260) 724-2604, Fax (260) 724-3104, info@decaturchamber.org, www.decaturchamber.org.

**Delphi** · *Delphi C/C* · Krista Watson, Pres., P.O. Box 178, 46923, P 4,300, M 71, (765) 564-3034, info@delphichamber.org, www.delphichamber.org

**DeMotte** · *DeMotte C/C* · Rodney Urbano, Pres., P.O. Box 721, 46310, P 4,200, M 155, (219) 987-5800, Fax (219) 987-5800, demottechamber@netnitco.net, www.townofdemotte.com

**Dillsboro** · *see Lawrenceburg*

**Dune Acres** · *see Chesterton*

**Dunkirk** · *see Portland*

**Dyer** · *Dyer C/C* · 1 Town Center, P.O. Box 84, 46311, P 15,000, M 125, (219) 865-1045, Fax (219) 865-4233, chamber@dyeronline.com, www.townofdyer.com

**East Chicago** · *see Hammond*

**Edinburgh** · *Edinburgh C/C* · Brad Peter, Chrmn., 107 S. Holland St., P.O. Box 65, 46124, P 5,000, M 67, (812) 526-3512, Fax (812) 526-3542, edinburghchamber@yahoo.com, www.edinburgh.in.us

**Elkhart** · *Greater Elkhart C/C* · Philip Penn, Pres./CEO, 418 S. Main St., P.O. Box 428, 46515, P 100,000, M 1,200, (574) 293-1531, Fax (574) 294-1859, info@elkhart.org, www.elkhart.org

**Elwood** · *Elwood C/C* · Melissa Alfrey, Exec. Dir., 108 S. Anderson St., 46036, P 9,700, M 150, (765) 552-0180, Fax (765) 552-1277, elwoodchamber@sbcglobal.net, www.elwoodchamber.org

**Evansville** · *C of C of Southwest Indiana* · Matt Meadors, Pres./CEO, 100 N.W. Second St., Ste. 100, 47708, P 300,000, M 1,800, (812) 425-8147, Fax (812) 421-5883, info@evansvillechamber.com, www.evansvillechamber.com

**Ferdinand** · *Ferdinand C/C* · Jim Hagedorn, Pres., P.O. Box 101, 47532, P 2,500, M 200, (812) 367-0550, Fax (812) 367-1303, www.ferdinandindiana.org

**Fishers** · *Fishers C/C* · Christi J. Wolf, Pres., 11601 Municipal Dr., P.O. Box 353, 46038, P 65,000, M 895, (317) 578-0700, Fax (317) 578-1097, info@fisherschamber.com, www.fisherschamber.com

**Fort Wayne** · *Greater Fort Wayne C/C* · Kristine Foate, Pres./CEO, 826 Ewing St., 46802, P 331,849, M 2,500, (260) 424-1435, Fax (260) 426-7232, mcallicoat@fwchamber.org, www.fwchamber.org.

**Fowler** · *Fowler C/C* · Mike Brewer, Pres., P.O. Box 293, 47944, P 2,600, M 70, www.townoffowler.com

**Francesville** · *see Winamac*

**Frankfort** · *Clinton County C/C* · Gina L. Sheets, CEO, 259 E. Walnut St., 46041, P 36,000, M 300, (765) 654-5507, Fax (765) 654-9592, chamber@ccinchamber.org, www.ccinchamber.org

**Franklin** · *Franklin C/C* · Tricia E. Bechman, Exec. Dir., 370 E. Jefferson St., 46131, P 22,500, M 375, (317) 736-6334, Fax (317) 736-9553, franklincoc@franklincoc.org, www.franklincoc.org.

**Fremont** · *Fremont Area C/C* · Chris Snyder, Pres., P.O. Box 462, 46737, P 1,700, M 65, (260) 495-9010, www.fremontchamber.org

**French Lick** · *French Lick-West Baden C/C* · Alan Barnett, Exec. Secy., 1 Monon St., P.O. Box 347, 47432, P 3,000, M 100, (812) 936-2405, Fax (812) 936-2904, flwbchamber@yahoo.com, www.flwbcc.com

**Garrett** · *Garrett C/C* · Amy Demske, 111 W. Keyser St., 46738, P 5,800, M 135, (260) 357-4600, Fax (260) 357-4600

**Gary** · *Gary C/C* · Charles Hughes, Exec. Dir., 839 Broadway #S103, 46402, P 102,000, M 400, (219) 885-7407, Fax (219) 885-7408, garychamber@garychamber.com, www.garychamber.com

**Gas City** · *Gas City Area C/C* · Scott Nicholson, Pres., 316 E. Main St., 46933, P 6,296, M 255, (765) 674-7545, Fax (765) 674-1152, gascity@comteck.com, www.gascity.com

**Gentryville** · *see Rockport*

**Goshen** · *Goshen C/C* · David B. Daugherty, Pres., 232 S. Main St., 46526, P 31,000, M 500, (574) 533-2102, (800) 307-4204, Fax (574) 533-2103, goshenchamber@goshen.org, www.goshen.org.

**Grabill** · *Grabill C/C* · 13717 1st St., Town Hall, 46741, P 1,113, M 62, (260) 627-5227, Fax (260) 627-0550, wittgrabill@yahoo.com, www.grabill.net

**Grandview** · *see Rockport*

**Greencastle** · *Greater Greencastle C/C* · Tammy Amor, Exec. Dir., 16 S. Jackson St., 46135, P 36,000, M 310, (765) 653-4517, Fax (765) 848-1015, gchamber@gogreencastle.com, www.gogreencastle.com

**Greendale** · *see Lawrenceburg*

**Greenfield** · *Greater Greenfield C/C* · Retta Livengood, Pres., One Courthouse Plaza, 46140, P 18,000, M 380, (317) 477-4188, Fax (317) 477-4189, info@greenfieldcc.org, www.greenfieldcc.org

**Greensburg** · *Greensburg/Decatur County C/C* · Jennifer Sturges, Exec. Dir., 125 N. Broadway, 47240, P 26,000, M 400, (812) 663-2832, Fax (812) 663-4275, info@greensburgchamber.com, www.greensburgchamber.com

**Greenwood** · *Greater Greenwood C/C* · Christian Maslowski, Exec. Dir., 550 U.S. 31 S., 46142, P 184,000, M 660, (317) 888-4856, Fax (317) 865-2609, info@greenwood-chamber.com, www.greenwood-chamber.com

**Griffith** · *Griffith C/C* · Joe Starkey, Pres., P.O. Box 204, 46319, P 17,914, M 90, (219) 838-2661, Fax (219) 838-2401, griffithchamber@sbcglobal.net, www.griffithchamber.org

**Hamilton** · *Hamilton C/C* · Mary Vail, Pres., P.O. Box 66, 46742, P 1,400, M 115, (260) 488-3607, www.hamiltonindiana.org

**Hammond** · *Lakeshore C/C* · Dave Ryan, Exec. Dir., 5246 Hohman Ave.. Ste. 100, 46320, P 103,000, M 470, (219) 931-1000, Fax (219) 937-8778, info@lakeshorechamber.com, www.lakeshorechamber.com

**Harrison County** · *see Corydon*

**Hartford City** · *Hartford City C/C* · Susan Gerard, Exec. Asst., 121 N. High St., P.O. Box 286, 47348, P 6,000, M 100, (765) 348-1905, Fax (765) 348-4945, sgerard@blackfordcoedc.org, www.blackfordcounty.org

**Hebron** · *Hebron C/C* · Donna Paulk, Pres., P.O. Box 672, 46341, P 3,610, M 40, (219) 996-5678, info@visithebron.org, www.visithebron.org

**Highland** · *Highland C/C* · Mary Luptak, Exec. Dir., 8536 Kennedy Ave., 46322, P 23,696, M 220, (219) 923-3666, Fax (219) 923-3704, mary@highlandchamber.com, www.highlandchamber.com

**Hobart** · *Hobart C/C* · Brenda Clemmons, Exec. Dir., 1001 Lillian St., 46342, P 25,363, M 420, (219) 942-5774, Fax (219) 942-4928, info@hobartchamber.com, www.hobartchamber.com

**Hope** · *Hope Area C/C* · P.O. Box 131, 47246, P 2,200, (812) 546-0980, www.hopechamber.com

**Huntingburg** · *Huntingburg C/C* · Connie Burgdorf, 309 N. Geiger St., 47542, P 6,200, M 150, (812) 683-5699, (866) 586-8494, info@huntingburg.org, www.huntingburgchamber.org

**Huntington** · *Huntington County C/C* · Bob Brown, Pres., 305 Warren St., 46750, P 18,000, M 400, (260) 356-5300, Fax (260) 356-5434, president@huntington-chamber.com, www.huntington-chamber.com.

**Indianapolis** · *Greater Indianapolis C/C* · Roland Dorson, Pres., 111 Monument Circle, Ste. 1950, 46204, P 1,503,368, M 4,200, (317) 464-2222, (317) 639-4153 Tourism, Fax (317) 464-2217, rdorson@indylink.com, www.indychamber.com.

**Jasper** • *Jasper C/C* • Nancy K. Eckerle, Exec. Dir., 302 W. 6th St., P.O. Box 307, 47547, P 14,000, M 400, (812) 482-6866, (812) 482-7716, Fax (812) 482-1883, chamber@jasperin.org, www.jasperin.org.

**Jeffersonville** • *see New Albany*

**Jonesboro** • *see Gas City*

**Kendallville** • *Kendallville Area C/C* • Anita Shepherd, Exec. Dir., 122 S. Main St., 46755, P 10,018, M 295, (260) 347-1554, (877) 347-1554, Fax (260) 347-1575, info@kendallvillechamber.com, www.kendallvillechamber.com.

**Kentland** • *Kentland Area C/C* • Curt Puetz, Pres., P.O. Box 273, 47951, P 2,000, M 60, (219) 474-5444, (219) 474-6050, Fax (219) 474-6097, novotnyreins@sugardog.com

**Knightstown** • *Knightstown C/C* • Sue Hood, Pres., P.O. Box 44, 46148, P 2,500, M 75, (765) 345-5290, (800) 668-1895, www.knightstownchamber.org

**Knox** • *Starke County C/C* • Anthony Manning, Dir., P.O. Box 5, 46534, P 25,000, M 160, (574) 772-5548, Fax (574) 772-0867, info@starkechamber.com, www.starkechamber.com

**Kokomo** • *Kokomo/Howard County C/C* • 325 N. Main St., 46901, P 85,000, M 550, (765) 457-5301, Fax (765) 452-4564, www.kokomochamber.com.

**Kouts** • *Kouts C/C* • Julie Jones, Exec. Dir., P.O. Box 330, 46347, P 1,698, M 80, (219) 766-2867, koutschamber@verizon.net, www.kouts.org

**Lafayette** • *The Lafayette-West Lafayette C/C* • Joseph Seaman, Pres./CEO, 337 Columbia St., P.O. Box 348, 47902, P 156,169, M 1,000, (765) 742-4041, Fax (765) 742-6276, information@lafayettechamber.com, www.lafayettechamber.com

**LaGrange** • *LaGrange County C/C* • Beth Sherman, Exec. Dir., 901 S. Detroit St. #A, 46761, P 39,000, M 300, (260) 463-2443, (877) 735-0340, Fax (260) 463-2683, info@lagrangechamber.org, www.lagrangechamber.org

**Lake Station** • *Lake Station C/C* • 2500 Pike, 46405, P 15,500, M 50, (219) 962-1159, Fax (219) 963-4030

**Lake Township** • *see Roselawn*

**Lake Village** • *see Roselawn*

**Lamar** • *see Rockport*

**LaPorte** • *Greater LaPorte C/C* • Michael B. Seitz, Pres., 414 Lincolnway, P.O. Box 486, 46352, P 22,260, M 325, (219) 362-3178, Fax (219) 324-7349, info@lpchamber.com, www.lpchamber.com

**Lawrence** • *Greater Lawrence C/C* • Sandi Ballard, Pres., 9120 Otis Ave. #100, 46216, P 42,000, M 280, (317) 541-9876, Fax (317) 541-9875, sandi@lawrencechamberofcommerce.org, www.lawrencechamberofcommerce.org

**Lawrenceburg** • *Dearborn County C/C* • Mike Rozow, Pres./COO, 320 Walnut St., 47025, P 50,000, M 422, (812) 537-0814, (800) 322-8198, Fax (812) 537-0845, mrozow@dearborncountychamber.org, www.dearborncountychamber.org

**Leavenworth** • *Crawford County C/C* • Gary Wiseman, Pres., 6225 E. Industrial Ln. #C, 47137, P 11,076, M 75, (812) 739-2246, (812) 739-2248, Fax (812) 739-4180, www.cccn.net

**Lebanon** • *Boone County C/C* • Michelle Wiltermood, Exec. Dir., 221 N. Lebanon St., 46052, P 50,847, M 280, (765) 482-1320, Fax (765) 482-3114, michelle@boonechamber.org, www.boonechamber.org

**Liberty** • *Liberty-Union County C/C* • Blanche Stelle, Exec. Dir., 5 W. High St., 47353, P 7,300, M 115, (765) 458-5976, Fax (765) 458-5976, ucdc@dslmyway.com, www.ucdc.us.

**Ligonier** • *Ligonier C/C* • Deb Imbody, Secy., P.O. Box 121, 46767, P 4,357, M 67, (260) 894-9909, Fax (260) 894-9913, www.ligonierindianachamber.org

**Lincoln Township** • *see Roselawn*

**Linton** • *Linton-Stockton C/C* • Cheryl Hamilton, Exec. Dir., 159 1st St. N.W., P.O. Box 208, 47441, P 6,438, M 226, (812) 847-4846, Fax (812) 847-0246, info@lintonchamber.org, www.lintonchamber.org

**Logansport** • *Logansport/Cass County C/C* • Brian Shafer, Pres., 300 E. Broadway, Ste. 103, 46947, P 40,930, M 400, (574) 753-6388, (800) 425-2071, Fax (574) 735-0909, info@logan-casschamber.com, www.logan-casschamber.com

**Loogootee** • *Martin County C/C* • Bernard Mattingly, 210 N. Line St., P.O. Box 257, 47553, P 10,381, M 100, (812) 295-4093, mccc@mcol.us, www.mcol.us/chamberofcommerce.htm

**Lowell** • *Lowell C/C* • Ruth Dunn, Secy., 428 E. Commercial Ave., 46356, P 8,400, M 115, (219) 696-0231, info@lowellinchamber.com, lowellinchamber.com

**Madison** • *Madison Area C/C* • David Collier, Exec. Dir., 975 Industrial Dr., Ste. 1, 47250, P 30,000, M 406, (812) 265-3135, Fax (812) 265-9784, info@madisonchamber.org, www.madisonchamber.org.

**Marion** • *Marion-Grant County C/C* • Michelle Bunker, Bus. Dev. Dir., 215 S. Adams St., 46952, P 75,000, M 500, (765) 664-5107, Fax (765) 668-5443, info@marionchamber.org, www.marionchamber.org.

**Markle** • *see Bluffton*

**Martinsville** • *Greater Martinsville C/C* • Jamie Thompson, Exec. Dir., 109 E. Morgan St., P.O. Box 1378, 46151, P 12,000, M 200, (765) 342-8110, Fax (765) 342-5713, info@martinsvillechamber.com, www.martinsvillechamber.com

**Medaryville** • *see Winamac*

**Mentone** • *Mentone C/C* • Rita Simpson, Pres., P.O. Box 366, 46539, P 900, M 40, (574) 353-7417, www.mentoneeggcity.com

**Merrillville** • *Merrillville C/C* • Edward C. Dernulc, Interim Exec. Dir., 255 W. 80th Pl., 46410, P 35,000, M 900, (219) 769-8180, Fax (219) 736-6223, geninq@merrillvillecoc.org, www.merrillvillecoc.org

**Michigan City** • *Michigan City Area C/C* • Tim Bietry, Pres., 200 E. Michigan Blvd., 46360, P 34,000, M 420, (219) 874-6221, Fax (219) 873-1204, info@mcachamber.com, www.michigancitychamber.com.

**Middlebury** • *Middlebury C/C* • Sam Pohl, Exec. Dir., P.O. Box 243, 46540, P 3,010, M 185, (574) 825-4300, Fax (574) 825-7541, info@middleburycoc.com, www.middleburycoc.com

**Mishawaka** • *see South Bend*

**Mitchell** • *Greater Mitchell C/C* • 533 W. Main St., P.O. Box 216, 47446, P 5,000, M 115, (812) 849-4441, Fax (812) 849-6669, mitchellchamber@verizon.net, www.mitchellchamberofcommerce.org

**Monon** • *Monon C/C* • Alicia Cox, P.O. Box 777, 47959, P 1,750, M 45, (219) 253-6441

**Monterey** • *see Winamac*

**Monticello** • *Greater Monticello C/C & Visitors Bur.* • Janet Dold, Exec. Dir., 116 N. Main St., P.O. Box 657, 47960, P 25,000, M 300, (574) 583-7220, Fax (574) 583-3399, janeto@sugardog.com, www.monticelloin.com

**Moores Hill** • *see Lawrenceburg*

**Mooresville** • *Mooresville C/C* • Mindy Taylor, Exec. Dir., 4 E. Harrison St., P.O. Box 62, 46158, P 13,000, M 320, (317) 831-6509, Fax (317) 831-9557, mindy@mooresvillechamber.com, www.mooresvillechamber.com

**Morocco** • *see Roselawn*

**Morristown** • *Morristown Area C/C* • Melody Hawk, Pres., P.O. Box 476, 46161, P 1,200, M 119, (765) 763-6012, (765) 745-0138, www.morristownchamber.com

**Mount Ayr** • *see Roselawn*

**Mount Vernon** • *Posey County C/C* • Sally Denning, Exec. Dir., 915 E. Fourth St., P.O. Box 633, 47620, P 80,000, M 600, (812) 838-3639, Fax (812) 838-6358, poseychamber@sbcglobal.net, www.ccswin.com.

**Muncie** • *Muncie-Delaware County C/C* • Dan Allen, Pres., 401 S. High St., P.O. Box 842, 47308, P 120,000, M 750, (765) 288-6681, (800) 336-1373, Fax (765) 751-9151, straub@muncie.com, www.muncie.com.

**Munster** • *Munster C/C* • Rhonda I. Damjanovich, Pres., 1040 Ridge Rd., 46321, P 23,000, M 252, (219) 836-5549, Fax (219) 836-5551, info@chambermunster.org, www.chambermunster.org

**Nappanee** • *Nappanee Area C/C* • Larry Andrews, Exec. Dir., 302 W. Market, 46550, P 7,000, M 200, (574) 773-7812, Fax (574) 773-4691, nappaneecofc@kconline.com, www.nappaneechamber.com

**Nashville** • *Brown County C/C* • Danyell Dahn, Exec. Dir., 211 Van Buren St., P.O. Box 164, 47448, P 15,000, M 275, (812) 988-0234, Fax (812) 988-1547, commerce@browncounty.org, www.browncounty.org

**New Albany** • *One Southern Indiana* • Michael Dalby, Pres./CEO, 4100 Charlestown Rd., 47150, P 173,590, M 1,050, (812) 945-0266, Fax (812) 948-4664, becky@1si.org, www.1si.org.

**New Castle** • *New Castle-Henry County C/C* • Mike McIntosh, Exec. Dir., 100 S. Main St., Ste. 108, 47362, P 50,000, M 300, (765) 529-5210, Fax (765) 521-7408, info@nchcchamber.com, www.nchcchamber.com

**New Haven** • *New Haven C/C* • Vince Buchanan, Pres./CEO, 435 Ann St., 46774, P 13,500, M 316, (260) 749-4484, Fax (260) 749-7900, info@newhavenindiana.org, www.newhavenindiana.org

**New Palestine** • *New Palestine Area C/C* • P.O. Box 541, 46163, P 1,000, M 140, (317) 861-2345, info@newpalchamber.com, www.newpalchamber.com

**New Paris** • *New Paris C/C* • Dave Parsons, Pres., P.O. Box 402, 46553, P 1,000, M 50, (574) 831-3600

**Newtonville** • *see Rockport*

**Noblesville** • *Noblesville C/C* • Sharon McMahon, Pres., 601 E. Conner St., 46060, P 55,000, M 550, (317) 773-0086, Fax (317) 773-1966, info@noblesvillechamber.com, www.noblesville chamber.com

**North Manchester** • *North Manchester C/C* • Kathy Roberts, Exec. Dir., 109 N. Market St., 46962, P 6,500, M 171, (260) 982-7644, Fax (260) 982-8718, nmcc@kconline.com, www.northman chesterchamber.com.

**North Vernon** • *Jennings County C/C* • Mandy Gauger, Pres., 524 N. State St., Ste. B, P.O. Box 340, 47265, P 28,000, M 310, (812) 346-2339, Fax (812) 346-2065, mgauger@jenningscounty chamber.com, www.jenningscountychamber.com

**North Webster** • *North Webster-Tippecanoe Twp. C/C* • Tonya Bowser, Pres., P.O. Box 19, 46555, P 1,100, M 120, (574) 834-1600, Fax (574) 834-2168, nwttchamber@earthlink.net, www.northwebster.com

**Orleans** • *Orleans C/C* • Robert Henderson, Exec. Dir., P.O. Box 9, 47452, P 2,273, M 90, (812) 865-9930, Fax (812) 865-3413, www.historicorleans.com

**Ossian** • *see Bluffton*

**Paoli** • *Paoli C/C* • Tom Motsinger, Pres., 210 S.W. Court St., P.O. Box 22, 47454, P 4,200, M 100, (812) 723-4769, Fax (812) 723-4307, paolichamber@verizon.net, www.paolichamber.org

**Pendleton** • *C/C in Pendleton* • Suzanne Hagan, Mgr., 100 W. State St., P.O. Box 542, 46064, P 3,000, M 50, (765) 778-1741, Fax (765) 642-0266, andersonchamber@ameritech.net, www.andersoninchamber.com

**Peru** • *Miami County C/C* • Sandy Chittum, Pres., 13 E. Main St., 46970, P 37,000, M 330, (765) 472-1923, Fax (765) 472-7099, info@miamicochamber.com, www.miamicochamber.com

**Petersburg** • *Pike County C/C* • 714 E. Main St., 47567, P 12,600, M 130, (812) 354-8155, Fax (812) 354-2335, chamber@verizon.net, www.pikecountyin.org

**Plainfield** • *Greater Plainfield C/C* • Kent McPhail, Dir., 210 W. Main St., P.O. Box 14, 46168, P 25,000, M 340, (317) 839-3800, (877) 597-4763, Fax (317) 839-9670, chamber@town.plainfield.in.us, www.plainfield-in.com

**Plymouth** • *Plymouth Area C/C* • Douglas C. Anspach, Exec. Dir., 120 N. Michigan St., 46563, P 10,000, M 500, (574) 936-2323, Fax (574) 936-6584, plychamber@plychamber.org, www.plychamber.org

**Poneto** • *see Bluffton*

**Portage** • *Greater Portage C/C* • Nick Bella Jr., Pres., 2642 Eleanor St., 46368, P 50,000, M 410, (219) 762-3300, Fax (219) 763-2450, info@portageinchamber.com, www.portageinchamber.com

**Porter** • *see Chesterton*

**Portland** • *Jay County C/C* • Vicki Tague, Exec. Dir., 118 S. Meridian St., Ste. A, 47371, P 21,500, M 280, (260) 726-4481, Fax (260) 726-3372, vickitague@jaycountychamber.com, www.jaycountychamber.com

**Princeton** • *Gibson County C/C* • Karen Thompson, Exec. Dir., 202 E. Broadway, 47670, P 33,000, M 260, (812) 385-2134, Fax (812) 385-2401, director@gibsoncountychamber.or, www.gibsoncountychamber.org

**Rensselaer** • *Greater Rensselaer C/C* • Deana Rule, Pres., 215 W. Washington, 47978, P 6,272, M 180, (219) 866-5884, Fax (219) 866-3010, chamber@embarqmail.com, www.rensselaerchamber.com

**Richmond** • *Wayne County Area C/C* • Dennis Andrews, Pres./CEO, 33 S. 7th St., Ste. 2, 47374, P 72,000, M 600, (765) 962-1511, Fax (765) 966-0882, chamber.of.commerce@rwchamber.org, www.rwchamber.org

**Rising Sun** • *Rising Sun-Ohio County C/C* • Karrah Miller, 215 Main, P.O. Box 158, 47040, P 5,000, M 45, (812) 438-3130, info@risingsunchamber.com, www.risingsunchamber.com

**Roanoke** • *Roanoke C/C* • Mike Gibson, Pres., P. O. Box 434, 46783, P 1,594, M 82, (260) 673-2951, www.discoverroanoke.org

**Rochester** • *Rochester & Lake Manitou C/C* • Alison Heyde, Exec. Dir., 822 Main St., 46975, P 7,000, M 270, (574) 224-2666, Fax (574) 224-2329, chamber@rtcol.com, www.contactrochester.org

**Rockport** • *Spencer County Reg. C/C* • Debbie Barrett, Exec. Dir., 2792 N. U.S. Hwy. 231, Ste. 100, 47635, P 20,000, M 160, (812) 649-2186, (800) 799-2186, Fax (812) 649-2246, scrcc@psci.net, www.spencercoin.org

**Rockville** • *Parke County C/C* • Alan Ader, Exec. Dir., 105 N. Market St., Ste. A, 47872, P 17,000, M 100, (765) 569-5565, Fax (765) 569-6767, info@parkecountychamber.com, www.parke countychamber.com

**Rome City** • *Rome City C/C* • Roberta Stone, Pres., P.O. Box 22, 46784, P 1,650, M 25, (260) 854-2412, romecitychamber.com

**Roselawn** · *North Newton Area C/C* · John Morgin, P.O. Box 197, 46372, P 4,200, M 48, (219) 345-2525

**Rushville** · *Rush County C/C* · Pamela Leisure, Exec. Dir., 315 N. Main St., 46173, P 18,500, M 279, (765) 932-2880, Fax (765) 932-4191, pamleisure@rushcounty.com, www.rushcounty.com/chamber.

**Saint John** · *Saint John C/C* · 9495 Keilman, Ste. 10, 46373, P 11,000, M 175, (219) 365-4686, Fax (219) 365-4602, info@stjohnchamber.com, www.stjohnchamber.com

**Saint Leon** · *see Lawrenceburg*

**Salem** · *Washington County C/C* · Laurie Carr, Exec. Secy., 201 E. Market St., Ste. 104, 47167, P 27,223, M 185, (812) 883-4303, Fax (812) 883-1467, info@washingtoncountychamber.org, www.washingtoncountychamber.org

**Santa Claus** · *see Rockport*

**Schererville** · *Schererville C/C* · 13 W. Joliet St., 46375, P 28,000, M 320, (219) 322-5412, Fax (219) 322-0598, info@46375.org, www.46375.org

**Scottsburg** · *Greater Scott County C/C* · Keith Colbert, Exec. Dir., 90 N. Main St., Ste. B, 47170, P 24,000, M 300, (812) 752-4080, Fax (812) 752-4307, scottcom@c3bb.com, www.scottchamber.org

**Seymour** · *Greater Seymour C/C* · Bill Bailey, Pres., 105 S. Chestnut St., 47274, P 20,000, M 475, (812) 522-3681, Fax (812) 524-1800, info@seymourchamber.org, www.seymourchamber.org.

**Shelbyville** · *Shelby County C/C* · Julie Metz, Exec. Dir., 501 N. Harrison St., 46176, P 44,300, M 455, (317) 398-6647, (800) 318-4083, Fax (317) 392-3901, chamberinfo@shelbychamber.net, www.shelbychamber.net

**Shipshewana** · *see LaGrange*

**South Bend** · *C/C of St. Joseph County* · Mark Dobson, Pres./CEO, 401 E. Colfax Ave., Ste. 310, P.O. Box 1677, 46634, P 265,000, M 1,300, (574) 234-0051, Fax (574) 289-0358, info@sjchamber.org, www.sjchamber.org.

**South Whitley** · *South Whitley C/C* · Susan Hicks, Pres., 214 S. State St., 46787, P 2,200, M 65, (260) 723-4842, Fax (260) 723-4845, xohearts@embarqmail.com, www.southwhitley.com

**Spencer** · *Owen County C/C & Eco. Dev. Corp.* · Denise Shaw, Exec. Dir., 205 E. Morgan St., Ste. D, P.O. Box 87, 47460, P 21,000, M 100, (812) 829-3245, Fax (812) 829-0936, occcedc@sbcglobal.net, www.owencountyindiana.org

**Sullivan** · *Sullivan County C/C* · Judy K. Harris, Pres., 31 W. Jackson, P.O. Box 325, 47882, P 19,000, M 100, (812) 268-2897, Fax (812) 268-2898, chamber@hotmail.com

**Summitville** · *Summitville C/C* · P.O. Box 396, 46070, P 1,300, M 40, (765) 536-2802

**Syracuse** · *Syracuse-Wawasee C/C* · Tammy Cotton, Exec. Dir., P.O. Box 398, 46567, P 3,200, M 185, (574) 457-5637, Fax (574) 528-6040, info@swchamber.com, www.swchamber.com

**Tell City** · *Perry County C/C* · Cheri Taylor, Exec. Dir., 601 Main St. #A, P.O. Box 82, 47586, P 18,899, M 305, (812) 547-2385, Fax (812) 547-8378, perrychamber@psci.net, www.perrycountychamber.com

**Terre Haute** · *Terre Haute C/C* · G. Roderick Henry CCE, Pres./CEO, 630 Wabash Ave., Ste. 105, P.O. Box 689, 47807, P 110,000, M 860, (812) 232-2391, Fax (812) 232-2905, rhenry@terrehautechamber.com, www.terrehautechamber.com

**Thayer** · *see Roselawn*

**Tipton** · *Tipton County C/C* · Jennifer Servies, Exec. Dir., 136 E. Jefferson St., 46072, P 16,819, M 150, (765) 675-7533, Fax (765) 675-8917, jservies@tds.net, www.tiptonchamber.com

**Topeka** · *Topeka Area C/C* · Mr. Chris Deisler, Pres., P.O. Box 284, 46571, P 1,200, M 20, (260) 593-2138

**Union City** · *Union City C/C* · Darlene Wymer, Exec. Dir., 101 E. Elm St., P.O. Box 424, 47390, P 5,900, M 150, (765) 964-5409, Fax same, ucchamber@embarqmail.com, www.myunioncity.com.

**Uniondale** · *see Bluffton*

**Upland** · *Upland C/C* · Patty Hart, Pres., P.O. Box 157, 46989, P 4,000, M 70, (765) 998-7439, (765) 998-6012

**Valparaiso** · *Greater Valparaiso C/C* · Rex Richards, Pres., 162 W. Lincolnway, 46383, P 40,000, M 700, (219) 462-1105, Fax (219) 462-5710, gvcc@valparaisochamber.org, www.valparaisochamber.org.

**Vera Cruz** · *see Bluffton*

**Versailles** · *Ripley County C/C* · Barry Lauber, Pres., 102 N. Main St., P.O. Box 576, 47042, P 27,550, M 155, (812) 689-6654, Fax (812) 689-3934, ripleycc@ripleycountychamber.org, www.ripleycountychamber.org

**Vevay** · *Switzerland County C/C* · P.O. Box 149, 47043, P 9,500, M 75, (800) 435-5688, Fax (812) 427-2184, visitsc@gmail.com, www.vevayin.com

**Vincennes** · *Knox County C/C* · Marc A. McNeece, Pres./CEO, 102 N. Third St., P.O. Box 553, 47591, P 40,000, M 375, (812) 882-6440, Fax (812) 882-6441, marc@knoxcountychamber.com, www.knoxcountychamber.com

**Wabash** · *Wabash County C/C* · Kimberly Pinkerton, Pres., 210 S. Wabash St., 46992, P 25,000, M 350, (260) 563-1168, Fax (260) 563-6920, info@wabashchamber.org, www.wabashchamber.org

**Wakarusa** · *Wakarusa C/C* · Deb Shively, Exec. Secy., 100 W. Waterford St., P.O. Box 291, 46573, P 1,700, M 100, (574) 862-4344, Fax (574) 862-2245, chamber@wakarusachamber.com, www.wakarusachamber.com

**Walkerton** · *Walkerton Area C/C* · Julie Keb, Pres., 612 Roosevelt Rd., 46574, P 2,274, M 100, (574) 586-3100, Fax (574) 586-3469, www.walkerton.org

**Warrick County** · *see Boonville*

**Warsaw** · *Warsaw/Kosciusko County C/C* · Joy McCarthy-Sessing, Pres., 313 S. Buffalo St., Ste. A, 46580, P 74,057, M 550, (574) 267-6311, (800) 776-6311, Fax (574) 267-7762, mgoble@wkchamber.com, www.wkchamber.com.

**Washington** · *Daviess County C/C* · Charles Selby, Exec. Dir., One Train Depot St., P.O. Box 430, 47501, P 32,000, M 319, (812) 254-5262, (800) 449-5262, Fax (812) 254-4003, chamber@dmrtc.net, www.daviesscounty.net

**Waterloo** · *Waterloo C/C* · Ken Surber, Pres., P.O. Box 551, 46793, P 2,200, M 45, (260) 837-5323, (260) 837-7428, www.waterloochamber.com

**West Baden** · *see French Lick*

**West Harrison** · *see Lawrenceburg*

**West Lafayette** · *see Lafayette*

**Westfield** · *Westfield C/C* · Julie Sole, Exec. Dir., 130 Penn St., P.O. Box 534, 46074, P 30,000, M 400, (317) 804-3030, Fax (317) 804-3035, info@westfield-chamber.org, www.westfield-chamber.org

**Westville** · *Westville Area C/C* · P.O. Box 215, 46391, P 2,500, M 50, www.westville.us

**Whiting** · *Whiting-Robertsdale C/C* · Mary Lu Gregor, Exec. Dir., 1417 119th St., 46394, P 11,000, M 170, (219) 659-0292, Fax (219) 659-5851, marylu.chamber@sbcglobal.net, www.whitingindiana.com

**Winamac** • *Pulaski County C/C* • Steve Morrison, Treas., 200 W. Main St., P.O. Box 113, 46996, P 13,000, M 200, (574) 946-7600, Fax (574) 946-7617, chamber@pulaskionline.org, www.pulaskionline.org

**Winchester** • *Winchester Area C/C* • Eric Fields, Pres., 112 W. Washington St., 47394, P 27,066, M 175, (765) 584-3731, Fax (765) 584-5544, chamber@globalsite.net, www.winchesterarea-chamber.org

**Zionsville** • *Zionsville C/C* • Ray Cortopassi, Exec. Dir., 135 S. Elm St., P.O. Box 148, 46077, P 12,000, M 350, (317) 873-3836, Fax (317) 873-3836, info@zionsvillechamber.org, www.zionsville chamber.org.

# Iowa

**Iowa Assn. of Bus. and Ind.** • Michael Ralston, Pres., 904 Walnut St., Ste. 100, Des Moines, 50309, P 2,988,046, M 1,200, (515) 280-8000, (800) 383-4224, Fax (515) 282-8085, abi@iowaabi.org, www.iowaabi.org

**Ackley** • *Ackley C/C* • Jolene Harms, P.O. Box 82, 50601, P 1,800, M 67, (641) 847-3332, www.ackleyiowa.net

**Adel** • *Adel Partners Main Street C/C* • Julie Bailey, Prog. Dir., 310 S. 10th, P.O. Box 73, 50003, P 4,300, M 200, (515) 993-5472, Fax (515) 993-3384, adel@netins.net, www.adeliowa.org

**Albia** • *Albia Area C/C* • Deborah Morgan, Exec. Dir., 18 S. Main St., 52531, P 3,706, M 180, (641) 932-5108, Fax (641) 932-3326, albiachamber@albiachamber.org, www.albiachamber.org.

**Algona** • *Algona Area C/C* • Vicki Mallory, Exec. Dir., 123 E. State St., 50511, P 6,000, M 250, (515) 295-7201, Fax (515) 295-5920, algonaiachamber@algona.org, www.algona.org

**Allerton** • *see Corydon*

**Altoona** • *Altoona Area C/C* • 119 2nd St. , 50009, P 13,500, M 350, (515) 967-3366, Fax (515) 967-3346, altoona@netins.net, www.altoonachamber.org

**Ames** • *Ames C/C* • Dan Culhane, Pres,/CEO, 1601 Golden Aspen Dr., Ste. 110, 50010, P 52,300, M 675, (515) 232-2310, Fax (515) 232-6716, chamber@ameschamber.com, www.ameschamber.com

**Anamosa** • *Anamosa C/C* • K.C. Kiner, Exec. Dir., 124 E. Main St., 52205, P 5,400, M 145, (319) 462-4879, acoc@commspeed.net, www.anamosachamber.org

**Ankeny** • *Ankeny Area C/C* • Julie Cooper, Exec. Dir., 210 S. Ankeny Blvd., P.O. Box 488, 50023, P 42,000, M 675, (515) 964-0685, Fax (515) 964-0487, chamber@ankeny.org, www.ankeny.org

**Arnolds Park** • *Iowa Great Lakes Area C/C* • Tom Kuhlman, Exec. V.P., 243 W. Broadway, P.O. Box 9, 51331, P 16,424, M 400, (712) 332-2107, (800) 839-9987, Fax (712) 332-7714, tom@okoboji chamber.com, www.vacationokoboji.com

**Atlantic** • *Atlantic Area C/C* • Ann McCurdy, Exec. Dir., 102 Chestnut St., 50022, P 7,600, M 245, (712) 243-3017, Fax (712) 243-4404, atlanticchamber@a-m-u.net, www.atlanticiowa.com.

**Audubon** • *Audubon C/C* • Barbara Smith, Secy., 800 Market St., P.O. Box 66, 50025, P 2,382, M 153, (712) 563-3780, Fax (712) 563-3780, audchmbr@iowatelecom.net, www.auduboniowa.org

**Bagley** • *Guthrie Center C/C* • Donna Fuller, Secy., 2549 150th St., 50026, P 1,713, M 85, (641) 332-2218, Fax (641) 332-2693, donnanana6@yahoo.com, www.guthriecenter.com

**Bedford** • *Bedford Area Dev. Center* • Deann Hensley, Exec. Dir., 601 Madison, 50833, P 1,600, M 85, (712) 523-3637, Fax (712) 523-3384, bedfordareadc@frontiernet.net, www.bedford-iowa.com

**Bellevue** • *Bellevue Area C/C* • 210 N. Riverview, 52031, P 2,350, M 110, (563) 872-5830, Fax (563) 872-3611, chamber@bellevueia.com, www.bellevueia.com

**Belmond** • *Belmond Area C/C & Ind. Dev.* • 235 E. Main St., 50421, P 2,600, M 100, (641) 444-3937, Fax (641) 444-3944, www.belmond.com

**Bettendorf** • *Bettendorf C/C* • Bob Lundin, Pres./CEO, 2117 State St., 52722, P 32,500, M 650, (563) 355-4753, Fax (563) 344-4203, mitzi.hook@bettendorfchamber.com, www.bettendorfchamber.com.

**Bloomfield** • *Bloomfield Area C/C* • Shannon Harry, Ofc. Asst., P.O. Box 159, 52537, P 9,500, M 80, (641) 664-1726, shannon@daviscounty.org, www.daviscounty.org

**Boone** • *Boone Area C/C* • Richard Baker, Exec. Dir., 903 Story St., 50036, P 12,813, M 325, (515) 432-3342, (800) 266-6312, Fax (515) 432-3343, boonechamber@iowatelecom.net, www.booneiowa.com

**Britt** • *Britt C/C* • Sue Miller Taylor, Exec. Dir., P.O. Box 63, 50423, P 2,200, M 82, (641) 843-3867, brittcoc@wctatel.net, www.brittiowa.com

**Brooklyn** • *Brooklyn Eco. Dev. Group* • 138 Jackson St., P.O. Box 187, 52211, P 1,400, (641) 522-5300, Fax (641) 522-5584, brkchmbr@netins.net, www.brooklyniowa.com

**Burlington** • *Burlington/West Burlington Area C/C* • Dennis Hinkle, Pres./CEO, 610 N. 4th St., Ste. 200, 52601, P 30,000, M 600, (319) 752-6365, (800) 82-RIVER, Fax (319) 752-6454, info@growburlington.com, www.growburlington.com.

**Carroll** • *Carroll C/C* • Jim Gossett, Exec. Dir., 407 W. 5th St., P.O. Box 307, 51401, P 10,106, M 450, (712) 792-4383, Fax (712) 792-4384, chamber@carrolliowa.com, www.carrolliowa.com

**Cedar Falls** • *Greater Cedar Valley C/C* • Bob Justis, Pres./CEO, 10 Main St., 50613, P 36,000, M 850, (319) 266-3593, Fax (319) 277-4325, kassey@greatercedarvalleychamber.com, www.greatercedarvalleychamber.com

**Cedar Rapids** • *Cedar Rapids Area C/C* • Shannon Meyer, Pres., 424 First Ave. N.E., 52401, P 135,000, M 1,500, (319) 398-5317, Fax (319) 398-5228, chamber@cedarrapids.org, www.cedarrapids.org

**Centerville** • *Centerville-Rathbun Area C/C* • Joyce Bieber, Exec. Dir., 128 N. 12th St., 52544, P 14,000, M 250, (641) 437-4102, (800) 611-3800, Fax (641) 437-0527, chamber@centervilleia.com, www.centervilleia.com.

**Chariton** • *Chariton C/C* • Ruth Comer, Exec. Dir., 104 N. Grand, P.O. Box 735, 50049, P 5,000, M 200, (641) 774-4059, Fax (641) 774-2801, ccdc@iowatelecom.net, www.charitonchamber.com

**Charles City** • *Charles City Area C/C* • Veronica Litterer, Dir., 401 N. Main, 50616, P 8,000, M 240, (641) 228-4234, Fax (641) 228-4744, info@charlescitychamber.com, www.charlescity chamber.com.

**Cherokee** • *Cherokee C/C* • Julie Hering-Kent, Exec. Dir., 416 W. Main St., Ste. I, 51012, P 5,600, M 210, (712) 225-6414, Fax (712) 225-2803, citykechamber@evertek.net, www.cherokeeiowa chamber.com

**Clarinda** • *Clarinda C/C* • Elaine Farwell, Exec. Dir., 115 E. Main St., 51632, P 5,700, M 150, (712) 542-2166, Fax (712) 542-4113, chamber@clarinda.org, www.clarinda.org.

**Clarion** • *Clarion Partnership for Growth* • Jill Harrington, Exec. Dir., 302 S. Main, P.O. Box 6, 50525, P 2,950, M 225, (515) 532-2256, Fax (515) 532-2511, clchamb@goldfieldaccess.net, www.clarion-iowa.com

**Clear Lake** · *Clear Lake Area C/C* · Gary Bright, Exec. Dir., 205 Main Ave., P.O. Box 188, 50428, P 8,200, M 430, (641) 357-2159, (800) 285-5338, Fax (641) 357-8141, info@clearlakeiowa.com, www.clearlakeiowa.com.

**Clinton** · *Clinton Area C/C* · Julie Allesee, Pres., 721 S. 2nd St., P.O. Box 1024, 52733, P 27,772, M 600, (563) 242-5702, Fax (563) 242-5803, chamber@clintonia.com, www.clintonia.com

**Clive** · *see Des Moines*

**Colfax** · *Colfax C/C* · P.O. Box 62, 50054, P 2,500, M 40, (515) 674-4033, info@colfaxiowachamber.com, www.colfaxiowachamber.com

**Conrad** · *Conrad Chamber-Main Street Inc.* · Keith Graff, Treas., P.O. Box 414, 50621, P 1,055, M 60, (641) 366-2108, Fax (641) 366-2109, cmspd@heartofiowa.net, www.conrad.govoffice.com

**Corning** · *Adams Comm. C/C* · Stacie Hull, Exec. Dir., 710 Davis Ave., 50841, P 1,800, M 140, (641) 322-3243, Fax (641) 322-4387, adamschamber@frontiernet.net, adamscountyiowa.com

**Corydon** · *Chamber of Commerce Corydon & Allerton* · P.O. Box 435, 50060, P 2,300, M 94, (641) 872-1338

**Council Bluffs** · *Council Bluffs Area C/C* · Bob Mundt, Pres./CEO, 7 N. 6th St., P.O. Box 1565, 51502, P 61,000, M 800, (712) 325-1000, (800) 228-6878, Fax (712) 322-5698, chamber@councilbluffsiowa.com, www.councilbluffsiowa.com

**Cresco** · *Cresco Area C/C* · Randy Mashek, Exec. Dir., 101 Second Ave. S.W., P.O. Box 403, 52136, P 9,932, M 200, (563) 547-3434, Fax (563) 547-2056, crescochamber@yahoo.com, www.cresco chamber.com

**Creston** · *Creston C/C* · Ellen Gerharz, Exec. Dir., 208 W. Taylor, P.O. Box 471, 50801, P 8,100, M 250, (641) 782-7021, Fax (641) 782-9927, chamber@crestoniowachamber.com, www.creston iowachamber.com

**Dakota City** · *see Humboldt*

**Davenport** · *Davenport One* · Tara Barney, Pres./CEO, 130 W. 2nd St., 52801, P 100,000, M 1,400, (563) 322-1706, Fax (563) 322-7804, tbarney@davenportone.com, www.davenportone.com

**Decorah** · *Decorah Area C/C* · Nikki Brevig, Exec. Dir., 507 W. Water St., 52101, P 8,700, M 406, (563) 382-3990, (800) 463-4692, Fax (563) 382-5515, director@decorah-iowa.com, www.decoraharea.com

**Denison** · *Chamber & Dev. Cncl. of Crawford County* · Don Luensmann, Dir., 18 S. Main, 51442, P 7,300, M 240, (712) 263-5621, Fax (712) 263-4789, dluensmann@cdcia.org, www.cdcia.org

**Des Moines** · *Greater Des Moines Partnership* · Martha Willits, Pres./CEO, 700 Locust St., Ste. 100, 50309, P 534,399, M 4,000, (515) 286-4950, (800) 376-9059, Fax (515) 286-4974, info@desmoinesmetro.com, www.desmoinesmetro.com

**Dewitt** · *Dewitt C/C* · JoElla O'Connell, Exec. Dir., 1010 6th Ave., 52742, P 5,064, M 245, (563) 659-8500, Fax (563) 659-2410, info@dewitt.org, www.dewitt.org.

**Dubuque** · *Dubuque Area C/C* · Molly Grover, Pres./CEO, 300 Main St., Ste. 200, 52004, P 90,000, M 1,200, (563) 557-9200, (800) 798-4748, Fax (563) 557-1591, office@dubuquechamber.com, www.dubuquechamber.com.

**Durant** · *Durant C/C* · Heather Wiskow, Pres., P.O. Box 1111, 52747, P 2,000, M 100, (563) 785-6099, www.durantchamber.com

**Dyersville** · *Dyersville Area C/C* · Karla Thompson, Exec. Dir., 1100 16th Ave. Ct. S.E., 52040, P 4,000, M 290, (563) 875-2311, (866) 393-7784, Fax (563) 875-8391, dyersvillechamber@dyersville.org, www.dyersville.org.

**Eagle Grove** · *Eagle Grove Area C/C* · Janine Nance, Exec. Dir., 120 N. Lucas, P.O. Box 2, 50533, P 3,700, M 175, (515) 448-4821, Fax (515) 448-4821, chamber@eaglegrove.com, www.eaglegrove.com

**Eldora** · *Greater Eldora C/C Inc.* · P.O. Box 303, 50627, P 3,038, M 57, (641) 939-3000, president@eldorachamber.com, www.eldorachamber.com

**Eldridge** · *Eldridge-North Scott C/C* · Carolyn Scheibe, Exec. Dir., 220 W. Davenport St., 52748, P 9,000, M 190, (563) 285-9965, Fax (563) 285-9964, info@northscottchamber.com, www.northscottchamber.com

**Elkader** · *Elkader Area C/C* · Mary Harstad, Exec. Secy., 207 N. Main, P.O. Box 599, 52043, P 1,600, M 85, (563) 245-2857, Fax (563) 245-2857, elkader@alpinecom.net, www.elkader-iowa.com

**Emmetsburg** · *Emmetsburg C/C* · Cecilia Miller, Exec. Dir., 1121 Broadway, 50536, P 4,000, M 150, (712) 852-2283, Fax (712) 852-2156, eburgchamber@kemb.org, www.emmetsburg.com

**Essex** · *Essex C/C-Comm. Club* · Dana Wensterand, Exec. Dir., .O. Box 334, 51638, P 884, M 160, (712) 586-4541

**Estherville** · *Estherville Area C/C* · Mrs. Dustin Embree, Exec. Dir., 620 First Ave. S., 51334, P 6,656, M 170, (712) 362-3541, Fax (712) 362-7742, echamber@ncn.net, www.estherville.org

**Fairfield** · *Fairfield Area C/C* · Brent Willett, Exec. Dir., 204 W. Broadway, 52556, P 15,500, M 360, (641) 472-2111, Fax (641) 472-6510, chamber@fairfieldiowa.com, www.fairfieldiowa.com

**Fayette** · *Fayette Betterment Found.* · Deb Boike, Pres., P.O. Box 94, 52142, P 1,351, M 20, (566) 425-3672, pmmurphy03@hotmail.com, www.fayetteia.com

**Forest City** · *Forest City Area C/C* · Kathy Rollefson, Exec. Dir., 145 East K St., 50436, P 4,300, M 165, (641) 585-2092, Fax (641) 585-2687, chamber1@wctatel.net, www.forestcityia.com

**Fort Dodge** · *Fort Dodge Area C/C* · Amy Bruno, Exec. Dir., 1406 Central Ave., P.O. Box T, 50501, P 26,309, M 575, (515) 955-5500, Fax (515) 955-3245, info@fortdodgechamber.com, www.fortdodgechamber.com

**Fort Madison** · *Fort Madison Area C/C* · Kirk Butler, Pres., 614 9th St., P.O. Box 277, 52627, P 11,500, M 284, (319) 372-5471, Fax (319) 372-6404, chamber@fortmadison.com, www.fortmadison.com

**Garner** · *Garner C/C* · Lisa Formanek, Exec. Dir., 211 State St., 50438, P 3,000, M 140, (641) 923-3993, Fax (641) 923-3993, chamber@qwestoffice.net, www.garneriachamber.com

**George** · *George C/C* · Arlyce Elias, Secy., 105 S. Main, 51237, P 1,100, M 65, (712) 475-2870, (712) 475-3612, www.george iowa.com

**Glenwood** · *Glenwood Area C/C & Glenwood/Mills County Eco. Dev. Found.* · Linda Washburn, Exec. Dir., 32 1/2 N. Walnut St., 51534, P 15,500, M 150, (712) 527-3298, Fax (712) 527-4349, glenwoodia@qwestoffice.net, www.glenwoodia.com

**Greenfield** · *Greenfield C/C* · Ginny Kuhfus, Exec. Dir., 201 S. First St., P.O. Box 61, 50849, P 2,195, M 146, (641) 743-8444, Fax (641) 743-8205, grfld_cc_ms_dev@iowatelecom.net, www.greenfieldiowa.com

**Grimes** · *Grimes Chamber & Eco. Dev.* · Brian Buethe, Exec. Dir., 101 N. Harvey, 50111, P 7,500, M 138, (515) 986-5770, Fax (515) 986-5776, brianb@ci.grimes.ia.us, www.grimesiowa.com

**Grinnell** · *Grinnell Area C/C* · Angela Harrington, Exec. Dir., 833 4th Ave., P.O. Box 538, 50112, P 9,300, M 280, (641) 236-6555, Fax (641) 236-3499, exec@grinnellchamber.org, www.grinnellchamber.org

**Griswold** · *Griswold C/C* · Janet Taylor, Pres., P.O. Box 376, 51535, P 1,200, M 80, (712) 778-2615, www.griswoldia.com

**Grundy Center** • *Grundy Center Chamber & Dev.* • Melanie Kirkpatrick & Kelly Riskedahl, Co-Dirs., 705 F Ave., 50638, P 2,700, M 150, (319) 825-3838, Fax (319) 825-6471, chamber@gcmuni. net, www.grundycenter.com

**Guthrie Center** • *see Bagley*

**Guttenberg** • *Naturally Guttenberg Inc.* • 323 S. River Park Dr., P.O. Box 536, 52052, P 2,000, M 75, (563) 252-2323, (877) 252-2323, Fax (563) 252-2378, guttenberg@alpinecom.net, www. guttenbergiowa.net

**Hampton** • *Hampton Area C/C* • Jennifer Gruelke, Exec. Dir., 5 First St. S.W., 50441, P 4,200, M 200, (641) 456-5668, Fax (641) 456-5660, hacc@hamptoniowa.org, www.hamptoniowa.org.

**Harlan** • *Shelby County C/C* • Dawn Cundiff, Dir., 1101 7th St., 51537, P 13,000, M 195, (712) 755-2114, (888) 876-1774, Fax (712) 755-2115, info@exploreshelbycounty.com, www. exploreshelbycounty.com

**Hartley** • *Hartley C/C* • Cindy Hennings, Pres., 56 2nd St. S.E., P.O. Box 146, 51346, P 1,733, M 75, (712) 928-4278, hartleychamber@ tcaexpress.net, www.hartleyiowa.com

**Hawarden** • *Hawarden Area Partnership for Progress* • Cathie Brown, Dir., 1150 Central Ave., 51023, P 2,500, M 100, (712) 551-4433, Fax (712) 551-4439, happ@cityofhawarden.com, www. happ-online.com

**Holstein** • *Holstein C/C* • 119 S. Main St., 51025, P 1,500, M 35, (712) 368-4898, holstein@netllc.net, www.holsteinchamber.com

**Hudson** • *Hudson C/C* • Mary Bucy, Pres., P.O. Box 493, 50643, P 2,117, M 53, (319) 988-4217, admin@hudsoniachamber.org, www.hudsoniachamber.org

**Humboldt** • *Humboldt-Dakota City C/C* • Tonya Harklau, Exec. Dir., 29 5th St. S., P.O. Box 247, 50548, P 5,000, M 150, (515) 332-1481, Fax (515) 332-1496, chamber@goldfieldaccess.net, www. ci.humboldt.ia.us

**Ida Grove** • *Ida Grove C/C* • Joan Bengford, Pres., 218 Main St., P.O. Box 252, 51445, P 2,500, M 100, (712) 364-3404, Fax (712) 364-2945, idagrovechamber@frontiernet.net, www.idagrove chamber.com

**Independence** • *Independence Area C/C* • Tammy Rasmussen, Dir., 112 1st St. E., P.O. Box 104, 50644, P 6,100, M 205, (319) 334-7178, Fax (319) 334-7394, indycommerce@indytel.com, www. indycommerce.com

**Indianola** • *Indianola C/C* • Denise Day, Exec. Dir., 515 N. Jefferson, Ste. D, 50125, P 14,000, M 270, (515) 961-6269, (866) 961-6269, Fax (515) 961-9753, chamber@indianolachamber.com, www.indianolachamber.com.

**Iowa City** • *Iowa City Area C/C* • Nancy Quellhorst, Pres., 325 E. Washington St., Ste. 100, 52240, P 114,000, M 1,000, (319) 337-9637, Fax (319) 338-9958, info@iowacityarea.com, www.iowacityarea.com

**Iowa Falls** • *Iowa Falls C of C/Main St.* • Diana Thies, Exec. Dir., 520 Rocksylvania, 50126, P 5,200, M 170, (641) 648-5549, Fax (641) 648-3702, chamber@iafalls.com, www.iowafallschamber.com

**Jefferson** • *Jefferson Area C/C* • Amy Milligan, Exec. Dir., 220 N. Chestnut St., 50129, P 4,626, M 175, (515) 386-2155, Fax (515) 386-2156, chamber@jeffersoniowa.com, gojacc.com

**Jesup** • *Jesup C/C* • Todd Rohlfsen, Pres., P.O. Box 592, 50648, P 2,212, M 62, (319) 827-3100, (319) 827-1522, Fax (319) 827-3510, www.jesupiowa.com

**Johnston** • *Johnston C/C* • Heather Wilcox, Admin., P.O. Box 61, 50131, P 14,000, M 250, (515) 276-9064, Fax (515) 309-0144, heather@growjohnston.com, www.johnstonchamber.com

**Kalona** • *Kalona Area C/C* • 514 B Ave., P.O. Box 615, 52247, P 2,300, M 85, (319) 656-2660, chamber@kctc.net, www.kalonachamber.com

**Keokuk** • *Keokuk Area C/C* • Katie O'Brien, Exec. Dir., 329 Main St., 52632, P 11,747, M 270, (319) 524-5055, Fax (319) 524-5016, www.keokukchamber.com

**Knoxville** • *Discover Knoxville Growth Alliance* • Roxanne Johnson, Exec. Dir., 309 E. Main St., 50138, P 8,270, M 275, (641) 828-7555, Fax (641) 828-7978, discoverknoxville@iowatelecom. net, discoverknoxville.com

**La Motte** • *see Bellevue*

**La Porte City** • *La Porte City C/C* • P.O. Box 82, 50651, P 2,500, M 35, (319) 342-3396, www.laportecityia.com

**Lake City** • *Lake City Betterment Assoc.* • Jenifer Villhauer, Dir., 700 N. Woodlawn, 51449, P 2,000, M 104, (712) 464-7611, lakecitybett@iowatelecom.net, www.lakecityiowa.com

**Lake Mills** • *Lake Mills Chamber Dev. Corp.* • Marilyn Hoffman, Exec. Dir., 203 N. 1st Ave. W., P.O. Box 182, 50450, P 2,140, M 120, (641) 592-5253, Fax (641) 592-5252, lmcdc@wctatel.net, www. lakemillsiowa.com

**Laurens** • *Laurens C/C* • Bill Mather, Pres., P.O. Box 33, 50554, P 1,500, M 50, (712) 845-2620, Fax (712) 845-2544, www. laurens-ia.com

**Le Claire** • *Le Claire C/C* • Lane Bleeker, Pres., P.O. Box 35, 52753, P 3,000, M 135, (563) 289-9970, info@leclairechamber.com, www.leclairechamber.com

**LeMars** • *LeMars Area C/C* • Neal Adler, Exec. Dir., 50 Central Ave. S.E., 51031, P 9,500, M 227, (712) 546-8821, Fax (712) 546-7218, lemarschamber@frontiernet.net, www.lemarsiowa.com

**Lenox** • *Lenox C/C* • Michelle Tullberg, Coord., 200 1/2 S. Main St., 50851, P 1,400, M 70, (641) 333-4272, lenoxchamber@frontiernet. net, www.lenoxia.com

**Leon** • *Leon C/C* • Laura Langholtz-Hill, Pres., c/o Leon City Hall, 50144, P 2,000, M 60, (641) 446-6221

**Lisbon** • *see Mount Vernon*

**Logan** • *Logan C/C* • Nikki Allen, P.O. Box 113, 51546, P 1,500, M 50, (712) 644-2280, Fax (712) 644-3124, www.loganiowa.com

**Manchester** • *Manchester Area C/C* • Jack Klaus, Exec. Dir., 200 E. Main St., 52057, P 5,300, M 200, (563) 927-4141, Fax (563) 927-2958, macc@manchesteriowa.org, www.manchesteriowa.org

**Manning** • *Manning C/C* • Dixon Cole, Pres., P.O. Box 345, 51455, P 1,500, M 58, (712) 655-3541, Fax (712) 655-2478, chamber@ mmctsu.com, www.manningia.com

**Manson** • *Manson Eco. Dev. Corp. and C/C* • Pat Essing, Secy., P.O. Box 561, 50563, P 2,000, M 35, (712) 469-3311, Fax (712) 469-3311, mansoniowa.com

**Maquoketa** • *Maquoketa Area C/C* • Cheryl Clark, Admin. Asst., 117 S. Main, 52060, P 6,100, M 210, (563) 652-4602, Fax (563) 652-3020, maqchamberassist@qwestoffice.net, www.maquoke-tachamber.com.

**Marengo** • *Marengo C/C* • P.O. Box 251, 52301, P 2,500, M 35, (319) 642-5506, www.marengoiowa.com

**Marion** • *Marion C/C* • Jill Hanna, Pres., 1225 6th Ave. #100, 52302, P 32,000, M 210, (319) 377-6316, Fax (319) 377-1576, chamber@marioncc.org, www.marioncc.org

**Marquette** • *see McGregor*

**Marshalltown** • *Marshalltown Area C/C* • Ken Anderson, Pres., 709 S. Center St., P.O. Box 1000, 50158, P 39,311, M 469, (641) 753-6645, Fax (641) 752-8373, kanderson@marshalltown.org, www.marshalltown.org.

**Mason City** · *Mason City Area C/C* · Robin Anderson, Exec. Dir., 25 W. State, Ste. B, 50401, P 30,000, M 655, (641) 423-5724, Fax (641) 423-5725, chamber@masoncityia.com, www.masoncityia.com

**McGregor** · *McGregor/Marquette C/C* · Sasha Dull, Exec. Dir., 146 Main St., P.O. Box 105, 52157, P 1,200, M 100, (563) 873-2186, (800) 896-0910, Fax (563) 873-2847, mac-marq@alpinecom.net, www.mcgreg-marq.org

**Milford** · *see Arnolds Park*

**Missouri Valley** · *Missouri Valley C/C* · Jeff Snyder, Exec. Dir., 100 S. 4th St., P.O. Box 130, 51555, P 3,000, M 132, (712) 642-2553, Fax (712) 642-3771, chamberofcommerce1@juno.com, www.missourivalleychamber.com

**Monona** · *Monona C/C* · P.O. Box 191, 52159, P 1,550, M 9, (563) 539-2355, mononachamber@hotmail.com

**Monticello** · *Monticello Area C/C* · Andrea Hunter, Pres., 204 E. 1st St., 52310, P 3,600, M 155, (319) 465-5626, Fax (319) 465-3527, chamber@macc-ia.us, www.macc-ia.us

**Mount Ayr** · *Mount Ayr C/C* · Sheila Shafer, Pres., P.O. Box 445, 50854, P 1,700, M 100, (641) 464-3704

**Mount Pleasant** · *Mount Pleasant Area Chamber Alliance* · Kiley Miller, Exec. V.P., 124 S. Main St., 52641, P 9,000, M 319, (319) 385-3101, (877) 385-3103, Fax (319) 385-3012, mpaca@mountpleasantiowa.org, www.mountpleasantiowa.org

**Mount Vernon** · *Mount Vernon-Lisbon Comm. Dev. Group* · Kristy SeBlonka, Dir., 311 First St. W., P.O. Box 31, 52314, P 6,000, M 135, (319) 895-8214, (319) 210-9935, kristy@visitmvl.com, www.visitmvl.com

**Muscatine** · *Greater Muscatine C/C & Ind.* · Bill Phelan, Pres./CEO, 102 Walnut St., 52761, P 24,000, M 400, (563) 263-8895, Fax (563) 263-7662, chamber@muscatine.com, www.muscatine.com

**Nevada** · *Nevada C/C* · Sara Clausen, Exec. Dir., 1015 6th St., 50201, P 6,658, M 180, (515) 382-6538, (800) 558-2288, Fax (515) 382-3803, chamber@midiowa.net, www.nevadaiowa.org

**New Hampton** · *New Horizons Chamber-MainStreet* · Jeannine Burgart, Exec. Dir., 15 W. Main, 50659, P 3,800, M 250, (641) 394-2021, nhc@iowatelecom.net, www.newhamptoniowa.com

**New London** · *New London C/C* · 213 W. Main St., 52645, P 1,937, M 50, (319) 367-2573

**Newton** · *Greater Newton Area C/C* · Annette West, Exec. Dir., 113 First Ave. W., 50208, P 15,311, M 200, (641) 792-5545, Fax (641) 791-0879, annettew@pcpartner.net, www.experiencenewton.com

**Northwood** · *Northwood Area C/C* · P.O. Box 71, 50459, P 2,000, M 85, (641) 324-1420, info@northwoodchamber.org, www.northwoodchamber.org

**Norwalk** · *Norwalk Area C/C* · Deb Mineart, Exec. Dir., P.O. Box 173, 50211, P 8,300, M 125, (515) 981-0619, Fax (515) 981-1890, norwalkchamber@msn.com, www.norwalkchamber.org

**Oelwein** · *Oelwein Chamber & Area Dev.* · Sally Falb, Exec. Dir., 25 W. Charles St., 50662, P 6,722, M 250, (319) 283-1105, Fax (319) 283-2890, ocad@oelwein.com, www.oelwein.com

**Okoboji** · *see Arnolds Park*

**Onawa** · *Onawa C/C* · Kevin Brandt, Pres., 707 Iowa Ave., 51040, P 3,000, M 100, (712) 423-1801, Fax (712) 433-4622, chamber@onawa.com, www.onawa.com

**Orange City** · *Orange City C/C* · Mike Hofman, Exec. Dir., 509 8th St. S.E., P.O. Box 36, 51041, P 6,200, M 260, (712) 707-4510, Fax (712) 707-4523, occhamberexec@orangecitycomm.net, www.orangecityiowa.com.

**Osage** · *Osage C/C* · Wendy Heuton, Exec. Dir., 808 Main St., 50461, P 3,500, M 120, (641) 732-3163, Fax (641) 732-3163, chamber@osage.net, www.osage.net/~chamber/

**Osceola** · *Osceola C/C* · Todd Thompson, Pres., 115 E. Washington, P.O. Box 425, 50213, P 4,700, M 155, (641) 342-4200, Fax (641) 342-6353, ocms@iowatelecom.net, osceolachamber.com

**Oskaloosa** · *Oskaloosa Area Chamber & Dev. Group* · Jon Sullivan, Dir., 124 N. Market St., 52577, P 21,522, M 300, (641) 672-2591, Fax (641) 672-2047, oskycofc@oacdg.org, www.oskaloosachamber.org

**Ottumwa** · *Ottumwa Area C/C* · Terry McNitt, Exec. Dir., 217 E. Main St., P.O. Box 308, 52501, P 35,000, M 400, (641) 682-3465, Fax (641) 682-3466, info@ottumwaiowa.com, www.ottumwaiowa.com

**Panora** · *Panora C/C* · Gayle Schackelford, Pres., P.O. Box 73, 50216, P 1,175, M 120, (641) 755-3300, train@netins.net, www.panora.org/chamber.html

**Parkersburg** · *Parkersburg C/C* · Norma Junker, Pres., 407 Coates, P.O. Box 565, 50665, P 1,900, M 75, (319) 346-1147

**Pella** · *Pella C/C* · Karen Eischen IOM, Exec. Dir., 518 Franklin St., 50219, P 10,000, M 300, (641) 628-2626, (888) 746-3882, Fax (641) 628-9697, pellacoc@pella.org, www.pella.org

**Perry** · *Perry C/C* · Wendy Goodale, Exec. Dir., 1102 Willis Ave., 50220, P 8,000, M 160, (515) 465-4601, Fax (515) 465-2256, perrychmbr@aol.com, www.perryia.org

**Pleasant Hill** · *Pleasant Hill C/C* · Carolyn Wilkins, Exec. Dir., 5160 Maple Dr., Ste. C, 50327, P 7,000, M 185, (515) 261-0466, phillchamber@qwestoffice.net, www.pleasanthillchamber.org

**Pleasantville** · *Pleasantville C/C* · 104 E. Monroe St., P.O. Box 672, 50225, P 1,600, M 50, (515) 848-3903, pleasantcc@iowatelecom.net, www.therealpleasantville.com

**Pocahontas** · *Pocahontas C/C* · Kelly Otto, Pres., P.O. Box 125, 50574, P 1,970, M 100, (712) 335-4775, chamber@pocahontasiowa.com, www.pocahontasiowa.com

**Rathbun** · *see Centerville*

**Red Oak** · *Red Oak C/C* · Jodie Smith, Interim Dir., 307 E. Reed St., 51566, P 6,000, M 240, (712) 623-4821, Fax (712) 623-4822, execdir@redoakiowa.com, www.redoakiowa.com.

**Remsen** · *Remsen C/C* · Karen Harnack, Secy./Treas., P.O. Box 225, 51050, P 1,700, M 100, (712) 786-2136, (712) 786-2416, chamber@remseniowa.net, www.remseniowa.net

**Rock Rapids** · *Rock Rapids Comm. Affairs Corp.* · Angie Jager, Exec. Dir., 206 1st Ave., P.O. Box 403, 51246, P 2,600, M 150, (712) 472-3456, Fax (712) 472-2764, chamber@rockrapids.com, www.rockrapids.com

**Rock Valley** · *Rock Valley C/C* · Curt Strouth, Exec. Dir., 1507 Main St., P.O. Box 89, 51247, P 3,000, M 94, (712) 476-9300, Fax (712) 476-9116, www.cityofrockvalley.com

**Rockwell** · *Rockwell C/C* · P.O. Box 156, 50469, P 1,000, M 35, (641) 822-4906, www.rockwell-ia.org

**Rockwell City** · *Rockwell City Chamber and Dev.* · Alyson Dietrich, Coord., 3012 270th St., 50579, P 1,900, M 80, (712) 297-8874, rcdev@iowatelecom.net, www.rockwellcity.com

**Sac City** · *Chamber-Main Street Sac City* · Laura Zimmerman, Prog. Dir., 615 W. Main St., 50583, P 2,516, M 150, (712) 662-7316, Fax (712) 662-7399, saccitymainstreet@prairieinet.net, www.saccity.org

**Saint Ansgar** · *Saint Ansgar C/C* · P.O. Box 133, 50472, P 1,100, M 60, (641) 736-4444, www.stansgar.org

**Saint Donatus** • *see Bellevue*

**Schaller** • *Schaller C/C* • Theresa Bailey, Secy./Treas., 1635 250th St., 51053, P 850, M 55, (712) 275-4251

**Sheldon** • *Sheldon Chamber & Dev. Corp.* • Mark Gaul, Exec. Dir., 416 9th St., P.O. Box 276, 51201, P 5,000, M 208, (712) 324-2813, Fax (712) 324-4602, mgaul@sheldoniowa.com, www. sheldoniowa.com

**Shenandoah** • *Shenandoah Chamber & Ind. Org.* • Gregg Connell, Exec. V.P., 100 S. Maple St., 51601, P 6,000, M 300, (712) 246-3455, Fax (712) 246-3456, chamber@simplyshenandoah.com, www.shenandoahiowa.net

**Sibley** • *Sibley C/C* • Carissa Janssen, Exec. Dir., 838 3rd Ave., 51249, P 2,800, M 120, (712) 754-3212, Fax (712) 754-3212, chamber@hickorytech.net, www.sibleyiowa.net

**Sidney** • *Sidney C/C* • Mike Ross, Pres., 400 Clay St., P.O. Box 401, 51652, P 1,300, M 60, (712) 374-3339, chamber@sidneyia.net, www.sidneyia.net

**Sioux Center** • *Sioux Center C/C* • Ardith Lein, Exec. Dir., 303 N. Main Ave., 51250, P 6,750, M 195, (712) 722-3457, Fax (712) 722-3465, scchambr@mtcnet.net, www.siouxcenterchamber.com

**Sioux City** • *Siouxland C/C* • Debi Durham, Pres., 101 Pierce St., 51101, P 143,000, M 1,000, (712) 255-7903, Fax (712) 258-7578, chamber@siouxlandchamber.com, www.siouxlandchamber.com

**Spencer** • *Spencer C/C* • Robert Rose, Exec. Dir., 122 W. 5th St., P.O. Box 7937, 51301, P 12,000, M 500, (712) 262-5680, Fax (712) 262-5747, spencerchamber@smunet.net, spenceriowa chamber.org.

**THE WORLD'S GREATEST COUNTY FAIR–"CLAY COUNTY FAIR" HELD EACH SEPTEMBER. ANNUAL FLAGFEST CELEBRATION AND FLY-IN BREAKFAST EACH JUNE.**

**Spirit Lake** • *Spirit Lake Mainsail C/C* • Blain Andera, Dir., 1710 Lincoln Ave., P.O. Box 155, 51360, P 5,000, M 160, (712) 336-4978, Fax (712) 336-4978, mainsail@mchsi.com, www.slmainsail.com.

**Storm Lake** • *Storm Lake C of C & Area Dev. Corp.* • Gary Lalone, Exec. Dir., 119 W. 6th St., P.O. Box 584, 50588, P 101,500, M 275, (712) 732-3780, (888) 572-4692, Fax (712) 732-1511, slc@stormlake.org, www.stormlakechamber.com

**Story City** • *Story City Greater Chamber Connection* • Carolyn Honeycutt, Exec. Dir., 602 Broad St., 50248, P 3,300, (515) 733-4214, Fax (515) 733-4504, chamber@storycity.net, www.storycity.net

**Strawberry Point** • *Strawberry Point C/C* • Dana Rowcliff, Secy., P.O. Box 404, 52076, P 1,368, M 60, (563) 933-2081

**Stuart** • *Stuart C/C* • Pat Sargent, Pres., 119 E. Front St., 50250, P 1,800, M 40, (515) 778-1569, (515) 523-1455, www.stuart ia.com

**Sumner** • *Sumner Commercial Club* • P.O. Box 262, 50674, P 3,000, M 65, (563) 578-5470

**Tama** • *see Toledo*

**Tipton** • *Tipton C/C* • John Todd, Comm. Dev. Dir., P.O. Box 5, 52772, P 3,200, M 100, (563) 886-6350, cddirector@iowatelecom. net, www.tiptoniowa.us

**Toledo** • *Tama-Toledo Area C/C* • Carolyn Dolezal, Coord., 103 S. Church St., P.O. Box 367, 52342, P 5,000, M 110, (641) 484-6661, tama.toledochamber@yahoo.com, www.tamatoledo.com

**Traer** • *Traer C/C* • Dahn Kennedy, Pres., P.O. Box 431, 50675, P 1,700, M 80, (319) 478-2346, Fax (319) 478-2346, traer chamber@hotmail.com, www.traer.com

**Tripoli** • *Tripoli Comm. Club* • Jay Ranard, Pres., P.O. Box 76, 50676, P 1,310, M 40, (319) 882-3002, n.ranard@butler-bremer.com

**Urbandale** • *Urbandale C/C* • Tiffany Menke IOM, Exec. Dir., 2900 Justin Dr., Ste. L, 50322, P 35,904, M 575, (515) 331-6855, Fax (515) 331-2987, info@urbandalechamber.com, www.uniquely urbandale.com

**Villisca** • *Villisca C/C* • Mr. Gayle Heard, Treas., 601 S. 3rd Ave., 50864, P 1,332, M 32, (712) 826-5222

**Vinton** • *Vinton Unlimited* • 310 A Ave., P.O. Box 387, 52349, P 5,500, M 220, (319) 472-3955, Fax (319) 472-4456, info@ vintonia.org, www.vintonia.org

**Washington** • *Washington C/C* • Tim Coffey, 205 W. Main St., 52353, P 7,200, M 235, (319) 653-3272, Fax (319) 653-5805, washcofc@iowatelecom.net, www.washingtoniowachamber.com

**Waterloo** • *Greater Cedar Valley C/C* • Bob Justis, Pres./CEO, 315 E. 5th St., 50703, P 68,747, M 850, (319) 233-8431, Fax (319) 233-4580, bob@greatercedarvalleychamber.com, www.greatercedar valleychamber.com

**Waukee** • *Waukee Area C/C* • Chad Airhart, Exec. Dir., 230 W. Hickman Rd., P.O. Box 23, 50263, P 9,500, M 200, (515) 978-7115, Fax (515) 987-1845, info@waukeechamber.com, www.waukee chamber.com

**Waukon** • *Waukon C/C* • Danny Schlitter, Exec. Dir., 101 W. Main St., 52172, P 4,800, M 165, (563) 568-4110, Fax (563) 568-6990, waukoncc@mchsi.com, www.waukon.org.

**Waverly** • *Waverly C/C* • Kelly Engelken, Exec. Dir., 118 E. Bremer Ave., 50677, P 9,000, M 200, (319) 352-4526, (800) 251-0360, Fax (319) 352-0136, waverly@waverlychamber.com, www. waverlyia.com.

**Webster City** • *Webster City Area Dev.* • Carrie Fitzgerald, Chamber Dir., 628 2nd St., P.O. Box 310, 50595, P 8,100, M 147, (515) 832-2564, Fax (515) 832-5130, info@webstercity-iowa.com, www.webstercity-iowa.com

**West Bend** • *West Bend C/C* • Tina Banwart, Secy., P.O. Box 366, 50597, P 834, M 45, (515) 887-2181, chamber@westbendiowa. com, www.westbendiowa.com

**West Des Moines** • *West Des Moines C/C* • Linda Hulleman, Exec. Dir., 4200 Mills Civic Pkwy., P.O. Box 65320, 50265, P 53,000, M 650, (515) 225-6009, Fax (515) 225-7129, info@wdmchamber. org, www.wdmchamber.org

**West Liberty** • *West Liberty C/C* • 405 N. Elm St., 52776, P 3,300, M 90, (319) 627-4876, Fax (319) 627-3087, wlchambr@ lcom.net

**West Union** • *West Union C/C* • Robin Bostrom, Exec. Dir., 101 N. Vine St., 52175, P 2,500, M 100, (563) 422-3070, Fax (563) 422-6322, wuchamber@alpinecom.net, www.westunion.com

**Williamsburg** • *Williamsburg C/C* • Barb Hopp, Exec. Asst., 208 W. State St., P.O. Box 982, 52361, P 2,700, M 100, (319) 668-1500, Fax (319) 668-9112, www.williamsburgiowa.org

**Wilton** • *Wilton C/C* • Eva Belitz, Exec. V.P., 118 W. 4th St., P.O. Box 280, 52778, P 2,900, M 110, (563) 732-2330, Fax (563) 732-2332, wiltoncc@netwtc.net, www.wiltoniowa.org

**Winfield** • *Winfield C/C* • Klay Edwards, Pres., P.O. Box H, 52659, P 1,131, M 30, (319) 257-3305

**Winterset** • *Madison County C/C* • 73 Jefferson St., 50273, P 15,000, M 175, (515) 462-1185, (800) 298-6119, Fax (515) 462-1393, chamber@madisoncounty.com, www.madisoncounty.com

# Kansas

**Kansas C of C** · 835 S.W. Topeka Blvd., Topeka, 66612, P 2,500,000, M 10,000, (785) 357-6321, Fax (785) 357-4732, info@kansaschamber.org, www.kansaschamber.org

**Abilene** · *Abilene Area C/C* · 500 Buckeye, 67410, P 6,800, M 275, (785) 263-1770, Fax (785) 263-1536, visitus1@sbcglobal. net, www.abileneks.com

**Alma** · *Alma C/C* · Trish Ringel, Secy., P.O. Box 234, 66401, P 900, M 45, (785) 765-3327, Fax (785) 765-3384

**Alta Vista** · *Alta Vista C/C* · Brier Kormanik, V.P., P.O. Box 115, 66834, P 500, M 20, (785) 499-5588

**Andover** · *Andover Area C/C* · Scott Wilson, Pres., 1607 E. Central, P.O. Box 339, 67002, P 9,500, M 150, (316) 733-0648, Fax (316) 733-8808, info@andoverchamber.com, www.andover chamber.com

**Anthony** · *Anthony C/C* · Gwen Warner, Exec. Dir., 227 W. Main, P.O. Box 354, 67003, P 2,400, M 160, (620) 842-5456, Fax (620) 842-3929, info@anthonychamber.com, www.anthonychamber.com

**Arkansas City** · *Arkansas City Area C/C* · Janet Siebert IOM, Pres./CEO, 106 S. Summit, P.O. Box 795, 67005, P 12,000, M 500, (620) 442-0230, Fax (620) 441-0048, ac-ceo@arkcitychamber.org, www.arkcity.org.

**Ashland** · *Ashland C/C* · P.O. Box 37, 67831, P 1,032, M 50, (620) 635-0427, (620) 635-2531, aac@ashlandks.com, www. ashlandks.com

**Atchison** · *Atchison Area C/C* · Jacque Pregont, Pres., 200 S. 10th St., P.O. Box 126, 66002, P 10,300, M 385, (913) 367-2427, (800) 234-1854, Fax (913) 367-2485, president@atchisonkansas. net, www.atchisonkansas.net

**Atwood** · *Atwood C/C* · Sarah Green, Exec. Dir., 303 Main St., P.O. Box 152, 67730, P 1,554, M 82, (785) 626-9630, atwood chamber@rawlinscounty.info, www.atwoodkansas.com

**Augusta** · *Augusta C/C & Conv. & Tourism Bur.* · Sharon Sudduth, Exec. Dir., 112 E. 6th Ave., 67010, P 8,500, M 160, (316) 775-6339, Fax (316) 775-1307, augustacoc@sbcglobal.net, www. chamberofaugusta.org

**Baldwin City** · *Baldwin City C/C* · 720 High St., P.O. Box 501, 66006, P 3,900, M 160, (785) 594-3200, info@baldwincity.com, www.baldwincitychamber.com

**Basehor** · *Basehor C/C* · Gayle Runnels, Pres., P.O. Box 35, 66007, P 2,700, (913) 724-9000, info@basehorchamber.org, www. basehorchamber.org

**Baxter Springs** · *Baxter Springs C/C* · 1004 Military Ave., 66713, P 5,000, M 110, (620) 856-3131, Fax (620) 856-3185, chamberdirector@baxtersprings.us, www.baxtersprings.us

**Belle Plaine** · *Belle Plaine Area C/C* · P.O. Box 721, 67013, P 1,800, M 36, (620) 488-2604, Fax (620) 488-3517, www.belle plainechamber.com

**Belleville** · *Belleville Area C/C* · Melinda Pierson, Dir., 1309 18th St., P.O. Box 280, 66935, P 2,239, M 100, (785) 527-5524, Fax (785) 527-5524, bellevcham@nckcn.com, www.bellevilleks.org

**Beloit** · *Beloit Area C/C* · 123 N. Mill, P.O. Box 582, 67420, P 4,100, M 162, (785) 738-2717, beloitchamber@nckcn.com, www.beloitchamberofcommerce.com

**Bird City** · *Bird City Comm. Club* · Jane Brubaker, P.O. Box 219, 67731, P 500, M 30, (785) 734-2616, www.birdcity.com

**Blue Rapids** · *Blue Rapids C/C* · P.O. Box 253, 66411, P 1,135, M 65, (785) 363-7991, bluerapidschamberofcommerce@yahoo. com, skyways.lib.ks.us/towns/BlueRapids

**Bonner Springs** · *Bonner Springs-Edwardsville Area C/C* · Charlene A. Biles, Exec. V.P./Exec. Secy., 129 N. Nettleton, P.O. Box 403, 66012, P 14,000, M 160, (913) 422-5044, Fax (913) 441-1366, www.lifeisbetter.org

**Burlingame** · *Burlingame Area C/C* · Kathy Kraus, Secy., P.O. Box 102, 66413, P 1,003, M 20, (785) 654-3322, www. burlingameks.gov

**Burlington** · *Coffey County C/C* · Kenda Rose, Exec. Dir., 110 N. 4th, 66839, P 9,000, M 135, (620) 364-2002, (877) 364-2002, Fax (620) 364-3048, www.coffeycountychamber.com

**Caldwell** · *Caldwell Area C/C* · LuAnn Jamison, Secy., P.O. Box 42, 67022, P 1,300, M 54, (620) 845-6666, (620) 845-2444, www. caldwellkansas.com

**Caney** · *Caney C/C* · Jackie Freisberg, Pres., 312 W. Fourth Ave., P.O. Box 211, 67333, P 2,300, M 85, (620) 879-5131, www.caney.com

**Canton** · *Canton C/C* · Bernard Rundstrum, Pres., 104 W. Allen, P.O. Box 275, 67428, P 800, M 25, (620) 628-4916, skyways.lib. ks.us/towns/Canton

**Cedar Vale** · *Cedar Vale C/C* · Priscilla Melton, P.O. Box 112, 67024, P 740, M 30, (620) 758-2244, (620) 758-2465

**Chanute** · *Chanute Area C/C & Ofc. of Tourism* · Jane Brophy, Exec. Dir., 21 N. Lincoln Ave., P.O. Box 747, 66720, P 10,000, M 400, (620) 431-3350, (877) 431-3350, Fax (620) 431-7770, director@ chanutechamber.com, www.chanutechamber.com

**Cheney** · *Cheney C/C* · P.O. Box 716, 67025, P 2,200, M 45, (316) 542-3142, (888) 522-7221, www.cheneychamber.com

**Cherryvale** · *Cherryvale C/C* · Tina Cunningham, Pres., P.O. Box 112, 67335, P 2,400, M 50, (620) 891-0072, cherryvalechamber@ hotmail.com, www.cherryvaleusa.com/chamber

**Chetopa** · *Chetopa C/C* · Mary Jane Houston, Secy., 917 Locust St., 67336, P 1,300, M 45, (620) 236-7371, (620) 236-7511, Fax (620) 236-7476, www.chetopacity.org

**Cimarron** · *Cimarron Area C/C* · TruDee Little, Secy./Treas., 119 S. Main, P.O. Box 602, 67835, P 2,000, M 50, (620) 855-2507, (620) 855-2215, www.cimarronkansas.net

**Clay Center** · *Clay Center Area C/C* · Andy Contreras, Pres./ CEO, 517 Court, 67432, P 5,000, M 130, (785) 632-5674, Fax same, ccchamber@eaglecom.net, www.claycenterkschamber.org.

**Clearwater** · *Clearwater C/C* · Jennifer Arnold, Exec. Dir., 130 E. Ross, Ste. 104, P.O. Box 627, 67026, P 2,300, M 90, (620) 584-3366, Fax (620) 584-2268, chamber@sktc.net, www.clearwaterks chamber.org

**Clyde** · *Clyde Comm. C/C* · Jamie Kegle, Pres., P.O. Box 5, 66938, P 750, M 45, (785) 446-2291, www.clydekansas.org

**Coffeyville** · *Coffeyville Area C/C* · Kimberly Millikin, Exec. Dir., 807 Walnut, P.O. Box 457, 67337, P 11,000, M 335, (620) 251-2550, (800) 626-3357, Fax (620) 251-5448, chamber@coffeyville. com, www.coffeyvillechamber.org

**Colby** · *Colby/Thomas County C/C* · Holly Stephens, Exec. Dir., 350 S. Range, Ste. 10, 67701, P 8,258, M 250, (785) 460-3401, Fax (785) 460-4509, colbychamber@thomascounty.com, www. oasisontheplains.com

**Coldwater** · *Coldwater C/C* · Johnita Stalcup, Treas., P.O. Box 333, 67029, P 700, M 30, (620) 582-2859, www.coldwaterkansas.com

**Columbus** • *Columbus C/C* • Jean Pritchett, Dir., 320 E. Maple, 66725, P 3,500, M 196, (620) 429-1492, Fax (620) 429-1492, columbuschamber@columbus-ks.com, www.columbus-kansas. com/chamber

**Concordia** • *Concordia Area C/C* • Roberta Lowrey, Pres., 606 Washington, 66901, P 6,000, M 170, (785) 243-4290, Fax (785) 243-2014, chamber@concordiakansas.org, www.concordiakansas.org

**Conway Springs** • *Conway Springs C/C* • Jon Ott, Pres., 208 W. Spring, P.O. Box 392, 67031, P 1,350, M 30, (620) 456-2252, jo@ statebankcs.com, www.chamberconway.com

**Cottonwood Falls** • *Chase County C/C* • Debbie Adcock, Admin. Dir., 318 Broadway, P.O. Box 362, 66845, P 3,100, M 75, (620) 273-8469, (800) 431-6344, chasechamber@sbcglobal.net, www. chasecountychamber.org

**Council Grove** • *Council Grove/Morris County Chamber & Tourism* • Tina Rae Scott, Exec. Dir., 207 W. Main, 66846, P 2,500, M 130, (620) 767-5413, (800) 732-9211, Fax (620) 767-5553, chamber@councilgrove.com, www.councilgrove.com

**Derby** • *Derby C/C* • Rhonda Cott, Pres., 330 E. Madison, Ste. 150, P.O. Box 544, 67037, P 22,000, M 375, (316) 788-3421, Fax (316) 788-6861, chamber@derbychamber.com, www.derby chamber.com

**Desoto** • *Desoto C/C* • Sara Ritter, Exec. Dir., P.O. Box 70, 66018, P 5,400, M 190, (913) 583-1585, sritter@desotoks.org, www. desotoks.org

**Dighton** • *Lane County Area C/C* • Chelle Anderson, Secy., 147 E. Long, P.O. Box 942, 67839, P 1,261, M 71, (620) 397-2211, Fax (620) 397-2416, info@dightonks.com, www.dightonkansas.com

**Dodge City** • *Dodge City Area C/C* • Cindy Malek, Pres., 311 W. Spruce, P.O. Box 939, 67801, P 31,000, M 525, (620) 227-3119, Fax (620) 227-2957, info@dodgechamber.com, www.dodge chamber.com

**Downs** • *Downs C/C* • Majean Scheider, Pres., 801 Morgan, P.O. Box 172, 67437, P 1,150, M 45, (785) 454-3416, www.downs-chamber.com

**El Dorado** • *El Dorado C/C* • Shirley Patton, Exec. Dir., 201 E. Central, 67042, P 12,600, M 297, (316) 321-3150, Fax (316) 321-5419, info@eldoradochamber.com, www.eldoradochamber.com

**Elkhart** • *Elkhart Area C/C* • Tim Hardy, Pres., 546 Morton, P.O. Box 696, 67950, P 2,500, M 125, (620) 697-4600, www.ci.elkhart.ks.us

**Ellinwood** • *Ellinwood C/C* • 110 1/2 N. Main St., P.O. Box 482, 67526, P 2,200, M 155, (620) 564-3300, (620) 566-7353, ellinwoodchamber@hotmail.com, www.ellinwoodchamber.com

**Ellis** • *Ellis C/C* • Dena Patee, Dir., 820 Washington, 67637, P 2,100, M 90, (785) 726-2660, Fax (785) 726-2661, ellischamber@eaglecom.net, www.ellischamberofcommerce.com

**Ellsworth** • *Ellsworth-Kanopolis Area C/C* • Nick Slechta, Dir., 114 1/2 N. Douglas, P.O. Box 315, 67439, P 2,600, M 120, (785) 472-4071, Fax (785) 472-5668, ecofc@eaglecom.net, www. ellsworthkschamber.net

**Emporia** • *Emporia Area C/C* • Jeanine McKenna, Pres./CEO, 719 Commercial St., 66801, P 28,000, M 500, (620) 342-1600, Fax (620) 342-3223, jmckenna@emporiakschamber.org, www. emporiakschamber.org.

**Eskridge** • *Eskridge C/C* • P.O. Box 313, 66423, P 600, M 45, (785) 449-7215

**Eudora** • *Eudora C/C* • P.O. Box 725, 66025, P 6,300, M 62, (785) 542-1212, Fax (785) 542-1235, contactus@eudorachamber.com, www.eudorachamber.com

**Eureka** • *Eureka Area C/C* • Anita Bjorling, Coord., Memorial Hall Bldg., P.O. Box 563, 67045, P 2,974, M 50, (620) 583-5452, Fax (620) 583-5452, www.eurekakansas.com

**Everest** • *Everest C/C* • Michael Wilburn, P.O. Box 6, 66424, P 300, M 30, (785) 548-7521

**Fairway** • *see Mission*

**Florence** • *Florence C/C* • Mary Jane Grimmett, Pres., 511 Main, 66851, P 670, M 30, (620) 878-4296, www.florenceks.com

**Fort Scott** • *Fort Scott Area C/C* • Vicki Pritchett, Pres./CEO, 231 E. Wall St., 66701, P 8,500, M 300, (620) 223-3566, (800) 245-FORT, Fax (620) 223-3574, fschamber@fortscott.com, www. fortscott.com

**Fredonia** • *Fredonia C/C* • Yvonne Hull, Exec. Dir., 402 N. 7th, P.O. Box 449, 66736, P 2,500, M 173, (620) 378-3221, Fax (620) 378-4833, fredoniakschamber@twinmounds.com, www.fredonia chamber.com

**Galena** • *Galena C/C* • Kathleen Anderson, Pres., P.O. Box 465, 66739, P 4,500, M 80, (620) 783-1395

**Garden City** • *Garden City Area C/C* • D. Paul Joseph, Pres., 1511 E. Fulton Terrace, 67846, P 34,000, M 520, (620) 276-3264, Fax (620) 276-3290, dpjoseph@gcnet.com, www.gardencity.net/ chamber.

**Gardner** • *Gardner Area C/C* • Peter Solie, Pres., 109 E. Main, P.O. Box 402, 66030, P 18,000, M 260, (913) 856-6464, Fax (913) 856-5274, solie@gardnerchamber.com, www.gardnerchamber.com

**Garnett** • *Garnett Area C/C* • Chris Maynard, Pres., 419 S. Oak, 66032, P 3,200, M 90, (785) 448-6767, Fax (785) 448-6767, www. garnettchamber.org

**Girard** • *Girard Area C/C* • Dr. Harold Bryan, Exec. Dir., 118 N. Ozark, P.O. Box 41, 66743, P 2,800, M 85, (620) 724-4715, girard chamber@ckt.net

**Glasco** • *Glasco Chamber Pride* • Mrs. Joan Northern, Secy., 405 E. Spaulding Ave., P.O. Box 572, 67445, P 550, M 20, (785) 568-0120, jnothern334@usd334.org, www.glascokansas.org

**Glen Elder** • *Glen Elder Community Club* • Megan Duskie, Pres., 105 S. Hobart, 67446, P 440, M 50, (785) 545-3180, megan_ duskie@yahoo.com, www.glenelder.com

**Goodland** • *Goodland Area C/C* • Jordie Mann, Interim Exec. Dir., 104 E. 10th, 67735, P 7,400, M 180, (785) 899-7130, Fax (785) 890-7130, gdlchmbr@eaglecom.net, www.goodland chamber.com

**JOIN US FOR OUR ANNUAL EVENTS: FREEDOM FEST–JULY, SHERMAN COUNTY FREE FAIR–AUG, FLATLANDERS FALL FEST–SEPT. HUNTERS ALWAYS WELCOME!**

**Great Bend** • *Great Bend C/C* • Jan Peters, Pres., 1125 Williams St., 67530, P 16,000, M 930, (620) 792-2401, Fax (620) 792-2404, gbcc@greatbend.org, www.greatbend.org.

**Greensburg** • *Kiowa County C/C* • Kim Alderfer, Pres., 101 S. Main, 67054, P 2,200, M 70, (620) 723-2400, tourism@bigwell. org, www.bigwell.org

**Halstead** • *Halstead C/C* • Mary Lee McDonald, Secy./Treas., P.O. Box 328, 67056, P 1,902, M 72, (316) 217-4996, chamber@ discoverhalstead.com, www.discoverhalstead.com

**Hanover** • *Hanover C/C* • Russ Behrends, 109 W. North, P.O. Box 283, 66945, P 652, M 45, (785) 337-2598

**Harper** • *Harper C/C* • 201 W. Main, P.O. Box 337, 67058, P 1,550, M 30, (620) 896-2511

**Havensville** • *see Onaga*

**Hays** · *Hays Area C/C* · Gina Riedel, Exec. Dir., 2700 Vine St., 67601, P 20,000, M 635, (785) 628-8201, Fax (785) 628-1471, hayscc@discoverhays.com, www.discoverhays.com

**Haysville** · *Haysville C/C* · Forrest Hummel, Pres., 150 Stewart, P.O. Box 372, 67060, P 10,000, M 150, (316) 529-2461, Fax (316) 554-2342, haysvillechamber@gmail.com, www.haysvillechamber.com

**Herington** · *Tri-County Area C/C* · Phyllis Smith, Exec. Dir., 106 N. Broadway, 67449, P 2,600, M 130, (785) 258-2115, Fax (785) 258-2799, hrngtnch@tctelco.net, www.tricountycofc.com

**Herndon** · *Herndon C/C* · Jayne Niermeier, Treas., P.O. Box 217, 67739, P 200, M 100, (785) 322-5619, Fax (785) 322-2020, skyways.lib.ks.us/towns/Herndon

**Hesston** · *Hesston C/C* · Janet Thrasher, Exec. Dir., 115 E. Smith, 67062, P 3,800, M 125, (620) 327-4102, (800) 442-1563, Fax (620) 327-4595, chamber@hesstonks.org, www.hesstonks.org

**Hiawatha** · *Hiawatha C/C & CVB* · Beth Spicer, Admin., 1711 Oregon St., 66434, P 3,600, M 140, (785) 742-7136, Fax (785) 742-3966, hiawathachamber@rainbowtel.net, www.hiawatha chamber.com.

**Hill City** · *Hill City C/C* · Carolyn Popp, Secy./Mgr., 801 W. Main St., P.O. Box 155, 67642, P 1,660, M 90, (785) 421-5621, hcchamber@ ruraltel.net, www.discoverhillcity.com

**Hillsboro** · *Hillsboro C/C* · Renee Gilkey, Exec. Dir., 109 S. Main, 67063, P 3,400, M 133, (620) 947-3506, Fax (620) 947-2585, hills borochamber@hillsboro-kansas.com, www.hillsboro-kansas.com

**Hoisington** · *Hoisington C/C* · Nancy Farmer, Pres., 123 N. Main St., 67544, P 3,000, M 100, (620) 653-4311, Fax (620) 653-4311, hoisingtoncofc@embarqmail.com, www.hoisingtonkansas.com

**Holton** · *Holton/Jackson County C/C* · Katie Ingles, Exec. Dlr, 105 W. 4th St., 66436, P 3,350, M 155, (785) 364-3963, chamber@ holtonks.net, www.holtonks.net/chamber

**Horton** · *Horton C/C* · Rita Higley, P.O. Box 105, 66439, P 2,000, M 70, (785) 486-3321, Fax (785) 486-3321, hortonchamber@ rainbowtel.net, www.hortonkansas.org

**Howard** · *Howard C/C* · Nadine Baumgartel, Treas., P.O. Box 545, 67349, P 850, M 75, (620) 374-2172

**Hugoton** · *Hugoton Area C/C* · Kristin Farnum, Dir., 630 S. Main St., 67951, P 5,463, M 80, (620) 544-4305, (620) 544-8531, Fax (620) 544-4610, hchamber@pld.com, www.hugotonchamber.com

**Humboldt** · *Humboldt C/C* · Don Copley, 105 S. 9th St., P.O. Box 133, 66748, P 2,000, M 45, (620) 473-3011, www.humboldtks.net

**Hutchinson** · *Hutchinson/Reno County C/C* · Dave Kerr, Pres., 117 N. Walnut, P.O. Box 519, 67504, P 65,000, M 1,400, (620) 662-3391, Fax (620) 662-2168, info@hutchchamber.com, www. hutchchamber.com.

**Independence** · *Independence C/C* · Gwen Wilburn, Pres./ CEO, 322 N. Penn, P.O. Box 386, 67301, P 10,000, M 350, (620) 331-1890, (800) 882-3606, Fax (620) 331-1899, chamber@ indkschamber.org, www.indkschamber.org.

**Inman** · *Inman C/C* · P.O. Box 511, 67546, P 1,200, M 65, (620) 585-2063, city@inmanks.org, www.inmanks.org

**Iola** · *Iola Area C/C* · Jana Taylor, Exec. Dir., 208 W. Madison, 66749, P 5,700, M 170, (620) 365-5252, Fax (620) 365-8078, chamber@iolaks.com, www.iolachamber.org.

**Jewell** · *Jewell C/C* · Becky Loomis, Pres., P.O. Box 235, 66949, P 450, M 50, (785) 428-3600, Fax (785) 428-3600

**Johnson** · *Stanton County C/C* · Karla Dimmitt, Exec. Dir., 206 S. Main St., P.O. Box 9, 67855, P 2,200, M 150, (620) 492-6606, stchamb@pld.com

**Junction City** · *Junction City Area C/C* · 814 N. Washington, P.O. Box 26, 66441, P 25,000, M 366, (785) 762-2632, Fax (785) 762-3353, jcchamber@junctionchamber.org, www.junctioncity chamber.org.

**Kanopolis** · *see Ellsworth*

**Kansas City** · *Kansas City Kansas Area C/C* · Cindy Cash, Pres./ CEO, 727 Minnesota Ave., P.O. Box 171337, 66117, P 160,000, M 840, (913) 371-3070, Fax (913) 371-3732, chamber@kckchamber.com, www.kckchamber.com.

**Kansas City** · *Women's C/C* · Therese Bysel, Pres., 727 Minnesota Ave., P.O. Box 171337, 66117, P 160,000, M 120, (913) 371-3165, Fax (913) 371-3732, www.womenschamberkck.org

**Kingman** · *Kingman Area C/C* · Greg Graffman, Pres., 322 N. Main, 67068, P 3,387, M 107, (620) 532-1853, info@kingmancc. com, www.kingmancc.com

**Kinsley** · *Edwards County C/C* · Carlene Engler, Pres., 200 E. 6th, P.O. Box 161, 67547, P 3,500, M 50, (620) 659-2711, Fax (620) 659-2711, ecedcweb@sbcglobal.net, www.edwardscountyks.org

**Kiowa** · *Kiowa C/C* · Kelly Stewart, Pres., 204 N. 5th St., 67070, P 1,160, M 80, (620) 825-4825

**LaCrosse** · *Rush County C/C* · Leslie Morgan, Secy., P.O. Box 716, 67548, P 3,200, M 60, (785) 222-2639, Fax (785) 222-2639, chamber67548@yahoo.com, www.rushcounty.org

**Lansing** · *see Leavenworth*

**Larned** · *Larned Area C/C* · Janet Hammond, Pres./CEO, 502 Broadway, 67550, P 7,600, M 176, (620) 285-6916, (800) 747-6919, Fax (620) 285-6917, larnedcofc@gbta.net, www.larnedks.org

**Lawrence** · *Lawrence C/C* · Tom Kern, Pres./CEO, 734 Vermont St., Ste. 101, P.O. Box 586, 66044, P 90,000, M 900, (785) 865-4411, Fax (785) 865-4400, lawrencechamber@lawrencechamber. com, www.lawrencechamber.com

**Leavenworth** · *Leavenworth-Lansing Area C/C* · Tim Holverson, Exec. V.P., 518 Shawnee St., P.O. Box 44, 66048, P 43,000, M 500, (913) 682-4112, Fax (913) 682-8170, info@ llchamber.com, www.llchamber.com.

**Leawood** · *Leawood C/C* · Kevin Jeffries, Pres./CEO, 4707 W. 135th St., Ste. 270, 66224, P 31,000, M 435, (913) 498-1514, Fax (913) 491-0134, chamber@leawoodchamber.org, www.leawood-chamber.org

**Lebanon** · *Lebanon Hub Club* · Lori Ladow, Pres., P.O. Box 125, 66952, P 230, M 16, (785) 389-3261, (785) 389-1141

**Lenexa** · *Lenexa C/C* · Blake Schreck, Pres., 11180 Lackman Rd., 66219, P 48,000, M 750, (913) 888-1414, Fax (913) 888-3770, bschreck@lenexa.org, www.lenexa.org.

**Lenora** · *Lenora C/C* · Box 331, 67645, P 306, M 20, (785) 567-4860, skyways.lib.ks.us/towns/Lenora

**Liberal** · *Liberal Area C/C* · Rozelle Webb, Exec. Dir., 4 Rock Island Rd., P.O. Box 676, 67905, P 20,000, M 400, (620) 624-3855, Fax (620) 624-8851, info@liberalkschamber.com, www.liberalks chamber.com

**Lincoln** · *Lincoln Area C/C* · Tammy Voeltz, Exec. Dir., 144 E. Lincoln Ave., 67455, P 1,500, M 80, (785) 524-4934, Fax same, lcoc137@sbcglobal.net, www.lincolnkansaschamber.com

**Lindsborg** · *Lindsborg C/C* · 104 E. Lincoln, 67456, P 3,300, M 150, (785) 227-3706, (888) 227-2227, lindsborgcofc@sbcglobal. net, www.lindsborg.org

**Louisburg** · *Louisburg C/C* · Patsy Bortner, Exec. Dir., P.O. Box 245, 66053, P 3,700, M 110, (913) 837-2826, chamber@louisburg kansas.com, www.louisburgkansas.com

**Lucas** • *Lucas Area C/C* • Connie Dougherty, 201 S. Main, P.O. Box 186, 67648, P 436, M 45, (785) 525-6288, lucascoc@wtciweb.com, www.lucaskansas.com

**Lyons** • *Lyons C/C* • Shannon Young, Mgr., 116 E. Ave. S., P.O. Box 127, 67554, P 3,500, M 100, (620) 257-2842, (866) 257-2842, Fax (620) 257-3426, lyonscc@lyons-chamber.com, www.lyons-chamber.com

**Madison** • *Madison Area C/C* • P.O. Box 58, 66860, P 800, M 55, (620) 437-3463, www.madisonkschamber.org

**Manhattan** • *Manhattan Area C/C* • Lyle A. Butler III, Pres./CEO, 501 Poyntz Ave., 66502, P 67,000, M 835, (785) 776-8829, Fax (785) 776-0679, chamber@manhattan.org, www.manhattan.org.

**Mankato** • *Mankato C/C* • Susan Abel-Diehl, Pres., 741 N. High St., 66956, P 976, M 50, (785) 378-3141, Fax (785) 378-3478, susan@nckcn.com, skyways.lib.ks.us/towns/Mankato

**Marion** • *Marion C/C* • Margo Yates, Exec. Secy., 203 N. 3rd, 66861, P 2,110, M 125, (620) 382-3425, Fax (620) 382-3993, chinga@eaglecom.net, www.marionks.com

**Marysville** • *Marysville C/C* • Brenda Staggenborg, Secy., 101 N. 10th, P.O. Box 16, 66508, P 3,200, M 172, (785) 562-3101, (800) 752-3965, Fax (785) 562-3101, marysvillechamber@sbcglobal.net, skyways.lib.ks.us/kansas/towns/Marysville

**McPherson** • *McPherson C/C* • Jennifer Burch, Exec. Dir., 306 N. Main, P.O. Box 616, 67460, P 13,770, M 403, (620) 241-3303, Fax (620) 241-8708, chamber@mcphersonks.org, www.mcphersonks. org, www.mcphersonchamber.org.

**Meade** • *Meade C/C* • Louis Podrebarac, Secy., P.O. Box 576, 67864, P 1,526, M 34, (620) 873-2979, www.meadechamber.com

**Medicine Lodge** • *Medicine Lodge Area C/C* • Jessica Rausch, Dir., 215 S. Iliff, P.O. Box 274, 67104, P 2,200, M 76, (620) 886-3417, mlchamber@sctelcom.net, www.medicinelodgechamber.com

**Merriam** • *see Mission*

**Miltonvale** • *Miltonvale C/C* • Carl Kennedy, 102 S.W. 6th, P.O. Box 98, 67466, P 500, M 25, (785) 427-3372, www.miltonvaleks.com

**Minneapolis** • *Minneapolis Area C/C* • Joyce Freel, Exec. Dir., 200 W. 2nd, 67467, P 2,001, M 100, (785) 392-3068, mplschamber@sbcglobal.net, www.minneapolisks.org

**Mission** • *Northeast Johnson County C/C* • Rob Johnson, Pres., 5800 Foxridge Dr., Ste. 100, 66202, P 77,000, M 350, (913) 262-2141, Fax (913) 262-2146, www.nejcchamber.com

**Mission Hills** • *see Mission*

**Mission Woods** • *see Mission*

**Moline** • *Moline C/C* • Stephanie Bogdahn, Pres., P.O. Box 253, 67353, P 470, M 28, (620) 647-3665, Fax (620) 647-8152, molinecity@sktc.net, www.molinekansas.com

**Mound City** • *Mound City C/C* • P.O. Box A, 66056, P 800, M 67, (913) 757-4551

**Moundridge** • *Moundridge Area C/C* • Lisa Teter, Dir., Box 312, 67107, P 1,740, M 50, (620) 345-6300, www.moundridge.com

**Mulvane** • *Mulvane C/C* • Kent Hixson, Pres., P.O. Box 67, 67110, P 5,400, M 68, (316) 777-4850, (316) 737-0534, evans3071@wheatstate.com, www.mulvanechamber.com

**Neodesha** • *Neodesha C/C* • Karen Porter, Exec. Dir., First & Main, P.O. Box 266, 66757, P 3,000, M 110, (620) 325-2055, karen@neodeshachamber.com, www.neodeshachamber.com

**Ness City** • *Ness City C/C* • Yvette Schlegel, Dir., 102 W. Main St., P.O. Box 262, 67560, P 1,400, M 86, (785) 798-2413, nccofc@gbta.net, www.skyways.org/towns/NessCity

**Newton** • *Newton Area C/C* • 500 N. Main, Ste. 101, 67114, P 20,000, M 385, (316) 283-2560, (800) 868-2560, Fax (316) 283-8732, billijo@thenewtonchamber.org, www.thenewtonchamber.org.

**Nickerson** • *Nickerson C/C* • Teresa Teufel, Pres., 15 N. Nickerson St., P.O. Box 3, 67561, P 1,135, M 37, (620) 422-3611, www.nickersonks.us

**North Overland Park** • *see Mission*

**Norton** • *Norton Area C/C* • Karla Reed, Exec. Dir., 104 S. State St., 67654, P 5,664, M 150, (785) 877-2501, Fax (785) 877-3300, nortoncc@ruraltel.net, www.us36.net/nortonkansas, www.discovernorton.com

**Oakley** • *Oakley Area C/C* • Carinda McConnell, Exec. Dir., 216 Center Ave., 67748, P 2,000, M 70, (785) 672-4862, Fax (785) 672-4766, oakleycc@st-tel.net, www.discoveroakley.com

**Oberlin** • *Decatur County Area C/C* • 104 S. Penn, Ste. 8, 67749, P 1,900, M 115, (785) 475-3441, Fax (785) 475-2128, dcacc@eaglecom.net, www.oberlinks.com

**Olathe** • *Olathe C/C* • L. Franklin Taylor, Pres., 18001 W. 106th St., Ste. 160, P.O. Box 98, 66051, P 120,000, M 2,400, (913) 764-1050, (800) 921-5678, Fax (913) 782-4636, info@olathe.org, www.olathe.org

**Onaga** • *Onaga Area C/C* • Dan Peters, P.O. Box 278, 66521, P 1,200, M 35, (785) 889-4211, www.onagakansas.org

**Osage City** • *Osage City C/C* • Robyn Williams, Pres., P.O. Box 56, 66523, P 3,050, M 83, (785) 528-8177, (785) 528-4090, chamber@osagecity.com, www.osagecity.com

**Osawatomie** • *Osawatomie C/C* • Jessica Shaddox, Exec. Dir., 628 Main St., P.O. Box 63, 66064, P 4,600, M 60, (913) 755-4114, Fax (913) 755-4114, osachamber@hotmail.com, www.osawatomiechamber.org

**Osborne** • *Osborne Area C/C* • Heather Poore, Dir., 130 N. First St., 67473, P 1,607, M 60, (785) 346-2670, (866) 346-2670, Fax (785) 346-2522, osborneed@ruraltel.net, www.discoverosborne.com

**Oswego** • *Oswego C/C* • Kevin Sheddrick, Pres., P.O. Box 8, 67356, P 2,100, M 120, (620) 795-2600, city@oswegokansas.com, www.oswegokansas.com

**Ottawa** • *Ottawa Area C/C* • Thomas R. Weigand, Pres./CEO, 109 E. 2nd, P.O. Box 580, 66067, P 27,000, M 350, (785) 242-1000, Fax (785) 242-4792, chambertw@ottawakansas.org, www.ottawakansas.org.

**Overland Park** • *Overland Park C/C* • Tracey Osborne CCE, Pres., 9001 W. 110th St., Ste. 150, 66210, P 500,000, M 900, (913) 491-3600, Fax (913) 491-0393, www.opchamber.org

**Oxford** • *Oxford C/C* • Cindy Gregor, Pres., 115 S. Sumner St., P.O. Box 841, 67119, P 1,200, M 29, (620) 455-3359, head2toeoxford@gmail.com, www.oxfordks.org.

**Paola** • *Paola C/C* • Carol Everhart, Exec. Dir., 3 W. Wea St., 66071, P 7,200, M 205, (913) 294-4335, Fax (913) 294-4336, mgr@paolachamber.org, www.paolachamber.org

**Park City** • *Park City C/C* • Rachel Fenske, 6110 N. Hydraulic St., 67219, P 7,000, M 120, (316) 744-2026, www.parkcityks.com

**Parsons** • *Parsons C/C* • Rikki Hess, Exec. V.P., 1715 Corning, 67357, P 11,500, M 250, (620) 421-6500, (800) 280-6401, Fax (620) 421-6501, chamber@parsonschamber.org, www.parsonschamber.org

**Phillipsburg** • *Phillipsburg Area C/C* • Jackie Swatzell, Dir., 270 State St., P.O. Box 326, 67661, P 2,800, M 105, (785) 543-2321, Fax (785) 543-0038, cvbcham@ruraltel.net, www.phillipsburgks.us

**Pittsburg** • *Pittsburg Area C/C* • Blake Benson, Pres., 117 W. 4th St., P.O. Box 1115, 66762, P 25,000, M 600, (620) 231-1000, Fax (620) 231-3178, bbenson@pittsburgareachamber.com, www.pittsburgareachamber.com.

**Pleasanton** • *Pleasanton C/C* • Jackie Taylor, Pres., P.O. Box 478, 66075, P 1,250, M 45, (913) 352-8257, www.linncountyks.com

**Prairie Village** • *see Mission*

**Pratt** • *Pratt Area C/C* • Brian Hoffman, Exec. Dir., 114 N. Main St., 67124, P 9,700, M 300, (620) 672-5501, (888) 886-1164, Fax (620) 672-5502, info@prattkan.com, www.prattkan.com

**Quinter** • *Quinter C/C* • Carolyn Tuttle, Secy., P.O. Box 35, 67752, P 900, M 61, (785) 754-3538, www.discoverquinter.com

**Richmond** • *Richmond C/C* • Sandi Ferguson, Pres., P.O. Box 267, 66080, P 400, M 6, (785) 835-6125

**Roeland Park** • *see Mission*

**Rose Hill** • *Rose Hill C/C* • Jason Jones, Pres., P.O. Box 375, 67133, P 3,950, M 50, (316) 776-2712

**Russell** • *Russell C/C & CVB* • Roy Stottlemyer, Dir., 507 N. Main, P.O. Box 58, 67665, P 4,600, M 120, (785) 483-6960, (800) 658-4686, Fax (785) 483-4535, chamber@russellks.org, www.russellks.org

**Sabetha** • *Sabetha C/C* • Judith Elliott, Secy., 805 Main, 66534, P 2,600, M 110, (785) 284-2158, sabethachamber@gmail.com, www.sabetha.com

**Saint Francis** • *St. Francis Area C/C* • Gloria Bracelin, Dir., 212 E. Washington, P.O. Box 793, 67756, P 1,500, M 65, (785) 332-2961, Fax (785) 332-8825, coc@cityofstfrancis.net, www.stfranciskansas.com

**Saint Marys** • *Saint Marys C/C* • Helen Pauly, Exec. Dir., 702 W. Bertrand, P.O. Box 3, 66536, P 2,500, M 120, (785) 437-2077, chamber@saintmarys.com, www.saintmarys.com

**Salina** • *Salina Area C/C* • Dennis Lauver, Pres./CEO, 120 W. Ash St., P.O. Box 586, 67402, P 47,000, M 1,200, (785) 827-9301, Fax (785) 827-9758, dlauver@salinakansas.org, www.salinakansas.org

**Satanta** • *Satanta C/C* • Brent Howie, P.O. Box 98, 67870, P 1,300, M 100, chamber@satanta.org, www.satanta.org

**Scott City** • *Scott City Area C/C & EDC* • 113 E. 5th, 67871, P 5,000, M 190, (620) 872-3525, Fax (620) 872-2242, sccc@wbsnet.org, www.scottcitycofc.com

**Sedan** • *Sedan Area C/C* • Jeanie Walker, Ofc. Mgr., 108 Sherman, P.O. Box 182, 67361, P 1,356, M 100, (620) 725-4033, sedanchamber@yahoo.com

**Seneca** • *Seneca C/C* • Harry Leem, Exec. Dir., 523 Main St., P.O. Box 135, 66538, P 2,354, M 110, (785) 336-2294, Fax (785) 336-6344, seneca_chamber@yahoo.com, www.seneca-kansas.us

**Shawnee** • *Shawnee C/C* • Linda Leeper, Pres., 15100 W. 67th St., Ste. 202, 66217, P 60,500, M 700, (913) 631-6545, Fax (913) 631-9628, lleeper@shawneekschamber.com, www.shawneekschamber.com

**Smith Center** • *Smith Center C/C* • Coleen Kirkendall, Dir., 219 S. Main, 66967, P 1,773, M 103, (785) 282-3895, Fax (785) 686-4116, ckirkendall@smithcenter.net, www.smithcenterks.com

**Spring Hill** • *Spring Hill C/C* • Ann Jensen, Exec. Dir., P.O. Box 15, 66083, P 5,000, M 160, (913) 592-3893, Fax (913) 592-3876, chamber@springhillks.org, www.springhillks.org

**Stafford** • *Stafford Area C/C* • Carolyn Claypool, Secy., 130 S. Main St., P.O. Box 24, 67578, P 1,350, M 50, (620) 234-5614, (620) 234-5011, www.cityofstafford.net

**Sterling** • *Sterling C/C* • Cheryl Buckman, Secy./Treas., 112 S. Broadway Ave., P.O. Box 56, 67579, P 2,200, M 72, (620) 278-3360, lcbuckman@cm.kscoxmail.com, www.sterling-kansas.org

**Stockton** • *Stockton C/C* • 115 S. Walnut, P.O. Box 1, 67669, P 1,407, M 55, (785) 425-6162, Fax (785) 425-6424, stocktoncofc@ruraltel.net, www.stocktonkansas.net

**Syracuse** • *Syracuse-Hamilton County C/C* • 118 N. Main, P.O. Box 678, 67878, P 2,666, M 110, (620) 384-5459, schamber@pld.com, www.syracusekschamber.com

**Tonganoxie** • *Tonganoxie C/C* • Cheryl Hanback, Exec. Dir., P.O. Box 838, 66086, P 5,500, M 95, (913) 845-9244, info@tonganoxichamber.org, www.tonganoxiechamber.org

**Topeka** • *Greater Topeka C/C* • Douglas Kinsinger, Pres./CEO, 120 S.E. 6th, Ste. 110, 66603, P 172,000, M 1,600, (785) 234-2644, Fax (785) 234-8656, topekainfo@topekachamber.org, www.topekachamber.org

**Troy** • *Doniphan County C/C & Eco. Dev. Comm.* • Lawrence Mays, Exec. Dir., 120 E. Chestnut, P.O. Box 250, 66087, P 8,400, M 100, (816) 244-6715, Fax (785) 985-3723, lmaysdoniphancounty@yahoo.com, www.dpcountyks.com

**Ulysses** • *Grant County C/C* • Evelina Flores, Chair, 113 S. Main St., Ste. B, 67880, P 7,500, M 450, (620) 356-4700, Fax (620) 424-2437, uchamber@pld.com, www.ulysseschamber.org

**Valley Center** • *Valley Center C/C* • Dawn Lechner, Exec. Dir., 214 W. Main St., P.O. Box 382, 67147, P 6,000, M 120, (316) 755-7340, Fax (316) 755-7341, vccc67147@yahoo.com, www.vckschamber.com

**Valley Falls** • *Valley Falls C/C* • P.O. Box 162, 66088, P 1,250, M 52, (785) 945-3245, Fax (785) 945-6269

**Wamego** • *Wamego Area C/C & Main Street Inc.* • Kourtney Brase, Exec. Dir., 529 Lincoln Ave., 66547, P 5,500, M 174, (785) 456-7849, Fax (785) 456-7427, wchamber@wamego.net, www.wamegochamber.com

**Waterville** • *Waterville C/C* • Barb Terry, Pres., P.O. Box 5, 66548, P 680, M 85, (785) 363-2629

**Wellington** • *Wellington Area C/C & CVB* • Jill Clark, Exec. Dir., 207 S. Washington, 67152, P 8,722, M 372, (620) 326-7466, Fax (620) 326-7467, jclark@sutv.com, www.wellingtonks.org.

**Wellsville** • *Wellsville C/C* • Kristin Adams, Pres., P.O. Box 472, 66092, P 1,700, M 80, (785) 883-2296, www.wellsvillechamber.com

**Westwood** • *see Mission*

**Westwood Hills** • *see Mission*

**Wheaton** • *see Onaga*

**Wichita** • *Wichita Metro C/C* • Bryan Derreberry, Pres./CEO, 350 W. Douglas Ave., 67202, P 584,000, M 1,800, (316) 265-7771, Fax (316) 265-7502, info@wichitachamber.org, www.wichitachamber.org.

**Wilson** • *Wilson C/C* • 2407 Ave. E, P.O. Box 328, 67490, P 850, M 50, (785) 658-2211, www.wilsonkansas.com

**Winfield** • *Winfield Area C/C* • Stephannie DeLong, Member Svcs. Coord., 123 E. 9th, P.O. Box 640, 67156, P 12,500, M 330, (620) 221-2420, Fax (620) 221-2958, win@winfieldchamber.org, www.winfieldchamber.org

**Winona** • *Winona C/C* • P.O. Box 54, 67764, P 250, M 20, (785) 846-7702

**Yates Center** • *Woodson County C/C* • Carey Spoon, Exec. Dir., 108 S. Main, P.O. Box 233, 66783, P 4,000, M 75, (620) 625-3235, Fax (620) 625-2416, chamber@wccc.kscoxmail.com, www.woodsoncountychamber.com.

# Kentucky

**Kentucky C of C ·** David Adkisson, Pres./CEO, 464 Chenault Rd., Frankfort, 40601, M 2,400, (502) 695-4700, Fax (502) 695-5051, kcc@kychamber.com, www.kychamber.com

**Adairville ·** *Adairville-South Logan C/C ·* Dick Dickerson, P.O. Box 266, 42202, P 2,500, M 100, (270) 539-2080

**Ashland ·** *Ashland Alliance ·* Jim Purgerson CEcD, Pres., 1733 Winchester Ave., P.O. Box 830, 41105, P 90,000, M 565, (606) 324-5111, Fax (606) 325-4607, bhammond@inicity.net, www.ashlandalliance.com

**Barbourville ·** *Knox County C/C ·* Janet Jones, Secy., 196 Daniel Boone Dr., Ste. 205, 40906, P 36,000, M 100, (606) 546-4300, Fax (606) 546-4300, chamber@barbourville.com, www.knoxco
chamber.com

**Bardstown ·** *Bardstown-Nelson County C/C ·* Dorothy White, Exec. Dir., One Court Square, 40004, P 40,000, M 550, (502) 348-9545, Fax (502) 348-6478, chamber@bardstown.com, www.bardstownchamber.com.

**Barren County ·** *see Glasgow*

**Beattyville ·** *Beattyville/Lee County C/C ·* Carole Kincaid, Pres., P.O. Box 676, 41311, P 7,500, M 70, (606) 464-1221, (606) 464-3607

**Benton ·** *Marshall County C/C ·* Debbie Buchanan, Exec. Admin., 17 U.S. Hwy. 68 W., 42025, P 30,250, M 280, (270) 527-7665, Fax (270) 527-9193, chamber@marshallcounty.net, www.marshall
county.net.

**Berea ·** *Berea C/C ·* David Rowlette, Exec. Dir., 926 W. Jefferson St., Ste. 1, 40403, P 12,000, M 320, (859) 986-9760, Fax (859) 986-2501, chamber@bereachamber.com, www.bereachamber.com

**Boone County ·** *see Fort Mitchell*

**Bowling Green ·** *Bowling Green Area C/C ·* Jim Hizer, Pres., 710 College St., P.O. Box 51, 42102, P 141,818, M 1,400, (270) 781-3200, Fax (270) 843-0458, jhizer@bgchamber.com, www.bgchamber.com

**Brandenburg ·** *Meade County Area C/C ·* Russ Powell, Exec. Dir., P.O. Box 483, 40108, P 28,500, M 125, (270) 422-3626, Fax (270) 422-1389, info@meadekychamber.org, www.meadeky
chamber.org

**Brooksville ·** *Bracken County C/C ·* Perry Poe, Pres., P.O. Box 7, 41004, P 8,750, M 65, (606) 735-3474, Fax (606) 735-3103, www.augustaky.com

**Buechel ·** *see Fern Creek*

**Burkesville ·** *Burkesville-Cumberland County C/C ·* Stephen Poindexter, Pres., P.O. Box 312, 42717, P 7,500, M 200, (270) 864-5890, chamber@burkesville.com, www.burkesville.com/chamber

**Cadiz ·** *Cadiz-Trigg County C/C ·* Kim Burkeen, Asst. Dir., 5748 Hopkinsville Rd., P.O. Box 647, 42211, P 15,000, M 165, (270) 522-3892, Fax (270) 522-6343, info@cadizchamber.com, www.cadizchamber.com.

**Calhoun ·** *McLean County C/C ·* 170 E. Second St., P.O. Box 303, 42327, P 10,000, M 90, (270) 273-9760, Fax (270) 273-9760

**Campbell County ·** *see Fort Mitchell*

**Campbellsville ·** *Campbellsville-Taylor County C/C ·* Judy Cox, Exec. Dir., 107 W. Broadway, P.O. Box 116, 42719, P 23,000, M 345, (270) 465-8601, Fax (270) 465-0607, chamber@teamtaylorcounty.com, www.campbellsvillechamber.com

**Carrollton ·** *Carroll County C/C ·* Nick Marsh, Pres., 511 Highland Ave., P.O. Box 535, 41008, P 10,000, M 120, (502) 732-7034, (502) 732-7035, Fax (502) 732-7028, chamber@carrollcountyky.com, www.carrollcountyky.com

**Cave City ·** *Cave City C/C & Welcome Center ·* Carol Degroft, Exec. Secy., 418 Mammoth Cave St., P.O. Box 460, 42127, P 4,000, M 129, (270) 773-5159, Fax (270) 773-7446, ccchamber@scrtc.com, www.cavecity.com

**Central City ·** *Greater Muhlenberg C/C ·* Judy Soderling, Exec. Secy., 214 N. 1st St., P.O. Box 671, 42330, P 32,000, M 220, (270) 754-2360, Fax (270) 754-2365, js.chamber@muhlon.com, www.muhlenbergchamber.org

**Clinton ·** *Hickman County C/C ·* Marla Pruitt, Pres., P.O. Box 298, 42031, P 5,300, M 45, (270) 653-4001, (270) 653-4369, marla.pruitt@clintonbankky.com

**Columbia ·** *Columbia-Adair County C/C ·* Sue C. Stivers, Exec. Dir., P.O. Box 116, 42728, P 17,206, M 200, (270) 384-6020, Fax (270) 384-2056, cacchamber@columbia-adaircounty.com, www.columbia-adaircounty.com

**Corbin ·** *Corbin C/C ·* Bruce Carpenter, Dir., 101 N. Depot St., 40701, P 25,000, M 260, (606) 528-6390, Fax (606) 523-6538, corbinchamber@corbinky.org, www.corbinky.org

**Covington ·** *see Fort Mitchell*

**Cumberland ·** *Tri-City C/C & Cumberland Tourist & Conv. Comm. ·* W. Bruce Ayers, Exec. Dir., 506 W. Main St., 40823, P 4,000, M 70, (606) 589-5812, Fax (606) 589-5812, tricity
chamber@windstrean.net, www.kingdomcome.org

**Cynthiana ·** *Cynthiana-Harrison County C/C ·* Patricia Grenier, Exec. Dir., 201 S. Main St., 41031, P 18,000, M 160, (859) 234-5236, Fax (859) 234-6647, cynchamber@setel.com, cynthiana
ky.com

**Danville ·** *Danville-Boyle County C/C ·* Paula Fowler Kilby, Exec. Dir., 304 S. Fourth St., 40422, P 28,000, M 500, (859) 236-2361, Fax (859) 236-3197, info@danvilleboylechamber.com, www.danvilleboylechamber.com

**Dawson Springs ·** *Dawson Springs C/C ·* 200 W. Arcadia Ave, P.O. Box 107, 42408, P 2,980, M 50, (270) 797-2781, Fax (270) 797-2221, www.dawsonspringsky.com

**Eddyville ·** *see Kuttawa*

**Edmonton ·** *Edmonton-Metcalfe County C/C ·* Gaye Shaw, Exec. Dir., P.O. Box 42, 42129, P 10,037, M 353, (270) 432-3222, Fax (270) 432-3224, metchamb@scrtc.com, www.metcalfechamber.com

**Elizabethtown ·** *Elizabethtown-Hardin County C/C ·* Tim Asher, Pres., 111 W. Dixie Ave., 42701, P 96,500, M 713, (270) 765-4334, (270) 769-2391, Fax (270) 737-0690, etownchamber@kvnet.org, www.elizabethtownchamber.org

**Falmouth ·** *Pendleton County C/C ·* Amanda Moore, Mgr., 230 Main St., P.O. Box 213, 41040, P 14,000, M 160, (859) 654-4189, Fax (859) 654-4189, pccoc@fuse.net, www.pendletoncounty
chamber.org

**Fern Creek ·** *Fern Creek Comm. Assn. & C/C ·* Carmen Ellington, Pres., P.O. Box 91564, Louisville, 40291, P 30,000, M 170, (502) 239-7550, Fax (502) 239-7650, fccacc@bellsouth.net, www.ferncreek.org

**Flatwoods ·** *see Ashland*

**Flemingsburg ·** *Fleming County C/C & EDO ·* Crystal Ruark, Exec. Dir., P.O. Box 24, 41041, P 14,000, M 300, (606) 845-1223, Fax (606) 845-1213, crystal@flemingkychamber.com, www.flemingkychamber.com

**Fort Mitchell** · *Northern Kentucky C/C* · Steve Stevens CCE, Pres., 300 Buttermilk Pike, Ste. 330, P.O. Box 17416, 41017, P 341,500, M 2,050, (859) 578-8800, Fax (859) 578-8802, info@nkychamber.com, www.nkychamber.com

**Frankfort** · *Frankfort Area C/C* · Carmen Inman, Exec. Dir., 100 Capital Ave., 40601, P 47,000, M 760, (502) 223-8261, Fax (502) 223-5942, chamber@frankfortky.info, www.frankfortky.info

**Franklin** · *Franklin-Simpson C/C* · Lee McBrayer, Pres., 201 S. Main St., P.O. Box 513, 42135, P 18,000, M 350, (270) 586-7609, Fax (270) 586-5438, cfreese@f-schamber.com, www.f-schamber.com

**Frenchburg** · *Frenchburg/Menifee County C/C* · Lola Thomas, Dir., 46 Back St., P.O. Box 333, 40322, P 6,500, M 97, (606) 768-9000, Fax (606) 768-9000, fchamber@mrtc.com, www.frenchburgmenifee.org

**Fulton** · *see South Fulton, TN*

**Georgetown** · *Georgetown-Scott County C/C* · John Conner, Exec. Dir., 160 E. Main St., 40324, P 39,550, M 601, (502) 863-5424, Fax (502) 863-5756, info@gtown.org, www.gtown.org

**Glasgow** · *Glasgow-Barren County C/C* · Ernie Myers, Exec. V.P., 118 E. Public Sq., 42141, P 39,200, M 471, (270) 651-3161, (800) 264-3161, Fax (270) 651-3122, chamber@glasgow-ky.com, www.glasgowbarrenchamber.com.

**Grand Rivers** · *Grand Rivers C of C & Tourism Comm.* · P.O. Box 181, 42045, P 350, M 65, (270) 362-0152, (888) 493-0152, info@grandrivers.com, www.grandrivers.com

**Grayson** · *Grayson Area C/C* · Don Combs, Pres., P.O. Box 612, 41143, P 18,000, M 130, (606) 474-4401, Fax same, don.combs@graysonrecc.com, www.graysonchamber.org

**Greensburg** · *Greensburg-Green County C/C* · John Henderson, Pres., 110 W. Court St., 42743, P 11,000, M 80, (270) 932-4298, Fax (270) 932-7778, director@greensburgonline.com, www.greensburgonline.com

**Greenville** · *Greater Muhlenberg C/C* · Dorothy Walker, Exec. Secy., 100 E. Main Cross, P.O. Box 313, 42345, P 32,000, M 220, (270) 338-5422, Fax (270) 338-5440, dw.chamber@muhlon.com, www.muhlenbergchamber.org

**Hardinsburg** · *Greater Breckinridge County C/C* · Sherry Stith, Exec. Dir., 224 S. Main St., P.O. Box 725, 40143, P 19,000, M 170, (270) 756-0268, Fax (270) 580-4783, chamber@breckinridgecountychamberky.com, www.breckinridgecountychamberky.com

**Harlan** · *Harlan County C/C* · Gladys Hoskins, Exec. Dir., 115 N. Cumberland Ave., P.O. Box 268, 40831, P 36,375, M 80, (606) 573-4717, Fax (606) 573-4717, chamber@harlanonline.com, www.harlancountychamber.com

**Harrison County** · *see Cynthiana*

**Harrodsburg** · *Mercer C/C* · Brenda Sexton, Exec. Dir., 488 Price Ave., Ste. 3, 40330, P 22,000, M 170, (859) 734-2365, info@mercerchamber.com, www.mercerchamber.com

**Hartford** · *Ohio County C/C* · P.O. Box 3, 42347, P 23,000, M 217, (270) 298-3551, Fax (270) 298-3331, ohiocochamber@ohiocounty.com, www.ohiocounty.com

**Hawesville** · *Hancock County C/C* · Edna Rice, Exec. Dir., P.O. Box 404, 42348, P 8,700, M 160, (270) 927-8223, Fax (270) 927-8223, erice@hancockky.us, www.hancockky.us

**Hazard** · *Hazard-Perry County C/C* · Betsy Clemons, Exec. Dir., 601 Main St., Ste. 3, 41701, P 32,000, M 140, (606) 439-2659, Fax (606) 436-6074, hazardcoc1@mikrotec.com, www.hazardperrychamber.com

**Henderson** · *Henderson-Henderson County C/C* · Brad Schneider, Pres., 201 N. Main St., 42420, P 46,500, M 500, (270) 826-9531, Fax (270) 827-4461, info@hendersonchamber.org, www.hendersonky.com

**Hickman** · *Hickman C/C* · P.O. Box 166, 42050, P 2,700, M 95, (270) 236-2902, hickmanchamber@galaxycable.net, www.hickmankychamber.org

**Highview** · *see Fern Creek*

**Hodgenville** · *LaRue County C/C* · Rita Williams, Exec. Dir., 60 Lincoln Sq., P.O. Box 176, 42748, P 13,150, M 150, (270) 358-3411, Fax (270) 358-3411, info@laruecountychamber.org, www.laruecountychamber.org

**Hopkinsville** · *Hopkinsville-Christian County C/C* · Betsy Shelton, Pres./CEO, 2800 Fort Campbell Blvd., 42240, P 73,000, M 600, (270) 885-9096, (800) 842-9959, Fax (270) 886-2059, chamber@hopkinsvillechamber.com, www.hopkinsvillechamber.com

**Irvine** · *Estill County Dev. Alliance* · P.O. Box 421, 40336, P 16,000, M 58, (606) 723-2450, info@estillcountyky.net, www.estillcountyky.net

**Jeffersontown** · *The Chamber Jeffersontown* · Carolyn Pfister, Mem. Dev. Dir., 10434 Watterson Trail, 40299, P 26,000, M 900, (502) 267-1674, Fax (502) 267-2070, info@jtownchamber.com, www.jtownchamber.com

**Kenton County** · *see Fort Mitchell*

**Kuttawa** · *Lyon County C/C* · Rick Fullard, Pres., 82 Days Inn Dr., 42055, P 9,200, M 160, (270) 388-4769, info@lyoncounty.com, www.lyoncounty.com

**La Center** · *Ballard County C/C & Tourism Center* · Barbara Jones, Dir., 547 W. Kentucky Dr., P.O. Box 322, 42056, P 8,900, M 245, (270) 665-8277, Fax (270) 665-8277, bcchamberinfo@brtc.net, www.ballardchamber.org

**LaGrange** · *Oldham County C/C* · Deana Epperly Karem, Exec. Dir., 412 E. Main St., 40031, P 50,000, M 406, (502) 222-1635, dkarem@oldhamcountychamber.com, www.oldhamcountychamber.com

**Lancaster** · *Garrard County C/C* · Susan Ledford, Secy./Treas., 208 Danville St., P.O. Box 462, 40444, P 18,000, M 80, (859) 792-2282, Fax (859) 792-2282, garrardchamber@gmail.com, www.garrardchamber.com

**Lawrenceburg** · *Anderson County C/C* · Catherine Myers, Exec. Dir., 100 N. Main St., Ste. 213, 40342, P 21,000, M 162, (502) 839-5564, Fax (502) 839-5106, chamber@lawrenceburgky.org, andersonchamberky.org

**Lebanon** · *Lebanon/Marion County C/C* · Dawna Kelch, Pres., 239 N. Spalding Ave., Ste. 201, 40033, P 18,000, M 220, (270) 692-9594, Fax (270) 692-2661, www.hamdays.com, lebanon@lebanon-ky.com, www.lebanon-ky.com

**Leitchfield** · *Grayson County C/C* · Caryn Lewis, Exec. Dir., 425 S. Main St., 42754, P 26,000, M 260, (270) 259-5587, (800) 667-5934, Fax (270) 259-9278, info@graysoncountychamber.com, www.graysoncountychamber.com

**Lexington** · *Commerce Lexington Inc.* · Robert L. Quick, Pres./CEO, 330 E. Main St., Ste. 100, 40507, P 450,000, M 2,100, (859) 254-4447, Fax (859) 233-3304, info@commercelexington.com, www.commercelexington.com

**Liberty** · *Liberty-Casey County C/C* · Jonathan Wilkerson, Pres., 518 Middleburg St., P.O. Box 278, 42539, P 15,250, M 60, (606) 787-6463, Fax (606) 787-7992, chamber@libertykentucky.org, www.libertykentucky.org/chamber.html

**London** · *London/Laurel County C/C* · Randy L. Smith, Exec. Dir., 409 S. Main St., 40741, P 60,000, M 550, (606) 864-4789, Fax (606) 864-7300, laurelco@windstream.net, www.london laurelchamber.com

**Louisville** · *Greater Louisville, Inc./The Metro Chamber* · Joe Reagan, Pres./CEO, 614 W. Main St., Ste. 6000, 40202, P 1,800,000, M 2,900, (502) 625-0000, Fax (502) 625-0010, info@greater louisville.com, www.greaterlouisville.com

**Madisonville** · *Madisonville-Hopkins County C/C* · Harriett Whitaker, Pres., 15 E. Center St., 42431, P 50,000, M 500, (270) 821-3435, Fax (270) 821-9190, c.commerce@newwavecomm.net, www.hopkinschamber.com

**Manchester** · *Manchester/Clay County C/C* · Joann Abner, Interim Dir., 277 White St., 40962, P 25,000, M 110, (606) 598-1754, Fax (606) 598-1545, claycochamber@windstream.net, www.kyclaycountychamber.org

**Marion** · *Crittenden County C/C* · Mark Bryant, Pres., 213 S. Main St., P.O. Box 164, 42064, P 9,400, M 138, (270) 965-5015, (800) 755-0361, Fax (270) 965-0058, chamber@marionkentucky. us, marionkentucky.us/chamber

**Mayfield** · *Mayfield & Graves County C/C* · Wendy Hunter, Exec. Dir., 201 E. College St., 42066, P 37,000, M 300, (270) 247-6101, Fax (270) 247-6110, chamber@mayfieldchamber.com, www. mayfieldchamber.com

**Maysville** · *Maysville-Mason County Area C/C* · Vicki Steigleder, Exec. Dir., 201 E. Third St., 41056, P 17,000, M 300, (606) 564-5534, (888) 875-MAYS, Fax (606) 564-5535, chamber@ maysvilleky.net, www.maysvillekentucky.com

**Middlesboro** · *Bell County C/C* · Nioma Lawson, Exec. Dir., N. 20th St., P.O. Box 788, 40965, P 30,060, M 230, (606) 248-1075, Fax (606) 248-8851, chamber@bellcountychamber.com, www. bellcountychamber.com

**Middletown** · *Louisville East-Middletown C/C* · Judy Francis, Pres./CEO, 12906 Shelbyville Rd., Ste. 250, 40253, P 8,500, M 300, (502) 244-8086, Fax (502) 244-0185, judy@middletownchamber. com, www.middletownchamber.com

**Monticello** · *Monticello-Wayne County C/C* · Penny Thompson, Admin. Asst., 120 S. Main St., Ste. 3, City Hall, P.O. Box 566, 42633, P 19,923, M 156, (606) 348-3064, (866) 348-3064, Fax (606) 348-3064, info@monticellokychamber.com, www.monticello kychamber.com

**Morehead** · *Morehead-Rowan County C/C* · Tracy Williams, Exec. Dir., 150 E. 1st St., 40351, P 26,000, M 380, (606) 784-6221, Fax (606) 783-1373, tcwilliams@moreheadchamber.com, www. moreheadchamber.com

**Morganfield** · *Morganfield C/C* · Becky Greenwell, Admin. Asst., P.O. Box 66, 42437, P 3,800, M 85, (270) 389-9777, Fax (270) 389-1112, mfieldchamber@bellsouth.net, www.morganfieldchamber.org

**Morgantown** · *Morgantown-Butler County C/C* · Amanda Hatcher, Exec. Dir., 112 S. Main, P.O. Box 408, 42261, P 13,010, M 135, (270) 526-6827, Fax (270) 526-6830, bcchamber07@ bellsouth.net, www.morgantown-ky.com

**Mount Sterling** · *Mt. Sterling-Montgomery County C/C* · Sandy Romenesko, Exec. Dir., 126 W. Main St., 40353, P 26,500, M 360, (859) 498-5343, Fax (859) 498-3947, sandy@mtsterling chamber.com, www.mtsterlingchamber.com.

**Munfordville** · *Hart County C/C* · Virginia Davis, Exec. Dir., 119 E. Union St., P.O. Box 688, 42765, P 18,887, M 260, (270) 524-2892, Fax (270) 524-1127, hart_co@scrtc.com, www.hartcountyky.org

**Murray** · *Murray-Calloway County C/C* · Lance Allison, Exec. Dir., 805 N. 12th St., P.O. Box 190, 42071, P 35,000, M 750, (270) 753-5171, (270) 753-5188, (800) 900-5171, Fax (270) 753-0948, chamber@mymurray.com, www.mymurray.com

**New Castle** · *Henry County C/C* · Pat Wallace, Exec. Dir., P.O. Box 355, 40050, P 15,093, M 225, (502) 845-0806, Fax (502) 845-5313, henrychamber@insightbb.com, chamber.henrycountyky.com

**Nicholasville** · *Jessamine County C/C* · Nancy Stone, Exec. Dir., 508 N. Main St., Ste. A, 40356, P 44,000, M 549, (859) 887-4351, Fax (859) 887-1211, jessaminechamber@windstream.net, www. jessamine-chamber.com

**Olive Hill** · *Olive Hill Area C/C* · P.O. Box 1570, 41164, P 2,500, M 197, (606) 286-6115, (606) 286-5533, ohcoc@atcc.net, www. atcc.net/chamber

**Owensboro** · *Greater Owensboro C/C* · Jody Wassmer, Pres., 200 E. 3rd St., Ste. 101, P.O. Box 825, 42302, P 92,000, M 900, (270) 926-1860, Fax (270) 926-3364, chamber@owensboro.com, www.owensboro.com

**Owingsville** · *Owingsville-Bath County C/C* · Jackie Watson, Pres., P.O. Box 360, 40360, P 11,000, M 60, (606) 674-2266, www. owingsville.com

**Paducah** · *Paducah Area C/C* · Elaine Spalding, Pres., 401 Kentucky Ave., P.O. Box 810, 42002, P 65,000, M 1,125, (270) 443-1746, Fax (270) 442-9152, info@paducahchamber.org, www.paducahchamber.org

**Paintsville** · *Paintsville-Johnson County C/C* · Fran Jarrell, Exec. Dir., 124 Main St., P.O. Box 629, 41240, P 24,000, M 90, (606) 422-8204, pjcchamber@foothills.net, www.pjcchamber.com

**Paris** · *Paris-Bourbon County C/C* · Lucy Cooper, Exec. Dir., 720 High St., 40361, P 20,000, M 200, (859) 987-3205, Fax (859) 987-4640, lcooper@parisky.org, www.parisky.org

**Pikeville** · *Pike County C/C* · Brad Hall, Pres./CEO, 787 Hambley Blvd., 41501, P 74,000, M 450, (606) 432-5504, Fax (606) 432-7295, info@pikecountychamber.org, www.pikecountychamber.org

**Prestonsburg** · *Floyd County C/C* · Mandy Stumbo, Exec. Dir., 113 S. Central Ave., P.O. Box 1508, 41653, P 44,000, M 200, (606) 886-0364, Fax (606) 886-0422, floydchamber@setel.com, www. floydcountykentucky.com

**Princeton** · *Princeton-Caldwell County C/C* · Kate Prince, 110 W. Washington St., 42445, P 13,000, M 200, (270) 365-5393, chamberofcommerce@pepb.net, www.princetonky.org

**Radcliff** · *Radcliff-Hardin County C/C* · Jo Emary, Exec. Dir., 306 N. Wilson Rd., 40160, P 25,000, M 360, (270) 351-4450, Fax (270) 352-4449, jo@radcliffchamber.org, www.radcliffchamber.org

**Richmond** · *Richmond C/C* · Mendi Goble, Exec. Dir., 201 E. Main St., 40475, P 27,000, M 743, (859) 623-1720, Fax (859) 623-0839, rchamber@richmondchamber.com, www.richmondchamber.com

**Russell Springs** · *Russell County C/C* · Debbie Conner, Admin. Asst., 650 S. Hwy. 127, P.O. Box 64, 42642, P 17,500, M 240, (270) 866-4333, (888) 833-4220, Fax (270) 866-4304, lake@russell countyky.com, www.russellcountyky.com

**Russellville** · *Logan County C/C* · Lisa Browning, Exec. Dir., 116 S. Main St., 42276, P 26,000, M 300, (270) 726-2206, Fax (270) 726-2237, lisa@loganchamber.com, www.loganchamber.com

**Scottsville** · *Scottsville-Allen County C/C* · Sue Shaver, Exec. Dir., 102 Public Sq., P.O. Box 416, 42164, P 18,706, M 250, (270) 237-4782, Fax (270) 237-5498, chamber@scottsvilleky.info, www. scottsvilleky.info

**Sebree** · *Sebree C/C* · Mike Walker, P.O. Box 245, 42455, P 1,510, M 45, (270) 835-7501

**Shelbyville** · *Shelby County C/C* · Shelley Goodwin, Exec. Dir., 316 Main St., P.O. Box 335, 40066, P 37,219, M 385, (502) 633-1636, Fax (502) 633-7501, info@shelbycountykychamber.com, www.shelbycountykychamber.com

**Shepherdsville** · *Bullitt County C/C* · Kristie Walls, Exec. Dir., 279 S. Buckman, P.O. Box 1656, 40165, P 70,000, M 450, (502) 955-9641, Fax (502) 543-1765, kwalls@bullittchamber.com, www.bullittchamber.com.

**Somerset** · *Somerset-Pulaski County C/C* · Jack Keeney, Exec. Dir., 445 S. Hwy. 27, Ste. 301, 42501, P 60,000, M 650, (606) 679-7323, Fax (606) 679-1744, info@spcchamber.com, www.spcchamber.com

**Springfield** · *Springfield/Washington County C/C* · Ralph Blandford, Pres., 124 W. Main St., Ste. 3, 40069, P 10,900, M 150, (859) 336-3810, Fax (859) 336-9410, info@springfieldkychamber.com, www.springfieldkychamber.com

**Stanford** · *Lincoln County C/C* · Andrea Miller, Exec. Dir., 201 E. Main St., Ste. 5, 40484, P 23,000, M 200, (606) 365-4118, Fax (606) 365-4118, director@lincolncountychamber.com, www.lincolncountychamber.com

**Stanton** · *Red River C/C* · James Combs, Pres., P.O. Box 1804, 40380, P 13,500, M 50, (606) 663-6631, Fax (606) 663-2267, www.kyredriverchamber.com

**Sturgis** · *Sturgis C/C* · Lisa Jones, Ofc. Mgr., 513 N. Main St., P.O. Box 125, 42459, P 2,184, M 65, (270) 333-9316, Fax (270) 333-9319, sturgisc@sturgischamberofcommerce.com, www.sturgischamberofcommerce.com

**Taylorsville** · *Taylorsville-Spencer County C/C* · Jerry L. Davis, Pres., P.O. Box 555, 40071, P 15,800, M 85, (502) 477-8369, www.spencercountyky.gov/chamber.html

**Tompkinsville** · *Tompkinsville/Monroe County C/C & Eco. Dev.* · Charles Emberton, 202 N. Magnolia St., 42167, P 11,000, M 100, (270) 487-1314, Fax (270) 487-0975, monroecountyedc@live.com, www.monroecountyky.com

**Versailles** · *Woodford County C/C* · Tami Vater, Exec. Dir., 141 N. Main St., 40383, P 25,000, M 340, (859) 873-5122, Fax (859) 873-4576, info@woodfordcountyinfo.com, www.woodfordcountyinfo.com

**Warsaw** · *Gallatin County C/C* · Steve Henderson, Pres., P.O. Box 1029, 41095, P 8,000, M 40, (859) 567-7900, www.gallatincountyky.com

**West Liberty** · *Morgan County C/C* · Hank Allen, Pres., 565 Main St., 41472, P 18,000, M 50, (606) 743-2300, (606) 743-3195, wliberty@mrtc.com, www.cityofwestliberty.com

**West Point** · *West Point C/C* · Roszelle Moore, P.O. Box 33, 40177, P 1,170, M 50, (502) 922-4505, roszelleh@hotmail.com, www.westpointky.org

**Whitesburg** · *Letcher County C/C* · Brenda DePriest, Pres., P.O. Box 127, 41858, P 27,000, M 35, (606) 832-4020, jbdep@yahoo.com, www.letchercountychamber.com

**Whitley City** · *McCreary County C/C* · Jimmie W. Greene, Pres., P.O. Box 548, 42653, P 17,200, M 110, (606) 376-5004, Fax (606) 376-9060, chamber7@highland.net, www.mccrearychamber.com

**Williamstown** · *Grant County C/C & Eco. Dev.* · Wade Gutman, P.O. Box 365, 41097, P 26,000, M 250, (859) 824-3322, (800) 824-2858, Fax (859) 824-7082, wgutman@grantcommerce.com, www.grantcommerce.com

**Winchester** · *Winchester-Clark County C/C* · Charmagne Castle, Pres./CEO, 2 S. Maple St., 40391, P 35,000, M 400, (859) 744-6420, Fax (859) 744-9229, charm@winchesterkychamber.com, www.winchesterkychamber.com

# Louisiana

**Louisiana Assn. of Bus. & Ind.** · Daniel Juneau, Pres., 3113 Valley Creek Dr., P.O. Box 80258, Baton Rouge, 70898, P 4,000,000, M 3,000, (225) 928-5388, Fax (225) 929-6054, labi@labi.org, www.labi.org

**Abbeville** · *Greater Abbeville-Vermilion C/C* · Lynn Guillory, Exec. Dir., 1907 Veterans Memorial Dr., 70510, P 52,000, M 240, (337) 893-2491, Fax (337) 893-1807, abbevillechamber@abbevillechamber.com, www.abbevillechamber.com

**Abita Springs** · *see Covington*

**Addis** · *West Baton Rouge C/C* · Deborah Biggs, Exec. Dir., 7520 Hwy. 1 S., P.O. Box 448, 70710, P 23,000, M 315, (225) 383-3140, Fax (225) 685-1044, info@wbrchamber.org, www.wbrchamber.org.

**Alexandria** · *Central Louisiana C/C* · Elton Pody, Pres., 1118 Third St., P.O. Box 992, 71309, P 400,000, M 1,000, (318) 442-6671, Fax (318) 442-6734, info@cenlachamber.org, www.cenlachamber.org

**Amite** · *Amite C/C* · Mike Case, Pres., 101 S.E. Central Ave., 70422, P 4,800, M 115, (985) 748-5537, Fax (985) 748-5537, amitecoc@I-55.com, www.amitechamberofcommerce.org

**Arcadia** · *Arcadia/Bienville Parish C/C* · Virginia Becker, Ofc. Mgr., 2440 Hazel St., P.O. Box 587, 71001, P 3,000, M 136, (318) 263-9897, Fax (318) 263-9897, arcadiachamber@bellsouth.net

**Arnaudville** · *Arnaudville C/C* · Todd Guilbeau, Pres., 292 Front St., P.O. Box 125, 70512, P 1,400, M 100, (337) 754-5316, Fax same, arnaudvillecc@aol.com, www.arnaudvillechamber.com

**Ascension** · *The Ascension C/C* · Sherrie Despino, Pres./CEO, 1006 W. Hwy. 30, P.O. Box 1204, Gonzales, 70707, P 100,000, M 500, (225) 647-7487, Fax (225) 647-5124, info@ascensionchamber.com, www.ascensionchamber.com.

**Baker** · *Baker C/C* · Monteal Carson-Margolis, Mktg. Dir., 3439 Groom Rd., 70714, P 15,000, M 160, (225) 775-3547, Fax (225) 775-8060, bakercoc@bellsouth.net

**Bastrop** · *Bastrop-Morehouse Parish C/C* · Dorothy Ford, Exec. Dir., 110 N. Franklin St., P.O. Box 1175, 71221, P 30,450, M 365, (318) 281-3794, Fax (318) 281-3781, director@bastroplacoc.org, www.bastroplacoc.org

**Baton Rouge** · *Baton Rouge Area C/C* · Adam Knapp, Pres./CEO, 564 Laurel St., 70801, P 780,000, M 1,500, (225) 381-7125, Fax (225) 336-4306, info@brac.org, www.brac.org

**Bogalusa** · *Bogalusa C/C* · Marilyn Bateman, Exec. Dir., 608 Willis Ave., 70427, P 15,200, M 250, (985) 735-5731, Fax (985) 735-6707, bogalusachamber@bellsouth.net, www.bogalusachamber.cc

**Bossier City** · *Bossier C/C* · Lisa Johnson, Exec. Dir., 710 Benton Rd., 71111, P 100,000, M 1,187, (318) 746-0252, Fax (318) 746-0357, info@bossierchamber.com, www.bossierchamber.com

**Breaux Bridge** · *Breaux Bridge Area C/C* · Tina Begnaud, Exec. Dir., 314 E. Bridge St., P.O. Box 88, 70517, P 8,000, M 230, (337) 332-5406, Fax (337) 332-5424, bbcc@centurytel.net, www.breauxbridgelive.com

**Bunkie** · *Bunkie C/C* · Phyllis Oquin, Secy., 110 N.W. Main St., P.O. Box 70, 71322, P 5,000, M 110, (318) 346-2575, Fax (318) 346-2576, bunkiechamber@bellsouth.net, www.bunkie.org

**Cameron** · *Cameron Parish C/C & Tourist Info. Center* · P.O. Box 1248, 70631, P 7,000, M 50, (337) 775-5222, info@cameronparish.com, www.cameronparish.com

**Central** · *City of Central C/C* · Juanita Ross, Admin. Asst., 13567 Hooper Rd., P.O. Box 78107, 70837, P 28,000, M 240, (225) 261-5818, Fax (225) 261-5122, chamber@cityofcentralchamber.com, www.cityofcentralchamber.com

**Claiborne** · *see Homer*

**Colfax** · *Grant Parish C/C* · W.T. McCain III, Pres., 277 Mead Rd., P.O. Box 32, 71417, P 20,000, M 100, (318) 627-2211, info@grantcoc.org, www.grantcoc.org

**Columbia** · *Caldwell Parish C/C* · Beth Hefner, Pres., P.O. Box 726, 71418, P 10,200, M 85, (318) 649-0726, Fax (318) 649-0509, msccth@yahoo.com, www.caldwellchamber.com

**Coushatta** · *Red River C/C* · 620 Rush St., P.O. Box 333, 71019, P 9,622, M 126, (318) 932-3289, Fax (318) 932-6919, redriver chamber@bellsouth.net, www.chamber.coushatta.net

**Covington** · *St. Tammany West C/C* · Lacey O. Toledano, Pres., 610 Hollycrest Blvd., 70433, P 220,000, M 1,100, (985) 892-3216, Fax (985) 893-4244, info@sttammanychamber.org, www.sttammanychamber.org

**Crowley** · *Crowley C/C* · Kayla Link, Pres./CEO, 11 N. Parkerson Ave., P.O. Box 2125, 70527, P 14,613, M 300, (337) 788-0177, Fax (337) 783-9507, kayla@crowleychamber.com, www.crowley chamber.com.

**Cut Off** · *see Larose*

**Denham Springs** · *Livingston Parish C/C* · Sherry Mely, Chrmn., 133 Hummell St., P.O. Box 591, 70727, P 102,000, M 385, (225) 665-8155, Fax (225) 665-2411, info@livingstonparishchamber.org, www.livingstonparishchamber.org

**DeQuincy** · *DeQuincy C/C* · P.O. Box 625, 70633, P 3,600, M 87, (337) 786-6451, Fax (337) 786-6451

**DeRidder** · *Greater Beauregard C/C* · Avon Knowlton, Exec. V.P., 111 N. Washington Ave., P.O. Box 309, 70634, P 32,986, M 400, (337) 463-5533, Fax (337) 463-2244, vicepresident@bellsouth.net, www.beauparish.org

**Donaldsonville** · *Donaldsonville Area C/C* · Becky Katz, Exec. Dir., 714 Railroad Ave., 70346, P 8,300, M 140, (225) 473-4814, Fax (225) 473-4817, dvillecoc@bellsouth.net, www.donaldson ville.org

**Dutchtown** · *see Ascension*

**Eunice** · *Eunice C/C* · Robin McGee, Exec. Dir., 200 S. C.C. Duson St., P.O. Box 508, 70535, P 12,000, M 200, (337) 457-2565, Fax (337) 546-0278, eunicecc@charterinternet.com, eunicechamber.com

**Farmerville** · *Union Parish C/C* · Jean Jones, Pres., 303 E. Water St., P.O. Box 67, 71241, P 24,000, M 126, (318) 368-3947, Fax (318) 368-3945, upcoc@bayou.com, www.unionparishchamber.org

**Ferriday** · *Ferriday C/C* · Liz Brookings, Pres., 218 Louisiana Ave., 71334, P 4,000, M 70, (318) 757-4297, www.ferridaychamber.org

**Folsom** · *see Covington*

**Franklin** · *St. Mary C/C* · Donna Meyer, Exec. Dir., 600 Main St., 70538, P 60,000, M 650, (985) 384-3830, Fax (337) 828-5606, info@stmarychamberofcommerce.com, www.stmarychamber ofcommerce.com

**Franklinton** · *Franklinton C/C* · Linda E. Crain, Exec. Dir., 1051 Main St., 70438, P 3,718, M 145, (985) 839-5822, franklinton chamber@franklinton.net, www.franklintonlouisiana.org

**Geismar** · *see Ascension*

**Gonzales** · *see Ascension*

**Grambling** · *Grambling C/C* · 2035 Martin Luther King Jr. Ave., P.O. Box 703, 71245, P 5,000, M 35, (318) 247-0803

**Gueydan** · *Gueydan C/C* · Jamie Gayle, Pres., P.O. Box 562, 70542, P 1,700, M 120, www.gueydan.org

**Hammond** · *Hammond C/C* · Charlotte Lenoir, Exec. Dir., 400 N.W. Railroad Ave., P.O. Box 1458, 70404, P 25,000, M 600, (985) 345-4457, Fax (985) 345-4749, director@hammondchamber.org, www.hammondchamber.org.

**Homer** · *Claiborne C/C* · John Watson, Exec. Dir., 519 S. Main St., 71040, P 17,000, M 160, (318) 927-3271, Fax (318) 927-3271, jdwatson_ccoc@bellsouth.net, www.claiborneone.org

**Houma** · *Houma-Terrebonne C/C* · Drake Pothier, Pres./CEO, 6133 Hwy. 311, 70360, P 107,491, M 825, (985) 876-5600, Fax (985) 876-5611, info@houmachamber.com, www.houmachamber.com.

**Jackson** · *Feliciana C/C* · Audrey Faciana, Exec. Dir., 1752 High St., P.O. Box 667, 70748, P 22,000, M 90, (225) 634-7155, Fax (225) 634-7155, tourism1@bellsouth.net, www.felicianatourism.org

**Jeanerette** · *Jeanerette C/C* · Peggy Parker, Exec. Dir., 500 E. Main St., P.O. Box 31, 70544, P 6,500, M 90, (337) 276-4293, Fax (337) 276-5911, sugarcity@msis.net, www.jeanerette.com

**Jennings** · *Jeff Davis Bus. Alliance* · Cynthia Hoffpauir, Pres./CEO, 246 N. Main St., P.O. Box 1209, 70546, P 32,000, M 411, (337) 824-0933, Fax (337) 824-0934, cynthia@jdbusinessalliance.com, www.jdbusinessalliance.com.

**Jonesboro** · *Jackson Parish C/C* · Wilda Smith, Dir., 102 Fourth St., 71251, P 16,000, M 171, (318) 259-4693, Fax (318) 395-8539, jacksonparishcoc@aol.com, www.jacksonparishchamber.org

**Kaplan** · *Kaplan Area C/C* · Nancy Matthews, Exec. Dir., 701 N. Cushing, 70548, P 5,000, M 86, (337) 643-2400, Fax (337) 643-2400, kchamber@kaplantel.net, www.kaplanchamber.org

**Kinder** · *Kinder C/C* · Pat Paxton, Secy., P.O. Box 853, 70648, P 2,800, M 150, (337) 738-5945, kindercc@centurytel.net, www.kinderchamber.com

**Lacombe** · *Lacombe C/C* · Patti Young, Pres., P.O. Box 889, 70445, P 9,000, M 120, (985) 882-7442, Fax (985) 882-8002

**Lafayette** · *Greater Lafayette C/C* · Robert M. Guidry, Pres./CEO, 804 E. St. Mary Blvd., P.O. Drawer 51307, 70505, P 202,569, M 1,400, (337) 233-2705, Fax (337) 234-8671, rguidry@lafcham ber.org, www.lafchamber.org.

**Lake Charles** · *The Chamber/Southwest Louisiana* · George Swift, Pres./CEO, 120 W. Pujo St., P.O. Box 3110, 70602, P 287,001, M 1,050, (337) 433-3632, Fax (337) 436-3727, gswift@allianc-eswla.org, www.chamberswla.org.

**Larose** · *C/C of Lafourche and the Bayou Region* · Lin Kiger, Pres./CEO, 107 W. 26th St., P.O. Box 1462, 70373, P 90,000, M 400, (985) 693-6700, Fax (985) 693-6702, lafchamber@lafourche chamber.com, www.lafourchechamber.com.

**Leesville** · *Greater Vernon C/C* · Eddie Wise, Exec. Dir., 9261 Shreveport Hwy., P.O. Box 1228, 71496, P 52,000, M 302, (337) 238-0349, (877) 234-0349, Fax (337) 238-0340, chambervernon parish@hotmail.com, www.chambervernonparish.com.

**Logansport** · *Logansport C/C* · 606 Main St., P.O. Box 320, 71049, P 1,700, M 35, (318) 697-0076, (318) 697-5359

**Madisonville** · *Greater Madisonville Area C/C* · Kimberly Hahn, P.O. Box 746, 70447, P 4,000, M 100, (985) 845-9824, bill@xlinc.net, www.madisonvillechamber.org

**Mandeville** · *see Covington*

**Mansfield** · *DeSoto Parish C/C* · James R. May, Exec. Dir., 115 N. Washington, 71052, P 26,000, M 195, (318) 872-1310, Fax (318) 871-1875, chamber75@bellsouth.net, www.desotoparish chamber.net

**Mansura** · *Mansura C/C* · P.O. Box 536, 71350, P 4,000, M 200, (318) 964-2887, (318) 964-2931, chamber@cochondelait.com, www.cochondelait.com

**Many** · *Sabine Parish C/C* · Liz Tramel, Dir., 1601 Texas Hwy., 71449, P 24,000, M 300, (318) 256-3523, Fax (318) 256-4137, spchamber@cp-tel.net, www.sabineparish.com.

**Marksville** · *Marksville C/C* · Eleanor Gremillion, Secy., P.O. Box 767, 71351, P 6,400, M 300, (318) 253-0284, (318) 253-9222, Fax (318) 253-0457

**Metairie** · *Jefferson C/C* · Glenn Hayes, Pres./CEO, 3421 N. Causeway Blvd., Ste. 203, 70002, P 525,000, M 900, (504) 835-3880, Fax (504) 835-3828, glenn@jeffersonchamber.org, www.jeffersonchamber.org

**Minden** · *Minden-South Webster Parish C/C* · Gina-Eubanks Almond, Chrmn., 110 Sibley Rd., 71055, P 28,689, M 360, (318) 377-4240, Fax (318) 377-4215, www.mindenchamber.com

**Monroe** · *Monroe C/C* · Sue Nicholson, Pres./CEO, 212 Walnut St., Ste. 100, 71201, P 150,000, M 910, (318) 323-3461, (888) 531-9535, Fax (318) 322-7594, monroe@monroe.org, www.monroe.org.

**Morgan City** · *St. Mary C/C* · Donna Meyer, Pres., 7332 Hwy. 182 E., P.O. Box 2606, 70381, P 60,000, M 650, (985) 384-3830, Fax (985) 384-0771, info@stmarychamber.com, www.stmarychamber.com

**Napoleonville** · *Assumption Area C/C* · Ella Metrejean, Exec. Dir., 123 Jefferson St., P.O. Box 718, 70390, P 24,000, M 180, (985) 369-2816, Fax (985) 369-2811, assumption@bellsouth.net, www.assumptionchamber.org

**Natchitoches** · *Natchitoches Area C/C* · Nick Pollacia Jr., Pres., 562 Second St., P.O. Box 3, 71458, P 39,080, M 324, (318) 352-6894, Fax (318) 352-5385, chamber@natchitoches.net, www.natchitocheschamber.com

**New Iberia** · *Greater Iberia C/C* · Mary Ellen Wilke, Pres./CEO, 111 W. Main St., 70560, P 75,000, M 700, (337) 364-1836, Fax (337) 367-7405, info@iberiachamber.org, www.iberiachamber.org

**New Orleans** · *New Orleans C/C* · Alex Lewis, Interim Dir., 1515 Poydras St., Ste. 1010, 70112, P 181,000, M 663, (504) 799-4260, Fax (504) 799-4259, alewis@neworleanschamber.org, www.neworleanschamber.org

**New Roads** · *Greater Pointe Coupee C/C* · Brian Adams, Pres., P.O. Box 555, 70760, P 23,000, M 150, (225) 638-3500, Fax (225) 638-9858, pointecoupeechamber@yahoo.com, www.pcchamber.org

**Oak Grove** · *West Carroll C/C* · Harold Russell, Pres., 306 E. Main St., P.O. Box 1336, 71263, P 15,000, M 86, (318) 428-8289, Fax (318) 428-4421, wcchamber@bellsouth.net

**Oakdale** · *Oakdale Area C/C* · Lisa Schaefer, Pres., 107 S. 12th St., P.O. Box 1138, 71463, P 8,137, M 153, (318) 335-1729, Fax (318) 215-1729, oakdaleareachamber@bellsouth.net, www.oakdalela.org

**Opelousas** · *Opelousas-Saint Landry C/C* · Ms. Frankie Bertrand, Pres./CEO, 109 W. Vine St., 70570, P 28,000, M 480, (337) 942-2683, Fax (337) 942-2684, opelousaschamber@charter.net, www.opelousaschamber.org

**Plaquemine** · *Iberville C/C* · Hank Grace, Exec. Dir., 23675 Church St., P.O. Box 248, 70765, P 33,400, M 260, (225) 687-3560, Fax (225) 687-3575, hgrace@ibervillechamber.com, www.ibervillechamber.com

**Ponchatoula** · *Ponchatoula C/C* · Jamene Dahmer, Secy., 109 W. Pine, P.O. Box 306, 70454, P 9,000, M 300, (985) 386-2533, (985) 386-2536, Fax (985) 386-2533, chamber@ponchatoulachamber.com, www.ponchatoulachamber.com

**Prairieville** · *see Ascension*

**Raceland** · *see Larose*

**Rayne** · *Rayne C/C* · Jan Cormier, Dir., 107 Oak St., P.O. Box 383, 70578, P 8,552, M 125, (337) 334-2332, Fax (337) 334-8341, raynechamber1@bellsouth.net, www.rayne.org/chamber.html

**Ruston** · *Ruston-Lincoln C/C* · Scott C. Terry, Pres., 2111 N. Trenton, P.O. Box 1383, 71273, P 43,000, M 493, (318) 255-2031, Fax (318) 255-3481, sterry@rustonlincoln.org, www.rustonlincoln.org.

**Sabine Parish** · *see Many*

**Saint Amant** · *see Ascension*

**Saint Francisville** · *Greater St. Francisville C/C* · Linda Osterberger, Dir., 11936 Ferdinand St., P.O. Box 545, 70775, P 15,111, M 200, (225) 635-6717, Fax (225) 635-6885, sfchamber@bellsouth.net, www.stfrancisvillechamber.com

**Saint Landry** · *see Opelousas*

**Saint Martinville** · *Saint Martinville C/C* · Marian Melancon, Exec. Dir., 120 New Market St., P.O. Box 436, 70582, P 8,000, M 120, (337) 394-7578, Fax (337) 394-4497, mbmtax@cox.net, www.stmartinvillechamber.com

**Shreveport** · *Greater Shreveport C/C* · Richard H. Bremer, Pres., 400 Edwards St., 71101, P 400,000, M 1,920, (318) 677-2500, (800) 448-5432, Fax (318) 677-2541, info@shreveportchamber.org, www.shreveportchamber.org

**Slidell** · *East St. Tammany C/C* · Dawn Sharpe Brackett, CEO, 118 W. Hall Ave., 70460, P 100,000, M 800, (985) 643-5678, (800) 471-3758, Fax (985) 649-2460, info@estchamber.com, www.estchamber.com

**Sorrento** · *see Ascension*

**South Webster Parish** · *see Minden*

**Springhill** · *Springhill-North Webster C/C* · Robert Bryan, Pres., 400 N. Giles St., 71075, P 5,700, M 150, (318) 539-4717, Fax (318) 539-2500, chamberc@cmaaccess.com, www.springhilllouisiana.net

**Sulphur** · *West Calcasieu Assn. of Commerce* · Sheron Faulk, Pres., 1906 Maplewood Dr., 70663, P 21,103, M 190, (337) 533-1040, associationw@bellsouth.net, www.westcal.org

**Thibodaux** · *Thibodaux C/C* · Kathy Benoit, Pres./CEO, 318 E. Bayou Rd., P.O. Box 467, 70302, P 38,000, M 650, (985) 446-1187, Fax (985) 446-1191, info@thibodauxchamber.com, www.thibodauxchamber.com.

**Vernon** · *see Leesville*

**Vidalia** · *Vidalia C/C* · Kathy Nunnery, Dir., 1401 Carter St., 71373, P 5,500, M 185, (318) 336-8223, Fax (318) 336-8215, chamber@vidaliala.com, www.vidaliala.com.

**Ville Platte** · *Ville Platte C/C* · Camille Fontenot, Exec. Dir., 306 W. Main St., P.O. Box 331, 70586, P 8,000, M 135, (337) 363-1878, Fax (337) 363-1894, villep001@centurytel.net, vpchamber.com

**Vinton** · *see Sulphur*

**Vivian** · *Vivian C/C* · Betty Matthews, Pres., 100 N.W. Front St., P.O. Box 182, 71082, P 4,031, M 40, (318) 375-5300, chamberofcom@centurytel.net, www.vivian.la.us

**Welsh** · *Welsh C/C* · 201S. Elms St., P.O. Box 786, 70591, P 3,500, M 50, (337) 734-4772, (337) 734-2231, welshla@centurytel.net, www.townofwelsh.com

**West Baton Rouge** · *see Addis*

**West Monroe** · *West Monroe-West Ouachita C/C* · Mary Ann Newton, Pres., 112 Professional Dr., 71291, P 15,000, M 661, (318) 325-1961, Fax (318) 325-4296, info@westmonroechamber.org, westmonroechamber.org.

**Westlake** · *see Sulphur*

**Winnfield** · *Winn C/C* · June Melton, Secy., 499 E. Main St., P.O. Box 565, 71483, P 17,714, M 150, (318) 628-4461, Fax (318) 628-2551, winnchamber@bellsouth.net, www.winnchamber ofcommerce.com

**Winnsboro** · *Winnsboro-Franklin Parish C/C* · Lindy Price, Pres., 3830 Front St., P.O. Box 1574, 71295, P 23,000, M 160, (318) 435-4488, Fax (318) 435-5398, winnsborochamber@bellsouth.net, www.winnsborochamber.com

**Zachary** · *Zachary C/C* · Ann Rasmussen, Exec. Dir., 4633 Main St., 70791, P 14,275, M 310, (225) 654-6777, Fax (225) 654-3957, arasmussen@zacharyla.com, www.zacharyla.com

# Maine

**Maine State C of C** · Dana F. Connors, Pres., 7 University Dr., Augusta, 04330, P 1,300,000, M 1,200, (207) 623-4568, Fax (207) 622-7723, rstoddard@mainechamber.org, www.mainechamber.org.

**Appleton** · *see Union*

**Auburn** · *see Lewiston*

**Augusta** · *Kennebec Valley C/C* · Peter G. Thompson, Pres., 21 University Dr., P.O. Box 676, 04332, P 70,000, M 650, (207) 623-4559, Fax (207) 626-9342, info@augustamaine.com, www.augustamaine.com.

**Bangor** · *Bangor Reg. C/C* · Candace Guerette, Pres., 519 Main St., P.O. Box 1443, 04402, P 104,000, M 850, (207) 947-0307, Fax (207) 990-1427, chamber@bangorregion.com, www.bangor region.com.

**Bar Harbor** · *Bar Harbor C/C* · Mr. Chris Fogg, CEO, P.O. Box 158, 04609, P 4,500, M 450, (207) 664-2940, (800) 288-5103, Fax (207) 667-9080, visitors@barharborinfo.com, www.barharborinfo.com

**Bath** · *see Topsham*

**Belfast** · *Belfast Area C/C* · Dawn Place, Pres., P.O. Box 58, 04915, P 7,000, M 310, (207) 338-5900, Fax (207) 338-5823, info@belfastmaine.org, www.belfastmaine.org

**Benedicta** · *see Island Falls*

**Bethel** · *Bethel Area C/C* · Robin Zinchuk, Exec. Dir., 8 Station Pl., Bethel Train Station, P.O. Box 1247, 04217, P 6,000, M 248, (207) 824-2282, (800) 442-5826, Fax (207) 824-7123, info@ bethelmaine.com, www.bethelmaine.com.

**Biddeford** · *see Saco*

**Bingham** · *Upper Kennebec Valley C/C* · Bruce A Pelletier, Pres., 356 Main St., P.O. Box 491, 04920, P 1,000, M 50, (207) 672-4100, upperkennebecvalleychamber.me

**Blue Hill** · *Blue Hill Peninsula C/C* · Susan Walsh, Exec. Dir., 107 Main St., P.O. Box 520, 04614, P 8,000, M 240, (207) 374-3242, chamber@bluehillpeninsula.org, www.bluehillpeninsula.org

**Boothbay** · *Boothbay C/C* · P.O. Box 187, 04537, P 5,000, M 190, (207) 633-4743, info@boothbay.org, www.boothbay.org

**Boothbay Harbor** · *Boothbay Harbor Reg. C/C* · Jaimie Logan, Exec. Dir., P.O. Box 356, 04538, P 7,500, M 360, (207) 633-2353, Fax (207) 633-7448, seamaine@boothbayharbor.com, www.boothbayharbor.com

**Bowdoinham** · *see Topsham*

**Bridgton** · *Greater Bridgton Lakes Reg. C/C* · Michael McClellan, Exec. Dir., 101 Portland Rd., P.O. Box 236, 04009, P 28,000, M 465, (207) 647-3472, Fax (207) 647-8372, info@ mainelakeschamber.com, www.mainelakeschamber.com

**Brighton** · *see Bingham*

**Brooklin** · *see Blue Hill*

**Brooksville** · *see Blue Hill*

**Brunswick** · *see Topsham*

**Bucksport** · *Bucksport Bay Area C/C* · Maureen Harris, Exec. Dir., P.O. Box 1676, 04416, P 5,000, M 225, (207) 469-6818, Fax (207) 469-2078, director@bucksportbaychamber.com, www.bucksportbaychamber.com

**Burlington** · *see Lincoln*

**Calais** · *St. Croix Valley C/C* · 39 Union St., 04619, P 4,000, M 100, (207) 454-2308, (888) 422-3112, Fax (207) 454-7979, visitstcroixvalley@verizon.net, www.visitstcroixvalley.com

**Camden** · *Camden-Rockport-Lincolnville C/C* · Dan Bookham, Exec. Dir., 2 Public Landing, P.O. Box 919, 04843, P 12,000, M 700, (207) 236-4404, (800) 223-5459, Fax (207) 236-4315, chamber@camdenme.org, www.visitcamden.com

**Caratunk** · *see Bingham*

**Caribou** · *Caribou C of C & Ind.* · Wendy Landes, Exec. Dir., 24 Sweden St., Ste. 101, 04736, P 8,500, M 244, (207) 498-6156, (800) 722-7648, Fax (207) 492-1362, ccci@cariboumaine.net, www.cariboumaine.net

**Carroll** · *see Lincoln*

**Casco** · *see Windham*

**Castine** · *see Blue Hill*

**Chester** · *see Lincoln*

**Corinna** · *see Newport*

**Crystal/Golden Ridge** · *see Island Falls*

**Damariscotta** · *Damariscotta Region C/C* · Lori Bryant, Op. Dir., 15 Courtyard St., Ste. 2, P.O. Box 13, 04543, P 2,000, M 300, (207) 563-8340, Fax (207) 563-8348, info@damariscottaregion.com, www.damariscottaregion.com

**Danforth** · *Greater East Grand Lake C/C* · Weston Lord, Chrmn., 123 Kneser Ln., P.O. Box 95, 04424, P 600, M 50, (207) 448-7739, (800) 498-7739, www.greenlandcovecabins.com, www.eastgrandlake.net

**Deer Isle** · *Deer Isle-Stonington C/C* · Christina Shipps, Pres., P.O. Box 490, 04627, P 3,000, M 130, (207) 348-6124, deerisle@deerisle.com, www.deerislemaine.com

**Detroit** · *see Newport*

**Dexter** · *see Newport*

**Dover-Foxcroft** · *Piscataquis C/C* · Russell Page, Exec. Dir., 1033 South St., P.O. Box 376, 04426, P 4,300, M 180, (207) 564-7533, Fax (207) 564-7533, exdir@piscataquischamber.com, www.piscataquischamber.com

**Durham** · *see Lewiston*

**Dyer Brook** · *see Island Falls*

**East Boothbay** · *see Boothbay Harbor*

**East Millinocket** · *see Millinocket*

**East Wilson** · *see Farmington*

**Eastport** · *Eastport Area C/C* · Karen Raye, Pres., 23A Water St., P.O. Box 254, 04631, P 1,800, M 65, (207) 853-4644, Fax (207) 853-4747, chamber@eastportme.net, www.eastport.net

**Edgecomb** · *see Boothbay Harbor*

**Eliot** · *see York*

**Ellsworth** · *Ellsworth Area C/C* · Margaret Sumpter, Exec. Dir., 163 High St., P.O. Box 267, 04605, P 7,000, M 670, (207) 667-5584, Fax (207) 667-2617, eacc@midmaine.com, www.ellsworthchamber.org

**Enfield** · *see Lincoln*

**Etna** · *see Newport*

**Exeter** · *see Newport*

**Farmington** · *Franklin County C/C* · Lorna Dee Nichols, Exec. Dir., 248 Wilton Rd., 04938, P 30,000, M 300, (207) 778-4215, Fax (207) 778-2438, info@franklincountymaine.org, www.franklin countymaine.org

**Farmington Falls** · *see Farmington*

**Fort Fairfield** · *Fort Fairfield C/C* · Janet Kelle, Exec. Dir., 18 Community Center Dr., 04742, P 4,000, M 75, (207) 472-3802, Fax (207) 472-3810, jkelle@fortfairfield.org, www.fortcc.org

**Fort Kent** · *Greater Fort Kent Area C/C* · Cheryl Harvey, Pres., 291 W. Main St., P.O. Box 430, 04743, P 5,000, M 189, (207) 834-5354, info@fortkentchamber.com, www.fortkentchamber.com

**Franklin** · *see Winter Harbor*

**Freeport** · *Freeport Merchants Assn.* · Myra Hopkins, Exec. Dir., 23 Depot St., P.O. Box 452, 04032, P 8,200, M 170, (207) 865-1212, (800) 865-1994, Fax (207) 865-0881, info@freeportusa.com, www.freeportusa.com

**Gouldsboro** · *see Winter Harbor*

**Gray** · *see Windham*

**Greene** · *see Lewiston*

**Greenville** · *Moosehead Lake Region C/C* · Bob Hamer, Exec. Dir., Rte. 15, P.O. Box 581, 04441, P 1,623, M 130, (207) 695-2702, (888) 876-2778, info@mooseheadlake.org, www.mooseheadlake. org

**Hallowell** · *Hallowell Bd. of Trade* · P.O. Box 246, 04347, P 2,532, M 90, (207) 620-7477, info@hallowell.org, www.hallowell.org

**Harpswell** · *see Topsham*

**Harrison** · *see South Paris*

**Hartland** · *see Newport*

**Hebron** · *see South Paris*

**Hersey** · *see Island Falls*

**Hope** · *see Union*

**Houlton** · *Greater Houlton C/C* · Lori Weston, Exec. Dir., 109 Main St., 04730, P 20,000, M 225, (207) 532-4216, Fax (207) 532-4961, chamber@greaterhoulton.com, www.greaterhoulton.com

**Howland** · *see Lincoln*

**Industry** · *see Farmington*

**Island Falls** · *Northern Katahdin Valley Reg. C/C* · Brenda Wheaton, Exec. Dir., P.O. Box 374, 04747, P 5,621, M 91, (207) 365-7700, Fax (207) 463-3500, nkvrcc@mfx.net, www.nkvmaine.com

**Jackman** · *Jackman-Moose River Region C/C* · P.O. Box 368, 04945, P 900, M 45, (207) 668-4171, (888) 622-5225, mooserus@ jackmanmaine.org, www.jackmanmaine.org

**Kennebunk** · *Kennebunk-Kennebunkport C/C* · Karen Duddy, Exec. Mktg. Dir., 17 Western Ave., P.O. Box 740, 04043, P 18,500, M 600, (207) 967-0857, Fax (207) 967-2867, info@visitthe kennebunks.com, www.visitthekennebunks.com

**Kittery** · *see York*

**Lakeville** · *see Lincoln*

**Lee** · *see Lincoln*

**Leeds** · *see Lewiston*

**Lewiston** · *Androscoggin County C/C* · Charles A. Morrison, Pres., 415 Lisbon St., P.O. Box 59, 04243, P 105,259, M 1,300, (207) 783-2249, Fax (207) 783-4481, info@androscoggincounty. com, www.androscoggincounty.com

**Limestone** · *Limestone C/C* · 93 Main St., 04750, P 2,400, M 45, (207) 325-4025, Fax (207) 325-3330, chamber@limestonemaine. org, www.limestonemaine.org

**Lincoln** · *Lincoln Lakes Region C/C* · Cheri Archer, Ofc. Mgr., 256 W. Broadway, P.O. Box 164, 04457, P 5,800, M 115, (207) 794-8065, Fax (207) 794-8065, llrcc@verizon.net, www.lincolnme chamber.org

**Lincolnville** · *see Camden*

**Lisbon** · *see Lewiston*

**Livermore** · *see Lewiston*

**Livermore Falls** · *see Lewiston*

**Machias** · *Machias Bay Area C/C* · Kathleen Shannon, Exec. Dir., 85 Main St., Ste. 2, P.O. Box 606, 04654, P 2,800, M 208, (207) 255-4402, Fax (207) 255-4402, info@machiaschamber.org, www. machiaschamber.org

**Madawaska** · *Greater Madawaska C/C* · Stephen Hughes, Exec. Dir., 356 Main St., P.O. Box 144, 04756, P 4,900, M 200, (207) 728-7000, Fax (207) 728-4696, valleyvisit@pwless.net, www. greatermadawaskachamber.com

**Magalloway** · *see Errol, NH*

**Mattamiscontis** · *see Lincoln*

**Mattawamkeag** · *see Lincoln*

**Mayfield** · *see Bingham*

**Mechanic Falls** · *see Lewiston*

**Medway** · *see Millinocket*

**Merrill** · *see Island Falls*

**Millinocket** · *Katahdin Area C/C* · Chip Lamson, Pres., 1029 Central St., 04462, P 5,300, M 130, (207) 723-4443, info@ katahdinmaine.com, www.katahdinmaine.com

**Minot** · *see Lewiston*

**Monada/Silver Ridge** · *see Island Falls*

**Moro Plantation** · *see Island Falls*

**Moscow** · *see Bingham*

**Mount Chase/Shin Pond** · *see Island Falls*

**Naples** · *see Windham*

**New Sharon** · *see Farmington*

**New Vineyard** · *see Farmington*

**Newport** · *Sebasticook Valley C/C* · Monica M. Bailey, Exec. Dir., P.O. Box 464, 04953, P 25,000, M 280, (207) 368-4698, Fax (207) 368-5312, svcc@midmaine.com, www.ourchamber.org

**Norridgewock** · *Norridgewock Area C/C* · Bob Gilcott, Pres., P.O. Box 184, 04957, P 3,990, M 125, (207) 431-5188, www. norridgewockareachamber.com

**Northeast Harbor** · *Mount Desert C/C* · 18 Harbor Dr., P.O. Box 675, 04662, P 6,000, M 140, (207) 276-5040, info@mountdesert chamber.org, www.mountdesertchamber.org

**Norway** · *see South Paris*

**Oakfield** · *see Island Falls*

**Ogunquit** · *Ogunquit C/C* · 36 Main St., P.O. Box 2289, 03907, P 1,200, M 345, (207) 646-2939, Fax (207) 641-0856, director@ ogunquit.org, www.ogunquit.org

**Old Orchard Beach** · *Old Orchard Beach C/C* · 11 First St., P.O. Box 600, 04064, P 9,000, M 230, (207) 934-2500, Fax (207) 934-4994, info@oldorchardbeachmaine.com, www.oldorchardbeachmaine.com

**Orland** · *see Bucksport*

**Otisfield** · *see South Paris*

**Oxbow** · *see Island Falls*

**Oxford** · *see South Paris*

**Palmyra** · *see Newport*

**Paris** · *see South Paris*

**Passadumkeag** · *see Lincoln*

**Patten** · *see Island Falls*

**Penobscot** · *see Blue Hill*

**Pittsfield** · *see Newport*

**Plymouth** · *see Newport*

**Poland** · *see Lewiston*

**Portland** · *Portland Reg. C/C* · W. Godfrey Wood, Pres./CEO, 60 Pearl St., 04101, P 275,000, M 1,500, (207) 772-2811, Fax (207) 772-1179, chamber@portlandregion.com, www.portlandregion.com

**Prentis** · *see Lincoln*

**Presque Isle** · *Presque Isle Area C/C* · Theresa Fowler, Exec. Dir., 3 Houlton Rd., P.O. Box 672, 04769, P 20,400, M 325, (207) 764-6561, Fax (207) 764-6571, piacc@mfx.net, www.pichamber.com

**Rangeley** · *Rangeley Lakes Region C/C* · Evelyn McAllister, Exec. Dir., 6 Park Rd., P.O. Box 317, 04970, P 1,600, M 230, (207) 864-5571, (800) 685-2537, Fax (207) 864-5366, info@rangeleymaine.com, www.rangeleymaine.com

**Raymond** · *see Windham*

**Rockland** · *Penobscot Bay Reg. C/C* · Shari Closter, Interim Exec. Dir., One Park Dr., P.O. Box 508, 04841, P 22,300, M 785, (207) 596-0376, (800) 562-2529, Fax (207) 596-6549, info@therealmaine.com, www.therealmaine.com

**Rockport** · *see Camden*

**Rumford** · *River Valley C/C* · Cherri Crockett, Admin., 10 Bridge St., 04276, P 17,000, M 200, (207) 364-3241, info@rivervalleychamber.com, www.rivervalleychamber.com

**Sabattus** · *see Lewiston*

**Saco** · *Biddeford-Saco C/C & Ind.* · 138 Main St., Ste. 101, 04072, P 45,000, M 503, (207) 282-1567, Fax (207) 282-3149, info@biddefordsacochamber.org, www.biddefordsacochamber.org

**Saint Albans** · *see Newport*

**Saint Francis** · *Saint Francis C/C* · P.O. Box 123, 04774, P 550, M 12, (207) 398-3358, jouelet@pivot.com

**Saint John** · *see Saint Francis*

**Sanford** · *Sanford-Springvale C/C & Eco. Dev.* · Richard Stanley, Pres., 917 Main St. #B, 04073, P 55,000, M 372, (207) 324-4280, Fax (207) 324-8290, sancoc@psouth.net, www.sanfordchamber.org

**ECONOMIC DEVELOPMENT CHAMBER PROVIDING DEMOGRAPHIC, INDUSTRIAL INFORMATION & ASSISTANCE IN SANFORD-SPRINGVALE AND SURROUNDING AREA.**

**Sebago Lake** · *see Windham*

**Seboeis** · *see Lincoln*

**Sedgwick** · *see Blue Hill*

**Sherman Mills** · *see Island Falls*

**Skowhegan** · *Skowhegan Area C/C* · 23 Commercial St., 04976, P 10,000, M 265, (207) 474-3621, Fax (207) 474-3306, info@skowheganchamber.com, www.skowheganchamber.com

**Smyrna Mills** · *see Island Falls*

**Solon** · *see Bingham*

**Sorrento** · *see Winter Harbor*

**South Berwick** · *see York*

**South China** · *China Area C/C* · Marlene Reed, Secy., P.O. Box 189, 04358, P 4,500, M 21, (207) 445-3183

**South Paris** · *Oxford Hills C/C* · Mindy Stewart, Mktg. Dir., 4 Western Ave., 04281, P 22,000, M 390, (207) 743-2281, Fax (207) 743-0687, info@oxfordhillsmaine.com, www.oxfordhillsmaine.com

**Southport** · *see Boothbay Harbor*

**Southwest Harbor** · *Southwest Harbor-Tremont C/C* · Bruce Carlson, Exec. Dir., 20 Village Green Way, P.O. Box 1143, 04679, P 2,500, M 154, (207) 244-9264, (800) 423-9264, Fax (207) 244-4185, quietside@acadiachamber.com, www.acadiachamber.com

**Springvale** · *see Sanford*

**Stacyville** · *see Island Falls*

**Standish** · *see Windham*

**Stetson** · *see Newport*

**Stonington** · *see Deer Isle*

**Sullivan** · *see Winter Harbor*

**Thomaston** · *see Rockland*

**Topsfield** · *see Lincoln*

**Topsham** · *Southern Midcoast Maine C/C* · Heather Collins, Exec. Dir., 2 Main St., 04086, P 60,000, M 625, (207) 725-8797, (877) 725-8797, Fax (207) 725-9787, chamber@midcoastmaine.com, www.midcoastmaine.com

**Trenton** · *see Ellsworth*

**Turner** · *see Lewiston*

**Union** · *Union Area C/C* · Martha Johnston-Nash, Pres., P.O. Box 603, 04862, P 22,000, M 80, (207) 785-3300, uacoc@tidewater.net, www.unionareachamber.org

**Upton** · *see Errol, NH*

**Van Buren** · *Greater Van Buren C/C* · Sheila Cannon, 51 Main St., Ste. 101, 04785, P 2,600, M 80, (207) 868-5059, Fax (207) 868-2222, vbchamber@pwless.net, www.vanburenmaine.com

**Verona** · *see Bucksport*

**Wales** · *see Lewiston*

**Warren** · *see Rockland*

**Washington** · *see Union*

**Waterford** · *see South Paris*

**Waterville** · *Mid-Maine C/C* · Kimberly N. Lindlof, Pres./CEO, One Post Office Sq., 04901, P 60,000, M 535, (207) 873-3315, Fax (207) 877-0087, info@midmainechamber.com, www.midmainechamber.com

**Webster Plantation** · *see Lincoln*

**Wellington** · *see Bingham*

**Wells** · *Wells C/C* · Eleanor Vadenais, Exec. Dir., 136 Post Rd., P.O. Box 356, 04090, P 10,000, M 330, (207) 646-2451, Fax (207) 646-8104, wellschamber@wellschamber.org, www.wellschamber.org

**West Enfield** · *see Lincoln*

**U.S. Chambers of Commerce**

**West Forks** • *The Forks Area C/C* • Pam Christopher, Exec. Dir., P.O. Box 1, 04985, P 2,150, M 35, (207) 663-2121, Fax (207) 663-2122, info@forksarea.com, www.forksarea.com

**West Paris** • *see South Paris*

**Whiting** • *Cobscook Bay Area C/C* • P.O. Box 42, 04691, P 8,000, M 80, (207) 733-2201, info@cobscookbay.com, www.cobscook bay.com

**Wilsons Mills** • *see Errol, NH*

**Wilton** • *see Farmington*

**Windham** • *Sebago Lakes Region C/C* • Barbara Clark, Exec. Dir., 746 Roosevelt Trail-Rte. 302, P.O. Box 1015, 04062, P 55,000, M 370, (207) 892-8265, Fax (207) 893-0110, info@sebagolakes chamber.com, www.sebagolakeschamber.com

**Winn** • *see Lincoln*

**Winter Harbor** • *Schoodic Area C/C* • Ed Brackett, Pres., P.O. Box 381, 04693, P 3,000, M 85, (207) 963-7658, info@acadia-schoodic. org, www.acadia-schoodic.org

**Winthrop** • *Winthrop Area C/C* • Jeffrey Seguin, Pres., P.O. Box 51, 04364, P 6,300, M 100, (207) 377-8020, Fax (207) 377-2767, info@winthropchamber.org, www.winthropchamber.org

**Yarmouth** • *Yarmouth C/C* • Carolyn Schuster, Mgr. Dir., 162 Main St., 04096, P 8,600, M 210, (207) 846-3984, Fax (207) 846-5419, info@yarmouthmaine.org, www.yarmouthmaine.org

**York** • *Greater York Region C/C* • Catherine R. Goodwin, Pres./ CEO, 1 Stonewall Ln., 03909, P 37,000, M 800, (207) 363-4422, Fax (207) 363-7320, info@yorkme.org, www.gatewaytomaine.org

# Maryland

**Maryland C of C** • Kathleen T. Snyder CCE, Pres./CEO, 60 West St., Ste. 100, Annapolis, 21401, P 5,300,000, M 800, (410) 269-0642, (301) 261-2858, Fax (410) 269-5247, mcc@mdchamber.org, www. mdchamber.org

**Aberdeen** • *Aberdeen C/C* • Janet Emmons, Dir., 214 W. Bel Air Ave., 21001, P 15,000, M 300, (410) 272-2580, Fax (410) 272-9357, aberdeenchamber@verizon.net, www.aberdeencc.com

**Annapolis** • *Annapolis and Anne Arundel County C/C* • Robert Burdon, Pres./CEO, 49 Old Solomons Island Rd., Ste. 204, P.O. Box 346, 21404, P 489,656, M 1,100, (410) 266-3960, Fax (410) 266-8270, info@aaaccc.org, www.annapolischamber.com

**Annapolis Junction** • *see Laurel*

**Anne Arundel County** • *see Annapolis and Laurel*

**Baltimore** • *Baltimore City C/C* • Charles Owens, Pres., 312 Martin Luther King Blvd., 21201, P 670,000, M 400, (410) 837-7101, Fax (410) 837-7104, baltcitycham@yahoo.com, www.baltimorecitychamber.org

**Baltimore County** • *Baltimore County C/C* • Keith Scott, Pres./CEO, 102 W. Pennsylvania Ave., Ste. 101, Towson, 21204, P 754,292, M 750, (410) 825-6200, Fax (410) 821-9901, info@ baltcountychamber.com, www.baltcountycc.com

**Bel Air** • *Harford County C/C* • William Seccurro, Pres./CEO, 108 S. Bond St., 21014, P 248,322, M 1,200, (410) 838-2020, (800) 682-8536, Fax (410) 893-4715, info@harfordchamber.org, www. harfordchamber.org

**Beltsville** • *see Laurel*

**Berlin** • *Berlin C/C* • Carol Kenney, Ofc. Mgr., P.O. Box 212, 21811, P 3,500, M 200, (410) 641-4775, Fax (410) 641-3118, inquire@ berlinmdcc.org, www.berlinmdcc.org

**Berwyn Heights** • *see Lanham*

**Bethesda** • *Greater Bethesda-Chevy Chase C/C* • Ginanne M. Italiano, Pres., 7910 Woodmont Ave., Ste. 1204, 20814, P 1,000,000, M 950, (301) 652-4900, Fax (301) 657-1973, staff@ bccchamber.org, www.bccchamber.org

**Bladensburg** • *see Lanham*

**Bowie** • *also see Lanham*

**Bowie** • *Greater Bowie C/C* • Jan Butler, Exec. Dir., 6911 Laurel Bowie Rd., Ste. 302, 20715, P 58,000, M 300, (301) 262-0920, Fax (301) 262-0921, kelly@bowiechamber.org, www.bowie chamber.org

**Brentwood** • *see Lanham*

**Burtonsville** • *see Laurel*

**BWI Airport** • *see Laurel*

**California** • *St. Mary's County C/C* • William E. Scarafia, Pres./CEO, 44200 Airport Rd., 20619, P 97,000, M 600, (301) 737-3001, Fax (301) 737-0089, info@smcchamber.com, www.smcchamber.com

**Cambridge** • *Dorchester County C/C* • Allen Nelson, Exec. Dir., 528 Poplar St., 21613, P 30,000, M 751, (410) 228-3575, Fax (410) 228-6848, allen@dorchesterchamber.org, www.dorchesterchamber.org

**Capitol Heights** • *see Lanham*

**Catonsville** • *Greater Catonsville C/C* • Teal Cary, Exec. Dir., 822-A Frederick Rd., P.O. Box 21100, 21228, P 40,000, M 375, (410) 719-9609, Fax (410) 744-6127, chamber@catonsville.org, www.catonsville.org

**Chester** • *Queen Anne's County C/C* • Linda Friday, Pres., 1561 Postal Rd., P.O. Box 511, 21619, P 45,000, M 625, (410) 643-8530, Fax (410) 643-8477, business@qacchamber.com, www.qac chamber.com

**Chestertown** • *Kent County C/C* • Cindy Genther, Exec. Dir., 122 N. Cross St., P.O. Box 146, 21620, P 19,200, M 280, (410) 810-2968, Fax (410) 778-1406, kentchamber@verizon.net, www.kentchamber.org

**Cheverly** • *see Lanham*

**Chevy Chase** • *see Bethesda*

**Churchton** • *Southern Ann Arundel C/C* • Carla Catterton, Exec. Dir., 5503 Muddy Creek Rd., 20764, P 32,000, M 320, (410) 867-3129, Fax (410) 867-3556, southcounty@toad.net, www. southcounty.org

**College Park** • *see Lanham and Laurel*

**Colmar Manor** • *see Lanham*

**Columbia** • *also see Laurel*

**Columbia** • *Howard County C/C* • Pamela Klahr CCE, Pres./CEO, 5560 Sterrett Pl., Ste. 105, 21044, P 286,950, M 840, (410) 730-4111, Fax (410) 730-4584, pklahr@howardchamber.com, www. howardchamber.com

**Cottage City** • *see Lanham*

**Crisfield** • *Crisfield Area C/C* • Valerie Mason, Exec. Dir., 906 W. Main St., P.O. Box 292, 21817, P 2,800, M 135, (410) 968-2500, (800) 782-3913, Fax (410) 968-0524, info@crisfieldchamber.com, www.crisfieldchamber.com

**Crofton** • *Greater Crofton C/C* • Bob Carr, Pres./CEO, P.O. Box 4146, 21114, P 27,500, M 185, (410) 721-9131, Fax (410) 721-0785, bob@tlcincorporated.com, www.croftonchamber.com

**Cumberland** • *Allegany County C/C* • Bell Tower Bldg., 24 Frederick St., 21502, P 74,930, M 425, (301) 722-2820, Fax (301) 722-5995, info@alleganycountychamber.com, www.allegany countychamber.com.

**Delmar** • *see Delmar, DE*

**District Heights** · *see Lanham*

**Dundalk** · *see Baltimore County*

**Eagle Harbor** · *see Lanham*

**East Baltimore** · *see Baltimore County*

**Easton** · *Talbot County C/C* · Alan I. Silverstein IOM, Pres./CEO, 101 Marlboro Ave., Ste. 53, P.O. Box 1366, 21601, P 35,550, M 850, (410) 822-4653, Fax (410) 822-7922, info@talbotchamber.org, www.talbotchamber.org

**Edgemere** · *see Baltimore County*

**Edmonston** · *see Lanham*

**Elkridge** · *see Laurel*

**Elkton** · *Cecil County C/C* · Laura Mayse, Exec. Dir., 233 E. Main St., 21921, P 100,000, M 640, (410) 392-3833, Fax (410) 392-6225, info@cecilchamber.com, www.cecilchamber.com

**Elkton** · *Elkton Chamber & Alliance* · Mary Jo Jablonski, Exec. Dir., 101 E. Main St., 21921, P 18,000, M 105, (410) 398-5076, Fax (410) 398-4971, info@elktonalliance.org, www.elktonalliance.org

**Essex** · *see Middle River*

**Essex** · *see Middle River*

**Fairmont Heights** · *see Lanham*

**Forest Heights** · *see Lanham*

**Fort Meade** · *see Laurel*

**Frederick** · *Frederick County C/C* · M. Richard Adams, Pres./CEO, 8420-B Gas House Pike, 21701, P 225,000, M 820, (301) 662-4164, Fax (301) 846-4427, info@frederickchamber.org, www.frederickchamber.org

**Gaithersburg** · *Gaithersburg-Germantown C/C* · Marilyn Balcombe, Pres., 4 Professional Dr., Ste. 132, 20879, P 150,000, M 500, (301) 840-1400, Fax (301) 963-3918, mbalcombe@ggchamber.org, www.ggchamber.org

**Germantown** · *Maryland Hispanic C/C* · Maria Welch, Chair, 20300 Century Blvd., Ste. 175, 20874, P 150,000, (240) 686-0450, customerservice@mdhcc.org, www.mdhcc.org

**Germantown** · *see Gaithersburg*

**Glen Burnie** · *Northern Anne Arundel County C/C* · Frances Schmidt, Exec. Dir., 7477 Baltimore-Annapolis Blvd., Ste. 203, 21061, P 500,000, M 400, (410) 766-8282, Fax (410) 766-5722, info@naaccc.com, www.naaccc.com

**Glenarden** · *see Lanham*

**Glyndon** · *see Reisterstown*

**Greenbelt** · *see Lanham and Laurel*

**Hagerstown** · *Hagerstown-Washington County C/C* · Brien Poffenberger, Pres., 28 W. Washington St., Ste. 200, 21740, P 131,923, M 575, (301) 739-2015, Fax (301) 739-1278, chamber@hagerstown.org, www.hagerstown.org

**Hancock** · *Hancock C/C* · Louis Close, Treas., 126 W. High St., 21750, P 1,725, M 77, (301) 678-5900, info@hancockmd.com, www.hancockmd.com

**Hanover** · *see Laurel*

**Harford County** · *see Bel Air*

**Havre de Grace** · *Havre de Grace C/C* · Cathy Vincenti, Exec. Dir., 450 Pennington Ave., 21078, P 14,000, M 260, (410) 939-3303, (800) 851-7756, Fax (410) 939-3490, hdegchamber1@comcast.net, www.hdgchamber.com

**Howard County** · *see Columbia and Laurel*

**Hyattsville** · *see Lanham*

**Jessup** · *see Laurel*

**Kingsville** · *see Baltimore County*

**Landover Hills** · *see Lanham*

**Lanham** · *Prince George's County C/C* · Rhonda Slade, Interim Pres./CEO, 4640 Forbes Blvd., Ste. 130, 20706, P 865,000, M 927, (301) 731-5000, Fax (301) 731-5013, info@pgcoc.org, www.pgcoc.org

**LaPlata** · *Charles County C/C* · Ken Gould, Exec. Dir., 101 Centennial, Ste. A, 20646, P 124,000, M 800, (301) 932-6500, (301) 870-3089, Fax (301) 932-3945, info@charlescountychamber.org, www.charlescountychamber.org

**Laurel** · *also see Lanham*

**Laurel** · *Baltimore Washington Corridor Chamber* · H. Walter Townshend III, Pres./CEO, 312 Marshall Ave., Ste. 104, 20707, P 2,200,000, M 650, (301) 725-4000, (410) 792-9714, Fax (301) 725-0776, bwcc@baltwashchamber.org, www.baltwashchamber.org.

**Maryland City** · *see Laurel*

**McHenry** · *Garrett County C/C & Visitors Center* · Charlie Ross, Pres./CEO, 15 Visitors Center Dr., 21541, P 30,000, M 750, (301) 387-4386, (301) 387-6171, Fax (301) 387-2080, info@garrettchamber.com, www.garrettchamber.com

**Middle River** · *Essex-Middle River-White Marsh C/C* · Hal Ashman, Pres., 405 Williams Ct., Ste. 108, 21220, P 95,000, M 450, (410) 686-2233, Fax (410) 687-9081, info@emrchamber.org, www.emrchamber.org.

**Montgomery County** · *see Rockville and Laurel*

**Morningside** · *see Lanham*

**Mount Airy** · *Greater Mount Airy C/C* · Dennis Emerson, V.P., P.O. Box 741, 21771, P 30,000, M 300, (301) 829-5426, inquiries@mtairybusiness.com, www.mtairybusiness.com

**Mount Rainier** · *see Lanham*

**North East** · *North East C/C* · Carolyn Crouch, Pres., P.O. Box 787, 21901, P 20,000, M 120, (410) 287-5252, (800) CECIL-95, info@northeastchamber.org, www.northeastchamber.org

**Oakland** · *see McHenry*

**Ocean City** · *Greater Ocean City C/C* · Melanie Purcel, Exec. Dir., 12320 Ocean Gateway, 21842, P 350,000, M 850, (410) 213-0552, (888) OC-MD-FUN, Fax (410) 213-7521, info@oceancity.org, www.oceancity.org

**Ocean Pines** · *Ocean Pines Area C/C* · Carol Ludwig, Exec. Dir., 10514 Racetrack Rd., Ste G, 21811, P 20,000, M 300, (410) 641-5306, Fax (410) 641-6176, info@oceanpineschamber.org, www.oceanpineschamber.org

**Odenton** · *West Anne Arundel County C/C* · Claire Louder, Pres./CEO, 8373 Piney Orchard Pkwy., Ste. 200, 21113, P 100,000, M 250, (410) 672-3422, Fax (410) 672-3475, info@westcountychamber.org, www.waaccc.org

**Olney** · *Olney C/C* · Ellen Coleman, 3460 Olney-Laytonsville Rd.. Ste. 211, P.O. Box 550, 20830, P 37,000, M 215, (301) 774-7117, Fax (301) 774-4944, chamber@olneymd.org, www.olneymd.org

**Owings Mills** · *see Reisterstown*

**Oxford** · *see Easton*

**Parkville** · *see Baltimore County*

**Perry Hall** · *see Baltimore County*

**Pikesville** · *Pikesville C/C* · Sherrie Becker, Exec. Dir., 7 Church Ln., Ste. 14, 21208, P 33,090, M 300, (410) 484-2337, Fax (410) 484-4151, pikesvillechamber@verizon.net, www.pikesvillechamber.org

**U.S. Chambers of Commerce**

**Pocomoke City** • *Pocomoke City C/C* • Roy Figgs, Pres., 144 Market St., P.O. Box 356, 21851, P 4,500, M 150, (410) 957-1919, Fax (410) 957-4784, pocomokechamber@gmail.com, www.pocomoke.com

**Poolesville** • *Poolesville Area C/C* • Maggie Nightingale, Exec. Secy., P.O. Box 256, 20837, P 5,000, M 140, (301) 349-5753, www.poolesvillechamber.com

**Potomac** • *Potomac C/C* • Adam Greenberg, Pres., P.O. Box 59160, 20859, P 50,000, M 80, (301) 299-2170, Fax (301) 299-4650, pcc@potomacchamber.org, www.potomacchamber.org

**Prince Frederick** • *Calvert County C/C* • Carolyn McHugh, Pres./CEO, 120 Dares Beach Rd., P.O. Box 9, 20678, P 75,000, M 500, (410) 535-2577, (301) 855-1930, Fax (410) 257-3140, calvertchamber@calvertchamber.org, www.calvertchamber.org

**Prince George County** • *see Lanham and Laurel*

**Princess Anne** • *Princess Anne C/C* • 11771 Beckford Ave., P.O. Box 642, 21853, P 2,313, M 50, (410) 651-2961, Fax (410) 651-3836

**Queen Anne's County** • *see Chester*

**Reisterstown** • *Reisterstown-Owings Mills-Glyndon C/C* • Brian Ditto, Exec. Dir., 100 Owings Ct., Ste. 9, 21136, P 60,000, M 350, (410) 702-7073, Fax (410) 702-7075, romg@romgchamber.org, www.romgchamber.org

**Rockville** • *Montgomery County C/C* • Georgette Godwin, Pres./CEO, 51 Monroe St., Ste. 1800, 20850, P 757,000, M 600, (301) 738-0015, Fax (301) 738-8792, www.montgomerycountychamber.com

**Rockville** • *Rockville C/C* • Andrea Jolly, Exec. Dir., 1 Research Ct., Ste. 450, 20850, P 47,000, M 185, (301) 424-9300, Fax (301) 762-7599, rockville@rockvillechamber.org, www.rockvillechamber.org

**Rosedale** • *see Baltimore County*

**Rossville** • *see Baltimore County*

**Saint Michaels** • *see Easton*

**Salisbury** • *Salisbury Area C/C* • Brad Bellacicco, Exec. Dir., 144 E. Main St., 21801, P 100,000, M 877, (410) 749-0144, Fax (410) 860-9925, chamber@salisburyarea.com, www.salisburyarea.com

**Sandy Spring** • *see Laurel*

**Savage** • *see Laurel*

**Severna Park** • *Greater Severna Park C/C* • Linda Zahn, Exec. Dir., 1 Holly Ave., 21146, P 40,000, M 650, (410) 647-3900, Fax (410) 647-3999, info@severnaparkchamber.com, www.severnaparkchamber.com

**Silver Spring** • *Greater Silver Spring C/C* • Jane Redicker, Pres., 8601 Georgia Ave., Ste. 203, 20910, P 235,000, M 750, (301) 565-3777, Fax (301) 565-3377, info@gsscc.org, www.gsscc.org

**Snow Hill** • *Snow Hill C/C* • Barry Laws, Pres., P.O. Box 176, 21863, P 3,200, M 55, (410) 632-0809, (410) 632-1700, blaws@taylorbank.com, www.snowhillmd.com

**Talbot County** • *see Easton*

**Taneytown** • *Taneytown C/C* • Donna Sako, Exec. Dir., 24 E. Baltimore St., P.O. Box 18, 21787, P 25,000, M 144, (410) 756-4234, Fax same, dlsako@verizon.net, www.taneytownchamber.org

**Tilghman Island** • *see Easton*

**Towson** • *see Baltimore County*

**Upper Marlboro** • *see Lanham*

**Westminster** • *Carroll County C/C* • Richard Haddad, Pres., 700 Corporate Center Ct., Ste. L, P.O. Box 871, 21158, P 170,000, M 525, (410) 848-9050, (410) 876-7212, Fax (410) 876-1023, info@carrollcountychamber.org, www.carrollcountychamber.org

**Wheaton** • *Wheaton-Kensington C/C* • Moshe Briel, Pres., 2401 Blueridge Ave., Ste. 101, 20902, P 153,000, M 150, (301) 949-0080, Fax (301) 949-0081, contactus@wkchamber.org, www.wkchamber.org

**White Marsh** • *see Middle River*

# Massachusetts

**Mass. Chamber of Bus. & Ind.** • Debra A. Boronski-Burack, Pres./CEO, 143 Shaker Rd., P.O. Box 414, East Longmeadow, 01028, (617) 512-9667, Fax (413) 525-1184, president@masscbi.com, www.masscbi.com.

**Abington** • *see Brockton*

**Acton** • *Middlesex West C/C* • Sarah Fletcher, Exec. Dir., 77 Great Rd., Ste. 214, 01720, P 92,000, M 400, (978) 263-0010, Fax (978) 264-0303, mdaigle@mwcoc.com, www.mwcoc.com

**Adams** • *see North Adams*

**Agawam** • *see Springfield*

**Alford** • *see Great Barrington*

**Amesbury** • *Amesbury C/C & Ind. Found. Inc.* • Stefanie McCowan, Exec. Dir., 5 Market Sq., 01913, P 18,000, M 300, (978) 388-3178, Fax (978) 388-4952, chamber@amesburychamber.com, www.amesburychamber.com

**Amherst** • *Amherst Area C/C* • Tony Maroulis, Exec. Dir., 28 Amity St., 01002, P 35,000, M 600, (413) 253-0700, Fax (413) 256-0771, info@amherstarea.com, www.amherstarea.com

**Arlington** • *Arlington C/C* • Michele Meagher, Exec. Dir., One Whittemore Park, 02474, P 42,389, M 310, (781) 643-4600, Fax (781) 646-5581, info@arlcc.org, www.arlcc.org

**Ashburnham** • *see North Central Mass.*

**Ashby** • *see North Central Mass.*

**Ashland** • *see Framingham*

**Ashley Falls** • *see Great Barrington*

**Ashley Falls** • *see Lakeville, CT*

**Athol** • *North Quabbin C/C* • Steve Raymond, Exec. Dir., 507 Main St., P.O. Box 157, 01331, P 28,000, M 201, (978) 249-3849, Fax (978) 249-7151, nqcc1@verizon.net, www.northquabbinchamber.com.

**Attleboro** • *United Reg. C/C* • Jack Lank, Pres., 42 Union St., 02703, M 1,050, (508) 222-0801, Fax (508) 222-1498, president@unitedregionalchamber.com, www.unitedregionalchamber.com

**Avon** • *see Brockton*

**Ayer** • *see Devens*

**Barnstable** • *see Hyannis*

**Barre** • *see Gardner*

**Becket** • *see Great Barrington*

**Bedford** • *Bedford C/C* • Maureen Sullivan, Exec. Dir., 12 Mudgeway, 01730, P 13,000, M 200, (781) 275-8503, bcoc@bedfordchamber.org, www.bedfordchamber.org

**Bellingham** • *see Milford*

**Belmont** • *see Watertown*

**Berkley** • *see Taunton*

**Berlin** • *see Hudson and Clinton*

**Beverly** • *Beverly C/C* • Sheila Field, Exec. Dir., 28 Cabot St., 01915, P 38,000, M 550, (978) 232-9559, Fax (978) 232-9372, director@beverlychamber.com, www.beverlychamber.com

**Blackstone** · *see Franklin*

**Bolton** · *see Hudson and Clinton*

**Boston** · *Greater Boston C/C* · Paul Guzzi, Pres./CEO, 265 Franklin St., 12th Flr., 02110, P 6,016,425, M 1,600, (617) 227-4500, Fax (617) 227-7505, info@bostonchamber.com, www.bostonchamber.com

**Bourne** · *see Cape Cod Canal*

**Boylston** · *see Clinton*

**Brewster** · *Brewster C of C & Bd. Of Trade United* · Suzie Roettig, Exec. Dir., P.O. Box 1241, 02631, P 10,519, M 200, (508) 896-3500, info@brewstercapecod.org, www.brewstercapecod.org

**Bridgewater** · *see Brockton and Middleborough*

**Brimfield** · *see Sturbridge*

**Brockton** · *Metro South C/C* · Christopher Cooney, Pres./CEO, Sixty School St., 02301, P 237,000, M 1,014, (508) 586-0500, Fax (508) 587-1340, info@metrosouthchamber.com, www.metrosouthchamber.com.

**HOME OF THE NORTHERN LEAGUE BASEBALL TEAM BROCKTON ROX, WORLD CHAMPION BOXERS MARVELOUS MARVIN HAGLER AND ROCKY MARCIANO. KNOWN AS THE CITY OF CHAMPIONS.**

**Brookline** · *Brookline C/C* · Roger Lipson, Pres., 251 Harvard St. #1, 02446, P 57,107, M 230, (617) 739-1330, Fax (617) 739-1200, info@brooklinechamber.com, www.brooklinechamber.com.

**Cambridge** · *Cambridge C/C* · Kelly Thompson Clark, Pres./CEO, 859 Massachusetts Ave., 02139, P 110,000, M 1,550, (617) 876-4100, Fax (617) 354-9874, ccinfo@cambridgechamber.org, www.cambridgechamber.org

**Canton** · *see Brockton and Norwood*

**Cape Cod** · *Cape Cod C of C & CVB* · Wendy Northcross, CEO, 5 ShootFlying Hill Rd., Centerville, 02632, P 228,000, M 1,376, (508) 362-3225, (888) 33-CAPECOD, Fax (508) 362-3698, info@capecodchamber.org, www.capecodchamber.org

**Cape Cod Canal** · *Cape Cod Canal Region C/C* · Marie Oliva, Pres./CEO, 70 Main St., Buzzards Bay, 02532, P 19,000, M 650, (508) 759-6000, Fax (508) 759-6965, info@capecodcanalchamber.org, www.capecodcanalchamber.org

**Carver** · *see Middleborough*

**Charlton** · *see Sturbridge*

**Chatham** · *Chatham C/C* · Lisa Franz, Exec. Dir., P.O. Box 793, 02633, P 6,800, M 400, (508) 945-5199, (800) 715-5567, Fax (508) 430-7919, chamber@chathaminfo.com, www.chathaminfo.com

**Chathamport** · *see Chatham*

**Chelmsford** · *see Lowell*

**Chelsea** · *Chelsea C/C* · Donald Harney, Exec. Dir., 308 Broadway, 02150, P 30,000, M 200, (617) 884-4877, Fax (617) 884-4878, dharney@chelseachamber.org, www.chelseachamber.org

**Chicopee** · *Chicopee C/C* · Gail A. Sherman, Pres., 264 Exchange St., 01013, P 57,100, M 450, (413) 594-2101, Fax (413) 594-2103, gailsherman@chicopeechamber.org, www.chicopeechamber.org

**Clinton** · *Wachusett C/C* · Maegen McCaffrey, Exec. Dir., 167 Church St., P.O. Box 703, 01510, P 54,000, M 500, (978) 368-7687, Fax (978) 368-7689, info@wachusettchamber.com, www.wachusettchamber.com.

**Cohasset** · *Cohasset C/C* · Darilynn Evans, Pres., P.O. Box 336, 02025, P 7,500, M 100, (781) 383-1010, Fax (781) 383-1141, info@cohassetchamber.org, www.cohassetchamber.org

**Concord** · *Concord C/C* · Stephanie Stillman, Exec. Dir., 15 Walden St., Ste. 7, 01742, P 16,000, M 360, (978) 369-3120, Fax (978) 369-1515, director@concordchamberofcommerce.org, www.concordchamberofcommerce.org

**Cotuit** · *see Hyannis*

**Danvers** · *North Shore C/C* · Robert G. Bradford, Pres., 5 Cherry Hill Dr. #100, 01923, P 300,000, M 1,500, (978) 774-8565, Fax (978) 774-3418, info@northshorechamber.org, www.northshorechamber.org

**Dedham** · *see Norwood*

**Deerfield** · *see Greenfield*

**Devens** · *Nashoba Valley C/C* · Melissa Fetterhoff, Exec. Dir., 100 Sherman Ave., Ste. 3, 01434, P 36,000, M 400, (978) 772-6976, Fax (978) 772-3503, director@nvcoc.com, www.nvcoc.com

**Dighton** · *see Taunton*

**Dracut** · *see Lowell*

**Dudley** · *see Worcester*

**East Boston** · *C/C of East Boston* · John Dudley, Exec. Dir., 296 Bennington St., 2nd Flr., 02128, P 32,000, M 300, (617) 569-5000, Fax (617) 569-1945, eastboston.chamber@verizon.net, www.eastbostonchamber.com

**East Bridgewater** · *see Brockton*

**East Longmeadow** · *see Springfield*

**Eastham** · *Eastham C/C* · Janet Demetri, Pres., P.O. Box 1329, 02642, P 5,000, M 175, (508) 240-7211, Fax (508) 240-7211, info@easthamchamber.com, www.easthamchamber.com

**Easthampton** · *Greater Easthampton C/C* · Eric Snyder, Exec. Dir., 33 Union St., 01027, P 23,000, M 340, (413) 527-9414, Fax (413) 527-1445, info@easthamptonchamber.org, www.easthamptonchamber.org

**Easton** · *see Brockton*

**Everett** · *Everett C/C* · Robert Laquidara, Exec. Dir., 467 Broadway, 02149, P 35,701, M 300, (617) 387-9100, Fax (617) 389-6655, ecocoffice@aol.com, www.everettmachamber.com

**Fall River** · *Fall River Area C/C & Ind.* · Robert Mellion, Pres./CEO, 200 Pocasset St., 02721, P 91,000, M 700, (508) 676-8226, Fax (508) 675-5932, info@fallriverchamber.com, www.fallriverchamber.com

**Falmouth** · *Falmouth C/C* · Jay Zavala, Pres., 20 Academy Ln., 02540, P 32,000, M 800, (508) 548-8500, (800) 526-8532 US & Canada, Fax (508) 548-8521, info@falmouthchamber.com, www.falmouthchamber.com

**Fitchburg** · *see North Central Mass.*

**Foxborough** · *see Mansfield*

**Framingham** · *MetroWest C/C* · A. Theodore Welte CCE, Pres., 1671 Worcester Rd., Ste. 201, 01701, P 220,000, M 875, (508) 879-5600, Fax (508) 875-9325, chamber@metrowest.org, www.metrowest.org.

**Franklin** · *United Reg. C/C* · Jack Lank, Pres./CEO, 620 Old West Central St., Ste. 202, 02038, P 150,000, M 1,050, (508) 528-2800, Fax (508) 520-7864, jack@unitedregionalchamber.org, www.unitedregionalchamber.com

**Gardner** · *Greater Gardner C/C* · Michael F. Ellis, Pres./CEO, 210 Main St., 01440, P 50,000, M 550, (978) 632-1780, Fax (978) 630-1767, www.gardnerma.com

**Gloucester** · *Cape Ann C/C* · Bob Hastings, Exec. Dir., 33 Commercial St., 01930, P 45,000, M 1,100, (978) 283-1601, Fax (978) 283-4740, info@capeannchamber.com, www.capeannvacations.com, www.capeannchamber.com

**Granby** · *see South Hadley*

**Great Barrington** · *Southern Berkshire C/C* · Christine B. Ludwiszewski, Exec. Dir., 40 Railroad St., Ste. 2, P.O. Box 810, 01230, P 16,027, M 550, (413) 528-4284, Fax (413) 528-2200, info@southern berkshirechamber.com, www.southernberkshirechamber.com

**Greenfield** · *Franklin County C/C* · Ann L. Hamilton, Pres., 395 Main St., P.O. Box 898, 01302, P 78,000, M 700, (413) 773-5463, Fax (413) 773-7008, fccc@crocker.com, www.franklincc.org.

**Groton** · *see North Central Mass.*

**Halifax** · *see Brockton and Middleborough*

**Hamilton** · *see Danvers*

**Hampden** · *see Springfield*

**Hanover** · *Hanover C/C* · Tom Burke, Pres., P.O. Box 68, 02339, P 15,000, M 185, (781) 826-8865, Fax (781) 826-7721, www. hanovermachamber.com

**Hanson** · *see Brockton*

**Harvard** · *see North Central Mass. and Clinton*

**Harwich Port** · *Harwich C/C* · Sandra Davidson, Exec. Dir., Rte. 28, One Schoolhouse Rd., 02646, P 14,000, M 325, (508) 432-1600, (508) 430-1165, (800) 4-HARWICH, Fax (508) 430-2105, info@ harwichcc.com, www.harwichcc.com

**Haverhill** · *Greater Haverhill C/C* · James P. Jajuga, Pres., 87 Winter St., 01830, P 62,000, M 700, (978) 373-5663, Fax (978) 373-8060, info@haverhillchamber.com, www.haverhillchamber.com.

**Holbrook** · *see Brockton*

**Holden** · *Holden Area C/C* · Jennifer Stanovich, Dir., 1174 Main St., 01520, P 30,000, M 170, (508) 829-9220, Fax (508) 829-9220, info@holdenareachamber.org, www.holdenareachamber.org

**Holland** · *see Sturbridge*

**Holliston** · *see Framingham and Milford*

**Holyoke** · *Greater Holyoke C/C* · Doris M. Ransford, Pres., 177 High St., 01040, P 39,838, M 525, (413) 534-3376, Fax (413) 534-3385, ransford@holycham.com, www.holyokechamber.com

**Hopedale** · *see Milford*

**Hopkinton** · *see Framingham and Milford*

**Housatonic** · *see Great Barrington*

**Hubbardston** · *see Gardner*

**Hudson** · *Assabet Valley C/C* · Sarah B. Cressy, Pres./CEO, 18 Church St., P.O. Box 578, 01749, P 34,000, M 560, (978) 568-0360, Fax (978) 562-4118, info@assabetvalleychamber.org, www. assabetvalleychamber.org

**Hull** · *Hull/Nantasket Beach C/C* · Geri Calos, Admin., P.O. Box 140, 02045, P 12,000, M 125, (781) 925-9980, info@hullchamber. com, www.hullchamber.com

**Hyannis** · *Hyannis Area C/C* · Deborah Converse, Pres./CEO, 397 Main St., P.O. Box 100, 02601, P 48,000, M 650, (508) 775-7778, Fax (508) 775-7131, hacc@hyannis.com, www.hyannis.com

**Ipswich** · *Ipswich C/C* · Ron Eklin, Pres., P.O. Box 94, 01938, P 13,500, M 260, (978) 356-9055, info@ipswichchamber.org, www.ipswichma.com

**Lakeville** · *see Middleborough*

**Lancaster** · *see North Central Mass. and Clinton*

**Lawrence** · *Merrimack Valley C/C* · Joseph J. Bevilacqua, Pres., 264 Essex St., 01840, P 200,000, M 1,000, (978) 686-0900, Fax (978) 794-9953, thechamber@merrimackvalleychamber.com, www.merrimackvalleychamber.com

**Lee** · *Lee C/C* · Exec. Dir., 3 Park Pl., 01238, P 9,000, M 152, (413) 243-0852, info@leechamber.org, www.leechamber.org

**Lenox** · *Lenox C/C* · 12 Housatonic St., P.O. Box 646, 01240, P 5,800, M 200, (413) 637-3646, Fax (413) 637-3626, info@lenox. org, www.lenox.org

**Leominster** · *see North Central Mass.*

**Lexington** · *Lexington C/C* · Mary Jo Bohart, Exec. Dir., 1875 Massachusetts Ave., 02420, P 31,000, M 300, (781) 862-2480, Fax (781) 862-5995, www.lexingtonchamber.org

**Lincoln** · *see Waltham*

**Lowell** · *Greater Lowell C/C* · Jeanne Osborn, Pres./CEO, 131 Merrimack St., 01852, P 200,000, M 1,000, (978) 459-8154, Fax (978) 452-4145, info@greaterlowellchamber.org, www.glcc.biz.

**Ludlow** · *see Springfield*

**Lunenburg** · *see North Central Mass.*

**Lynn** · *Lynn Area C/C* · Leslie Gould, Exec. Dir., 100 Oxford St., 01901, P 89,050, M 450, (781) 592-2900, Fax (781) 592-2903, info@lynnareachamber.com, www.lynnareachamber.com.

**Lynnfield** · *see Danvers and Lynn*

**Malden** · *Malden C/C* · Edward Coates, Exec. Dir., Malden Government Center, 200 Pleasant St., Ste. 416, 02148, P 56,000, M 500, (781) 322-4500, Fax (781) 322-4866, info@malden chamber.org, www.maldenchamber.org

**Mansfield** · *Tri-Town C/C* · Kara Griffin, Exec. Dir., 15 West St., 02048, P 45,000, M 400, (508) 339-5655, Fax (508) 339-8333, office@tri-townchamber.org, www.tri-townchamber.org.

**SERVING FOXBOROUGH, MANSFIELD AND NORTON. HOME TO GILLETTE STADIUM, PATRIOT PLACE, TPC BOSTON, DEUTSCHE BANK CHAMPIONSHIP, COMCAST CENTER. STRIVING TO IMPROVE THE ECONOMIC DEVELOPMENT IN ALL OUR COMMUNITIES.**

**Marblehead** · *Marblehead C/C* · Ann Marie Casey, Exec. Dir., 62 Pleasant St., 01945, P 20,000, M 450, (781) 631-2868, Fax (781) 639-8582, info@marbleheadchamber.org, www.marblehead chamber.org

**Marlborough** · *Marlborough Reg. C/C* · Susanne Morreale-Leeber CCE, Pres./CEO, 11 Florence St., 01752, P 40,000, M 750, (508) 485-7746, Fax (508) 481-1819, susannem@marlborough chamber.org, www.marlboroughchamber.org.

**Marshfield** · *Marshfield C/C* · Richard Roberts, Pres., 2021 Ocean St., 02050, P 25,000, M 165, (781) 834-8911, office@ marshfieldchamberofcommerce.com, www.marshfieldchamber ofcommerce.com.

**Marstons Mills** · *see Hyannis*

**Martha's Vineyard** · *see Vineyard Haven*

**Mashpee** · *Mashpee C/C* · 520 Main St., P.O. Box 1245, 02649, P 15,000, M 200, (508) 477-0792, Fax (508) 477-5541, info@ mashpeechamber.com, www.mashpeechamber.com

**Maynard** · *see Hudson*

**Medfield** · *see Norwood*

**Medford** · *Medford C/C* · Cheryl White, Exec. Dir., 1 Shipyard Way, Ste. 302, 02155, P 70,000, M 400, (781) 396-1277, Fax (781) 396-1278, director@medfordchamberma.com, www.medford chamberma.com

**Medway** · *see Milford*

**Melrose** · *Melrose C/C* · Joan Mongeau, Exec. Dir., One W. Foster St., Ste. 5, 02176, P 27,000, M 300, (781) 665-3033, Fax (781) 665-5595, info@melrosechamber.org, www.melrosechamber.org

**Mendon** · *see Milford*

**Middleborough** · *Cranberry Country C/C* · Jean Scarborough, Pres., 40 N. Main St., Ste. F-1, P.O. Box 409, 02346, P 125,000, M 300, (508) 947-1499, Fax (508) 947-1446, info@cranberrycountry.org, www.cranberrycountry.org

**Milford** · *Milford Area C/C* · Barry Feingold, Pres./CEO, 258 Main St., Ste. 306, P.O. Box 621, 01757, P 135,000, M 750, (508) 473-6700, Fax (508) 473-8467, chamber@milfordchamber.org, www.milfordchamber.org

**Millis** · *see Milford*

**Monterey** · *see Great Barrington*

**Mount Washington** · *see Great Barrington*

**Nahunt** · *see Lynn*

**Nantucket** · *Nantucket Island C/C* · Tracy Bakalar, Exec. Dir., Zero Main St., 2nd Flr., 02554, P 12,000, M 680, (508) 228-3643, Fax (508) 325-4925, info@nantucketchamber.org, www.nantucketchamber.org

**Natick** · *see Framingham*

**Needham** · *see Newton*

**New Bedford** · *New Bedford Area C/C* · Roy Nascimento, Pres., 794 Purchase St., P.O. Box 8827, 02742, P 250,000, M 900, (508) 999-5231, Fax (508) 999-5237, info@newbedfordchamber.com, www.newbedfordchamber.com.

**Newburyport** · *Greater Newburyport C/C* · Ann Ormond, Pres., 38 R Merrimac St., 01950, P 17,000, M 850, (978) 462-6680, Fax (978) 465-4145, info@newburyportchamber.org, www.newburyportchamber.org

**Newton** · *Newton-Needham C/C* · Thomas O'Rourke, Pres., 281 Needham St., Upper Level, 02464, P 112,000, M 700, (617) 244-5300, Fax (617) 244-5302, info@nnchamber.com, www.nnchamber.com

**Norfolk** · *see Franklin*

**North Adams** · *Berkshire C/C* · Michael Supranowicz, Pres./CEO, 6 W. Main St., 01247, P 135,150, M 1,200, (413) 499-4000, Fax (413) 447-9641, info@berkshirechamber.com, www.berkshirechamber.com

**North Attleboro** · *United Reg. C/C* · Jack Lank, Pres./CEO, 31 N. Washington St., Ste. 5, P.O. Box 1071, 02761, M 1,050, (508) 695-6011, Fax (508) 695-6096, info@napcc.org, www.napcc.org

**North Central Mass.** · *North Central MA C/C* · David L. McKeehan CCE, Pres., 860 South St., Fitchburg, 01420, P 200,000, M 1,500, (978) 353-7600, Fax (978) 353-4896, chamber@massweb.org, northcentralmass.com

**North Chatham** · *see Chatham*

**North Easton** · *see Brockton*

**North Egremont** · *see Great Barrington*

**North Reading** · *see Reading*

**North Truro** · *Truro C/C* · Jane Peters, P.O. Box 26, 02652, P 2,087, (508) 487-1288, info@trurochamberofcommerce.com, www.trurochamberofcommerce.com

**Northampton** · *Greater Northampton C/C* · Suzanne Beck, Exec. Dir., 99 Pleasant St., 01060, P 30,000, M 750, (413) 584-1900, Fax (413) 584-1934, info@explorenorthampton.com, www.explorenorthampton.com

**Northborough** · *see Westborough*

**Northfield** · *see Greenfield*

**Norton** · *see Mansfield*

**Norwell** · *Norwell C/C* · Tom Malames, P.O. Box 322, 02061, P 10,000, M 100, info@norwellchamberofcommerce.com, www.norwellchamberofcommerce.com

**Norwood** · *Neponset Valley C/C* · Sue McQuaid, Pres./CEO, 190 Vanderbilt Ave., 02062, P 180,000, M 1,000, (781) 769-1126, Fax (781) 769-0808, sue@nvcc.com, www.nvcc.com

**Orleans** · *Orleans C/C* · Mary J. Corr, Exec. Dir., 44 Main St., P.O. Box 153, 02653, P 6,800, M 285, (508) 255-1386, Fax (508) 255-2774, info@capecod-orleans.com, www.capecod-orleans.com

**Osterville** · *see Hyannis*

**Otis** · *see Great Barrington*

**Oxbury** · *see Worcester*

**Palmer** · *Quaboag Hills C/C* · Lenny Weake, Pres., 3 Converse St., Ste. 103, 01069, P 85,000, M 330, (413) 283-2418, Fax (413) 289-1355, info@qhcc.biz, www.qhcc.biz

**Peabody** · *Peabody C/C* · Deanne Healey, Exec. Dir., 24 Main St., 01960, P 49,000, M 400, (978) 531-0384, Fax (978) 532-7227, pcc@peabodychamber.com, www.peabodychamber.com

**Pepperell** · *see North Central Mass.*

**Pittsfield** · *Berkshire C/C - Pittsfield Ofc.* · Michael Supranowicz, Pres./CEO, 75 North St., Ste. 360, 01201, P 135,150, M 1,200, (413) 499-4000, Fax (413) 447-9641, info@berkshirechamber.com, www.berkshirechamber.com.

**Plainville** · *see North Attleboro*

**Plymouth** · *Plymouth Area C/C* · Denis Hanks, Exec. Dir., 10 Cordage Park Circle, Ste. 231, 02360, P 152,000, M 800, (508) 830-1620, Fax (508) 830-1621, info@plymouthchamber.com, www.plymouthchamber.com

**Plympton** · *see Middleborough*

**Princeton** · *see North Central Mass.*

**Provincetown** · *Provincetown C/C* · Candice Collins-Boden, Exec. Dir., 307 Commerical St., P.O. Box 1017, 02657, P 3,800, M 350, (508) 487-3424, Fax (508) 487-8966, info@ptownchamber.com, www.ptownchamber.com

**Quincy** · *South Shore C/C* · Peter Forman, Pres./CEO, 36 Miller Stile Rd., P.O. Box 690625, 02169, P 220,000, M 2,000, (617) 479-1111, Fax (617) 479-9274, info@southshorechamber.org, www.southshorechamber.org.

**Randolph** · *Randolph C/C* · 1 Credit Union Way, Ste. 210, 02368, P 31,000, M 190, (781) 963-6862, Fax (781) 963-5252, info@randolphchamberofcommerce.org, www.randolphchamberofcommerce.org

**Raynham** · *see Taunton*

**Reading** · *Reading-North Reading C/C* · Irene Collins, Exec. Dir., P.O. Box 771, 01867, P 37,000, M 265, (781) 944-8824, (978) 664-5060, Fax (781) 944-6125, rnrchambercom@aol.com, www.readingnreadingchamber.org

**Rehoboth** · *see Taunton*

**Revere** · *Revere C/C* · 270 Broadway, Ste. 10, 02151, P 53,000, M 175, (781) 289-8009, Fax (781) 289-2166, info@reverechamber.org, www.reverechamber.org

**Rochester** · *see Middleborough*

**Rockland** · *Rockland C/C* · John Ward, Pres., P.O. Box 45, 02370, P 18,000, M 70, (781) 681-7204, www.rocklandchamberofcommerce.com

**Rockport** · *Rockport C/C* · Peter Webber, Mgr., 170 Main St., P.O. Box 67, 01966, P 7,931, M 230, (978) 546-6575, Fax (978) 283-4740, info@rockportusa.com, www.rockportusa.com

**Salem** · *Salem C/C* · Rinus Oosthoek, Exec. Dir., 265 Essex St., 01970, P 42,000, M 650, (978) 744-0004, Fax (978) 745-3855, info@salem-chamber.org, www.salem-chamber.org

**Salisbury** · *Salisbury 'By the Sea' C/C* · Maria Miles, Town Hall, Beach Rd., P.O. Box 1000, 01952, P 8,000, M 250, (978) 465-3581, Fax (978) 465-3581, salisburychamber@aol.com, www.salisburychamber.com

**Sandisfield** · *see Great Barrington*

**Sandwich** · *see Cape Cod Canal*

**Saugus** · *Saugus C/C* · 394 Lincoln Ave., 01906, P 25,000, M 300, (781) 233-8407, Fax (781) 231-1145, sauguschamber@verizon.net, www.sauguschamber.org

**Scituate** · *Scituate C/C* · Elaine Bongarzone, Pres., P.O. Box 401, 02066, P 18,779, M 125, (781) 545-4000, info@scituatechamber.org, www.scituatechamber.org

**Sheffield** · *see Great Barrington*

**Sheffield** · *see Lakeville, CT*

**Shelburne** · *see Greenfield*

**Sherborn** · *see Framingham*

**Shirley** · *see North Central Mass.*

**Shrewsbury** · *see Westborough*

**Somerville** · *Somerville C/C* · Stephen V. Mackey, Pres./CEO, 2 Alpine St., P.O. Box 440343, 02144, P 78,000, M 325, (617) 776-4100, smackey@somervillechamber.org, www.somervillechamber.org

**South Chatham** · *see Chatham*

**South Egremont** · *see Great Barrington*

**South Hadley** · *South Hadley & Granby C/C* · Susan Stockman, Exec. Dir., 116 Main St., Ste. 4, 01075, P 17,000, M 125, (413) 532-6451, mail@shchamber.com, www.southhadleygranbychamber.com

**South Yarmouth** · *Yarmouth Area C/C* · Robert E. DuBois, Exec. Dir., P.O. Box 479, 02664, P 24,700, M 465, (508) 778-1008, (800) 732-1008, Fax (508) 778-5114, info@yarmouthcapecod.com, www.yarmouthcapecod.com

**Southborough** · *see Framingham and Westborough*

**Southbridge** · *see Sturbridge*

**Spencer** · *see Sturbridge*

**Springfield** · *Affiliated Chambers of Commerce of Greater Springfield, Inc.* · Russell F. Denver, Pres., 1441 Main St., Ste. 133, 1st Flr., 01103, P 157,000, M 1,800, (413) 787-1555, Fax (413) 731-8530, denver@myonlinechamber.com, www.myonlinechamber.com.

**Sterling** · *see North Central Mass. and Clinton*

**Stockbridge** · *Stockbridge C/C* · Barbara Zanetti, Exec. Dir., 50 Main St., P.O. Box 224, 01262, P 2,500, M 100, (413) 298-5200, Fax (413) 931-3128, info@stockbridgechamber.org, www.stockbridgechamber.org

**Stoneham** · *Stoneham C/C* · Sharon Iovanni, Exec. Dir., 271 Main St., Ste. L-02, 02180, P 24,000, M 280, (781) 438-0001, Fax (781) 438-0007, info@stonehamchamber.org, www.stonehamchamber.org

**Stoughton** · *Stoughton C/C* · Terry Schneider, Exec. Dir., P.O. Box 41, 02072, P 30,000, M 175, (781) 297-7450, chamber@stoughtonma.com, www.stoughtonma.com

**Stow** · *see Hudson*

**Sturbridge** · *Central Mass South C/C* · Alexandra McNitt, Exec. Dir., 380 Main St., 01566, P 60,000, M 475, (508) 347-2761, (800) 628-8379, Fax (508) 347-5218, info@sturbridgetownships.org, cmschamber.org

**Sudbury** · *see Framingham*

**Swampscott** · *see Lynn*

**Taunton** · *Taunton Area C/C* · Kerrie Babin, Pres./CEO, 12 Taunton Green, Ste. 201, 02780, P 70,000, M 500, (508) 824-4068, Fax (508) 884-8222, info@tauntonareachamber.org, www.tauntonareachamber.org.

**Templeton** · *see Gardner*

**Tewksbury** · *see Lowell*

**Three Rivers** · *Three Rivers C/C* · P.O. Box 233, 01080, P 3,500, M 60, (413) 283-6425, www.threeriverschamber.org

**Townsend** · *see North Central Mass.*

**Truro** · *see North Truro*

**Tyngsboro** · *see Lowell*

**Upton** · *see Milford*

**Vineyard Haven** · *Martha's Vineyard C/C* · Nancy Gardella, Exec. Dir., Beach Rd., P.O. Box 1698, 02568, P 15,000, M 1,050, (508) 693-0085, (800) 505-4815, Fax (508) 693-7589, www.mvy.com

**Wakefield** · *Wakefield C/C* · Nancy Bertrand, Exec. Dir., 467 Main St., P.O. Box 585, 01880, P 25,000, M 300, (781) 245-0741, chamber@wakefieldma.org, www.wakefieldma.org

**Wales** · *see Sturbridge*

**Walpole** · *Walpole C/C* · Virginia Griffin, Pres., P.O. Box 361, 02081, P 23,000, M 200, (508) 668-0081, office@walpolechamber.com, www.walpolechamber.com

**Waltham** · *Waltham West Suburban C/C* · John Peacock, Exec. Dir., 84 South St., 02453, P 60,000, M 650, (781) 894-4700, Fax (781) 894-1708, info@walthamchamber.com, www.walthamchamber.com.

**Wareham** · *see Cape Cod Canal and Middleborough*

**Watertown** · *Watertown-Belmont C/C* · Brenda Fanara, Exec. Dir., 182 Main St., P.O. Box 45, 02471, P 52,000, M 450, (617) 926-1017, Fax (617) 926-2322, info@wbcc.org, www.wbcc.org

**Wayland** · *see Framingham*

**Webster** · *see Worcester*

**Wellesley** · *Wellesley C/C* · Maura O'Brien, Pres./CEO, One Hollis St. #232, 02482, P 26,615, M 250, (781) 235-2446, Fax (781) 235-7326, www.wellesleychamber.org

**Wellfleet** · *Wellfleet C/C* · Maureen Schraut, Exec. Secy., Off Rte. 6, P.O. Box 571, 02667, P 3,000, M 230, (508) 349-2510, Fax (508) 349-3740, info@wellfleetchamber.com, www.wellfleetchamber.com

**Wenham** · *see Danvers*

**West Barnstable** · *see Hyannis*

**West Boylston** · *see Clinton*

**West Bridgewater** · *see Brockton*

**West Chatham** · *see Chatham*

**West Dennis** · *Dennis C/C* · Spyro Mitrokostas, Exec. Dir., 238 Swan River Rd., P.O. Box 1001, 02670, P 16,000, M 400, (508) 398-3568, Fax (508) 760-5212, info@dennischamber.com, www.dennischamber.com

**West Springfield** · *see Springfield*

**West Stockbridge** · *see Great Barrington*

**West Yarmouth** · *see South Yarmouth*

**Westborough** · *also see Framingham*

**Westborough** · *Corridor Nine Area C/C* · Barbara Clifford, Pres., 30 Lyman St., Ste. 6, P.O. Box 1555, 01581, P 73,000, M 800, (508) 836-4444, Fax (508) 836-2652, events@corridornine.org, www.corridornine.org

**Westfield** · *see Springfield*

**Westford** · *see Lowell*

**Westminster** · *see North Central Mass.*

**Weston** · *see Waltham*

**Westwood** · *see Norwood*

**Whitinsville** · *Blackstone Valley C/C* · Jeannie Hebert, Pres./CEO, 110 Church St., 01588, P 95,000, M 500, (508) 234-9090, Fax (508) 234-5152, www.blackstonevalley.org

**Whitman** · *see Brockton*

**Wilbraham** · *see Springfield*

**Williamstown** · *Williamstown C/C* · Judy Giamborino, Exec. Dir., P.O. Box 357, 01267, P 8,300, M 200, (413) 458-9077, Fax (413) 458-2666, info@williamstownchamber.com, www.williamstownchamber.com

**Wilmington** · *Wilmington C/C* · 226 Lowell St., P.O. Box 463, 01887, P 21,000, M 150, (978) 657-7211, Fax (978) 657-0139, wilmingtonchamber@verizon.net, www.wilmingtonbusiness.com

**Winchendon** · *see Gardner*

**Winchester** · *Winchester C/C* · Catherine S. Alexander, Exec. Dir., 25 Waterfield Rd., 01890, P 21,000, M 210, (781) 729-8870, Fax (781) 729-8884, winchamb@aol.com, www.winchesterchamber.com

**Winthrop** · *Winthrop C/C* · Eric Gaynor, Exec. Dir., 207 Hagman Rd., 02152, P 18,000, M 425, (617) 846-9898, Fax (617) 846-9922, info@winthropchamber.com, www.winthropchamber.com

**Woburn** · *North Suburban C/C* · Maureen A. Rogers, Pres., 76R Winn St., Ste. 3-D, 01801, P 100,000, M 427, (781) 933-3499, Fax (781) 933-1071, info@northsuburbanchamber.com, www.northsuburbanchamber.com

**Worcester** · *Worcester Reg. C/C* · Richard Kennedy, Pres./CEO, 446 Main St., Ste. 200, 01608, P 174,000, M 3,800, (508) 753-2924, Fax (508) 754-8560, rkennedy@worcesterchamber.org, www.worcesterchamber.org

**Wrentham** · *see Franklin*

**Yarmouth** · *see South Yarmouth*

# Michigan

**Michigan C of C** · Rich Studley, Pres./CEO, 600 S. Walnut St., Lansing, 48933, P 9,200,000, M 7,000, (517) 371-2100, (800) 748-0266, Fax (517) 371-7224, info@michamber.com, www.michamber.com

**Adrian** · *Adrian Area C/C* · Ann Hughes, Pres./CEO, 128 E. Maumee St., 49221, P 22,000, M 450, (517) 265-2320, Fax (517) 265-2432, info@adrianareachamber.com, www.adrianareachamber.com

**Albion** · *Greater Albion C/C* · Sue Marcos, Pres., 416 S. Superior St., P.O. Box 238, 49224, P 10,000, M 220, (517) 629-5533, Fax (517) 629-4284, sue@greateralbionchamber.org, www.greateralbionchamber.org

**Algonac** · *Greater Algonac C/C* · 1396 St. Clair River Dr., P.O. Box 375, 48001, P 4,500, M 106, (810) 794-5511, Fax (866) 643-0023, execdirector@algonacchamber.com, www.algonacchamber.com

**Allegan** · *Allegan Area C/C* · Mary Hedberg, Exec. Dir., 221 Trowbridge St., Ste. B, 49010, P 5,000, M 200, (269) 673-2479, Fax (269) 673-7190, mail@alleganchamber.com, www.alleganchamber.com

**Allen Park** · *Allen Park C/C* · Margaret Lezotte, Exec. Dir., 6543 Allen Rd., 48101, P 29,000, M 155, (313) 382-7303, Fax (313) 382-4409, info@allenparkchamber.org, www.allenparkchamber.org

**Allendale** · *Allendale Area C/C* · Amy Millard, Dir., 6101 Lake Michigan Dr., Ste. B300, PMB #167, 49401, P 15,000, M 225, (616) 892-2632, Fax (616) 895-2600, aacc@allendalechamber.org, www.allendalechamber.org

**Alma** · *Gratiot Area C/C* · Patricia Nelson, Exec. Dir., 110 W. Superior St., P.O. Box 516, 48801, P 39,000, M 450, (989) 463-5525, Fax (989) 463-6588, chamber@gratiot.org, www.gratiot.org

**Alpena** · *Alpena Area C/C* · Jackie Krawczak, Exec. Dir., 235 W. Chisholm, 49707, P 31,314, M 580, (989) 354-4181, (800) 4-ALPENA, Fax (989) 356-3999, alpenachamber@chartermi.net, www.alpenachamber.com

**Ann Arbor** · *Ann Arbor Area C/C* · Jesse Bernstein, Pres., 115 W. Huron St., 3rd Flr., 48104, P 114,000, M 1,400, (734) 665-4433, Fax (734) 665-4191, info@annarborchamber.org, www.annarborchamber.org

**Armada** · *see Romeo*

**Ashley** · *see Alma*

**Atlanta** · *Atlanta C/C* · Phil LaMore, Pres., P.O. Box 410, 49709, P 2,500, M 200, (989) 785-3400, Fax (989) 785-3400, atlantamotel@i2k.com, www.atlantamichigan.com

**Au Gres** · *Au Gres Area C/C* · J.R. Stoltz, Pres., P.O. Box 455, 48703, P 1,000, M 73, (989) 876-6688, staff@augreschamber.com, www.augreschamber.com

**Au Sable** · *see Oscoda*

**Auburn** · *Auburn Area C/C* · Cherri Allen, Pres., P.O. Box 215, 48611, P 4,000, M 65, (989) 662-4001, Fax (989) 662-3333, www.auburnchambermi.org

**Auburn Hills** · *Auburn Hills C/C* · Susan Rothfuss, Exec. Dir., P.O. Box 214083, 48321, P 20,000, M 300, (248) 853-7862, Fax (248) 853-0763, info@auburnhillschamber.com, www.auburnhillschamber.com

**Bad Axe** · *Bad Axe C/C* · P.O. Box 87, 48413, P 3,642, M 120, (989) 269-6936, Fax (989) 269-2611, chamberinfo@badaxechamber.com, www.badaxemich.com

**Baldwin** · *Lake County C/C & Tourist Center* · 911 Michigan Ave., P.O. Box 130, 49304, P 10,000, M 200, (231) 745-4331, (800) 245-3240, info@lakecountymichigan.com, www.lakecountymichigan.com

**Bannister** · *see Alma*

**Battle Creek** · *Battle Creek Area C/C* · Kathleen Mechem, Pres./CEO, 77 E. Michigan Ave., Ste. 80, Commerce Pointe, 49017, P 134,000, M 950, (269) 962-4076, Fax (269) 962-6309, chamber@battlecreek.org, www.battlecreek.org

**Bay City** · *Bay Area C/C* · Michael Seward, Pres./CEO, 901 Saginaw St., 48708, P 110,000, M 750, (989) 893-4567, Fax (989) 895-5594, chamber@baycityarea.com, www.baycityarea.com

**Beaver Island** · *Beaver Island C/C* · Steve West, Exec. Dir., P.O. Box 5, 49782, P 2,000, M 120, (231) 448-2505, chamber@beaverisland.org, www.beaverisland.org

**Belding** · *Belding Area C/C* · 120 Covered Village Mall, 48809, P 6,000, M 80, (616) 794-9890, info@beldingchamber.org, www.beldingchamber.org

**Bellaire** · *Bellaire Area C/C* · Patricia Savant, Exec. Dir., 308 E. Cayuga, P.O. Box 205, 49615, P 1,164, M 100, (231) 533-6023, Fax (231) 533-8764, info@bellairechamber.org, www.bellaire chamber.org

**Belleville** · *Belleville Area C/C* · Lianne Clair, Exec. Dir., 248 Main St., 48111, P 43,000, M 450, (734) 697-7151, Fax (734) 697-1415, bellechamber@bellevillech.org, www.bellevillech.org.

**Benton Harbor** · *Cornerstone C/C* · Pat Moody, Exec. V.P., 38 W. Wall St., P.O. Box 428, 49023, P 79,000, M 700, (269) 925-6100, Fax (269) 925-4471, info@cornerstonechamber.com, www. cornerstonechamber.com.

**Benzonia** · *Benzie County C/C* · Mary Carroll, Exec. Dir., 826 Michigan Ave., P.O. Box 204, 49616, P 17,000, M 425, (231) 882-5801, Fax (231) 882-9249, director@benzie.org, www.benzie.org.

**Bergland** · *Lake Gogebic Area C/C* · P.O. Box 114-T, 49910, P 600, M 81, (888) GO-GEBIC, info@lakegogebicarea.com, www. lakegogebicarea.com

**Berkley** · *Greater Berkley C/C* · Julie Melrose, Exec. Dir., P.O. Box 72-1253, 48072, P 15,500, M 100, (248) 414-9157, Fax (248) 246-6290, julie@berkleychamber.com, www.berkleychamber.com

**Berrien Springs** · *Berrien Springs-Eau Claire C/C* · Scott Bormann, Pres., P.O. Box 177, 49103, P 11,000, M 100, (269) 471-2484, www.bsechamber.org

**Bessemer** · *Bessemer C/C* · Candice Snyder, Secy., U.S. Hwy. 2, P.O. Box 243, 49911, P 2,148, M 110, (906) 663-0026, bessemer chamber@hotmail.com, www.bessemerchamber.org

**Big Rapids** · *Mecosta County Area C/C* · Anja J. Wing, Exec. Dir., 246 N. State St., 49307, P 40,000, M 500, (231) 796-7649, Fax (231) 796-1625, info@mecostacounty.com, www.mecostacounty.com

**Birch Run** · *Birch Run Area C/C & CVB* · Tammey Inman, CEO, 11600 N. Beyer Rd., 48415, P 10,815, M 160, (989) 624-9193, (888) 624-9193, Fax (989) 624-5337, info@birchrunchamber.com, www.birchrunchamber.com

**Birmingham** · *Birmingham-Bloomfield C/C* · Carrie Zarotney, Pres., 124 W. Maple Rd., 48009, P 75,000, M 700, (248) 644-1700, Fax (248) 644-0286, thechamber@bbcc.com, www.bbcc.com

**Blissfield** · *Blissfield Area C/C* · Frank Baker, Pres., 105 N. Lane, 49228, P 3,200, M 90, (517) 486-3642, info@blissfieldchamber. org, www.blissfieldchamber.org

**Boyne City** · *Boyne Area C/C* · Jim Baumann, Exec. Dir., 28 S. Lake St., 49712, P 3,500, M 300, (231) 582-6222, Fax (231) 582-6963, info@boynechamber.com, www.boynechamber.com

**Breckenridge** · *see Alma*

**Bridgeport** · *Bridgeport Area C/C* · Jan Crane, Exec. Secy., P.O. Box 564, 48722, P 1,300, M 107, (989) 777-1801, Fax (989) 777-2223, execsecbridgeportcoc@yahoo.com, bridgeportchambermi.org

**Brighton** · *Greater Brighton Area C/C* · Pamela McConeghy, Pres./CEO, 131 Hyne St., 48116, P 85,000, M 1,200, (810) 227-5086, Fax (810) 227-5940, info@brightoncoc.org, www. brightoncoc.org

**Brooklyn** · *Brooklyn-Irish Hills C/C* · Cindy Hubbell, Exec. Dir., 131 N. Main St., P.O. Box 805, 49230, P 25,000, M 215, (517) 592-8907, Fax same, info@brooklynmi.com, www.brooklynmi.com/.

**Bruce Township** · *see Romeo*

**Buchanan** · *Buchanan Area C/C* · Monroe Lemay, Exec. Dir., 103 W. Front St., 49107, P 5,000, M 110, (269) 695-3291, Fax (269) 695-3813, bacc@buchanan.mi.us, www.buchanan.mi.us

**Burr Oak** · *Burr Oak C/C* · Margie Barrington, Secy./Treas., P.O. Box 308, 49030, P 900, M 20, (616) 489-5075, Fax (616) 489-2731

**Cadillac** · *Cadillac Area C/C* · Bill Tencza, Pres., 222 Lake St., 49601, P 35,000, M 500, (231) 775-9776, Fax (231) 775-1440, info@cadillac.org, www.cadillac.org

**Canton** · *Canton C/C* · Dianne Cojei, Pres., 45525 Hanford Rd., 48187, P 85,000, M 670, (734) 453-4040, Fax (734) 453-4503, info@cantonchamber.com, www.cantonchamber.com

**Capac** · *Capac Area C/C* · P.O. Box 386, 48014, P 1,600, M 50, (810) 395-8350, info@capacchamber.org, www.capacchamber.org

**Caro** · *Caro C/C* · Brenda Caruthers, Exec. Dir., 157 N. State St., 48723, P 4,200, M 150, (989) 673-5211, Fax (989) 673-2517, executivedirector@carochamber.org, www.carochamber.org

**Caseville** · *Caseville Area C/C* · Mrs. Dena Withey, Ofc. Mgr., P.O. Box 122, 48725, P 2,700, M 155, (989) 856-3818, (800) 606-1347, Fax (989) 856-2596, ccofc@avci.net, www.casevillechamber.com

**Cass City** · *Cass City C/C* · Dee Ann Mulligan, Admin., 6506 Main St., 48726, P 2,643, M 151, (989) 872-4618, (866) 266-3822, Fax (989) 872-4855, ccc@casscitychamber.com, www.casscity chamber.com

**Cedarville** · *Les Cheneaux Islands C/C* · Amy Polk, Coord., P.O. Box 10, 49719, P 2,200, M 117, (906) 484-3935, (888) 364-7526, Fax (906) 484-9941, lcichamber@lescheneaux.net, www. lescheneaux.net

**Center Line** · *see Mount Clemens*

**Central Lake** · *Central Lake Area C/C* · Jackie White, Pres., 2587 N. M-88 Hwy., P.O. Box 428, 49622, P 1,000, M 90, (231) 544-3322, clcc@torchlake.com, www.central-lake.com

**Charlevoix** · *Charlevoix Area C/C* · Erin Bemis, Exec. Dir., 109 Mason St., 49720, P 26,000, M 500, (231) 547-2101, info@ charlevoix.org, www.charlevoix.org

**Charlotte** · *Charlotte C/C* · Ann Garvey, Dir., 126 N. Bostwick, P.O. Box 356, 48813, P 10,500, M 320, (517) 543-0400, Fax (517) 543-9638, agarvey@charlottechamber-mi.org, www.charlotte chamber-mi.org

**Cheboygan** · *Cheboygan Area C/C* · Kimberlee Pappas, Exec. Dir., 124 N. Main St., P.O. Box 69, 49721, P 29,000, M 417, (231) 627-7183, (800) 968-3302, Fax (231) 627-2770, kpappas@ cheboygan.com, www.cheboygan.com

**Chelsea** · *Chelsea Area C/C* · Bob Pierce, Exec. Dir., 310 N. Main St., Ste. 120, 48118, P 8,000, M 275, (734) 475-1145, Fax (734) 475-6102, bpierce@chelseamichamber.org, www.chelseami chamber.org

**Chesaning** · *Chesaning C/C* · Steven Keck, Pres., 218 N. Front St., P.O. Box 83, 48616, P 4,904, M 170, (989) 845-3055, (800) 255-3055, Fax (989) 845-6006, info@chesaningchamber.org, www. chesaningchamber.org

**Chesterfield Twp** · *see Mount Clemens and New Baltimore*

**Clare** · *Clare Area C/C* · Jennifer Heinzman, Ofc. Mgr., 429 N. McEwan, 48617, P 3,050, M 270, (989) 386-2442, (888) AT-CLARE, Fax (989) 386-3173, manager@claremichigan.com, www.clare michigan.com

**Clarkston** · *Clarkston Area C/C* · Penny Shanks, Exec. Dir., 5856 S. Main St., 48346, P 32,000, M 600, (248) 625-8055, Fax (248) 625-8041, info@clarkston.org, www.clarkston.org

**Clarksville** · *see Lake Odessa*

**Clawson** · *Clawson C/C* · Sheryl Geralds, Exec. Dir., P.O. Box 217, 48017, P 13,000, M 140, (248) 435-6500,.Fax (248) 435-6868, sheryl@clawsonchamber.com, www.clawsonchamber.com

**Clinton Twp** · *see Mount Clemens*

**Clio** · *Clio Area C/C* · Janet Towns, Ofc. Mgr., 192 W. Vienna St., P.O. Box 543, 48420, P 30,000, M 260, (810) 686-4480, clio chamber@sbcglobal.net, www.cliomi.org

**Coldwater** · *Branch County Area C/C* · Hillary Eley, Pres., 20 Division St., 49036, P 45,000, M 600, (517) 278-5985, Fax (517) 278-8369, info@branchareachamber.com, www.brancharea chamber.com

**Coloma** · *Coloma-Watervliet Area C/C* · Lee Scherwitz, Pres., P.O. Box 418, 49038, P 15,000, M 140, (269) 468-9160, Fax (269) 468-7088, info@coloma-watervliet.org, www.coloma-watervliet.org

**Commerce Twp** · *see Lakes Area*

**Coopersville** · *Coopersville Area C/C* · Cynthia Timmerman, Exec. Dir., 289 Danforth St., 49404, P 4,000, M 250, (616) 997-5164, Fax (616) 997-6679, ctimmerman@cityofcoopersville.com, www.coopersville.com.

**Corunna** · *see Owosso*

**Curtis** · *Curtis Area C/C* · Pat MacLachlan, Pres., P.O. Box 477, 49820, P 1,500, M 150, (906) 586-3700, curtiscofc@sbcglobal.net, www.curtischamber.com

**Davison** · *Davison Area C/C* · LaDawn Hastings, Exec. Dir., 709 S. State Rd., Ste. A, 48423, P 30,000, M 250, (810) 653-6266, Fax (810) 653-0669, ladawn@davisonchamberofcommerce.com, www.davisonchamberofcommerce.com

**Dearborn** · *Dearborn C/C* · Jennifer Giering, Pres., 15544 Michigan Ave., 48126, P 100,000, M 600, (313) 584-6100, Fax (313) 584-9818, jgiering@dearbornchamber.org, www.dear bornchamber.org

**Dearborn Heights** · *Dearborn Heights C/C* · Wendy Fichter, Exec Dir., 25147 W. Warren Ave., 48127, P 58,000, M 120, (313) 274-7480, Fax (313) 724-0757, info@dearbornheightschamber.com, www.dearbornheightschamber.com

**Decatur** · *Greater Decatur C/C* · David Moormann, Pres., P.O. Box 211, 49045, P 1,900, M 60, (269) 423-2411, Fax (269) 423-2411, info@decaturmi.org, www.decaturmi.org

**Delton** · *see Hastings*

**Detroit** · *Detroit Reg. Chamber* · Richard E. Blouse Jr. CCE, Pres./CEO, One Woodward Ave., Ste. 1900, P.O. Box 33840, 48232, P 5,200,000, M 23,000, (313) 964-4000, Fax (313) 964-0183, www.detroitchamber.com

**Dexter** · *Dexter Area C/C* · Judy Feldmann, Ofc. Mgr., 3215 Central St., 48130, P 3,700, M 230, (734) 426-0887, Fax (734) 426-6055, info@dexterchamber.org, www.dexterchamber.org

**Dowagiac** · *Greater Dowagiac C/C* · Vickie Phillipson, Prog. Dir., 200 Depot Dr., 49047, P 6,400, M 225, (269) 782-8212, vickie@ dowagiacchamber.com, www.dowagiacchamber.com

**Durand** · *Durand Area C/C* · Patricia Post, Exec. Dir., 100 W. Clinton St., 48429, P 5,000, M 125, (989) 288-3715, Fax (989) 288-5177, office@durandchamber.com, www.durandchamber.com

**East Jordan** · *East Jordan Area C/C* · Mary H. Faculak, Pres., 100 Main St. #B, P.O. Box 137, 49727, P 3,500, M 290, (231) 536-7351, Fax (231) 536-0966, info@ejchamber.org, www.ejchamber.org

**Eastpointe** · *Eastpointe-Roseville C/C* · Catherine Green, Exec. Dir., 24840 Gratiot Ave., Ste. B, 48021, P 36,000, M 225, (586) 776-5520, Fax (586) 776-7808, director@epchamber.com, www. epchamber.com

**Eaton Rapids** · *Eaton Rapids Area C/C* · Donald Wyckoff, Exec. Dir., 147 S. Main St., 48827, P 5,330, (517) 663-6480, Fax (517) 663-3500, don@eatonrapidschamber.com, www.eatonrapids chamber.com

**Eau Claire** · *see Berrien Springs*

**Edmore** · *Edmore Area C/C* · Kristin Callow, Pres., P.O. Box 102, 48829, P 1,300, M 60, (989) 289-2428, kristincallow@yahoo.com

**Edwardsburg** · *Edwardsburg Area C/C* · Karen Sinkiewicz, Admin., 69139 M-62 Hwy., P.O. Box 575, 49112, P 5,200, M 85, (269) 663-6344, (800) 942-8413, Fax (269) 663-5344, adminis tration@edwardsburg.biz, edwardsburg.biz

**Elk Rapids** · *Elk Rapids C/C* · Sheila Marker, Ofc. Admin., 305 U.S. 31 N., 49629, P 2,500, M 420, (231) 264-8202, (800) 626-7328, Fax (231) 264-6591, info@elkrapidschamber.org, www. elkrapidschamber.org

**Elwell** · *see Alma*

**Escanaba** · *Delta County Area C/C* · Vickie Micheau, Dir., 230 Ludington St., 49829, P 37,780, M 700, (906) 786-2192, (888) DELTAMI, Fax (906) 786-8830, info@deltami.org, www.deltami.org

**Evart** · *Evart Area C/C* · Herb Phelps, Pres., P.O. Box 688, 49631, P 1,745, M 75, (231) 734-9799, Fax (231) 734-9799, fairman@ netonecom.net, www.evart.org

**Fair Haven** · *see Algonac*

**Farmington Hills** · *Farmington/Farmington Hills C/C* · Mary Engelman, Pres., 27555 Executive Dr., Ste. 145, 48331, P 90,000, M 850, (248) 474-3440, Fax (248) 474-9235, mary@ffhchamber. com, www.ffhchamber.com

**Farwell** · *Farwell Area C/C* · Wanda Agle, Ofc. Mgr., 221 W. Main, P.O. Box 771, 48622, P 31,000, M 95, (989) 588-0580, Fax (989) 588-0580, facc@farwellareachamber.com, www.farwellarea chamber.com.

**Fennville** · *Greater Fennville C/C* · Jim Lytle, Pres., P.O. Box 484, 49408, P 1,500, M 91, (269) 561-8321, (269) 686-6854, jlytle@ fenvillenews.com, www.greaterfennville.com

**Fenton** · *Fenton Reg. C/C* · Shelly Day, Pres., 114 N. Leroy St., 48430, P 33,000, M 450, (810) 629-5447, Fax (810) 629-6608, info@fentonchamber.com, www.fentonchamber.com.

**Ferndale** · *Ferndale C/C* · Jennifer Roosenberg, Exec Dir., 407 E. Nine Mile Rd., 48220, P 25,000, M 275, (248) 542-2160, Fax (248) 542-8979, info@ferndalechamber.com, www.ferndalechamber.com

**Ferrysburg** · *see Grand Haven*

**Fife Lake** · *Fife Lake C/C* · P.O. Box 59, 49633, P 468, M 40, (231) 879-4154, president@fifelake.org, www.fifelake.com/chamber

**Flint** · *Genesee Reg. C/C* · Tim Herman, CEO, 519 S. Saginaw St. #200, 48502, P 430,459, M 1,400, (810) 600-1404, Fax (810) 600-1461, info@thegrcc.org, www.thegrcc.org

**Flushing** · *Flushing Area C/C* · Susan Little, Exec. Dir., 133 E. Main St., P.O. Box 44, 48433, P 18,000, M 200, (810) 659-4141, Fax (810) 659-6964, flushingchamber@sbcglobal.net, www. flushingchamber.com.

**Frankenmuth** · *Frankenmuth C/C* · Jamie Furbush, Pres./CEO, 635 S. Main St., 48734, P 4,800, M 401, (989) 652-6106, (800) 386-8696, Fax (989) 652-3841, chamber@frankenmuth.org, www. frankenmuth.org

**Frankfort** · *Frankfort-Elberta Area C/C* · Joanne Bartley, Exec. Dir., 517 Main St., P.O. Box 566, 49635, P 1,703, M 185, (231) 352-7251, Fax (231) 352-6750, fcofc@frankfort-elberta.com, www. frankfort-elberta.com.

**Fraser** · *see Saint Clair Shores*

**Freeland** · *Freeland Area C/C* · Dwight Kelsey, Pres., P.O. Box 217, 48623, P 7,700, M 90, (989) 695-6620, info@freeland chamber.com, www.freelandchamber.com

**Freeport** · *see Hastings & Lake Odessa*

**Fremont** · *Fremont Area C/C* · Ron Vliem, Exec. Dir., 7 E. Main St., 49412, P 12,000, M 300, (231) 924-0770, Fax (231) 924-9248, info@fremontcommerce.com, www.fremontcommerce.com

**Garden City** · *Garden City C/C* · Amelia Oliverio, Exec. Dir., 30120 Ford Rd., Ste. D, 48135, P 32,000, M 210, (734) 422-4448, Fax (734) 422-1601, www.gardencity.org

**Gaylord** · *Gaylord/Otsego County C/C* · Bob Kasprzak, Exec. Dir., 101 W. Main St., P.O. Box 513, 49734, P 23,301, M 600, (989) 732-6333, Fax (989) 732-7990, info@gaylordchamber.com, www.gaylordchamber.com

**Gladwin** · *Gladwin County C/C* · Tom Tucholski, Exec. Dir., 608 W. Cedar Ave., 48624, P 26,287, M 210, (989) 426-5451, (800) 789-4812, Fax (989) 426-1074, chamber@ejourney.com, www.gladwincountychamber.com

**Glen Arbor** · *Glen Lake C/C* · David Marshall, Pres., P.O. Box 217, 49636, P 1,200, M 130, (231) 334-3238, gollinglen@aol.com, www.visitglenarbor.com

**Grand Beach** · *see New Buffalo*

**Grand Blanc** · *Grand Blanc C/C* · Jet Kilmer, Pres., 512 E. Grand Blanc Rd., 48439, P 45,000, M 525, (810) 695-4222, Fax (810) 695-0053, www.grandblancchamber.com

**Grand Haven** · *The Chamber-Grand Haven, Spring Lake, Ferrysburg* · Joy A. Gaasch, Pres., One S. Harbor Dr., P.O. Box 509, 49417, P 49,000, M 700, (616) 842-4910, Fax (616) 842-0379, areainfo@grandhavenchamber.org, www.grandhavenchamber.org.

**Grand Ledge** · *Grand Ledge Area C/C* · Susan Sasse, Secy./Treas., 222 S. Bridge St., 48837, P 7,000, M 125, (517) 627-2383, Fax (517) 627-9213, glacc@grandledgemi.com, www.gran-dledgemi.com

**Grand Marais** · *Grand Marais C/C* · Steve Bell, Pres., P.O. Box 139, 49839, P 400, M 36, (906) 494-2447, president@grandmaraismichigan.com, www.grandmaraismichigan.com

**Grand Rapids** · *Grand Rapids Area C/C* · Jeanne Englehart, Pres./CEO, 111 Pearl St. N.W., 49503, P 547,000, M 2,800, (616) 771-0300, Fax (616) 771-0318, info@grandrapids.org, www.grandrapids.org

**Grandville** · *Grandville C/C* · Sandy LeBlanc, Exec. Dir., 2905 Wilson, Ste. 202-A, 49468, P 17,000, M 300, (616) 531-8890, gcc@grandvillechamber.org, www.grandvillechamber.org

**Grayling** · *Grayling Reg. C/C* · Theresa Compton, Ofc. Mgr., 213 N. James St., P.O. Box 406, 49738, P 13,000, M 305, (989) 348-2921, Fax (989) 348-7315, board@graylingchamber.com, www.graylingchamber.com

**Greenbush** · *Greenbush C/C* · Nebbie Kushmaul, Pres., 4115 S. U.S. 23, 48738, P 1,373, M 200, (989) 739-7635

**Greenville** · *Greenville Area C/C* · Kathy Jo VanderLaan & Candy Kerschen, Co-Dirs., 108 N. Lafayette, Ste. A, 48838, P 12,000, M 300, (616) 754-5697, Fax (616) 754-4710, info@greenvillechamber.net, www.greenvillechamber.net.

**Grosse Pointes** · *see Saint Clair Shores*

**Gwinn** · *Gwinn-Sawyer Area C/C* · Jeanette Maki, Pres., 248 Wellington Dr., 49841, P 8,000, M 165, (906) 346-9666, (888) 346-4946, Fax (906) 346-9695, gccdir@gwinnmi.com, www.gwinnmi.com

**Hamburg** · *see Brighton*

**Hamtramck** · *Hamtramck C/C* · 2926 Caniff, 48212, P 22,600, M 100, (313) 875-7877

**Harbert** · *see New Buffalo*

**Harbor Beach** · *Harbor Beach C/C* · Bob Montana, P.O. Box 113, 48441, P 2,089, M 100, (989) 479-6477, (800) HB-MICH-5, Fax (989) 479-6477, visitor@harborbeachchamber.com, www.harborbeachchamber.com

**Harbor Springs** · *Harbor Springs Area C/C* · Scott A. Herceg, Exec. Dir., 368 E. Main St., 49740, P 1,100, M 450, (231) 526-7999, Fax (231) 526-5593, info@harborspringschamber.com, www.harborspringschamber.com

**Harper Woods** · *see Saint Clair Shores*

**Harrison** · *Harrison Area C/C* · Tammy Carlstrom, Ofc. Mgr., 809 N. First St., P.O. Box 682, 48625, P 2,213, M 187, (989) 539-6011, Fax (989) 539-6099, harrisonchamber@sbcglobal.net, www.harrisonchamber.com

**Harrison Twp** · *see Mount Clemens*

**Harrisville** · *Huron Shores C/C* · P.O. Box 581, 48740, P 10,000, M 130, (989) 724-5107, (800) 432-2823, Fax (989) 724-6656, www.huronshoreschamber.com

**Harsens Island** · *see Algonac*

**Hart** · *Hart-Silver Lake-Mears C/C & Visitor Bur.* · 2388 N. Comfort Dr., 49420, P 28,200, M 210, (231) 873-2247, (800) 870-9786, Fax (231) 873-1683, www.thinkdunes.com, info@hartsilverlakemears.com, www.hartsilverlakemears.com

**Hartland** · *Hartland Area C/C* · Barbara Walker, Pres., 3508 Avon St., P.O. Box 427, 48353, P 15,194, M 155, (810) 632-9130, Fax (810) 632-9133, info@hartlandchamber.org, www.hartlandchamber.org

**Hastings** · *Barry County C/C* · Valerie Byrnes, Dir., 221 W. State St., 49058, P 58,774, M 400, (269) 945-2454, Fax (269) 945-3839, valerie@barrychamber.com, www.barrychamber.com

**Hazel Park** · *see Madison Heights*

**Hesperia** · *Hesperia Area C/C* · Rick Roberson, Pres., P.O. Box 32, 49421, P 900, M 70, (231) 854-3695, www.hesperiachamberofcommerce.org

**Hessel** · *see Cedarville*

**Highland** · *see Milford*

**Hillman** · *Hillman Area C/C* · P.O. Box 506, 49746, P 10,000, M 120, (989) 742-3739, www.hillmanchamber.com

**Hillsdale** · *Hillsdale County C/C* · Karri Doty, Pres./Exec. Dir., 22 N. Manning, 49242, P 48,000, M 500, (517) 437-6401, Fax (517) 437-6408, karri@hillsdalecountychamber.com, www.hillsdale-countychamber.com

**Holland** · *Holland Area C/C* · Jane Clark, Pres., 272 E. 8th St., 49423, P 100,000, M 1,300, (616) 392-2389, Fax (616) 392-7379, info@hollandchamber.org, www.hollandchamber.org

**Holly** · *Holly Area C/C* · Sandra Kleven, Pres., 202 S. Saginaw St., 2nd Flr., P.O. Box 214, 48442, P 35,000, M 150, (248) 215-7099, Fax (248) 215-7106, staffhollychamber@yahoo.com, www.hollychamber.com

**Houghton** · *Keweenaw Peninsula C/C* · 902 College Ave., P.O. Box 336, 49931, P 38,000, M 600, (906) 482-5240, (866) 304-5722, Fax (906) 482-5241, info@keweenaw.org, www.keweenaw.org.

**Houghton Lake** · *Houghton Lake C/C* · Kim Rathbun, 1625 W. Houghton Lake Dr., 48629, P 25,000, M 400, (989) 366-5644, (800) 248-5253, Fax (989) 366-9472, hlcc@houghtonlakechamber.org, www.houghtonlakechamber.org

**Howard City** · *Montcalm County Panhandle Area C/C* · Terry Reeves, Pres., P.O. Box 474, 49329, P 10,000, M 110, (231) 937-5681, m46@jhoil.com, www.panhandlechamber.com

**Howell** · *Howell Area C/C* · Vicki Hartman, Chrmn. of the Bd., 123 E. Washington St., 48843, P 75,000, M 919, (517) 546-3920, Fax (517) 546-4115, chamber@howell.org, www.howell.org

**Hudson** · *Hudson Area C/C* · Dave Sheely, Pres., 121 N. Church St., 49247, P 2,545, M 50, (517) 448-8983, Fax (517) 448-7339, www.hudsonmich.com

**Hudsonville** · *Hudsonville Area C/C* · Laurie Van Haitsma, Dir., 5340 Plaza Ave., P.O. Box 216, 49426, P 7,300, M 160, (616) 662-0900, Fax (616) 662-4557, hcc@netpenny.net, www.hudson villechamber.com

**Imlay City** · *Imlay City Area C/C* · Sally Reinhardt, Exec. Dir., 150 N. Main St., P.O. Box 206, 48444, P 4,000, M 150, (810) 724-1361, info@imlaycitymich.com, www.imlaycitymich.com

**Indian River** · *Indian River Resort Reg. C/C* · Rebecca Behm, Exec. Dir., 3435 S. Straits Hwy., P.O. Box 57, 49749, P 4,500, M 280, (231) 238-9325, (800) EXIT-310, Fax (231) 238-0949, info@irchamber.com, www.irchamber.com

**Interlochen** · *Interlochen Area C/C* · Laura M. Franke, Dir., P.O. Box 13, 49643, P 6,000, M 150, (231) 276-7141, interlochen chamber@juno.com, www.interlochenchamber.org

**Ionia** · *Ionia Area C/C* · Tina Conner Wellman, Exec. Dir., 439 W. Main St., 48846, P 10,500, M 240, (616) 527-2560, Fax (616) 527-0894, info@ioniachamber.net, www.ioniachamber.org

**Ira Twp** · *see New Baltimore*

**Iron Mountain** · *Dickinson Area Partnership* · Lynda Zanon, Exec. Dir., 600 S. Stephenson Ave., 49801, P 27,400, M 402, (906) 774-2002, Fax (906) 774-2004, dchamber@dickinsonchamber. com, www.dickinsonchamber.com

**Iron River** · *Iron County C/C* · William Leonoff, Exec. Dir., 50 E. Genesee St., 49935, P 13,138, M 308, (906) 265-3822, (888) TRY-IRON, Fax (906) 265-5605, info@iron.org, www.iron.org

**Ironwood** · *Ironwood Area C/C* · Kim Kolesar, Exec. Dir., 150 N. Lowell, P.O. Box 45, 49938, P 18,000, M 200, (906) 932-1122, Fax (906) 932-2756, chamber@ironwoodmi.org, www.ironwoodmi.org

**Ishpeming** · *Ishpeming Ofc. Of Lake Superior Comm Partnership* · Amy Clickner, CEO, 119 W. Division St., 49849, P 64,616, M 900, (906) 486-4841, (888) 57-UNITY, Fax (906) 486-4850, info@marquette.org, www.marquette.org

**Ithaca** · *see Alma*

**Jackson** · *Greater Jackson C/C & Jackson County CVB* · Mindy Bradish, Pres./Exec. Dir., 141 S. Jackson St., 49201, P 162,400, M 725, (517) 782-8221, Fax (517) 780-3688, mindy@gjcc.org, www.gjcc.org

**Jenison** · *Jenison Area C/C* · Chad Tuttle, P.O. Box 405, 49429, P 46,000, M 195, (616) 322-7090, info@jenison.com, www.jenison.com

**Kalamazoo** · *Kalamazoo Reg. C/C* · Steward Sandstrom, Pres./CEO, 346 W. Michigan Ave., 49007, P 260,000, M 1,800, (269) 381-4000, Fax (269) 343-0430, steward@kazoochamber.com, www.kazoochamber.com

**Kalkaska** · *Kalkaska Area C/C* · April Smith, Admin. Asst., 353 S. Cedar St., P.O. Box 291, 49646, P 16,571, M 150, (231) 258-9103, (800) 487-6880, Fax (231) 258-6155, kalkaska@tcchamber.org, www.kalkaskami.com

**Kentwood** · *see Wyoming*

**Lake City** · *Lake City Area C/C* · Kim Mosher, Admin. Asst., 107 S. Main St., P.O. Drawer H, 49651, P 14,478, M 215, (231) 839-4969, Fax (231) 839-5991, lcacc@centurytel.net, www.lakecitymich.com

**Lake Odessa** · *Lakewood Area C/C* · Lisa Spurgis, Exec. Dir., Page Memorial Bldg., 839 4th Ave., 48849, P 12,000, M 60, (616) 374-0766, director@lakewoodareacoc.org, www.lakewoodareacoc.org

**Lake Orion** · *Orion Area C/C* · Donna Heyniger, Exec. Dir., P.O. Box 484, 48361, P 30,000, M 250, (248) 693-6300, Fax (248) 693-9227, info@lakeorionchamber.com, www.lakeorionchamber.com

**Lakeland** · *see Brighton*

**Lakeside** · *see New Buffalo*

**Lakeview** · *Lakeview Area C/C* · Brian Brasser, Pres., P.O. Box 57, 48850, P 1,200, M 50, (989) 352-1200, www.lakeviewmichigan.com

**L'Anse** · *Baraga County C/C* · Karen DeKleyn, Secy./Treas., P.O. Box 122, 49946, P 3,300, M 87, (906) 353-8808, baragachamber@baragacountycc.org, www.baragacountycc.org

**Lansing** · *Lansing Reg. C/C* · Tim Daman, Pres./CEO, 500 E. Michigan Ave., Ste. 200, P.O. Box 14030, 48901, P 447,728, M 1,500, (517) 487-6340, Fax (517) 484-6910, tdaman@lansing-chamber.org, www.lansingchamber.org.

**Lapeer** · *Lapeer Area C/C* · Neda Payne, Exec. Dir., 108 W. Park St., 48446, P 92,510, M 400, (810) 664-6641, Fax (810) 664-4349, staff@lapeerareachamber.org, www.lapeerareachamber.org, www.lapeerdays.com

**Leelanau Peninsula** · *see Suttons Bay*

**Lenox Twp** · *see New Baltimore*

**LeRoy** · *LeRoy C/C* · Adam Johnson, Pres., 98 Underwood Ave., P.O. Box 28, 49655, P 3,500, M 35, (231) 768-4558, pres@leroy michigan.org, www.leroymichigan.org

**Les Cheneaux** · *see Cedarville*

**Leslie** · *Leslie Area C/C* · Bruce Crockett, Pres., P.O. Box 214, 49251, P 4,371, M 125, (517) 589-8642, (517) 589-8222, www.lesliechamber.com

**Lewiston** · *Lewiston Area C/C* · 2946 Kneeland St., P.O. Box 656, 49756, P 3,500, M 180, (989) 786-2293, Fax (989) 786-4515, lewistonchamber@i2k.com, www.lewistonchamber.com

**Lexington** · *Greater Croswell-Lexington C/C* · Marcy Bartniczak, Pres., P.O. Box 142, 48450, P 6,500, M 170, (810) 359-2262, croslex@greatlakes.net, www.cros-lex-chamber.com

**Lincoln Park** · *Lincoln Park C/C* · Karen Maniaci, Exec. Dir., 1335 Southfield Rd., P.O. Box 382, 48146, P 43,000, M 100, (313) 386-0140, Fax (313) 386-0140, info@lpchamber.org, www.lpchamber.org

**Linden** · *see Fenton*

**Litchfield** · *Litchfield C/C* · P.O. Box 236, 49252, P 1,483, M 50, (517) 542-2921, Fax (517) 542-2491, clerk@cityoflitchfield.org, www.cityoflitchfield.org

**Livonia** · *Livonia C/C* · Dan West, Pres., 33233 Five Mile Rd., 48154, P 100,000, M 815, (734) 427-2122, Fax (734) 427-6055, dwest@livonia.org, www.livonia.org

**Lowell** · *Lowell Area C/C* · Liz Baker, Exec. Dir., 113 Riverwalk Plaza, P.O. Box 224, 49331, P 4,000, M 300, (616) 897-9161, Fax (616) 897-9101, info@lowellchamber.org, www.discoverlowell.org

**Ludington** · *Ludington & Scottville C/C* · Kathryn Maclean, Pres./CEO, 5300 W. U.S. 10, 49431, P 25,000, M 442, (231) 845-0324, Fax (231) 845-6857, chamberinfo@ludington.org, www.ludington.org

**Mackinaw City** · *Mackinaw City C/C* · Dawn Edwards, Exec. Dir., 216 E. Central Ave., P.O. Box 856, 49701, P 850, M 225, (231) 436-5574, (888) 455-8100, dedwards@mackinawchamber.com, www.mackinawchamber.com

**Macomb Twp** · *see Mount Clemens*

**Madison Heights** • *Madison Heights-Hazel Park C/C* • Mary Lou Sames, Exec. Dir., 724 W. 11 Mile Rd., 48071, P 52,000, M 550, (248) 542-5010, Fax (248) 542-6821, mary@mhhpchamber.org, www.mhhpchamber.org.

**Mancelona** • *Mancelona Area C/C* • P.O. Box 558, 49659, P 1,400, M 100, (231) 587-5500, www.mancelonachamber.org

**Manchester** • *Manchester Area C/C* • Ray Berg, Pres., P.O. Box 521, 48158, P 2,000, M 105, (734) 476-4565, www.48158.com

**Manistee** • *Manistee Area C/C* • 11 Cypress St., 49660, P 23,330, M 408, (231) 723-2575, (800) 288-2286, Fax (231) 723-1515, www.manisteechamber.com.

**Manistique** • *Schoolcraft County C/C* • Lenore Derouin, Exec. Dir., 1000 W. Lakeshore Dr., 49854, P 8,576, M 241, (906) 341-5010, Fax (906) 341-1549, chamber@reiters.netLenore Derovin, www.schoolcraftcountychamber.com.

**Manton** • *Manton C/C* • Chuck Brandt, Pres., P.O. Box 313, 49663, P 1,300, M 115, (231) 824-4158, Fax (231) 824-3664, info@mantonmichigan.org, www.mantonmichigan.org

**Maple Valley** • *see Howard City*

**Marine City** • *Marine City C/C* • Judith White, 226 S. Water St., 48039, P 5,000, M 141, (810) 765-4501, Fax (810) 765-4501, chamberoffice@marinecitychamber.net, www.marinecitychamber.net

**Marion** • *Marion Area C/C* • Anndrea McCrimmon, Pres., P.O. Box 294, 49665, P 816, M 40, (231) 743-2461, Fax (231) 743-2461

**Marlette** • *Marlette Area C/C* • Virginia Labelle, Pres., P.O. Box 222, 48453, P 4,200, M 100, (989) 635-7448, cityofmarlette.com

**Marquette** • *Marquette Area C/C-Lake Superior Comm. Partnership* • Amy Clickner, CEO, 501 S. Front St., 49855, P 64,616, M 900, (906) 226-6591, (888) 57-UNITY, Fax (906) 226-2099, info@marquette.org, www.marquette.org

**Marshall** • *Marshall Area C/C* • Monica Anderson, Pres./CEO, 424 E. Michigan Ave., 49068, P 15,000, M 350, (269) 781-5163, (800) 877-5163, Fax (269) 781-6570, info@marshallmi.org, www.marshallmi.org

**Marysville** • *Marysville C/C* • Laura J. Crawford, Exec. Dir., 2055 Gratiot Blvd., Ste. D, 48040, P 10,000, M 150, (810) 364-6180, Fax (810) 364-9388, chamber@marysvillechamber.com, www.marysvillechamber.com

**Mason** • *Mason Area C/C* • Doug Klein, Exec. Dir., 148 E. Ash St., 48854, P 8,000, M 280, (517) 676-1046, (517) 676-4816, Fax (517) 676-8504, masonchamber@masonchamber.org, www.masonchamber.org.

**Mears** • *see Hart*

**Memphis** • *Memphis C/C* • Judy Weaver, Pres., P.O. Box 41006, 48041, P 1,200, M 20, (810) 392-2385, (810) 392-2394

**Menominee** • *see Marinette, WI*

**Mesick** • *Mesick Area C/C* • Jeff Ellens, P.O. Box 548, 49668, P 1,500, M 30, (231) 885-3200, www.mesick-michigan.org

**Metamora** • *Metamora C/C* • Wes Wickham, Pres., P.O. Box 16, 48455, M 90, (810) 678-6222, Fax (810) 678-3312, info@metamorachamber.org, www.metamorachamber.org

**Michiana** • *see New Buffalo*

**Middleton** • *see Alma*

**Middleville** • *see Hastings*

**Midland** • *Midland Area C/C* • Sid Allen, Pres., 300 Rodd St., Ste. 101, 48640, P 84,000, M 825, (989) 839-9901, Fax (989) 835-3701, chamber@macc.org, www.macc.org.

**Milan** • *Milan Area C/C* • Christine Mann, Pres., 153 E. Main, P.O. Box 164, 48160, P 5,500, M 122, (734) 439-7932, Fax (734) 241-3520, info@milanchamber.org, www.milanchamber.org

**Milford** • *Huron Valley C/C* • Joell Beether, Exec. Dir., 317 Union St., Ste. F, 48381, P 60,000, M 500, (248) 685-7129, Fax (248) 685-9047, info@huronvcc.com, www.huronvcc.com

**Mio** • *C/C for Oscoda County* • Kendle Nichols, P.O. Box 670, 48647, P 10,000, M 160, (989) 826-3331, (800) 800-6133, Fax (989) 826-6679, info@oscodacountymi.org, www.oscodacountymi.org

**Monroe** • *Monroe County C/C* • Michelle S. Dugan, Exec. Dir., 1645 N. Dixie Hwy., Ste. 2, 48162, P 160,000, M 530, (734) 384-3366, Fax (734) 384-3367, chamber@monroecountychamber.com, www.monroecountychamber.com

**Montague** • *see Whitehall*

**Montrose** • *Montrose Area C/C* • Jerry Whitney, Pres., P.O. Box 628, 48457, P 8,000, M 50, (810) 639-4357, www.montroseareachamber.org

**Morrice** • *see Perry*

**Mount Clemens** • *Macomb County Chamber* • Grace M. Shore, CEO/COO, 28 First St., Ste. B, 48043, P 850,000, M 1,000, (586) 493-7600, Fax (586) 493-7602, grace@macombcountychamber.com, www.macombcountychamber.com

**Mount Pleasant** • *Mt. Pleasant Area C/C* • Lisa Hadden, Pres./CEO, 114 E. Broadway, 48858, P 64,663, M 716, (989) 772-2396, Fax (989) 773-2656, lhadden@mt-pleasant.net, www.mt-pleasant.net

**Munising** • *Alger C/C* • Jim Erwin, Pres., 114 W. Superior St., P.O. Box 405, 49862, P 3,000, M 200, (906) 387-2138, Fax (906) 387-1858, chamber@algercounty.org, www.algercounty.org

**Muskegon** • *Muskegon Area C/C* • Cindy Larsen, Pres., 380 W. Western Ave., Ste. 202, 49440, P 171,765, M 1,230, (231) 722-3751, Fax (231) 728-7251, macc@muskegon.org, www.muskegon.org

**Napoleon** • *Napoleon C/C* • Paula Jester, Co-Pres., P.O. Box 224, 49261, P 9,000, M 38, (517) 536-0547

**Nashville** • *see Hastings*

**Negaunee** • *see Ishpeming*

**New Baltimore** • *also see Mount Clemens*

**New Baltimore** • *Anchor Bay C/C* • Lisa M. Edwards, Pres., 36341 Front St., Ste. 2, 48047, P 58,436, M 230, (586) 725-5148, Fax (586) 725-5369, info@anchorbaychamber.com, www.anchorbaychamber.com

**New Boston** • *Huron Township C/C* • Teresa Trosin, Exec. Ofc. Mgr., 37236 Huron River Dr., P.O. Box 247, 48164, P 15,000, M 50, (734) 753-4220, Fax (734) 753-4602, township@provide.net, www.members.tripod.com/htcc48164

**New Buffalo** • *Harbor Country C/C* • 530 S. Whittaker, Ste. F, 49117, P 8,000, M 502, (269) 469-5409, (800) 362-7251, Fax (269) 469-2257, chamber@harborcountry.org, www.harborcountry.org

**New Haven** • *see New Baltimore*

**New Haven Center** • *see Alma*

**Newaygo** • *Newaygo Area C/C* • Terrie Ortwein, Exec. Dir., 28 State St., P.O. Box 181, 49337, P 16,500, M 100, (231) 652-3068, Fax (231) 652-9489, info@newaygonaturally.com, www.newaygonaturally.com

**Newberry** • *Newberry Area C/C* • Angela Harris, Pres., 4947 E. County Rd. 460, P.O. Box 308, 49868, P 8,000, M 117, (906) 293-5562, (800) 831-7292, Fax (906) 293-5739, newberry@lighthouse.net, www.newberrychamber.net

**Niles** · *Four Flags Area C/C* · Ronald J. Sather, Pres./CEO, 321 E. Main St., P.O. Box 10, 49120, P 40,000, M 700, (269) 683-3720, Fax (269) 683-3722, chamber@nilesmi.com, www.nilesmi.com.

**Northstar** · *see Alma*

**Northville** · *Northville Comm. C/C* · Jody Humphries, Pres., 195 S. Main St., 48167, P 28,000, M 500, (248) 349-7640, Fax (248) 349-8730, chamber@northville.org, www.northville.org

**Novi** · *Novi C/C* · Linda Daly, Exec. Dir., 41875 W. 11 Mile Rd., Ste. 201, 48375, P 50,000, M 550, (248) 349-3743, Fax (248) 349-9719, info@novichamber.com, www.novichamber.com

**Oakland County** · *see Detroit*

**Onaway** · *Onaway Area C/C* · Beverly Brougham, Exec. Dir., 20774 State St., P.O. Box 274, 49765, P 990, M 100, (989) 733-2874, (800) 711-3685, Fax (989) 733-2874, info@onawaychamber.com, www.onawayarea.com

**Ontonagon** · *Ontonagon County C/C* · Edith Basile, Corresponding Secy., P.O. Box 266, 49953, P 7,918, M 100, (906) 884-4735, ontcofc@up.net, www.ontonagonmi.org

**Ortonville** · *Greater Ortonville Area C/C* · Fred Waybrant, Pres., P.O. Box 152, 48462, P 12,000, M 84, (248) 627-8079, Fax (248) 627-8079, president@ortonvillechamber.com, www.ortonvillechamber.com

**Oscoda** · *Oscoda-Au Sable C/C* · Marilyn Flanagan, Ofc. Mgr., 4440 N. U.S. 23, 48750, P 9,000, M 248, (989) 739-7322, (800) 235-4625, Fax (989) 739-9195, marilynf@oscodachamber.com, oscodachamber.com

**Otsego** · *Otsego C/C* · Steven Lick, Exec. Dir., 135 E. Allegan St., 49078, P 4,000, M 110, (269) 694-6880, Fax (269) 694-4866, director@otsegochamber.org, otsegochamber.org

**Owosso** · *Shiawassee Reg. C/C* · Renita Mikolajczyk, Pres., 215 N. Water St., 48867, P 71,000, M 600, (989) 723-5149, Fax (989) 723-8353, customerservice@shiawasseechamber.org, www.shiawasseechamber.org.

**Oxford** · *Oxford Area C/C* · Holly Bills, Exec. Dir., P.O. Box 142, 48371, P 13,500, M 250, (248) 628-0410, Fax (248) 628-0430, info@oxfordchamberofcommerce.com, www.oxfordchamberofcommerce.com

**Paradise** · *Paradise C/C* · P.O. Box 82, 49768, P 1,000, M 50, (906) 492-3219, paradisecoc@jamadots.com, www.paradisemichigan.org

**Paw Paw** · *Greater Paw Paw C/C* · Mary Springer, Dir., 129 S. Kalamazoo St., 49079, P 7,500, M 248, (269) 657-5395, Fax (269) 655-8755, ppccdda@btc-bci.com, pawpawchamber.com

**Pearl Beach** · *see Algonac*

**Pentwater** · *Pentwater C/C* · Mary Mohr, Exec. Dir., P.O. Box 614, 49449, P 12,000, M 260, (231) 869-4150, (866) 869-4150, Fax (231) 869-5286, travelinfo@pentwater.org, www.pentwater.org

**Perrinton** · *see Alma*

**Perry** · *Perry/Morrice Area C/C* · P.O. Box 803, 48872, P 5,600, M 40, (517) 625-8122, www.perry.mi.us

**Petoskey** · *Petoskey Reg. C/C* · Carlin Smith, Pres., 401 E. Mitchell St., 49770, P 31,000, M 755, (231) 347-4150, Fax (231) 348-1810, chamber@petoskey.com, www.petoskey.com

**Pierson** · *see Howard City*

**Pigeon** · *Pigeon C/C* · Tamara Gnagey, Admin. Asst., P.O. Box 618, 48755, P 1,200, M 100, (989) 453-7400, pgncofc@avci.net, www.pigeonchamber.com

**Pinckney** · *see Brighton*

**Pinconning** · *Pinconning Area C/C* · P.O. Box 856, 48650, P 7,000, M 105, (989) 879-2816, (989) 879-2360

**Plainwell** · *Plainwell C/C* · Katie Bell Moore, Pres., 798 E. Bridge, Ste. A, 49080, P 4,000, M 100, (269) 685-8877, Fax (269) 685-1844, plainwellchamber@sbcglobal.net, www.plainwellchamber.org

**Plymouth** · *Plymouth Comm. C/C* · G. Wesley Graff, Exec. Dir., 850 W. Ann Arbor Trail, 48170, P 37,000, M 650, (734) 453-1540, Fax (734) 453-1724, chamber@plymouthmich.org, www.plymouthmich.org

**Pontiac** · *Pontiac Reg. C/C* · Dawnaree Demrose, Pres., 402 N. Telegraph, 48341, P 71,000, M 400, (248) 335-9600, Fax (248) 335-9601, info@pontiacchamber.com, www.pontiacchamber.com

**Port Austin** · *Greater Port Austin Area C/C* · Joyce Stanek, Exec. Dir., 2 W. Spring St., P.O. Box 274, 48467, P 1,747, M 110, (989) 738-7600, pacofc@airadvantage.net, www.portaustinarea.com

**Port Huron** · *Blue Water Area C/C* · Vickie Ledsworth, Pres./CEO, 512 McMorran Blvd., 48060, P 162,000, M 400, (810) 985-7101, (800) 361-0526, Fax (810) 985-7311, info@bluewaterchamber.com, www.bluewaterchamber.com

**Portland** · *Portland Area C/C* · RJ Niklas, Pres., 1126 E. Grand River Ave., P.O. Box 303, 48875, P 3,000, M 100, (517) 647-2100, Fax (517) 647-2100, pacc@power-net.net, www.portlandareachamber.com

**Potterville** · *Potterville Area Chamber of Businesses* · P.O. Box 76, 48876, P 2,300, M 40, (517) 645-2313, Fax (517) 645-7889, www.gizzardfest.com, info@gizzardfest.com, www.pottervillechamber.org

**Prescott** · *see Skidway Lake*

**Quincy** · *Quincy C/C* · P.O. Box 132, 49082, P 4,411, M 65, (517) 639-8369, www.quincy-mi.org

**Ravenna** · *Ravenna C/C* · Larry D. Gardiner, Pres., P.O. Box 332, 49451, P 1,200, M 50, (231) 853-2360, www.ravennami.com

**Ray Township** · *see Romeo*

**Redford** · *Redford Twp. C/C* · Mary Jo Mullen, Exec. Dir., 26050 Five Mile, 48239, P 51,000, M 320, (313) 535-0960, Fax (313) 535-6356, RTCC@wanemail.com, redfordchamber.org

**Reed City** · *Reed City Area C/C* · Suzie Williams, Exec. Dir., 200 N. Chestnut, 49677, P 2,400, M 250, (231) 832-5431, (877) 832-7332, Fax (231) 832-5431, chambergeneral@reedcitycrossroads.com, www.reedcitycrossroads.com

**Reese** · *Reese Area C/C* · Kay Bierlein, Dir., P.O. Box 113, 48757, P 1,500, M 65, (989) 868-4291, kabierlein@gmail.com, www.villageofreese.net

**Reynolds** · *see Howard City*

**Richmond** · *Richmond Area C/C* · Kim Galante, Exec. Dir., 68371 Oak, 48062, P 5,906, M 175, (586) 727-3266, Fax (586) 727-3635, kim@robn.org, www.robn.org

**Riverdale** · *see Alma*

**Rochester** · *Rochester Reg. C/C* · Sheri L. Heiney, Exec. Dir., 71 Walnut, Ste. 110, 48307, P 80,000, M 1,400, (248) 651-6700, Fax (248) 651-5270, info@rrc-mi.com, www.rrc-mi.com.

**Rockford** · *Rockford C/C* · Brenda Davis, Exec. Dir., 598 Byrne Industrial Dr., P.O. Box 520, 49341, P 30,000, M 290, (616) 866-2000, Fax (616) 866-2141, info@rockfordmichamber.com, www.rockfordmichamber.com

**Rogers City** · *Rogers City Area C/C* · Dave Snow, Exec. Dir., 292 S. Bradley Hwy., 49779, P 3,300, M 201, (989) 734-2535, (800) 622-4148, Fax (989) 734-7767, rcchamber@lhi.net, www.rogerscity.com

**Romeo** • *Romeo-Washington C/C* • Jennifer Groomes, Exec. Dir., 228 N. Main, Ste. D, P.O. Box 175, 48065, P 38,850, M 395, (586) 752-4436, Fax (586) 752-2835, contact@rwchamber.com, www.rwchamber.com.

**Romulus** • *Greater Romulus C/C* • Karen LaBelle, Exec. Dir., 11189 Shook St., Ste. 200, 48174, P 23,000, M 180, (734) 893-0694, Fax (734) 893-0696, info@romuluschamber.org, www.romuluschamber.org

**Roscommon** • *Higgins Lake-Roscommon C/C* • Connie Allen, Ofc. Coord., 709 Lake St., P.O. Box 486, 48653, P 25,469, M 150, (989) 275-8760, Fax (989) 275-2029, info@hlrcc.com, www.hlrcc.com

**Rose City** • *Rose City-Lupton Area C/C* • Mike Dunn, Pres., P.O. Box 100, 48654, P 1,200, M 74, (989) 685-2936, info@rosecityluptonchamber.com, www.rosecityluptonchamber.com

**Roseville** • *see Saint Clair Shores*

**Royal Oak** • *Greater Royal Oak C/C* • Bill Allen, Exec. Dir., 200 S. Washington Ave., 48067, P 60,000, M 700, (248) 547-4000, Fax (248) 547-0504, coc@royaloakchamber.com, www.royaloakchamber.com

**Saginaw** • *Saginaw County C/C* • Bob Van Deventer, Pres., 515 N. Washington Ave., 2nd Flr., 48607, P 210,039, M 900, (989) 752-7161, Fax (989) 752-9055, info@saginawchamber.org, www.saginawchamber.org

**Saint Charles** • *Saint Charles Area C/C* • P.O. Box 26, 48655, P 2,215, M 75, (989) 865-8289, Fax (989) 865-6480, www.stcmi.com

**Saint Clair Shores** • *Metro East C/C* • Heather Lynn, Admin., 27601 Jefferson, 48081, P 250,000, M 450, (586) 777-2741, Fax (586) 777-4811, info@metroeastchamber.org, www.metroeastchamber.org

**Saint Helen** • *Saint Helen C/C* • Jan Waltz, Pres., P.O. Box 642, 48656, P 3,500, M 100, (989) 389-3725, sainthelen_chamber@yahoo.com, www.sainthelenchamber.net

**Saint Johns** • *Clinton County C/C* • Brenda Terpening, Exec. Dir., 1013 S. U.S. 27, P.O. Box 61, 48879, P 65,000, M 325, (989) 224-7248, Fax (989) 224-7667, ccchamber@power-net.net, www.clintoncountychamber.org

**Saline** • *Saline Area C/C* • Larry Osterling, Exec. Dir., 141 E. Michigan Ave., P.O. Box 198, 48176, P 55,000, M 490, (734) 429-4494, Fax (734) 944-6835, salinechamber@aol.com, www.salinechamber.com

**Sandusky** • *Sandusky C/C* • 26 W. Speaker St., 48471, P 2,800, M 135, (810) 648-4445, Fax (810) 648-3959, quieann78@yahoo.com, www.ci.sandusky.mi.us

**Sanford** • *Sanford Area C/C* • Mr. Pat Wortley, Pres., P.O. Box 98, 48657, P 1,000, M 21, (989) 687-2800, (989) 687-5000, info@sanfordmi.com, sanfordmi.com/chamber

**Sault Sainte Marie** • *Sault Sainte Marie C/C* • Leisa Mansfield, Exec. Dir., 2581 I-75 Business Spur, 49783, P 38,000, M 400, (906) 632-3301, Fax (906) 632-2331, info@saultstemarie.org, www.saultstemarie.org

**Sawyer** • *see Gwinn*

**Scottville** • *see Ludington*

**Sebewaing** • *Sebewaing C/C* • Jeff Sigmund, Pres., P.O. Box 622, 48759, P 2,000, M 60, (989) 883-2150, Fax (989) 883-9367, www.sebewaingchamber.com

**Shelby Township** • *see Sterling Heights*

**Shepherd** • *Shepherd Area C/C* • P.O. Box 111, 48883, P 1,400, M 45, (989) 828-6442, (989) 828-5175

**Silver Lake** • *see Hart*

**Skidway Lake** • *Skidway Lake Area C/C* • Mary Cline, Mgr., P.O. Box 4041, 48756, P 5,000, M 70, (989) 873-4150

**South Haven** • *Greater South Haven Area C/C* • Rachel Vochaska, Exec. Dir., 606 Phillips St., 49090, P 19,202, M 429, (269) 637-5171, Fax (269) 639-1570, cofc@southhavenmi.com, www.southhavenmi.com

**South Lyon** • *C/C for the South Lyon Area* • Laura Hogan, Ofc. Mgr., 125 N. Lafayette, 48178, P 60,000, M 350, (248) 437-3257, Fax (248) 437-4116, laura@southlyonchamber.com, www.southlyonchamber.com

**Southfield** • *Southfield Area C/C* • Ed Powers, Pres., 17515 W. 9 Mile Rd., Ste. 190, 48075, P 78,000, M 350, (248) 557-6661, Fax (248) 557-3931, southfieldchamber@yahoo.com, www.southfieldchamber.com

**Sparta** • *Sparta C/C* • Elizabeth Gorski, Exec.Dir., 156 E. Division St., P.O. Box 142, 49345, P 8,000, M 135, (616) 887-2454, www.spartachamber.com

**Spring Lake** • *see Grand Haven*

**St. Clair** • *St. Clair C/C* • David Gillis, Exec. V.P., 201 N. Riverside Ave., P.O. Box 121, 48079, P 5,800, M 248, (810) 329-2962, Fax (810) 329-2422, info@stclairchamber.com, www.stclairchamber.com

**St. Ignace** • *St. Ignace C/C* • Janet Peterson, Exec. Dir., 560 N. State St., 49781, P 2,700, M 210, (906) 643-8717, (800) 970-8717, Fax (906) 643-9380, sicc@lighthouse.net, www.saintignace.org.

**St. Joseph** • *see Benton Harbor*

**St. Louis** • *see Alma*

**Standish** • *Standish Area C/C* • Andrew Radatz, Pres., 108 E. Cedar St., P.O. Box 458, 48658, P 3,300, M 100, (989) 846-7867, www.standishchamber.com

**Stanton** • *Heart of Montcalm C/C* • P.O. Box 792, 48888, P 5,000, M 40, (989) 831-5794, Fax (989) 555-5556, info@heartofmontcalmchamber.com, www.heartofmontcalmchamber.com

**Sterling Heights** • *also see Mount Clemens*

**Sterling Heights** • *Sterling Heights Area C/C* • Wayne Oehmke, Pres., 12900 Hall Rd., Ste. 190, 48313, P 230,000, M 2,000, (586) 731-5400, Fax (586) 731-3521, woehmke@suscc.com, www.suscc.com.

**Stevensville** • *Lakeshore C/C* • Griffin Ott, Pres., 4290 Red Arrow Hwy., P.O. Box 93, 49127, P 15,465, M 165, (269) 429-1170, Fax (269) 429-8882, info@lakeshorechamber.org, www.lakeshorechamber.org

**Sturgis** • *Sturgis Area C/C* • Cathi Garn Abbs, Exec. Dir., 200 W. Main, P.O. Box 189, 49091, P 12,000, M 360, (269) 651-5758, Fax (269) 651-4124, sturgischamber@charter.net, www.sturgischamber.com.

**Sumner** • *see Alma*

**Sumpter Township** • *see Belleville*

**Sunfield** • *see Lake Odessa*

**Suttons Bay** • *Leelanau Peninsula C/C* • 5046 S. West Bayshore Dr., Ste. G, 49682, P 20,000, M 475, (231) 271-9895, (800) 980-9895, Fax (231) 271-9896, info@leelanauchamber.com, www.leelanauchamber.com

**Suttons Bay** • *Suttons Bay C/C* • Jim Munro, Pres., P.O. Box 46, 49682, P 1,000, M 125, (231) 271-5077, www.suttonsbayarea.com

**Swartz Creek** • *see Flint*

**Tawas City** • *Tawas Area C/C* • Laura Loeffler, Mgr., 402 E. Lake St., P.O. Box 608, 48764, P 6,000, M 252, (989) 362-8643, (800) 55-TAWAS, Fax (989) 362-7880, info@tawas.com, www.tawas.com.

**Taylor** · *Southern Wayne County Reg. C/C* · Alan Anderson, Pres., 20600 Eureka Rd. #315, 48180, P 450,000, M 1,200, (734) 284-6000, Fax (734) 284-0198, info@swcrc.com, www.swcrc.com

**Tecumseh** · *Tecumseh Area C/C* · 132 W. Chicago Blvd., 49286, P 15,000, M 230, (517) 423-3740, (888) 261-3367, Fax (517) 423-5748, chamber@qtwave.net, www.tecumsehchamber.org

**Three Oaks** · *see New Buffalo*

**Three Rivers** · *Three Rivers Area C/C* · 57 N. Main St., 49093, P 21,000, M 325, (269) 278-8193, Fax (269) 273-1751, info@trchamber.com, www.trchamber.com

**Traverse City** · *Traverse City Area C/C* · Douglas Luciani, Pres./CEO, 202 E. Grandview Pkwy., 49684, P 84,952, M 2,425, (231) 947-5075, Fax (231) 946-2565, info@tcchamber.org, www.tcchamber.org

**Troy** · *Troy C/C* · Michele Hodges, Pres., 4555 Investment Dr. #300, 48098, P 82,000, M 720, (248) 641-8151, Fax (248) 641-0545, theteam@troychamber.com, www.troychamber.com

**Trufant** · *Trufant Area C/C* · Ralph Krantz, Pres., P.O. Box 129, 49347, P 500, M 87, (616) 984-2555, (616) 984-2396, Fax (616) 984-6311

**Union Pier** · *see New Buffalo*

**Utica** · *see Sterling Heights*

**VanBuren Township** · *see Belleville*

**Vassar** · *Vassar C/C* · P.O. Box 126, 48768, P 2,600, M 86, (989) 823-2601, (989) 823-8517, www.cityofvassar.org

**Wakefield** · *Wakefield C/C* · Suzanne Backman, Pres., P.O. Box 93, 49968, P 2,100, M 65, (906) 224-2222, www.visitwakefield.com

**Walled Lake** · *Lakes Area C of C* · Jo Alley, Exec. Dir., 305 N. Pontiac Trail #B, 48390, P 126,356, M 500, (248) 624-2826, Fax (248) 624-2892, info@lakesareachamber.com, www.lakesareachamber.com

**Walled Lake** · *see Lakes Area*

**Warren** · *see Mount Clemens*

**Washington Township** · *see Romeo*

**Waterford** · *Waterford C/C* · Marie Hauswirth, Exec. Dir., 2309 Airport Rd., 48327, P 74,000, M 400, (248) 666-8600, Fax (248) 666-3325, info@waterfordchamber.org, www.waterfordchamber.org

**Waterford Twp** · *see Lakes Area*

**Wayland** · *Wayland Area C/C* · Denise Behm, Exec. Dir., 117 S. Main St. #6, 49348, P 4,000, M 195, (269) 792-9246, Fax (269) 509-4512, info@waylandchamber.org, www.waylandchamber.org

**Wayne** · *Wayne C/C* · Joe Dauget, Exec. Dir., 34844 W. Michigan Ave., 48184, P 19,899, M 210, (734) 721-0100, Fax (734) 721-3070, www.waynechamber.net

**West Bloomfield** · *West Bloomfield C/C* · Ann Corwell, Exec. Dir., 6668 Orchard Lake Rd. #207, 48322, P 64,862, M 250, (248) 626-3636, Fax (248) 626-4218, wbcc@sbcglobal.net, www.westbloomfieldchamber.com

**West Branch** · *West Branch C/C* · Steven G. Leonard, Exec. Dir., 422 W. Houghton Ave., 48661, P 22,000, M 320, (989) 345-2821, (800) 755-9091, Fax (989) 345-9075, chamber@westbranch.com, www.wbacc.com.

**Westland** · *Westland C/C* · 36900 Ford Rd., 48185, P 85,000, M 400, (734) 326-7222, Fax (734) 326-6040, info@westlandchamber.com, www.westlandchamber.com

**Wheeler** · *see Alma*

**White Cloud** · *White Cloud Area C/C* · Sherry Adams, Secy., 12 N. Charles, P.O. Box 260, 49349, P 1,240, M 104, (231) 689-6607, Fax (231) 689-6744, kb8ife@ncats.net, www.whitecloudchamber.org

**White Lake Twp** · *see Lakes Area*

**Whitehall** · *White Lake Area C/C* · Amy VanLoon, Exec. Dir., 124 W. Hanson St., 49461, P 18,000, M 334, (231) 893-4585, (800) 879-9702, Fax (231) 893-0914, info@whitelake.org, www.whitelake.org

**Whitmore Lake** · *see Brighton*

**Whittemore** · *Whittemore Area C/C* · 405 E. Sherman Rd., 48770, P 2,000, M 18, (989) 756-5231, (989) 756-3011

**Williamston** · *Williamston Area C/C* · Barbara Burke, Exec. Dir., 369 W. Grand River Ave., P.O. Box 53, 48895, P 5,000, M 150, (517) 655-1549, Fax (517) 655-8859, info@williamston.org, www.williamston.org

**Winfield** · *see Howard City*

**Wixom** · *see Lakes Area*

**Wolverine Village** · *see Lakes Area*

**Woodland** · *see Hastings & Lake Odessa*

**Wyoming** · *Wyoming-Kentwood Area C/C* · John J. Crawford, Pres., 590 32nd St. S.E., 49548, P 119,000, M 580, (616) 531-5990, Fax (616) 531-0252, john@southkent.org, www.southkent.org

**Yale** · *Yale Area C/C* · Judy Dowling, Pres., P.O. Box 59, 48097, P 3,000, M 80, (810) 387-9253, yale@yalechamber.com, www.yalechamber.com

**Ypsilanti** · *Ypsilanti Area C/C* · Diane Keller, Pres./CEO, 301 W. Michigan Ave., Ste. 101, 48197, P 160,000, M 600, (734) 482-4920, Fax (734) 482-2021, trish@ypsichamber.org, www.ypsichamber.org

**Zeeland** · *Zeeland C/C* · Ann L. Query, Pres., 149 Main Pl., 49464, P 22,000, M 380, (616) 772-2494, Fax (616) 772-0065, zchamber@zeelandchamber.org, www.zeelandchamber.org.

# Minnesota

**Minnesota C of C** · David Olson, Pres., 400 Roberts St. N., Ste. 1500, Saint Paul, 55101, P 4,500,000, M 2,600, (651) 292-4650, (800) 821-2230, Fax (651) 292-4656, www.mnchamber.com

**Ada** · *Ada C/C* · Lee Ann Hall, Secy./Treas., P.O. Box 1, 56510, P 1,700, M 73, (218) 784-3542, Fax (218) 784-3890, leeannko@loretel.net, www.ci.ada.mn.us

**Aitkin** · *Aitkin Area C/C* · Sue Marxen, Exec. Dir., 114 Minnesota Ave. N., P.O. Box 127, 56431, P 2,000, M 288, (218) 927-2316, (800) 526-8342, Fax (218) 927-4494, upnorth@aitkin.com, www.aitkin.com

**Albany** · *Albany C/C* · Kim Fish, Exec. Secy., P.O. Box 634, 56307, P 1,796, M 100, (320) 845-7777, Fax (320) 845-2346, albanycc@albanytel.com, www.albanymnchamber.com

**Albert Lea** · *Albert Lea-Freeborn County C/C* · Randy Kehr, Exec. Dir., 701 Marshall St., 56007, P 33,000, M 530, (507) 373-3938, Fax (507) 373-0344, alfccoc@albertlea.org, www.albertlea.org.

**Albertville** · *see Rogers*

**Aldrich** · *see Staples*

**Alexandria** · *Alexandria Lakes Area C/C* · Coni McKay, Exec. Dir., 206 Broadway, 56308, P 30,000, M 670, (320) 763-3161, (800) 245-ALEX, Fax (320) 763-6857, info@alexandriamn.org, www.alexandriamn.org.

**Andover** · *see Anoka*

**Angle Inlet** · *see Baudette*

**Annandale** · *Annandale Area C/C* · David Burd, P.O. Box 417, 55302, P 2,700, M 180, (320) 274-2474, www.annandalechamber.org

**Anoka** · *Anoka Area C/C* · Peter Turok, Pres., 12 Bridge Sq., 55303, P 100,000, M 700, (763) 421-7130, Fax (763) 421-0577, mail@anokaareachamber.com, www.anokaareachamber.com

**Apple Valley** · *Apple Valley C/C & CVB* · Edward Kearney, Pres., 14800 Galaxie Ave., Ste. 101, 55124, P 51,300, M 350, (952) 432-8422, (800) 301-9435, Fax (952) 432-7964, info@apple valleychamber.com, www.applevalleychamber.com

**Appleton** · *Appleton Area C/C* · Becca Bucholz, 127 W. Soreson, P.O. Box 98, 56208, P 2,800, M 60, (320) 289-1527, appletonmn@mchsi.com, www.appletonmn.com

**Arden Hills** · *see Saint Paul*

**Arlington** · *Arlington Area C/C* · Jim Highland, Pres., P.O. Box 543, 55307, P 2,048, M 60, (507) 964-5177, libertystation@frontiernet.net, www.arlingtonmn.com

**Atwater** · *Atwater C/C* · Goldie Smith, P.O. Box 59, 56209, P 1,079, M 50, (320) 974-8760, Fax (320) 974-8760, www.atwaterchamber.com

**Austin** · *Austin Area C/C* · Sandy Forstner, Exec. Dir., 329 N. Main St., Ste. 102, 55912, P 23,300, M 380, (507) 437-4561, (888) 319-5655, Fax (507) 437-4869, execdir@austincoc.com, www.austincoc.com

**Avon** · *Avon Area C/C* · Mary Eisenschenk, Pres., P.O. Box 293, 56310, P 1,400, M 75, (320) 356-7922, avonmnchamber@hotmail.com, www.avonmnchamber.com

**Barnesville** · *Barnesville Main Street Program* · Ryan Tonsfeldt, Pres., 202 Front St. N., P.O. Box 550, 56514, P 2,200, M 152, (218) 354-2479, mainstreet@bvillemn.net, www.barnesvillemn.com

**Baudette** · *Baudette-Lake of the Woods Area C/C* · 930 W. Main, P.O. Box 659, 56623, P 4,000, M 100, (218) 634-1174, (800) 382-3474, Fax (218) 634-2915, lakwoods@wiktel.com, www.lakeofthewoodsmn.com

**Bay Lake** · *see Crosby*

**Becker** · *Becker Area C/C* · Kimberly Schmidt, Pres., P.O. Box 313, 55308, P 5,000, M 134, (763) 262-2420, Fax (763) 262-2150, info@beckerchamber.org, www.beckerchamber.org

**Belle Plaine** · *Belle Plaine C/C* · 204 N. Meridian St., 56011, P 5,200, M 90, (952) 873-4295, Fax (952) 873-4142, bellepln@frontiernet.net, www.belleplainemn.com

**Bemidji** · *Bemidji Area C/C* · Lori Paris, Pres., 300 Bemidji Ave., P.O. Box 850, 56619, P 25,000, M 500, (218) 444-3541, (800) 458-2223, Fax (218) 444-4276, info@bemidji.org, www.bemidji.org

**Benson** · *Benson Area C/C* · 1228 Atlantic Ave., 56215, P 3,500, M 135, (320) 843-3618, Fax (320) 843-3618, bensonchamber@embarqmail.com, www.bensonareachamber.com

**Bethel** · *see Blaine*

**Big Lake** · *Big Lake C/C* · Karen Barta, Pres., 160 N. Lake St., P.O. Box 241, 55309, P 20,000, M 150, (763) 263-7800, (877) 363-0549, Fax (763) 263-7668, blchamber@sherbtel.net, www.biglakechamber.com

**Birchdale** · *see Baudette*

**Birchwood Village** · *see White Bear Lake*

**Blaine** · *MetroNorth C/C* · Thomas Snell, Exec. Dir., 9380 Central Ave., Ste. 320, 55434, P 350,000, M 800, (763) 783-3553, Fax (763) 783-3557, chamber@metronorthchamber.org, www.metronorthchamber.org

**Blooming Prairie** · *Blooming Prairie C/C* · Becky Noble, Exec. Dir., 138 Hwy. 218 S., P.O. Box 805, 55917, P 1,900, M 100, (507) 583-4472, Fax (507) 583-4520, bpcofc@frontiernet.net, www.bloomingprairie.com

**Bloomington** · *Bloomington C/C* · Maureen Scallen Failor, Exec. Dir., 9633 Lyndale Ave. S., Ste. 200, 55420, P 88,700, M 1,250, (952) 888-8818, Fax (952) 888-0508, mscallenfailor@bloomington chamber.org, www.minneapolischamber.org

**Blue Earth** · *Blue Earth Area C/C* · Shelly Greimann, Dir., 113 S. Nicollet, 56013, P 4,000, M 200, (507) 526-2916, Fax (507) 526-2244, chamber@bevcomm.net, www.blueearthchamber.com

**Brainerd** · *Brainerd Lakes C/C* · 124 N. 6th St., 56401, P 22,000, M 1,200, (218) 829-2838, (800) 450-2838, Fax (218) 829-8199, info@explorebrainerdlakes.com, www.explorebrainerdlakes.com

**Breckenridge** · *see Wahpeton, ND*

**Breezy Point** · *see Pequot Lakes*

**Brooklyn Center** · *see Plymouth - TwinWest C/C*

**Brooklyn Park** · *see Osseo*

**Buffalo** · *Buffalo Area C/C* · Sally Custer, Pres., 205 Central Ave., 55313, P 14,000, M 280, (763) 682-4902, Fax (763) 682-5677, sally@buffalochamber.org, www.buffalochamber.org

**Burnsville** · *Burnsville C/C* · Daron Van Helden, Pres., 101 W. Burnsville Pkwy., Ste. 150, 55337, P 60,220, M 650, (952) 435-6000, Fax (952) 435-6972, chamber@burnsvillechamber.com, www.burnsvillechamber.com

**Caledonia** · *Caledonia Area C/C & Tourism Center* · Mike Werner, 214 E. Main St., 55921, P 2,965, M 69, (507) 725-5477, (877) 439-4893, caledoniacc@acegroup.cc, www.caledoniamn.gov

**Cambridge** · *Cambridge Area C/C* · Nicki Klanderud, Pres., 140 N. Buchanan St., Ste. 174, P.O. Box 343, 55008, P 36,000, M 250, (763) 689-2505, Fax (763) 552-2505, info@cambridge-chamber.com, www.cambridge-chamber.com

**Canby** · *Canby Area C/C* · Amy Szumal, 123 First St. E., 56220, P 1,903, M 150, (507) 223-7775, www.canbychamber.com

**Cannon Falls** · *Cannon Falls Area C/C* · Patricia A. Anderson, Pres., 103 N. 4th St., P.O. Box 2, 55009, P 4,000, M 190, (507) 263-2289, tourism@cannonfalls.org, www.cannonfalls.org

**Carver** · *see Chaska*

**Cass Lake** · *Cass Lake C/C* · P.O. Box 548, 56633, P 1,000, M 93, (218) 335-2250, (800) 356-8615, info@casslake.com, www.casslake.com

**Center City** · *see Lindstrom*

**Centerville** · *see Circle Pines*

**Champlin** · *see Anoka*

**Chanhassen** · *see Chaska*

**Chaska** · *SouthWest Metro C/C* · Deb McMillan, Pres., 564 Bavaria Ln., Ste. 100, 55318, P 58,000, M 450, (952) 448-5000, Fax (952) 448-4261, info@swmetrochamber.com, www.swmetrochamber.com

**Chatfield** · *Chatfield Commerical Club* · 21 2nd St. S.E., 55923, P 2,800, M 50, (507) 867-3810, www.ci.chatfield.mn.us

**Chisago City** · *see Lindstrom*

**Chisholm** · *Chisholm Area C/C* · Shannon Kishel-Roche, Exec. Dir., 223 W. Lake St., 55719, P 5,000, M 175, (218) 254-7930, (800) 422-0806, Fax (218) 254-7932, info@chisholmchamber.com, www.chisholmchamber.com

**Circle Pines** · *Quad Area C/C* · P.O. Box 430, 55014, P 40,000, M 60, (651) 815-2750, annamwicks@msn.com, www.quadchamber.org

**Claremont** · *Claremont Area C/C* · Dean Schuette, Pres./CEO, P.O. Box 236, 55924, P 670, M 40, (507) 456-3899, Fax (507) 528-2126, schuette@myclearwave.net, www.claremontmn.com

**Clarissa** · *Clarissa Commercial Club* · Ray Benning, P.O. Box 188, 56440, P 600, M 25, (218) 756-2131

**Clementson** · *see Baudette*

**Cloquet** · *Cloquet Area C/C & Tourism* · 225 Sunnyside Dr., 55720, P 12,000, M 285, (218) 879-1551, (800) 554-4350, Fax (218) 878-0223, chamber@cloquet.com, www.cloquet.com

**Cokato** · *Cokato C/C* · Louann Worden, Secy., 255 Broadway Ave. S., P.O. Box 819, 55321, P 2,700, M 85, (320) 286-5505, Fax (320) 286-5876, depclerk@cokato.mn.us, www.cokato.mn.us

**Cold Spring** · *Cold Spring Area C/C* · 215 1st St. S., Ste. 200, 56320, P 3,000, M 95, (320) 685-4186, Fax (320) 685-4186, info@coldspringmn.com, www.coldspringmn.com

**Columbia Heights** · *see Mounds View*

**Cook** · *Cook Area C/C* · Ellie Brunner, Pres., P.O. Box 296, 55723, P 800, M 75, (218) 666-5850, (800) 648-5897, Fax (218) 666-6073, info@cookminnesota.com, www.cookminnesota.com

**Coon Rapids** · *see Blaine*

**Corcoran** · *see Rogers*

**Cottage Grove** · *Cottage Grove Area C/C* · Geanee Junker, Pres., 7064 W. Point Douglas Rd. S., P.O. Box 16, 55016, P 35,000, M 140, (651) 458-8334, Fax (651) 458-8383, office@cottagegrove chamber.org, www.cottagegrovechamber.org

**Crookston** · *Crookston Area C/C* · Lori Wagner, Pres./CEO, 107 W. 2nd St., P.O. Box 115, 56716, P 8,198, M 220, (218) 281-4320, (800) 809-5997, Fax (218) 281-4349, lwagner@visitcrookston. com, www.visitcrookston.com.

**Crosby** · *Cuyuna Range C/C* · Johnna Johnson, Dir., P.O. Box 23, 56441, P 9,600, M 140, (218) 546-8131, Fax (218) 546-2618, info@cuyunacountry.net, www.cuyunacountry.net

**Crosslake** · *Crosslake Office of Brainerd Lakes C/C* · P.O. Box 315, 56442, P 5,000, M 1,200, (218) 692-1828, (800) 450-2838, info@explorebrainerdlakes.com, www.explorebrainerdlakes.com

**Crystal** · *see Plymouth - TwinWest C/C*

**Cuyuna** · *see Crosby*

**Dakota County** · *Dakota County Reg. C/C* · Ruthe Batulis, Pres., 1121 Town Centre Dr., Ste. 102, Eagan, 55123, P 150,000, M 600, (651) 452-9872, Fax (651) 452-8978, info@dcrchamber.com, www.dcrchamber.com

**Dawson** · *Dawson Area C/C* · Janet Liebl, P.O. Box 382, 56232, P 1,700, M 100, (320) 769-2981, www.dawsonmn.com

**Dayton** · *see Anoka and Rogers*

**Deer River** · *Deer River C/C* · P.O. Box 505, 56636, P 903, M 125, (218) 246-8055, (888) 701-2226, drchamb@deerriver.org, www. deerriver.org

**Deerwood** · *see Crosby*

**Delano** · *Delano Area C/C* · J. Kopp, Exec. Dir., 265 N. River St., Ste. 109, P.O. Box 27, 55328, P 5,100, M 135, (763) 972-6756, Fax (763) 972-9326, info@delanochamber.com, www.delanochamber.com

**Dellwood** · *see White Bear Lake*

**Detroit Lakes** · *Detroit Lakes Reg. C/C* · Ms. Kris Tovson, Pres., 700 Summit Ave., P.O. Box 348, 56502, P 10,000, M 500, (218) 847-9202, (800) 542-3992, Fax (218) 847-9082, dlchamber@ visitdetroitlakes.com, www.visitdetroitlakes.com.

**Duluth** · *Duluth Area C/C* · David Ross, Pres./CEO, 5 W. First St., Ste. 101, 55802, P 84,167, M 1,150, (218) 722-5501, Fax (218) 722-3223, inquiry@duluthchamber.com, www.duluthchamber.com

**Eagan** · *see Dakota County*

**East Bethel** · *see Blaine*

**East Grand Forks** · *The Chamber Grand Forks - East Grand Forks* · Barry Wilfahrt, Pres./CEO, P.O. Box 315, 56721, P 65,000, M 875, (701) 772-7271, Fax (701) 772-9238, info@gochamber.org, www.gochamber.org.

**Eden Prairie** · *Eden Prairie C/C* · Pat MulQueeny, Pres., 11455 Viking Dr., Ste. 270, 55344, P 58,000, M 460, (952) 944-2830, Fax (952) 944-0229, adminj@epchamber.org, www.epchamber.org

**Eden Valley** · *Eden Valley C/C* · Chad Stanwick, Pres., P.O. Box 557, 55329, P 866, M 47, (320) 453-5251, www.edenvalley chamber.com

**Edina** · *Edina C/C* · Ms. Arrie Larsen Manti, Pres., 7710 Computer Ave., Ste. 134, 55435, P 47,000, M 400, (952) 806-9060, Fax (952) 806-9065, chamber@edina.org, www.edinachamber.com

**Elbow Lake** · *Elbow Lake C/C* · Edie Johnson, Managing Dir., P.O. Box 1083, 56531, P 1,275, M 120, (218) 685-5380, Fax (218) 685-5381, chamber@runestone.net, www.elbowlakechamber.com

**Elk River** · *Elk River Area C/C* · Debbi Rydberg, Pres., 509 Hwy. 10, 55330, P 21,000, M 400, (763) 441-3110, Fax (763) 441-3409, eracc@elkriverchamber.org, www.elkriverchamber.org.

**Ely** · *Ely C/C* · Linda Fryer, Admin. Dir., 1600 E. Sheridan St., 55731, P 3,968, M 280, (218) 365-6123, (800) 777-7281, Fax (218) 365-5929, fun@ely.org, www.ely.org

**Elysian** · *Elysian Area C/C* · Ron Greenwald, Pres., P.O. Box 95, 56028, P 550, M 80, (507) 267-4708, (507) 267-4040, Fax (507) 267-4750, www.elysianmn.com

**Eveleth** · *see Virginia*

**Excelsior** · *South Lake/Excelsior C/C* · Linda Murrell, Exec. Dir., P.O. Box 32, 55331, P 15,000, M 170, (952) 474-6461, eacc@isd. net, www.southlake-excelsiorchamber.com

**Fairfax** · *Fairfax Civic & Commerce* · P.O. Box 114, 55332, P 1,275, M 60

**Fairmont** · *Fairmont Area C/C* · Bob Wallace, Pres., 323 E. Blue Earth Ave., P.O. Box 826, 56031, P 11,000, M 277, (507) 235-5547, Fax (507) 235-8411, info@fairmontchamber.org, www.fairmont chamber.org

**Falcon Heights** · *see Saint Paul*

**Faribault** · *Faribault Area C/C* · Kymn Anderson, Pres., 530 Wilson Ave., P.O. Box 434, 55021, P 28,000, M 490, (507) 334-4381, (800) 658-2354, Fax (507) 334-1003, chamber@faribaultmn. org, www.faribaultmn.org

**Farmington** · *see Dakota County*

**Fergus Falls** · *Fergus Falls Area C/C* · Lisa Workman, Exec. Dir., 202 S. Court St., 56537, P 14,000, M 300, (218) 736-6951, Fax (218) 736-6952, chamber@prtel.com, www.fergusfalls.com

**Flag Island** · *see Baudette*

**Floodwood** · *Floodwood Bus./Comm. Partnership* · Deb Arro, Pres., P.O. Box 337, 55736, P 500, M 45, (218) 476-3210, fbcp55736@yahoo.com, www.floodwood.govoffice.com

**Forest Lake** · *Forest Lake Area C/C* · Colleen Eddy, Pres., 56 E. Broadway Ave., Ste. 204, P.O. Box 474, 55025, P 45,000, M 330, (651) 464-3200, Fax (651) 464-3201, chamber@flacc.org, www. flacc.org

**Frankfort Twp.** · *see Rogers*

**Fridley** · *see Mounds View*

**Gaylord** · *Gaylord C/C* · Ellen Felmlee, Pres., 332 Main, P.O. Box 7, 55334, P 2,300, M 50, (507) 237-5869, Fax (507) 237-5121, gaylordeda@gaylord.govoffice.com, www.gaylord.govoffice.com

**Gem Lake** · *see White Bear Lake*

**Gilbert** · *see Virginia*

**Glencoe** · *Glencoe Area C/C* · Dan Ehrke, Pres., 630 10th St., 55336, P 5,700, M 150, (320) 864-3650, Fax (320) 864-6405, chamber@glencoechamber.com, www.glencoechamber.com

**Glenwood** · *Glenwood Lakes Area C/C* · Cody Rogahn, Diir., 2 E. Minnesota Ave., Ste. 100, 56334, P 11,236, M 175, (320) 634-3636, (866) 634-3636, Fax (320) 634-3637, chamber@glenwoodlakesarea.info, www.glenwoodlakesarea.info

**Golden Valley** · *see Plymouth - TwinWest C/C*

**Grand Marais** · *Greater Grand Marais C/C* · Bev Wolke, Exec. Dir., 13 N. Broadway, P.O. Box 805, 55604, P 1,800, M 100, (218) 387-9112, (218) 387-2524, Fax (888) 922-5000, gmcc@boreal.org, www.grandmaraismn.com

**Grand Rapids** · *Grand Rapids Area C/C* · Bud Stone, Pres./CEO, One N.W. Third St., 55744, P 40,000, M 600, (218) 326-6619, (800) 472-6366, Fax (218) 326-4825, info@grandmn.com, www.grandmn.com

**Granite Falls** · *Granite Falls Area C/C* · Nicole Richter, Exec. Dir., 646 Prentice St., 56241, P 3,451, M 125, (320) 564-4039, Fax (320) 564-3843, gfchamber@mvtvwireless.com, www.granitefallschamber.com

**Greenfield** · *see Rogers*

**Hackensack** · *Hackensack C/C* · Jean Dawson, Coord., 100 Fleisher Ave. S., P.O. Box 373, 56452, P 275, M 135, (218) 675-6135, (800) 279-6932, Fax (218) 675-6135, chamber@hackensackchamber.com, www.hackensackchamber.com

**Ham Lake** · *Ham Lake C/C* · Kim Hogdal, Dir., 1207 Constance Blvd. N.E., 55304, P 12,029, M 100, (763) 434-3011, Fax (763) 434-6668, admin@hamlakecc.org, www.hamlakecc.org

**Hamel** · *see Rogers*

**Hanover** · *see Rogers*

**Hassan Twp.** · *see Rogers*

**Hastings** · *Hastings Area C/C & Tourism Bur.* · Michelle Jacobs, Pres., 111 E. Third St., 55033, P 22,000, M 300, (651) 437-6775, (888) 612-6122, Fax (651) 437-2697, info@hastingsmn.org, www.hastingsmn.org

**Hayfield** · *Hayfield C/C* · Tom Monahan, P.O. Box 1113, 55940, P 1,325, M 90, (507) 477-3535, (507) 477-3492, www.hayfieldmn.com

**Hermantown** · *Hermantown Area C/C* · Michael Lundstrom, Exec. Dir., 4940 Lightning Dr., 55811, P 9,760, M 310, (218) 729-6843, Fax (218) 729-7132, www.hermantownchamber.com

**Hibbing** · *Hibbing Area C/C* · Lory Fedo, Pres./CEO, 211 E. Howard St., P.O. Box 727, 55746, P 17,000, M 400, (218) 262-3895, (800) 4-HIBBING, Fax (218) 262-3897, hibbcofc@hibbing.org, www.hibbing.org

**Hilltop** · *see Blaine*

**Hinckley** · *Hinckley Area C/C* · Betty Miller, Dir., 108 Main St. E., P.O. Box 189, 55037, P 1,400, M 80, (320) 384-7837, info@hinckleychamber.com, www.hinckleychamber.com

**Hopkins** · *see Plymouth - TwinWest C/C*

**Houston** · *Houston C/C* · Karla Kinstler, Secy., 215 W. Plum St., P.O. Box 3, 55943, P 3,000, M 50, (507) 896-4668, nature@acegroup.cc, www.houstonmnchamber.com

**Hoyt Lakes** · *Hoyt Lakes C/C* · Robert Bartholomew, Pres., P.O. Box 429, 55750, P 2,700, M 100, (218) 225-2787, www.hoytlakes.com

**Hugo** · *see White Bear Lake*

**Hutchinson** · *Hutchinson Area C/C* · Bill Corby, Pres., 2 Main St. S., 55350, P 13,977, M 350, (320) 587-5252, Fax (320) 587-4752, info@explorehutchinson.com, www.explorehutchinson.com

**International Falls** · *International Falls Area C/C* · Betsy Jensen, Pres., 301 2nd Ave., 56649, P 7,000, M 250, (218) 283-9400, (800) FALLS-MN, Fax (218) 283-3572, betsy@intlfalls.org, www.ifallschamber.com

**Inver Grove Heights** · *River Heights C/C* · Jennifer Gale, Pres., 5782 Blackshire Path, 55076, P 53,470, M 350, (651) 451-2266, Fax (651) 451-0846, info@riverheights.com, www.riverheights.com

**Ironton** · *see Crosby*

**Isanti** · *Isanti Area C/C* · Jan Peterson, Exec. Dir., 12 W. Main St., P.O. Box 203, 55040, P 6,000, M 165, (763) 444-8515, admin@isantichamber.com, www.isantichamber.com

**Jackson** · *Jackson Area C/C* · Marilyn Reese, Exec. Dir., 82 W. Ashley St., 56143, P 3,501, M 130, (507) 847-3867, Fax (507) 847-3869, chamber@jacksonmn.com, www.jacksonmn.com

**Janesville** · *Janesville C/C* · Paul Pfenning, Pres., P.O. Box 0, 56048, P 2,200, M 40, (507) 234-5110, Fax (507) 234-5236, janesville.govoffice.com

**Jordan** · *Jordan Area C/C* · 315 Broadway St. S., P.O. Box 102, 55352, P 5,000, M 140, (952) 492-2355, Fax (952) 492-3739, info@jordanchamber.org, www.jordanchamber.org

**Kasson** · *Kasson C/C* · Cathy Pletta, P.O. Box 326, 55944, P 5,200, M 100, (507) 634-7618, kassonchamber@kmtel.com, www.kassonchamber.org

**Kimball** · *Kimball C/C* · Leo Wirth, Pres., P.O. Box 214, 55353, P 650, M 55, (320) 398-8211, www.kimballareachamber.com

**La Crescent** · *La Crescent C of C & Tourist Info. Center* · Eileen Krenz, Exec. Secy., 109 S. Walnut, Ste. B, P.O. Box 132, 55947, P 5,100, M 140, (507) 895-2800, (800) 926-9480, Fax (507) 895-2619, LaCrescent.Chamber@acegroup.cc, www.lacrescentmn.com

**Lake Benton** · *Lake Benton Area C/C & CVB* · 110 S. Center St., P.O. Box 205, 56149, P 700, M 55, (507) 368-9577, lbenton@itctel.com, www.lakebentonminnesota.com

**Lake City** · *Lake City Area C/C* · Mary Huselid, Exec. Dir., 101 W. Center St., 55041, P 5,000, M 220, (651) 345-4123, (800) 369-4123, Fax (651) 345-4195, lcchamber@lakecity.org, www.lakecitymn.org

**Lake Crystal** · *Lake Crystal Area C/C* · Sara Nilson, Coord., 129 S. Main, P.O. Box 27, 56055, P 2,500, M 100, (507) 726-6088, lcchambr@hickorytech.net, www.lakecrystalchamber.com

**Lake Lillian** · *Lake Lillian Civic & Commerce* · Dirk Siems, P.O. Box 205, 56253, P 300, M 15, (320) 664-4111, www.lakelillian.govoffice.com

**Lake Minnetonka** · *see Spring Park*

**Lakeville** · *Lakeville Area C/C* · Todd J. Bornhauser, Exec. Dir., 19950 Dodd Blvd., Ste. 101, 55044, P 55,000, M 450, (952) 469-2020, Fax (952) 469-2028, info@lakevillechambercvb.org, www.lakevillechambercvb.org

**Lamberton** · *Lamberton Comm. Club* · Steve Flaig, P.O. Box 356, 56152, P 900, M 68, (507) 752-7601, www.rrcnet.org/~lambrton/

**Lanesboro** • *Lanesboro Area C/C* • Julie Kiehne, Dir., 100 Milwaukee Rd., P.O. Box 348, 55949, P 788, M 135, (507) 467-2696, (800) 944-2670, Fax (507) 467-3060, lvc@acegroup.cc, www.lanesboro.com

**Lauderdale** • *see Saint Paul*

**Le Center** • *Le Center Area C/C* • Don Hayden, Exec. Dir., 10 W. Tyrone St., P.O. Box 54, 56057, P 2,200, M 100, (507) 357-6737, Fax (507) 357-6888, donlc@frontiernet.net

**Le Sueur** • *Le Sueur Area C/C* • Julie Boyland, Exec. Dir., 500 N. Main St., 56058, P 4,300, M 185, (507) 665-2501, Fax (507) 665-4372, julieb@lesueurchamber.org, www.lesueurchamber.org

**Lewiston** • *Lewiston C/C* • Craig Porter, Pres., P.O. Box 423, 55952, P 1,800, M 70, (507) 523-2300

**Lexington** • *see Circle Pines*

**Lilydale** • *see Dakota County*

**Lindstrom** • *Chisago Lakes Area C/C* • Tangi Schaapveld, Exec. Dir., 30525 Linden St., P.O. Box 283, 55045, P 10,000, M 200, (651) 257-1177, Fax (651) 257-1770, clacc@frontiernet.net, www.chisagolakeschamber.com

**Lino Lakes** • *see Circle Pines*

**Litchfield** • *Litchfield C/C* • Dee Schutte, Exec. Dir., 219 Sibley Ave. N., 55355, P 6,500, M 300, (320) 693-8184, Fax (320) 593-8184, litch@litch.com, www.litch.com

**Little Canada** • *see Saint Paul*

**Little Falls** • *Little Falls Area C/C* • Debora Boelz, Pres./CEO, 200 N.W. First St., 56345, P 32,900, M 350, (320) 632-5155, Fax (320) 632-2122, assistance@littlefallsmnchamber.com, www.littlefallsmnchamber.com.

**Littlefork** • *Littlefork C/C* • 313 Main St., P.O. Box 131, 56653, P 700, M 40, (218) 278-6617, www.littlefork.org

**Long Lake** • *Long Lake C/C* • Roxie Albers, Pres., P.O. Box 662, 55356, P 2,200, M 100, (952) 473-0873, www.longlake-orono.org

**Long Prairie** • *Long Prairie Area C/C* • Lyle Danielson, Mgr., 42 N. 3rd St., 56347, P 3,040, M 115, (320) 732-2514, info@longprairie.org, www.longprairie.org

**Longville** • *Longville C/C* • John Weins, Coord., P.O. Box 33, 56655, P 300, M 90, (218) 363-2630, (800) 756-7583, chamber@longville.com, www.longville.com

**Lonsdale** • *Lonsdale Area C/C* • Barb Cole, Pres., 102 5th Ave. N.W., P.O. Box 37, 55046, P 2,600, M 80, (507) 744-4962, Fax (507) 744-2388, information@lonsdalechamber.com, www.lonsdalechamber.com

**Loretto** • *see Rogers*

**Luverne** • *Luverne Area C/C* • Jane Wildung Lanphere, Exec. Dir., 213 E. Luverne, 56156, P 4,500, M 190, (507) 283-4061, (888) 283-4061, Fax (507) 283-4061, luvernechamber@iw.net, www.luvernechamber.com.

**Madelia** • *Madelia Area C/C* • Brent Christiansen, Pres., 127 W. Main St., P.O. Box 171, 56062, P 2,400, M 100, (507) 642-8822, (888) 941-7283, Fax (507) 642-8832, chamber@madeliamn.com, www.visitmadelia.com

**Madison** • *Madison Area C/C* • Maynard R. Meyer, Coord., 623 W. 3rd St., P.O. Box 70, 56256, P 2,000, M 100, (320) 598-7301, Fax (320) 598-7955, klqpfm@farmerstel.net, www.madisonmn.info

**Mahnomen** • *Mahnomen County C/C* • Tom Ryan, Pres., P.O. Box 36, 56557, P 5,250, M 65, (218) 935-2573

**Mahtomedi** • *see White Bear Lake*

**Mankato** • *Greater Mankato Growth Inc.* • Jonathan Zierdt, Pres./CEO, 1961 Premier Dr., Ste. 100, 56001, P 50,000, M 770, (507) 385-6640, (800) 697-0652, Fax (507) 345-8899, info@greatermankato.com, www.greatermankato.com.

**Maple Grove** • *see Osseo*

**Maple Plain** • *West Hennepin C/C* • P.O. Box 363, 55359, P 25,000, M 130, (763) 479-1988, Fax (952) 472-8828, info@whcc-mn.org, www.whcc-mn.org

**Mapleton** • *Mapleton Area C/C* • Rhonda Roesch, Coord., P.O. Box 288, 56065, P 2,500, M 50, (507) 524-4756, r.roesch@mapletonchamber.com, www.mapletonchamber.com

**Maplewood** • *see Saint Paul*

**Marshall** • *Marshall Area C/C* • Dan Schenkein, Pres./CEO, 317 W. Main, P.O. Box 352-B, 56258, P 12,500, M 350, (507) 532-4484, Fax (507) 532-4485, chamber@starpoint.net, www.marshall-mn.org.

**McGregor** • *McGregor Area C/C* • Kathy Larson, Pres., P.O. Box 68, 55760, P 500, M 100, (218) 768-3692, chamber@mcgregormn.com, www.mcgregormn.com

**Medicine Lake** • *see Plymouth - TwinWest C/C*

**Medina** • *see Rogers*

**Melrose** • *Melrose Area C/C* • 223 E. Main St., P.O. Box 214, 56352, P 3,293, M 110, (320) 256-7174, Fax (320) 256-7177, chamber@meltel.net, www.melrosemn.org

**Mendota Heights** • *see Dakota County*

**Milaca** • *Milaca Area C/C* • Becky Bergstrom, Coord., 255 1st St. E., P.O. Box 155, 56353, P 2,800, M 100, (320) 983-3140, Fax (320) 983-3142, chamber@milacacity.com, www.cityofmilaca.org

## Minneapolis Area

**Minneapolis Reg.C/C** • Todd Klingel, Pres./CEO, 81 S. 9th St., Ste. 200, 55402, P 2,968,806, M 1,250, (612) 370-9100, Fax (612) 370-9195, info@minneapolischamber.org, www.minneapolischamber.org.

**Hispanic C/C of MN** • Val Vargas, CEO, 3000 N. 2nd St., 55411, P 400,000, M 300, (612) 312-1692, Fax (612) 312-1693, gustavo@hispanicmn.org, www.hispanicmn.org

**Northeast Minneapolis C/C** • Christine Levens, Exec. Dir., 2329 Central Ave. N.E., 55418, M 1,250, (612) 378-0050, Fax (612) 378-8870, info@minneapolischamber.org, www.minneapolischamber.org

**Minneota** • *Minneota Area C/C* • Rick Konold, Pres., P.O. Box 413, 56264, P 1,500, M 75, (507) 872-6144, www.minneotamn.com

**Minnesota Lake** • *Minnesota Lake Comm.Club* • Sally Roesler, Pres., P.O. Box 128, 56068, P 670, M 100, (507) 462-3277, mnlake@bevcomm.net, www.minnesotalake.com

**Minnetonka** • *see Plymouth*

**Minnetrista** • *see Spring Park*

**Montevideo** • *Montevideo Area C/C* • 202 N. 1st St., Ste. 150, 56265, P 5,500, M 250, (320) 269-5527, (800) 269-5527, Fax (320) 269-5696, generalinfo@montechamber.com, www.montechamber.com

**Monticello** • *Monticello C/C* • Sandy Suchy, Dir., 205 Pine St., P.O. Box 192, 55362, P 13,000, M 285, (763) 295-2700, Fax (763) 295-2705, info@monticellocci.com, www.monticellocci.com

**Montrose** • *Montrose-Waverly C/C* • Jim Tourville, P.O. Box 421, 55363, P 2,700, (612) 508-6474, jamestourville@msn.com, www.montrosewaverlychamber.com

**Moorhead** • *C/C of Fargo Moorhead* • David K. Martin, Pres./CEO, 202 1st Ave. N., 56560, P 190,000, M 1,900, (218) 233-1100, Fax (218) 233-1200, info@fmchamber.com, www.fmchamber.com.

**Moose Lake** · *Moose Lake Area C/C* · Dean Paulson, Exec. Dir., 4524 Arrowhead Ln., P.O. Box 110, 55767, P 4,000, M 140, (218) 485-4145, (800) 635-3680, mlchamber@moose-tec.com, www.mooselake-mn.com

**Mora** · *Kanabec Area C/C* · Karen Amundson, Exec. Dir., 200 S. Hwy. 65, Ste. 1, 55051, P 4,000, M 125, (320) 679-5792, (800) 291-5792, Fax (320) 679-3279, karen@kanabecchamber.org, www.kanabecchamber.org

**Morris** · *Morris Area C/C* · Karen Arnold, Interim Dir., 507 Atlantic Ave., 56267, P 5,068, M 170, (320) 589-1242, Fax (320) 585-4814, mchamber@fedtel.net, www.morrismnchamber.org

**Morton** · *Morton Area C/C & Tourism Bur.* · Shirley Dove, P.O. Box 0127, 56270, P 448, M 30, (507) 697-6912, mortoncityhall@mchsi.com, www.mortonmnchamber.com

**Motley** · *see Staples*

**Mound** · *see Spring Park*

**Mounds View** · *Twin Cities North C/C* · Tim Roche, Pres., 5394 Edgewood Dr., Ste. 100, 55112, P 87,000, M 500, (763) 571-9781, Fax (763) 572-7950, info@twincitiesnorth.org, www.twincitiesnorth.org

**Mountain Iron** · *see Virginia*

**Mountain Lake** · *Mountain Lake C/C* · Rob Anderson, Dir., 930 Third Ave., P.O. Drawer C, 56159, P 2,000, M 60, (507) 427-2999, Fax (507) 427-3327, eda@mountainlake.govoffice.com, www.mountainlakemn.com

**Nashwauk** · *Nashwauk Area C/C* · Mike Olson, Pres., P.O. Box 156, 55769, P 1,000, M 70, (218) 885-2714, (218) 885-3010, www.nashwaukchamber.com

**Navarre** · *see Spring Park*

**New Brighton** · *see Mounds View*

**New Hope** · *see Plymouth - TwinWest C/C*

**New London** · *see Willmar*

**New Prague** · *New Prague C/C* · Kristy Mach, Exec. Dir., 101 E. Main St., P.O. Box 191, 56071, P 6,200, M 185, (952) 758-4360, Fax (952) 758-5396, info@newprague.com, www.newprague.com

**New Ulm** · *New Ulm Area C/C* · Sharon Weinkauf, Pres./CEO, 1 N. Minnesota St., P.O. Box 384, 56073, P 14,000, M 370, (507) 233-4300, (888) 4-NEW-ULM, Fax (507) 354-1504, nuchamber@newulmtel.net, www.newulm.com

**New York Mills** · *New York Mills Civic & Commerce Assn.* · Duane Koehler, Pres., P.O. Box 176, 56567, P 1,200, M 70, (218) 385-3339, info@explorenewyorkmills.com, www.explorenewyorkmills.com

**Nisswa** · *Nisswa C/C* · 25532 Main St., P.O. Box 185, 56468, P 2,000, M 330, (218) 963-2620, (800) 950-9610, Fax (218) 963-1420, requests@nisswa.com, www.nisswa.com

**North Branch** · *North Branch Area C/C* · Kathy Lindo, Exec. Dir., 6063 Main St., P.O. Box 577, 55056, P 10,000, M 300, (651) 674-4077, Fax (651) 674-2600, nbachamber@izoom.net, northbranchchamber.com

**North Maplewood** · *see White Bear Lake*

**North Oaks** · *see Saint Paul and White Bear Lake*

**North Saint Paul** · *see Saint Paul*

**Northfield** · *Northfield Area C/C* · Kathy Feldbrugge, Exec. Dir., 205 Third St. W., Ste A, P.O. Box 198, 55057, P 18,900, M 275, (507) 645-5604, (800) 658-2548, Fax (507) 663-7782, info@northfieldchamber.com, www.northfieldchamber.com.

**Norwood Young America** · *Norwood Young America C/C* · John P. Fahey, Exec. Dir., P.O. Box 292, 55368, P 7,000, M 80, (952) 467-4003, nyachamberofcommerce@yahoo.com, www.nyachamber.org

**Oak Grove** · *see Blaine*

**Oak Island** · *Northwest Angle & Island C/C* · Debra Kellerman, P.O. Box 11, 56741, P 400, M 150, (218) 223-4611, Fax (218) 223-4612, www.lakeofthewoodsresorts.com

**Oakdale** · *see Saint Paul*

**Olivia** · *Olivia Area C/C* · Nancy Standfuss, Exec. Dir., 909 W. DePue Ave., P.O. Box 37, 56277, P 2,600, M 100, (320) 523-1350, (888) 265-CORN, Fax (320) 523-1514, oliviachamber@tds.net, www.oliviachamber.org

**Orono** · *see Spring Park*

**Orr** · *Orr C/C* · P.O. Box 64, 55771, P 300, M 30, (218) 757-3288, info@orrchamber.com, www.orrchamber.com

**Ortonville** · *Big Stone Lake Area C/C* · Donnette Herberg, Dir., 987 US Hwy. 12, 56278, P 2,158, M 175, (320) 839-3284, (800) 568-5722, Fax (320) 839-2621, chamber@bigstonelake.com, www.bigstonelake.com

**Osakis** · *Osakis C/C* · Jan Moore, Exec. Dir., P.O. Box 327, 56360, P 1,615, M 80, (320) 859-3777, (866) 784-8941, Fax (320) 859-4794, chamber@visitosakis.com, www.visitosakis.com

**Osseo** · *North Hennepin Area C/C* · Jill Johnson, Pres., 229 1st Ave. N.E., 55369, P 120,000, M 450, (763) 424-6744, info@nhachamber.com, www.nhachamber.com

**Otsego** · *see Rogers*

**Owatonna** · *Owatonna Area C/C & Tourism* · Brad Meier, Pres., 320 Hoffman Dr., 55060, P 25,090, M 610, (507) 451-7970, (800) 423-6466, Fax (507) 451-7972, oacct@owatonna.org, www.owatonna.org

**Park Rapids** · *Park Rapids Lakes Area C/C* · Katherine Magozzi, Exec. Dir., 1204 S. Park, Hwy. 71 S., P.O. Box 249, 56470, P 30,000, M 400, (218) 732-4111, (800) 247-0054, Fax (218) 732-4112, chamber@parkrapids.com, www.parkrapids.com

**Paynesville** · *Paynesville Area C/C* · Linda Musel, Ofc. Mgr., P.O. Box 4, 56362, P 2,267, M 125, (320) 243-3233, (800) 547-9034, chamber@lakedalelink.net, www.paynesvillechamber.org

**Pelican Rapids** · *Pelican Rapids Area C/C* · Angela Harvala-Asleson, Exec. Dir., 25 N. Broadway, P.O. Box 206, 56572, P 2,374, M 170, (218) 863-1221, Fax (218) 863-4606, tourism@loretel.net, www.pelicanrapidschamber.com

**Pequot Lakes** · *Pequot Lakes Ofc.of Brainerd Lakes C/C* · P.O. Box 208, 56472, P 1,802, M 1,200, (218) 568-8911, (800) 950-0291, Fax (218) 568-8910, info@explorebrainerdlakes.com, www.explorebrainerdlakes.com

**Perham** · *Perham Area C/C* · Don Schroeder, Exec. Dir., 185 E. Main St., 56573, P 12,000, M 262, (218) 346-7710, (800) 634-6112, Fax (218) 346-7712, chamber@perham.com, www.perham.com

**Pillager** · *see Staples*

**Pine City** · *Pine City Area C/C* · Rick Herzog, Pres., 900 4th St. S.E., Ste. 85, 55063, P 3,400, M 150, (320) 629-4565, info@pinecitychamber.com, www.pinecitychamber.com

**Pine River** · *Pine River C/C* · John Wetrosky, Dir., P.O. Box 131, 56474, P 4,000, M 125, (218) 587-4000, (800) 728-6926, Fax (218) 587-4096, prcofc@uslink.net, www.pinerivermn.com

**Pipestone** · *Pipestone Area C/C* · Mick Myers, Exec. Dir., 117 8th Ave. S.E., P.O. Box 8, 56164, P 4,549, M 160, (507) 825-3316, Fax (507) 825-3317, pipecham@pipestoneminnesota.com, www.pipestoneminnesota.com

**Plymouth** · *also see Rogers*

**Plymouth** · *TwinWest C/C* · Bruce Nustad, Pres., 10700 Old County Rd. 15, Ste. 170, 55441, P 250,000, M 1,000, (763) 450-2220, Fax (763) 450-2221, bruce@twinwest.com, www.twinwest.com

**Princeton** · *Princeton Area C/C* · Cheryl Brindle, Exec. Dir., 705 2nd St. N., 55371, P 4,600, M 132, (763) 389-1764, Fax (763) 631-1764, pacc@sherbtel.net, www.princetonmnchamber.org

**Prior Lake** · *Prior Lake Area C/C* · Sandi Fleck, Exec. Dir., 4785 Dakota St., P.O. Box 114, 55372, P 21,000, M 250, (952) 440-1000, Fax (952) 440-1611, sandi@priorlakechamber.com, www.prior lakechamber.com

**Proctor** · *Proctor Area C/C* · Glen Johnson, P.O. Box 1016, 55810, P 3,200, M 100, (218) 628-6297 x290, info@proctorchamber.com, www.proctorchamber.com

**Ramsey** · *see Anoka*

**Raymond** · *Raymond Civic & Commerce* · Larry Macht, P.O. Box 353, 56282, P 800, M 60, (320) 967-4439, Fax (320) 967-4439, raymondminnesota@yahoo.com, www.raymondminnesota.com

**Red Wing** · *Red Wing Area C/C* · Marie Mikel, Pres., 439 Main St., 55066, P 16,500, M 350, (651) 388-4719, marie@redwing-chamber.com, www.redwingchamber.com

**Redwood Falls** · *Redwood Area Chamber & Tourism* · Jean Hallberg, Exec. Dir., 200 S. Mill St., 56283, P 5,459, M 180, (507) 637-2828, (800) 657-7070, Fax (507) 637-5202, chamber@ redwoodfalls.org, www.redwoodfalls.org.

**Remer** · *Remer Area C/C* · Bob Stoekel, Pres., P.O. Box 101, 56672, P 342, M 70, (218) 566-1680, (800) 831-5262, info@ remerchamber.com, www.remerchamber.com

**Renville** · *Renville C/C* · P.O. Box 706, 56284, P 1,300, M 50, (320) 329-8403, Fax (320) 329-8403, www.ci.renville.mn.us

**Rice** · *Rice C/C* · Barb Johnson, P.O. Box 22, 56367, P 1,151, M 65, (320) 393-2280, chamber@riceminnesota.com, www. riceminnesota.com

**Richfield** · *Richfield C/C* · Steven Lindgren, Pres., 6601 Lyndale Ave. S., Ste. 106, 55423, P 34,496, M 200, (612) 866-5100, Fax (612) 861-8302, info@richfieldchambercvb.org, richfield chambercvb.org

**Richmond** · *Richmond Civic & Commerce* · Anita Riechert, Pres., P.O. Box 355, 56368, P 1,200, M 75, (320) 597-5300, www. richmondmn.com

**Riverton** · *see Crosby*

**Robbinsdale** · *Robbinsdale C/C* · Francince Wilson, Pres., P.O. Box 22646, 55422, P 14,500, M 68, (763) 531-1279, dkiser@ twelve.tv, www.robbinsdalemn.com/chamber.htm

**Rochester** · *Rochester Area C/C* · John Wade, Pres., 220 S. Broadway, Ste. 100, 55904, P 100,000, M 1,250, (507) 288-1122, Fax (507) 282-8960, chamber@rochestermnchamber.com, www. rochestermnchamber.com

**Rockford** · *see Rogers*

**Rogers** · *I-94 West C/C* · Kathleen Poate, Pres., 21370 John Milless Dr., P.O. Box 95, 55374, P 35,000, M 775, (763) 428-2921, Fax (763) 428-9068, requests@i94westchamber.org, www. i94westchamber.org

**Roosevelt** · *see Baudette*

**Roseau** · *Roseau Civic & Commerce* · Jack McDonald, P.O. Box 304, 56751, P 4,000, M 128, (218) 463-1184, (800) 815-1824, Fax (218) 463-1252, www.city.roseau.mn.us

**Rosemount** · *see Dakota County*

**Roseville** · *see Saint Paul*

**Rush City** · *Rush City Area C/C* · P.O. Box 713, 55069, P 2,000, M 75, (320) 358-4639, director@rushcitychamber.com, www. rushcitychamber.com

**Rushford** · *Rushford Area C/C* · Valencia Gaddis, Exec. Dir., P.O. Box 338, 55971, P 3,000, M 85, (507) 864-3338, chamber@ acegroup.cc, www.rushfordchamber.com

**Saint Anthony** · *Saint Anthony C/C* · 3301 Silver Lake Rd., 55418, P 8,000, M 65, (612) 782-3301, info@saintanthony chamber.org, www.saintanthonychamber.org

**Saint Bonifacius** · *see Spring Park*

**Saint Cloud** · *Saint Cloud Area C/C* · Teresa Bohnen, Pres., 110 S. 6th Ave., P.O. Box 487, 56302, P 85,000, M 1,100, (320) 251-2940, Fax (320) 251-0081, information@stcloudareachamber.com, www.stcloudareachamber.com.

**Saint Francis** · *see Anoka*

**Saint James** · *Saint James Area C/C* · Lori Nusbaum, Exec. Dir., 516 1st Ave. S., P.O. Box 346, 56081, P 4,900, M 125, (507) 375-3333, (866) 375-2480, chamber@stjamesmn.org, www. stjameschamberofcommerce.com

**Saint Joseph** · *Saint Joseph C/C* · Jean Dotzler, Pres., P.O. Box 696, 56374, P 5,100, M 80, (320) 363-7721, www.stjoseph chamber.com

**Saint Louis Park** · *see Plymouth - TwinWest C/C*

**Saint Michael** · *see Rogers*

**Saint Paul** · *Saint Paul Area C/C* · Kris Johnson, Pres., 401 N. Robert St., Ste. 150, 55101, P 373,000, M 2,000, (651) 223-5000, Fax (651) 223-5119, info@saintpaulchamber.com, www. saintpaulchamber.com

**Saint Peter** · *Saint Peter Area C/C* · Emily Peck, Admin., 101 S. Front St., 56082, P 10,000, M 300, (507) 934-3400, (800) 473-3404, Fax (507) 934-8960, spchamb@hickorytech.net, www. tourism.st-peter.mn.us

**Sandstone** · *Sandstone Area C/C* · 402 N. Main, P.O. Box 23, 55072, P 2,200, M 58, (320) 245-2271, info@sandstonechamber. com, www.sandstonechamber.com

**Sartell** · *Sartell Area C/C* · P.O. Box 82, 56377, P 10,500, M 135, (320) 258-6061, Fax (320) 258-6061, info@sartellchamber.com, www.sartellchamber.com

**Sauk Centre** · *Sauk Centre Area C/C* · Cindy Uhlenkamp, Jct. I-94 & Hwy. 71, P.O. Box 222, 56378, P 4,200, M 150, (320) 352-5201, Fax (320) 352-5202, chamber@saukcentrechamber.com, www.saukcentrechamber.com

**Savage** · *Savage C/C* · Lori Anderson, Exec. Dir., 14141 Glendale Rd. #210, 55378, P 25,000, M 225, (952) 894-8876, Fax (952) 894-9906, mail@savagechamber.com, www.savagechamber.com

**Shafer** · *see Lindstrom*

**Shakopee** · *Shakopee Area C/C* · Carol Schultz, Pres., 1801 E. Cty. Rd. 101, P.O. Box 717, 55379, P 32,000, M 250, (952) 445-1660, Fax (952) 445-1669, cschultz@shakopee.org, www. shakopee.org.

**Sherburn** · *Sherburn Area Civic & Commerce Org.* · P.O. Box 108, 56171, P 1,082, M 40, (507) 764-4491, sherburn.govoffice.com

**Shoreview** · *see Saint Paul*

**Silver Bay** · *see Two Harbors*

**Slayton** · *Slayton Area C/C* · Berneva Johnson, 2635 Broadway Ave., 56172, P 2,100, M 95, (507) 836-6902, Fax (507) 836-6650

**Sleepy Eye** · *Sleepy Eye Area C/C* · Julie Schmitt, Exec. Dir., 115 2nd Ave. N.E., 56085, P 3,600, M 125, (507) 794-4731, (800) 290-0588, Fax (507) 794-4732, secofc@sleepyeyetel.net, www. sleepyeyechamber.com

**Soudan** · *see Tower*

**South Saint Paul** · *see Inver Grove Heights*

**Spring Lake Park** · *see Mounds View*

**Spring Park** · *Lake Minnetonka Area C/C* · John Waldron, Pres., 4165 Shoreline Dr., Ste. 130, 55384, P 30,000, M 200, (952) 471-5492, Fax (952) 471-5449, chamber@lakeminnetonkachamber. com, www.lakeminnetonkachamber.com

**Spring Valley** · *Spring Valley Area C/C* · Jayson Smith, Pres., P.O. Box 13, 55975, P 2,600, M 42, (507) 346-1015, (507) 346-7367, springvalley.govoffice.com

**Springfield** · *Springfield Area C/C* · Marlys Vanderwerf, Exec. Secy., 33 S. Cass Ave., P.O. Box 134, 56087, P 2,178, M 110, (507) 723-3508, spfdchamber@newulmtel.net, www.springfieldmn-chamber.org

**Staples** · *Staples-Motley Area C/C* · P.O. Box 133, 56479, P 4,000, M 120, (218) 894-3974, info@staples-motleyarea.com, www.staples-motleyarea.com

**Starbuck** · *Starbuck C/C* · Lori Vaadeland, Mgr., P.O. Box 234, 56381, P 1,300, M 125, (320) 239-4220, Fax (320) 239-4250, starbuckchamber@hcinet.net, www.starbuckmn.org

**Stewartville** · *Stewartville Area C/C* · Lynne Benedict, Chamber Coord., 417 S. Main St., P.O. Box 52, 55976, P 6,000, M 87, (507) 533-6006, Fax (507) 533-6006, www.stewartville chamber.com

**Stillwater** · *Greater Stillwater C/C* · Jennifer Severson, Exec. Dir., 106 S. Main St., P.O. Box 516, 55082, P 19,000, M 450, (651) 439-4001, Fax (651) 439-4035, info@ilovestillwater.com, www. ilovestillwater.com

**Sunfish Lake** · *see Dakota County*

**Thief River Falls** · *Thief River Falls C/C* · 2017 Hwy. 59 S.E., 56701, P 8,334, M 250, (218) 681-3720, (800) 827-1629, Fax (218) 681-3739, trfchamb@wiktel.com, www.visitthiefriverfalls.com

**Tower** · *Lake Vermilion Area C/C* · Barb Burgess, Secy./Treas., Box 776, 55790, P 3,500, M 75, (218) 753-2301, (800) 869-3766, troy@lakevermilioncommerce.com, www.lakevermilion commerce.com

**Tracy** · *Tracy Area C/C* · Val Roskens Lubben, Dir., 372 Morgan St., 56175, P 2,268, M 90, (507) 629-4021, Fax (507) 629-5530, tracychamber@iw.net, www.tracymnchamber.com

**Trimont** · *Trimont Area C/C* · Jerry McGee, Treas., P.O. Box 278, 56176, P 750, M 50, (507) 639-2981, trimontchamber@hotmail. com, www.trimont.govoffice.com

**Trommald** · *see Crosby*

**Two Harbors** · *Two Harbors Area C/C* · Gordy Anderson, Pres./ CEO, 1330 Hwy. 61, 55616, P 3,630, M 260, (218) 834-2600, Fax (218) 834-2600, thchamber@twoharborschamber.com, www. twoharborschamber.com

**Tyler** · *Tyler Area Commercial Club* · P.O. Box 445, 56178, P 1,253, M 50, (507) 247-3905

**Vadnais Heights** · *see Saint Paul and White Bear Lake*

**Victoria** · *see Chaska*

**Virginia** · *Laurentian C/C* · Jim Currie, Pres./CEO, 403 1st St. North, 55792, P 15,000, M 350, (218) 741-2717, Fax (218) 749-4913, jcurrie@laurentianchamber.org, www.laurentianchamber.org

**Wabasha** · *Wabasha-Kellogg Chamber/CVB* · Director, 137 W. Main St., P.O. Box 105, 55981, P 3,200, M 120, (651) 565-4158, (800) 565-4158, Fax (651) 565-2808, www.wabashamn.org

**Waconia** · *Waconia Area C/C* · Kellie Sites, Pres., 209 S. Vine St., 55387, P 10,000, M 200, (952) 442-5812, Fax (952) 856-4476, ksites@destinationwaconia.org, www.destinationwaconia.org

**Wadena** · *Wadena Area C/C* · Shirley Uselman, Dir., 5 Aldrich Ave. S.E., P.O. Box 107, 56482, P 4,292, M 185, (218) 632-7704, (877) 631-7704, Fax (218) 632-7705, www.wadena.org

**Walker** · *Leech Lake Area C/C* · Brian Hein, Pres., 205 Minnesota Ave., P.O. Box 1089, 56484, P 1,100, M 250, (218) 547-1313, (800) 833-1118, Fax (218) 547-1338, walker@eot.com, www.leech-lake.com

**Warren** · *Warren C/C* · Mike Williams, 120 E. Bridge Ave., 56762, P 1,675, M 65, (218) 745-5343, Fax (218) 745-5344, www. warrenminnesota.com

**Warroad** · *Warroad Area C/C* · Jon Cole, Pres., P.O. Box 551, 56763, P 2,300, M 100, (218) 386-3543, (800) 328-4455, Fax (218) 386-3454, wcoc@wiktel.com, www.warroad.org

**Waseca** · *Waseca Area C/C* · Kim Foels, Pres., 111 N. State St., 56093, P 9,827, M 240, (507) 835-3260, (888) 9-WASECA, Fax (507) 835-3267, info@wasecachamber.com, www.waseca chamber.com

**Watertown** · *Watertown C/C* · Evonne Dennis, Exec. Secy., P.O. Box 994, 55388, P 4,000, M 68, (952) 955-5175, secretary@ watertown-chamber.com, www.watertown-chamber.com

**Waterville** · *Waterville Area C/C* · Marlys Meskan, Exec. Secy., 213 Blowers, 56096, P 1,800, M 55, (507) 362-8403, (507) 362-4609, lmesk@frontiernet.net, www.watervillemn.com

**Waverly** · *see Montrose*

**Wayzata** · *Greater Wayzata Area C/C* · Peggy Douglas, Pres., 402 E. Lake St., 55391, P 4,100, M 380, (952) 473-9595, Fax (952) 473-6266, info@wayzatachamber.com, www.wayzatachamber. com

**Wells** · *Wells Area C/C* · Matt Zebro, Pres., 28 S. Broadway, P.O. Box 134, 56097, P 2,494, M 80, (507) 553-6450, (866) 553-6450, Fax (507) 553-6451, wellscc@bevcomm.net, www.cityofwells.net

**West Saint Paul** · *see Dakota County*

**Wheaton** · *Wheaton Area C/C* · P.O. Box 493, 56296, P 1,619, M 60, (320) 563-4460, www.cityofwheaton.com

**White Bear Lake** · *White Bear Area C/C* · William Dinkel, Exec. Dir., 4801 Hwy. 61, Ste. 305, 55110, P 86,000, M 300, (651) 429-8593, Fax (651) 429-8592, info@whitebearchamber.com, www. whitebearchamber.com

**White Bear Lake Township** · *see White Bear Lake*

**Willernie** · *see White Bear Lake*

**Williams** · *see Baudette*

**Willmar** · *Willmar Lakes Area C/C* · Ken Warner, Pres., 2104 E. Hwy. 12, 56201, P 42,000, M 600, (320) 235-0300, Fax (320) 231-1948, chamber@willmarareachamber.com, www.willmar areachamber.com.

**Windom** · *Windom Area C/C & Visitors Bur.* · Cheryl Hanson, Pres., 303 9th St., 56101, P 5,000, M 200, (507) 831-2752, (800) 7-WINDOM, Fax (507) 831-2755, windomchamber@windomnet. com, www.winwacc.com

**Winnebago** · *Winnebago C/C* · Scott Robertson, Pres., P.O. Box 516, 56098, P 1,500, M 40, (507) 893-4600, Fax (507) 893-3473, www.winnebago.govoffice.com

**Winona** · *Winona Area C/C* · Della Schmidt, Pres., 67 Main St., P.O. Box 870, 55987, P 27,069, M 560, (507) 452-2272, Fax (507) 454-8814, info@winonachamber.com, www.winonachamber.com

**Winsted** · *Winsted Area C/C* · Tom Ollig, Pres., P.O. Box 352, 55395, P 2,400, M 75, (320) 485-2351, info@winstedchamber.com, www.winstedchamber.com

**Winthrop** · *Winthrop Area C/C* · Doug Hanson, Exec. Secy., P.O. Box 594, 55396, P 1,800, M 85, (507) 647-2627, (800) 647-9461, winthropchamber@hotmail.com

**Woodbury** · *Woodbury C/C* · Nancy Kennedy, Ofc. Mgr., 7650 Currell Blvd., Ste. 360, 55125, P 60,000, M 260, (651) 578-0722, Fax (651) 578-7276, chamber@woodburychamber.org, www.woodburychamber.org

**Worthington** · *Worthington Area C/C* · Darlene Macklin, Exec. Dir., 1121 Third Ave., 56187, P 11,230, M 310, (507) 372-2919, Fax (507) 372-2827, wcofc@frontiernet.net, www.worthingtonmn chamber.com.

**Zimmerman** · *Greater Zimmerman Area C/C* · Deb Kazle, Admin., 12980 Fremont Ave., Ste. C, 55398, P 10,000, M 92, (763) 856-4404, Fax (763) 856-4787, zimmchamber@sherbtel.net, www.zimmermanchamber.com

# Mississippi

**Mississippi Eco.Cncl.** · Blake Wilson, Pres., P.O. Box 23276, Jackson, 39225, M 8,000, (601) 969-0022, Fax (601) 353-0247, www.mec.ms

**Aberdeen** · *Monroe County C/C* · Tony Green, Exec. Dir., 124 W. Commerce St., P.O. Box 727, 39730, P 38,014, M 300, (662) 369-6488, Fax (662) 369-6489, chamber@gomonroe.org, www.gomonroe.org.

**Amory** · *Monroe County C/C* · Tony Green, Exec. Dir., 1619 Hwy. 25 N., 38821, P 38,014, M 300, (662) 256-7194, Fax (662) 256-9671, tony@gomonroe.org, www.gomonroe.org

**Baldwyn** · *Baldwyn Mainstreet Chamber* · Lori Tucker, Exec. Dir., P.O. Box 40, 38824, P 3,600, M 85, (662) 365-1050, Fax (662) 365-3969, www.baldwyn.ms

**Batesville** · *Panola Partnership Inc.* · Sonny Simmons, CEO, 150A Public Sq., 38606, P 34,250, M 260, (662) 563-3126, (888) 872-6652, Fax (662) 563-0704, sonnysimmons@cableone.net, www.panolacounty.com.

**Bay Saint Louis** · *Hancock County C/C* · Tish Williams, Dir., 412 Hwy. 90, Ste. 6, 39520, P 42,000, M 690, (228) 467-9048, Fax (228) 467-6033, www.hancockchamber.org

**Belzoni** · *Belzoni-Humphreys Dev. Found.* · 110 Magnolia St., P.O. Box 145, 39038, P 11,000, M 60, (662) 247-4838, Fax (662) 247-4805, catfish@belzonicable.com, www.catfishcapital online.com

**Biloxi** · *Biloxi Bay C/C* · Tina Ross-Seamans, Exec. Dir., P.O. Box 889, 39533, P 60,000, M 1,200, (228) 435-6149, info@biloxi baychamber.org, www.biloxibaychamber.org

**Bolivar County** · *see Cleveland*

**Booneville** · *Booneville Area C/C* · Rhonda Greening, Exec. Dir., 100 W. Church St., P.O. Box 927, 38829, P 9,000, M 200, (662) 728-4130, (800) 300-9302, Fax (662) 728-4134, chamber@booneville mississippi.com, www.boonevillemississippi.com

**Brandon** · *Rankin County C/C* · Gale Martin, Exec. Dir., 101 Service Dr., P.O. Box 428, 39043, P 118,000, M 1,000, (601) 825-2268, Fax (601) 825-1977, information@rankinchamber.com, www.rankinchamber.com

**Brookhaven** · *Brookhaven-Lincoln County C/C* · Cliff Brumfield, Exec. V.P., 230 S. Whitworth Ave., P.O. Box 978, 39602, P 33,000, M 600, (601) 833-1411, Fax (601) 833-1412, info@ brookhavenchamber.com, www.brookhavenchamber.com

**Bruce** · *Bruce C/C* · 102 Public Sq., P.O. Box 1013, 38915, P 2,200, M 49, (662) 983-2222, Fax (662) 983-7300, chamber@ brucetelephone.com

**Burnsville** · *Burnsville C/C* · Kim Grisson, Pres., P.O. Box 211, 38833, P 1,000, M 40, (662) 427-9526

**Byhalia** · *Byhalia Area C/C* · Sarah Sawyer, Exec. Dir., 2452 Church St., P.O. Box 910, 38611, P 36,000, M 300, (662) 838-8127, Fax (662) 838-8128, info@gobyhalia.com, www.gobyhalia.com

**Calhoun City** · *Calhoun City C/C* · James Franklin, 102 S. Monroe St., P.O. Box 161, 38916, P 2,000, M 75, (662) 628-6990, Fax (662) 628-8931, www.calhouncity.net

**Canton** · *Canton C/C* · Deborah Anderson, Exec. Dir., 100 Depot Dr., P.O. Box 74, 39046, P 14,000, M 260, (601) 859-5816, Fax (601) 855-0149, ccoc@canton-mississippi.com, www.canton-mississippi.com.

**Carthage** · *Leake County C/C* · Renodda Dorman, Exec. Dir., 103 N. Pearl St., P.O. Box 209, 39051, P 20,940, M 200, (601) 267-9231, Fax (601) 267-8123, director@leakems.com, www.leakems.com

**Clarksdale** · *Clarksdale-Coahoma County C/C & Ind. Found.* · Ronald E. Hudson, Exec. Dir., P.O. Box 160, 38614, P 20,000, M 300, (662) 627-7337, Fax (662) 627-1313, chamberofcommerce@ clarksdale-ms.com, www.clarksdale-ms.com.

**Cleveland** · *Cleveland-Bolivar County C/C* · Judson Thigpen III, Exec. Dir., 600 Third St., P.O. Box 490, 38732, P 42,000, M 400, (662) 843-2712, Fax (662) 843-2718, judson@clevelandms chamber.com, www.clevelandmschamber.com

**Clinton** · *Clinton C/C* · Dianne Newman Carson, Exec. Dir., 100 E. Leake, P.O. Box 143, 39060, P 25,000, M 570, (601) 924-5912, (800) 611-9980, Fax (601) 925-4009, public-relations@clinton-chamber.org, www.clintonchamber.org

**Coffeeville** · *Coffeeville Area C/C* · Beverly Freer, Treas., P.O. Box 184, 38922, P 1,000, M 20, (662) 675-8385, www.coffeeville ms.com

**Collins** · *Covington County C/C* · Marie Shoemake, Exec. Dir., 500 Komo St., P.O. Box 1595, 39428, P 19,600, M 200, (601) 765-6012, Fax (601) 765-1740, ms@covingtonchamber.com, www.covingtonchamber.com

**Columbia** · *Marion County Dev. Partnership* · Carolyn Burton, V.P. of Chamber, 412 Courthouse Sq., P.O. Box 272, 39429, P 27,000, M 350, (601) 736-6385, Fax (601) 736-6392, info@ mcdp.info, www.mcdp.info

**Columbus** · *Columbus-Lowndes Dev. Link* · Joe Max Higgins Jr., CEO, 1102 Main St., P.O. Box 1328, 39703, P 63,000, M 680, (662) 328-8369, (800) 748-8882, Fax (662) 327-3417, info@cldlink.org, www.cldlink.org.

**Como** · *see Batesville*

**Corinth** · *The Alliance* · Gary Chandler, Pres./COO, 810 Tate St., P.O. Box 1089, 38835, P 35,000, M 360, (662) 287-5269, (877) 347-0545, Fax (662) 287-5260, alliance@corinth.ms, www.corinth.ms.

**Courtland** · *see Batesville*

**Crenshaw** · *see Batesville*

**Crystal Springs** · *Crystal Springs C/C* · Donna Y. Wells, Exec. Dir., 286 E. Railroad Ave., P.O. Box 519, 39059, P 6,005, M 145, (601) 892-2711, Fax (601) 892-4870, crystalspringschamber@gmail.com.

**Decatur** · *Greater Decatur C/C* · Brenda Harper, Pres., P.O. Box 474, 39327, P 1,420, M 60, (601) 635-2761

**DeKalb** · *Kemper County C/C* · Juanice Evans, Exec. Dir., 14064 Industrial Park Dr., P.O. Box 518, 39328, P 10,000, M 300, (601) 743-2754, Fax (601) 743-2760, www.kempercounty.com

**D'Iberville** · *D'Iberville-St. Martin Area C/C* · Carol Heyliger, Pres., P.O. Box 6054, 39540, P 10,000, M 265, (228) 392-2293, Fax (228) 396-3216, dsmchmbr@datasync.com, www.dsmchamber.com

**Drew** · *Drew C/C* · 129 Shaw Ave., 38737, P 2,500, M 90, (662) 745-8975, www.drew-ms.netfirms.com

**Flora** · *see Ridgeland-Madison County C/C*

**Forest** · *Forest Area C/C* · Mandi Arinder, Exec. Dir., 120 S. Davis St., P.O. Box 266, 39074, P 6,000, M 200, (601) 469-4332, Fax (601) 469-3224, chamberguide@bellsouth.net, www.forest mschamber.com

**Fulton** · *Itawamba County Dev. Cncl.* · Greg Deakle, Exec. Dir., 107 W. Wiygul St., P.O. Box 577, 38843, P 22,000, M 320, (662) 862-4571, (800) 371-8642, Fax (662) 862-5637, icdc@itawamba.com, www.itawamba.com

**Greenville** · *Delta Eco. Dev. Center* · Sheree Hobart, Exec. Dir., 342 Washington Ave., Ste. 101, P.O. Box 933, 38702, P 72,000, M 600, (662) 378-3141, Fax (662) 378-3143, generalinfo@deltaedc.com, www.greenvilleareachamber.com

**Greenwood** · *Greenwood-Leflore County C/C* · Beth Stevens, Exec. Dir., 402 Hwy. 82 W., P.O. Box 848, 38935, P 19,000, M 700, (662) 453-4152, Fax (662) 453-8003, info@greenwoodms.com, www.greenwoodms.com.

**Grenada** · *Grenada County C/C* · Phillip Heard, Exec. Dir., P.O. Box 628, 38902, P 23,263, M 400, (662) 226-2571, (800) 373-2571, Fax (662) 226-9745, www.grenadamississippi.com

**Gulfport** · *Mississippi Gulf Coast C/C* · Kimberly Nastasi, Exec. V.P./CEO, 11975 Seaway Rd., Ste. B-120, 39503, P 141,000, M 1,100, (228) 604-0014, Fax (228) 604-0105, info@mscoast chamber.com, www.mscoastchamber.com

**Hattiesburg** · *Area Dev. Partnership* · Angie Godwin, Pres., One Convention Center Plaza, 39401, P 138,932, M 1,500, (601) 296-7500, (800) 238-HATT, Fax (601) 296-7505, adp@theadp.com, www.theadp.com.

**Hazlehurst** · *Hazlehurst Area C/C* · Randall Day, Exec. Dir., P.O. Box 446, 39083, P 4,500, M 100, (601) 894-3752, Fax (601) 894-3752, hazlechamber@bellsouth.net

**Hernando** · *Hernando Main Street Chamber of Commerce* · Angie Hicks, Exec. Dir., 2465 Hwy. 51 S., 38632, P 13,800, M 340, (662) 429-9055, Fax (662) 429-2909, chamber@hernandoms.org, www.hernandoms.org

**Holly Springs** · *Holly Springs C/C* · Amy S. Heaton, Exec. Dir., 148 E. College Ave., 38635, P 8,000, M 200, (662) 252-2943, Fax (662) 252-2934, director@hschamber.org, www.hschamber.org

**Horn Lake** · *Horn Lake C/C* · Larry Witherspoon, Exec. Dir., 3010 Goodman Rd. W., Ste. B, 38637, P 25,000, M 310, (662) 393-9897, Fax (662) 393-2942, info@hornlakechamber.com, www.horn lakechamber.com

**Houston** · *Chickasaw Dev. Found.* · Joyce East, Exec. Dir., 635 Starkville Rd., 38851, P 19,000, M 160, (662) 456-2321

**Indianola** · *Indianola C/C* · Sheila R. Waldrup, Exec. Dir., P.O. Box 151, 38751, P 12,000, M 225, (662) 887-4454, (877) 816-7581, Fax (662) 887-4454, icoc@tecinfo.com, www.indianolams.org

**Inverness** · *Inverness C/C* · Beth Evans, P.O. Box 13, 38753, P 1,153, M 105, (662) 265-6060, (662) 265-5741, bethevans@in-ms.org, www.in-ms.org

**Jackson** · *Greater Jackson Chamber Partnership* · Duane O'Neill, Pres./CEO, 201 S. President St., Post Office Box 22548, 39225, P 512,000, M 2,200, (601) 948-7575, Fax (601) 352-5539, doneill@greaterjacksonpartnership.com, www.greaterjackson partnership.com.

**Laurel** · *Jones County C/C* · Donna Williams, Dir., 153 Base Dr., Ste. 3, P.O. Box 527, 39441, P 64,958, M 450, (601) 428-0574, Fax (601) 428-2047, www.jonescounty.com, info@edajones.com, www.edajones.com.

**Leland** · *Leland C/C* · Robert Neill, Exec. Dir., 206 Broad St., P.O. Box 67, 38756, P 5,000, M 100, (662) 686-2687, Fax (662) 686-2689, lcoc@tecinfo.com, www.lelandms.org

**Lexington** · *Holmes County C/C* · Jean Carson, Exec. Dir., 104 W. China St., Ste. A, 39095, P 21,609, M 75, (662) 834-3372, Fax (662) 834-4544

**Liberty** · *Liberty Area C/C* · Cheryl Blalock, Secy./Treas., P.O. Box 18, 39645, P 700, M 50, (601) 657-8051

**Long Beach** · *see Gulfport*

**Louisville** · *Louisville-Winston County C/C* · Linda Skelton, Dir., 311 W. Park St., P.O. Box 551, 39339, P 20,160, M 200, (662) 773-3921, Fax (662) 773-8909, linda@winstoncounty.com, www.winstoncounty.com

**Lucedale** · *George County C/C & Eco. Dev. Found.* · Mike Smith, Pres., 116 Beaver Dam Rd., P.O. Box 441, 39452, P 21,828, M 130, (601) 947-2755, Fax (601) 947-2650, georgecountyedf@bellsouth.net

**Lyman** · *see Gulfport*

**Macon** · *Noxubee County C/C & Eco. Dev. Ofc.* · Jim Robbins, 503 S. Washington St., P.O. Box 308, 39341, P 12,548, M 100, (662) 726-4456, (800) 487-0165, Fax (662) 726-1041, noxubeecounty chamber@yahoo.com

**Madison** · *Madison C/C* · Rosie Vassallo, Exec. Dir., 1239 Hwy. 51 N, P.O. Box 544, 39130, P 20,000, M 800, (601) 856-7060, Fax (601) 856-4852, info@madisonthecitychamber.com, www.madisonthecitychamber.com.

**Magee** · *Magee C/C* · Beulah Stephens, Dir., 117 N.W. 1st Ave., 39111, P 5,000, M 200, (601) 849-2517, Fax (601) 849-2517, commercechamber@bellsouth.net

**Magnolia** · *South Pike Area C/C* · Sherri O'Brian, Secy., 180 S. Cherry, 39652, P 2,071, M 45, (601) 783-5267, (601) 783-0550

**McComb** · *Pike County C/C & Eco. Dev. Dist.* · J. Britt Herrin, Exec. Dir., 112 N. Railroad Blvd., P.O. Box 83, 39648, P 38,000, M 450, (601) 684-2291, Fax (601) 684-4899, pcedd@pikeinfo.com, www.pikeinfo.com

**Meadville** · *Franklin C/C* · Brad Jones, Pres., 36 Main St., P.O. Box 400, 39653, P 9,000, M 200, (601) 384-2305, www.franklin countyms.com

**Mendenhall** · *Mendenhall Area C/C* · Marsha Bratcher, Secy., P.O. Box 635, 39114, P 2,555, M 125, (601) 847-1725

**Meridian** · *East Mississippi Bus. Dev. Corp.* · Wade Jones, Pres., 1901 Front St., Ste. A, P.O. Box 790, 39302, P 78,000, M 700, (601) 693-1306, Fax (601) 693-5638, info@embdc.org, www.embdc.org.

**Monticello** · *Lawrence County C/C* · Bob Smira, Pres./CEO, 517 Broad St. E., P.O. Box 996, 39654, P 13,000, M 80, (601) 587-3007, Fax (601) 587-0765, bsmira@lccda.org, www.lccda.org

**Moorhead** · *Moorhead C/C* · Byron Wright, V.P., P.O. Box 177, 38761, P 3,500, M 22, (662) 207-0084, bryonsr@hotmail.com

**Morton** · *Morton C/C* · Brenda M. McCaughn, Exec. Dir., P.O. Box 530, 39117, P 3,500, M 100, (601) 732-6135, Fax (601) 732-7188, www.cityofmorton.com

**Natchez** · *Natchez-Adams County C/C* · Debbie Hudson, Pres./ CEO, 211 Main St., Ste. A, P.O. Box 1403, 39121, P 35,000, M 350, (601) 445-4611, Fax (601) 445-9361, chamber@natchezchamber. com, www.natchezchamber.com

**Newton** · *Newton C/C* · Kay Crenshaw, Pres., P.O. Box 301, 39345, P 4,000, M 150, (601) 683-2201, Fax (601) 683-2201, chamber newton@bellsouth.net, www.newtonmschamber.com

**Ocean Springs** · *Ocean Springs C/C* · Margaret Miller, Exec. Dir., 1000 Washington Ave., 39564, P 18,000, M 600, (228) 875-4424, Fax (228) 875-0332, mail@oceanspringschamber.com, www. oceanspringschamber.com

**Okolona** · *Okolona Area C/C-Main Street Program* · Linda M. Carnathan, Dir., 219 Main St., P.O. Box 446, 38860, P 3,056, M 150, (662) 447-5913, Fax (662) 447-0254, linda@okolonams.org, www. okolonams.org

**Olive Branch** · *Olive Branch C/C* · Vickie DuPree, Exec. Dir., 9123 Pigeon Roost, P.O. Box 608, 38654, P 34,000, M 560, (662) 895-2600, Fax (662) 895-2625, info@olivebranchms.com, www. olivebranchms.com.

**Orange Grove** · *see Gulfport*

**Oxford** · *Oxford-Lafayette County C/C* · Max D. Hipp CID, Pres./ CEO, 299 W. Jackson, P.O. Box 147, 38655, P 40,000, M 700, (662) 234-4651, Fax (662) 234-4655, info@oxfordms.com, www. oxfordms.com

**Pascagoula** · *Jackson County C/C* · Carla Todd, Pres./CEO, 720 Krebs Ave., P.O. Box 480, 39568, P 134,000, M 850, (228) 762-3391, Fax (228) 769-1726, chamber@jcchamber.com, www.jcchamber.com

**Pass Christian** · *see Gulfport*

**Pearl** · *Pearl C/C* · Kathy Deer, Exec. Dir., 110 George Wallace Dr., P.O. Box 54125, 39288, P 27,000, M 350, (601) 939-3338, Fax (601) 936-5717, chamber@pearlms.org, www.pearlms.org

**Petal** · *Petal Area C/C* · Deborah Reynolds, Pres., 712 S. Main St., Ste. B, P.O. Box 421, 39465, P 10,000, M 250, (601) 583-3306, Fax (601) 583-3312, dacofc@aol.com, www.petalchamber.com

**Philadelphia** · *Community Dev. Partnership* · David Vowell, Pres., 256 W. Beacon St., P.O. Box 330, 39350, P 30,000, M 220, (601) 656-1000, (877) 752-2643, Fax (601) 656-1066, info@ neshoba.org, www.neshoba.org

**Picayune** · *Greater Picayune Area C/C* · April Parsons, Exec. Dir., 201 Hwy. 11 N., P.O. Box 448, 39466, P 29,000, M 465, (601) 798-3122, Fax (601) 798-3122, chambercommerce1@bellsouth. net, www.picayunechamber.org.

**Pontotoc** · *Pontotoc County C/C* · Cecilia Derrington, Exec. Dir., 109 N. Main, P.O. Box 530, 38863, P 28,581, M 200, (662) 489-5042, Fax (662) 489-5263, chamber@pontotocchamber.com, www.pontotocchamber.com

**Pope** · *see Batesville*

**Poplarville** · *Poplarville C/C* · Teresa Penton, Pres., P.O. Box 367, 39470, P 3,000, M 100, (601) 795-0578, Fax (601) 795-0578, poplarvillechamber@gmail.com, www.poplarville.org

**Port Gibson** · *Port Gibson-Claiborne County C/C* · Judith Scruggs, Exec. Dir., 1601 Church St., P.O. Box 491, 39150, P 11,831, M 60, (601) 437-4351, judyscruggs@bellsouth.net, www.port gibsononthemississippi.com

**Prentiss** · *Jefferson Davis County C/C* · Missy Chain, Secy., P.O. Box 1797, 39474, P 1,400, M 100, (601) 792-5142, Fax (601) 792-5190

**Quitman** · *Clarke County C/C* · Tony Fleming, Pres., P.O. Box 172, 39355, P 17,877, M 160, (601) 776-5701, Fax (601) 776-5745, clarkechamber@att.net, www.visitclarkecounty.com

**Raymond** · *Raymond C/C* · John Barber, Exec. Dir., P.O. Box 1162, 39154, P 4,000, M 75, (601) 857-8942, www.raymondchamber.com

**Ridgeland** · *City of Ridgeland C/C* · Linda T. Bynum, Exec. Dir., 754 Pear Orchard Rd., P.O. Box 194, 39158, P 26,000, M 950, (601) 991-9996, Fax (601) 991-9997, admin@ridgelandchamber.com, www.ridgelandchamber.com.

**Ridgeland** · *Madison County C/C* · Dianne Dyar, Exec. Dir., 618 Crescent Blvd., Ste. 101, 39157, P 72,000, M 450, (601) 605-2554, Fax (601) 605-2260, info@madisoncountychamber.com, www. madisoncountychamber.com

**Ruleville** · *Ruleville C/C* · Thelma Johnson, Pres., 200 N. Front Ave., P.O. Box 552, 38771, P 3,500, M 75, (662) 402-0727, (662) 756-2249, Fax (662) 756-0187, jofroth@cableone.net

**Sardis** · *Sardis-Sardis Lake C/C* · P.O. Box 377, 38666, P 2,250, M 75, (662) 487-3451, Fax (662) 487-3451, www.sardislake.com

**Senatobia** · *Tate County C/C, Eco. Dev. Found. & Main St.* · J.E. Mortimer, Exec. Dir., 135 N. Front St., 38668, P 27,000, M 260, (662) 562-8715, Fax (662) 562-5786, www.tate-county.com, jemortimer@cityofsenatobia.com, www.cityofsenatobia.com

**Southaven** · *Southaven C/C* · Ginger Adams, Exec. Dir., 8700 Northwest Dr., P.O. Box 211, 38671, P 40,000, M 600, (662) 342-6114, (800) 272-6551, Fax (662) 342-6365, info@southaven chamber.com, www.southavenchamber.com

**Starkville** · *Greater Starkville Dev. Partnership/Chamber* · Allison Matthews, V.P. of Mbrshp. Dev., 200 E. Main St., 39759, P 38,375, M 387, (662) 323-3322, Fax (662) 323-5815, info@ starkville.org, www.starkville.org.

**Tunica** · *Tunica County C/C* · Lyn Arnold, Pres./CEO, 1301 Main St., P.O. Box 1888, 38676, P 10,930, M 323, (662) 363-2865, Fax (662) 357-0378, larnold@tunicachamber.com, www.tunica chamber.com

**Tupelo** · *Comm. Dev. Found.* · David Rumbarger, Pres./CEO, 300 W. Main St., P.O. Box A, 38802, P 40,000, M 1,400, (662) 842-4521, Fax (662) 841-0693, info@cdfms.org, www.cdfms.org

**Tylertown** · *Walthall County C/C* · Jewel Magee, Pres., P.O. Box 227, 39667, P 15,380, M 172, (601) 876-2680, Fax (601) 876-2680, walthallchamber@bellsouth.net, www.walthallcountychamber.org

**Union** · *Union C/C* · John Knoop, Pres., P.O. Box 90, 39365, P 2,105, M 150, (601) 774-9586, Fax (601) 774-9586, union commerce@bellsouth.net, www.unionms.com.

**Vicksburg** · *Vicksburg-Warren County C/C* · Christi Kilroy, Exec. Dir., 2020 Mission 66, 39180, P 50,000, M 400, (601) 636-1012, Fax (601) 636-4422, info@vicksburgchamber.org, www.vicksburg chamber.org

**Water Valley** · *Water Valley Area C/C* · Bonnie Cox, Ofc. Mgr., 206 Main St., P.O. Box 726, 38965, P 4,100, M 73, (662) 473-1122, (877) 604-5462, Fax (662) 473-1477, wvchamber@bellsouth.net, www.watervalleychamber.info

**Waynesboro** · *Wayne County C/C* · Tim Williams, Pres., 802 Station St., P.O. Box 864, 39367, P 20,000, M 100, (601) 735-3311, (601) 735-5050, waynesboroinfo@gmail.com, www.waynesboro info.com

**Wesson** · *Wesson C/C* · Clara Crow, V.P., P.O. Box 557, 39191, P 1,693, M 75, (601) 643-5000, Fax (601) 643-5000

**Winston County** · *see Louisville*

**Yazoo City** · *Yazoo County C/C* · Henry Cote, Exec. Dlr., 212 E. Broadway, P.O. Box 172, 39194, P 28,000, M 175, (662) 746-1273, Fax (662) 746-7238, ccyazoo@bellsouth.net, www.yazoochamber.org

# Missouri

**Missouri C of C & Ind.** · Daniel P. Mehan, Pres./CEO, 428 E. Capitol Ave., P.O. Box 149, Jefferson City, 65102, P 4,500,000, M 2,864, (573) 634-3511, Fax (573) 634-8855, dmehan@ mochamber.com, www.mochamber.com

**Affton** · *Affton C/C* · Joan Edleson, Exec. Dir., 10203 Gravois Rd., 63123, P 40,000, M 320, (314) 849-6499, info@afftonchamber. com, www.afftonchamber.com

**Albany** · *Albany C/C* · Connie Worden, Pres., 106 E. Clay St., 64402, P 2,000, M 55, (660) 726-3935, cityhall@albanymo.net, www.albanymo.net

**Anderson** · *Anderson Area C/C* · Susan McCormick, P.O. Box 1217, 64831, P 3,000, M 120, (417) 845-8200, (417) 845-3351, chamber@andersonmo.org, www.andersonmo.org

**Arnold** · *Arnold C/C* · Bob Gruenewald, Pres., 1838 Old Lemay Ferry Rd., 63010, P 20,000, M 150, (636) 296-1910, kelly@arnold chamber.org, www.arnoldchamber.org

**Augusta** · *Greater Augusta C/C* · Vic Brown, Pres., P.O. Box 31, 63332, P 216, M 55, (636) 228-4005, Fax (636) 228-0000, anchor millinn@msn.com, www.augusta-chamber.org

**Aurora** · *Aurora C/C* · Shannon Walker, Exec. Dir., 121 E. Olive, P.O. Box 257, 65605, P 7,014, M 185, (417) 678-4150, Fax (417) 678-1387, auroracoc@mo-net.com, www.auroramochamber.com

**Ava** · *Ava Area C/C* · 810 S.W. 13th Ave., P.O. Box 1103, 65608, P 13,500, M 126, (417) 683-4594, Fax (417) 683-9464, director@ avachamber.org, www.avachamber.org

**Ballwin** · *see Manchester*

**Belton** · *Belton C/C* · Terri McEneany, Exec. Dir., 323 Main, P.O. Box 350, 64012, P 22,000, M 316, (816) 331-2420, Fax (816) 331-8736, chamber@beltonmochamber.com, www.beltonmochamber.com

**Berkeley** · *see Ferguson*

**Bethany** · *Bethany Area C/C* · Jeff Nichols, Pres., 116 N. 16th St., 64424, P 3,100, M 74, (660) 425-6358, Fax (660) 425-0123, staff@ bethanyareachamber.com, www.bethanyareachamber.com

**Blue Springs** · *Blue Springs C/C* · Lara Vermillion, Exec. Dir., 1000 S.W. Main, 64015, P 53,000, M 400, (816) 229-8558, Fax (816) 229-1244, info@bluespringschamber.com, www. bluespringschamber.com

**Bolivar** · *Bolivar Area C/C* · Diana Leslie, Exec. Dir., 454 S. Springfield, P.O. Box 202, 65613, P 10,500, M 250, (417) 326-4118, Fax (417) 777-9080, bolchamb@windstream.net, www.bolivar chamber.com

**Bonne Terre** · *Bonne Terre C/C* · Marty Umfleet, Pres., 11 S.W. Main St., P.O. Box 175, 63628, P 4,003, M 146, (573) 358-4000, Fax (573) 358-0071, btchamberofcommerce@yahoo.com, www. bonneterrechamber.com

**Boonville** · *Boonville Area C/C* · Lisa McClary, Exec. Dir., 320 First St., Ste. A, 65233, P 8,202, M 350, (660) 882-2721, Fax (660) 882-5660, execdir2200@sbcglobal.net, www.boonvillemo chamberofcommerce.com

**Bowling Green** · *Bowling Green C/C & CVB* · Donna Colbert, Exec. Dir., 16A W. Church St., 63334, P 5,166, M 80, (573) 324-3733, bgmocc@att.net, www.bgchamber.org

**Branson** · *Branson/Lakes Area C/C* · Ross Summers, Pres./ CEO, 269 State Hwy. 248, P.O. Box 1897, 65615, P 30,000, M 1,000, (417) 334-4084, (800) 214-3661, Fax (417) 334-4139, info@ bransoncvb.com, www.explorebranson.com

**Braymer** · *Braymer C/C* · MaryLou Tuck, Treas., 2nd & Main St., 64624, P 900, M 50, (660) 645-2802

**Breckenridge Hills** · *see Bridgeton*

**Brentwood** · *Brentwood C/C* · Christine Albrecht, Secy., 8754 Rosalie Ave., 63144, P 9,000, M 150, (314) 963-9007, chamber@ brentwoodmo.org, www.brentwoodmochamber.org

**Bridgeton** · *Northwest C/C* · Larry Perney, Exec. Dir., 11965 St. Charles Rock Rd., Ste. 203, 63044, P 90,000, M 350, (314) 291-2131, Fax (314) 291-2153, tina@northwestchamber.com, www. northwestchamber.com

**Brookfield** · *Brookfield Area C/C* · Fran Graff, Dir., 101 S. Main St., 64628, P 4,888, M 143, (660) 258-7255, Fax (660) 258-7255, chamber@brookfieldmochamber.com, www.brookfieldmo chamber.com

**Brunswick** · *Brunswick Area C/C* · Colleen Johnson, Secy., P.O. Box 104, 65236, P 925, M 41, (660) 548-3171, (660) 548-3028, info@brunswickmo.com, www.brunswickmo.com

**Buckner** · *Buckner C/C* · Patrick Farrell, Pres., P.O. Box 325, 64016, P 2,725, M 50, (816) 650-5535

**Buffalo** · *Buffalo Area C/C* · Kathy Kesler, Exec. Dir., 101 N. Maple, P.O. Box 258, 65622, P 2,781, M 100, (417) 345-2852, Fax same, chamber@buffalococ.com, www.buffalococ.com

**Butler** · *Butler Area C/C* · Pat Decker, Exec. Dir., 7 W. Dakota, 64730, P 5,000, M 150, (660) 679-3380, Fax (660) 679-6636, executive director@butlermochamber.org, www.butlermochamber.org.

**Cabool** · *Cabool Area C/C* · Debbie Lemon, Dir., P.O. Box 285, 65689, P 2,006, M 82, (417) 962-3002, Fax (417) 962-3002, cabool_2@hotmail.com, caboolchamber.com

**California** · *California Area C/C* · Ruth Ellis, Exec. Secy., P.O. Box 85, 65018, P 4,200, M 120, (573) 796-3040, Fax (573) 796-8309, office@calmo.com, www.calmo.com

**Camdenton** · *Camdenton Area C/C* · Bruce Mitchell, Exec. Dir., 739 W. U.S. Hwy. 54, P.O. Box 1375, 65020, P 15,000, M 500, (573) 346-2227, (800) 769-1004, Fax (573) 346-3496, info@camdenton chamber.com, www.camdentonchamber.com.

**Cameron** · *Cameron Area C/C* · Artis Stoebener, Exec. Dir., 205 N. Main St., 64429, P 9,788, M 170, (816) 632-2005, office@ cameronmochamber.com, cameronmochamber.com

**Canton** · *Canton C/C* · Jarrod Phillips, Pres., P.O. Box 141, 63435, P 2,600, M 75, (573) 288-2686, www.showmecanton.com

**Cape Fair** · *Cape Fair C/C* · Chuck Mills, Pres., P.O. Box 104, 65624, P 600, M 45, (417) 538-2222, info@capefairchamber.com, www.capefairchamber.com

**Cape Girardeau** · *Cape Girardeau Area C/C* · John E. Mehner, Pres./CEO, 1267 N. Mount Auburn Rd., 63701, P 75,000, M 1,300, (573) 335-3312, Fax (573) 335-4686, info@capechamber.com, www.capechamber.com.

**Carl Junction** · *Carl Junction Area C/C* · Jerry Botts, Pres., P.O. Box 301, 64834, P 6,200, M 60, (417) 649-7255, www.carljunctioncc.com, www.carljunction.org

**Carrollton** · *Carrollton C/C* · Sharon Metz, Exec. Dir., 111 N. Mason, 64633, P 4,100, M 150, (660) 542-0922, Fax (660) 542-3489, director@carrolltonareachamber.org, www.carrollton areachamber.org

**Carthage** · *Carthage C/C* · John Bode, Pres., 402 S. Garrison Ave., 64836, P 15,000, M 350, (417) 358-2373, Fax (417) 358-7479, info@carthagechamber.com, www.carthagechamber.com

**Caruthersville** · *Caruthersville C/C* · Bobby Culler, Pres., 200 W. 3rd, P.O. Box 806, 63830, P 6,760, M 200, (573) 333-1222, Fax (573) 333-4586, chamber@caruthersvillecity.com, www.caruthersvillecity.com

**Cassville** · *Cassville Area C/C* · Amy White, Exec. Dir., 504 Main St., 65625, P 3,500, M 200, (417) 847-2814, cassville@mo-net.com, www.cassville.com

**Centralia** · *Centralia C/C* · Ginny Zoellers, Exec. Dir., 101 W. Singleton, P.O. Box 235, 65240, P 3,800, M 91, (573) 682-2272, Fax (573) 682-1111, centralia.missouri.org

**Chaffee** · *Chaffee C/C* · Leslie Horman, Pres., P.O. Box 35, 63740, P 3,500, M 60, (573) 887-3558

**Charlack** · *see Bridgeton*

**Charleston** · *Charleston C/C* · Claudia Arington, Exec. Dir., 110 E. Commercial St., P.O. Box 407, 63834, P 4,600, M 190, (573) 683-6509, Fax (573) 683-6799, chamber@charlestonmo.org, www.charlestonmo.org

**Chesterfield** · *Chesterfield C/C* · Joan Schmelig, Pres., 101 Chesterfield Business Pkwy., 63005, P 50,000, M 950, (636) 532-3399, tourism (888) 242-4262, Fax (636) 532-7446, joan@chesterfieldmochamber.com, www.chesterfieldmochamber.com.

**Chillicothe** · *Chillicothe Area C/C* · Garni Churan, Exec. Dir., 514 Washington St., P.O. Box 407, 64601, P 10,000, M 300, (660) 646-4050, (877) 224-4554, Fax (660) 646-3309, chamber@chillicothemo.com, www.chillicothemo.com

**Clarksville** · *Main Street Clarksville* · Marge Greenwell, Chair, 104 Howard St., P.O. Box 238, 63336, P 480, M 25, (573) 242-3993, (573) 242-3994, mainstclarksville@att.net, www.clarksvillemo.com

**Clayton** · *Clayton C/C* · Ellen Gale, Exec. Dir., 225 S. Meramec Ave., Ste. 300, 63105, P 13,000, M 450, (314) 726-3033, Fax (314) 726-0637, ccc@claytoncommerce.com, www.claytoncommerce.com

**Clinton** · *Clinton Area C/C* · Charles Dibble, Exec. Dir., 200 S. Main, The Depot, 64735, P 10,000, M 370, (660) 885-8166, (800) 222-5251, Fax (660) 885-8168, information@clintonmochamber.com, www.clintonmochamber.com.

**Cole Camp** · *Cole Camp C/C* · Judy Harris, 108 S. Maple, P.O. Box 3, 65325, P 1,100, M 60, (660) 668-2295, www.colecampmo.com

**Columbia** · *Columbia C/C* · Donald M. Laird, Pres., 300 S. Providence Rd., P.O. Box 1016, 65205, P 150,000, M 1,300, (573) 874-1132, Fax (573) 443-3986, dlaird@columbiamochamber.com, www.columbiamochamber.com.

**Concord** · *see South County*

**Concordia** · *Concordia Area C/C* · Cara Harris, Exec. Dir., 802 S. Gordon, P.O. Box 143, 64020, P 2,360, M 100, (660) 463-2454, Fax (660) 463-2845, concordiachamber@centurytel.net, www.concordiamo.com

**Cool Valley** · *see Ferguson*

**Crane** · *Crane C/C* · Andrea Jackson, Pres., P.O. Box 287, 65633, P 1,250, M 40, (417) 723-0031, www.cranechamber.com

**Crestwood** · *Crestwood-Sunset Hills Area C/C* · Mary Ann McWilliams, Exec. Dir., 9058-A Watson, 63126, P 20,000, M 275, (314) 843-8545, Fax (314) 843-8526, info@ourchamber.com, www.ourchamber.com

**Creve Coeur** · *Creve Coeur-Olivette C/C* · Nancy M. Gray, Exec. V.P., 677 N. New Ballas, Ste. 214, 63141, P 20,000, M 300, (314) 569-3536, Fax (314) 569-3073, info@ccochamber.com, www.ccochamber.com

**Crocker** · *Crocker Comm. C/C* · Marty White, Secy., P.O. Box 833, 65452, P 1,077, M 35, (573) 736-2156, Fax (573) 736-5438

**Crystal City** · *see Festus*

**Cuba** · *Cuba Area C/C & Visitor Center* · Norma Bretz, Secy., 71 Hwy. P, P.O. Box 405, 65453, P 3,500, M 165, (573) 885-2531, (877) 212-8429, Fax (573) 885-0988, cuba@misn.com, www.cubamochamber.com

**De Soto** · *De Soto C/C* · Cindy Valle, Ofc. Coord., 412 S. Main St., 63020, P 6,300, M 150, (636) 586-5591, Fax (636) 586-5591, chamber@desotomo.com, www.desotomo.com

**Dellwood** · *see Ferguson*

**Des Peres** · *see Kirkwood*

**Desloge** · *Desloge C/C* · Debbie Kester, 200 N. Lincoln, 63601, P 4,802, M 50, (573) 431-3006, deslogechamber@sbcglobal.net, www.deslogechamber.com

**Dexter** · *Dexter C/C* · Janet Coleman, Exec. Dir., 515 W. Market, P.O. Box 21, 63841, P 13,000, M 313, (573) 624-7458, (800) 332-8857, Fax (573) 624-7459, info@dexterchamber.com, www.dexterchamber.com.

**Doniphan** · *Ripley County C/C* · Tracey Holden, Exec. Dir., 101 Washington St., 63935, P 13,781, M 130, (573) 996-2212, Fax (573) 351-1441, ripleyco@semo.net, www.ripleycountymissouri.org

**Earth City** · *see Bridgeton*

**East Prairie** · *East Prairie C/C* · Clinton Wolford, Pres., 106 S. Washington, 63845, P 3,713, M 100, (573) 649-5243, Fax (573) 649-2024, eastprairiechamber@yahoo.com, www.eastprairiemo.net

**Edgerton** · *Edgerton C/C* · Bobby Eckstein, V.P., 20453 Hwy. B, 64444, P 533, M 32, (816) 790-3296

**Edmundson** · *see Bridgeton*

**El Dorado Springs** · *El Dorado Springs C/C* · DeeDee Hunter, Exec. Dir., 1303 S. Hwy. 32, 64744, P 4,000, M 125, (417) 876-4154, Fax (417) 876-4154, info@eldomo-cofc.org, www.eldomo-cofc.org

**Eldon** · *Eldon Area C/C* · Diane Gollihugh, Chamber Coord., 203 E. First St., P.O. Box 209, 65026, P 5,000, M 250, (573) 392-3752, Fax (573) 392-0634, diane@eldonchamber.com, www.eldonchamber.com.

**Ellington** · *Ellington C/C* · David Burns, Pres., P.O. Box 515, 63638, P 1,000, M 55, (573) 663-7997, chamber@ellingtonmo.com, www.ellingtonmo.com

**Ellisville** · *see Manchester*

**Elsberry** · *Elsberry C/C* · Michael Short, Pres., P.O. Box 32, 63343, P 2,400, M 40, (573) 898-2318, chamber.info@elsberrycofc.org, www.elsberrycofc.org

**Elvins** · *see Park Hills*

**Eminence** · *Eminence Area C/C* · Carol Chrisco, Pres., P.O. Box 415, 65466, P 600, M 80, (573) 226-3318, chamber@eminencemo.com, www.eminencemo.com

**Esther** · *see Park Hills*

**Eureka** · *Eureka C/C* · Tracie Bibb, Pres., 208 N. Central Ave., Ste. D, 63025, P 9,500, M 300, (636) 938-6062, assocdirector@eurekachamber.us, www.eurekachamber.us

**Excelsior Springs** · *Excelsior Springs C/C* · Terry Smelcer, Exec. Dir., 461 S. Thompson, P.O. Box 632, 64024, P 11,800, M 226, (816) 630-6161, Fax (816) 630-7500, escoc@sbcglobal.net, www.exspgschamber.com

**Fair Grove** · *Fair Grove Area C/C* · Renee Bradford, Pres., P.O. Box 91, 65648, P 1,107, M 62, (417) 759-2807, info@87main.com, www.fairgrovemo.org

**Farmington** · *Farmington C/C* · Ursula Kthiri, Exec. Dir., 302 N. Washington St., P.O. Box 191, 63640, P 14,000, M 400, (573) 756-3615, Fax (573) 756-1003, ursulak@farmingtonmo.org, www.farmingtonmo.org

**Fayette** · *Fayette Area C/C* · Michael Dimond, Pres., P.O. Box 414, 65248, P 4,000, M 50, (573) 449-2561, info@fayettemochamber.com, www.fayettemochamber.com

**Fenton** · *Fenton Area C/C* · Jeannie Braun, Exec. Dir., 964 S. Hwy. Dr. #103, 63026, P 54,000, M 440, (636) 717-0200, Fax (636) 717-0214, exdir@fentonmochamber.com, www.fentonmochamber.com

**Ferguson** · *North County C/C* · Jean Montgomery, Exec. Dir., 119 Church St., Ste. 135, 63135, P 60,003, M 1,400, (314) 521-6000, Fax (314) 521-2897, nccc@northcountycc.com, www.northcountycc.org

**Festus** · *Twin City Area C/C* · Claudia Kirn, Admin., 114 Main St., 63028, P 20,000, M 350, (636) 937-7697, (636) 931-7697, Fax (636) 937-0925, twincity.chamber@sbcglobal.net, www.twincity.org.

**Flat River** · *see Park Hills*

**Florissant** · *Greater North County C/C* · Diana Weidinger, Pres., 420 Washington St., 63031, P 140,000, M 650, (314) 831-3500, Fax (314) 831-9682, diana@greaternorthcountychamber.com, www.greaternorthcountychamber.com

**Forsyth** · *Forsyth C/C* · Donna Bassett, Exec. Dir., 16075 U.S. Hwy. 160, P.O. Box 777, 65653, P 1,700, M 160, (417) 546-2741, Fax (417) 546-4192, forsyth.chamber@yahoo.com, www.forsythmissouri.org.

**Fredericktown** · *Madison County C/C* · Christina Mattingly, Exec. Dir., P.O. Box 505, 63645, P 15,728, M 100, (573) 783-2604, Fax (573) 783-2645, ftownchamber@sbcglobal.net, www.fredericktownmissouri.net

**Frontenac** · *see Town & Country*

**Fulton** · *Kingdom of Callaway C/C* · Nancy Lewis, Exec. Dir., 409 Court St., 65251, P 40,766, M 285, (573) 642-3055, (800) 257-3554, Fax (573) 642-5182, cocommerce@sbcglobal.net, callawaychamber.com.

**Gainesville** · *Ozark County C/C* · Cleta Tevebaugh, Ofc. Mgr., P.O. Box 605, 65655, P 1,000, M 85, (417) 679-4913, www.ozarkcounty.net

**Gerald** · *Gerald Area C/C* · Pat Holland, Pres., P.O. Box 274, 63037, P 1,300, M 105, (573) 764-4627, www.fidnet.com/~geraldcc

**Gladstone** · *Gladstone Area C/C* · Amy Harlin, Pres., 6913 N. Cherry St., 64118, P 28,000, M 395, (816) 436-4523, Fax (816) 436-4352, info@gladstonechamber.com, www.gladstonechamber.com

**Glasgow** · *Glasgow C/C* · Stephanie Fuemmeler, P.O. Box 192, 65254, P 1,300, M 50, (660) 338-2300, www.glasgowmo.com

**Grain Valley** · *Grain Valley C/C* · Cindy Panza, Exec. Dir., P.O. Box 195, 64029, P 11,000, M 138, (816) 847-2627, Fax (816) 847-2555, info@grainvalleychamber.org, www.grainvalleychamber.org

**Grandview** · *Grandview Area C/C* · Kim Curtis, Pres., 12500 S. 71 Hwy., Ste. 100, 64030, P 25,500, M 280, (816) 761-6505, Fax (816) 763-8460, ksc@grandview.org, www.grandview.org

**Grant City** · *Grant City C/C* · Amber Monticue, Secy./Treas., P.O. Box 134, 64456, P 1,000, M 25, (660) 564-4000

**Green City** · *Green City C/C* · Dee Squire, Pres., P.O. Box 35, 63345, P 700, M 20, (660) 874-4412

**Greenfield** · *Greenfield C/C* · Nancy Lowe, Pres., P.O. Box 63, 65661, P 1,500, M 100, (417) 637-2040, mamalowe@hotmail.com, www.greenfieldmochamber.com

**Hannibal** · *Hannibal Area C/C* · Terry R. Sampson, Exec. Dir., 623 Broadway, P.O. Box 230, 63401, P 17,757, M 450, (573) 221-1101, Fax (573) 221-3389, info@hannibalchamber.org, www.hannibalchamber.org

**Harrisonville** · *Harrisonville Area C/C* · Ann Britt, Exec. Dir., 2819 Cantrell Rd., 64701, P 8,900, M 230, (816) 380-5271, (866) 380-5271, Fax (816) 884-4291, info@harrisonvillechamber.com, www.harrisonvillechamber.com.

**Hazelwood** · *see Bridgeton*

**Hermann** · *Hermann Area C/C* · June Diebal, Mgr., 312 Market St., 65041, P 2,700, M 199, (573) 486-2313, Fax (573) 486-3066, hermannchamber@centurytel.net, www.hermannmo.info

**Hermitage** · *Pomme de Terre Lake Area C/C* · Victor Domzalski, Pres., P.O. Box 36, 65668, P 6,500, M 115, (417) 745-2299, (800) 235-9519, Fax (417) 745-2293, vacation@pommedeterrechamber.com, www.pommedeterrechamber.com

**Higginsville** · *Higginsville C/C* · Teri Ray, Exec. Dir., 2102 S. Main St., P.O. Box 164, 64037, P 5,000, M 200, (660) 584-3030, Fax (660) 584-3033, chamber@ctcis.net, www.higginsvillechamber.org

**High Ridge** · *Northwest Jefferson County C/C* · Susan Tuggle, Pres., P.O. Box 371, 63049, P 50,000, M 130, (636) 671-8010, nwjcounty@sbcglobal.net, www.nwchamberweb.org

**Hillsboro** · *Greater Hillsboro C/C* · Mandy Alley, Admin., P.O. Box 225, 63050, P 2,000, M 75, (636) 789-4920, Fax (636) 789-4920, chamberoffice@sbcglobal.net, www.hillsboromo.org

**Holden** · *Holden C/C* · JoAnn Alpert, Pres., 100 E. 2nd, 64040, P 2,500, M 67, (816) 732-6844, info@holdenchamber.org, www.holdenchamber.com

**Hollister** · *Hollister Area C/C* · P.O. Box 674, 65673, P 3,867, M 175, (417) 334-3050, Fax (417) 334-5501, info@hollisterchamber.net, www.hollisterchamber.net

**Houston** · *Houston Area C/C* · Kim Scroggins, Exec. Dir., P.O. Box 374, 65483, P 2,100, M 200, (417) 967-2220, Fax (417) 967-2178, chamber004@centurytel.net, www.houstonmochamber.com

**Humansville** · *Humansville C/C* · Ken Turner, Pres., P.O. Box 195, 65674, P 1,000, M 60, (417) 754-2501, www.humansville.net

**Independence** · *Independence C/C* · Rick Hemmingsen, Pres., 210 W. Truman Rd., P.O. Box 1077, 64051, P 114,000, M 1,000, (816) 252-4745, Fax (816) 252-4917, rhemmingsen@independencechamber.org, www.independencechamber.org

**Ironton** · *Arcadia Valley C/C* · Jan Young, Pres., 630-21 Hwy., P.O. Box 343, 63650, P 3,500, M 100, (573) 546-7117, Fax (573) 546-7019, www.arcadiavalley.biz

**Jackson** · *Jackson C/C* · Brian Gerau, Exec. Dir., 125 E. Main, P.O. Box 352, 63755, P 11,947, M 400, (573) 243-8131, (888) 501-8827, Fax (573) 243-0725, director@jacksonmochamber.org, www.jacksonmochamber.org

**Jamesport** · *Jamesport Community Assn.* · P.O. Box 215, 64648, P 505, M 50, (660) 684-6146, jamesportmo@yahoo.com, www.jamesportmissouri.org

**Jefferson City** · *Jefferson City Area C/C* · Randall Allen, Pres./CEO, 213 Adams St., P.O. Box 776, 65102, P 50,000, M 1,000, (573) 634-3616, Fax (573) 634-3805, randyallen@jcchamber.org, www.jeffersoncitychamber.org.

**Jennings** · *see Ferguson*

**Joplin** • *Joplin Area C/C* • Rob O'Brian CEcD, Pres., 320 E. 4th St., 64801, P 169,031, M 1,100, (417) 624-4150, Fax (417) 624-4303, info@joplincc.com, www.joplincc.com.

**Kahoka** • *Kahoka/Clark County C/C* • Beverly Laffoon, Pres., 250 N. Morgan St., 63445, P 8,000, M 76, (660) 727-3143, (660) 727-3750

## Kansas City Area

**Black C/C of Greater Kansas City Inc.** • 1501 E. 18th St., 64108, P 640,000, M 539, (816) 474-9901, Fax (816) 842-1748, info@bcckc.org, www.bcckc.org

**Greater Kansas City C/C** • Dick Gibson, CAO, 911 Main St., Ste. 2600, 64105, P 1,800,000, M 8,000, (816) 221-2424, Fax (816) 221-7440, chamber@kcchamber.com, www.kcchamber.com

**Northeast Kansas City C/C** • Rebecca Koop, Exec. Dir., 6400 Independence Ave., P.O. Box 240392, 64124, P 40,000, M 107, (816) 231-3312, Fax (816) 231-2101, nekcchamber@aol.com, www.nekcchamber.com

**Northland Reg. C/C** • Sheila Tracy, Pres., 634 N.W. Englewood Rd., 64118, P 296,000, M 800, (816) 455-9911, Fax (816) 455-9933, northland@northlandchamber.com, www.northland chamber.com

**South Kansas City C/C** • Vickie Wolgast, Exec. Dir., 5908 E. Bannister Rd., 64134, P 72,000, M 250, (816) 761-7660, Fax (816) 761-7340, vwolgast@southkcchamber.com, www.southkc chamber.com

**Kearney** • *Kearney C/C* • Phyllis Strobel, Pres., P.O. Box 242, 64060, P 8,700, M 240, (816) 628-4229, Fax (816) 902-1234, kearneychamber@exop.net, www.kearneychamber.org

**Kennett** • *Kennett C/C* • Jan McElwrath, Exec. Dir., 1601 First St., P.O. Box 61, 63857, P 12,000, M 400, (573) 888-5828, (866) 848-5828, Fax (573) 888-9802, info@kennettmo.com, www. kennettmo.com

**Kimberling City** • *Table Rock Lake Area C/C* • Wyli Barnes, Pres., 14226 State Hwy. 13, P.O. Box 495, 65686, P 20,000, M 550, (417) 739-2564, Fax (417) 739-2580, trlchamber@visittablerocklake. com, www.visittablerocklake.com.

**Kirksville** • *Kirksville Area C/C* • Alisa Kigar, Exec. Dir., 304 S. Franklin, P.O. Box 251, 63501, P 17,304, M 400, (660) 665-3766, Fax (660) 665-3767, kvacoc@cableone.net, www.kirksville chamber.com

**Kirkwood** • *Kirkwood-Des Peres Area C/C* • Jim Wright, Pres./ CEO, 108 W. Adams, St. Louis, 63122, P 50,000, M 670, (314) 821-4161, Fax (314) 821-5229, jim@thechamber.us, www.kirkwood desperes.com.

**LaGrange** • *LaGrange C/C* • Ken Schuetz, Pres., P.O. Box 67, 63448, P 1,000, M 70, (573) 655-2297, www.cityoflagrangemo.gov

**Lake Ozark** • *Lake Area C/C* • Trisha Creach, Exec. Dir., 1 Willmore Ln., P.O. Box 1570, 65049, P 5,300, M 950, (573) 964-1008, (800) 451-4117, Fax (573) 964-1010, info@lakearea chamber.com, www.lakeareachamber.com

**Lake Saint Louis** • *Lake Saint Louis-Dardenne Prairie Area C/C* • Angela Campbell, Exec. Dir., 121 Civic Center Dr., Ste. 161, 63367, P 13,000, M 220, (636) 699-0045, info@lsldpchamber.com, www.lsldpchamber.com

**Lamar** • *Barton County C/C* • Nancy Curless, Exec. Dir., 102 W. 10th St., P.O. Box 577, 64759, P 12,600, M 200, (417) 682-3595, Fax (417) 682-9566, nancy@bartoncounty.com, www.barton county.com.

**Lebanon** • *Lebanon Area C/C* • Debbie Wikowsky, Exec. Dir., 186 N. Adams, P.O. Box 505, 65536, P 12,000, M 431, (417) 588-3256, (888) 588-5710, Fax (417) 588-3251, stephanie@lebanonmissouri. com, www.lebanonmissouri.com.

**Lee's Summit** • *Lee's Summit C/C* • Nancy K. Bruns, Pres., 220 S.E. Main, 64063, P 94,000, M 950, (816) 524-2424, Fax (816) 524-5246, lscoc@lschamber.com, www.lschamber.com.

**Lexington** • *Lexington Area C/C* • Carol Baker, Exec. Dir., 1029 Franklin Ave., 64067, P 5,000, M 200, (660) 259-3082, Fax (660) 259-7776, chamberdirector@historiclexington.com, www. historiclexington.com

**Liberty** • *Liberty Area C/C* • Gayle Potter, Pres., 9 S. Leonard, 64068, P 27,234, M 425, (816) 781-5200, Fax (816) 781-4901, info@libertychamber.com, libertychamber.com.

**Licking** • *Licking C/C* • Kyle Smith, Pres., P.O. Box 89, 65542, P 3,000, M 50, (573) 674-2510, Fax (573) 674-2914

**Lincoln** • *Lincoln C/C* • Janice Swearngin, V.P., P.O. Box 246, 65338, P 1,200, M 40, (660) 547-2718, (877) 947-9954, www. lincolnmissouri.com

**Louisiana** • *Louisiana C/C* • 202 S. 3rd, Ste. 120, 63353, P 4,000, M 112, Fax (573) 754-5921, lamochamber@sbcglobal.net, www. louisiana-mo.com

**Macon** • *Macon Area C/C* • 1407 N. Missouri St., 63552, P 5,920, M 176, (660) 385-2811, Fax (660) 385-6543, director@macon mochamber.com, www.maconmochamber.com

**Malden** • *Malden C/C* • Olivia Hamra, Pres., 123 W. Main, 63863, P 4,782, M 153, (573) 276-4519, Fax (573) 276-4925, info@ maldenchamber.com, www.maldenchamber.com

**Manchester** • *West St. Louis County C/C* • Lori Kelling, Exec. Dir., 134 Enchanted Pkwy., Ste. 204, 63021, P 200,000, M 320, (636) 230-9900, Fax (636) 230-9912, info@westcountychamber.com, www.westcountychamber.com

**Mansfield** • *Mansfield Area C/C* • Darrel Adamson, Pres., P.O. Box 322, 65704, P 1,400, M 40, (417) 924-3525, mansfieldcofc@ gmail.com, www.mansfieldchamber.com

**Maplewood** • *Maplewood C/C* • Jeannine Beck, Exec. Dir., 2915 Sutton Blvd., 63143, P 10,000, M 130, (314) 781-8588, Fax (314) 781-5397, info@maplewood-chamber.com, www.maplewood-chamber.com

**Marceline** • *Marceline C/C* • Jed Frost, Pres., P.O. Box 93, 64658, P 2,500, M 50, (660) 376-2332, www.marceline.com

**Marshall** • *Marshall C/C* • Ken Yowell, Exec. Dir., 214 N. Lafayette, 65340, P 13,000, M 203, (660) 886-3324, Fax (660) 831-0349, ken@marshallchamber.com, www.marshallchamber.com

**Marshfield** • *Marshfield C/C* • Pam Cook, Exec. Secy., 1350 Spur Dr., Ste. 190, 65706, P 7,100, M 225, (417) 859-3925, Fax (417) 468-3944, mfldcoc@fidnet.com, www.marshfieldmochamber ofcommerce.com

**Marthasville** • *Marthasville Area C/C* • Larry Brewe, Pres., P.O. Box 95, 63357, P 1,000, M 74, (636) 433-5242

**Maryland Heights** • *Maryland Heights C/C* • Kim Braddy, Dir., 547 West Port Plaza, St. Louis, 63146, P 26,000, M 450, (314) 576-6603, Fax (314) 576-6855, www.mhcc.com

**Maryville** • *Maryville C/C* • 423 N. Market, 64468, P 11,000, M 260, (660) 582-8643, Fax (660) 582-3071, chamber@asde.net, www.maryvillechamber.com

**Maysville** • *Maysville C/C* • John Murphy, Pres., 701 W. Main St., P.O. Box 521, 64469, P 1,200, M 40, (816) 449-2062

**Mehlville** • *see South County*

**Mexico** · *Mexico Area C/C* · Sue Caine, Exec. V.P., 100 W. Jackson St., 65265, P 12,500, M 400, (573) 581-2765, (800) 581-2765, Fax (573) 581-6226, scaine@mexico-chamber.org, www.mexico-chamber.org.

**Moberly** · *Moberly Area C/C* · Deborah Dean-Miller, Exec. V.P., 211 W. Reed St., 65270, P 25,438, M 275, (660) 263-6070, Fax (660) 263-9443, chamber@moberly.com, moberlychamber.com

**Moline Acres** · *see Ferguson*

**Monett** · *Monett C/C* · Suzy McElmurry, Exec. Dir., 200 E. Broadway, P.O. Box 47, 65708, P 8,000, M 275, (417) 235-7919, Fax (417) 235-4076, chamber@monett-mo.com, www.monett-mo.com

**Monroe City** · *Mark Twain Lake C/C* · Doug Smith, Pres., P.O. Box 182, 63456, P 20,000, M 70, (573) 565-2228, mtlcoc@socket.net, www.visitmarktwainlake.org

**Monroe City** · *Monroe City Area C/C* · Loree Quinn, Pres., 314 S. Main St., P.O. Box 22, 63456, P 2,588, M 90, (573) 735-4391, mcchamber@centurytel.net, www.monroecitymo.com

**Montgomery City** · *Montgomery City Area C/C* · David Gaines, Exec. Dir., P.O. Box 31, 63361, P 12,000, M 124, (573) 564-2712, Fax (573) 564-3802, www.montgomerycity.org

**Mound City** · *Mound City Area C/C* · Adam Johnson, Pres., P.O. Box 175, 64470, P 5,000, M 44, (660) 442-5423, moundcitynews@socket.com, www.moundcitynews.com

**Mount Vernon** · *Mount Vernon C/C* · Doris McBride, Exec. Secy., 425 E. Mt. Vernon Blvd., P.O. Box 373, 65712, P 4,500, M 243, (417) 466-7654, Fax (417) 466-7654, mtvchamber@mchsi.com, www.mtvernonchamber.com

**Mountain Grove** · *Mountain Grove C/C* · Mary Armstrong, Exec. Dir., 205 W. 3rd, Ste. 8, P.O. Box 434, 65711, P 4,500, M 200, (417) 926-4135, Fax (417) 926-5440, chamber@mountaingrovechamber.com, www.mountaingrovechamber.com

**Mountain View** · *Mountain View C/C* · Linda Lewis, Exec. Dir., 117 E. 2nd. St., 65548, P 2,400, M 218, (417) 934-2794, Fax (417) 934-2882, mvcoc@centurytel.net, www.mountainviewmo.com

**Neosho** · *Neosho Area C/C* · Shana Griffin, Exec. Dir., 216 W. Spring, P.O. Box 605, 64850, P 10,505, M 400, (417) 451-1925, Fax (417) 451-8097, director@neoshocc.com, www.neoshocc.com.

**Nevada** · *Nevada-Vernon County C/C* · Cat McGrath-Farmer, Exec. Dir., 225 W. Austin, Ste. 200, 64772, P 21,000, M 325, (417) 667-5300, Fax (417) 667-3492, chamber@nevada-mo.com, www.nevada-mo.com

**New Haven** · *New Haven Area C/C* · P.O. Box 201, 63068, P 2,000, M 100, (573) 237-3830, info@newhavenmo.com, www.newhavenmo.com

**New Madrid** · *New Madrid C/C* · Christina McWaters, Dir., 537 Mott St., P.O. Box 96, 63869, P 3,340, M 95, (573) 748-5300, (877) 748-5300, Fax (573) 748-5402, chambernm@yahoo.com, www.new-madrid.mo.us

**New Melle** · *New Melle C/C* · Chris Ryan, Pres., P.O. Box 212, 63365, P 300, M 100, (636) 828-5600, Fax (636) 433-2012, info@newmellechamber.com, www.newmellechamber.com

**Nixa** · *Nixa Area C/C* · Sharon Whitehill Gray, Pres./CEO, 105 Sherman Way, Ste. 108, 65714, P 18,000, M 488, (417) 725-1545, Fax (417) 725-4532, director@nixachamber.com, www.nixachamber.com

**Oak Grove** · *Oak Grove C/C* · Jerry Lewis, Pres., 103 S.E. 12th St., 64075, P 6,000, M 70, (816) 690-4147, Fax (816) 690-4147, oakgrovechamber@yahoo.com, www.ogchamber.org

**Oakland** · *see Kirkwood*

**Oakville** · *see South County*

**Odessa** · *Odessa C/C* · D.J. Davis, Ofc. Mgr., 309A Park Ln., 64076, P 5,000, M 78, (816) 633-4044, Fax (816) 633-4044, odessacoc@embarqmail.com, www.odessamochamber.com

**O'Fallon** · *OFallon C/C* · Rose Mack, Pres./CEO, 1299 Bryan Rd., 63366, P 70,000, M 530, (636) 240-1818, info@ofallonchamber.org, www.ofallonchamber.org

**Olivette** · *see Creve Coeur*

**Oran** · *Oran C/C* · Ed Evans, Pres., P.O. Box 49, 63771, P 1,284, M 17, (573) 262-3942

**Osceola** · *Osceola Comm. C/C* · Peter Hauer, Pres., P.O. Box 422, 64776, P 834, M 50, (417) 646-2727, martha.hauer@gmaill.com, www.osceolamochamber.com

**Overland** · *see Bridgeton*

**Owensville** · *Owensville C/C* · Michelle Jet, Pres., P.O. Box 77, 65066, P 2,500, M 100, (573) 437-4270, Fax (573) 437-4270, chamber1@fidnet.com, www.owensvillemissouri.com

**Ozark** · *Ozark Area C/C* · Chris Stone, Exec. Dir., 191 N. 18th St., P.O. Box 1450, 65721, P 10,200, M 260, (417) 581-6139, Fax (417) 581-0639, info@ozarkmissouri.com, ozarkchamber.com

**Pacific** · *Pacific C/C* · Al Baldwin, Pres., 333 Chamber Dr., 63069, P 6,600, M 170, (636) 271-6639, Fax (636) 257-2109, exdir@pacificchamber.com, www.pacificchamber.com

**Palmyra** · *Palmyra C/C* · Josh Wilson, Pres., 400 S. Main, Ste. 2300, 63401, P 3,500, M 65, (573) 769-0777, palmyrachamber@centurytel.net, www.showmepalmyra.com

**Paris** · *Paris Area C/C* · Vanessa Forrest, Exec. Dir., 208 N. Main St., 65275, P 1,500, M 67, (660) 327-4450, Fax (660) 327-1376, chamber@parismo.net, www.parismo.net

**Park Hills** · *Park Hills-Leadington C/C* · Tamara Burns, Exec. Dir., 5 Municipal Dr., 63601, P 9,000, M 150, (573) 431-1051, Fax (573) 431-2327, phlcoc@sbcglobal.net, phlcoc.com

**Peculiar** · *Peculiar C/C* · Kim Duey, Pres., P.O. Box 669, 64078, P 6,000, M 72, (816) 779-5212, (816) 863-6077, kimduey@firstchoicerealty.info, www.peculiarchamber.com

**Perryville** · *Perryville C/C* · Melissa Hemmann, Exec. Dir., 2 W. Ste. Maries St., 63775, P 7,667, M 460, (573) 547-6062, Fax (573) 547-6071, perryvillemo@sbcglobal.net, www.perryvillemo.com

**Piedmont** · *Greater Piedmont Area C/C* · Rober Gayle, Pres., P.O. Box 101, 63957, P 2,500, M 120, (573) 223-4046, Fax (573) 223-4046, contact@piedmontchamber.com, piedmontchamber.com

**Platte City** · *Platte City Area Chamber/Eco. Dev. Council* · Karen Wagoner, Exec. Dir., 620 3rd St., P.O. Box 650, 64079, P 9,000, M 240, (816) 858-5270, www.plattecitymo.com

**Plattsburg** · *Plattsburg C/C* · Tonya Sloan, Pres., 101 S. Main, 64477, P 2,500, M 75, (816) 539-2649, Fax (816) 539-3539, chamber@plattsburgmo.com, www.plattsburgmo.com

**Poplar Bluff** · *Greater Poplar Bluff Area C/C* · Steve Halter, Pres., 1111 W. Pine, 63901, P 17,000, M 720, (573) 785-7761, Fax (573) 785-1901, info@poplarbluffchamber.org, www.poplarbluffchamber.org

**Portageville** · *Portageville C/C* · Sandy Stewart, Pres., 301 E. Main, P.O. Box 409, 63873, P 4,000, M 130, (573) 379-5789, Fax (573) 379-3080, www.portagevillemo.com

**Potosi** · *Washington County & Potosi C/C* · Kris Richards, Pres., 501 E. High St., P.O. Box 404, 63664, P 4,000, M 75, (573) 438-4517, Fax (573) 438-3676, www.potosichamber.com

**Raymore** • *Raymore C/C* • Cherie Turney, 1000 W. Foxwood Dr., P.O. Box 885, 64083, P 18,000, M 175, (816) 322-0599, Fax (816) 322-7127, raymorechamber@sbcglobal.net, www.raymorechamber.com

**Raytown** • *Raytown Area C/C* • Vicki Turnbow, Pres., 5909 Raytown Trafficway, 64133, P 30,388, M 300, (816) 353-8500, Fax (816) 353-8525, staff@raytownchamber.com, www.raytown chamber.com.

**Republic** • *Republic Area C/C* • Ruby Gum, Ofc. Mgr., 145 W. Hwy. 174, 65738, P 13,000, M 220, (417) 732-5200, Fax (417) 732-2851, info@republicchamber.com, www.republicchamber.com

**Rich Hill** • *Rich Hill C/C* • Don Swope, Pres., P.O. Box 165, 64779, P 1,461, M 40, (417) 395-2275

**Richmond** • *Richmond C/C* • Scott Marshall, Pres., 104 W. North Main, 64085, P 6,116, M 192, (816) 776-6916, Fax (816) 776-6917, cofcommerce@mchsi.com, www.richmondchamber.org

**Richmond Heights** • *Richmond Heights C/C* • Virginia Pennington, Exec. Dir., 1249 Boland Pl., 63117, P 10,000, M 100, (314) 647-6483, www.richmondheights.org

**Rivermines** • *see Park Hills*

**Riverside** • *Riverside Area C/C* • Cynthia Rice, Exec. Dir., P.O. Box 9074, 64168, P 3,000, M 170, (816) 746-1577, riversidechamber@msn.com, www.riversidemochamber.com

**Rock Port** • *Rock Port C/C* • 321 S. Main, P.O. Box 134, 64482, P 1,500, M 40, (660) 744-2222

**Rogersville** • *Rogersville Area C/C* • Gwen Mackey, Admin. Asst., P.O. Box 77, 65742, P 2,500, M 130, (417) 753-7538, Fax (417) 753-2606, rogersvillecoc@sbcglobal.net, www.rogersvillechamber.com

**Rolla** • *Rolla Area C/C* • Stevie Kearse, Exec. Dir., 1311 Kingshighway, 65401, P 18,000, M 500, (573) 364-3577, Fax (573) 364-5222, stevie@rollachamber.org, www.rollachamber.org.

**Saint Ann** • *see Bridgeton*

**Saint Charles** • *Saint Charles C/C* • Scott Tate, Pres./CEO, 2201 First Capitol Dr., 63301, P 66,000, M 630, (636) 946-0633, Fax (636) 946-0301, info@stcharleschamber.org, www.stcharles chamber.org.

**Saint Clair** • *St. Clair Area C/C* • Terry Triphahn, Exec. Dir., 920 Plaza Dr., Ste. F, 63077, P 4,392, M 150, (636) 629-1889, Fax (636) 629-5510, chamber@stclairmo.com, www.stclairmo.com

**Saint James** • *Saint James C/C* • Dominic DeLuca, Pres., 111 S. Jefferson, P.O. Box 358, 65559, P 3,700, M 153, (573) 265-6649, Fax (573) 265-6650, info@stjameschamber.net, www.stjames chamber.net

**Saint Johns** • *see Bridgeton*

**Saint Joseph** • *St. Joseph Area C/C* • Ted Allison, Pres./CEO, 3003 Frederick Ave., 64506, P 76,107, M 975, (816) 232-4461, Fax (816) 364-4873, chamber@saintjoseph.com, www.saintjoseph.com.

**Saint Louis** • *Lemay C/C* • Barbara Hehmeyer, Exec. Dir., P.O. Box 6642, 63125, P 20,000, M 250, (314) 631-2796, Fax (314) 638-9500, lemaychamber@sbcglobal.net, www.lemaychamber.com

**Saint Louis** • *St. Louis Reg. Chamber & Growth Assn.* • Richard C.D. Fleming, Pres./CEO, One Metropolitan Square, Ste. 1300, 63102, P 2,561,400, M 4,000, (314) 231-5555, Fax (314) 444-1122, inforcga@stlrcga.org, www.stlrcga.org.

**Saint Mary** • *Saint Mary C/C* • Bob Bartels, Pres., P.O. Box 38, 63673, P 377, M 20, (573) 543-2230, saintmarymo.com

**Saint Peters** • *Saint Peters C/C* • Ed Weeks, Pres./CEO, 1236 Jungermann Rd., Ste. C, 63376, P 57,000, M 740, (636) 447-3336, Fax (636) 447-9575, info@stpeterschamber.com, www.stpeters chamber.com

**Salem** • *Salem Area C/C* • Patty Shults, Dir., 200 S. Main St., 65560, P 5,000, M 200, (573) 729-6900, Fax (573) 729-6741, chamber@salemmo.com, www.salemmo.com

**Salisbury** • *Salisbury Area C/C* • Melody Eads, Pres., P.O. Box 5, 65281, P 1,800, M 52, (660) 388-6116, salisburymo@yahoo.com, www.c-magic.com/salisbury

**Sarcoxie** • *Sarcoxie Area C/C* • Johnny Hankins, Pres., P.O. Box 171, 64862, P 1,400, M 97, (417) 548-6130, (417) 548-6390, j_hankins@mo-net.com, www.sarcoxiemo.com

**Savannah** • *Savannah Area C/C* • Christy Sipes, Coord., 411 Court, P.O. Box 101, 64485, P 5,100, M 135, (816) 324-3976, Fax (816) 324-5728, sacc@savannahmochamber.com, www.savannahmochamber.com

**Scott City** • *Scott City Area C/C* • Chodra Mason, Secy./Treas., 215 Chester Ave., 63780, P 4,600, M 40, (573) 264-2157, scottcitymo.org

**Sedalia** • *Sedalia Area C/C & Conv. & Visitors Bur.* • Deborah Biermann, Exec. Dir., 600 E. Third St., 65301, P 36,000, M 300, (660) 826-2222, Fax (660) 826-2223, dbiermann@visitsedaliamo.com, www.sedaliachamber.com

**Seligman** • *Seligman Greater Area C/C* • David VanPetty, Pres., P.O. Box 250, 65745, P 10,000, M 48, (417) 662-3611, www.seligmanchamber.com

**Seneca** • *Seneca C/C* • Josh Dodson, Pres., P.O. Box 332, 64865, P 2,300, M 90, (417) 776-2100, chamberpresident@senecamo chamber.com, www.senecamochamber.com

**Seymour** • *Greater Seymour Area C/C* • Charity Kane, Pres., P.O. Box 700, 65746, P 2,200, M 35, (417) 935-9300, www.seymour mochamber.com

**Shelbina** • *Shelbina C/C* • Leslie Thompson, Pres., P.O. Box 646, 63468, P 2,000, M 75, (573) 588-1506, lthompson@cerroflow.com, www.cityofshelbina.com

**Shell Knob** • *Shell Knob C/C* • Sheila House, Exec. Dir., #6 TimbeRoc Village, P.O. Box 193, 65747, P 8,000, M 190, (417) 858-3300, Fax (417) 858-9428, info@shellknob.com, www.shellknob.com

**Sikeston** • *Sikeston Area C/C* • Missy Marshall, Exec. Dir., One Industrial Dr., 63801, P 21,000, M 540, (573) 471-2498, Fax (573) 471-2499, chamber@sikeston.net, www.sikeston.net

**Slater** • *Slater C/C* • Keith Wright, Pres., P.O. Box 24, 65349, P 2,100, M 70, (660) 529-2271, Fax (660) 529-2593, info@city ofslater.com, www.cityofslater.com

**Smithville** • *Smithville Area C/C* • Kim Palmer, Exec. Dir., 105 W. Main, 64089, P 6,200, M 225, (816) 532-0946, Fax (816) 532-3513, smithvillechamber@sbcglobal.net, smithvillechamber.org

**South County** • *South County C/C* • Donna Abernathy, Exec. Dir., 6921 S. Lindbergh, St. Louis, 63125, P 140,000, M 380, (314) 894-6800, Fax (314) 894-6888, dascounty@sbcglobal.net, www.southcountychamber.net

**Springfield** • *Springfield Area C/C* • James B. Anderson, Pres., 202 S. John Q. Hammons Pkwy., P.O. Box 1687, 65801, P 407,092, M 1,198, (417) 862-5567, Fax (417) 862-1611, info@springfield chamber.com, www.springfieldchamber.com.

**St. Robert** • *Waynesville-St. Robert Area C/C* • Cecilia Murray, Exec. Dir., 137 St. Robert Blvd., Ste. B, 65584, P 9,087, M 474, (573) 336-5121, Fax (573) 336-5472, chamber@wsrchamber.com, www.wsrchamber.com

**Ste. Genevieve** • *Ste. Genevieve C/C* • Dena Kreitler, Exec. Dir., 251 Market St., 63670, P 17,782, M 350, (573) 883-3686, Fax (573) 883-7092, stegenchamber@sbcglobal.net, www.sainte genevieve.org

**Steele** • *Steele C/C* • Leigh Ann Powell, V.P., 101 S. Walnut St., 63877, P 2,200, M 22, (573) 695-4710, (573) 695-4732, www.cityofsteele.org

**Steelville** • *Steelville C/C* • Liz Bennett, Pres., P.O. Box 956, 65565, P 1,500, M 75, (573) 775-5533, Fax (573) 775-5521, chamber@misn.com, www.steelville.com

**Stockton** • *Stockton Area C/C* • Charlotte Haden, P.O. Box 410, 65785, P 2,000, M 135, (417) 276-5213, stocktonchamber@windstream.net, www.stocktonmochamber.com

**Stover** • *Stover C/C* • Bill Fairbiarn, Pres., P.O. Box 370, 65078, P 968, M 48, (573) 377-4510, Fax (573) 377-2521

**Strafford** • *Strafford Area C/C* • Alice Delcour, Pres., P.O. Box 21, 65757, P 8,000, M 60, (417) 522-6935, (417) 736-2154, rt66campbell@yahoo.com, www.strafford-mo.com

**Sullivan** • *Sullivan Area C/C* • Debbe Campbell, Exec. Dir., 2 Springfield, 63080, P 6,300, M 300, (573) 468-3314, Fax (573) 860-2313, chamber@fidnet.com, www.sullivanmo.com.

**Summersville** • *Summersville C/C* • Cathy Tuttle, Pres., P.O. Box 251, 65571, P 544, M 20, (417) 932-5373, Fax (417) 932-4791, catron@hotmail.com, www.summersvillemo.com

**Sunrise Beach** • *Lake of the Ozarks West C/C* • Mike Kenagy, Exec. Dir., P.O. Box 340, 65079, P 16,000, M 455, (573) 374-5500, (877) 227-4086, Fax (573) 374-8576, info@lakewestchamber.com, www.lakewestchamber.com

**Sweet Springs** • *Sweet Springs C/C* • Tara Brewer, Pres., P.O. Box 255, 65351, P 1,700, M 50, (660) 335-6321, Fax (660) 335-4592

**Table Rock Lake** • *see Kimberling City*

**Tarkio** • *Tarkio C/C* • Lori Seymour, Pres., P.O. Box 222, 64491, P 1,935, M 75, (660) 736-5772, www.tarkiomo.com

**Thayer** • *Thayer Area C/C* • Faith Holt, Pres., P.O. Box 14, 65791, P 2,300, M 88, (417) 264-7324, www.thayerareachamber.org

**Theodosia** • *Theodosia Area C/C* • P.O. Box 11, 65761, P 300, M 75, (417) 273-0005, (417) 273-4245, theodosiachamber@yahoo.com, www.missourichamber.com

**Tipton** • *Tipton C/C* • Mark Koechner, Pres., P.O. Box 307, 65081, P 3,000, M 85, (660) 433-6377, chamber@tiptonmo.com, www.tiptonmo.com

**Town & Country** • *Town & Country/Frontenac C/C* • 13443 Clayton Rd., Ste. 2, 63131, P 11,000, M 130, (314) 469-3335, Fax (314) 259-1778, tccoc@aol.com, www.tcfchamber.com

**Trenton** • *Trenton Area C/C* • Terri Henderson, Pres., 617 Main St., 64683, P 6,500, M 200, (660) 359-4324, Fax (660) 359-4606, trentonchamber@grundyec.net, www.trentonmochamber.com

**Union** • *Union C/C* • Tammy Stowe, Exec. Dir., 103 S. Oak St., P.O. Box 168, 63084, P 9,000, M 325, (636) 583-8979, Fax (636) 583-4001, director@unionmochamber.org, www.unionmochamber.org

**Vandalia** • *Vandalia Area C/C* • 200 E. Park St., 63382, P 3,963, M 70, (573) 594-6186, www.vandaliamo.net

**Versailles** • *Versailles Area C/C* • Cecilia Dunham, Secy., 109 N. Monroe, P.O. Box 256, 65084, P 2,500, M 125, (573) 378-4401, Fax (573) 378-2499, info@versailleschamber.com, www.versailleschamber.com

**Vinita Park** • *see Bridgeton*

**Warrensburg** • *Greater Warrensburg Area C/C & Visitors Center* • Tammy Long, Exec. Dir., 100 S. Holden St., 64093, P 18,500, M 375, (660) 747-3168, Fax (660) 429-5490, chamber@warrensburg.org, www.warrensburg.org

**Warrenton** • *Warrenton Area C/C* • Allan Dreyer, Pres., 111 Steinhagen, 63383, P 6,500, M 200, (636) 456-2530, Fax (636) 456-2329, info@warrentoncoc.com, www.warrentoncoc.com

**Warsaw** • *Warsaw Area C/C* • Sandi Schmitt, Exec. V.P., 816 E. Main, P.O. Box 264, 65355, P 2,000, M 200, (660) 438-5922, (800) WARSAW-4, Fax (660) 438-3493, warsawcc@embarqmail.com, www.warsawmo.org.

**Warson Woods** • *see Kirkwood*

**Washington** • *Washington Area C/C* • Mark Wessels, Pres./CEO, 323 W. Main St., 63090, P 14,000, M 600, (636) 239-2715, Fax (636) 239-1381, mwessels@washmo.org, www.washmo.org

**Waynesville** • *see St. Robert*

**Webb City** • *Webb City Area C/C* • Dixie Meredith, Exec. Dir., 555 S. Main St., P.O. Box 287, 64870, P 10,764, M 201, (417) 673-1154, Fax (417) 673-2856, dixie@webbcitychamber.com, www.webbcitychamber.com

**Webster Groves** • *Webster Groves/Shrewsbury Area C/C* • Diane Lamboley, Pres./CEO, 357 Marshall Ave., Ste. 3, 63119, P 30,000, M 300, (314) 962-4142, Fax (314) 962-9398, chamber info@go-webster.com, www.webstershrewsburychamber.com

**Wentzville** • *Wentzville C/C* • Erin Williams, Exec. Dir., P.O. Box 11, 63385, P 24,000, M 400, (636) 327-6914, info@wentzvillechamber.com, www.wentzvillechamber.com

**West Plains** • *Greater West Plains Area C/C* • Joanne Wix, Exec. Dir., 401 Jefferson Ave., 65775, P 11,000, M 550, (417) 256-4433, Fax (417) 256-8711, info@wpchamber.com, wpchamber.com.

**Weston** • *Weston C/C* • Mary Jo Heidrick, Pres., 526 Main St., 64098, P 1,631, M 100, (816) 640-2909, Fax (816) 640-2909, westonmo@kc.rr.com, www.westonmo.com

**Westport** • *see Maryland Heights*

**Wildwood** • *see Manchester*

**Willard** • *Willard Area C/C* • Dr. Devon Jarvis, Pres., P.O. Box 384, 65781, P 4,500, M 84, (888) 523-6392, www.cityofwillard.org, willardchamber@yahoo.com, www.willardmo.org

**Willow Springs** • *Willow Springs Area C/C* • Jeannie Murrell, Exec. Dir., 112 E. Main St., 65793, P 2,400, M 95, (417) 469-5519, Fax (417) 469-3192, wschamber@live.com, www.willowspringsmo.com

**Winchester** • *see Manchester*

**Windsor** • *Windsor Area C/C* • Terri Kline, Pres., 102 N. Main, 65360, P 3,087, M 90, (660) 647-2318, windsorm@iland.net, www.windsormo.org

**Woodson Terrace** • *see Bridgeton*

**Wright City** • *Wright City Area C/C* • Phil Cartwright, Pres., P.O. Box 444, 63390, P 8,000, M 100, (636) 745-7855, wcchamber@wrightcitychamber.com, www.wrightcitychamber.com

# Montana

**Montana C of C** • Webb Brown, Pres./CEO, P.O. Box 1730, Helena, 59624, P 800,000, M 1,500, (406) 442-2405, Fax (406) 442-2409, leah@montanachamber.com, www.montanachamber.com

**Alder** • *see Twin Bridges*

**Anaconda** • *Anaconda C/C* • Edith Fransen, Exec. Dir., 306 E. Park St., 59711, P 9,400, M 195, (406) 563-2400, Fax (406) 563-2400, www.anacondamt.org

**Baker** • *Baker C of C & Ag.* • Karol Zachmann, Pres., P.O. Box 849, 59313, P 1,850, M 88, (866) 862-2537, (406) 778-3382, www.bakermt.com

**Belgrade** · *Belgrade C/C* · Debra Youngberg, Exec. Dir., 10 E. Main, 59714, P 10,000, M 372, (406) 388-1616, Fax (406) 388-2090, dyoungberg@belgradechamber.org, www.belgrade chamber.org

**Big Sandy** · *Big Sandy C/C* · Conrad Heimbigner, Pres., P.O. Box 411, 59520, P 700, M 40, (406) 378-2418, www.bigsandymt.org

**Big Sky** · *Big Sky C/C* · Marne Hayes, Exec. Dir., 3091 Pine Dr., P.O. Box 160100, 59716, P 2,200, M 450, (406) 995-3000, (800) 943-4111, Fax (406) 995-3054, info@bigskychamber.com, www. bigskychamber.com

**Big Timber** · *Sweet Grass County C/C & Visitor Info. Center* · 1350 Hwy. 10 W., P.O. Box 1012, 59011, P 3,500, M 80, (406) 932-5131, info@bigtimber.com, www.bigtimber.com

**Bigfork** · *Bigfork Area C/C* · Diane Kautzman, Pres., 8155 MT Hwy. 35, P.O. Box 237, 59911, P 2,000, M 335, (406) 837-5888, Fax (406) 837-5808, chamber@bigfork.org, www.bigfork.org

**Billings** · *Billings Area C/C* · John Brewer, Pres./CEO, 815 S. 27th St., P.O. Box 31177, 59107, P 130,000, M 1,100, (406) 245-4111, Fax (406) 245-7333, info@billingschamber.com, www.billings chamber.com

**Birney** · *see Lame Deer*

**Bozeman** · *Bozeman Area C/C* · David R. Smith, Pres./CEO, 2000 Commerce Way, 59715, P 82,000, M 1,265, (406) 586-5421, Fax (406) 586-8286, info@bozemanchamber.com, www.bozeman chamber.com

**Broadus** · *Powder River C/C* · Phoebe Amsden, Pres., P.O. Box 484, 59317, P 1,900, M 82, (406) 436-2778, prchamber9@yahoo.com

**Browning** · *Browning Area C/C* · Joe Bremner, Chair, P.O. Box 469, 59417, P 1,200, M , (406) 338-2344, (406) 338-4015, info@ browningchamber.com, www.browningmontana.com

**Busby** · *see Lame Deer*

**Butte** · *Butte-Silver Bow C/C & Conv. Bur.* · Marko Lucich, Exec. Dir., 1000 George St., 59701, P 34,000, M 700, (406) 723-3177, (800) 735-6814, Fax (406) 723-1215, www.buttecvb.com, chamber@buttecvb.com, www.buttechamber.org

**Checkerboard** · *see White Sulpher Springs*

**Chester** · *Liberty County C/C* · Lynda Vande Sandt, Coord., 30 Main St., P.O. Box 632, 59522, P 2,100, M 105, (406) 759-4848, Fax (406) 759-5523, lynda@libertycountycc.com, www.liberty countycc.com

**Chinook** · *Chinook C/C* · Larry Surber, Pres., P.O. Box 744, 59523, P 1,350, M 90, (406) 357-3459, info@chinookmontana.com, www. chinookmontana.com

**Choteau** · *Choteau C/C* · P.O. Box 897, 59422, P 1,800, M 100, (406) 466-5316, (800) 823-3866, choteauchamber@choteau montana.com, www.choteaumontana.com

**Circle** · *Circle C of C & Ag.* · P.O. Box 321, 59215, P 700, M 60, (406) 485-2741, www.circle-montana.com

**Colstrip** · *Colstrip C/C* · Cathy Franks, Pres., P.O. Box 1100, 59323, P 2,000, M 50, www.colstripchamber.com

**Columbia Falls** · *Columbia Falls Area C/C* · Carol Pike, Exec. Dir., 233 13th St. E., P.O. Box 312, 59912, P 4,200, M 200, (406) 892-2072, info@columbiafallschamber.com, www.columbiafalls chamber.com.

**Columbus** · *Stillwater County C/C* · Charles Sangmeister, Pres., P.O. Box 783, 59019, P 8,500, M 100, (406) 322-4505, admin@ stillwatercountychamber.com, www.stillwatercountychamber.com

**Conrad** · *Conrad Area C/C* · Barbie Killion, Exec. Dir., 7 Sixth Ave. S.W., 59425, P 3,000, M 130, (406) 271-7791, Fax (406) 271-2924, chamber@3rivers.net, www.conradmt.com

**Cooke City** · *Colter Pass, Cooke City, Silver Gate C/C* · Bev Chatelain, Pres., 109 W. Main, P.O. Box 1071, 59020, P 100, M 45, (406) 838-2495, Fax (406) 838-2495, info@cookecitychamber.org, www.cookecitychamber.org

**Culbertson** · *Culbertson C/C* · P.O. Box 639, 59218, P 800, M 50, (406) 787-5821, culbertsonmt@hotmail.com, www.culbert sonmt.com

**Cut Bank** · *Cut Bank Area C/C* · Jeff Billman, P.O. Box 1243, 59427, P 3,400, M 120, (406) 873-4041, info@cutbankchamber. com, www.cutbankchamber.com

**Deer Lodge** · *Powell County C/C* · 1109 Main St., 59722, P 6,789, M 105, (406) 846-2094, Fax (406) 846-2094, chamber@ powellcountymontana.com, www.powellcountymontana.com

**Dillon** · *Beaverhead C/C* · Melissa Hannah, Exec. Dir., 10 W. Reeder, P.O. Box 425, 59725, P 4,000, M 245, (406) 683-5511, Fax (406) 683-9233, info@beaverheadchamber.org, www.beaver headchamber.org

**Drummond** · *Drummond C/C* · Mary Ellen McGowan, Pres., P.O. Box 364, 59832, P 348, M 20, (406) 288-3297, www.drummond montana.com

**East Glacier Park** · *East Glacier C/C* · Terry Sherburne, Pres., Hwy. 49 N., P.O. Box 260, 59434, P 396, M 20, (406) 226-4403, Fax (406) 226-4403, mtnpine@3rivers.net, www.eastglacierpark.info

**Ekalaka** · *Carter County C/C* · Rhonda Knapp, Pres., P.O. Box 108, 59324, P 1,500, M 30, (406) 775-6886, www.cartercounty chamberofcommerce.com

**Ennis** · *Ennis Area C/C* · Pamela Kimmey, Exec. Dir., P.O. Box 291, 59729, P 1,000, M 225, (406) 682-4388, Fax (406) 682-4328, info@ennischamber.com, www.ennischamber.com

**Eureka** · *Eureka Area C/C* · Randy McIntyre, Exec. Dir., P.O. Box 186, 59917, P 4,000, M 152, (406) 889-4636, www.eurekaevents. com, randy@welcome2eureka.com, www.welcome2eureka.com

**Fairfield** · *Fairfield C/C* · Marci Shaw, Pres., P.O. Box 776, 59436, P 700, M 76, (406) 467-2493, (406) 590-1042, ffchamber@ hotmail.com

**Fairview** · *Fairview C/C* · Ray Trumpower, Pres., P.O. Box 374, 59221, P 800, M 60, (406) 742-5259, Fax (406) 742-5259, trumpower@midrivers.com, www.midrivers.com/~fairview

**Forsyth** · *Forsyth Area C/C & Ag.* · Stephanie Nielson, Pres., P.O. Box 448, 59327, (406) 347-5656, Fax (406) 346-2492, forsyth montana.org

**Fort Benton** · *Fort Benton C/C & Info. Center* · Stella Scott, Pres., P.O. Box 12, 59442, P 1,400, M 60, (406) 622-3864, info@ fortbenton.com, www.fortbenton.com

**Gardiner** · *Gardiner C/C* · Keren Walters, Exec. Dir., 222 Park St., P.O. Box 81, 59030, P 851, M 130, (406) 848-7971, Fax (406) 848-2446, info@gardinerchamber.com, www.gardinerchamber.com

**Glasgow** · *Glasgow Area C/C & Ag.* · Diane Brandt, Exec. Dir., 23 E. Hwy. 2, P.O. Box 832, 59230, P 3,500, M 200, (406) 228-2222, Fax (406) 228-2244, chamber@glasgowmt.net, www.glasgowmt.net

**Glendive** · *Glendive C of C & Ag.* · Kim Trangmoe, Exec. Dir., 808 N. Merrill, 59330, P 5,000, M 265, (406) 377-5601, (800) 859-0824, Fax (406) 377-5602, chamber@midrivers.com, www. glendivechamber.com.

**Great Falls** · *Great Falls Area C/C* · Steve Malicott, Pres./ CEO, 100 1st Ave. N., 59401, P 79,385, M 650, (406) 761-4434, Fax (406) 761-6129, smalicott@greatfallschamber.org, www. greatfallschamber.org

**Hamilton** · *Bitterroot Valley C/C* · Rick O'Brien, Exec. Dir., 105 E. Main St., 59840, P 40,500, M 600, (406) 363-2400, Fax (406) 363-2402, localinfo@bvchamber.com, www.bitterrootvalleychamber.com.

**Hardin** · *Hardin Area C/C & Ag.* · Dorothy Stenerson, Secy., 10 E. Railway, P.O. Box 446, 59034, P 3,300, M 95, (406) 665-1672, Fax (406) 665-3577, hardinchamber@bhwi.net, www.hardinmt chamber.com

**Harlowton** · *Harlowton Area C/C & Ag.* · Kim Guesanduru, Exec. Dir., P.O. Box 694, 59036, P 1,000, M 80, (406) 632-4694, chamber@ harlowtonchamber.com, www.harlowtonchamber.com

**Havre** · *Havre Area C/C* · Debbie Vandeberg, Exec. Dir., 130 5th Ave., P.O. Box 308, 59501, P 10,800, M 225, (406) 265-4383, Fax (406) 265-7748, chamber@havremt.net, www.havremt.com.

**Helena** · *Helena Area C/C* · Cathy Burwell, Pres./CEO, 225 Cruse Ave., Ste. A, 59601, P 45,000, M 850, (406) 442-4120, (800) 743-5362, Fax (406) 447-1532, lhegstad@helenachamber.com, www. helenachamber.com

**Hot Springs** · *Hot Springs C/C* · Sandra Prongua, Secy., P.O. Box 580, 59845, P 530, M 60, (406) 741-2662, hscofc@hotspringsmt. net, www.hotspringsmtchamber.org

**Hysham** · *Hysham C/C* · Cora Marks, Secy., P.O. Box 63, 59038, P 800, M 25, (406) 342-5457, www.hysham.org

**Jordan** · *Garfield County C/C & Ag.* · Rocky Nelson, Pres., 434 Main St., P.O. Box 370, 59337, P 1,600, M 125, (406) 557-6158, Fax same, chamber@garfieldcounty.com, www.garfieldcounty.com

**Kalispell** · *Kalispell Area C/C* · Joe Unterreiner, Pres./CEO, 15 Depot Park, 59901, P 87,000, M 700, (406) 758-2800, Fax (406) 758-2805, info@kalispellchamber.com, www.kalispellchamber.com.

**Lakeside** · *Lakeside-Somers C/C* · Dave Christensen, Pres., P.O. Box 177, 59922, P 3,500, M 150, (406) 844-3715, info@lakeside somers.org, www.lakesidesomers.org

**Lame Deer** · *Lame Deer C/C* · Suzanne Trusler, Pres., P.O. Box 991, 59043, P 3,000, M 15, (406) 477-8844

**Laurel** · *Laurel C/C* · Joanne Flynn, Exec. Secy., 108 E. Main, 59044, P 7,000, M 131, (406) 628-8105, chamber@laurelmontana. org, www.laurelmontana.org

**Laurin** · *see Twin Bridges*

**Lennep** · *see White Sulpher Springs*

**Lewistown** · *Lewistown Area C/C* · Connie Fry, Exec. Dir., 408 N.E. Main, 59457, P 7,000, M 300, (406) 535-5436, Fax (406) 535-5437, lewchamb@midrivers.com, www.lewistownchamber.com.

**Libby** · *Libby Area C/C* · Dusti Thompson, Exec. Dir., 905 W. 9th St., P.O. Box 704, 59923, P 10,000, M 275, (406) 293-4167, Fax (406) 293-2197, libbyacc@libbychamber.org, www.libbychamber.org

**Lincoln** · *Lincoln Valley C/C* · Ron Erickson, Pres., P.O. Box 985, 59639, P 1,500, M 62, (406) 362-4949, lincolnmontana@gmail. com, www.lincolnmontana.com

**Livingston** · *Livingston Area C/C* · LouAnn Nelson, Ofc. Mgr., 303 E. Park St., 59047, P 7,500, M 450, (406) 222-0850, Fax (406) 222-0852, info@livingston-chamber.com, www.livingston-chamber.com

**Malta** · *Malta Area C/C* · Krista Fahlgren, Secy., 10 1/2 S. 4 E., P.O. Box 1420, 59538, P 4,900, M 125, (406) 654-1776, Fax (406) 654-1776, malta@mtintouch.net, www.maltachamber.com

**Manhattan** · *Manhattan Area C/C* · Karen Lauersdorf, Exec. Secy., P.O. Box 606, 59741, P 1,500, M 111, (406) 284-4162, Fax (406) 284-4162, manhattanmontana@yahoo.com, www.man hattanmontana.com

**Martinsdale** · *see White Sulpher Springs*

**Miles City** · *Miles City Area C/C* · John Laney, Exec. Dir., 511 Pleasant St., 59301, P 8,700, M 306, (406) 234-2890, Fax (406) 234-6914, mcchamber@mcchamber.com, www.milescitymt.org

**Missoula** · *Missoula Area C/C* · Kim Latrielle, CEO, 825 E. Front, P.O. Box 7577, 59807, P 100,086, M 1,000, (406) 543-6623, Fax (406) 543-6625, info@missoulachamber.com, www.missoula chamber.com

**Philipsburg** · *Philipsburg C/C* · P.O. Box 661, 59858, P 915, M 30, (406) 859-3388, chamber@philipsburgmt.com, www. philipsburgmt.com

**Plains** · *Plains-Paradise C/C* · P.O. Box 1531, 59859, P 1,500, M 90, (406) 826-4700, www.wildhorseplainschamber.com

**Plentywood** · *Sheridan County C/C* · Richard Rice, Pres., P.O. Box 104, 59254, P 4,000, M 100, (406) 765-1733, Fax (406) 765-2106, rrice1733@aol.com, www.sheridancountychamber.org

**Polson** · *Polson C/C* · 418 Main St., P.O. Box 667, 59860, P 4,600, M 222, (406) 883-5969, Fax (406) 883-1716, chamber@polson chamber.com, www.polsonchamber.com

**Red Lodge** · *Red Lodge Area C/C* · Gwen Williams, Pres., 601 N. Broadway, P.O. Box 988, 59068, P 2,500, M 200, (406) 446-1718, (888) 281-0625, Fax (406) 446-1720, info@redlodgechamber.org, www.redlodgechamber.org

**Ringling** · *see White Sulpher Springs*

**Ronan** · *Ronan C/C* · P.O. Box 254, 59864, P 1,800, M 100, (406) 676-8300, info@ronanchamber.com, www.ronanchamber.com

**Roundup** · *Roundup C/C* · Meryl Hunt, Pres., P.O. Box 751, 59072, P 2,049, M 69, (406) 323-1966, Fax (406) 323-1966, roundupc@midrivers.com, www.roundupchamber.net

**Saco** · *Saco C/C* · Joy Linn, Pres., P.O. Box 75, 59261, P 200, M 10, (406) 527-3434

**Saint Ignatius** · *Saint Ignatius C/C* · Amy Miller, 333 Mountain View, P.O. Box 566, 59865, P 700, M 40, (406) 745-3900, Fax (406) 745-5038, stignatiusinfo@stignatius.net, www. stignatiusmontana.com

**Scobey** · *Daniels County C/C & Ag.* · 120 Main St., P.O. Box 91, 59263, P 1,082, M 43, (406) 487-2061, scobey@nemontel.net, www.scobeymt.com

**Seeley Lake** · *Seeley Lake Area C/C* · Cheryl Thompson, Exec. Dir., 2920 Hwy. 83 N., P.O. Box 516, 59868, P 2,500, M 95, (406) 677-2880, Fax (406) 677-2880, slchamber@blackfoot.net, www. seeleylakechamber.com

**Shelby** · *Shelby Area C/C* · Holly Rogers, Pres., P.O. Box 865, 59474, P 3,500, M 110, (406) 434-7184, shelbycoc@3rivers.net, www.shelbymtchamber.org

**Sheridan** · *see Twin Bridges*

**Sidney** · *Sidney C of C and Ag.* · Wade Vanevery, Exec. Dir., 909 S. Central Ave., 59270, P 9,800, M 240, (406) 433-1916, Fax (406) 433-1127, schamber@midrivers.com, www.sidneymt.com

**Silver Gate** · *see Cooke City*

**Silver Star** · *see Twin Bridges*

**St. Regis** · *see Superior*

**Superior** · *Mineral County C/C* · Jim Hollenbeck, Pres., P.O. Box 483, 59872, P 4,000, M 50, (406) 649-6400, mccoc@blackfoot.net, www.montanarockies.org

**Swan Lake** · *Swan Lake C/C* · Diane Kautzman, Pres., P.O. Box 5096, 59911, P 300, M 110, (406) 886-2303

**Terry** · *Prairie County C/C* · Glenda Ueland, Pres., P.O. Box 667, 59349, P 1,200, M 50, (406) 635-5513, (406) 635-2126, Fax (406) 635-5513, www.terrytribune.com

**Thompson Falls** · *Thompson Falls C/C* · Melissa Wilson, Mgr., P.O. Box 493, 59873, P 1,800, M 110, (406) 827-4930, tfchamber@ thompsonfallschamber.com, www.thompsonfallschamber.com

**Three Forks** · *Three Forks C/C & Visitor Center* · Barbara Frost, Pres., P.O. Box 1103, 59752, P 1,800, M 113, (406) 285-4753, (406) 285-3011, tfchamber@aol.com, www.threeforksmontana.com

**Townsend** · *Townsend Area C/C* · M.A. Upton, Secy., P.O. Box 947, 59644, P 4,000, M 90, (406) 266-4101, (877) 266-4101, Fax (406) 266-4042, townsendchamber@mt.net

**Troy** · *Troy C/C* · Melody Condron, Pres., P.O. Box 3005, 59935, P 1,000, M 51, (406) 295-1064, troymtchamber@hotmail.com, www.troymtchamber.org

**Twin Bridges** · *Greater Ruby Valley C/C* · Karen W. Town, Pres., P.O. Box 134, 59754, P 1,500, M 160, (406) 684-5678, info@ rubyvalleychamber.com, www.rubyvalleychamber.com

**Virginia City** · *Virginia City Area C/C* · P.O. Box 218, 59755, P 140, M 70, (406) 843-5555, (800) 829-2969, info@virginiacity. com, www.virginiacity.com

**West Yellowstone** · *West Yellowstone C/C & Visitors Center* · 30 Yellowstone Ave., P.O. Box 458, 59758, P 1,020, M 224, (406) 646-7701, Fax (406) 646-9691, visitorservices@westyellowstone chamber.com, www.westyellowstonechamber.com

**White Sulphur Springs** · *Meagher County C/C* · Kelly Huffield, Pres., P.O. Box 356, 59645, P 1,000, M 60, (406) 547-2250, info@ meagherchamber.com, www.meagherchamber.com

**Whitefish** · *Whitefish C/C* · Sheila Bowen, Pres./CEO, 520 E. 2nd St., P.O. Box 1120, 59937, P 8,000, M 540, (406) 862-3501, Fax (406) 862-9494, visit@whitefishchamber.org, www.whitefish chamber.org

**Whitehall** · *Whitehall C/C* · P.O. Box 72, 59759, P 2,000, M 50, (406) 287-2260, www.whitehallmt.com

**Wibaux** · *Wibaux County C/C* · Renee Nelson, Pres., P.O. Box 159, 59353, P 900, M 20, (406) 796-2412

**Wolf Point** · *Wolf Point C of C & Ag.* · Kt Northington, Exec. Dir., 218 3rd Ave. S. #B, 59201, P 3,200, M 125, (406) 653-2012, wpchmber@nemont.net, www.wolfpointchamber.org

# Nebraska

**Nebraska C of C & Ind.** · Barry L. Kennedy CAE IOM, Pres., P.O. Box 95128, Lincoln, 68509, P 1,800,000, M 1,300, (402) 474-4422, Fax (402) 474-5681, nechamber@nechamber.com, www. nechamber.com.

**Ainsworth** · *Ainsworth Area C/C & North Central Dev. Center* · Lesley Holmes, Exec. Secy., 335 N. Main St., 69210, P 3,000, M 150, (402) 387-2740, chamber@threeriver.net, www. ainsworthchamber.com

**Albion** · *Albion C/C* · Abby Johnson, Dir., 420 W. Market, 68620, P 1,700, M 115, (402) 395-6723, ccalbn@hotmail.com, www. cityofalbion-ne.com

**Alliance** · *Alliance Area C/C* · Dixie Nelson, Exec. Dir., 111 W. 3rd, P.O. Box 571, 69301, P 9,000, M 274, (308) 762-1520, (800) 738-0648, Fax (308) 762-4919, chamber@bbc.net, www. alliancechamber.com.

**Alma** · *Alma C/C* · Bonnie Nurnberg, Pres., P.O. Box 52, 68920, P 1,200, M 60, (308) 928-2992, Fax (308) 928-2683, alma@ megavision.com, www.ci.alma.ne.us

**Arapahoe** · *Arapahoe C/C* · Tammie Middagh, Secy., P.O. Box 624, 68922, P 1,028, M 65, (308) 962-7777, chamber@arapahoe-ne.com, www.arapahoe-ne.com

**Arnold** · *Arnold C/C* · Bob Westbrook, Pres., P.O. Box 166, 69120, P 680, M 79, (308) 848-2522

**Arthur** · *Arthur C/C* · Ron Jageler, Pres., 103 N. Hwy. 61, 69121, P 120, M 4, (308) 764-2367

**Ashland** · *Ashland C/C* · Bob Luebbe, Pres., P.O. Box 5, 68003, P 2,500, M 85, (402) 944-2050, www.historicashland.com

**Atkinson** · *Atkinson C/C* · Bonnie Lech, Secy./Treas., P.O. Box 871, 68713, P 1,200, M 70, (402) 925-5571, bonnielech@morcomm. net, www.atkinsonne.com

**Auburn** · *Auburn C/C* · Kendall Neiman, Pres., 1211 J St., 68305, P 3,500, M 200, (402) 274-3521, Fax (402) 274-4020, auburn chamberofcommerce@gmail.com, www.auburnneb.com

**Aurora** · *Aurora Area Chamber & Dev. Corp.* · Christian Evans, Exec. Dir., 1604 L St., P.O. Box 146, 68818, P 4,400, M 275, (402) 694-6911, Fax (402) 694-5766, aacd@hamilton.net, www. auroranebraska.com

**Axtell** · *Axtell C/C* · Jim Messer, Secy., P.O. Box 26, 68924, P 696, M 75, (308) 743-2437, www.axtellne.com

**Bassett** · *Bassett/Rock County C/C* · Bill Sanger, Pres., P.O. Box 537, 68714, P 1,700, M 73, (402) 684-3649, (402) 684-2268, www.bassettnebr.com

**Beatrice** · *Beatrice Area C/C* · Lori Warner, Pres./CEO, 226 S. 6th St., 68310, P 12,894, M 430, (402) 223-2338, (800) 755-7745, Fax (402) 223-2339, info@beatricechamber.com, www.beatrice chamber.com

**Beaver City** · *Beaver City C/C* · Linda Tomlinson, Coord., P.O. Box 303, 68926, P 680, M 40, (308) 268-9966, Fax (308) 268-9966, beaverchamber@swnebr.net

**Beaver Crossing** · *Beaver Crossing C/C* · Kathy Fisher, V.P., 413 Martin Ave., 68313, P 475, M 30, (402) 532-3875, chamber@ beavercrossingne.com, www.beavercrossingne.com

**Bellevue** · *Bellevue C/C* · Megan Lucas, Pres./CEO, 1102 Galvin Rd. S., 68005, P 50,000, M 520, (402) 898-3000, Fax (402) 291-8729, bellevue@bellevuenebraska.com, www.bellevuenebraska.com.

**Benkelman** · *Benkelman C/C* · P.O. Box 661, 69021, P 1,000, M 36, (308) 423-5210, benkchamber@bwtelcom.neet

**Bennington** · *see Elkhorn*

**Big Springs** · *Big Springs C/C* · Ron Hendrickson, P.O. Box 436, 69122, P 400, M 24, (308) 889-3681, www.ci.big-springs.ne.us

**Blair** · *Blair Area C/C* · Harriet Waite, Exec. Dir., 1646 Washington St., 68008, P 7,800, M 240, (402) 533-4455, Fax (402) 533-4456, mail@blairchamber.org, www.blairchamber.org

**Bloomfield** · *Bloomfield C/C* · Jason Hefner, Pres., P.O. Box 292, 68718, P 1,126, M 60, (402) 373-4321, Fax (402) 373-4597, www. ci.bloomfield.ne.us

**Blue Hill** · *Blue Hill Comm. Club* · P.O. Box 63, 68930, P 867, M 25, (402) 756-2056

**Bridgeport** · *Prairie Winds C/C* · Jack Berg, Pres., P.O. Box 640, 69336, P 1,600, M 100, (308) 262-1825, www.bridgeport-ne.com

**Broken Bow** · *Broken Bow C/C* · Denise Russell, Exec. Dir., 444 S. 8th Ave., 68822, P 3,800, M 200, (308) 872-5691, Fax (308) 872-6137, info@brokenbow-ne.com, www.brokenbow-ne.com

**Burwell** · *Burwell C/C* · David Sawyer, Dir., P.O. Box 131, 68823, P 1,300, M 110, (308) 346-5210, Fax (308) 346-5121, www.burwellchamber.net

**Callaway** · *Callaway C/C* · Shirley Trout, Pres./CEO, P.O. Box 272, 68825, P 700, M 70, (308) 836-2245, www.callaway-ne.com

**Cambridge** · *Cambridge C/C* · Bev Smith, Secy., P.O. Box 8, 69022, P 1,100, M 50, (308) 697-3120, www.swnebr.net

**Campbell** · *Campbell Area C/C* · William Pearson, P.O. Box 219, 68932, P 440, M 66, (402) 756-8851, www.campbellnebraska.org

**Central City** · *Central City Area C/C* · Kendra Jefferson, Exec. Dir., 1515 17th St., P.O. Box 418, 68826, P 3,000, M 200, (308) 946-3897, cchamber@cablene.com, www.centralcitychamber.com

**Chadron** · *Chadron C/C* · Collette Fernandez, Exec. Dir., 706 W. 3rd, P.O. Box 646, 69337, P 5,588, M 200, (308) 432-4401, (800) 603-2937, Fax (308) 432-4757, chamber@chadron.com, www.chadron.com

**Chappell** · *Chappell C/C* · P.O. Box 121, 69129, P 980, M 50, (308) 874-9912, chamber69129@yahoo.com, www.chappellchamber.com

**Clearwater** · *Clearwater C/C* · Curt Thiele, Pres., 85314 516th Ave., 68726, P 400, M 100, (402) 485-2348, (402) 485-2365, www.clearwaterne.com

**Columbus** · *Columbus Area C/C* · K.C. Belitz, Pres., 764 33rd Ave., P.O. Box 515, 68602, P 22,000, M 738, (402) 564-2769, Fax (402) 564-2026, chamber@megavision.com, www.thecolumbuspage.com

**Cozad** · *Cozad Area C/C* · Judy Andres, 135 W. 8th St., 69130, P 4,200, M 205, (308) 784-3930, Fax (308) 784-3026, cozadchmbr@cozadtel.net, www.cozadnebraska.net

**Crawford** · *Crawford C/C* · Tim Krieder, Pres., P.O. Box 145, 69339, P 1,000, M 65, (308) 665-1817, crawfordchamber@yahoo.com, www.crawfordnebraska.biz

**Creighton** · *Creighton Area C/C* · Steve Morrill, P.O. Box 502, 68729, P 1,200, M 90, (402) 358-3293, (402) 360-4148, creightonchamber@gpcom.net, www.creighton.org

**Crete** · *Crete C/C* · Char Sieck, 1341 Main Ave., 68333, P 6,200, M 125, (402) 826-2136, Fax (402) 826-2136, cretechamber@neb.rr.com, www.crete-ne.com

**Crofton** · *Crofton Comm. Club* · Doug Moser, Pres., P.O. Box 81, 68730, P 800, M 45, (402) 388-4583, ccclub@gpcom.net, www.crofton-ne.com

**Curtis** · *Medicine Creek C/C* · P.O. Box 463, 69025, P 800, M 30, (308) 367-4122, medcreekchamber@curtis-ne.com, www.curtis-ne.com/chamber.html

**David City** · *Butler County C/C* · Stephanie Dubbs, Exec. Dir., 457 D St., 68632, P 2,600, M 100, (402) 367-4238, dcchamber@windstream.net, www.davidcityne.com

**Deshler** · *Deshler C/C* · P.O. Box 449, 68340, P 879, M 50, (402) 365-7211, www.deshlernebraska.com

**Dorchester** · *Dorchester C/C* · Judith Ottmann, 1146 County Rd. F, 68343, P 620, M 15, (402) 946-4821

**Elgin** · *Elgin C/C* · Greg Tharnish, Pres., P.O. Box C, 68636, P 700, M 50, (402) 843-2411, www.elginne.com

**Elkhorn** · *Western Douglas County C/C* · Jim Tomanek, Pres., 20801 Elkhorn Dr., P.O. Box 202, 68022, P 10,000, M 250, (402) 289-9560, Fax (402) 289-9560, jtomanek.wdccc@gmail.com, www.wdccc.org

**Elm Creek** · *Elm Creek C/C* · Jan Hinrichsen, Pres., P.O. Box 103, 68836, P 950, M 40, (308) 856-4913

**Elwood** · *Elwood C/C* · Jim Varvel, Pres., P.O. Box 92, 68937, P 700, M 56, (308) 785-3366, jvarvel@security1stbank.com, www.elwoodnebraska.com

**Eustis** · *Eustis C/C* · Sharon Larsen, Secy., P.O. Box 372, 69028, P 450, M 50, (308) 486-5615, www.eustisnebraska.com

**Fairbury** · *Fairbury C/C* · Sharon Priefert, Exec. Dir., 518 E St., P.O. Box 274, 68352, P 4,262, M 147, (402) 729-3000, Fax (402) 729-3076, fairburychamber@diodecom.net, www.fairburychamber.org

**Falls City** · *Falls City Area C/C* · 1705 Stone St., 68355, P 4,600, M 155, (402) 245-4228, Fax (402) 245-4228, fcchamber@sentco.net, www.fallscityonline.com

**Fremont** · *Fremont Area C/C* · Allan Hale, Pres., 605 N. Broad St., P.O. Box 182, 68026, P 25,184, M 675, (402) 721-2641, Fax (402) 721-9359, info@fremontne.org, www.fremontne.org.

**Friend** · *Friend C/C* · Vickie Himmelberg, 122 S. Main, 68359, P 1,200, M 52, www.ci.friend.ne.us.

**Geneva** · *Geneva C/C* · Lori Loontjer, Dir., 145 N. 9th St., P.O. Box 85, 68361, P 2,300, M 85, (402) 759-1155, Fax (402) 759-3629, chamber@cityofgeneva.org, www.cityofgeneva.org/chamber/

**Genoa** · *Genoa C/C* · P.O. Box 331, 68640, P 982, M 20, (402) 993-2330, www.ci.genoa.ne.us

**Gering** · *see Scottsbluff*

**Gibbon** · *Gibbon C/C* · Kelli Peterson, Pres., P.O. Box 56, 68840, P 1,759, M 60, (308) 468-6118, gibbonchamber@nctc.net, www.gibbonchamber.org

**Gordon** · *Gordon Area C/C* · P.O. Box 160, 69343, P 1,500, M 106, (308) 282-0730, gcc@gordonchamber.com, www.gordonchamber.com

**Gothenburg** · *Gothenburg Area C/C* · Anne Anderson, Exec. Dir., 1021 Lake Ave., P.O. Box 263, 69138, P 3,746, M 230, (308) 537-3505, (800) 482-5520, Fax (308) 537-2541, chamber@gothenburgdelivers.com, www.gothenburgdelivers.com

**Grand Island** · *Grand Island Area C/C* · Cindy Johnson, Pres., 309 W. 2nd St., P.O. Box 1486, 68802, P 43,000, M 735, (308) 382-9210, Fax (308) 382-1154, info@gichamber.com, www.gichamber.com

**Grant** · *Perkins County C/C* · P.O. Box 767, 69140, P 3,000, M 80, chamber@gpcom.net, www.perkinscountychamber.com

**Greeley** · *Greeley C/C* · P.O. Box 306, 68842, P 585, M 15, (308) 428-3925, www.cnbgreeley.com

**Gretna** · *Gretna Area C/C* · P.O. Box 431, 68028, P 5,000, M 174, (402) 332-3535, info@gretnachamber.com, www.gretnachamber.com

**Hartington** · *Hartington C/C* · Stephanie Skoggan, Pres., P.O. Box 742, 68739, P 1,640, M 120, (402) 254-6357, Fax (402) 254-6391, www.ci.hartington.ne.us

**Hastings** · *Hastings Area C/C* · Tom Hastings, Pres., 301 S. Burlington, P.O. Box 1104, 68902, P 24,064, M 738, (402) 461-8400, Fax (402) 461-4400, hastings@hastingschamber.com, www.hastingschamber.com.

**Hay Springs** · *Hay Springs C/C* · Jane Diers, Treas., P.O. Box 264, 69347, P 650, M 60, (308) 638-4416, Fax (308) 638-4418

**Hebron** · *Hebron C/C* · Tina Reed, Exec. Dir., 216 Lincoln Ave., P.O. Box 172, 68370, P 1,565, M 80, (402) 768-7156, Fax (402) 768-6176, hebronchamber@yahoo.com, www.hebronnebraska.us

**Hemingford** · *Hemingford C/C* · Amy Raben, Pres., P.O. Box 51, 69348, P 993, M 40, (308) 487-5578, www.bbc.net/chamber

**Henderson** · *Henderson C/C* · Kelsey Bergen, Dir., P.O. Box 225, 68371, P 1,000, M 90, (402) 723-4228, hcchamber@mainstaycomm.net, www.cityofhenderson.org

**Holdrege** · *Holdrege Area C/C* · Trenna Lawrence, Admin. Asst., 316 East Ave., P.O. Box 200, 68949, P 5,650, M 225, (308) 995-4444, Fax (308) 995-4445, chamber@justtheplacenebraska.com, www.justtheplacenebraska.com

**Humboldt** · *Humboldt C/C* · Kathy Kanel, Secy., P.O. Box 125, 68376, P 941, M 70, (402) 862-2821

**Hyannis** · *Sandhills C/C* · 313 Morton St., P.O. Box, 69350, P 500, M 8, (308) 458-2716

**Imperial** · *Imperial C/C* · Sue Moore, P.O. Box 87, 69033, P 2,000, M 65, (308) 882-5444, www.imperialchamber.com

**Kearney** · *Kearney Area C/C* · Greg Shea, Exec. Dir., 1007 2nd Ave., P.O. Box 607, 68848, P 28,250, M 950, (308) 237-3101, (800) 227-8340, Fax (308) 237-3103, gshea@kearneycoc.org, www.kearneycoc.org

**Kimball** · *Kimball-Banner County C/C* · Kim Baliman, Dir., 122 S. Chestnut, 69145, P 2,600, M 202, (308) 235-3782, Fax (308) 235-3825, kbccc@megavision.com, www.ci.kimball.ne.us

**LaVista** · *LaVista Area C/C* · Kim Madrigal, Exec. Dir., 8040 S. 84th St., 68128, P 15,000, M 300, (402) 339-2078, Fax (402) 339-2026, info@lavistachamber.org, www.lavistachamber.org

**Lexington** · *Lexington Area C/C* · Susan Bennett, Exec. Dir., 302 E. 6th, P.O. Box 97, 68850, P 10,000, M 350, (308) 324-5504, Fax (308) 324-5505, www.visitlexington.org, julie@lexcoc.com, www.lexcoc.com

**Lincoln** · *Lincoln C/C* · Wendy Birdsall, Pres., 1135 M St., P.O. Box 83006, 68501, P 250,000, M 1,450, (402) 436-2350, Fax (402) 436-2360, info@lcoc.com, www.lcoc.com.

**Long Pine** · *Long Pine C/C* · P.O. Box 234, 69217, P 346, M 22, (402) 273-4395, www.cityoflongpine.org

**Loup City** · *Loup City C/C* · Chamber Coord., P.O. Box 24, 68853, P 1,000, M 100, (308) 745-0430, lcchamber@cornhusker.net, www.loupcity.com

**Madison** · *Madison Area C/C* · Linda Haack, Exec. Dir., P.O. Box 287, 68748, P 2,400, M 75, (402) 454-2251, Fax (402) 454-2262, chamber@ncfcomm.com, www.ci.madison.ne.us

**McCook** · *McCook Area C/C* · Pamela Harsh, Exec. Dir., 107 Norris Ave., P.O. Box 337, 69001, P 8,000, M 230, (308) 345-3200, Fax (308) 345-3201, info@aboutmccook.com, www.aboutmccook.com

**Milford** · *Milford C/C* · Susan Nitzsche, Pres., P.O. Box 174, 68405, P 2,000, M 75, (402) 761-3247, chamber@milford-ne.com, www.milfordnechamber.com

**Minden** · *Minden C/C* · 325 N. Colorado Ave., P.O. Box 375, 68959, P 3,000, M 180, (308) 832-1811, Fax (308) 832-1811, info@mindenne.org, www.mindenne.org

**Mitchell** · *Mitchell C/C* · Brenda Muhr, Pres., P.O. Box 72, 69357, P 1,800, M 31, (308) 623-1523, www.mitchellcity.net

**Nebraska City** · *Nebraska City Tourism & Commerce Inc.* · Rose Ralstin, Exec. Dir., 806 1st Ave., 68410, P 7,400, M 352, (402) 873-6654, (800) 514-9113, Fax (402) 873-6701, roser@nebraskacity.com, www.nebraskacity.com

**Neligh** · *Neligh C/C* · Walter Storey, Pres., P.O. Box 266, 68756, P 1,700, M 100, (402) 887-4447, Fax (402) 887-4399, www.neligh.net

**Norfolk** · *Norfolk Area C/C* · 405 Madison Ave., P.O. Box 386, 68702, P 24,183, M 600, (402) 371-4862, Fax (402) 371-0182, exec@norfolk.ne.us, www.norfolk.ne.us

**North Bend** · *North Bend C/C* · Katy Bode, Pres., P.O. Box 361, 68649, P 1,200, M 65, (402) 652-3221, Fax (402) 652-8601, www.northbendne.org

**North Platte** · *North Platte Area C/C & Dev.* · Dan Mauk, Pres./CEO, 502 S. Dewey, 69101, P 24,800, M 650, (308) 532-4966, Fax (308) 532-4827, cameron@northplattechamber.com, www.northplattechamber.com.

**Oakland** · *Oakland C/C* · Andy Rennerfeldt, Pres., 212 N. Oakland Ave., 68045, P 1,300, M 150, (402) 685-6282

**Ogallala** · *Ogallala/Keith County C/C* · Marion Kroeker, Exec. Dir., 204 E. A St., P.O. Box 628, 69153, P 8,877, M 395, (308) 284-4066, (800) 658-4390, Fax (308) 284-3126, info@visitogallala.com, www.visitogallala.com, www.lakemcconaughy.com.

**Omaha** · *Greater Omaha C/C* · David Brown, Pres./CEO, 1301 Harney St., 68102, P 828,741, M 3,500, (402) 346-5000, Fax (402) 346-7050, info@omahachamber.org, www.omahachamber.org.

**O'Neill** · *O'Neill Area C/C* · Pat Fritz, Exec. Dir., 125 S. 4th St., 68763, P 5,000, M 250, (402) 336-2355, Fax (402) 336-4563, oneill@morcomm.net, www.oneillchamber.org

**Ord** · *Ord Area C/C* · Caleb Pollard, Exec. Dir., 1514 K St., 68862, P 2,600, M 200, (308) 728-7875, Fax (308) 728-7691, valleycountyed@frontiernet.net, www.ordnebraska.com

**Orleans** · *Orleans C/C* · Tom Arnett, Pres., P.O. Box 464, 68966, P 450, M 50, (308) 473-4825, www.orleansne.com

**Osceola** · *Osceola C/C* · Doug Rathjen, P.O. Box 136, 68651, P 1,000, M 40, (402) 747-2251, www.ci.osceola.ne.us

**Oshkosh** · *Garden County C/C* · Terri O'Brien, Pres., P.O. Box 256, 69154, P 1,900, M 60, (308) 772-9990, chamber@gardencone.com, www.gardencone.com

**Papillion** · *Sarpy County C/C* · Jane Nielsen, Pres., 7775 Olson Dr., Ste. 207, 68046, P 147,000, M 575, (402) 339-3050, Fax (402) 339-9968, chamber@sarpychamber.org, www.sarpychamber.org

**Pawnee City** · *Pawnee City C/C* · Steve Glen, P.O. Box 6, 68420, P 1,000, (402) 852-2444, www.pawneecity.com

**Pender** · *Pender Thurston C/C* · Connie Wichman, P.O. Box 250, 68047, P 1,500, M 52, (402) 385-3200, www.penderthurston.com

**Peru** · *Peru C/C* · Ruth Hazwood, Pres., P.O. Box 246, 68421, P 922, M 20, growchamberofcommerce@windstream.com, www.ci.peru.ne.us

**Pierce** · *Pierce C/C* · Rick Higgins, Pres., P.O. Box 82, 68767, P 1,800, M 50, (402) 329-6879, www.piercenebraska.com

**Plainview** · *Plainview C/C* · 306 W. Park Ave., P.O. Box 813, 68769, P 1,400, M 65, (402) 582-4433

**Plattsmouth** · *Plattsmouth C/C* · Lisa Davis, Exec. Dir., 918 Washington Ave., 68048, P 7,070, M 230, (402) 296-6021, Fax (402) 296-6974, lisad@plattsmouthchamber.com, www.plattsmouthchamber.com

**Ralston** · *Ralston Area C/C* · Marlene Hansen, Pres., 5505 Miller Ave., 68127, P 6,200, M 275, (402) 339-7737, Fax (402) 339-7954, chamber@cityofralston.com, www.ralstonareachamber.org

**Ravenna** · *Ravenna C/C* · Margaret Treffer, Secy./Treas., P.O. Box 56, 68869, P 1,347, M 77, (402) 910-4231, (308) 452-3225, Fax (308) 452-3296, ravchamber@towncountrybank.net, www.ci.ravenna.ne.us

**Red Cloud** · *Red Cloud C/C* · Ken Van Wey, Co-Pres., P.O. Box 327, 68970, P 1,131, M 40, (402) 746-3238, redcloudchamberofcommerce@gmail.com, www.redcloudnebraska.com

**Saint Paul** · *Saint Paul Area C/C* · 619 Howard Ave., 68873, P 2,200, M 130, (308) 754-5558, Fax (308) 754-5558, stpaulcham@qwestoffice.net, www.stpaulnebraska.com

**Schuyler** · *Schuyler Area C/C* · Marie Myrick, Exec. Dir., 1107 B St., 68661, P 5,100, M 182, (402) 352-5472, Fax (402) 615-3659, www.ci.schuyler.ne.us/chamber.asp

**Scottsbluff** · *Scottsbluff/Gering United C/C* · Karen Anderson, Exec. Dir., 1517 Broadway #104, 69361, P 23,000, M 480, (308) 632-2133, (800) 788-9475, Fax (308) 632-7128, chamber@scottsbluffgering.net, www.scottsbluffgering.net.

**Scribner** · *Scribner C/C* · Deb Eggleston, P.O. Box 25, 68057, P 970, M 65, (402) 664-2561, www.scribnernebraska.com

**Seward** · *Seward Area C/C* · Ms. Pat Coldiron, Dir., 616 Bradford, 68434, P 6,700, M 200, (402) 643-4189, Fax (402) 643-4713, sewcham@sewardne.com, www.sewardne.com.

**Shelby** · *Shelby C/C* · P.O. Box 27, 68662, P 690, M 60, (402) 527-5198, www.ci.shelby.ne.us

**Sidney** · *Cheyenne County C/C* · Megan McGown, Exec. Dir., 740 Illinois St., 69162, P 9,830, M 260, (308) 254-5851, (800) 421-4769, Fax (308) 254-3081, ccchamber@hamilton.net, www.cheyennecountychamber.com

**South Sioux City** · *South Sioux City Area C/C* · Pat Anderson, Pres., 3900 Dakota Ave., Ste. 11, 68776, P 12,000, M 360, (402) 494-1626, Fax (402) 494-5010, www.southsiouxchamber.org.

**Stamford** · *Stamford C/C* · Rolena Novak, Secy., P.O. Box 34, 68977, P 202, (308) 868-2401, rnovak@accessdirectwb.net

**Stratton** · *Stratton Area C/C* · P.O. Box 264, 69043, P 396, M 24, (308) 276-2184, chamber@stratton-ne.org, www.stratton-ne.org

**Superior** · *Superior Area C/C* · 354 N. Commercial Ave., 68978, P 2,055, M 120, (402) 879-3419, Fax (402) 879-4562, superiorcc@windstream.net, www.ci.superior.ne.us

**Sutherland** · *Sutherland C/C* · Bob Lantis, Pres., P.O. Box 81, 69165, P 1,200, M 36, (308) 386-4345

**Syracuse** · *Syracuse C/C* · Carolyn Gigstad, Exec. Dir., P.O. Box J, 68446, P 1,710, M 75, (402) 269-3373, chamber@syracusene.com, www.syracusene.com

**Table Rock** · *Table Rock Comm. Club* · 712 State, 68447, P 270, (402) 839-2180

**Tecumseh** · *Tecumseh C/C* · Eloise Bartels, Secy., P.O. Box 126, 68450, P 1,720, M 64, (402) 335-3400, Fax (402) 335-3235, tecumsehchamber@windstream.net, www.tecumsehne.com

**Tekamah** · *Tekamah C/C* · Harriet Schafer, Secy., P.O. Box 231, 68061, P 1,900, M 110, (402) 374-2020, Fax (402) 374-1392, www.tekamahchamberofcommerce.com

**Valentine** · *Valentine C/C* · Dean Jacobs, Exec. Dir., 239 S. Main St., P.O. Box 201, 69201, P 3,000, M 200, (402) 376-2969, (800) 658-4024, Fax (402) 376-2688, valentinecc@sandhillswireless.net, www.visitvalentine.com

**Valley** · *see Elkhorn*

**Wahoo** · *Wahoo C/C* · Doug Watts, Exec. Dir., 640 N. Broadway, P.O. Box 154, 68066, P 4,045, M 350, (402) 443-4001, Fax (402) 443-3077, watts@wahoo.ne.us, www.wahoo.ne.us

**Waterloo** · *see Elkhorn*

**Waverly** · *Waverly C/C* · Tina Sondgeroth, Pres., P.O. Box 331, 68462, P 2,500, M 50, (402) 786-2555, www.waverlyne.org

**Wayne** · *Wayne Area C/C & Eco. Dev.* · Wes Blecke, Asst. Dir., 108 W. 3rd St., 68787, P 6,000, M 200, (402) 375-2240, (866) 929-6363, Fax (402) 375-2246, wblecke@waedi.org, www.wayneworks.org

**Weeping Water** · *Weeping Water C/C* · Keith Hammons, Pres., P.O. Box 286, 68463, P 1,107, M 50, (402) 267-5152, www.weepingwaternebraska.com

**West Point** · *West Point C/C* · Tina Welding, Exec. Dir., P.O. Box 125, 68788, P 3,660, M 125, (402) 372-2981, Fax (402) 372-1105, info@westpointchamber.com, www.westpointchamber.com

**Wilber** · *Wilber Area C/C* · Tim Linscott, Pres., P.O. Box 1164, 68465, P 1,700, M 40, (402) 821-2732, Fax (402) 821-2691, www.ci.wilber.ne.us

**Winnetoon** · *see Creighton*

**Wisner** · *Wisner Area C/C* · Layne Matthes, Pres., P.O. Box 296, 68791, P 1,300, M 64, (402) 529-3338, wisnerareachamber@yahoo.com, www.wisnerareachamberofcommerce.com

**York** · *Greater York Area C/C* · Todd Kirshenbaum, Exec. Dir., 603 Lincoln Ave., 68467, P 8,000, M 284, (402) 362-5531, Fax (402) 362-5953, yorkcc@yorkchamber.net, www.yorkchamber.org.

# Nevada

**Nevada State C of C** · One E. First St. #1600, P.O. Box 3499, Reno, 89505, P 1,781,750, M 1,500, (775) 337-3030, Fax (775) 337-3038, info@renosparkschamber.org, www.renosparkschamber.org

**Women's Chamber of Commerce of Nevada** · June Beland, Pres./CEO, 2300 W. Sahara Ave., Ste. 800, Las Vegas, 89102, P 2,400,000, M 401, (702) 733-3955, Fax (702) 733-1172, info@womenschamberofnevada.org, www.womenschamberofnevada.org

**Amargosa Valley** · *Amargosa Valley C/C* · HC 69 Box 401W, 89020, P 1,300, M 30, (775) 372-1515, Fax (775) 372-5362, amargosachamber.com

**Austin** · *Greater Austin C/C* · Phillip Williams, Pres., 122 Main St., P.O. Box 212, 89310, P 350, M 37, (775) 964-2200, Fax (775) 964-2200, austinnvchamber@yahoo.com, www.austinnevada.com

**Battle Mountain** · *Battle Mountain C/C* · Sarah Burkhart, Exec. Dir., P.O. Box 333, 89820, P 5,500, M 127, (775) 635-8245, Fax (775) 635-8064, bmcommerce@yahoo.com, www.shopbattlemountain.com

**Beatty** · *Beatty C/C* · Ann Marchand, Pres., P.O. Box 956, 89003, P 1,000, M 50, (775) 553-2424, Fax (775) 553-2424, beattychamber@sbcglobal.net, www.beattynevada.org

**Boulder City** · *Boulder City C/C* · Jill Rowland-Lagan, CEO, 465 Nevada Way, 89005, P 15,000, M 410, (702) 293-2034, Fax (702) 293-0574, info@bouldercitychamber.com, www.bouldercitychamber.com.

**Carson City** · *Carson City Area C/C* · Ronni Hannaman, Exec. Dir., 1900 S. Carson St. #200, 89701, P 57,000, M 800, (775) 882-1565, Fax (775) 882-4179, support@carsoncitychamber.com, www.carsoncitychamber.com

**Crystal Bay** · *see Lake Tahoe, CA*

**Dayton** · *Dayton Area C/C* · Susan Skaggs, Exec. Dir., P.O. Box 2408, 89403, P 17,000, M 200, (775) 246-7909, Fax (775) 246-5838, info@daytonnvchamber.org, www.daytonnvchamber.org

**Elko** · *Elko Area C/C* · LaVon Thomsen, CEO, 1405 Idaho St., 89801, P 38,000, M 550, (775) 738-7135, (800) 428-7143, Fax (775) 738-7136, chamber@elkonevada.com, www.elkonevada.com

**Ely** · *White Pine C/C* · Evie Pinneo, Exec. Dir., 636 Aultman St., 89301, P 15,000, M 220, (775) 289-8877, Fax (775) 289-6144, elycc@whitepinechamber.com, www.whitepinechamber.com, www.elynevada.net

**Fallon** · *Fallon C/C* · Rick Dentino, Exec. Dir., 85 N. Taylor, 89406, P 26,247, M 240, (775) 423-2544, Fax (775) 423-0540, info@fallonchamber.com, www.fallonchamber.com

**Fernley** · *Fernley C/C* · Chris Beni, Pres., 70 N. West St., P.O. Box 1606, 89408, P 20,000, M 302, (775) 575-4459, Fax (775) 575-2626, fernleychamber@sbcglobal.net, www.fernleychamber.org

**Gardnerville** · *Carson Valley C/C & Visitors Auth.* · Bill Chernock, Exec. Dir., 1477 Hwy. 395 #A, 89410, P 46,000, M 450, (775) 782-8144, (800) 727-7677, Fax (775) 782-1025, info@carsonvalleynv.org, www.carsonvalleynv.org

**Gold Hill** · *see Virginia City*

**Goldfield** · *Goldfield C/C* · Donald Miguez, Pres., P.O. Box 204, 89013, P 300, M 35, (775) 485-3560, Fax (775) 485-3560, goldfieldchamber@yahoo.com, www.geocities.com/goldfieldchamber

**Hawthorne** · *Mineral County C/C* · Jefferson Gibson, Pres., 822 5th St., P.O. Box 2250, 89415, P 3,500, M 60, (775) 945-2507, info@mineralcountychamber.com, www.mineralcountychamber.com

**Henderson** · *Henderson C/C* · Alice Martz, CEO, 590 S. Boulder Hwy., 89015, P 280,000, M 1,500, (702) 565-8951, Fax (702) 565-3115, info@hendersonchamber.com, www.hendersonchamber.com

**Incline Village** · *see Lake Tahoe, CA*

**Lake Tahoe** · *see Stateline*

**Las Vegas** · *Las Vegas C/C* · Kara Kelley, Pres./CEO, 6671 Las Vegas Blvd. S., Ste. 300, 89119, P 2,000,000, M 7,000, (702) 641-5822, Fax (702) 735-2273, info@lvchamber.com, www.lvchamber.com

**Laughlin** · *Laughlin C/C* · Janet Medina, Exec. Dir., 1585 Casino Dr., 89029, P 8,500, M 425, (702) 298-2214, (800) 227-5245, Fax (702) 298-5708, director@laughlinchamber.com, www.laughlinchamber.com

**Lovelock** · *Greater Pershing Partnership* · 350 Main St., P.O. Box 821, 89419, P 5,000, M 196, (775) 273-7213, Fax (775) 273-1732, info@pershingcountynevada.com, www.pershingcountynevada.com

**Mesquite** · *Mesquite Area C/C* · Bill McClure, Exec. Dir., 12 W. Mesquite Blvd. #107, 89027, P 20,000, M 400, (702) 346-2902, Fax (702) 346-6138, contact@mesquite-chamber.com, www.mesquite-chamber.com

**North Las Vegas** · *North Las Vegas C/C* · Sharon Powers, Pres./CEO, 3365 W. Craig Rd., Ste. 25, 89032, P 200,000, M 900, (702) 642-9595, Fax (702) 642-0439, contact@nlvchamber.org, www.northlasvegaschamber.com

**Overton** · *Moapa Valley C/C* · Vernon Robison, P.O. Box 361, 89040, P 10,000, M 78, (702) 398-7160, chamber@moapavalley.com, www.moapavalley.com

**Pahrump** · *Pahrump Valley C/C* · Luci Ivins, CEO, 1301 S. Hwy. 160, 2nd Flr., P.O. Box 42, 89041, P 37,000, M 570, (775) 727-5800, (866) 722-5800, Fax (775) 727-3909, info@pahrumpchamber.com, www.pahrumpchamber.com

**Pioche** · *Pioche C/C* · Barbara Constantine, Pres., P.O. Box 127, 89043, P 750, M 40, (775) 962-5544, (775) 962-5207, info@piochenevada.com, www.piochenevada.com

**Reno** · *Reno Sparks C/C* · Doug Kurkul, CEO, One E. First St. #1600, P.O. Box 3499, 89505, P 374,000, M 15,000, (775) 337-3030, Fax (775) 337-3038, info@renosparkschamber.org, www.renosparkschamber.org

**Silver Springs** · *Silver Springs Area C/C* · Vida Keller, Pres., 1190 Hwy. 50 #1, P.O. Box 617, 89429, P 11,500, M 60, (775) 577-4336, Fax (775) 577-4399, sschamber@silverspringsnevada.com, www.silverspringsnevada.com

**Sparks** · *Sparks C/C* · Len Stevens, Exec. Dir., 634 Pyramid Way, P.O. Box 1776, 89432, P 86,000, M 1,500, (775) 358-1976, Fax (775) 358-1992, l.stevens@sparkschamber.org, www.sparkschamber.org

**Stateline** · *Lake Tahoe South Shore C/C* · Betty Gorman, Pres., 169 Hwy. 50, 3rd Flr., P.O. Box 7139, 89449, P 40,000, M 775, (775) 588-1728, Fax (775) 588-1941, info@tahoechamber.org, www.tahoechamber.org

**Tonopah** · *Tonopah C/C* · Denise Nelson, 200 S. Main St., P.O. Box 869, 89049, P 3,000, M 60, (775) 482-3859, Fax (775) 482-9846, tonopahcofc@live.com, www.tonopahchamberofcommerce.com

**Virginia City** · *Virginia City/Gold Hill C/C* · Jet Aguillar, Pres., P.O. Box 464, 89440, P 800, M 31, (775) 847-0311, info@virginiacity-nv.net, www.virginiacity-nv.net

**Wells** · *Wells C/C* · Thad Ballard, Pres., 395 6th St., P.O. Box 615, 89835, P 1,450, M 75, (775) 752-3540, coc@wellsnevada.com, www.wellsnevada.com

**Winnemucca** · *Humboldt County C/C* · Debbie Stone, Exec. Dir., 30 W. Winnemucca Blvd., 89445, P 8,000, M 250, (775) 623-2225, (877) 326-1916, Fax (775) 623-6478, chamber@winnemucca.net, www.humboldtcountychamber.com.

**Yerington** · *Yerington-Mason Valley C/C* · Joy Tibbals, Pres., 227 S. Main St., 89447, P 8,800, M 150, (775) 463-2245, Fax (775) 463-2284, info@masonvalleychamber.org, www.masonvalleychamber.org

# New Hampshire

**Bus. & Ind. Assn. of N.H.** · Jim Roche, Pres., 122 N. Main, Concord, 03301, P 1,200,000, M 400, (603) 224-5388, Fax (603) 224-2872, www.nhbia.org

**Acworth** · *see Bellows Falls, VT*

**Amherst** · *Souhegan Valley C/C* · May Balsama, Exec. Dir., 69 Route 101A, 03031, P 60,000, M 300, (603) 673-4360, Fax (603) 673-5018, may@souhegan.net, www.souhegan.net

**Berlin** · *Androscoggin Valley C/C* · William York, Exec. Dir., 961 Main St., 03570, P 17,000, M 200, (603) 752-6060, (800) 992-7480, Fax (603) 752-1002, info@androscogginvalleychamber.com, www.androscogginvalleychamber.com.

**Bethlehem** · *Bethlehem C/C* · Victor Hoffman, 2182 Main St., P.O. Box 748, 03574, P 2,200, M 67, (603) 869-3409, info@bethlehemwhitemtns.com, www.bethlehemwhitemtns.com

**Brentwood** · *see Exeter*

**Bretton Woods** · *see Twin Mountain*

**Bristol** · *Newfound Region C/C* · 45 Pleasant St., P.O. Box 454, 03222, P 3,300, M 92, (603) 744-2150, newfoundchamber@metrocast.net, www.newfoundchamber.com

**Brookline** · *see Amherst*

**Cambridge** · *see Errol*

**Campton** · *Waterville Valley Region C/C* · Christopher Bolan, Pres., 12 Vintinner Rd., 03223, P 15,000, M 230, (603) 726-3804, (800) 237-2307, Fax (603) 726-4058, info@watervillevalleyregion.com, www.watervillevalleyregion.com

**Center Harbor** · *see Meredith*

**Center Ossipee** · *Greater Ossipee Area C/C* · P.O. Box 323, 03814, P 12,000, M 175, (603) 539-6201, (866) 683-6295, Fax (603) 941-0133, info@ossipeevalley.org, www.ossipeevalley.org

**Charlestown** · *see Claremont*

**Claremont** · *Greater Claremont C/C* · Shelly Hudson, Exec. Dir., 24 Opera House Sq. #100, 03743, P 13,902, M 250, (603) 543-1296, Fax (603) 542-1469, claremontchamber@myfairpoint.net, www.claremontnhchamber.org

**Colebrook** · *North Country C/C* · Luc Lambert, Pres., P.O. Box 1, 03576, P 5,000, M 200, (603) 237-8939, (800) 698-8939, Fax (603) 237-4573, nccoc@ncia.net, www.northcountrychamber.org

**Concord** · *Greater Concord C/C* · Timothy G. Sink, Pres., 40 Commercial St., 03301, P 43,000, M 900, (603) 224-2508, Fax (603) 224-8128, info@concordnhchamber.com, www.concord nhchamber.com

**Conway** · *Conway C/C* · Laura Gorman, Pres., P.O. Box 1019, 03818, P 5,000, M 130, (603) 447-2639, info@conwaychamber. com, www.conwaychamber.com

**Cornish** · *see Windsor*

**Derry** · *Greater Derry Londonderry C/C* · Gina Gulino-Payne, Exec. Dir., 29 W. Broadway, 03038, P 35,000, M 280, (603) 432-8205, Fax (603) 432-7938, derrychamber@earthlink.net, www. derry-chamber.org

**Dover** · *Greater Dover C/C* · Kirt Schuman, Exec. Dir., 550 Central Ave., 03820, P 30,000, M 500, (603) 742-2218, info@dovernh.org, www.dovernh.org

**Dummer** · *see Berlin*

**East Kingston** · *see Exeter*

**Easton** · *see Franconia*

**Effingham** · *see Center Ossipee*

**Epping** · *see Exeter*

**Errol** · *Umbagog Area C/C* · Frank Lawson, Pres., P.O. Box 113, 03579, P 300, M 30, (603) 482-3906, Fax (603) 482-9804, umbagog@ncia.net, www.umbagogchambercommerce.com

**Exeter** · *Exeter Area C/C* · Thomas A. Kraus, Pres., 24 Front St. #101, P.O. Box 278, 03833, P 51,000, M 500, (603) 772-2411, Fax (603) 772-9965, info@exeterarea.org, www.exeterarea.org

**Franconia** · *Franconia Notch C/C* · Frank Grima, Pres., 421 Main St., P.O. Box 780, 03580, P 2,500, M 115, (603) 823-5661, info@ franconianotch.org, www.franconianotch.org

**Freedom** · *see Center Ossipee*

**Gorham** · *see Berlin*

**Greenfield** · *see Amherst*

**Greenville** · *see Amherst*

**Hampton** · *Hampton Area C/C* · B.J. Noel, Pres., 1 Lafayette Rd., P.O. Box 790, 03843, P 36,000, M 425, (603) 926-8718, Fax (603) 926-9977, info@hamptonchamber.com, www.hamptonchamber.com.

**Hanover** · *Hanover Area C/C* · Janet Rebman, Exec. Dir., 216 Nugget Bldg., P.O. Box 5105, 03755, P 100,000, M 370, (603) 643-3115, Fax (603) 643-5606, hacc@hanoverchamber.org, www. hanoverchamber.org

**Hillsborough** · *Hillsborough C/C* · Andrea Kaubris, Admin., P.O. Box 541, 03244, P 5,000, M 150, (603) 464-5858, Fax (603) 464-9166, hcofc@conknet.com, www.hillsboroughnhchamber.com

**Hollis** · *see Amherst*

**Hudson** · *Hudson C/C* · Brenda Collins, Exec. Dir., 71 Lowell Rd., 03051, P 22,000, M 140, (603) 889-4731, Fax (603) 889-7939, info@hudsonchamber.com, www.hudsonchamber.com

**Jackson** · *Jackson Area C/C* · Kathleen Driscoll, Exec. Dir., Jackson Falls Market Pl., 03846, P 900, M 100, (603) 383-9356, (800) 866-3334, Fax (603) 383-0931, info@jacksonnh.com, www. jacksonnh.com

**Jaffrey** · *Jaffrey C/C* · Cathy Furze, Pres., P.O. Box 2, 03452, P 5,700, M 210, (603) 532-4549, Fax (603) 532-8823, info@ jaffreychamber.com, www.jaffreychamber.com

**Jefferson** · *see Berlin*

**Keene** · *Greater Keene C/C* · Tom Dowling, Pres., 48 Central Sq., 03431, P 73,825, M 440, (603) 352-1303, Fax (603) 358-5341, info@keenechamber.com, www.keenechamber.com

**Kensington** · *see Exeter*

**Kinston** · *see Exeter*

**Laconia** · *Lakes Region C/C* · Doug Holmes, Exec. Dir., 383 S. Main St., 03246, P 18,000, M 550, (603) 524-5531, Fax (603) 524-5534, info@laconia-weirs.org, www.laconia-weirs.org

**Lake Sunapee** · *see New London*

**Lancaster** · *Northern Gateway C/C* · Marilyn DeLozier, Dir., P.O. Box 537, 03584, P 13,000, M 125, (603) 788-2530, (877) 788-2530 New England only, info@northerngatewaychamber.org, www.northerngatewaychamber.org

**Lebanon** · *Lebanon C/C* · Paul R. Boucher, Pres./CEO, 1 School St., P.O. Box 97, 03766, P 12,500, M 450, (603) 448-1203, Fax (603) 448-6489, lebanonchamber@lebanonchamber.com, www. lebanonchamber.com.

**Lincoln** · *Lincoln-Woodstock C/C* · Mark LaClair, Exec. Dir., Rte. 112, P.O. Box 1017, 03251, P 3,000, M 240, (603) 745-6621, Fax (603) 745-4908, info@lincolnwoodstock.com, www.lincolnwood stock.com

**Littleton** · *Littleton Area C/C* · Chad Stearns, Member Svcs. Coord., P.O. Box 105, 03561, P 6,200, M 325, (603) 444-6561, Fax (603) 444-2427, info@littletonareachamber.com, www.littleton areachamber.com

**Londonderry** · *see Manchester*

**Lyndeborough** · *see Amherst*

**Madison** · *see Center Ossipee*

**Manchester** · *Greater Manchester C/C* · Robin Comstock, Pres./ CEO, 889 Elm St., 3rd Flr., 03101, P 107,000, M 1,000, (603) 666-6600, Fax (603) 626-0910, info@Manchester-Chamber.org, www. Manchester-Chamber.org.

**Mason** · *see Amherst*

**Meredith** · *Meredith Area C/C* · Susan Cerutti, Exec. Dir., P.O. Box 732, 03253, P 20,000, M 340, (603) 279-6121, Fax (603) 279-4525, meredith@lr.net, www.meredithcc.org

**Merrimack** · *Merrimack C/C* · Deb Courtemanche, Exec. Dir., 301 Daniel Webster Hwy., P.O. Box 254, 03054, P 28,000, M 200, (603) 424-3669, Fax (603) 429-4325, info@merrimackchamber.org, www.merrimackchamber.org

**Milan** · *see Berlin*

**Milford** · *see Amherst*

**Millsfield** · *see Errol*

**Mont Vernon** · *see Amherst*

**Moultonboro** · *see Meredithdave's test's*

**Nashua** · *Greater Nashua C/C* · Chris Williams, Pres., 151 Main St., 03060, P 188,000, M 750, (603) 881-8333, Fax (603) 881-7323, chamber@nashuachamber.com, www.nashuachamber.com

**New Ipswich** · *see Amherst*

**New London** · *Lake Sunapee Region C/C* · Rob Bryant, Exec. Dir., P.O. Box 532, 03257, P 18,000, M 175, (603) 526-6575, (877) 526-6575, chamberinfo@nhvt.net, www.lakesunapeenh.org

**Newfields** · *see Exeter*

**Newmarket** · *see Exeter*

**Newport** • *Newport Area C/C* • Ella M. Casey, Exec. Dir., 2 N. Main St., 03773, P 6,200, M 120, (603) 863-1510, Fax (603) 863-9486, chamber@newportnhchamber.org, www.newport nhchamber.org.

**North Conway** • *Mount Washington Valley C/C & Visitors Bur.* • Janice Crawford, Exec. Dir., P.O. Box 2300, 03860, P 15,000, M 750, (603) 356-5701, (800) 367-3364, Fax (603) 356-7069, info@mtwashingtonvalley.org, www.mtwashingtonvalley.org

**North Walpole** • *see Bellows Falls, VT*

**Ossipee** • *see Center Ossipee*

**Peterborough** • *Greater Peterborough C/C* • Jack Burnett, Exec. Dir., P.O. Box 401, 03458, P 6,200, M 350, (603) 924-7234, Fax (603) 924-7235, info@peterboroughchamber.com, www. peterboroughchamber.com

**Plainfield** • *see Windsor*

**Plymouth** • *Plymouth C/C* • Sarah Kilfoyle, Exec. Dir., 1 Foster St. #A, P.O. Box 65, 03264, P 6,000, M 240, (603) 536-1001, (800) 386-3678, Fax (603) 536-4017, info@plymouthnh.org, www. plymouthnh.org

**Portsmouth** • *Greater Portsmouth C/C* • Douglas Bates, Pres., 500 Market St., P.O. Box 239, 03802, P 125,000, M 1,025, (603) 436-3988, Fax (603) 436-5118, info@portsmouthchamber.org, www.portsmouthchamber.org

**Randolph** • *see Berlin*

**Raymond** • *see Exeter*

**Rindge** • *Rindge C/C* • Betty Anders, Pres., P.O. Box 911, 03461, P 5,615, M 80, (603) 899-5051, info@rindgechamber.org, www. rindgechamber.org

**Rochester** • *Greater Rochester C/C* • Laura Ring, Pres., 18 S. Main St., 03867, P 30,527, M 470, (603) 332-5080, Fax (603) 332-5216, chamber@rochesternh.org, www.rochesternh.org

**Salem** • *Greater Salem C/C* • Donna Morris, Exec. Dir., 224 N. Broadway, 03079, P 70,000, M 350, (603) 893-3177, Fax (603) 894-5158, donna@gschamber.com, www.gschamber.com

**Sandwich** • *see Center Ossipee*

**Shelburne** • *see Berlin*

**Somersworth** • *Greater Somersworth C/C* • Jennifer Soldati, Pres., 58 High St., P.O. Box 615, 03878, P 11,500, M 200, (603) 692-7175, Fax (603) 692-4501, jennifer@somersworthchamber. com, www.somersworthchamber.com

**Stratham** • *see Exeter*

**Sugar Hill** • *see Franconia*

**Sunapee** • *see New London*

**Tamworth** • *see Center Ossipee*

**Temple** • *see Amherst*

**Twin Mountain** • *Twin Mountain-Bretton Woods C/C* • P.O. Box 194, 03595, P 800, M 50, (800) 245-TWIN, info@twin mountain.org, www.twinmountain.org

**Wakefield** • *Greater Wakefield C/C* • Thomas Lavender, Pres., P.O. Box 111, 03872, P 4,569, M 95, (603) 522-6106, postmaster@ wakefieldnh.org, www.wakefieldnh.org

**Walpole** • *see Bellows Falls, VT*

**Waterville Valley** • *see Campton*

**Weirs Beach** • *see Laconia-Lakes Region C/C*

**West Ossipee** • *see Center Ossipee*

**Westmoreland** • *see Bellows Falls, VT*

**Wilton** • *see Amherst*

**Wolfeboro** • *Wolfeboro Area C/C* • Mary DeVries, Exec. Dir., P.O. Box 547, 03894, P 6,000, M 300, (603) 569-2200, (800) 516-5324, Fax (603) 569-2275, wolfeborochamber@conknet.com, www. wolfeborochamber.com

# New Jersey

**New Jersey C of C** • Joan Verplanck, Pres., 216 W. State St., Trenton, 08608, P 8,500,000, M 1,600, (609) 989-7888, Fax (609) 989-9696, linda@njchamber.com, www.njchamber.com.

**Aberdeen** • *see Matawan*

**Allumuchy** • *see Washington*

**Alpha** • *see Washington*

**Asbury Park** • *Greater Asbury Park C/C* • Cindi D'Onofrio, Exec. Dir., 308 Main St., P.O. Box 649, 07712, P 20,000, M 200, (732) 775-7676, Fax (732) 775-7675, cindi@asburyparkchamber.com, www.asburyparkchamber.com

**Atlantic City** • *Greater Atlantic City C/C* • Joseph Kelly, Pres., 12 S. Virginia Ave., 08401, P 252,552, M 1,000, (609) 345-4524, Fax (609) 345-1666, acchamber@aol.com, www.acchamber.com

**Atlantic Highlands** • *see Hazlet*

**Avalon** • *Avalon C/C* • Edward Galante, Pres., 30th & Ocean Dr., P.O. Box 22, 08202, P 2,162, M 250, (609) 967-3936, Fax (609) 967-1815, chamber@avalonbeach.com, www.avalonbeach.com

**Basking Ridge** • *Bernards Twp. C/C* • Albert LiCata, Exec. Dir., P.O. Box 11, 07920, P 28,000, M 210, (908) 766-6755, www. bernardstownshipchamber.org

**Bay Head** • *see Point Pleasant Beach*

**Bayonne** • *Bayonne C/C* • Janis Demellier, Gen. Mgr., 621 Ave. C, P.O. Box 266, 07002, P 64,000, M 120, (201) 436-4333, Fax (201) 436-8546

**Bayville** • *see Toms River*

**Belford** • *see Hazlet*

**Belmar** • *Belmar C/C* • Tracy Keller, Exec. Dir., 1005 1/2 Main St., 07719, P 7,340, M 125, (732) 681-2900, Fax (732) 681-8471, info@belmarchamber.com, www.belmarchamber.com

**Belvidere** • *see Washington*

**Bergen** • *see Hasbrouck Heights*

**Berkeley Heights** • *see Summit*

**Bernardsville** • *Bernardsville C/C* • Caesar Mistretta Sr., Pres., P.O. Box 672, 07924, P 7,400, M 160, (908) 766-9900, bvillechamber.com

**Blairstown** • *see Washington*

**Bloomfield** • *Suburban Essex C/C* • Donna Pietroiacovo, Exec. Admin., 256 Broad St., Rm 2F, 07003, P 48,000, M 250, (973) 748-2000, Fax (973) 748-2450, admin@suburbanessexchamber.com, www.suburbanessexchamber.com

**Bloomingdale** • *Tri-Boro Area C/C* • Gerald Vinci, Pres., P.O. Box 100, 07403, P 30,922, M 70, (973) 838-5678, Fax (973) 838-5229, triborochamber@aol.com, www.triborochamber.org

**Bogota** • *C/C of Bogota* • Louis Knaube, Pres., P.O. Box 81, 07603, P 8,000, M 48, (201) 487-8983, tres@bogotachamber.org, www. bogotachamber.org

**Boonton** • *Tri-Town C/C* • Gina Ramich, Exec. Dir., P.O. Box 496, 07005, P 16,300, M 170, (973) 334-4117, Fax (973) 263-4164, info@tritownchamber.org, www.tritownchamber.org

**Bordentown** • *Northern Burlington Reg. C/C* • Diane DiSpaldo, Exec. Secy., P.O. Box 65, 08505, P 8,000, M 100, (609) 298-7774, Fax (609) 291-5008, info@nbrchamber.org, www.nbrchamber.org

**Bound Brook** · *Bound Brook Area C/C* · Deanne Confalone, P.O. Box 227, 08805, P 11,000, M 80, (732) 356-7273

**Brick** · *Brick Twp. C/C* · Michele Eventoff, Exec. Dir., 270 Chambers Bridge Rd., 08723, P 85,000, M 600, (732) 477-4949, Fax (732) 477-5788, info@brickchamber.com, www.brickchamber.com.

**Bridgeton** · *Bridgeton Area C/C* · Anthony Stanzione, Exec. Dir., 76 Magnolia Ave., P.O. Box 1063, 08302, P 38,000, M 190, (856) 455-1312, Fax (856) 453-9795, bacc@baccnj.com, www.baccnj.com

**Bridgewater** · *Somerset County Bus. Partnership* · Tom Sharpe, Pres./CEO, 360 Grove St. at Rte. 22 E., P.O. Box 833, 08807, P 315,000, M 610, (908) 218-4300, Fax (908) 722-7823, info@somersetbusinesspartnership.com, www.scbp.org

**Brielle** · *Brielle C/C* · P.O. Box 162, 08730, P 4,900, M 100, (732) 528-0377, info@briellechamber.com, www.briellechamber.com

**Brigantine Beach** · *Brigantine Beach C/C* · P.O. Box 484, 08203, P 12,000, M 115, (609) 266-3437, info@brigantine chamber.com, www.brigantinechamber.com

**Broadway** · *see Washington*

**Budd Lake** · *Mt. Olive Area C/C* · Rick Ege, Pres., P.O. Box 192, 07828, P 26,000, M 130, (973) 691-0109, info@mtolivechambernj.com, www.mtolivechambernj.com

**Burlington** · *Greater Burlington C/C* · Sue Woolman, Secy., P.O. Box 67, 08016, P 35,000, M 55, (609) 387-4528, swoolman@cornerstonebank.com

**Burlington County** · *see Mount Laurel*

**Butler** · *see Bloomingdale and Wayne*

**Caldwell** · *see West Caldwell*

**Camden** · *see Cherry Hill*

**Cape May** · *C/C of Greater Cape May* · Bob Steenrod, Pres., P.O. Box 556, 08204, P 5,000, M 300, (609) 884-5508, Fax (609) 884-2054, request@capemaychamber.com, www.capemaychamber.com

**Cape May County** · *Cape May County C/C* · Vicki Clark, Pres., P.O. Box 74, Cape May Court House, 08210, P 98,000, M 965, (609) 465-7181, Fax (609) 465-5017, info@cmcchamber.com, www.capemaycountychamber.com

**Cape May Court House** · *Middle Township C/C* · Barbara Peltzer, Pres., P.O. Box 6, 08210, P 15,000, M 125, (609) 463-1655, middletownshipchamberofcommerce.org

**Carneys Point** · *Salem County C/C* · Jennifer A. Jones, Exec. Dir., 91A S. Virginia Ave., 08069, P 65,000, M 400, (856) 299-6699, Fax (856) 299-0299, sccoc@verizon.net, www.salemnjchamber.homestead.com

**Cedar Grove** · *see West Caldwell*

**Cedar Knolls** · *see Florham Park*

**Chatham** · *Chatham Area C/C* · Carolyn Cherry, Exec. Dir., P.O. Box 231, 07928, P 40,000, M 200, (973) 635-2444, Fax (973) 635-2953, chathamchamber@gmail.com, www.chathamchambernj.org

**Cherry Hill** · *Cherry Hill Reg. C/C* · Arthur Campbell, Pres., 1060 Kings Hwy. N., Ste. 200, 08034, P 70,000, M 950, (856) 667-1600, Fax (856) 667-1464, info@cherryhillregional.com, www.cherryhillregional.com

**Cliffside Park** · *Cliffside Park C/C* · Lynne Nesbihal, Exec. Dir., 645 Anderson Ave., 07010, P 24,000, M 350, (201) 941-9505, Fax (201) 941-8499, info@cliffsideparkchamber.org, www.cliffsideparkonline.com/chamber

**Clifton** · *North Jersey Reg. C/C* · Gloria Martini, Pres., 1033 Rte. 46 E., Ste. A103, 07013, P 150,000, M 600, (973) 470-9300, Fax (973) 470-9245, staff@njrcc.org, www.njrcc.org

**Clinton** · *see Flemington*

**Colts Neck** · *see Freehold*

**Columbia** · *see Washington*

**Cranford** · *Cranford C/C* · J. Robert Hoeffler, Exec. Dir., 8 Springfield Ave., P.O. Box 165, 07016, P 22,000, M 200, (908) 272-6114, Fax (908) 272-3742, cranfordchamber@comcast.net, www.cranford.com/chamber.

**Dennis Township** · *see Ocean View*

**Denville** · *Denville C/C* · Alan Verbeke, Pres., P.O. Box 333, 07834, P 14,000, M 155, (973) 625-1171, www.denville-nj.com

**Dover** · *Dover Area C/C* · P.O. Box 506, 07802, P 16,000, M 100, (973) 989-4000, Fax (973) 673-5828, www.doverareachamber.com

**Dumont** · *Dumont C/C* · 50 Washington Ave., 07628, P 18,000, M 25, (201) 384-6090, info@dumontchamber.com

**Dunellen** · *see Piscataway*

**East Brunswick** · *East Brunswick Reg. C/C* · Lauren Mosko, Mktg. Dir., P.O. Box 56, 08816, P 100,000, M 190, (732) 257-3009, Fax (732) 257-0949, mosko@ebchamber.org, www.ebchamber.org

**East Hanover** · *see Florham Park*

**East Millstone** · *see Franklin Twp.*

**East Newark** · *see Jersey City*

**East Orange** · *East Orange C/C* · Raymond Scott, Pres., P.O. Box 2418, 07019, P 80,000, M 50, (973) 674-0900, info@eastorangechamber.biz, www.eastorangechamber.biz

**East Orange** · *Jefferson Twp. C/C* · Raymond Fernandez, Pres., 604 Central Ave., 07018, P 80,000, M 100, (973) 663-2240, www.jeffersontownshipchamber.org

**East Windsor** · *see Mercerville*

**Eatontown** · *see Red Bank*

**Edison** · *Edison C/C* · Barbara C. Roos, Pres./CEO, 336 Raritan Center Pkwy., Campus Plaza 6, 08837, P 100,000, M 350, (732) 738-9482, Fax (732) 738-9485, president@edisonchamber.com, www.edisonchamber.com.

**Egg Harbor City** · *Egg Harbor City C/C* · Lloyd Wimberg, Exec. Dir., P.O. Box 129, 08215, P 4,545, M 100, (609) 965-0001

**Elizabeth** · *Gateway Reg. C/C* · James R. Coyle, Pres., 135 Jefferson Ave., P.O. Box 300, 07207, P 504,000, M 1,800, (908) 352-0900, Fax (908) 352-0865, jamescoyle@gatewaychamber.com, www.gatewaychamber.com

**Elizabeth** · *Greater Elizabeth C/C* · Gordon Haas, Pres./CEO, 456 N. Broad St., 2nd Flr., 07208, P 127,000, M 550, (908) 355-7600, Fax (908) 436-2054, gecc@juno.com, www.elizabethchamber.com.

**Englewood** · *Englewood C/C* · Karen Rawl, Exec. Dir., 2-10 N. Van Brunt St., 07631, P 26,000, M 175, (201) 567-2381, Fax (201) 871-4549, karen.rawl@gmail.com, www.englewood-chamber.com

**Englishtown** · *see Freehold*

**Essex County** · *see Wayne and West Caldwell*

**Essex Fells** · *see West Caldwell*

**Ewing** · *see Mercerville*

**Fair Haven** · *see Red Bank*

**Fair Lawn** · *Fair Lawn C/C* · Debbie Berowitz, Exec. Dir., 18-00 Fair Lawn Ave., 07410, P 33,000, M 250, (201) 796-7050, Fax (201) 475-0619, info@fairlawnchamber.org, www.fairlawnchamber.org

**Fairfield** · *see Wayne and West Caldwell*

**Fairview** · *Fairview C/C Inc.* · Manuel Tridgiano, Secy./Treas., 202 Anderson Ave., 07022, P 12,000, M 48, (201) 945-3707

**Farmingdale** • *Farmingdale C/C* • Debra Davis, Pres., 11 Asbury Ave., 07727, P 1,587, M 60, (732) 938-4077, Fax (732) 938-2023

**Flemington** • *Hunterdon County C/C* • Christopher J. Phelan, Pres./CEO, 1 Church St., Ste. 73, 08822, P 121,000, M 550, (908) 782-7115, Fax (908) 782-7283, info@hunterdon-chamber.org, www.hunterdon-chamber.org

**Florham Park** • *also see Morristown*

**Florham Park** • *Hanover Area C/C* • Steven F. Miller, Pres., P.O. Box 168, 07932, P 25,000, (973) 884-3278, info@hanoverarea chamber.org, www.hanoverareachamber.org

**Fort Lee** • *Greater Fort Lee C/C* • Judith Auerbach-Adamo, Exec. Dir., 210 Whiteman St., 07024, P 36,000, M 300, (201) 944-7575, Fax (201) 944-5168, gflcoc@verizon.net, www.greaterfortlee-chamber.com

**Franklin Lakes** • *Franklin Lakes C/C* • Mina Kozma, Exec. Admin., P.O. Box 81, 07417, P 9,200, M 50, (201) 560-1289, info@flcoc.org, www.flcoc.org

**Franklin Twp.** • *Franklin Twp. C/C* • Bill DiNicola, Exec. Dir., 675 Franklin Blvd., Somerset, 08873, P 50,000, M 200, (732) 545-7044, Fax (732) 745-7043, director@franklinchamber.com, www.franklinchamber.com

**Freehold** • *Greater Monmouth C/C* • Loretta Kuhnert, Pres., 17 Broad St., 07728, P 183,096, M 675, (732) 462-3030, Fax (732) 462-2123, info@wmchamber.com, www.wmchamber.com

**Garfield** • *C/C of Garfield* • P.O. Box 525, 07026, P 27,000, M 201, (973) 773-7500, info@chamberofgarfield.com, www.chamberofgarfield.com

**Gibbstown** • *see Cherry Hill*

**Glassboro** • *Greater Glassboro C/C* • Karal Corradetti, P.O. Box 651, 08028, P 19,870, M 90, (856) 881-7900, Fax (856) 881-7755, info@glassborochamber.com, www.glassborochamber.com

**Glen Brook** • *see Piscataway*

**Glen Rock** • *Glen Rock C/C* • Pam Wolak, Pres., 199 Rock Rd., 07452, P 11,000, M 55, (201) 447-3434, www.glenrockchamber.com

**Gloucester County** • *see Cherry Hill*

**Great Meadows** • *see Washington*

**Griggstown** • *see Franklin Twp.*

**Guttenberg** • *see Jersey City*

**Hackensack** • *Greater Hackensack C/C* • Darlene Damstrom, Exec. Dir., 5 University Plaza Dr., 07601, P 42,000, M 225, (201) 489-3700, Fax (201) 489-1741, office@hackensackchamber.org, www.hackensackchamber.org

**Hackettstown** • *see Washington*

**Haddonfield** • *see Voorhees*

**Haledon** • *see Wayne*

**Hammonton** • *Greater Hammonton C/C* • Michele Samanic, Exec. Dir., 10 S. Egg Harbor Rd., P.O. Box 554, 08037, P 13,280, M 130, (609) 561-9080, Fax (609) 561-9411, msamanic@hammontonnj.us, www.hammontonnj.us

**Hanover Twp.** • *see Florham Park*

**Hardwick** • *see Washington*

**Harrison** • *see Jersey City*

**Hasbrouck Heights** • *Hasbrouck Heights C/C* • Ray Vorisek, Pres., P.O. Box 1, 07604, P 12,000, M 100, (201) 288-5464, www.hasbrouck-heights.com

**Hawthorne** • *Hawthorne C/C* • Joann Ciampa, Exec. Secy., 471 Lafayette Ave., P.O. Box 331, 07507, P 17,000, M 230, (973) 427-5078, Fax (973) 427-6066, hawcofc@aol.com, www.hawthorne cofc.com

**Hazlet** • *Northern Monmouth C/C* • Regina Hyatt, Exec. Dir., 1340 Hwy. 36, Ste. 22, P.O. Box 5007, 07730, P 90,000, M 350, (732) 203-0340, Fax (732) 203-0341, director@northernmon mouthchamber.com, www.northernmonmouthchamber.com

**Highlands** • *see Hazlet*

**Hightstown** • *see Mercerville*

**Hillside** • *Hillside C/C* • Irene Goldie-Petras, Exec. Dir., P.O. Box 965, 07205, P 23,000, M 100, (908) 964-6659, Fax (908) 964-3951, lgoldie@earthlink.net, www.hillsidechamber.com

**Hoboken** • *Hoboken C/C* • Robert Mahnken, Pres., P.O. Box 349, 07030, P 38,000, M 160, (201) 222-1100, Fax (201) 222-9120, hobchamber@aol.com, www.hobokenchamber.com

**Hohokus** • *Ho-Ho-kus C/C* • Steve Eiman, Pres., P.O. Box 115, 07423, P 4,000, M 75, (201) 444-6664, Fax (201) 444-6292, slightson@verizon.net, www.hohokuschamber.com

**Holmdel** • *see Hazlet*

**Hope** • *Hope Area C/C* • P.O. Box 2, 07844, P 7,000, M 45, (908) 475-8322, www.hopenj.org

**Hopewell Township** • *see Mercerville*

**Howell** • *Howell C/C* • Susan Dominguez, Exec. Dir., 103 W. 2nd St., Ste. 2, P.O. Box 196, 07731, P 50,000, M 246, (732) 363-4114, Fax (732) 363-8747, info@howellchamber.com, www.howell chamber.com

**Irvington** • *Irvington C/C* • Luz Carde, Exec. Dir., P.O. Box 323, 07111, P 65,000, M 150, (973) 372-4100, Fax (973) 673-5828, email@irvington-nj.com, www.irvington-nj.com

**Iselin** • *see Woodbridge*

**Jackson** • *Jackson C/C* • Clara Glory, Pres., 1021 W. Commodore Blvd., 08527, P 51,870, M 245, (732) 833-0005, Fax (732) 833-7033, jcinfo@jacksonchamber.com, www.jacksonchamber.com

**Jersey City** • *Hudson County C/C* • 660 Newark Ave., Ste. 220, 07306, P 500,000, M 500, (201) 386-0699, Fax (201) 386-8480, info@hudsonchamber.org, www.hudsonchamber.org

**Johnsonburg** • *see Washington*

**Keansburg** • *see Hazlet*

**Kearny** • *see Jersey City*

**Kingston** • *see Franklin Twp.*

**Kinnelon** • *see Bloomingdale and Wayne*

**Lake Hiawatha** • *Parsippany Area C/C* • Robert Peluso, Pres., 12-14 N. Beverwyck Rd., 07034, P 52,000, M 300, (973) 402-6400, president@parsippanychamber.org, www.parsippanychamber.org

**Lakewood** • *Lakewood C/C* • Maureen Stankowitz, Exec. Dir., 395 Rte. 70 W., Ste. 125, 08701, P 60,350, M 490, (732) 363-0012, Fax (732) 367-4453, maureen@mylakewoodchamber.com, www.mylakewoodchamber.com

**Lambertville** • *Lambertville Area C/C* • Ellen Pineno, Ofc. Mgr., 60 Wilson St., 08530, P 4,000, M 200, (609) 397-0055, info@lambertville.org, www.lambertville.org

**Landing** • *see Ledgewood*

**Lavallette** • *see Toms River*

**Lawrenceville** • *see Mercerville*

**Lebanon** • *see Flemington*

**Ledgewood** · *Roxbury Area C/C* · Richard Willets, Pres., P.O. Box 436, 07852, P 22,000, M 120, (973) 770-0740, elaineracc@verizon. net, www.roxburynjchamber.org

**Leonardo** · *see Hazlet*

**Lincoln Park** · *see Wayne*

**Little Falls** · *see Clifton, Wayne & West Caldwell*

**Little Silver** · *see Red Bank*

**Livingston** · *Livingston Area C/C* · Beth Lippman, Exec. Dir./ Admin., 25 S. Livingston Ave., 2nd Flr., Ste. E, 07039, P 27,000, M 160, (973) 992-4343, Fax (973) 992-8024, info@livingston chambernj.com, www.livingstonchambernj.com

**Lodi** · *Lodi C/C* · Charles Pinto, P.O. Box 604, 07644, P 28,000, M 101, (973) 778-6573, info@lodichamberofcommerce.org, www. lodichamberofcommerce.org

**Long Branch** · *Greater Long Branch C/C* · Nancy Kleiberg, Exec. Dir., 228 Broadway, P.O. Box 628, 07740, P 32,000, M 260, (732) 222-0400, Fax (732) 571-3385, longbranchchamber@verizon.net, www.longbranchchamber.org

**Madison** · *Madison C/C* · Susan Marcy, Exec. Dir., P.O. Box 152, 07940, P 17,000, M 200, (973) 377-7830, Fax (973) 822-3336, info@madisonnjchamber.org, www.madisonnjchamber.org

**Mahwah** · *Mahwah Reg. C/C* · Sharon Rounds, Exec. Dir., 65 Ramapo Valley Rd., Ste. 211, 07430, P 26,000, M 520, (201) 529-5566, Fax (201) 529-8122, info@mahwah.com, www.mahwah.com

**Manahawkin** · *see Ship Bottom*

**Manalapan** · *see Freehold*

**Manasquan** · *Manasquan C/C* · John Newman, Pres., 107 Main St., 08736, P 6,000, M 150, (732) 223-8303, Fax (732) 223-8303, info@manasquanchamber.org, www.manasquanchamber.org

**Manville** · *see Franklin Twp.*

**Maplewood** · *Maplewood C/C* · Rene Conlon, Exec. Secy., P.O. Box 423, 07040, P 24,000, M 150, (973) 761-4333, Fax (973) 762-9105, www.maplewoodchamber.org

**Marlboro** · *see Freehold*

**Marlton** · *see Mount Laurel*

**Matawan** · *Matawan-Aberdeen C/C* · Charles Mylod, Pres., P.O. Box 522, 07747, P 30,000, M 133, (732) 290-1125, Fax same, macocnj@yahoo.com, www.macocnj.com

**Maywood** · *Maywood C/C* · Dr. Timothy Eustace, Pres., 140 W. Pleasant Ave., 07607, P 9,536, M 75, (201) 843-3111, teustace@ aol.com, www.maywoodnj.org

**Meadowlands** · *see Rutherford-Meadowlands Reg. C/C*

**Medford** · *see Burlington*

**Mercerville** · *Mercer Reg. C/C* · Michele Siekerka, Pres./CEO, 1A Quakerbridge Plaza Dr., Ste. 2, 08619, P 359,463, M 1,300, (609) 689-9960, Fax (609) 586-9989, michele@mercerchamber.org, www.mercerchamber.org

**Metuchen** · *Metuchen Area C/C* · Caroline Woodruff, Ofc. Admin., 323 Main St., Ste. B, 08840, P 13,000, M 300, (732) 548-2964, Fax (732) 548-4094, metuchenchamber@metuchen chamber.com, www.metuchenchamber.com

**Middlesex** · *see Piscataway*

**Middlesex County** · *see New Brunswick*

**Middletown** · *see Hazlet*

**Midland Park** · *Midland Park C/C* · Mr. Chris Rossi, Pres., P.O. Box 267, 07432, P 8,000, M 75, (201) 445-0100, www.mpnj.com

**Millburn** · *Millburn-Short Hills C/C* · Karol McNulty, Exec. Dir., 343 Millburn Ave., Ste. 303, P.O. Box 651, 07041, P 18,600, M 250, (973) 379-1198, Fax (973) 376-5678, info@millburnchamber.com, www.millburnchamber.com

**Millstone** · *see Freehold*

**Millville** · *Greater Millville C/C* · Earl Sherrick, Exec. Dir., 4 City Park Dr., P.O. Box 831, 08332, P 26,000, M 200, (856) 825-2600, Fax (856) 825-5333, chamber@millville-nj.com, www.millville-nj.com

**Monmouth Beach** · *see Red Bank*

**Montclair** · *see West Caldwell*

**Montville** · *Montville Twp. C/C* · Carol Ann De Vito, Secy., 195 Changebridge Rd., 07045, P 20,863, M 190, (973) 263-3310, Fax (973) 263-3453, info@montvillechamber.com, www.montville chamber.com

**Moorestown** · *see Mount Laurel*

**Mooresville** · *see Mount Laurel*

**Morris County** · *see Morristown*

**Morristown** · *Morris County C/C* · Paul Boudreau, Pres., 25 Lindsley Dr., Ste. 105, 07960, P 421,361, M 800, (973) 539-3882, Fax (973) 539-3960, www.morrischamber.org

**Mount Freedom** · *Randolph Area C/C* · Bill Burke, Pres., P.O. Box 391, 07970, P 26,000, M 80, (973) 361-3462, www.randolph chamber.org

**Mount Laurel** · *Burlington County C/C* · Kristi Howell-Ikeda, Pres., 100 Technology Way, Ste. 110, 08054, P 396,000, M 425, (856) 439-2520, Fax (856) 439-2523, bccoc@bccoc.com, www. bccoc.com

**Mount Olive** · *see Budd Lake*

**Mountain Lakes** · *see Boonton*

**Mountainside** · *see Elizabeth*

**Navesink** · *see Hazlet*

**New Brunswick** · *Middlesex County Reg. C/C* · Katie Watson, Pres., 109 Church St., 08901, P 750,162, M 750, (732) 745-8090, Fax (732) 745-8098, www.gocentraljersey.com, info@mcrcc.org, www.mcrcc.org

**New Providence** · *see Summit*

**Newark** · *Newark Reg. Bus. Partnership* · Chip Hallock, Pres., National Newark Bldg., 744 Broad St., 26th Flr., 07102, P 280,000, M 500, (973) 522-0099, Fax (973) 824-6587, info@newarkrbp.org, www.newarkrbp.org.

**Newark** · *Statewide Hispanic C/C of NJ* · Daniel Jara, Pres./CEO, 1 Gateway Center, Ste. 615, 07102, P 500,000, M 4,000, (201) 451-9512, Fax (201) 451-9547, shccnj@att.net, www.shccnj.org

**Newton** · *Sussex County C/C* · Tammie Horsfield, Pres., 120 Hampton House Rd., 07860, P 135,000, M 700, (973) 579-1811, Fax (973) 579-3031, mail@sussexcountychamber.org, www. sussexcountychamber.org

**North Bergen** · *see Jersey City*

**North Caldwell** · *see West Caldwell*

**Northfield** · *see Atlantic City*

**Nutley** · *Nutley C/C* · Richard Spector, Ofc. Mgr., 299 Franklin Ave., 07110, P 28,000, M 150, (973) 667-5300, chamber@nutley chamber.com, www.nutleychamber.com

**Oakhurst** · *Greater Ocean Twp. C/C* · Penny Daniels, Bus. Mgr., 2002 Bellmore St., P.O. Box 656, 07755, P 30,000, M 250, (732) 660-1888, Fax (732) 660-1688, info@oceantwpchamber.org, www.oceantwpchamber.org

**Oakland** • *Oakland C/C* • Michael Fox, Pres., P.O. Box 8, 07436, P 12,000, M 100, (973) 439-2569, www.oakland-nj.org

**Ocean City** • *Ocean City C/C* • Michele Gillian, Exec. Dir., 16 E. 9th St., 08226, P 15,000, M 500, (609) 399-1412, (800) BEACH-NJ, Fax (609) 398-3932, info@oceancitychamber.com, www.ocean cityvacation.com

**Ocean County** • *see Toms River*

**Ocean Grove** • *Ocean Grove Area C/C* • Lois Hetfield, Admin., 45 Pilgrim Pathway, P.O. Box 415, 07756, P 7,500, M 122, (732) 774-1391, (800) 388-4768, Fax (732) 774-3799, info@oceangrovenj. com, www.oceangrovenj.com

**Ocean Twp.** • *see Oakhurst*

**Ocean View** • *Dennis Twp. C/C* • Kim Gansert, Pres., P.O. Box 85, 08230, P 7,000, M 125, (609) 624-0990, info@dennistwpchamber. com, www.dennistwpchamber.com

**Oceanport** • *see Red Bank*

**Old Bridge** • *The C/C serving Old Bridge, Sayreville & South Amboy* • Reggie Butler, Pres., P.O. Box 5241, 08857, P 150,000, M 160, (732) 607-6340, Fax (732) 607-6341, info@obssachamber. org, www.obssachamber.org

**Oradell** • *see River Edge*

**Orange** • *Orange C/C* • Robert Masoud, Pres., P.O. Box 1178, 07050, P 39,000, M 100, (973) 676-8725, Fax (973) 673-5828, www.orangechamber.biz

**Ortley Beach** • *see Toms River*

**Oxford** • *see Washington*

**Paramus** • *Greater Paramus C/C* • Fred Rohdieck, Pres., 58 E. Midland Ave., P.O. Box 325, 07652, P 25,100, M 400, (201) 261-3344, Fax (201) 261-3346, office2005@paramuschamber.com, www.paramuschamber.com.

**Parsippany** • *see Lake Hiawatha*

**Passaic** • *see Clifton*

**Passaic County** • *see Wayne*

**Paterson** • *Greater Paterson C/C* • James Dykes II, Pres., 100 Hamilton Plz., Ste. 1201, 07505, P 170,000, M 650, (973) 881-7300, Fax (973) 881-8233, gpcc@greaterpatersoncc.org, www. greaterpatersoncc.org

**Paulsboro** • *Greater Paulsboro C/C* • Virginia Scott, P.O. Box 181, 08066, P 6,000, M 50, (856) 423-7600, www.paulsborochamber.com

**Pennington** • *see Mercerville*

**Pequannock** • *see Bloomingdale and Wayne*

**Perth Amboy** • *Perth Amboy C/C* • Mario Herns, Admin. Asst., 69A Smith St., 08862, P 35,000, M 150, (732) 442-7400, Fax (732) 442-7450, pachamerofcommerce@verizon.net, www.perthamboy chamber.com

**Phillipsburg** • *Phillipsburg Area C/C* • J. Michael Dowd, Exec. Dir., 314 S. Main, 08865, P 29,000, M 170, (908) 859-5161, Fax (908) 859-6861, miked@lehighvalleychamber.org, www.lehigh valleychamber.org.

**Pine Beach** • *see Toms River*

**Piscataway** • *Piscataway/Middlesex/South Plainfield C/C* • Linda Griggs, Dir., 2 Lakeview Ave., Ste. 303, 08854, P 70,000, M 150, (732) 394-0220, Fax (732) 394-0223, chamber@pmspcoc. org, www.pmspcoc.org

**Plainfield** • *Plainfield C/C* • 320 Park Ave., 07060, P 48,600, M 200, (908) 753-2296, Fax (908) 753-6609, info@positively plainfield.org, www.positivelyplainfield.org

**Point Pleasant Beach** • *Point Pleasant Beach C/C* • Carol Vaccaro, Exec. Dir., 517A Arnold Ave., 08742, P 6,000, M 310, (732) 899-2424, (888) PPB-FUN-2, Fax (732) 899-0103, info@ pointpleasantbeachnj.com, www.pointpleasantbeachnj.org.

**Pompton Lakes** • *Pompton Lakes C/C* • Art Kaffka, Pres., P.O. Box 129, 07442, P 11,000, M 95, (973) 839-0187, Fax (973) 839-0187, info@pomptonchamber.com, www.pomptonlakeschamber.com

**Port Murray** • *see Washington*

**Princeton** • *Princeton Reg. C/C* • Peter Crowley, Pres./CEO, 9 Vandeventer Ave., 08542, P 150,000, M 950, (609) 924-1776, Fax (609) 924-5776, info@princetonchamber.org, www.princeton chamber.org

**Princeton Junction** • *see Princeton*

**Randolph** • *see Mount Freedom*

**Readington** • *see Flemington*

**Red Bank** • *Eastern Monmouth Area C/C* • Lynda Rose, Pres./ COO, 47 Reckless Pl., Ste. 1, 07701, P 100,000, M 650, (732) 741-0055, Fax (732) 741-6778, emacc@emacc.org, www.emacc.org

**Ridgewood** • *Ridgewood C/C* • Joan Groome, 199 Dayton St., 07450, P 25,000, M 250, (201) 445-2600, Fax (201) 251-1958, info@ridgewoodchamber.com, www.ridgewoodchamber.com

**Ringwood** • *Ringwood C/C* • Michael Coppola, Pres., P.O. Box 62, 07456, P 13,000, M 200, info@ringwoodchamber.com, www. ringwoodchamber.com

**River Edge** • *River Edge C/C* • P.O. Box 15, 07661, P 11,000, M 75, (201) 576-9400, info@riveredgechamber.org, www.riveredge chamber.org

**Riverdale** • *see Bloomingdale and Wayne*

**Rochelle Park** • *see Paramus*

**Roseland** • *see West Caldwell*

**Roselle** • *Roselle C/C* • Valerie Dering, Pres., 135 E. Highland Pkwy., 07203, P 22,000, M 50, (908) 298-0123, rosellechamber ofcommerce@comcast.net, www.rosellechamberofcommerce.org.

**Roxbury** • *see Ledgewood*

**Rumson** • *see Red Bank*

**Rutherford** • *Meadowlands Reg. Chamber* • James Kirkos, Pres./CEO, 201 Route 17 N., 07070, P 1,000,000, M 730, (201) 939-0707, Fax (201) 939-0522, office@meadowlands.org, www. meadowlands.org

**Rutherford** • *Rutherford C/C* • P.O. Box 216, 07070, P 19,000, M 75, (201) 933-5230

**Saddle Brook** • *Greater Saddle Brook C/C* • Kevin Konovitch, Pres./Chrmn., 527 N. Midland Ave., 07663, P 17,500, M 50, sbccpres@yahoo.com, www.saddlebrookchamber.com

**Salem** • *see Carneys Point*

**Sandy Hook** • *see Hazlet*

**Sayreville** • *see Old Bridge*

**Scotch Plains** • *see Westfield*

**Sea Bright** • *see Red Bank*

**Sea Girt** • *see Wall*

**Sea Isle City** • *Greater Sea Isle City C/C* • Peggy McDermott, Secy., P.O. Box 635, 08243, P 3,000, M 85, (609) 263-9090, Fax (609) 263-9090, www.seaislechamber.com

**Seaside Heights** • *see Toms River*

**Seaside Park** • *see Toms River*

**Secaucus** • *see Jersey City*

**Ship Bottom** · *Southern Ocean County C/C* · Rick Reynolds, Exec. Dir., 265 W. 9th St., 08008, P 50,000, M 700, (609) 494-7211, (800) 292-6372, Fax (609) 494-5807, info@discoversouthern ocean.com, www.discoversouthernocean.com

**Short Hills** · *see Millburn*

**Shrewsbury** · *see Red Bank*

**Somerset** · *see Franklin Twp.*

**Somerville** · *see Bridgewater*

**South Amboy** · *see Old Bridge*

**South Orange** · *South Orange C/C* · Leslie Pogany, Exec. Dir., P.O. Box 621, 07079, P 17,000, M 60, (973) 762-4333, Fax (973) 763-0943, director@southorangechamber.com, www.south orangechamber.com

**South Plainfield** · *see Piscataway*

**Spring Lake** · *Greater Spring Lake C/C* · 302 Washington Ave., P.O. Box 694, 07762, P 25,000, M 140, (732) 449-0577, www. springlake.org

**Stewartsville** · *see Washington*

**Stone Harbor** · *Stone Harbor C/C* · Karl Giulian, Pres., P.O. Box 422, 08247, P 1,100, M 200, (609) 368-6101, Fax (609) 368-6102, www.stoneharborbeach.com

**Summit** · *Suburban C/C* · Maureen Kelly, Pres., 71 Summit Ave., P.O. Box 824, 07902, P 75,000, M 300, (908) 522-1700, Fax (908) 522-9252, info@suburbanchambers.org, www.suburbanchambers.org

**Sussex County** · *see Newton*

**Teaneck** · *Teaneck C/C* · Karen Careccio, Exec. Dir., 555 Cedar Ln., Ste. 4, 07666, P 39,255, M 100, (201) 801-0012, Fax (201) 907-0870, teaneckchamber@aol.com, www.teaneckchamber.org

**Tinton Falls** · *see Red Bank*

**Toms River** · *Toms River-Ocean County C/C* · Lucy Greene, Pres., 1200 Hooper Ave., 08753, P 135,000, M 800, (732) 349-0220, Fax (732) 349-1252, info@oc-chamber.com, www.oc-chamber.com.

**Totowa** · *see Clifton and Wayne*

**Turnersville** · *Washington Twp. C/C* · John P. Campbell, Pres., 5001 Rte. 42, Ste. C, P.O. Box 734, 08012, P 49,000, M 175, (856) 227-1776, Fax (856) 227-1225, www.washingtontownship chamber.org

**Union** · *Union Twp. C/C* · James R. Brody, Exec. Dir., 355 Chestnut St., 2nd Flr., 07083, P 54,500, M 300, (908) 688-2777, Fax (908) 688-0338, info@unionchamber.com, www.union chamber.com.

**Union Beach** · *see Hazlet*

**Union City** · *see Jersey City*

**Vernon** · *Vernon C/C* · P.O. Box 308, 07462, P 25,000, (973) 764-0764, info@vernonchamber.com, www.vernonchamber.com

**Verona** · *see West Caldwell*

**Vineland** · *Greater Vineland C/C* · Paige Desiere, Exec. Dir., 2115 S. Delsea Dr., 08360, P 60,000, M 600, (856) 691-7400, Fax (856) 691-2113, info@vinelandchamber.org, www.vineland chamber.org

**Voorhees** · *Chamber of Commerce Southern NJ* · Debra DiLorenzo, Pres./CEO, Piazza 6014 at Main St., 08043, P 2,500,000, M 2,000, (856) 424-7776, Fax (856) 424-8180, info@chambersnj. com, www.chambersnj.com

**Wall** · *Southern Monmouth C/C* · Evelyn Mars, Exec. Dir., P.O. Box 1305, 07719, P 90,000, M 350, (732) 280-8800, Fax (732) 280-8505, info@smcconline.org, www.smcconline.org

**Wanaque** · *Wanaque C/C* · Michael Ryan, Pres., P.O. Box 93, 07465, P 11,000, M 55, (973) 248-8634, (973) 839-3000, info@ afamilytown.org, www.afamilytown.org

**Washington** · *Warren County Reg. C/C* · Robert Goltz, Pres./ CEO, 10 Brass Castle Rd., 07882, P 105,765, M 396, (908) 835-9200, Fax (908) 835-9296, info@warrencountychamber.org, www. warrencountychamber.org.

**Washington Township** · *see Turnersville*

**Wayne** · *Tri-County C/C* · Kathe Crimmins, Pres., 2055 Hamburg Tpk., 07470, P 120,000, M 440, (973) 831-7788, Fax (973) 831-9112, kathec@tricounty.org, www.tricounty.org

**Weehawken** · *see Jersey City*

**West Caldwell** · *North Essex C/C* · Meryl Layton, Exec. Dir., 3 Fairfield Ave., 07006, P 52,000, M 650, (973) 226-5500, Fax (973) 403-9335, email@northessexchamber.com, www.northessex chamber.com

**West Milford** · *West Milford C/C* · P.O. Box 234, 07480, P 25,000, M 100, (973) 728-3150, www.westmilford.com

**West New York** · *West New York C/C* · 425 60th St., 07093, P 47,500, M 210, (201) 295-5065, www.wnynj.com

**West Orange** · *West Orange C/C* · Micky Wagner, Exec. Dir., P.O. Box 83, 07052, P 45,000, M 190, (973) 731-0360, Fax (973) 736-3156, mail@westorangechamber.com, www.westorange chamber.com

**West Patterson** · *see Clifton and Wayne*

**West Windsor** · *see Mercerville*

**Westfield** · *Westfield Area C/C* · Naomi McElynn, Exec. Dir., 173 Elm St., 3rd Flr., 07090, P 28,870, M 325, (908) 233-3021, Fax (908) 654-8183, info@westfieldareachamber.com, www.west fieldareachamber.com

**Whippany** · *see Florham Park*

**Wildwood** · *Greater Wildwood C/C* · Patricia McGuigan, Ofc. Mgr., 3306 Pacific Ave., 08260, P 12,000, M 650, (609) 729-4000, Fax (609) 729-4003, info@gwcoc.com, www.gwcoc.com

**Willingboro** · *see Mount Laurel*

**Woodbridge** · *Woodbridge Metro C/C* · Carol S. Hila, Pres., 52 Main St., 07095, P 101,000, M 450, (732) 636-4040, Fax (732) 636-3492, woodbridgechamber@comcast.net, www.woodbridge chamber.com.

**Woodbury** · *Greater Woodbury C/C* · Shirley Bierbrunner, Exec. Dir., P.O. Box 363, 08096, P 10,500, M 300, (856) 845-4056, Fax (856) 848-4445, www.greaterwoodburychamber.com

**Wyckoff** · *Wyckoff C/C* · Diane Kuiken, Bus. Admin., P.O. Box 2, 07481, P 20,000, M 130, (201) 891-3616, info@wyckoffchamber. com, www.wyckoffchamber.com

**Zarepath** · *see Franklin Twp.*

# New Mexico

**Assn. Of Commerce & Ind. Of New Mexico** · Dr. Beverlee McClure, Pres., P.O. Box 9706, Albuquerque, 87119, P 1,800,000, M 1,300, (505) 842-0644, Fax (505) 842-0734, info@aci-nm.org, www.aci-nm.org

**Alamogordo** · *Alamogordo C/C* · Mike Espiritu, Exec. Dir., 1301 N. White Sands Blvd., 88310, P 37,000, M 718, (575) 437-6120, (800) 826-0294, Fax (575) 437-6334, chamber@alamogordo.com, www.alamogordo.com.

## Albuquerque Area

**Greater Albuquerque C/C** • Mrs. Terri L. Cole CCE, Pres./CEO, 115 Gold Ave. S.W., Ste. 201, P.O. Box 25100, 87125, P 724,000, M 5,300, (505) 764-3700, Fax (505) 764-3714, infospec@abq-chamber.com, www.abqchamber.com

**Albuquerque Hispano C/C** • Alex O. Romero, Pres./CEO, 1309 4th St. S.W., 87102, P 600,000, M 1,500, (505) 842-9003, (888) 451-7824, Fax (505) 764-9664, alex@ahcnm.org, www.ahcnm.org

**American Indian C/C of New Mexico** • Theodore Pedro, Exec. Dir., 2401 12th St. NW #5-S, 87104, M 375, (505) 766-9545, Fax (505) 766-9499, www.aiccnm.com

**Algodones** • see Rio Rancho

**Angel Fire** • *Angel Fire C/C* • Tom Bowles, Pres., 3407 Hwy. 434, Centro Plaza, P.O. Box 547, 87710, P 1,600, M 235, (575) 377-6661, (800) 446-8117, Fax (575) 377-3034, askus@angelfirechamber.org, www.angelfirechamber.org

**Anthony** • *Anthony C/C* • Jenny Ayres, Pres., P.O. Box 1086, 88021, P 12,000, M 30, (575) 882-5677, www.leapyearcapital.com

**Artesia** • *Greater Artesia C/C & Visitors Center* • Hayley Klein, Exec. Dir., 107 N. 1st St., P.O. Box 99, 88211, P 16,000, M 368, (575) 746-2744, (800) 658-6251, Fax (575) 746-2745, chamber@artesiachamber.com, www.artesiachamber.com.

**Aztec** • *Aztec C of C & Visitor Center* • Becki Christensen, Exec. Dir., 110 N. Ash, 87410, P 6,378, M 250, (505) 334-9551, (888) 868-9551, Fax (505) 334-7648, director@aztecchamber.com, www.aztecchamber.com

**Belen** • *Greater Belen C/C* • Cindy Clark, Exec. Dir., 712 Dalies Ave., 87002, P 7,000, M 300, (505) 864-8091, Fax (505) 864-7461, belenchamber@belenchamber.com, www.belenchamber.com

**Bernalillo** • see Rio Rancho

**Bloomfield** • *Bloomfield C/C* • Bernadette Smith, Exec. Dir., 224 W. Broadway, 87413, P 7,500, M 170, (505) 632-0880, (800) 461-1245, Fax (505) 634-1431, askme@bloomfieldnm.info, www.bloomfieldnm.info

**Bosque Farms** • see Los Lunas

**Capitan** • *Capitan C/C & Visitors Center* • Peter Renich, 433 Smokey Bear Blvd., P.O. Box 441, 88316, P 1,500, M 40, (575) 354-2273, Fax (575) 354-3666, chamber@villageofcapitan.com, www.villageofcapitan.com

**Carlsbad** • *Carlsbad C/C and C & VB* • Lisa Boeke, Tourism Dir., 302 S. Canal, P.O. Box 910, 88220, P 27,000, M 500, (575) 887-6516, (800) 221-1224, Fax (575) 885-1455, lboeke@carlsbadchamber.com, www.carlsbadchamber.com

**Carrizozo** • *Carrizozo C/C* • Pres., P.O. Box 567, 88301, P 1,030, M 80, (575) 648-2732, zozoccc@tularosa.net, www.carrizozochamber.org

**Chama** • *Chama Valley C/C* • Scott Flury, Pres., P.O. Box 306, 87520, P 1,400, M 182, (575) 756-2306, (800) 477-0149, Fax (575) 756-2892, info@chamavalley.com, www.chamavalley.com

**Cimarron** • *Cimarron C/C* • Carol Baker, 104 N. Lincoln Ave., P.O. Box 604, 87714, P 900, M 50, (575) 376-2417, (888) 376-2417, Fax (575) 376-2417, cimarronnm@gmail.com, www.cimarronnm.com

**Clayton** • *Clayton-Union County C/C* • Rose Ramirez, Exec. Dir., 1103 S. 1st St., P.O. Box 476, 88415, P 2,524, M 100, (575) 374-9253, (800) 390-7858, Fax (575) 374-9250, cuchamber@plateautel.net, www.claytonnewmexico.org

**Cloudcroft** • *Cloudcroft C/C* • Jason Baldwin, Dir., P.O. Box 1290, 88317, P 768, M 185, (575) 682-2733, (866) 874-4447, Fax (575) 682-6028, cloudcroft@cloudcroft.net, www.cloudcroft.net

**Clovis** • *Clovis/Curry County C/C* • Mrs. Ernie Kos, Exec. Dir., 105 E. Grand Ave., 88101, P 45,000, M 700, (575) 763-3435, (800) 261-7656, Fax (575) 763-7266, clovisnm@clovisnm.org, www.clovisnm.org.

**Cuba** • *Cuba C/C* • Adan Delgado, Dir., P.O. Box 1000, 87013, P 8,000, M 75, (575) 289-3514, (575) 289-0302, info@cubanewmexico.com, www.cubanewmexico.com

**Deming** • *Deming-Luna County C/C* • Cyndi Longoria, Exec. Dir., 800 E. Pine, P.O. Box 8, 88031, P 26,000, M 230, (575) 546-2674, (800) 848-4955, Fax (575) 546-9569, info@demingchamber.com, www.demingchamber.com.

**Eagle Nest** • *Eagle Nest C/C* • Nancy Barry, Ofc. Mgr., P.O. Box 322, 87718, P 360, M 60, (575) 377-2420, Fax (575) 377-2420, info@eaglenestchamber.org, www.eaglenestchamber.org

**Edgewood** • *Edgewood C/C* • Myra Oden, Exec. Dir., P.O. Box 457, 87015, P 2,000, M 110, (505) 286-2577, info@edgewoodchambernm.com, www.edgewoodchambernm.com

**Elephant Butte** • *Elephant Butte C/C* • Kim Skinner, Chrmn. of the Bd., 608 Hwy. 195, P.O. Box 1355, 87935, P 2,200, M 110, (575) 744-4708, (877) 744-4900, Fax (575) 744-0044, info@elephantbuttechamberofcommerce.com, www.elephantbuttechamberofcommerce.com

**Espanola** • *Espanola Valley C/C* • Alice D. Lucero, Exec. Dir., 1 Calle de las Espanolas, Ste. F & G, P.O. Box 190, 87532, P 50,000, M 280, (505) 753-2831, Fax (505) 753-1252, info@espanolanmchamber.com, www.espanolanmchamber.com.

**Eunice** • *Eunice C/C* • Fay Thompson, Pres., 1021 Main, P.O. Box 838, 88231, P 3,000, M 100, (575) 394-2755, Fax (575) 394-3937, eunicecofc@windstream.net, www.cityofeunice.org

**Farmington** • *Farmington C/C* • Dorothy Nobis, Pres./CEO, 100 W. Broadway, 87401, P 45,000, M 750, (505) 325-0279, (888) 325-0279, Fax (505) 327-7556, chamber@gofarmington.com, www.gofarmington.com

**Fort Sumner** • *Fort Sumner/DeBaca County C/C* • Sandy Paul, Exec. Dir., P.O. Box 28, 88119, P 2,300, M 121, (575) 355-7705, Fax (575) 355-2850, ftsumnercoc@plateautel.net, www.ftsumnerchamber.com

**Gallup** • *Gallup-McKinley County C/C* • Bill Lee, Exec. Dir., 103 W. Hwy. 66, 87301, P 22,000, M 300, (505) 722-2228, (800) 380-4989, Fax (505) 863-2280, bill@thegallupchamber.com, www.thegallupchamber.com

**Grants** • *Grants/Cibola County C/C* • Star Gonzales, Exec. Dir., 100 N. Iron Ave., P.O. Box 297, 87020, P 28,000, M 250, (505) 287-4802, (800) 748-2142, Fax (505) 287-8224, discover@grants.org, www.grants.org

**Hatch** • *Hatch Valley C/C* • Marcia Nordyke, Pres., P.O. Box 38, 87937, P 1,673, M 70, (575) 267-5050, mnordyke@zianet.com, www.villageofhatch.org, www.hatchchilefest.com

**Jal** • *Jal C/C* • Amelia Trevino, 100 W. Idaho, P.O. Box 1205, 88252, P 2,000, M 125, (575) 395-2620, Fax same, jalchamber@leaco.net, www.jalnm.com

**Las Cruces** • *Greater Las Cruces C/C* • Jim Berry, Pres./CEO, 760 W. Picacho Ave., P.O. Drawer 519, 88004, P 100,000, M 996, (575) 524-1968, Fax (575) 527-5546, jberry@lascruces.org, www.lascruces.org

**Las Cruces** • *Hispano C/C de Las Cruces* • Rachel Garcia-Banegas, Exec. Dir., 308 E. Griggs Ave., P.O. Box 1964, 88004, P 80,000, M 300, (575) 523-2681, Fax (575) 523-4639, office@hispano-chamberlc.org, www.hispanochamberlc.org

**Las Vegas** • *Las Vegas-San Miguel C/C* • Diane Ortiz, Exec. Dir., 503 6th St., P.O. Box 128, 87701, P 17,000, M 350, (505) 425-8631, (800) 832-5947, Fax (505) 425-3057, lvexec@qwestoffice.net, www.lasvegasnewmexico.com

**Logan** • *Logan/Ute Lake C/C* • P.O. Box 277, 88426, P 1,000, M 45, (575) 487-2722, www.utelake.com

**Lordsburg** • *Lordsburg-Hidalgo County C/C* • 117 E. 2nd St., 88045, P 6,000, M 90, (575) 542-9864, Fax (575) 542-9059, lordsburgcoc@aznex.net, .

**Los Alamos** • *Los Alamos C/C* • Katy Korkos, Member Svcs. Coord., 109 Central Park Sq., P.O. Box 460, 87544, P 18,000, M 300, (505) 662-8105, Fax (505) 662-8399, chamber@losalamos.com, www.losalamoschamber.com

**Los Lunas** • *Valencia County C/C* • Rachel Pugh, Exec. Dir., 3447 Lambros, P.O. Box 13, 87031, P 14,000, M 300, (505) 352-3596, Fax (505) 352-3591, chamberdirector@loslunasnm.gov, www.loslunasnm.gov/chamber

**Lovington** • *Lovington C/C* • Ky Atwood, Exec. Dir., 201 S. Main, 88260, P 9,500, M 180, (575) 396-5311, Fax (575) 396-2823, kyatwood@lovingtoncoc.org, www.lovingtonchamber.org

**Magdalena** • *Magdalena C/C* • Danielle Fitzpatrick, Pres., P.O. Box 281, 87825, P 970, M 60, (866) 854-3217, info@magdalena-nm.com, www.magdalena-nm.com

**Melrose** • *Melrose C/C* • Randy Lesly, Pres., P.O. Box 216, 88124, P 750, M 100, (575) 253-4274

**Mora** • *Mora Valley C/C* • Craig Wolf, Pres., P.O. Box 800, 87732, P 5,500, M 60, (575) 387-6072, www.morachamber.com

**Moriarty** • *Moriarty C/C* • Debbie Ortiz, Exec. Dir., P.O. Box 96, 87035, P 1,900, M 125, (505) 832-4087, Fax (505) 832-5436, moriartycc@moriartychamber.com, www.moriartychamber.com

**Mountainair** • *Mountainair C/C* • Kevin Turner, Pres., P.O. Box 595, 87036, P 1,200, M 40, (505) 847-2795, mcc@mountainair chamber.com, www.mountainairchamber.com

**Placitas** • *see Rio Rancho*

**Portales** • *Roosevelt County/Portales C/C* • Sharon King, Exec. Dir., 100 S. Ave. A, 88130, P 20,000, M 300, (575) 356-8541, (800) 635-8036, Fax (575) 356-8542, chamber@portales.com, www.portales.com

**Raton** • *Raton Chamber & Eco. Dev. Cncl.* • Jennifer Wiseman, Exec. Dir., 100 Clayton Rd., P.O. Box 1211, 87740, P 7,282, M 143, (575) 445-3689, (800) 638-6161, Fax (575) 445-3680, raton chamber@bacavalley.com, www.raton.info

**Red River** • *Red River C/C* • Rebecca Sanchez, Exec. Dir., P.O. Box 870, 87558, P 500, M 176, (575) 754-2366, (800) 348-6444, Fax (575) 754-3104, rrinfo@redrivernewmex.com, www.redrivernewmex.com

**Rio Rancho** • *Rio Rancho Reg. C/C* • Debbi Moore, Pres./CEO, 4001 Southern Blvd. S.E., 87124, P 80,000, M 500, (505) 892-1533, Fax (505) 892-6157, info@rrrcc.org, www.rrrcc.org.

**Roswell** • *Roswell C/C* • Bernarr Treat, Exec. Dir., 131 W. Second St., P.O. Drawer 70, 88202, P 52,000, M 550, (575) 623-5695, (877) 849-7679, Fax (575) 624-6870, information@roswellnm.org, www.roswellnm.org

**Ruidoso** • *Ruidoso Valley C/C & Visitors Center* • Sandi Aguilar, Dir., 720 Sudderth Dr., 88345, P 9,000, M 600, (575) 257-7395, (877) 784-3676, Fax (575) 257-4693, info@ruidosonow.com, www.ruidosonow.com

**San Miguel** • *see Las Vegas*

**Sandia Pueblo** • *see Rio Rancho*

**Santa Ana Pueblo** • *see Rio Rancho*

**Santa Fe** • *Santa Fe C/C* • Simon Brackley, Pres./CEO, 8380 Cerrillos Rd., Ste. 302, P.O. Box 1928, 87504, P 139,000, M 1,250, (505) 988-3279, Fax (505) 984-2205, info@santafechamber.com, www.santafechamber.com

**Silver City** • *Silver City-Grant County C/C* • Lola Polley, Exec. Dir., 201 N. Hudson St., 88061, P 31,000, M 550, (575) 538-3785, (800) 548-9378, Fax (575) 538-3786, info@silvercity.org, www.silvercity.org

**Socorro** • *Socorro County C/C* • 101 Plaza, P.O. Box 743, 87801, P 18,000, M 250, (575) 835-0424, Fax (575) 835-9744, chamber@socorro-nm.com, www.socorro-nm.com

**Taos** • *Taos County C/C* • Steve Fuhlendorf, CEO, 108 F Kit Carson Rd., P.O. Box 1300, 87571, P 32,152, M 550, (575) 751-8800, (800) 732-8267, Fax (575) 758-3872, info@taoschamber.com, www.taoschamber.com

**Tatum** • *Tatum C/C* • Marilyn Burns, Pres., P.O. Box 355, 88267, P 800, M 30, (575) 398-5455, Fax (575) 398-5455, mburns@leaco.net, www.tatumschool.org

**Tijeras** • *East Mountain C/C* • Bill Walters, Pres., P.O. Box 2436, 87059, P 1,060, M 80, (505) 281-1999, info@eastmountain chamber.com, www.eastmountainchamber.com

**Truth or Consequences** • *Truth or Consequences & Sierra County C/C* • Jessica Mackenzie, Pres., 207 S. Foch St., P.O. Box 31, 87901, P 13,270, M , (575) 894-3536, contact@truthor consequencesnm.net, www.truthorconsequencesnm.net

**Tucumcari** • *Tucumcari-Quay County C/C* • Thomas Even, Exec. Dir., 404 W. Rte. 66, P.O. Drawer E, 88401, P 5,700, M 150, (575) 461-1694, Fax (575) 461-3884, chamber@tucumcarinm.com, www.tucumcarinm.com

**White's City** • *see Carlsbad*

# New York

**No State Chamber**

**Adams** • *South Jefferson C/C* • Crystal Cobb, Pres., 10924 U.S. Rte. 11, Ste. 2, 13605, P 10,634, M 204, (315) 232-4215, Fax (315) 232-3967, chamrep@northnet.org, www.southjeffersonchamber.com

**Adirondack Region** • *see Glens Falls*

**Albany** • *Albany-Colonie Reg. C/C* • Mark Eagan, Pres./CEO, One Computer Dr. S., 12205, P 294,281, M 3,000, (518) 431-1400, Fax (518) 431-1402, info@acchamber.org, www.acchamber.org.

**Albion** • *Orleans County C/C* • Kelly Kiebala, Exec. Dir., 102 N. Main St., Ste. 1, 14411, P 43,735, M 550, (585) 589-7727, Fax (585) 589-7326, kkiebala@orleanschamber.com, www.orleans chamber.com

**Alden** • *Alden C/C* • Barbara Hoskyns, Exec. Secy., P.O. Box 149, 14004, P 12,000, M 300, (716) 937-6177, secretary@aldenny.org, www.aldenny.org

**Alexandria Bay** • *Alexandria Bay C/C* • Susan Boyer, Exec. Dir., 7 Market St., 13607, P 10,000, M 250, (315) 482-9531, (800) 541-2110, Fax (315) 482-5434, info@alexbay.org, www.alexbay.org

**Amenia** • *see Lakeville, CT*

**Amherst** • *Amherst C/C* • Colleen DiPirro, Pres./CEO, 350 Essjay Rd., Ste. 200, Williamsville, 14221, P 116,000, M 2,300, (716) 632-6905, Fax (716) 632-0548, www.amherst.org

**Amityville** • *Amityville C/C* • John Diliberto, Pres., P.O. Box 885, 11701, P 15,000, M 170, (631) 598-0695, www.amityville chamber.org

**Amsterdam** • *see Fonda*

**Angola** • *Evans-Brant C/C* • Carolyn Schiedel, Mgr., 70 N. Main St., 14006, P 18,000, M 250, (716) 549-3221, information@ebccny. org, www.ebccny.org

**Arcade** • *Arcade Area C/C* • Dorie Clinch, Exec. Secy., 684 W. Main St., 14009, P 3,800, M 400, (585) 492-2114, Fax (585) 492-5103, www.arcadechamber.org

**Athens** • *see Coxsackie*

**Auburn** • *Cayuga County C/C* • 36 South St., 13021, P 81,400, M 600, (315) 252-7291, Fax (315) 255-3077, www.cayugacounty chamber.com

**Avoca** • *see Bath*

**Avon** • *Avon C/C* • Kelly Cole, Pres., 74 Genesee St., 14414, P 6,600, M 150, (585) 226-8080, www.avon-ny.org

**Baldwin** • *Baldwin C/C* • Doris Rios Duffy & Virginia Foley, Co-Pres., P.O. Box 804, 11510, P 31,000, M 100, (516) 223-8080, info@baldwinchamber.com, www.baldwinchamber.com

**Baldwinsville** • *Greater Baldwinsville C/C* • Lee Wilder, Exec. Dir., 3 Marble St., 13027, P 35,000, M 300, (315) 638-0550, bchamber07@verizon.net, www.baldwinsvillechamber.com

**Ballston Lake** • *see Clifton Park*

**Ballston Spa** • *see Clifton Park*

**Batavia** • *Genesee County C/C* • LN Freeman, Pres., 210 E. Main St., 14020, P 61,000, M 1,000, (585) 343-7440, (800) 622-2686, Fax (585) 343-7487, chamber@geneseeny.com, www.geneseeny.com

**Bath** • *Greater Bath Area C/C* • 10 Pulteney Sq. W., 14810, P 30,250, M 250, (607) 776-7122, Fax (607) 776-7122, email@ bathnychamber.com, www.bathnychamber.com

**Bay Shore** • *C/C of Greater Bay Shore* • Donna Periconi, Pres., 77 E. Main St., P.O. Box 5110, 11706, P 30,000, M 300, (631) 665-7003, Fax (631) 665-5204, www.bayshorecommerce.com

**Beacon** • *see Wappingers Falls*

**Bedford Hills** • *Bedford Hills C/C* • Gregory J. Riley, P.O. Box 162, 10507, P 6,500, M 100, (914) 381-3356, Fax (914) 241-8719, www.bedfordhills.org

**Bellmore** • *C/C of the Bellmores* • Joni Caputo, Exec. Dir., P.O. Box 861, 11710, P 25,000, M 350, (516) 679-1875, Fax (516) 409-0544, bellmorecc@aol.com, www.bellmorechamber.com

**Bellport** • *Bellport C/C* • P.O. Box 246, 11713, M 105, (631) 776-9268, email@bellportchamber.com, www.bellportchamber.com

**Bethlehem** • *see Delmar*

**Bethpage** • *Bethpage C/C* • Gary Bretton, Pres., P.O. Box, 11714, P 8,000, M 120, (516) 433-0010, bethpagechamber@yahoo.com, www.bethpagecommunity.com/chamber

**Binghamton** • *Greater Binghamton C/C* • Lou Santoni, Pres./ CEO, Metrocenter, 49 Court St., P.O. Box 995, 13902, P 200,536, M 900, (607) 772-8860, (800) 836-6740, Fax (607) 722-4513, chambergreater@binghamtonchamber.com, www.greater binghamtonchamber.com

**Blue Mountain Lake** • *see Indian Lake*

**Bolton Landing** • *Bolton Landing C/C* • Andrea Maranville, Pres., 4928 Lakeshore Dr., P.O. Box 368, 12814, P 2,117, M 150, (518) 644-3831, Fax (518) 644-5951, www.boltonchamber.com

**Boonville** • *Boonville Area C/C* • Kim Lynch, Pres., 122 Main St., P.O. Box 163, 13309, P 4,400, M 180, (315) 942-5112, Fax (315) 942-6823, info@boonvillechamber.com, www.boonvillechamber.com

**Bradford** • *see Bath*

**Brant** • *see Angola*

**Brewerton** • *Fort Brewerton/Greater Oneida Lake C/C* • Pearl Wilson, Exec. Secy., P.O. Box 655, 13029, P 15,000, M 125, (315) 668-3408, www.oneidalakechamber.com

**Brewster** • *Brewster C/C* • Beth Murtha, Exec. Dir., 16 Mount Ebo Rd. S., Ste. 12A, 10509, P 19,000, M 200, (845) 279-2477, Fax (845) 278-8349, chamber@brewsterchamber.com, www. brewsterchamber.com

**Brockport** • *Greater Brockport C/C* • Elaine Bader, Pres., P.O. Box 119, 14420, P 13,716, M 90, (585) 234-1512, (585) 637-5997, www.brockportchamber.org

**Bronx** • *Bronx C/C* • Lenny Caro, Pres./CEO, 1200 Waters Pl. #305, 10461, P 1,320,000, M 600, (718) 828-3900, Fax (718) 409-3748, lenny@bronxchamber.org, www.bronxchamber.org.

**Bronxville** • *Bronxville C/C* • Ruth Wood, Exec. Dir., 81 Pondfield Rd., Ste. 7, 10708, P 6,200, M 250, (914) 337-6040, Fax (914) 337-6040, bronxvillechamber@verizon.net, www.bronxvillechamber.com.

**Brooklyn** • *Brooklyn C/C* • Carl Hum, Pres./CEO, 25 Elm Pl., Ste. 200, 11201, P 2,500,000, M 1,200, (718) 875-1000, Fax (718) 237-4274, info@brooklynchamber.com, www.ibrooklyn.com

**Brooklyn** • *Coney Island C/C* • 1015 Surf Ave., 11224, P 130,000, M 150, (718) 266-1234, info@coneyislandchamberofcommerce. com, www.coneyislandchamberofcommerce.com

**Broome County** • *see Binghamton*

**Buffalo** • *Buffalo Niagara Partnership* • Andrew J. Rudnick, Pres./CEO, 665 Main St., Ste. 200, 14203, P 1,292,000, M 2,200, (716) 852-7100, (800) 241-0474, Fax (716) 852-2761, www. thepartnership.org

**Burnt Hills** • *see Clifton Park*

**Cambria** • *see Sanborn*

**Camden** • *Camden Area C/C* • Diane Miller, Pres., P.O. Box 134, 13316, P 6,200, M 130, (315) 245-5000, www.camdennycham ber.com

**Camillus** • *Greater Camillus C/C* • Kathy Kitt, Secy., P.O. Box 415, 13031, P 25,000, M 200, (315) 247-5992, kathykitt@gmail.com, www.camilluschamber.com

**Campbell** • *see Bath*

**Canajoharie** • *see Fonda*

**Canandaigua** • *Canandaigua C/C* • Alison Grems, Pres./CEO, 113 S. Main St., 14424, P 20,000, M 750, (585) 394-4400, Fax (585) 394-4546, chamber@canandaiguachamber.com, www. canandaiguachamber.com.

**Canastota** • *Canastota C/C* • Rick Stevens, Pres., 222 S. Peterboro St., P.O. Box 206, 13032, P 5,000, M 85, (315) 697-3677, www.canastota.org

**Candor** • *Candor C/C* • Butch Crowe, Pres., P.O. Box 802, 13743, P 5,000, M 90, (607) 659-7450, www.candorny.org

**Canton** • *Canton C/C* • Sally Hill, Exec. Dir., P.O. Box 369, 13617, P 11,600, M 200, (315) 386-8255, Fax (315) 386-8255, cantoncc@ northnet.org, www.cantonnychamber.org

**Canton** • *St. Lawrence County C/C* • Patricia McKeown, Exec. Dir., 101 Main St., 1st Flr., 13617, P 111,000, M 800, (315) 386-4000, (877) 228-7810, Fax (315) 379-0134, slccoc@northnet.org, www. northcountryguide.com

**Cape Vincent** · *Cape Vincent C/C* · 175 N. James St., P.O. Box 482, 13618, P 1,200, M 250, (315) 654-2481, Fax (315) 654-4141, thecape@tds.net, www.capevincent.org

**Carmel** · *Carmel-Kent C/C* · Bill Nulk, Treas., P.O. Box 447, 10512, P 20,000, M 150, (845) 278-3004, Fax (845) 225-7835

**Carthage** · *Carthage Area C/C* · Edie Roggie, Dir., 120 S. Mechanic St., 13619, P 10,000, M 230, (315) 493-3590, Fax (315) 493-3590, carthage@gisco.net, www.carthageny.com

**Catskill** · *Greene County C/C* · Tracy McNally, Exec. Dir., 1 Bridge St., 2nd Flr., 12414, P 49,000, M 350, (518) 943-4222, Fax (518) 943-1700, tmcnally@greenecounty-chamber.com, www.greenecounty-chamber.com

**Catskill** · *Heart of Catskill Assn. - Catskill C/C* · 327 Main St., P.O. Box 248, 12414, P 12,000, M 450, (518) 943-0989, catskillchamber@mhcable.com, www.catskillny.org

**Cayuga County** · *see Auburn*

**Cazenovia** · *Greater Cazenovia Area C/C* · 59 Albany St., 13035, P 6,500, M 350, (315) 655-9243, (888) 218-6305, cazchamber@windstream.net, www.cazenoviachamber.com

**Center Moriches** · *Moriches C/C* · Dr. Judith Savino-Burd, Pres., P.O. Box 686, 11934, P 15,000, M 140, (631) 874-3849, info@surpassyourdreams.com, www.moricheschamber.com

**Centereach** · *The Greater Middle Country C/C* · Jeff Freund, Pres., P.O. Box 65, 11720, P 65,000, M 150, (631) 585-9393, info@middlecountrychamber.com, www.middlecountrychamber.com

**Chaumont** · *see Three Mile Bay*

**Chautauqua** · *see Mayville*

**Cheektowaga** · *Cheektowaga C/C* · Debra Liegl, Pres./CEO, 2875 Union Rd., Ste. 50, 14227, P 99,314, M 900, (716) 684-5838, Fax (716) 684-5571, chamber@cheektowaga.org, www.cheektowaga.org

**Chemung County** · *see Elmira*

**Cherry Valley** · *Greater Cherry Valley C/C* · Jackie Hall, Pres., P.O. Box 37, 13320, P 1,600, M 90, (607) 264-3100, Fax (607) 264-3447, www.cherryvalleychamber.org

**Cicero** · *Greater Cicero C/C* · P.O. Box 1269, 13039, P 32,000, (315) 699-1358, www.cicerochamber.net

**Clarence** · *Clarence C/C* · David Hartzel, Pres., 8975 Main St., 14031, P 28,500, M 600, (716) 631-3888, Fax (716) 631-3946, info@clarence.org, www.clarence.org

**Clarkson** · *see Brockport*

**Clayton** · *1000 Islands-Clayton Area C/C* · Karen Goetz, Exec. Dir., 517 Riverside Dr., 13624, P 4,500, M 275, (315) 686-3771, (800) 252-9806, Fax (315) 686-5564, info@1000islands-clayton.com, www.1000islands-clayton.com

**Clifton Park** · *The Chamber of Southern Saratoga County* · Peter L. Aust, Pres./CEO, 15 Park Ave., Ste. 7, P.O. Box 399, 12065, P 104,300, M 950, (518) 371-7748, Fax (518) 371-5025, info@southernsaratoga.org, www.southernsaratoga.org

**Clifton Springs** · *Clifton Springs Area C/C* · Brian Morris, Pres., 2 E. Main St, P.O. Box 86, 14432, P 2,300, M 70, (315) 462-8200, info@cliftonspringschamber.com, www.cliftonspringschamber.com

**Clinton** · *Clinton C/C* · Ferris Betrus Jr., Exec. V.P., P.O. Box 142, 13323, P 10,000, M 270, (315) 853-1735, Fax (315) 853-1735, info@clintonnychamber.org, www.clintonnychamber.org

**Clyde** · *Clyde C/C* · Rudolph DeLisio, Pres., P.O. Box 69, 14433, P 2,400, M 75, (315) 923-9862, Fax (315) 923-9862, www.clydeontheerie.com

**Cohoes** · *see Albany*

**Cold Spring** · *Cold Spring Area C/C* · Maureen McGrath, Exec. Dir., P.O. Box 36, 10516, P 10,000, M 180, (845) 265-3200, chamberdirector@gmail.com, www.coldspringchamber.com

**Colonie** · *see Albany*

**Columbia County** · *Columbia County C/C* · David Colby, Pres./CEO, 507 Warren St., Hudson, 12534, P 63,000, M 1,000, (518) 828-4417, Fax (518) 822-9539, mail@columbiachamber-ny.com, www.columbiachamber-ny.com.

**Coney Island** · *see Brooklyn-Coney Island C/C*

**Conklin** · *see Binghamton*

**Cooperstown** · *Cooperstown C/C* · Susan O'Handley, Exec. Dir., 31 Chestnut St., 13326, P 2,160, M 600, (607) 547-9983, Fax (607) 547-6006, susan@cooperstownchamber.org, www.cooperstownchamber.org

**Copiague** · *Copiague C/C* · Sharon Fattoruso, Pres., 1285 Montauk Hwy., P.O. Box 8, 11726, P 26,000, (631) 226-2956, www.copiaguechamber.org

**Corning** · *Corning Area C/C* · Denise Ackley, Pres., 1 W. Market St., Ste. 302, 14830, P 30,000, M 325, (607) 936-4686, Fax (607) 936-4685, info@corningny.com, www.corningny.com

**Cortland** · *Cortland County C/C* · Garry VanGorder, Exec. Dir., 37 Church St., 13045, P 49,000, M 440, (607) 756-2814, Fax (607) 756-4698, info@cortlandchamber.com, www.cortlandchamber.com

**Coxsackie** · *Coxsackie Area C/C* · Doug Calkins, Pres., P.O. Box 251, 12051, P 14,000, M 130, (518) 731-7300, info@coxsackieareachamber.com, www.coxsackieareachamber.com

**Crompond** · *see Yorktown Heights*

**Croton-on-Hudson** · *see Peekskill*

**Cutchogue** · *see Southold*

**Dansville** · *Dansville C/C* · William Bacon, Pres., 126 Main St., P.O. Box 105, 14437, P 5,000, M 400, (585) 335-6920, (800) 949-0174, dansvillechamber@hotmail.com

**Delhi** · *Delaware County C/C* · Mary Beth Silano, Exec. Dir., 5 1/2 Main St., 13753, P 47,000, M 720, (607) 746-2281, Fax (607) 746-3571, info@delawarecounty.org, www.delawarecounty.org

**Delmar** · *Bethlehem C/C* · Marty DeLaney, Pres., 318 Delaware Ave., Ste. 11, 12054, P 33,000, M 650, (518) 439-0512, (888) 439-0512, Fax (518) 475-0910, info@bethlehemchamber.com, www.bethlehemchamber.com.

**Depew** · *see Lancaster*

**Deposit** · *Deposit on the Delaware C/C* · P.O. Box 222, 13754, P 2,000, M 60, www.depositchamber.com

**Dunkirk** · *Chautauqua County C/C* · 10785 Bennett Rd., 14048, P 139,000, M 1,350, (716) 366-6200, Fax (716) 366-4276, cccc@chautauquachamber.org, www.chautauquachamber.org

**East Amherst** · *see Amherst*

**East Aurora** · *Greater East Aurora C/C* · Gary D. Grote, Exec. Dir., 431 Main St., 14052, P 38,550, M 633, (716) 652-8444, Fax (716) 652-8384, eanycc@verizon.net, www.eanycc.com

**East Fishkill** · *see Wappingers Falls*

**East Hampton** · *East Hampton C/C* · Marina Van, Exec. Dir., 42 Gingerbread Ln., 11937, P 22,000, M 315, (631) 324-0362, Fax (631) 329-1642, info@easthamptonchamber.com, www.easthamptonchamber.com

**East Islip** · *East Islip Comm. Chamber* · Mike Visgauss, Pres., P.O. Box 225, 11730, P 13,000, M 40, (631) 581-1200, secretary@eastislipcc.com, www.eastislipcc.com

**East Meadow** · *see Garden City*

**East Moriches** • *see Center Moriches*

**East Quogue** • *see Southampton*

**East Setauket** • *Three Village C/C* • David Woods, Exec. Dir., P.O. Box 6, 11733, (631) 689-8838, Fax (631) 246-9037, director@ threevillagechamber.com, www.threevillagechamber.com

**East Williston** • *see Williston Park*

**East Yaphank** • *East Yaphank C/C* • Michael Giacomaro, Pres., 524 Birch Hollow Dr., 11967, P 5,000, M 132, (631) 345-0805, Fax (631) 924-8193

**Eastchester** • *Eastchester-Tuckahoe C/C* • Nicole Pushkal & Kathy Muscat, Co-Pres., P.O. Box 66, 10709, P 24,000, M 120, (914) 779-7344, cetcoc@aol.com, eastchestertuckahoechamber ofcommerce.com

**Eastport** • *Eastport C/C* • Andrea Milano, Pres., P.O. Box 458, 11941, P 10,000, M 110, (631) 325-5911

**Eden** • *Eden C/C* • Patrick O'Brien, Pres., 8584 S. Main St., P.O. Box 2, 14057, P 3,600, M 200, (716) 992-4799, Fax (716) 992-4751, edenchamber@yahoo.com, www.edenny.org

**Ellenville** • *Ellenville-Wawarsing C/C* • Janet McDonnell, Ofc. Secy., 124 Canal St., P.O. Box 227, 12428, P 16,000, M 130, (845) 647-4620, info@ewcoc.com, www.ewcoc.com

**Ellicottville** • *Ellicottville C/C* • Brian McFadden, 9 W. Washington St., P.O. Box 456, 14731, P 1,700, M 350, (716) 699-5046, Fax (716) 699-5636, info@ellicottvilleny.com, www. ellicottvilleny.com

**Elma** • *see Lancaster*

**Elmira** • *Chemung County C/C* • Kevin D. Keeley, Pres./CEO, 400 E. Church St., 14901, P 96,000, M 800, (607) 734-5137, Fax (607) 734-4490, info@chemungchamber.org, www.chemungchamber.org

**Evans** • *see Angola*

**Fair Haven** • *Fair Haven Area C/C* • Alan Avrich, Pres., P.O. Box 13, 13064, P 6,000, M 55, (315) 947-6037, info@fairhavenny.com, www.fairhavenny.com

**Farmington** • *Farmington C/C* • Calvin T. Cobb, Pres., 1000 County Rd. 8, 14425, P 11,000, M 289, (315) 986-8100, (585) 398-2331, Fax (315) 986-4377, www.farmingtoncofc.com

**SHOVEL READY SITES. LOCATED ALONG I-90 NY STATE THRUWAY, MIDWAY BETWEEN BUFFALO & SYRACUSE, WITH INFRASTRUCTURE, RAIL ACCESS AND STABLE TAXES.**

**Farnham** • *see Angola*

**Fayetteville** • *Fayetteville C/C* • Bernice Tarolli, Admin., 404 E. Genesee St., 13066, P 4,200, M 85, (315) 637-5544, fayette villechamber@twcny.rr.com, www.fayettevillechamber.org

**Fire Island Pines** • *Greater Fire Island Pines C/C* • Christine Pfoh, Secy., P.O. Box 695, Sayville, 11782, P 3,000, M 51, (631) 597-3058, info@pineschamber.com, www.pineschamber.com

**Fishkill** • *see Wappingers Falls*

**Fleischmanns** • *Fleischmanns C/C* • P.O. Box 126, 12430, P 300, M 20, (845) 254-4884, www.fleischmannsny.com

**Floral Park** • *Floral Park C/C* • Robert Rouge, Pres., P.O. Box 20093, 11002, P 16,000, M 177, (516) 641-1200, Fax (516) 488-5107, www.floralparkchamber.org

**Flushing** • *see Queens*

**Fonda** • *Montgomery County C/C* • Deborah Auspelmyer, Pres., 12 S. Bridge St., P.O. Box 836, 12068, P 49,708, M 485, (518) 853-1800, Fax (518) 853-1813, chamber@montgomerycountyny.com, www.montgomerycountyny.com

**Forest Hills** • *Forest Hills C/C* • Leslie Brown, Pres., P.O. Box 751123, 11375, P 100,000, M 200, (718) 268-6565, www. foresthillschamber.org

**Fort Edward** • *Fort Edward C/C* • P.O. Box 267, 12828, P 6,000, M 80, (518) 747-3000, Fax (518) 747-3000, info@fortedward chamber.com, www.fortedwardchamber.com

**Fort Plain** • *see Fonda*

**Franklin** • *Greater Franklin C/C* • P.O. Box 814, 13775, P 2,700, M 72, (607) 829-5890, franklinnychamber@yahoo.com, www. franklinny.org

**Fredonia** • *see Dunkirk*

**Freeport** • *Freeport C/C* • Francisco Jorge, Pres., 300 Woodcleft Ave., 11520, P 43,000, M 213, (516) 223-8840, Fax (516) 223-1211, www.freeportchamberofcommerce.com

**Fulton** • *see Oswego*

**Fulton County** • *see Gloversville*

**Fultonville** • *see Fonda*

**Garden City** • *Garden City C/C* • Althea Robinson, Exec. Dir., 230 Seventh St., 11530, P 21,000, M 390, (516) 746-7724, Fax (516) 746-7725, gcchamber@verizon.net, www.gardencitychamber.org

**Garden City** • *Nassau Cncl. Of Chambers of Commerce* • E. Christopher Murray, Pres., 1305 Franklin Ave., P.O. Box 119, 11530, P 3,200,000, M 6,000, (516) 396-0200, Fax (516) 396-5097, www. ncchambers.org

**Genesee County** • *see Batavia*

**Geneseo** • *Livingston County C/C* • Cynthia Oswald, Pres., 4635 Millennium Dr., 14454, P 67,000, M 1,200, (585) 243-2222, Fax (585) 243-4824, coswald@frontiernet.net, www.livingstoncounty chamber.com

**Geneva** • *Geneva Area C/C* • Rob Gladden, Pres., 35 Lakefront Dr., P.O. Box 587, 14456, P 15,000, M 630, (315) 789-1776, Fax (315) 789-3993, info@genevany.com, www.genevany.com.

**Getzville** • *see Amherst*

**Glen Cove** • *Glen Cove C/C* • Phyllis Gorham, Exec. Dir., 19 Village Sq., 11542, P 25,000, M 227, (516) 676-6666, Fax (516) 676-5490, info@glencovechamber.org, www.glencovechamber.org

**Glens Falls** • *Adirondack Reg. C/C* • Todd L. Shimkus CCE, Pres./ CEO, 5 Warren St., 12801, P 145,580, M 1,040, (518) 798-1761, Fax (518) 792-4147, tshimkus@adirondackchamber.org, www. adirondackchamber.org.

**Gloversville** • *Fulton County Reg. C/C & Ind.* • Wally Hart, Pres., 2 N. Main St., 12078, P 55,500, M 942, (518) 725-0641, (800) 676-3858, Fax (518) 725-0643, info@fultoncountyny.org, www. fultoncountyny.org, www.44lakes.com

**Goshen** • *Goshen C/C* • Lynn Cione, Exec. Dir., 44 Park Place, P.O. Box 506, 10924, P 13,500, M 200, (845) 294-7741, Fax (845) 294-3998, gcc1@frontiernet.net, www.goshennychamber.com

**Gouverneur** • *Gouverneur C/C* • Donna M. Lawrence, Exec. Dir., 214 E. Main St., Lawrence Manor Bldg., 13642, P 8,000, M 130, (315) 287-0331, Fax (315) 287-3694, www.gouverneurchamber.net

**Gowanda** • *Gowanda Area C/C* • Rev. Travis Grubbs, Pres., P.O. Box 45, 14070, P 19,000, M 150, (716) 532-2834, Fax (716) 532-2834, www.gowandachamber.org

**Grand Island** • *Grand Island C/C* • John Bonora, Pres., 2257 Grand Island Blvd., 14072, P 20,000, M 300, (716) 773-3651, Fax (716) 773-3316, info@gichamber.org, www.gichamber.org

**Granville** · *Granville Area C/C* · 1 Main St., 12832, P 5,000, M 125, (518) 642-2815, info@granvillechamber.com, www. granvillechamber.com

**Great Neck** · *Great Neck C/C* · Valerie Link, Pres., P.O. Box 220432, 11022, P 60,000, M 300, (516) 487-2000, www.great neckchamber.org

**Greece** · *Greece C/C* · Jodie Perry, Pres./CEO, 2496 W. Ridge Rd., Ste. 201, 14626, P 94,000, M 760, (585) 227-7272, Fax (585) 227-7275, jodie@greecechamber.org, www.greecechamber.org

**Greene** · *Greater Greene C/C* · Deb & Joe Eggleston, Co-Dirs., P.O. Box 441, 13778, P 6,000, (607) 656-8225, info@greenenys.com, www.greenenys.com

**Greenport** · *see Southold*

**Greenvale** · *Greenvale C/C* · P.O. Box 123, 11548, P 1,800, M 60, (516) 621-2110, www.greenvalechamber.com

**Greenwich** · *Greater Greenwich C/C* · Kathy Nichols-Tomkins, Secy., 6 Academy St., 12834, P 10,000, M 245, (518) 692-7979, Fax (518) 692-7979, info@greenwichchamber.org, www.green wichchamber.org

**Greenwich Village** · *see New York-Greenwich Village-Chelsea C/C*

**Guilderland** · *Guilderland C/C* · Kathy Burbank, Exec. Dir., 2050 Western Ave., Ste. 109, Albany, 12084, P 37,000, M 600, (518) 456-6611, Fax (518) 456-6690, info@guilderlandchamber.com, www.guilderlandchamber.com

**Hague** · *Hague-on-Lake George C/C* · P.O. Box 615, 12836, P 850, www.hagueticonderoga.com

**Halfmoon** · *see Clifton Park*

**Hamburg** · *Hamburg C/C* · Betty Newell, Pres./CEO, 8 S. Buffalo St., 14075, P 57,000, M 800, (716) 649-7917, (877) 322-6890, Fax (716) 649-6362, hccmail@hamburg-chamber.org, www. hamburg-chamber.org

**Hammond** · *Black Lake C/C* · P.O. Box 12, 13646, M 60, (315) 375-8640, info@blacklakeny.com, www.blacklakeny.com

**Hammondsport** · *Hammondsport C/C* · John Jensen, Pres., 47 Shethar St., P.O. Box 539, 14840, P 8,000, M 165, (607) 569-2989, Fax (607) 569-2989, info@hammondsport.org, www.hammond sport.org

**Hampton Bays** · *Hampton Bays C/C* · Stan Glinka, Pres., 140 W. Main St., Ste. 1, 11946, P 13,092, M 115, (631) 728-2211, Fax (631) 728-0308, hamptonbayschamber@verizon.net, www. hamptonbayschamber.com

**Hancock** · *Hancock Area C/C* · P.O. Box 525, 13783, P 1,400, M 45, (607) 637-4756, (800) 668-7624, hancockchamber@ hancock.net, www.hancockareachamber.com

**Harlem** · *see New York-Greater Harlem C/C*

**Harrison** · *Harrison C/C* · Ada Angarano, Pres./CEO, 1 Heineman Pl., 10528, P 20,000, M 140, (914) 835-7039, Fax (914) 835-7039, harrisoncc04@yahoo.com, www.theharrisoncofc.org

**Hartland** · *see Sanborn*

**Hastings-On-Hudson** · *Hastings-On-Hudson C/C* · Ravi Wadera, Pres., 32 Main St., 10706, P 8,000, M 34, (914) 478-2101, info@hohchamber.com, www.hohchamber.com

**Haverstraw** · *Greater Haverstraw C/C* · Matthew S. Clement, Pres., 4 Broadway, P.O. Box 159, 10927, P 10,000, M 150, (845) 947-5646, info@haverstrawchamber.org, www.haverstraw chamber.org

**Hempstead** · *Hempstead C/C* · Leo Fernandez, Pres., 1776 Denton Green Park, P.O. Box 4264, 11550, P 50,000, M 125, (516) 483-2000, Fax (516) 483-2000, president@hempsteadchamber. com, www.hempsteadchamber.com

**Henderson Harbor** · *Henderson Harbor C/C* · P.O. Box 468, 13651, P 1,300, M 110, (315) 938-5568, (888) 938-5568, thechambertreasurer@gmail.com, www.hendersonharborny.com

**Hicksville** · *Hicksville C/C* · Lionel J. Chitty, Pres., 10 W. Marie St., 11801, P 51,000, M 190, (516) 931-7170, Fax (516) 931-8546, hicksvillechamber@earthlink.net, www.hicksvillechamber.com

**Highland** · *Southern Ulster County C/C* · William Farrell, Pres., 20 Milton Ave., Ste. 3, 12528, P 40,000, M 110, (845) 691-6070, Fax (845) 691-9194, info@southernulsterchamber.org, www. southernulsterchamber.org

**Hinsdale** · *see North Syracuse*

**Holbrook** · *Holbrook C/C* · Rick Ammirati, Pres., P.O. Box 585, 11741, P 25,000, M 250, (631) 471-2725, Fax (631) 343-4816, info@holbrookchamber.com, www.holbrookchamber.com

**Holtsville** · *Farmingville/Holtsville C/C* · Wayne Carrington, Pres., P.O. Box 66, 11742, P 35,000, M 60, (631) 926-8259

**Honeoye** · *Honeoye Lake C/C* · Tina Ketchum, Secy., P.O. Box 305, 14471, P 20,000, M 500, (585) 229-4226, www.honeoyechamber ofcommerce.com

**Hopewell Junction** · *see Wappingers Falls*

**Hornell** · *Hornell Area C/C* · James W. Griffin, Pres., 40 Main St., 14843, P 11,000, M 450, (607) 324-0310, Fax (607) 324-3776, griff@hornellny.com, www.hornellny.com.

**Hudson** · *see Columbia County*

**Hunter** · *Town of Hunter C/C* · P.O. Box 177, 12442, P 2,100, M 124, (518) 263-4900, Fax (518) 589-0117, chamberinfo@ hunterchamber.org, www.hunterchamber.org

**Huntington** · *Huntington Twp. C/C* · Ellen O'Brien, Exec. Dir., 164 Main St., 11743, P 197,000, M 700, (631) 423-6100, Fax (631) 351-8276, ellen@huntingtonchamber.com, www.huntington chamber.com

**Hyde Park** · *Hyde Park C/C* · Elizabeth Roger, Pres., P.O. Box 17, 12538, P 21,000, M 200, (845) 229-8612, Fax (845) 229-8638, www.hydeparkchamber.org

**Indian Lake** · *Indian Lake C/C* · 5 Main St., P.O. Box 724, 12842, P 4,900, (518) 648-5112, www.indian-lake.com

**Inlet** · *Inlet Info. Ofc.* · Adele Burnett, Tourism Dir., 160 Rte. 28, Box 266, 13360, P 485, M 106, (315) 357-5501, (866) GO-INLET, Fax (315) 357-3570, info@inletny.com, www.inletny.com

**Islip** · *Islip C/C* · P.O. Box 112, 11751, P 16,000, M 200, (631) 581-2720, Fax (631) 581-2720, info@islipchamberofcommerce.com, www.islipchamberofcommerce.com

**Ithaca** · *Tompkins County C/C* · Jean McPheeters, Pres., 904 E. Shore Dr., 14850, P 106,000, M 710, (607) 273-7080, Fax (607) 272-7617, jean@tompkinschamber.org, tompkinschamber.org

**Jamaica** · *Jamaica C/C* · Robert M. Richards, Pres., 90-25 161st St., Rm. 505, 11432, P 770,000, M 500, (718) 657-4800, Fax (718) 658-4642, jamaicachamber@aol.com, www.jccnewyork.net

**Jamestown** · *Chautauqua County C/C* · Todd Tranum, Exec. Dir., 101 W. Fifth St., 14701, P 139,000, M 1,600, (716) 484-1101, Fax (716) 487-0785, cccc@chautauquachamber.org, www.chautauqua chamber.org

**Jefferson Valley** · *see Yorktown Heights*

**Jeffersonville** • *Jeffersonville Area C/C* • P.O. Box 463, 12748, P 300, (845) 482-5688, info@jeffersonvilleny.com, www.jeffersonvilleny.com

**Kanona** • *see Bath*

**Katonah** • *Katonah C/C* • Jennifer Cook & Sara Zipp, Co-Pres., P.O. Box 389, 10536, P 5,000, M 135, (914) 232-2668, info@katonahchamber.org, www.katonahchamber.org

**Kenmore** • *Kenmore-Town Of Tonawanda C/C* • Tracey M. Lukasik, Exec. Dir., 3411 Delaware Ave., 14217, P 82,414, M 850, (716) 874-1202, Fax (716) 874-3151, info@ken-ton.org, www.ken-ton.org

**Kings Park** • *Kings Park C/C* • Charles Gardner, Pres., P.O. Box 322, 11754, P 25,000, M 140, (631) 269-7678, www.kingsparkli.com

**Kingston** • *C of C of Ulster County* • Ward Todd, Pres., 55 Albany Ave., 12401, P 178,000, M 1,300, (845) 338-5100, Fax (845) 338-0968, info@ulsterchamber.org, www.ulsterchamber.org

**Lackawanna** • *Lackawanna Area C/C* • Michael Sobaszek, Exec. Dir., 638 Ridge Rd., 14218, P 20,000, M 350, (716) 823-8841, Fax (716) 823-8848, info@lackawannachamber.com, www.lackawannachamber.com

**Lake George** • *Lake George Reg. C/C* • Janice Fox, Pres., 2176 State Rte. 9, P.O. Box 272, 12845, P 3,900, M 400, (518) 668-5755, (800) 705-0059, Fax (518) 668-4286, info@lakegeorgechamber.com, www.lakegeorgechamber.com

**Lake Placid** • *Lake Placid C/C* • James McKenna, Pres./CEO, Olympic Center, 49 Parkside Dr., 12946, P 8,000, M 600, (800) 447-5224, (518) 523-2445, Fax (518) 523-2605, info@lakeplacid.com, www.lakeplacid.com

**Lake Pleasant** • *see Speculator*

**Lakewood** • *see Jamestown*

**Lancaster** • *Lancaster Area C/C* • Kathy Konst, Pres./CEO, 41 Central Ave., P.O. Box 284, 14086, P 50,000, M 550, (716) 681-9755, Fax (716) 684-3385, laccny@aol.com, www.laccny.org

**Latham** • *Colonie C/C* • Tom Nolte, Exec. Dir., 950 New Loudon Rd., 12110, P 78,000, M 550, (518) 785-6995, Fax (518) 785-7173, info@coloniechamber.org, www.coloniechamber.org

**Levittown** • *Levittown C/C* • P.O. Box 207, 11756, P 50,000, M 150, (516) 520-8000, Fax (516) 520-8000, info@levittownchamber.com, www.levittownchamber.com

**Liberty** • *see Monticello*

**Liverpool** • *Greater Liverpool C/C* • Lucretia Hudzinski, Exec. Dir., 314 2nd St., 13088, P 55,000, M 400, (315) 457-3895, Fax (315) 234-3226, chamber@liverpoolchamber.com, www.liverpoolchamber.com

**Lockport** • *see Sanborn*

**Long Beach** • *Long Beach C/C* • Michael J. Kerr, Pres., 350 National Blvd., 11561, P 35,000, M 300, (516) 432-6000, Fax (516) 432-0273, www.longbeachnychamber.com

**Long Island City** • *see Queens*

**Long Island City** • *Sunnyside C/C* • Luke Adams, Consultant, c/o LaGuardia Comm. College, 3110 Thomson Ave., Ste. M222, 11101, M 100, (718) 482-6053, luke@sunnysidechamber.org, www.sunnysidechamber.org

**Lowville** • *Lewis County C of C* • Anne Merrill, Exec. Dir., 7559 S. State St., 13367, P 26,796, M 465, (315) 376-2213, Fax (315) 376-0326, anne@lewiscountychamber.org, www.lewiscountychamber.org

**Lyme** • *see Three Mile Bay*

**Lynbrook** • *Lynbrook C/C* • Bill Gaylor, Pres., P.O. Box 624, 11563, P 19,000, M 210, (516) 599-7777, www.lynbrookusa.com

**Lyons** • *Lyons C/C* • P.O. Box 39, 14489, P 5,000, M 60, (315) 946-6691, www.lyonsny.com

**Mahopac** • *Greater Mahopac-Carmel C/C* • 953 S. Lake Blvd., P.O. Box 160, 10541, P 31,886, M 435, (845) 628-5553, Fax (845) 628-5962, info@mahopaccarmelchamber.com, www.mahopaccarmelchamber.com.

**Malone** • *Malone C/C* • Minique Barnett, Exec. Dir., 497 E. Main St., 12953, P 14,000, M 238, (518) 483-3760, (877) 625-6631, Fax (518) 483-3172, director@visitmalone.com, www.visitmalone.com

**Malta** • *see Clifton Park*

**Mamaroneck** • *Mamaroneck C/C* • Jennifer M. Graziano, Pres., 430 Center Ave., 10543, P 19,000, M 200, (914) 698-4400, chamber10543@optonline.net, www.mamaroneckchamberofcommerce.org

**Manhattan** • *see New York-Manhattan C/C*

**Manorville** • *Manorville C/C* • P.O. Box 232, 11949, M 75, (631) 487-3504, info@manorvillechamber.org, www.manorvillechamber.org

**Marcy** • *Marcy C/C* • Everett Smith, Secy./Treas., P.O. Box 429, 13403, P 10,000, M 140, (315) 865-6144, Fax (315) 865-6144, www.marcychamber.com

**Margaretville** • *Central Catskills C/C* • Georgi Fairlie, P.O. Box 605, 12455, P 700, M 131, (845) 586-3300, Fax (845) 586-3161, georgi.fairlie@margaretville.org, www.centralcatskills.org

**Massapequa** • *C/C of the Massapequas* • Robert R. Barrett, Pres., 674 Broadway, 11758, P 77,590, M 325, (516) 541-1443, masscoc@aol.com, www.massapequachamber.com

**Massena** • *Greater Massena C/C* • Michael Gleason, Exec. Dir., 50 Main St., 13662, P 14,000, M 365, (315) 769-3525, Fax (315) 769-5295, chamber@massenaworks.com, www.massenaworks.com/chamber

**Mastic** • *see Shirley*

**Mattituck** • *Mattituck C/C* • Terry McShane, Pres., P.O. Box 1056, 11952, P 5,400, M 170, (631) 298-5230, (631) 298-5757, info@mattituckchamber.org, www.mattituckchamber.org

**Mattydale** • *see North Syracuse*

**Mayville** • *Mayville/Chautauqua Area C/C* • Deborah Marsala, Coord., P.O. Box 22, 14757, P 4,554, M 80, (716) 753-3113, Fax (716) 753-3113, maychautchamber@yahoo.com, www.mayville-chautauquachamber.org

**Mechanicville** • *Mechanicville Area C/C* • Barbara Corsale, Pres., 312 N. 3rd Ave., 12118, P 5,500, M 180, (518) 664-7791, Fax (518) 664-0826, mechanicvillechamber@verizon.net

**Medford** • *Medford C/C* • Jim Gubitosi, Pres., P.O. Box 926, 11763, P 20,000, (631) 475-3374, www.medfordchamberny.org

**Medina** • *Orleans County C/C* • Kelly Kiebala, Exec. Dir., 433 Main St., 14103, P 43,735, M 450, (585) 798-4287, Fax (585) 798-4371, kkiebala@orleanschamber.com, www.orleanschamber.com

**Melville** • *Long Island Assn.* • Matthew Crosson, Pres., 300 Broadhollow Rd., Ste. 110W, 11747, P 2,754,718, M 3,000, (631) 493-3000, info@liaonline.org, www.liaonline.org

**Mexico** • *Greater Mexico C/C* • Robert Loforte, Pres., P.O. Box 158, 13114, P 7,500, M 60, (315) 963-1042, www.mexicony.net

**Miller Place** · *CDM C/C - Council of Dedicated Merchants* · Dr. Thomas J. Ianniello, Pres., P.O. Box 512, 11764, P 35,000, M 290, (631) 821-1313, Fax (631) 331-0027, cdmpresident@yahoo.com, www.cdmlongisland.com

**Millerton** · *see Lakeville, CT*

**Mineola** · *Mineola C/C* · Steve Ford, Pres., P.O. Box 62, 11501, P 25,000, M 200, (516) 746-3944, www.mineolachamber.com

**Mohawk** · *Herkimer County C/C* · John Scarano, Exec. Dir., 28 W. Main St., P.O. Box 129, 13407, P 64,400, M 450, (315) 866-7820, (877) 984-4636, Fax (315) 866-7833, hcccomm@ntcnet.com, www.herkimercountychamber.com.

**Mohegan Lake** · *see Yorktown Heights*

**Montauk** · *Montauk C/C* · Laraine Creegan, Exec. Dir., 742 Montauk Hwy., 11954, P 5,500, M 280, (631) 668-2428, Fax (631) 668-9363, www.montaukchamber.com

**Montgomery** · *Orange County C/C* · Dr. John A. D'Ambrosio, Pres., 30 Scotts Corner Dr., 12549, P 350,000, M 2,200, (845) 457-9700, Fax (845) 457-8799, drjohn@orangeny.com, www.orangeny.com.

**Montgomery** · *Town of Montgomery C/C* · P.O. Box 662, 12549, P 18,500, M 150, (845) 778-0514, (845) 457-2660, Fax (845) 457-9981

**Monticello** · *Sullivan County C/C* · Terri Ward, Pres./CEO, 457 W. Broadway, Ste. 1, 12701, P 74,000, M 1,000, (845) 791-4200, Fax (845) 791-4220, chamber@catskills.com, www.catskills.com

**Morehouse** · *see Speculator*

**Moriches** · *see Center Moriches*

**Mount Kisco** · *Mount Kisco C/C* · Janet Deane, Exec. Dir., 3 N. Moger Ave., 10549, P 10,000, M 200, (914) 666-7525, Fax (914) 666-7663, mtkiscochamber@aol.com, www.mtkisco.com

**Mount Sinai** · *see Miller Place*

**Mount Vernon** · *African American C/C* · Frank Fraley, Pres., 100 Stevens Ave., Ste. 202, 10550, M 250, (914) 699-9050, Fax (914) 699-6279, robinlisadouglas@cs.com, www.aaccnys.org

**Mount Vernon** · *Mount Vernon C/C* · Martin Rego, Pres., P.O. Box 351, 10604, P 68,000, M 210, (914) 667-7500, Fax (914) 699-0139, mtvcoc@hotmail.com, www.mtvernonchamber.org

**Narrowsburg** · *Narrowsburg C/C* · Jane Luchsinger, Pres., P.O. Box 300, 12764, P 1,000, M 55, (845) 252-7234, www.narrowsburg.org

**New Baltimore** · *see Coxsackie*

**New City** · *New City C/C* · Doug Staley, Pres., 65 N. Main St., 2nd Flr., 10956, P 36,000, M 120, (845) 638-1395, Fax (845) 638-4636, www.newcitychamberofcommerce.org

**New Hartford** · *New Hartford C/C* · Mark Turnbull, P.O. Box 372, 13413, P 23,000, M 150, (315) 735-1974, Fax (315) 266-1231, info@newhartfordchamber.com, www.newhartfordchamber.com

**New Hyde Park** · *Greater New Hyde Park C/C* · P.O. Box 247, 11040, P 25,000, M 225, (516) 775-4716, Fax (516) 358-7770, contact@nhpchamber.com, www.nhpchamber.com

**New Paltz** · *New Paltz Reg. C/C* · Joyce M. Minard, Pres., 124 Main St., 12561, P 12,830, M 800, (845) 255-0243, Fax (845) 255-5189, info@newpaltzchamber.org, www.newpaltzchamber.org.

**New Rochelle** · *C/C of New Rochelle* · Denise Lally, Exec. Dir., 459 Main St., 10801, P 69,500, M 500, (914) 632-5700, Fax (914) 632-0708, chamber@newrochellechamber.org, www.newrochellechamber.org

**New Suffolk** · *see Southold*

## New York Area

**Greater New York C/C** · Mark S. Jaffe, Pres., 20 W. 44th St., 4th Flr., 10036, P 15,000,000, M 2,000, (212) 686-7220, Fax (212) 686-7232, info@chamber.com, www.chamber.com.

**THE GREATER NY CHAMBER IS AN APPROVED NYS NOT-FOR-PROFIT REGIONAL CHAMBER; RECOGNIZED BY THE US CHAMBER, SERVING NYC AND THE NY METROPOLITAN AREA. IT PROVIDES VALUABLE SERVICES TO ALMOST 10,000 BUSINESS AND CIVIC LEADERS. IT ALSO MAINTAINS A CHARITABLE FOUNDATION APPROVED BY THE IRS TO ASSIST LOCAL CHAMBERS, TRADE ORGANIZATIONS & CIVIC GROUPS; AS WELL AS A POLITICAL ACTION COMMITTEE TO HELP IMPROVE THE BUSINESS CLIMATE AND QUALITY OF LIVING!**

**Greater Harlem C/C** · Lloyd Williams, Pres./CEO, 200A W. 136th St., 10030, P 500,000, M 1,900, (212) 862-7200, Fax (212) 862-8745, www.harlemdiscover.com

**Greenwich Village-Chelsea C/C** · Dirk McCall, Exec. Dir., 154 Christopher St., 10014, M 200, (212) 337-5923, www.villagechelsea.com

**Manhattan C/C** · Nancy Ploeger, Pres., 1375 Broadway, 3rd Flr., 10018, P 8,000,000, M 1,500, (212) 479-7772, Fax (212) 473-8074, info@manhattancc.org, www.manhattancc.org

**West Manhattan C/C** · Andrew Albert, Exec. Dir., P.O. Box 1028, Planetarium Station, 10024, P 300,000, M 400, (212) 787-1112, Fax (212) 787-1115, mail@westmanhattanchamber.org, www.westmanhattanchamber.org

**Newark** · *Newark C/C* · John Tickner, Pres., 199 Van Buren St., 14513, P 15,000, M 215, (315) 331-2705, Fax (315) 331-2705, newarkchamber@rochester.rr.com, www.newarknychamber.org

**Newburgh** · *see Montgomery*

**Newfane** · *see Sanborn*

**Niagara Falls** · *see Sanborn*

**North Creek** · *Gore Mountain Reg./North Creek C/C* · Ed Milner, Pres., P.O. Box 84, 12853, P 2,450, M 130, (518) 251-2612, goremtn@frontiernet.net, www.gorechamber.com

**North Syracuse** · *Plank Road C/C* · John Mehlek, Pres., P.O. Box 324, 13212, M 125, (315) 458-4181, smay@twcny.rr.com, www.plankroadchamber.com

**North Tonawanda** · *C/C of the Tonawandas* · Joyce Santiago, Exec. Dir., 15 Webster St., 14120, P 49,398, M 610, (716) 692-5120, Fax (716) 692-1867, chamber@the-tonawandas.com, www.the-tonawandas.com

**Northport** · *Northport C/C* · Lori Leonardo, Pres., P.O. Box 33, 11768, P 7,800, M 200, (631) 757-0086, chamber@northportny.com, www.northportny.com

**Norwich** · *Commerce Chenango* · Maureen Carpenter, Pres./CEO, 19 Eaton Ave., 13815, P 52,000, M 500, (607) 334-1400, (877) CHENANGO, Fax (607) 336-6963, info@chenangony.org, www.chenangony.org

**Nyack** · *C/C of the Nyacks* · Carol Fleischmann, Pres., P.O. Box 677, 10960, P 7,500, M 195, (845) 353-2221, Fax (845) 353-4204, info@nyackchamber.com, www.nyackchamber.com

**Ocean Beach** · *Fire Island-Ocean Beach C/C* · Harvey Levine, 468 Denhoff Walk, 11770, M 300, (631) 583-8295

**Oceanside** · *Oceanside C/C* · Joseph Garay, Pres., P.O. Box 1, 11572, P 36,000, M 175, (516) 763-9177, (516) 620-8006, info@oceansidechamber.org, www.oceansidechamber.org

**Ogdensburg** • *Greater Ogdensburg C/C* • Sandra Porter, Exec. Dir., 330 Ford St., 13669, P 12,364, M 280, (315) 393-3620, Fax (315) 393-1380, chamber@gisco.net, www.ogdensburgny.com

**Old Field** • *see East Setauket*

**Olean** • *C/C of Olean & Vicinity* • Margaret Kenney, Exec. Dir., 319 N. Union St., 14760, P 25,000, M 460, (716) 373-4230, (800) 381-5463, Fax (716) 372-1204, margek9061@aol.com, www.oleanny.org.

**Olean** • *Greater Olean Area C/C* • John Sayegh, COO, 120 N. Union St., 14760, P 35,000, M 722, (716) 372-4433, Fax (716) 372-7912, jsayegh@oleanny.com, www.oleanny.com.

HOME AND GARDEN SHOW, ART IN THE PARK, SANTA CLAUS LANE, RALLY IN THE VALLEY, TASTE OF OLEAN, REC/SPORT SHOW, AND MORE.

**Oneida** • *Oneida C/C* • Ms. Brett Bogardus, Exec. Dir., 136 Lenox Ave., 13421, P 11,000, M 200, (315) 363-4300, Fax (315) 361-4558, executivedirector@oneidachamber.com, www.oneidachamber.com

**Oneonta** • *The Otsego County Chamber* • Rob Robinson, Pres./CEO, 189 Main St., Ste. 201, 13820, P 61,676, M 600, (607) 432-4500, Fax (607) 432-4506, tocc@otsegocountychamber.com, www.otsegocountychamber.com

**Ontario** • *Ontario C/C* • Donna Burolla, Dir., P.O. Box 100, 14519, P 10,000, M 159, (315) 524-5886, Fax (315) 524-7465, burolla@ontariotown.org, www.ontariotown.org

**Orange County** • *see Montgomery*

**Orchard Park** • *Orchard Park C/C* • Nancy L. Conley, Exec. Dir., 4211 N. Buffalo St., Ste. 14, 14127, P 30,000, M 625, (716) 662-3366, Fax (716) 662-5946, opcc@orchardparkchamber.com, www.orchardparkchamber.com

**Ossining** • *Greater Ossining C/C* • Jerry Gershner, Pres., 2 Church St., 10562, P 35,000, M 150, (914) 941-0009, info@ossiningchamber.org, www.ossiningchamber.org

**Oswego** • *Greater Oswego-Fulton C/C* • Beth Hilton, Exec. Dir., 44 E. Bridge St., 13126, P 20,000, M 650, (315) 343-7681, Fax (315) 342-0831, gofcc@oswegofultonchamber.com, www.oswegofultonchamber.com.

**Owego** • *Tioga County C/C* • Martha Sauerbrey, Pres./CEO, 80 North Ave., 13827, P 52,000, M 300, (607) 687-2020, Fax (607) 687-9028, business@tiogachamber.com, www.tiogachamber.com

**Oxford** • *Promote Oxford Now* • Bill Troxell & David Emerson, Co-Dirs., P.O. Box 11, 13830, P 4,500, M 100, (607) 843-8722, (607) 843-9538, www.oxfordny.com

**Oyster Bay** • *Oyster Bay C/C* • Alex Gallego, Pres., P.O. Box 21, 11771, P 12,000, M 150, (516) 922-6464, obchamber@gmail.com, www.visitoysterbay.com

**Painted Post** • *Painted Post Area Bd. Of Trade* • Thomas Magnusen, Pres., P.O. Box 128, 14870, P 2,000, M 100, www.paintedpostny.com

**Palatine Bridge** • *see Fonda*

**Patchogue** • *Greater Patchogue C/C* • Gail Hoag, Exec. Dir., 15 N. Ocean Ave., 11772, P 20,000, M 400, (631) 207-1000, Fax (631) 475-1599, info@patchoguechamber.com, www.patchoguechamber.com

**Patterson** • *Patterson C/C* • Anthony LoMeli, Pres., P.O. Box 316, 12563, P 11,500, M 75, (845) 878-4696, info@pcofc.org, www.pcofc.org

**Pawling** • *Pawling C/C* • Peter Cris, Pres., P.O. Box 19, 12564, P 5,000, M 200, (845) 855-0500, www.pawlingchamber.org

**Pearl River** • *Pearl River C/C* • 4 E. Central Ave., P.O. Box 829, 10965, P 17,000, (845) 735-5324, prchamberofcommerce@yahoo.com, www.pearlriverny.org

**Peekskill** • *Hudson Valley Gateway C/C* • Ron Forehand, Pres./CEO, One S. Division St., 10566, P 57,000, M 550, (914) 737-3600, Fax (914) 737-0541, info@hvgatewaychamber.com, www.hvgatewaychamber.com

**Pelham** • *Pelham C/C* • John Decicco, Pres., P.O. Box 965, 10803, P 13,000, M 110, (914) 738-7380, Fax (914) 712-3682, www.pelhamchamberofcommerce.com

**Pendleton** • *see Sanborn*

**Penn Yan** • *Yates County C/C* • Michael Linehan, Pres./CEO, 2375 Route 14A, 14527, P 24,500, M 425, (315) 536-3111, (800) 868-9283, Fax (315) 536-3791, info@yatesny.com, www.yatesny.com.

**Perry** • *Perry Area C/C* • Lorraine Sturm, Secy., P.O. Box 35, 14530, P 7,000, M 200, (585) 237-5040, joinus@perrychamber.com, www.perrychamber.com

**Perry** • *Wyoming County C/C* • James Pierce, Exec. Dir., 6470 Route 20A, Ste. 2, 14530, P 45,000, M 503, (585) 237-0230, Fax (585) 237-0231, info@wycochamber.org, www.wycochamber.org

**Phelps** • *Phelps C/C* • Chuck Molloy, Pres., P.O. Box 1, 14532, P 2,000, M 90, (315) 548-5481, chamber@phelpsny.com, www.phelpsny.com

**Phoenix** • *see Fulton*

**Piseco** • *see Speculator*

**Plainview** • *Plainview-Old Bethpage C/C* • P.O. Box 577, 11803, P 37,000, (516) 937-5646, info@pobcoc.com, www.pobcoc.com

**Plattsburgh** • *Plattsburgh-North Country C/C* • Garry Douglas, Pres., 7061 Rte. 9, P.O. Box 310, 12901, P 200,000, M 3,200, (518) 563-1000, Fax (518) 563-1028, chamber@westelcom.com, www.northcountrychamber.com

**Pleasantville** • *Pleasantville C/C* • William Flooks, Jr., Pres., P.O. Box 94, 10570, P 7,000, M 165, (914) 747-6419, Fax (914) 769-0037, info@pleasantvillechamber.com, www.pleasantville.com

**Poquott** • *see East Setauket*

**Port Chester** • *see Rye Brook*

**Port Jefferson** • *Greater Port Jefferson C/C* • Susan Balch, Pres., 118 W. Broadway, 11777, P 7,850, M 270, (631) 473-1414, Fax (631) 474-4540, info@portjeffchamber.com, www.portjeffchamber.com

**Port Jervis** • *Tri-State C/C* • Gary Linton, Exec. Dir., P.O. Box 121, 12771, P 9,800, M 362, (845) 856-6694, Fax (845) 856-6695, info@tristatechamber.org, www.tristatechamber.org

**Port Washington** • *Port Washington C/C* • Warren Schein, Pres., 329 Main St., P.O. Box 121, 11050, P 35,000, M 250, (516) 883-6566, Fax (516) 883-6591, pwcoc@optonline.net, www.pwguide.com

**Potsdam** • *Potsdam C/C* • Brenda Thornton, Exec. Dir., One Market St., P.O. Box 717, 13676, P 17,000, M 300, (315) 274-9000, Fax (315) 274-9222, potsdam@slic.com, www.potsdamchamber.com

**Poughkeepsie** • *Dutchess County Reg. C/C* • Charles North, Pres./CEO, 1 Civic Center Plaza, 12601, P 275,000, M 1,400, (845) 454-1700, Fax (845) 454-1702, office@pokchamb.org, www.pokchamb.org.

**Prattsburg** • *see Bath*

**Pulaski** • *Pulaski/Eastern Shore C/C* • Margaret Clerkin, Pres., 3044 State Rte. 13, P.O. Box 34, 13142, P 2,500, M 89, (315) 298-2213, pulaski@dreamscape.com, www.pulaskinychamber.com

**Queens** • *C/C of the Borough of Queens* • Jack Friedman, Exec. V.P., 75-20 Astoria Blvd., Ste. 140, Jackson Heights, 11370, P 2,100,000, M 1,700, (718) 898-8500, Fax (718) 898-8599, info@queenschamber.org, www.queenschamber.org.

**Red Hook** • *Red Hook Area C/C* • P.O. Box 254, 12571, P 10,000, M 220, (845) 758-0824, info@redhookchamber.org, www.redhookchamber.org

**Rensselaer County** • *see Troy*

**Rhinebeck** • *Rhinebeck Area C/C* • Nancy Amy, Exec. Dir., 23F E. Market St., P.O. Box 42, 12572, P 45,000, M 430, (845) 876-5904, Fax (845) 876-8624, info@rhinebeckchamber.com, www.rhinebeckchamber.com.

**Richfield Springs** • *Richfield Area C/C* • Harriet Sessler, Pres., P.O. Box 909, 13439, P 1,800, M 90, (315) 858-0031, hsessler@stny.rr.com

**Riverhead** • *Riverhead C/C* • 542 E. Main St., Ste. 2, 11901, P 27,000, M 350, (631) 727-7600, Fax (631) 727-7946, info@riverheadchamber.com, www.riverheadchamber.com

**Rochester** • *Rochester Business Alliance* • Sandra Parker, CEO, 150 State St., 14614, P 1,062,420, M 2,400, (585) 244-1800, Fax (585) 244-4864, www.rochesterbusinessalliance.com

**Rockaway Park** • *C/C of the Rockaways Inc.* • John Lepore, Pres., 253 Beach 116th St., 11694, P 150,000, M 275, (718) 634-1300, Fax (718) 634-9623, rockawaychamber@aol.com, www.rockawaychamberofcommerce.com

**Rockville Centre** • *Rockville Centre C/C* • Lawrence Siegel, P.O. Box 226, 11571, P 24,568, M 175, (516) 766-0666, mailbox@rvcchamber.org, www.rvcchamber.com

**Rocky Point** • *see Miller Place*

**Rome** • *Rome Area C/C* • William K. Guglielmo, Pres., 139 W. Dominick St., 13440, P 35,000, M 600, (315) 337-1700, Fax (315) 337-1715, info@romechamber.com, www.romechamber.com.

**Ronkonkoma** • *Ronkonkoma C/C* • Steve Browne, Pres., P.O. Box 2546, 11779, P 15,400, M 195, (631) 471-0302, info@ronkonkomachamber.com, www.ronkonkomachamber.com

**Roscoe** • *Roscoe-Rockland C/C* • Rick Baxter, Pres., P.O. Box 443, 12776, P 1,800, M 75, (607) 498-5765, info@roscoeny.com, www.roscoeny.com

**Round Lake** • *see Clifton Park*

**Royalton** • *see Sanborn*

**Rye** • *Rye Merchants Assn.* • Cai Palmer, Exec. Dir., P.O. Box, 10580, P 15,500, M 120, (914) 921-5950, Fax (914) 921-5952, wineatfive@verizon.net, www.ryemerchantsassociation.com

**Rye Brook** • *Port Chester-Rye Brook-Rye Town C/C* • Ken Manning, Exec. Dir., 122 N. Ridge St., 10573, P 35,000, M 400, (914) 939-1900, Fax (914) 437-7779, pcrbchamber@gmail.com, www.pcrbchamber.com

**Sabael** • *see Indian Lake*

**Sackets Harbor** • *Sackets Harbor C/C* • Tim Scee, Pres., 301 W. Main, P.O. Box 17, 13685, P 1,500, M 75, (315) 646-1700, shvisit@gisco.net, www.sacketsharborchamberofcommerce.com

**Sag Harbor** • *Sag Harbor C/C* • Bob Evjen, Pres., The Windmill, P.O. Box 2810, 11963, P 2,500, M 200, (631) 725-2100, (631) 725-0011, sagchamber@peconic.net, www.sagharborchamber.com

**Saint James** • *Saint James C/C* • P.O. Box 286, 11780, P 15,000, M 125, (631) 584-8510, Fax (631) 862-9839, info@stjameschamber.org, www.stjameschamber.org

**Salamanca** • *Salamanca Area C/C* • Jayne Fenton, Pres., 26 Main St., 14779, P 6,800, M 125, (716) 945-2034, Fax (716) 945-2034, sal.cofc@verizon.net, www.salamancachamber.com

**Sanborn** • *Niagara USA Chamber* • Deanna Alterio Brennen, Pres./CEO, 6311 Inducon Corporate Dr., 14132, P 210,000, M 1,200, (716) 285-9141, Fax (716) 285-0941, dalteriobrennen@niagarachamber.org, www.niagarachamber.org

**Saranac Lake** • *Saranac Lake Area C/C* • Sylvie D. Nelson, Exec. Dir., 132 River St., 12983, P 5,000, M 490, (518) 891-1990, (800) 347-1992, Fax (518) 891-7042, info@saranaclake.com, www.saranaclake.com

**Saratoga Springs** • *Saratoga County C/C* • Joseph W. Dalton Jr. CCE, Pres., 28 Clinton St., 12866, P 200,000, M 3,003, (518) 584-3255, Fax (518) 587-0318, info@saratoga.org, www.saratoga.org.

**Savona** • *see Bath*

**Sayville** • *Greater Sayville C/C* • Dan Lent, Lincoln Ave. & Montauk Hwy., P.O. Box 235, 11782, P 17,000, M 200, (631) 567-5257, Fax (631) 218-0881, info@sayvillechamber.com, www.sayvillechamber.com

**Scarsdale** • *Scarsdale C/C* • P.O. Box 635, 10583, P 18,000, (914) 725-1602, info@scarsdalechamber.com, www.scarsdalechamber.org

**Schenectady** • *Schenectady County C/C* • Charles Steiner, Pres., 306 State St., 12305, P 150,000, M 1,500, (518) 372-5656, (800) 962-8007, Fax (518) 370-3217, info@schenectadychamber.org, www.schenectadychamber.org

**Schoharie** • *Schoharie County C/C* • Jodie Rutt, Exec. Dir., 113 Park Pl., Ste. 2, 12157, P 33,000, M 375, (518) 295-6550, (800) 41-VISIT, Fax (518) 295-7453, info@schohariechamber.com, www.schohariechamber.com

**Schroon Lake** • *Schroon Lake Area C/C* • Laura Donaldson, Pres., 1075 U.S. Rte. 9, P.O. Box 726, 12870, P 2,000, M 125, (518) 532-7675, (888) SCHROON, Fax (518) 532-7675, schroon@capital.net, www.schroonlake.org, www.schroonlakechamber.com

**Schuylerville** • *Schuylerville Area C/C* • Dave Roberts, Pres., P.O. Box 19, 12871, P 25,000, M 100, (518) 695-5268, info@schuylervillechamber.org, www.schuylervillechamber.org

**Seneca Falls** • *Seneca County C/C* • Alfred Gaffney, Exec. Dir., 2020 Rtes. 5 & 20 W., P.O. Box 70, 13148, P 33,486, M 500, (315) 568-2906, Fax (315) 568-1730, info@senecachamber.org, www.senecachamber.org

**Setauket** • *see East Setauket*

**Shelter Island** • *Shelter Island C/C* • P.O. Box 598, 11964, P 1,234, (631) 749-0399, www.shelterislandchamber.com

**Shirley** • *Mastics-Shirley C/C* • Mark Smothergill, Pres., 211 Hounslow Rd., 11967, P 53,000, M 145, (631) 399-2228

**Shoreham** • *see Wading River*

**Shrub Oak** • *see Yorktown Heights*

**Sidney** • *Sidney C/C* • John Marano, Pres., 24 River St., P.O. Box 2295, 13838, P 4,000, M 160, (607) 561-2642, Fax (607) 561-2644, office@sidneychamber.org, www.sidneychamber.org

**Skaneateles** • *Skaneateles C/C* • Susan Dove, Exec. Dir., 22 Jordan St., P.O. Box 199, 13152, P 8,000, M 400, (315) 685-0552, Fax (315) 685-0552, info@skaneateles.com, www.skaneateles.com

**Sleepy Hollow** • *see Tarrytown*

**Smithtown** • *Smithtown C/C* • Barbara Franco, Exec. Dir., P.O. Box 1216, 11787, P 14,000, M 375, (631) 979-8069, Fax (631) 979-2206, info@smithtownchamber.com, www.smithtownchamber.com

**Snyder** • *see Amherst*

**Sodus** • *Sodus Town C/C* • Mary Jane Mumby, Pres., P.O. Box 187, 14551, P 10,000, M 100, (315) 576-3818, Fax (315) 483-0059, chamber14551@yahoo.com, www.sodusny.com

**Somers** · *Somers C/C* · P.O. Box 602, 10589, P 20,000, M 150, (914) 276-3904, info@somerschamber.org, www.somerschamber.org

**Somerset** · *see Sanborn*

**Sound Beach** · *see Miller Place*

**South Setauket** · *see East Setauket*

**Southampton** · *Southampton C/C* · Millie A. Fellingham, Exec. Dir., 76 Main St., 11968, P 50,000, M 577, (631) 283-0402, Fax (631) 283-8707, info@southamptonchamber.com, www.southamptonchamber.com

**Southern Dutchess** · *see Wappingers Falls*

**Southold** · *North Fork C/C* · Joseph Corso, Pres., P.O. Box 1415, 11971, P 22,000, M 300, (631) 765-3161, (631) 477-1383, Fax (631) 765-3161, info@northforkchamber.org, www.northforkchamberofcommerce.org

**Speculator** · *Adirondacks Speculator Region C/C* · Lisa Turner, Dir. of Tourism, Rtes. 30 & 8, P.O. Box 184, 12164, P 5,000, M 200, (518) 548-4521, Fax (518) 548-4905, info@speculatorchamber.com, www.speculatorchamber.com

**Sprakers** · *see Fonda*

**Springville** · *Springville Area C/C* · Katherine Moody, Exec. Dir., 23 N. Buffalo St., Ste. 23, P.O. Box 310, 14141, P 12,000, M 175, (716) 592-4746, information@springvillechamber.com, www.springvillechamber.com

**St. Johnsville** · *see Fonda*

**Staten Island** · *Staten Island C/C* · Linda M. Baran, Pres./CEO, 130 Bay St., 10301, P 477,377, M 900, (718) 727-1900, Fax (718) 727-2295, info@sichamber.com, www.sichamber.com.

**Stillwater** · *see Clifton Park*

**Stony Brook** · *see East Setauket*

**Suffern** · *Suffern C/C* · Aury Licata, Pres., 71 Lafayette Ave., P.O. Box 291, 10901, P 10,000, M 125, (845) 357-8424, suffernchamberofcommerce@yahoo.com, www.suffernchamberofcommerce.org

**Sugarloaf** · *SugarLoaf C/C* · Ada Hunter, Pres., P.O. Box 125, 10981, P 12,000, M 40, (845) 469-9181, info@sugarloafnewyork.com, www.sugarloafnewyork.com

**Sweden** · *see Brockport*

**Syracuse** · *Greater Syracuse C/C* · Darlene Kerr, Pres., 572 S. Salina St., 13202, P 458,336, M 2,200, (315) 470-1800, Fax (315) 471-8545, info@syracusechamber.com, www.syracusechamber.com.

**Tarrytown** · *Sleepy Hollow Tarrytown C/C* · Katharine M. Swibold, Exec. Dir., 54 Main St., 10591, P 19,000, M 250, (914) 631-1705, Fax (914) 366-4291, info@sleepyhollowchamber.com, www.sleepyhollowtarrytownchamber.com.

**Terryville** · *see Port Jefferson*

**Three Mile Bay** · *Chaumont-Three Mile Bay C/C* · P.O. Box 24, 13693, P 2,500, (315) 649-3404, chaumontchamber@yahoo.com, www.chaumontchamber.com

**Ticonderoga** · *Ticonderoga Area C/C* · Joseph Conway, Exec. Dir., 94 Montcalm St., Ste. 1, 12883, P 6,000, M 200, (518) 585-6619, Fax (518) 585-9184, tacc@bluemoo.net, www.ticonderogany.com

**Tioga County** · *see Owego*

**Tonawanda** · *see North Tonawanda*

**Troy** · *Rensselaer County Reg. C/C* · Linda Hillman, Pres., 255 River St., 12180, P 192,000, M 1,125, (518) 274-7020, Fax (518) 272-7729, info@renscochamber.com, www.renscochamber.com.

**Trumansburg** · *Trumansburg Area C/C* · P.O. Box 478, 14886, P 2,000, M 60, (607) 387-9254, info@trumansburgchamber.com, www.trumansburgchamber.com

**Tupper Lake** · *Tupper Lake C/C* · Marti Mozdzier, Exec. Dir., 121 Park St., P.O. Box 987, 12986, P 6,000, M 242, (518) 359-3328, Fax (518) 359-2434, tuppercc@adelphia.net, www.tupperlakeinfo.com

**Ulster County** · *see Kingston*

**Unadilla** · *Unadilla C/C* · Chris Wilson, Treas., P.O. Box 275, 13849, P 10,000, M 150, (607) 563-8600, www.unadillachamber.org

**Utica** · *Mohawk Valley C/C* · Frank Elias, Pres., 200 Genesee St., Radisson Hotel Ste. 1, 13502, P 228,000, M 900, (315) 724-3151, Fax (315) 724-3177, info@mvchamber.org, www.mvchamber.org

**Valley Stream** · *Valley Stream C/C* · Debbie Gyulay, Pres., P.O. Box 1016, 11582, P 35,000, M 200, (516) 825-1741, Fax (516) 825-1741, valleystreamcc@gmail.com, www.valleystreamchamber.org

**Victor** · *Victor C/C* · Mitch Donovan, Pres., 37 E. Main St., 14564, P 10,000, M 350, (585) 742-1476, Fax (866) 857-6338, info@victorchamber.com, www.victorchamber.com

**Victory** · *see Schuylerville*

**Waddington** · *Waddington Area C/C* · Alicia Murphy, Pres., P.O. Box 291, 13694, P 2,000, M 67, (315) 388-4079, www.waddingtonny.us

**Wading River** · *Wading River-Shoreham C/C* · Mike Roth, Pres., P.O. Box 348, 11792, M 60, (631) 929-8201, info@wrschamber.org, www.wrschamber.org

**Walden** · *see Montgomery*

**Walton** · *Walton C/C* · Maureen Wacha, Pres., 129 North St., 13856, P 8,500, M 125, (607) 865-6656, walton_chamber@yahoo.com, www.waltonchamber.com

**Wantagh** · *Wantagh C/C* · Marc Nadelman, Exec. Dir., P.O. Box 660, 11793, P 19,000, M 215, (516) 679-0100, www.wantaghchamber.com

**Wappingers Falls** · *Greater Southern Dutchess C/C* · Ann Meagher, Pres., 2582 South Ave., 12590, P 260,000, M 1,100, (845) 296-0001, Fax (845) 296-0006, info@gsdcc.org, www.gsdcc.org

**Warrensburg** · *Warrensburg C/C* · Lynn Smith, Pres., 3847 Main St., 12885, P 4,000, M 120, (518) 623-2161, Fax (518) 623-2184, info@warrensburgchamber.com, www.warrensburgchamber.com

**Warsaw** · *Greater Warsaw C/C* · Becky Ryan, Pres., P.O. Box 221, 14569, P 5,000, M 200, (585) 786-3730, (585) 786-3080, info@warsawchamber.com, www.warsawchamber.com

**Warwick** · *Warwick Valley C/C* · Michael A. Johndrow, Exec. Dir., South St., 'Caboose', P.O. Box 202, 10990, P 32,000, M 425, (845) 986-2720, Fax (845) 986-6982, info@warwickcc.org, www.warwickcc.org

**Washingtonville** · *Blooming Grove/Washingtonville C/C* · P.O. Box 454, 10992, P 20,000, M 100, (845) 497-7717

**Waterford** · *see Clifton Park*

**Watertown** · *Greater Watertown-North Country C/C* · Karen K. Delmonico, Pres., 1241 Coffeen St., 13601, P 110,943, M 1,007, (315) 788-4400, Fax (315) 788-3369, chamber@watertownny.com, www.watertownny.com

**Watkins Glen** · *Watkins Glen Area C/C* · Crystal M. Ricks IOM, Pres./CEO, 100 N. Franklin St., 14891, P 19,662, M 354, (607) 535-4300, (800) 607-4552, Fax (607) 535-6243, info@watkinsglenchamber.com, www.watkinsglenchamber.com.

**U.S. Chambers of Commerce**

**Waverly** · *see Sayre, PA*

**Webster** · *Webster C/C* · Elizabeth Bernard, Admin., 1110 Crosspointe Ln., Ste. C, 14580, P 45,000, M 600, (585) 265-3960, Fax (585) 265-3702, bbernard@websterchamber.com, www. websterchamber.com.

**Wells** · *see Speculator*

**Wellsville** · *Wellsville Area C/C* · Steve Havey, Exec. Dir., 114 N. Main St., 14895, P 49,500, M 280, (585) 593-5080, Fax (585) 593-5088, info@wellsvilleareachamber.com, www.wellsville areachamber.com

**West Amherst** · *see Amherst*

**West Islip** · *West Islip C/C* · P.O. Box 58, 11795, P 30,000, M 400, (631) 661-3838, www.westislip.org

**West Seneca** · *West Seneca C/C* · Kathleen Gullo, Admin. Dir., 950A Union Rd., Ste. 5, 14224, P 50,000, M 400, (716) 674-4900, Fax (716) 674-5846, kgullochamber@westseneca.org, www. westseneca.org

**Westbury** · *Westbury-Carle Place C/C* · Steven Levy, Pres., P.O. Box 474, 11590, P 16,000, M 150, (516) 997-3966, info@ wcpchamber.com, www.wcpchamber.com

**Westchester County** · *Bus. Cncl. Of Westchester* · Marsha Gordon, Pres./CEO, 108 Corporate Park Dr., Ste. 101, White Plains, 10604, P 923,000, M 1,400, (914) 948-2110, Fax (914) 948-0122, www.westchesterny.org.

**Westfield** · *Westfield Barcelona C/C* · P.O. Box 125, 14787, P 5,200, M 100, (716) 326-4000, www.westfieldny.com

**Westhampton Beach** · *Greater Westhampton C/C* · 7 Glover's Ln., P.O. Box 1228, 11978, P 3,300, M 180, (631) 288-3337, Fax (631) 288-3322, info@whbcc.org, www.whbcc.org

**Westport** · *Westport C/C* · P.O. Box 394, 12993, P 1,200, M 100, (518) 962-8383, chamber@westportny.com, www.westportny.com

**White Plains** · *see Westchester County*

**Whitehall** · *Whitehall C/C* · Scott Ray, Pres., P.O. Box 97, 12887, P 5,200, M 110, (518) 499-2292, Fax (518) 499-9145, scott. whitehall-chamber@live.com, whitehall-chamber.org

**Williamson** · *Williamson C/C* · Lorraine Mason, Pres., P.O. Box 907, 14589, P 7,000, (315) 589-2857, williamsoncofc@aol.com, www.williamsonchamberofcommerce.org

**Williamsville** · *see Amherst*

**Williston Park** · *C/C of the Willistons* · Raymond Haller, P.O. Box 207, 11596, P 7,500, M 100, (516) 739-1943, Fax (516) 294-1444, www.chamberofthewillistons.org

**Wilson** · *see Sanborn*

**Windham** · *Windham C/C* · P.O. Box 613, 12496, P 1,660, M 115, (518) 734-3852, info@windhamchamber.org, www.windham chamber.org

**Woodstock** · *Woodstock C/C* · Joyce Beymer, Pres., P.O. Box 36, 12498, P 6,290, M 260, (845) 679-6234, info@woodstockchamber. com, www.woodstockchamber.com

**Yonkers** · *Yonkers C/C* · Kevin Cacace, Pres., 55 Main St., 2nd Flr., 10701, P 195,000, M 800, (914) 963-0332, Fax (914) 963-0455, info@yonkerschamber.com, www.yonkerschamber.com.

**Yorktown Heights** · *New Yorktown C/C* · Arlette Rossignol, Dir. of Ops., P.O. Box 632, 10598, P 38,000, M 400, (914) 245-4599, Fax (914) 734-7171, info@yorktownchamber.org, www.yorktown chamber.org

# North Carolina

**North Carolina Chamber** · S. Lewis Ebert, Pres./CEO, 701 Corporate Center Dr., Ste. 400, Raleigh, 27607, P 9,222,414, M 1,900, (919) 836-1400, Fax (919) 836-1425, info@nccbi.org, www.ncchamber.net

**Ahoskie** · *Ahoskie C/C* · Jerry W. Castelloe, Exec. V.P., 310 S. Catherine Creek Rd., P.O. Box 7, 27910, P 25,000, M 200, (252) 332-2042, Fax (252) 332-8617, ahoskiechamber@ahoskie.net, www.ahoskiechamber.com

**Albemarle** · *Stanly County C/C* · Tom Ramseur, Pres./CEO, 116 E. North St., P.O. Box 909, 28002, P 60,000, M 500, (704) 982-8116, Fax (704) 983-5000, info@stanlychamber.org, www.stanlychamber.org

**Andrews** · *Andrews C/C* · Tom Nash, Dir. of Tourism, 345 Locust St., P.O. Box 800, 28901, P 1,900, M 135, (828) 321-3584, (877) 558-0005, Fax (828) 321-3584, info@andrewschamber.com, www. andrewschambercommerce.com

**Angier** · *Angier C/C* · Jamie Strickland, Exec. Dir., 24 E.Depot St., P.O. Box 47, 27501, P 4,000, M 250, (919) 639-2500, Fax (919) 639-8826, angiercc@angierchamber.org, www.angierchamber.org

**Apex** · *Apex C/C* · Brenda Steen, Exec. Dir., 220 N. Salem St., 27502, P 34,000, M 543, (919) 362-6456, (800) 345-4504, Fax (919) 362-9050, info@apexchamber.com, www.apexchamber.com

**Archdale** · *Archdale-Trinity C/C* · Beverly M. Nelson, Pres., 213 Balfour Dr., P.O. Box 4634, 27263, P 25,000, M 265, (336) 434-2073, Fax (336) 431-5845, info@archdaletrinitychamber.com, www.archdaletrinitychamber.com

**Asheboro** · *Asheboro/Randolph C/C* · George Gusler Jr., Pres., 317 E. Dixie Dr., 27203, P 162,857, M 650, (336) 626-2626, Fax (336) 626-7077, chamber@asheboro.com, chamber.asheboro.com

**Asheville** · *Asheville Area C/C* · Rick Lutovsky, Pres., 36 Montford Ave., P.O. Box 1010, 28802, P 224,000, M 2,000, (828) 258-6101, Fax (828) 251-0926, asheville@ashevillechamber.org, www.ashevillechamber.org

**Aurora** · *Aurora Richland Twp. C/C* · Christy Carpenter, Exec. Dir., P.O. Box 326, 27806, P 4,700, M 68, (252) 322-4405, aurorachamber@ embarqmail.com, www.aurorarichlandchamber.com

**Ayden** · *Ayden C/C* · Stacy Gaskins, Interim Dir., P.O. Box 31, 28513, P 4,622, M 85, (252) 746-2266, Fax (252) 746-2266, chamber@ayden.com, www.aydenchamber.com

**Banner Elk** · *Avery County C/C* · Barry G. Sutton, Pres., 4501 Tynecastle Hwy. #2, 28604, P 19,980, M 315, (828) 898-5605, (800) 972-2183, Fax (828) 898-8287, chamber@averycounty.com, www.averycounty.com

**Beech Mountain** · *Beech Mountain Area C/C* · Peggy Koscia, Ofc. Mgr., 403A Beech Mountain Pkwy., 28604, P 380, M 100, (828) 387-9283, (800) 468-5506, Fax (828) 387-3572, chamber@ beechmtn.com, www.beechmtn.com

**Belhaven** · *Belhaven Comm. C/C* · Gary Dean, Exec. Dir., 125 W. Main St., P.O. Box 147, 27810, P 1,900, M 75, (252) 943-3770, Fax (252) 943-3769, belhaveninfo@gotricounty.com, www. belhavenchamber.com

**Belmont** · *Belmont C/C* · Ted Hall, Pres., 32 N. Main St., P.O. Box 368, 28012, P 9,000, M 240, (704) 825-5307, Fax (704) 825-5550, info@belmontchamber.com, www.belmontchamber.com

**Benson** · *Benson Area C/C* · Loretta Byrd, Exec. Dir., 303 E. Church St., P.O. Box 246, 27504, P 3,500, M 350, (919) 894-3825, Fax (919) 894-1052, info@benson-chamber.com, www.benson-chamber.com

**Bessemer City** • *Bessemer City Area C/C* • Joan Bolen, 201 W. Washington Ave., P.O. Box 1342, 28016, P 6,500, M 75, (704) 629-3900, www.bessemercity.com/chamber.html

**Black Mountain** • *Black Mountain-Swannanoa C/C* • Bob McMurray, Exec. Dir., 201 E. State St., 28711, P 7,511, M 400, (828) 669-2300, (800) 669-2301, Fax (828) 669-1407, BMChamber@juno.com, www.exploreblackmountain.com

**Blowing Rock** • *Blowing Rock C/C* • Charles Hardin, Exec. Dir., 7738 Valley Blvd., P.O. Box 406, 28605, P 1,600, M 520, (828) 295-7851, (800) 295-7851, Fax (828) 295-4643, info@blowingrock.com, www.blowingrock.com

**Bolivia** • *see Southport*

**Boone** • *Boone Area C/C* • Dan Meyer, Pres./CEO, 208 Howard St., 28607, P 43,000, M 975, (828) 264-2225, Fax (828) 264-6644, info@boonechamber.com, www.boonechamber.com

**Boonville** • *see Yadkinville*

**Brevard** • *Brevard-Transylvania C/C* • Libby Freeman, Exec. Dir., 175 E. Main St., 28712, P 30,354, M 480, (828) 883-3700, Fax (828) 883-8550, libby@brevardncchamber.org, www.brevardncchamber.org

**Bryson City** • *Swain County C/C* • Karen Wilmot, Exec. Dir., 210 Main St., P.O. Box 509, 28713, P 13,000, M 360, (828) 488-3681, (800) 867-9246, Fax (828) 488-6858, chamber@greatsmokies.com, www.greatsmokies.com

**Burgaw** • *Burgaw Area C/C* • Donna Best-Klingel, Exec. Dir., 203 S. Dickerson St., P.O. Box 1096, 28425, P 5,000, M 175, (910) 259-9817, info@burgawchamber.com, www.burgawchamber.com

**Burlington** • *Alamance County Area C/C* • Mac Williams, Pres., 610 S. Lexington Ave., P.O. Box 450, 27216, P 138,000, M 800, (336) 228-1338, Fax (336) 228-1330, info@alamancechamber.com, www.thecarolinacorridor.com

**Cabarrus County** • *see Kannapolis*

**Canton** • *see Waynesville*

**Carolina Beach** • *Pleasure Island C/C* • Gail McCloskey, Exec. Dir., 1121 N. Lake Park Blvd., 28428, P 10,000, M 387, (910) 458-8434, Fax (910) 458-7969, visitor@pleasureislandnc.org, www.pleasureislandnc.org

**Carrboro** • *see Chapel Hill*

**Carteret County** • *see Morehead City*

**Cary** • *Cary C/C* • Howard S. Johnson, Pres., 307 N. Academy St., P.O. Box 4351, 27519, P 135,000, M 1,300, (919) 467-1016, (800) 919-2279, Fax (919) 469-2375, hjohnson@carychamber.com, www.carychamber.com

**Cashiers** • *Cashiers Area C/C* • Sue Bumgarner, Exec. Dir., P.O. Box 238, 28717, P 2,500, M 450, (828) 743-5191, Fax (828) 743-9446, cashcham@dnet.net, www.cashiers-nc.com

**Catawba County** • *see Hickory*

**Chadbourn** • *Greater Chadbourn C/C* • P.O. Box 200, 28431, P 2,200, M 85, (910) 654-3445, www.ncstrawberryfestival.com

**Chapel Hill** • *Chapel Hill-Carrboro C/C* • Aaron Nelson, Pres./CEO, 104 S. Estes Dr., P.O. Box 2897, 27515, P 60,000, M 900, (919) 967-7075, Fax (919) 968-6874, info@carolinachamber.org, www.carolinachamber.org

**Charlotte** • *Charlotte C/C* • Bob Morgan, Pres., 330 S. Tryon St., P.O. Box 32785, 28232, P 871,432, M 3,800, (704) 378-1300, Fax (704) 374-1903, www.charlottechamber.com

**Cherokee** • *Cherokee C/C* • Mary Jane Ferguson, Dir., 498 Tsali Blvd., P.O. Box 460, 28719, P 13,500, M 400, (828) 497-9195, (800) 438-1601, Fax (828) 497-2505, www.cherokee-nc.com

**Cherryville** • *Cherryville C of C & EDC* • Richard Randall, Exec. Dir., 220 E. Main St., P.O. Box 305, 28021, P 5,500, M 130, (704) 435-3451, Fax (704) 435-4200, cherryvi@bellsouth.net, www.cherryvillechamber.com

**Chimney Rock** • *Hickory Nut Gorge C/C* • Laurel Hewson, Mbrshp. & Bus. Mgr., P.O. Box 32, 28720, P 2,800, M 350, (828) 625-2725, (877) 625-2725, Fax (828) 625-9601, director@hickorynut.org, www.hickorynut.org.

**Clayton** • *Clayton Area C/C* • Tony McKinney, Pres., 301 E. Main St., P.O. Box 246, 27528, P 14,000, M 500, (919) 553-6352, Fax (919) 553-1758, sally@claytonchamber.com, www.claytonchamber.com

**Clinton** • *Clinton-Sampson C/C* • Amber Cava, Exec. Dir., 414 Warsaw Rd., P.O. Box 467, 28329, P 60,000, M 430, (910) 592-6177, Fax (910) 592-5770, info@clintonsampsonchamber.org, www.clintonsampsonchamber.org

**Coats** • *Coats Area C/C* • Carolyn Spears, Exec. Dir., 127 S. McKinley St., P.O. Box 667, 27521, P 2,580, M 200, (910) 897-6213, Fax (910) 897-4672, chamber@coatschamber.com, www.coatschamber.com

**Columbus** • *see Tryon*

**Concord** • *see Kannapolis*

**Cornelius** • *Lake Norman C/C* • W.E. 'Bill' Russell, Pres., 19900 W. Catawba Ave., Ste. 102, P.O. Box 760, 28031, P 65,000, M 1,100, (704) 892-1922, Fax (704) 892-5313, chamber@lakenorman.org, www.lakenormanchamber.org

**Currituck County** • *see Kill Devil Hills*

**Dare County** • *see Kill Devil Hills*

**Davidson** • *see Cornelius*

**Davie County** • *see Mocksville*

**Denton** • *Denton Area C/C* • 27 E. Salisbury St., P.O. Box 1268, 27239, P 1,650, M 100, (336) 859-5922, Fax (336) 859-5922, dentonacc@alltel.net, www.dentonnorthcarolina.com

**Dunn** • *Dunn Area C/C* • Tammy Williams, Exec. V.P., 209 W. Divine St., P.O. Box 548, 28335, P 10,000, M 460, (910) 892-4113, Fax (910) 892-4071, tammy@dunnchamber.com, www.dunnchamber.com.

**Durham** • *Greater Durham C/C* • Casey Steinbacher, Pres./CEO, 300 W. Morgan St., Ste. 1400, P.O. Box 3829, 27702, P 252,089, M 1,100, (919) 682-2133, Fax (919) 688-8351, info@durhamchamber.org, www.durhamchamber.org.

**Eden** • *Eden C/C* • Lou Trollinger, Admin. Asst., 678 S. Van Buren Rd., 27288, P 16,500, M 475, (336) 623-3336, (336) 623-8800, Fax (336) 623-8800, info@edenchamber.com, www.edenchamber.com

**Edenton** • *Edenton-Chowan C/C* • Richard Bunch, Exec. Dir., 116 E. King St., P.O. Box 245, 27932, P 16,000, M 300, (252) 482-3400, Fax (252) 482-7093, www.visitedenton.com

**Elizabeth City** • *Elizabeth City Area C/C* • Jennifer Palestrant, Pres., 502 E. Ehringhaus St., P.O. Box 426, 27907, P 39,000, M 600, (252) 335-4365, Fax (252) 335-5732, information@elizabethcitychamber.org, www.elizabethcitychamber.org

**Elizabethtown** • *Elizabethtown-White Lake Area C/C* • Lisa Fisher, Mbrshp. Dir., 805 W. Broad St., P.O. Box 306, 28337, P 15,000, M 185, (910) 862-4368, Fax (910) 862-2425, chamber28337@embarqmail.com, www.elizabethtownwhitelake.com

**Elkin** • *Yadkin Valley C/C* • Laurette Leagon, Pres./CEO, 116 E. Market St., P.O. Box 496, 28621, P 7,000, M 300, (336) 526-1111, Fax (336) 526-1879, www.yadkinvalley.org

**Erwin** · *Erwin Area C/C* · Sarah Jackson, Admin., 100 West F St., P.O. Box 655, 28339, P 5,000, M 165, (910) 897-7300, Fax (910) 897-5543, contact@erwinchamber.org, www.erwinchamber.org

**Fair Bluff** · *Fair Bluff C/C* · Karen Grainger, Pres., P.O. Box 648, 28439, P 1,100, M 30, (910) 649-7202, www.fairbluff.com

**Farmville** · *Farmville C/C* · P.O. Box 150, 27828, P 4,500, M 77, (252) 753-4670, Fax (252) 753-7313, chamber@farmville-nc.com, www.farmville-nc.com

**Fayetteville** · *Fayetteville-Cumberland County C/C* · Douglas Peters, Pres./CEO, 201 Hay St., P.O. Box 9, 28302, P 306,518, M 1,400, (910) 483-8133, Fax (910) 483-0263, chamberreceptionist@fayettevillencchamber.org, www.fayettevillencchamber.org

**Franklin** · *Franklin Area C/C* · Linda Harbuck, Exec. Dir., 425 Porter St., 28734, P 33,000, M 560, (828) 524-3161, (800) 336-7829, Fax (828) 369-7516, facc@franklin-chamber.com, www.franklin-chamber.com

**Franklin County** · *Franklin County C/C* · Brenda Fuller, Exec. Dir., 112 E. Nash St., P.O. Box 62, Louisburg, 27549, P 55,000, M 275, (919) 496-3056, Fax (919) 496-0422, bfuller@franklin-chamber.org, www.franklin-chamber.org

**Fuquay-Varina** · *Fuquay-Varina Area C/C* · Ron Tropcich, Exec. Dir., 121 N. Main St., 27526, P 16,000, M 450, (919) 552-4947, Fax (919) 552-1029, director@fuquay-varina.com, www.fuquay-varina.com

**Garner** · *Garner C/C* · Neal Padgett, Pres., 401 Circle Dr., 27529, P 24,400, M 580, (919) 772-6440, Fax (919) 772-6443, info@garnerchamber.com, www.garnerchamber.com

**Gastonia** · *Gaston Reg. C/C* · Elyse Cochran, Pres./CEO, 601 W. Franklin Blvd., P.O. Box 2168, 28053, P 190,000, M 970, (704) 864-2621, Fax (704) 854-8723, elyse@gastonchamber.com, www.gastonchamber.com

**Goldsboro** · *C/C of Wayne County* · Steve Hicks, Pres., 308 N. William St., P.O. Box 1107, 27533, P 140,000, M 786, (919) 734-2241, Fax (919) 734-2247, steveh@waynecountychamber.com, www.waynecountychamber.com.

**Grantsboro** · *Pamlico County C/C* · Carla Byrnes, Pres., 10642 Hwy. 55, P.O. Box 92, 28529, P 13,000, M 270, (252) 745-3008, Fax (252) 745-3090, pamlicochamber@embarqmail.com, www.pamlicochamber.com

**Greensboro** · *Greensboro C/C* · Rob Clapper, Pres., 342 N. Elm St., P.O. Box 3246, 27402, P 240,000, M 1,900, (336) 387-8300, Fax (336) 275-9299, info@greensboro.org, www.greensboro-chamber.com.

**Greenville** · *Greenville-Pitt County C/C* · Susanne D. Sartelle CCE, Pres., 302 S. Greene St., 27834, P 165,000, M 1,000, (252) 752-4101, Fax (252) 752-5934, chamber@greenvillenc.org, www.greenvillenc.org

**Grifton** · *Grifton C/C* · Jennifer Barr, Secy., P.O. Box 133, 28530, P 2,374, M 25, (252) 524-5169, Fax (252) 524-5826, grifton4u2@embarqmail.com, www.grifton.com

**Hampstead** · *Greater Hampstead C/C* · Liz Schoenleber, Exec. Dir., P.O. Box 211, 28443, P 8,000, M 235, (910) 270-9642, (800) 833-2483, Fax (910) 270-4000, hampsteadcoc1@bellsouth.net, www.hampsteadchamber.com

**Havelock** · *Havelock C/C* · George Cook, Chrmn., 201 Tourist Center Dr., P.O. Box 21, 28532, P 23,000, M 250, (252) 447-1101, Fax (252) 447-0241, info1@havelockchamber.org, www.havelockchamber.org.

**Hayesville** · *Clay County C/C* · Marcile Smith, Exec. Dir., 388 Bus. Hwy. 64, 28904, P 10,500, M 325, (828) 389-3704, Fax (828) 389-1033, info@ncmtnchamber.com, www.ncmtnchamber.com

**Henderson** · *Henderson-Vance County C/C* · Bill Edwards, Pres., 414 S. Garnett St., P.O. Box 1302, 27536, P 44,700, M 467, (252) 438-8414, Fax (252) 492-8989, chamber@hendersonvance.org, www.hendersonvance.org

**Hendersonville** · *Henderson County C/C* · Bob Williford, Pres., 204 Kanuga Rd., 28739, P 101,000, M 1,100, (828) 692-1413, Fax (828) 693-8802, chamber@hendersoncountychamber.org, www.hendersoncountychamber.org

**Hertford** · *Perquimans County C/C* · Sid Eley, Dir., 118 W. Market St., 27944, P 12,000, M 285, (252) 426-5657, Fax (252) 426-7542, chamber@perquimans.com, www.visitperquimans.com

**Hickory** · *Catawba County C/C* · G. Daniel Hearn CCE, Pres./CEO, 1055 Southgate Corp. Park S.W., P.O. Box 1828, 28603, P 153,000, M 1,100, (828) 328-6111, Fax (828) 328-1175, www.catawba chamber.org.

**High Point** · *High Point C/C* · Thomas W. Dayvault, Pres./CEO, 1634 N. Main St., P.O. Box 5025, 27262, P 98,490, M 1,100, (336) 882-5000, Fax (336) 889-9499, tom@highpointchamber.org, www.highpointchamber.org

**Highlands** · *Highlands Area C/C* · Bob Kieltyka, Exec. Dir., 269 Oak St., P.O. Box 62, 28741, P 3,000, M 240, (828) 526-5841, Fax (828) 526-5803, visitor@highlandschamber.org, www.highlands chamber.org

**Hillsborough** · *Hillsborough/Orange County C/C* · Margaret Cannell, Exec. Dir., 102 N. Churton St., 27278, P 125,000, M 325, (919) 732-8156, Fax (919) 732-4566, info@hillsboroughchamber.com, www.hillsboroughchamber.com

**Holly Springs** · *Holly Springs C/C* · Chris Scoop Green, Exec. Dir., 344 Raleigh St., Ste. 100, P.O. Box 695, 27540, P 22,646, M 311, (919) 567-1796, Fax (919) 567-1380, director@hollysprings chamber.org, hollyspringschamber.org

**Hope Mills** · *Hope Mills Area C/C* · Jan Spell, Pres., 5546 Trade St., P.O. Box 451, 28348, P 13,000, M 180, (910) 423-4314, Fax (910) 423-6796, hmacc@hopemillschamber.com, www.hope millschamber.com

**Hot Springs** · *see Mars Hill*

**Huntersville** · *see Cornelius*

**Jackson** · *Northampton County C/C* · Judy Collier, Dir., 102 E. Jefferson St., P.O. Box 1035, 27845, P 22,000, M 125, (252) 534-1383, Fax (252) 534-1739, jcolliernhcoc@embarqmail.com, www.northamptonchamber.org

**Jacksonville** · *Jacksonville Onslow C/C* · Mona Padrick, Pres., 1099 Gum Branch Rd., 28540, P 167,000, M 800, (910) 347-3141, Fax (910) 347-4705, info@jacksonvilleonline.org, www.jacksonville online.org

**Jonesville** · *see Elkin*

**Kannapolis** · *Cabarrus Reg. C/C* · John S. Cox, CEO, 3003 Dale Earnhardt Blvd., 28083, P 160,000, M 1,000, (704) 782-4000, Fax (704) 782-4050, jcox@cabarrus.biz, www.cabarrus.biz

**Kenansville** · *Kenansville Area C/C* · Cristal Jenkins, Secy./Treas., P.O. Box 358, 28349, P 1,215, M 60, (910) 296-0369, www.kenansvillechamber.com

**Kenly** · *Kenly Area C/C* · P.O. Box 190, 27542, P 1,700, M 150, (919) 284-5510, Fax (919) 284-1179, kacc@embarqmail.com, www.kenlynorthcarolina.com

**Kernersville** · *Kernersville C/C* · Bruce Boyer, Pres./CEO, 136 E. Mountain St., 27284, P 22,000, M 520, (336) 993-4521, Fax (336) 993-3756, kchamber@kernersvillenc.com, www.kernersvillenc.com

**Kill Devil Hills** · *Outer Banks C/C* · John Bone, Pres./CEO, 101 Town Hall Dr., P.O. Box 1757, 27948, P 51,000, M 1,100, (252) 441-8144, Fax (252) 441-0338, chamber@outer-banks.com, www.outerbankschamber.com.

**King** · *King C/C* · Deanne Moore, Exec. Dir., 124 S. Main St., P.O. Box 863, 27021, P 6,353, M 184, (336) 983-9308, Fax (336) 983-9526, kingchamber@windstream.net, www.kingnc.com

**Kings Mountain** · *Kings Mountain-Branch of Cleveland County C/C* · Shirley Brutko, Dir., 150 W. Mountain St., P.O. Box 794, 28086, P 12,000, M 145, (704) 739-4755, Fax (704) 739-8149, shirley@clevelandchamber.org, www.clevelandchamber.org

**Kinston** · *Kinston-Lenoir County C/C* · Laura Lee Sylvester, Pres., 301 N. Queen St., P.O. Box 157, 28502, P 60,000, M 650, (252) 527-1131, Fax (252) 527-1914, info@kinstonchamber.com, www.kinstonchamber.com

**Kitty Hawk** · *see Kill Devil Hills*

**Knightdale** · *Knightdale C/C* · Jennifer Bryan, Exec. Dir., 207 Main St., 27545, P 10,322, M 415, (919) 266-4603, Fax (919) 266-8010, knightdalechamber@knightdalechamber.org, www.knightdalechamber.org

**LaGrange** · *see Kinston*

**Lake Gaston** · *see Littleton*

**Lake Lure** · *see Chimney Rock*

**Laurinburg** · *Laurinburg/Scotland County Area C/C* · Theresa Lamson, Pres., 606 Atkinson St., P.O. Box 1025, 28353, P 35,050, M 465, (910) 276-7420, Fax (910) 277-8785, tlamson@laurinburg chamber.com, www.laurinburgchamber.com

**Leland** · *North Brunswick C/C* · Terry Grillo, Exec. Dir., 151 Poole Rd., Ste. 3, 28451, P 15,000, M 300, (910) 383-0553, (888) 383-0553, Fax (910) 383-1992, nbchamber@nbchamber.net, www.nbchamberofcommerce.com

**Lenoir** · *Caldwell County C/C* · Deborah Ashley, Pres./CEO, 1909 Hickory Blvd. S.E., 28645, P 80,000, M 500, (828) 726-0616, (828) 726-0323, Fax (828) 726-0385, visitors@caldwellcochamber.org, www.caldwellcochamber.org

**Lexington** · *Lexington Area C/C* · Radford Thomas, Pres./CEO, 16 E. Center St., P.O. Box C, 27293, P 21,000, M 450, (336) 248-5929, Fax (336) 248-2161, chamber@lexingtonchamber.net, www.lexingtonchamber.net.

**Liberty** · *Liberty C/C* · A. Pike Johnson, Exec. Dir., 112 S. Greensboro, P.O. Box 986, 27298, P 3,000, M 100, (336) 622-4937, libertychamber@rtelco.net

**Lillington** · *Lillington Area C/C* · Aneta Brewer, Exec. Dir., 24 W. Front St., P.O. Box 967, 27546, P 3,600, M 190, (910) 893-3751, Fax (910) 893-3751, contact@lillington.org, www.lillingtonchamber.org

**Lincolnton** · *Lincolnton-Lincoln County C/C* · Ken Kindley, Pres., 101 E. Main St., P.O. Box 1617, 28093, P 75,457, M 700, (704) 735-3096, Fax (704) 735-5449, lincolnchambernc@bellsouth.net, www.lincolnchambernc.org.

**Littleton** · *Lake Gaston C/C & Visitors Center Inc.* · Almira Papierniak, Exec. Dir., 2475 Eaton Ferry Rd., 27850, P 8,500, M 280, (252) 586-5711, Fax (252) 586-3152, lgcc@earthlink.net, www.lakegastonchamber.com

**Louisburg** · *see Franklin County*

**Lumberton** · *Lumberton Area C/C* · Cindy S. Kern, Exec. Dir., 800 N. Chestnut St., P.O. Box 1008, 28359, P 28,000, M 500, (910) 739-4750, Fax (910) 671-9722, lumbertonchamber@bellsouth.net, www.lumbertonchamber.com

**Madison** · *Western Rockingham C/C* · Donnie Joyce, Exec. Dir., 112 W. Murphy St., 27025, P 30,000, M 300, (336) 548-6248, Fax (336) 548-4466, wrcc1@embarqmail.com, www.westernrockinghamchamber.com

**Maggie Valley** · *Maggie Valley Area C/C & CVB* · Teresa Smith, Pres., 2511 Soco Rd., P.O. Box 279, 28751, P 647, M 225, (828) 926-1686, (800) 624-4431, Fax (828) 926-9398, cmaggie@maggievalley.org, www.maggievalley.org

**Manteo** · *see Kill Devil Hills*

**Marion** · *McDowell C/C* · John R. Birdsong, Exec. Dir., 1170 W. Tate St., 28752, P 43,247, M 425, (828) 652-4240, Fax (828) 659-9620, mountains@mcdowellchamber.com, www.mcdowellchamber.com.

**Mars Hill** · *Madison County C/C* · Maxine Brown, Pres., 635-4 Carl Eller Rd., P.O. Box 1527, 28754, P 20,000, M 250, (828) 689-9351, (877) 2-MADISON, madisonchamber@main.nc.us, www.madisoncounty-nc.com

**Marshall** · *see Mars Hill*

**Marshville** · *Marshville C/C* · Robert Palmer, 201 W. Main, P.O. Box 337, 28103, P 2,893, M 65, (704) 624-3183

**Matthews** · *Matthews C/C* · Tina Whitley, Exec. Dir., 210 Matthews Stations St., P.O. Box 601, 28106, P 24,000, M 480, (704) 847-3649, Fax (704) 847-3364, tbwhitley@matthewschamber.com, www.matthewschamber.com

**Mayodan** · *see Madison*

**Mocksville** · *Davie County C/C* · Joan Carter, Pres., 135 S. Salisbury St., 27028, P 40,000, M 420, (336) 751-3304, Fax (336) 751-5697, chamber@daviecounty.com, www.daviecounty.com

**Monroe** · *Union County C/C* · James G. Carpenter, Pres., 903 Skyway Dr., P.O. Box 1789, 28111, P 175,000, M 650, (704) 289-4567, Fax (704) 282-0122, jim@unioncountycoc.com, www.unioncountycoc.com

**Montgomery County** · *see Troy*

**Mooresville** · *Mooresville-South Iredell C/C* · Karen Shore, Pres./CEO, 149 E. Iredell Ave., P.O. Box 628, 28115, P 65,000, M 1,000, (704) 664-3898, Fax (704) 664-2549, info@mooresvillenc.org, www.mooresvillenc.org

**Morehead City** · *Carteret County C/C* · Mike Wagoner, Pres., 801 Arendell St. #1, 28557, P 63,800, M 950, (252) 726-6350, (800) 622-6278, Fax (252) 726-3505, cart.coc@nccoastchamber.com, www.nccoastchamber.com

**Morganton** · *Burke County C/C* · Anissa Starnes, Pres./CEO, 110 E. Meeting St., 28655, P 89,361, M 515, (828) 437-3021, Fax (828) 437-1613, info@burkecounty.org, www.burkecounty.org

**Morrisville** · *Morrisville C/C* · Sharon Rosche, Pres., 260 Town Hall Dr. #A, 27560, P 13,827, M 500, (919) 463-7150, Fax (919) 380-9021, chamber@morrisvillenc.com, www.morrisvillenc.com

**Mount Airy** · *Greater Mount Airy C/C* · Betty Ann Collins, Pres., 200 N. Main St., P.O. Box 913, 27030, P 11,179, M 500, (336) 786-6116, Fax (336) 786-1488, president1@mtairyncchamber.org, www.mtairyncchamber.org, www.visitmayberry.com.

**Mount Olive** · *Mount Olive Area C/C* · Tyler Barwick, Pres., 123 N. Center St., 28365, P 4,800, M 200, (919) 658-3113, Fax (919) 658-3125, moacc@bellsouth.net, www.moachamber.com

**Murfreesboro** · *Murfreesboro C/C* · Sherry Sullens, Exec. Dir., 116 W. Main St., P.O. Box 393, 27855, P 3,500, M 60, (252) 398-4886, Fax (252) 398-5871, murfreesborochamber@gmail.com, townofmurfreesboro.com

**Murphy** • *Cherokee County C/C* • Phylis J. Blackmon, Exec. Dir., 805 W. U.S. 64, 28906, P 27,000, M 500, (828) 837-2242, Fax (828) 837-6012, info@cherokeecountychamber.com, www.cherokeecountychamber.com

**Nags Head** • *see Kill Devil Hills*

**Nashville** • *Nashville C/C* • Crystal Hyman, P.O. Box 1003, 27856, P 4,300, M 100, (252) 459-4050, www.townofnashville.com

**New Bern** • *New Bern Area C/C* • Kevin Roberts, Pres., 316 S. Front St., P.O. Drawer C, 28563, P 91,599, M 910, (252) 637-3111, Fax (252) 637-7541, nbchamber@newbernchamber.com, www.newbernchamber.com

**North Wilkesboro** • *Wilkes C/C* • Linda S. Cheek, Pres., 717 Main St., P.O. Box 727, 28659, P 67,310, M 702, (336) 838-8662, Fax (336) 838-3728, info@wilkesnc.org, www.wilkesnc.org

**Oak Island** • *see Southport*

**Ocracoke Island** • *see Kill Devil Hills*

**Old Fort** • *Old Fort C/C* • 25 W. Main St., P.O. Box 1447, 28762, P 5,000, M 50, (828) 668-7223, chamber@oldfortchamber.com, www.oldfortchamber.com

**Outer Banks** • *see Kill Devil Hills*

**Oxford** • *Granville County C/C* • Ginnie D. Currin, Exec. Dir., 124 Hillsboro St., P.O. Box 820, 27565, P 50,000, M 480, (919) 693-6125, Fax (919) 693-6126, granvillechamber@embarqmail.com, www.granville-chamber.com

**Pembroke** • *Pembroke Area C/C* • Denise Fuller, P.O. Box 1978, 28372, P 3,000, M 50, (910) 522-2162, Fax (910) 521-3122, pembrokechamber@aol.com, www.pembrokechamber.com

**Pinehurst** • *see Southern Pines*

**Pittsboro** • *see Siler City*

**Plymouth** • *Washington County C/C* • Shaylee Wright, Exec. Dir., 701 Washington St., 27962, P 14,000, M 180, (252) 793-4804, Fax (252) 793-2143, chamber@washconc.org, www.washconc.org

**Raeford** • *Raeford-Hoke C/C* • Jackie Lynch, Bus. Admin., 101 N. Main St., 28376, P 37,000, M 200, (910) 875-5929, Fax (910) 875-1010, rae-hokchamber@embarqmail.com, www.raeford-hokechamber.com

**Raleigh** • *Greater Raleigh C/C* • Harvey A. Schmitt, Pres./CEO, 800 S. Salisbury St., P.O. Box 2978, 27602, P 782,283, M 2,800, (919) 664-7000, Fax (919) 664-7099, info@raleighchamber.org, www.raleighchamber.org.

**Randleman** • *Randleman C/C* • David Caughron, Exec. Dir., 102 W. Naomi St., P.O. Box 207, 27317, P 5,000, M 130, (336) 495-1100, Fax (336) 495-1133, www.randlemanchamber.com

**Red Springs** • *Red Springs C/C* • Fran Ray, Exec. Dir., 225 S. Main, 28377, P 4,000, M 160, (910) 843-5441, Fax (910) 843-2975, franrschamber@aol.com

**Reidsville** • *Reidsville C/C* • Beth Simmons, Pres./CEO, 513 S. Main St., P.O. Box 1020, 27323, P 15,300, M 335, (336) 349-8481, Fax (336) 349-8495, info@reidsvillechamber.org, www.reidsville chamber.org

**Roanoke Rapids** • *Roanoke Valley C/C* • Allen Purser, Pres., 260 Premier Blvd., P.O. Box 519, 27870, P 75,000, M 709, (252) 537-3513, Fax (252) 535-5767, apurser@rvchamber.com, www.rvchamber.com

**Robeson County** • *see Lumberton*

**Rockingham** • *Richmond County C/C* • Emily Tucker, Pres., 101 W. Broad Ave., P.O. Box 86, 28379, P 44,518, M 400, (910) 895-9058, (800) 858-1688, Fax (910) 895-9056, info@richmond countychamber.com, www.richmondcountychamber.com.

**Rocky Mount** • *Rocky Mount Area C/C* • Edward J. Baysden, CEO, 100 Coast Line St., 2nd Flr., P.O. Box 392, 27802, P 145,000, M 700, (252) 446-0323, Fax (252) 446-5103, www.rockymount chamber.org.

**Roxboro** • *Roxboro Area C/C* • Marcia A. O'Neil, Pres./CEO, 211 N. Main St., 27573, P 40,000, M 400, (336) 599-8333, Fax (336) 599-8335, chamber@roxboronc.com, www.roxboronc.

**Rutherfordton** • *Rutherford County C/C* • Bill Hall, Exec. Dir., 162 N. Main St., 28139, P 64,000, M 500, (828) 287-3090, Fax (828) 287-0799, info@rutherfordcoc.com, www.rutherfordcoc.com

**Saint Pauls** • *Saint Pauls C/C* • Paul Terry, Exec. Dir., P.O. Box 243, 28384, P 2,137, M 80, (910) 865-3890, spnccofc@aol.com

**Salisbury** • *Rowan County C/C* • Robert H. Wright, Pres., 204 E. Innes St., P.O. Box 559, 28145, P 138,000, M 1,000, (704) 633-4221, Fax (704) 639-1200, info@rowanchamber.com, www.rowanchamber.com.

**Sanford** • *Sanford Area C/C* • Bob Joyce, Pres., 143 Charlotte Ave., P.O. Box 519, 27331, P 55,000, M 650, (919) 775-7341, Fax (919) 776-6244, info@sanford-nc.com, www.sanford-nc.com

**Selma** • *see Smithfield*

**Shallotte** • *Brunswick County C/C* • Cathy Altman, Pres./CEO, 4948 Main St., P.O. Box 1185, 28459, P 95,000, M 775, (910) 754-6644, (800) 426-6644, Fax (910) 754-6539, info@brunswick countychamber.org, www.brunswickcountychamber.org.

**Shelby** • *Cleveland County C/C* • Michael Chrisawn, Pres., 200 S. Lafayette St., P.O. Box 879, 28151, P 96,287, M 725, (704) 487-8521, Fax (704) 487-7458, info@clevelandchamber.org, www.clevelandchamber.org.

**Siler City** • *Chatham C/C* • Cindy Poindexter, Dir., 1609 E. Eleventh St., 27344, P 66,000, M 300, (919) 742-3333, Fax (919) 742-1333, info@ccucc.net, www.ccucc.net

**Smithfield** • *Greater Smithfield-Selma Area C/C* • Richard W. Childrey, Pres., 1115 Industrial Park Dr., P.O. Box 467, 27577, P 25,000, M 550, (919) 934-9166, Fax (919) 934-1337, rchildrey@smithfieldselma.com, www.smithfieldselma.com.

**Snow Hill** • *Greene County C/C* • Angie Turnage, Dir., P.O. Box 364, 28580, P 19,000, M 90, (252) 747-8090, Fax (52) 747-8090, gcdirector@greenechamber.com, www.greenechamber.com

**Southern Pines** • *Moore County C/C* • Patrick J. Coughlin CCE, Pres./CEO, 10677 Hwy. 15-501, 28387, P 84,000, M 900, (910) 692-3926, Fax (910) 692-0619, info@moorecountychamber.com, www.moorecountychamber.com

**Southern Shores** • *see Kill Devil Hills*

**Southport** • *Southport-Oak Island Area C/C* • Karen Sphar, Exec. V.P., 4841 Long Beach Rd. S.E., 28461, P 16,000, M 630, (910) 457-6964, (800) 457-6964, Fax (910) 457-0598, info@southport-oakisland.com, www.southport-oakisland.com

**Sparta** • *Alleghany County C/C* • Bob Bamberg, Exec. Dir., 58 S. Main St., P.O. Box 1237, 28675, P 10,875, M 350, (336) 372-5473, (800) 372-5473, Fax (336) 372-8251, info@sparta-nc.com, www.sparta-nc.com

**Spinedale** • *see Rutherfordton*

**Spring Hope** • *Spring Hope Area C/C* • P.O. Box 255, 27882, P 1,400, M 60, (252) 478-1919, swissmilen@aol.com, www.springhopechamber.com

**Spring Lake** • *Spring Lake C/C* • John Thomas, Pres., P.O. Box 333, 28390, P 8,040, M 102, (910) 497-8821, Fax (910) 497-1897, sprlkchamber@faynet.com, www.springlakenc.org

**Spruce Pine** · *Mitchell County C/C* · Shirley Hise, Dir., 79 Parkway Maintenance Rd., P.O. Box 858, 28777, P 15,900, M 450, (828) 765-9483, (800) 227-3912, Fax (828) 765-0202, getinfo@mitchell-county.com, www.mitchell-county.com

**Statesville** · *Greater Statesville C/C* · David Bradley, Pres., 115 E. Front St., 28677, P 68,000, M 875, (704) 873-2892, Fax (704) 871-1552, smclaughlin@statesvillechamber.org, www.statesville chamber.org.

**Stoneville** · *see Madison*

**Surf City** · *Greater Topsail Area C/C & Tourism* · P.O. Box 2486, 28445, P 5,808, M 333, (910) 329-4446, (800) 626-2780, Fax (910) 329-4432, info@topsailcoc.com, www.topsailcoc.com

**Swan Quarter** · *Greater Hyde County C/C* · 20646 U.S. Hwy. 264, 27885, P 5,826, M 220, (252) 926-9171, (888) 493-3826, Fax (252) 926-9041, hydecocc@embarqmail.com, www.hydecounty chamber.org

**Sylva** · *Jackson County C/C* · Julie Spiro, Exec. Dir., 773 W. Main St., 28779, P 36,000, M 475, (828) 586-2155, (800) 962-1911, Fax (828) 586-4887, jctta@nc-mountains.com, www.mountain lovers.com

**Tabor City** · *Greater Tabor City C/C* · Cynthia Nelson, Exec. V.P., P.O. Box 446, 28463, P 4,000, M 125, (910) 653-2031, Fax (910) 653-2031, tccofc@earthlink.net, www.taborcitync.org

**Tarboro** · *Tarboro Edgecombe C/C* · Sally Davis, Pres., 509 Trade St., P.O. Drawer F, 27886, P 30,000, M 230, (252) 823-7241, Fax (252) 823-1499, sdavis08@embarqmail.com, www.tarboro chamber.com

**Taylorsville** · *Alexander County C/C* · Denise Elder, Exec. Dir., 16 W. Main Ave., 28681, P 35,858, M 275, (828) 632-8141, Fax (828) 632-1096, delder@alexandercountychamber.com, www.alexandercountychamber.com

**Thomasville** · *Thomasville Area C/C* · Doug Croft, Pres., 6 W. Main St., P.O. Box 1400, 27361, P 26,917, M 300, (336) 475-6134, Fax (336) 475-4802, tvillecoc@northstate.net, www.thomasville hamber.net

**Troy** · *Montgomery County C/C* · Judy Stevens, Dir., 444 N. Main St., P.O. Box 637, 27371, P 26,822, M 200, (910) 572-4300, Fax (910) 572-5193, chamber@montgomery-county.com, www.montgomery-county.com

**Tryon** · *Polk County C/C* · Janet Sciacca, Exec. Dir., 2753 Lynn Rd., Ste. A, 28782, P 19,500, M 397, (828) 859-6236, Fax (828) 859-2301, info@polkchamber.org, polkchamber.org.

**Wadesboro** · *Anson County C/C* · Lynn Edwards, Exec. Dir., 107-A E. Wade St., P.O. Box 305, 28170, P 25,275, M 279, (704) 694-4181, Fax (704) 694-3830, ansonchamber@windstream.net, www.ansoncounty.org

**Wake Forest** · *Wake Forest Area C/C* · Jodi LaFreniere, Exec. Dir., 350 S. White St., 27587, P 28,000, M 700, (919) 556-1519, Fax (919) 556-8570, info@wakeforestchamber.org, www.wakeforest chamber.org

**Wallace** · *Wallace C/C* · Lou Powell, Dir., P.O. Box 427, 28466, P 3,800, M 165, (910) 285-4044, lou@wallacechamber.com, www.wallacechamber.com

**Warrenton** · *C/C of Warren County* · 130 N. Main St., P.O. Box 826, 27589, P 20,000, M 165, (252) 257-2657, Fax (252) 257-2657, info@warren-chamber.org, www.warren-chamber.org

**Warsaw** · *Warsaw C/C* · Linda F. Kitchin, Exec. Dir., 121 S. Front St., P.O. Box 585, 28398, P 3,066, M 90, (910) 293-7804, Fax (910) 293-6773, warsawchamber@embarqmail.com, townofwarsawnc.com

**Washington** · *Washington-Beaufort County C/C* · Catherine Glover, Exec. Dir., 102 Stewart Pkwy., P.O. Box 665, 27889, P 47,000, M 325, (252) 946-9168, Fax (252) 946-9169, cglover@wbcchamber.com, www.wbcchamber.com

**Waynesville** · *Haywood County C/C* · CeCe Hipps IOM, Dir., P.O. Drawer 600, 28786, P 57,000, M 600, (828) 456-3021, Fax (828) 452-7265, info@haywood-nc.com, www.haywood-nc.com

**Wendell** · *Wendell C/C* · Ula Mae Life, Exec. Dir., 115 N. Pine St., P.O. Box 562, 27591, P 4,700, M 225, (919) 365-6318, Fax (919) 366-2010, wendellcc@ncrrbiz.com, www.wendellchamber.com

**West Jefferson** · *Ashe County C/C & Visitors Center* · Cabot Hamilton, Exec. Dir., P.O. Box 31, 28694, P 25,775, M 471, (336) 846-9550, (888) 343-2743, Fax (336) 846-8671, ashechamber@skybest.com, www.ashechamber.com

**Whiteville** · *Greater Whiteville C/C* · Janice Young, Exec. V.P., 601 S. Madison St., 28472, P 5,400, M 400, (910) 642-3171, (888) 533-7196, Fax (910) 642-6047, chambercow@weblnk.net, www.whitevillechamber.org.

**Wilkesboro** · *see North Wilkesboro*

**Williamston** · *Martin County C/C* · Ashley Smith, Exec. Dir., 419 E. Blvd., 27892, P 26,000, M 299, (252) 792-4131, (252) 792-0755, Fax (252) 792-1013, info@martincountync.com, www.MartinCountyNC.com

**Wilmington** · *Greater Wilmington C/C* · Connie Majure-Rhett CCE, Pres./CEO, One Estell Lee Pl., 28401, P 220,000, M 1,700, (910) 762-2611, Fax (910) 762-9765, info@wilmingtonchamber.org, www.wilmingtonchamber.org.

**Wilson** · *Wilson C/C* · Bruce Beasley, Pres., 200 West Nash St., P.O. Box 1146, 27894, P 78,000, M 550, (252) 237-0165, Fax (252) 243-7931, bbeasley@wilsonncchamber.com, www.wilsonnc chamber.com.

**Windsor** · *Windsor/Bertie County C/C* · Collins Cooper, Exec. Dir., 102 N. York St., P.O. Box 572, 27983, P 25,000, M 172, (252) 794-4277, Fax (252) 794-5070, windsorchamber@embarqmail.com, www.windsorbertie.com

**Winston-Salem** · *Greater Winston-Salem C/C* · Gayle Anderson, Pres., 601 W. Fourth St., P.O. Box 1408, 27102, P 338,774, M 1,800, (336) 728-9200, Fax (336) 721-2209, info@winstonsalem.com, www.winstonsalem.com.

**Yadkinville** · *Yadkin County C/C* · Bobby Todd, Dir., 205 S. Jackson St., P.O. Box 1840, 27055, P 36,348, M 202, (336) 679-2200, Fax (336) 679-3034, BTODD@yadkinchamber.org, www.yadkinchamber.org

**Yanceyville** · *Caswell County C/C* · Sharon Sexton, Dir., 15 Main St. E., P.O. Box 29, 27379, P 22,000, M 150, (336) 694-6106, Fax (336) 694-7454, sharon@caswellchamber.com, www.caswell chamber.com

**Zebulon** · *Zebulon C/C* · Tammy Russo, Exec. Dir., 815 N. Arendell Ave., P.O. Box 546, 27597, P 4,700, M 275, (919) 269-6320, Fax (919) 269-6350, zebcoc@bellsouth.net, www.zebulonchamber.org

# North Dakota

**North Dakota C of C** · Dave Maciver, Pres., 2000 Schafer St., P.O. Box 2639, Bismarck, 58502, P 639,715, M 1,100, (701) 222-0929, (800) 382-1405, Fax (701) 222-1611, ndchamber@ndchamber.com, www.ndchamber.com

**Ashley** · *Ashley C/C* · Chellie Kaseman, Pres., P.O. Box 334, 58413, P 882, M 60, (701) 288-2124, perfextion@drtel.net

**Beach** · *Beach Area C/C* · Jacob Holkup, Pres., P.O. Box 757, 58621, P 1,100, M 75, (701) 872-3121, beachchamber@yahoo. com, www.beachnd.com

**Belfield** · *Belfield Area C/C* · Terry Johnson, 515 6th St. N.E., P.O. Box 959, 58622, P 800, M 30, (701) 575-8135, www.belfieldnd.com

**Beulah** · *Beulah C/C* · Steffanie Boeckel, Exec. Dir., 120 Central Ave. N., P.O. Box 730, 58523, P 3,200, M 125, (701) 873-4585, (800) 441-2649, Fax (701) 873-5361, chamber@westriv.com, www.beulahnd.org

**Bismarck** · *Bismarck-Mandan C/C* · Kelvin Hullet, Pres., 1640 Burnt Boat Dr., P.O. Box 1675, 58502, P 101,138, M 1,120, (701) 223-5660, Fax (701) 255-6125, info@bismarckmandan.com, www. bismarckmandan.com.

**Bottineau** · *Bottineau C/C* · Clint Reinoehl, Exec. Dir., 519 Main St., 58318, P 2,400, M 175, (701) 228-3849, (800) 735-6932, Fax (701) 228-5130, bcc@utma.com, www.bottineau.com

**Bowman** · *Bowman Area C/C* · Josh Lindstrom, Pres., P.O. Box 1143, 58623, P 1,800, M 160, (701) 523-5880, Fax (701) 523-3322, chamber@bowmannd.com, www.bowmannd.com

**Cando** · *Cando Area C/C* · Jamie Halverson, Pres., P.O. Box 396, 58324, P 1,150, M 46, www.candond.com

**Carrington** · *Carrington Area C/C* · Laurie Dietz, Exec. Dir., 871 Main St., P.O. Box 439, 58421, P 2,300, M 130, (701) 652-2524, (800) 641-9668, Fax (701) 652-2391, chambergal@daktel.com, www.cgtn-nd.com

**Cavalier** · *Cavalier Area C/C* · Shari Hanson, Exec. Dir., 206 Division Ave. S., P.O. Box 271, 58220, P 1,501, M 100, (701) 265-8188, Fax (701) 265-8720, cacc@polarcomm.com, www. cavaliernd.com

**Crosby** · *Crosby C/C* · Sandra Simonson, Pres., P.O. Box 635, 58730, P 1,200, M 50, (701) 965-6091, www.crosbynd.com

**Devils Lake** · *Devils Lake Area C/C* · John Campbell, Exec. Dir., 208 Hwy. 2 W., P.O. Box 879, 58301, P 8,000, M 300, (701) 662-4903, (800) 233-8048, Fax (701) 662-2147, chamber@gondtc.com, www.devilslakend.com

**Dickinson** · *Dickinson Area C/C* · Lexi Sebastian, Exec. Dir., 314 3rd Ave. W., P.O. Box C, 58602, P 22,832, M 490, (701) 225-5115, Fax (701) 225-5116, team@dickinsonchamber.org, www. dickinsonchamber.org.

**Drayton** · *Drayton Comm. C/C* · Larry Ritzo, Pres., P.O. Box 265, 58225, P 1,000, M 53, (701) 454-3474, chamber@draytonnd.com, www.draytonnd.com

**Fargo** · *C/C of Fargo Moorhead* · David K. Martin, Pres./CEO, P.O. Box 2443, 58108, P 190,000, M 1,900, (218) 233-1100, Fax (218) 233-1200, info@fmchamber.com, www.fmchamber.com.

**Garrison** · *Garrison C/C* · Diane Affeldt, Secy./Treas., P.O. Box 459, 58540, P 1,318, M 80, (701) 463-2600, Fax (701) 463-7400, garrisonchamber@rtc.coop, garrisonnd.com

**Grafton** · *Grafton Area C/C* · Tabatha Widner, Exec. V.P., 432 Hill Ave., 58237, P 4,500, M 150, (701) 352-0781, Fax (701) 352-3043, gracha@polarcomm.com, www.graftonchamber.com

**Grand Forks** · *The Chamber Grand Forks-East Grand Forks* · Barry Wilfahrt, Pres., 202 N. Third St., 58203, P 65,000, M 875, (701) 772-7271, Fax (701) 772-9238, info@gochamber.org, www. gochamber.org

**Harvey** · *Harvey Area C/C* · 120 W. 8th St. #3, 58341, P 1,998, M 145, (701) 324-2604, Fax (701) 324-2674, chamber@harveynd. com, www.harveynd.com

**Hazen** · *Hazen C/C* · Myra Axtman, Exec. Dir., 146 E. Main, P.O. Box 423, 58545, P 2,600, M 115, (701) 748-6848, Fax (701) 748-2559, hazenchamber@westriv.com, www.hazennd.org

**Hettinger** · *Hettinger Area C/C* · Earleen Friez, Secy., P.O. Box 1031, 58639, P 2,500, M 135, (701) 567-2531, Fax (701) 567-2690, adamschmbr@ndsupernet.com, www.hettingernd.com

**Jamestown** · *Jamestown Area C/C* · JoDee Rasmusson, Exec. Dir., 120 2nd St. S.E., P.O. Box 1530, 58402, P 22,000, M 355, (701) 252-4830, Fax (701) 952-4837, info@jamestownchamber.com, www.jamestownchamber.com

**Kenmare** · *Kenmare Assn. of Commerce* · Jamie Livingston, Pres., P.O. Box 324, 58746, P 1,200, M 90, www.kenmarend.com

**Langdon** · *Langdon C/C* · Barb Mehlhoff, Exec. Dir., 324 8th Ave., 58249, P 2,300, M 100, (701) 256-3079, Fax (701) 256-2156, langdonchamber@cityoflangdon.com, www.cityoflangdon.com

**Lisbon** · *Lisbon Civic & Comm.* · Sherri Geyer, Secy./Treas., P.O. Box 812, 58054, P 2,300, M 120, (701) 683-5680, Fax (701) 683-5680, lisbonciviccommerce@yahoo.com, www.lisbonnd.com

**Mandan** · *see Bismarck*

**Medora** · *Medora C/C* · Jennifer Ondracek, Pres., P.O. Box 186, 58645, P 100, M 40, (701) 623-4910, medorachamber@midstate. net, www.medorandchamber.com

**Minot** · *Minot Area C/C* · L. John MacMartin CCE, Pres., 1020 20th Ave. S.W., P.O. Box 940, 58702, P 36,567, M 700, (701) 852-6000, Fax (701) 838-2488, chamber@minotchamber.org, www. minotchamber.org

**Mott** · *Mott Area C/C & Dev. Assistance* · Mary Messer, Secy./ Treas., P.O. Box 37, 58646, P 700, M 45, (701) 824-2891, www. discovermott.com

**New England** · *New England Commercial Club* · Butch Frank, Pres., P.O. Box 151, 58647, P 555, M 40, (701) 579-8001, Fax (701) 579-8033, www.newenglandcommercialclub.com

**New Rockford** · *New Rockford Area C/C* · Jeanette Perleberg, Chair, P.O. Box 67, 58356, P 1,500, M 42, (701) 947-2211, www. newrockford-nd.com

**New Town** · *New Town C/C* · Brad Reese, Pres., P.O. Box 422, 58763, P 1,367, M 91, (701) 627-4812, Fax (701) 627-4316, ntchamb@rtc.coop, www.newtownchamber.com

**Oakes** · *Oakes Area C/C* · Audrey O'Brien, Ofc. Mgr., 412 Main, 58474, P 2,000, M 160, (701) 742-3508, (888) 259-6448, Fax (701) 742-3139, oakesnd@drtel.net, www.oakesnd.com

**Ray** · *Ray C/C* · John Halseth, Pres., P.O. Box 153, 58849, P 580, M 23, (701) 568-3343, www.raynd.com

**Rolla** · *Rolla C/C* · Bethany McCloud, P.O. Box 712, 58367, P 1,471, M 84, (701) 477-5800, rolla.nd.utma.com

**Rugby** · *Geographical Center of North America C/C* · Dondi Sobolik, Exec. Dir., 224 Hwy. 2 S.W., 58368, P 3,000, M 150, (701) 776-5846, Fax (701) 776-6390, rugbychamber@gondtc.com, www.rugbynorthdakota.com

**Stanley** · *Stanley Commercial Club* · Box 974, 58784, P 1,277, M 67, (701) 628-2225, Fax (701) 628-2232, www.stanleynd.com

**Tioga** · *Tioga C/C* · Harlan Germundson, Pres., P.O. Box 52, 58852, P 1,200, M 60, (701) 664-2807, Fax (701) 664-2543, tiogand.net

**Valley City** · *Valley City Area C/C & CVB* · Dean Ihla, Exec. V.P., 250 W. Main St., P.O. Box 724, 58072, P 7,100, M 250, (701) 845-1891, (888) 288-1891, Fax (701) 845-1892, chamber@hellovalley. com, www.hellovalley.com/valleycitynd.com

**Velva** · *Velva Assn. of Commerce* · Mr. Cory Schmaltz, Pres., P.O. Box 334, 58790, P 1,200, M 44, (701) 338-2816, www.velva.net

**Wahpeton** · *Wahpeton Breckenridge Area C/C* · Jim Oliver, Exec. V.P., 118 6th St. N., 58075, P 12,127, M 285, (701) 642-8744, (800) 892-6673, Fax (701) 642-8745, info@wahpetonbreckenridgechamber.com, www.wahpetonbreckenridgechamber.com.

**Walhalla** · *Walhalla Area C/C* · Liann Zeller, Exec. Dir., P.O. Box 34, 58282, P 1,131, M 100, (701) 549-3939, Fax (701) 549-2410, walchmbr@utma.com, tradecorridor.com/walhalla/

**Watford City** · *Watford City Area C/C* · Mandy Foreman, Exec. Secy., P.O. Box 458, 58854, P 1,500, M 90, (701) 675-2526, Fax (701) 675-2526, tforeman@ruggedwest.com, www.4eyes.net

**West Fargo** · *West Fargo Area C/C* · Chris Barton, Exec. Dir., 109 3rd St. E., P.O. Box 753, 58078, P 24,000, M 460, (701) 282-4444, (701) 282-4550, Fax (701) 282-3665, chamber@westfargochamber.com, www.westfargochamber.com

**Williston** · *Williston Area C/C* · Diane Hagen, Exec. Dir., 10 Main St., P.O. Box G, 58802, P 14,000, M 450, (701) 577-6000, Fax (701) 577-8591, wchamber@nemont.net, www.willistonchamber.net.

# Ohio

**Ohio C of C** · Andrew E. Doehrel, Pres., 230 E. Town, P.O. Box 15159, Columbus, 43215, P 11,000,000, M 4,000, (614) 228-4201, (800) 622-1893, Fax (614) 228-6403, www.ohiochamber.com

**Ada** · *Ada Area C/C* · Jo Nell Hanratty, Secy./Treas., P.O. Box 225, 45810, P 3,500, M 59, (419) 634-0936, www.adafirst.com

**Akron** · *Greater Akron C/C* · Daniel C. Colantone, Pres./CEO, One Cascade Plaza, 17th Flr., 44308, P 833,000, M 2,000, (330) 376-5550, Fax (330) 379-3164, info@greaterakronchamber.org, www.greaterakronchamber.org

**Alliance** · *Alliance Area C/C* · R. Mark Locke, Pres., 210 E. Main St., 44601, P 50,000, M 450, (330) 823-6260, Fax (330) 823-4434, info@allianceohiochamber.org, www.allianceohiochamber.org

**Andover** · *Andover Area C/C* · Michael Creed, Pres., P.O. Box 503, 44003, P 2,400, M 75, (440) 293-5895, Fax (440) 293-7374, www.andoverohio.com

**Antwerp** · *Antwerp C/C* · Cheryl Lichty, Secy., P.O. Box 1111, 45813, P 1,741, M 65, (419) 258-1722, www.antwerpohio.org

**Archbold** · *Archbold Area C/C* · Nanette Buehrer, Dir., 300 N. Defiance St., P.O. Box 102, 43502, P 4,300, M 200, (419) 445-2222, Fax (419) 445-0205, aacc@rtecexpress.net, www.archboldchamber.com

**Ashland** · *Ashland Area C/C* · Marla Akridge, Pres., 10 W. 2nd St., 2nd Flr., 44805, P 52,000, M 425, (419) 281-4584, Fax (419) 281-4585, chamber@ashlandoh.com, www.ashlandohio.com

**Ashtabula** · *Ashtabula Area C/C* · Jim Timonere, Pres./CEO, 4536 Main Ave., 44004, P 28,000, M 420, (440) 998-6998, Fax (440) 992-8216, jim@ashtabulachamber.net, www.ashtabulachamber.net

**Athens** · *Athens Area C/C* · Wendy W. Jakmas, Pres./CEO, 449 E. State St., 45701, P 64,000, M 500, (740) 594-2251, Fax (740) 594-2252, info@athenschamber.com, www.athenschamber.com

**Aurora** · *Aurora Area C/C* · Jennifer Natale, Exec. Dir., 12 W. Garfield, Office Park 1, 44202, P 15,000, M 200, (330) 562-3355, Fax (330) 995-9052, jennifer@allaboutaurora.com, www.allaboutaurora.com

**Avon** · *see Avon Lake*

**Avon Lake** · *North Coast Reg. C/C* · John Sobolewski, Exec. Dir., P.O. Box 275, 44012, P 40,000, M 300, (440) 933-9311, contact@northcoastchamber.com, www.northcoastchamber.com

**Baltimore** · *Baltimore Area C/C* · Tony Caito, P.O. Box 193, 43105, P 5,000, M 85, (740) 438-0837

**Barberton** · *Barberton-South Summit C/C* · Joe Fazek, CEO, 503 W. Park Ave., 44203, P 27,899, M 315, (330) 745-3141, Fax (330) 777-0597, southsummitcc@att.net, www.southsummitchamber.org

**Barnesville** · *Barnesville Area C/C* · Barbara Roby, Ofc. Mgr., 130 W. Main St., 43713, P 4,326, M 115, (740) 425-4300, Fax (740) 425-1048, bacc@sbcglobal.net, www.barnesvilleohio.com

**Beachwood** · *Beachwood C/C* · Wayne Lawrence, Exec. Dir., 3 Commerce Park Sq., 23230 Chagrin Blvd., Ste. 900, 44122, P 15,000, M 640, (216) 831-0003, Fax (216) 360-7333, info@beachwood.org, www.beachwood.org

**Beavercreek** · *Beavercreek C/C* · Clete Buddelmeyer, Exec. Dir., 3299 Kemp Rd., 45431, P 60,000, M 650, (937) 426-2202, Fax (937) 426-2204, clete@beavercreekchamber.org, www.beavercreekchamber.org

**Bedford** · *Bedford C/C* · 33 S. Park St., 44146, P 15,000, M 130, (440) 232-0115, Fax (440) 232-0521, bedfordchamberoh@sbcglobal.net, www.bedfordchamberoh.org

**Bedford Heights** · *Bedford Heights C/C* · Pres., 24816 Aurora Rd., Ste. C, 44146, P 12,000, M 100, (440) 232-3369, Fax (440) 232-4862, bedfordhtscofc@aol.com, www.bedfordheightschamber.com

**Belden** · *see Jackson Twp.*

**Bellaire** · *Bellaire Area C/C* · Michael W. Doyle, Pres., P.O. Box 428, 43906, P 4,898, M 70, (740) 676-9723, Fax (740) 676-9723, belleairechamber@yahoo.com, www.bellairechamber.com

**Bellbrook** · *Bellbrook-Sugarcreek Area C/C* · Chris Ewing, Exec. Dir., 64 W. Franklin St., 45305, P 14,000, M 195, (937) 848-4930, Fax (937) 848-4930, info@bellbrooksugarcreekchamber.com, www.bellbrooksugarcreekchamber.com

**Bellefontaine** · *Logan County C/C* · Ed Wallace, Pres./CEO, 100 S. Main St., 43311, P 46,000, M 450, (937) 599-5121, Fax (937) 599-2411, ewallace@logancountyohio.com, www.logancountyohio.com

**Bellevue** · *Bellevue Area C/C* · Richard Stegman, Exec. Dir., 110 W. Main St., 44811, P 8,900, M 200, (419) 483-2182, Fax (419) 483-4259, chamber@cross.net, www.bellevuechambercrossnet.com

**Bellville** · *Bellville C/C* · Joan Jones, Pres., 142 Park Place, 44813, P 1,773, M 35, (419) 886-2245, Fax (419) 886-2297, www.bellvilleohio.net

**Belpre** · *Belpre Area C/C* · Jackie Cassady, Ofc. Mgr., 713 Park Dr., P.O. Box 8, 45714, P 10,000, M 300, (740) 423-8934, Fax (740) 423-6616, jackie@belprechamber.com, www.belprechamber.com

**Berea** · *Berea C/C* · Judy Groty, Exec. Dir., 173 Front St., P.O. Box 232, 44017, P 18,970, M 232, (440) 243-8415, Fax (440) 243-8470, bereachamber@sbcglobal.net, www.bereaohio.com/business

**Beverly** · *Muskingum Valley Area C/C* · Glen Miller, Chrmn., P.O. Box 837, 45715, P 60,000, M 150, (740) 984-8259, www.mvacc.com

**Bexley** · *Bexley Area C/C* · Becky Hohmann, Exec. Dir., 2770 E. Main St., Ste. 5, 43209, P 13,203, M 150, (614) 470-4500, bexleyareachamber@gmail.com, www.bexleyareachamber.org

**Blanchester** · *Blanchester Area C/C* · Mr. Chris Owen, Pres., P.O. Box 274, 45107, P 5,000, M 80, (937) 783-3601, blanchesterchamber@hotmail.com, www.blanchesterohio.org

**Bluffton** · *Bluffton Area C/C* · Fred Steiner, CEO, P.O. Box 142, 45817, P 3,900, M 126, (419) 358-5675, blufftonchamber@gmail.com, www.explorebluffton.com

**Bowling Green** · *Bowling Green C/C* · Earlene Kilpatrick, Exec. Dir., 163 N. Main St., P.O. Box 31, 43402, P 29,636, M 545, (419) 353-7945, Fax (419) 353-3693, chamber@bgchamber.net, www. bgchamber.net

**Brecksville** · *Brecksville C/C* · Michael Gorman, Pres., 49 Public Sq., 44141, P 13,000, M 175, (440) 526-7350, Fax (440) 526-7889, brecksvillecoc@sbcglobal.net, www.brecksvillechamber.com

**Bremen** · *Bremen C/C* · Connie Moyer, Pres., 119 Main St., P.O. Box 45, 43107, P 1,400, M 50, (740) 569-9150, (740) 569-4121, bremen_ chamberofcommerce@msn.com, www.bremenvillage.com

**Bridgeport** · *Bridgeport Area C/C* · Ann Gallagher, Secy., 410 Bennett St., P.O. Box 86, 43912, P 5,000, M 104, (740) 635-3377

**Brimfield** · *see Kent-Brimfield Area C/C*

**Broadview Heights** · *Broadview Heights C/C* · Tom Craft, Exec. Dir., P.O. Box 470211, 44147, P 16,000, M 250, (440) 838-4510, Fax (440) 717-0500, bhcc@broadviewhts.org, www.broadviewhts.org

**Brook Park** · *Brook Park C/C* · Sharon Zimmer, Exec. Dir., 5855 Smith Rd., Ste. 5, 44142, P 22,500, M 95, (216) 898-9755, Fax (216) 898-9755, bpchamber@sbcglobal.net, www.bpcoc.com

**Brooklyn Heights** · *see Independence*

**Brookville** · *Brookville C/C* · Jeff Sewert, Pres., 245 Sycamore St., P.O. Box 84, 45309, P 5,900, M 93, (937) 833-2375, Fax (937) 833-2375, brookvillechamber@verizon.net, www.brookvilleohio.com

**Brunswick** · *Brunswick Area C/C* · Melissa Krebs, Pres./CEO, 3511 Center Rd., Ste. AB, 44212, P 38,000, M 285, (330) 225-8411, Fax (330) 273-8172, office@brunswickareachamber.org, www. brunswickareachamber.org

**Bryan** · *Bryan Area C/C* · Daniel S. Yahraus, Exec. Dir., 138 S. Lynn St., 43506, P 17,000, M 375, (419) 636-2247, Fax (419) 636-5556, bryancc@cityofbryan.net, www.bryanchamber.org.

**Buckeye Lake** · *Greater Buckeye Lake C/C* · P.O. Box 5, 43008, P 3,049, M 142, (740) 928-2048, info@buckeyelakecc.com, www. buckeyelakecc.com

**Bucyrus** · *Bucyrus Area C/C* · Deb Pinion, Exec. Dir., 122 W. Rensselaer St., 44820, P 13,500, M 300, (419) 562-4811, Fax (419) 562-9966, bacc@bucyrusohio.com, www.bucyrusohio.com.

**Burton** · *Burton C/C* · Brian Brockway, Pres., E. Park St., P.O. Box 537, 44021, P 4,500, M 200, (440) 834-4204, info@burtonchamber ofcommerce.org, www.burtonchamberofcommerce.org

**Butler** · *see Vandalia*

**Cadiz** · *Harrison Reg. C/C* · Ed Coultrap, Exec. Dir., 37840 Cadiz Dennison Rd., 43907, P 16,000, M 90, (740) 942-3350, Fax (740) 942-0009, hrcctour@eohio.net, pages.eohio.net/harrisonchamber

**Calcutta** · *Calcutta Area C/C* · Lori Kline, Exec. Dir., 15442 Pugh Rd., Ste. 2A, 43920, P 8,175, M 89, (330) 386-6060, Fax (330) 386-6060, calcuttaareachamber@stclairtwp.com, www.calcut-taohiochamber.com

**Caldwell** · *Noble County C/C* · Herman Gray, Pres., P.O. Box 41, 43724, P 14,058, M 100, (740) 732-5288, www.noblecountyohio.com

**Cambridge** · *Cambridge Area C/C* · Mike Kachilla, Pres., 918 Wheeling Ave., 43725, P 40,000, M 320, (740) 439-6688, Fax (740) 439-6689, info@cambridgeohiochamber.com, www. cambridgesupersite.com

**Camden** · *Camden Area C/C* · Karen Feix, V.P., P.O. Box 90, 45311, P 3,600, M 85, (937) 452-1684, aldunkinc@yahoo.com

**Canal Fulton** · *Canal Fulton Area C/C* · Don Lemmon, Ofc. Mgr., P.O. Box 636, 44614, P 20,000, M 50, (330) 854-9095, Fax (330) 854-9095, cfcc@sssnet.com, www.discovercanalfulton.com

**Canal Winchester** · *Canal Winchester Area C/C* · Kim Rankin, Pres., 20 N. High St., 43110, P 6,000, M 300, (614) 837-1556, Fax (614) 837-9901, chamber@canalwinchester.com, www.canal winchester.com

**Canton** · *Canton Reg. C/C* · Dennis P. Saunier, Pres., 222 Market Ave. N., 44702, P 379,000, M 1,550, (330) 456-7253, (800) 533-4302, Fax (330) 452-7786, dennys@cantonchamber.org, www. cantonchamber.org

**Carey** · *Carey Area C/C* · Nancy Robison, Exec. Dir., 119 W. Findlay St., P.O. Box 94, 43316, P 4,000, M 107, (419) 396-7856, Fax same, careychamber@udata.com, www.careychamber.com.

**Carlisle** · *Carlisle Area C/C* · Barb Williams, Pres., P.O. Box 8238, 45005, P 5,121, M 30, (937) 743-8737, (937) 746-0555

**Carrollton** · *Carroll County C/C & Eco. Dev.* · Wayne Chunat, Exec. Dir., 61 N. Lisbon St., P.O. Box 277, 44615, P 29,500, M 180, (330) 627-4811, (800) 956-4684, Fax (330) 627-3647, carroll chamber@eohio.net, www.carrollohchamber.com

**Celina** · *Celina-Mercer County C/C* · Pam Buschur, Exec. Dir., 226 N. Main St., 45822, P 40,471, M 350, (419) 586-2219, Fax (419) 586-8645, info@celinamercer.com, www.celinamercer.com

**Chagrin Falls** · *Chagrin Valley C/C* · Darci Spilman, Exec. Dir., 79 N. Main St., 44022, P 4,000, M 445, (440) 247-6607, darci@ cvcc.org, www.cvcc.org

**Chardon** · *Chardon Area C/C* · Erna Leagan-Mabel, Exec. Secy., 111 South St., 44024, P 14,000, M 200, (440) 285-9050, Fax (440) 286-8964, emabel@chardonchamber.com, www.chardonchamber.com

**Chesterland** · *Chesterland C/C* · Kelly Monaco, Sales/Mktg. Mgr., 8228 Mayfield Rd., Ste. 4B, 44026, P 13,000, M 225, (440) 729-7297, Fax (440) 729-2690, ccoc@chesterlandchamber.com, www.chesterlandchamber.com

**Chillicothe** · *Chillicothe Ross C/C* · Marvin E. Jones, Pres./CEO, 45 E. Main, 45601, P 74,500, M 670, (740) 702-2722, Fax (740) 702-2727, mjones@chillicotheohio.com, www.chillicotheohio.com

## Cincinnati Area

**Cincinnati USA Reg. Chamber** · Ellen van der Horst, Pres./CEO, 300 Carew Tower, 441 Vine St., 45202, P 1,900,000, M 6,000, (513) 579-3100, Fax (513) 579-3101, info@cincinnatichamber.com, www.cincinnatichamber.com

**Anderson Area C/C** · Eric Miller, Exec. Dir., 7850 Five Mile Rd., 45230, P 42,000, M 450, (513) 474-4802, Fax (513) 474-4857, info@andersonareachamber.org, www.andersonareachamber.org

**Clermont C/C** · Matthew Van Sant, Pres./CEO, 4355 Ferguson Dr., Ste. 150, 45245, P 175,000, M 1,100, (513) 576-5000, Fax (513) 576-5001, clermontchamber@clermontchamber.com, www. clermontchamber.com

**Greater Cincinnati & No. KY African American C/C** · Sean Rugless, Pres./CEO, 2945 Gilbert Ave., 45206, M 350, (513) 751-9900, Fax (513) 751-9100, admin@gcaacc.org, www.gcaacc.org

**Hamilton County C/C** · J. Gruber, Exec. Dir., P.O. Box 42250, 45242, P 1,700,000, M 1,200, (513) 984-6555, Fax (513) 793-1063, hccc@fuse.net, .

**Over-the-Rhine C/C** · Cheryl Curtis, V.P., 1401 Main St., 45202, P 9,000, M 500, (513) 241-2690, Fax (513) 241-6770, otrchamber@ zoomtown.com, www.otrchamber.com

**Circleville** · *Pickaway County C/C* · Amy Elsea, Pres./CEO, 325 W. Main St., 43113, P 52,000, M 350, (740) 474-4923, Fax (740) 477-6800, aelsea@pickaway.com, www.pickaway.com

**Clermont County** · *see Cincinnati-Clermont C/C*

**Cleveland** · *Greater Cleveland Partnership* · Joe Roman, Pres./CEO, 100 Public Sq., Ste. 210, 44113, P 2,945,831, M 17,000, (216) 621-3300, (888) 304-GROW, Fax (216) 621-6013, customer service@gcpartnership.com, www.gcpartnership.com

**Cleveland Heights** · *Heights Reg. C/C* · Angie Pohlman, Exec. Dir., 3109 Mayfield Rd., Ste. 202, 44118, P 155,000, M 350, (216) 397-7322, Fax (216) 397-7353, info@hrcc.org, www.hrcc.org

**Coldwater** · *Coldwater Area C/C* · Mark Obringer, Pres., P.O. Box 67, 45828, P 4,482, M 150, (419) 678-4881, www.coldwater chamberofcommerce.com

**Columbiana** · *Columbiana Area C/C* · Rick Noel, Pres., 328 N. Main St., 44408, P 6,900, M 199, (330) 482-3822, Fax (330) 482-3960, info@columbianachamber.com, www.columbianachamber.com

**Columbus** · *Clintonville Area C/C* · Donna Leigh-Osborne, Pres., 4219 N. High St., 43214, P 30,000, M 350, (614) 262-2790, Fax (614) 262-2791, info@clintonvillechamber.com, www.clintonvillechamber.com

**Columbus** · *Greater Columbus C/C* · Ty Marsh, Pres., 150 S. Front St., Ste. 200, 43215, P 1,200,000, M 2,500, (614) 221-1321, Fax (614) 221-1408, membership@columbus.org, www.columbus.org

**Columbus Grove** · *Columbus Grove Area C/C* · Ed Cassidy, Pres., P.O. Box 3, 45830, P 2,600, M 60, (419) 659-2366, (419) 659-2365, www.columbusgrove.org

**Conneaut** · *Conneaut Area C/C* · Stephanie Nesbitt, Pres., 235 Main St., 44030, P 12,485, M 200, (440) 593-2402, Fax (440) 599-1514, conneautchamber@suite224.net, www.conneautchamber.org

**Coshocton** · *Coshocton County C/C* · Carol Remington, Exec. Dir., 401 Main St., 43812, P 36,131, M 300, (740) 622-5411, Fax (740) 622-9902, info@coshocton.com, www.visitcoshocton.com

**Covington** · *Covington Area C/C* · Jay Wackler, Pres., P.O. Box 183, 45318, P 2,567, M 75, (937) 473-3420, (937) 473-3165, covington chamber@yahoo.com, www.covingtonohiochamber.com

**Crestline** · *Crestline Area C/C* · P.O. Box 355, 44827, P 5,000, M 75, (419) 683-3818, www.crestlineoh.com

**Cuyahoga Falls** · *Cuyahoga Falls C/C* · Laura Petrella, CEO, 151 Portage Trl., Ste. 1, 44221, P 50,000, M 300, (330) 929-6756, info@cfchamber.com, www.cfchamber.com

**Dalton** · *Dalton Area C/C* · Kerry Pickett, Pres., P.O. Box 168, 44618, P 1,600, M 80, (330) 828-2323, klwee@aol.com, www. daltonohchamber.com

**Dayton** · *Dayton Area C/C* · Phillip L. Parker, Pres./CEO, One Chamber Plaza, 45402, P 970,000, M 3,000, (937) 226-1444, Fax (937) 226-8254, info@dacc.org, www.daytonchamber.org

**Deerfield** · *Deerfield C/C* · Sandie Welch, Pres., P.O. Box 193, 44411, P 2,263, M 14, (330) 584-8440, sandie.welch@yahoo.com

**Defiance** · *Defiance Area C/C* · R. Timothy Small, Pres., 615 W. Third St., 43512, P 39,350, M 750, (419) 782-7946, Fax (419) 782-0111, commerce@defiancechamber.com, www.defiancechamber.com

**Delaware** · *Delaware Area C/C* · Holly Quaine, Pres., 23 N. Union St., 43015, P 110,000, M 475, (740) 369-6221, Fax (740) 369-4817, dachamber@delawareohiochamber.com, www. delawareohiochamber.com

**Delphos** · *Delphos Area C/C* · Jennifer Moenter, Exec. Dir., 310 N. Main, 45833, P 8,000, M 270, (419) 695-1771, Fax (419) 692-1751, info@delphoschamber.com, www.delphoschamber.com

**Delta** · *Delta C/C* · Marcy LeFevre, Pres., 401 Main St., P.O. Box 96, 43515, P 3,000, M 90, (419) 822-3089, Fax same, www.deltaohio.com

**Dennison** · *see Uhrichsville*

**Deshler** · *Deshler C/C* · Jackie Arps, Secy./Treas., P.O. Box 123, 43516, P 2,000, M 55, (419) 278-8129, www.deshlerohiochamber.com

**Dublin** · *Dublin C/C* · Margery S. Amorose, Exec. Dir., 129 S. High St., 43017, P 40,000, M 1,200, (614) 889-2001, Fax (614) 889-2888, info@dublinchamber.org, www.dublinchamber.org

**East Liverpool** · *East Liverpool Area C/C* · Pamela Y. Hoppel, CEO, 529 Market St., P.O. Box 94, 43920, P 15,000, M 200, (330) 385-0845, Fax (330) 385-0581, office@elchamber.com, www. elchamber.com

**East Palestine** · *East Palestine Area C/C* · Don Elzer, Pres., P.O. Box 329, 44413, P 5,058, M 61, (330) 426-2128, contact@east palestinechamber.com, www.eastpalestinechamber.com

**Eastlake** · *see Wickliffe*

**Eaton** · *Eaton-Preble County C/C* · Virginia Lindsey, Ofc. Mgr., 122 W. Decatur St., P.O. Box 303, 45320, P 42,944, M 220, (937) 456-4949, Fax (937) 456-4949, chamberoffices@preblecountyohio. com, www.preblecountyohio.com

**Edgerton** · *Edgerton C/C* · Roger Strup, Secy., P.O. Box 399, 43517, P 2,300, M 75, (419) 298-2335

**Edon** · *Edon Area C/C* · Nikki Poorman, Pres., P.O. Box 153, 43518, P 1,000, M 50, (419) 272-3394, www.edon-ohio.com

**Elyria** · *Lorain County C/C* · Frank DeTillio, Pres., 226 Middle Ave., 5th Flr., 44035, P 282,465, M 500, (440) 328-2550, Fax (440) 328-2557, fdetillio@loraincountychamber.com, loraincounty chamber.com

**Englewood** · *Northmont Area C/C* · Cathy Hutton, CEO, P.O. Box 62, 45322, P 33,700, M 300, (937) 836-2550, Fax (937) 836-2485, cathy.hutton@northmont-area-coc.com, www.northmont-area-coc.com.

**Euclid** · *Euclid C/C* · David L. Carlson, Chrmn., 22639 Euclid Ave., 44117, P 52,000, M 200, (216) 731-9322, Fax (216) 731-8354, info@euclidchamber.com, www.euclidchamber.com

**Fairborn** · *Fairborn Area C/C* · John Siehl, Pres., 12 N. Central Ave., 45324, P 32,500, M 500, (937) 878-3191, Fax (937) 878-3197, chamber@fairborn.com, www.fairborn.com

**Fairfield** · *Fairfield C/C* · Kert Radel, Pres./CEO, 670 Wessel Dr., 45014, P 44,000, M 470, (513) 881-5500, Fax (513) 881-5503, president@fairfieldchamber.com, www.fairfieldchamber.com

**Fairlawn** · *Fairlawn Area C/C* · Polly Riffle, Exec. Dir., P.O. Box 13388, 44334, P 7,302, M 350, (330) 777-0032, Fax (330) 777-0032, info@fairlawnareachamber.org, www.fairlawnareachamber.org

**Fayette** · *Fayette Area C/C* · Lowell Beaverson, Exec. Secy., P.O. Box 8, 43521, P 1,300, M 45, (419) 237-2036, Fax (419) 237-9043

**Findlay** · *Findlay-Hancock County C/C-Greater Findlay Inc.* · Dionne K. Neubauer, COO, 123 E. Main Cross St., 45840, P 72,000, M 850, (419) 422-3313, Fax (419) 422-9508, info@greaterfindlay inc.com, www.greaterfindlayinc.com.

**Fort Recovery** · *Fort Recovery C/C* · Bob Walters, Pres., P.O. Box 671, 45846, P 1,300, M 75, (419) 375-2530, Fax (419) 375-4709, www.fortrecovery.org

**Fostoria** · *Fostoria Area C/C* · Sheri Fleegle, Exec. Dir., 121 N. Main St., 44830, P 14,000, M 245, (419) 435-0486, Fax (419) 435-0936, chamberfost@aol.com, www.fostoriachamber.com

**Franklin** · *Franklin Area C/C* · Peggy Darragh-Jeromos, Exec. Dir., 340 S. Main St., P.O. Box 721, 45005, P 28,000, M 120, (937) 746-8457, chamber45005@gmail.com, www.chamber45005.org

**Fremont** · *C/C of Sandusky County* · Holly Stacy, Pres./CEO, 101 S. Front St., 43420, P 62,000, M 450, (419) 332-1591, Fax (419) 332-8666, communications@scchamber.org, www.scchamber.org

**Gahanna** · *Gahanna Area C/C* · Leslee Blake, Pres., 181 Granville St., Ste. 200, 43230, P 35,000, M 460, (614) 471-0451, Fax (614) 471-5122, info@gahannaareachamber.com, www.gahannaareachamber.com

**Galion** · *Galion Area C/C* · Joe Kleinknecht, Pres./CEO, 106 Harding Way E., 44833, P 11,341, M 300, (419) 468-7737, Fax (419) 462-5487, galionchamber@galionchamber.org, www.galionchamber.org.

**Gallipolis** · *Gallia County C/C* · Lorie Neal, Exec. Dir., 16 State St., P.O. Box 465, 45631, P 32,000, M 200, (740) 446-0596, Fax (740) 446-7031, lneal@galliacounty.org, www.galliacounty.org.

**Garfield Heights** · *Garfield Heights C/C* · Mary Stamler, Exec. Dir., 5284 Transportation Blvd., P.O. Box 25412, 44125, P 31,000, M 200, (216) 475-7775, Fax (216) 475-2237, mstamler@garfieldchamber.com, www.garfieldchamber.com

**Garrettsville** · *Garrettsville Area C/C* · P.O. Box 1, 44231, P 3,000, M 132, (330) 527-2411, patricks@apk, www.garrettsvillearea.com

**Geneva** · *Geneva Area C/C* · Sue Ellen Foote, Exec. Dir., 866 E. Main St., P.O. Box 84, 44041, P 26,000, M 325, (440) 466-8694, Fax (440) 466-0823, info@genevachamber.org, www.genevachamber.org

**Geneva-on-the-Lake** · *Geneva-on-the-Lake C/ C & CVB* · 5536 Lake Rd., 44041, P 1,600, M 112, (440) 466-8600, (800) 862-9948, Fax (440) 466-8911, gotl@roadrunner.com, www.visitgenevaonthelake.com

**Genoa** · *Genoa Area C/C* · Gaylord Sheldon, Pres., P.O. Box 141, 43430, P 3,300, M 150, media@genoachamber.com, www.genoachamber.com

**Georgetown** · *Brown County C/C* · Ray Becraft, Exec. Dir., 110 E. State St., 45121, P 45,000, M 312, (937) 378-4784, (888) 276-9664, Fax (937) 378-1634, brchcom@bright.net, www.browncountyohiochamber.com

**Germantown** · *Germantown C/C* · Jeff Fannin, Pres., P.O. Box 212, 45327, P 8,000, M 55, (937) 855-3471

**Girard** · *Greater Girard Area C/C* · Jeff Kay, Pres., P.O. Box 418, 44420, P 15,000, M 75, (330) 545-8108, www.girardchamber.org

**Gnadenhutten** · *Gnadenhutten C/C* · Dick Brown, P.O. Box 155, 44629, P 1,280, (740) 254-4307, www.gnaden.tusco.net

**Grand Rapids** · *Grand Rapids Area C/C* · P.O. Box 391, 43522, P 1,200, M 50, (419) 832-1106, Fax (419) 832-1106, information@grandrapidsohio.com, www.grandrapidsohio.com

**Grandview Heights** · *Grandview/Marble Cliff Area C/C* · 1258B Grandview Ave., 43212, P 7,000, M 225, (614) 486-0196, Fax (614) 486-4656, info@grandviewchamber.org, www.grandviewchamber.org

**Granville** · *Granville Area C/C* · Maggie Barno, Dir., P.O. Box 603, 43023, P 5,000, M 120, (740) 587-4490, gacc@alltel.net, www.granvilleoh.com

**Greentown** · *see Hartville*

**Greenville** · *Darke County C/C* · Sharon Deschambeau, Pres., 622 S. Broadway, 45331, P 53,309, M 385, (937) 548-2102, Fax (937) 548-5608, info@darkecountyohio.com, www.darkecountyohio.com.

**Greenwich** · *see Willard*

**Grove City** · *Grove City Area C/C* · William H. Diehl, Exec. Dir., 4069 Broadway, 43123, P 35,000, M 550, (614) 875-9762, (877) 870-5393, Fax (614) 875-1510, e.dir@gcchamber.org, www.gcchamber.org

**Groveport** · *Southeastern Franklin County C/C* · Susan Brobst, Exec. Dir., 5151 Berger Rd., 43125, P 5,000, M 200, (614) 836-1138, Fax (614) 836-1138, chambersefc@aol.com, www.chambersefc.com

**Hamilton** · *Greater Hamilton C/C* · Kenny Craig, Pres./CEO, 201 Dayton St., 45011, P 62,000, M 600, (513) 844-1500, Fax (513) 844-1999, info@hamilton-ohio.com, www.hamilton-ohio.com

**Hartville** · *Lake Township C/C* · Christa Kozy, Pres./CEO, P.O. Box 1207, 44632, P 25,892, M 175, (330) 877-5500, Fax (330) 877-2149, president@lakechamber.com, www.lakechamber.com

**Hicksville** · *Hicksville Area C/C* · P.O. Box 244, 43526, P 4,000, M 94, (419) 542-6161

**Highland Hills** · *see Warrensville Heights*

**Hilliard** · *Hilliard Area C/C* · Libby Gierach, Pres./CEO, 4081 Main St., 43026, P 25,000, M 400, (614) 876-7666, Fax (614) 876-3113, info@hilliardchamber.org, www.hilliardchamber.org

**Hillsboro** · *Highland County C/C* · Katy Farber, Pres., 1575 N. High St., Ste. 400, 45133, P 41,000, M 350, (937) 393-1111, Fax (937) 393-9604, hccoc@cinci.rr.com, www.highlandcountychamber.com

**Hinckley** · *Hinckley C/C* · Amanda M. Phahl, Pres., P.O. Box 354, 44233, P 7,100, M 35, (330) 278-2066, Fax (330) 225-0239, www.hinckleytwp.org

**Holland** · *Holland/Springfield C/C* · Pat Hicks, Exec. Dir., 940 Clarion St., P.O. Box 986, 43528, P 23,000, M 200, (419) 865-2110, Fax (419) 865-3740, info@hollandspringfieldcoc.org, www.hollandspringfieldcoc.org

**Hubbard** · *Hubbard Area C/C* · Deborah Shields, Exec. Dir., 105B N. Main St., P.O. Box 177, 44425, P 17,000, M 70, (330) 534-5120, Fax (330) 534-5120, hacc44425@yahoo.com

**Huber Heights** · *Huber Heights C/C* · Pat Stephens, Exec. Dir., 4756 Fishburg Rd., 45424, P 40,000, M 300, (937) 233-5700, Fax (937) 233-5769, hhchamber@sbcglobal.net, www.huberheightschamber.com

**Hudson** · *Hudson Area C/C* · Carolyn Konefal, Pres., 245 N. Main St., Ste. 100, 44236, P 24,000, M 300, (330) 650-0621, Fax (330) 656-1646, info@hudsoncoc.org, www.explorehudson.com

**Huron** · *Huron C/C* · Sheila Ehrhardt, Dir., 509 Huron St., P.O. Box 43, 44839, P 10,000, M 285, (419) 433-5700, Fax same, chamber@huron.net, www.huron.net

**Independence** · *Cuyahoga Valley C/C* · Lynette Slama, Exec. Dir., P.O. Box 31326, 44131, P 9,000, M 250, (216) 573-2707, Fax (216) 524-9280, cvcc@cuyahogavalleychamber.org, www.cuyahogavalleychamber.org

**Ironton** · *see South Point*

**Jackson** · *Jackson Area C/C* · Randy Heath, Exec. Dir., 234 Broadway St., 45640, P 6,500, M 275, (740) 286-2722, Fax (740) 286-8443, rheath@zoomnet.net, www.jacksonohio.org

**Jackson Twp.** · *Jackson-Belden C/C* · Ruthanne Wilkof, Pres./CEO, 5735 Wales Ave. N.W., 44646, P 42,500, M 650, (330) 833-4400, Fax (330) 833-4456, info@jbcc.org, www.jbcc.org.

**Jamestown** · *Jamestown C/C* · Joe Baught, P.O. Box 66, 45335, P 4,000, M 60, (937) 372-5468, (937) 675-5311

**Jefferson** · *Jefferson Area C/C* · Michelle Thompson, Corresp. Secy., P.O. Box 100, 44047, P 6,000, M 120, (440) 576-0133, Fax (440) 576-4352, chamber@jeffersonchamber.com, www.jeffersonchamber.com

**Kelleys Island** · *Kelleys Island C/C* · Marvin Robinson, Dir., P.O. Box 783-F, 43438, P 300, M 65, (419) 746-2360, Fax (419) 746-2360, kelleyschamber@aol.com, www.kelleysislandchamber.com

**Kent** · *Brimfield Area C/C* · Scott Mikula, Pres., P.O. Box 3414, 44240, P 9,500, M 67, (330) 677-6439, smikula@homesavingsbnk. com, www.brimfieldchamber.com

**Kent** · *Kent Area C/C & Info. Center* · Bill Hoover, Exec. Dir., 138 E. Main St., 44240, P 27,906, M 280, (330) 673-9855, Fax (330) 673-9860, bhoover@kentbiz.com, www.kentbiz.com

**Kenton** · *Hardin County Chamber & Bus. Alliance* · Jannette Jacobs, V.P. of Chamber & Tourism, 225 S. Detroit St., 43326, P 31,945, M 245, (419) 673-4131, Fax (419) 674-4876, alliance@ hardinohio.org, www.hardinohio.org

**Kettering** · *Kettering-Moraine-Oakwood C/C* · Ann-Lisa Rucker, Exec. Dir., 2977 Far Hills Ave., 45419, P 80,000, M 875, (937) 299-3852, Fax (937) 299-3851, info@kmo-coc.org, www. kmo-coc.org

**Lakewood** · *Lakewood C/C* · Kathy Berkshire, Pres./CEO, 16017 Detroit Ave., 44107, P 56,000, M 350, (216) 226-2900, Fax (216) 226-1340, kberkshire@lakewoodchamber.org, www.lakewood chamber.org

**Lancaster** · *Lancaster-Fairfield County C/C* · Travis Markwood, Pres., 109 N. Broad St., Ste. 100, P.O. Box 2450, 43130, P 136,000, M 750, (740) 653-8251, Fax (740) 653-7074, info@lancoc.org, www.lancoc.org

**Lawrence County** · *see South Point*

**Lebanon** · *Lebanon Area C/C* · Sara Arseneau, Exec. Dir., 20 N. Broadway, 45036, P 20,000, M 375, (513) 932-1100, Fax (513) 932-9050, info@lebanonchamber.org, www.lebanonchamber.org

**Leipsic** · *Leipsic Area C/C* · Cammie Flores, Pres., 142 E. Main St., 45856, P 2,300, M 60, (419) 943-2009, www.leipsic.com

**Lewisburg** · *Lewisburg Area C/C* · Diane Odo, P.O. Box 697, 45338, P 2,000, M 42, (937) 962-4377, www.lewisburg.net

**Lexington** · *see Mansfield*

**Lima** · *Lima/Allen County C/C* · Jed E. Metzger, Pres./CEO, 144 S. Main St., Ste. 100, 45801, P 108,473, M 1,150, (419) 222-6045, Fax (419) 229-0266, chamber@limachamber.com, www. limachamber.

**Lisbon** · *Lisbon Area C/C* · Marilyn McCullough, Exec. Dir., 120 N. Market St., P.O. Box 282, 44432, P 3,082, M 86, (330) 424-1803, lacoc2@sbcglobal.net, www.lisbonchamber.com

**Lodi** · *Lodi Area C/C* · Kate Heil, Admin., P.O. Box 6, 44254, P 3,000, M 95, (330) 948-8047, info@lodiohiochamber.com, www.lodiohiochamber.com

**Logan** · *Logan-Hocking C/C* · Bill Rienhart, Exec. Dir., 4 E. Hunter St., P.O. Box 838, 43138, P 28,700, M 250, (740) 385-6836, (800) 414-6731, Fax (740) 385-7259, lo-hockchamber@hocking. net, www.logan-hockingchamber.com

**Logan County** · *see Bellefontaine*

**London** · *Madison County C/C* · Sean Hughes, Exec. Dir., 730 Keny Blvd., 43140, P 47,000, M 365, (740) 852-2250, Fax (740) 852-5133, sean@madisoncountychamber.org, www.madison countychamber.org

**Lorain** · *see Elyria*

**Loudonville** · *Loudonville-Mohican C/C* · Jeanne Leckrone, Ofc. Mgr., 131 W. Main St., 44842, P 2,900, M 160, (419) 994-4789, Fax (419) 994-5950, info@loudonville-mohican.com, www. loudonville-mohican.com

**Louisville** · *Louisville Area C/C* · Cheryle Casar, CEO, 229 E. Main St., P.O. Box 67, 44641, P 8,900, M 120, (330) 875-7371, Fax (330) 875-3839, lcoc@neo.rr.com, www.louisvilleohchamber.com

**Loveland** · *Loveland Area C/C* · Paulette Leeper, Exec. Dir., 442 W. Loveland Ave., 45140, P 20,000, M 350, (513) 683-1544, Fax (513) 683-5449, info@lovelandchamber.org, www.lovelandchamber.org

**Lyndhurst** · *see Beachwood*

**Madison** · *Madison-Perry Area C/C* · Cynthia Girdler IOM CCEO-AP, Pres., 5965 N. Ridge Rd., P.O. Box 4, 44057, P 25,000, M 335, (440) 428-3760, Fax (440) 428-6668, exec@mpacc.org, www.mpacc.org

**Mansfield** · *Mansfield-Richland Area C/C* · Kevin Nestor, Pres., 55 N. Mulberry St., 44902, P 129,000, M 1,000, (419) 522-3211, Fax (419) 526-6853, info@mrachamber.com, www.mrachamber.com

**Marblehead** · *Marblehead Peninsula C/C* · Judy Balsom, Exec. Asst., 5681 E. Harbor Rd., 43440, P 4,000, M 170, (419) 734-9777, Fax (419) 734-9777, info@marbleheadpeninsula.com, www. marbleheadpeninsula.com

**Marietta** · *Marietta Area C/C* · Charlotte Keim, Pres., 100 Front St., Ste. 200, 45750, P 62,000, M 558, (740) 373-5176, Fax (740) 373-7808, info@mariettachamber.com, www.mariettachamber.com

**Marion** · *Marion Area C/C* · Pamela S. Hall, Pres., 205 W. Center St., 43302, P 66,217, M 621, (740) 382-2181, Fax (740) 387-7722, phall@marionareachamber.org, www.marionareachamber.org

**Martins Ferry** · *Martins Ferry Area C/C* · Dorothy Powell, Exec. Dir., 108 S. Zane Hwy., 43935, P 7,500, M 100, (740) 633-2565, Fax (740) 633-2641, m.chamber@att.net, www.martinsferry chamber.com

**Marysville** · *Union County C/C* · Eric S. Phillips, CEO/Dir., 227 E. Fifth St., 43040, P 40,909, M 531, (937) 642-6279, (800) 642-0087, Fax (937) 644-0422, chamber@unioncounty.org, www.whereprideresides.org.

**Mason** · *NE Cincinnati C/C* · John Harris, Pres., 316 W. Main St., 45040, P 48,000, M 880, (513) 398-2188, (513) 336-0125, Fax (513) 398-6371, jharris@necchamber.org, www.necchamber.org

**Massillon** · *Massillon Area C/C* · Bob Sanderson, Pres., 137 Lincoln Way E., 44646, P 33,000, M 450, (330) 833-3146, Fax (330) 833-8944, info@massillonohchamber.com, www.massillon ohchamber.com.

**Maumee** · *Maumee C/C* · Brenda Clixby, Exec. Dir., 605 Conant St., 43537, P 15,752, M 450, (419) 893-5805, Fax (419) 893-8699, info@maumeechamber.com, www.maumeechamber.com

**Mayfield Heights** · *Mayfield Area C/C* · 1280 SOM Ctr. Rd., Ste. 308, 44124, P 55,000, M 175, (216) 556-4598, jasspring@mayfield areachamber.org, www.mayfieldareachamber.org

**McArthur** · *Vinton County C/C* · Brandi Betts, Mktg. Dir., 104 W. Main St., P.O. Box 307, 45651, P 13,429, M 130, (740) 596-5033, Fax (740) 596-9262, info@vintoncounty.com, www.vintoncounty.com

**McConnelsville** · *Morgan County C/C* · Amy Grove, Bd. Member, 155 E. Main St., P.O. Box 508, 43756, P 14,000, M 130, (740) 962-3200, (740) 962-4854, Fax (740) 962-3516, info@morgancounty. org, www.morgancounty.org

**Medina** · *Greater Medina C/C* · Debra Lynn-Schmitz, Pres./CEO, 145 N. Court St., 44256, P 30,000, M 590, (330) 723-8773, Fax (330) 722-6844, info@medinaohchamber.com, www.medinaoh chamber.com.

**Mentor** · *Mentor Area C/C* · Marie S. Pucak, Exec. Dir., 6972 Spinach Dr., 44060, P 52,000, M 675, (440) 255-1616, Fax (440) 255-1717, info@mentorchamber.org, www.mentorchamber.org

**Miami Twp.** · *see Milford-Milford-Miami Twp. C/C*

**Middleburg Heights** · *Middleburg Heights C/C* · Doris J. Wroble, Exec. Dir., 16000 Bagley Rd., P.O. Box 30161, 44130, P 15,790, M 210, (440) 243-5599, Fax (440) 243-8660, doris@middleburg heightschamber.org, www.middleburgheightschamber.com

**Middlefield** · *Middlefield C/C* · Lynnette Bramley, Exec. Secy., P.O. Box 801, 44062, P 2,500, M 100, (440) 632-5705, Fax (440) 632-5705, mccinfo@middlefieldcc.com, www.middlefieldcc.com

**Middletown** · *The C/C serving Middletown, Monroe & Trenton* · Bill Triick, Pres./CEO, 1500 Central Ave., 45044, P 125,000, M 500, (513) 422-4551, Fax (513) 422-6831, info@ thechamberofcommerce.org, www.thechamberofcommerce.org.

**Milan** · *Milan C/C* · Kelly Guseman, Secy., P.O. Box 544, 44846, P 1,500, M 200, (419) 499-4909, Fax (419) 499-1389, secretary@ milanohio.com, www.milanohio.com

**Milford** · *Milford-Miami Twp. C/C* · Karen Huff, CEO, 983 Lila Ave., 45150, P 43,000, M 320, (513) 831-2411, Fax (513) 831-3547, director@milfordmiamitownship.com, www.milfordmiami township.com

**Millersburg** · *Holmes County C/C & Tourism Bur.* · Shasta Mast, Exec. Dir., 35 N. Monroe St., 44654, P 42,000, M 400, (330) 674-3975, Fax (330) 674-3976, info@holmescountychamber.com, www.holmescountychamber.com.

**Minerva** · *Minerva Area C/C* · 203 N. Market St., 44657, P 4,000, M 120, (330) 868-7979, Fax (330) 868-3347, minervachamber@ adelphia.net, www.minervachamber.com

**Minster** · *see New Bremen*

**Monroe** · *see Middletown*

**Montpelier** · *Montpelier Area C/C* · Ms. Terry Buntain, Exec. Dir., 410 W. Main St., 43543, P 4,700, M 172, (419) 485-4416, Fax (419) 485-4416, macofc@verizon.net, www.montpelierchamber.com

**Moraine** · *see Kettering*

**Morrow** · *Little Miami C/C* · Norma Rayl, Secy./Treas., P.O. Box 164, 45152, P 4,282, M 76, (513) 899-4466, (513) 932-3299, Fax (513) 932-3299, malcolm@goconcepts.com, www.morrow-today.org

**Mount Gilead** · *Morrow County C/C & Visitors Bur.* · Rosemary Levings, Exec. Dir., 17 1/2 W. High St., P.O. Box 174, 43338, P 34,000, M 220, (419) 946-2821, Fax (419) 946-3861, chamuway@bright. net, www.morrowcochamber.com

**Mount Vernon** · *Mount Vernon-Knox County C/C* · Carol Grubaugh, Chamber Mgr., 400 S. Gay St., 43050, P 60,000, M 379, (740) 393-1111, Fax (740) 393-1590, chamber@knoxchamber. com, www.knoxchamber.com

**Munroe Falls** · *see Stow*

**Napoleon** · *Napoleon/Henry County C/C* · Joel Miller, Exec. Dir., 611 N. Perry St., 43545, P 29,893, M 290, (419) 592-1786, Fax (419) 592-4945, hcncoc@ohiohenrycounty.com, www.naphc chamber.com

**Nelsonville** · *Nelsonville Area C/C* · Keller Blackburn, Pres., P.O. Box 276, 45764, P 5,444, M 88, (740) 753-4346, rocky brands@nelsonvilletv.com, www.nelsonvillechamber.com

**New Albany** · *New Albany C/C* · Eileen Leuby, Pres., 220 Market St., Ste. 204, P.O. Box 202, 43054, P 25,000, M 500, (614) 855-4400, Fax (614) 855-4446, director@newalbanychamber.com, www.newalbanychamber.com

**New Bremen** · *Southwestern Auglaize County C/C* · James S. Coons, Dir., 107 W. Monroe St., Ste. 2, P.O. Box 3, 45869, P 8,000, M 300, (419) 629-0313, Fax (419) 629-0411, info@auglaize.org, www.auglaize.org

**New Carlisle** · *New Carlisle Area C/C* · Linda Campbell, P.O. Box 483, 45344, P 5,735, M 60, (937) 845-3911, www.newcarlisle.net

**New Concord** · *New Concord Bd. Of Trade* · Renee Coll, Pres., 200 S. Friendship Dr., P.O. Box 90, 43762, P 4,000, M 150, (740) 826-5074, rhcoll@fabri-form.com, www.ncboardoftrade.com

**New Lexington** · *Perry County C/C* · John Ulmer, Exec. Dir., 121 S. Main St., 43764, P 33,000, M 170, (740) 342-3547, Fax (740) 342-9124, pcccofc@yahoo.com, www.perrycountyohiocofc.com

**New Paris** · *New Paris Area C/C* · Amy Aldridge, Pres., P.O. Box 101, 45347, P 1,600, M 65, (937) 437-2511, www.newparisoh.com

**New Philadelphia** · *Tuscarawas County C/C* · Jill R. McCartney IOM, Pres., 1323 Fourth St. N.W., 44663, P 90,000, M 600, (330) 343-4474, Fax (330) 343-6526, info@tuschamber.com, www. tuschamber.com

**Newark** · *Licking County C/C* · Cheri Hottinger, Pres., 50 W. Locust St., P.O. Box 702, 43058, P 149,000, M 700, (740) 345-9757, Fax (740) 345-5141, chottinger@lickingcountychamber.com, www.lickingcountychamber.com

**Newcomerstown** · *Newcomerstown C/C* · Gary Chaney, Treas., P.O. Box 456, 43832, P 8,000, M 100, (740) 498-7244, Fax (740) 498-6310, gjc@sota-oh.com

**Niles** · *see Youngstown*

**North Baltimore** · *North Baltimore Area C/C* · Susan Kronbach, Pres., P.O. Box 284, 45872, P 3,300, M 50, (419) 257-5050, (419) 257-3514, nbacc@wcnet.org, www.nbacc.org

**North Canton** · *North Canton Area C/C* · Doug Lane, Pres., 121 S. Main St., 44720, P 22,000, M 400, (330) 499-5100, Fax (330) 499-7181, dlane@northcantonchamber.org, www.northcanton chamber.org

**North Olmsted** · *North Olmsted C/C* · John Sobolewski, Exec. Dir., 28938 Lorain Rd., Ste. 204, 44070, P 34,204, M 250, (440) 777-3368, Fax (440) 777-9361, nocc@nolmstedchamber.org, www.nolmstedchamber.org

**North Randall** · *see Warrensville Heights*

**North Ridgeville** · *North Ridgeville C/C & Visitor Bur.* · Ms. Dayle Noll, Exec. Dir., 34845 Lorain Rd., 44039, P 26,000, M 185, (440) 327-3737, Fax (440) 327-1474, nrcoc@nrchamber.com, www.nrchamber.com

**North Royalton** · *North Royalton C/C* · Kevin Lynch, Pres., 13737 State Rd., P.O. Box 33122, 44133, P 32,500, M 220, (440) 237-6180, Fax (440) 237-6181, rrnews@aol.com, www.nroyalton chamber.com

**Northfield** · *Nordonia Hills C/C* · Laura Sparano, Exec. Dir., P.O. Box 34, 44067, P 22,000, M 310, (330) 467-8956, Fax (330) 468-4901, laura@nordoniahillschamber.org, www.nordoniahills chamber.org

**Norwalk** · *Norwalk -Huron County C/C* · Melissa James, Exec. Dir., 10 W. Main St., 44857, P 60,000, M 480, (419) 668-4155, Fax (419) 663-6173, chamber@accnorwalk.com, www.norwalkarea chamber.com

**Oak Harbor** · *Oak Harbor Area C/C* · Laurene Moore, Exec. Dir., 178 W. Water St., 43449, P 3,000, M 163, (419) 898-0479, Fax (419) 898-2429, chamber@oakharborohio.net, www.oakharbor ohio.net

**Oak Hill** · *Oak Hill Area C/C* · Kurtis Strickland, Pres., P.O. Box 354, 45656, P 1,700, M 70, (740) 682-8414, www.oakhillchamber.org

**Oakwood** · *see Kettering*

**Oberlin** • *Oberlin Area C/C* • Annie Cunningham, Exec. Dir., 13 S. Main St., 2nd Flr., 44074, P 8,200, M 130, (440) 774-6262, Fax (440) 775-2423, oberlinchamber@oberlin.net, www.oberlin chamber.org

**Olmsted Falls** • *Olmsted C/C* • Al Stringer, Pres., P.O. Box 38043, 44138, P 8,600, M 45, (440) 235-0032, www.olmstedchamber.org

**Oregon** • *Eastern Maumee Bay C/C* • Deb Warnke, Exec. Dir., 2460 Navarre Ave., Ste. 1, 43616, P 25,000, M 200, (419) 693-5580, Fax (419) 693-9990, director@embchamber.org, www.embchamber.org

**Orrville** • *Orrville Area C/C* • Jennifer Reusser, Pres., 132 S. Main St., 44667, P 8,900, M 260, (330) 682-8881, Fax (330) 682-8383, chamberoffice@orrvillechamber.com, www.orrvillechamber.com.

**Orwell** • *Orwell-Grand Valley Area C/C* • Diane Giel, Pres., P.O. Box 261, 44076, P 1,600, M 53, (440) 437-5782, orwellgv@fairpoint.net, www.orwellgvchamber.org

**Ottawa** • *Ottawa Area C/C* • Mary Jo Bockrath, Exec. Dir., 129 Court St., P.O. Box 68, 45875, P 4,367, M 270, (419) 523-3141, Fax (419) 523-5860, ottawachamber@earthlink.net, ottawachamber.org

**Ottoville** • *Ottoville Area C/C* • P.O. Box 275, 45876, P 1,000, M 69, (419) 453-2426

**Oxford** • *Oxford C/C* • JoNell Rowan, Pres., 30 W. Park Pl., 2nd Flr., 45056, P 26,000, M 250, (513) 523-5200, Fax (513) 523-2308, jonell@oxfordchamber.org, www.oxfordchamber.org

**Painesville** • *Painesville Area C/C* • Linda Reed, Exec. Dir., One Victoria Pl., Ste. 265A, 44077, P 50,000, M 400, (440) 357-7572, Fax (440) 357-8752, exec@painesvilleohchamber.org, www.painesvilleohchamber.org

**Pandora** • *Pandora Area C/C* • Stan Schneck, Village Admin., P.O. Box 333, 45877, P 1,188, M 35, (419) 384-3112, Fax (419) 384-3110, villageadministrator@bright.net, www.pandoraoh.com

**Parkman** • *Parkman C/C* • Faith Kumber, Pres., P.O. Box 525, 44080, P 3,200, M 26, (440) 476-4337, (440) 548-5213, www.parkmanohio.com

**Parma** • *Parma Area C/C* • Lisa Masotti, Exec. Dir., 7908 Day Dr., Parmatown Mall, 44129, P 125,000, M 620, (440) 886-1700, Fax (440) 886-1770, chamber@parmaareachamber.org, www.parmaareachamber.org

**Parma Heights** • *see Parma*

**Pataskala** • *Pataskala Area C/C* • J. Scott Smith, Pres., P.O. Box 132, 43062, P 20,000, M 215, (740) 964-6100, PACC132@embarq mail.com, www.pataskalachamber.com

**Paulding** • *Paulding C/C* • Conrad Clippinger, Exec. Dir., Corner Main & Caroline St., P.O. Box 237, 45879, P 3,650, M 210, (419) 399-5215, Fax (419) 399-2047, pcoc@paulding-net.com, www.pauldingchamber.com

**Perrysburg** • *Perrysburg Area C/C* • Sandy Latchem, Exec. Dir., 105 W. Indiana Ave., 43551, P 28,000, M 325, (419) 874-9147, Fax (419) 872-9347, director@perrysburgchamber.com, www.perrysburgchamber.com

**Picaway County** • *see Circleville*

**Pickerington** • *Pickerington Area C/C* • Helen Mayle, Pres., 13 W. Columbus St., 43147, P 38,000, M 425, (614) 837-1958, Fax (614) 837-6420, president@pickeringtonchamber.com, www.pickeringtonchamber.com

**Pioneer** • *Pioneer Area C/C* • Susie Osburn, Pres., P.O. Box 633, 43554, P 1,500, M 80, (419) 737-2614, Fax (419) 737-2066, www.pioneerchamber.com

**Piqua** • *Piqua Area C/C* • Lisa Whitaker, Pres., 326 N. Main, P.O. Box 1142, 45356, P 22,000, M 400, (937) 773-2765, Fax (937) 773-8553, lisa.whitaker@piquaareachamber.com, www.piqua areachamber.com

**Plymouth** • *see Willard*

**Pomeroy** • *Meigs County C/C* • Michelle Donovan, Exec. Dir., 238 W. Main St., 45769, P 25,000, M 200, (740) 992-5005, Fax (740) 992-7942, michelle@meigscountychamber.com, www.meigscountychamber.com

**Port Clinton** • *Port Clinton Area C/C* • Laura Schlachter, Pres./CEO, 110 Madison St., 43452, P 6,300, M 464, (419) 734-5503, Fax (419) 734-4768, pcacc@cros.net, www.portclintonchamber.com

**Portsmouth** • *Portsmouth Area C/C* • Robert Huff, Pres./CEO, 342 2nd St., P.O. Box 509, 45662, P 20,909, M 700, (740) 353-7647, (800) 648-2574, Fax (740) 353-5824, rhuff@portsmouth.org, www.portsmouth.org

**Powell** • *Greater Powell Area C/C* • Steve Lutz, Pres., 50 S. Liberty St., Ste. 170, 43065, P 20,000, M 250, (614) 888-1090, Fax (614) 888-4803, powellchamber@columbus.rr.com, www.powellchamber.com

**Put-In-Bay** • *Put-In-Bay C/C & Visitors Bur.* • 148 Delaware Ave., P.O. Box 250, 43456, P 550, M 185, (419) 285-2832, Fax (419) 285-4702, questions@visitput-in-bay.com, www.put-in-bay.com

**Ravenna** • *Ravenna Area C/C* • Jack Ferguson, Exec. Dir., 135 E. Main St., 44266, P 12,000, M 153, (330) 296-3886, Fax (330) 296-6986, ravennachamber@n2net.net, www.ravennaareachamber.com

**Reading** • *Reading C/C* • Jim Stewart, Pres., P.O. Box 15164, 45215, P 12,000, M 100, (513) 786-7274, www.readingohiochamber.org

**Reynoldsburg** • *Reynoldsburg Area C/C* • Jan Hills, Pres./CEO, 1580 Brice Rd., 43068, P 33,000, M 350, (614) 866-4753, Fax (614) 866-7313, jan@reynoldsburgchamber.com, www.reynoldsburg chamber.com

**Richland** • *see Mansfield*

**Richmond Heights** • *see Beachwood*

**Rittman** • *Rittman Area C/C* • Kimberly Field, Exec. Dir., 12 N. Main St., Ste. 2, 44270, P 6,500, M 91, (330) 925-4828, Fax (330) 925-4828, rittmanchamber@ohio.net, www.rittmanchamber.com

**Riverside** • *Riverside Area C/C* • Brett Domescik, Chrmn., 5100 Springfield St., Ste. 105, 45431, P 24,000, (937) 253-6479, Fax (937) 253-9508, brett@riversidechamber.com, www.riversidechamber.com

**Rockford** • *Rockford C/C* • Bob Thompson, P.O. Box 175, 45882, P 1,200, M 90, (419) 363-9779

**Rocky River** • *Rocky River C/C* • Liz Manning, Exec. Dir., 20220 Center Ridge Rd., Ste. 100, 44116, P 20,500, M 350, (440) 331-1140, Fax (440) 331-3485, info@rockyriverchamber.com, www.rockyriverchamber.com

**Rootstown** • *Rootstown Area C/C* • Jackie Waltz, Pres., P.O. Box 254, 44272, P 7,690, M 59, www.rootstownchamber.org

**Russells Point** • *Indian Lake Area C/C* • Pam Miller, Exec. Dir., 8200 State Rte. 366, Ste. D, P.O. Box 717, 43348, P 14,500, M 385, (937) 843-5392, Fax (937) 843-9051, office@indianlakechamber.org, www.indianlakechamber.org

**Saint Bernard** • *Saint Bernard C/C* • Bob Sawtell, Pres., 110 Washington Ave., 45217, P 5,000, M 65, (513) 242-7770, Fax (513) 641-1840, www.cityofstbernard.org

**Saint Clairsville** • *Saint Clairsville Area C/C* • Amy Aspenwall, Admin., 130 W. Main St., 43950, P 12,000, M 340, (740) 695-9623, info@stcchamber.com, www.stcchamber.com

**Saint Marys** · *Saint Marys Area C/C* · Kelly Kill, Exec. Dir., 301 E. Spring St., 45885, P 8,000, M 250, (419) 300-4611, Fax (419) 300-6202, amy@stmarysohio.org, www.stmarysohio.org.

**Salem** · *Salem Area C/C* · Audrey Null, Exec. Dir., 713 E. State St., 44460, P 16,000, M 340, (330) 337-3473, Fax (330) 337-3474, acnull@salemohiochamber.org, www.salemohiochamber.org

**Sandusky** · *Erie County C/C* · John Moldovan, Pres., 225 W. Washington Row, 44870, P 80,000, M 520, (419) 625-6421, Fax (419) 625-7914, director@eriecountyohiocofc.com, www.eriecountyohiocofc.com

**Sebring** · *Sebring Area C/C* · Gayle Agnew, Pres., 135 E. Ohio Ave., 44672, P 4,912, M 90, (330) 938-1243, www.sebringohio.net

**Seven Hills** · *see Parma*

**Seville** · *Seville Area C/C* · Kate Heil, CEO, P.O. Box 471, 44273, P 1,900, M 70, (330) 769-1522, sevilleareaohiochamber@gmail.com, www.villageofseville.com

**Shadyside** · *Shadyside Area C/C* · Pat Heller, Pres., P.O. Box 115, 43947, P 3,700, M 50, (740) 676-3202

**Shaker Heights** · *see Beachwood*

**Sharonville** · *Sharonville C/C* · Richard Arnold, Pres., 4015 Executive Park Dr., Ste. 302, 45241, P 36,800, M 230, (513) 554-1722, Fax (513) 554-1307, info@sharonvillechamber.com, www.sharonvillechamber.com

**Sheffield Lake** · *see Avon Lake*

**Sheffield Village** · *see Avon Lake*

**Shelby** · *Shelby C/C* · Carol Knapp, Pres., 142 N. Gamble, Ste. A, 44875, P 9,600, M 165, (419) 342-2426, (888) 245-2426, Fax (419) 342-2189, carol.knapp@shelbyoh.com, www.shelbyoh.com

**Sidney** · *Sidney-Shelby County C/C* · Jeff Raible, Pres., 101 S. Ohio Ave., Flr. 2, 45365, P 47,910, M 630, (937) 492-9122, Fax (937) 498-2472, office@sidneyshelbychamber.com, www.sidneyshelbychamber.com

**Solon** · *Solon C/C* · Nancy S. Traum, Pres./CEO, 33595 Bainbridge Rd., Ste. 101, 44139, P 23,000, M 550, (440) 248-5080, Fax (440) 248-9121, staff@solonchamber.com, www.solonchamber.com

**South Euclid** · *see Beachwood*

**South Point** · *Greater Lawrence County Area C/C* · Bill Dingus, PhD, Exec. Dir., 216 Collins Ave., P.O. Box 488, 45680, P 64,000, M 300, (740) 377-4550, (800) 408-1334, Fax (740) 377-2091, cofcagency@zoominternet.net, www.lawrencecountyohio.org

**Spencerville** · *Spencerville C/C* · P.O. Box 32, 45887, P 2,300, (419) 647-5368, www.spencervilleoh.org

**Spring Valley** · *Spring Valley Area C/C* · Judy Madden, Pres., P.O. Box 396, 45370, P 2,800, M 80, (937) 862-4110, www.springvalleyoh.com

**Springboro** · *Springboro Area C/C* · Anne Stremanos, Exec. Dir., 325 S. Main St., 45066, P 28,000, M 460, (937) 748-0074, Fax (937) 748-0525, chamber@springboroohio.org, www.springboroohio.org

**Springfield** · *Greater Springfield C/C* · Michael McDorman, Pres., 20 S. Limestone St., Ste. 100, 45502, P 168,000, M 820, (937) 325-7621, (800) 803-1553, Fax (937) 325-8765, mmcdorman@greaterspringfield.com, www.greaterspringfield.com

**Steubenville** · *Jefferson County C/C* · Gary Folden, Pres., 630 Market St., 43952, P 73,894, M 500, (740) 282-6226, Fax (740) 282-6285, info@jeffersoncountychamber.com, www.jeffersoncountychamber.com.

**Stow** · *Stow-Munroe Falls C/C* · Cindy Smith Lewis, Exec. Dir., 4381 Hudson Dr., 44224, P 32,000, M 350, (330) 688-1579, Fax (330) 688-6234, smfcc@smfcc.com, www.smfcc.com.

**Streetsboro** · *Streetsboro Area C/C* · Meghan Urban, Exec. Dir., 9205 State Rte. 43, Ste. 106, 44241, P 14,000, M 230, (330) 626-4769, Fax (330) 422-1118, sacc@streetsborochamber.org, www.streetsborochamber.org

**Strongsville** · *Strongsville C/C* · Gordon Glissman, Pres., 18829 Royalton Rd., 44136, P 44,000, M 550, (440) 238-3366, Fax (440) 238-7010, info@strongsvillechamber.com, www.strongsvillechamber.com

**Stryker** · *Stryker C/C* · Mel Pace, Pres., P.O. Box 58, 43557, P 1,500, M 100, (419) 682-2301, (419) 682-1108, web@strykerchamber.org, www.strykerchamber.org

**Sunbury** · *Sunbury/Big Walnut Area C/C* · Cindy Hall, Admin., 45. S. Columbus St., P.O. Box 451, 43074, P 11,000, M 250, (740) 965-2860, Fax (740) 965-2860, chall@sunburybigwalnutchamber.com, www.sunburybigwalnutchamber.com

**Swanton** · *Swanton Area C/C* · Neil Toeppe, Exec. Dir., 100 Broadway St., 43558, P 16,000, M 140, (419) 826-1941, Fax (419) 826-3242, swantoncc@aol.com, www.swantonareacoc.com

**Sylvania** · *Sylvania Area C/C* · Ms. Pat Nowak, Exec. Dir., 5632 N. Main St., 43560, P 50,000, M 550, (419) 882-2135, Fax (419) 885-7740, info@sylvaniachamber.org, www.sylvaniachamber.org

**Tallmadge** · *Tallmadge C/C* · Mary Cea, Exec. Dir., 80 Community Rd., 44278, P 18,000, M 200, (330) 633-5417, Fax (330) 633-5415, tallmadgechamber@onecommail.com, www.tallmadge-chamber.com

**Tiffin** · *Tiffin Area C/C* · 62 S. Washington St., 44883, P 25,000, M 328, (419) 447-4141, Fax (419) 447-5141, info@tiffinchamber.com, www.tiffinchamber.com

**Tipp City** · *Tipp City Area C/C* · Matt Owen, Pres./CEO, 12 S. Third St., 45371, P 16,200, M 212, (937) 667-8300, Fax (937) 667-8862, mowen@tippcitychamber.com, www.tippcitychamber.org

**Toledo** · *Toledo Reg. C/C* · Mark A. V'Soske CAE, Pres., 300 Madison Ave., Enterprise Ste. 200, 43604, P 658,000, M 3,550, (419) 243-8191, (419) CHAMBER, Fax (419) 241-8302, joinus@toledochamber.com, www.toledochamber.com.

**Toronto** · *Toronto Ohio C/C* · Heather Steffens, Pres., 214 Main St., P.O. Box 158, 43964, P 6,127, M 86, (740) 537-4355, Fax (740) 537-4355, torontoohiochamber@att.net, www.toronto-ohio-chamber.com

**Trenton** · *see Middletown*

**Trotwood** · *Trotwood C/C* · Marie Battle, Exec. Dir., 4444 Lake Center Dr., P.O. Box 26507, 45426, P 30,000, M 115, (937) 837-1484, Fax (937) 837-1508, trotwoodchamber@earthlink.net, www.trotwoodchamber.org

**Troy** · *Troy Area C/C* · Charles Cochran, Pres., 405 S.W. Public Sq., Ste. 330, 45373, P 32,000, M 430, (937) 339-8769, (937) 339-1716, Fax (937) 339-4944, tacc@troyohiochamber.com, www.troyohiochamber.com

**Twinsburg** · *Twinsburg C/C & Visitor Center* · Douglas H. Johnson, Exec. Dir., 9044 Church St., 44087, P 18,000, M 300, (330) 963-6249, Fax (330) 963-6995, djohnson@twinsburgchamber.com, www.twinsburgchamber.com

**Uhrichsville** · *Twin City C/C* · Teri Edwards, Exec. Dir., P.O. Box 49, 44683, P 8,000, M 250, (740) 922-5623, Fax (740) 922-1371, twincitychamber@sbcglobal.net, www.twincitychamber.org

**Uniontown** · *see Hartville*

**University Heights** · *see Beachwood*

**Upper Arlington** • *Upper Arlington Area C/C* • Becky Hajost, Pres., 2120 Tremont Center, 43221, P 33,000, M 584, (614) 481-5710, Fax (614) 481-5711, admin@uachamber.org, www.uachamber.org

**Upper Sandusky** • *Upper Sandusky Area C/C* • Aaron Korte, Exec. Dir., 108 E. Wyandot Ave., P.O. Box 223, 43351, P 22,800, M 250, (419) 294-3349, Fax (419) 294-3531, upperchamber@udata.com, www.uppersanduskychamber.com

**Urbana** • *Champaign County C/C & Visitors Bur.* • Tina Knotts, Exec. Dir., 113 Miami St., 43078, P 38,900, M 250, (937) 653-5764, (877) 873-5764, Fax (937) 652-1599, info@champaignohio.com, www.champaignohio.com

**Valley City** • *Valley City C/C* • Cindy Kintop, Pres., P.O. Box 304, 44280, P 4,500, M 109, (330) 483-1111, chamberofcommerce@valleycity.org, www.valleycity.org

**Valley View** • *see Independence*

**Van Wert** • *Van Wert Area C/C* • Kate Gribble, Pres./CEO, 1199 Professional Dr., 45891, P 30,000, M 335, (419) 238-4390, Fax (419) 238-4589, chamber@vanwertchamber.com, www.vanwertchamber.com

**Vandalia** • *Vandalia-Butler C/C* • Will Roberts, Exec. Dir., 262 James Bohanan Dr., P.O. Box 224, 45377, P 25,000, M 400, (937) 898-5351, Fax (937) 898-5491, info@vandaliabutlerchamber.org, www.vandaliabutlerchamber.org

**Vermilion** • *Vermilion C/C* • Pam Cooper, Pres., 5495 Liberty Ave., 44089, P 12,500, M 350, (440) 967-4477, Fax (440) 967-2877, vermilionchamber@centurytel.net, www.vermilionohio.com

**Wadsworth** • *Wadsworth C/C* • Michelle Masica, CEO, 125 W. Boyer St., Ste. B, 44281, P 19,000, M 369, (330) 336-6150, Fax (330) 336-2672, business@wadsworthchamber.com, www.wadsworthchamber.com

**Walton Hills** • *see Independence*

**Wapakoneta** • *Wapakoneta Area C/C* • Dan Graf, Exec. Dir., 30 E. Auglaize St., P.O. Box 208, 45895, P 10,000, M 287, (419) 738-2911, Fax (419) 738-2977, chamber@wapakoneta.com, www.wapakoneta.com

**Warren** • *see Youngstown*

**Warrensville Heights** • *Tri-City C/C* • Steve Petti, Pres./CEO, P.O. Box 22098, 44122, P 45,000, M 135, (216) 454-0199, Fax (216) 378-7371, steve@tricitychamber.com, www.tricitychamber.com

**Washington Court House** • *Fayette County C/C* • Roger Blackburn, Pres., 101 E. East St., 43160, P 32,000, M 340, (740) 335-0761, (800) 479-7797, Fax (740) 335-0762, fayettechamber@yahoo.com, www.fayettecountyohio.com

**Waterville** • *Waterville Area C/C* • Dawn Bly, Exec. Dir., 122 Farnsworth Rd., P.O. Box 74, 43566, P 5,000, M 115, (419) 878-5188, Fax (419) 878-5199, admin@watervillechamber.com, www.watervillechamber.com

**Wauseon** • *Wauseon C/C* • Debbie Nelson, Dir., 115 N. Fulton St., P.O. Box 217, 43567, P 7,200, M 230, (419) 335-9966, Fax (419) 335-7693, debbie@wauseonchamber.com, www.wauseonchamber.com

**Waverly** • *Pike County C/C* • 12455 St. Rte. 104, P.O. Box 107, 45690, P 27,695, M 275, (740) 947-7715, Fax (740) 947-7716, info@pikechamber.org, www.pikechamber.org

**Waynesburg** • *Waynesburg Area Bus. Assn.* • Steve Chandler, Pres., P.O. Box 394, 44688, P 1,000, M 61, (330) 866-3435

**Waynesville** • *Waynesville Area C/C* • Dawn Schroeder, Exec. Dir., 10-B N. Main St., P.O. Box 281, 45068, P 2,800, M 230, (513) 897-8855, Fax (513) 897-9833, waynsville@aol.com, www.waynesvilleohio.com

**Wellington** • *Wellington Area C/C* • Virginia Haynes, Pres., P.O. Box 42, 44090, P 4,500, M 70, (440) 647-2222, www.villageofwellington.com

**Wellston** • *Wellston Area C/C* • J. Edgar Evans, Pres., 203 E. Broadway St., 45692, P 6,500, M 135, (740) 384-3051, Fax (740) 384-3357, www.jacksonohio.org

**Wellsville** • *Wellsville Area C/C* • Randy Allmon, Pres., 1200 Main St., P.O. Box 636, 43968, P 4,000, M 70, (330) 532-2120, rallmon@hotmail.com, www.wellsvilleohiochamber.com

**West Chester** • *West Chester Chamber Alliance* • Joseph A. Hinson, Pres./CEO, 7617 Voice of America Centre Dr., 45069, P 100,000, M 900, (513) 777-3600, Fax (513) 777-0188, www.westchesterchamberalliance.com

**West Lafayette** • *West Lafayette C/C* • Christie Maurer, Pres., P.O. Box 113, 43845, P 2,200, M 61, (740) 545-9370, www.westlafayettevillage.com

**West Union** • *Adams County C/C* • Delsey Wilson, Exec. Dir., 110 N. Manchester St., P.O. Box 398, 45693, P 27,000, M 230, (937) 544-5454, Fax (937) 544-6957, acchamber@verizon.net, www.adamscountyohchamber.org

**West Unity** • *West Unity Area C/C* • P.O. Box 263, 43570, P 1,760, M 49, (419) 924-2952, Fax (419) 924-2952, wucoc@williams-net.com, www.westunity.org

**Westerville** • *Westerville Area C/C* • Janet Tressler-Davis, Pres./CEO, 99 Commerce Park Dr., 43082, P 40,000, M 700, (614) 882-8917, Fax (614) 882-2085, info@westervillechamber.com, www.westervillechamber.com

**Westlake** • *West Shore C/C* • John Sobolewski, Exec. Dir., West Lake Holiday Inn, 1100 Crocker Rd., 44145, P 32,000, M 375, (440) 835-8787, Fax (440) 835-8798, sandy@westshorechamber.org, www.westshorechamber.org

**Whitehall** • *Whitehall Area C/C* • Johnny L. Jackson, Exec. Dir., P.O. Box 13607, 43213, P 25,000, M 125, (614) 237-7792, Fax (614) 238-3863, info@whitehallchamber.org, www.whitehallchamber.org

**Whitehouse** • *Whitehouse C/C* • Josh Torres, Pres., P.O. Box 2746, 43571, P 2,400, M 100, (419) 877-2747, admin@whitehouseohchamber.com, www.whitehouseohchamber.com

**Wickliffe** • *Western Lake County Area C/C* • Karen W. Tercek, Pres., The Provo House, 28855 Euclid Ave., 44092, P 100,000, M 200, (440) 943-1134, Fax (440) 943-1114, ktercek@westernlakecountychamber.org, www.westernlakecountychamber.org

**Willard** • *Willard Area C/C* • Todd Shininger, Dir., 16 Myrtle Ave., P.O. Box 73, 44890, P 6,800, M 135, (419) 935-1888

**Willoughby** • *Willoughby Area C/C* • Nikki Matala, Exec. Dir., 28 Public Sq., 44094, P 38,000, M 460, (440) 942-1632, Fax (440) 942-0586, nikki@willoughbyareachamber.com, www.willoughbyareachamber.com

**Willowick** • *see Wickliffe*

**Wilmington** • *Wilmington Clinton County C/C* • Kimberly Danker & Bobbi Long, Co-Pres., 40 N. South St., 45177, P 40,000, M 330, (937) 382-2737, Fax (937) 383-2316, wccadmast@wccchamber.com, www.wccchamber.com

**Woodsfield** • *Monroe County C/C* • Melissa Perkins-Smithberger, Pres., 117 N. Main St., P.O. Box 643, 43793, P 15,500, M 165, (740) 472-5499, Fax same, monroechamber@gmn4u.com, www.monroechamber.com

**Wooster** • *Wooster Area C/C* • Jeff Griffin, Pres., 377 W. Liberty St., 44691, P 25,000, M 810, (330) 262-5735, Fax (330) 262-5745, wchamber@bright.net, www.woosterchamber.com

**Worthington** · *Worthington Area C/C* · Kathryn Paugh, Exec. Dir., 25 W. New England Ave., Ste. 100, 43085, P 62,000, M 740, (614) 888-3040, Fax (614) 841-4842, connect@worthington chamber.org, www.worthingtonchamber.org

**Xenia** · *Xenia Area C/C* · Alan D. Liming, Pres./CEO, 334 W. Market St., 45385, P 27,000, M 475, (937) 372-3591, Fax (937) 372-2192, xacc@xacc.com, www.xacc.com.

**Yellow Springs** · *Yellow Springs C/C* · Karen Wintrow, Exec. Dir., 101 Dayton St., 45387, P 4,000, M 269, (937) 767-2686, Fax (937) 767-7876, info@yellowspringsohio.org, www.yellowspringsohio.org

**Youngstown** · *Youngstown Warren Reg. C/C* · Thomas M. Humphries, Pres./CEO, 11 Central Sq., Ste. 1600, 44503, P 796,905, M 2,974, (330) 744-2131, Fax (330) 746-0330, tom@regional-chamber.com, www.regionalchamber.com

**Zanesville** · *Zanesville-Muskingum County C/C* · Thomas C. Poorman, Pres., 205 N. Fifth St., 43701, P 83,388, M 835, (740) 455-8282, Fax (740) 454-2963, tpoorman@zmchamber.com, www.zmchamber.com

# Oklahoma

**The State Chamber of Oklahoma** · Richard P. Rush CCE, Pres./CEO, 330 N.E. 10th St., Oklahoma City, 73104, P 3,600,000, M 3,000, (405) 235-3669, Fax (405) 235-3670, drush@okstate chamber.com, www.okstatechamber.com.

**Ada** · *Ada Area C/C* · Karen Hudson, Pres./CEO, 209 W. Main, P.O. Box 248, 74820, P 34,100, M 497, (580) 332-2506, Fax (580) 332-3265, adachamber@adachamber.com, www.adachamber.com

**Adair** · *Adair Area C/C* · Secy., P.O. Box 377, 74330, P 850, M 50, (918) 785-4242, adairchamber@upperspace.net, www.adairok.com

**Aline** · *Aline C/C* · Carolyn Rexroat, 33 Heritage Rd., 73716, P 300, M 25, (580) 463-2563, www.1aj.org

**Allen** · *Allen C/C* · Cindy Davis, Pres., P.O. Box 396, 74825, P 1,000, M 40, (580) 857-2687, www.allenoklahoma.com

**Altus** · *Altus C/C* · Holley Urbanski, Pres., 301 W. Commerce St., P.O. Box 518, 73522, P 24,000, M 425, (580) 482-0210, Fax (580) 482-0223, altuschamber@altuschamber.com, www.altuschamber.com.

**Alva** · *Alva Area C/C* · Alexandra Mantz Drenning, Dir., 502 Oklahoma Blvd., 73717, P 5,200, M 260, (580) 327-1647, chamber@alvaok.net, www.alvaok.net

**Anadarko** · *Anadarko C/C* · Carla Hall, Exec. Dir., 516 W. Kentucky, P.O. Box 366, 73005, P 6,635, M 130, (405) 247-6651, Fax (405) 247-6652, coc@anadarko.org, www.anadarko.org

**Antlers** · *Pushmataha County C/C* · Ylonda McAllister, Exec. Dir., 119 W. Main St., 74523, P 11,667, M 150, (580) 298-5770, Fax (580) 298-5770, pushchamber@gmail.com, www.pushchamber.org

**Apache** · *Apache C/C* · Ronnie Orf, Pres., P.O. Box 461, 73006, P 3,000, M 100, (580) 588-3440, www.apache-ok.com

**Ardmore** · *Ardmore C/C* · Mita Bates, V.P., 410 W. Main, P.O. Box 1585, 73402, P 35,000, M 850, (580) 223-7765, Fax (580) 223-7825, mbates@ardmore.org, www.ardmore.org.

**Atoka** · *Atoka County C/C* · Brian Cathey, Pres., 415 E. Court, P.O. Box 778, 74525, P 4,200, M 189, (580) 889-2410, Fax (580) 889-2410, chamber1atoka@sbcglobal.net, www.atokachamber.com

**Barnsdall** · *Barnsdall C/C* · Mitzi Whinery, Pres., P.O. Box 443, 74002, P 1,260, M 50, (918) 847-2202, barnsdallchamber@yahoo.com

**Bartlesville** · *Bartlesville Reg. C/C* · Emily Call, Interim Pres., 201 S.W. Keeler, P.O. Box 2366, 74005, P 34,748, M 700, (918) 336-8708, Fax (918) 337-0216, ecall@bartlesville.com, www.bartlesville.com

**Beaver** · *Beaver County C/C* · Charlene Marshall, Secy./Mgr., 33 W. 2nd St., P.O. Box 878, 73932, P 2,000, M 83, (580) 625-4726, Fax (580) 625-4726, bvrchamber@ptsi.net, www.beavercountychamberofcommerce.com

**Beggs** · *Beggs C/C* · Crystal Simmons, Pres., P.O. Box 270, 74421, P 1,500, M 35, (918) 267-4935, (918) 267-5240, information@beggschamber.org, www.beggschamber.org

**Bethany** · *Northwest C/C* · Jill McCartney, Pres./CEO, 7440 N.W. 39th Expy., P.O. Box 144, 73008, P 22,000, M 350, (405) 789-1256, Fax (405) 789-2478, thenorthwestchamber@coxinet.net, www.thenorthwestchamber.com

**Bixby** · *Bixby C/C* · Lisa Navrkal, Pres., 4 E. Dawes, 74008, P 19,000, M 300, (918) 366-9445, Fax (918) 366-9443, chamber@bixbychamber.com, www.bixbychamber.com

**Blackwell** · *Blackwell C/C* · Shane Frye, Exec. Dir., 120 S. Main, P.O. Box 230, 74631, P 7,619, M 300, (580) 363-4195, Fax (580) 363-1704, info@blackwellchamber.com, www.blackwellchamber.org

**Blanchard** · *Blanchard C/C* · Crystal Griffis, Exec. Dir., 113 W. Broadway, P.O. Box 1190, 73010, P 12,000, M 125, (405) 485-8787, Fax (405) 485-8707, office@blanchardchamber.com, www.blanchardchamber.com

**Boise City** · *Cimarron County C/C* · John Smith, Co-Pres., 6 N.E. Square, P.O. Box 1027, 73933, P 3,000, M 50, (580) 544-3344, cccc@ptsi.net, www.ccccok.org

**Boley** · *Boley C/C* · Dr. Francis Shelton, Pres., P.O. Box 31, 74829, P 1,100, M 200, (918) 667-3477, chamber@boley-ok.com, www.boley-ok.com

**Broken Arrow** · *Broken Arrow Area C/C & EDC* · Mickey Thompson CEcD, Pres./CEO, 123 N. Main, 74012, P 100,000, M 830, (918) 251-1518, Fax (918) 251-1777, info@brokenarrowchamber.com, www.brokenarrowchamber.com

**Broken Bow** · *Broken Bow C/C* · Charity O'Donnell, Dir., 113 W. Martin Luther King Dr., 74728, P 4,898, M 275, (580) 584-3393, (800) 528-7337, Fax (580) 584-7698, bchamber@pine-net.com, www.brokenbowchamber.com, www.mccurtaincountygetaways.com.

**Burns Flat** · *Burns Flat C/C* · Brian Mooney, Pres., P.O. Box 68, 73624, P 2,500, M 35, (580) 562-3356, Fax (580) 562-3113, www.burnsflat-ok.com

**Canton** · *Canton C/C* · Johnnie Jones, Pres., P.O. Box 307, 73724, P 800, M 50, (580) 886-2434

**Carnegie** · *Carnegie C/C* · Terri Johnson, Pres., P.O. Box 615, 73015, P 1,637, M 73, (580) 654-2121

**Catoosa** · *Catoosa C/C* · Jonnie Mott, Mgr., 650 S. Cherokee #C, P.O. Box 297, 74015, P 5,000, M 215, (918) 266-6042, Fax (918) 266-6314, catoosachamber@sbcglobal.net, www.catoosachamber.com

**Chandler** · *Chandler C/C* · 804 Manvel, 74834, P 3,000, M 110, (405) 258-0673, Fax (405) 258-0377, chandlerchamber@sbcglobal.net, www.chandlerok.com

**Checotah** · *Checotah C/C* · Lloyd Jernigan, Exec. Dir., 201 N. Broadway, 74426, P 4,000, M 100, (918) 473-2070, Fax (918) 473-1453, checotahchamber@valornet.com, www.checotah.com

**Chelsea** · *Chelsea Area C/C* · Rick Johnson, Pres., 618 Pine, 74016, P 2,100, M 60, (918) 789-2220, Fax (918) 789-5899, chelseaokchamber@earthlink.net, www.chelseachamber.com

**Cherokee** · *Cherokee Mainstreet C/C* · Susie Koontz, Prog. Mgr., 121 E. Main St., 73728, P 1,505, M 120, (580) 596-3575 x122, (580) 596-6111, Fax (580) 596-2464, mainstreet@akslc.net, www.cherokeeoklahoma.com

**Cheyenne** · *Cheyenne-Roger Mills C/C & Tourism* · Gene Eakins, Exec. V.P., 101 S. LL Males Ave., P.O. Box 57, 73628, P 948, M 75, (580) 497-3318, cheyennecoc@yahoo.com, www.cheyenneokcoc.com, www.rogermills.org

**Chickasha** · *Chickasha C/C* · Bud Andrus, Pres., 221 Chickasha Ave., P.O. Box 1717, 73023, P 17,000, M 420, (405) 224-0787, Fax (405) 222-3730, mandy@chickashachamber.com, www.chickashachamber.com

**Choctaw** · *Choctaw C/C* · Tracy Mosley, 2437 Main St., P.O. Box 1000, 73020, P 11,500, M 213, (405) 390-3303, Fax (405) 390-3330, chocchamber@tds.net, www.choctawchamber.com

**Chouteau** · *Chouteau C/C* · Neil Patel, Pres., P.O. Box 332, 74337, P 2,200, M 60, (918) 476-8222, www.chouteauok.net

**Claremore** · *Claremore Area C/C* · Dell Davis, Pres./CEO, 419 W. Will Rogers Blvd., 74017, P 18,500, M 450, (918) 341-2818, Fax (918) 342-0663, chamber@claremore.org, www.claremore.org

**Cleveland** · *Cleveland Area C/C* · Diana Tilley-Esparza, Exec. Dir., 113 N. Broadway St., P.O. Box 240, 74020, P 3,282, M 93, (918) 358-2131, Fax (918) 358-5710, info@chamberofcleveland.com, www.chamberofcleveland.com

**Clinton** · *Clinton C/C* · Erin Adams, Pres., 101 S. 4th St., 73601, P 10,000, M 350, (580) 323-2222, Fax (580) 323-2931, office@clintonok.org, www.clintonok.org

**Coalgate** · *Coal County C/C* · Mary Riley, Pres., P.O. Box 323, 74538, P 5,000, M 80, (580) 927-2119, coalcommerce@yahoo.com

**Colcord** · *Colcord Area C/C* · Bridgette Nichols, Pres., P.O. Box 265, 74338, P 1,000, M 25, (918) 326-4778, (918) 326-1033

**Collinsville** · *Collinsville C/C* · Mr. Cory Slagle, Pres., 1023 W. Main St., P.O. Box 245, 74021, P 5,000, M 200, (918) 371-4703, Fax (918) 371-4703, cvillechamber3477@sbcglobal.net, www.collinsvillechamber.net

**Cordell** · *Cordell C/C* · Claudia Gray, Exec. Secy., 116 S. College, 73632, P 2,867, M 125, (580) 832-3538, (888) CORDELL, Fax (580) 832-5432, chamberqueen_2000@yahoo.com, www.cordellchamber.com

**Coweta** · *Coweta C/C* · 107 S. Broadway, P.O. Box 70, 74429, P 10,000, M 200, (918) 486-2513, Fax (918) 279-0829, cowetachamber1@windstream.net, www.cowetachamber.com

**Crescent** · *Crescent C/C* · Ethan Keiffer, Treas., P.O. Box 333, 73028, P 1,651, M 60, (405) 969-2814

**Cushing** · *Cushing C of C & Ind.* · Mr. Bobby Bryant, Exec. Dir., 1301 E. Main, 74023, P 8,400, M 270, (918) 225-2400, Fax (918) 225-2903, bobby@cushingchamber.org, www.cushingchamber.org

**Davenport** · *Davenport C/C* · Steve Guest, Secy., P.O. Box 66, 74026, P 1,000, M 125, (918) 377-2241, Fax (918) 377-2506, davenportcoc@brightok.net, www.davenportok.org

**Davis** · *Davis C/C* · Trinity Damron, Exec. Dir., 100 E. Main, P.O. Box 5, 73030, P 2,800, M 163, (580) 369-2402, Fax (580) 369-3719, davischamber@sbcglobal.net, www.davisok.org

**Del City** · *Del City C/C* · Helen Watson, Asst. Dir., 4505 S.E. 15th St., P.O. Box 15643, 73155, P 23,000, M 150, (405) 672-5285, Fax (405) 677-2275, delcitychamber@sbcglobal.net, delcitychamber.com

**Drumright** · *Drumright C/C* · Darrel Morris, Pres., 103 E. Broadway, P.O. Box 828, 74030, P 3,000, M 110, (918) 352-2204, Fax (918) 352-2065, drumright.net/chamber.htm, drumright chamber@aol.com, www.drumright.com

**Duncan** · *Duncan C of C & Ind.* · Debra Burch, Pres./CEO, 911 Walnut, P.O. Box 699, 73534, P 24,000, M 393, (580) 255-3644, Fax (580) 255-6482, duncancc@texhoma.net, www.duncanchamber.com

**Durant** · *Durant Area C/C* · Janet Reed, Exec. Dir., 215 N. 4th Ave., 74701, P 20,000, M 500, (580) 924-0848, Fax (580) 924-0348, director@durantchamber.org, www.durantchamber.org.

**Edmond** · *Edmond Area C/C* · Ken Moore, Pres., 825 E. 2nd #100, 73034, P 78,000, M 1,100, (405) 341-2808, Fax (405) 340-5512, info@edmondchamber.com, www.edmondchamber.com

**El Reno** · *El Reno C/C* · Karmon Stanley, Exec. Dir., 206 N. Bickford, 73036, P 17,000, M 180, (405) 262-1188, Fax (405) 262-1189, elrenochamber@swbell.net, www.elrenochamber.com

**Elgin** · *Elgin C/C* · Gilmer J. Capps, Pres., P.O. Box 362, 73538, P 1,220, M 25, (580) 492-5290, www.elginchamber.net

**Elk City** · *Elk City C/C* · Susie Cupp, Exec. Dir., P.O. Box 972, 73648, P 13,500, M 300, (580) 225-0207, (800) 280-0207, Fax (580) 225-1008, elkcitychamber@itlnet.net, www.elkcitychamber.com

**Enid** · *Greater Enid C/C* · Jon Blankenship, Pres./CEO, 210 Kenwood Blvd., P.O. Box 907, 73702, P 47,000, M 600, (580) 237-2494, Fax (580) 237-2497, brittany@enidchamber.com, www.enidchamber.com.

**Erick** · *Erick C/C* · Paula Harris, Pres., P.O. Box 1232, 73645, P 1,100, M 40, (580) 526-3332, erickchamber@yahoo.com, www.erickchamber.com

**Eufaula** · *Eufaula Area C/C* · Ms. Jimmie Phelan, Exec. Dir., 321 N. Main, P.O. Box 738, 74432, P 50,000, M 200, (918) 689-2791, Fax (918) 689-7746, chamber@eufaulachamberofcommerce.com, www.eufaulachamberofcommerce.com

**Fairfax** · *Fairfax C/C* · Carol Irons, Pres., 242 N. Main St., P.O. Box 35, 74637, P 2,000, M 40, (918) 642-1271, (918) 642-5266, bob_stephens@msn.com, www.fairfaxchamber.com

**Fairview** · *Fairview C/C* · Jeannie Marlin, Exec. Dir., 624 N. Main, P.O. Box 180, 73737, P 2,700, M 145, (580) 227-2527, Fax (580) 227-2258, fairviewchamber@att.net, www.fairviewokchamber.com

**Fort Gibson** · *Fort Gibson C/C* · Gary Perkins, Exec. Dir., 112 N. Lee St., P.O. Box 730, 74434, P 4,300, M 120, (918) 478-4780, Fax (918) 478-4780, fortgibson@sbcglobal.net, www.fortgibson.com

**Fort Sill** · *see Lawton*

**Frederick** · *Frederick C/C & Ind.* · Sharon Bennett, Exec. Dir., 100 S. Main St., 73542, P 4,000, M 200, (580) 335-2126, Fax (580) 335-3767, frederickcc@pldi.net, www.frederickokchamber.org

**Freedom** · *Freedom C/C* · Mark Nixon, Secy./Treas., P.O. Box 125, 73842, P 300, M 120, (580) 621-3276, Fax (580) 621-3275, freedomchamberofcommerce@yahoo.com, www.freedomokla.com

**Gage** · *Gage C/C* · Ferrall Barnes, P.O. Box 328, 73843, P 400, M 15, (580) 923-7727

**Garber** · *Garber Comm. Improvement Assn.* · P.O. Box 574, 73738, P 700, M 30, (580) 863-2279

**Geary** · *Geary C/C* · Kay Hagerman, Pres., P.O. Box 273, 73040, P 1,350, M 30, (405) 884-2765

**Glenpool** · *Glenpool C/C* · Carol Campbell, Exec. Dir., 494 E. 141st St., P.O. Box 767, 74033, P 9,000, M 135, (918) 322-3505, Fax (918) 322-3505, director@glenpoolchamber.org, www.glenpoolchamber.org

**Gore** · *Gore C/C* · Shannon Smith, Pres., P.O. Box 943, 74435, P 900, M 70, (918) 489-2534, goreokchamber@yahoo.com, www.goreok.net

**Grove** · *Grove Area C/C* · Lisa Friden, Pres., 310 S. Main, 74344, P 16,640, M 400, (918) 786-9079, Fax (918) 786-2909, grovecc@sbcglobal.net, www.groveok.org.

**Guthrie** · *Guthrie C/C* · Mary Coffin, Pres., 212 W. Oklahoma Ave., P.O. Box 995, 73044, P 13,000, M 275, (405) 282-1947, (800) 299-1889, Fax (405) 282-0061, info@guthrieok.com, www.guthrieok.com

**Guymon** · *Guymon C/C* · Ronni Malone, Exec. Dir., 711 S.E. Hwy. 3, Rte. 5, Box 120, 73942, P 13,000, M 196, (580) 338-3376, Fax (580) 338-0014, guycofc@ptsi.net, www.guymoncofc.org

**Harrah** · *Harrah C/C* · Scott Dull, Pres., P.O. Box 907, 73045, P 4,800, M 125, (405) 454-2190, www.harrahchamberofcommerce.com

**Hartshorne** · *Hartshorne C/C* · Jerry Earp, Pres., P.O. Box 343, 74547, P 2,200, M 55, (918) 297-2055, (918) 297-3651, www.cityofhartshorneok.com

**Haskell** · *Haskell Area C/C* · Rocky Purdum, Pres., P.O. Box 252, 74436, P 6,000, M 63, (918) 482-1245, Fax (918) 482-5619, info@haskellchamber.com, www.haskellchamber.com

**Healdton** · *Healdton C/C* · Amy Grace, Pres., 315 E. Main, 73438, P 2,700, M 100, (580) 229-0900, Fax (580) 229-0900, healdton chamber@suddenlinkmail.com, www.healdtonchamber.com

**Heavener** · *Heavener C/C* · Diane Brand, 501 W. 1st St., 74937, P 3,600, M 100, (918) 653-4303, Fax (918) 653-2438, manager@havenerok.org, www.heavenerok.org

**Henryetta** · *Henryetta C/C* · Roy Madden, Exec. Dir., 115 S. 4th, 74437, P 6,000, M 120, (918) 652-3331, Fax (918) 652-3332, chamber@henryetta.org, www.henryetta.org

**Hinton** · *Hinton C/C* · Beverly Ball, Pres., P.O. Box 48, 73047, P 2,000, M 70, (405) 542-6428, www.hintonok.com

**Hobart** · *Hobart C/C* · Dewaina Edge, Dir., 106 W. 4th St., 73651, P 4,000, M 200, (580) 726-2553, Fax same, hobartchamber@cableone.net, www.hobartok.com

**Holdenville** · *Holdenville C/C* · Shelly Griggs, Exec. Dir., 105 S. Hinckley, P.O. Box 70, 74848, P 5,493, M 100, (405) 592-4221, Fax (405) 379-6968, chamber@holdenville.org, www.holdenville.org

**Hollis** · *Harmon County C/C* · P.O. Box 188, 73550, P 3,400, M 76, (580) 688-9246, Fax (580) 688-9247

**Hominy** · *Hominy C/C* · Jerry Stumpff, Pres., P.O. Box 99, 74035, P 3,200, M 50, (918) 885-4939, Fax (918) 885-4939, hominy chamberofcommerce@windstream.net

**Hooker** · *Hooker C/C* · Linda Martin, Pres., P.O. Box 989, 73945, P 1,788, M 80, (580) 652-2809

**Hugo** · *Hugo Area C/C* · 200 S. Broadway, 74743, P 6,000, M 200, (580) 326-7511, Fax (580) 326-7512, hugo-chamber@sbcglobal.net, www.hugochamber.org

**Idabel** · *Idabel C of C & Ag.* · Betty L. Johnson, Exec. Dir., 7 S.W. Texas St., 74745, P 7,000, M 214, (580) 286-3305, Fax (580) 286-6708, idabelchamber@yahoo.com, www.idabel chamberofcommerce.com

**Jay** · *Jay C/C* · Becki Farley, Pres., P.O. Box 806, 74346, P 2,482, M 62, (918) 253-8698

**Jenks** · *Jenks C/C* · Annette Bowles, Pres., 224 E. A St., P.O. Box 902, 74037, P 16,500, M 350, (918) 299-5005, Fax (918) 299-5799, info@jenkschamber.com, www.jenkschamber.com

**Kaw City** · *Kaw City Area C/C* · Rosa Lee Kirk, Pres., P.O. Box 241, 74641, P 400, M 54, (580) 269-2984, kawcitychamber@kawcityok.net, www.kawcitychamber.org

**Kingfisher** · *Kingfisher C/C* · Judy Whipple, Mgr., 123 W. Miles, 73750, P 5,000, M 125, (405) 375-4445, Fax (405) 375-5304, chamber@pldi.net, www.kingfisher.org

**Kingston** · *see Madill*

**Konawa** · *Konawa C/C* · P.O. Box 112, 74849, P 1,500, M 65, (580) 925-3220

**Langley** · *Grand Lake Area C/C* · Jim Sellers, Exec. Dir., P.O. Box 215, 74350, P 25,000, M 350, (918) 782-3214, Fax (918) 782-3215, admin istrator@grandlakechamber.org, www.grandlakechamber.org

**Laverne** · *Laverne Area C/C* · Lindy L. Cronister, Exec. Dir., 108 W. Jane Jayroe, P.O. Box 634, 73848, P 1,100, M 60, (580) 921-3612, (580) 921-5121, lvrnokcc@ptsi.net, www.laverneok.com

**Lawton** · *Lawton-Fort Sill C/C & Ind.* · Dana Davis, Pres./CEO, 629 S.W. C Ave. #A, P.O. Box 1376, 73502, P 112,000, M 880, (580) 355-3541, (800) 872-4540, Fax (580) 357-3642, bhinkle@lawton fortsillchamber.com, www.lawtonfortsillchamber.com

**Lindsay** · *Lindsay C/C* · Paula Barker, Mgr., 107 N. Main St., P.O. Box 504, 73052, P 3,000, M 123, (405) 756-4312, Fax (405) 756-8657, lchamber@oriok.net, www.lindsayokchamberofcommerce.com

**Locust Grove** · *Locust Grove Area C/C* · P.O. Box 525, 74352, P 1,400, M 60, (918) 479-6336

**Lone Grove** · *Lone Grove C/C* · Pam Keeton, Chrmn., P.O. Box 746, 73443, P 4,600, M 75, (580) 657-3113

**Madill** · *Marshall County C/C* · Jeff Hudson, Exec. Dir., 400 W. Overton, P.O. Box 542, 73446, P 20,000, M 220, (580) 795-2431, Fax (580) 795-5870, info@mccoconline.org, www.mccoconline.org

**Mangum** · *Greer County C/C* · Wayne Vaughn, Dir., 222 W. Jefferson, 73554, P 6,095, M 165, (580) 782-2444, Fax (580) 782-2444, info@greercountychamber.com, www.greercounty chamber.com

**Mannford** · *Mannford Area C/C* · Rita Bougher, Pres., P.O. Box 487, 74044, P 15,000, M 100, (918) 865-2000, Fax (918) 865-3187, info@mannfordchamberofcommerce.com, www.mannfordcham berofcommerce.com

**Marietta** · *Love County C/C* · Gwen Wyatt, Secy., P.O. Box 422, 73448, P 3,000, M 100, (580) 276-3102, lovecountychamber@yahoo.com, www.lovecountyokla.org

**Marlow** · *Marlow C/C* · Debbe Ridley, Mgr., 223 W. Main, 73055, P 4,592, M 300, (580) 658-2212, marlowchamber@starcomm.net, www.marlowchamber.org

**Maysville** · *Maysville C/C* · Johnny Bob Williams, Pres., P.O. Box 313, 73057, P 1,240, M 40, (405) 867-4485, (405) 867-5850

**McAlester** · *McAlester Area C/C & Ag.* · Tanaye Harvanek, Mbrshp. Svcs. Coord., 345 E. Adams, P.O. Box 759, 74501, P 20,000, M 482, (918) 423-2550, Fax (918) 423-1345, info@mcalester.org, www.mcalester.org

**McLoud** · *McLoud C/C* · Jayne Sconyers, Exec. Dir., P.O. Box 254, 74851, P 3,548, M 70, (405) 964-6566, Fax (405) 964-6566, jayne@mcloudchamber.com, www.mcloudchamber.com

**Miami** · *Miami C/C* · Cindy Morris, Exec. Dir., 111 N. Main, P.O. Box 760, 74355, P 14,800, M 300, (918) 542-4481, Fax (918) 540-1260, info@miamiokchamber.com, www.miamiokchamber.com

**Midwest City** · *Midwest City C/C* · Bonnie Cheatwood, Exec. Dir., 5905 Trosper Rd., P.O. Box 10980, 73140, P 55,000, M 529, (405) 733-3801, Fax (405) 733-5633, information@midwestcityok.com, www.midwestcityok.com

**Minco** · *Minco C/C* · John Hacker, Pres., P.O. Box 451, 73059, P 1,579, M 26, (405) 352-4382

**Moore** · *Moore C/C* · Brenda Roberts, Exec. Dir., 305 W. Main, P.O. Box 6305, 73153, P 50,000, M 525, (405) 794-3400, Fax (405) 794-8555, brendar@moorechamber.com, www.moorechamber.com

**Muldrow** · *Muldrow C/C* · Katherine Jones, Mayor, 100 S. Main, P.O. Box 429, 74948, P 4,000, (918) 427-7668

**Muskogee** · *Greater Muskogee Area C/C & Tourism* · Sue Harris, Pres., 310 W. Broadway, P.O. Box 797, 74402, P 40,000, M 800, (918) 682-2401, (866) 381-6543, Fax (918) 682-2403, info@muskogeechamber.org, www.muskogeechamber.org.

**Mustang** · *Mustang C/C* · Becky Julian, Exec. Dir., 1201 N. Mustang Rd., P.O. Box 213, 73064, P 17,000, M 280, (405) 376-2758, Fax (405) 376-4764, info@mustangchamber.com, www.mustangchamber.com

**Newcastle** · *Newcastle C/C* · Kim Brown, Exec. Dir., P.O. Box 1006, 73065, P 7,200, M 160, (405) 387-3232, Fax (405) 387-3885, www.newcastleok.org

**Newkirk** · *Newkirk C/C* · 104 W. 7th St., 74647, P 2,243, M 115, (580) 362-2155, Fax (580) 362-3774, ncof104@sbcglobal.net, www.oknewkirk.com

**Nicoma Park** · *Nicoma Park C/C* · Bud Green, Exec. V.P., P.O. Box 4520, 73066, P 2,500, M 42, (405) 769-6635, Fax (405) 769-1041, npccbud@swbell.net

**Noble** · *Noble C/C* · Christine Frank, Exec. Dir., 114 S. Main, P.O. Box 678, 73068, P 5,000, M 100, (405) 872-5535, Fax (405) 872-2020, info@nobleok.org, www.nobleok.org

**Norman** · *Norman C/C* · Anna-Mary Suggs, Exec. Dir., 115 E. Gray, P.O. Box 982, 73070, P 108,000, M 1,350, (405) 321-7260, Fax (405) 360-4679, normanchamber@normanchamber.com, www.normanchamber.com.

**Nowata** · *Nowata Area C/C* · 126 S. Maple, P.O. Box 202, 74048, P 5,000, M 130, (918) 273-2301, nowatachamber@sbcglobal.net, www.nowatachamber.org

**Oilton** · *Oilton C/C* · Kay Lewis, P.O. Box 624, 74052, P 1,600, M 35, (918) 862-3202

**Okeene** · *Okeene C/C* · Sherri Feely, Exec. Dir., 116 W. E St., P.O. Box 704, 73763, P 1,200, M 75, (580) 822-3005, okchamber@pldi.net, www.okeene.com

**Okemah** · *Okemah C/C* · Roger Thompson, Pres., 407 W. Broadway, P.O. Box 508, 74859, P 5,000, M 225, (918) 623-2440, okemahchamber@okemah.org, www.okemah.org

**Oklahoma City** · *Greater Oklahoma City C/C* · Roy Williams, Pres./CEO, 123 Park Ave., 73102, P 1,172,300, M 4,200, (405) 297-8900, Fax (405) 297-8916, rwilliams@okcchamber.com, www.okcchamber.com

**Oklahoma City** · *South Oklahoma City C/C* · Elaine Lyons, Pres., 701 S.W. 74th St., 73139, P 140,246, M 750, (405) 634-1436, Fax (405) 634-1462, info@southokc.com, www.southokc.com

**Okmulgee** · *Okmulgee C/C* · Nolan Crowley, Exec. Dir., 112 N. Morton, 74447, P 13,000, M 200, (918) 756-6172, Fax (918) 756-6441, okmulgeeinfo@okmulgeechamber.org, www.okmulgeeonline.com

**Oologah** · *Oologah Area C/C* · Amos Berry, Pres., P.O. Box 109, 74053, P 1,500, M 160, (918) 443-2790, Fax (918) 443-2790, chamber@oologah.org, www.oologah.org

**Owasso** · *Owasso C/C* · Gary Akin, Pres., 315 S. Cedar, 74055, P 45,000, M 500, (918) 272-2141, Fax (918) 272-8564, susan@owassochamber.com, www.owassochamber.com.

**Pauls Valley** · *Pauls Valley C/C* · Della Wilson, Exec. Dir., 112 E. Paul, P.O. Box 638, 73075, P 6,900, M 270, (405) 238-6491, Fax (405) 238-2335, pvchamber@sbcglobal.net, www.paulsvalley.com.

**Pawhuska** · *Pawhuska C/C* · Michael McCartney, Exec. Dir., 210 W. Main, P.O. Box 5, 74056, P 3,825, M 144, (918) 287-1208, Fax (918) 287-3159, pawhuskachamber@sbcglobal.net, www.pawhuskachamber.com

**Pawnee** · *Pawnee C/C* · Bill Gosnell, Mgr., 613 Harrison St., 74058, P 2,200, M 105, (918) 762-2108, pawneechamber@cowboy.net, www.cityofpawnee.com

**Perkins** · *Perkins C/C* · Becky Reedy, Pres., P.O. Box 502, 74059, P 2,500, M 88, (405) 747-6809, www.cityofperkins.net

**Perry** · *Perry C/C* · Brett Powers, Exec. Dir., 300 N. 6th St., P.O. Box 426, 73077, P 5,200, M 250, (580) 336-4684, Fax (580) 336-3522, information@perrychamber.org, www.perryokchamber.com

**Piedmont** · *Piedmont C/C* · Eric Anderson, Pres., P.O. Box 501, 73078, P 5,000, M 132, (405) 373-2234, piedmontokchamber@wavelinx.net, www.piedmontokchamber.org

**Ponca City** · *Ponca City Area C/C* · Rich Cantillon, Pres./CEO, 420 E. Grand Ave., P.O. Box 1109, 74602, P 26,000, M 600, (580) 765-4400, Fax (580) 765-2798, rich@poncacitychamber.com, www.poncacitychamber.com.

**Poteau** · *Poteau C/C* · Karen Wages, Pres./CEO, 201 S. Broadway, 74953, P 9,000, M 364, (918) 647-9178, Fax (918) 647-4099, poteauchamber@windstream.net, www.poteauchamber.com.

**Prague** · *Prague C/C* · 820 Jim Thorpe Blvd., P.O. Box 111, 74864, P 2,300, M 95, (405) 567-2616, Fax (405) 567-2616, praguecoc@windstream.net, www.pragueok.org

**Pryor** · *Pryor Area C/C* · Barbara Hawkins, Pres., 100 E. Graham Ave., P.O. Box 367, 74362, P 9,500, M 310, (918) 825-0157, Fax (918) 825-0158, info@pryorchamber.com, www.pryorchamber.com

**Purcell** · *Heart of Oklahoma C/C* · Mark Alfonso, Exec. Dir., 302 W. Main St. #104, 73080, P 5,500, M 200, (405) 527-3093, Fax (405) 527-4351, purcellchamber@cebridge.net, www.theheartofoklahomachamber.com

**Roff** · *Roff C/C* · Nelda Burrows, Pres., P.O. Box 303, 74865, P 720, M 20, (580) 456-7774, hjcrawford@cableone.net

**Roland** · *Roland C/C* · Keith Wasson, Acting Pres., P.O. Box 492, 74954, P 4,000, M 45, (479) 651-0321, info@rolandchamber.com, www.rolandchamber.com

**Sallisaw** · *Sallisaw C/C* · Judy Martens, Exec. Dir., 301 E. Cherokee, P.O. Box 251, 74955, P 8,500, M 200, (918) 775-2558, Fax (918) 775-4021, sallisawchamber@yahoo.com, www.sallisawchamber.com

**Sand Springs** · *Sand Springs Area C/C* · Mr. J.C. Kinder, Pres., 121 N. Main, 74063, P 18,000, M 250, (918) 245-3221, Fax (918) 245-2530, info@sandspringschamber.com, www.sandspringschamber.com

**Sapulpa** · *Sapulpa Area C/C* · Suzanne Shirey, Exec. Dir., 101 E. Dewey, 74066, P 22,500, M 329, (918) 224-0170, Fax (918) 224-0172, info@sapulpachamber.com, www.sapulpachamber.com.

**Sayre** · *Sayre C/C* · Niki Callahan, Dir., 117 N. 4th, P.O. Box 474, 73662, P 3,500, M 115, (580) 928-3386, Fax (580) 928-3158, sayrechamber@att.net, www.sayrechamber.com

**Seiling** · *Seiling C/C* · P.O. Box 794, 73663, P 900, M 30, www.seilingchamber.com

**Seminole** · *Seminole C/C* · Amy Britt, Exec. Dir., 326 E. Evans, P.O. Box 1190, 74818, P 6,950, M 150, (405) 382-3640, Fax (405) 382-3529, info@seminoleokchamber.org, www.seminoleokchamber.org.

**Sentinel** · *Sentinel C/C* · John Werhan, P.O. Box 131, 73664, P 850, M 60, (580) 393-2171

**Shattuck** · *Shattuck C/C* · David Romine, Dir., 115 S. Main, P.O. Box 400, 73858, P 1,250, M 52, (580) 938-2818, Fax (580) 938-2852, shattuckcc@pldi.net, www.shattuckchamber.org

**Shawnee** · *Greater Shawnee Area C/C* · Nancy Keith, Pres./CEO, 131 N. Bell, P.O. Box 1613, 74802, P 32,000, M 520, (405) 273-6092, Fax (405) 275-9851, nkeith@shawneechamber.com, www.shawneechamber.com.

**Shidler** · *Shidler C/C* · Molly Bivin, P.O. Box 281, 74652, P 500, M 56, (918) 793-4171, www.shidleroklahoma.com

**Skiatook** · *Skiatook C/C* · Stephanie Upton, Exec. Dir., 304 E. Rogers Blvd., P.O. Box 272, 74070, P 8,500, M 130, (918) 396-3702, Fax (918) 396-3577, info@skiatookchamber.com, www.skiatookchamber.com

**Spencer** · *Spencer C/C* · Tony Wangler, Exec. Dir., 8606 Main St., P.O. Box 53, 73084, P 3,550, M 87, (405) 771-9933

**Spiro** · *Spiro Area C/C* · Marcia Day, Exec. Dir., 210 S. Main St., 74959, P 2,300, M 100, (918) 962-3816, Fax (918) 962-3816, spirocc@sbcglobal.net, www.myspiro.com

**Stigler** · *Stigler/Haskell County C/C* · Janice Williams, Exec. Dir., 204 E. Main St., 74462, P 12,000, M 70, (918) 967-8681, Fax (918) 967-4319, chamber@tulsaconnect.com, .

**Stillwater** · *Stillwater C/C* · Larry Brown, Pres./CEO, 409 S. Main, P.O. Box 1687, 74076, P 46,976, M 650, (405) 372-5573, Fax (405) 372-4316, info@stillwaterchamber.org, www.stillwaterchamber.org

**Stilwell** · *Stilwell Area C/C* · P.O. Box 845, 74960, P 3,000, M 100, (918) 696-7845, www.strawberrycapital.com

**Stratford** · *Stratford C/C* · Kim Gray, Pres., P.O. Box 491, 74872, P 1,600, M 35, (580) 759-3300

**Stroud** · *Stroud C/C* · David Timmons, Pres., 216 W. Main, 74079, P 2,700, M 145, (918) 968-3321, Fax (918) 968-4113, stroudch@brightok.net, www.stroudok.com

**Sulphur** · *Sulphur C/C* · Shelly Sawatzky, Exec. Dir., 717 W. Broadway, 73086, P 5,000, M 230, (580) 622-2824, Fax (580) 622-4217, sulphur@brightok.net, www.sulphurokla.com

**Tahlequah** · *Tahlequah Area C/C* · David Moore, Exec. Dir., 123 E. Delaware St., 74464, P 46,000, M 500, (918) 456-3742, (800) 456-4860, Fax (918) 456-3751, tahlequahchamber@swbell.net, www.tahlequahchamber.com

**Talihina** · *Talihina C/C* · 900 2nd St., Ste. 12, 74571, P 1,297, M 65, (918) 567-3434, Fax (918) 567-3388, chamber@talihinacc.com, www.talihinacc.com

**Tecumseh** · *Tecumseh C/C* · Autumn Brown, Exec. Dir., 114 N. Broadway St., 74873, P 6,200, M 95, (405) 598-8666, Fax (405) 598-6760, chambertecumseh@windstream.net, www.tecumsehchamber.com

**Temple** · *Temple C/C* · Virginia Dupler, Pres., P.O. Box 58, 73568, P 1,200, M 67, (580) 342-6991

**Texhoma** · *Texhoma C/C* · P.O. Box 564, 73949, P 1,300, M 15, (580) 423-7114

**Tipton** · *Tipton C/C* · Linton Deskins, Pres., P.O. Box 403, 73570, P 1,200, M 130, (580) 305-8549

**Tishomingo** · *Johnston County C/C* · Janis Stewart, Exec. Dir., 106 W. Main, 73460, P 11,000, M 150, (580) 371-2175, Fax (580) 371-2175, chamber@johnstoncountyok.org, www.johnstoncountyok.org

**Tonkawa** · *Tonkawa C/C* · Jared Grell, Pres., 102 E. Grand Ave., 74653, P 3,299, M 160, (580) 628-2220, Fax (580) 628-2221, info@tonkawachamber.org, www.tonkawachamber.org

**Tulsa** · *American Indian C/C of Oklahoma* · 5103 S. Sheridan Rd. #695, 74145, Fax (918) 343-3578, chamber@aicco.org, www.aicco.org

**Tulsa** · *Tulsa Metro C/C* · Mike Neal, Pres./CEO, Two W. Second St. #150, 74103, P 916,079, M 2,900, (918) 585-1201, Fax (918) 599-6122, webmaster@tulsachamber.com, www.tulsachamber.com.

**Tuttle** · *Tuttle Area C/C* · Lara Douglas, Mgr., P.O. Box 673, 73089, P 5,500, M 100, (405) 381-4600, Fax (405) 381-4600, lara@tuttlechamber.org, www.tuttlechamber.org

**Vici** · *Vici C/C* · Molly Randall, Secy., 107 E. Broadway, P.O. Box 2, 73859, P 750, M 40, (580) 995-3425, Fax (580) 995-4987, vicichamber@vicihorizon.com, www.viciok.com

**Vinita** · *Vinita Area C/C* · BJ Mooney, Exec. Dir., 125 S. Scraper, P.O. Box 882, 74301, P 15,000, M 230, (918) 256-7133, Fax (918) 256-8261, chamber@vinita.com, www.vinita.com

**Wagoner** · *Wagoner Area C/C* · Meredith Zehr, Exec. Dir., 301 S. Grant, 74467, P 8,900, M 265, (918) 485-3414, Fax (918) 485-2523, chamber@thecityofwagoner.org, www.thecityofwagoner.org

**Walters** · *Walters C/C* · Lavera Thompson, Secy., 116 N. Broadway, P.O. Box 352, 73572, P 2,657, M 75, (580) 875-3335, Fax (580) 875-3652, www.waltersok.us

**Warner** · *Warner C/C* · Roger Thomason, Pres., P.O. Box 170, 74469, P 1,600, M 30, (918) 463-2696, www.warnerok.com

**Watonga** · *Watonga C/C* · Travis Bradt, Pres., P.O. Box 537, 73772, P 7,500, M 175, (580) 623-5452, Fax (580) 623-5428, cwatonga@pldi.net, www.watongachamber.com

**Waurika** · *Waurika C/C* · Brad Scott, Pres., P.O. Box 366, 73573, P 1,900, M 75, (580) 228-2041, www.jeffcoinfo.org

**Waynoka** · *Waynoka C/C* · Wayne LaMunyon, Pres., P.O. Box 173, 73860, P 1,000, M 100, (580) 824-4741, (580) 824-2261, waynokachamber@gmail.com, www.waynokachamber.com

**Weatherford** · *Weatherford Area C/C* · Marie Hanza, Exec. Dir., 522 W. Rainey, P.O. Box 857, 73096, P 14,000, M 307, (580) 772-7744, (800) 725-7744, Fax (580) 772-7751, director@weatherfordchamber.com, www.weatherfordchamber.com

**Wellston** · *Wellston C/C* · P.O. Box 188, 74881, P 925, M 35, (405) 356-2476

**Westville** · *Westville C/C* · Patsy Winn, Comm. Bldg., P.O. Box 1020, 74965, P 1,600, M 25, (918) 723-3243, Fax (918) 723-4936, pswinn58@hotmail.com

**Wetumka** · *Wetumka C/C* · Vernon Stout, 202 N. Main, 74883, P 1,700, M 50, (405) 452-3237, wetumkacoc@hotmail.com, www.wetumka.net

**Wewoka** · *Wewoka C/C* · Tara Morgan, Mgr., 101 W. Park, P.O. Box 719, 74884, P 4,000, M 200, (405) 257-5485, Fax (405) 257-2662, wewokachamber@sbcglobal.net, www.wewokachamber.samsbiz.com

**Wilburton** · *Wilburton C/C* · 302 W. Main, 74578, P 3,500, M 88, (918) 465-2759, Fax (918) 465-2759, wilburtonchamber@sbcglobal.net, www.wilburtonchamber.com

**Woodward** · *Woodward C/C* · CJ Montgomery, Pres., 1006 Oklahoma Ave., P.O. Box 1026, 73802, P 15,000, M 400, (580) 256-7411, (800) 364-5352, Fax (580) 254-3585, wwchamber@sbcglobal.net, www.woodwardchamber.com

**Wynnewood** · *Wynnewood C/C* · Tabatha Hayes, Pres., P.O. Box 616, 73098, P 2,400, M 50, (405) 665-4466, wynnewoodokla@sbcglobal.net, www.wynnewoodokla.com

**Yale** · *Yale C/C* · Cindy White, Pres., P.O. Box 132, 74085, P 1,342, M 30, (918) 387-2406, (918) 387-2444

**Yukon** · *Yukon C/C* · Sandy Meier, Dir., 510 Elm, 73099, P 25,000, M 400, (405) 354-3567, Fax (405) 350-0724, chamber@yukoncc.com, www.yukoncc.com

# Oregon

**Oregon State C of C** · Dave Hauser, Admin., P.O. Box 1107, Eugene, 97440, M 33,000, (541) 484-1314, Fax (541) 484-4942, www.oregonstatechamber.org.

**Albany** · *Albany Area C/C* · Janet Steele, Pres., 435 W. First Ave., P.O. Box 548, 97321, P 48,000, M 710, (541) 926-1517, Fax (541) 926-7064, info@albanychamber.com, www.albanychamber.com.

**Arlington** · *Arlington C/C* · Julius Courtney, Pres., P.O. Box 202, 97812, P 550, M 30, (541) 454-2636, www.visitarlington.us

**Ashland** · *Ashland C/C* · Sandra Slattery, Exec. Dir., 110 E. Main St., P.O. Box 1360, 97520, P 20,000, M 700, (541) 482-3486, Fax (541) 482-2350, katharine@ashlandchamber.com, www.ashland chamber.com

**Astoria** · *Astoria-Warrenton Area C/C* · Skip Hauke, Exec. Dir., 111 W. Marine Dr., P.O. Box 176, 97103, P 16,000, M 650, (503) 325-6311, (800) 875-6807, Fax (503) 325-9767, oldoregon@ charterinternet.com, www.oldoregon.com.

**Baker City** · *Baker County Chamber & Visitor Bur.* · Debi Bainter, Exec. Dir., 490 Campbell St., 97814, P 10,000, M 420, (541) 523-5855, (800) 523-1235, Fax (541) 523-9187, info@ visitbaker.com, www.visitbaker.com

**Bandon** · *Bandon C/C* · Julie Miller, Dir., 300 S.E. Second, P.O. Box 1515, 97411, P 3,000, M 385, (541) 347-9616, Fax (541) 347-7006, bandoncc@mycomspan.com, www.bandon.com

**Banks** · *Banks C/C* · Ray Deeth, Admin., P.O. Box 206, 97106, P 1,400, M 60, (503) 324-1081, www.oregonbankschamber.com

**Beaver** · *see Cloverdale*

**Beaverton** · *Beaverton Area C/C* · Lorraine Clarno, Pres., 12655 S.W. Center St. #140, 97005, P 88,000, M 725, (503) 644-0123, Fax (503) 526-0349, info@beaverton.org, www.beaverton.org

**Bend** · *Bend C/C* · Tim Casey, Pres./CEO, 777 N.W. Wall St. #200, 97701, P 80,000, M 1,550, (541) 382-3221, (800) 905-BEND, Fax (541) 385-9929, info@bendchamber.org, www.bendchamber.org

**Blaine** · *see Cloverdale*

**Boardman** · *Boardman C/C* · Diane Wolfe, CEO, 206 N. Main St., P.O. Box 1, 97818, P 3,400, M 178, (541) 481-3014, Fax (541) 481-2733, boardmanchamber@centurytel.net, www.boardman chamber.com.

**Boring** · *see Milwaukie*

**Brookings** · *Brookings-Harbor C/C* · Les Cohen, Pres./CEO, 16330 Lower Harbor Rd., P.O. Box 940, 97415, P 13,500, M 370, (541) 469-3181, (800) 535-9469, Fax (541) 469-4094, www. brookingsor.com

**Brownsville** · *Brownsville Comm. C/C* · Sharon McCoy, Pres., P.O. Box 161, 97327, P 1,700, M 55, (541) 466-5709, brownsvil-lechamber@hotmail.com, www.historicbrownsville.com

**Burns** · *Harney County C/C* · 484 N. Broadway, 97720, P 7,300, M 210, (541) 573-2636, Fax (541) 573-3408, director@harney-county.com, www.harneycounty.com

**Canby** · *Canby Area C/C* · Bev Doolittle, Exec. Dir., 191 S.E. 2nd Ave., P.O. Box 35, 97013, P 16,000, M 325, (503) 266-4600, Fax (503) 266-4338, chamber@canby.com, www.canbyareachamber.org.

**Cannon Beach** · *Cannon Beach C/C & Info. Center* · Kim Bosse, Dir., 207 Spruce St., P.O. Box 64, 97110, P 1,600, M 265, (503) 436-2623, Fax (503) 436-0910, chamber@cannonbeach.org, www.cannonbeach.org

**Canyonville** · *Canyonville C/C* · Judy Coleman, Pres., P.O. Box 1028, 97417, P 1,649, M 50, (541) 839-4282, www.canyonville chamber.org

**Cave Junction** · *Illinois Valley C/C* · Don Moore, Pres., P.O. Box 312, 97523, P 18,000, M 150, (541) 592-3326, Fax (541) 592-4077, ivchamberofcommerce@cavenet.com, www.cavejunctionoregon.com

**Central Point** · *Central Point C/C & Visitors Center* · Cindy Hudson, Admin., 150 Manzanita St., 97502, P 19,500, M 180, (541) 664-5301, Fax (541) 664-3667, cpchamber@qwestoffice.net, www.centralpointchamber.org

**Christmas Valley** · *Christmas Valley C/C* · Lindy Simmons, Pres., P.O. Box 65, 97641, P 3,000, M 135, (541) 576-3838, Fax (541) 576-3838, info@christmasvalley.org, www.christmasvalley.org

**Clackamas** · *African American C/C of Oregon* · Roy Jay, Pres./ CEO, P.O. Box 2979, 97015, P 1,300,000, M 916, (503) 244-5794, (800) 909-2882, Fax (503) 293-2094, blackchamber@usa.net, www.blackchamber.info

**Clackamas** · *see Milwaukie*

**Clatskanie** · *Clatskanie C/C* · John Moore, Pres., 155 W. Columbia River Hwy., P.O. Box 635, 97016, P 1,800, M 60, (503) 728-2502, Fax (503) 728-2135, www.clatskanie.com

**Cloverdale** · *Pacific City-Nestucca Valley C/C* · Kitty Poore, Pres., P.O. Box 75, 97112, P 1,027, M 112, (503) 392-4340, Fax (503) 965-6579, manager@pcnvchamber.org, www.pacificcity.com

**Columbia City** · *see St. Helens*

**Condon** · *Condon C/C* · Nichole Schott, Pres., 128 S. Main St., P.O. Box 315, 97823, P 750, M 50, (541) 384-7777, condonchamber@ hotmail.com, www.discovercondon.com

**Coos Bay** · *Bay Area C/C & Visitors Center* · Timm Slater, Exec. Dir., 145 Central Ave., 97420, P 32,000, M 650, (541) 266-0868, (800) 824-8486, Fax (541) 267-6704, timmslater@oregonsba-yarea.org, www.oregonsbayarea.org

**Coquille** · *Coquille C of C & Visitor Info. Center* · Terry Mai, Dir., 119 N. Birch St., 97423, P 4,300, M 100, (541) 396-3414, Fax (541) 824-0103, coquillechamber@myspan.com, www.coquillechamber.org

**Cornelius** · *Cornelius C/C* · Jenny Garner, Exec. Dir., 120 N. 13th Ave., P.O. Box 681, 97113, P 10,785, M 70, (503) 359-4037, Fax (503) 992-1997, info@corneliuschamber.com, www.cornelius chamber.com

**Corvallis** · *Corvallis Benton Chamber Coalition* · Mysty Rusk, Pres., 420 N.W. 2nd St., 97330, P 54,890, M 700, (541) 757-1505, Fax (541) 766-2996, info@cbchambercoalition.com, www. cbchambercoalition.com

**Cottage Grove** · *Cottage Grove Area C/C* · Marc Bass, Exec. Dir., 700 E. Gibbs #C, 97424, P 9,100, M 255, (541) 942-2411, Fax (541) 767-0783, info@cgchamber.com, www.cgchamber.com.

**Creswell** · *Creswell C/C* · Wendy Locke, Ofc. Mgr., 99 S. 1st St., P.O. Box 577, 97426, P 4,500, M 100, (541) 895-5161, Fax (541) 895-5161, creswell-cc@centurytel.net, www.creswellchamber. com

**Crooked River Ranch** · *Crooked River Ranch C/C* · Hope Johnson, Exec. Dir., P.O. Box 1502, 97760, P 4,500, M 150, (541) 923-2679, info@crrchamber.com, www.crrchamber.com

**Dallas** · *Dallas Area C/C & Visitors Center* · Chelsea Pope, Exec. Dir., 119 S.W. Court St., P.O. Box 377, 97338, P 15,000, M 260, (503) 623-2564, Fax (503) 623-8936, chamber@dallasoregon.org, www.dallasoregon.org

**Damascus** · *see Milwaukie*

**Deer Island** · *see St. Helens*

**Depoe Bay** · *Depoe Bay C/C* · Carole Barkhurst, Mgr., 223 S.W. Hwy. 101 #B, P.O. Box 21, 97341, P 1,174, M 160, (541) 765-2889, Fax (541) 765-2836, info@depoebaychamber.org, www.depoe baychamber.org.

WHALE WATCHING CAPITOL OF OREGON. APRIL– WOODEN BOAT SHOW. SEPTEMBER–INDIAN SALMON BAKE. YEAR-ROUND STORMS AND SUNSETS.

**Drain** · *Drain C/C* · Becky Drescher, Pres., P.O. Box 885, 97435, P 1,100, M 60, (541) 836-2166, www.354.com/drain

**Eagle Point** · *Eagle Point C/C* · Pat Jacobson, Pres., P.O. Box 1539, 97524, P 8,700, M 55, (541) 826-6945, info@eaglepoint chamber.org, www.eaglepointchamber.org

**Elgin** · *Elgin C/C* · P.O. Box 1001, 97827, P 1,700, M 40, (541) 786-1770

**Enterprise** · *Wallowa County C/C* · Vicki Searles, Exec. Dir., 115 Tejaka Ln., P.O. Box 427, 97828, P 7,200, M 325, (541) 426-4622, (800) 585-4121, Fax (541) 426-2032, info@wallowacounty.org, www.wallowacountychamber.com.

**Estacada** · *Estacada-Clackamas River Area C/C* · Rob Gaskill, Pres., 475 S.E. Main, P.O. Box 298, 97023, P 2,855, M 164, (503) 630-3483, estacadachamber@cascadeaccess.com, www.estacada chamber.org

**Eugene** · *Eugene Area C/C* · David Hauser CCE, Pres., 1401 Willamette St., P.O. Box 1107, 97440, P 154,620, M 1,230, (541) 484-1314, Fax (541) 484-4942, info@eugenechamber.com, www.eugenechamber.com.

**Florence** · *Florence Area C/C* · Kady Sneddon, Dir., 290 Hwy. 101, 97439, P 20,000, M 349, (541) 997-3128, Fax (541) 997-4101, florence@oregonfast.net, www.florencechamber.com

**Forest Grove** · *Forest Grove C/C* · Terri Koerner, Exec. Dir., 2417 Pacific Ave., 97116, P 20,000, M 215, (503) 357-3006, Fax (503) 357-2367, info@fgchamber.org, www.fgchamber.org.

**Gladstone** · *see Milwaukie*

**Gold Beach** · *Gold Beach C/C* · Elyse Power, Dir., 29692 Ellensburg Ave. #7, Gold Rush Center, 97444, P 2,500, M 270, (541) 247-0923, Fax (541) 247-4394, info@goldbeachchamber. com, www.goldbeachchamber.com

**Grants Pass** · *Grants Pass/Josephine County C/C* · Jon Jordan, Pres./CEO, 1995 N.W. Vine St., P.O. Box 970, 97528, P 78,000, M 800, (541) 476-7717, (800) 547-5927, Fax (541) 476-9574, gpcoc@grantspasschamber.org, www.grantspasschamber.org

**Gresham** · *Gresham Area C/C* · Carol Nielsen-Hood, CEO, 701 N.E. Hood Ave., P.O. Box 1768, 97030, P 99,000, M 800, (503) 665-1131, Fax (503) 666-1041, gacc@greshamchamber.org, www.greshamchamber.org.

**Happy Valley** · *see Milwaukie*

**Harney County** · *see Burns*

**Harrisburg** · *see Junction City*

**Hebo** · *see Cloverdale*

**Hemlock** · *see Cloverdale*

**Heppner** · *Heppner C/C* · Sheryl Bates, Exec. Dir., 123 W. May St., P.O. Box 1232, 97836, P 1,450, M 80, (541) 676-5536, Fax (541) 676-9650, heppnerchamber@centurytel.net, www.heppnerchamber.com

**Hermiston** · *Greater Hermiston C/C* · Debbie Pedro, Exec. Dir., 415 S. Hwy. 395, P.O. Box 185, 97838, P 15,785, M 400, (541) 567-6151, Fax (541) 564-9109, info@hermistonchamber.com, www. hermistonchamber.com

**Hillsboro** · *Hillsboro C/C* · Deanna Palm, Pres., 5193 N.E. Elam Young Pkwy. #A, 97124, P 89,285, M 800, (503) 648-1102, Fax (503) 681-0535, info@hillchamber.org, www.hillchamber.org.

**Hood River** · *Hood River County C/C* · Mary Closson, Exec. Dir., 720 E. Port Marina Dr., 97031, P 21,000, M 490, (541) 386-2000, (800) 366-3530, Fax (541) 386-2057, info@hoodriver.org, www. hoodriver.org

**Huntington** · *Huntington C/C* · Claudia Stacy, Pres., P.O. Box 280, 97907, P 500, M 7, (541) 869-2111

**Illinois Valley** · *see Cave Junction*

**Independence** · *see Monmouth*

**Jacksonville** · *Jacksonville C of C & Visitors Info.* · Sandi Torrey, Dir. of Visitor Center, P.O. Box 33, 97530, P 2,800, M 130, (541) 899-8118, Fax (541) 899-4462, chamber@jacksonvilleoregon.org, www.jacksonvilleoregon.org

**John Day** · *Grant County C/C & Visitors Center* · Sharon Mogg, Exec. Dir., 301 W. Main St., 97845, P 7,750, M 150, (541) 575-0547, (800) 769-5664, Fax (541) 575-1932, grant@grantcounty.cc, www. grantcounty.cc

**Johnson City** · *see Milwaukie*

**Joseph** · *Joseph C/C* · 102 E. 1st, P.O. Box 13, 97846, P 1,280, M 110, (541) 432-1015, Fax (541) 432-1015, cjdays@eoni.com, www.chiefjosephdays.com

**Junction City** · *Junction City-Harrisburg C/C* · Taryl Perry, Exec. Dir., 585 Greenwood St., 97448, P 9,500, M 230, (541) 998-6154, Fax (541) 998-1037, info@jch-chamber.org, www.jch-chamber.org.

**Keizer** · *Keizer C/C* · Christine Dieker, Exec. Dir., 980 Chemawa Rd. N.E., 97303, P 34,719, M 426, (503) 393-9111, Fax (503) 393-1003, info@keizerchamber.com, www.keizerchamber.com.

**Klamath Falls** · *Klamath County C/C* · Charles Massie, Exec. Dir., 203 Riverside Dr., 97601, P 69,000, M 610, (541) 884-5193, (877) KLAMATH, Fax (541) 884-5195, inquiry@klamath.org, www. klamath.org.

**La Grande** · *Union County C/C* · Judy Hector, Exec. Dir., 102 Elm St., 97850, P 26,000, M 400, (541) 963-8588, (800) 848-9969, Fax (541) 963-3936, director@unioncountychamber.org, www. unioncountychamber.org

**La Pine** · *La Pine C of C & Visitor Center* · Dan Varcoe, Exec. Dir., 51425 Hwy. 97 #A, P.O. Box 616, 97739, P 16,600, M 250, (541) 536-9771, Fax (541) 536-8410, director@lapine.org, www.lapine.org

**Lake Oswego** · *Lake Oswego C/C* · Jerry L. Wheeler Sr., CEO, 242 B Ave., P.O. Box 368, 97034, P 39,000, M 722, (503) 636-3634, (866) 341-5253, Fax (503) 636-7427, info@lake-oswego.com, www.lake-oswego.com

**Lakeside** · *Lakeside C/C* · Mrs. Jonie Reeder, Treas., P.O. Box 333, 97449, P 1,200, M 50, (541) 759-3981, lkchamber@presys.com, www.lakesideoregonchambers.com

**Lakeview** · *Lake County C/C* · Caro Johnson, Exec. Dir., 126 North E St., 97630, P 7,600, M 225, (541) 947-6040, (877) 947-6040, Fax (541) 947-4892, information@lakecountychamber.org, www.lakecountychamber.org

**Lebanon** · *Lebanon Area C/C* · Shelley Garrett, Pres./CEO, 1040 Park St., 97355, P 15,000, M 326, (541) 258-7164, (877) 447-8873, Fax (541) 258-7166, shelley@lebanon-chamber.org, www. lebanon-chamber.org

**Lincoln City** · *Lincoln City C/C* · Gian Paolo Mammone, Exec. Dir., 4039 N.W. Logan Rd. & Hwy. 101, P.O. Box 787, 97367, P 7,437, M 420, (541) 994-3070, Fax (541) 994-8339, info@lcchamber.com, www.lcchamber.com

**Madras** · *Madras-Jefferson County C/C* · Holli VanWert, Exec. Dir., 274 S.W. 4th St., P.O. Box 770, 97741, P 21,065, M 350, (541) 475-2350, (800) 967-3564, Fax (541) 475-4341, office@madras chamber.com, www.madraschamber.com

**Manzanita** · *see Wheeler*

**McMinnville** · *McMinnville C/C* · 417 N.W. Adams St., 97128, P 32,000, M 460, (503) 472-6196, Fax (503) 472-6198, chamber info@mcminnville.org, www.mcminnville.org.

**Medford** · *The Chamber of Medford/Jackson County* · Brad S. Hicks, Pres./CEO, 101 E. 8th St., 97501, P 202,310, M 1,650, (541) 779-4847, Fax (541) 776-4808, business@medfordchamber.com, www.medfordchamber.com.

**Mill City** · *North Santiam C/C* · Nicole Miller, Exec. Dir., P.O. Box 222, 97360, P 7,500, M 100, (503) 897-4500, www.nschamber.org

**Milton-Freewater** · *Milton-Freewater Area C/C* · Cheryl York, Exec. Dir., 157 S. Columbia, 97862, P 6,500, M 160, (541) 938-5563, Fax (541) 938-5564, www.mfchamber.com

**Milwaukie** · *North Clackamas County C/C* · Wilda Parks ACE, Pres./CEO, 7740 S.E. Harmony Rd., 97222, P 170,000, M 700, (503) 654-7777, Fax (503) 653-9515, info@yourchamber.com, www.yourchamber.com

**Molalla** · *Molalla Area C/C* · Sheri Kelly, Exec. Dir., 105 E. Main St. #3, P.O. Box 578, 97038, P 7,130, M 200, (503) 829-6941, Fax (503) 829-7949, macc@molalla.net, www.molallachamber.com

**Monmouth** · *Monmouth-Independence C/C* · Amberly Van Winkle, Mgr., 309 N. Pacific Ave., 97361, P 16,500, M 175, (503) 838-4268, Fax (503) 838-6658, micc@micc-or.org, www.mitownchamber.org.

**Mount Angel** · *Mount Angel C/C* · Mary Grant, Pres., P.O. Box 221, 97362, P 3,700, M 120, (503) 845-9440, Fax (503) 845-6190, maureen@mtangeltel.org, www.mtangelchamber.org

**Mount Hood** · *see Welches*

**Myrtle Creek** · *Myrtle Creek - Tri City Area C/C* · Linda Johnson, Pres., P.O. Box 31, 97457, P 8,000, M 100, (541) 863-3037, president@ myrtlecreekchamber.com, www.myrtlecreekchamber.com

**Nehalem** · *see Wheeler*

**Neskowin** · *see Cloverdale*

**Newberg** · *Chehalem Valley C/C* · Sheryl Kelsh, Exec. Dir., 415 E. Sheridan St., 97132, P 20,500, M 460, (503) 538-2014, Fax (503) 538-2463, info@chehalemvalley.org, www.chehalemvalley.org

**Newport** · *Greater Newport C/C* · Lorna Davis, Exec. Dir., 555 S.W. Coast Hwy., 97365, P 10,000, M 730, (541) 265-8801, (800) 262-7844, Fax (541) 265-5589, info@newportchamber.org, www.newportchamber.org.

**North Bend** · *see Coos Bay*

**North Plains** · *North Plains C/C* · P.O. Box 152, 97133, P 1,700, M 51, (503) 647-2207, www.northplainschamberofcommerce.org

**Nyssa** · *Nyssa C/C* · Larry Wilson, Pres., 105 Main St., 97913, P 3,300, M 80, (541) 372-3091, Fax (541) 372-3091, nyssa chamber@nyssachamber.com, www.nyssachamber.com

**Oakridge** · *Oakridge-Westfir Area C/C* · Randy Dreiling, Exec. Dir., P.O. Box 217, 97463, P 5,000, M 75, (541) 782-4146, www. oakridgechamber.com

**Ontario** · *Ontario C/C* · John Breidenbach, Exec. Dir., 876 S.W. 4th Ave., 97914, P 11,000, M 370, (541) 889-8012, (866) 989-8012, Fax (541) 889-8331, ontvcb@fmtc.com, www.ontariochamber.com

**Oregon City** · *Oregon City C/C* · Amber Holveck, Exec. Dir., 1201 Washington St., P.O. Box 226, 97045, P 30,000, M 350, (503) 656-1619, Fax (503) 656-2274, chamberinfo@oregoncity.org, www. oregoncity.org

**Pacific City** · *see Cloverdale*

**Pendleton** · *Pendleton C/C* · Leslie Carnes, Exec. Dir., 501 S. Main, 97801, P 16,600, M 470, (541) 276-7411, (800) 547-8911, Fax (541) 276-8849, pendleton@pendletonchamber.com, www. pendletonchamber.com

**Philomath** · *Philomath Area C/C* · Mona Luebbert, Exec. Dir., 2395 Main St., P.O. Box 606, 97370, P 4,400, M 100, (541) 929-2454, director@philomathchamber.org, www.philomathchamber.org

**Phoenix** · *Phoenix C of C & Info. Center* · 205 Fern Valley Rd. #M-1, P.O. Box 998, 97535, P 4,740, M 120, (541) 535-6956, Fax (541) 535-5210, phoenixoregonchamber@opusnet.com, www. phoenixoregonchamber.org

**Port Orford** · *Port Orford C/C* · 520 W. Jefferson St., P.O. Box 637, 97465, P 1,200, M 102, (541) 332-8055, chamber@ portorfordchamber.com, www.portorfordchamber.com, www. discoverportorford.com

**Portland** · *Portland Bus. Alliance-Greater Portland's C/C* · Sandra McDonough, Pres./CEO, 200 S.W. Market St. #1770, 97201, P 2,121,910, M 1,300, (503) 224-8684, Fax (503) 323-9186, info@ portlandalliance.com, www.portlandalliance.com

**Prineville** · *Prineville-Crook County C/C & Visitors Center* · Brandi Hereford, Exec. Dir., 390 N.E. Fairview, 97754, P 20,000, M 425, (541) 447-6304, Fax (541) 447-6537, info@visitprineville. com, www.visitprineville.com

**Ranier** · *Ranier C/C* · Judith Taylor, Pres., P.O. Box 1085, 97048, P 1,750, M 50, (503) 556-7212, Fax (503) 556-1855, www. rainier97048.org

**Redmond** · *Redmond Chamber & CVB* · Eric Sande, Exec. Dir., 446 S.W. 7th St., 97756, P 25,000, M 780, (541) 923-5191, Fax (541) 923-6442, info@visitredmondoregon.com, www.visit redmondoregon.com.

**Reedsport** · *Reedsport/Winchester Bay C/C* · Robin Dollar, Ofc. Mgr., 855 Hwy. Ave., P.O. Box 11, 97467, P 5,000, M 150, (541) 271-3495, (800) 247-2155, Fax (541) 271-3496, reewbycc@ charterinternet.com, www.reedsportcc.org.

**Rockaway Beach** · *Rockaway Beach C/C* · Lynda Holm, V.P., 103 S. 1st St., P.O. Box 198, 97136, P 1,200, M 75, (503) 355-8108, info@rockawaybeach.net, www.rockawaybeach.net.

**Rogue River** · *Rogue River Area C/C* · 8898 Rogue River Hwy., P.O. Box 457, 97537, P 2,085, M 100, (541) 582-0242, info@ rrchamber.cc, www.rrchamber.cc

**Roseburg** · *Roseburg Area C/C* · Debbie Fromdahl, Exec. Dir., 410 S.E. Spruce St., P.O. Box 1026, 97470, P 40,000, M 660, (541) 672-2648, (800) 444-9584, Fax (541) 673-7868, debbie@roseburg areachamber.org, www.roseburgareachamber.org.

**Salem** · *Salem Area C/C* · Michael T. McLaran, CEO, 1110 Commercial St. N.E., 97301, P 146,000, M 1,350, (503) 581-1466, Fax (503) 581-0972, info@salemchamber.org, www.salemchamber.org.

**Sandlake** · *see Cloverdale*

**Sandy** · *Sandy Area C/C* · Hollis MacLean-Wenzel, Exec. Dir., 39345 Pioneer Blvd., P.O. Box 536, 97055, P 7,700, M 325, (503) 668-4006, chamber@sandyoregonchamber.org, www.sandy oregonchamber.org

**Scappoose** · *see St. Helens*

**Seaside** · *Seaside C/C* · Al Smiles, Exec. Dir., 7 N. Roosevelt, P.O. Box 7, 97138, P 6,300, M 360, (503) 738-6391, (800) 444-6740, Fax (503) 738-5732, info@seasidechamber.com, www.seaside chamber.com

U.S. Chambers of Commerce

**Sherwood** · *Sherwood C/C* · Elizabeth Eckstein, Ofc. Mgr., 16065 S.W. Railroad St., P.O. Box 805, 97140, P 16,700, M 380, (503) 625-7800, Fax (503) 625-7550, chamber@sherwoodchamber.org, www.sherwoodchamber.org

**Silverton** · *Silverton Area C/C* · Stacy Palmer, Exec. Dir., 426 S. Water St., P.O. Box 257, 97381, P 9,500, M 290, (503) 873-5615, Fax (503) 873-7144, info@silvertonchamber.org, www.silverton chamber.org.

**Sisters** · *Sisters Area C/C* · Erin Borla, Exec. Dir., 291 E. Main Ave., P.O. Box 430, 97759, P 9,000, M 400, (541) 549-0251, Fax (541) 549-4253, info@sisterschamber.com, www.sisterschamber.com

**Springfield** · *Springfield Area C/C* · Dan Egan, Exec. Dir., 101 South A St., P.O. Box 155, 97477, P 58,000, M 936, (541) 746-1651, Fax (541) 726-4727, general@springfield-chamber.org, www. springfield-chamber.org

**St. Helens** · *South Columbia County C/C* · 2194 Columbia Blvd., 97051, P 25,000, M 250, (503) 397-0685, Fax (503) 397-7196, info@sccchamber.org, www.sccchamber.org

**Stayton** · *Stayton-Sublimity C/C* · Kelly Schreiber, Exec. Dir., 175 E. High St., P.O. Box 121, 97383, P 10,000, M 320, (503) 769-3464, Fax (503) 769-3463, sscoc@wvi.com, www.stayton sublimitychamber.org

**Sunriver** · *Sunriver Area C/C* · P.O. Box 3246, 97707, P 4,500, M 250, (541) 593-8149, Fax (541) 593-3581, info@sunriver chamber.com, www.sunriverchamber.com

**Sutherlin** · *Sutherlin C/C* · Gary Lund, Pres., 100 W. Central, P.O. Box 1404, 97479, P 7,300, M 111, (541) 580-1122, www. sutherlinchamber.com

**Sweet Home** · *Sweet Home C/C* · Andrea Culy, Int. Exec. Dir., 1575 Main St., 97386, P 8,300, M 150, (541) 367-6186, Fax (541) 367-6150, shchamber@comcast.net, www.sweethomechamber.org

**The Dalles** · *The Dalles Area C/C* · Dana Schmidling, Exec. Dir., 404 W. 2nd St., 97058, P 22,000, M 500, (541) 296-2231, (800) 255-3385, Fax (541) 296-1688, info@thedalleschamber.com, www.thedalleschamber.com.

**Tierra del Mar** · *see Cloverdale*

**Tigard** · *Tigard Area C/C* · Christopher Zoucha, CEO, 12345 S.W. Main St., 97223, P 49,500, M 430, (503) 639-1656, Fax (503) 639-6302, info@tigardchamber.org, www.tigardchamber.org

**Tillamook** · *Tillamook Area C/C* · Andy Neal, Exec. Dir., 3705 Hwy. 101 N., 97141, P 4,500, M 300, (503) 842-7525, Fax (503) 842-7526, tillchamber@oregoncoast.com, www.gotillamook.com.

**Toledo** · *Toledo C/C* · P.O. Box 249, 97391, P 3,580, M 117, (541) 336-3183, info@visittoledooregon.com, www.visittoledooregon.com

**Troutdale** · *West Columbia Gorge C/C* · Alice Freuler, Exec. Dir., 107 E. Historic Columbia River Hwy., P.O. Box 245, 97060, P 15,000, M 200, (503) 669-7473, Fax (503) 492-3613, info@westcolumbia gorgechamber.com, www.westcolumbiagorgechamber.com

**Tualatin** · *Tualatin C/C* · Linda Moholt, CEO, 18791 S.W. Martinazzi Ave., P.O. Box 701, 97062, P 26,000, M 325, (503) 692-0780, Fax (503) 692-6955, info@tualatinchamber.com, www.tualatinchamber.com

**Umatilla** · *Umatilla C/C* · CJ Saunders-Cribbs, Ofc. Mgr., P.O. Box 67, 97882, P 6,000, M 65, (541) 922-4825, Fax (541) 922-4825, umatillachamber@eoni.com, www.umatillachamber.com

**Vale** · *Vale C/C* · Brian Wolfe, Pres., 252 B St. W., P.O. Box 661, 97918, P 1,990, M 80, (541) 473-3133, www.valeoregon.org

**Veneta** · *Fern Ridge C/C* · Charlie Hamada, Pres., 24949 Hwy. 126, P.O. Box 335, 97487, P 4,700, M 140, (541) 935-8443, Fax (541) 935-1164, staff@fernridgechamber.com, www.fernridge chamber.com

**Vernonia** · *Vernonia Area C/C* · Donna Webb, Pres., 1001 Bridge St., 97064, P 2,300, M 65, (503) 429-6081, info@vernoniachamber. org, www.vernoniachamber.org

**Waldport** · *Waldport C/C & Visitor Center* · Patty Glas, Pres., 620 N.W. Spring St., P.O. Box 669, 97394, P 2,000, M 120, (541) 563-2133, Fax (541) 563-6326, chamber@peak.org, www. waldport-chamber.com

**Warren** · *see St. Helens*

**Wedderburn** · *see Gold Beach*

**Welches** · *Mount Hood Area C/C* · Carol Burk, Pres., 24403 E. Welches Rd. #103, P.O. Box 819, 97067, P 8,000, M 138, (503) 622-3017, Fax (503) 622-3163, chamber@mthood.org, www. mthood.org

**West Linn** · *West Linn C/C* · 21420 Willamette Dr., 97068, P 24,482, M 240, (503) 655-6744, chamberinfo@westlinnchamber. com, www.westlinnchamber.com

**Westfir** · *see Oakridge*

**Wheeler** · *Nehalem Bay Area C/C* · Deanna Hendricks, Dir., P.O. Box 601, 97147, P 1,200, M 95, (503) 368-5100, Fax (503) 368-4641, nehalem@nehalemtel.net, www.nehalembaychamber.com

**Willamina** · *Willamina Coastal Hills C/C* · P.O. Box 569, 97396, P 1,850, M 35, (503) 876-5777, Fax (503) 876-6132, www. willamina.org

**Wilsonville** · *Wilsonville C/C* · Steve Gilmore, CEO, 29600 S.W. Park Pl., P.O. Box 3737, 97070, P 16,850, M 390, (503) 682-0411, (800) 647-3843, Fax (503) 682-4189, info@wilsonvillechamber. com, www.wilsonvillechamber.com.

**Winchester Bay** · *see Reedsport*

**Winston** · *Winston-Dillard Area C/C & Visitors Info. Center* · Dan Strasser, Pres., 30 N.W. Glenhart, P.O. Box 68, 97496, P 10,000, M 125, (541) 679-0118, Fax (541) 679-4270, winstonvic@charter. net, www.winstonoregon.net

**Woodburn** · *Woodburn Area C/C* · Don Judson, Exec. Dir., 124 W. Lincoln St., P.O. Box 194, 97071, P 22,000, M 300, (503) 982-8221, Fax (503) 982-8410, welcome@woodburnchamber.org, www. woodburnchamber.org.

**Woods** · *see Cloverdale*

**Yachats** · *Yachats Area C/C & Visitors Center* · P.O. Box 728, 97498, P 650, M 205, (541) 547-3530, (800) 929-0477, info@ yachats.org, www.yachats.org

# Pennsylvania

**Harrisburg Reg. C/C** · David E. Black, Pres./CEO, 3211 N. Front St., Ste. 201, Harrisburg, 17110, P 550,000, M 1,700, (717) 232-4099, (877) 883-8339, Fax (717) 232-5184, frontdesk@hbgrc.org, www.HarrisburgRegionalChamber.org

**Adams County** · *see Gettysburg*

**Allegheny** · *see Pittsburgh*

**Allentown** · *Greater Lehigh Valley C/C* · Tony Iannelli, Pres., 840 Hamilton St., Ste. 205, 18101, P 579,156, M 5,000, (610) 841-4582, Fax (610) 437-4907, info@lehighvalleychamber.org, www. lehighvalleychamber.org

**Altoona** · *Blair County C/C* · Joseph D. Hurd, Exec. Dir., 3900 Industrial Park Dr., Ste. 12, 16602, P 135,000, M 1,000, (814) 943-8151, Fax (814) 943-5239, chamber@blairchamber.com, www.blairchamber.com

**Ambridge** · *Ambridge Area C/C* · 562 Merchant St., 15003, P 8,000, M 160, (724) 266-3040, www.ambridgechamberof commerce.com

**Antrim** · *see Greencastle*

**Archbald** · *see Carbondale*

**Aspinwall** · *Aspinwall C/C* · Harold Sankey, Pres., 217 Commercial Ave., 15215, P 2,960, M 75, (412) 781-0213, www.aspinwallpa.com

**Athens** · *see Sayre*

**Audubon** · *see King of Prussia*

**Baldwin** · *see Pittsburgh-Brentwood Baldwin Whitehall C/C*

**Bangor** · *see Pen Argyl*

**Beaver** · *Beaver County C/C* · Diane Dornenburg, Pres., 300 S. Walnut Ln., Ste. 202, 15009, P 185,000, M 600, (724) 775-3944, Fax (724) 728-9737, info@bcchamber.com, www.bcchamber.com

**Bedford** · *Bedford County C/C* · Carol H. Snyder, Exec. Dir., 137 E. Pitt St., 15522, P 50,000, M 610, (814) 623-2233, Fax (814) 623-6089, info@bedfordcountychamber.org, www.bedfordcounty chamber.org.

**Bellefonte** · *Bellefonte Intervalley Area C/C* · Gary Hoover, Exec. Dir., Train Station, 320 W. High St., 16823, P 30,000, M 230, (814) 355-2917, Fax (814) 355-2761, bellefontecoc@aol.com, www.bellefonte.com

**Bellevue** · *North Suburban C/C* · Connie Rankin, 547 Lincoln Ave., 15202, P 30,000, M 60, (412) 761-2113, www.borough. bellevue.pa.us

**Bensalem** · *see Fairless Hills*

**Berlin** · *see Somerset*

**Berwick** · *see Bloomsburg*

**Bethlehem** · *see Allentown*

**Birdsboro** · *see Pottstown*

**Bloomsburg** · *Columbia Montour C/C* · Edward G. Edwards, Pres., 238 Market St., 17815, P 63,000, M 400, (570) 784-2522, Fax (570) 784-2661, chamber@columbiamontourchamber.com, www.columbiamontourchamber.com

**Boyertown** · *see Pottstown*

**Brackenridge** · *Allegheny Valley C/C* · Mary Bowlin, Pres., 1030 Broadview Blvd., Ste. 1, 15014, P 50,000, M 400, (724) 224-3400, Fax (724) 224-3442, staff@alleghenyvalleychamber.com, www.alleghenyvalleychamber.com

**Bradford** · *Bradford Area C/C* · Diane Sheeley, Exec. Dir., 121 Main St., 16701, P 19,435, M 300, (814) 368-7115, Fax (814) 368-6233, info@bradfordchamber.com, www.bradfordchamber.com

**Brentwood** · *see Pittsburgh-Brentwood Baldwin Whitehall C/C*

**Bridgeport** · *see King of Prussia*

**Bridgeville** · *see Pittsburgh-South West Comm. C/C*

**Brockway** · *see DuBois*

**Brookville** · *Brookville Area C/C* · 173 Main St., Ste. 100, 15825, P 4,200, M 285, (814) 849-8448, Fax (814) 849-8455, executive director@brookvillechamber.com, www.brookvillechamber.com

**Brownsville** · *Greater Brownsville Area C/C* · 325 Market St., 15417, P 6,000, M 70, (724) 785-4160, Fax (724) 785-5631

**Butler** · *Butler County C/C* · Stan Kosciuszko, Pres., 101 E. Diamond St., Ste. 116, P.O. Box 1082, 16003, P 184,000, M 650, (724) 283-2222, Fax (724) 283-0224, www.butlercountychamber.com.

**California** · *California Area C/C* · Mark Koehler, Pres., P.O. Box 311, 15419, P 5,207, M 20, (724) 938-2305

**Camp Hill** · *West Shore C/C* · Edward M. Messner, Pres., 4211 Trindle Rd., 17011, P 172,000, M 1,100, (717) 761-0702, Fax (717) 761-4315, wschamber@wschamber.org, www.wschamber.org.

**Canonsburg** · *Greater Canonsburg C/C* · Consuelo Fossum, Admin. Secy., 169 E. Pike St., 15317, P 12,000, M 200, (724) 745-1812, Fax (724) 745-5211, info@canonchamber.com, www.canonchamber.com

**Canton** · *Canton Area C/C* · Jodi Wesneski, Pres., P.O. Box 153, 17724, P 2,000, M 54, (570) 364-2600, cantonareachamberofcom merce@yahoo.com, www.cantonareachamberofcommerce.com

**Carbondale** · *Greater Carbondale C/C* · Lorraine Parise, Pres., 27 N. Main St., 18407, P 11,000, M 400, (570) 282-1690, Fax (570) 282-1206, info@carbondale-pa-coc.com, www.carbondale-pa-coc.com

**Carlisle** · *Greater Carlisle Area C/C* · Michelle Crowley, Pres., 212 N. Hanover St., P.O. Box 572, 17013, P 72,000, M 670, (717) 243-4515, Fax (717) 243-4446, info@carlislechamber.org, www.carlislechamber.org.

**Cecil** · *see Canonsburg*

**Chambersburg** · *Greater Chambersburg C/C* · David G. Sciamanna, Pres., 100 Lincoln Way East #A, 17201, P 50,000, M 1,025, (717) 264-7101, Fax (717) 267-0399, chamber@chambersburg.org, www.chambersburg.org

**Champion** · *see Donegal*

**Charleroi** · *Mon Valley Reg. C/C* · Debra Keefer, Exec. Dir., One Chamber Plaza, 15022, P 50,000, M 250, (724) 483-3507, Fax (724) 489-1045, info@mvrchamber.org, www.mvrchamber.org

**Chester County** · *see Malvern*

**Childs** · *see Carbondale*

**Clairton** · *see McKeesport*

**Clarion** · *Clarion Area Chamber of Bus. & Ind.* · Tracy J. Becker, Exec. Dir., 21 N. 6th Ave., 16214, P 43,000, M 272, (814) 226-9161, Fax (814) 226-4903, tracy@clarionpa.com, www.clarionpa.com.

**Clearfield** · *Clearfield C/C* · Amy Potter, Exec. Dir., 125 E. Market St., 16830, P 18,000, M 380, (814) 765-7567, Fax (814) 765-6948, info@clearfieldchamber.com, www.clearfieldchamber.com

**Clifford** · *see Carbondale*

**Clinton County** · *see Lock Haven*

**Coatesville** · *Western Chester County C/C* · Donna Siter, Dir., 50 S. First Ave., 19320, P 12,000, M 275, (610) 384-9550, Fax (610) 384-9550, info@westernchestercounty.com, www.western chestercounty.com

**Collegeville** · *Perkiomen Valley C/C* · Amy Purcell, Dir. of PR, 351 E. Main St., 19426, P 65,000, M 500, (610) 489-6660, Fax (610) 454-1270, info@pvchamber.net, www.pvchamber.net

**Collier Twp.** · *see Pittsburgh-South West Comm. C/C*

**Columbia** · *Susquehanna Valley C/C & Visitors Bur.* · Melissa Glenn, Exec. Dir., 445 Linden St., P.O. Box 510, 17512, P 18,000, M 300, (717) 684-5249, Fax (717) 684-5142, svcc@parivertowns.com, www.parivertowns.com

**Confluence** · *see Somerset*

**Connellsville** · *Greater Connellsville C/C* · June Newill, Ofc. Mgr., 923 W. Crawford Ave., 15425, P 30,000, M 215, (724) 628-5500, Fax (724) 628-5676, info@greaterconnellsville.org, www.greaterconnellsville.org

**Coraopolis** · *see Pittsburgh Airport Area C/C*

**Corry** · *Corry Area C/C* · Pam Brown, Exec. Dir., 221 N. Center St., 16407, P 7,300, M 110, (814) 665-9925, Fax same, cacc@velocity.net, www.corrychamber.org

**Coudersport** · *Coudersport Area C/C* · 6 E. 2nd St., P.O. Box 261, 16915, P 3,000, M 120, (814) 274-8165, Fax (814) 274-8165, cacoc@coudersport.org, www.coudersport.org

**Cranberry Township** · *Cranberry Area C/C* · Kari Ambrass Geyer, Pres., 2525 Rochester Rd. #200, 16066, P 28,200, M 550, (724) 776-4949, Fax (724) 776-5344, info@cranberrychamber.com, www.cranberrychamber.com

**Crescent Township** · *see Pittsburgh Airport Area C/C*

**Cresson** · *Borough of Cresson C/C* · Veronica Harkins, Secy., P.O. Box 113, 16630, P 5,000, M 65, (814) 886-8100, info@cressonarea.com, www.cressonarea.com

**Cressona** · *see Pottsville*

**Danville** · *see Bloomsburg*

**Delmont** · *see Greensburg*

**Donegal** · *Mountain Laurel C/C* · Sarah Harkam, Pres., P.O. Box 154, 15628, P 15,000, M 180, (724) 593-8900, (888) 455-8900, Fax (724) 593-8900, mlcc@lhtot.com, www.mountainlaurelchamber.com

**Donora** · *Donora C/C* · 638 McKean Ave., 15033, P 6,500, M 100, (724) 379-5929

**Dormont** · *see Pittsburgh-South Hills C/C*

**Downingtown** · *Downingtown Area C/C* · Alane Butler, Exec. Dir., 38 W. Lancaster Ave., 19335, P 9,000, M 300, (610) 269-1523, Fax (610) 269-8713, info@downingtownchamber.org, www.downingtownchamber.org

**Doylestown** · *Central Bucks C/C* · Dr. Vail P. Garvin, Exec. Dir., Baliwick #23, 252 W. Swamp Rd., 18901, P 44,984, M 2,600, (215) 348-3913, (215) 345-7051, Fax (215) 348-7154, info@centralbuckschamber.com, www.centralbuckschamber.com.

**Dravosburg** · *Borough of Dravosburg* · Brenda Honick, 226 Maple Ave., 15034, P 2,000, (412) 466-5200, Fax (412) 466-6027

**DuBois** · *DuBois Area C/C & Eco. Dev. Corp.* · Nancy Micks, Pres./CEO, 3 S. Brady St., Ste. 205, 15801, P 38,000, M 480, (814) 371-5010, Fax (814) 371-5005, dacc@duboispachamber.com, www.duboispachamber.com

**Duquesne** · *see McKeesport*

**Eagleville** · *Montgomery County C/C* · Albert Paschall, Managing Dir./CEO, 101 Bill Smith Blvd./Historic King of Prussia Inn, P.O. Box 200, 19408, P 400,000, M 1,800, (610) 265-1776, Fax (610) 265-0473, info@montgomerycountychamber.org, www.montgomerycountychamber.org

**East Bangor** · *see Pen Argyl*

**East Greenville** · *Upper Perkiomen Valley C/C* · Luanne Stauffer, Exec. Dir., 300 Main St., 18041, P 18,638, M 300, (215) 679-3336, Fax (215) 679-2624, info@upvchamber.org, www.upvchamber.org

**Easton** · *see Allentown*

**Elizabethtown** · *Elizabethtown C/C* · Beth Wood Bergman, Exec. Dir., 29 S. Market St., Ste. 101, 17022, P 30,000, M 220, (717) 361-7188, Fax (717) 361-7666, info@elizabethtowncoc.com, www.elizabethtowncoc.com

**Elizabethville** · *Northern Dauphin Reg. C/C* · Mandy Margerum, Secy., 2 W. Main St., P. O. Box 218, 17023, P 15,000, M 70, (717) 362-1240, Fax (717) 362-1392, ndrcc@epix.net, www.ndrcc.org

**Ellwood City** · *Ellwood City Area C/C* · Thomas Stachura, Exec. Dir., 314 Fifth St., 16117, P 8,800, M 205, (724) 758-5501, Fax (724) 758-2143, info@ellwoodchamber.org, www.ellwoodchamber.org.

**Emmaus** · *see Allentown*

**Emporium** · *Cameron County C/C* · Tina Lorson, Exec. Dir., 34 E. Fourth St., 15834, P 5,913, M 92, (814) 486-4314, cameroncountychamber@alltel.net, www.cameroncountychamber.org

**Ephrata** · *Ephrata Area C/C* · Dave Klotz, Pres., 16 E. Main St., Ste. 1, 17522, P 125,000, M 232, (717) 738-9010, Fax (717) 738-9012, info@ephrata-area.org, www.ephrata-area.org

**Erie** · *Erie Reg. Chamber & Growth Partnership* · Jim Dible, Pres./CEO, 208 E. Bayfront Pkwy. #100, 16507, P 276,000, M 850, (814) 454-7191, Fax (814) 459-0241, www.eriepa.com.

**Export** · *see Greensburg*

**Exton** · *Exton Region C/C* · Robert Johnston, Pres., 967 E. Swedesford Rd. #409, 19341, P 50,000, M 650, (610) 644-4985, Fax (610) 644-2370, chamber@ercc.net, www.ercc.net

**Eynon** · *see Carbondale*

**Fairless Hills** · *Lower Bucks County C/C* · Clark L. Shuster, Pres./CEO, 409 Hood Blvd., 19030, P 600,000, M 1,600, (215) 943-7400, Fax (215) 943-7404, info@lbccc.org, www.lbccc.org

**Falls Creek** · *see DuBois*

**Findlay Township** · *see Pittsburgh Airport Area C/C*

**Forest City** · *see Carbondale*

**Forest Hills** · *see McKeesport*

**Franklin** · *Franklin Area C/C* · Lynn Cochran, Exec. Dir., 1259 Liberty St., 16323, P 7,200, M 550, (814) 432-5823, Fax (814) 437-2453, www.franklinapplefest.com, chamber@franklin-pa.org, www.franklinareachamber.org

**Frazer** · *see Malvern-Great Valley Reg. C/C*

**Freeland** · *Freeland C/C* · Charles Reczkowski, Pres., P.O. Box 31, 18224, P 4,200, M 55, (570) 636-0670, www.freelandchamber.org

**Galeton** · *Galeton Area C/C* · John Tubbs, Pres., P.O. Box 154, 16922, P 3,000, M 60, (814) 435-8737, visitgaleton@yahoo.com, www.visitgaleton.com

**Gettysburg** · *Gettysburg Adams C/C* · Carri Stuart, Pres., 18 Carlisle St., Ste. 203, 17325, P 99,749, M 610, (717) 334-8151, Fax (717) 334-3368, info@gettysburg-chamber.org, www.gettysburg-chamber.org

**Gibsonia** · *Twp. of Richland* · Herbert C. Dankmyer, Chrmn., 4019 Dickey Rd., 15044, P 9,231, (724) 443-5921, Fax (724) 443-8860, www.richland.pa.us

**Girard** · *Girard-Lake City C/C* · 522 Main St., 16417, P 6,000, (814) 774-3535, www.girard-lakecity.com

**Glenside** · *Greater Glenside C/C* · Barbara Nye, Pres., 452 N. Easton Rd., 19038, P 44,000, M 370, (215) 887-3110, info@glensidechamber.org, www.glensidechamber.org

**Gratz** · *see Elizabethville*

**Greencastle** · *Greencastle-Antrim C/C* · Bill Gour, Exec. Dir., 217 E. Baltimore St., P.O. Box 175, 17225, P 17,500, M 350, (717) 597-4610, Fax (717) 597-0709, bill@greencastlepachamber.org, www.greencastlepachamber.org.

**Greensburg** • *Westmoreland C/C* • Thomas L. Sochacki, Pres., 241 Tollgate Hill Rd., 15601, P 250,000, M 1,000, (724) 834-2900, Fax (724) 837-7635, info@westmorelandchamber.com, www.westmorelandchamber.com

**Greentown** • *see Hamlin*

**Greenville** • *Greenville Area C/C* • Douglas Riley, Exec. Dir., 182 Main St., P.O. Box 350, 16125, P 15,000, M 280, (724) 588-7150, Fax (724) 588-2013, gacc@nauticom.net, www.greenvillechamber-pa.com

**Grove City** • *Grove City Area C/C* • Beth Black, Exec. Dir., 119 S. Broad St., 16127, P 16,000, M 280, (724) 458-6410, Fax (724) 458-6841, gcchamber@shopgrovecity.com, www.shopgrovecity.com.

**Halifax** • *see Elizabethville*

**Hamlin** • *Southern Wayne Reg. C/C* • Patty Blaum, Exec. Dir., P.O. Box 296, 18427, P 15,000, M 225, (570) 689-4199, Fax (570) 689-4391, swrchamber@swrchamber.org, www.swrchamber.org

**Hanover** • *Hanover Area C/C* • Gary Laird, Pres., 146 Carlisle St., 17331, P 55,000, M 650, (717) 637-6130, Fax (717) 637-9127, office@hanoverchamber.com, www.hanoverchamber.com

**Harmony** • *see Zelienople*

**Harrisburg** • *The Pennsylvania Chamber of Bus. & Ind.* • Floyd W. Warner, Pres., 417 Walnut St., 17101, P 12,000,000, M 9,000, (717) 255-3252, (800) 225-7224, Fax (717) 255-3298, info@pachamber.org, www.pachamber.org

**Hatboro** • *Greater Hatboro C/C* • Bill George, Prs., P.O. Box 244, 19040, P 7,300, M 600, (215) 956-9540, Fax (215) 956-9635, office@hatborochamber.org, www.hatboro-pa.com

**Hatfield** • *Hatfield C/C* • Larry Stevens, Exec. Dir., P.O. Box 445, 19440, P 20,000, M 500, (215) 855-3335, Fax (215) 855-3335, admin@hatfieldchamber.com, www.hatfieldchamber.com

**Hawley** • *Hawley-Lake Wallenpaupack C/C* • U.S. Rte. 6, P.O. Box 150, 18428, P 20,000, M 265, (570) 226-3191, Fax (570) 226-9387, hlwchmbr@ptd.net, www.hawleywallenpaupackcc.com.

**Hazleton** • *Greater Hazleton C/C* • Donna Palermo, Pres., 20 W. Broad St., 18201, P 80,351, M 750, (570) 455-1509, Fax (570) 450-2013, info@hazletonchamber.org, www.hazletonchamber.org.

**Hershey** • *see Harrisburg*

**Homestead** • *see Steel Valley*

**Honesdale** • *Wayne County C/C* • Donna LaBar, Exec. Dir., 32 Commercial St., 18431, P 48,000, M 500, (570) 253-1960, (800) 433-9008, Fax (570) 253-1517, exec@waynecountycc.com, www.waynecountycc.com

**Horsham** • *see Lansdale*

**Houston** • *see Canonsburg*

**Hummelswharf** • *see Milton*

**Huntingdon** • *Huntingdon County C/C* • Yvonne Martin, Exec. Dir., 500 Allegheny St., 16652, P 46,000, M 370, (814) 643-1110, Fax (814) 643-1115, mail@huntingdonchamber.com, www.huntingdonchamber.com

**Indiana** • *Indiana County C/C* • Dana P. Henry, Pres., 1019 Philadelphia St., 15701, P 90,000, M 800, (724) 465-2511, Fax (724) 465-3706, dphenry@wpia.net, www.indianapa.com/chamber

**Irwin** • *Norwin C/C* • Rosanne Barry Novotnak, Pres., 321 Main St., 15642, P 34,000, M 350, (724) 863-0888, Fax (724) 863-5133, info@norwinchamber.com, www.norwinchamber.com

**Jeannette** • *see Greensburg*

**Jefferson Borough** • *see McKeesport*

**Jenkintown** • *Eastern Montgomery County C/C* • Wendy Klinghoffer, Exec. V.P., 436 Old York Rd., 19046, P 100,000, M 700, (215) 887-5122, info@emccc.org, www.emccc.org

**Jermyn** • *see Carbondale*

**Jim Thorpe** • *see Lehighton*

**Johnsonburg** • *Johnsonburg C/C* • Bill Simon, Exec. Dir., 501 High St., 15845, P 3,583, M 95, (814) 965-4793, Fax (814) 965-3215

**Johnstown** • *Greater Johnstown/Cambria County C/C* • Robert F. Layo, Pres., 245 Market St. #100, 15901, P 175,000, M 700, (814) 536-5107, (800) 790-4522, Fax (814) 539-5800, chamber@johnstownchamber.com, www.johnstownchamber.com

**Jones Mills** • *see Donegal*

**Kane** • *Kane C/C* • 54 Fraley St., 16735, P 4,100, M 135, (814) 837-6565, Fax (814) 837-6565, kanepa.chamber@verizon.net, www.kanepa.com

**Kennett Square** • *Southern Chester County C/C* • Roxane Ferguson, Exec. Dir., 217 W. State St., P.O. Box 395, 19348, P 38,000, M 600, (610) 444-0774, Fax (610) 444-5105, info@scccc.com, www.scccc.com.

**Kittanning** • *Armstrong County C/C* • Lynda Pozzuto, Exec. Dir., 124 Market St., 16201, P 72,514, M 305, (724) 543-1305, Fax (724) 548-2951, accc1@alltel.net, www.armstrongchamber.org

**Kutztown** • *Northeast Berks C/C* • Liz P. Weiss, Exec. Dir., 110 W. Main St., P.O. Box 209, 19530, P 25,000, M 280, (610) 683-8860, Fax (610) 683-8544, nbcc@ptd.net, www.northeastberkschamber.com

**Lake Ariel** • *see Hamlin*

**Lake Wallenpaupack** • *see Hawley*

**Lancaster** • *Lancaster C of C & Ind.* • Thomas T. Baldrige, Pres., 100 S. Queen St., P.O. Box 1558, 17608, P 482,000, M 2,700, (717) 397-3531, Fax (717) 293-3159, info@lcci.com, www.lancasterchamber.com

**Lansdale** • *North Penn - Suburban C/C* • R. Michael Owens, Pres./CEO, 229 S. Broad St., 19446, P 125,000, M 1,300, (215) 362-9200, Fax (215) 362-0393, info@northpenn.org, www.northpenn.org

**Lansford** • *see Lehighton*

**Laporte** • *see Muncy Valley*

**Latrobe** • *Latrobe Area C/C* • Andrew M. Stofan, Pres., 326 McKinley Ave., Ste. 102, 15650, P 50,000, M 400, (724) 537-2671, Fax (724) 537-2690, info@latrobearea.com, www.latrobearea.com.

**Lebanon** • *Lebanon Valley C/C* • Larry A. Bowman CCE, Pres./CEO, 728 Walnut St., P.O. Box 899, 17042, P 128,000, M 850, (717) 273-3727, Fax (717) 273-7940, info@lvchamber.org, www.lvchamber.org.

**Lehighton** • *Carbon County C/C* • Michael Heery, Pres., 110 N. Third St. #217, 18235, P 60,000, M 530, (610) 379-5000, Fax (610) 379-0130, mheery@carboncountychamber.org, www.carboncountychamber.org

**Lewisburg** • *see Shamokin Dam*

**Lewistown** • *Juniata Valley Area C/C* • Jim Tunall, Pres., Historic Courthouse, One W. Market St., Ste. 119, 17044, P 68,463, M 420, (717) 248-6713, Fax (717) 248-6714, jvacc@juniatavalleychamber.org, www.juniatavalleychamber.org

**Ligonier** • *Ligonier Valley C/C* • Rachel Roehrig, Exec. Dir., 120 E. Main St., 15658, P 10,000, M 310, (724) 238-4200, Fax (724) 238-4610, thechamber@ligonier.com, www.ligonier.com

**Linesville** • *Linesville Area C/C* • Virginia Headley, Pres., P.O. Box 651, 16424, P 1,155, M 100, (814) 683-1006

**Littlestown** · *Littlestown Area C/C* · Matthew Turley, Pres., P.O. Box 384, 17340, P 4,500, M 60, (717) 359-7006, Fax (717) 334-3368, littlestownchamber@yahoo.com, www.littlestownpa.info/chamber

**Lock Haven** · *Clinton County Eco. Partnership* · Peter Lopes, Chamber/Tourism Dir., 212 N. Jay St., P.O. Box 506, 17745, P 37,000, M 385, (570) 748-5782, Fax (570) 893-0433, tourism@kcnet.org, www.clintoncountyinfo.com.

**Lower Mount Bethel** · *see Pen Argyl*

**Malvern** · *Chester County Chamber of Bus. & Ind.* · Nancy Keefer CCE, Pres./CEO, 1600 Paoli Pike, 19355, P 442,815, M 1,600, (610) 725-9100, Fax (610) 725-8479, info@cccbi.org, www.cccbi.org

**Malvern** · *Great Valley Reg. C/C* · Mary Ann Severance, Pres., 7 Great Valley Pkwy., 19355, P 30,000, M 270, (610) 889-2069, Fax (610) 889-2063, greatchamber@gvrcc.org, www.great valleyonline.com

**Manheim** · *Manheim Area C/C* · Teresa Shelly, Exec. Dir., 13 E. High St., 17545, P 18,000, M 115, (717) 665-6330, Fax (717) 665-7656, info@manheimchamber.com, www.manheimchamber.com

**Mansfield** · *Greater Mansfield Area C/C* · Gale Hall, Pres., 51-B S. Main St., 16933, P 15,000, M 125, (570) 662-3442, info@mansfield.org, www.mansfield.org

**Marietta** · *see Columbia*

**Mayfield** · *see Carbondale*

**McConnellsburg** · *Fulton County C/C* · Brenda Gordon, Exec. Dir., 201 Lincolnway W. #101, P.O. Box 141, 17233, P 14,900, M 183, (717) 485-4064, info@fultoncountypa.com, www.fulton countypa.com

**McDonald** · *see Canonsburg*

**McKeesport** · *Reg. Chamber Alliance* · Howard Carpenter, Pres./CEO, 201 Lysle Blvd., 15132, P 180,000, M 500, (412) 678-2450, Fax (412) 678-2451, howard@rba-pa.com, www.rba-pa.com

**McMurray** · *Peters Twp. C/C* · Carol A. Foley, Exec. Dir., 3909 Washington Rd. #321, P.O. Box 991, 15317, P 21,430, M 440, (724) 941-6345, Fax (724) 942-2345, info@peterstownshipchamber.com, www.peterstownshipchamber.com.

**Meadowlands** · *see Canonsburg*

**Meadville** · *Meadville-Western Crawford County C/C* · Charlie Anderson, Pres./CEO, 211 Chestnut St., 16335, P 13,900, M 548, (814) 337-8030, Fax (814) 337-8022, info@meadvillechamber.com, www.meadvillechamber.com

**Mechanicsburg** · *Mechanicsburg C/C* · Jeff Palm, Exec. Dir., 6 W. Strawberry Ave., 17055, P 60,000, M 400, (717) 796-0811, Fax (717) 796-1977, info@mechanicsburgchamber.org, www.mechanicsburgchamber.org

**Media** · *Delaware County C/C* · Jeff Vermeulen, Pres., 602 E. Baltimore Pike, 19063, P 547,641, M 2,300, (610) 565-3677, Fax (610) 565-1606, info@delcochamber.org, www.delcochamber.org

**Mercer** · *Mercer Area C/C* · Deborah Plant, Exec. Dir., 143 N. Diamond St., 16137, P 3,000, M 219, (724) 662-4185, Fax (724) 662-0211, mercerchamber@zoominternet.net, www.mercer areachamber.com

**Mercersburg** · *Mercersburg Area C/C* · Mary-Anne Gordon, Exec. Dir., 19 N. Main St., 17236, P 1,817, M 172, (717) 328-5827, Fax (717) 328-4814, mercersburgchamber@embarqmail.com, www.mercersburg.org

**Meyersdale** · *see Somerset*

**Middleburg** · *see Milton*

**Middletown** · *see Harrisburg*

**Mifflinburg** · *see Shamokin Dam*

**Milford** · *Pike County C/C* · Danielle Jordan, Exec. Dir., 209 E. Harford St., 18337, P 54,000, M 550, (570) 296-8700, Fax (570) 296-3921, info@pikechamber.com, www.pikechamber.com

**Millersburg** · *see Elizabethville*

**Milton** · *Central Pennsylvania C/C* · Maria Culp, Pres./CEO, 700 Hepburn St. #4, 17847, P 9,056, M 300, (570) 742-7341, Fax (570) 742-2008, info@centralpachamber.com, www.centralpachamber.com

**Monessen** · *Monessen C/C* · Gary Boatman, East Gate 11, Ste. 154, 15062, P 9,500, M 100, (724) 684-3200, Fax (724) 684-8470, info@monessenchamberofcommerce.com, www.monessen chamberofcommerce.com

**Monongahela** · *Monongahela Area C/C* · Teresa Cypher, Dir., 173 W. Main St., 15063, P 13,310, M 170, (724) 258-5919, Fax (724) 258-5919, www.cityofmonongahela.com/chamberofcommerce

**Monroeville** · *Monroeville Area C/C* · Chad Amond, Pres., Chamber of Commerce Bldg., 4268 Northern Pike, 15146, P 30,000, M 695, (412) 856-0622, Fax (412) 856-1030, macc@monroeville chamber.com, www.monroevillechamber.com.

**Montrose** · *Montrose Area C/C* · Marilyn Morgan, Pres., P.O. Box 423, 18801, P 1,700, (570) 278-1174, marilyn@montrosearea.com, www.montrosearea.com

**Moon Township** · *see Pittsburgh Airport Area C/C*

**Mount Carmel** · *see Shamokin*

**Mount Joy** · *Mount Joy C/C* · Nancy Shonk, Exec. Dir., 62 E. Main, Ste. 1, 17552, P 7,000, M 230, (717) 653-0773, Fax (717) 653-0773, info@mountjoychamber.com, www.mountjoychamber.com

**Mount Lebanon** · *see Pittsburgh-South Hills C/C*

**Mount Pleasant** · *Laurel Highlands C/C* · 537 W. Main St., 15666, P 30,000, M 380, (724) 547-7521, marjorie@laurelhigh landschamber.com, www.laurelhighlandschamber.com

**Mount Union** · *Mount Union Area C/C* · Jonathan Shapiro, P.O. Box 12, 17066, P 2,500, M 60, (814) 542-9413, www.muacoc.com

**Muncy Valley** · *Sullivan County C/C* · Florence Suarez, Admin. Dir., 1240 Rte. 220, Ste. 3, P.O. Box 134, 17758, P 6,500, M 125, (570) 482-4088, Fax (570) 482-4089, sulchamc@epix.net, www.sullivanpachamber.com

**Munhall** · *see Steel Valley*

**Murrysville** · *see Greensburg*

**Nanticoke** · *South Valley C/C* · Mill House, 495 E. Main St., 18634, P 11,000, M 100, (570) 735-6990, Fax (570) 735-6990, svcc495@verizon.net

**Natrona Heights** · *see Brackenridge*

**Nazareth** · *Nazareth Area C/C* · Tina Smith, Pres., 201 N. Main St., 18064, P 25,000, M 400, (610) 759-9188, Fax (610) 759-5262, bsmith@nazarethchamber.com, www.nazarethchamber.com

**Nesquehoning** · *see Lehighton*

**Neville Island** · *see Pittsburgh Airport Area C/C*

**New Bethlehem** · *Red Bank Valley C/C* · 309 Broad St., Ste. 2, 16242, P 10,000, M 96, (814) 275-3929, nbchamber@alltel.net, www.newbethlehemarea.com

**New Castle** · *Lawrence County C/C* · Robert McCracken, Exec. V.P., Shenango Street Station, 138 W. Washington St., 16101, P 94,643, M 900, (724) 654-5593, Fax (724) 654-3330, info@lawrencecountychamber.org, www.lawrencecountychamber.org

**New Hope** • *Greater New Hope C/C* • Stephanie Nagy, Admin., P.O. Box 633, 18938, P 3,000, M 200, (215) 862-9990, info@enjoynewhope.com, www.enjoynewhope.com

**New Kensington** • *New Kensington Area C/C* • John Ciesielski, 858 4th Ave., 15068, P 14,300, M 160, (724) 339-6616, Fax (724) 339-3346, admin@nwchamber.org, www.nwchamber.org

**New Oxford** • *New Oxford Area C/C* • P.O. Box 152, 17350, P 1,700, M 200, (717) 624-2800, info@newoxford.org, www.newoxford.org

**New Stanton** • *see Greensburg*

**Newfoundland** • *see Hamlin*

**Norristown** • *see King of Prussia*

**North East** • *North East Area C/C* • Sue Spacht, Comm. Coord., 21 S. Lake St., 16428, P 11,000, M 250, (814) 725-4262, Fax (814) 725-3994, info@nechamber.org, www.nechamber.org

**North Fayette Twp.** • *see Pittsburgh Airport Area C/C*

**North Huntingdon** • *see Irwin*

**Northampton** • *see Allentown*

**Northern Allegheny County** • *see Wexford*

**Ohiopyle** • *see Donegal*

**Oil City** • *Venango Area C/C* • Susan Williams, Exec. Dir., 41 Main St., P.O. Box 376, 16301, P 51,000, M 484, (814) 676-8521, Fax (814) 676-8185, chamber@venangochamber.org, www.venangochamber.org

**Oxford** • *Oxford Area C/C* • Eleanor Roper, Exec. Secy., P.O. Box 4, 19363, P 20,364, M 215, (610) 932-0740, Fax (610) 932-0827, oxfordchamber@zoominternet.net, www.oxfordpa.org

**Palmerton** • *Palmerton Area C/C* • Peter Kern, Pres., 410 Delaware Ave., 18071, P 14,000, M 160, (610) 824-6954, www.palmertonpa.com/chamber

**Paoli** • *see Malvern-Great Valley Reg. C/C*

**Patton** • *Patton Area C/C* • Ken Bailey, Pres., P.O. Box 72, 16668, P 2,200, M 25, (814) 674-3641

**Pen Argyl** • *Slate Belt C/C* • Laura McLain, Ofc. Mgr., 856 W. Pennsylvania Ave., P.O. Box 5, 18072, P 34,250, M 270, (610) 863-0315, Fax same, sbcc@frontiernet.net, www.slatebeltchamber.org

**Penfield** • *see DuBois*

**Penn Twp.** • *see Greensburg*

**Perkasie** • *Pennridge C/C* • Betty Graver, Exec. Dir., 538 W. Market St., 18944, P 42,000, M 460, (215) 257-5390, Fax (215) 257-6840, pennridgecc@pennridge.com, www.pennridge.com

**Peters Twp.** • *see McMurray*

## Philadelphia Area

**Greater Philadelphia C/C** • Mark Schweiker, Pres./CEO, 200 S. Broad St., Ste. 700, 19102, P 6,000,000, M 5,000, (215) 545-1234, Fax (215) 790-3600, www.greaterphilachamber.com

**African American C/C of PA, NJ & DE** • Kim Johnson, Exec. Dir., 30 S. 15th St., Ground Floor, 19106, M 400, (215) 751-9501, Fax (215) 751-9509, info@aachamber.org, www.aachamber.org

**Greater Northeast Philadelphia C/C** • Al Taubenberger, Pres., 8601 Roosevelt Blvd., 19152, P 550,000, M 900, (215) 332-3400, Fax (215) 332-6050, gnpccoffice@aol.com, www.gnpcc.org.

**Philipsburg** • *Moshannon Valley Eco. Dev. Partnership* • Stanley LaFuria, Exec. Dir., 200 Shady Ln., 16866, P 34,000, M 170, (814) 342-2260, Fax (814) 342-2878, slafuria@mvedp.org, www.mvedp.org

**Phoenixville** • *Phoenixville Reg. C/C* • Kim Cooley, Exec. Dir., 171 E. Bridge St., 19460, P 20,000, M 500, (610) 933-3070, Fax (610) 917-0503, info@phoenixvillechamber.org, www.phoenixvillechamber.org

**Pitcairn** • *see McKeesport*

## Pittsburgh Area

**Greater Pittsburgh C/C** • 425 Sixth Ave., Ste. 1100, 15219, P 2,394,800, M 1,200, (412) 392-4500, Fax (412) 392-4520, info@pittsburghchamber.com, www.pittsburghchamber.com

**Brentwood Baldwin Whitehall C/C** • Dottie Coll, 3501 Brownsville Rd., 15227, P 15,000, M 174, (412) 884-1233, secretary@bbwchamber.com, www.bbwchamber.com

**East Liberty Quarter C/C** • Paul G. Brecht, Exec. Dir., 5907 Penn Ave., Ste. 305, 15206, P 65,000, M 150, (412) 661-9660, Fax (412) 661-9661, pbrecht@eastlibertychamber.org, www.eastlibertychamber.org

**Northside Northshore C/C** • Robin Rosemary Miller, Exec. Dir., 809 Middle St., 15212, P 54,600, M 215, (412) 231-6500, Fax (412) 321-6760, nsccrobin@hotmail.com, www.northsidechamberofcommerce.com

**Penn Hills C/C** • 13049 Frankstown Rd., 15235, P 47,000, M 320, (412) 795-8741, Fax (412) 795-7993, s.werner@pennhillschamber.org, www.pennhillschamber.org

**Pittsburgh Airport Area C/C** • Sally Haas, Pres., 850 Beaver Grade Rd., Moon Twp., 15108, P 170,000, M 1,000, (412) 264-6270, Fax (412) 264-1575, shaas@paacc.com, www.paacc.com

**South Hills C/C** • Angie Kazmeraski, Exec. Dir., 1910 Cochran Rd., Manor Oak One, Ste. 140, 15220, P 225,000, M 574, (412) 306-8090, Fax (412) 306-8093, office@shchamber.org, www.shchamber.org

**South Side C/C** • Tom Smith, 1910 E. Carson St., P.O. Box 42380, 15203, P 15,000, M 150, (412) 431-3360, Fax (412) 431-0630, office@southsidechamber.org, www.southsidechamber.org

**South West Communities C/C** • Emerald VanBuskirk, Exec. Dir., 990 Washington Pike, Bridgeville, 15017, P 20,615, M 437, (412) 221-4100, Fax (412) 257-1210, info@swccoc.org, www.swccoc.org

**Pittston** • *Greater Pittston C/C* • Rosemary Dessoye, Exec. V.P., 104 Kennedy Blvd., P.O. Box 704, 18640, P 49,672, M 500, (570) 655-1424, Fax (570) 655-0336, info@pittstonchamber.org, pittstonchamber.org.

**Plainfield** • *see Pen Argyl*

**Pleasant Hills** • *see McKeesport*

**Plum Borough** • *see Greensburg*

**Pocono Mountains** • *see Stroudsburg*

**Portland** • *see Pen Argyl*

**Pottstown** • *TriCounty Area C/C* • P. Timothy Phelps, Pres., 152 High St., Ste. 360, 19464, P 175,000, M 800, (610) 326-2900, Fax (610) 970-9705, tim@tricountyareachamber.com, www.tricountyareachamber.com

**Pottsville** • *Schuylkill C/C* • Bob Carl, Exec. Dir., 91 S. Progress Ave., 17901, P 150,336, M 750, (570) 622-1942, (800) 755-1942, Fax (570) 622-1638, info@schuylkillchamber.com, www.schuylkillchamber.com.

**Punxsutawney** • *Punxsutawney Area C/C* • Marlene Lellock, Exec. Dir., 102 W. Mahoning St., 15767, P 6,800, M 300, (814) 938-7700, (800) 752-PHIL, Fax (814) 938-4303, chamber@punxsutawney.com, www.punxsutawney.com

**Quakertown** · *Upper Bucks C/C* · Tara King, Exec. Dir., 2170 Portzer Rd., 18951, P 50,000, M 700, (215) 536-3211, Fax (215) 536-7767, info@ubcc.org, www.ubcc.org

**Quarryville** · *Southern Lancaster County C/C* · Catherine Horn, Exec. Secy., P.O. Box 24, 17566, P 2,500, M 110, (717) 786-1911, (717) 786-8361, www.southernlancasterchamber.org

**Reading** · *Greater Reading C/C & Ind.* · Ellen T. Horan, Pres./CEO, 601 Penn St., 19601, P 373,638, M 1,800, (610) 376-6766, Fax (610) 376-4135, info@greaterreadingchamber.org, www.greaterreadingchamber.org

**Richmondale** · *see Carbondale*

**Ridgway** · *Ridgway-Elk County C/C* · 300 Main St., 15853, P 5,000, M 170, (814) 776-1424, Fax (814) 772-9150, ridgwaychamber@ncentral.com, www.ridgwaychamber.com

**Robinson Township** · *see Pittsburgh Airport Area C/C*

**Rochester** · *Rochester C/C* · 350 Adams St., Ste. 4C, 15074, P 4,000, M 169, (724) 728-4998, rochesterpachamber@yahoo.com

**Rockwood** · *see Somerset*

**Roseto** · *see Pen Argyl*

**Royersford** · *Spring-Ford C/C* · Beth Haverson, Exec. Dir., P.O. Box 26, 19468, P 6,000, M 235, (610) 948-1771, Fax (610) 948-1783, beth@springfordchamber.com, www.springfordchamber.com

**Saint Marys** · *St. Marys Area C/C* · Sally J. Wilson, Exec. Dir., 53 S. St. Marys Street, 15857, P 15,000, M 325, (814) 781-3804, Fax (814) 781-7302, swilson@stmaryschamber.org, www.stmaryschamber.org.

**Saltlick** · *see Donegal*

**Saxton** · *Broad Top C/C* · Robert Jenkins, Pres., P.O. Box 121, 16678, P 10,000, M 50, (814) 635-3430

**Sayre** · *Greater Valley C/C* · Greg Joseph, Pres., 703 S. Elmer Ave., 18840, P 20,000, M 233, (570) 888-2217, Fax (570) 888-6558, gvcc@cqservices.com, www.greatervalleychamberofcommerce.com

**Scottdale** · *Scottdale Area C/C* · Joan Brown, Pres., 318 Pittsburgh St., 15683, P 5,000, M 75, (724) 887-3611, scottdalechamber@gmail.com, www.scottdale.com

**Scranton** · *Greater Northeast C/C* · John Gleason, Chrmn., P.O. Box 3893, 18505, M 200, (570) 457-1130, Fax (570) 300-1645, info@gnecc.com, www.gnecc.com

**Scranton** · *Greater Scranton C/C* · Austin J. Burke, Pres., 222 Mulberry St., P.O. Box 431, 18501, P 212,029, M 2,200, (570) 342-7711, Fax (570) 347-6262, info@scrantonchamber.com, www.scrantonchamber.com

**Selinsgrove** · *see Shamokin Dam*

**Sellersville** · *see Doylestown*

**Shamokin** · *Brush Valley Reg. C/C* · Sandy Winhofer, Dir., 2 E. Arch St. #313A, 17872, P 45,000, M 235, (570) 648-4675, Fax (570) 648-0679, swinhofer@censop.com, www.brushvalleychamber.com

**Shamokin Dam** · *Greater Susquehanna Valley C/C* · Dave Hall, Pres./CEO, 2859 N. Susquehanna Trail, P.O. Box 10, 17876, P 130,000, M 720, (570) 743-4100, Fax (570) 743-1221, info@gsvcc.org, www.gsvcc.org.

**Shanksville** · *see Somerset*

**Sharon** · *Shenango Valley C/C* · George Gerhart, Exec. Dir./CEO, 41 Chestnut St., 16146, P 66,495, M 500, (724) 981-5880, Fax (724) 981-5480, george@svchamber.com, www.svchamber.com.

**Shenandoah** · *see Schuylkill*

**Shippensburg** · *Shippensburg Area C/C* · Bruce Hockersmith, Exec. Dir., 53 W. King St., 17257, P 30,000, M 290, (717) 532-5509, Fax (717) 532-7501, chamber@shippensburg.org, www.shippensburg.org

**Simpson** · *see Carbondale*

**Smethport** · *Smethport C/C* · P.O. Box 84, 16749, P 1,700, M 60, (814) 887-6020, www.smethportchamber.com

**Somerset** · *Somerset County C/C* · Ron Aldom, Exec. Dir., 601 N. Center Ave., 15501, P 80,023, M 750, (814) 445-6431, Fax (814) 443-4313, info@somersetcountychamber.com, www.somerset-countychamber.com.

**Souderton** · *Indian Valley C/C* · Sharon Minninger, Exec. Dir., P.O. Box 64077, 18964, P 50,000, M 475, (215) 723-9472, Fax (215) 723-2490, ivchamber@indianvalleychamber.com, www.indianvalleychamber.com

**South Fayette Twp.** · *see Pittsburgh-South West Comm. C/C*

**South Sterling** · *see Hamlin*

**South Waverly** · *see Sayre*

**Spring City** · *see Pottstown*

**Stahlstown** · *see Donegal*

**State College** · *Chamber of Bus. & Ind. Of Centre County* · John F. Coleman Jr., Pres./CEO, 200 Innovation Blvd. #150, 16801, P 124,000, M 1,086, (814) 234-1829, Fax (814) 234-5869, cbicc@cbicc.org, www.cbicc.org

**Steel Valley** · *Steel Valley C/C* · John J. Karafa, Pres., 3910 Main St., Munhall, 15120, P 44,892, M 125, (412) 461-4141, Fax (412) 461-9804, www.steelvalleychamber.com

**Sterling** · *see Hamlin*

**Stroudsburg** · *Greater Pocono C/C* · Robert Phillips IOM, Pres./CEO, 556 Main St., 18360, P 200,000, M 1,650, (570) 421-4433, Fax (570) 424-7281, rphillips@greaterpoconochamber.com, www.greaterpoconochamber.com.

**Summit Hill** · *see Lehighton*

**Sunbury** · *see Shamokin Dam*

**Tamaqua** · *Tamaqua Area C/C* · Linda J. Yulanavage, Exec. Dir., 114 W. Broad St., 18252, P 7,500, M 170, (570) 668-1880, Fax (570) 668-0826, chamber@tamaqua.net, www.tamaqua.net.

**Telford** · *see Souderton*

**Titusville** · *Titusville Area C/C* · Jerry Schill, Exec. Dir., 202 W. Central Ave., 16354, P 6,000, M 300, (814) 827-2941, Fax (814) 827-2914, jerrys@titusvillechamber.com, www.titusvillechamber.com

**Towanda** · *Central Bradford County C/C* · Sharon Kaminsky, Secy., P.O. Box 146, 18848, P 6,000, M 115, (570) 268-2732, Fax (570) 265-4558, sharon@bcrac.org, www.cbradchamber.org

**Trafford** · *see McKeesport*

**Trooper** · *see King of Prussia*

**Tunkhannock** · *Wyoming County C/C* · Maureen E. Dispenza, Dir., 81B Warren St., P.O. Box 568, 18657, P 28,000, M 350, (570) 836-7755, Fax (570) 836-6049, maureen@wyccc.com, www.wyccc.com

**Turtle Creek** · *see McKeesport*

**Tyrone** · *Tyrone Area C/C* · Rose Black, Exec. Dir., 1004 Logan Ave., 16686, P 5,400, M 200, (814) 684-0736, Fax (814) 684-6070, rose@tyronechamber.com, www.tyronechamber.com

**Uniontown** · *Fayette C/C* · Muriel J. Nuttall, Exec. Dir., 65 W. Main St., 15401, P 55,000, M 535, (724) 437-4571, (800) 916-9365, Fax (724) 438-3304, faycham@faycham.org, www.faycham.org.

**Upper Mount Bethel** · *see Pen Argyl*

**Upper St. Clair** • *Upper St. Clair C/C* • Rosemary Siddall, Exec. Dir., 71 McMurray Rd., Ste. 201, P.O. Box 12619, 15241, P 20,000, M 100, (412) 833-9111, www.uscchamber.org

**Valley Forge** • *see King of Prussia*

**Vandergrift** • *StrongLand C/C* • A. Allan Walzak, Pres., Box 10 #108, 1129 Industrial Park Rd., 15690, P 65,000, M 400, (724) 845-5426, Fax (724) 845-5428, strongland@windstream.net, www.strongland.org.

**Vandling** • *see Carbondale*

**Warminster** • *Greater Warminster C/C* • 228C York Rd., 18974, P 36,000, M 350, (215) 672-6633, Fax (215) 672-7637, www.greaterwcc.com

**Warren** • *Warren County Chamber of Bus. & Ind.* • James Decker, Pres./CEO, 308 Market St., 16365, P 42,000, M 285, (814) 723-3050, Fax (814) 723-6024, info@wccbi.org, www.wccbi.org

**Washington** • *Washington County C/C* • Jeff M. Kotula, Pres., 20 E. Beau St., 15301, P 203,000, M 850, (724) 225-3010, Fax (724) 228-7337, info@washcochamber.com, www.washcochamber.com

**Watsontown** • *see Milton*

**Wayne** • *Main Line C/C* • R. Stanley Schuck, Pres./CEO, 175 Strafford Ave. #130, 19087, P 265,000, M 1,800, (610) 687-6232, Fax (610) 687-8085, info@mlcc.org, www.mlcc.org.

**Waynesboro** • *Greater Waynesboro C/C* • Carlene Willhide, Exec. Dir., 5 Roadside Ave., 17268, P 40,000, M 430, (717) 762-7123, Fax (717) 762-7124, carlene@waynesboro.org, www.waynesboro.org

**Waynesburg** • *Waynesburg Area C/C* • Melody R. Longstreth, Exec. Dir., 143 E. High St., 15370, P 15,000, M 300, (724) 627-5926, Fax (724) 627-8017, waynesburgchamber@windstream.net, www.waynesburgchamber.com.

**Wellsboro** • *Wellsboro Area C/C* • Julie VanNess, Exec. Dir., 114 Main St., P.O. Box 733, 16901, P 3,500, M 300, (570) 724-1926, Fax (570) 724-5084, info@wellsboropa.com, www.wellsboropa.com

**West Chester** • *C/C of Greater West Chester Inc.* • Katie Walker, Pres., 119 N. High St., 19380, P 81,000, M 800, (610) 696-4046, Fax (610) 696-9110, info@gwcc.org, www.greaterwestchester.com.

**West Elizabeth** • *see McKeesport*

**West Homestead** • *see Steel Valley*

**West Mifflin** • *see McKeesport and Steel Valley*

**Westfield** • *Westfield Area C/C* • P.O. Box 232, 16950, P 3,000, M 80, (814) 367-2617, chamber@westfieldpa.org, www.westfieldpa.org

**Westinghouse Valley** • *see McKeesport*

**Wexford** • *Northern Allegheny County C/C* • Mary Margaret Fisher, Exec. Dir., 5000 Brooktree Rd., Ste. 100, 15090, P 12,000, M 830, (724) 934-9700, Fax (724) 934-9710, naccc@naccc.com, www.naccc.com.

**Whitaker** • *see Steel Valley*

**White Oak** • *see McKeesport*

**Wilkes-Barre** • *Greater Wilkes-Barre Chamber of Bus. & Ind.* • Todd Vonderheid, Pres./CEO, Two Public Square, P.O. Box 5340, 18710, P 353,000, M 1,150, (570) 823-2101, Fax (570) 822-5951, wbcofc@wilkes-barre.org, www.wilkes-barre.org.

**Wilkinsburg** • *Wilkinsburg C/C* • Valerie Tierno, Pres., P.O. Box 8638, 15221, P 20,680, M 100, (412) 242-0234, info@wilkinsburgchamber.com, www.wilkinsburgchamber.com

**Williamsport** • *Williamsport/Lycoming C/C* • Vincent J. Matteo, Pres./CEO, 100 W. Third St., 17701, P 130,000, M 900, (570) 326-1971, Fax (570) 321-1208, chamber@williamsport.org, www.williamsport.org.

**Willow Grove** • *see Lansdale*

**Wind Gap** • *see Pen Argyl*

**Windber** • *see Somerset*

**Wrightsville** • *see Columbia*

**Wyalusing** • *Greater Wyalusing C/C & IDC* • Debbie Howard, Pres., 121 Main St., P.O. Box 55, 18853, P 5,000, M 150, (570) 746-4922, Fax (570) 746-0235, wchamber@epix.net, www.wyalusing.net

**Wysox** • *Wysox Comm. C/C* • Walter Warburton, Pres., P.O. Box 63, 18854, P 1,800, M 80, (570) 265-7511, info@wysoxpacc.com, www.wysoxpacc.com

**York** • *York County C/C* • Thomas E. Donley, Pres., 96 S. George, Ste. 300, 17401, P 401,613, M 2,000, (717) 848-4000, Fax (717) 843-6737, info@YorkChamber.com, www.YorkChamber.com.

**Zelienople** • *Zelienople-Harmony Area C/C* • Marnie Repasky, Exec. Dir., 111 W. New Castle St., P.O. Box 464, 16063, P 10,000, M 190, (724) 452-5232, Fax (724) 452-5712, zhcc@zoominternet.net, www.zelienopleharmonychamber.com

# Puerto Rico

**Puerto Rico C of C** • Edgardo Bigas, Exec. V.P., P.O. Box 9024033, San Juan, 00902, P 3,850,000, M 2,000, (787) 721-6060, Fax (787) 723-1891, camarapr@camarapr.org, www.camarapr.org.

**Mayaguez** • *C/C of the West of Puerto Rico* • Jose Justiniano, Pres., P.O. Box 9, 00681-0009, P 2,000,000, M 250, (787) 832-3749, Fax (787) 832-4287, ccopr@coqui.net, www.ccopr.org

**Ponce** • *Southern Puerto Rico C/C* • Elena M. Colon Parrilla, Pres., P.O. Box 7455, 00732-7455, P 2,000,000, M 510, (787) 844-4400, Fax (787) 844-4705, camarasur@prtc.net, www.camarasur.org

# Rhode Island

**Barrington** • *see Warren*

**Block Island** • *Block Island C/C* • Kathleen Szabo, Exec. Dir., P.O. Box D, 02807, P 950, M 250, (401) 466-2982, info@blockislandchamber.com, www.blockislandchamber.com

**Bristol** • *see Warren*

**Burrillville** • *see Lincoln*

**Central Falls** • *see Lincoln*

**Centredale** • *see Johnston*

**Charlestown** • *Charlestown C/C* • Jack Marshall, Exec. Dir., 4945 Old Post Rd., P.O. Box 633, 02813, P 8,000, M 400, (401) 364-3878, Fax (401) 364-8794, charlestowncoc@earthlink.net, www.charlestownrichamber.com

**Cranston** • *Cranston C/C* • Susan Pagnoczi, Pres., 48A Rolfe Square, 02910, P 79,000, M 500, (401) 785-3780, Fax (401) 785-3782, susan@cranstonchamber.com, www.cranstonchamber.com

**Cumberland** • *see Lincoln*

**East Greenwich** • *East Greenwich C/C* • Jerry Meyer, Exec. Dir., 580 Main St., P.O. Box 514, 02818, P 12,948, M 420, (401) 885-0020, Fax (401) 885-0048, info@eastgreenwichchamber.com, www.eastgreenwichchamber.com

**East Providence** · *East Providence Area C/C* · Laura A. McNamara, Exec. Dir., 1005 Waterman Ave., 02914, P 48,000, M 400, (401) 438-1212, Fax (401) 435-4581, office@eastprov chamber.com, www.eastprovchamber.com

**Foster** · *see Johnston*

**Glocester** · *see Johnston*

**Jamestown** · *Jamestown C/C* · Exec. Dir., P.O. Box 35, 02835, P 6,200, M 135, (401) 423-3650, info@jamestownrichamber.com, www.jamestownrichamber.com

**Johnston** · *North Central C/C* · Robert Lafond IOM, Pres., 255 Greenville Ave., 02919, P 150,000, M 350, (401) 349-4674, Fax (401) 349-4676, chamber@ncrichamber.com, www.ncrichamber.com

**Lincoln** · *Northern Rhode Island C/C* · John C. Gregory, Pres./ CEO, 6 Blackstone Valley Pl. #301, 02865, P 250,000, M 900, (401) 334-1000, Fax (401) 334-1009, general@nrichamber.com, www. nrichamber.com

**Middletown** · *Newport County C/C* · Keith Stokes, Exec. Dir., 35 Valley Rd., 02842, P 100,000, M 1,300, (401) 847-1600, Fax (401) 849-5848, info@newportchamber.com, www.newportchamber.com

**Narragansett** · *Narragansett C/C* · Deborah Kelso, Exec. Dir., P.O. Box 742, 02882, P 16,000, M 400, (401) 783-7121, (401) 788-0684, Fax (401) 789-0220, dkelso@narragansett.com, www. narragansettri.com/chamber

**Newport** · *see Middletown*

**North Kingstown** · *North Kingstown C/C* · Karla P. Driscoll, Exec. Dir., 8045 Post Rd., 02852, P 26,000, M 500, (401) 295-5566, Fax (401) 295-5582, info@northkingstown.com, www. northkingstown.com

**North Providence** · *see Johnston*

**North Smithfield** · *see Lincoln*

**Pawcatuck** · *see Westerly*

**Pawtucket** · *see Lincoln*

**Providence** · *Greater Providence C/C* · Laurie L. White, Pres., 30 Exchange Terrace, 02903, P 180,000, M 2,300, (401) 521-5000, Fax (401) 621-6109, chamber@provchamber.com, www. providencechamber.com

**Scituate** · *see Johnston*

**Smithfield** · *see Johnston and Lincoln*

**South Kingstown** · *see Wakefield*

**Wakefield** · *South Kingstown C/C* · Pres./CEO, 230 Old Tower Hill Rd., 02879, P 35,000, M 655, (401) 783-2801, Fax (401) 789-3120, info@skchamber.com, www.skchamber.com

**Warren** · *East Bay C/C* · Betty J. Pleacher, Pres., 16 Cutler St. #102, 02885, P 50,000, M 500, (401) 245-0750, Fax (401) 245-0110, info@eastbaychamberri.org, www.eastbaychamberri.org

**Warwick** · *Central Rhode Island C/C* · Lauren Slocum, Pres./ CEO, 3288 Post Rd., 02886, P 150,000, M 1,200, (401) 732-1100, Fax (401) 732-1107, business@centralrichamber.com, www. centralrichamber.com

**West Warwick** · *Pawtuxet Valley C/C* · Diane Wilson, Exec. Dir., 1192 Main St., 02893, P 75,000, M 280, (401) 823-3349, Fax (401) 823-8162, diane@pawtuxetvalleychamber.org, www. pvccommerce.org

**Westerly** · *Greater Westerly-Pawcatuck Area C/C* · Lisa Konicki, Exec. Dir., 1 Chamber Way, 02891, P 24,798, M 963, (401) 596-7761, (800) 732-7636, Fax (401) 596-2190, info@westerly chamber.org, www.westerlychamber.org

**Woonsocket** · *see Lincoln*

# South Carolina

**South Carolina C of C** · Otis Rawl, Pres./CEO, 1201 Main St., Ste. 1700, Columbia, 29201, P 3,700,000, M 2,300, (803) 799-4601, Fax (803) 779-6043, chamber@scchamber.net, www.scchamber.net.

**Abbeville** · *Greater Abbeville C/C* · 107 Court Sq., 29620, P 26,000, M 177, (864) 366-4600, Fax (864) 366-4068, abv chamber@wctel.com, www.visitabbevillesc.com

**Aiken** · *Greater Aiken C/C* · David Jameson, Pres./CEO, 121 Richland Ave. E., P.O. Box 892, 29802, P 165,000, M 875, (803) 641-1111, Fax (803) 641-4174, chamber@aikenchamber.net, www.aikenchamber.net

**Allendale** · *Allendale County C/C* · Michaele Goodson, Exec. Dir, P.O. Box 517, 29810, P 12,000, M 81, (803) 584-0082, Fax same, info@allendalechamber.com, www.allendalecountychamber.com

**Anderson** · *Anderson Area C/C* · Lee R. Luff, Pres., 907 N. Main St., Ste. 200, 29621, P 181,098, M 850, (864) 226-3454, Fax (864) 226-3300, info@andersonscchamber.com, www.andersonsc chamber.com

**Andrews** · *see Georgetown*

**Aynor** · *Aynor C/C* · Jeremy Johnson, Pres., P.O. Box 175, 29511, P 500, M 75, (843) 358-4808, www.aynorscchamber.org

**Bamberg** · *Bamberg County C/C* · Mr. Ronnie Maxwell, Pres., 604 Airport Rd., 29003, P 16,991, M 94, (803) 245-4427, Fax (803) 245-4428, info@bambergcountychamber.org, www.bamberg countychamber.org

**Barnwell** · *Barnwell County C/C* · 367 Fuldner Rd., P.O. Box 898, 29812, P 23,478, M 200, (803) 259-7446, Fax (803) 259-0030, bcchamber@bellsouth.net, www.barnwellcountychamber.com

**Batesburg-Leesville** · *Greater Batesburg-Leesville C/C* · Jim Wiszowaty, Pres./CEO, 112 E. Columbia Ave., P.O. Box 2178, 29070, P 6,500, M 250, (803) 532-4339, Fax (803) 532-3978, jim@batesburg-leesvillechamber.sc, www.batesburg-leesvillechamber.sc

**Beaufort** · *Beaufort Reg. C/C & Visitors Center* · Carlotta Ungaro, Pres., 1106 Carteret St., P.O. Box 910, 29901, P 147,000, M 900, (843) 525-8531, Fax (843) 986-5405, carlotta@beaufortsc. org, www.beaufortsc.org

**Bennettsville** · *Bennettsville C/C* · 304 W. Main, P.O. Box 1036, 29512, P 30,000, M 200, (843) 479-3941, Fax (843) 479-4859, info@visitbennettsville.com, www.visitbennettsville.com

**Bishopville** · *Lee County C/C* · Pam Kelley, Exec. Dir., 219 N. Main St., P.O. Box 187, 29010, P 22,000, M 160, (803) 484-5145, Fax (803) 484-4270, kingcotton@ftc-i.net, www.leecountychambersc.com

**Bluffton** · *Hilton Head Island-Bluffton C/C* · William G. Miles, Pres./CEO, 9 Oak Forest Rd., Ste. 202, 29910, P 42,000, M 1,700, (843) 757-1624, Fax (843) 757-6021, bluffton@hiltonheadisland. org, www.hiltonheadisland.org

**Bowman** · *see Saint George*

**Branchville** · *see Saint George*

**Camden** · *Kershaw County C/C & Visitors Center* · Liz Horton, Exec. Dir., 607 S. Broad St., P.O. Box 605, 29020, P 58,000, M 600, (803) 432-2525, (800) 968-4037, Fax (803) 432-4181, camden cvb@bellsouth.net, www.camden-sc.org

**Cayce** · *West Metro C/C* · Lisa Ingram, Pres., 1006 12th St., 29033, P 33,000, M 334, (803) 794-6504, (866) 720-5400, Fax (803) 794-6505, westmetrochamber@aol.com, www.west metrochamber.sc

**Central** · *see Clemson*

**Chapin** • *Greater Chapin C/C* • Norma Hammer, Pres./CEO, 302 Columbia Ave., P.O. Box 577, 29036, P 145,000, M 340, (803) 345-1100, Fax (803) 345-0266, director@chapinchamber.com, www.chapinchamber.com

**Charleston** • *Charleston Metro C/C* • Charles H VanRysselberge CCE, CEO, 2750 Speissegger Dr., Ste. 100, P.O. Box 975, 29402, P 530,000, M 2,400, (843) 577-2510, Fax (843) 723-4853, mail@charlestonchamber.org, www.charlestonchamber.net.

**Cheraw** • *Greater Cheraw C/C* • Patsy J. Hendley, Pres., 221 Market St., 29520, P 9,999, M 400, (843) 537-7681, Fax (843) 537-5886, cherawchamber@bellsouth.net, www.cherawchamber.com

**Chester** • *Chester County C/C* • Jim Fuller, Pres., 109 Gadsden St., P.O. Box 489, 29706, P 34,000, M 300, (803) 581-4142, Fax (803) 581-2431, preschamber@truvista.net, www.chesterchamber.com

**Chesterfield** • *Greater Chesterfield C/C* • Donna Curtis, Exec. Dir., 100 Main St., P.O. Box 230, 29709, P 1,404, M 200, (843) 623-2343, Fax (843) 623-2424, info@chesterfieldscchamber.com, www.chesterfieldscchamber.com

**Clemson** • *Clemson Area C/C* • Chris Hardy, Pres., 1105 Tiger Blvd., P.O. Box 1622, 29633, P 11,096, M 565, (864) 654-1200, (800) 542-0746, Fax (864) 654-5096, info@clemsonchamber.org, www.clemsonchamber.org

**Clover** • *Greater Clover C/C* • 118 Bethel St., P.O. Box 162, 29710, P 4,500, M 145, (803) 222-3312, Fax (803) 222-8396, scclover chamber@aol.com, www.cloversc.info

**Columbia** • *Greater Columbia C/C* • Ike McLeese, Pres., 930 Richland St., P.O. Box 1360, 29202, P 650,000, M 2,500, (803) 733-1110, Fax (803) 733-1149, info@columbiachamber.com, www.columbiachamber.com

**Conway** • *Conway Area C/C* • Alicia Harper, Exec. Dir., 203 Main St., P.O. Box 831, 29526, P 12,500, M 550, (843) 248-2273, Fax (843) 248-0003, info@conwayscchamber.com, www.conwaysc chamber.com

**Cross** • *see Saint George*

**Darlington** • *Greater Darlington C/C* • Susan Alexander, Exec. Dir., 38 Public Sq., 29532, P 66,000, M 300, (843) 393-2641, Fax (843) 393-8059, darlcoc@bellsouth.net, www.darlingtonchamber.net

**Dillon** • *Dillon County C/C* • Johnnie Luehrs, Pres./CEO, 100 N. MacArthur Ave., P.O. Box 1304, 29536, P 31,000, M 200, (843) 774-8551, (800) 444-6838, Fax (843) 774-0114, dillonchamber@bellsouth.net, www.dilloncitysc.com

**Dorchester** • *see Saint George*

**Easley** • *Greater Easley C/C* • Kent Dykes, Pres., 2001 E. Main St., P.O. Box 241, 29641, P 57,000, M 470, (864) 859-2693, Fax (864) 859-1941, ecc@easleychamber.org, www.easleychamber.org.

**Edisto Island** • *Edisto C/C* • Dan Carter, Exec. Dir., P.O. Box 206, 29438, P 3,500, M 145, (843) 869-3867, (888) 333-2781, eichamber@aol.com, www.edistochamber.com

**Elloree** • *see Orangeburg*

**Eutawville** • *see Saint George*

**Florence** • *Greater Florence C/C* • Tom Marschel, Pres., 610 W. Palmetto St., P.O. Box 948, 29503, P 125,000, M 842, (843) 665-0515, Fax (843) 662-2010, info@flochamber.com, www.flochamber.com.

**Fort Mill** • *see Rock Hill*

**Fountain Inn** • *Fountain Inn C/C* • Maria Bentley, Dir., 315 N. Main St., 29644, P 7,300, M 168, (864) 862-2586, Fax (864) 862-1086, www.fountaininnchamber.org

**Gaffney** • *Cherokee County C/C* • Gene Moorhead, Exec. Dir., 225 S. Limestone St., 29340, P 53,000, M 500, (864) 489-5721, Fax (864) 487-3399, comcher@bellsouth.net, www.cherokeechamber.org

**Garden City** • *see Georgetown*

**Georgetown** • *Georgetown County C/C* • Annette Fisher, Pres., 531 Front St., P.O. Box 1776, 29442, P 50,000, M 650, (843) 546-8436, Fax (843) 520-4876, info@visitgeorge.com, www.georgetownchamber.com

**Greeleyville** • *see Kingstree*

**Greenville** • *Greenville C/C* • Ben Haskew, Pres./CEO, 24 Cleveland St., 29601, P 401,000, M 2,400, (864) 242-1050, (866) 485-5262, Fax (864) 282-8509, info@greenvillechamber.org, www.greenvillechamber.org

**Greenwood** • *Greenwood Area C/C* • Angelle LaBorde, Pres., 110 Phoenix St., P.O. Box 980, 29648, P 67,000, M 625, (864) 223-8431, Fax (864) 229-9785, info@greenwoodscchamber.org, www.greenwoodscchamber.org

**Greer** • *Greater Greer C/C* • John Kimbrell, Pres./CEO, 111 Trade St., 29651, P 20,000, M 560, (864) 877-3131, Fax (864) 877-0961, info@greerchamber.com, www.greerchamber.com

**Grover** • *see Saint George*

**Hampton** • *Hampton County C/C* • Sal Arzillo, Pres., P.O. Box 122, 29924, P 21,386, M 120, (803) 943-3784, Fax (803) 943-7538, info@hardeevillechamber.com, www.hardeevillechamber ofcommerce.com

**Hardeeville** • *Greater Hardeeville C/C* • Sal Arzillo, Pres., 6 Ulmer St., P.O. Box 307, 29927, P 21,000, M 103, (843) 784-3606, Fax (843) 784-2781, bill@billtamiso.com, www.hardeevillechamber.com

**Harleyville** • *see Saint George*

**Hartsville** • *Greater Hartsville C/C* • Sharman Poplava, Pres., P.O. Box 578, 29551, P 31,472, M 337, (843) 332-6401, Fax (843) 332-8017, president@hartsvillechamber.org, www.hartsville chamber.org

**Hemingway** • *see Kingstree*

**Hilton Head Island** • *Hilton Head Island-Bluffton C/C* • William G. Miles, Pres./CEO, One Chamber of Commerce Dr., P.O. Box 5647, 29938, P 42,000, M 1,700, (843) 785-3673, (800) 523-3373, Fax (843) 785-7110, info@hiltonheadisland.org, www.hiltonheadisland.org

**Holly Hill** • *Tri-County Reg. C/C* • Teresa Mizzell Hatchell, Exec. Dir., 8603 Old State Rd., P.O. Box 1012, 29059, P 88,000, M 315, (803) 496-3831, (888) 568-5646, Fax (803) 496-3831, tcrcc@bellsouth.net, www.tri-crcc.com

**Inman** • *Greater Inman Area C/C* • Bessie Fisher, Pres., P.O. Box 227, 29349, P 2,500, M 72, (864) 472-3654, bessie50@gmail.com, www.inmanscchamber.org

**Irmo** • *Greater Irmo C/C* • Meredith Allan, Pres./CEO, 1248 Lake Murray Blvd., P.O. Box 1246, 29063, P 90,000, M 790, (803) 749-9355, Fax (803) 732-7986, info@greaterirmochamber.com, www.irmochamber.com

**Jasper County** • *see Ridgeland*

**Johnston** • *Edgefield County C/C* • 416 Calhoun St., 29832, P 25,000, M 175, (803) 275-0010, Fax (803) 275-3586, info@edgefieldcountychamber.org, info@edgefieldcountychamber.org, www.edgefieldcountychamber.org

**Kingstree** • *Williamsburg HomeTown C/C* • Leslee Spivey, Exec. Dir., 130 E. Main St., P.O. Box 696, 29556, P 37,000, M 250, (843) 355-6431, Fax (843) 355-3343, whtc@FTC-i.net, www.williamsburgsc.org

**Lake City** • *Greater Lake City C/C* • Rita Smith, Exec. Dir., 144 S. Acline Ave., P.O. Box 669, 29560, P 7,500, M 225, (843) 374-8611, Fax (843) 374-7938, lccoc1@ftc-i.net, www.lakecitysc.org

**Lake Wylie** • *Lake Wylie C/C* • P.O. Box 5233, 29710, P 25,000, M 400, (803) 831-2827, Fax (803) 831-2460, info@lakewyliesc.com, www.lakewyliesc.com

**Lancaster** • *Lancaster County C/C* • 604 N. Main St., P.O. Box 430, 29721, P 72,000, M 570, (803) 283-4105, Fax (803) 286-4360, lanchamber@infoave.net, www.lancasterchambersc.org

**Lane** • *see Kingstree*

**Langley** • *Midland Valley Area C/C* • Al McKay, Chrmn., P.O. Box 310, 29834, P 15,000, M 200, (803) 593-3030, Fax (803) 593-0085, ernieace@yahoo.com, www.midlandvalleyarea.com

**Laurens** • *Laurens County C/C* • Greg Alexander, Pres./CEO, P.O. Box 248, 29360, P 72,000, M 475, (864) 833-2716, Fax (864) 833-6935, mail@laurenscounty.org, www.laurenscounty.org

**Leesville** • *see Batesburg-Leesville*

**Lexington** • *Greater Lexington C/C* • Randy Halfacre, Pres./CEO, 321 S. Lake Dr., P.O. Box 44, 29071, P 65,000, M 800, (803) 359-6113, Fax (803) 359-0634, chamber@lexingtonsc.org, www.lexingtonsc.org.

**Liberty** • *Liberty C/C* • P.O. Box 123, 29657, P 3,500, M 30, (864) 843-3021, info@libertychamberofcommerce.com, www.libertychamberofcommerce.com

**Litchfield Beach** • *see Georgetown*

**Little River** • *Little River C/C* • Mary Martin, Exec. Dir., 1180 Hwy. 17 N., Ste. 1, P.O. Box 400, 29566, P 8,000, M 400, (843) 249-6604, (866) 817-8082, Fax (843) 249-9788, mary@littleriverchamber.org, www.littleriverchamber.org

**Loris** • *Loris Chamber and Visitors & Conv. Bur.* • James Edwards, Pres., 4242 Main St., P.O. Box 356, 29569, P 4,300, M 180, (843) 756-6030, Fax (843) 756-5661, info@lorischambersc.com, www.lorischambersc.com

**Manning** • *Clarendon County C/C* • Dawn Griffith, Exec. Dir., 19 N. Brooks St., 29102, P 32,000, M 320, (803) 435-4405, (800) 731-LAKE, Fax (803) 435-4406, chamber@clarendoncounty.com, www.clarendoncounty.com

**Marion** • *Marion C/C* • Judy J. Johnson, Exec. V.P., 209 E. Bobby Gerald Pkwy., P.O. Box 35, 29571, P 8,000, M 300, (843) 423-3561, Fax (843) 423-0963, marionsc@bellsouth.net, www.marionscchamber.com

**Mauldin** • *Greater Mauldin C/C* • Pat Pomeroy, Exec. Dir., P.O. Box 881, 29662, P 20,000, M 390, (864) 297-1323, Fax (864) 297-5645, info@mauldinchamber.org, www.mauldinchamber.org.

**Mc Cormick** • *Mc Cormick County C/C* • Rita Smith, Chrmn., 100 S. Main St., P.O. Box 938, 29835, P 10,410, M 166, (864) 852-2835, Fax (864) 852-2382, mccchamber@wctel.net, www.mccormickscchamber.org

**Moncks Corner** • *Berkeley County C/C* • Bill McCall, Pres., 1004 Old Hwy. 52, P.O. Box 968, 29461, P 146,000, M 650, (843) 761-8238, (800) 882-0337, Fax (843) 899-6491, info@berkeleysc.org, www.berkeleysc.org

**Mullins** • *Greater Mullins C/C* • Cindy Lesieur, Exec. Dir., 1 N. Main St., P.O. Box 595, 29574, P 5,000, M 250, (843) 464-6651, Fax same, mullinschamber@bellsouth.net, www.mullinsscchamber.com

**Murrells Inlet** • *see Georgetown*

**Myrtle Beach** • *Myrtle Beach Area C/C* • Dana Lilly, V.P., 1200 N. Oak St., P.O. Box 2115, 29578, P 150,000, M 2,400, (843) 626-7444, (800) 356-3016, Fax (843) 448-3010, info@visitmyrtlebeach.com, www.visitmyrtlebeach.com

**Newberry** • *Newberry County C/C* • Sheryl Starnes, Exec. Dir., 1109 Main St., P.O. Box 396, 29108, P 36,100, M 300, (803) 276-4274, Fax (803) 276-4373, chamber@newberrycounty.org, www.newberrycounty.org

**Ninety Six** • *Ninety Six C/C* • Diane Quinn, Secy., P.O. Box 8, 29666, P 1,935, M 115, (864) 543-2047, Fax (864) 543-4304, 96chamber@gmail.com

**North Augusta** • *North Augusta C/C* • Bill Bassham, Pres., 406 West Ave., P.O. Box 6246, 29861, P 25,000, M 400, (803) 279-2323, Fax (803) 279-0003, chamber@northaugusta.net, www.northaugustachamber.net

**North Myrtle Beach** • *North Myrtle Beach C/C* • Marc Jordan, Pres./CEO, 270 Hwy. 17 N., 29582, P 15,000, M 1,200, (843) 281-2662, (877) 332-2662, Fax (843) 280-2930, info@northmyrtlebeachchamber.com, www.northmyrtlebeachchamber.com.

**Orangeburg** • *Orangeburg County C/C* • David Coleman, Pres., 155 Riverside Dr., P.O. Box 328, 29116, P 92,167, M 450, (803) 534-6821, Fax (803) 531-9435, chamber@orangeburgsc.net, www.orangeburgchamber.com.

**Pageland** • *Pageland C/C* • Sondra Price, 128 N. Pearl St., P.O. Box 56, 29728, P 3,000, M 100, (843) 672-6400, Fax (843) 672-6401, pagelandcham@shtc.net, www.pagelandchamber.com

**Pawleys Island** • *see Georgetown*

**Pickens** • *Greater Pickens C/C* • Jim Capaldi, Exec. Dir., 222 W. Main St., P.O. Box 153, 29671, P 18,049, M 214, (864) 878-3258, Fax (864) 878-7317, info@pickenschamber.org, www.pickenschamber.org

**Pine Ridge** • *see Cayce*

**Providence** • *see Saint George*

**Reevesville** • *see Saint George*

**Ridgeland** • *Jasper County C/C* • Kendall Malphrus, Exec. Dir., 451-B E. Wilson St., P.O. Box 1267, 29936, P 21,809, M 270, (843) 726-8126, Fax (843) 726-6290, jasperchamber@jaspersc.org, www.jaspersc.org

**Ridgeville** • *see Saint George*

**Rock Hill** • *York County Reg. C/C* • Rob Youngblood, Pres., 116 E. Main St., P.O. Box 590, 29731, P 200,000, M 1,050, (803) 324-7500, Fax (803) 324-1889, info@yorkcountychamber.com, www.yorkcountychamber.com

**Saint George** • *Tri-County Reg. C/C* • Teresa Mizzell Hatchell, Exec. Dir., 225 Parler Ave., 29477, P 88,000, M 315, (843) 563-9091, Fax same, tcrcc@bellsouth.net, www.tri-crcc.com.

**Saint Matthews** • *Calhoun County C/C* • Jane Dyches, Exec. Dir., Courthouse Annex, Rm. 114, 29135, P 15,185, M 110, (803) 655-5650, Fax (803) 655-6110, calhounchamber@sc.rr.com, www.calhouncountychamber.org

**Saluda** • *Saluda County C/C* • Teresa Hendrix, Secy./Treas., P.O. Box 246, 29138, P 19,000, M 100, (864) 445-4100, saludacountychamber@embarqmail.com, www.saludacountychamber.sc

**Santee** • *see Orangeburg and Saint George*

**Santee** • *see Orangeburg and Saint George*

**Seneca** • *Oconee County C/C* • Patrick Lee, Dir., 108 E. N.1st St., P.O. Box 855, 29679, P 25,000, M 350, (864) 882-2097, Fax (864) 882-2881, oconeechamberofc@bellsouth.net, www.oconeecountychamber.com

**Simpsonville** · *Simpsonville Area C/C* · Deborah Hardwick, Pres., 211 N. Main St., P.O. Box 605, 29681, P 16,000, M 400, (864) 963-3781, Fax (864) 228-0003, dhardwick@simpsonvillechamber.com, www.simpsonvillechamber.com

**South Congaree** · *see Cayce*

**Spartanburg** · *Spartanburg Area C/C* · David Cordeau, Pres./CEO, 105 N. Pine St., P.O. Box 1636, 29304, P 253,791, M 1,685, (864) 594-5000, Fax (864) 594-5055, spartanburgchamber@spartanburgchamber.com, www.spartanburgchamber.com

**Springdale** · *see Cayce*

**Summerville** · *Greater Summerville C/C* · Rita Berry, Pres./CEO, 402 N. Main St., P.O. Box 670, 29484, P 113,000, M 575, (843) 873-2931, Fax (843) 875-4464, rberry@greatersummerville.org, www.greatersummerville.org.

**Sumter** · *Greater Sumter C/C* · Grier U. Blackwelder, Pres., 32 E. Calhoun St., 29150, P 108,000, M 1,200, (803) 775-1231, Fax (803) 775-0915, info@sumterchamber.com, www.sumterchamber.com.

**Tega Cay** · *see Rock Hill*

**Union** · *Union County C/C* · Torance Inman, Exec. Dir., 135 W. Main St., 29379, P 29,000, M 210, (864) 427-9039, (877) 202-8755, Fax (864) 427-9030, torance@unionsc.com, www.unionsc.com

**Vance** · *see Saint George*

**Walhalla** · *Greater Area Walhalla C/C* · Barbara Justus, Exec. Dir., 214 E. Main St., 29691, P 5,000, M 140, (864) 638-2727, Fax (864) 638-2727, walhallacoc@bellsouth.net, walhallasc.com

**Walterboro** · *Walterboro-Colleton C/C* · David M. Smalls, Pres./CEO, 109-C Benson St., P.O. Box 426, 29488, P 40,000, M 325, (843) 549-9595, Fax (843) 549-5775, info@walterboro.org, www.walterboro.org.

**West Columbia** · *see Cayce*

**Westminster** · *Westminster C/C* · Sandra Powell, Dir., 135 E. Main St., P.O. Box 155, 29693, P 3,000, M 112, (864) 647-5316, Fax (864) 647-5316, wcoc@nuvox.net, www.westminstersc.com

**Winnsboro** · *Fairfield County C/C* · Terry N. Vickers, Pres., Town Clock-Congress St., P.O. Box 297, 29180, P 24,500, M 185, (803) 635-4242, Fax (803) 712-2996, fchamber@truvista.net, www.fairfieldchamber.sc

**Woodruff** · *see Spartanburg*

**York** · *Greater York C/C* · Paul Boger, Exec. Dir., 203 E. Liberty St., P.O. Box 97, 29745, P 8,000, M 310, (803) 684-2590, (877) 684-2590, Fax (803) 684-2575, info@greateryorkchamber.com, www.greateryorkchamber.com

# South Dakota

**South Dakota C of C & Ind.** · David Owen, Pres., P.O. Box 190, Pierre, 57501, P 765,000, M 450, (605) 224-6161, (800) 742-8112, Fax (605) 224-7198, contactus@sdchamber.biz, www.sdchamber.biz

**Aberdeen** · *Aberdeen Area C/C* · Gail Ogdahl, Pres., 516 S. Main, P.O. Box 1179, 57402, P 28,000, M 635, (605) 225-2860, (800) 874-9038, Fax (605) 225-2437, info@aberdeen-chamber.com, www.aberdeen-chamber.com.

**Badlands** · *see Wall*

**Belle Fourche** · *Belle Fourche C/C* · Teresa Schanzenbach, Exec. Dir., 415 5th Ave., 57717, P 5,000, M 350, (605) 892-2676, (888) 345-JULY, Fax (605) 892-4633, director@bellefourchechamber.org, www.bellefourchechamber.org

**Beresford** · *Beresford C/C* · Nicole Hyronimus, Exec. Dir., P.O. Box 167, 57004, P 2,000, M 75, (605) 763-2021, Fax (605) 763-2021, chamber@bmtc.net, www.bmtc.net

**Brandon** · *Brandon Valley Area C/C* · Kim Cerwick, Exec. Dir., P.O. Box 182, 57005, P 8,100, M 250, (605) 582-7400, Fax (605) 582-8941, brancofc@alliancecom.net, www.brandonvalleychamber.com

**Britton** · *Britton Area C/C* · Julie Zuehlke, Secy./Treas., P.O. Box 96, 57430, P 1,500, M 80, (605) 448-5323, brittonchamber@venturecomm.net, www.brittonsouthdakota.com

**Brookings** · *Brookings Area C/C* · Al Heuton, Exec. Dir., 414 Main Ave., P.O. Box 431, 57006, P 25,000, M 435, (605) 692-6125, Fax (605) 697-8109, chamber@brookings.net, www.brookingssd.com.

**Buffalo** · *Harding County C/C* · Diane Haivala, Pres., P.O. Box 113, 57720, P 1,000, M 25, (605) 375-3844, (605) 375-3130, Fax (605) 375-3119

**Canton** · *Canton C/C* · Lisa Alden, Coord., P.O. Box 34, 57013, P 3,110, M 100, (605) 764-7864, lisa.canton@iw.net, www.cantonsouthdakota.org

**Centerville** · *Centerville C/C* · Doug Voss, Pres., P.O. Box 266, 57014, P 920, M 60, (605) 563-2291, Fax (605) 563-2615, doug.voss@k12.sd.us, www.centervillesd.org

**Chamberlain** · *Chamberlain-Oacoma Area C/C & CVB* · April Reis, Dir., 115 W. Lawler, 57325, P 2,900, M 154, (605) 234-4416, Fax (605) 234-4418, chamber@chamberlainsd.org, www.chamberlainsd.org

**Custer** · *Custer Area C/C* · David Ressler, Exec. Dir., 615 Washington St., P.O. Box 5018, 57730, P 1,860, M 310, (605) 673-2244, (800) 992-9818, Fax (605) 673-3726, info@custersd.com, www.custersd.com

**Deadwood** · *Deadwood C/C & Visitors Bur.* · George Milos, Exec. Dir., 767 Main St., 57732, P 1,300, M 400, (605) 578-1876, (800) 999-1876, Fax (605) 578-2429, visit@deadwood.org, www.deadwood.org

**Dell Rapids** · *Dell Rapids C/C* · Loretta Mattern, Coord., P.O. Box 81, 57022, P 3,500, M 80, (605) 428-4167, Fax (605) 428-4167, chamber@dellrapids.org, www.dellrapids.org

**DeSmet** · *DeSmet C/C* · Connie Halberson, P.O. Box 105, 57231, P 1,300, M 72, (605) 854-3652, www.desmetsd.com

**Edgemont** · *Edgemont C/C* · Bill Curran, Pres., P.O. Box 797, 57735, P 799, M 70, (605) 662-5900, edgemontchamber@gwtc.net, www.edgemont-sd.com

**Eureka** · *Eureka C/C* · Jim Schumacher, Pres., P.O. Box 272, 57437, P 1,100, M 50, (605) 284-2639, www.eurekasd.com

**Faith** · *Faith C/C* · Sandy Rasmussen, Pres., 205 E. 1st St., P.O. Box 246, 57626, P 500, M 80, (605) 967-2001, Fax (605) 967-2002, faithchamber@faithsd.com, www.faithsdchamber.com

**Flandreau** · *Flandreau Civic & Commerce Assn.* · 1005 W. Elm Ave., P.O. Box 343, 57028, P 2,400, M 65, (605) 997-2492, Fax (605) 997-2915, fdc@mcis.com, www.flandreau.org

**Fort Pierre** · *Fort Pierre C/C* · Pat Sutley, 310 Casey Tibbs St., P.O. Box 426, 57532, P 2,000, (605) 223-2178, www.fortpierre.com

**Freeman** · *Freeman Chamber/Comm. Dev.* · Shane Vetch, Pres., P.O. Box 43, 57029, P 1,300, M 100, (605) 925-4444, Fax (605) 925-7920, dennis@cityoffreeman.org, www.freemansd.com

**Garretson** · *Garretson Commercial Club* · Ron Luke, Pres., P.O. Box 349, 57030, P 1,165, M 60, (605) 594-3411, kvegas@alliancecom.net, www.garretsonsd.com

**Gettysburg** · *Gettysburg C/C* · Molly McRoberts, Secy., 110 S. Exene St., P.O. Box 33, 57442, P 1,300, M 60, (605) 765-2528, gburgchamber@venturecomm.net, www.gettysburgsd.net

**Gregory** · *Gregory Commercial Club* · Guyla Husman, Secy., 1313 Main St., 57533, P 1,350, M 90, (605) 835-8229, Fax (605) 835-9023, guylahusman@hotmail.com, www.cityofgregory.com

**Hill City** · *Hill City Area C/C* · Mike Verchio, Exec. Dir., P.O. Box 253, 57745, P 3,780, M 243, (605) 574-2368, (800) 888-1798, Fax (605) 574-2055, hcacoc@hills.net, www.hillcitysd.com

**Hot Springs** · *Hot Springs Area C/C* · George Kotti, Exec. Dir., 801 S. 6th St., P.O. Box 342, 57747, P 4,300, M 285, (605) 745-4140, (800) 325-6991, Fax (605) 745-5849, hschamber@gwtc.net, www.hotsprings-sd.com.

**NAMED ONE OF AMERICA'S DOZEN DISTINCTIVE DESTINATIONS IN 2009. HOME OF THE MAMMOTH SITE. LEAN HORSE ULTRA MARATHON IN AUG; BADGER CLARK COWBOY POETRY AND MUSIC GATHERING IN SEPT.**

**Huron** · *Huron Area C/C* · Peggy Woolridge, Exec. Dir., 1725 Dakota Ave. S., 57350, P 11,500, M 400, (605) 352-0000, (800) 487-6673, Fax (605) 352-8321, cvb@huronsd.com, www.huronsd.com

**Keystone** · *Keystone C/C* · Bonnetta Eich, Exec. Dir., P.O. Box 653, 57751, P 350, M 92, (605) 666-4896, (800) 456-3345, Fax (605) 666-4896, info@keystonechamber.com, www.keystonechamber.com

**Kimball** · *Kimball C/C* · Erin Bergeleen, Pres., P.O. Box 2, 57355, P 750, (605) 778-6218, erinbergeleen@midstatesd.net, www.kimballsd.org

**Lead** · *Lead Area C/C* · Melissa Johnson, Exec. Dir., 160 W. Main, 57754, P 3,100, M 250, (605) 584-1100, Fax (605) 584-2209, leadcoc@rushmore.com, www.leadmethere.org

**Lemmon** · *Lemmon Area C/C* · Stacy Dailey, Coord., 100 3rd St. W., 57638, P 1,350, M 120, (605) 374-5716, Fax (605) 374-5789, lchamber@sdplains.com, www.lemmonsd.com

**Lennox** · *Lennox Commercial Club* · Justin Weiland, City Admin., P.O. Box 181, 57039, P 2,700, M 25, (605) 647-2286, Fax (605) 647-2281, www.cityoflenoxsd.com

**Madison** · *Madison Area C/C* · Julie Gross, Exec. Dir., 315 S. Egan Ave., P.O. Box 467, 57042, P 6,540, M 250, (605) 256-2454, Fax (605) 256-9606, director@chamberofmadisonsd.com, www.chamberofmadisonsd.com

**Milbank** · *Milbank Area C/C* · Laura Foss, Exec. Dir., 1001 E. 4th Ave. #101, 57252, P 3,500, M 198, (605) 432-6656, (800) 675-6656, Fax (605) 432-6507, chamber@milbanksd.com, www.milbanksd.com

**Miller** · *Miller Civic & Commerce Assn.* · Greg Palmer, Pres., 103 W. 3rd St., 57362, P 1,500, M 80, (605) 853-3098, Fax (605) 853-3276, amy@millersd.net, millersd.net

**Mitchell** · *Mitchell Area C/C* · Bryan Hisel, Exec. Dir., 601 N. Main St., P.O. Box 1026, 57301, P 18,741, M 610, (605) 996-5567, (866) 273-CORN, Fax (605) 996-8273, info@mitchellchamber.com, www.mitchellchamber.com.

**Mobridge** · *Mobridge C/C* · Cindy Melcher, Exec. Dir., 103 Main St., 57601, P 3,500, M 176, (605) 845-2387, (888) 614-3474, Fax (605) 845-3223, info@mobridge.org, www.mobridge.org.

**Murdo** · *Murdo C/C* · Sherry Philips, P.O. Box 242, 57559, P 600, M 80, (605) 669-3333, murdoinfo@murdosd.com, www.murdosd.com

**Oacoma** · *see Chamberlain*

**Philip** · *Philip C/C* · P.O. Box 378, 57567, P 800, M 100, (605) 859-2645, Fax (605) 859-2622, ccphilip@gwtc.net, www.philip southdakota.com

**Pierre** · *Pierre Area C/C* · Laura Schoen Carbonneau, CEO, 800 W. Dakota Ave., P.O. Box 548, 57501, P 16,000, M 400, (605) 224-7361, (800) 962-2034, Fax (605) 224-6485, contactchamber@ pierre.org, www.pierre.org

**Platte** · *Platte Area C/C* · Laura VandenBerg, Exec. Dir., P.O. Box 393, 57369, P 1,367, M 130, (605) 337-2275, (888) 297-8175, Fax (605) 337-3988, plattechamber@midstatesd.net, www.plattesd.org

**Presho** · *Presho Area C/C* · P.O. Box 415, 57568, P 600, M 50, (605) 895-9445, preshochamber@kennebectelephone.com, www.presho.net

**Rapid City** · *Rapid City Area C/C* · Linda Rabe IOM CCE, Pres./CEO, 444 Mt. Rushmore Rd. N., P.O. Box 747, 57709, P 89,000, M 1,400, (605) 343-1744, Fax (605) 343-6550, info@rapidcity chamber.com, www.rapidcitychamber.com.

**Redfield** · *Redfield Area C/C* · Cathy Fink, Exec. Dir., 626 Main St., 57469, P 2,800, M 100, (605) 472-0965, Fax (605) 472-4553, redfieldchamber@redfield-sd.com, www.redfield-sd.com

**Sioux Falls** · *Sioux Falls Area C/C* · Evan C. Nolte, Pres., 200 N. Phillips Ave. #102, P.O. Box 1425, 57101-1425, P 227,171, M 2,261, (605) 336-1620, Fax (605) 336-6499, sfacc@siouxfalls.com, www.siouxfalls.com

**Sisseton** · *Sisseton Area C/C & Visitors Bur.* · Ruth Ceroll, Ofc. Dir., 1608 SD Hwy. 10, Ste. A, 57262, P 2,572, M 80, (605) 698-7261, (888) 512-1966, sissetonchamber@venturecomm.net, www.sisseton.com

**Spearfish** · *Spearfish Area C/C* · Lisa Langer IOM, Exec. Dir., 106 W. Kansas, P.O. Box 550, 57783, P 13,500, M 596, (605) 642-2626, (800) 626-8013, Fax (605) 642-7310, info@spearfishcham ber.com, www.spearfishchamber.org, www.visitspearfish.travel

**Sturgis** · *Sturgis Area C/C & VB* · Michele Loobey-Gertsch, Exec. Dir., 2040 Junction Ave., P.O. Box 504, 57785, P 6,500, M 350, (605) 347-2556, Fax (605) 347-6682, info@sturgis-sd.org, www.sturgis-sd.org.

**Vermillion** · *Vermillion Area C/C & Dev. Co.* · Steve Howe, Exec. Dir., 906 E. Cherry St., 57069, P 13,000, M 300, (605) 624-5571, (800) 809-2071, Fax (605) 624-0094, vcdc@vermillionchamber.com, www.vermillionchamber.com

**Wagner** · *Wagner C/C* · Craig Kronaizle, Pres., 60 Main Ave. S.E., P.O. Box 40, 57380, P 1,558, M 65, (605) 384-3741, Fax (605) 384-3403, developwagner@hcinet.net, www.wagnersd.org

**Wall** · *Wall Badlands Area C/C* · Carla Seybold, Exec. Dir., 501 Main St., P.O. Box 527, 57790, P 825, M 105, (605) 279-2665, (888) 852-9255, Fax (605) 279-2067, wallchamber@gwtc.net, www.wall-badlands.com

**Watertown** · *Watertown Area C/C* · Megan Olson, Pres./CEO, 20 S. Maple, P.O. Box 1113, 57201, P 21,000, M 715, (605) 886-5814, Fax (605) 886-5957, coc@watertownsd.com, www.watertownsd.com

**Webster** · *Webster Area C/C* · Marcia Lefman, Secy./Treas., P.O. Box 123, 57274, P 2,000, M 175, (605) 345-4668, (888) 571-7582, wchamber@itctel.com, www.webstersd.com, www.proudanglers.com

**Wessington Springs** · *Wessington Springs Area C/C* · Jerry Caffee, Pres., P.O. Box 513, 57382, P 1,011, M 45, (605) 539-1929, wsprings@venturecomm.net, www.wessingtonsprings.com

**White River** · *Mellette County C/C* · Rose West, Treas., 202 N. Main St, P.O. Box 223, 57579, P 2,083, M 41, (605) 259-3651, mellettecounty@yahoo.com

**Winner** · *Winner C/C* · Amy Moe, Exec. Dir., 201 Monroe St., P.O. Box 268, 57580, P 3,500, M 200, (605) 842-1533, (800) 658-3079, Fax (605) 842-1512, thechamber@gwtc.net, www.winnersd.org.

**Yankton** • *Yankton Area C/C* • Bob Cappel, Dir. of Chamber Svcs., 803 E. Fourth St., P.O. Box 588, 57078, P 20,000, M 400, (605) 665-3636, (800) 888-1460 visitor info, Fax (605) 665-7501, visitorinfo@yanktonsd.com, www.yanktonsd.com

# Tennessee

**Tennessee C of C & Ind.** • Deb Woolley, Pres., 611 Commerce St. #3030, Nashville, 37203, M 600, (615) 256-5141, Fax (615) 256-6726, www.tnchamber.org

**Alamo** • *Crockett County C/C* • Melissa Cox, Exec. Dir., 29 N. Bells St., 38001, P 14,000, M 162, (731) 696-5120, Fax (731) 696-4855, contact@crockettchamber.com, www.crockettchamber.com

**Ardmore** • *Ardmore C/C* • 29910 Ardmore Ave., P.O. Box 845, 38449, P 2,224, M 124, (256) 423-7588, Fax (256) 423-8950

**Arlington** • *Arlington C/C* • Glen Bascom II, Pres., 6220 Greenlee St. #3B, P.O. Box 545, 38002, P 10,000, M 145, (901) 867-0545, Fax (901) 867-4066, info@arlingtontnchamber.com, arlingtontnchamber.com

**Ashland City** • *Cheatham County C/C* • Mary MacRae, Interim Exec. Dir., 575 S. Main St. #101, P.O. Box 354, 37015, P 39,000, M 400, (615) 792-6722, (615) 792-1335, Fax (615) 792-5001, info@cheathamchamber.org, www.cheathamchamber.org

**Athens** • *Athens Area C/C* • Rob Preston, Pres./CEO, 13 N. Jackson St., 37303, P 15,000, M 600, (423) 745-0334, Fax (423) 745-0335, info@athenschamber.org, www.athenschamber.org

**Bartlett** • *Bartlett Area C/C* • John P. Threadgill, Pres., 2969 Elmore Park Rd., P.O. Box 34193, 38184, P 48,000, M 615, (901) 372-9457, Fax (901) 372-9488, info@bartlettchamber.org, www.bartlettchamber.org.

**Bellevue** • *Bellevue C/C* • Cindy Tremblay, Exec. Dir., 177-A Belle Forest Circle, 37221, P 35,000, M 290, (615) 662-2737, (877) 660-2737, Fax (615) 662-0197, info@thebellevuechamber.com, www.thebellevuechamber.com

**Benton** • *Polk County C/C* • P.O. Box 560, 37307, P 18,000, M 200, (423) 338-5040, (800) 633-7655, Fax (423) 338-0056, westoffice@ocoeecountry.com, www.ocoeecountry.com

**Bolivar** • *Hardeman County C/C* • Anne Crighton, Pres., 500 W. Market St., P.O. Box 313, 38008, P 28,105, M 180, (731) 658-6554, Fax (731) 658-6874, info@hardemancountychamber.org, www.hardemancountychamber.org

**Brentwood** • *Brentwood Cool Springs C/C* • Cindi Parmenter, Interim Pres./CEO, 5211 Maryland Way #1080, 37027, P 150,000, M 1,000, (615) 373-1595, Fax (615) 373-8810, info@brentwoodcoolsprings.org, www.brentwoodcoolsprings.org

**Bristol** • *see Bristol, VA*

**Brownsville** • *Brownsville-Haywood County C/C* • Joe Ing, Exec. Dir., 121 W. Main, 38012, P 20,000, M 320, (731) 772-2193, Fax (731) 772-2195, brownsvillechamber@newwavecomm.net, www.haywoodcountybrownsville.com

**Bybee** • *see Newport*

**Byrdstown** • *Byrdstown-Pickett County C/C* • Desiree Peterson, Exec. Dir., 109 W. Main St., P.O. Box 447, 38549, P 5,000, M 140, (931) 864-7195, (888) 406-4704, Fax (931) 864-6845, dpeterson@twlakes.net, www.dalehollow.com

**Camden** • *Benton County/Camden C/C* • Bill Kee, Exec. Dir., 266 Hwy. 641 N., 38320, P 16,328, M 209, (731) 584-8395, (877) 584-8395, Fax (731) 584-5544, chamber1@usit.net, www.bentoncountycamden.com.

**Carthage** • *Smith County C/C* • Regina Brooks, Admin. Dir., 939 Upper Ferry Rd., P.O. Box 70, 37030, P 17,712, M 171, (615) 735-2093, Fax (615) 735-2093, info@smithcountychamber.org, www.smithcountychamber.org

**Celina** • *Clay County C/C* • Ray Norris, Exec. Dir., 424 Brown St., 38551, P 8,000, M 130, (931) 243-3338, Fax (931) 243-6809, claychamber@twlakes.net, www.dalehollowlake.net

**Centerville** • *Hickman County C/C* • Nancy Roland, Exec. Dir., 405 W. Public Sq., P.O. Box 126, 37033, P 25,000, M 150, (931) 729-5774, Fax (931) 729-0874, hccc@mlec.net, www.hickmanco.org

**Chattanooga** • *Chattanooga Area C/C* • Tom Edd Wilson, Pres./CEO, 811 Broad St. #100, 37402, P 496,854, M 1,550, (423) 756-2121, Fax (423) 267-7242, info@chattanoogachamber.com, www.chattanoogachamber.com

**Chester County** • *see Henderson*

**Church Hill** • *East Hawkins County C/C* • Steve Loller, P.O. Box 1314, 37642, P 20,000, M 30, (423) 357-6365, (423) 357-2943

**Clarksville** • *Clarksville Area C/C* • James Chavez, Pres./CEO, 25 Jefferson St. #300, P.O. Box 883, 37040, P 122,000, M 1,000, (931) 647-2331, Fax (931) 645-1574, cacc@clarksville.tn.us, www.clarksvillechamber.com

**Cleveland** • *Cleveland/Bradley C/C* • Gary Farlow, Pres./CEO, 225 Keith St. S.W., P.O. Box 2275, 37320, P 92,538, M 800, (423) 472-6587, Fax (423) 472-2019, info@clevelandchamber.com, www.clevelandchamber.com.

**Clinton** • *Anderson County C/C* • Jackie L. Nichols, Pres., 245 N. Main St., Ste. 200, 37716, P 71,587, M 450, (865) 457-2559, (865) 457-2977, Fax (865) 463-7480, jackie@andersoncountychamber.org, www.andersoncountychamber.org

**Collierville** • *Collierville C/C* • Fran Persechini, Pres., 485 Halle Park Dr., 38017, P 43,000, M 683, (901) 853-1949, Fax (901) 853-2399, info@colliervillechamber.com, www.colliervillechamber.com

**Collinwood** • *Wayne County C/C* • Rena' Purdy, Exec. Dir., 219 E. Broadway, 38450, P 18,000, M 125, (931) 724-4337, Fax (931) 724-4347, chamber@netease.net, www.waynecountychamber.org

**Columbia** • *Maury Alliance* • Frank M. Tamberrino, Pres., 106 W. 6th St., P.O. Box 1076, 38402, P 80,000, M 600, (931) 388-2155, Fax (931) 380-0335, scobb@mauryalliance.com, www.mauryalliance.com.

**Cookeville** • *Cookeville Area-Putnam County C/C* • George Halford, Pres./CEO, 1 W. First St., 38501, P 68,000, M 900, (931) 526-2211, (800) 264-5541, Fax (931) 526-4023, info@cookevillechamber.com, www.cookevillechamber.com

**Cool Springs** • *see Brentwood*

**Copperhill** • *Polk County C/C* • P.O. Box 960, 37317, P 16,050, M 200, (423) 496-9000, (877) 790-2157, Fax (423) 496-5415, eastoffice@ocoeecountry.com, www.ocoeecountry.com

**Cosby** • *see Newport*

**Covington** • *Covington-Tipton County C/C* • Lee Johnston, Exec. Dir., 106 W. Liberty, P.O. Box 683, 38019, P 56,000, M 340, (901) 476-9727, Fax (901) 476-0056, tiptoncounty_covingto@comcast.net, www.covington-tiptoncochamber.com

**Crossville** • *Crossville-Cumberland County C/C* • Beth Alexander, Pres./CEO, 34 S. Main St., 38555, P 51,346, M 550, (931) 484-8444, (877) 465-3861, Fax (931) 484-7511, thechamber@crossville-chamber.com, www.crossville-chamber.com.

**Dandridge** • *Jefferson County C/C* • Don Cason, Pres./CEO, P.O. Box 890, 37725, P 47,000, M 450, (865) 397-9642, Fax (865) 397-0164, info@jeffersoncountytennessee.com, www.jeffersoncountytennessee.com.

**Dayton** · *Dayton C/C* · Cynthia Rodriguez, Admin. Asst., 107 Main St., 37321, P 30,000, M 240, (423) 775-0361, Fax (423) 570-0105, chamber@volstate.net, www.rheacountyetc.com, www.tnstrawberryfestival.com.

**Del Rio** · *see Newport*

**Dickson** · *Dickson County C/C* · David Hamilton, Pres./CEO, 119 Hwy. 70 E., 37055, P 52,500, M 450, (615) 446-2349, Fax (615) 441-3112, contactus@dicksoncountychamber.com, www.dickson countychamber.com.

**Donelson** · *see Nashville - Donelson-Hermitage*

**Dover** · *Stewart County C/C* · Laura Shemwell, Pres., 117 Moore Rd., P.O. Box 147, 37058, P 13,500, M 150, (931) 232-8290, Fax (931) 232-4973, stewartcountycha@bellsouth.net, www.stewart countyvacation.com

**Dresden** · *Weakley County C/C* · Barbara Virgin, Exec. Dir., 114 W. Maple, N. Court Sq., P.O. Box 67, 38225, P 34,895, M 400, (731) 364-3787, Fax (731) 364-2099, wccc@crunet.com, www.weakley countychamber.com.

**Dunlap** · *Sequatchie County-Dunlap C/C* · Howard Hatcher, Exec. Dir., 15643 Rankin Ave., P.O. Box 1653, 37327, P 5,000, M 250, (423) 949-7608, Fax (423) 949-8052, sequatchie@bledsoe.net, www.sequatchie.com

**Dyersburg** · *Dyersburg/Dyer County C/C* · Allen Hester CCE, Pres./CEO, 2000 Commerce Ave., 38024, P 40,000, M 620, (731) 285-3433, Fax (731) 286-4926, chamber@ecsis.net, www.dyerchamber.com

**Elizabethton** · *Elizabethton/Carter County C/C* · Candy Crayg, Exec. Dir., 500 Veterans Memorial Pkwy., P.O. Box 190, 37644, P 59,000, M 320, (423) 547-3850, Fax (423) 547-3854, director@elizabethtonchamber.com, www.elizabethtonchamber.com

**Erin** · *Houston County C/C* · Betsy Ligon, Pres., P.O. Box 603, 37061, P 8,000, M 110, (931) 289-5100, Fax (931) 289-5600, irish@peoplestel.net, www.houstoncochamber.com

**Erwin** · *Unicoi County C/C* · Amanda Bennett, Exec. Dir., 100 S. Main Ave., P.O. Box 713, 37650, P 18,000, M 200, (423) 743-3000, Fax (423) 743-0942, amanda@unicoicounty.org, www.unicoicounty.org

**Etowah** · *Etowah Area C/C* · Durant Tullock, Exec. Dir., L & N Depot, P.O. Box 458, 37331, P 40,000, M 200, (423) 263-2228, Fax (423) 263-1670, info@etowahcoc.org, www.etowahcoc.org

**Fairview** · *Fairview Area C/C* · Mitzi Mangrum, Ofc. Mgr., 7200 City Center Cirle, P.O. Box 711, 37062, P 12,000, M 145, (615) 799-9290, Fax (615) 799-9290, fairviewchamber@bellsouth.net, www.fairviewchamber.org

**Fayetteville** · *Fayetteville-Lincoln County C/C* · Carolyn Denton, Exec. Dir., 208 Elk Ave. S., P.O. Box 515, 37334, P 32,000, M 365, (931) 433-1234, (888) 433-1238, Fax (931) 433-9087, flcchamber@fpunet.com, www.fayettevillelincolncountychamber.com.

**Franklin** · *Williamson County-Franklin C/C* · Nancy P. Conway, Pres./CEO, 134 2nd Ave. N., P.O. Box 156, 37065, P 157,000, M 1,550, (615) 794-1225, (800) 356-3445, Fax (615) 790-5337, info@wcfchamber.com, williamson-franklinchamber.com

**Gainesboro** · *Jackson County C/C* · Carla Khouri, Pres., P.O. Box 827, 38562, P 10,000, M 80, (931) 268-0971, Fax (931) 268-3540, www.gainesboro-jcchamber.com

**Gallatin** · *Gallatin C/C* · Paige Brown Strong, Dir., 118 W. Main St., P.O. Box 26, 37066, P 28,000, M 500, (615) 452-4000, (800) 452-5286, Fax (615) 452-4021, info@gallatintn.org, www.gallatintn.org

**Gatlinburg** · *Gatlinburg C/C* · Victoria Simms, Exec. Dir., 811 East Pkwy., P.O. Box 527, 37738, P 3,550, M 596, (865) 436-4178, (800) 568-4748, Fax (865) 430-3876, info@gatlinburg.com, www.gatlinburg.com

**Germantown** · *Germantown Area C/C* · Pat Scroggs, Exec. Dir., 2195 S. Germantown Rd., Ste. 100, 38138, P 40,000, M 700, (901) 755-1200, Fax (901) 755-9168, info@germantownchamber.com, www.germantownchamber.com

**Gleason** · *see Dresden*

**Goodlettsville** · *Goodlettsville Area C/C* · David Wilson, Exec. Dir., 117 N. Main St., 37072, P 13,800, M 500, (615) 859-7979, Fax (615) 859-1480, david@goodlettsvillechamber.com, www.goodlettsvillechamber.com

**Greeneville** · *Greene County Partnership* · Randy Harrell, Pres./CEO, 115 Academy St., 37743, P 65,945, M 500, (423) 638-4111, Fax (423) 638-5345, gcp@greenecop.com, www.GreeneCountyPartnership.com

**Greenfield** · *see Dresden*

**Gruetli** · *see Monteagle*

**Hartford** · *see Newport*

**Hartsville** · *Hartsville-Trousdale County C/C* · Seth H. Thurman, Exec. Dir., 240 Broadway, 37074, P 7,500, M 300, (615) 374-9243, Fax (615) 374-0068, sthurman@hartsvilletrousdale.com, www.hartsvilletrousdale.com.

**Helenwood** · *Scott County C/C* · Almeda Peavyhouse, Exec. Dir., 12025 Scott Hwy., P.O. Box 766, 37755, P 21,217, M 240, (423) 663-6900, (800) 645-6905, Fax (423) 663-6906, scchamber@highland.net, www.scottcountychamber.com.

**Henderson** · *Chester County-City of Henderson C/C* · Kristen Hicks, Exec. Dir., 130 E. Main St., P.O. Box 1976, 38340, P 16,000, M 200, (731) 989-5222, Fax (731) 983-5518, khester@chestercountychamber.com, www.chestercountychamber.com

**Hendersonville** · *Hendersonville Area C/C* · Brenda Payne, Pres., 100 Country Club Dr. #104, 37075, P 43,866, M 780, (615) 824-2818, Fax (615) 250-3637, brenda@hendersonvillechamber.com, www.hendersonvillechamber.com

**Hohenwald** · *Hohenwald-Lewis County C/C* · Mark Graves, Pres., 106 N. Court St., 38462, P 12,000, M 145, (931) 796-4084, Fax (931) 796-6020, director@hohenwaldlewischamber.com, www.hohenwaldlewischamber.com

**Humboldt** · *Humboldt C/C* · Gil Fletcher, Dir., 1200 Main St., 38343, P 9,500, M 267, (731) 784-1842, Fax (731) 784-1573, gil@humboldttnchamber.org, www.humboldttnchamber.org

**Huntingdon** · *Carroll County C/C* · Brad Hurley, Pres., 20740 E. Main St., P.O. Box 726, 38344, P 29,322, M 320, (731) 986-4664, Fax (731) 986-2029, cchamber@earthlink.net, carrollcounty-tn-chamber.com.

**Jacksboro** · *Campbell County C/C* · E.L. Morton, Exec. Dir., 1016 Main St., P.O. Box 305, 37757, P 39,854, M 230, (423) 566-0329, Fax (423) 566-4896, chamber@campbellcountygov.com, co.campbell.tn.us

**Jackson** · *Jackson Area C/C* · Paul Latture III, Pres./CEO, 197 Auditorium St., P.O. Box 1904, 38302, P 95,894, M 1,198, (731) 423-2200, Fax (731) 424-4860, chamber@jacksontn.com, www.jacksontn.com

**Jamestown** · *Fentress County C/C* · Walter Page CTTP, Exec. Dir., 114 Central Ave. W., P.O. Box 1294, 38556, P 17,000, M 212, (931) 879-9948, (800) 327-3945, Fax (931) 879-6767, wpage@jamestowntn.org, www.jamestowntn.org

**Jasper** • *Marion County C/C* • Debbie Stewart, Exec. Dir., 302 Betsy Pack Dr., 37347, P 27,942, M 167, (423) 942-5103, Fax (423) 942-0098, marioncoc@bellsouth.net, www.marioncountychamber.com

**Jefferson City** • *see Dandridge*

**Johnson City** • *Johnson City/Jonesborough/Washington County C/C* • Gary M. Mabrey III CCE, Pres./CEO, 603 E. Market St., P.O. Box 180, 37605, P 151,000, M 850, (423) 461-8000, Fax (423) 461-8047, mabrey@johnsoncitytnchamber.com, www.johnsoncitytnchamber.com.

**Jonesborough** • *see Johnson City*

**Kingsport** • *Kingsport Area C/C* • Miles Burdine, Pres./CEO, 151 E. Main St., P.O. Box 1403, 37662, P 50,000, M 700, (423) 392-8800, Fax (423) 246-7234, info@kingsportchamber.org, www.kingsportchamber.org.

**Kingston** • *Roane Alliance* • Leslie Henderson, Pres./CEO, 1209 N. Kentucky, 37763, P 52,000, M 400, (865) 376-5572, Fax (865) 376-4978, info@roanealliance.org, www.roanealliance.org

**Knoxville** • *Knoxville Area Chamber Partnership* • Mike Edwards, Pres./CEO, 17 Market Sq., Ste. 201, 37902, P 385,572, M 2,000, (865) 637-4550, Fax (865) 523-2071, partnership@kacp.com, www.knoxvillechamber.com

**La Vergne** • *Rutherford County C/C* • Stephanie Brackman, Interim Pres., 5093 Murfreesboro Rd., 37086, P 223,000, M 2,200, (615) 793-5444, Fax (615) 793-6025, chamber@lavergne.org, www.rutherfordchamber.org

**Lafayette** • *Macon County C/C* • Lona Vinson, Exec. Secy., 685 Hwy. 52 Bypass W., 37083, P 22,800, M 178, (615) 666-5885, Fax (615) 666-6969, mchamber@nctc.com, www.maconcountytn.com

**Lake City** • *Lake City C/C* • Janet Phillips, Pres./CEO, 506 S. Main St., P.O. Box 1054, 37769, P 2,000, M 100, (865) 426-9595, lcchambe@bellsouth.net

**Lawrenceburg** • *Lawrence County C/C* • Chad Chancellor, Exec. Dir., 1609 N. Locust Ave., P.O. Box 86, 38464, P 40,000, M 350, (931) 762-4911, (877) 388-4911, Fax (931) 762-3153, info@selectlawrence.com, www.selectlawrence.com

**Lebanon** • *Lebanon-Wilson County C/C* • Sue Vanatta, Pres./CEO, 149 Public Sq., 37087, P 88,000, M 800, (615) 444-5503, (615) 444-7132, Fax (615) 443-0596, lebchamb@bellsouth.net, lebanonwilsontnchamber.org.

**Lenoir City** • *see Loudon*

**Lewisburg** • *Marshall County C/C* • Ritaanne Weaver, Exec. Dir., 227 Second Ave. N., 37091, P 30,000, M 280, (931) 359-3863, Fax (931) 359-8411, director@marshallchamber.org, www.marshallchamber.org

**Lexington** • *Henderson County C/C* • Vicki Bunch, Exec. Dir., 149 Eastern Shores Dr., 38351, P 27,000, M 300, (731) 968-2126, Fax (731) 968-7006, vickibunch@hctn.org, www.hctn.org

**Livingston** • *Livingston-Overton County C/C* • John Roberts, Exec. Dir., 222 E. Main St., P.O. Box 354, 38570, P 20,523, M 231, (931) 823-6421, Fax (931) 823-6422, chamber@twlakes.net, overtonco.com.

**Loudon** • *Loudon County C/C* • Michael Bobo, Pres., 318 Angel Row, P.O. Box 87, 37774, P 45,000, M 450, (865) 458-2067, Fax (865) 458-1206, michael@loudoncountychamber.com, www.loudoncountychamber.com

**Lynchburg** • *Lynchburg-Moore County C/C* • Dr. Becker, Pres., P.O. Box 421, 37352, P 7,500, M 80, (931) 759-4111, info@lynchburgtn.com, www.lynchburgtn.com

**Madison** • *Madison-Rivergate Area C/C* • Debbie Pace, Exec. Dir., P.O. Box 97, 37116, P 36,000, M 350, (615) 865-5400, Fax (615) 865-0448, president@madisonrivergatechamber.com, www.madisonrivergatechamber.com

**Madisonville** • *Monroe County C/C* • William Wells III, Pres./CEO, 520 Cook St. #A, 37354, P 43,000, M 385, (423) 442-4588, Fax (423) 442-9016, info@monroecountychamber.org, www.monroecountychamber.org

**Manchester** • *Manchester Area C/C* • Susie McEacharn, Exec. Dir., 110 E. Main St., 37355, P 10,000, M 380, (931) 728-7635, Fax (931) 723-0736, manchestercoc@macoc.org, www.macoc.org

**Martin** • *see Dresden*

**Maryville** • *Blount County C/C* • Fred H. Forster, Pres./CEO, 201 S. Washington St., 37804, P 118,186, M 1,370, (865) 983-2241, Fax (865) 984-1386, info@blountchamber.com, www.blountchamber.com.

**Maynardville** • *Union County C/C* • Julie Graham, Exec. Dir., P.O. Box 848, 37807, P 25,000, M 115, (865) 992-2811, Fax (865) 992-9812, info@comeherecomehome.com, www.comeherecomehome.com

**McEwen** • *see Waverly*

**McMinnville** • *McMinnville-Warren County C/C* • Alicea Weddington, Pres., 110 S. Court Sq., P.O. Box 574, 37111, P 39,000, M 350, (931) 473-6611, Fax (931) 473-4741, aweddington@warrentn.com, www.warrentn.com.

**Memphis** • *Memphis Reg. C/C* • John Moore, Pres./CEO, 22 N. Front St., Ste. 200, P.O. Box 224, 38101, P 1,280,000, M 2,300, (901) 543-3500, (901) 543-5333, Fax (901) 543-3510, info@memphischamber.com, www.memphischamber.com

**Milan** • *Milan C/C* • Tara Bradford, Exec. V.P., 1061 S. Main St., 38358, P 7,891, M 180, (731) 686-7494, Fax (731) 686-7495, chamber@cityofmilantn.com, www.cityofmilantn.com.

**Millington** • *Millington Area C/C* • Cary Vaughn, Pres./CEO, 7743 Church St., 38053, P 10,500, M 346, (901) 872-1486, Fax (901) 872-0727, info@millingtonchamber.com, www.millingtonchamber.com

**Monteagle** • *Monteagle Mountain C/C* • Maxine Wade, Exec. Dir., P.O. Box 353, 37356, P 5,000, M 200, (931) 924-5353, Fax (931) 924-2264, info@monteaglechamber.com, www.monteaglechamber.com

**Morristown** • *Morristown Area C/C* • C. Thomas Robinson CCE CEcD, Pres./CEO, 825 W. First N. St., P.O. Box 9, 37815, P 66,000, M 740, (423) 586-6382, Fax (423) 586-6576, macc@morristownchamber.com, www.morristownchamber.com.

**Mount Carmel** • *see Rogersville*

**Mount Juliet** • *Mount Juliet/West Wilson County C/C* • Mark Hinesley, Pres./CEO, 46 W. Caldwell St., 37122, P 25,000, M 475, (615) 758-3478, Fax (615) 754-8595, mtjuliet@tds.net, www.mtjulietchamber.com.

**Mount Pleasant** • *see Columbia*

**Mountain City** • *Johnson County C/C* • David Sexton, Pres., P.O. Box 66, 37683, P 18,000, M 250, (423) 727-5800, Fax (423) 727-4943, info@johnsoncountychamber.org, www.johnsoncountychamber.org

**Munford** • *South Tipton County C/C* • Rosemary Bridges, Pres., P.O. Box 1198, 38058, P 57,000, M 340, (901) 837-4600, Fax (901) 837-4602, chamber@southtipton.com, www.southtipton.com

**Murfreesboro** • *Rutherford County C/C* • Stephanie Brackman, Interim Pres., 501 Memorial Blvd., P.O. Box 864, 37133, P 223,000, M 2,200, (615) 893-6565, (800) 716-7560, Fax (615) 890-7600, info@rutherfordchamber.org, www.rutherfordchamber.org

**Nashville** · *Donelson-Hermitage C/C* · Lori Weir, Exec. Dir., P.O. Box 140200, 37214, P 78,000, M 450, (615) 883-7896, Fax (615) 391-4880, lweir@d-hchamber.com, www.d-hchamber.com

**Nashville** · *Nashville Area C/C* · 211 Commerce St. #100, 37201, P 580,450, M 2,500, (615) 743-3000, Fax (615) 256-3074, info@nashvillechamber.com, www.nashvillechamber.com

**New Johnsonville** · *see Waverly*

**Newport** · *Newport/Cocke County C/C* · Sherry Butler, V.P. of Op., 433-B Prospect Ave., 37821, P 35,000, M 300, (423) 623-7201, Fax (423) 623-7216, ccpchamber@bellsouth.net, www.cockecounty.org

**Norris** · *see Clinton*

**Oak Ridge** · *Oak Ridge C/C* · Parker Hardy CCE, Pres./CEO, 1400 Oak Ridge Turnpike, 37830, P 28,000, M 700, (865) 483-1321, Fax (865) 483-1678, lchristman@orcc.org, www.orcc.org

**Oliver Springs** · *see Clinton*

**Oneida** · *see Helenwood*

**Paris** · *Paris-Henry County C/C* · Jennifer Wheatley, Exec. Dir., 2508 E. Wood St., 38242, P 31,115, M 500, (731) 642-3431, (800) 345-1103, Fax (731) 642-3454, pariscoc@charterbn.com, www.paristnchamber.com.

**Parrottsville** · *see Newport*

**Parsons** · *Decatur County C/C* · Bridgette Scallion, Exec. Dir., 139 Tenn. Ave. N., P.O. Box 245, 38363, P 11,000, M 207, (731) 847-4202, Fax (731) 847-4222, dccc@netease.net, www.decaturcountytennessee.org

**Pigeon Forge** · *City of Pigeon Forge Dept. of Tourism* · 2450 Pkwy., P.O. Box 1390-I, 37868, P 5,784, M 976, (865) 453-8574, (800) 251-9100, Fax (865) 429-7362, inquire@mypigeonforge.com, www.mypigeonforge.com

**Pigeon Forge** · *Pigeon Forge C/C* · Cathy Sizemore, Exec. Dir., 3171 Pkwy. #A, 37863, P 5,083, M 150, (865) 453-5700, (800) 221-9858, Fax (865) 492-9040, pifchamber@kmsfia.com, www.pigeonforgechamber.com

**Pikeville** · *Pikeville-Bledsoe County C/C* · Hank Williams, P.O. Box 205, 37367, P 14,000, M 85, (423) 447-2791, directors@pikeville-bledsoe.com, www.pikeville-bledsoe.com

**Portland** · *Portland C/C* · Amy Wald, Exec. Dir., 106 Main St., P.O. Box 387, 37148, P 12,000, M 200, (615) 325-9032, Fax (615) 325-8399, portcofc@bellsouth.net, www.portlandcofc.com

**Pulaski** · *Giles County C/C* · Donna Baker, Exec. Dir., 110 N. Second St., 38478, P 29,447, M 300, (931) 363-3789, Fax (931) 363-7279, director@gilescountychamber.com, www.gilescountychamber.com.

**Ridgely** · *Ridgely C/C* · 140 N. Main, 38080, P 1,700, M 35, (731) 264-0330

**Ripley** · *Lauderdale Chamber/ECD* · Lisa Hankins, Exec. Dir., 123 S. Jefferson St., 38063, P 27,101, M 275, (731) 635-9541, (731) 635-8463, Fax (731) 635-9064, mail@lauderdalecountytn.org, www.lauderdalecountytn.org

**Rogersville** · *Rogersville/Hawkins County C/C* · Nancy Barker, Exec. Dir., US Bank Bldg., 107 E. Main St. #100, 37857, P 57,054, M 300, (423) 272-2186, Fax (423) 272-2186, hawkinschamber@chartertn.net, www.rogersvillechamber.us, www.hawkinscounty.org.

**Savannah** · *Hardin County C/C* · Beth Pippin, Exec. Dir., 320 Main St., P.O. Box 996, 38372, P 27,000, M 300, (731) 925-2363, Fax (731) 925-8069, info@hardincountychamber.com, www.hardincountychamber.com

**Selmer** · *McNairy County C/C & EDC* · Matthew Ernst, Exec. Dir., 144 Cypress Ave., P.O. Box 7, 38375, P 26,000, M 375, (731) 645-6360, Fax (731) 645-7663, mcnairy@charterinternet.com, www.mcnairy.com

**Sevierville** · *Sevierville C/C* · Brenda McCroskey, Exec. Dir., 110 Gary Wade Blvd., 37862, P 11,000, M 585, (865) 453-6411, Fax (865) 453-9649, info@seviervillechamber.com, www.visitsevierville.com.

**Sewanee** · *see Monteagle*

**Sharon** · *see Dresden*

**Shelbyville** · *Shelbyville-Bedford County C/C* · Walter W. Wood CEcD, CEO, 100 N. Cannon Blvd., 37160, P 40,253, M 520, (931) 684-3482, (888) 662-2525, Fax (931) 684-3483, bedfordchamber@bellsouth.net, www.shelbyvilletn.com

**Smithville** · *Smithville-DeKalb County C/C* · Suzanne Williams, Exec. Dir., 301 N. Public Sq., P.O. Box 64, 37166, P 17,500, M 200, (615) 597-4163, Fax (615) 597-4164, chamber@dekalbtn.com, www.dekalbtn.com

**Smyrna** · *Rutherford County C/C* · Stephanie Brackman, Interim Pres., 315 S. Lowry St., 37167, P 38,073, M 2,200, (615) 355-6565, Fax (615) 355-5715, chamber@townofsmyrna.org, www.rutherfordchamber.org

**Somerville** · *Fayette County C/C* · Julie Perrine, Exec. Dir., 13145 N. Main St., P.O. Box 411, 38068, P 35,000, M 280, (901) 465-8690, Fax (901) 465-6497, fcc@fayettecountychamber.net, www.fayettecountychamber.com

**South Fulton** · *C/C of the Twin Cities* · Thea Reams, Exec. Dir., 515 Siegel Dr., P.O. Box 5077, 38257, P 6,000, M 135, (731) 479-7029, Fax (731) 479-7026, twincitieschamber@bellsouth.net, www.fultonsouthfultonchamber.com.

**Sparta** · *Sparta-White County C/C* · Wallace G. Austin, Pres., 16 W. Bockman Way, 38583, P 26,066, M 260, (931) 836-3552, Fax (931) 836-2216, sparta-chamber@sparta-chamber.net, www.sparta-chamber.net

**Spencer** · *Greater Van Buren County-Spencer C/C* · P.O. Box 814, 38585, P 6,000, M 100, (931) 946-7033, vbchamber@blomand.net, www.vanburenchamber.com

**Spring City** · *Spring City C/C* · Nancy Miller, Bus. Mgr., 390 Front St., P.O. Box 355, 37381, P 3,500, M 140, (423) 365-5210, Fax (423) 365-9790, scchamber@bellsouth.net, www.springcitychamberofcommerce.com

**Spring Hill** · *Spring Hill C/C* · Stacy Neisler, Chair, P.O. Box 1815, 37174, P 23,000, M 200, (931) 486-0625, info@springhillchamber.net, www.springhillchamber.net

**Springfield** · *Robertson County C/C* · Margot Fosnes, Exec. Dir., 503 W. Court Sq., 37172, P 59,380, M 400, (615) 384-3800, Fax (615) 384-1260, mfosnes@robertsonchamber.org, www.robertsonchamber.org

**Tazewell** · *Claiborne County C/C* · Dennis Shipley, Exec. Dir./V.P., 1732 Main St. #1, P.O. Box 649, 37879, P 32,000, M 220, (423) 626-4149, (800) 332-8164 TN only, Fax (423) 626-1611, chamber@claibornecounty.com, www.claibornecounty.com

**Tiptonville** · *Reelfoot Area C/C* · Marcia Mills, Exec. Dir., 130 S. Court St., 38079, P 7,954, M 45, (731) 253-8144, Fax (731) 253-9923, info@reelfootareachamber.com, www.reelfootareachamber.com

**Townsend** · *see Maryville*

**Tracy City** · *see Monteagle*

**Trenton** · *Greater Gibson County Area C/C* · 200 E. Eaton St., P.O. Box 464, 38382, P 48,152, M 250, (731) 855-0973, Fax (731) 855-0979, gibsonchamber@wiwt.com, www.gibsoncountytn.com

**Tullahoma** • *Tullahoma Area C/C* • Diane Bryant, Exec. Dir., 135 W. Lincoln St., P.O. Box 1205, 37388, P 25,332, M 524, (931) 455-5497, Fax (931) 455-5350, tullahomachamber@tullahoma. org, www.tullahoma.org.

**Union City** • *Obion County C/C* • 214 E. Church St., 38261, P 33,000, M 450, (731) 885-0211, Fax (731) 885-7155, www. obioncounty.org

**Wartburg** • *Morgan County C/C* • P.O. Box 539, 37887, P 20,000, M 65, (423) 346-5740, Fax (423) 346-9707, www.morgancounty chamber.com

**Wartrace** • *Wartrace C/C* • Pearl Change, Secy., P.O. Box 543, 37183, P 575, M 29, (931) 389-9999, www.wartracechamber.org

**Washington County** • *see Johnson City*

**Watertown** • *Watertown-East Wilson County C/C* • Jerry Lee, Pres., P.O. Box 5, 37184, P 1,400, M 140, (615) 237-0270, info@ watertowntn.com, www.watertowntn.com

**Waverly** • *Humphreys County Area C/C* • Wendy Lee, Dir., 124 E. Main St., P.O. Box 733, 37185, P 17,192, M 213, (931) 296-4865, Fax (931) 296-2285, hcchamber@bellsouth.net, waverly.net/ hcchamber

**Waynesboro** • *see Collinwood*

**Westmoreland** • *Westmoreland C/C* • David Harrison, Pres., P.O. Box 536, 37186, P 2,132, M 75, (615) 644-6397, www.westmore landtn.com

**White House** • *White House Area C/C* • Julie Bolton, Exec. Dir., 414 Hwy. 76, P.O. Box 521, 37188, P 9,000, M 245, (615) 672-3937, Fax (615) 672-2828, whcoc@bellsouth.net, www.whitehousetn.com

**Winchester** • *Franklin County C/C* • Judy DeWeese Taylor, Exec. Dir., 44 Chamber Way, P.O. Box 280, 37398, P 43,000, M 400, (931) 967-6788, Fax (931) 967-9418, judy@franklincountychamber.com, www.franklincountychamber.com

**Woodbury** • *Historic Cannon County C/C* • Carolyn Motley, Svcs. Coord., 313 Main St., P.O. Box 140, 37190, P 13,500, M 101, (615) 563-2222, cannontn@dtccom.net, www.cannoncounty.info

# Texas

**Texas Assn. of Bus.** • Bill Hammond, Pres., 1209 Nueces St., Austin, 78701, P 20,851,820, M 5,000, (512) 477-6721, Fax (512) 477-0836, info@txbiz.org, www.txbiz.org

**Women's C/C of Texas** • Rose Batson, Pres., P.O. Box 26051, Austin, 78755, M 500, (512) 338-0839, austin@womenschamber texas.com, www.womenschambertexas.com

**Abilene** • *Abilene C/C* • Mike McMahan, Pres., 174 Cypress, Ste. 200, P.O. Box 2281, 79604, P 115,000, M 1,200, (325) 677-7241, Fax (325) 677-0622, info@abilenechamber.com, www.abilene chamber.com.

**Alamo** • *Alamo C/C* • Carrol Moering, Exec. Dir., 130 S. 8th St., 78516, P 17,000, M 75, (956) 787-2117, alamo.chamber@yahoo. com, www.alamochamber.com

**Alamo Heights** • *Alamo Heights C/C* • Julie Blanda, Pres., P.O. Box 6141, 78209, P 10,000, M 150, (210) 822-7027, admin@ alamoheightschamber.org, www.alamoheightschamber.org

**Albany** • *Albany C/C* • Chuck Senter, Exec. Dir., #2 Railroad, P.O. Box 185, 76430, P 1,921, M 220, (325) 762-2525, Fax (325) 762-3125, chamberc@bitstreet.com, www.albanytexas.com

**Aldine** • *see Houston-- North Houston-Greenspoint C/C*

**Aledo** • *see Willow Park*

**Alice** • *Alice C/C* • Juan Navejar, Mgr., 612 E. Main St., P.O. Box 1609, 78333, P 19,000, M 411, (361) 664-3454, Fax (361) 664-2291, jnavejar@alicetx.org, www.alicetx.org

**Allen** • *Allen C/C* • Sharon Mayer, Pres./CEO, 210 W. McDermott, 75013, P 76,000, M 530, (972) 727-5585, Fax (972) 727-9000, sharon@allenchamber.com, www.allenchamber.com

**Alpine** • *Alpine C/C* • Mark Hannan, Pres., 106 N. 3rd St., 79830, P 6,300, M 200, (432) 837-2326, (800) 561-3712, Fax (432) 837-1259, alpinechamber@alpinetexas.com, www.alpinetexas.com

**Alvarado** • *Alvarado C/C* • Jacob Wheat, Pres., P.O. Box 712, 76009, P 3,700, M 45, (817) 783-2233, www.alvaradoarea chamber.org

**Alvin** • *Alvin-Manvel Area C/C* • Connie Elies, Pres., 105 W. Willis, 77511, P 33,000, M 500, (281) 331-3944, (800) 331-4063, Fax (281) 585-8662, chamber@alvintexas.org, www.alvinmanvel chamber.org

**Amarillo** • *Amarillo C/C* • Gary Molberg, Pres./CEO, 1000 S. Polk St., P.O. Box 9480, 79105, P 190,000, M 1,700, (806) 373-7800, Fax (806) 373-3909, chamber@amarillo-chamber.org, www. amarillo-chamber.org.

**Anahuac** • *Anahuac Area C/C* • Robbie King, Exec. Dir., P.O. Box R, 77514, P 3,000, M 250, (409) 267-4190, Fax (409) 267-3907, www.texasgatorfest.com, anahuacchamber@windstream.net, www.anahuacarea.com

**Andrews** • *Andrews C/C & CVB* • Julia Wallace, Exec. Dir., 700 W. Broadway, 79714, P 13,000, M 250, (432) 523-2695, Fax (432) 523-2375, achamber@andrewstx.com, www.andrewstx.com

**Angleton** • *Greater Angleton C/C* • Beth Journeay, Pres./CEO, 445 E. Mulberry, 77515, P 20,000, M 600, (979) 849-6443, Fax (979) 849-4520, chamber@angletonchamber.org, www.angleton chamber.org

**Annetta** • *see Willow Park*

**Anson** • *Anson C/C* • Sarah Shaw, Mgr., 1132 W. Court Plz., P.O. Box 351, 79501, P 2,556, M 150, (325) 823-3259, Fax (325) 823-4326

**Anthony** • *see Anthony, NM*

**Aransas Pass** • *Aransas Pass C/C* • Rosemary Vega, CEO, 130 W. Goodnight, 78335, P 1,000, M 250, (361) 758-2750, (800) 633-3028, Fax (361) 758-8320, info@aransaspass.org, www. aransaspass.org

**Argyle** • *Argyle C/C* • Kim Hinnrichs, Exec. Dir., P.O. Box 245, 76226, P 3,300, M 150, (940) 464-9990, chamber@argylechamber.org

**Arlington** • *Arlington C/C* • Wes Jurey, Pres./CEO, 505 E. Border, 76010, P 375,000, M 1,200, (817) 275-2613, Fax (817) 701-0893, info@arlingtontx.com, www.arlingtontx.com

**Arp** • *Arp Area C/C* • P.O. Box 146, 75750, P 1,000, M 70, (903) 859-6131, (903) 859-2055, bigsandytx.net

**Aspermont** • *Aspermont C/C & Eco. Dev. Corp.* • Martha McDowell, Exec. Dir., 612 Washington, P.O. Box 556, 79502, P 1,693, M 47, (940) 989-3197, Fax (940) 989-2517, www. aspermonttexas.com

**Athens** • *Athens C/C* • Mary Waddell, Pres., 1206 S. Palestine, 75751, P 12,800, M 610, (903) 675-5181, (800) 755-7878, Fax (903) 675-5183, mwaddell@athenscc.org, www.athenscc.org.

**Atlanta** • *Atlanta Area C/C* • Roy Raney, Mgr., 101 N. East St., P.O. Box 29, 75551, P 10,000, M 200, (903) 796-3296, Fax (903) 796-5711, atlantaareacoc@sbcglobal.net, www.atlantatexas.net.

**Aubrey** · *Aubrey Area C/C* · Judy Higgs, Pres., 901 S. Hwy. 377, 76227, P 4,000, M 365, (940) 365-9781, Fax (940) 365-9781, www.aubreycoc.org

## Austin Area

**Greater Austin C/C** · Michael W. Rollins CCE, Pres./CEO, 210 Barton Springs Rd., Ste. 400, 78704, P 1,400,000, M 2,600, (512) 478-9383, Fax (512) 478-6389, info@austinchamber.com, www.austinchamber.com

**Greater Austin Hispanic C/C** · Andrew Martinez, Pres., 2800 IH 35, Ste. 260, 78704, M 650, (512) 476-7502, Fax (512) 476-6417, amartinez@gahcc.org, www.gahcc.org

**Lake Travis C/C** · Laura Mitchell, Pres., 1415 RR 620 S., Ste. 202, P.O. Box 340034, 78734, P 20,000, M 450, (512) 263-5833, (877) 263-0073, Fax (512) 263-1355, info@laketravischamber.com, www.laketravischamber.com

**Avinger** · *Avinger C/C* · W.J. Salmon Jr., Pres., 8 Main St., P.O. Box 218, 75630, P 420, M 25, (903) 562-1000, (903) 562-1325, www.avingerareachamber.com

**Azle** · *Azle Area C/C* · Whitney Bettis, Exec. Dir., 252 W. Main St. #A, 76020, P 30,000, M 312, (817) 444-1112, Fax (817) 444-1143, info@azlechamber.com, www.azlechamber.com

**Bacliff** · *see San Leon*

**Baird** · *Baird C/C* · 328 Market St., 79504, P 1,651, M 100, (325) 854-2003, Fax (325) 854-2003, chamber@bairdtexas.com, www.bairdtexas.com

**Balch Springs** · *Balch Springs C/C* · Sandra Wood, Pres., 3636 Shepherd Ln., P.O. Box 800095, 75180, P 22,000, M 132, (972) 557-0988, info@balchspringschamber.org, www.balchspringschamber.org

**Ballinger** · *Ballinger C/C* · Tammie Virden, Exec. V.P., 700 Railroad Ave., P.O. Box 577, 76821, P 4,200, M 160, (325) 365-2333, Fax (325) 365-3445, chamber@ballingertx.org, www.ballingertx.org

**Bandera** · *Bandera County C/C* · Cerise Ripps, Exec. Admin., P.O. Box 2445, 78003, P 19,000, M 325, (830) 796-3280, Fax (830) 796-3970, cowboy@banderatex.com, www.banderatex.com

**Bartlett** · *Bartlett Area C/C* · Jose Alejo, Pres., P.O. Box 103, 76511, P 1,675, M 50, (254) 527-4141, www.bartlettchamberof commerce.org

**Bastrop** · *Bastrop C/C* · Susan Weems Wendel IOM, Pres./CEO, 927 Main St., 78602, P 8,025, M 580, (512) 303-0558, Fax (512) 303-0305, info@bastropchamber.us, www.bastropchamber.com.

**Bay City** · *Bay City C/C & Ag.* · Mitch Thames, Pres., 201 Seventh St., P.O. Box 768, 77404, P 20,000, M 500, (979) 245-8333, (800) 806-8333, Fax (979) 245-1622, mitchthames@visitbaycity.org, www.baycitychamber.org

**Baytown** · *Baytown C/C* · Tracey S. Wheeler, Pres./CEO, 1300 Rollingbrook, Ste. 400, P.O. Box 330, 77522, P 70,000, M 1,400, (281) 422-8359, Fax (281) 428-1758, info@baytownchamber.com, www.baytownchamber.com

**Bayview** · *see San Leon*

**Beaumont** · *Greater Beaumont C/C* · Jim Rich, Pres., 1110 Park St., P.O. Box 3150, 77704, P 115,000, M 1,500, (409) 838-6581, Fax (409) 833-6718, jimrich@bmtcoc.org, www.bmtcoc.org.

**Bedford** · *Hurst-Euless-Bedford C/C* · Mary Martin Frazior, Pres./CEO, 2109 Martin Dr., P.O. Box 969, 76095, P 135,000, M 1,000, (817) 283-1521, Fax (817) 267-5111, chamber@heb.org, www.heb.org

**Beeville** · *Bee County C/C* · Pam Priour Stuart, Pres./CEO, 1705 N. St. Marys St., 78102, P 32,300, M 333, (361) 358-3267, Fax (361) 358-3966, info@beecountychamber.org, www.beecountychamber.org

**Bellaire** · *Greater Southwest Houston C/C* · Toni Franklin, Pres./CEO, 6900 S. Rice Ave., 77401, P 350,000, M 600, (713) 666-1521, Fax (713) 666-1523, info@gswhcc.org, www.gswhcc.org

**Bellmead** · *Bellmead C/C* · 3400 Bellmead Dr., P.O. Box 154615, 76715, P 10,500, M 200, (254) 799-1552, Fax (254) 799-9370, chamberoffice@clearwire.net, www.bellmeadchamber.com

**Bellville** · *Bellville C/C* · Tammy Hall, Exec. Dir., 13 E. Main St., 77418, P 4,000, M 300, (979) 865-3407, Fax (979) 865-9760, bellvillechamber@sbcglobal.net, www.bellville.com

**Belton** · *Belton Area C/C* · Stephanie O'Banion, Pres./CEO, 412 E. Central Ave., P.O. Box 659, 76513, P 18,000, M 500, (254) 939-3551, Fax (254) 939-1061, www.beltonchamber.com

**Benbrook** · *Benbrook Area C/C* · Debbie Watkins, Exec. Dir., 8507 Benbrook Blvd., P.O. Box 26745, 76126, P 27,000, M 278, (817) 249-4451, Fax (817) 249-3307, chamberinfo@benbrook chamber.org, www.benbrookchamber.org

**Bertram** · *Bertram C/C* · P.O. Box 508, 78605, P 1,200, M 40, (512) 355-2197, www.bertramtx.org

**Big Lake** · *Big Lake C/C* · Tina Robertson, Mgr., 120 N. Main, P.O. Box 905, 76932, P 2,885, M 50, (325) 884-2980, blcoc@verizon.net, www.biglaketx.com

**Big Sandy** · *Big Sandy C/C* · 100 N. Tyler St., P.O. Box 175, 75755, P 1,200, M 25, (903) 636-2238, info@bigsandytx.com, bigsandytx.net

**Big Spring** · *Big Spring Area C/C* · Debbye Valverde IOM, Exec. Dir., 215 W. 3rd St., P.O. Box 1391, 79721, P 25,000, M 375, (432) 263-7641, Fax (432) 264-9111, debbyev@bigspringchamber.com, www.bigspringchamber.com.

**Bishop** · *Bishop C/C* · Betty Paschal, Exec. Dir., 213 E. Main, P.O. Box 426, 78343, P 3,305, M 70, (361) 584-2214, Fax (361) 584-2214, bishopcc@intcomm.net, www.bishoptx.org

**Blanco** · *Blanco C/C* · Julie Dill, Dir., P.O. Box 626, 78606, P 1,500, M 184, (830) 833-5101, Fax (830) 833-5101, blanco@moment.net, www.blancochamber.com

**Boerne** · *Greater Boerne C/C* · Paula White, Pres./CEO, 126 Rosewood Ave., P.O. Box 2328, 78006, P 10,354, M 830, (830) 249-8000, Fax (830) 249-9639, boerne@gvtc.com, www.boerne.org.

**Bonham** · *Bonham Area C/C* · Bill Jones, Exec. Dir., 327 N. Main St., 75418, P 13,092, M 300, (903) 583-4811, Fax (903) 583-7972, bonhamchamber@cableone.net, www.bonhamchamber.com

**Booker** · *Booker C/C* · Darrin Chisum, Pres., P.O. Box 22, 79005, P 1,300, M 50, (806) 658-4579

**Borger** · *Borger C/C* · Beverly Benton, Pres., 613 N. Main St., P.O. Box 490, 79008, P 14,000, M 300, (806) 274-2211, Fax (806) 273-3488, borgerchamber@amaonline.com, www.borgerchamber.org

**Bovina** · *Bovina C/C* · Mindy Neal-Witner, Pres., P.O. Box 607, 79009, P 1,800, M 65, (806) 251-1116, (806) 251-1300

**Bowie** · *Bowie-Montague County C/C* · Bonnie Julius Hamilton, Exec. V.P., 309 N. Smythe St., 76230, P 5,700, M 248, (940) 872-1173, (866) 872-1173, Fax (940) 872-3291, info@bowietxchamber.org, www.bowietxchamber.org.

**Brackettville** · *Kinney County C/C* · Mary Martin, Pres., P.O. Box 386, 78832, P 3,119, M 140, (830) 563-2466, Fax (830) 563-2239

**Brady** · *Brady/McCulloch County C/C* · Wendy Ellis, Dir., 101 E. 1st St., 76825, P 8,000, M 192, (325) 597-3491, Fax (325) 792-9181, info@bradytx.com, www.bradytx.com

**Brazoria** • *Brazoria C/C* • Kristen Pierce, Exec. Dir., 202 A Smith St., P.O. Box 992, 77422, P 2,932, M 175, (979) 798-6100, Fax (979) 798-6101, brazoriachamber@brazoriainet.com, www.brazoriachamber.net

**Brazosport** • *Brazosport Area C/C* • Sandra Shaw, Pres./CEO, 300 Abner Jackson Pkwy., 77566, P 75,000, M 710, (979) 285-2501, (888) 477-2505, Fax (979) 285-2505, chamber2@sbcglobal.net, www.brazosport.org

**Breckenridge** • *Breckenridge C/C* • Maryann Olson, Exec. Dir., 100 E. Elm, P.O. Box 1466, 76424, P 6,000, M 330, (254) 559-2301, Fax (254) 559-7104, chamber@breckenridgetexas.com, www.breckenridgetexas.com.

**Bremond** • *Bremond C/C* • Marie Abraham, Dir., P.O. Box 40, 76629, P 900, M 40, (254) 746-7421, www.cityofbremond.com

**Brenham** • *Washington County C/C* • Page Michel, Pres./CEO, 314 S. Austin St., 77833, P 31,000, M 760, (979) 836-3695, (888) BRENHAM, Fax (979) 836-2540, info@brenhamtexas.com, www.brenhamtexas.com.

**Bridge City** • *Bridge City C/C* • Janelle Sehon, Exec. V.P., 150 W. Roundbunch, 77611, P 8,651, M 193, (409) 735-5671, Fax (409) 735-7017, bcchamber@sbcglobal.net, www.bridgecitychamber.org

**Bridgeport** • *Bridgeport Area C/C* • Teri Bland, Exec. Dir., 1107 8th St., P.O. Box 1104, 76426, P 5,800, M 305, (940) 683-2076, Fax (940) 683-3969, bridgeportchamber@embarqmail.com, www.bridgeportchamber.org.

**Brooks City-Base** • *South San Antonio C/C* • Cindy Taylor, Pres., 7902 Challenge Dr., 78235, P 350,000, M 450, (210) 533-1600, Fax (210) 533-1611, ctaylor@southsachamber.org, www.southsachamber.org

**Brookshire** • *see Pattison*

**Brownfield** • *Brownfield C/C & Visitor Center* • Tory Decker Hook, Exec. Dir., 211 Lubbock Rd., P.O. Box 211, 79316, P 9,000, M 200, (806) 637-2564, Fax (806) 637-2565, www.brownfieldchamber.com.

**Brownsboro** • *see Chandler*

**Brownsville** • *Brownsville C/C* • Angela R. Burton, Pres./CEO, 1600 University Blvd., 78520, P 180,000, M 1,192, (956) 542-4341, Fax (956) 504-3348, info@brownsvillechamber.com, www.brownsvillechamber.com

**Brownwood** • *Brownwood Area C/C* • Laura Terhune, Exec. V.P., 600 Depot St., P.O. Box 880, 76804, P 36,000, M 500, (325) 646-9535, Fax (325) 643-6686, information@brownwoodchamber.org, www.brownwoodchamber.org.

**Bryan** • *Bryan-College Station C/C* • Royce Hickman, Pres./CEO, 4001 E. 29th St., Ste. 175, P.O. Box 3579, 77805, P 159,830, M 1,500, (979) 260-5200, Fax (979) 260-5208, receptionist@bcschamber.org, www.bcschamber.org

**Buchanan Dam** • *Lake Buchanan-Inks Lake C/C & Tourist Center* • Ray McCasland, Pres., Hwy. 29 between Burnet & Llano, TX, P.O. Box 282, 78609, P 3,500, M 250, (512) 793-2803, Fax (512) 793-2112, info@buchanan-inks.com, www.buchanan-inks.com

**Buda** • *Buda Area C/C* • Dick Schneider, Pres., 203 Railroad St., Ste. 1C, P.O. Box 904, 78610, P 5,075, M 350, (512) 295-9999, Fax (512) 295-3569, bacc@austin.rr.com, www.budachamber.com

**Buffalo** • *Buffalo C/C* • 942 N. Hill St., P.O. Box 207, 75831, P 2,982, M 120, (903) 322-5810, www.buffalotex.com

**Bullard** • *Bullard Area C/C* • Bryan Capps, Pres., 114 S. Phillips, P.O. Box 945, 75757, P 3,500, M 85, (903) 894-4238, www.bullardtexaschamber.com

**Bulverde** • *see Spring Branch*

**Buna** • *Buna C/C* • Andy Whitehead, Pres., P.O. Box 1782, 77612, P 9,000, M 100, (409) 994-5586, bunatexas@att.net, www.bunatexas.net

**Burkburnett** • *Burkburnett C/C* • Dick Vallon, Dir., 104 W. Third, 76354, P 11,000, M 130, (940) 569-3304, Fax (940) 569-3306, dvallon@burkburnett.org, www.burkburnett.org

**Burleson** • *Burleson Area C/C* • Dan-O Strong, Pres., P.O. Box 9, 76097, P 35,000, M 1,000, (817) 295-6121, Fax (817) 295-6192, dstrong@burleson.org, www.burlesonareachamber.com

**Burnet** • *Burnet C/C* • Patti Alford, Mgr., 229 S. Pierce, 78611, P 5,000, M 450, (512) 756-4297, Fax (512) 756-2548, info@burnetchamber.org, www.burnetchamber.org

**Caldwell** • *Burleson County C/C-Caldwell Office* • Weldon Peters, Pres., 301 N. Main, 77836, P 18,000, M 289, (979) 567-0000, (979) 567-7979, Fax (979) 567-0818, info@burlesoncountytx.com, www.burlesoncountytx.com.

**Calvert** • *Calvert C/C* • 300 Main St., P.O. Box 132, 77837, P 1,400, M 75, (979) 364-2559, www.calverttx.com

**Cameron** • *Cameron Area C/C* • Brandy McLerran, Mgr., 102 E. 1st St., P.O. Drawer 432, 76520, P 5,700, M 204, (254) 697-4979, Fax (254) 697-2345, chamber@cameron-tx.com, www.cameron-tx.com.

**Camp Wood** • *Nueces Canyon C/C* • P.O. Box 369, 78833, P 1,300, M 49, (830) 597-6241, nc-coc@mycampwood.com, www.mycampwood.com

**Canadian** • *Canadian-Hemphill County C/C* • Jackie McPherson, Dir., 119 N. 2nd St., 79014, P 2,500, M 130, (806) 323-6234, Fax (806) 323-9243, canadiantx@sbcglobal.net, www.canadiantx.com.

**Canton** • *Canton C/C* • Rona Watson, Pres., 119 N. Buffalo, 75103, P 5,146, M 412, (903) 567-2991, Fax (903) 567-5708, info@chambercantontx.com, www.chambercantontx.com

**Canyon** • *Canyon C/C* • Cheryl Malcolm, Exec. Dir., 1518 5th Ave., 79015, P 13,000, M 300, (806) 655-7815, (800) 999-9481, Fax (806) 655-4608, info@canyonchamber.org, www.canyonchamber.org.

**Canyon Lake** • *Canyon Lake Area C/C & Visitor Center* • Amanda Stewart, Pres., 3934 FM 2673, 78133, P 40,000, M 525, (830) 964-2223, (800) 528-2104, Fax (830) 964-3209, admin@canyonlakechamber.com, www.canyonlakechamber.com

**Carrizo Springs** • *Dimmit County C/C* • P.O. Box 699, 78834, P 10,248, M 90, (830) 876-5205, Fax (830) 876-5206, chambermanager@dimmitcountytx.com, www.dimmitcountytx.com

**Carrollton** • *Metrocrest C/C* • Greg Vaughn, Pres./CEO, 1204 Metrocrest Dr., 75006, P 158,000, M 600, (972) 416-6600, Fax (972) 416-7874, greg@metrocrestchamber.com, www.metrocrestchamber.com

**Carthage** • *Panola County C of C/Carthage CVB* • Ms. Tommie Ritter Smith, Pres., 300 W. Panola St., 75633, P 25,000, M 350, (903) 693-6634, Fax (903) 693-8578, chamber@carthagetexas.com, www.carthagetexas.com

**Castroville** • *Castroville Area C/C* • Ashlee Bates, Mgr., 100 Karm St., P.O. Box 572, 78009, P 2,664, M 270, (830) 538-3142, (800) 778-6775, Fax (830) 538-3295, chamber@castroville.com, www.castroville.com

**Cedar Creek Lake** • *see Mabank*

**Cedar Hill** • *Cedar Hill C/C* • Amanda Skinner, Pres., 300 Houston St., 75104, P 43,000, M 450, (972) 291-7817, Fax (972) 291-8101, info@cedarhillchamber.org, www.cedarhillchamber.org

**Cedar Park** • *Cedar Park C/C* • Harold Dean, Pres., 1460 E. Whitestone Blvd., Ste. 180, P.O. Box 805, 78630, P 50,000, M 670, (512) 260-7800, Fax (512) 260-9269, deanl@cedarparkchamber.org, www.cedarparkchamber.org

**Celina** · *Greater Celina C/C* · Alyssa Tingle, Pres./Exec. Dir., 211 W. Pecan, P.O. Box 1476, 75009, P 5,000, M 100, (972) 382-3600, Fax (972) 382-3606, alyssa.tingle@celinachamber.org, www.celinachamber.org

**Center** · *Shelby County C/C* · Pam Phelps, Exec. Dir., 100 Courthouse Sq. #A-101, 75935, P 25,000, M 316, (936) 598-3682, Fax (936) 598-8163, info@shelbycountychamber.com, www.shelbycountychamber.com

**Centerville** · *Centerville C/C* · Bobby Walters, Pres., P.O. Box 422, 75833, P 1,000, M 100, (903) 536-7261, centerville75833@yahoo.com, www.centervilletexas.com

**Chandler** · *Chandler Brownsboro C/C* · Bertha Pritchard, Ofc. Mgr., 811 Hwy. 31 E., P.O. Box 1500, 75758, P 27,000, M 87, (903) 849-5930, cbacc2@embarqmail.com, www.cbacc.net

**Channelview** · *see Houston-North Channel Area C/C*

**Childress** · *Childress C/C* · Susan J. Leary, Exec. Dir., 237 Commerce St., P.O. Box 35, 79201, P 7,200, M 160, (940) 937-2567, Fax (940) 937-8836, childresschamber@childresstexas.net, www.childresstexas.net.

**Christoval** · *Christoval Comm. C/C* · 4702 McKee St., 76935, P 1,500, M 100, (325) 896-1065

**Cibolo** · *see Selma*

**Cisco** · *Cisco C/C* · Carrie Goodman, Exec. Dir., 309 Conrad Hilton Ave., 76437, P 3,851, M 173, (254) 442-2537, Fax (254) 442-2553, ciscoinfo@ciscotx.com, www.ciscotx.com/homepage.htm

**Clarendon** · *Clarendon-Donley County C/C* · Judith P. Burlin, Exec. Dir., 318 Kearney, P.O. Box 730, 79226, P 2,200, M 103, (806) 874-2421, (800) 579-4023, Fax (806) 874-2911, clarendon@donleytx.com, www.donleytx.com

**Clarksville** · *Historic Red River County C/C* · Shelley Benton, Pres., 101 N. Locust, 75426, P 3,879, M 144, (903) 427-2645, Fax (903) 427-5454, redrivercc@1starnet.com, www.red-river.net

**Clear Lake Shores** · *see Dickinson*

**Cleburne** · *Cleburne C/C* · Cathy Marchel, Pres., 1511 W. Henderson St., P.O. Box 701, 76033, P 29,395, M 947, (817) 645-2455, Fax (817) 641-3069, info@cleburnechamber.com, www.cleburnechamber.com.

**Cleveland** · *Greater Cleveland C/C* · Tracey Walters, CEO, 210 Peach Ave., Ste. B, 77327, P 7,605, M 400, (281) 592-8786, Fax (281) 592-6949, info@clevelandtxchamber.com, www.clevelandtxchamber.com

**Clifton** · *Clifton C/C* · Brenda Herzog, Exec. Dir., 115 N. Ave. D, 76634, P 3,800, M 325, (254) 675-3720, Fax (254) 675-4630, info@cliftontexas.org, www.cliftontexas.org

**Clyde** · *Clyde C/C* · Tim Laws, Pres., 614 N. 1st St., P.O. Box 257, 79510, P 3,500, M 100, (325) 893-4221, Fax (325) 893-2778, clydecoc@camalott.com

**Coldspring** · *Coldspring-San Jacinto County C/C* · Barbara Brock, Pres., 31 N. Butler, P.O. Box 980, 77331, P 22,500, M 145, (936) 653-2184, Fax (936) 653-2184, ccc@coldspringtexas.org, www.coldspringtexas.org

**Coleman** · *Coleman County C/C, Ag. & Tourist Bur.* · Mary Griffis, Exec. Dir., 218 Commercial, P.O. Box 796, 76834, P 5,127, M 210, (325) 625-2163, Fax (325) 625-2164, chamber@colemantexas.org, www.colemantexas.org

**College Station** · *see Bryan*

**Colleyville** · *Colleyville Area C/C* · Mary Smith, Pres., 6700 Colleyville Blvd., 76034, P 22,000, M 800, (817) 488-7148, Fax (817) 488-4242, info@colleyvillechamber.org, www.colleyvillechamber.org

**Colorado City** · *Colorado City Area C/C* · Sue Lowrance, Exec. Dir., 157 W. 2nd St., P.O. Box 242, 79512, P 7,000, M 168, (325) 728-3403, Fax (325) 728-2911, ccitychamber@sbcglobal.net, www.coloradocitychamberofcommerce.com

**Columbus** · *Columbus Area C/C* · George Fox, Exec. Dir., 425 Spring St., 78934, P 5,000, M 225, (979) 732-8385, Fax (979) 732-5881, spring@intertex.net, www.columbuscofc.org

**Comanche** · *Comanche C/C* · Christine Perkins, Exec. Dir., 100 Indian Creek Dr., P.O. Box 65, 76442, P 4,823, M 227, (325) 356-3233, Fax (325) 356-2940, comanchechamber@verizon.net, www.comanchechamber.org

**Comfort** · *Comfort C/C* · Regina Alexander, Ofc. Mgr., 630 Hwy. 27, P.O. Box 777, 78013, P 2,400, M 225, (830) 995-3131, Fax (830) 995-5252, info@comfort-texas.com, www.comfortchamberofcommerce.com

**Commerce** · *Commerce C/C* · Barbara Kersey, Mgr., 1114 Main St., P.O. Box 290, 75429, P 8,000, M 300, (903) 886-3950, Fax (903) 886-8012, cchambr@koyote.com, www.commerce-chamber.com.

**Conroe** · *Greater Conroe/Lake Conroe Area C/C* · E.S. 'Stew' Darsey, Pres., 505 W. Davis, P.O. Box 2347, 77305, P 42,000, M 1,275, (936) 756-6644, Fax (936) 756-6462, darsey@conroe.org, www.conroe.org.

**Converse** · *see Selma*

**Cooper** · *Delta County C/C* · Gracie Young, Ofc. Mgr., P.O. Box 457, 75432, P 6,000, M 160, (903) 395-4314, Fax (903) 395-4318, deltacounty@neto.com, www.deltacounty.org

**Coppell** · *Coppell C/C* · Beverly Widner, Pres., 509 W. Bethel Rd. #200, P.O. Box 452, 75019, P 39,000, M 420, (972) 393-2829, Fax (972) 393-0659, info@coppellchamber.org, www.coppellchamber.org

**Copperas Cove** · *Copperas Cove C of C & Visitors Bur.* · Mrs. Marty Smith, Pres., 204 E. Robertson Ave., 76522, P 32,000, M 475, (254) 547-7571, Fax (254) 547-5015, chamber@copperascove.com, www.copperascove.com

**Corpus Christi** · *Corpus Christi C/C* · Foster Edwards, Pres./CEO, 1201 N. Shoreline Blvd., 78401, P 308,000, M 1,350, (361) 881-1800, Fax (361) 882-4256, foster@theccchamber.org, www.corpuschristichamber.org.

**Corpus Christi** · *Corpus Christi Hispanic C/C* · Bob Vela, Interim Dir., 615 N. Upper Broadway, Ste. 410, P.O. Box 5523, 78465, P 387,500, M 750, (361) 887-7408, Fax (361) 888-9473, rvela@cchispanicchamber.org, www.cchispanicchamber.org

**Corsicana** · *Corsicana/Navarro County C/C* · Paul Hooper, Exec. Dir., 120 N. 12th St., 75110, P 50,000, M 600, (903) 874-4731, (877) 376-7477, Fax (903) 874-4187, chamber@corsicana.org, www.corsicana.org.

**Cotulla** · *Cotulla-LaSalle County C/C* · Stacie Hillje, Mgr., 290 N. IH-35 Access Rd., 78014, P 5,100, M 125, (830) 879-2326, (800) 256-2326, Fax (830) 879-2326, chamber@cotulla-chamber.com, www.cotulla-chamber.com

**Crandall** · *Greater Crandall C/C* · Denny Mackey, Pres., P.O. Box 669, 75114, P 3,800, M 60, (972) 472-8663, coordinator@crandallchamber.net, www.crandallchamber.net

**Crane** · *Crane County C/C* · Micah Ortiz, Mgr., 409 S. Gaston, 79731, P 3,100, M 54, (432) 558-2311, Fax (432) 558-2311, craneccc@sbcglobal.net, www.cranechamber.net

**Crockett** · *Crockett Area C/C* · Jeana Culp, Exec. Dir., 1100 Edmiston Dr., P.O. Box 307, 75835, P 23,000, M 360, (936) 544-2359, (888) 269-2359, Fax (936) 544-4355, jessizwar@crockettareachamber.org, www.crockettareachamber.org

**Crosby** · *Crosby/Huffman C/C* · Judy Richard & Christy Schubert, Co-Coord., 5611 S. Main St., P.O. Box 452, 77532, P 34,000, M 250, (281) 328-6984, Fax (281) 328-7296, chamber@crosbyhuffmancc.org, www.crosbyhuffmancc.org

**Crosbyton** · *Crosbyton C/C* · 124 S. Berkshire, 79322, P 1,894, M 100, (806) 675-2261, Fax same, www.crosbytoncoc.com

**Cross Plains** · *Cross Plains C/C* · Joe Kemp, Pres., 209 N.W. Main, P.O. Box 233, 76443, P 1,068, M 50, (254) 725-7251, Fax (254) 725-6747, www.crossplains.com/COC.htm

**Crowell** · *Crowell C/C* · JoAnna Mills, Pres., 107 N. Main, P.O. Box 164, 79227, P 1,600, M 100, (940) 684-1310, www.crowelltex.com

**Crowley** · *Crowley Area C/C* · Eileen Yarborough, Pres., 200 E. Main #D, 76036, P 11,000, M 320, (817) 297-4211, Fax (817) 297-7334, info@crowleyareachamber.org, www.crowleyareachamber.org

**Crystal Beach** · *Bolivar Peninsula C/C* · Anne Willis, Pres., 1750 Hwy. 87, P.O. Box 1170, 77650, P 4,500, M 175, (409) 684-3345, info@bolivarchamber.org, www.bolivarchamber.org

**Cuero** · *Cuero C of C & Ag.* · Kay Lapp, Exec. Dir., 124 E. Church, 77954, P 7,000, M 340, (361) 275-2112, Fax (361) 275-6351, cuerocc@cuero.org, www.cuero.org.

**Cypress** · *Cy-Fair Houston C/C* · 11734 Barker Cypress, Ste. 105, 77433, P 600,000, M 755, (281) 373-1390, Fax (281) 373-1394, staff@cyfairchamber.com, www.cyfairchamber.com.

**Daingerfield** · *Daingerfield C/C* · 102 Coffey St., 75638, P 2,572, M 127, (903) 645-2646, Fax (903) 645-7847, daingerfieldchamberofcommerce@cebridge.net, www.daingerfieldtx.net

**Dalhart** · *Dalhart Area C/C* · Kristine Olsen, Pres., 102 E. 7th St., P.O. Box 967, 79022, P 10,000, M 270, (806) 244-5646, Fax (806) 244-4945, chamber@dalhart.org, www.dalhart.org

## Dallas Area

**Dallas Reg. C/C** · James C. Oberwetter, Pres., 700 N. Pearl #1200, 75201, P 3,000,000, M 3,000, (214) 746-6600, Fax (214) 746-6799, information@dallaschamber.org, www.dallaschamber.org

**Dallas Black C/C** · Reginald Gates, Pres., 2838 MLK Jr. Blvd., 75215, M 1,800, (214) 421-5200, Fax (214) 421-5510, www.dbcc.org

**Greater East Dallas C/C** · Greg Solomon, Pres., 9543 Losa Dr. #118, 75218, P 250,000, M 350, (214) 328-4100, Fax (214) 328-4124, president@eastdallaschamber.com, www.eastdallaschamber.com.

**North Dallas C/C** · Stephen E. Taylor, Pres., 10707 Preston Rd., 75230, P 500,000, M 900, (214) 368-6485, Fax (214) 691-5584, www.ndcc.org

**Oak Cliff C/C** · Ed Oakley, Chrmn., 400 S. Zang Blvd. #110, 75208, P 330,000, M 650, (214) 943-4567, Fax (214) 943-4582, occ@oakliffchamber.org, www.oakliffchamber.org

**Southeast Dallas C/C** · Carl Raines, Chrmn., P.O. Box 170132, 75217, P 100,000, M 300, (214) 398-9590, Fax (214) 398-9591, info@sedcc.org, www.sedcc.org

**Dayton** · *also see Liberty*

**Dayton** · *Dayton C/C* · Tammy Pratka, Pres., 107 W. Clayton, 77535, P 30,000, M 220, (936) 257-2393, Fax (936) 257-2394, tpratka@daytontxchamber.com, www.daytontxchamber.com

**Decatur** · *Decatur C/C* · Misty Hudson, Exec. Dir., 308 W. Main, P.O. Box 474, 76234, P 6,250, M 340, (940) 627-3107, Fax (940) 627-3771, mhudson@decaturtx.com, www.decaturtx.com

**Deer Park** · *Deer Park C/C* · Sharon McLean, Pres., 110 Center St., 77536, P 28,520, M 600, (281) 479-1559, Fax (281) 476-4041, info@deerpark.org, www.deerpark.org

**DeKalb** · *DeKalb C/C* · Judd Johns, Pres., P.O. Box 219, 75559, P 2,000, M 150, (903) 667-9000, www.dekalbtexas.org

**Del Rio** · *Del Rio C/C* · Linda Henderson, Exec. Dir., 1915 Veterans Blvd., 78840, P 45,000, M 600, (830) 775-3551, (800) 889-8149, Fax (830) 774-1813, info@drchamber.com, www.drchamber.com, www.usachamber.com/delrio.

**DeLeon** · *DeLeon C/C & Ag.* · Linda Levens, Exec. Dir., 109 S. Texas St., 76444, P 2,500, M 143, (254) 893-2083, Fax (254) 893-3702, chamber@deleontexas.com, www.deleontexas.com

**Dell City** · *Dell Valley C/C* · P.O. Box 225, 79837, P 400, M 40, (915) 964-2344, www.dellcity.com

**Denison** · *Denison Area C/C* · Anna H. McKinney, Pres./CEO, 313 W. Woodard, P.O. Box 325, 75020, P 24,000, M 503, (903) 465-1551, Fax (903) 465-8443, information@denisontexas.us, www.denisontexas.us.

**Denton** · *Denton C/C* · C.W. Carpenter, Pres., 414 Parkway St., 76201, P 115,550, M 865, (940) 382-9693, (940) 382-7895, Fax (940) 382-0040, info@denton-chamber.org, www.denton-chamber.org.

**Denver City** · *Denver City C of C & CVB* · Daun McLeroy, Exec. V.P., 120 N. Main St., 79323, P 4,000, M 132, (806) 592-5424, Fax (806) 592-7613, denvercitycofc@valornet.com, www.denvercitychamber.com.

**DeSoto** · *DeSoto C/C* · Cammy Jackson, Pres., 2010 N. Hampton, Ste. #200, 75115, P 47,250, M 450, (972) 224-3565, Fax (972) 354-1022, info@desotochamber.org, www.desotochamber.org.

**Devine** · *Greater Devine C/C* · Fran Taylor, Pres., 200 E. Hondo Ave., P.O. Box 443, 78016, P 4,600, M 100, (830) 663-2739, Fax same, chamber@devinechamber.com, www.devinechamber.com

**Dickinson** · *North Galveston County C/C* · Brenda Holcomb, Pres., 218 FM 517 W., P.O. Box 426, 77539, P 217,399, M 280, (281) 534-4380, Fax (281) 534-4389, contact@northgalvestoncountychamber.com, www.northgalvestoncountychamber.com.

**Dimmitt** · *Dimmitt C/C* · Lourdes Chavez, Exec. Dir., 115 W. Bedford, 79027, P 4,375, M 210, (806) 647-2524, Fax (806) 647-2469, dimmittchamber@amaonline.com, www.dimmittchamber.com

**Dripping Springs** · *Dripping Springs C/C* · Kim Johnson, Pres., 600 Hwy. 290 E., P.O. Box 206, 78620, P 2,000, M 300, (512) 858-4740, Fax (512) 858-4144, dschamber@verizon.net, www.drippingspringstx.org

**Dublin** · *Dublin C/C* · Karen Wright, Exec. Dir., 108 S. Patrick, P.O. Box 309, 76446, P 3,800, M 120, (254) 445-3422, Fax (254) 445-0394, dublintxchamber@embarqmail.com, www.dublintxchamber.com

**Dumas** · *Dumas/Moore County C/C & Visitor Center* · Sam Cartwright, Pres./CEO, 1901 S. Dumas Ave., P.O. Box 735, 79029, P 21,000, M 300, (806) 935-2123, Fax (806) 935-2124, sam@dumaschamber.com, www.dumaschamber.com.

**Duncanville** · *Duncanville C/C* · Sara Dedeluk, Pres., 300 E. Wheatland Rd., 75116, P 36,500, M 450, (972) 780-4990, Fax (972) 298-9370, info@duncanvillechamber.org, www.duncanvillechamber.org

**Eagle Lake** · *Eagle Lake C/C* · Barbara Class, Pres., 303 E. Main, 77434, P 3,664, M 90, (979) 234-2780, chamber@elc.net, www.VisitEagleLake.com

**Eagle Pass** · *Eagle Pass C/C* · Sandra Martinez, Exec. Dir., 400 Garrison St., P.O. Box 1188, 78853, P 53,000, M 300, (830) 773-3224, (888) 355-3224, Fax (830) 773-8844, chamber@eaglepasstexas.com, www.eaglepasstexas.com

**Early** · *Early C/ C & Conv. & Tourism Bur.* · Wanda Furgason, CDC, 104 E. Industrial Dr., 76802, P 2,588, M 253, (325) 649-9317, (877) 643-7243, Fax (325) 643-4746, wanda@earlytx.com, www.earlychamber.com

**East Bernard** · *East Bernard C/C* · Dusty Leopold, Treas., P.O. Box 567, 77435, P 2,300, M 100, (979) 335-6558, www.ebchamber.com

**East Tawakoni** · *see Quinlan*

**Eastland** · *Eastland C/C* · Nellie Chalmers, Mgr., 209 W. Main St., Ste. A, 76448, P 4,000, M 200, (254) 629-2332, (877) 2-OLDRIP, Fax (254) 629-1629, ecofc@eastland.net, www.eastlandtexas.com

**Eden** · *Eden C/C* · Leigh Dycus, P.O. Box 367, 76837, P 1,700, M 50, (325) 869-3336, Fax (325) 869-5075, edenchamber@verizon.net, www.edentexas.com

**Edinburg** · *Edinburg C/C* · Letty Gonzalez, Pres., 602 W. University Dr., P.O. Box 85, 78540, P 48,000, M 600, (956) 383-4974, (800) 800-7214, Fax (956) 383-6942, chamber@edinburg.com, www.edinburg.com.

**Edna** · *Jackson County C/C & Ag.* · Clinton Tegeler, Exec. Dir., 317 W. Main St., P.O. Box 788, 77957, P 14,500, M 310, (361) 782-7146, Fax (361) 782-2811, jcchamber@att.net, www.jacksoncountytx.com

**El Campo** · *El Campo C/C & Ag.* · Rebecca Munos, Exec. Sec., 201 E. Jackson, P.O. Box 1400, 77437, P 10,946, M 747, (979) 543-2713, Fax (979) 543-5495, rebecca@elcampochamber.com, www.elcampochamber.com

**El Paso** · *El Paso Hispanic C/C* · Cindy Ramos-Davidson, Pres./CEO, 2401 E. Missouri St., 79903, P 875,000, M 1,137, (915) 566-4066, Fax (915) 566-9714, ephcc01@whc.net, www.ephcc.org

**El Paso** · *Greater El Paso C/C* · Richard E. Dayoub, Pres./CEO, 10 Civic Center Plaza, 79901, P 734,000, M 1,500, (915) 534-0500, Fax (915) 534-0510, gepccreceptionist@elpaso.org, www.elpaso.org

**Electra** · *Electra C/C* · Sherry Strange, Exec. Dir., 112 W. Cleveland, 76360, P 3,168, M 45, (940) 495-3577, Fax (940) 495-3022, electracoc@electratel.net, www.electratexas.org

**Elgin** · *Greater Elgin C/C* · Gena Carter, Pres., 114 Central Ave., P.O. Box 408, 78621, P 7,200, M 205, (512) 285-4515, Fax (512) 281-3393, elginchamber@hotmail.com, www.elgintx.com

**Emory** · *Rains County C/C* · Anne Butler, Mgr., 199 Texas St., P.O. Box 538, 75440, P 11,500, M 120, (903) 473-3913, Fax (903) 473-3913, rainschamber@verizon.net, www.rainschamber.com, www.eaglefest.org

**Ennis** · *Ennis Area C/C* · Jeannette J. Patak, Pres., 108 Chamber of Commerce Dr., P.O. Box 1177, 75120, P 19,000, M 450, (972) 878-2625, Fax (972) 875-1473, manager@ennis-chamber.com, www.ennis-chamber.com

**Euless** · *see Bedford*

**Eustace** · *see Mabank*

**Everman** · *see Forest Hill*

**Fairfield** · *Fairfield C/C* · Gail Farish, Pres., 900 W. Commerce, P.O. Box 899, 75840, P 3,306, M 165, (903) 389-5792, Fax (903) 389-8382, chamber@fairfieldtx.com, www.fairfieldtexaschamber.com

**Falfurrias** · *Falfurrias C/C* · Gus Barrera, Exec. Dir., 124 N. St. Mary St., P.O. Box 476, 78355, P 8,300, M 140, (361) 325-3333, Fax (361) 325-2956, c_of_commerce@yahoo.com

**Falls City** · *Falls City C/C* · Arlene Jurgajtis, Pres., P.O. Box 298, 78113, P 500, M 50, (830) 745-2154

**Farmers Branch** · *Farmers Branch C/C* · Lara Orlic, Dir. of Chamber Relations, 12875 Josey Ln. #150, 75234, P 28,000, M 350, (972) 243-8966, Fax (972) 243-8968, lorlic@fbchamber.com, www.fbchamber.com

**Farmersville** · *Farmersville C/C & Visitors Center* · Cynthia Craddock-Clark, Ofc. Mgr., 201 S. Main, 75442, P 3,319, M 103, (972) 782-6533, Fax (972) 782-6603, chamber@farmersvilletx.net, www.farmersvillechamber.org

**Farwell** · *Farwell C/C* · P.O. Box 1005, 79325, P 1,400, M 50, (806) 481-3620

**Fayetteville** · *Fayetteville C/C* · P.O. Box 217, 78940, P 350, M 60, (888) 575-4553, fayettevilletx@cvtv.net, www.fayettevilletx.com

**Flatonia** · *Flatonia C/C* · Tammy Parisher, Exec. Dir., 208 E. N. Main, P.O. Box 610, 78941, P 1,300, M 125, (361) 865-3920, Fax (361) 865-2451, flatoniacofc@sbcglobal.net, www.flatoniachamber.com

**Florence** · *Florence C/C* · Robert Chambers, Pres., c/o City Hall, P.O. Box 201, 76527, P 1,066, M 25, (512) 635-5170, mail@florencetexaschamberofcommerce.org, www.florencetexaschamberofcommerce.org/

**Floresville** · *Floresville C/C* · Traci Jaskinia, Exec. Dir., 910 10th St., 78114, P 6,000, M 125, (830) 393-0074, (866) 279-6778, Fax (830) 393-9224, visitors@felpsis.net, www.floresvillechamber.com

**Flower Mound** · *Flower Mound C/C* · Katy Taggart, Pres., 700 Parker Square #100, 75028, P 63,000, M 800, (972) 539-0500, Fax (972) 539-4307, k.taggart@flowermoundchamber.com, www.flowermoundchamber.com

**Floydada** · *Floydada C/C & Ag.* · Patti Sanchez, Mgr., 125 E. California, P.O. Box 147, 79235, P 3,676, M 154, (806) 983-3434, Fax (806) 983-3535, chamber2005@sbcglobal.net, www.floydadachamber.com

**Forest Hill** · *South Tarrant County C/C* · David Miller, Chrmn., 6800 Forest Hill Dr., 76140, P 30,000, M 150, (817) 568-2685, Fax (817) 568-3049, info@southtarrantchamber.com, www.southtarrantchamber.com

**Forney** · *Forney Area C/C* · Laurie Barkham, Pres., 100 U.S. Hwy. 80, Ste. 110, P.O. Box 570, 75126, P 15,000, M 200, (972) 564-2233, Fax (972) 564-3677, lauriebarkham@sbcglobal.net, www.forneychamber.com

**Fort Davis** · *Fort Davis C/C* · Lisa Nugent, Exec. Dir., P.O. Box 378, 79734, P 2,100, M 120, (432) 426-3015, (800) 524-3015, Fax (432) 426-3978, info@fortdavis.com, www.fortdavis.com

**Fort Hood** · *see Killeen*

**Fort Stockton** · *Fort Stockton C/C* · Arna McCorkle, Exec. Dir., 1000 Railroad Ave., 79735, P 7,600, M 325, (432) 336-2264, (800) 336-2166, Fax (432) 336-6114, www.fortstockton.org.

**Fort Worth** · *Fort Worth C/C* · Bill Thornton, Pres./CEO, 777 Taylor, Ste. 900, 76102, P 618,600, M 3,500, (817) 336-2491, Fax (817) 877-4034, bthornton@fortworthchamber.com, www.fortworthchamber.com

**Fort Worth** · *Fort Worth Hispanic C/C* · Rosa Navejar, Pres., 1327 N. Main St., 76164, P 450,000, M 850, (817) 625-5411, Fax (817) 625-1405, rosa.navejar@fwhcc.org, www.fwhcc.org

**Franklin** · *Franklin C/C* · Peggy Baxter, Exec, Dir, 351 Cooks Ln., P.O. Box 126, 77856, P 1,800, M 300, (979) 828-3276, Fax (979) 828-1816, franklincc@valornet.com, www.franklintexas.com

**Frankston** · *Lake Palestine C/C* · Larry Paxton, Pres., P.O. Box 1002, 75763, P 1,850, M 44, (903) 876-5310, info@lakepalestinechamber.com, www.lakepalestinechamber.com

**Fredericksburg** · *Fredericksburg C/C* · Peggy Crenwelge, Exec. V.P., 302 E. Austin, 78624, P 10,432, M 800, (830) 997-6523, Fax (830) 997-8588, www.fredericksburg-texas.com.

**Freer** · *Freer C/C* · Angel Ybarez, Exec. Dir., P.O. Box 717, 78357, P 3,271, M 150, (361) 394-6891, Fax (361) 394-6891, freercofc@yahoo.com

**Friendswood** · *Friendswood C/C* · Carol Jones, Pres., 1100 S. Friendswood Dr., P.O. Box 11, 77546, P 31,500, M 550, (281) 482-3329, Fax (281) 482-3911, fwdchmbr@swbell.net, www.friendswood-chamber.com.

**Friona** · *Friona C/C & Ag.* · Chris Alexander, Exec. V.P., 621 Main St., 79035, P 3,800, M 200, (806) 250-3491, Fax (806) 250-2348, fedc@wtrt.net, www.frionachamber.com

**Frisco** · *Frisco C/C* · Tony Felker, Pres./CEO, 6843 Main St., 75034, P 101,000, M 1,300, (972) 335-9522, Fax (972) 335-6654, info@friscochamber.com, www.friscochamber.com

**Fulshear** · *see Pattison*

**Gainesville** · *Gainesville Area C/C* · John Broyles, Dir., 101 S. Culberson St., P.O. Box 518, 76241, P 33,000, M 460, (940) 665-2831, (888) 585-4468, Fax (940) 665-2833, john@gogainesville.net, www.gogainesville.net

**Galena Park** · *see Houston-North Channel Area C/C*

**Galveston** · *Galveston C/C* · Gina Spagnola, Pres., 519 25th St., 77550, P 57,247, M 850, (409) 763-5326, Fax (409) 763-8271, gcc@galvestonchamber.com, www.galvestonchamber.com.

**Garden Oaks** · *see Houston-- North Houston-Greenspoint C/C*

**Garden Ridge** · *see Selma*

**Garland** · *Garland C/C* · Paul Mayer, CEO, 520 N. Glenbrook Dr., 75040, P 240,876, M 453, (972) 272-7551, Fax (972) 276-9261, paul.mayer@garlandchamber.com, www.garlandchamber.com

**Gatesville** · *Gatesville Area C/C & Agribusiness* · 2307 Hwy. 36 S., 76528, P 8,000, M 230, (254) 865-2617, Fax (254) 865-5581, chamber@gatesvilletx.info, www.gatesvilletx.info.

**George West** · *George West C/C* · Becky Allen, Exec. Dir., P.O. Box 359, 78022, P 2,524, M 100, (361) 449-2033, Fax (361) 449-1871, chamber@georgewest.org, www.georgewest.org

**Georgetown** · *Georgetown C/C* · Mel Pendland, Pres., 100 Stadium Dr., P.O. Box 346, 78627, P 48,000, M 1,100, (512) 930-3535, Fax (512) 930-3587, info@georgetownchamber.org, www.georgetownchamber.org.

**Giddings** · *Giddings Area C/C* · Denice Harlan, Exec. Dir., 171 E. Hempstead, 78942, P 5,500, M 270, (979) 542-3455, Fax (979) 542-7060, giddingsofc@verizon.net, www.giddingstx.com

**Gilmer** · *Gilmer Area C/C* · Joan Small, Exec. Dir., 106 Buffalo St., P.O. Box 854, 75644, P 35,000, M 300, (903) 843-2413, Fax (903) 843-3759, upchamber@aol.com, www.gilmerareachamber.com

**Gladewater** · *Gladewater C/C* · Marsha Valdetero, Mgr., 215 N. Main St., P.O. Box 1409, 75647, P 6,078, M 230, (903) 845-5501, (800) 627-0315, Fax (903) 845-6326, gladewatercoc@suddenlinkmail.com, www.gladewaterchamber.com.

**Glen Rose** · *Glen Rose-Somervell County C/C* · Darrell Best, Chrmn., 1505 Hwy. 67, P.O. Box 605, 76043, P 7,500, M 300, (254) 897-2286, Fax (254) 897-7670, grcc@glenrosechamber.com, www.glenrosechamber.com

**Goldthwaite** · *Mills County-Goldthwaite C/C* · Becca Miles, Exec. Dir., 1001 Fisher St., P.O. Box 308, 76844, P 5,000, M 132, (325) 648-3619, gcc@centex.net, www.goldthwaite.biz

**Goliad** · *Goliad C/C* · Mona Foust, Mgr. Dir., 231 S. Market St., P.O. Box 606, 77963, P 7,200, M 185, (361) 645-3563, Fax (361) 645-3579, goliadcc@goliad.net, www.goliadcc.org

**Gonzales** · *Gonzales C/C* · Barbara Hand, Exec. Dir., 414 St. Lawrence St., 78629, P 7,202, M 290, (830) 672-6532, Fax (830) 672-6533, info@gonzalestexas.com, www.gonzalestexas.com.

**Gorman** · *Gorman C/C* · Terry Treadway, Secy./Mgr., P.O. Box 266, 76454, P 1,236, M 50, (254) 639-2317, Fax (254) 639-2317, terry@cctc.net

**Graford** · *Possum Kingdom Lake C/C* · Gayla Chambers, Exec. Dir., 362 N. FM 2353, 76449, P 2,500, M 240, (940) 779-2424, pkchamber@possumkingdomlake.com, www.possumkingdomlake.com

**Graham** · *Graham C/C* · DeAnna Bullock Armstrong, Exec. Dir., 608 Elm St., P.O. Box 299, 76450, P 8,716, M 350, (940) 549-3355, (800) 256-4844, Fax (940) 549-6391, info@grahamtxchamber.com, www.grahamtxchamber.com

**Granbury** · *Granbury C/C* · Mike Scott, CEO, 3408 Hwy. 377 E., 76049, P 54,900, M 920, (817) 573-1622, Fax (817) 573-0805, info@granburychamber.com, www.granburychamber.com.

**Grand Prairie** · *Grand Prairie C/C* · Lynn McGinley, Pres., 900 Conover Dr., 75051, P 170,000, M 900, (972) 264-1558, Fax (972) 264-3419, info@grandprairiechamber.org, www.grandprairiechamber.org.

**Grand Saline** · *Grand Saline C/C* · Lisa Morrison, Secy., 203 N.E. Pacific, 75140, P 3,200, M 125, (903) 962-7147, chamber@grandsaline.com, www.grandsaline.com

**Grandfalls** · *Grandfalls-Royalty C/C* · Mary Lynn Geurin, Pres., P.O. Box 269, 79742, P 400, M 40, (432) 547-2360, (432) 547-2331

**Grandview** · *Greater Grandview C/C* · Chuck McGowen, Pres., P.O. Box 276, 76050, P 1,300, (817) 866-4881, info@grandviewchamber.net, www.grandviewchamber.net

**Grapevine** · *Grapevine C/C* · RaDonna Hessel, Pres., 200 E. Vine St., 76051, P 49,635, M 880, (817) 481-1522, Fax (817) 424-5208, info@grapevinechamber.org, www.grapevinechamber.org.

**Greenspoint** · *see Houston-- North Houston-Greenspoint C/C*

**Greenville** · *Greenville C/C* · Sally Bird, Pres., 2713 Stonewall St., P.O. Box 1055, 75403, P 26,500, M 575, (903) 455-1510, Fax (903) 455-1736, chamber@greenvillechamber.com, www.greenvillechamber.com.

**Groesbeck** · *Groesbeck C/C* · 115 N. Ellis St., P.O. Box 326, 76642, P 4,200, M 120, (254) 729-3894, Fax (254) 729-8310, www.groesbecktexas.org

**Groves** · *Groves C of C & Tourist Center* · Ronnie Boneau, Exec. Mgr., 4399 Main Ave., 77619, P 15,733, M 133, (409) 962-3631, (800) 876-3631, Fax (409) 963-0745, gchamberofcommer@gt.rr.com, www.grovescofc.com.

**Groveton** · *Trinity County C/C* · Paul E. Snyder, Pres., 135 Main St., P.O. Box 366, 75845, P 1,106, M 61, (936) 642-1715, Fax (936) 642-2144, tccoc@valornet.com, .

**Gruver** · *Gruver C/C* · Steve McKay, Mgr., 201 E. Broadway, P.O. Box 947, 79040, P 1,162, M 40, (806) 733-5114, Fax (806) 733-5038, www.gruvertexas.com

**Gun Barrel City** · *see Mabank*

**Gunter** · *Gunter Area C/C* · Andrea Allen, P.O. Box 830, 75058, P 1,300, M 75, (903) 433-2050, ww.guntertxchamber.com

**Hale Center** · *Hale Center C/C* · 702 Main St., P.O. Box 487, 79041, P 2,200, M 106, (806) 839-2642

**Hallettsville** · *Hallettsville C/C* · 1614 N. Texana, P.O. Box 313, 77964, P 2,531, M 200, (361) 798-2662, Fax (361) 798-1553, visit@hallettsville.com, www.hallettsville.com

**Hallsville** · *Hallsville Area C/C* · P.O. Box 535, 75650, P 2,905, M 185, (903) 668-5990

**Haltom City** · *Northeast Tarrant C/C* · Robert Hamilton, Pres./CEO, 5001 Denton Hwy., 76117, P 135,000, M 1,200, (817) 281-9376, Fax (817) 281-9379, tnaini@netarrant.org, www.netarrant.org

**Hamilton** · *Hamilton C/C* · Steve Almquist, Mgr., 204 E. Main St., P.O. Box 429, 76531, P 3,000, M 144, (254) 386-3216, Fax (254) 386-3563, cofc@htcomp.net, www.hamiltontexas.com

**Hamlin** · *Hamlin C/C* · Amanda Bell, Pres., P.O. Box 402, 79520, P 2,200, M 100, (325) 576-3501

**Harker Heights** · *Harker Heights C/C* · Bill Kozlik, Pres., 552 E. FM 2410, Ste. B, 76548, P 26,000, M 900, (254) 699-4999, Fax (254) 699-5194, bill@hhchamber.com, www.hhchamber.com

**Harlingen** · *Harlingen Area C/C & Visitor Bur.* · Crisanne Zamponi, Exec. Dir., 311 E. Tyler St., 78550, P 84,832, M 900, (956) 423-5440, (800) 531-7346, Fax (956) 425-3870, czamponi@harlingen.com, www.harlingen.com

**Harlingen** · *Harlingen Hispanic C/C* · Frank Puente Jr., Chrmn., 2309 N. Ed Carey Dr., P.O. Box 530967, 78553, P 65,000, M 400, (956) 421-2400, Fax (956) 364-1879, hhcoc@harlingenchamber.com, www.harlingenchamber.com

**Harper** · *Harper C/C* · P.O. Box 308, 78631, P 2,000, M 110, (830) 864-5656, Fax (830) 864-4799, www.harpertexas.com

**Haskell** · *Haskell C/C* · Sally Rueffer, Gen. Mgr., 510 S. 2nd St., P.O. Box 316, 79521, P 3,200, M 90, (940) 864-2477, www.haskelltxchamber.com

**Haslet** · *see Roanoke*

**Hawkins** · *Hawkins Area C/C* · Dr. H.L. Peace, Mgr., P.O. Box 345, 75765, P 1,331, M 119, (903) 769-4482, Fax (903) 769-4320

**Hemphill** · *Sabine County C/C* · Jim Binns, Exec. Dir., 717 Sabine St., P.O. Box 717, 75948, P 11,000, M 225, (409) 787-2732, Fax (409) 787-2158, sabinetx@sabinenet.com, www.sabinecountytexas.com

**Hempstead** · *Hempstead C/C* · John Stanley, Pres., 733 12th St., 77445, P 7,500, M 175, (979) 826-8217, www.hempsteadtxchamber.com

**Henderson** · *Henderson Area C/C* · Judy Sewell, Exec. Dir., 201 N. Main St., 75652, P 47,255, M 355, (903) 657-5528, Fax (903) 657-9454, info@hendersontx.com, www.hendersontx.com

**Henrietta** · *Henrietta/Clay County C/C* · Hank Bullinger, Pres., 202 W. Omega St., P.O. Box 75, 76365, P 3,800, M 100, (940) 538-5261, claycountychamber@sbcglobal.net, www.hcccchamber.com

**Hereford** · *Deaf Smith County C/C* · Sid C. Shaw, Exec. V.P., 701 N. Main, P.O. Box 192, 79045, P 20,000, M 500, (806) 364-3333, Fax (806) 364-3342, deafs@wtrt.net, www.herefordtx.org

**Hewitt** · *Greater Hewitt C/C* · 101 Third St., P.O. Box 661, 76643, P 14,000, M 310, (254) 666-1200, Fax (254) 666-3181, info@hewitt-texas.com, www.hewitt-texas.com

**Hico** · *Hico Civic Club* · P.O. Box 93, 76457, P 1,341, M 80

**Hidalgo** · *Hidalgo C/C* · 611 E. Coma, 78557, P 7,500, M 570, (956) 843-2734, Fax (956) 843-2722, chamber@hidalgotexas.com, www.hidalgotexas.com

**Highlands** · *Greater Highlands & Lynchburg C/C* · Beverly Culbreath, Exec. Dir., 127 San Jacinto St., 77562, P 10,000, M 100, (281) 426-7227, Fax (281) 426-7227

**Hillje** · *see Louise*

**Hillsboro** · *Hillsboro C/C* · 115 N. Covington St., P.O. Box 358, 76645, P 8,500, M 360, (254) 582-2481, Fax (254) 582-0465, chamber@hillsborochamber.org, www.hillsborochamber.org.

**Hitchcock** · *Hitchcock C/C* · Teresa Weishuhn, Exec. Dir., 8300 Hwy. 6, Ste. A, P.O. Box 389, 77563, P 6,386, M 200, (409) 986-9224, Fax (409) 986-6317, hcofc662@verizon.net, www.hitchcocktexaschamber.com

**Hondo** · *Hondo Area C/C* · Evelyne Barbutti, Exec. Dir., 1607 Ave. K, 78861, P 8,500, M 250, (830) 426-3037, Fax (830) 426-5357, hondochamber@sbcglobal.net, www.hondochamber.com

**Honey Grove** · *Honey Grove C/C* · P.O. Box 92, 75446, P 1,800, M 74, (903) 378-7211, www.honeygrovechamber.com

## Houston Area

**Greater Houston Partnership** · Maria Velasquez, Mgr. of Intl. Bus. Programs, 1200 Smith St., Ste. 700, 77002, P 5,087,127, M 2,000, (713) 844-3636, Fax (713) 844-0236, mvelasquez@houston.org, www.houston.org

**Clear Lake Area C/C** · Cindy Harreld, Pres./CEO, 1201 NASA Pkwy., 77058, P 250,000, M 1,800, (281) 488-7676, Fax (281) 488-8981, chamber@clearlakearea.com, www.clearlakearea.com

**Galleria C/C** · Don Sweat, Pres., 5005 Woodway, Ste. 215, 77056, P 210,000, M 765, (713) 629-5555, Fax (713) 629-6403, info@galleriachamber.com, www.galleriachamber.com

**Greater Heights Area C/C** · David Santana, Pres., 545 W. 19th St., 77008, P 350,000, M 400, (713) 861-6735, Fax (713) 861-9310, president@heightschamber.com, www.heightschamber.com

**Houston East End C/C** · Diane Lipton, Pres., 550 Gulf Gate Center Mall, 77087, P 110,000, M 500, (713) 926-3305, Fax (713) 926-0960, diane@eecoc.org, www.eecoc.org

**Houston Northwest C/C** · Barbara Thomason, Pres., 14511 Falling Creek, Ste. 205, 77014, P 865,000, M 700, (281) 440-4160, Fax (281) 440-5302, chamberinfo@houstonnwchamber.org, www.houstonnwchamber.org

**Houston West C/C** · Jeannie Bollinger, Pres./CEO, 10370 Richmond, Ste. 125, 77042, P 700,000, M 560, (713) 785-4922, Fax (713) 785-4944, info@hwcoc.org, www.hwcoc.org

**North Channel Area C/C** · Wayne R. Oquin, Pres./CEO, 13301 I-10 E. Frwy., Ste. 100, P.O. Box 9759, 77213, P 210,000, M 700, (713) 450-3600, Fax (713) 450-0700, wayneoq@flash.net, www.northchannelarea.com.

**North Houston-Greenspoint C/C** · Reggie Gray, Pres., 250 N. Sam Houston Pkwy. E., Ste. 200, 77060, P 900,000, M 500, (281) 260-3163, Fax (281) 260-3161, www.nhgcc.org

**South Belt-Ellington C/C** · Sally Mitchell, Exec. Dir., 10500 Scarsdale, 77089, P 81,000, M 400, (281) 481-5516, Fax (281) 922-7045, info@southbeltchamber.com, www.southbeltchamber.com

**Hubbard** · *City of Hubbard C/C* · Margo Foster, Corresponding Secy., P.O. Box 221, 76648, P 1,600, M 100, (254) 576-2521, Fax (254) 576-2688, mfoster396@aol.com, www.hubbardchamber.com

**Hudson Oaks** · *see Willow Park*

**Huffman** · *see Crosby*

**Hughes Springs** · *Hughes Springs C/C* · Judi Howell, Exec. Dir., 603 E. 1st St., P.O. Box 218, 75656, P 2,000, M 110, (903) 639-2351, Fax (903) 639-3769, jhowell@hughesspringstx.net, www.hughesspringstx.net

**Humble** · *Humble Area C/C* · Mike Byers, Pres., 110 W. Main St., P.O. Box 3337, 77347, P 270,000, M 1,300, (281) 446-2128, Fax (281) 446-7483, mbyers@humbleareachamber.org, www.humbleareachamber.org

**Huntsville** • *Huntsville-Walker County C/C* • Dee Everett, Pres./ CEO, 1327 11th St., P.O. Box 538, 77342, P 62,000, M 650, (936) 295-8113, (800) 289-0389, Fax (936) 295-0571, chamber@chamber. huntsville.tx.us, www.chamber.huntsville.tx.us

**Hurst** • *see Bedford*

**Hutto** • *Hutto C/C* • 122 East St., P.O. Box 99, 78634, P 17,200, M 260, (512) 759-4400, Fax (512) 846-1618, info@hutto.org, www.hutto.org

**Ingleside** • *Ingleside C/C* • 2867 Ave. J, P.O. Box 686, 78362, P 9,338, M 182, (361) 776-2906, (888) 899-2906, Fax (361) 776-0678, ingchamber@cableone.net, www.inglesidetxchamber.org

**Ingram** • *West Kerr County C/C* • Joanne Gray, Exec. Dir., 3186 Junction Hwy., P.O. Box 1006, 78025, P 10,000, M 158, (830) 367-4322, wkccc1@ktc.com, www.wkcc.com

**Iowa Park** • *Iowa Park C/C* • David Owen, Dir. of Eco. Dev., 102 N. Wall St., 76367, P 6,500, M 125, (940) 592-5441, dowen@ iowapark.com, www.iowapark.com

**Iraan** • *Iraan-Sheffield C/C* • 501 W. 6th, P.O. Box 153, 79744, P 1,250, M 60, (432) 639-2232, mail@iraantx.com, www.iraantx.com

**Iredell** • *Iredell C/C* • P.O. Box 111, 76649, P 360, M 12, (254) 364-2436

**Irving** • *Greater Irving-Las Colinas C/C* • Chris Wallace, Pres., 5221 N. O'Connor Blvd. #100, 75039, P 200,000, M 1,250, (214) 217-8484, Fax (214) 389-2513, cwallace@irvingchamber.com, www.irvingchamber.com

**Jacksboro** • *Jacksboro C/C* • Kevin Kelly, Ofc. Mgr., 112 W. Belknap, P.O. Box 606, 76458, P 4,533, M 120, (940) 567-2602, Fax (940) 567-2602, jacksborocofc@sbcglobal.net, www.jacks borochamber.com

**Jacksonville** • *Jacksonville C/C* • Peggy Renfro, Pres., 526 E. Commerce, P.O. Box 1231, 75766, P 14,090, M 435, (903) 586-2217, Fax (903) 586-6944, chamber@jacksonvilletexas.com, www. jacksonvilletexas.com

**Jasper** • *Jasper-Lake Sam Rayburn Area C/C* • Elizabeth Street, Exec. Dir., 246 E. Milam, 75951, P 8,500, M 395, (409) 384-2762, Fax (409) 384-4733, jaspercc@jaspercoc.org, www.jaspercoc.org

**Jefferson** • *Marion County C/C* • 101 N. Polk St., 75657, P 2,200, M 224, (903) 665-2672, (888) GO-RELAX, Fax (903) 665-8233, jef-fersonchamber@sbcglobal.net, www.jefferson-texas.com

**Jewett** • *Jewett Area C/C* • Kim Pritchard, Pres., 111 N. Robinson, P.O. Box 220, 75846, P 1,250, M 95, (903) 626-4202, Fax (903) 626-6599, jewettchamber@sbcglobal.net, www.jewetttexas.com

**Johnson City** • *Johnson City Chamber & Visitors Center* • Dale Hardy, Dir., 100 E. Main, P.O. Box 485, 78636, P 1,350, M 140, (830) 868-7684, Fax (830) 868-5700, info@johnstoncitytexas chamber.com, www.lbjcountry.com

**Joshua** • *Joshua Area C/C* • Tana Howell, Pres., 104 N. Main St., P.O. Box 1292, 76058, P 8,200, M 187, (817) 558-2821, josh chamber@att.net, www.joshuachamber.org

**Jourdanton** • *Jourdanton C/C* • P.O. Box 747, 78026, P 3,700, M 50, (830) 769-2866, www.jourdanton.net

**Junction** • *Kimble County C/C* • Connie Booth, Exec. Dir., 402 Main St., 76849, P 5,000, M 275, (325) 446-3190, (800) KIMBLE-4, Fax (325) 446-2871, junctiontx@cebridge.net, www.junction texas.net.

**Karnack** • *Caddo Lake Area C/C* • Jay Webb, Pres., 984 TJ Taylor Ave., P.O. Box 228, 75661, P 700, M 58, info@caddolake.org, www. caddolake.org

**Karnes City** • *Karnes City Comm. C/C* • Maggie Hunt, Exec. Dir., 210 E. Calvert St., 78118, P 3,578, M 110, (830) 780-3112, Fax (830) 780-3112, office@karnescitychamber.net, www.karnescity chamber.net

**Kashmere** • *see Houston-- North Houston-Greenspoint C/C*

**Katy** • *Katy Area C/C* • Ann Hodge, Pres./CEO, 23501 Cinco Ranch Blvd., Ste. B206, 77494, P 214,000, M 800, (281) 391-5289, Fax (281) 391-7423, info@katychamber.com, www. katychamber.com

**Kaufman** • *Greater Kaufman C/C* • Anne Glasscock, Pres./CEO, 2100 S. Washington, P.O. Box 146, 75142, P 7,120, M 275, (972) 932-3118, Fax (972) 932-8373, info@kaufmanchamber.com, www.kaufmantx.com

**Keene** • *Keene C/C* • Paul Gnadt, Pres., P.O. Box 817, 76059, P 6,000, M 125, (817) 556-2995, info@keenechamber.org, www. keenechamber.org

**Keller** • *Greater Keller C/C* • Susanne Johnson, Pres./CEO, 200 S. Main, P.O. Box 761, 76244, P 36,000, M 700, (817) 431-2169, Fax (817) 431-3789, kellerinfo@kellerchamber.com, www. kellerchamber.com

**Kemah** • *see Dickinson*

**Kemp** • *see Mabank*

**Kenedy** • *Kenedy C/C* • Carolyn McDonald, Exec. Dir., 205 S. 2nd St., 78119, P 3,400, M 130, (830) 583-3223, Fax same, info@ kenedychamber.com, www.kenedychamber.org

**Kennedale** • *Kennedale C/C* • Pat Doescher, Chrmn., P.O. Box 1552, 76060, P 6,500, M 170, (817) 985-2109, kennedalecham ber@yahoo.com, www.kennedalechamber.com

**Kerens** • *Kerens C/C* • Rita West, Secy., P.O. Box 117, 75144, P 1,681, M 100, (903) 396-2391, kerenschamber@txun.net, www. ci.kerens.tx.us

**Kermit** • *Kermit C/C* • Stefanie Haley, Pres., 112 N. Poplar, 79745, P 6,200, M 130, (432) 586-2507, Fax (432) 586-2508, kermit chamber@cebridge.net

**Kerrville** • *Kerrville Area C/C* • Brian J. Bondy IOM, Pres./CEO, 1700 Sidney Baker St., Ste. 100, 78028, P 44,000, M 1,222, (830) 896-1155, Fax (830) 896-1175, president@kerrvilletx.com, www. kerrvilletx.com

**Kilgore** • *Kilgore C/C* • Michael Coston, Pres., 813 N. Kilgore St., P.O. Box 1582, 75663, P 11,990, M 550, (903) 984-5022, (866) 984-0400, Fax (903) 984-4975, info@kilgorechamber.com, www. kilgorechamber.com

**Killeen** • *Greater Killeen C/C* • John Crutchfield, Pres., One Santa Fe Plaza, P.O. Box 548, 76540, P 112,000, M 1,200, (254) 526-9551, Fax (254) 526-6090, chamber@gkcc.com, www.gkcc.com.

**Kingsland** • *Kingsland/Lake LBJ C/C* • Vern Magnuson, Ofc. Mgr., P.O. Box 465, 78639, P 12,500, M 250, (325) 388-6211, Fax (325) 388-5391, kchamber@zeecon.com, www.kingslandchamber.org

**Kingsville** • *Kingsville C/C* • Alice Byers, Exec. Dir., 635 E. King St., P.O. Box 1030, 78364, P 26,331, M 350, (361) 592-6438, Fax (361) 592-0866, chamber@kingsville.org, www.kingsville.org

**Kirby** • *see Selma*

**Kirbyville** • *Kirbyville C/C* • Angie Brown, Secy., 105 S. Elizabeth, 75956, P 2,000, M 100, (409) 423-5827, Fax (409) 423-3353, abrownkcc@yahoo.com, www.digitalkirbyville.com

**Knox City** • *Knox City C/C* • 123 Central Ave., P.O. Box 91, 79529, P 1,219, M 75, (940) 658-3442, Fax (940) 658-1247, www. knoxcountytexas.com

**Kountze** · *Kountze C/C* · Ann Boyett, Pres., P.O. Box 878, 77625, P 2,119, M 88, (409) 246-3413, (866) 4-KOUNTZ, Fax (409) 246-4659, www.kountzechamber.com

**Kyle** · *Kyle Area C/C & Visitors Bur.* · Ray Hernandez, Exec. Dir., 100 N. Front St., P.O. Box 900, 78640, P 30,000, M 250, (512) 268-4220, (800) 903-1564, Fax (512) 268-4220, ray@kylechamber.org, www.kylechamber.org

**La Grange** · *La Grange Area C/C* · 171 S. Main, 78945, P 12,000, M 325, (979) 968-5756, (800) LAGRANGE, Fax (979) 968-8000, chamber@lagrangetx.org, www.lagrangetx.org.

**La Porte** · *La Porte-Bayshore C/C* · Colleen Hicks, Pres., 712 W. Fairmont Pkwy., P.O. Box 996, 77572, P 38,000, M 450, (281) 471-1123, Fax (281) 471-1710, info-lpcc@laportechamber.org, www.laportechamber.org

**La Vernia** · *Greater La Vernia C/C* · P.O. Box 1055, 78121, P 1,000, M 100, (830) 779-4522, info@lavernia.org, www.lavernia.org

**Ladonia** · *Ladonia C/C* · Chris Porter, Pres., P.O. Box 44, 75449, P 667, M 30, (903) 367-7011, chamber@cityofladonia.com, www.cityofladonia.com

**Lago Vista** · *Lago Vista C/C & CVB* · P.O. Box 4946, 78645, P 5,800, M 221, (512) 267-7952, (888) 328-LAGO, Fax (512) 267-2338, info@lagovista.org, www.lagovista.org

**Lake Conroe** · *see Conroe*

**Lake Dallas** · *Lake Cities C/C* · John Lugenheim, Pres., 450 Main St., P.O. Box 1028, 75065, P 26,000, M 309, (940) 497-3097, Fax (972) 534-1375, lccc@lakecitieschamber.com, www.lakecitieschamber.com

**Lake Tawakoni** · *see Quinlan*

**Lake Worth** · *Northwest Tarrant C/C* · Larry Thompson, Exec. Dir., 3918 Telephone Rd., Ste. 200, P.O. Box 136333, 76136, P 10,000, M 175, (817) 237-0060, Fax (817) 237-2365, lthompson@nwtcc.org, www.nwtcc.org

**Lakewood** · *see Houston-- North Houston-Greenspoint C/C*

**Lamesa** · *Lamesa Area C/C* · Larry Allison, Exec. V.P., 123 Main St., P.O. Box 880, 79331, P 15,000, M 240, (806) 872-2181, Fax (806) 872-5700, lamesaareacoc@growlamesa.com, www.growlamesa.com

**Lampasas** · *Lampasas County C/C* · Jill Carroll, Dir., 205 S. U.S. Hwy. 281, P.O. Box 627, 76550, P 18,500, M 310, (512) 556-5172, Fax (512) 556-2195, info@lampasaschamber.org, www.lampasaschamber.org

**Lancaster** · *Lancaster C/C* · Joe Johnson, Pres., 100 N. Dallas Ave., P.O. Box 1100, 75146, P 35,000, M 290, (972) 227-2579, Fax (972) 227-9555, jjohnson@lancastertx.org, www.lancastertx.org

**Laredo** · *Laredo-Webb County C/C* · Miguel Conchas, Pres./CEO, 2310 San Bernardo Ave., P.O. Box 790, 78042, P 224,997, M 831, (956) 722-9895, Fax (956) 791-4503, chamber@laredochamber.com, www.laredochamber.com

**League City** · *League City C/C* · Debbie Thomas, Pres./CEO, 260 Park Ave., 77573, P 62,000, M 700, (281) 338-7339, Fax (281) 554-8103, info@leaguecitychamber.com, www.leaguecitychamber.com

**Leakey** · *Frio Canyon C/C* · P.O. Box 743, 78873, P 399, M 90, (830) 232-5222, www.friocanyonchamber.com

**Leander** · *Greater Leander C/C* · Mary E. Bradshaw, Pres., 103 N. Brushy St., P.O. Box 556, 78641, P 27,500, M 345, (512) 259-1907, Fax (512) 259-9114, contactus@leandercc.org, www.leandercc.org

**Leonard** · *Leonard C/C* · Allecia Booher, Pres., P.O. Box 117, 75452, P 1,846, M 75, (903) 587-0174, Fax (903) 587-2580

**Levelland** · *Levelland Area C/C* · Mary Siders, Pres., 1101 Ave. H, 79336, P 14,000, M 261, (806) 894-3157, msiders@levelland.com, www.levelland.com

**Lewisville** · *Lewisville C/C* · Matt McCormick, Pres., 551 N. Valley Pkwy., 75067, P 91,000, M 850, (972) 436-9571, Fax (972) 436-5949, matt@lewisvillechamber.org, www.lewisvillechamber.org

**Liberty** · *Liberty-Dayton Area C/C* · Mary Anne Campbell, Pres., 1801 Trinity, P.O. Box 1270, 77575, P 25,000, M 450, (936) 336-5736, Fax (936) 336-1159, chamber@imsday.com, www.libertydaytonchamber.com

**Liberty Hill** · *Liberty Hill C/C* · Zack Milam, Chrmn., P.O. Box 586, 78642, P 1,400, M 90, (512) 548-6343, membership@mylibertyhill.net, www.mylibertyhill.net

**Lindale** · *Lindale Area C/C* · Shelbie Glover, Exec. Dir., 110 E. Hubbard, P.O. Box 670, 75771, P 4,900, M 450, (903) 882-7181, Fax (903) 882-7190, info@lindalechamber.org, www.lindalechamber.org

**Linden** · *Linden Area C/C* · Steven Webb, Pres., 201 N. Main St., P.O. Box 993, 75563, P 2,400, M 50, (903) 756-3106, Fax (903) 756-7842, www.lindentexas.org

**Littlefield** · *Littlefield C/C* · Gini Coffman, Exec. V.P., 4th & LFD Dr., P.O. Box 507, 79339, P 6,500, M 130, (806) 385-5331, Fax (806) 385-0108, chamber@littlefieldchamber.org, .

**Live Oak** · *see Selma*

**Livingston** · *Polk County C/C* · Sydney Murphy, Exec. Dir., U.S. Hwy. 59 Loop N., P.O. Box 600, 77351, P 50,000, M 478, (936) 327-4929, (800) 918-1305, Fax (936) 327-2660, chamberadmin@livingston.net, www.polkchamber.com.

**Llano** · *Llano C/C & Visitor Center* · Tony Griffith, Exec. Dir., 100 Train Station Dr., 78643, P 3,500, M 300, (325) 247-5354, (866) 539-5535, Fax (325) 248-6917, info@llanochamber.org, www.llanochamber.org.

**Lockhart** · *Lockhart C/C* · Wayne Bock, Pres./CEO, 631 S. Colorado, P.O. Box 840, 78644, P 13,500, M 300, (512) 398-2818, Fax (512) 376-2632, wbock@lockhartchamber.com, www.lockhartchamber.com.

**Lockney** · *Lockney C/C* · Melissa Kunselman, Pres., P.O. Box 477, 79241, P 2,200, M 150, (806) 652-2355, www.lockneychamber.com

**Lone Oak** · *see Quinlan*

**Lone Star** · *Lone Star C/C* · Robert Rodden, Pres., P.O. Box 0505, 75668, P 1,615, M 47, (903) 656-2595

**Longview** · *Longview Partnership* · Kelly Hall, Pres., 410 N. Center St., 75601, P 75,000, M 1,300, (903) 237-4000, Fax (903) 237-4049, info1@longviewtx.com, www.longviewtx.com.

**Los Fresnos** · *Los Fresnos C/C* · Michael Garza, Exec. Dir., 203 N. Arroyo Blvd., Ste. A, 78566, P 5,000, M 115, (956) 233-4488, (956) 350-3000, www.losfresnoschamber.com

**Louise** · *Louise-Hillje C/C* · John Crowell, Pres., P.O. Box 156, 77455, P 1,000, M 75, (979) 648-2615, (979) 648-2691, Fax (979) 648-2598

**Lubbock** · *Lubbock C/C* · Eddie McBride, Pres., 1301 Broadway, Ste. 101, 79401, P 212,000, M 2,200, (806) 761-7000, (800) 321-5822, Fax (806) 761-7013, eddie.mcbride@lubbockbiz.org, www.lubbockchamber.com

**Lufkin** · *Angelina County C/C* · Jerry Huffman, Pres./CEO, 1615 S. Chestnut, P.O. Box 1606, 75901, P 85,000, M 1,400, (936) 634-6644, Fax (936) 634-8726, chamber@lufkintexas.org, www.lufkintexas.org.

**Luling** • *Luling Area C/C & Visitors Center* • Rita Moore, Exec. Dir., 421 E. Davis St., P.O. Box 710, 78648, P 5,500, M 250, (830) 875-3214, Fax (830) 875-2082, lulingcc@austin.rr.com, www. lulingcc.org.

**Lumberton** • *Lumberton C/C* • Tammy Melvin, Exec. Dir., 826 N. Main, P.O. Box 8574, 77657, P 20,000, M 200, (409) 755-0554, Fax (409) 755-2516, lcoc@lumbertoncoc.com, www.lumbertoncoc.com

**Lytle** • *Greater Lytle C/C* • Brad Boyd, Pres., P.O. Box 2131, 78052, P 2,500, M 30, (830) 772-5843, www.lytlechamber.com

**Mabank** • *Greater Cedar Creek Lake Area C/C* • JoAnn Hanstrom, Pres., 604 S. Third St., Ste. E, P.O. Box 581, 75147, P 51,065, M 475, (903) 887-3152, Fax (903) 887-3695, info@cedarcreeklakechamber.com, www.cedarcreeklakechamber.com

**Madisonville** • *Madison County C/C* • 113 W. Trinity, 77864, P 4,400, M 180, (936) 348-3591, Fax (936) 348-2212, info@madisoncountytxchamber.com, www.madisoncountytxchamber.com.

**Magnolia** • *Magnolia Area C/C* • Anne Sundquist, Pres., 18935 FM 1488, P.O. Box 399, 77353, P 75,000, M 450, (281) 356-1488, info@magnoliatexas.org, www.magnoliatexas.org

**Malakoff** • *Malakoff Area C/C* • P.O. Box 1042, 75148, P 2,100, M 70, (903) 489-1518, Fax same, malakoffcofc@embarqmail.com, www.malakoffchamber.com

**Mansfield** • *Mansfield Area C/C* • Lucretia Mills, Exec. Dir., 114 N. Main St., 76063, P 60,000, M 700, (817) 473-0507, Fax (817) 473-8687, lucretia@mansfieldchamber.org, www.mansfield chamber.org.

**Marathon** • *Marathon C/C* • 105 Hwy. 90 W., 79842, P 600, M 85, (432) 386-4516, www.marathontexas.com

**Marble Falls** • *Marble Falls-Lake LBJ C/C* • Christian Fletcher, Exec. Dir., 916 Second St., 78654, P 30,000, M 800, (830) 693-2815, (800) 759-8178, Fax (830) 693-1620, info@marblefalls.org, www.marblefalls.org.

**Marfa** • *Marfa C/C* • Daniel Browning, Pres., 207 N. Highland, P.O. Box 635, 79843, P 2,424, M 112, (432) 729-4942, (800) 650-9696, Fax (432) 729-4956, info@marfacc.com, www.marfacc.com

**Marion** • *see Selma*

**Marlin** • *Marlin C/C* • Cynthia Dees, Ofc. Mgr., 245 Coleman St., P.O. Box 369, 76661, P 6,683, M 150, (254) 803-3301, Fax (254) 883-2171, marlintxchamber@aol.com, www.marlintexas.com.

**Marquez** • *Marquez Area C/C* • P.O. Box 751, 77865, P 220, M 35, (903) 529-1419

**Marshall** • *Marshall C/C* • Connie Ware, Pres./CEO, 213 W. Austin St., P.O. Box 520, 75670, P 26,000, M 900, (903) 935-7868, (800) 953-7868, Fax (903) 935-9982, www.marshalltxchamber.com

**Mart** • *Mart C/C & Ag.* • Jim Read, Pres., P.O. Box 59, 76664, P 2,200, M 100, (254) 876-2561

**Mason** • *Mason County C/C* • Sherry Alm, Ofc. Mgr., 108 Ft. McKavitt, P.O. Box 156, 76856, P 3,800, M 220, (325) 347-5758, Fax (325) 347-5259, masontexas@verizon.net, www.masontxcoc.com

**Mathis** • *Mathis Area C/C* • 211 E. San Patricio Ave., 78368, P 6,000, M 60, (361) 547-0289, Fax (361) 547-7802, www. mathischamber.org, www.mathischamber.org

**McAllen** • *McAllen C/C* • Steve Ahlenius, Pres./CEO, 1200 Ash Ave., P.O. Box 790, 78505, P 120,000, M 1,600, (956) 682-2871, (877) 622-5536, Fax (956) 687-2917, steve@mcallenchamber.com, www.mcallenchamber.com

**McCamey** • *McCamey C/C* • Crystal Glenn, Sec., 201 E. 6th St., P.O. Box 906, 79752, P 1,805, M 83, (432) 652-8202, info@mccamey chamber.com, www.mccameychamber.com

**McGregor** • *McGregor C/C* • Meghan Mullens, Exec. V.P., 303 S. Main St., 76657, P 5,000, M 105, (254) 840-0123, Fax (254) 840-4703, mcgregorchamber@mcgregor-texas.com, www.mcgregor-texas.com

**McKinney** • *McKinney C/C* • Terrie Keith, Pres., 1650 W. Virginia St. #110, 75069, P 105,000, M 1,100, (972) 542-0163, Fax (972) 548-0876, info@mckinneytx.org, www.mckinneytx.org.

**Melissa** • *Melissa Area C/C* • Tina Helmberger, Exec. Dir., 1501 W. Harrison St., P.O. Box 121, 75454, P 4,800, M 161, (972) 837-4277, melissaareachamber@gmail.com, www.melissatx.org

**Memphis** • *Memphis C/C* • Judy Stewart, Pres., 515 W. Main, 79245, P 2,500, M 75, (806) 259-3144, Fax (806) 259-3144, memphistexaschamber@valornet.com

**Menard** • *Menard County C/C* • Tina Hodge, Ofc. Mgr., 100 E. San Saba, P.O. Box 64, 76859, P 1,600, M 135, (325) 396-2365, Fax (325) 396-4545, info@menardchamber.com, www.menardchamber.com

**Mercedes** • *Mercedes Area C/C* • Donna Jackson, Ofc. Mgr., 320 S. Ohio, P.O. Box 37, 78570, P 13,660, M 140, (956) 565-2221, Fax same, donna@mercedeschamber.com, www.mercedeschamber.com

**Meridian** • *Meridian C/C* • Rick Goon, Pres., P.O. Box 758, 76665, P 1,539, M 135, (254) 435-2966, meridian-chamber@sbcglobal. net, www.meridian-chamber.com

**Merkel** • *Merkel C/C* • P.O. Box 536, 79536, P 2,715, M 50, (325) 928-5722, Fax (325) 928-5722, coc@merkeltx.com, www. merkeltx.com

**Mesquite** • *Mesquite C of C & CVB* • Terry McCullar, Pres., 617 N. Ebrite, 75149, P 134,000, M 650, (972) 285-0211, (800) 541-2355, Fax (972) 285-3535, info@mesquitechamber.com, www. mesquitechamber.com

**Mexia** • *Mexia C/C* • Linda Archibald, Exec. Dir., 405 E. Milam, Ste. 2, 76667, P 7,000, M 175, (254) 562-5569, (888) 535-5476, Fax (254) 562-7138, linda@mexiachamber.com, www.mexiachamber.com

**Miami** • *Miami/Roberts County C/C* • P.O. Box 355, 79059, P 588, M 75

**Midland** • *Midland C/C* • Rob Cunningham, Pres./CEO, 109 N. Main St., 79701, P 119,500, M 1,431, (432) 683-3381, (800) 624-6435, Fax (432) 686-3556, info@midlandtxchamber.com, www. midlandtxchamber.com.

**Midlothian** • *Midlothian C/C* • Amanda Miller, Pres./CEO, 310 N. 9th St., 76065, P 13,000, M 500, (972) 723-8600, Fax (972) 723-9300, amiller@midlothianchamber.org, www.midlothian chamber.org

**Mineola** • *Mineola Area C/C* • Shirley Chadwick, Exec. Dir., 101 E. Broad St., P.O. Box 68, 75773, P 5,611, M 270, (903) 569-2087, Fax (903) 569-5510, chamber@mineola.com, www.mineolachamber.org

**Mineral Wells** • *Mineral Wells Area C/C* • Beth Watson, Pres., 511 E. Hubbard, P.O. Box 1408, 76068, P 29,000, M 420, (940) 325-2557, (800) 252-6989, Fax (940) 328-0850, info@mineralwellstx. com, www.mineralwellstx.com.

**Mission** • *Greater Mission C/C* • Arlene Rivera, Pres./CEO, 202 W. Tom Landry, 78572, P 75,000, M 525, (956) 585-2727, (800) 580-2700, Fax (956) 585-3044, receptionist@missionchamber. com, www.missionchamber.com

**Monahans** • *Monahans C/C* • Teresa Burnett, Exec. Dir., 401 S. Dwight, 79756, P 7,500, M 200, (432) 943-2187, Fax (432) 943-6868, chamber@monahans.org, www.monahans.org

**Mont Belvieu** • *West Chambers County C/C* • M.G. Malechek, Pres., 11340 Eagle Dr., Ste. 4, P.O. Box 750, 77580, P 3,000, M 350, (281) 576-5440, Fax (281) 576-2135, www.westchamberscoc.com

**Morton** · *Morton Area C/C* · Bryant Sears, Pres., 201 E. Wilson, 79346, P 2,000, M 30, (806) 266-5200

**Moulton** · *Moulton C/C* · P.O. Box 482, 77975, P 1,000, M 150, (361) 596-7205, Fax (361) 596-4384, chamber@moultontexas.com, www.moultontexas.com

**Mount Pleasant** · *Mount Pleasant-Titus County C/C & CVB* · Natalie Davis, Exec. Dir., 1604 N. Jefferson, 75455, P 14,000, M 385, (903) 572-8567, Fax (903) 572-0613, info@mtpleasanttx.com, www.mtpleasanttx.

**Mount Vernon** · *Franklin County C/C* · Patricia Oertel, Mgr., 109 S. Kaufman St., P.O. Box 554, 75457, P 9,458, M 163, (903) 537-4365, Fax (903) 537-4160, chamber@mt-vernon.com, www.franklincountytx.com

**Muenster** · *Muenster C/C* · Margie Starke, Exec. Dir., 1000 E. Division St., Ste. D, P.O. Box 714, 76252, P 2,000, M 135, (940) 759-2227, (800) 942-8037, Fax (940) 759-2228, chamber@ntin.net, www.muensterchamber.com.

**35TH "GERMANFEST"—35,000 PEOPLE ENJOY THIS FEST. LAST FULL WEEKEND OF APRIL. SANCTIONED BAR-B-QUE COOK-OFF, LOTS OF GOOD ENTERTAINMENT, GERMAN FOOD, BIKE RALLY, FUN RUN, ARTS & CRAFTS.**

**Muleshoe** · *Muleshoe C/C* · Celie Parham, Pres., 115 E. American Blvd., P.O. Box 356, 79347, P 4,530, M 110, (806) 272-4248, Fax (806) 272-4614, chamber@fivearea.com, www.muleshoe.org

**Munday** · *Munday C/C and Ag.* · 121 E. B St., P.O. Drawer L, 76371, P 1,525, M 150, (940) 422-4540, Fax (940) 422-4540, munday-chamberofcommerce@valornet.com, www.mundaytexas.com

**Nacogdoches** · *Nacogdoches County C/C* · Bruce R. Partain, Pres., 2516 North St., 75965, P 60,000, M 800, (936) 560-5533, Fax (936) 560-3920, chamber@nactx.com, www.nacogdoches.org, www.texasblueberryfestival.com.

**THE MOST DELICIOUS FESTIVAL IN TEXAS! FRESH BLUEBERRIES, BLUEBERRY PANCAKES, BLUEBERRY PIE/COBBLER, LIVE ENTERTAINMENT, KIDS AREA. FUN FOR EVERYONE!**

**Naples** · *Naples C/C* · 101 WL Doc Dodson E., 75568, P 1,700, M 25, (903) 897-2041

**Navasota** · *Navasota/Grimes County C/C* · Sandra D. Niobles, Exec. Dir., 117 S. LaSalle, P.O. Box 530, 77868, P 23,500, M 350, (936) 825-6600, Fax (936) 825-3699, director@navasotagrimeschamber.com, www.navasotagrimeschamber.com

**Nederland** · *Nederland C/C* · Cindy Clifton, Exec. V.P., 1515 Boston Ave., P.O. Box 891, 77627, P 17,400, M 320, (409) 722-0279, Fax (409) 722-0615, nedcofc@nederlandtx.com, www.nederlandtx.com.

**Needville** · *Needville Area C/C* · Glenn Schmidt, Pres., 8903 Line St., P.O. Box 1200, 77461, P 2,600, M 250, (979) 793-5700, www.needville.org

**New Boston** · *New Boston C/C* · Deborah Cook, Exec. Dir., 100 N. Center St., 75570, P 4,808, M 183, (903) 628-2581, Fax same, chamber@newbostontx.org, www.newbostontx.org.

**New Braunfels** · *New Braunfels C/C* · Michael Meek, Pres., 390 S. Seguin Ave., P.O. Box 311417, 78131, P 54,000, M 2,040, (830) 625-2385, (800) 572-2626, Fax (830) 625-7918, nbcc@nbcham.org, www.nbcham.org.

**New Caney** · *Comm. C/C of East Montgomery County* · Andy Dill, Pres., 21575 U.S. Hwy. 59 N., Ste. 100, 77357, P 74,000, M 400, (281) 354-0051, Fax (281) 354-0091, info@communitychamberemc.com, www.communitychamber.com

**Newton** · *Newton County C/C* · Susan Karpel, Secy., 313 Rusk St., P.O. Box 66, 75966, P 18,500, M 100, (409) 379-5527, chamber@newton-texas.com, www.newton-texas.com

**Nocona** · *Nocona Area C/C* · Wanda Wood, Exec. Dir., 100 E. Hwy. 82, P.O. Box 27, 76255, P 3,198, M 100, (940) 825-3526, Fax (940) 825-5389, www.nocona.org

**Normangee** · *Normangee Area C/C* · P.O. Box 436, 77871, P 704, M 70, (936) 396-3611

**North Richland Hills** · *see Haltom City*

**Northlake** · *see Roanoke*

**Northline** · *see Houston-- North Houston-Greenspoint C/C*

**Odessa** · *Odessa C/C* · Mike George, Pres./CEO, 700 N. Grant, Ste. 200, P.O. Box 3626, 79760, P 96,948, M 1,900, (432) 332-9111, (800) 780-4678, Fax (432) 333-7858, info@odessachamber.com, www.odessachamber.com.

**Olney** · *Olney C/C* · Malinda Morrow, Coord., 108 E. Main, 76374, P 3,400, M 165, (940) 564-5445, Fax (940) 564-3610, chamber@brazosnet.com, www.olneytexas.com

**Olton** · *Olton C of C & Ag.* · 518 8th St., P.O. Box 487, 79064, P 2,288, M 49, (806) 285-2292, Fax (806) 285-2292, www.oltontexas.com

**Omaha** · *Omaha C/C* · Cheryl Durrett, Pres., P.O. Box 816, 75571, P 999, M 50, (903) 884-3600, www.cityofomahatx.com

**Onalaska** · *Onalaska C/C* · Greg Smith, Pres., P.O. Box 1300, 77360, P 1,500, M 35, (936) 646-5000, www.cityofonalaska.us

**Orange** · *Greater Orange Area C/C* · Sabrina Gray, Pres./CEO, 1012 Green Ave., 77630, P 52,000, M 475, (409) 883-3536, Fax (409) 886-3247, thechamber@sbcglobal.net, www.goacc.org

**Overton** · *Overton-New London Area C/C* · Don Wayt, Pres., 121 E. Henderson, P.O. Box 6, 75684, P 2,105, M 95, (903) 834-3542, Fax (903) 834-3063, onlchamber@earthlink.net, www.onlchamber.com

**Ozona** · *Ozona C/C & Visitor Center* · Shanon Biggerstaff, Exec. Dir., 505 15th St., P.O. Box 1135, 76943, P 3,800, M 160, (325) 392-3737, Fax (325) 392-3485, oztxcoc@aol.com, www.ozona.com

**Paducah** · *Paducah C/C* · Freda Brooks, Pres., P.O. Box 863, 79248, P 1,650, M 57, (806) 492-2044, (806) 492-2167, www.co.cottle.tx.us

**Palacios** · *Palacios C/C* · Judith Chavez, Pres., 420 Main St., 77465, P 5,153, M 134, (361) 972-2615, (800) 611-4567, Fax (361) 972-9980, palcoc@tisd.net, www.palacioschamber.com

**Palestine** · *Palestine Area C/C* · Kathi Masonheimer, Exec. Dir., 401 W. Main St., P.O. Box 1177, 75802, P 55,000, M 476, (903) 729-6066, Fax (903) 729-2083, info@palestinechamber.org, www.palestinechamber.org.

**Pampa** · *Greater Pampa Area C/C* · 200 N. Ballard, P.O. Box 1942, 79066, P 18,000, M 350, (806) 669-3241, Fax (806) 669-3244, harvest@pampachamber.com, www.pampachamber.com.

**Panhandle** · *Panhandle C/C* · Clint Walker, Pres., P.O. Box 1021, 79068, P 2,600, M 74, (806) 537-4325, chamber@panhandletx.com, www.panhandletx.com

**Paris** · *Lamar County C/C* · Peter Kampfer, Pres., 1125 Bonham St., 75460, P 50,016, M 700, (903) 784-2501, (800) 727-4789, Fax (903) 784-2503, chamber@paristexas.com, www.paristexas.com

**Pasadena** · *Pasadena C/C* · Sherry Trainer, Pres./CEO, 4334 Fairmont Pkwy., 77504, P 150,000, M 900, (281) 487-7871, Fax (281) 487-5530, info@pasadenachamber.org, www.pasadenachamber.org.

**Pattison** • *West I-10 C/C* • P.O. Box 100, 77466, P 5,000, M 80, (281) 375-8100, Fax (281) 934-2012, chamber@westi10chamber. org, www.westi10chamber.org

**Pearland** • *Pearland C/C* • Carol R. Artz, Pres., 6117 Broadway, P.O. Box 97, 77581, P 85,000, M 750, (281) 485-3634, Fax (281) 485-2420, chamber@pearlandchamber.org, www.pearlandchamber.com

**Pearsall** • *Pearsall C/C* • 317 S. Oak St., 78061, P 7,864, M 51, (830) 334-9414, pearsall@granderiver.net, www.pearsalltexas.com

**Pecos** • *Pecos Area C/C* • Linda Gholson, Exec. Dir., 111 S. Cedar, P.O. Box 27, 79772, P 9,501, M 120, (432) 445-2406, Fax (432) 445-2407, pcoc@cebridge.net, www.pecostx.com.

**Perryton** • *Perryton-Ochiltree C/C* • Marilyn Reiswig, Pres., 2000 S. Main, P.O. Drawer 789, 79070, P 10,000, M 400, (806) 435-6575, Fax (806) 435-9821, pococ@ptsi.net, www.perryton.org.

**Pflugerville** • *Greater Pflugerville C/C* • Patricia Gervan-Brown IOM, Pres./CEO, 101 S. 3rd St., P.O. Box 483, 78691, P 200,000, M 400, (512) 251-7799, Fax (512) 251-7802, gpcc2@sbcglobal.net, www.pfchamber.com

**Pharr** • *Pharr C/C* • Louis A. Bazon, Pres./CEO, 308 W. Park, P.O. Box 1715, 78577, P 54,000, M 400, (956) 787-1481, Fax (956) 787-7972, info@pharrchamberofcommerce.com, www.visitpharr.com

**Pilot Point** • *Pilot Point C/C* • Karen Walterscheid, Exec. Dir., 300 S. Washington, P.O. Box 497, 76258, P 5,100, M 150, (940) 686-5385, Fax (940) 686-9392, chamber.ofcommerce@cebridge. net, www.pilotpoint.org

**Pittsburg** • *Pittsburg/Camp County C/C* • 202 Jefferson St., 75686, P 15,000, M 200, (903) 856-3442, Fax (903) 856-3570, info@pittsburgchamber.com, www.pittsburgchamber.com

**Plains** • *Plains C/C* • Terry Howard, Pres., P.O. Box 364, 79355, P 1,450, M 20, (806) 456-2288

**Plainview** • *Plainview C/C* • Dee Blevins, Exec. Dir., 710 W. 5th St., 79072, P 21,000, M 430, (806) 296-7431, (800) 658-2685, Fax (806) 296-0819, info@plainviewtexaschamber.com, www. plainviewtexaschamber.com.

**Plano** • *Plano C/C* • Brad Shanklin, Pres., 1200 E. 15th St., 75074, P 250,000, M 1,500, (972) 424-7547, Fax (972) 422-5182, info@ planochamber.org, www.planochamber.org.

**Pleasanton** • *Pleasanton C/C* • Jessie Schievelbein, Mgr., 605 Second St., P.O. Box 153, 78064, P 9,500, M 180, (830) 569-2163, Fax same, www.pleasantoncofc.com

**Point** • *see Quinlan*

**Port Aransas** • *Port Aransas C/C* • Ann B. Vaughan, Exec. Dir., 403 W. Cotter, 78373, P 3,370, M 379, (361) 749-5919, Fax (361) 749-4672, info@portaransas.org, www.portaransas.org

**Port Arthur** • *Greater Port Arthur C/C* • Mary Ann Reid, Pres., 4749 Twin City Hwy., Ste. 300, 77642, P 60,000, M 920, (409) 963-1107, Fax (409) 962-1997, portarthurchamber@portarthurtexas. com, www.portarthurtexas.com

**Port Isabel** • *Port Isabel C/C* • Betty Wells, Exec. Dir., 421 Queen Isabella Blvd., 78578, P 5,021, M 275, (956) 943-2262, (800) 527-6102, Fax (956) 943-4001, director@portisabel.org, www. portisabel.org

**Port Lavaca** • *Port Lavaca C/C* • 2300 Hwy. 35, 77979, P 20,000, M 425, (361) 552-2959, (800) 556-PORT, Fax (361) 552-1288, lacey@portlavacatx.org, www.portlavacatx.org

**Port Mansfield** • *Port Mansfield C/C* • Ron Dobson, Pres., 101 E. Port Dr., P.O. Box 75, 78598, P 400, M 110, (956) 944-2354, Fax (956) 944-2515, pmft@granderiver.net, www.portmansfield.us

**Port Neches** • *Port Neches C/C* • Debbie Plaia, Exec. Dir., 1110 Port Neches Ave., P.O. Box 445, 77651, P 15,000, M 240, (409) 722-9154, Fax (409) 722-7380, pncoc@swbell.net, www.port necheschamber.com

**Port O'Connor** • *Port O'Connor C/C* • Linda Butler, Pres., 207 Trevor St., P.O. Box 701, 77982, P 1,200, M 150, (361) 983-2898, Fax (361) 983-2898, poccc@tisd.net, www.portoconnorchamber.com

**Portland** • *Portland C/C* • David L. Pinter, Exec. Dir., 1605-A Hwy. 181, P.O. Box 388, 78374, P 17,100, M 350, (361) 643-2475, Fax (361) 643-7377, chamber@portlandtx.org, www.portlandtx.org

**Post** • *Post Area C/C* • Janice Plummer, Mgr., 131 E. Main, P.O. Box 610, 79356, P 3,960, M 94, (806) 495-3461, Fax (806) 495-0414, chamberofcommerce@postcitytexas.com, www.postcitytexas.com

**Poteet** • *Poteet C/C* • Diana Martinez, Pres., P.O. Box 577, 78065, P 3,100, M 40, (830) 742-8144, (888) 742-8144, Fax (830) 742-3608, www.strawberryfestival.com

**Poth** • *Poth C/C* • Ronald Eckel, Pres., P.O. Box 128, 78147, P 1,850, M , (830) 484-2111, (830) 484-3314

**Pottsboro** • *Pottsboro Area C/C* • Rosemary Hall, Mgr., 615 Hwy. 120 E., P.O. Box 995, 75076, P 10,000, M 300, (903) 786-6371, Fax (903) 786-4965, info@pottsborochamber.com, www.pottsboro chamber.com

**Prairie View** • *Prairie View C/C* • George Higgs, Pres., P.O. Box 847, 77446, P 4,000, M 55, (936) 857-5817, (936) 857-3226, Fax (936) 857-5806

**Premont** • *Premont C/C* • Epi Vargas, Pres., P.O. Box 1107, 78375, P 3,000, M 45, (361) 348-3933

**Presidio** • *Presidio C/C* • Imelda Contreras, Exec. Dir., 202 W. O'Reilly, P.O. Box 2497, 79845, P 5,000, M 90, (432) 229-3199, Fax (432) 229-4008, presidiochamber@yahoo.com

**Princeton** • *Princeton Area C/C* • Virginia Gathright, Pres., 275 W. Princeton Dr. #105, 75407, P 15,500, M 85, (972) 736-6462, Fax (972) 736-3309, info@princetontxchamber.com, www. princetontxchamber.com

**Prosper** • *Prosper Area C/C* • Judy Rucker, Facilitator, P.O. Box 432, 75078, P 4,500, M 105, (972) 580-4200, prosperchamber@ grandecom.net, www.prosperchamber.org

**Quanah** • *Quanah C/C* • Bertha Woods, Dir., 220 S. Main, P.O. Box 158, 79252, P 3,114, M 131, (940) 663-2222, Fax (940) 663-2222, quanahcoc@cebridge.net, www.quanah.net

**Quinlan** • *Lake Tawakoni Reg. C/C & CVB* • Jim Johnson, Pres., P.O. Box 1149, 75474, P 20,000, M 150, (903) 447-3020, Fax (903) 447-3820, laketawakonichamber@yahoo.com, www.laketawakoni chamber.org

**Quitaque** • *Quitaque C/C* • P.O. Box 487, 79255, P 432, M 30, (806) 455-1225, www.quitaque.org

**Quitman** • *Greater Quitman Area C/C* • Mary Bass, Exec. Dir., P.O. Box 426, 75783, P 2,261, M 170, (903) 763-4411, (866) 302-3884, Fax (903) 763-2764, qtmncoc@peoplescom.net, www.quitman.com

**Ralls** • *Ralls C/C* • 808 Ave. I, 79357, P 2,318, M 100, (806) 253-2342

**Ranger** • *Ranger C/C* • P.O. Box 57, 76470, P 2,852, M 50, (254) 647-3091, rangerchamber@sbcglobal.net

**Raymondville** • *Raymondville C/C* • Elma Chavez, Mgr., 142 S. 7th St., P.O. Box 746, 78580, P 20,000, M 180, (956) 689-3171, (888) 603-6994, Fax (956) 689-1243, chamber@granderiver.net, www.raymondvillechamber.com

**Red Oak** · *Red Oak Area C/C* · Shelley Oglesby, Pres., P.O. Box 2098, 75154, P 20,000, M 235, (972) 617-0906, Fax (972) 576-3737, admin@redoakareachamber.org, www.redoakareachamber.org

**Refugio** · *Refugio County C/C* · Lenny Anzaldua, 301 N. Alamo, 78377, P 8,000, M 100, (361) 526-2835, Fax (361) 526-1289, refugiochamber@sbcglobal.net, www.refugiocountytx.org

**Rhome** · *South Wise County C/C* · Toni Kelly Richardson, Pres., P.O. Box 558, 76078, P 20,000, M 280, (817) 636-2783, www.southwisechamber.com

**Richardson** · *Richardson C/C* · Bill Sproull, Pres./CEO, 411 Belle Grove Dr., 75080, P 97,467, M 1,200, (972) 792-2800, Fax (972) 792-2825, bill@richardsonchamber.com, www.richardsonchamber.com

**Richland Hills** · *see Haltom City*

**Richmond** · *see Rosenberg*

**Rio Grande** · *Rio Grande City C/C* · Maria Berrera, Mgr., P.O. Box 2, 78582, P 19,700, M 130, (956) 487-0672, www.cityofrgc.com

**River Oaks** · *Tri-City Area C/C* · Jack Adkison, Pres., P.O. Box 10005, 76114, P 11,100, M 115, (817) 377-4227, www.tricityareachamber.org

**Roanoke** · *Northwest Metroport C/C* · Sally Michalak, Pres., 99 Trophy Club Dr., P.O. Box 74, 76262, P 18,000, M 300, (817) 491-1222, Fax (817) 430-5822, sally@nwmetroportchamber.org, www.nwmetroportchamber.org

**Robstown** · *Robstown Area Dev. Comm.* · Ken Faughn, Exec. Dir., 1150 E. Main Ave., P.O. Box 111, 78380, P 14,000, M 100, (361) 387-3933, Fax (361) 387-7280, radc@verizon.net, www.robstownadc.com

**Rockdale** · *Rockdale C/C* · Denice Doss, Pres., 1203 W. Cameron Ave., 76567, P 6,000, M 280, (512) 446-2030, Fax (512) 446-5969, ddoss@rockdalechamber.com, www.rockdalechamber.com

**Rockport** · *Rockport-Fulton Area C/C* · Diane Probst, Pres./CEO, 404 Broadway, 78382, P 24,000, M 750, (361) 729-6445, (800) 242-0071, Fax (361) 729-7681, president@lrockport.org, www.rockport-fulton.org.

**Rocksprings** · *Edwards County C/C* · 411 Well St., 78880, P 2,295, M 100, (830) 683-6466, Fax (830) 683-3182, info@rockspringstexas.net, www.rockspringstexas.net

**Rockwall** · *Rockwall Area County C/C* · Cher Seibert, Ofc. Mgr., 697 E. I-30, P.O. Box 92, 75087, P 50,000, M 900, (972) 771-5733, Fax (972) 772-3642, admin@rockwallchamber.org, www.rockwallchamber.org

**Rosebud** · *Rosebud C/C & Ag.* · Royce Spivey, Pres., 402 W. Main, P.O. Box 369, 76570, P 1,493, M 100, (254) 583-7979, Fax (254) 583-2157, www.rosebudtx.org

**Rosenberg** · *Rosenberg-Richmond Area C/C* · Gail Parker, Pres., 4120 Ave. H, 77471, P 528,392, M 750, (281) 342-5464, Fax (281) 342-2990, gparker@roserichchamber.org, www.roserichchamber.org

**Round Rock** · *Round Rock C/C* · Tom Manskey, Pres., 212 E. Main St., 78664, P 96,000, M 945, (512) 255-5805, (800) 747-3479, Fax (512) 255-3345, tmanskey@roundrockchamber.org, www.roundrockchamber.org

**Round Top** · *Round Top C/C* · Laurie Fisbeck, Dir., P.O. Box 216, 78954, P 7,700, M 200, (979) 249-4042, Fax (979) 249-2085, info@roundtop.org, www.roundtop.org

**Rowlett** · *Rowlett C/C* · Mary Alice Ethridge, Exec. Dir., 3910 Main St., P.O. Box 610, 75030, P 55,000, M 430, (972) 475-3200, Fax (972) 463-1699, maryalice@rowlettchamber.com, www.rowlettchamber.com

**Royse City** · *Royse City C/C* · Julia Bryant, Exec. Dir., 216 N. Arch St. #A, P.O. Box 547, 75189, P 10,000, M 225, (972) 636-5000, Fax (972) 636-0051, info@roysecitychamber.com, www.roysecitychamber.com

**Rule** · *Rule C/C* · Orheana Greeson, Secy., 701 Union Ave., P.O. Box 58, 79547, P 698, M 15, (940) 997-2141

**Runaway Bay** · *Greater Runaway Bay Alliance* · Bettye Parker, Pres., 51 Runaway Bay Dr., 76426, P 1,200, M 100, (940) 575-4745, www.greaterrunawaybayalliance.com

**Rusk** · *Rusk C/C* · Bob Goldsberry, Dir., 184 S. Main St., P.O. Box 67, 75785, P 5,085, M 200, (903) 683-4242, Fax (903) 683-1054, chamber@rusktx.com, www.ruskchamber.com

**Sabinal** · *Sabinal C/C* · P.O. Box 55, 78881, P 1,600, M 20, (830) 988-2010, sab@sabinalchamber.com, www.sabinalchamber.com

**Sachse** · *Sachse C/C* · Tina Stelnicki IOM, Pres., 2924 5th St., 75048, P 18,000, M 290, (972) 496-1212, Fax (972) 496-7916, info@sachsechamber.com, www.sachsechamber.com

**Saginaw** · *Saginaw Area C/C* · Wally Key, Pres., 301 S. Saginaw Blvd., 76179, P 18,400, M 460, (817) 232-0500, Fax (817) 232-2311, info@saginawtxchamber.org, www.saginawtxchamber.org

**Saint Jo** · *Saint Jo C/C* · Howard Davies, Pres., 108 S. Broad, P.O. Box 130, 76265, P 1,000, M 40, (940) 995-2188, info@saintjo-chamber.com, www.saintjochamber.com

**Salado** · *Salado C/C* · 881 N. Main St., P.O. Box 849, 76571, P 3,000, M 200, (254) 947-5040, Fax (254) 947-3126, saladochamber@vvm.com, www.salado.com

**San Angelo** · *San Angelo C/C & Visitor Center* · Phil Neighbors, Pres., 418 W. Ave. B, 76903, P 90,483, M 1,400, (325) 655-4136, Fax (325) 658-1110, chamber@sanangelo.org, www.sanangelo.org.

## San Antonio Area

**Greater San Antonio C/C** · Richard Perez, Pres., 602 E. Commerce, P.O. Box 1628, 78296, P 2,000,000, M 1,800, (210) 229-2100, Fax (210) 229-1600, info@sachamber.org, www.sachamber.org.

**Alamo City Black C/C** · Theresa Britts, Chrmn., 600 Hemisfair Plaza Way, Bldg. 406-10, 78205, P 1,750,000, M 250, (210) 226-9055, Fax (210) 226-0524, info@alamocitychamber.com, www.alamocitychamber.org.

**North San Antonio C/C** · E. Duane Wilson, Pres./CEO, 12930 Country Pkwy., 78216, P 1,500,000, M 1,350, (210) 344-4848, Fax (210) 525-8207, dzucker@northsachamber.com, www.northsachamber.com

**San Antonio Hispanic C/C** · Ramiro A. Cavazos, Pres./CEO, 318 W. Houston, Ste. 300, 78205, M 1,600, (210) 225-0462, Fax (210) 225-2485, www.sahcc.org

**San Augustine** · *San Augustine County C/C* · Liz Ware, Exec. Dir., 611 W. Columbia St., 75972, P 9,000, M 225, (936) 275-3610, Fax (936) 288-0380, liz.sa.chamber@sbcglobal.net, www.sanaugustinetx.com

**San Benito** · *San Benito C/C* · Zeke Padilla, Pres., 401 N. Sam Houston Blvd., 78586, P 28,600, M 200, (956) 399-5321, Fax (956) 399-5421, chamber@cityofsanbenito.com, www.sanbenitochamber.org.

**San Juan** · *San Juan C/C* · Miki McCarthy, Exec. Dir., 430 N. Standard, 78589, P 34,968, M 80, (956) 783-9957, Fax (956) 783-5413, miki@sanjuan-edc.com, www.sanjuan-edc.com

**San Leon** · *San Leon-Bacliff-Bayview C/C* · Joe Sullivan, Pres., P.O. Box 5281, 77539, P 10,000, M 91, (281) 559-3121

**San Marcos** • *San Marcos Area C/C* • Phyllis Snodgrass, Pres., 202 N. CM Allen Pkwy., P.O. Box 2310, 78667, P 50,317, M 1,039, (512) 393-5900, Fax (512) 393-5912, chamber@sanmarcostexas.com, www.sanmarcostexas.com.

**San Saba** • *San Saba County C/C* • Fern Reed, Exec. Dir., 302 E. Wallace St., 76877, P 2,700, M 142, (325) 372-5141, Fax (325) 372-5141, executive.director@sansabachamber.com, www.sansabachamber.com

**Sanderson** • *Sanderson C/C* • P.O. Box 734, 79848, P 800, M 10, (432) 345-2324, Fax (432) 345-2678, chamber@sandersonchamberofcommerce.info, www.sandersonchamberofcommerce.info

**Sanger** • *Sanger Area C/C* • 300 Bolivar St., P.O. Box 537, 76266, P 6,500, M 170, (940) 458-7702, Fax (940) 458-7823, chamber@sangertexas.com, www.sangertexas.com

**Santa Anna** • *Santa Anna C/C* • 303 S. Houston, 76878, P 1,249, M 35, (325) 348-3535

**Santa Fe** • *Santa Fe C/C* • Fay Picard, Pres./CEO, 12406 Hwy. 6, 77510, P 10,000, M 200, (409) 925-8558, Fax (409) 925-8551, sfchamber@comcast.net, www.santafetexaschamber.com

**Schertz** • *see Selma*

**Schulenburg** • *Greater Schulenburg C/C* • Mike Stroup, Exec. Dir., 618 N. Main, P.O. Box 65, 78956, P 2,700, M 300, (979) 743-4514, (866) 504-5294, Fax (979) 743-9155, info@schulenburgchamber.org, www.schulenburgchamber.org

**Seadrift** • *Seadrift C/C* • Cindy Alford, Pres., P.O. Box 3, 77983, P 1,352, M 60, (361) 655-9690, Fax (361) 785-2208, www.seadriftchamber.com

**Seagoville** • *Seagoville C/C* • Phil Greenawalt, Exec. Dir., 107 Hall Rd., 75159, P 11,400, M 170, (972) 287-5184, Fax (972) 287-5815, seagovillechamber@sbcglobal.net, www.seagovillecoc.org

**Seagraves** • *Seagraves Area C/C* • 401 Main, P.O. Box 1257, 79359, P 2,334, M 75, (806) 387-2609, seagraveschamber@yahoo.com

**Sealy** • *Sealy C/C* • Nancy James, Pres., 309 Main St., P.O. Box 586, 77474, P 6,000, M 300, (979) 885-3222, Fax (979) 885-7184, sealycoc@sbcglobal.net, www.sealychamber.com

**Seguin** • *Seguin Area C/C* • Shanta Kuhl, Pres., 116 N. Camp, P.O. Box 710, 78156, P 90,000, M 800, (830) 379-6382, Fax (830) 379-6971, cofc@seguinchamber.com, www.seguinchamber.com

**Selma** • *Randolph Metrocom C/C* • Mr. Pat O'Brien, Chrmn. of the Bd., 9374 Valhalla St., 78154, P 200,000, M 475, (210) 658-8322, Fax (210) 658-1817, admin@metrocomchamber.org, www.metrocomchamber.org

**Seminole** • *Seminole Area C/C* • Shelby Concotelli, Pres./CEO, 119 S.E. Ave. B, P.O. Box 1198, 79360, P 6,700, M 260, (432) 758-2352, Fax (432) 758-6698, seminolechamber@warpdriveonline.com, www.seminoletxchamber.org.

**Seven Points** • *see Mabank*

**Seymour** • *Seymour C/C* • Myra Busby, Exec. Dir., 400 N. Main St., P.O. Box 1379, 76380, P 3,500, M 80, (940) 889-2921, Fax (940) 889-8882, scoc@nts-online.net, www.seymourtxchamber.org

**Shamrock** • *Shamrock C/C* • 105 E. 12th St., 79079, P 2,000, M 65, (806) 256-2501, Fax (806) 256-2224, irishedb@hotmail.com, www.shamrocktx.net

**Sheffield** • *see Iraan*

**Shepherd** • *Greater Shepherd C/C* • Olene Reaves, Pres., W. Hwy. 150, P.O. Box 520, 77371, P 3,000, M 45, (936) 628-3890, Fax (936) 628-3890, shepherdchamber@netzero.net

**Sherman** • *Sherman C/C* • Traci Carlson, Pres., 307 W. Washington St. #100, P.O. Box 1029, 75091, P 40,000, M 600, (903) 893-1184, Fax (903) 893-4266, info@shermanchamber.us, www.shermanchamber.us

**Shiner** • *Shiner C/C* • Marilyn Parker, Pres., P.O. Box 221, 77984, P 2,000, M 200, (361) 594-4180, shinerchamber@sbcglobal.net, www.shinertx.com

**Silsbee** • *Silsbee C/C* • Jason Fuller, Pres., 835 Hwy. 96 S., 77656, P 15,000, M 400, (409) 385-5562, Fax (409) 385-5695, schambercommerce@gt.rr.com, www.silsbeechamber.com

**Sinton** • *Sinton C/C* • Jo Liz Villarreal, Exec. Dir., 218 W. Sinton St., 78387, P 6,000, M 175, (361) 364-2307, Fax (361) 364-3538, sintonchamber@sbcglobal.net, www.sintontexas.org.

**Slaton** • *Slaton C/C* • Leslie Robinson, Mgr., 200 W. Garza, P.O. Box 400, 79364, P 6,000, M 100, (806) 828-6238, Fax (806) 828-6239, slatoncoc@sbcglobal.net, www.slatonchamberofcommerce.org

**Smithville** • *Smithville Area C/C* • Adena Lewis, Pres., 100 First St., P.O. Box 716, 78957, P 5,000, M 315, (512) 237-2313, Fax (512) 237-2605, chamber@smithvilletx.org, www.smithvilletx.org

**Snyder** • *Snyder C/C* • Stephanie Bretz, Exec. Dir., 2302 Ave. R, P.O. Box 840, 79550, P 10,783, M 245, (325) 573-3558, Fax (325) 573-9721, snychcom@snydertex.com, www.snyderchamber.org

**Somerville** • *Burleson County C/C-Somerville Office* • Weldon Peters, Pres./CEO, P.O. Box 596, 77879, P 18,000, M 250, (979) 596-2383, Fax (979) 596-3036, weldon@burlesoncountytx.com, www.burlesoncountytx.com

**Sonora** • *Sonora C/C* • Donna Garrett, Exec. Dir., 205 Hwy. 277 N., Ste. B, P.O. Box 1172, 76950, P 4,000, M 250, (325) 387-2880, Fax (325) 387-5357, soncoc@sonoratx.net, www.sonoratx-chamber.com.

**South Houston** • *City of South Houston C/C* • JoAnn Parish, Pres., 58 Spencer Hwy., 77587, P 15,000, M 200, (713) 943-0244, Fax (713) 943-3978, sohochamber@sbcglobal.net, www.southhoustonchamber.org

**South Padre Island** • *South Padre Island C/C* • Roxanne Guenzel, Pres., 600 Padre Blvd., 78597, P 2,500, M 500, (956) 761-4412, Fax (956) 761-2739, info@spichamber.com, www.spichamber.com

**Southlake** • *Southlake C/C* • Giovanna Phillips, Pres., 1501 Corporate Circle #100, 76092, P 28,000, M 650, (817) 481-8200, Fax (817) 749-8202, info@southlakechamber.com, www.southlakechamber.com

**Spearman** • *Spearman C/C* • Alvin Byers, Pres., 211 Main St., P.O. Box 161, 79081, P 3,197, M 150, (806) 659-5555, Fax (806) 659-5923, spearcc@hotmail.com, www.spearman.org

**Spring Branch** • *Bulverde-Spring Branch Area C/C* • Stefanie Doyer, Admin. Asst., P.O. Box 1132, 78070, P 20,000, M 315, (830) 438-4285, (866) 285-8373, Fax (830) 438-8572, bsbacoc@gvtc.com, www.bulverdespringbranchchamber.com

**Springtown** • *Springtown Area C/C* • Ann McDorman, Exec. Dir., 112 S. Main, P.O. Box 296, 76082, P 40,000, M 300, (817) 220-7828, Fax (817) 523-3268, chamber@springtowntexas.com, www.springtowntexas.com

**Spur** • *Spur Area C/C* • Fernella Gilcrease, Pres., P.O. Box 103, 79370, P 1,088, M 48, (806) 271-3466, inspur@caprock-spur.com

**Stamford** • *Stamford C/C* • Dawn Ham, Exec. Dir., 113 S. Wetherbee, 79553, P 3,600, (325) 773-2411, Fax (325) 773-2411, stamfordcoc@sbcglobal.net, www.stamfordcoc.org

**Stanton** • *Martin County C/C* • Kim Baker, Exec. Dir., 209 N. St. Peter, P.O. Box 615, 79782, P 4,735, M 100, (432) 756-3386, www.stantontex.com

**Stephenville** · *Stephenville C/C* · July Danley, Pres./CEO, 187 W. Washington St., P.O. Box 306, 76401, P 16,100, M 600, (254) 965-5313, Fax (254) 965-3814, info@stephenvilletexas.org, www.stephenvilletexas.org.

**Stockdale** · *Stockdale C/C* · P.O. Box 578, 78160, P 1,300, (830) 996-3128, www.stockdaletx.org

**Stonewall** · *Stonewall C/C* · Mike Talley, Pres., 250 Peach St., P.O. Box 1, 78671, P 300, M 200, (830) 644-2735, Fax (830) 644-2165, chamber@stonewalltexas.com, www.stonewalltexas.com

**Stratford** · *Stratford C/C* · 305 N. Main St., P.O. Box 570, 79084, P 3,000, M 167, (806) 366-2260

**Sugar Land** · *Fort Bend C/C* · Louis Garvin, Pres./CEO, 445 Commerce Green Blvd., 77478, P 510,000, M 1,500, (281) 491-0800, Fax (281) 491-0112, www.fortbendchamber.com

**Sulphur Springs** · *Hopkins County C/C* · Meredith Caddell, Pres./CEO, 300 Connally St., P.O. Box 347, 75483, P 32,000, M 600, (903) 885-6515, Fax (903) 885-6516, meredithcaddell@suddenlinkmail.com, www.sulphursprings-tx.com.

**Sweeny** · *Sweeny C/C & Eco. Dev. Corp.* · Sue Netherly, Exec. Dir., 111 W. 3rd, 77480, P 5,000, M 150, (979) 548-3249, Fax (979) 548-3251, sweenychamber@windstream.net, .

**Sweetwater** · *Sweetwater C/C* · Jacque McCoy, Exec. V.P., 810 E. Broadway, P.O. Box 1148, 79556, P 12,000, M 250, (325) 235-5488, (800) 658-6757, Fax (325) 235-1026, jacque@sweetwatertexas.org, www.sweetwatertexas.org

**Taft** · *Taft C/C* · Mary Griffin, Secy., 503 Green Ave., P.O. Box 123, 78390, P 5,117, M 51, (361) 528-3230, Fax (361) 528-3515

**Taylor** · *Taylor C/C* · Rob Bauman, Pres., 1519 N. Main St., 76574, P 17,225, M 350, (512) 352-6364, Fax (512) 352-6366, president@taylorchamber.org, www.taylorchamber.org

**Teague** · *Teague C/C* · Marilyn Michaud, Ofc. Mgr., 316 Main St., P.O. Box 484, 75860, P 4,000, M 85, (254) 739-2061, Fax (254) 739-2061

**Temple** · *Temple C/C* · Ken Higdon, Pres., 2 N. 5th St., P.O. Box 158, 76503, P 60,000, M 1,400, (254) 773-2105, Fax (254) 773-0661, temple@templetx.org, www.templetx.org.

**Terrell** · *Terrell C/C* · Danny R. Booth, Pres./CEO, 1314 W. Moore Ave., P.O. Box 97, 75160, P 19,000, M 580, (972) 563-5703, (877) TERRELL, Fax (972) 563-2363, danny@terrelltexas.com, www.terrelltexas.com.

**Texarkana** · *Texarkana C/C* · Jeff Sandford, Pres., 819 State Line Ave., P.O. Box 1468, 75504, P 61,230, M 1,400, (903) 792-7191, Fax (903) 793-4304, chamber@texarkana.org, www.texarkana.org

**Texas City** · *Texas City-La Marque C/C* · Jimmy Hayley, Pres., 9702 Emmett F. Lowry Expy., P.O. Box 1717, 77592, P 57,000, M 850, (409) 935-1408, (877) 986-8719 TX only, Fax (409) 316-0901, dedra@texascitychamber.com, www.texascitychamber.com.

**The Colony** · *The Colony C/C* · Allison Mihavics, Exec. Dir., 6900 Main St., P.O. Box 560006, 75056, P 40,000, M 300, (972) 625-8027, Fax (972) 625-8027, info@thecolonychamber.org, www.thecolonychamber.com

**The Woodlands** · *South Montgomery County Woodlands C/C* · Karen Hoylman, Pres./CEO, 1400 Woodloch Forest Dr., Ste. 300, 77380, P 394,517, M 2,000, (281) 367-5777, Fax (281) 292-1655, karen.hoylman@woodlandschamber.org, www.woodlandschamber.org

**Thorndale** · *Thorndale Area C/C* · P.O. Box 668, 76577, P 1,278, M 90, (512) 898-2523

**Three Rivers** · *Three Rivers C/C* · Murrell Foster, Exec. Dir., P.O. Box 1648, 78071, P 2,200, M 100, (361) 786-4330, www.threeriverstx.org

**Throckmorton** · *Throckmorton County C/C & Ag.* · P.O. Box 711, 76483, P 1,800, M 32, (940) 849-0222, Fax (940) 849-0222, www.throckmortontx.com

**Timpson** · *Timpson C/C* · Marilyn Corder, Pres., 191 Bremond St., P.O. Box 987, 75975, P 1,100, M 70, (936) 254-3500

**Tomball** · *Greater Tomball Area C/C* · Bruce E. Hillegeist, Pres., 29201 Quinn Rd., Ste. B, P.O. Box 516, 77377, P 11,002, M 840, (281) 351-7222, (866) 670-7222, Fax (281) 351-7223, admin@tomballchamber.org, www.tomballchamber.org

**Tool** · *see Mabank*

**Trinity** · *Trinity Peninsula C/C* · 702 S. Robb, P.O. Box 549, 75862, P 15,000, M 100, (936) 594-3856, Fax (936) 594-0558, info@trinitychamber.org, www.trinitychamber.org

**Trophy Club** · *see Roanoke*

**Troup** · *Troup C/C* · Gene Whitsell, Exec. V.P., P.O. Box 336, 75789, P 1,949, M 85, (903) 842-4113, www.trouptexas.org

**Tulia** · *Tulia C/C* · Joe Weaver, Dir., 127 S.W. 2nd, P.O. Box 267, 79088, P 5,117, M 200, (806) 995-2296, Fax (806) 995-4426, exec@tuliachamber.com, www.tuliachamber.com

**Tyler** · *Tyler Area C/C* · Henry M. Bell III, COO, 315 N. Broadway, P.O. Box 390, 75710, P 183,833, M 2,000, (903) 592-1661, Fax (903) 593-2746, hbell@tylertexas.com, www.tylertexas.com.

**Tyler** · *Tyler Metro Black C/C* · Darryl Bowdre, Pres./COO, 2000 W. Gentry Pkwy., P.O. Box 4362, 75712, P 90,000, M 100, (903) 593-6026, Fax (903) 593-6995, dbowdre@tylermetrochamber.org, www.tylermetrochamber.org

**Universal City** · *see Selma*

**Uvalde** · *Uvalde C/C* · Wendy Speer, Exec. Dir., 300 E. Main, 78801, P 18,500, M 350, (830) 278-3361, Fax (830) 278-3363, director@uvalde.org, www.uvalde.org

**Van** · *Van Area C/C* · Lynn Ward, P.O. Box 55, 75790, P 2,362, M 130, (903) 963-5051, Fax (903) 963-8883, vanchamber@vantexas.com, www.vantexas.com

**Van Alstyne** · *Van Alstyne Area C/C* · Larry Jordan, Pres., 205 E. Marshall, 75495, P 3,300, M 125, (903) 482-6066, Fax (903) 712-0966, info@vanalstynechamber.org, www.vanalstynechamber.org

**Van Horn** · *Van Horn C/C* · P.O. Box 488, 79855, P 2,400, M 20, (866) 424-6939, info@vanhorntexas.org, www.vanhorntexas.org

**Vega** · *Oldham County C/C* · Linda Drake, Mgr., P.O. Box 538, 79092, P 2,200, M 170, (806) 267-2828, Fax (806) 267-2645, oldhamco@arn.net, www.oldhamcofc.org

**Vernon** · *Vernon C/C* · Sheri Morriss, Exec. Dir., 1614 Main St., P.O. Box 1538, 76385, P 11,660, M 190, (940) 552-2564, (800) 687-3137, Fax (940) 552-0654, vernonchamber@sbcglobal.net, www.vernontexas.org

**Victoria** · *Victoria C/C* · Randy Vivian, Pres./CEO, 3404 N. Ben Wilson, P.O. Box 2465, 77902, P 81,550, M 1,132, (361) 573-5277, Fax (361) 573-5911, info@victoriachamber.org, www.victoriachamber.org

**Vidor** · *Vidor C/C* · Jane Carter, Exec. Secy., 385 N. Main St., 77662, P 20,000, M 220, (409) 769-6339, Fax (409) 769-0227, vidorchamber@sbcglobal.net, www.vidorchamber.com

**Waco** · *CenTex Hispanic C/C* · J.R. Marquez, Pres., 915 LaSalle Ave., 76706, P 112,000, M 170, (254) 754-7111, Fax (254) 754-3456, joe@wacohispanicchamber.com, www.wacohispanicchamber.com

**Waco** · *Greater Waco C/C* · James G. Vaughan Jr., Pres./CEO, 101 S. 3rd St., P.O. Box 1220, 76703, P 226,189, M 1,508, (254) 752-6551, Fax (254) 752-6618, info@wacochamber.com, www.wacochamber.com

**Waller** • *Waller Area C/C* • Trey Duhon, Pres., 2313 Main St., P.O. Box 53, 77484, P 15,000, M 145, (936) 372-5300, info@waller chamber.com, www.wallerchamber.com

**Watauga** • *see Haltom City*

**Waxahachie** • *Waxahachie C/C* • Debra Wakeland, Pres./CEO, 102 YMCA Dr., 75165, P 30,000, M 800, (972) 937-2390, (972) 938-9617, Fax (972) 938-9827, dwakeland@waxahachiechamber. com, www.waxahachiechamber.com

**Weatherford** • *Weatherford C/C* • Timmy Gazzola, Pres., 401 Ft. Worth Hwy., P.O. Box 310, 76086, P 25,000, M 750, (817) 594-3801, (888) 594-3801, Fax (817) 613-9216, info@weatherford-chamber.com, www.weatherford-chamber.com.

**Weimar** • *Weimar Area C/C* • Sandra Michna, Exec. Secy., 109 E. Main, P.O. Box 90, 78962, P 1,981, M 128, (979) 725-9511, Fax (979) 725-6890, weimarcc@cvtv.net, www.weimartx.org

**Wellington** • *Wellington C/C* • P.O. Box 267, 79095, P 2,800, M 100, (806) 447-5848

**Weslaco** • *Rio Grande Valley C/C* • Bill Summers, Pres./CEO., 322 S. Missouri, P.O. Box 1499, 78599, P 1,100,000, M 850, (956) 968-3141, Fax (956) 968-0210, mail@valleychamber.com, www. valleychamber.com

**Weslaco** • *Weslaco Area C/C* • Martha Noell, Pres./CEO, 301 W. Railroad St., P.O. Box 8398, 78599, P 32,000, M 575, (956) 968-2102, Fax (956) 968-6451, chamber@weslaco.com, www. weslaco.com

**West** • *West C/C* • Toni Kaska, Pres., 308 N. Washington, P.O. Box 123, 76691, P 2,752, M 100, (254) 826-3188, Fax (254) 826-3188, westchamber@sbcglobal.net, www.westtxchamber.com

**West Columbia** • *West Columbia C/C* • Rita Terrell, Exec. Dir., 202 E. Brazos Ave., P.O. Box 837, 77486, P 4,400, M 225, (979) 345-3921, Fax (979) 345-6526, rita@westcolumbiachamber.org, www.westcolumbiachamber.com

**West Tawakoni** • *see Quinlan*

**Westlake** • *see Roanoke*

**Wharton** • *Wharton C/C* • John Perches, Bd. Chair, 225 N. Richmond Rd., 77488, P 10,200, M 350, (979) 532-1862, Fax (979) 532-0102, helpdesk@whartonchamber.com, www.whartontexas.com

**Wheeler** • *Wheeler C/C* • Frankie Jackson, Pres., 505 Alan L. Bean, P.O. Box 221, 79096, P 1,391, M 50, (806) 826-3408, www. wildlifetexas.com

**White Settlement** • *White Settlement Area C/C* • Roger Chambers, Chamber Mgr., 8224 White Settlement Rd., Ste. 100, P.O. Box 150578, 76108, P 16,150, M 114, (817) 246-1121, Fax (817) 246-1121, wsacc@whitesettlement-tx.com, www. whitesettlement-tx.com

**Whitehouse** • *Whitehouse Area C/C* • Mike Peterson, Pres., P.O. Box 1041, 75791, P 7,000, M 147, (903) 839-8200, info@ whitehousetx.com, www.whitehousetx.com

**Whitesboro** • *Whitesboro Area C/C* • Melodie Jackson, Pres., 2535 Hwy. 82 E., Ste. C, P.O. Box 522, 76273, P 4,400, M 300, (903) 564-3331, Fax (903) 564-3397, chamber@whitesborotx.com, www.whitesborotx.com

**Whitewright** • *Whitewright Area C/C* • Aaron Mangrum, Pres., 113 W. Grand, P.O. Box 189, 75491, P 1,760, M 94, (903) 364-2000, Fax (903) 364-1079, wacc@isp.com, www.whitewright.org

**Whitney** • *Lake Whitney C/C* • H. Findley, Exec. Secy., 102 W. Railroad Ave., P.O. Box 604, 76692, P 20,000, M 200, (254) 694-2540, Fax (254) 694-3005, bluewater@lakewhitneychamber.com, www.lakewhitneychamber.com

**Wichita Falls** • *Wichita Falls Bd. of Comm. & Ind.* • Tim Chase, Pres./CEO, 900 8th St. #218, P.O. Box 1860, 76307, P 104,000, M 1,200, (940) 723-2741, Fax (940) 723-8773, wfbci@wf.net, www.wichitafallscommerce.com.

**Willow Park** • *East Parker County C/C* • Lisa Flowers, Exec. Dir., 100 Chuck Wagon Tr., 76087, P 30,000, M 400, (817) 441-7844, Fax (817) 441-1544, info@eastparkerchamber.com, www.east parkerchamber.com

**Wills Point** • *Wills Point C/C* • Karen Samples, Pres., 307 N. 4th St., 75169, P 4,000, M 200, (903) 873-3111, (903) 873-3588, Fax (903) 873-2199, karen@willspoint.org, www.willspoint.org

**Wilmer** • *Wilmer C/C* • Ann Hester, Secy./Treas., 211 S. Dallas Ave., 75172, P 3,600, M 20, (972) 441-3787

**Wimberley** • *Wimberley Chamber & Visitor Center* • Jenelle Flocke, Chrmn., P.O. Box 12, 78676, P 9,000, M 425, (512) 847-2201, Fax (512) 847-3189, info@wimberley.org, www.wimberley.org

**Windcrest** • *see Selma*

**Wink** • *Wink C/C* • Bill Beckham, Pres., P.O. Box 401, 79789, P 919, M 8, (432) 527-3365, Fax (432) 527-3949

**Winnie** • *Winnie Area C/C* • Melissa Hodges, Ofc. Mgr., 327 E. LeBlanc Rd., P.O. Box 1715, 77665, P 5,275, M 200, (409) 296-2231, Fax (409) 296-4213, winnie@winnietexas.com, www. winnietexas.com.

**Winnsboro** • *Winnsboro Area C/C* • Larry Wright, Pres., 100 E. Broadway, 75494, P 3,800, M 250, (903) 342-3666, Fax (903) 342-3666, info@winnsboro.com, www.winnsboro.com

**Winters** • *Winters Area C/C* • Jean Boles, Gen. Mgr., 100 W. Dale St., P.O. Box 662, 79567, P 3,200, M 95, (325) 754-5210, wacc@ wtxs.net, www.winters-texas.us, www.winterschamber.org

**Wolfforth** • *Wolfforth Area C/C & Ag.* • Julie Merrill & Shawndell Kreger, Co-Pres., P.O. Box 35, 79382, P 3,300, M 100, (806) 866-4215, Fax (806) 866-4217, chamber@wolfforthtx.us, www.wolfforthtx.us

**Woodville** • *Tyler County C/C* • Jimmie Cooley, Pres., 717 W. Bluff St., 75979, P 30,000, M 210, (409) 283-2632, Fax (409) 283-6884, tylerctychamber@sbcglobal.net, www.tylercountychamber.com

**Wylie** • *Wylie C/C* • Mike Agnew, Pres., 108-A W. Marble, 75098, P 41,000, M 392, (972) 442-2804, Fax (972) 429-0139, info@ wyliechamber.org, www.wyliechamber.org.

**Yoakum** • *Yoakum Area C/C* • Bill Lopez, Pres., 105 Huck St., P.O. Box 591, 77995, P 5,700, M 150, (361) 293-2309, Fax (361) 293-3507, info@yoakumareachamber.com, www.yoakumareachamber.com.

**Yorktown** • *Yorktown C/C* • Melissa Armstrong, Exec. Dir., 141 S. Riedel St., P.O. Box 488, 78164, P 2,271, M 150, (361) 564-2661, Fax (361) 564-2518, 4yorktown@sbcglobal.net, www.yorktowntx.com

**Zapata** • *Zapata County C/C* • Paco Mendoza, Exec. Dir., 601 N. Hwy. 83, P.O. Box 1028, 78076, P 16,000, M 209, (956) 765-4871, (800) 292-LAKE, Fax (956) 765-5434, pacomendoza.zapata chamber@yahoo.com, www.zapatausa.com.

# Utah

**Utah State C of C** • Donna Brown, Chair, 175 E. 400 S. #600, Salt Lake City, 84111, P 2,758,000, M 15,500, (801) 328-5090, Fax (801) 328-5093, www.utahstatechamber.org

**American Fork** • *American Fork C/C* • Debby Lauret, Exec. Dir., 51 E. Main St., P.O. Box 162, 84003, P 60,000, M 240, (801) 756-5110, chamber@afcity.net, www.afchamber.org

**Beaver** • *Beaver C/C & Travel Cncl.* • Ursula Carstensen, Pres., P.O. Box 272, 84713, P 2,500, M 50, (435) 438-5438, (888) 848-5081, bctravel@infowest.com

**Bluffdale** • *see Riverton*

**Bountiful** • *see Kaysville*

**Brian Head** • *Brian Head C/C* • Angie Haderlie, Dir./Treas., P.O. Box 190325, 84719, P 150, M 100, (888) 677-2810, Fax (435) 677-2154, angie@brianheadchamber.com, www.brianheadchamber.com

**Brigham City** • *Brigham City Area C/C* • Monica Holdaway, Exec. Dir., 6 N. Main, 84302, P 35,000, M 360, (435) 723-3931, Fax (435) 723-5761, www.brighamchamber.com.

**Cedar City** • *Cedar City Area C/C* • Scott Jolley, Exec. Dir., 581 N. Main St. #B, 84720, P 27,000, M 435, (435) 586-4484, Fax (435) 586-4022, director@infowest.com, www.chambercedarcity.org

**Centerville** • *see Kaysville*

**Clearfield** • *see Kaysville*

**Clinton** • *see Kaysville*

**Cottonwood Heights** • *see Salt Lake City-Chamber East*

**Delta** • *Delta Area C/C* • Lorie L. Skeem, Ofc. Mgr., 80 N. 200 W., 84624, P 8,000, M 100, (435) 864-4316, Fax (435) 864-4313, chamber@deltautah.com, www.millardcounty.org

**Draper** • *Draper Area C/C* • William Rappleye, Pres./CEO, 1160 E. Pioneer Rd., P.O. Box 1002, 84020, P 35,000, M 200, (801) 553-0928, Fax (801) 816-0478, wrappleye@integraonline.com, www.draperchamber.com

**Farmington** • *see Kaysville*

**Fillmore** • *Fillmore Area C/C* • Michael King, Pres., P.O. Box 164, 84631, P 2,300, M 30, (435) 743-7803, www.fillmoreutah chamber.com

**Fruit Heights** • *see Kaysville*

**Garden City** • *Bear Lake Rendezvous C/C* • Angie McPhie, Pres., P.O. Box 55, 84028, P 450, M 60, (800) 448-2327, info@bearlake chamber.com, www.bearlakechamber.com

**Green River** • *Green River C/C* • Keith Brady, Chrmn., 45 S. Walnut St., 84525, P 997, M 30, (435) 564-3490, (877) 564-3490, www.greenriverutah.org

**Heber City** • *Heber Valley C/C* • Jason Giles, Exec. Dir., 475 N. Main St., 84032, P 20,000, M 300, (435) 654-3666, Fax (435) 654-3667, info@gohebervalley.com, www.gohebervalley.com

**Herriman** • *see Riverton*

**Hurricane** • *Hurricane Valley C/C* • Eric Heideman, Pres., 545 W. State St. #9, 84737, P 15,000, M 95, (435) 635-3402, Fax (435) 635-3402, billbrown@hvchamber.com, www.hvchamber.com

**Kanab** • *Kanab Area C/C* • Sheldon Honey, 78 S. 100 E., 84741, P 6,500, M 125, (435) 644-5033, Fax (435) 644-5923, www.kanabchamber.com

**Kaysville** • *Davis C/C* • John Pitt, Pres./CEO, 450 S. Simmons Way #220, 84037, P 265,000, M 900, (801) 593-2200, Fax (801) 593-2212, daviscc@davischamberofcommerce.com, www.davis chamberofcommerce.com

**Kearns** • *see West Valley City*

**Layton** • *see Kaysville*

**Lehi** • *Lehi Area C/C* • Rose Klingonsmith, Pres., 235 E. State St., P.O. Box 154, 84043, P 48,000, M 150, (801) 766-9657, (801) 836-0836, Fax (801) 766-8599, rosek@lehiareachamber.org, www.lehiareachamber.org

**Logan** • *Cache Valley C/C* • Sandra Emile, Pres., 160 N. Main St., 84321, P 105,000, M 630, (435) 752-2161, Fax (435) 753-5825, semile@cachechamber.com, www.cachechamber.com

**Manila** • *Flaming Gorge Area C/C* • Tina Benington, Pres., 84046, P 920, M 50, (435) 784-3184

**Midvale** • *see Salt Lake City-Chamber East*

**Millcreek** • *see Salt Lake City-Chamber East*

**Moab** • *Moab Area C/C* • Kammy Wells, Exec. Dir., 217 E. Center St. #250, 84532, P 9,000, M 273, (435) 259-7814, Fax (435) 259-8519, info@moabchamber.com, www.moabchamber.com

**Monticello** • *Monticello C/C* • Jeremy Hoggard, Pres., P.O. Box 217, 84535, P 2,000, M 50, (435) 587-2992, info@monticello utahchamber.com, www.monticelloutahchamber.com

**Mount Pleasant** • *Mount Pleasant Main Street Comm.* • Monte Bona, Dir., 115 W. Main St., City Hall, 84647, P 2,800, M 55, (435) 462-2456, Fax (435) 462-2581, www.utahheritage.com

**Murray** • *Murray Area C/C* • Scott Baker, Pres., 5250 S. Commerce Dr. #180, 84107, P 48,000, M 400, (801) 263-2632, Fax (801) 263-8262, scott@murraychamber.net, www.murraychamber.org

**North Salt Lake** • *see Kaysville*

**Ogden** • *Ogden-Weber C/C* • Dave Hardman, Pres./CEO, 2484 Washington Blvd., Ste. 400, 84401, P 197,000, M 2,287, (801) 621-8300, Fax (801) 392-7609, chamber@echamber.cc, www.echamber.cc.

**Orem** • *see Provo*

**Park City** • *Park City C/C* • Bill Malone, Exec. Dir., 1910 Prospector Ave., P.O. Box 1630, 84060, P 24,500, M 1,075, (435) 649-6100, Fax (435) 649-4132, info@parkcityinfo.com, www.parkcityinfo.com

**Payson** • *Payson C/C* • Carolyn Bowman, Exec. Dir., 20 S. Main, P.O. Box 176, 84651, P 17,500, M 100, (801) 465-2634, Fax (801) 465-5173, paysonchamber@yahoo.com, www.paysoncitychamber.org

**Pleasant Grove** • *Pleasant Grove Bus. Alliance* • Jennifer Wright, Secy., 70 S. 100 E., 84062, P 31,000, M 250, (801) 380-3179, (801) 785-5045, Fax (801) 785-8925, info@pgbusiness alliance.com, www.pgbusinessalliance.com

**Price** • *Carbon County C/C* • Ann Evans, Coord., 81 N. 200 E. #3, 84501, P 22,000, M 300, (435) 637-2788, Fax (435) 637-7010, cccc@priceutah.net, www.carboncountychamber.com

**Provo** • *Provo Orem C/C* • Steven T. Densley, Pres., 51 S. University Ave. #215, 84601, P 200,000, M 820, (801) 851-2555, Fax (801) 851-2557, info@thechamber.org, www.thechamber.org.

**Richfield** • *Richfield Area C/C* • Lorraine Gregerson, Exec. Dir., 250 N. Main #B42, 84701, P 7,200, M 145, (435) 896-4241, Fax (435) 896-4313, richfieldchamber@infowest.com, www.richfield areachamber.com

**Riverdale** • *see Ogden*

**Riverton** • *Southwest Valley C/C* • Susan Schilling, 4168 W. 12600 S., P.O. Box 330, 84065, P 80,000, M 135, (801) 280-0595, Fax (801) 280-3674, susan@swvchamber.org, www.swvchamber.org

**Roosevelt** • *Duchesne County Area C/C* • Irene Hansen, Exec. Dir., 50 E. 200 S., P.O. Box 1417, 84066, P 18,000, M 250, (435) 722-4598, Fax (435) 722-4579, dcac@ubtanet.com, www.duchesne.net

**Roy** • *see Ogden*

**Salem** • *see Spanish Fork*

**Salt Lake City** • *Chamber East* • Marie Marshall, Pres./CEO, 3335 S. 900 E. #220, 84106, P 150,000, M 400, (801) 561-3880, info@chambereast.com, www.chambereast.com

**Salt Lake City** · *Salt Lake C/C* · Lane Beattie, Pres./CEO, 175 E. University Blvd. (400 S.) #600, 84111, P 978,701, M 4,200, (801) 364-3631, Fax (801) 328-5098, info@slchamber.com, www.slchamber.com.

**THE SALT LAKE CHAMBER IS UTAH'S LARGEST BUSINESS ASSOCIATION AND UTAH'S BUSINESS LEADER.**

**Sandy** · *Sandy Area C/C* · Nancy Workman, Pres./CEO, 8807 S. 700 E., 84070, P 100,000, M 450, (801) 566-0344, Fax (801) 566-0346, nancy.workman@sandychamber.com, www.sandychamber.com

**Smithfield** · *Greater Smithfield C/C* · Rigo Chaparro, Pres., P.O. Box 31, 84335, P 7,000, M 40, (435) 563-3236, www.smithfieldchamber.com

**South Jordan** · *South Jordan C/C* · Yvonne Margis, Admin., 1665 W. 10600 S., Ste. 2, 84095, P 53,000, M 200, (801) 253-5200, Fax (801) 253-5201, info@southjordanchamber.org, www.southjordanchamber.org

**South Salt Lake City** · *South Salt Lake C/C* · Stacey Liddiard, Pres./CEO, P.O. Box 65001, 84165, P 23,000, M 200, (801) 466-3377, Fax (801) 467-3322, info@sslchamber.com, www.sslchamber.com

**South Weber** · *see Kaysville*

**Spanish Fork** · *Spanish Fork Area C/C* · Patti Witham, Exec. Dir., 40 S. Main #10, 84660, P 30,000, M 225, (801) 798-8352, Fax (801) 798-6594, sfchamberdirector@gmail.com, www.spanishforkchamber.com

**Springville** · *Springville Area C/C* · Andy Shelline, Exec Dir., 224 S. Main #440, 84663, P 25,000, M 135, (801) 489-4681, Fax (801) 489-4811, springvillechamber@qwestoffice.net, www.springvilleareachamber.com

**St. George** · *St. George Area C/C* · Russell G. Behrmann, Pres., 97 E. St. George Blvd., 84770, P 142,000, M 900, (435) 628-1658, Fax (435) 673-1587, hotspot@stgeorgechamber.com, www.stgeorgechamber.com

**Sugar House** · *see Salt Lake City-Chamber East*

**Sunset** · *see Kaysville*

**Syracuse** · *see Kaysville*

**Taylorsville** · *see West Valley City*

**Tooele** · *Tooele County C/C* · Debbie Winn, Exec. Dir., 86 S. Main, P.O. Box 460, 84074, P 54,300, M 300, (435) 882-0690, (800) 378-0690, Fax (435) 833-0946, chamber@tooelechamber.com, www.tooelechamber.com

**Tremonton** · *Bear River Valley C/C* · P.O. Box 311, 84337, P 15,000, M 200, (435) 257-7585, Fax (435) 279-2947, www.bearriverchamber.org

**Vernal** · *Vernal Area C/C* · Michael Kitzmiller, Exec. Dir., 134 W. Main, 84078, P 27,000, M 250, (435) 789-1352, Fax (435) 789-1355, staff@vernalchamber.com, www.vernalchamber.com

**West Bountiful** · *see Kaysville*

**West Jordan** · *West Jordan C/C* · N. Craig Dearing, Pres./CEO, 8000 S. Redwood Rd., 84088, P 100,000, M 360, (801) 569-5151, Fax (801) 569-5153, info@westjordanchamber.com, www.westjordanchamber.com

**West Point** · *see Kaysville*

**West Valley City** · *ChamberWest* · Alan Anderson, Pres./CEO, 1241 Village Main Dr. #B, 84119, P 200,000, M 420, (801) 977-8755, Fax (801) 977-8329, chamber@chamberwest.org, www.chamberwest.org

**Woods Cross** · *see Kaysville*

# Vermont

**Vermont C of C** · Christopher Barbieri, Interim Pres., P.O. Box 37, Montpelier, 05601, P 639,000, M 1,500, (802) 223-3443, Fax (802) 223-4257, info@vtchamber.com, www.vtchamber.com.

**Arlington** · *see Manchester Center*

**Ascutney** · *see Windsor*

**Athens** · *see Bellows Falls*

**Barre** · *Central Vermont C/C* · George Malek, Exec. V.P., P.O. Box 336, 05641, P 60,000, M 450, (802) 229-5711, (877) 887-3678, Fax (802) 229-5713, cvchamber@aol.com, www.central-vt.com.

**Barton** · *Barton Area C/C* · Nancy Rodgers, Pres., P.O. Box 776, 05822, P 5,000, M 130, (802) 239-4147, info@centerofthekingdom.com, www.centerofthekingdom.com

**Bellows Falls** · *Great Falls Reg. C/C* · Roger Riccio, Exec. Dir., 17 Depot St., P.O. Box 554, 05101, P 12,000, M 290, (802) 463-4280, Fax (802) 463-4280, info@gfrcc.org, www.gfrcc.org

**Bennington** · *Bennington Area C/C* · Joann Erenhouse, Dir., 100 Veterans Memorial Dr., 05201, P 15,000, M 500, (802) 447-3311, (800) 229-0252, Fax (802) 447-1163, chamber@bennington.com, www.bennington.com

**Berlin** · *see Barre*

**Bethel** · *see Randolph*

**Bradford** · *see Wells River*

**Braintree** · *see Randolph*

**Brandon** · *Brandon Area C/C* · Janet Mondlak, Exec. Dir., P.O. Box 267, 05733, P 4,000, M 175, (802) 247-6401, info@brandon.org, www.brandon.org

**Brattleboro** · *Brattleboro Area C/C* · Jerry Goldberg, Exec. Dir., 180 Main St., 05301, P 35,000, M 610, (802) 254-4565, (877) 254-4565, Fax (802) 254-5675, info@brattleborochamber.org, www.brattleborochamber.org

**Bristol** · *see Middlebury*

**Brookfield** · *see Randolph*

**Burke Hollow** · *see East Burke*

**Burlington** · *Lake Champlain Reg. C/C* · Tom Torti, Pres., 60 Main St. #100, 05401, P 149,286, M 2,500, (802) 863-3489, (877) 686-5253, Fax (802) 863-1538, vermont@vermont.org, www.vermont.org

**Chelsea** · *see Randolph*

**Chester** · *see Ludlow*

**Dorset** · *Dorset C/C* · Roger Squire, P.O. Box 121, 05251, P 2,000, M 65, chamber@dorsetvt.com, www.dorsetvt.com

**East Burke** · *Burke Area C/C* · Hannah Collins, Pres., P.O. Box 347, 05832, P 2,000, M 50, (802) 626-4124, burkechamber@burkevermont.com, www.burkevermont.com

**Fair Haven** · *Fair Haven Area C/C* · Mr. Kerry Fowler, Pres., P.O. Box 206, 05743, P 8,000, M 60, (802) 265-8600, contact@fairhavenchambervt.com, www.fairhavenchambervt.com

**Grafton** · *see Bellows Falls*

**Hancock** · *see Randolph*

**Hardwick** · *Hardwick Area C/C* · Ronald Sanville, Pres., P.O. Box 111, 05843, P 7,000, M 125, (802) 472-5906, chamber@heartofvt.com, www.heartofvt.com

**Hartland** · *see Windsor*

**Island Pond** · *Island Pond C/C* · Patricia Whitney, Admin., P.O. Box 255, 05846, P 2,000, M 20, (802) 723-9889 welcome center, info@islandpondchamber.org, www.islandpondchamber.org

**Jeffersonville** · *Smugglers Notch Area C/C* · Ray Saloomey, Pres., P.O. Box 364, 05464, P 3,000, M 98, (802) 644-8232, info@smugnotch.com, www.smugnotch.com

**Killington** · *Killington C/C* · Christopher Karr, Pres., P.O. Box 114, 05751, P 1,000, M 200, (802) 773-4181, (800) 337-1928, Fax (802) 775-7070, info@killingtonchamber.com, www.killington chamber.com

**Lake Champlain Islands** · *see North Hero*

**Lincoln** · *see Middlebury*

**Londonderry** · *Londonderry Area C/C* · James J. Lind, Exec. Dir., P.O. Box 58, 05148, P 1,500, M 106, (802) 824-8178, londcham@aol.com

**Ludlow** · *Okemo Valley Reg. C/C* · Marji Graf, Exec. Dir., P.O. Box 333, 05149, P 3,000, M 300, (802) 228-5830, mgraf@yourplace invermont.com, www.yourplaceinvermont.com

**Lyndonville** · *Lyndon Area C/C* · Steve Nichols, Pres., P.O. Box 886, 05851, P 9,000, M 90, (802) 626-9696, Fax (802) 626-1167, info@lyndonvermont.com, www.lyndonvermont.com

**Manchester Center** · *Manchester & The Mountains Reg. C/C* · Jay Hathaway, Exec. Dir., 5046 Main St., 05255, P 3,800, M 730, (802) 362-2100, (800) 362-4144, (802) 362-6313, Fax (802) 362-3451, visitor@manchesterchamber.net, www.manchestervermont.net

**Middlebury** · *Addison County C/C* · Andrew Mayer, Pres., 2 Court St., 05753, P 37,000, M 700, (802) 388-7951, (800) 733-8376, Fax (802) 388-8066, info@addisoncounty.com, www. addisoncounty.com

**Monkton** · *see Middlebury*

**Montpelier** · *see Barre*

**Morrisville** · *Lamoille Valley C/C* · Cindy Locke, Exec. Dir., 34 Pleasant St. #1, P.O. Box 445, 05661, P 21,225, M 390, (802) 888-7607, (800) 849-9985, Fax (802) 888-5006, info@lamoillevalley chamber.com, www.lamoillevalleychamber.com

**New Haven** · *see Middlebury*

**Newbury** · *see Wells River*

**Newport** · *Vermont's North Country C/C* · Tod Pronto, Exec. Dir., 246 The Causeway, 05855, P 25,000, M 200, (802) 334-7782, (800) 635-4643, Fax (802) 334-7238, chamber@vtnorthcountry.org, www.vtnorthcountry.org

**North Hero** · *Lake Champlain Islands C/C* · Ruth Wallman, Exec. Dir., P.O. Box 213, 05474, P 7,000, M 200, (802) 372-8400, (800) 262-5226, Fax (802) 372-5107, info@champlainislands.com, www.champlainislands.com

**Northfield** · *see Barre*

**Poultney** · *Poultney Area C/C* · Valerie Broughton, Pres., P.O. Box 151, 05764, P 3,500, M 140, (802) 287-2010, poultneyvt@yahoo.com, www.poultneyvt.com

**Putney** · *see Bellows Falls*

**Randolph** · *Randolph Area C/C* · Deborah Jones, Exec. Dir., 31 VT Rte. 66, P.O. Box 9, 05060, P 30,000, M 195, (802) 728-9027, Fax (802) 728-4705, mail@randolph-chamber.com, www. randolph-chamber.com

**Reading** · *see Windsor*

**Rochester** · *see Randolph*

**Rockingham** · *see Bellows Falls*

**Royalton** · *see Randolph*

**Rutland** · *Rutland Region C/C* · Thomas L. Donahue, Exec. V.P., 256 N. Main St., 05701, P 18,230, M 600, (802) 773-2747, (800) 756-8880, Fax (802) 773-2772, rrccvt@aol.com, www.rutland vermont.com

**Saint Albans** · *Franklin County Reg. C/C* · Jim Walsh, Exec. Dir., 2 N. Main St. #101, 05478, P 45,000, M 600, (802) 524-2444, (877) 524-2445, Fax (802) 527-2256, fcrcc@myfairpoint.net, www.fcrccvt.com/www.stalbanschamber.com

**Saint Johnsbury** · *Northeast Kingdom C/C* · Darcie McCann, Exec. Dir., 51 Depot Sq. #3, 05819, P 63,612, M 425, (802) 748-3678, (800) 639-6379, Fax (802) 748-0731, nekinfo@nekchamber.com, www.nekchamber.com

**Saxton's River** · *see Bellows Falls*

**Sharon** · *see Randolph*

**Smugglers Notch** · *see Jeffersonville*

**Springfield** · *Springfield Reg. C/C* · Patricia Chaffee, Exec. V.P., 56 Main St. #2, 05156, P 9,550, M 330, (802) 885-2779, Fax (802) 885-6826, chamber@springfieldvt.com, www.springfieldvt.com

**Starksboro** · *see Middlebury*

**Stockbridge** · *see Randolph*

**Stowe** · *Stowe Area Assn.* · Ed Stahl, Exec. Dir., 51 Main St., P.O. Box 1320, 05672, P 4,300, M 315, (802) 253-7321, (877) GO-STOWE, Fax (802) 253-6628, askus@gostowe.com, www.gostowe.com

**Swanton** · *Swanton C/C* · Adam Paxman, Pres., P.O. Box 237, 05488, P 6,000, M 62, (802) 868-7200, adam_paxman@comcast.net, www.swantonchamber.com

**Tunbridge** · *see Randolph*

**Vergennes** · *see Middlebury*

**Waitsfield** · *Mad River Valley C/C* · Susan Klein, Dir., P.O. Box 173, 05673, P 3,800, M 200, (802) 496-3409, (800) 828-4748, Fax (802) 496-5420, chamber@madriver.com, www.madrivervalley.com

**Waterbury** · *see Barre*

**Wells River** · *Lower Cohase Reg. C/C* · P.O. Box 35, 05081, P 9,000, M 152, (802) 757-2549, info@cohase.org, www.cohase.org

**West Burke** · *see East Burke*

**West Windsor** · *see Windsor*

**Westminster** · *see Bellows Falls*

**White River Junction** · *Hartford Area C/C* · Gayle Ottmann, Exec. Dir., 100 Railroad Row, 05001, P 11,000, M 400, (802) 295-7900, (800) 295-5451, Fax (802) 296-8280, info@hartfordvt chamber.com, www.hartfordvtchamber.com

**White River Junction** · *Upper Valley Bi-State Reg. C/C* · Geoffrey Ross, P.O. Box 697, 05001, P 10,000, M 250, (802) 295-6200, Fax (802) 295-3779, director@uppervalleychamber.com, www.uppervalleychamber.com

**Wilmington** · *Mt. Snow Valley C/C* · Laura Sibilia, Exec. Dir., 21 West Main St., P.O. Box 3, 05363, P 3,500, M 300, (802) 464-8092, (877) 887-6884, Fax (802) 464-0287, info@visitvermont.com, www.visitvermont.com

**Windsor** · *Windsor-Mount Ascutney Region C/C* · Nate Larson, Pres., P.O. Box 41, 05089, P 15,000, M 156, (802) 674-5910, Fax (802) 674-5910, info@windsorvt.com, www.windsorvt.com

**Woodstock** · *Woodstock Area C/C* · Elizabeth Finlayson, Dir., 61 Central St., P.O. Box 486, 05091, P 3,232, M 305, (802) 457-3555, (888) 496-6378, Fax (802) 457-1601, info@woodstockvt.com, www.woodstockvt.com

# Virgin Islands

**St. Croix** · *St. Croix C/C* · Michael Dembeck, Exec. Dir., 3009 Orange Grove Suite 12, Christiansted, 00820, P 55,000, M 325, (340) 773-1435, Fax (340) 773-8172, info@stxchamber.org, www.stxchamber.org

**St. Thomas** · *St. Thomas-St. John C/C* · Joe S. Aubain, Exec. Dir., P.O. Box 324, 00804, P 57,514, M 500, (340) 776-0100, Fax (340) 776-0588, chamber.vi@gmail.com, www.usvichamber.com

# Virginia

**Virginia C of C** · Hugh D. Keogh, Pres./CEO, 9 S. Fifth St., Richmond, 23219, M 1,000, (804) 644-1607, Fax (804) 783-6112, m.crowder@vachamber.com, www.vachamber.com

**Abingdon** · *Washington County C/C* · Suzanne G. Lay, Exec. V.P., 179 E. Main St., 24210, P 51,000, M 650, (276) 628-8141, Fax (276) 628-3984, chamber@eva.org, www.washingtonva chamber.org.

**Alexandria** · *Alexandria C/C* · Joseph Shumard, Interim Pres./CEO, 801 N. Fairfax St., Ste. 402, 22314, P 132,000, M 1,000, (703) 549-1000, Fax (703) 739-3805, info@alexchamber.com, www.alexchamber.com

**Altavista** · *Altavista Area C/C* · Patty Eller, Pres., 414 Washington St., P.O. Box 606, 24517, P 3,500, M 220, (434) 369-6665, Fax (434) 369-4202, altavistachamber@embarqmail.com, www.altavistachamber.org

**Amherst** · *Amherst County C/C* · Amy Allen, Pres., 154 S. Main St., P.O. Box 560, 24521, P 32,000, M 200, (434) 946-0990, Fax (434) 946-0879, information@amherstvachamber.com, www.amherstvachamber.com

**Annandale** · *also see Fairfax County C/C*

**Annandale** · *Annandale C/C* · Vicki Burman, Exec. Dir., 7263 Maple Pl. #207, 22003, P 130,000, M 240, (703) 256-7232, Fax (703) 256-7233, info@annandalechamber.com, www.annandalechamber.com

**Appomattox** · *Appomattox County C/C* · J. Patrick Richardson, Pres., P.O. Box 704, 24522, P 13,705, M 150, (434) 352-2621, Fax (434) 352-0294, chamber@appomattoxchamber.org, www.appomattoxchamber.org.

**Arlington** · *Arlington C/C* · Richard V. Doud Jr., Pres., 2009 N. 14th St., Ste. 111, 22201, P 200,000, M 800, (703) 525-2400, Fax (703) 522-5273, chamber@arlingtonchamber.org, www.arlingtonchamber.org.

**Ashland** · *Hanover Assn. of Businesses & C/C* · Kris Holt, Ofc. Admin., 106 Robinson St., P.O. Box 16, 23005, P 100,000, M 400, (804) 798-8130, Fax (804) 798-0014, admin@habcc.com, www.habcc.com

**Augusta County** · *see Fishersville*

**Baileys Crossroads** · *see Fairfax County*

**Bedford** · *Bedford Area C/C* · Susan Martin, Pres., 305 E. Main St., 24523, P 66,000, M 680, (540) 586-9401, Fax (540) 587-6650, www.bedfordareachamber.com

**Berryville** · *see Winchester*

**Blacksburg** · *Montgomery County C/C* · Shane Adams, Pres./CEO, 103 Professional Park Dr., 24060, P 100,000, M 1,100, (540) 552-2636, Fax (540) 552-2639, chamber@montgomerycc.org, www.montgomerycc.org.

**Blackstone** · *Blackstone C/C* · Stacey Lynn, Exec. Dir., 300 Church St., P.O. Box 295, 23824, P 4,000, M 150, (434) 292-1677, Fax (434) 292-1588, chamber@blackstoneva.com, www.blackstoneva.com

**Blairs** · *Danville-Pittsylvania County C/C* · Laurie S. Moran CCE, Pres., 8653 U.S. Hwy. 29, P.O. Box 99, 24527, P 110,000, M 725, (434) 836-6990, Fax (434) 836-6955, chamber@dpchamber.org, www.dpchamber.org

**Bland County** · *see Wytheville*

**Botetourt County** · *see Fincastle*

**Bowling Green** · *Caroline C/C* · Eileen Beach, Exec. Dir., P.O. Box 384, 22427, P 26,000, M 140, (804) 448-5264, Fax (804) 448-0844, chamber@bealenet.com, www.carolinechamber.com

**Bristol** · *Bristol C/C* · Lisa Meadows, Pres./CEO, 20 Volunteer Pkwy., P.O. Box 519, 24203, P 43,000, M 800, (423) 989-4850, Fax (423) 989-4867, frontdesk@bristolchamber.org, www.bristolchamber.org.

**Broadway** · *see Timberville*

**Brookneal** · *Brookneal Area C/C* · P.O. Box 387, 24528, P 1,300, M 56, (434) 376-7111, www.brooknealchamber.org

**Buckingham County** · *see Dillwyn*

**Burke** · *see Fairfax County*

**Burkeville** · *see Crewe*

**Callao** · *Northumberland County C/C* · Ann Lekander, Exec. Dir., P.O. Box 149, 22435, P 12,500, M 160, (804) 529-5031, Fax (804) 529-5031, northumberlandcoc@verizon.net, www.northumberlandcoc.org

**Cape Charles** · *see Eastville*

**Centreville** · *see Fairfax County*

**Chantilly** · *Dulles Reg. C/C* · Eileen Curtis, Pres./CEO, 3901 Centerview Dr., Ste. R, 20151, P 50,000, M 930, (571) 323-5300, Fax (703) 787-8859, info@dullesregionalchamber.org, www.dullesregionalchamber.org

**Charlottesville** · *Charlottesville Reg. C/C* · Timothy Hulbert, Pres., Fifth & E. Market St., P.O. Box 1564, 22902, P 120,000, M 1,200, (434) 295-3141, Fax (434) 295-3144, desk@cvillechamber.com, www.cvillechamber.com.

**Chase City** · *Chase City C/C* · RC Hartley, Exec. Dir., 316 N. Main St., 23924, P 2,460, M 100, (434) 372-0379, Fax (434) 372-4699, chasecityva@meckcom.net, www.chasecitychamberofcomm.com

**Chatham** · *see Blairs*

**Cheriton** · *see Eastville*

**Chesapeake** · *see Hampton Roads*

**Chesterfield** · *Chesterfield County C/C* · Lenita Gilreath, Pres., 9330 Iron Bridge Rd., Ste. B, 23832, P 300,000, M 650, (804) 748-6364, Fax (804) 425-5669, lenita@chesterfieldchamber.com, www.chesterfieldchamber.com

**Chincoteague** · *Chincoteague C/C* · Suzanne Taylor, Exec. Dir., 6733 Maddox Blvd., P.O. Box 258, 23336, P 4,000, M 260, (757) 336-6161, Fax (757) 336-1242, chincochamber@verizon.net, www.chincoteaguechamber.com

**Christiansburg** · *see Blacksburg*

**Clarksville** · *Clarksville Lake Country C/C* · Linda Williams, Exec. Dir., 105 2nd St., P.O. Box 1017, 23927, P 6,000, M 200, (434) 374-2436, (800) 557-5582, Fax (434) 374-8174, clarksville@kerrlake.com, www.clarksvilleva.com

**Clifton** · *see Fairfax County*

**Clifton Forge** · *see Covington*

**Clintwood** · *Dickenson County C/C* · Rita Surratt, Pres./CEO, 194 Main St., P.O. Box 1990, 24228, P 16,400, M 350, (276) 926-6074, chamber@dcwin.org, www.dickensonchamber.net

**Colonial Beach** · *Colonial Beach C/C* · Carey Geddes, Pres., 6 N. Irving Ave., P.O. Box 475, 22443, P 3,300, M 120, (804) 224-8145, Fax (804) 224-8145, info@colonialbeach.org, www.colonialbeach.org

**Colonial Heights** · *Colonial Heights C/C* · Roger Green, Exec. Dir., 201 Temple Ave., Ste. E, 23834, P 17,700, M 400, (804) 526-5872, Fax (804) 526-9637, chchamber@colonialheights.cc, www.colonial-heights.com

**Covington** · *Alleghany Highlands C/C* · Teresa A. Hammond, Exec. Dir., 241 W. Main St., 24426, P 23,025, M 230, (540) 962-2178, (888) 430-5786, Fax (540) 962-2179, info@ahchamber.com, www.ahchamber.com.

**Crewe** · *Crewe-Burkeville C/C* · Eddie Higgins, Pres., P.O. Box 305, 23930, P 2,300, M 60, (434) 645-8509, Fax (434) 645-7232, chamber@creweburkeville.org, www.creweburkeville.org

**Culpeper** · *Culpeper County C/C & Visitor Center* · Jim Charapich, Pres./CEO, 109 S. Commerce St., 22701, P 45,372, M 600, (540) 825-8628, (888) CULPEPER, Fax (540) 825-1449, info@culpepervachamber.com, www.culpepervachamber.com

**Dahlgren** · *King George County C/C* · Stanley Palivoda, Pres., P.O. Box 1073, 22448, P 20,000, M 95, (540) 663-2000, Fax (540) 663-0385

**Danville** · *see Blairs*

**Dillwyn** · *Buckingham County C/C* · Sandra Moss, P.O. Box 951, 23936, P 17,000, M 165, (434) 983-2372, info@buckingham chamber.org, www.buckinghamchamber.org

**Dublin** · *Pulaski County C/C* · Peggy White, Exec. Dir., 4440 Cleburne Blvd., 24084, P 36,000, M 450, (540) 674-1991, Fax (540) 674-4163, pcchamber2@swva.net, www.pulaskichamber.info

**Eastville** · *Northampton County C/C* · Linda Baylis Spence, Exec. Dir., 16429A Courthouse Rd., P.O. Box 475, 23347, P 14,000, M 300, (757) 678-0010, chamber@northamptoncountychamber. com, www.northamptoncountychamber.com

**Edinburg** · *Edinburg Area C/C* · Tracy Miller, Pres., P.O. Box 511, 22824, P 860, M 130, (540) 984-8318, www.edinburgchamber.com

**Emporia** · *Emporia-Greensville C/C* · Emporia Train Depot, 400 Halifax St., 23847, P 18,000, M 385, (434) 634-9441, Fax (434) 634-3485, ontrack@telpage.net, www.emporia-greensville chamber.com

**Exmore** · *see Eastville*

**Fairfax** · *Central Fairfax C/C* · Melissa Choate, Pres./CEO, 11166 Fairfax Blvd. #407, 22030, P 200,000, M 750, (703) 591-2450, info@cfcc.org, www.cfcc.org

**Fairfax County** · *Fairfax County C/C* · William D. Lecos, Pres./ CEO, 8230 Old Courthouse Rd. #350, Vienna, 22182, P 1,041,200, M 1,800, (703) 749-0400, Fax (703) 749-9075, fairfaxchamber.org

**Falls Church** · *also see Fairfax County C/C*

**Falls Church** · *Greater Falls Church C/C* · Sally Cole, Exec. Dir., 417 W. Broad St. #205, 22046, P 10,000, M 250, (703) 532-1050, Fax (703) 237-7904, info@fallschurchchamber.org, www. fallschurchchamber.org

**Farmville** · *Farmville Area C/C* · 405 D E. Third St., P.O. Box 361, 23901, P 17,500, M 240, (434) 392-3939, Fax (434) 392-3818, wwhitus@farmvilleareachamber.org, www.farmvillearea chamber.org

**Fincastle** · *Botetourt County C/C* · Dan Naff, Exec. Dir., 13 W. Main St., P.O. Box 81, 24090, P 32,000, M 400, (540) 473-8280, Fax (540) 473-8365, bccoc@rbnet.com, www.bot-co-chamber.com

**Fishersville** · *Greater Augusta Reg. C/C* · Benjamin E. Carter IOM CAE, Pres./CEO, 30 Ladd Rd., P.O. Box 1107, 22939, P 104,000, M 1,104, (540) 324-1133, (540) 949-8203, Fax (540) 324-1136, chamber@ntelos.net, www.augustachamber.org

**Floyd** · *Floyd County C/C* · John McEnhill, Pres., 202 S. Locust, P.O. Box 510, 24091, P 14,000, M 200, (540) 745-4407, chamber@ swva.net, www.visitfloyd.org

**Forest** · *Bedford Area C/C-Forest Satellite Office* · Susan Martin, Pres., 14805 Forest Rd., Ste. 107, 24551, P 66,000, M 680, (434) 525-7860, Fax (434) 525-7862, chamberinfo@bedfordarea chamber.com, www.bedfordareachamber.com

**Franklin** · *Franklin-Southampton Area C/C* · Teresa Beale, Exec. Dir., 108 W. Third Ave., P.O. Box 531, 23851, P 25,500, M 250, (757) 562-4900, Fax (757) 562-6138, join@fsachamber.com, www.fsachamber.com

**Franklin County** · *see Rocky Mount*

**Frederick County** · *see Winchester*

**Fredericksburg** · *Fredericksburg Reg. C/C* · Robert Hagan, Pres., 2300 Fall Hill Ave., Ste. 240, P.O. Box 7476, 22404, P 290,600, M 1,100, (540) 373-9400, Fax (540) 373-9570, bob@fredericksburg chamber.org, www.fredericksburgchamber.org

**Front Royal** · *Front Royal-Warren County C/C* · Niki Findley, Pres., 104 E. Main St., 22630, P 34,000, M 605, (540) 635-3185, Fax (540) 635-9758, info@frontroyalchamber.com, www.front royalchamber.com

**Galax** · *Twin County Reg. C/C* · Judy Brannock, Exec. Dir., 405 N. Main St., 24333, P 53,900, M 320, (276) 236-2184, Fax (276) 236-1338, info@twincountychamber.com, www.twincountychamber.com.

**Gate City** · *Scott County C/C* · Penny Horton, Exec. Secy., 180 W. Jackson St., P.O. Box 609, 24251, P 23,403, M 110, (276) 386-6665, Fax (276) 386-6158, scottcc@mountnet.com, www.scottcountyva.org

**Giles County** · *Giles County C/C* · Barbara M. Stafford, Exec. Dir., 101 S. Main St., Pearisburg, 24134, P 17,000, M 150, (540) 921-5000, Fax (540) 921-3892, gcc@i-plus.net, www.gilescounty.org.

**Gloucester** · *Gloucester County C/C* · Beverly Teichs, Exec. Dir., 6688 Main St., 23061, P 35,000, M 300, (804) 693-2425, Fax (804) 693-7193, beverly@gloucestervachamber.org, www.gloucester vachamber.org

**Goochland** · *Goochland County C/C* · Doris Elderman, Exec. Dir., 2941 River Rd. W., P.O. Box 123, 23063, P 18,500, M 400, (804) 556-3811, Fax (804) 556-2131, director@goochlandchamber.org, www.goochlandchamber.org.

**Gretna** · *see Blairs*

**Grundy** · *Buchanan County C/C* · Mary M. Belcher, Exec. Dir., 20786A Riverside Dr., P.O. Box 2818, 24614, P 27,000, M 129, (276) 935-4147, bcchamber1@verizon.net

**Hampton** · *Virginia Peninsula C/C* · Dorothy Jordan, Pres./CEO, 21 Enterprise Pkwy., Ste. 100, 23666, P 450,000, M 2,800, (757) 262-2000, (800) 556-1822, Fax (757) 262-2009, vpcc@vpcc.org, www.vpcc.org.

**Hampton Roads** · *Hampton Roads C/C-Headquarters* · John A. Hornbeck Jr. CCE, Pres./CEO, 420 Bank St., P.O. Box 327, Norfolk, 23501, P 1,316,300, M 2,500, (757) 622-2312, Fax (757) 622-5563, info@hrccva.com, www.hamptonroadschamber.com.

**Harrisonburg** • *Harrisonburg-Rockingham C/C* • James Berg IOM, Pres./CEO, 800 Country Club Rd., 22802, P 113,900, M 850, (540) 434-3862, Fax (540) 434-4508, president@hrchamber.org, www.hrchamber.org

**Herndon** • *see Chantilly*

**Hillsville** • *Carroll County C/C* • 515 N. Main St., P.O. Box 1184, 24343, P 29,000, M 100, (276) 728-5397, Fax (276) 728-7825

**Hopewell** • *Hopewell-Prince George C/C* • Becky McDonough, Exec. V.P., 210 N. 2nd Ave., P.O. Box 1297, 23860, P 50,000, M 470, (804) 458-5536, Fax (804) 458-0041, becky@hpgchamber.org, www.hpgchamber.org

**Hot Springs** • *Bath County C/C* • Melinda Nichols, Exec. Dir., 2696 Main St., Ste. 6, P.O. Box 718, 24445, P 4,800, M 186, (540) 839-5409, (800) 628-8092, Fax (540) 839-5409, bathco@tds.net, www.discoverbath.com

**Huntington** • *see Fairfax County*

**Hurt** • *see Blairs*

**Irvington** • *Irvington Improvement Assn. & C/C* • Larry Worth, Pres., P.O. Box 282, 22480, P 450, M 100, (804) 438-9371, www.townofirvington.com

**Isle of Wight** • *see Smithfield*

**James City County** • *see Williamsburg and Hampton*

**Kenbridge** • *see Lunenburg*

**Kilmarnock** • *Kilmarnock C/C* • William Smith, Pres., P.O. Box 1357, 22482, P 1,200, M 80, (804) 435-2850, www.kilmarnock chamber.org

**Kilmarnock** • *Lancaster County C/C* • Edie Jett, Exec. Dir., 506 N. Main St., P.O. Box 1868, 22482, P 12,000, M 250, (804) 435-6092, Fax (804) 435-3092, info@lancasterva.com, www.lancasterva.com

**Lawrenceville** • *Brunswick C/C* • Mary Lucy, Exec. Dir., 400 N. Main St., 23868, P 18,400, M 115, (434) 848-3154, Fax (434) 848-9356, brunschamber@lawrencevilleweb.com, www.brunswick chamber.com

**Lebanon** • *Russell County C/C* • Linda Tate, Exec. Dir., 331 W. Main St., P.O. Box 926, 24266, P 30,000, M 200, (276) 889-8041, Fax (276) 889-8002, lindatate@bvunet.net, www.russellcountyva.org

**Leesburg** • *Loudoun County C/C* • Tony Howard, Pres., 19301 Winmeade Dr., Ste. 210, P.O. Box 1298, 20177, P 275,000, M 1,300, (703) 777-2176, Fax (703) 777-1392, info@loudounchamber.org, www.loudounchamber.org

**Lexington** • *Lexington-Rockbridge County C/C* • James Samuel Moore, Dir., 100 E. Washington St., 24450, P 35,000, M 520, (540) 463-5375, Fax (540) 463-3567, chamber@lexrockchamber.com, www.lexrockchamber.com

**VISIT HISTORIC LEXINGTON & ROCKBRIDGE COUNTY. HOME OF ROBERT E. LEE, 'STONEWALL' JACKSON, W&L, VMI, VA HORSE CTR, NATURAL BRIDGE, VIRGINIA HOSPITALITY**

**Loudoun County** • *see Leesburg*

**Louisa** • *Louisa County C/C* • Deana Meredith, Exec. Dir., 214 Fredericksburg Ave., P.O. Box 955, 23093, P 29,500, M 160, (540) 967-0944, info@louisachamber.org, www.louisachamber.org

**Lunenburg** • *Lunenburg County C/C* • General Delivery, 23952, P 13,194, M 100, (434) 696-2282, info@lunenburgva.org, www.lunenburgva.org

**Luray** • *Luray-Page County C/C* • 18 Campbell St., 22835, P 20,000, M 350, (540) 743-3915, (888) 743-3915, Fax (540) 743-3944, pcounty@embarqmail.com, www.luraypage.com

**Lynchburg** • *Lynchburg Reg. C/C* • Rex Hammond, Pres., 2015 Memorial Ave., 24501, P 230,000, M 960, (434) 845-5966, Fax (434) 522-9592, info@lynchburgchamber.org, www.lynchburg chamber.org.

**Madison** • *Madison C/C & Visitor Center* • Tracey Gardner, Exec. Dir., 110A N. Main, P.O. Box 373, 22727, P 13,000, M 210, (540) 948-4455, Fax (540) 948-3174, chamber@madison-va.com, www.madison-va.com

**Manassas** • *Prince William County-Greater Manassas C/C* • Deborah L. Jones, Pres., 8963 Center St., P.O. Box 495, 20108, P 400,000, M 1,000, (703) 368-6600, Fax (703) 368-4733, djones@pwcgmcc.org, www.pwcgmcc.org

**Marion** • *C/C of Smyth County* • Jerry Jones, Exec. Dir., 214 W. Main St., P.O. Box 924, 24354, P 33,081, M 500, (276) 783-3161, Fax (276) 783-8003, info@smythchamber.org, www.smythchamber.org.

**Martinsville** • *Martinsville-Henry County C/C* • Amanda Witt, Pres., 115 Broad St., P.O. Box 709, 24114, P 72,000, M 638, (276) 632-6401, (866) 632-3378, Fax (276) 632-5059, mhccoc@mhc chamber.com, www.martinsville.com.

**Massaponax** • *see Eastville*

**Mathews** • *Mathews County C/C* • Joe Syslo, Pres., P.O. Box 1126, 23109, P 9,100, M 107, (804) 725-9000, Fax (804) 725-9009, postmaster@mathewschamber.org, www.mathewschamber.org

**McLean** • *Greater McLean C/C* • Matthew Wallace, Pres., 1437 Balls Hill Rd., 22101, P 66,000, M 400, (703) 356-5424, Fax (703) 356-9244, info@mcleanchamber.org, www.mcleanchamber.org

**Melfa** • *Eastern Shore of Virginia C/C* • Jeff Davis, Pres., 19056 Parkway, P.O. Box 460, 23410, P 53,000, M 740, (757) 787-2460, Fax (757) 787-8687, info@esvachamber.org, www.esvachamber.org

**Merrifield** • *see Fairfax County*

**Moneta** • *Smith Mountain Lake C/C* • Vicki Gardner, Exec. Dir., 16430 Booker T. Washington Hwy. #2, Bridgewater Plaza, 24121, P 20,000, M 770, (540) 721-1203, (800) 676-8203, Fax (540) 721-7796, smlchamber@yahoo.com, www.visitsmithmountainlake.com

**Monterey** • *Highland County C/C* • Carolyn Pohowsky, Exec. Dir., 61 Highland Center Dr., Ste. 1, P.O. Box 223, 24465, P 2,635, M 196, (540) 468-2550, Fax (540) 468-2551, info@highlandcounty.org, www.highlandcounty.org

**Montross** • *Westmoreland County C/C* • Kay Campbell, Pres., P.O. Box 785, 22520, P 16,000, M 60, (804) 333-1974, www.wcchamber.com

**Mount Jackson** • *Mount Jackson Area C/C* • Stephen Kirchner, Pres., 5901 Main St., P.O. Box 111, 22842, P 1,800, M 100, (540) 477-3275, mjcc@shentel.net, www.mountjacksonva.org

**Mount Vernon-Lee** • *Mount Vernon-Lee C/C* • Holly Hicks Dougherty, Exec. Dir., 8804-D Pear Tree Village Ct., Alexandria, 22309, P 250,000, M 400, (703) 360-6925, Fax (703) 360-6928, info@MtVernon-LeeChamber.org, www.MtVernon-LeeChamber.org

**New Kent** • *New Kent C/C* • Scotty N. Hager, Pres., 7324 Vineyard Pkwy., 23124, P 15,000, M 150, (804) 966-8581, president@newkentchamber.org, www.newkentchamber.org

**New Market** • *New Market Area C/C* • Judy Delaughter, Pres., 100 W. Lee St., P.O. Box 57, 22844, P 1,800, M 106, (540) 740-3212, (877) 740-3212, Fax (540) 740-4234, nmchambr@shentel.net, www.newmarketcoc.net.

**Newington** • *see Fairfax County*

**Newport News** • *see Hampton*

**Norfolk** • *see Hampton Roads*

**Norton** · *Wise County C/C* · Joyce M. Payne, Exec. Dir., 765 Park Ave., P.O. Box 226, 24273, P 44,000, M 560, (276) 679-0961, Fax (276) 679-2655, wisecountycoc@verizon.net, www.wisecounty chamber.org.

**Oakton** · *see Fairfax County and Vienna*

**Orange** · *Orange County C/C* · Barbara Bannar, Exec. Dir., 103 N. Madison Rd., P.O. Box 146, 22960, P 29,000, M 250, (540) 672-5216, Fax (540) 672-2304, barbara@orangevachamber.com, www.orangevachamber.com

**Palmyra** · *Fluvanna County C/C* · Robert Mayfield, Pres., 177 Main St., P.O. Box 93, 22963, P 30,000, M 180, (434) 589-3262, Fax (434) 589-6212, fluvannacountycoc@embarqmail.com, www.fluvannachamber.org

**Pennington Gap** · *Lee County Area C/C* · P.O. Box 417, 24277, P 25,000, M 100, (276) 546-2233, info@leecountyvachamber.org, www.leecountyvachamber.org

**Petersburg** · *Petersburg C/C* · Cynthia Raitt Devereaux, Pres./CEO, 325 E. Washington St., P.O. Box 928, 23804, P 33,000, M 500, (804) 733-8131, Fax (804) 733-9891, info@petersburgvachamber.com, www.petersburgvachamber.com

**Poquoson** · *see Hampton*

**Portsmouth** · *see Hampton Roads*

**Powhatan** · *Powhatan C/C* · Tina Bustos, Exec. Dir., 3829 Old Buckingham Rd., P.O. Box 643, 23139, P 28,000, M 240, (804) 598-2636, Fax (804) 598-2636, powhatanchamber@verizon.net, www.powhatanchamberofcommerce.org

**Prince William** · *Prince William Reg. C/C* · Laurie Wieder, Pres., 4320 Ridgewood Center Dr., 22192, P 350,000, M 1,200, (703) 590-5000, Fax (703) 590-9815, pwrcc@regionalchamber.org, www.regionalchamber.org

**Pulaski** · *see Dublin*

**Radford** · *Radford C/C* · 27 W. Main St., 24141, P 16,000, M 300, (540) 639-2202, Fax (540) 639-2228, info@radfordchamber.com, www.radfordchamber.com

**Reston** · *also see Fairfax County C/C*

**Reston** · *Greater Reston C/C, Bus. & Visitors Center* · 1763 Fountain Dr., 20190, P 67,910, M 1,000, (703) 707-9045, Fax (703) 707-9049, restonbiz@restonchamber.org, www.restonchamber.org

**Richlands** · *Richlands Area/Tazewell County C/C* · Ginger H. Branton, Exec. Dir., 1413 Front St., 24641, P 5,400, M 300, (276) 963-3385, Fax (276) 963-4278, richlandschamber@roadrunner.com, richlandschamber.com

**Richmond** · *Greater Richmond C/C* · Kim Scheeler, Pres./CEO, 600 E. Main St., Ste. 700, P.O. Box 1598, 23218, P 1,000,000, M 2,000, (804) 648-1234, Fax (804) 783-9366, www.grcc.com.

**Roanoke** · *Roanoke Reg. C/C* · Joyce Waugh, Pres., 210 S. Jefferson St., 24011, P 295,529, M 1,400, (540) 983-0700, Fax (540) 983-0723, business@roanokechamber.org, www.roanokechamber.org.

**Rocky Mount** · *Franklin County C/C* · Janie Hopkins, Exec. Dir., 52 Franklin St., P.O. Box 158, 24151, P 52,841, M 350, (540) 483-9542, Fax (540) 483-0653, info@franklincounty.org, www.franklincounty.org

**Salem** · *Salem-Roanoke County C/C* · Debbie Kavitz, Exec. Dir., 611 E. Main St., P.O. Box 832, 24153, P 110,773, M 500, (540) 387-0267, Fax (540) 387-4110, chamber@s-rcchamber.org, www.s-rcchamber.org

**Scottsville** · *Scottsville Comm. C/C* · Brian LaFontaine, Pres., P.O. Box 11, 24590, P 560, M 110, (434) 286-6000, sccc@bnsi.net, www.scottsvilleva.com

**Seven Corners** · *see Fairfax County*

**Smithfield** · *Isle of Wight-Smithfield-Windsor C/C* · Constance Rhodes, Pres., 100 Main St., P.O. Box 38, 23431, P 35,000, M 450, (757) 357-3502, (888) 284-3475, Fax (757) 357-6884, chamber@theisle.org, www.theisle.org

**South Boston** · *Halifax County C/C* · Nancy Pool, Pres., 515 Broad St., P.O. Box 399, 24592, P 37,500, M 415, (434) 572-3085, Fax (434) 572-1733, info@halifaxchamber.net, www.halifaxchamber.net.

**South Hill** · *South Hill C/C* · Frank Malone, Exec. Dir., 201 S. Mecklenburg Ave., 23970, P 5,000, M 300, (434) 447-4547, Fax (434) 447-4461, frank@southhillchamber.com, www.southhillchamber.com

**Spotsylvania** · *see Fredericksburg*

**Springfield** · *Greater Springfield C/C* · Nancy-jo Manney, Exec. Dir., 6434 Brandon Ave. #3A, 22150, P 90,000, M 300, (703) 866-3500, Fax (703) 866-3501, admin@springfieldchamber.org, www.springfieldchamber.org

**Stafford** · *see Fredericksburg*

**Staunton** · *see Fishersville*

**Stony Creek** · *Sussex County C/C* · Debbie Robinson, Exec. Dir., P.O. Box 466, 23882, P 10,000, M 40, (804) 248-2223, Fax (804) 248-2223, info@sussexvachamber.org, www.sussexvachamber.org

**Strasburg** · *Strasburg C/C* · Jackie Thompson, Admin. Asst., 160 E. King St., P.O. Box 42, 22657, P 5,000, M 150, (540) 465-3187, Fax (540) 465-2812, schamber@shentel.net, www.strasburgvachamber.com

**Stuart** · *Patrick County C/C* · Tom Bishop, Exec. Dir., 20475 Jeb Stuart Hwy., P.O. Box 577, 24171, P 19,407, M 300, (276) 694-6012, Fax (276) 694-3582, patcchamber@embarqmail.com, www.patrickchamber.com

**Suffolk** · *see Hampton Roads*

**Surry** · *Surry County C/C* · 267 Church St., P.O. Box 353, 23883, P 6,800, M 35, (757) 294-0066, (877) 290-0066, www.surrychamber.org

**Tappahannock** · *Tappahannock-Essex County C/C* · Linda E. Lumpkin, Exec. Secy., P.O. Box 481, 22560, P 10,000, M 200, (804) 443-5241, Fax (804) 443-4157, www.essex-virginia.org

**Tazewell** · *Tazewell Area C/C* · Rebecca Duncan, Dir., Tazewell Mall, Box 6, 24651, P 47,070, M 250, (276) 988-5091, Fax (276) 988-5093, info@tazewellchamber.org, www.tazewellchamber.org

**Timberville** · *Broadway-Timberville C/C* · Crystal Collins, Secy., 233 McCauley Dr., 22853, P 4,000, M 100, (540) 896-7413, Fax (540) 896-2825, secretary@btchamber.org, www.btchamber.org

**Tysons Corner** · *see Vienna*

**Victoria** · *see Lunenburg*

**Vienna** · *Vienna-Tysons Reg. C/C* · Diane Poldy, Pres., 513 Maple Ave. W., 2nd Flr., 22180, P 1,000,000, M 446, (703) 281-1333, Fax (703) 242-1482, info@vtrcc.org, www.vtrcc.org

**Vinton** · *Vinton Area C/C* · Judy Cunningham, Exec. Dir., 116 S. Poplar St., Ste. 2, 24179, P 8,000, M 180, (540) 343-1364, www.vintonchamber.com

**Virginia Beach** · *see Hampton Roads*

**Warren County** · *see Front Royal*

**Warrenton** · *Fauquier County C/C* · Karen Henderson, Pres., 205-1 Keith St., P.O. Box 127, 20188, P 57,000, M 639, (540) 347-4414, Fax (540) 347-7510, mailbox@fauquierchamber.org, www.fauquierchamber.org

**Warsaw** • *Warsaw-Richmond County C/C* • Cheryl Alderman, Dir., P.O. Box 1141, 22572, P 8,000, M 80, (804) 313-2252, cheryl.alderman@vec.virginia.gov, www.warsaw-rcchamber.com

**Waynesboro** • *see Fishersville*

**West Point** • *West Point/Tri-Rivers C/C* • John Crowder, Pres., 621 Main St., P.O. Box 1035, 23181, P 3,000, M 60, (804) 843-4620, wptrcc@oasisonline.com, www.westpointvachamber.com

**Williamsburg** • *Greater Williamsburg C/C & Tourism Alliance* • Richard Schreiber, Pres./CEO, 421 N. Boundary St., P.O. Box 3495, 23187, P 130,000, M 967, (757) 229-6511, (800) 368-6511, Fax (757) 229-2047, wacc@williamsburgcc.com, www.williamsburgcc.com

**Winchester** • *Top of Virginia Reg. Chamber* • Randy Collins IOM, Pres./CEO, 407 S. Loudon St., 22601, P 90,000, M 1,200, (540) 662-4118, Fax (540) 722-6365, cocinfo@regionalchamber.biz, www.regionalchamber.biz

**Windsor** • *see Smithfield*

**Wise County** • *see Norton*

**Woodstock** • *Woodstock C/C* • Alma F. Hottle, Exec. Secy., 140 N. Main St., P.O. Box 605, 22664, P 4,000, M 245, (540) 459-2542, Fax (540) 459-2513, www.woodstockvachamber.com.

**Wythe County** • *see Wytheville*

**Wytheville** • *Wytheville-Wythe-Bland C/C* • Jennifer W. Jones, Exec. Dir., 150 E. Monroe St., P.O. Box 563, 24382, P 34,470, M 456, (276) 223-3365, Fax (276) 223-3412, chamber@wytheville.org, www.wwbchamber.com.

**York County** • *see Hampton and Williamsburg*

**Yorktown** • *York County C/C* • William Jarrett, Pres., 5030 George Washington Mem. Hwy., 23692, P 40,000, M 360, (757) 877-5920, Fax (757) 969-5190, ycccadmin@yorkcountycc.org, www.yorkcountychamberva.org

# Washington

**Assn. Of Washington Business** • Don Brunell, Pres., 1414 Cherry St. S.E., P.O. Box 658, Olympia, 98507, P 5,400,000, M 6,200, (360) 943-1600, (800) 521-9325, Fax (360) 943-5811, members@awb.org, www.awb.org

**Washington C of C Execs.** • Robert Green, Admin., P.O. Box 1349, Enumclaw, 98022, M 125, (360) 802-4595, Fax (877) 381-8834, information@wcce.org, www.wcce.org.

**Aberdeen** • *Grays Harbor C/C* • LeRoy Tipton, Pres., 506 Duffy St., 98520, P 68,400, M 650, (360) 532-1924, (800) 321-1924, Fax (360) 533-7945, info@graysharbor.org, www.graysharbor.org.

**Airway Heights** • *see Cheney*

**Allyn** • *see Belfair*

**Amboy** • *see La Center*

**Anacortes** • *Anacortes C/C* • Mitch Everton, Exec. Dir., 819 Commercial Ave., Ste. F, 98221, P 20,000, M 437, (360) 293-7911, (360) 293-3832, Fax (360) 293-1595, info@anacortes.org, www.anacortes.org

**Arlington** • *Arlington-Smokey Point C/C* • Jennifer Shaw, Exec. Dir., 3710 168th St. N.E., Ste. C101, 98223, P 17,000, M 300, (360) 659-5453, Fax (360) 657-1002, jennifer@arlington-smokeypointchamber.com, www.arlington-smokeypointchamber.com

**Asotin** • *Asotin C/C* • Wes Vaughn, Pres., P.O. Box 574, 99402, P 1,200, M 20, (509) 243-4242, Fax (509) 243-4243, www.cityofasotin.org

**Auburn** • *Auburn Area C/C* • Nancy Wyatt, Pres./CEO, 108 S. Division #B, 98001, P 67,000, M 600, (253) 833-0700, Fax (253) 735-4091, auburncc@auburnareawa.org, www.auburnareawa.org.

**Bader** • *see Winlock*

**Bainbridge Island** • *Bainbridge Island C/C* • Kevin Dwyer, Exec. Dir., 590 Winslow Way E., 98110, P 23,000, M 1,000, (206) 842-3700, Fax (206) 842-3713, info@bainbridgechamber.com, www.bainbridgechamber.com

**Ballard** • *see Seattle-Ballard C/C*

**Battle Ground** • *Battle Ground C/C* • Diane Rivera, Exec. Dir., 2210 W. Main St., Ste. 107, Box 345, 98604, P 16,000, M 374, (360) 687-1510, Fax (360) 687-4505, info@battlegroundchamber.org, www.battlegroundchamber.org

**Beacon Hill** • *see Seattle-Beacon Hill C/C*

**Belfair** • *North Mason C/C* • Frank Kenny, Pres./CEO, 23910 N.E. State Rte. 3, P.O. Box 416, 98528, P 22,000, M 350, (360) 275-4267, Fax (360) 277-0679, communications@northmasonchamber.com, www.northmasonchamber.com

**Bellevue** • *Bellevue C/C* • Betty Nokes, Pres./CEO, 302 Bellevue Sq., 98004, P 117,000, M 1,100, (425) 454-2464, Fax (425) 462-4660, staffteam@bellevuechamber.org, www.bellevuechamber.org

**Bellingham** • *Bellingham/Whatcom C/C & Ind.* • Ken Oplinger, Pres./CEO, 119 N. Commercial Street, Ste. 110, P.O. Box 958, 98227, P 175,000, M 800, (360) 734-1330, Fax (360) 734-1332, chamber@bellingham.com, www.bellingham.com

**Benton City** • *Benton City C/C* • Robbin Hall, Pres., P.O. Box 401, 99320, P 2,800, M 60, (509) 588-4984, info@bentoncitychamber.org, www.bentoncitychamber.org

**Bingen** • *see White Salmon*

**Birch Bay** • *Birch Bay C/C & Visitors Info. Center* • Lisa Guthrie, Pres., 4550 Birch Bay Lynden Rd., PMB B119, 98230, P 6,800, M 160, (360) 371-5004, Fax (360) 371-5004, info@birchbaychamber.com, www.birchbaychamber.com

**Blaine** • *Blaine Comm. C/C* • Ron Spanjer, Pres., 728 Peace Portal Dr., 98230, P 4,800, M 70, (360) 332-6484, (800) 624-3555, Fax (360) 332-4544, info@blainechamber.com, www.blainechamber.com

**Bonney Lake** • *Bonney Lake C/C* • Lora Butterfield, Exec. Dir., P.O. Box 7171, 98391, P 13,000, M 111, (253) 222-5945, lora@bonneylake.com, www.bonneylake.com

**Bothell** • *Greater Bothell C/C* • Lori Cadwell, Exec. Dir., P.O. Box 1203, 98041, P 30,000, M 275, (425) 485-4353, Fax (425) 368-0396, info@bothellchamber.com, www.bothellchamber.com

**Bremerton** • *Bremerton Area C/C* • Silvia Klatman, Exec. Dir., 286 Fourth St., P.O. Box 229, 98337, P 39,000, M 550, (360) 479-3579, Fax (360) 479-1033, chamber@bremertonchamber.org, www.bremertonchamber.org.

**Brewster** • *Brewster C/C* • JD Smith, Bd. Member, P.O. Box 1087, 98812, P 2,195, M 66, (509) 689-3464, info@brewsterchamber.org, www.brewsterchamber.org

**Bridgeport** • *Bridgeport Area C/C* • Charlene Knox, Pres., P.O. Box 1060, 98813, P 2,150, M 25, (509) 686-0369, Fax (509) 686-2221, bridgeportchamber@yahoo.com, www.bridgeport-washington.com

**Brier** • *see Lynnwood*

**Brinnon** • *see Quilcene*

**Buckley** • *Buckley C/C* • 121 N. Cottage St., P.O. Box 168, 98321, P 4,000, M 75, (360) 829-0975, Fax (360) 829-6543, www.buckleychamber.org

**Burien** • *see Seattle-Southwest King County C/C*

**Burlington** · *Burlington C/C* · Linda Aufrecht, 111 S, Cherry St., P.O. Box 1087, 98233, P 8,421, M 380, (360) 757-0994, Fax (360) 757-0821, info@burlington-chamber.com, www.burlington-chamber.com

**Camano Island** · *Camano Island C/C* · Karen Daum, Dir. of Tourism & Op., 370 N. East Camano Dr., Ste. 5-80, 98282, P 18,000, M 130, (360) 629-7136, Fax (360) 629-7136, chamber@camano island.org, www.camanoisland.org

**Camas** · *Camas-Washougal C/C* · Brent Erickson, Exec. Dir., 422 N.E. 4th Ave., P.O. Box 919, 98607, P 37,000, M 345, (360) 834-2472, info@cwchamber.com, www.cwchamber.com.

**Carnation** · *Carnation C/C* · Kirsten Greenlaw, Pres., P.O. Box 603, 98014, P 1,900, M 50, (425) 444-9314, www.carnationchamber.com

**Cashmere** · *Cashmere C/C* · Sara Urdahl, Mgr., 204 Cottage Ave., P.O. Box 834, 98815, P 2,900, M 100, (509) 782-7404, Fax (509) 782-1265, info@cashmerechamber.com, www.cashmerechamber.com

**Cathlamet** · *Wahkiakum County C/C & Visitors Info. Center* · Ashley Eckert, Chamber Coord., 102 Main St., Ste. 205, P.O. Box 52, 98612, P 4,000, M 180, (360) 795-9996, Fax (360) 795-3944, wchamber@cni.net, www.cathlametchamber.com

**Centralia** · *see Chehalis*

**Chehalis** · *Centralia-Chehalis C/C* · Vernadel Peterson, Pres./ CEO, 500 N.W. Chamber of Commerce Way, 98532, P 72,500, M 775, (360) 748-8885, Fax (360) 748-8763, thechamber@ chamberway.com, www.chamberway.com.

**Chelan** · *Lake Chelan C/C* · Mike Steele, Exec. Dir., 102 E. Johnson Ave., P.O. Box 216, 98816, P 10,000, M 525, (509) 682-3503, (800) 4-CHELAN, Fax (509) 682-3538, info@lakechelan.com, www.lakechelan.com

**Cheney** · *West Plains C/C* · Matthew Pederson, Exec. Dir., 201 First St., 99004, P 60,000, M 200, (509) 235-8480, (509) 299-8480, Fax (509) 235-9338, chamberoffice@westplainschamber.org, www.westplainschamber.org

**Chewelah** · *Chewelah C/C* · Jeanne Nixon, Mgr., 214 E. Main St., P.O. Box 94, 99109, P 2,500, M 120, (509) 935-8595, Fax (509) 935-8520, info@chewelah.org, www.chewelah.org

**Chimacum** · *see Port Hadlock*

**Clallam Bay** · *Clallam Bay-Sekiu C/C & Visitor Center* · Brian Adler, Pres., 16795 Hwy. 112, P.O. Box 355, 98326, P 1,000, M 70, (360) 963-2339, (877) 694-9433, chamber@clallambay.com, www.clallambay.com

**Clarkston** · *Clarkston C/C* · Kristin Kemak, Exec. Dir., 502 Bridge St., 99403, P 8,000, M 450, (509) 758-7712, (800) 933-2128, Fax (509) 751-8767, info@clarkstonchamber.org, www.clarkston chamber.org.

**Cle Elum** · *Cle Elum - Roslyn C/C* · Judy Moen Tokarsyck, Exec. Dir., 401 W. 1st, P.O. Box 43, 98922, P 3,200, M 157, (509) 674-5958, Fax (509) 674-1674, cle_elum@cleelum.com, www. cleelumroslyn.org

**Colfax** · *Colfax C/C* · Judy Liddle, Secy., 109 E. Wall, 99111, P 3,000, M 120, (509) 397-3712, Fax (509) 397-4458, chamber@ colfax.com, www.visitcolfax.com

**Colville** · *Colville C/C* · Tricia Woods, Mgr., 121 E. Astor, 99114, P 5,000, M 300, (509) 684-5973, Fax (509) 684-1344, colvillecoc@ colville.com, www.colville.com

**Conconully** · *Town of Conconully C/C* · Tom Gibson, Pres., P.O. Box 309, 98819, P 210, M 58, (509) 826-9050, (877) 826-9050, conconullychamber@yahoo.com, www.conconully.com

**Concrete** · *Concrete C/C* · Valerie Stafford, Pres., 45909 Main St., P.O. Box 743, 98237, P 4,500, M 45, (360) 853-7042, ccof@ concrete-wa.com, www.concrete-wa.com

**Connell** · *Greater Connell Area C/C* · Monica Pruett, Admin., 600 S. Columbia, P.O. Box 401, 99326, P 3,100, M 70, (509) 234-8731, Fax (509) 234-8722, cityofconnell.com

**Cosmopolis** · *see Aberdeen*

**Coulee City** · *Coulee City C/C* · Alan Fox, Pres., P.O. Box 896, 99115, P 550, M 50, (509) 632-5043

**Coupeville** · *Central Whidbey C/C & Visitors Info. Center* · Lynda Eccles, Exec. Dir., 107 S. Main St., Bldg. E, P.O. Box 152, 98239, P 2,000, M 165, (360) 678-5434, (360) 678-5664, Fax (360) 678-5564, director@centralwhidbeychamber.com, www. centralwhidbeychamber.com

**Crescent Bar** · *see Quincy*

**Dallesport** · *see White Salmon*

**Davenport** · *Davenport C/C* · Danita Hammond, Pres., P.O. Box 869, 99122, P 1,780, M 90, (509) 725-6711, www.davenportwa.org

**Dayton** · *Dayton C of C & Visitor Center* · Lisa Ronnberg, Exec. Dir., 166 E. Main, 99328, P 4,100, M 196, (509) 382-4825, (800) 882-6299, Fax (509) 382-1969, chamber@historicdayton.com, www.historicdayton.com

**Deer Park** · *Deer Park C/C* · Cordelia Jeffery, Ofc. Mgr., 316 E. Crawford, Ste. A, P.O. Box 518, 99006, P 3,150, M 110, (509) 276-5900, Fax (509) 276-5900, info@DeerParkChamber.com, www. DeerParkChamber.com

**Dungeness Valley** · *see Sequim*

**Duvall** · *Duvall C/C* · Peggy Kahler, Pres., 15321 Main St. N.E. #320B, 98019, P 5,600, M 180, (425) 788-9182, (425) 788-8384, info@duvallchamberofcommerce.com, www.duvallchamber ofcommerce.com

**East Wenatchee** · *see Wenatchee*

**Eastsound** · *Orcas Island C/C* · Lance Evans, Exec. Dir., 65 N. Beach Rd., P.O. Box 252, 98245, P 5,000, M 315, (360) 376-2273, Fax (360) 376-8889, info@orcasislandchamber.com, www.orcas islandchamber.com

**Eatonville** · *Greater Eatonville C/C* · P.O. Box 845, 98328, P 2,100, M 97, (360) 832-4000, info@eatonvillechamber.com, www.eatonvillechamber.com

**Edmonds** · *Greater Edmonds C/C* · Jan Vance, Exec. Dir., 121 5th Ave. N., P.O. Box 146, 98020, P 40,000, M 420, (425) 670-1496, Fax (425) 712-1808, admin@edmondswa.com, www.edmondswa. com, www.everythingedmonds.com

**Ellensburg** · *Ellensburg C/C* · Marshall Madsen, Exec. Dir., 609 N. Main St., 98926, P 18,000, M 500, (509) 925-2002, (888) 925-2204, Fax (509) 962-6148, info@ellensburg-chamber.com, www. ellensburg-chamber.com.

**Elma** · *Elma C/C* · Kerry Dickman, Pres., P.O. Box 798, 98541, P 3,400, M 100, (360) 482-3055, www.elmachamber.org

**Enumclaw** · *Enumclaw Area C/C* · Cathy Rigg IOM, Exec. Dir., 1421 Cole St., 98022, P 11,400, M 250, (360) 825-7666, Fax (360) 825-8369, info@enumclawchamber.com, www.enumclawchamber.com

**Enumclaw** · *Washington C of C Execs.* · Robert Green, Admin., P.O. Box 1349, 98022, M 125, (360) 802-4595, Fax (877) 381-8834, information@wcce.org, www.wcce.org.

**Ephrata** · *Ephrata C/C* · Tia Tracy, Dir., 1 Basin St. S.W., P.O. Box 275, 98823, P 7,101, M 265, (509) 754-4656, Fax (509) 754-5788, info@ephratawachamber.com, www.ephratawachamber.com

**Everett** · *Everett Area C/C* · Louise Stanton-Masten, Pres./ CEO, 2000 Hewitt Ave., Ste. 205, 98201, P 101,000, M 600, (425) 257-3222, Fax (425) 257-2074, info@everettchamber.com, www.everettchamber.com

**Everson** · *Everson Nooksack C/C* · Kelly Isfeld, Pres., 103 W. Main St., P.O. Box 234, 98247, P 3,000, M 90, (360) 966-3407, info@eversonnooksackchamber.org, www.eversonnooksackchamber.org

**Fairfield** · *Hangman Creek C/C* · Ken Fuchs, Pres., P.O. Box 345, 99012, P 1,719, M 43, (509) 283-2414, hangmancreekchamber.com

**Fall City** · *see North Bend*

**Federal Way** · *Federal Way C/C* · Tom Pierson, Pres./CEO, 31919 1st Ave. S., Ste. 202, P.O. Box 3440, 98003, P 85,000, M 600, (253) 838-2605, Fax (253) 661-9050, federalway@federalwaychamber. com, www.federalwaychamber.com

**Ferndale** · *Ferndale C/C* · Guy Occhiogrosso, Dir., 5683 2nd Ave., P.O. Box 1264, 98248, P 10,800, M 170, (360) 384-3042, Fax (360) 384-3009, info@ferndale-chamber.com, www.ferndale-chamber.com

**Fife** · *Fife Reg. C/C* · P.K. MacLean, Exec. Dir., 5303 Pacific Hwy. E., PMB 272, 98424, P 15,000, M 350, (253) 922-9320, Fax (253) 922-1638, info@fifechamber.org, www.fifechamber.org.

**Forks** · *Forks C/C* · Marcia Bingham, Dir., 1411 S. Forks Ave., P.O. Box 1249, 98331, P 5,500, M 300, (360) 374-2531, (800) 44-FORKS, Fax (360) 374-9253, info@forkswa.com, www.forkswa.com

**Frederickson** · *see Puyallup*

**Freeland** · *Freeland C/C* · Renate Audette, Admin., 1664 E. Main St., P.O. Box 361, 98249, P 1,700, M 160, (360) 331-1980, Fax (360) 331-1980, freeland@whidbey.com, www.freeland-wa.org

**Friday Harbor** · *San Juan Island C/C* · Debbie Pigman, Exec. Dir., 135 Spring St., P.O. Box 98, 98250, P 8,000, M 360, (360) 378-5240, Fax (360) 370-5289, chamberinfo@sanjuanisland.org, www.sanjuanisland.org

**George** · *see Quincy*

**Gig Harbor** · *Gig Harbor Peninsula Area C/C* · Warren Zimmerman, Exec. Dir., 3311 Harborview Dr., Ste. 101, P.O. Box 102, 98335, P 66,000, M 500, (253) 851-6865, (800) 359-8804, executivedirector@gigharborchamber.com, www.gigharborchamber.com

**Glenwood** · *see White Salmon*

**Goldendale** · *Greater Goldendale Area C/C* · Mindy Blomquist, Exec. Dir., 903 E. Broadway, 98620, P 6,000, M 150, (509) 773-3400, Fax (509) 773-3411, info@goldendalechamber.org, www.goldendalechamber.org

**Graham** · *see Puyallup*

**Grand Coulee** · *Grand Coulee Dam Area C/C* · Susan Miller, Exec. Dir., 306 Midway, P.O. Box 760, 99133, P 4,000, M 100, (509) 633-3074, (800) 268-5332, Fax (509) 633-2366, chamber@grandcouleedam.org, www.grandcouleedam.org

**Grandview** · *Grandview C/C* · 133 W. 2nd St., 98930, P 9,150, M 350, (509) 882-2100, Fax (509) 882-5014, grancofc@grandviewchamber.com, www.grandviewchamber.com

**Granger** · *Granger C/C* · P.O. Box 250, 98932, P 3,000, M 45, (509) 854-7304, grangerchamber@gmail.com, www.grangerchamber.org

**Grapeview** · *see Belfair*

**Grayland** · *Cranberry Coast C/C* · Beverly Ripley, P.O. Box 305, 98547, P 3,000, M 60, (360) 267-2003, (800) 473-6018, Fax (360) 267-2003, info@2thebeach.org, www.2thebeach.org, www.cranberrycoastcoc.com

**Grays Harbor** · *see Aberdeen*

**Grays River** · *see Cathlamet*

**Greenbank** · *see Coupeville*

**Hockinson** · *see La Center*

**Hoquiam** · *see Aberdeen*

**Husum** · *see White Salmon*

**Irondale** · *see Port Hadlock*

**Issaquah** · *Issaquah C/C* · Matthew Bott, CEO, 155 N.W. Gilman Blvd., 98027, P 24,710, M 450, (425) 392-7024, Fax (425) 392-8101, info@issaquahchamber.com, www.issaquahchamber.com

**Kalama** · *Kalama C/C* · Vic Leatzow, Pres., P.O. Box 824, 98625, P 3,000, M 80, (360) 673-6299, kalamachamber@kalama.com, www.cityofkalama.com

**Kelso** · *see Longview*

**Kenmore** · *see Bothell*

**Kennewick** · *Tri City Reg. C/C* · Lori Mattson, Pres./CEO, 7130 W. Grandridge Blvd., Ste. C, 99336, P 275,000, M 1,350, (509) 736-0510, Fax (509) 783-1733, info@tricityregionalchamber.com, www.tricityregionalchamber.com

**Kent** · *Kent C/C* · 524 W. Meeker #1, P.O. Box 128, 98035, P 86,660, M 500, (253) 854-1770, Fax (253) 854-8567, info@kentchamber.com, www.kentchamber.com

**Kettle Falls** · *Kettle Falls Area C/C* · Cheryl Largent, Pres., 425 W. 3rd, P.O. Box 119, 99141, P 1,600, M 80, (509) 738-2300, www.kettlefalls.com

**Kingston** · *Greater Kingston C/C* · Linda Fyfe, Exec. Dir., 11201 N.E. State Hwy. 104, P.O. Box 78, 98346, P 4,900, M 220, (360) 297-3813, Fax (360) 297-3813, exec@kingstonchamber.com, www.kingstonchamber.com

**Kirkland** · *Greater Kirkland C/C* · Bill Vadino, Exec. Dir., 401 Parkplace #102, 98033, P 65,000, M 400, (425) 822-7066, Fax (425) 827-4878, info@kirklandchamber.org, www.kirklandchamber.org

**Klickitat** · *see White Salmon*

**La Center** · *La Center North Clark County C/C* · Wendy McGraw, Pres., P.O. Box 83, 98629, P 6,000, M 50, (360) 263-4636, wendy@lacenternorthclarkcountychamber.com, www.lacenternorthclarkcountychamber.com

**La Conner** · *La Conner C/C* · Marci Plank, Exec. Dir., 606 Morris St., P.O. Box 1610, 98257, P 900, M 160, (360) 466-4778, (888) 642-9284, Fax (360) 466-0204, info@laconnerchamber.com, www.laconnerchamber.com

**Lacey** · *Lacey C/C* · Jenny Thorsell, Exec. Dir., 8300 Quinault Dr. N.E., Ste. A, 98516, P 35,000, M 350, (360) 491-4141, Fax (360) 491-9403, info@laceychamber.com, www.laceychamber.com

**Lake Stevens** · *Greater Lake Stevens C/C* · Donna Foster, Ofc. Mgr., 9327 4th St. N.E., Ste. 7, P.O. Box 439, 98258, P 36,000, M 200, (425) 334-0433, info@lakestevenschamber.com, www.lakestevenschamber.com

**Lakewood** · *Lakewood C/C* · Linda K. Smith, Pres./CEO, 4650 Steilacoom Blvd. S.W., Bldg. 19, Ste. 109, 98499, P 60,000, M 500, (253) 582-9400, Fax (253) 581-5241, chamber@lakewood-wa.com, www.lakewood-wa.com.

**Langley** · *Langley C/C & Visitor Info. Center* · Sherry Mays, Exec. Dir., 208 Anthes Ave., P.O. Box 403, 98260, P 15,700, M 205, (360) 221-6765, www.visitlangley.com

**Latah** · *see Fairfield*

**Leavenworth** • *Leavenworth C/C* • Nancy Smith, Exec. Dir., 940 Hwy. 2, Ste. B, P.O. Box 327, 98826, P 2,300, M 540, (509) 548-5807, Fax (509) 548-1014, info@leavenworth.org, www. leavenworth.org

**Liberty Lake** • *see Spokane Valley*

**Lind** • *Lind C/C* • P.O. Box 561, 99341, P 500, M 20, (509) 677-3655, lindchamber@ritzcom.net, www.lindwa.com

**Longview** • *Kelso Longview C/C* • Rick Winsman, Pres./CEO, 1563 Olympia Way, 98632, P 46,000, M 785, (360) 423-8400, Fax (360) 423-0432, info@kelsolongviewchamber.org, www. kelsolongviewchamber.org

**Lopez Island** • *Lopez Island C/C* • Lia Noreen, Ofc. Mgr., P.O. Box 102, 98261, P 2,300, M 130, (360) 468-4664, (877) 433-2789, lopezchamber@lopezisland.com, www.lopezisland.com

**Lyle** • *see White Salmon*

**Lynden** • *Lynden C/C* • Gary Vis, Dir., 518 Front St., 98264, P 12,000, M 340, (360) 354-5995, Fax (360) 354-0401, lynden@ lynden.org, www.lynden.org

**Lynnwood** • *South Snohomish County C/C* • Jean Hales, Pres./ CEO, 3815 196th St. S.W. #136, 98036, P 150,000, M 500, (425) 774-0507, Fax (425) 774-4636, info@s2c3.com, www.s2c3.com

**Maple Valley** • *Greater Maple Valley-Black Diamond C/C* • Melanie Johnson, Ofc. Mgr., 22035 S.E. Wax Rd., P.O. Box 302, 98038, P 35,000, M 343, (425) 432-0222, Fax (425) 413-8017, chamber@maplevalley.com, www.maplevalley.com

**Marcus** • *see Kettle Falls*

**Marysville** • *see Tulalip*

**Maury Island** • *see Vashon*

**McCleary** • *McCleary Comm. C/C* • Destiny Frahm, Pres., 100 S. 3rd St., P.O. Box 53, 98557, P 1,600, M 30, (360) 495-3667, www. mcclearychamber.org

**McKenna** • *see Yelm*

**Medical Lake** • *see Cheney*

**Mercer Island** • *Mercer Island C/C* • Terry Moreman, Exec. Dir., 7605 S.E. 27th #109, P.O. Box 108, 98040, P 23,000, M 225, (206) 232-3404, Fax (206) 232-8903, mi_chamber@msn.com, www. mercerislandchamber.org

**Metaline Falls** • *Metalines C/C* • Don Wilson, Pres., P.O. Box 388, 99153, P 350, M 40, (509) 446-1721

**Mill Creek** • *see Bothell*

**Millwood** • *see Spokane Valley*

**Milton** • *see Puyallup*

**Monroe** • *Monroe C of C & Visitor Info. Center* • Neil Watkins, Exec. Dir., 111 W. Main St., 98272, P 16,700, M 410, (360) 794-5488, Fax (360) 794-2044, neil@chamber-monroe.org, www. monroewachamber.com

**Montesano** • *Montesano C/C & Visitor Info. Center* • P.O. Box 688, 98563, P 3,300, M 100, (360) 249-5522, info@montesano chamber.org, www.montesanochamber.org

**Morton** • *Morton C/C* • 1391 Main St., P.O. Box 10, 98356, P 1,200, M 50, (360) 496-6086, Fax (360) 496-6210, chamber@ lewiscounty.com, mortonchamber.lewiscounty.com

**Moses Lake** • *Moses Lake Area C/C* • Debbie Doran-Martinez, Exec. Dir., 324 S. Pioneer Way, 98837, P 35,000, M 400, (509) 765-7888, (800) 992-6234, Fax (509) 765-7891, information@ moseslake.com, www.moseslake.com

**Mount St. Helens** • *see Touttle*

**Mount Vernon** • *Mount Vernon C/C* • Kristen Whitener IOM, Pres./CEO, 105 E. Kincaid St., Ste. 101, P.O. Box 1007, 98273, P 32,000, M 485, (360) 428-8547, Fax (360) 424-6237, info@ mountvernonchamber.com, www.mountvernonchamber.com

**Mountlake Terrace** • *see Lynnwood*

**Mukilteo** • *see Lynnwood*

**Naselle** • *see Cathlamet*

**Newport** • *Newport Oldtown C/C* • David Livingston, Exec. Dir., 325 W. 4th St., 99156, P 2,040, M 117, (509) 447-5812, (877) 818-1008, Fax (509) 447-5812, chamber@conceptcable.com, www. newportoldtownchamber.org

**Nooksack** • *see Everson*

**Normandy Park** • *see Seattle-Southwest King County C/C*

**North Bend** • *Snoqualmie Valley C/C* • Karen Granger, Exec. Dir., P.O. Box 357, 98045, P 39,000, M 350, (425) 888-4440, Fax (425) 888-4665, info@snovalley.org, www.snovalley.org

**North Creek Area** • *see Bothell*

**Oak Harbor** • *Greater Oak Harbor C/C & Visitor Info. Center* • Jill Johnson, Exec. Dir., 32630 S.R. 20, P.O. Box 883, 98277, P 42,000, M 480, (360) 675-3535, (360) 675-3755, Fax (360) 679-1624, info@oakharborchamber.com, www.oakharbor chamber.com.

**Oakville** • *Oakville C/C* • Janice Howell, Pres., P.O. Box 331, 98568, P 1,000, M 30, (360) 273-2702, info@oakville-wa.org, www.oakville-wa.org

**Ocean City** • *Washington Coast C/C* • Patricia Cox, Publ. Rel., 2616-A State Rte. 109, 98569, P 4,000, M 50, (360) 289-4552, info@ washingtoncoastchamber.org, www.washingtoncoastchamber.org

**Ocean Park** • *Ocean Park Area C/C* • Phyllis Knight, Pres., 1715 Bay Ave., P.O. Box 403, 98640, P 1,400, M 75, (360) 665-4448, (888) 751-9354, opchamber@opwa.com, www.opwa.com

**Ocean Shores** • *Ocean Shores/North Beach C/C* • Leslie Reedy, Exec. Dir., 873 Pt. Brown Ave. N.W., P.O. Box 382, 98569, P 4,800, M 236, (360) 289-2451, (888) 48-BEACH, Fax (360) 289-5005, chamber@oceanshores.org, www.oceanshores.org.

**Odessa** • *Odessa C/C* • Ed Hayden, Pres., P.O. Box 355, 99159, P 970, M 73, (509) 982-0049, www.odessachamber.net

**Okanogan** • *Okanogan C/C* • Bonnie Rawson, Pres., P.O. Box 1125, 98840, P 2,415, M 67, (509) 422-2383, (888) 782-1134, Fax (509) 422-1541, okchamber@communitynet.org

**Olympia** • *Thurston County C/C* • David Schaffert, Pres./CEO, 809 Legion Way, P.O. Box 1427, 98507, P 238,000, M 1,450, (360) 357-3362, Fax (360) 357-3376, info@thurstonchamber.com, www. thurstonchamber.com

**Omak** • *Omak C/C* • Corina Radford, Pres., 401 Omak Ave., P.O. Box 3100, 98841, P 5,000, M 213, (509) 826-1880, (800) 225-6625, omakchamber@northcascades.net, www.omakchamber.com

**Orcas Island** • *see Eastsound*

**Oroville** • *Oroville C of C & Visitor Welcome Center* • Rich Solberg, Pres., 1730 Main St., P.O. Box 2140, 98844, P 1,670, M 80, (509) 476-2739, Fax (509) 476-2739, orovillewashington@gmail. com, orovillewashington.com

**Orting** • *see Puyallup*

**Othello** • *Greater Othello C/C* • John Reneau, Pres., 33 E. Larch St., P.O. Box 2813, 99344, P 16,000, M 150, (509) 488-2683, (800) 684-2556, Fax (509) 488-3123, manager@othellochamber.com, www.othellochamber.com

**Palouse** • *Palouse C/C* • Bev Pearce, Pres., P.O. Box 174, 99161, P 1,000, M 50, (509) 878-1811, palousechamber@visitpalouse.com, www.visitpalouse.com

**Pasco** • *Pasco C/C* • Nikki Gerds, Exec. Dir., 1925 N. 20th Ave., 99301, P 54,255, M 400, (509) 547-9755, Fax (509) 547-9756, info@pascochamber.org, www.pascochamber.org

**Pateros** • *Pateros C/C* • Jen Stennes, Pres., P.O. Box 613, 98846, P 625, M 30, (509) 923-9203, info@pateros.com, www.pateros.com

**Point Roberts** • *Point Roberts C/C* • Heather McPhee, Secy., P.O. Box 128, 98281, P 1,340, M 57, (360) 945-2313, Fax (360) 945-2956, info@pointrobertschamber.com, www.pointroberts chamber.com

**Pomeroy** • *Pomeroy C/C* • P.O. Box 916, 99347, P 1,515, M 55, (509) 843-5110, pomeroychamber@pomeroy-wa.com, www.pomeroychamberofcommerce.com

**Port Angeles** • *Port Angeles C/C & Visitor Center* • Russell Veenema, Exec. Dir., 121 E. Railroad Ave., 98362, P 20,000, M 550, (360) 452-2363, Fax (360) 457-5380, pangeles@olypen.com, www.portangeles.org

**Port Hadlock** • *Port Hadlock Tri-Area C/C* • P.O. Box 1223, 98339, P 10,000, M 65, (360) 379-5380, chamberinfo@port hadlock.org, www.porthadlock.org

**Port Ludlow** • *Port Ludlow C/C* • Kathie Sharp & Paula Zimmerman, Co-Pres., P.O. Box 65305, 98365, P 3,500, M 70, (360) 437-9798, info@portludlowchamber.org, www.portludlowchamber.org

**Port Orchard** • *Port Orchard C/C* • Coreen Haydock Johnson, Exec. Dir., 1014 Bay St., Ste. 8, 98366, P 8,310, M 350, (360) 876-3505, Fax (360) 895-1920, office@portorchard.com, www.portorchard.com

**Port Townsend** • *Port Townsend C/C* • Jennifer MacGillonie, Exec. Dir., 440 12th St., 98368, P 9,000, M 370, (360) 385-7869, (360) 385-2722, admin@ptchamber.org, www.ptchamber.org

**Poulsbo** • *Greater Poulsbo C/C* • Adele T. Heinrich, Exec. Dir., 19351 8th Ave., Ste. 108, P.O. Box 1063, 98370, P 7,500, M 438, (360) 779-4999, (360) 779-4848, (877) 768-5726, Fax (360) 779-3115, info@poulsbochamber.com, www.poulsbochamber.com

**Prosser** • *Prosser C/C & Visitor Info. Center* • Jim Milne, Exec. Dir., 1230 Bennett Ave., 99350, P 5,600, M 200, (509) 786-3177, (800) 408-1517, Fax (509) 786-2399, jimmilne@prosserchamber.org, www.prosserchamber.org

**Pullman** • *Pullman C/C* • Tammy Lewis, Exec. Dir., 415 N. Grand Ave., 99163, P 27,000, M 460, (509) 334-3565, (800) 365-6948, Fax (509) 332-3232, chamber@pullmanchamber.com, www.pullmanchamber.com.

**Puyallup** • *Puyallup/Sumner C/C* • Sally Zeiger Hanson, Exec. Dir., 323 N. Meridian, Ste. A, P.O. Box 1298, 98371, P 175,000, M 650, (253) 845-6755, Fax (253) 848-6164, info@puyallupsumnerchamber.com, www.puyallupsumnerchamber.com

**Quilcene** • *Quilcene & Brinnon C/C & Visitors Center* • Mike McFadden, Pres., P.O. Box 774, 98376, P 1,200, M 90, (360) 765-4999, visitorscenter@embarqmail.com, www.emeraldtowns.com

**Quincy** • *Quincy Valley C/C* • Erin Jones, Exec. Dir., 119 F St. S.E., P.O. Box 668, 98848, P 13,000, M 270, (509) 787-2140, Fax (509) 787-4500, qvcc@quincyvalley.org, www.quincyvalley.org

**Rainier** • *see Yelm*

**Raymond** • *see South Bend*

**Redmond** • *Greater Redmond C/C* • Christine Hoffmann, Pres./CEO, 16210 N.E. 80th St., P.O. Box 628, 98073, P 48,500, M 550, (425) 885-4014, Fax (425) 882-0996, chrish@redmondchamber.org, www.redmondchamber.org

**Renton** • *Renton C/C* • Bill Taylor, Pres., 300 Rainier Ave. N., 98057, P 80,708, M 600, (425) 226-4560, Fax (425) 226-4287, info@gorenton.com, www.gorenton.com.

**Republic** • *Republic Area C/C* • Daria Gerig, Pres., P.O. Box 502, 99166, P 9,000, M 100, (509) 775-2704, info@republicchamber.org, www.republicchamber.org

**Richfield** • *see La Center*

**Richland** • *see Kennewick*

**Ritzville** • *Ritzville Area C/C & Visitor Info. Center* • Mary Graves, Admin., 111 W. Main, P.O. Box 122, 99169, P 1,800, M 115, (509) 659-1936, Fax (509) 659-0142, chamber@ritzville.com, www.ritzville.com/chamber.

**Rockford** • *see Fairfield*

**Rosalia** • *Rosalia C/C* • Dr. James Sharp, Pres., P.O. Box 132, 99170, P 642, M 55, (509) 523-3506, staff@rosaliachamber.com, www.rosaliachamber.com

**Rosburg** • *see Cathlamet*

**Roslyn** • *see Cle Elum*

**Roy** • *see Yelm*

**Salmon Creek** • *see La Center*

**Sammamish** • *Sammamish C/C* • Deborah Sogge, Exec. Dir., 704 228th Ave. N.E., Ste. 123, 98074, P 40,000, M 235, (425) 681-4910, info@sammamishchamber.org, www.sammamishchamber.org

**San Juan Island** • *see Friday Harbor*

**Sea Tac** • *see Seattle-Southwest King County C/C*

# Seattle Area

**Greater Seattle C/C** • 1301 5th Ave., Ste. 2500, 98101, P 3,500,000, M 2,400, (206) 389-7200, Fax (206) 389-7288, info@seattlechamber.com, www.seattlechamber.com

**Ballard C/C** • Beth Williamson Miller, Exec. Dir., 2208 N.W. Market St., Ste. 100, 98107, P 70,000, M 350, (206) 784-9705, Fax (206) 783-8154, info@ballardchamber.com, www.ballard chamber.com

**Beacon Hill C/C** • 3801 Beacon Ave. S., 98144, M 165, (206) 264-1996

**Fremont C/C** • Jessica Vets, Exec. Dir., P.O. Box 31139, 98103, P 15,000, M 210, (206) 632-1500, Fax (206) 632-7156, director@fremont.com, www.fremont.com

**Seattle** • *Greater Lake City C/C* • Diane Haugen, Exec. Dir., 12345 30th Ave. N.E. Ste.F-G, 98125, P 40,000, M 200, (206) 363-3287, Fax (206) 363-6456, chamber@lakecitychamber.org, www.lakecitychamber.org

**Greater Queen Anne C/C** • Jill Arnow, Exec. Dir., P.O. Box 19386, 98109, P 80,000, M 300, (206) 282-4539, (206) 283-6876, www.qachamber.org

**Greater University C/C** • Teresa Lord Hugel, Exec. Dir., 4710 University Way N.E., Ste. 114, 98105, P 70,000, M 170, (206) 547-4417, Fax (206) 547-5266, director@udistrictchamber.org, www.udistrictchamber.org

**Magnolia C/C** • Mark Johnston, Pres., 3214 W. McGraw St., Ste. 301B, 98199, P 21,500, M 250, (206) 284-5836, Fax (206) 352-7494, info@magnoliachamber.org, www.magnoliachamber.org

**Northgate C/C** • Theresa Poalucci, Pres., 9594 First Ave. N.E., Ste. 296, 98115, P 500,000, M 100, (206) 733-0115, info@northgate chamber.com, www.northgatechamber.com

## Seattle Area, *continued*

**Southwest King County C/C** · Nancy Hinthorne, Pres./CEO, 14220 Interurban Ave. S., Ste. 134, Tukwila, P.O. Box 58591, 98138, P 105,000, M 400, (206) 575-1633, (800) 638-8613, Fax (206) 575-2007, staff@swkcc.org, www.swkcc.org

**Wallingford C/C** · Kara Ceriello, Pres., 2100-A N. 45th St., 98103, P 20,000, M 110, (206) 632-0645, chamber@wallingford.org, www.wallingfordchamber.org

**Washington State Hispanic C/C** · 1100 Dexter Ave N., Ste. 100, 98109, M 1,000, (206) 273-7519, info@wshcc.com, www.wshcc.com

**West Seattle C/C** · Patricia Mullen, Pres./CEO, 3614A California Ave. S.W., 98116, P 125,000, M 286, (206) 932-5685, Fax (206) 938-7437, info@wschamber.com, www.wschamber.com

**White Center C/C** · 1612 S.W. 114th PMB 108, 98146, P 30,000, M 125, (206) 763-4196, Fax (206) 763-1042, wcchamber@hotmail.com, www.whitecenterchamber.org

**Sedro-Woolley** · *Sedro-Woolley C/C* · 714-B Metcalf St., 98284, P 9,064, M 214, (360) 855-1841, (888) 225-8365, Fax (360) 855-1582, swchamber@sedro-woolley.com, www.sedro-woolley.com.

**Selah** · *Selah C/C* · Shirley M. Wasilewski, Admin. Asst., 216 S. 1st St., P.O. Box 415, 98942, P 6,000, M 106, (509) 698-7303, Fax (509) 698-7309, selahchamber@elltel.net, www.selahchamber.com

**Sequim** · *Sequim-Dungeness Valley C/C & Visitor Info. Center* · Vickie Maples, Exec. Dir., 1192 E. Washington, P.O. Box 907, 98382, P 25,000, M 425, (360) 683-6197, Fax (360) 683-6349, info@sequimchamber.com, www.sequimchamber.com

**Shelton** · *Shelton-Mason County C/C* · Dick Taylor, Exec. Dir., 215 W. Railroad Ave., P.O. Box 2389, 98584, P 54,000, M 350, (360) 426-2021, (800) 576-2021, Fax (360) 426-8678, info@shelton-chamber.org, sheltonchamber.org.

**Shoreline** · *Shoreline C/C* · Sharon Knight, Mgr., 18560 1st Ave. N.E., 98155, P 58,000, M 205, (206) 361-2260, Fax (206) 361-2268, info@shorelinechamber.com, www.shorelinechamber.com

**Silverdale** · *Silverdale C/C* · Darla Murker, Exec. Dir., 3100 Buckland Hill, Ste. 100, P.O. Box 1218, 98383, P 16,000, M 450, (360) 692-6800, Fax (360) 692-1379, info@silverdalechamber.com, www.silverdalechamber.com

**Skamokawa** · *see Cathlamet*

**Smokey Point** · *see Arlington*

**Snohomish** · *Snohomish C/C* · Pam Osborne, Mgr., 127 Ave. A, P.O. Box 135, 98291, P 8,500, M 220, (360) 568-2526, Fax (360) 568-3869, manager@cityofsnohomish.com, www.cityofsnohomish.com

**Snoqualmie** · *see North Bend*

**Snoqualmie Pass** · *see North Bend*

**Soap Lake** · *Soap Lake C/C* · P.O. Box 433, 98851, P 1,733, M 52, (509) 246-1821, slcoc@soaplakecoc.org, www.soaplakecoc.org

**South Bend** · *Willapa Harbor C/C & Visitor Info.* · Ms. Pat Shults, Dir., P.O. Box 1249, 98586, P 4,800, M 160, (360) 942-5419, Fax (360) 942-5419, visitorinfo@willapabay.org, www.visit.willapabay.org

**South Hill** · *see Puyallup*

**Spangle** · *see Fairfield*

**Spokane** · *Greater Spokane Inc.* · Richard Hadley, Pres./CEO, 801 W. Riverside Ave., Ste. 100, 99201, P 510,000, M 1,500, (509) 624-1393, Fax (509) 747-0077, info@greaterspokane.org, www.greaterspokane.org.

**Spokane Valley** · *Greater Spokane Valley C/C* · Eldonna Shaw, Pres./CEO, 9507 E. Sprague Ave., 99206, P 104,000, M 1,032, (509) 924-4994, (866) 475-1436, Fax (509) 924-4992, info@spokanevalleychamber.org, www.spokanevalleychamber.org.

**SERVING THE BUSINESS COMMUNITIES IN EASTERN SPOKANE COUNTY SINCE 1921. CALL US FOR INFO ABOUT THE NEW CITIES OF SPOKANE VALLEY, LIBERTY LAKE AND MILLWOOD.**

**Sprague** · *Sprague C/C* · Sylvia Fox, Pres., P.O. Box 17, 99032, P 500, M 30, (509) 979-3539, president@spraguechamber.org, www.spraguechamber.org

**Springdale** · *Springdale Area C/C* · Linda Ritts, Pres., P.O. Box 275, 99173, P 300, M 53, (509) 258-7805, springdalecommunitynews@hotmail.com, www.higherelevations.com/springdale_chamber.htm

**Stanwood** · *Stanwood C/C* · Stacy Johnson, Exec. Dir., 8725 271st St. N.W., P.O. Box 641, 98292, P 28,000, M 125, (360) 629-0562, www.stanwoodchamber.org

**Steilacoom** · *Steilacoom C/C* · Cindy McKitrick, Pres., P.O. Box 88584, 98388, P 6,000, M 120, (253) 353-6982, Fax (253) 353-6982, cinmck@mindspring.com, www.steilacoom.org

**Stevenson** · *Skamania County C/C* · Casey Roeder, Exec. Dir., 167 N.W. Second St., P.O. Box 1037, 98648, P 10,000, M 265, (509) 427-8911, (800) 989-9178, Fax (509) 427-5122, info@skamania.org, www.skamania.org

**Sultan** · *Sky Valley Visitor Info. Center & C/C* · Debbie Copple, Dir., 320 Main St., P.O. Box 46, 98294, P 9,000, M 80, (360) 793-0983, Fax (360) 793-3241, debbie@skyvalleyvic.net, www.skyvalleychamber.com

**Sumas** · *Sumas C/C* · Tony Kelley, Pres., P.O. Box 268, 98295, P 1,200, M 30, (360) 988-2028, www.sumaschamber.com

**Summit** · *see Puyallup*

**Sumner** · *see Puyallup*

**Sunland Estates** · *see Quincy*

**Sunnyside** · *Sunnyside C/C* · Pam Turner, Exec. Dir., 230 E. Edison, P.O. Box 360, 98944, P 14,500, M 250, (509) 837-5939, (800) 457-8089, Fax (509) 837-8015, pturner@sunnysidechamber.com, www.sunnysidechamber.com

**Tacoma** · *Tacoma-Pierce County C/C* · David W. Graybill, Pres./CEO, 950 Pacific Ave., Ste. 300, P.O. Box 1933, 98401, P 790,500, M 1,300, (253) 627-2175, Fax (253) 597-7305, info@tacomachamber.org, www.tacomachamber.org.

**Tahuya** · *see Belfair*

**Tenino** · *Tenino C/C* · Janet Duncan, Pres., P.O. Box 506, 98589, P 1,600, M 60, (360) 264-4116, Fax (360) 264-4436, www.teninochamberofcommerce.com

**Toledo** · *South Lewis County C/C* · Mary Garrison, Pres., 408 Silver St., P.O. Box 607, 98591, P 5,000, M 95, (360) 864-8844, Fax (360) 864-8846, slcc@toledotel.com, www.slcchamberofcommerce.com

**Tonasket** · *Tonasket C/C* · Kari Alexander, Pres., P.O. Box 523, 98855, P 1,010, M 76, (509) 486-4543, (866) 440-8828, Fax (509) 486-4543, www.ci.tonasket.wa.us, info@tonasketwa.org, www.tonasketwa.org

**Toppenish** · *Toppenish C/C & Visitor Info. Center* · Susan Treneer, Dir., 504 S. Elm St., P.O. Box 28, 98948, P 9,000, M 100, (509) 865-3262, (800) 863-6375, Fax (509) 865-3549, chamber@toppenish.net, www.toppenish.net

**Toutle** • *Mount St. Helens C/C* • Greg Drew, Pres., 5304 Spirit Lake Hwy., 98649, P 2,500, M , (360) 274-8920

**Trout Lake** • *see White Salmon*

**Tukwila** • *see Seattle-Southwest King County C/C*

**Tulalip** • *Greater Marysville Tulalip C/C* • Caldie Rogers IOM, Pres./CEO, 8825 34th Ave. N.E., Ste. C, 98271, P 60,000, M 400, (360) 659-7700, Fax (360) 653-7539, caldie@marysvilletulalip chamber.com, www.marysvilletulalipchamber.com.

**Tumwater** • *Tumwater C/C* • Sandra Kozlowski, Exec. Dir., 5304 Littlerock Rd. S.W., 98512, P 13,000, M 250, (360) 357-5153, Fax (360) 786-1685, office@tumwaterchamber.com, www.tumwater chamber.com

**Twisp** • *Twisp C/C* • Vicki Wilson, Mgr./Treas., P.O. Box 686, 98856, P 1,000, M 85, (509) 997-2020, Fax (509) 997-2290, info@twisp info.com, www.twispinfo.com

**Vancouver** • *Greater Vancouver C/C* • Kim J. Capeloto, Pres./CEO, 1101 Broadway, Ste. 100, 98660, P 400,000, M 1,100, (360) 694-2588, Fax (360) 693-8279, info@vancouverusa.com, www.vancouverusa.com

**Vashon** • *Vashon-Maury Island C/C* • Lee Ockinga, Exec. Dir., 19021 Vashon Hwy. S.W., P.O. Box 1035, 98070, P 11,000, M 210, (206) 463-6217, Fax (206) 463-7590, discover@vashonchamber.com, www.vashonchamber.com

**Victor** • *see Belfair*

**Walla Walla** • *Walla Walla Valley C/C* • Dave Warkentin, Pres./CEO, 29 E. Sumach, P.O. Box 644, 99362, P 57,500, M 800, (509) 525-0850, Fax (509) 522-2038, info@wwvchamber.com, www.wwvchamber.com

**Washougal** • *see Camas*

**Waterville** • *Waterville C/C* • Royal DeVaney, Mayor, P.O. Box 628, 98858, P 1,170, M 20, (509) 745-8871, waterville@nwi.net, www.ci.waterville.wa.us

**Waverly** • *see Fairfield*

**Wenatchee** • *Northcentral Washington Hispanic C/C* • Claudia De Robles, Pres., P.O. Box 2001, 98807, M 63, (509) 662-2116, Fax (509) 663-2022, informacion@wenatchee.org, www.ncwhcc.org

**Wenatchee** • *Wenatchee Valley C/C* • Craig Larsen, Exec. Dir., 300 S. Columbia St., 3rd Flr., P.O. Box 850, 98807, P 70,000, M 750, (509) 662-2116, Fax (509) 663-2022, info@wenatchee.org, www.wenatchee.org

**West Richland** • *West Richland Area C/C* • May Hays, Exec. Dir., 6102 W. Van Giesen, P.O. Box 4023, 99353, P 12,000, M 175, (509) 967-0521, Fax (509) 967-2950, wrcc@westrichlandchamber.org, www.westrichlandchamber.org

**West Seattle** • *see Seattle-West Seattle C/C*

**West Spokane County** • *see Cheney*

**Westport** • *Westport/Grayland C/C* • Leslie Eichner, Exec. Dir., 2985 S. Montesano St., P.O. Box 306, 98595, P 6,000, M 130, (360) 268-9422, (800) 345-6223, Fax (360) 268-1990, westport@techline.com, www.westportgrayland-chamber.org

**Whidbey Island** • *see Coupeville, Langley and Oak Harbor*

**White Salmon** • *Mt. Adams C/C* • Marsha Holliston, Ofc. Admin., One Heritage Plaza, P.O. Box 449, 98672, P 7,000, M 223, (509) 493-3630, (866) 493-3630, info@mtadamschamber.com, www.mtadamschamber.com

**Wilbur** • *Wilbur C/C* • Penny West, Pres., P.O. Box 111, 99185, P 900, M 60, (509) 647-5551, Fax (509) 647-5552, www.wilburwa.com

**Winchester** • *see Quincy*

**Winthrop** • *Winthrop C/C* • 202 Hwy. 20, P.O. Box 39, 98862, P 350, M 140, (509) 996-2125, (888) 463-8469, info@winthrop washington.com, www.winthropwashington.com

**Woodinville** • *Greater Woodinville C/C* • Randy Small, Exec. Dir., 14421 Woodinville-Redmond Rd. N.E., 98072, P 12,000, M 350, (425) 481-8300, Fax (425) 481-9743, info@woodinvillechamber.org, www.woodinvillechamber.org

**Woodland** • *Woodland C/C* • Sharon Knight, Dir., 900 Goerig St., P.O. Box 1012, 98674, P 5,000, M 285, (360) 225-9552, Fax (360) 225-3490, info@woodlandwachamber.com, www.woodland wachamber.com

**Woodway** • *see Lynnwood*

**Yakima** • *Greater Yakima C/C* • Mike Morrisette, Pres./CEO, 10 N. Ninth St., P.O. Box 1490, 98907, P 233,000, M 1,050, (509) 248-2021, Fax (509) 248-0601, chamber@yakima.org, www.yakima.org

**Yelm** • *Yelm Area C/C* • Cecelia Jenkins, Exec. Dir., 701 Prairie Park Lane S.E., Ste. A, P.O. Box 444, 98597, P 12,000, M 400, (360) 458-6608, Fax (360) 458-6383, info@yelmchamber.com, www.yelmchamber.com

**Zillah** • *Zillah C/C* • Ken Waymire, Pres., P.O. Box 1294, 98953, P 2,720, M 50, (509) 829-5055, zillahchamber@zillahchamber.com, www.zillahchamber.com

# West Virginia

**West Virginia C of C** • Stephen Roberts, Pres., 1624 Kanawha Blvd. E., P.O. Box 2789, Charleston, 25330, P 1,818,470, M 1,800, (304) 342-1115, Fax (304) 342-1130, forjobs@wvchamber.com, www.wvchamber.com.

**Barrackville** • *see Fairmont*

**Beckley** • *Beckley-Raleigh County C/C* • Ellen M. Taylor, Pres./CEO, 245 N. Kanawha St., 25801, P 76,819, M 350, (304) 252-7328, Fax (304) 252-7373, chamber@brccc.com, www.brccc.com.

**Berkeley Springs** • *Berkeley Springs-Morgan County C/C* • Andrea Curtin, Exec. Dir., 127 Fairfax St., 25411, P 16,000, M 193, (304) 258-3738, chamber@berkeleysprings.com, www.berkeleyspringschamber.com

**Bluefield** • *Greater Bluefield C/C* • Marc Meachum, Pres./CEO, 619 Bland St., P.O. Box 4098, 24701, P 13,000, M 635, (304) 327-7184, Fax (304) 325-3085, info@bluefieldchamber.com, www.bluefieldchamber.com.

**Buckhannon** • *Buckhannon-Upshur C/C* • Dee Heater-Tomblyn, Pres., 16 S. Kanawha St., P.O. Box 442, 26201, P 23,000, M 160, (304) 472-1722, Fax (304) 472-4938, buckhannon@3wlogic.net, www.buchamber.com

**Charles Town** • *Jefferson County C/C* • Heather Morgan, Exec. Dir., 29 Keyes Ferry Rd., P.O. Box 426, 25414, P 50,000, M 500, (304) 725-2055, (800) 624-0577, Fax (304) 728-8307, chamber@jeffersoncounty.com, www.jeffersoncounty.com

**Charleston** • *Charleston Area Alliance* • Matthew G. Ballard, Pres./CEO, 1116 Smith St., 25301, P 273,000, M 600, (304) 340-4253, Fax (304) 340-4275, info@charlestonareaalliance.org, www.charlestonareaalliance.org

**Chester** • *Chester-Newell Area C/C* • David Nurmi, Exec. Dir., 449 Carolina Ave., P.O. Box 2, 26034, P 3,000, M 95, (304) 387-2025, Fax (304) 387-2025, chester-newellchamber@verizon.net

**Clarksburg** • *Harrison County C/C* • Katherine Wagner PCED IOM, Pres., 520 W. Main St., 26301, P 79,000, M 550, (304) 624-6331, Fax (304) 624-5190, info@harrisoncountychamber.com, www.harrisoncountychamber.com

**Davis** • *Tucker County C/C* • Bill Smith, Dir., 410 William Ave. & 4th St., P.O. Box 565, 26260, P 7,800, M 60, (304) 259-5315, Fax (304) 259-4210, tuckerchamber@canaanvalley.org

**Delbarton** • *see Williamson*

**Elkins** • *Elkins-Randolph County C/C* • Ellen Spears, Exec. Dir., 200 Executive Plaza, 26241, P 28,000, M 268, (304) 636-2717, Fax (304) 636-8046, chamber@elkinsrandolphcountywv.com, erccc.com

**Fairmont** • *Marion County C/C* • Tina Shaw, Pres., 110 Adams St., P.O. Box 208, 26555, P 57,000, M 500, (304) 363-0442, (800) 296-3379, Fax (304) 363-0480, mccc@marionchamber.com, www.marionchamber.com

**Fairview** • *see Fairmont*

**Farmington** • *see Fairmont*

**Follansbee** • *Follansbee C/C* • Tony Paesano, Pres., P.O. Box 606, 26037, P 4,000, M 60, (304) 527-1330, Fax (304) 527-2615, www.follansbeewv.com

**Gilbert** • *see Williamson*

**Grant Town** • *see Fairmont*

**Harrisville** • *Ritchie County C/C* • Richard Edman, Pres., 217 W. Main St., P.O. Box 177, 26362, P 10,500, M 47, (304) 643-2500, Fax (304) 643-2502, ritchiechamber@zoominternet.net, www.ritchiechamber.com

**Hinton** • *Summers County C/C* • Mary Haley, Pres., 200 Ballengee St., 25951, P 14,204, M 90, (304) 466-5332, Fax (304) 466-5301, sccc200@verizon.net, www.summerscounty.org

**Huntington** • *Huntington Reg. C/C* • Mark Bugher, Pres./CEO, 720 Fourth Ave., P.O. Box 1509, 25716, P 51,000, M 550, (304) 525-5131, Fax (304) 525-5158, info@huntingtonchamber.org, www.huntingtonchamber.org.

**Hurricane** • *see Teays*

**Kermit** • *see Williamson*

**Keyser** • *Mineral County C/C* • Anne Palmer, Exec. Dir., Grand Central Plaza, Ste. 2011, 26726, P 27,234, M 150, (304) 788-2513, Fax (304) 788-3887, www.mineralchamber.com

**Kingwood** • *Preston County C/C* • Sheila Haney, Exec. Dir., 200 1/2 W. Main St., 26537, P 30,000, M 225, (304) 329-0576, Fax (304) 329-1407, info@prestonchamber.com, www.prestonchamber.com

**Lewisburg** • *Greater Greenbrier C/C* • Katie C. Ickes, Exec. Dir., 540 N. Jefferson St., Box 17, Ste. N, 24901, P 35,000, M 325, (304) 645-2818, Fax (304) 647-3001, info@greenbrierwvchamber.org, www.greenbrierwvchamber.org

**Logan** • *Logan County C/C* • Debrina J. Williams, Mgr. Dir., 214 Stratton St., P.O. Box 218, 25601, P 37,710, M 200, (304) 752-1324, Fax (304) 752-5988, logancountychamber@verizon.net, www.logancountychamberofcommerce.com

**Mannington** • *see Fairmont*

**Marlinton** • *Pocahontas County C/C* • David J. Cain, Treas., P.O. Box 411, 24954, P 9,000, M 70, (304) 799-4476, info@pccocwv.com, www.pccoc.com

**Martinsburg** • *Martinsburg-Berkeley County C/C* • Tina Combs, Pres./CEO, 198 Viking Way, 25401, P 107,347, M 530, (304) 267-4841, (800) 332-9007, Fax (304) 263-4695, chamber@berkeleycounty.org, www.berkeleycounty.org.

**Matewan** • *see Williamson*

**Monongah** • *see Fairmont*

**Morgantown** • *Morgantown Area C/C* • Ken Busz, Pres./CEO, 1029 University Ave, Ste. 101, P.O. Box 658, 26507, P 88,640, M 367, (304) 292-3311, (800) 618-2525, Fax (304) 296-6619, info@morgantownchamber.org, www.morgantownchamber.org

**Moundsville** • *Marshall County C/C* • David W. Knuth, Exec. Dir., 609 Jefferson Ave., 26041, P 34,800, M 251, (304) 845-2773, Fax (304) 845-2773, dknuth@marshallcountychamber.com, www.marshallcountychamber.com

**Mullens** • *Mullens Area C/C* • Kay King, Pres., P.O. Box 235, 25882, P 2,000, M 30, (304) 294-6714, ekayking@verizon.net

**New Martinsville** • *Wetzel County C/C* • Don Riggenbach, Pres., 201 Main St., P.O. Box 271, 26155, P 18,000, M 110, (304) 455-3825, Fax (304) 455-3637, chamber@wetzelcountychamber.com, www.wetzelcountychamber.com

**Oak Hill** • *Fayette County C/C* • Sharon Cruikshank, Exec. Dir., 310 Oyler Ave., 25901, P 48,655, M 350, (304) 465-5617, (800) 927-0263, Fax (304) 465-5618, fayette@wvdsl.net, www.fayettecounty.com.

**Oceana** • *Oceana Area C/C* • P.O. Box 190, 24870, P 4,000, M 20, (304) 682-6231

**Parkersburg** • *C/C of the Mid-Ohio Valley* • Robin Ollis, Chair, 214 8th St., 26101, P 132,000, M 631, (304) 422-3588, Fax (304) 422-3580, info@movchamber.org, www.parkersburgchamber.com

**Petersburg** • *Grant County C/C* • Tammy Kesner, Pres., 126 N. Main St., 26847, P 11,300, M 129, (304) 257-2722, gowv@gowv.com, www.gowv.com

**Philippi** • *Barbour County C/C* • Donald A. Smith, Exec. Dir., 101 College Hill Dr., Box 2124, 26416, P 16,000, M 150, (304) 457-1958, Fax (304) 457-6239, info@barbourchamber.com, www.barbourchamber.com

**Pineville** • *Pineville Area C/C* • Tim Ellison, Mayor, P.O. Box 116, 24874, P 1,500, M 37, (304) 732-6255, Fax (304) 732-0024, info@pinevillechamber.com, www.pinevillechamber.com

**Point Pleasant** • *Mason County Area C/C* • Marsha Smith, Exec. Dir., 305 Main St., 25550, P 25,178, M 90, (304) 675-1050, Fax (304) 675-1601, mccofc@pointpleasantwv.org, www.masoncountychamber.org

**Princeton** • *Princeton-Mercer County C/C* • Robert Farley, Pres./CEO, 1522 N. Walker St., 24740, P 64,000, M 345, (304) 487-1502, Fax (304) 425-0227, pmccc@frontiernet.net, www.pmccc.com.

**Ravenswood** • *Greater Ravenswood C/C* • Kathy Meadows, Pres., P.O. Box 743, 26164, P 4,500, M 50, (304) 942-2282, (304) 273-2621

**Reedsville** • *see Fairmont*

**Richwood** • *Richwood Area C/C* • Raymond Chapman, Dir., 1 E. Main St., P.O. Box 267, 26261, P 2,200, M 100, (304) 846-6790, Fax (304) 846-6790, rwdchamber@verizon.net, www.richwoodwv.com

**Romney** • *Hampshire County C/C* • Patricia Maxwell, 91 S. High St., 26757, P 21,000, M 170, (304) 822-7221, Fax (304) 822-7221, hampshirechamberofcommerce@citlink.net, www.hampshire-countychamber.com

**Saint Albans** • *St. Albans Area C/C* • Janet Painter, Exec. Dir., P.O. Box 675, 25177, P 13,000, M 75, (304) 727-7251, Fax (304) 727-7251, stacoc@netzero.net, www.stalbanswv.com

**Salem** • *Salem Area C/C* • Dr. Joseph Audia, Pres., P.O. Box 191, 26426, P 2,000, M 50, (304) 782-1005, chamber@salemwv.com, www.salemwv.com

**South Charleston** • *South Charleston C/C* • Kelly Kirk, Chrmn., 401 D St., P.O. Box 8595, 25303, P 15,000, M 145, (304) 744-0051, Fax (304) 744-1649, soccoc@wvdsl.net, www.southcharleston chamber.org

**Spencer** • *Roane County C/C* • Kim Davis, Admin. Asst., P.O. Box 1, 25276, P 15,446, M 80, (304) 927-1780, Fax (304) 927-5953, rchamber@commission.state.wv.us, www.roanechamberwv.org

**Summersville** • *Summersville Area C/C* • P.O. Box 567, 26651, P 26,662, M 120, (304) 872-1588, (800) 760-6158, Fax (304) 883-2588, info@summersvillechamber.com, www.summers villechamber.com

**Teays** • *Putnam County C/C* • Marty Chapman, Pres., P.O. Box 553, 25569, P 55,000, M 550, (304) 757-6510, Fax (304) 757-6562, chamber@putnamcounty.org, www.putnamcounty.org.

**Weirton** • *Weirton Area C/C* • Brenda Mull, Pres., 3174 Pennsylvania Ave., Ste. 1, 26062, P 19,250, M 400, (304) 748-7212, Fax (304) 748-0241, info@weirtonchamber.com, www. weirtonchamber.com.

**Welch** • *McDowell C/C* • Reba Honaker, Pres., 92 McDowell St., Ste. 100, 24801, P 27,000, M 152, (304) 436-4260, (866) 571-0746, www.mcdowellchamberofcommerce.com

**Wellsburg** • *Wellsburg C/C* • Candy Monroe, Exec. Dir., P.O. Box 487, 26070, P 3,500, M 120, (304) 737-1065, Fax (304) 748-1832, candyvmonroe@verizon.net, www.wellsburgchamber.com

**Weston** • *Lewis County C/C* • Gerhard St. John, Exec. Dir., 115 E. Second St., 26452, P 17,000, M 149, (304) 269-2608, Fax (304) 517-1608, lcinfo@lcchamber.org, www.lcchamber.org

**Wheeling** • *Wheeling Area C/C* • Terry A. Sterling, Pres., 1310 Market St., 26003, P 154,000, M 700, (304) 233-2575, Fax (304) 233-1320, terrysterling@wheelingchamber.com, www.wheeling chamber.com

**White Sulphur Springs** • *see Lewisburg*

**Williamson** • *Tug Valley C/C* • 2nd Ave. & Court St., P.O. Box 376, 25661, P 42,000, M 150, (304) 235-5240, Fax (304) 235-4509, tvcc1@verizon.net, www.tugvalleychamberofcommerce.com

**Winfield** • *see Teays*

**Worthington** • *see Fairmont*

# Wisconsin

**Wisconsin Manufacturers & Commerce** • James S. Haney, Pres., 501 E. Washington Ave., P.O. Box 352, Madison, 53701, P 4,900,000, M 4,000, (608) 258-3400, Fax (608) 258-3413, wmc@wmc.org, www.wmc.org

**Abbotsford** • *Abbotsford C/C* • 100 W. Spruce St., P.O. Box 418, 54405, P 2,000, M 65, (715) 223-3444

**Adams** • *Adams County C/C & Tourism* • Alice Parr, Exec. Dir., 252 S. Main St., P.O. Box 576, 53910, P 20,060, M 160, (608) 339-6997, (888) 339-6997, Fax (608) 339-8079, chamber@ visitadamscountywi.com, www.visitadamscountywi.com

**Algoma** • *Algoma Area C/C* • Pam Ritchie, Exec. Dir., 1226 Lake St., 54201, P 3,500, M 210, (920) 487-2041, (800) 498-4888, Fax (920) 487-5519, chamber@itol.com, www.algoma.org

**Almena** • *Almena Commercial Club* • Jessica Vohs, Pres., P.O. Box 175, 54805, P 736, M 30, (715) 357-3592

**Antigo** • *Antigo/Langlade County C/C* • 1005 S. Superior, 54409, P 19,500, M 220, (715) 623-4134, (888) 526-4523, Fax (715) 623-4135, antigocc@verizon.net, www.antigochamber.com.

**Appleton** • *Fox Cities C/C & Ind.* • William J. Welch, Pres., 125 N. Superior St., P.O. Box 1855, 54912, P 207,660, M 1,750, (920) 734-7101, Fax (920) 734-7161, information@foxcitieschamber. com, www.foxcitieschamber.com

**Arbor Vitae** • *see Minocqua*

**Ashland** • *Ashland Area C/C* • Mary McPhetridge, Exec. Dir., 805 W. Lake Shore Dr., P.O. Box 746, 54806, P 8,700, M 300, (715) 682-2500, (800) 284-9484, Fax (715) 682-9404, ashchamb@centurytel. net, www.travelashlandcounty.com

**Baileys Harbor** • *Baileys Harbor Comm. Assn.* • P.O. Box 31, 54202, P 1,100, M 100, (920) 839-2366, bhinfo@dcwis.com, www.baileysharbor.com

**Baldwin** • *Baldwin Area C/C & Visitor Bur.* • Tracy Carlson, Pres., P.O. Box 142, 54002, P 2,667, M 90, (715) 684-2221, baldwin chamber@baldwin-telecom.net, www.baldwinareachamber.org

**Bangor** • *Bangor Bus. Club* • Chad Wehrs, Pres., P.O. Box 154, 54614, P 1,571, M 40

**Baraboo** • *Baraboo Area C/C* • Gene Dalhoff, Exec. Dir., 600 W. Chestnut St., P.O. Box 442, 53913, P 14,500, M 370, (608) 356-8333, (800) BARABOO, Fax (608) 356-8422, gpdalhoff@baraboo. com, www.baraboo.com.

**Bayfield** • *Bayfield C/C & Visitor Bur.* • Cari Obst, Exec. Dir., 42 S. Broad St., P.O. Box 138, 54814, P 615, M 400, (715) 779-3335, (800) 447-4094, Fax (715) 779-5080, chamber@bayfield.org, www.bayfield.org

**Beaver Dam** • *Beaver Dam Area C/C* • Philip Fritsche, Exec. Dir., 127 S. Spring St., 53916, P 21,000, M 325, (920) 887-8879, Fax (920) 887-9750, info@beaverdamchamber.com, www.beaver damchamber.com.

**Belgium** • *Belgium Area C/C* • Lila M. Mueller, Secy., P.O. Box 215, 53004, P 2,500, M 58, (262) 285-7887, (262) 285-7931, www.belgiumchamberofcommerce.com

**Belleville** • *Belleville C/C* • Brad Freitag, Pres., P.O. Box 392, 53508, P 2,000, M 50, (608) 424-3336, www.belleville-wi.com

**Beloit** • *Greater Beloit C/C* • Amy Loudenbeck, Interim Pres., 500 Public Ave., 53511, P 65,000, M 325, (608) 365-8835, Fax (608) 365-6850, info@greaterbeloitchamber.com, greaterbeloitchamber.com.

**Black River Falls** • *Black River Area C/C* • Barbara Brower, Exec. Dir., 120 N. Water St., 54615, P 5,000, M 320, (715) 284-4658, (800) 404-4008, Fax (715) 284-9476, chamber@blackrivercountry. net, www.blackrivercountry.net

**Blanchardville** • *Blanchardville Comm. Pride* • 208 Mason St., P.O. Box 52, 53516, P 800, M 10, (608) 523-2274, www. blanchardville.com

**Bloomer** • *Bloomer C/C* • 1421 Main St., P.O. Box 273, 54724, P 3,400, M 145, (715) 568-3339, Fax (715) 568-3346, bchamber@ bloomer.net, www.bloomerchamber.com

**Boscobel** • *Boscobel C/C* • Terri Evans, Secy./Treas., 800 Wisconsin Ave., 53805, P 3,076, M 75, (608) 375-2672, chamber@ boscobelwisconsin.com, www.boscobelwisconsin.com

**Boulder Junction** • *Boulder Junction C/C* • Theresa Smith, Exec. Secy., P.O. Box 286 W, 54512, P 1,000, M 118, (715) 385-2400, (800) 466-8759, Fax (715) 385-2379, boulderjct@boulderjct.org, www.boulderjct.org

**Brillion** • *Brillion C/C* • Doug Bubholz, Pres., P.O. Box 123, 54110, P 3,000, M 75, (920) 756-2181, www.brillionchamber.com

**Brodhead** • *Brodhead C/C* • Nancy Sutherland, Secy., P.O Box 16, 53520, P 5,000, M 60, (608) 897-8411, info@brodheadchamber. org, www.brodheadchamber.org

**Brookfield** • *Greater Brookfield C/C* • Carol White, Pres., 1305 N. Barker Rd., Ste. 5, 53045, P 35,000, M 400, (262) 786-1886, Fax (262) 786-1959, carol@brookfieldchamber.com, www.brookfield chamber.com

**Brooklyn** • *Brooklyn Area C/C* • LaVorn Dvorak, Pres., 100 E. Main, P.O. Box 33, 53521, P 1,165, M 18, (608) 455-1627, info@ brooklynwisconsin.com, www.brooklynwisconsin.com

**Bryant** • *see Antigo*

**Burlington** • *Burlington Area C/C* • Janice Ludtke, Exec. Dir., 113 E. Chestnut St., P.O. Box 156, 53105, P 16,000, M 490, (262) 763-6044, Fax (262) 763-3631, info@burlingtonchamber.org, www.burlingtonchamber.org.

**Butler** • *Butler Area C/C* • Linda Ryfinski, Exec. Dir., 12808 W. Hampton Ave., 53007, P 1,900, M 100, (262) 781-5195, Fax (262) 781-7870, linda@butlerchamber,org, www.butlerchamber.org

**Cable** • *Cable Area C/C* • James Bolen, Exec. Dir., 13380 County Hwy. M, P.O. Box 217, 54821, P 2,000, M 190, (715) 798-3833, (800) 533-7454, Fax (715) 798-4456, info@cable4fun.com, www. cable4fun.com

**Cadott** • *Cadott Area C/C* • Huntz Geissler, Pres., P.O. Box 84, 54727, P 1,352, M 100, (715) 289-3338, info@cadottchamber.org, www.cadottchamber.org

**Cambridge** • *Cambridge C/C* • P.O. Box 572, 53523, P 1,300, M 111, (608) 423-3780, Fax (608) 423-7558, chamber@small bytes.net, www.cambridgewi.com

**Campbellsport** • *Campbellsport C/C* • Julie Roth, Treas., P.O. Box 535, 53010, P 1,800, M 52, (920) 533-8386, campbellsport@ care2.com, www.campbellsport.org

**Cedarburg** • *Cedarburg C/C* • Kristine Hage, Exec. Dir., W61 N480 Washington Ave., P.O. Box 104, 53012, P 16,000, M 300, (262) 377-5856, (262) 377-9620, Fax (262) 377-6470, info@ cedarburg.org, www.cedarburg.org

**Chetek** • *Chetek Area C/C* • P.O. Box 747, 54728, P 3,800, M 109, (715) 924-3200, (800) 317-1720, info@chetekwi.net, www. chetekwi.net

**Chilton** • *Chilton C/C* • Tammy Pethan, Secy., P.O. Box 351, 53014, P 3,708, M 170, (920) 418-1650, info@chiltonchamber.com, chiltonchamber.com.

**Chippewa Falls** • *Chippewa Falls Area C/C* • Mike D. Jordan, Pres., 10 S. Bridge St., 54729, P 13,000, M 440, (715) 723-0331, (888) 723-0024, Fax (715) 723-0332, info@chippewachamber.org, www.chippewachamber.org.

**Clam Lake** • *see Cable*

**Cleveland** • *Cleveland C/C* • Tim Schueler, Pres., P.O. Box 56, 53015, P 1,600, (920) 693-8256

**Clintonville** • *Clintonville Area C/C* • Joanne Doornink, Exec. Dir., 18 S. Main St., P.O. Box 56, 54929, P 4,700, M 150, (715) 823-4606, Fax (715) 823-7318, cvlchmbr@frontiernet.net, clintonvillewi.org/chamber

**Colby** • *Colby C/C* • Todd Schmidt, Pres., P.O. Box 444, 54421, P 1,750, M 75, (715) 223-4435, Fax (715) 223-3109, colbych@ charter.net

**Columbus** • *Columbus Area C/C* • P.O. Box 362, 53925, P 4,500, M 90, (920) 623-3699, www.columbuswichamber.com

**Combined Locks** • *see Kaukauna*

**Conover** • *Conover C/C* • P.O. Box 32, 54519, P 1,235, M 78, (715) 479-4928, (866) 394-4386, vacation@conover.org, www.conover.org

**Crandon** • *Crandon Area C/C* • Melinda Otto, Exec. Dir., 201 S. Lake Ave., P.O. Box 88, 54520, P 10,000, M 110, (715) 478-3450, (800) 334-3387, Fax (715) 478-3388, crandon@newnorth.net, www.visitforestcounty.com

**Cross Plains** • *Cross Plains Area Bus. Assn.* • Amy Hansen, Exec. Dir., P.O. Box 271, 53528, P 3,000, M 90, (608) 843-3166, cpbaexecdir@yahoo.com, www.cpba.hm

**Cuba City** • *Cuba City C/C* • Tim Gile, Pres., 108 N. Main St., 53807, P 2,156, M 70, (608) 744-3456

**Cudahy** • *Cudahy C/C* • Raymond Glowacki, Pres., 3569 E. Barnard Ave., 53110, P 19,000, M 150, (414) 483-8615, Fax (414) 486-9918, www.cudahywichamber.com.

**Cumberland** • *Cumberland C/C* • P.O. Box 665, 54829, P 2,000, M 150, (715) 822-3378, bagafest@cumberland-wisconsin.com, www.cumberland-wisconsin.com

**Danbury** • *Danbury Area C/C* • Jenny Hill, P.O. Box 173, 54830, P 400, M 14, (715) 656-3100

**Darboy** • *see Kaukauna*

**Darlington** • *Darlington Chamber Main Street* • Suzi Osterday, Prog. Mgr., 447 Main St., 53530, P 2,400, M 100, (608) 776-3067, Fax (608) 776-3067, mainstprogram@centurytel.net, www. darlingtonwi.org

**De Forest** • *De Forest Area C/C* • Lisa Beck, Exec. Dir., 201 De Forest St., 53532, P 8,300, M 190, (608) 846-2922, Fax (608) 846-9521, dacc1@centurytel.net, www.deforestarea.com

**Deer Park** • *see New Richmond*

**Deerbrook** • *see Antigo*

**Delafield** • *Delafield C/C* • Deborah Smith, Exec. Dir., P.O. Box 180171, 53018, P 6,996, M 250, (262) 646-8100, (888) 294-1082, Fax (262) 646-8237, info@delafieldchamber.org, www.delafield chamber.org

**Delavan** • *Delavan-Delavan Lake Area C/C* • Jackie Busch, Exec. Dir., 52 E. Walworth Ave., 53115, P 12,000, M 230, (262) 728-5095, Fax (262) 728-9199, info@delavanwi.org, www.delavanwi.org

**Denmark** • *Denmark Comm. Bus. Assn.* • Mark Looker, Pres., P.O. Box 97, 54208, P 2,132, M 54, (920) 863-8423, Fax (920) 863-3237, www.dcbawis.com

**Dodgeville** • *Dodgeville Area C/C* • Bob Berglin, Exec. Dir., 338 N. Iowa St., 53533, P 4,220, M 180, (608) 935-9200, (877) 863-6343, Fax (608) 930-5324, info@dodgeville.com, www.dodgeville.com

**Dousman** • *Dousman C/C* • Mary Mecikalski, Pres., P.O. Box 2, 53118, P 1,500, M 100, (262) 965-2115, mary.mecikalski@ associatedbank.com, www.dousmanchamber.org

**Drummond** • *see Cable*

**Dundas** • *see Kaukauna*

**Eagle River** • *Eagle River C/C* • Conrad Heeg, Exec. Dir., 201 N. Railroad St., P.O. Box 1917, 54521, P 1,500, M 400, (715) 479-6400, (800) 359-6315, Fax (715) 479-1960, info@eagleriver.org, www.eagleriver.org

**Eagle River** • *Vilas County C/C* • Stephanie McClelland, Pres., 330 Court St., 54521, P 21,033, M 12, (715) 479-3649, Fax (715) 479-1978

**East Troy** • *East Troy Area C/C* • Katie Matteson, Exec. Dir., 2096 Church St., Ste. A, P.O. Box 312, 53120, P 9,604, M 188, (262) 642-3770, Fax (262) 642-8769, info@easttroywi.org, www.easttroywi.org

**Eau Claire** • *Eau Claire Area C/C* • Bob McCoy, Pres./CEO, 101 N. Farwell St., Ste. 101, P.O. Box 1107, 54703, P 99,000, M 1,160, (715) 834-1204, Fax (715) 834-1956, information@eauclaire chamber.org, www.eauclairechamber.org.

**Edgerton** • *Edgerton Area C/C* • Kathy Citta, Admin., 20 S. Main St., P.O. Box 5, 53534, P 5,000, M 120, (608) 884-4408, Fax (608) 884-4408, edgertonchamber@verizon.net, www.edgertonwisconsin.com

**Elcho** • *see Antigo*

**Elkhart Lake** • *Elkhart Lake Area C/C* • Lola Roeh, Pres., 41 E. Rhine St., P.O. Box 425, 53020, P 1,028, M 120, (920) 876-2922, (877) 355-3554, Fax (920) 876-3659, elcoc@verizon.net, www.elkhartlake.com

**Elkhorn** • *Elkhorn Area C/C & Tourism Center* • 203 E. Walworth St., P.O. Box 41, 53121, P 9,020, M 275, (262) 723-5788, Fax (262) 723-5784, elkchamber@elkhorn-wi.org, www.elkhorn-wi.org

**Ellsworth** • *Ellsworth Area C/C* • Tami Langer, Pres., P.O. Box 927, 54011, P 3,078, M 125, (715) 273-6442, Fax (715) 273-6442, info@ellsworthchamber.com, www.ellsworthchamber.com

**Elroy** • *Elroy Area Advancement Corp.* • Kris Yager, P.O. Box 52, 53929, P 1,623, M 50, (608) 462-2400, gyager000@centurytel.net, www.elroychamber.com

**Elton** • *see Antigo*

**Evansville** • *Evansville C/C* • Ellen Brown, Exec. Dir., P.O. Box 51, 53536, P 4,600, M 128, (608) 882-5131, info@evansvillechamber.org, www.evansvillechamber.org.

**Fennimore** • *Fennimore Area C/C* • Linda Parrish, Promo. Coord., 850 Lincoln Ave., 53809, P 2,500, M 80, (608) 822-3599, (800) 822-1131, Fax (608) 822-4354, promo@fennimore.com, fennimore.com

**Fish Creek** • *Fish Creek Civic Assn.* • James DeGroot, Ofc. Mgr., 4097 Main St., P.O. Box 74, 54212, P 1,000, M 140, (920) 868-2316, (800) 577-1880, manager@fishcreekinfo.com, www.fishcreekinfo.com

**Fitchburg** • *Fitchburg C/C* • Angela Kinderman, Exec. Dir., 5540 Research Park Dr., 53711, P 22,000, M 315, (608) 288-8284, akinderman@fitchburgchamber.com, www.fitchburgchamber.com

**Florence** • *Florence County C/C* • Russ Trip, Pres., P.O. Box 643, 54121, P 5,500, M 100, (715) 528-5377, www.florencewisconsin.com

**Fond du Lac** • *Fond du Lac Area Assn. of Commerce* • Joseph R. Reitemeier CCE, Pres./CEO, 207 N. Main St., 54935, P 97,000, M 900, (920) 921-9500, Fax (920) 921-9559, info@fdlac.com, www.fdlac.com

**Fontana** • *Geneva Lake West C/C* • Jim Saxton, Pres., 175 Valley View Dr., P.O. Box 118, 53125, P 8,000, M 130, (262) 275-5102, info@genevalakewest.com, www.genevalakewest.com

**Forest Junction** • *see Kaukauna*

**Fort Atkinson** • *Fort Atkinson Area C/C* • Dianne A. Hrobsky, Exec. V.P., 244 N. Main St., 53538, P 12,000, M 400, (920) 563-3210, (888) 733-3678, Fax (920) 563-8946, facoc@fortchamber.com, www.fortchamber.com

**Fox Lake** • *Fox Lake Area C/C* • Julie Quade, Pres., P.O. Box 94, 53933, P 1,500, M 75, (920) 928-3777, (800) 858-4904, Fax (920) 928-2033, foxlake@powercom.net, www.cityoffoxlake.org

**Franklin** • *see Oak Creek*

**Frederic** • *Frederic Area C/C* • Rebecca Harlander, Secy./Treas., P.O. Box 250, 54837, P 1,267, M 125, (715) 327-4836, www.frederic-wi.com

**Freedom** • *see Kaukauna*

**Fremont** • *Fremont Area C/C* • P.O. Box 114, 54940, P 750, M 81, (920) 446-3838, www.fremontwis.com

**Friendship** • *see Adams*

**Friesland** • *Friesland C/C* • Don DeYoung, Pres., P.O. Box 127, 53935, P 300, M 11, (920) 348-5267, Fax (920) 348-6040, friesland@centurytel.net

**Galesville** • *Galesville Area C/C* • Bob Smith, Pres., P.O. Box 196, 54630, P 1,440, M 100, (608) 582-2868, info@galesvillewi.com, www.galesvillewi.com

**Germantown** • *Germantown Area C/C* • Lynn Grgich, Exec. Dir., W 156 N 11251 Pilgrim Rd., P.O. Box 12, 53022, P 20,000, M 225, (262) 255-1812, Fax (262) 255-9033, executivedirector@germantownchamber.org, www.germantownchamber.org

**Glendale** • *Glendale C/C* • Dale Schmidt, Pres./CEO, P.O. Box 170056, 53217, P 13,337, M 220, (414) 332-0900, www.glendale-chamber.com

**Grafton** • *Grafton Area C/C* • Nancy Hundt, Exec. Dir., 1624 Wisconsin Ave., P.O. Box 132, 53024, P 11,500, M 280, (262) 377-1650, Fax (262) 375-7087, chamber@grafton-wi.org, www.grafton-wi.org

**Grand View** • *see Cable*

**Grantsburg** • *Grantsburg C/C* • Ronda Taber, Pres., 316 S. Brad St., P.O. Box 451, 54840, P 1,400, M 75, (715) 463-2405, Fax (715) 463-5555, www.grantsburgwi.com

**Green Bay** • *Green Bay Area C/C* • Paul Jadin, Pres., 300 N. Broadway, Ste. 3A, P.O. Box 1660, 54305, P 220,000, M 1,400, (920) 437-8704, Fax (920) 437-1024, info@titletown.org, www.titletown.org.

**Green Lake** • *Green Lake Area C/C* • Ellen Koeppen, Exec. Dir., 550 Mill St., P.O. Box 337, 54941, P 1,100, M 200, (920) 294-3231, (800) 253-7354, Fax (920) 294-3415, info@visitgreenlake.com, www.visitgreenlake.com

**Greendale** • *Greendale C/C* • Lynn Magner, Pres., P.O. Box 467, 53129, P 16,861, M 50, (414) 423-3900, info@greendalechamber.com, www.greendalechamber.com

**Greenfield** • *Greenfield C/C* • Judy Baxter, Pres., 4818 S. 76th St., Ste., Ste. 129, 53220, P 34,000, M 125, (414) 327-8500, gcc@thegreenfieldchamber.com, www.thegreenfieldchamber.com

**Greenleaf** • *see Kaukauna*

**Greenwood** • *Greenwood C/C* • Pat Linder, Pres., 212 S. Main St., P.O. Box 86, 54437, P 1,000, M 60, (715) 267-7221

**Hartford** • *Hartford Area C/C* • Kim Infalt, Exec. Dir., 225 N. Main St., P.O. Box 270305, 53027, P 12,278, M 280, (262) 673-7002, Fax (262) 673-7057, info@hartfordchamber.org, www.hartfordchamber.org.

**Hartland** • *Hartland C/C* • Lynn Minturn, Exec. Dir., 116 W. Capitol Dr., 53029, P 8,000, M 200, (262) 367-7059, Fax (262) 367-2980, admin@hartland-wi.org, www.hartland-wi.org

**Hayward** • *Hayward Area C/C* • Kevin Ruetten, Exec. Dir., P.O. Box 726, 54843, P 8,000, M 310, (715) 634-8662, (800) 724-2992, Fax (715) 634-8498, info@haywardareachamber.com, www.haywardareachamber.com

**Holland** • *see Kaukauna*

**Holmen** • *see Onalaska*

**Horicon** • *Horicon C/C* • 407 E. Lake St., P.O. Box 23, 53032, P 3,914, M 85, (920) 485-3200, writeus@horiconchamber.com, www.horiconchamber.com

**Hudson** • *Hudson Area C/C & Tourism Bur.* • Kim Heinemann, Pres., 502 Second St., 54016, P 20,000, M 650, (715) 386-8411, (800) 657-6775, Fax (715) 386-8432, info@hudsonwi.org, www.hudsonwi.org

**Hurley** • *Hurley Area C/C* • Sarah Robinson, Exec. Dir., 316 Silver St., 54534, P 1,818, M 180, (715) 561-4334, (866) 340-4334, www.hurleywi.com.

**Iola** · *Iola-Scandinavia Area C/C* · Chris Aasen, Pres., P.O. Box 167, 54945, P 1,289, M 65, (715) 445-4000, Fax (715) 445-4169, info@iolaoldcarshow.com, www.ischamber.org

**Iron River** · *Iron River Area C/C* · Shelley Knabe, Exec. Dir., P.O. Box 448, 54847, P 2,000, M 140, (715) 372-8558, Fax (715) 372-8558, info@visitironriver.com, www.visitironriver.com

**Janesville** · *Forward Janesville Inc.* · John Beckord, Pres., 14 S. Jackson St., 53548, P 62,000, M 600, (608) 757-3160, Fax (608) 757-3170, forward@forwardjanesville.com, www.forwardjanesville.com

**Jefferson** · *Jefferson C/C* · Janet M. Werner, Exec. Dir., 122 W. Garland St., 53549, P 7,787, M 220, (920) 674-4511, Fax (920) 674-1499, coc@jefnet.com, www.jeffersonchamberwi.com.

**Johnson Creek** · *Johnson Creek Area C/C* · Connie Oestreich, Exec. Dir., 204 Union St., P.O. Box 527, 53038, P 2,044, M 82, (920) 699-4949, admin@johnsoncreekchamber.com, www.johnson creekchamber.com

**Juneau** · *Juneau C/C* · Gretchen Last, Pres., P.O. Box 4, 53039, P 2,500, M 75, (920) 386-3359, www.juneauwi.org

**Kaukauna** · *Heart of the Valley C/C* · Bobbie Beckman, Exec. Dir., 101 E. Wisconsin Ave., 54130, P 13,000, M 550, (920) 766-1616, Fax (920) 766-5504, bbeckman@heartofthevalleychamber.com, www.heartofthevalleychamber.com

**Kempster** · *see Antigo*

**Kenosha** · *Kenosha Area C/C* · Lou Molitor, Exec. Dir., 600 52nd St., Ste. 130, 53140, P 150,934, M 700, (262) 654-1234, Fax (262) 654-4655, info@kenoshaareachamber.com, www.kenoshaarea chamber.com

**Kewaskum** · *Kewaskum Area C/C* · P.O. Box 300, 53040, P 3,500, M 70, (262) 626-3336, www.kewaskum.org

**Kewaunee** · *Kewaunee Area C/C* · Jamie Sperber, Exec. Coord., 308 N. Main, P.O. Box 243, 54216, P 3,000, M 120, (920) 388-4822, (800) 666-8214, info@kewaunee.org, www.kewaunee.org

**Kiel** · *Kiel Area Assn. of Commerce* · P.O. Box 44, 53042, P 3,450, M 125, (920) 894-4638, www.kielwi.org

**Kimberly** · *see Kaukauna*

**La Crosse** · *La Crosse Area C/C* · Dick Granchalek, Pres., 712 Main St., 54601, P 110,743, M 900, (608) 784-4880, (800) 889-0539, Fax (608) 784-4919, lse_chamber@centurytel.net, www.lacrossechamber.com.

**Lac du Flambeau** · *Lac du Flambeau C/C* · 602 Peace Pipe Rd., P.O. Box 456, 54538, P 2,200, M 75, (715) 588-3346, (877) 588-3346, Fax (715) 588-9408, info@lacduflambeauchamber.com, www.lacduflambeauchamber.com

**Ladysmith** · *Greater Ladysmith Area C/C* · Ron Moore, Pres., 209 W. 5th St. S., 54848, P 4,000, M 200, (715) 532-7328, Fax (715) 532-2649, ladysmithchamber@centurytel.net, www.ladysmithchamber.com

**Lake Geneva** · *Geneva Lake Area C/C* · George F. Hennerley, Exec. V.P., 201 Wrigley Dr., 53147, P 7,400, M 355, (262) 248-4416, Fax (262) 248-1000, lgcc@lakegenevawi.com, www.lakegenevawi.com

**Lake Mills** · *Lake Mills Area C/C* · 200C Water St., 53551, P 5,000, M 100, (920) 648-3585, Fax (920) 648-6751, chamber@lakemills.org, www.lakemills.org

**Lake Nebagamon** · *Nebagamon Comm. Assn.* · Catherine Coletta, Prog. Chair, 11507 E. Waterfront Dr., 54849, P 1,000, M 50, (715) 374-2283, (715) 374-3101, Fax (715) 374-3766, ccoletta@centurytel.net, www.lakenebagamonwi.com

**Lakewood** · *Lakewood Area C/C* · 15386 State Hwy. 32, P.O. Box 87, 54138, P 2,300, M 120, (715) 276-6500, info@lakewoodarea chamber.com, www.lakewoodareachamber.com

**Lancaster** · *Lancaster Area C/C* · Marge Sherwin, Exec. Dir., 206 S. Madison St., P.O. Box 292, 53813, P 4,200, M 100, (608) 723-2820, Fax (608) 723-7409, chamber@lancasterwisconsin.com, www.lancasterwisconsin.com

**Land O'Lakes** · *Land O'Lakes C/C* · Mark Gostisha, Pres., 6484 Hwy. 45 N., P.O. Box 599, 54540, P 800, M 135, (715) 547-3432, (800) 236-3432, Fax (715) 547-8010, infolandolakes@gmail.com, www.landolakes-wi.org

**LaPointe** · *Madeline Island C/C* · P.O. Box 274, 54850, P 272, M 100, (715) 747-2801, (888) 475-3386, Fax (715) 747-2800, info@madelineisland.com, www.madelineisland.com

**Lena** · *Lena Comm. Dev. Corp.* · A.H. Schuettpelz, Secy./Treas., 304 N. Rosera, P.O. Box 59, 54139, P 600, M 45, (920) 829-5525

**Little Chute** · *see Kaukauna*

**Lodi** · *Lodi C/C* · Dori Bilse, Exec. Asst., P.O. Box 43, 53555, P 3,200, M 80, (608) 592-4412, Fax (608) 592-4412, information@lodiwisconsin.com, www.lodiwisconsin.com

**Lomira** · *Lomira Area C/C* · Jiim Bisek, Pres., P.O. Box 386, 53048, P 2,200, M 100, (920) 269-7229, (920) 269-4112, www.lomira.com

**Luxemburg** · *Luxemburg C/C* · Tim Ledvina, Pres., P.O. Box 141, 54217, P 2,200, M 200, (920) 845-1005, Fax (920) 845-1018, www.luxemburgusa.com

**Madison** · *Greater Madison C/C* · Jennifer Alexander, Pres., 615 E. Washington Ave., 2nd Flr., P.O. Box 71, 53701, P 460,000, M 1,750, (608) 256-8348, Fax (608) 256-0333, info@greater madisonchamber.com, www.greatermadisonchamber.com

**Manawa** · *Manawa Area C/C* · Ken Groholski, Pres., P.O. Box 221, 54949, P 1,400, M 45, (920) 596-2495, manawachamber@wolfnet.net, www.manawachamber.com

**Manitowish Waters** · *Manitowish Waters C/C* · Jodi McMahon, Dir., 4 S. U.S. Hwy. 51, P.O. Box 251, 54545, P 698, M 130, (715) 543-8488, (888) 626-9877, Fax (715) 543-2519, funinfo@mani-towishwaters.org, www.manitowishwaters.org

**Manitowoc** · *Chamber of Manitowoc County* · Karen Szyman, Exec. Dir., 1515 Memorial Dr., P.O. Box 903, 54221, P 34,000, M 500, (920) 684-5575, (866) 727-5575, Fax (920) 684-1915, info@chambermanitowoccounty.org, www.chambermanitowoc county.org

**Marinette** · *Marinette/Menominee Area C/C* · Mary D. Johns, Exec. Dir., 601 Marinette Ave., 54143, P 21,000, M 410, (715) 735-6681, (906) 863-2679, Fax (715) 735-6682, chamber@centurytel.net, www.mandmchamber.com

**Markesan** · *Markesan Area C/C* · Clyde Olson, Pres., P.O. Box 327, 53946, P 1,397, M 55, (920) 398-8023, (888) LT-GREEN, www.markesanwi.com

**Marshfield** · *Marshfield Area C/C & Ind.* · Scott Larson, Exec. Dir., 700 S. Central Ave., P.O. Box 868, 54449, P 20,000, M 600, (715) 384-3454, Fax (715) 387-8925, info@marshfieldchamber.com, www.marshfieldchamber.com

**Mauston** · *Greater Mauston Area C/C* · Virginia Hustad, Ofc. Admin., 503 State Rd. 82 E., P.O. Box 171, 53948, P 4,143, M 175, (608) 847-4142, Fax (608) 847-4142, chamber@mauston.com, www.mauston.com

**Mayville** · *Mayville Area C/C* · Linda Turk, 119 S. Main St., P.O. Box 185, 53050, P 5,000, M 100, (920) 387-5776, (800) 256-7670, Fax (920) 387-5776, info@mayvillechamber.com, www.mayville chamber.com

**Mazomanie** · *Greater Mazomanie Area C/C* · Bob Brumley, Pres., P.O. Box 211, 53560, P 1,550, M 25, (608) 795-2789, (608) 795-9824, info@mazomaniechamber.com, www.mazomanie chamber.com

**McFarland** · *McFarland C/C* · Jim Hartman, Pres., 4869 Larson Beach Rd., Ste. B, P.O. Box 372, 53558, P 7,000, M 125, (608) 838-4011, Fax (608) 838-4011, info@mcfarlandchamber.com, www. mcfarlandchamber.com

**Medford** · *Medford Area C/C* · Susan Emmerich, Exec. Dir., 104 E. Perkins St., P.O. Box 172, 54451, P 4,300, M 325, (715) 748-4729, (888) 682-9567, Fax (715) 748-6899, chamber@dwave.net, www. medfordwis.com

**Menomonee Falls** · *Menomonee Falls C/C* · Suzanne Jeskewitz, Exec. Dir., N88 W16621 Appleton Ave., P.O. Box 73, 53052, P 34,600, M 400, (262) 251-2430, Fax (262) 251-0969, sue@ fallschamber.com, www.menomoneefallschamber.com.

**Menomonie** · *Greater Menomonie Area C/C* · Lisa Montgomery, Exec. Dir., 342 E. Main St., 54751, P 15,100, M 500, (715) 235-9087, Fax (715) 235-2824, info@menomoniechamber.org, www. menomoniechamber.org.

**Mequon** · *see Thiensville*

**Mercer** · *Mercer C/C* · Tina Brunell, Ofc. Mgr., 5150 N. Hwy. 51, 54547, P 1,808, M 125, (715) 476-2389, Fax (715) 476-2389, info@mercercc.com, www.mercercc.com

**Merrill** · *Merrill Area C/C* · Jane Ann Savaske, Exec. Dir., 705 N. Center Ave., 54452, P 25,000, M 290, (715) 536-9474, (877) 90-PARKS, Fax (715) 539-2043, info@merrillchamber.com, www. merrillchamber.com

**Middleton** · *Middleton C/C* · Van Nutt, Exec. Dir., 7507 Hubbard Ave., 53562, P 17,000, M 550, (608) 827-5797, Fax (608) 831-7765, chamber@middletonchamber.com, www.middletonchamber.com

**Milltown** · *Milltown Comm. Club* · P.O. Box 402, 54858, P 900, M 20, (715) 825-2222, (715) 825-3258, info@milltown-wi.com, www.milltown-wi.com

**Milton** · *Milton Area C/C, Ind. & Tourism* · Christina Slaback, Exec. Dir., 508 Campus St., P.O. Box 222, 53563, P 6,000, M 150, (608) 868-6222, info@maccit.com, www.maccit.com

**Milwaukee** · *Metro Milwaukee Assn. of Commerce* · Timothy Sheehy, Pres., 756 N. Milwaukee St., Ste. 400, 53202, P 1,500,000, M 2,000, (414) 287-4100, Fax (414) 271-7753, www.mmac.org.

**Mineral Point** · *Mineral Point C/C* · Joy Gieseke, Exec. Dir., 225 High St., 53565, P 2,617, M 150, (608) 987-3201, (888) POINT-WI, Fax (608) 987-4425, info@mineralpoint.com, www.mineralpoint.com

**Minocqua** · *Minocqua-Arbor Vitae-Woodruff Area C/C* · Diane Hapka, Exec. Dir., 8216 Hwy. 51 S., P.O. Box 1006, 54548, P 10,000, M 450, (715) 356-5266, (800) 446-6784, Fax (715) 358-2446, mavwacc@minocqua.org, www.minocqua.org.

**Mishicot** · *Mishicot Area Growth & Improvement Committee* · P.O. Box 237, 54228, P 1,400, M 40, (920) 755-3411, magic@ tm.net, www.mishicot.org

**Mondovi** · *Mondovi Business Assn.* · Nan Wolfe, Pres., P.O. Box 25, 54755, P 2,700, M 40, (715) 926-6001, www.mondovi.com

**Monona** · *Monona C/C* · Terri Groves, Exec. Dir., 6320 Monona Dr., 53716, P 8,100, M 261, (608) 222-8565, Fax (608) 222-8596, chamber@monona.com, www.monona.com

**Monroe** · *Monroe C/C & Ind.* · Pamela Christopher, Exec. Dir., 1505 9th St., 53566, P 10,842, M 200, (608) 325-7648, Fax (608) 328-2241, mcci@tds.net, www.monroechamber.org.

**Montello** · *Marquette Now* · Laureen McHugh, V.P., P.O. Box 219, 53949, P 14,000, M 264, (608) 297-7420, (888) 318-0362, accentsbylaureen@aol.com, www.marquettenow.com

**Mosinee** · *Mosinee Area C/C* · Tammy Campo, Exec. Dir., 301 Main St., Ste. 102, 54455, P 4,008, M 120, (715) 693-4330, Fax (715) 693-9555, macoc@mtc.net, www.mosineechamber.org

**Mount Horeb** · *Mount Horeb Area C/C* · Melissa Theisen, Exec. Dir., 300 E. Main St., 53572, P 8,000, M 200, (608) 437-5914, 88-TROLLWAY, Fax (608) 437-1427, info@trollway.com, www.trollway.com

**Mountain** · *see Lakewood*

**Mukwonago** · *Mukwonago Area C/C & Tourism Center* · Mary Blott, Exec. Dir., 121 Wolf Run, Ste. 4, 53149, P 15,000, M 377, (262) 363-7758, Fax (262) 363-7730, director@mukwonago chamber.org, www.mukwonagochamber.org.

**Muscoda** · *Muscoda Chamber & Ind. Dev. Corp.* · Mark Jelinek, Pres., P.O. Box 587, 53573, P 1,500, M 65, (608) 739-9158, (608) 739-4234

**Muskego** · *Muskego Area C/C* · Kathy Chiaverotti, Exec. Dir., S. 74 W. 16894 Janesvile Rd., P.O. Box 234, 53150, P 23,000, M 240, (414) 422-1155, Fax (414) 422-1415, info@muskego.org, www. muskego.org

**Namakagon** · *see Cable*

**Necedah** · *Necedah C/C* · Roger Herried, Admin., 101 Center St., P.O. Box 244, 54646, P 888, M 61, (608) 565-2261, necedahadmin@ necedah.us, www.necedah.us

**Neenah** · *see Appleton*

**Neillsville** · *Neillsville Area C/C* · Cindy Schwanz, Exec. Dir., 106 W. Division, P.O. Box 52, 54456, P 2,800, M 171, (715) 743-6444, Fax (715) 743-8262, nacc@tds.net, www.neillsville.org

**New Berlin** · *New Berlin Chamber & Visitors Bur.* · Bob Bruemmer, Pres., 2140 S. Calhoun Rd., 53151, P 39,000, M 185, (262) 786-5280, Fax (262) 786-9165, office@nb-chamber.org, www.nb-chamber.org

**New Glarus** · *New Glarus C/C* · 418 Railroad St., 53574, P 2,000, M 125, (608) 527-2095, (800) 527-6838, Fax (608) 527-4991, info@swisstown.com, www.swisstown.com

**New Holstein** · *New Holstein Area C/C* · Robert Bosma, Pres., P.O. Box 17, 53061, P 3,300, M 115, (920) 898-5771, nhsecretary@ newholstein.org, www.newholstein.org

**New Lisbon** · *New Lisbon Area C/C* · Tina Brounacker, Exec. Secy., 218 E. Bridge St., P.O. Box 79, 53950, P 1,500, M 120, (608) 562-3555, Fax (608) 562-5625, nlchambr@mwt.net, www. newlisbonchamber.com

**New London** · *New London Area C/C* · Laurie Shaw, Exec. Dir., 301 E. Beacon Ave., 54961, P 7,000, M 250, (920) 982-5822, Fax (920) 982-6344, chamber@newlondonwi.org, www.newlondon chamber.com

**New Richmond** · *New Richmond Area C/C & Visitors Bur.* · Russ Korpela, Exec. Dir., 245A S. Knowles Ave., 54017, P 8,000, M 250, (715) 246-2900, (800) 654-6380, Fax (715) 246-7100, nrchamber@pressenter.com, www.newrichmondchamber.com

**Oak Creek** · *South Suburban C/C* · Barbara Wesener CAE, Exec. Dir., 8580 S. Howell Ave., 53154, P 55,000, M 420, (414) 768-5845, Fax (414) 768-5848, info@southsuburbanchamber.com, www. southsuburbanchamber.com

**Oconomowoc** · *Oconomowoc Area C/C* · Pat Ornberg, Exec. Dir., 152 E. Wisconsin Ave., 53066, P 14,000, M 368, (262) 567-2666, Fax (262) 567-3477, chamber@oconomowoc.org, www. oconomowoc.org.

**Oconto** · *Oconto Area C/C* · Nancy Rhode, Secy., 110 Brazeau Ave., P.O. Box 174, 54153, P 4,900, M 140, (920) 834-6254, www.ocontocounty.org

**Oconto Falls** · *Oconto Falls Area C/C* · Michele Ripley, P.O. Box 24, 54154, P 2,900, M 115, (920) 846-8306, Fax (920) 846-4516, ofchamber@centurytel.net, www.ocontofallschamber.com

**Omro** · *Omro Area C/C* · Jesse Koonce, Dir., 130 W. Larrabee St., 54963, P 3,500, M 125, (920) 685-6960, Fax (920) 685-0384, omrochamber@charterinternet.net, www.omro-wi.com

**Onalaska** · *Center for Commerce & Tourism* · Jean Lunde, Dir., 1101 Main St., 54650, P 16,425, (608) 781-9570, (800) 873-1901, Fax (608) 781-9572, info@discoveronalaska.com, www.discover onalaska.com

**Oostburg** · *Center for Commerce & Tourism* · P.O. Box 700198, 53070, P 3,000, M 50, (920) 564-2336, www.oostburg.org

**Oregon** · *Oregon Area C/C* · Marechiel Santos-Lang, Exec. Dir., 733 N. Main St., Lower Level, P.O. Box 123, 53575, P 8,000, M 206, (608) 835-3697, Fax (608) 835-2475, director@oregonwi.com, www.oregonwi.com

**Osceola** · *Osceola Area C/C* · Paul Anderson, Pres., 310 Chieftain St., P.O. Box 251, 54020, P 2,700, M 70, (715) 755-3300, (800) 947-0581, Fax (715) 294-2210, chamber@vil.osceola.wi.us, www.osceolachamber.org

**Oshkosh** · *Oshkosh C/C* · John A. Casper, Pres./CEO, 120 Jackson St., 54901, P 64,132, M 1,050, (920) 303-2266, Fax (920) 303-2263, info@oshkoshchamber.com, www.oshkoshchamber.com

**Owen** · *Owen-Withee Area C/C* · Sid Borgeson, Pres., P.O. Box 186, 54460, P 1,600, M 64, (715) 229-2697, info@owenwithee chamber.org, www.owenwitheechamber.org

**Palmyra** · *Palmyra Area C/C* · Kathy Walters, Pres., P.O. Box 139, 53156, P 1,704, M 40, (262) 495-8316, (414) 531-4357, information@ palmyrawi.com, www.palmyrawi.com

**Pardeeville** · *Pardeeville Area Bus. Assn.* · P.O. Box 337, 53954, P 2,100, M 50, (608) 429-9888

**Park Falls** · *Park Falls Area C/C* · Sue Holm, Exec. Dir., 400 4th Ave. S., 54552, P 3,104, M 180, (715) 762-2703, (877) 762-2703, Fax (715) 762-4130, chamber@parkfalls.com, www.parkfalls.com.

**Parrish** · *see Antigo*

**Pearson** · *see Antigo*

**Pelican Lake** · *Pelican Lake C/C* · Chet Haatvedt, Pres., P.O. Box 45, 54463, P 650, M 60, (715) 487-5222, pelicanlakecc@frontier net.net, www.pelicanlakewi.org

**Peshtigo** · *Peshtigo C/C* · Cindy Hagert, Secy., P.O. Box 36, 54157, P 4,100, M 100, (715) 582-0327, Fax (715) 582-0327, peshtigochamber@centurytel.net, www.peshtigochamber.com

**Pewaukee** · *Pewaukee C/C* · Laura Podd, Exec. Dir., 214 Oakton Ave., 53072, P 15,000, M 200, (262) 691-8851, Fax (262) 691-0922, info@pewaukeechamber.org, www.pewaukeechamber.org

**Phelps** · *Phelps C/C* · P.O. Box 217, 54554, P 1,400, M 78, (715) 545-3800, (877) 669-7077, www.phelpscofc.org

**Phillips** · *Phillips Area C/C* · Judith Boers, Exec. Dir., 305 S. Lake Ave., 54555, P 1,748, M 180, (715) 339-4100, (888) 408-4800, Fax (715) 339-4190, pacc@pctcnet.net, phillipswisconsin.net

**Phlox** · *see Antigo*

**Pickerel** · *see Antigo*

**Platteville** · *Platteville C/C* · Kathy Kopp, Exec. Dir., 275 Bus. Hwy. 151 W., P.O. Box 16, 53818, P 10,007, M 280, (608) 348-8888, Fax (608) 348-8890, chamber@platteville.com, www.platteville.

**Plover** · *see Stevens Point*

**Plymouth** · *Plymouth C/C* · Lisa Hurley, Exec. Dir., 647 Walton Dr., P.O. Box 584, 53073, P 8,500, M 340, (920) 893-0079, (888) 693-8263, Fax (920) 893-8473, plymouthchamber@excel.net, www.plymouthwisconsin.com

**Polar** · *see Antigo*

**Port Washington** · *Port Washington C/C* · Mary Monday, Exec. Dir., 126 E. Grand Ave., P.O. Box 514, 53074, P 10,500, M 200, (262) 284-0900, (800) 719-4881, Fax (262) 284-0591, mary@ portwashingchamber.com, www.portwashingchamber.com

**Portage** · *Portage Area C/C* · Marianne Hanson, Exec. Dir., 104 W. Cook St., 53901, P 14,306, M 340, (608) 742-6242, (800) 474-2525, Fax (608) 742-3799, pacc@portagewi.com, www.portagewi.com.

**Potosi** · *Potosi-Tennyson Area C/C* · Marilyn Hauth, Pres., P.O. Box 11, 53820, P 711, M 40, (608) 763-2261, (608) 763-2539, www.potosi.wisconsin.com

**Poynette** · *Lake Wisconsin C/C* · P.O. Box 441, 53955, P 6,000, M 92, (608) 635-8700, info@lakewisconsin.org, www.lake wisconsin.org

**Poynette** · *Poynette Area C/C* · Brit Schoeneberg, Pres., P.O. Box 625, 53955, P 2,496, M 90, (608) 635-2425, britlivw@aol.com, www.poynettechamber.com

**Prairie du Chien** · *Prairie du Chien Area C/C* · Robert Moses, Exec. Dir., 211 S. Main St., P.O. Box 326, 53821, P 6,000, M 285, (608) 326-8555, (800) 732-1673, Fax (608) 326-7744, pdccoc@ mhtc.net, www.prairieduchien.org

**Prairie du Sac** · *Sauk Prairie Area C/C* · Leslie Bruner, Exec. Dir., 421 Water St. #105, 53578, P 7,500, M 170, (608) 643-4168, (800) 683-2453, Fax (608) 643-3544, saukprairie@verizon.net, www.saukprairie.com

**Prescott** · *Prescott Area C/C* · Trisha Huber, Coord., 237 Broad St. N., 54021, P 4,000, M 115, (715) 262-3284, Fax (715) 262-5943, info@prescottwi.com, www.prescottwi.com

**Presque Isle** · *Presque Isle C/C* · P.O. Box 135, 54557, P 600, M 50, (715) 686-2910, (888) 835-6508, Fax (715) 686-2913, presqueisle@centurytel.net, www.presqueisle.com

**Princeton** · *Greater Princeton Area C/C* · P.O. Box 45, 54968, P 1,500, M 150, (920) 295-3877, Fax (920) 295-4375, info@ princetonwi.com, www.princetonwi.com

**Pulaski** · *Pulaski Area C/C* · Gloria Morgan, Exec. Dir., 159 W. Pulaski St., P.O. Box 401, 54162, P 3,300, M 95, (920) 822-4400, Fax (920) 822-4455, pacc@netnet.net, www.pulaskichamber.org

**Racine** · *Racine Area Mfg. & Commerce* · Roger Caron, Pres., 300 Fifth St., 53403, P 189,000, M 750, (262) 634-1931, Fax (262) 634-7422, ramac@racinechamber.com, www.racinechamber.com.

**Randolph** · *Randolph C/C* · Joyce Gorr, Secy./Treas., P.O. Box 66, 53956, P 1,800, M 65, (920) 326-4769

**Reedsburg** · *Reedsburg Area C/C* · Kristine Koenecke, Exec. Dir., 240 Railroad St., P.O. Box 142, 53959, P 8,883, M 210, (608) 524-2850, (800) 844-3507, Fax (608) 524-5392, reedsbrg@rucls.net, www.reedsburg.org

**Rhinelander** · *Rhinelander Area C/C* · Kim Swisher, Exec. Dir., 450 W. Kemp St., P.O. Box 795, 54501, P 9,000, M 285, (715) 365-7464, (800) 236-4386, Fax (715) 365-7467, info@rhinelander-chamber.com, www.rhinelanderchamber.com.

**Rice Lake** · *Rice Lake Area C/C* · Karen Heram, Exec. Dir., 37 S. Main St., 54868, P 10,000, M 300, (715) 234-2126, (877) 234-2126, Fax (715) 234-2085, chamber@rice-lake.com, www.ricelakechamber.org

**Richland Center** · *Richland Area C/C* · Susan Price, Exec. Dir., 397 W. Seminary, P.O. Box 128, 53581, P 17,000, M 150, (608) 647-6205, info@richlandchamber.com, www.richlandchamber.com

**Ripon** · *Ripon Area C/C* · Paula Price, Exec. Dir., 127 Jefferson St., P.O. Box 305, 54971, P 7,542, M 235, (920) 748-6764, Fax (920) 748-6784, chamber@ripon-wi.com, www.ripon-wi.com

**River Falls** · *River Falls Area C/C & Tourism Bur.* · Rosanne Bump, CEO, 214 N. Main St., 54022, P 13,000, M 275, (715) 425-2533, Fax (715) 425-2305, info@rfchamber.com, www.rfchamber.com

**Saint Croix Falls** · *Falls C/C* · Shelley Staeven, Exec. Dir., 106 S. Washington, P.O. Box 178, 54024, P 3,000, M 150, (715) 483-3580, (800) 447-4958, Fax (715) 483-3580, info@scfwi.com, www.scfwi.com

**Saint Germain** · *Saint Germain C/C* · William Neider, Dir., 473 Hwy. 70 E., P.O. Box 155, 54558, P 2,000, M 160, (715) 477-2205, (800) 727-7203, Fax (715) 542-3423, info@st-germain.com, www.st-germain.com

**Sauk City** · *see Prairie Du Sac*

**Saukville** · *Saukville C/C* · Stacey Frey, Exec. Dir., P.O. Box 80238, 53080, P 4,200, M 110, (262) 268-1970, Fax (262) 268-1970, saukvillechamber@earthlink.net, www.saukvillechamber.org

**Sayner** · *Sayner-Starlake C/C* · P.O. Box 191, 54560, P 550, M 50, (715) 542-3789, saynerstarlake@wildblue.net, www.sayner-starlake.org

**Sharon** · *Sharon Main Street C/C* · 194 Baldwin St., P.O. Box 528, 53585, P 1,552, (262) 736-6246, info@villageofsharon.com, www.villageofsharon.com/chamber

**Shawano** · *Shawano Country C/C* · Nancy Smith, Exec. Dir., 1263 S. Main St., P.O. Box 38, 54166, P 40,000, M 430, (715) 524-2139, (800) 235-8528, Fax (715) 524-3127, chamber@shawano.com, www.shawanocountry.com.

**Sheboygan** · *Sheboygan County C/C* · Delores E. Olsen, Exec. Dir., 712 Riverfront Dr., Ste. 101, 53081, P 113,000, M 850, (920) 457-9491, Fax (920) 457-6269, olsen@sheboygan.org, www.sheboygan.org

**Sheboygan Falls** · *Sheboygan Falls C/C* · Nancy Verstrate, Exec. Dir., 504 Broadway St., 53085, P 7,000, M 178, (920) 467-6206, Fax (920) 467-9571, chambermnst@sheboyganfalls.org, www.sheboyganfalls.org

**Sherwood** · *see Kaukauna*

**Siren** · *Siren Area C/C* · Gary Kannenberg, Pres., P.O. Box 57, 54872, P 900, M 90, (715) 349-8399, info@visitsiren.com, www.visitsiren.com

**Slinger** · *Slinger Advancement Assn.* · Dr. Don Crego, Pres., P.O. Box 422, 53086, P 5,000, M 55, (262) 644-5866, www.slingersaa.com

**Somerset** · *also see New Richmond*

**Somerset** · *Somerset Area C/C* · Kathy Land, P.O. Box 357, 54025, P 1,556, M 36, (715) 247-3366, schamber@somtel.net, www.somerset-chamber.com

**South Milwaukee** · *South Milwaukee Assn. of Commerce* · Bryan Lorentzen, Pres., 2424 15th Ave., P.O. Box 207, 53172, P 21,315, M 165, (414) 762-2222, Fax (414) 768-9505, laurac@smaconline.com, www.smaconline.com

**Sparta** · *Sparta Area C/C* · Sharon Folcey, Exec. Dir., 111 Milwaukee St., 54656, P 9,160, M 345, (608) 269-4123, (800) 354-2453, Fax (608) 269-3350, spartachamber@centurytel.net, www.spartachamber.org

**Spencer** · *Spencer Area C/C* · Dan Schwantes, Pres., P.O. Box 52, 54479, P 1,941, M 62, (715) 659-5423

**Spooner** · *Spooner Area C/C* · Ted Schmitz, Pres., 122 N. River St., 54801, P 2,500, M 100, (715) 635-2168, (800) 367-3306, Fax (715) 635-5170, spoonerareachamber@centurytel.net, www.spoonerchamber.org

**Spring Green** · *Spring Green Area C/C* · Dawn Eno, Ofc. Mgr., P.O. Box 3, 53588, P 8,000, M 125, (608) 588-2054, sgacc@verizon.net, www.springgreen.com

**Spring Valley** · *Spring Valley C/C* · P.O. Box 351, 54767, P 1,189, M 60, (715) 778-5015, www.springvalleywisconsin.org

**Stanley** · *Stanley Area C/C* · Dale Johnson, Treas., 117 N. Broadway St., P.O. Box 123, 54768, P 3,378, M 70, (715) 644-3336

**Star Prairie** · *see New Richmond*

**Starlake** · *see Sayner*

**Stevens Point** · *Portage County Bus. Cncl.* · Lori Dehlinger, Exec. Dir., 5501 Vern Holmes Dr., 54481, P 69,000, M 526, (715) 344-1940, Fax (715) 344-4473, info@portagecountybiz.com, www.portagecountybiz.com

**Stone Lake** · *Stone Lake C/C* · Karen Skwira, Pres., P.O. Box 75, 54876, P 300, M 20, (715) 865-3378, (715) 865-3302, www.stonelakewi.us

**Stoughton** · *Stoughton C/C* · David B. Phillips, Exec. Dir., 532 E. Main St., 53589, P 13,000, M 250, (608) 873-7912, (888) 873-7912, Fax (608) 873-7743, administrator@stoughtonwi.com, www.stoughtonwi.com

**Stratford** · *Stratford C/C* · Dan Hartwig, Pres., P.O. Box 312, 54484, P 1,600, M 100, (715) 687-4466, www.stratfordwi.com

**Summit Lake** · *see Antigo*

**Sun Prairie** · *Sun Prairie C/C* · Ann Smith, Exec. Dir., 109 E. Main St., 53590, P 25,000, M 376, (608) 837-4547, Fax (608) 837-8765, spchamber@verizon.net, www.sunprairiechamber.com

**Superior** · *Superior-Douglas County C/C* · David W. Minor, Pres./CEO, 205 Belknap St., 54880, P 45,000, M 450, (715) 394-7716, (800) 942-5313, Fax (715) 394-3810, chamber@superiorchamber.org, www.superiorchamber.org

**Sussex** · *Sussex Area C/C* · Sheri Pellechia, Exec. Dir., N64 W24050 Main St., P.O. Box 24, 53089, P 9,812, M 120, (262) 246-4940, Fax (262) 246-7350, info@sussexareachamber.org, www.sussexareachamber.org

**Thiensville** · *Mequon-Thiensville Area C/C* · Linda Oakes, Exec. Dir., 250 S. Main St., 53092, P 25,000, M 550, (262) 512-9358, Fax (262) 512-9359, lindao@mtchamber.org, www.mtchamber.org

**Thorp** · *Thorp Area C/C* · Randy Reeg, Pres., P.O. Box 16, 54771, P 1,650, M 45, (715) 669-5321

**Three Lakes** · *Three Lakes Area C/C* · Terilyn Fritz, Exec. Dir., 1704 Superior St., P.O. Box 268, 54562, P 2,400, M 120, (715) 546-3344, (800) 972-6103, Fax (715) 546-2103, vacation@threelakes.com, www.threelakes.com

**Tomah** · *Greater Tomah Area C/C* · Christopher Hanson, Exec. Dir., 901 Kilbourn Ave., P.O. Box 625, 54660, P 8,000, M 310, (608) 372-2166, (800) 94-TOMAH, Fax (608) 372-2167, info@tomahwisconsin.com, www.tomahwisconsin.com

**Tomahawk** · *Tomahawk Reg. C/C* · 208 N. 4th St., P.O. Box 412, 54487, P 3,770, M 300, (715) 453-5334, (800) 569-2160, Fax (715) 453-1178, chambert@gototomahawk.com, www.gototomahawk.com.

**Townsend** · *see Lakewood*

**Trempealeau** · *Trempealeau C/C* · Jean Galasinski, Pres., 24455 3rd St., P.O. Box 242, 54661, P 1,400, M 45, (608) 534-6780, chamber@trempealeau.net, www.trempealeau.net

**Twin Lakes** · *Twin Lakes Area Chamber & Bus. Assn. Inc.* · Joanne Oreilly, Ofc. Admin., 349 E. Main St., P.O. Box 64, 53181, P 5,164, M 125, (262) 877-2220, Fax (262) 877-9437, info@twinlakeschamber.com, www.twinlakeschamber.com

**Two Rivers** · *see Manitowoc*

**Union Grove** · *Greater Union Grove Area C/C* · Terri Gray, Exec. Dir., 925 15th Ave., P.O. Box 44, 53182, P 15,000, M 110, (262) 878-4606, Fax (262) 878-9125, ugchamber@att.net, www.uniongrovechamber.org

**Verona** · *Verona Area C/C* · Karl Curtis, Exec. Dir., 205 S. Main, P.O. Box 930003, 53593, P 10,000, M 296, (608) 845-5777, Fax (608) 845-2519, info@veronawi.com, www.veronawi.com

**Viroqua** · *Viroqua C/C Main St.* · Rebecca Eby, Exec. Dir., 220 S. Main St., 54665, P 4,335, M 200, (608) 637-2575, infodesk@viroqua-wisconsin.com, www.viroqua-wisconsin.com

**Wabeno** · *Wabeno C/C* · Ron Drott, P.O. Box 105, 54566, P 1,500, M 49, (715) 473-5400

**Washburn** · *Washburn Area C/C* · Bruce Hanson, Exec. Dir., P.O. Box 74, 54891, P 2,350, M 135, (715) 373-5017, (800) 253-4495, Fax (715) 373-0240, info@washburnchamber.com, www.washburnchamber.com

**Washington Island** · *Washington Island C/C* · Marianna Gibson, Secy./Treas., 2206 W. Harbor Rd., 54246, P 670, M 100, (920) 847-2179, www.washingtonislandchamber.com

**Waterford** · *Waterford Area C/C* · Raegan Dexter, Exec. Dir., 102 E. Main St., P.O. Box 203, 53185, P 7,000, M 220, (262) 534-5911, Fax (262) 534-6507, chamber@waterford-wi.org, www.waterford-wi.org

**Waterloo** · *Waterloo C/C* · 117 E. Madison St., P.O. Box 1, 53594, P 3,000, M 65, (920) 478-2500, wchamber@hurleycomputers.com, www.waterloowis.com

**Watertown** · *Watertown Area C/C* · Randy Roeseler, Exec. Dir., 519 E. Main St., 53094, P 23,200, M 350, (920) 261-6320, watncofc@powercom.net, www.watertownchamber.com

**Waukesha** · *Waukesha County C/C* · Patti Wallner, Pres., 2717 N. Grandview Blvd., Ste. 204, 53188, P 100,000, M 825, (262) 542-4249, Fax (262) 542-8068, chamber@waukesha.org, www.waukesha.org

**Waunakee** · *Waunakee/Westport C/C* · Ellen K. Schaaf, Exec. Dir., 100 E. Main St., P.O. Box 41, 53597, P 11,105, M 280, (608) 849-5977, Fax (608) 849-9825, wwchamber@tds.net, www.waunakee.com

**Waupaca** · *Waupaca Area C/C* · Terri Schulz, Pres., 221 S. Main St., 54981, P 15,000, M 395, (715) 258-7343, (888) 417-4040, Fax (715) 258-7868, discoverwaupaca@waupacaareachamber.com, www.waupacaareachamber.com, www.waupacamemories.com.

**Waupun** · *Waupun Area C/C* · 16 S. Mill St., 53963, P 10,986, M 150, (920) 324-3491, Fax (920) 324-4357, info@waupunchamber.com, www.waupunchamber.com

**Wausau** · *Wausau Region C/C* · Roger A. Luce, Exec. Dir., 200 Washington St., Ste. 120, P.O. Box 6190, 54402, P 127,000, M 1,200, (715) 845-6231, Fax (715) 845-6235, info@wausau-chamber.com, www.wausauchamber.com

**Wautoma** · *Waushara Area C/C* · Kit Kudukis, Exec. Secy., 440 W. Main St., P.O. Box 65, 54982, P 24,000, M 240, (920) 787-3488, (877) WAUTOMA, Fax (920) 787-3788, info@visitwaushara.com, www.wausharachamber.com

**Wauwatosa** · *West Suburban C/C* · Sharon Scaccia, Pres./CEO, 2300 N. Mayfair Rd., Ste. 380, 53226, P 50,000, M 400, (414) 453-2330, Fax (414) 453-2336, info@westsuburbanchamber.com, www.westsuburbanchamber.com

**Webster** · *Webster Area C/C* · P.O. Box 48, 54893, P 681, M 100, (715) 866-4856, websterfacts@websterwisconsin.com, www.websterwisconsin.com

**West Allis** · *West Allis/West Milwaukee C/C* · Diane Brandt, Exec. Dir., 7447 W. Greenfield Ave., 53214, P 70,000, M 400, (414) 302-9901, Fax (414) 302-9918, contact@wawmchamber.com, www.wawmchamber.com

**West Bend** · *West Bend Area C/C* · Craig Farrell, Exec. Dir., 548 S. Main St., 53095, P 30,000, M 500, (262) 338-2666, info@wbachamber.org, www.wbachamber.org

**West Milwaukee** · *see West Allis*

**West Salem** · *see Onalaska*

**Westby** · *Westby Area C/C* · Trish Evenstad, Exec. Dir., P.O. Box 94, 54667, P 2,045, M 100, (608) 634-4011, westbycoc@mwt.net, www.westbywi.com

**Westfield** · *Westfield C/C* · Roger Peterson, Pres., P.O. Box 393, 53964, P 1,230, M 65, (608) 296-4146, www.westfieldwi.com

**Westport** · *see Waunakee*

**Weyauwega** · *Weyauwega Area C/C* · Becca Eckhardt, Pres., P.O. Box 531, 54983, P 1,806, M 61, (920) 867-2500, info@weyauwega.com, www.weyauwegachamber.com

**White Lake** · *see Antigo*

**Whitehall** · *Whitehall Area C/C* · Karen Witte, Treas., P.O. Box 155, 54773, P 1,671, M 45, (715) 538-4353, www.whitehall-chamber.com

**Whitewater** · *Whitewater Area C/C* · Deb Williamson, Exec. Dir., 171 W. Main St., P.O. Box 34, 53190, P 15,000, M 175, (262) 473-4005, (866) 4-WW-TOUR, Fax (262) 753-0067, wacc@idcnet.com, www.whitewaterchamber.com

**Williams Bay** · *see Fontana*

**Wind Lake** · *Wind Lake C/C* · Nancy Hoppe, Pres., 26422 Oakridge Dr., 53185, P 7,643, M 50, (262) 895-7566, www.windlake-wi.org

**Winneconne** · *Winneconne Area C/C* · 31 S. 2nd St., P.O. Box 126, 54986, P 2,510, M 90, (920) 582-4775, chamberoffice@winneconne.org, www.winneconne.org

**Winter** · *Winter Area C/C* · P.O. Box 245, 54896, P 1,500, M 90, (715) 266-2204, www.winterwi.com

**Wisconsin Rapids** · *Heart of Wisconsin Bus. & Eco. Alliance* · Connie Loden, Exec. Dir., 1120 Lincoln St., 54494, P 40,000, M 490, (715) 423-1830, Fax (715) 423-1865, info@heartofwi.com, www.heartofwi.com

**Wittenberg** · *Wittenberg Area C/C* · P.O. Box 284, 54499, P 1,150, M 50, (715) 253-3525, wittcham@wittenbergchamber.org, www.wittenbergchamber.org

**Woodruff** · *see Minocqua*

**Wrightstown** · *see Kaukauna*

# Wyoming

**No State Chamber**

**Afton** · *see Thayne*

**Basin** · *Basin Area C/C* · Barbara Anne Green, P.O. Box 883, 82410, P 1,224, M 60, (307) 568-3055, basincc@tctwest.net, www.basincc.com.

**Buffalo** • *Buffalo C/C* • Angela Jarvis, Exec. Dir., 55 N. Main St., 82834, P 5,500, M 250, (307) 684-5544, (800) 227-5122, Fax (307) 684-0291, info@buffalowyo.com, www.buffalowyo.com.

**Casper** • *Casper Area C/C* • Lori Becker, Exec. Dir., 500 N. Center St., P.O. Box 399, 82602, P 50,000, M 843, (307) 234-5311, (866) 234-5311, Fax (307) 265-2643, chamber@casperwyoming.org, www.casperwyoming.org

**Cheyenne** • *Greater Cheyenne C/C* • Dale G. Steenbergen, Pres., One Depot Sq., 121 W. 15th St. #204, 82001, P 80,000, M 825, (307) 638-3388, Fax (307) 778-1407, info@cheyennechamber.org, www.cheyennechamber.org.

**Chugwater** • *see Wheatland*

**Cody** • *Cody Country C/C* • Kimberly Jones, Exec. Dir., 836 Sheridan Ave., 82414, P 9,000, M 600, (307) 587-2777, Fax (307) 527-6228, info@codychamber.org, www.codychamber.org.

**Cokeville** • *Cokeville C/C* • P.O. Box 358, 83114, P 509, M 30, (307) 279-3200, Fax (307) 279-3105, cvchamber@allwest.net, www.cokevillewy.com

**Diamondville** • *see Kemmerer*

**Douglas** • *Douglas Area C/C* • Helga Bull, Dir., 121 Brownfield Rd., 82633, P 5,600, M 210, (307) 358-2950, Fax (307) 358-2972, chamber@jackalope.org, www.douglaschamber.com.

**Dubois** • *Dubois C/C* • 616 W. Ramshorn, P.O. Box 632, 82513, P 1,000, M 185, (307) 455-2556, duboiscc@dteworld.com, www.duboiswyoming.org

**Evanston** • *Evanston C/C* • Summer Meagher, Exec. Dir., 1020 Front St., P.O. Box 365, 82931, P 12,500, M 300, (307) 783-0370, (800) 328-9708, Fax (307) 789-4807, chamber@etownchamber.com, www.etownchamber.com.

**Gillette** • *Campbell County C/C* • Julie Simon, Pres., 314 S. Gillette Ave., 82716, P 36,110, M 590, (307) 682-3673, Fax (307) 682-0538, frontoffice@gillettechamber.com, www.gillettechamber.com.

**Glendo** • *see Wheatland*

**Glenrock** • *Glenrock Area C/C* • Mary Kay Kindt, Dir., 506 W. Birch, P.O. Box 411, 82637, P 2,200, M 157, (307) 436-5652, Fax (307) 436-5477, glenrockchamber@sdwinc.com, www.glenrockchamber.com

**Green River** • *Green River C/C* • Janet Hartford, Exec. Dir., 1155 W. Flaming Gorge Way, 82935, P 15,000, M 250, (307) 875-5711, (800) 354-6743, Fax (307) 875-8993, jhartford@sweetwaterhsa.com, www.grchamber.com.

**Greybull** • *Greybull Area C/C* • Jade Smith, Pres., 521 Greybull Ave., 82426, P 1,900, M 80, (307) 765-2100, chamber@greybull.com, www.greybull.com

**Guernsey** • *see Wheatland*

**Hartville** • *see Wheatland*

**Hulett** • *Hulett C/C* • Rose Ann Olson, Pres., P.O. Box 421, 82720, P 425, M 95, (307) 467-5747, Fax (307) 467-5765, www.hulett-wyoming.com

**Jackson** • *Jackson Hole C/C* • Tim O'Donoghue, Exec. Dir., 980 W. Broadway, P.O. Box 550, 83001, P 19,000, M 904, (307) 733-3316, Fax (307) 733-5585, info@jacksonholechamber.com, www.jacksonholechamber.com

**Kaycee** • *Kaycee Area C/C* • Christy Cleveland, Secy., 100 Park Ave., P.O. Box 147, 82639, P 250, M 80, (307) 738-2444, Fax (307) 738-2444, kayceechamber@rtconnect.net, www.kayceewyoming.org

**Kemmerer** • *Kemmerer/Diamondville Area C/C* • Teri Picerno, Exec. Dir., 800 Pine Ave., Triangle Park, 83101, P 4,000, M 100, (307) 877-9761, (888) 300-3413, Fax (307) 877-9762, chamber@hamsfork.net, www.kemmererchamber.com.

**Lander** • *Lander Area C/C* • Scott Goetz, Exec. Dir., 160 N. 1st St., 82520, P 7,500, M 328, (307) 332-3892, (800) 433-0662, Fax (307) 332-3893, info@landerchamber.org, www.landerchamber.org

**Laramie** • *Laramie Area C/C* • Peggy Rounds, Exec. Dir., 800 S. Third St., 82070, P 27,000, M 500, (307) 745-7339, (866) 876-1012, Fax (307) 745-4624, chamberofcommerce@laramie.org, www.laramie.org

**Lovell** • *Lovell Area C/C* • Suzanne Winterholler, Secy., 287 E. Main, 82431, P 2,361, M 80, (307) 548-7552, lovell@tctwest.net, www.lovellchamber.com

**Lusk** • *Niobrara C/C* • Jackie Bredthauer, Exec. Dir., 224 S. Main, P.O. Box 457, 82225, P 2,500, M 120, (307) 334-2950, (800) 223-LUSK, Fax (307) 334-2951, luskchamberofcommerce@yahoo.com, www.luskwyoming.com

**Lyman** • *Greater Bridger Valley C/C* • Chuck James, Dir., P.O. Box 1506, 82937, P 8,000, M 90, (307) 787-6738, Fax (307) 787-6100, bvchamber@bvea.net, www.bridgervalleychamber.com

**Marbleton** • *see Pinedale*

**Moorcroft** • *Moorcroft C/C* • Susan Millard, P.O. Box 932, 82721, P 1,500, M 35, (307) 756-3526

**Newcastle** • *Newcastle Area C/C* • Norma Shelton, Dir., 1323 Washington Blvd., 82701, P 3,064, M 174, (307) 746-2739, (800) 835-0157, Fax (307) 746-2739, nacoc@rtconnect.net, www.newcastlewyo.com.

**Pine Bluffs** • *Pine Bluffs Area C/C* • Cate Cundall, P.O. Box 429, 82082, P 1,163, M 65, (307) 245-3746, Fax (307) 245-3883, pinebluffs@rtconnect.net, www.pinebluffs.org

**Pinedale** • *Sublette C/C* • Terrie Swift, Exec. Dir., 19 E. Pine, P.O. Box 176, 82941, P 7,000, M 220, (307) 367-2242, (888) 285-7282, Fax (307) 367-2248, director@sublettechamber.com, www.sublettechamber.com

**Platte County** • *see Wheatland*

**Powell** • *Powell Valley C/C* • Naomi Burns, Exec. Dir., 111 S. Day St., P.O. Box 1258, 82435, P 5,300, M 250, (307) 754-3494, (800) 325-4278, Fax (307) 754-3483, info@powellchamber.org, www.powellchamber.org.

**Rawlins** • *Rawlins-Carbon County C/C* • Dennis Schuster, Exec. Dir., 519 W. Cedar St., P.O. Box 1331, 82301, P 10,000, M 230, (307) 324-4111, Fax (307) 324-5078, chamberdirector@qwest.net, www.rawlinschamberofcommerce.org.

**Riverton** • *Riverton C/C* • Jim Davis, Exec. Dir., 213 W. Main St., Ste.C, 82501, P 10,000, M 345, (307) 856-4801, (800) 325-2732, Fax (307) 857-0873, info@rivertonchamber.org, www.rivertonchamber.org.

**Rock Springs** • *Rock Springs C/C* • Dave Hanks, Exec. Dir., 1897 Dewar Dr., P.O. Box 398, 82901, P 28,000, M 600, (307) 362-3771, (800) 46-DUNES, Fax (307) 362-3838, rschamber@sweetwaterhsa.com, www.rockspringschamber.com

**Saratoga** • *Saratoga-Platte Valley C/C* • Stacy Crimmins, Dir., 210 W. Elm St., P.O. Box 1095, 82331, P 1,726, M 180, (307) 326-8855, Fax (307) 326-8850, info@saratogachamber.info, www.saratogachamber.info

**Sheridan** • *Sheridan County C/C* • Janelle Martinsen, Exec. Dir., P.O. Box 707, 82801, P 26,500, M 575, (307) 672-2485, (800) 453-3650, Fax (307) 672-7321, info@sheridanwyomingchamber.org, www.sheridanwyomingchamber.org.

**U.S. Chambers of Commerce**

**Shoshoni** • *Shoshoni C/C* • Oscar Lawson, Pres., 206 E. 6th St., P.O. Box 324, 82649, P 800, M 110, (307) 876-2591

**Sundance** • *Sundance Area C/C* • Jeff Moberg, Pres, P.O. Box 1004, 82729, P 1,100, M 40, (307) 283-1000, (800) 477-9340, chamber@sundancewyoming.com, www.sundancewyoming.com

**Ten Sleep** • *see Worland*

**Thayne** • *Star Valley C/C* • Melanie S. Wilkes, Dir., 606 N. Main St., P.O. Box 1171, 83127, P 12,000, M 135, (307) 883-2759, (800) 426-8833, Fax (307) 883-2758, info@starvalleychamber.com, www.starvalleychamber.com

**Thermopolis** • *Thermopolis-Hot Springs C/C* • Kathy Wallingford, Exec. Dir., 220 Park St., P.O. Box 768, 82443, P 3,300, M 238, (307) 864-3192, (877) 864-3192, Fax (307) 864-3128, thercc@rtconnect.net, www.thermopolis.com.

**Torrington** • *Goshen County C/C* • Rhonda Schulte, Exec. Dir., 350 W. 21st Ave., 82240, P 12,600, M 237, (307) 532-3879, Fax (307) 534-2360, goshencountychamber@yahoo.com, www.goshencountychamber.com

**Upton** • *Upton C/C* • P.O. Box 756, 82730, P 872, M 60, (307) 468-2228

**Wheatland** • *Platte County C/C* • Stacy Benson, Exec. Dir., 65 16th St., P.O. Box 427, 82201, P 8,800, M 242, (307) 322-2322, Fax (307) 322-3419, info@plattechamber.com, www.plattechamber.com

**Worland** • *Worland-Ten Sleep C/C* • Terry Sutherland, Exec. Dir., 120 N. 10th St., 82401, P 5,250, M 245, (307) 347-3226, Fax (307) 347-3025, wtschamber@rtconnect.net, www.worlandchamber.com.

**Wright** • *Wright Area C/C* • P.O. Box 430, 82732, P 1,425, M 106, (307) 464-1312, Fax (307) 464-6115, wrightchamberofcommerce@orbitcom.biz, www.wrightareachamber.org

# Notes

# Notes

# State Boards of Tourism

**Alabama** · *Alabama Tourism Dept.* · Lee Sentell, Dir., 401 Adams Ave., Ste. 126, P.O. Box 4927, Montgomery, 36103, (334) 242-4169, Fax (334) 242-4554, (800) ALABAMA, info@tourism.alabama.gov, www.alabama.travel

**Alaska** · *Alaska Travel Industry Assn.* · 2600 Cordova St., Ste. 201, Anchorage, 99503, (907) 929-2200, Fax (907) 561-5727, info@AlaskaTIA.org, www.travelalaska.com

**Arizona** · *Arizona Office of Tourism* · Margie Emmermann, Dir., 1110 W. Washington St., Ste. 155, Phoenix, 85007, (602) 364-3700, (866) 275-5816, Fax (602) 364-3702, www.arizonaguide.com

**Arkansas** · *Arkansas Dept. of Parks & Tourism* · Joe David Rice, Dir. of Tourism, One Capitol Mall, Little Rock, 72201, (501) 682-1088, Fax (501) 682-2523, info@arkansas.com, www.arkansas.com

**California** · *California Travel & Tourism* · Carolyn Beteta, Dir., P.O. Box 1499, Sacramento, 95812, (916) 444-4429, (877) 225-4367, Fax (916) 444-0410, www.visitcalifornia.com

**Colorado** · *Colorado Office of Tourism* · Don Elliman, Exec. Dir., 1625 Broadway, Ste. 2700, Denver, 80202, (303) 892-3885, Fax (303) 892-3848, (800) COLORADO, info@colorado.com, www.colorado.com

**Connecticut** · *Connecticut Office of Tourism* · One Constitution Plaza, 2nd Flr., Hartford, 06103, (860) 256-2800, Fax (860) 270-8077, (888) CT-VISIT, www.ctvisit.com

**Delaware** · *Delaware Tourism Office* · Alan Levin, Dir., 99 Kings Hwy., Dover, 19901, (302) 739-4271, (866) 284-7483, Fax (302) 739-5749, www.visitdelaware.com

**Florida** · *Visit Florida* · Bud Nocera, CEO, 2540 W. Executive Center Cir., Ste. 200, Tallahassee, 32301, (850) 488-5607, (877) 435-2872, Fax (850) 224-9589, www.visitflorida.com, www.visitflorida.org

**Georgia** · *Georgia Dept. of Eco. Dev.* · Ken Stuart, Commissioner of Tourism, 75 Fifth St. N.W., Ste. 1200, Atlanta, 30308, (404) 962-4000, Fax (404) 651-9462, (800) VISIT-GA, www.exploregeorgia.org

**Hawaii** · *Hawaii Tourism Auth.* · Rex Johnson, Pres./CEO, 1801 Kalakaua Ave., Honolulu, 96815, (808) 973-2255, Fax (808) 973-2253, www.hawaiitourismauthority.org

**Idaho** · *Idaho Div. of Tourism Dev.* · Karen Ballard, Admin., 700 W. State St., P.O. Box 83720, Boise, 83720, (208) 334-2470, (800) 635-7820, Fax (208) 334-2631, karen.ballard@tourism.idaho.gov, www.visitid.org

**Illinois** · *Illinois Bur. of Tourism* · Warren Ribley, Dir., DCEO, 620 E. Adams St., Springfield, 62701, (217) 557-2407, Fax (217) 785-6336, warren.ribley@illinois.gov, www.enjoy illinois.com

**Indiana** · *Indiana Office of Tourism Dev.* · Amy Vaughan, Dir., One N. Capitol, Ste. 600, Indianapolis, 46204, (317) 232-8860, (800) 677-9800, Fax (317) 233-6887, www.visitindiana.com

**Iowa** · *Iowa Tourism Office* · Nancy Landess, Mgr., 200 E. Grand Ave., Des Moines, 50309, (888) 472-6035, Fax (515) 242-4795, (800) 345-IOWA, nancy.landess@iowalifechanging.com, www.traveliowa.com

**Kansas** · *Kansas Travel & Tourism* · Becky Blake, Div. Dir., 1000 S.W. Jackson St., Ste. 100, Topeka, 66612, (785) 296-2009, Fax (785) 296-6988, (800) 2KANSAS, travtour@kansascommerce. com, www.travelks.com

**Kentucky** · *Kentucky Dept. of Tourism* · Mike Cooper, Commissioner, Capital Plaza Tower, 22nd Flr., 500 Mero St., Frankfort, 40601, (502) 564-4930, (800) 225-8747, Fax (502) 564-5695, www.kentuckytourism.com

**Louisiana** · *Louisiana Office of Tourism* · P.O. Box 94291, Baton Rouge, 70804, (225) 342-8100, Fax (225) 342-1051, www.louisianatravel.com

**Maine** · *Maine Office of Tourism* · Patricia Eltman, Dir., 59 State House Station, Augusta, 04333, (207) 287-5711, (888) 624-6345, Fax (207) 287-8070, www.visitmaine.com

**Maryland** · *Maryland Div. of Tourism* · Hannah Byron, Asst. Secy., 401 E. Pratt St., 14th Flr., Baltimore, 21202, (410) 767-3400, (866) 639-3526, Fax (410) 333-6643, info@visitmaryland. org, www.visitmaryland.org

**Massachusetts** · *Massachusetts Office of Travel & Tourism* · Betsy Wall, Exec. Dir., 10 Park Plaza, Ste. 4510, Boston, 02116, (617) 973-8500, Fax (617) 973-8525, (800) 227-MASS, VacationInfo@state.ma.us, www.massvacation.com

**Michigan** · *Travel Michigan* · George Zimmermann, V.P., 300 N. Washington Sq., 2nd Flr., Lansing, 48913, (888) 784-7328, Fax (517) 373-0059, www.michigan.org

**Minnesota** · *Minnesota Office of Tourism* · John Edman, Dir., 121 7th Pl. E., Ste. 100, Saint Paul, 55101, (651) 296-2755, (800) 868-7476, Fax (651) 296-7095, explore@state.mn.us, www.exploreminnesota.com

**Mississippi** · *Mississippi Div. of Tourism* · Craig Ray, Dir., P.O. Box 849, Jackson, 39205, (601) 359-3297, Fax (601) 359-5757, tourdiv@mississippi.org, www.visitmississippi.org

**Missouri** · *Missouri Div. Of Tourism* · Blaine Luetkemeyer, Dir., P.O. Box 1055, Jefferson City, 65102, (573) 751-4133, Fax (573) 751-5160, tourism@ded.mo.gov, www.visitmo.com

**Montana** · *Travel Montana* · Betsy Baumgart, Travel Dir., 301 S. Park Ave., Helena, 59620, (406) 841-2870, (800) 847-4868, Fax (406) 841-2871, www.visitmt.com

**Nebraska** · *Nebraska Tourism* · Christian Hornbaker, Dir., P.O. Box 98906, Lincoln, 68509, (402) 471-3796, (877) 632-7275, Fax (402) 471-3026, tourism@visitnebraska.org, www.visit nebraska.org

**Nevada** · *Nevada Commission on Tourism* · 401 N. Carson St., Carson City, 89701, (775) 687-4322, (800) 237-0774, Fax (775) 687-6779, ncot@travelnevada.com, www.travelnevada.com

**New Hampshire** · *New Hampshire Div. of Travel & Tourism Dev.* · Alice DeSouza, Dir., P.O. Box 1856, Concord, 03302, (603) 271-2665, Fax (603) 271-6870, travel@dred.state.nh.us, www.visitnh.gov

**New Jersey** · *New Jersey Commerce Commission., Office of Travel & Tourism* · Nancy Byrne, Exec. Dir., 20 W. State St. 4th Flr., P.O. Box 820, Trenton, 08625, (609) 292-2470, Fax (609) 633-7418, (800) VISIT-NJ, www.visitnj.org

**New Mexico** · *New Mexico Tourism Dept.* · Mike Cerletti, Cabinet Secy., 491 Old Santa Fe Trail, Santa Fe, 87501, (505) 827-7400, (800) 545-2070, Fax (505) 827-7402, Mike.Cerletti@state.nm.us, www.newmexico.org

**New York** · *New York State Div. Of Tourism* · Lisa Yarusso, Supervisor, 30 S. Pearl St., 5th Flr., P.O. Box 2603, Albany, 12220, (518) 474-4116, (800) 847-4862, Fax (518) 292-5893, www.iloveny.com

**North Carolina** · *North Carolina Div. of Tourism, Film & Sports Dev.* · Lynn Minges, Asst. Secy. for Tourism, 301 N. Wilmington St., Raleigh, 27601, (919) 733-4171, (800) 847-4862, Fax (919) 733-8582, lminges@nccommerce.com, www.visitnc.com

**North Dakota** · *North Dakota Tourism Div.* · Sara Otte Coleman, Dir., 1600 E. Century Ave., Ste. 2, P.O. Box 2057, Bismarck, 58502, (701) 328-2525, (800) 435-5663, Fax (701) 328-4878, tourism@nd.gov, www.ndtourism.com

**Ohio** · *Ohio Div. of Travel & Tourism* · Jim Greenhalge, Asst. Tourism Dir., 77 S. High St., P.O. Box 1001, Columbus, 43216, (614) 466-8844, Fax (614) 466-6744, (800) BUCKEYE, www.discoverohio.com

**Oklahoma** · *Oklahoma Tourism & Rec. Dept.* · Sandy Pantlik, Dir., P.O. Box 52002, Oklahoma City, 73102, (405) 230-8400, (800) 652-6552, Fax (405) 230-8600, information@travelok.com, www.travelok.com

**Oregon** · *Oregon Tourism Commission* · Todd Davidson, CEO, 670 Hawthorne Ave. S.E., Ste. 240, Salem, 97301, (503) 378-8850, (800) 547-7842, Fax (503) 378-4574, www.traveloregon.com

**Pennsylvania** · *Pennsylvania Tourism Office* · Richard Bonds, Dir. of Mktg., Commonwealth Keystone Bldg., 400 North St., 4th Flr., Harrisburg, 17120, (717) 787-5453, Fax (717) 787-0687, (800) VISIT-PA, www.visitpa.com

**Rhode Island** · *Rhode Island Tourism* · David DePetrillo, Dir., 315 Iron Horse Way., Ste. 101, Providence, 02908, (401) 278-9100, (800) 250-7384, Fax (401) 273-8270, www.visitrhodeisland.com

**South Carolina** · *South Carolina Dept. of Parks & Rec & Tourism* · Chad Prosser, Dir., 1205 Pendleton St., Columbia, 29201, (803) 734-1700, Fax (803) 734-1409, www.discoversouthcarolina.com

**South Dakota** · *South Dakota Dept. of Tourism & State Dev.* · Melissa Bump, Dir., 711 E. Wells Ave., Pierre, 57501, (605) 773-3301, Fax (605) 773-3256, (800) SDAKOTA, sdinfo@state.sd.us, www.travelsd.com

**Tennessee** · *Tennessee Dept. of Tourist Dev.* · Susan Whitaker, Commissioner, 312 8th Ave. N., 25th Flr., Nashville, 37243, (615) 741-2159, Fax (615) 741-9071, (800) GO2-TENN, tourdev@tn.gov, www.tnvacation.com

**Texas** · *Office of Gov. Eco. Dev. & Tourism Dev.* · Julie Chase, Dir. of Tourism, P.O. Box 12428, Austin, 78711, (512) 936-0100, Fax (512) 936-0303, www.traveltex.com

**Utah** · *Utah Office of Tourism* · Leigh Von Der Esch, Dir., 300 N. State. St., Salt Lake City, 84114, (801) 538-1030, (800) 200-1160, Fax (801) 538-1399, travel@utah.gov, www.utah.com

**Vermont** · *Vermont Dept. of Tourism & Mktg.* · Bruce Hyde, Commissioner, National Life Bldg., 6th Flr., Montpelier, 05620, (802) 828-3237, Fax (802) 828-3233, info@vermontvacation.com, www.vermontvacation.com

**Virginia** · *Virginia Tourism Corp.* · 901 E. Byrd St., Richmond, 23219, (804) 786-2051, Fax (804) 545-5501, (800) VISIT-VA, VAinfo@helloinc.com, www.virginia.org

**Washington** · *Washington State Tourism* · 128 10th Ave. S.W., P.O. Box 42525, Olympia, 98504, (360) 725-4028, (800) 544-1800, Fax (360) 753-4470, tourism@cted.wa.gov, www.experiencewashington.com

**West** *Virginia* · *West Virginia Div. Of Tourism* · Betty Carver, Commissioner, 90 MacCorkle Ave. S.W., South Charleston, 25303, (304) 558-2200, (800) 225-5982, Fax (304) 558-2956, bcarver@wvtourism.com, www.wvtourism.com

**Wisconsin** · *Wisconsin Dept. of Tourism* · Kelli Trumble, Secy., P.O. Box 8690, Madison, 53708, (608) 266-7621, (800) 432-8747, Fax (608) 266-3403, tourinfo@travelwisconsin.com, www.travelwisconsin.com

**Wyoming** · *Wyoming Div. Of Tourism* · Diane Shober, Dir., I-25 at College Dr., Cheyenne, 82002, (307) 777-7777, (800) 225-5996, Fax (307) 777-2877, info@visitwyo.gov, www.wyomingtourism.org

# C&VB Convention and Visitors Bureaus

## Alabama

**Anniston** · *Calhoun County CVB* · Mike Galloway, Dir. of Tourism, 1330 Quintard Ave., P.O. Box 1087, 36202, P 117,000, (256) 237-3536, (800) 489-1087, Fax (256) 237-0126, www.calhounchamber.com

**Auburn** · *Auburn/Opelika Tourism Bur.* · John Wild, Pres., 714 E. Glenn Ave., 36830, P 118,000, (334) 887-8747, (866) 880-8747, Fax (334) 821-5500, info@aotourism.com, www.aotourism.com

**Birmingham** · *Greater Birmingham CVB* · James Smither, Pres., 2200 9th Ave. N., 35203, P 1,000,000, (205) 458-8000, (800) 458-8085, Fax (205) 458-8086, info@birminghamal.org, www.birminghamal.org

**Decatur** · *Decatur-Morgan County CVB* · Tami Reist, Pres., 719 6th Ave. S.E., P.O. Box 2349, 35602, P 55,000, (256) 350-2028, (800) 524-6181, Fax (256) 350-2054, info@decaturcvb.org, www.decaturcvb.org

**Dothan** · *Dothan Area CVB* · Bob Hendrix, Exec. Dir., 3311 Ross Clark Circle, P.O. Box 8765, 36304, P 63,000, (334) 794-6622, (888) 449-0212, Fax (334) 712-2731, dothancvb@ala.net, www.dothanalcvb.com

**Eufaula** · *Eufaula/Barbour County Tourism Cncl.* · Corey Kirkland, Tourism Dir., 333 E. Broad St., 36027, P 29,000, (334) 687-7099, (800) 524-7529, Fax (334) 687-5240, info@eufaulachamber.com, www.eufaulachamber.com

**Fort Payne** · *DeKalb County Tourist Assn.* · John Dersham, Exec. Dir., P.O. Box 681165, 35968, P 65,000, M 200, (256) 845-3957, (888) 805-4740, Fax (256) 845-3946, info@tourdekalb.com, www.tourdekalb.com

**Gulf Shores** · *Alabama Gulf Coast CVB* · Herbert Malone Jr., Pres./CEO, 900 Commerce Loop, 36542, P 11,000, (251) 974-1510, (800) 745-7263, Fax (251) 974-1509, info@gulfshores.com, www.gulfshores.com, www.orangebeach.com

**Guntersville** · *Marshall County CVB* · Lisa Socha, Exec. Dir., 200 Gunter Ave., P.O. Box 711, 35976, P 85,000, (256) 582-7015, (800) 582-6282, Fax (256) 582-3682, marshallcountycvb@charterinternet.com, www.marshallcountycvb.com

**Huntsville** · *Huntsville-Madison County CVB* · Judy S. Ryals, Pres./CEO, 500 Church St., Ste 1, 35801, P 300,000, (256) 551-2230, (800) 772-2348, Fax (256) 551-2324, info@huntsville.org, www.huntsville.org.

**Mobile** · *Mobile Bay CVB* · Leon Maisel, Pres./CEO, 1 S. Water St., P.O. Box 204, 36601, P 400,000, (251) 208-2000, Fax (251) 208-2060, (800) 5-MOBILE, lmaisel@mobile.org, www.mobile.org.

**Montgomery** · *Montgomery Area CVB* · Dawn Hathcock, V.P., 300 Water St., P.O. Box 79, 36101, P 335,000, (334) 261-1100, (800) 240-9452, Fax (334) 261-1111, tourism@montgomerychamber.com, www.visitingmontgomery.com

**Orange Beach** · *see Gulf Shores*

**Scottsboro** · *Greater Jackson County CVB* · John Parsons, V.P. Destination Mktg., 407 E. Willow St., P.O. Box 973, 35768, P 75,000, (256) 259-5500, (800) 259-5508, Fax (256) 259-4447, tourjackson@scottsboro.org, www.jacksoncountychamber.com

**Selma** · *Selma CVB* · Lauri S. Cothran, Pres., 912 Selma Ave., 36701, P 46,365, (334) 875-7241, Fax (334) 875-7142, (800) 45-SELMA, info@SelmaAlabama.com, www.SelmaAlabama.com

**Tuscaloosa** · *Tuscaloosa CVB* · Robert Ratliff, Exec. Dir., 1305 Greensboro Ave., P.O. Box 3167, 35403, P 170,000, (205) 391-9200, (800) 538-8696, Fax (205) 759-9002, robert@tcvb.org, www.tcvb.org

**Tuscumbia** · *Colbert County Tourism CVB* · Susann Hamlin, Exec. Dir., P.O. Box 740425, 35674, P 150,000, (256) 383-0783, (800) 344-0783, Fax (256) 383-2080, colberttourism@comcast.net, www.colbertcountytourism.org

## Alaska

**Anchorage** · *Anchorage CVB* · Julie Saupe, Pres./CEO, 524 W. Fourth Ave., 99501, P 277,000, M 1,500, (907) 276-4118, (800) 446-5352, Fax (907) 278-5559, info@anchorage.net, www.anchorage.net

**Fairbanks** · *Fairbanks CVB* · 101 Dunkel St., Ste. 111, 99701, P 84,000, M 300, (907) 456-5774, (800) 327-5774, Fax (907) 459-3757, info@explorefairbanks.com, www.explorefairbanks.com

**Gustavus** · *Gustavus Visitors Assn.* · P.O. Box 167, 99826, P 420, M 33, info@gustavusak.com, www.gustavusak.com

**Haines** · *Haines CVB* · Lori Stepansky, Dir., P.O. Box 530, 99827, P 2,300, (907) 766-2234, (800) 458-3579, Fax (907) 766-3155, hcvb@haines.ak.us, www.haines.ak.us

**Homer** · *Homer Visitor Info. Center* · Tina Day, Exec. Dir., 201 Sterling Hwy., 99603, P 5,400, (907) 235-7740, Fax (907) 235-8766, info@homeralaska.org, www.homeralaska.org

**Iliamna** · *Iliamna Cncl. Visitor Info.* · P.O. Box 286, 99606, P 150, (907) 571-1246, Fax (907) 571-1256, ilivc@aol.com

**Juneau** · *Juneau CVB* · Lorene Palmer, Pres./CEO, One Sealaska Plaza, Ste. 305, 99801, P 32,000, M 300, (907) 586-1737, (800) 587-2201, Fax (907) 586-1449, info@traveljuneau.com, www.traveljuneau.com

**Kenai** · *Kenai CVB* · Natasha Ala, Exec. Dir., 11471 Kenai Spur Hwy., 99611, P 7,000, M 250, (907) 283-1991, Fax (907) 283-2230, info@visitkenai.com, www.visitkenai.com

**Ketchikan** · *Ketchikan Visitors Bur.* · Patricia Mackey, Exec. Dir., 131 Front St., 99901, P 14,000, M 287, (907) 225-6166, (800) 770-3300, Fax (907) 225-4250, info@visit-ketchikan.com, www.visit-ketchikan.com

**King Salmon** · *King Salmon Visitor Center* · King Salmon Airport, P.O. Box 298, 99613, P 350, (907) 246-4250, Fax (907) 246-8550

**Kodiak** · *Kodiak Island CVB* · Janet Buckingham, Exec. Dir., 100 Marine Way, Ste. 200, 99615, P 13,479, M 215, (907) 486-4782, (800) 789-4782, Fax (907) 486-6545, visit@kodiak.org, www.kodiak.org

**Nome** · *Nome CVB* · Mitchell Erickson, Dir., 301 Front St., P.O. Box 240, 99762, P 3,500, (907) 443-6655, Fax (907) 443-5966, tourinfo@ci.nome.ak.us, www.nomealaska.org

**Palmer** · *Mat-Su CVB* · Bonnie Quill, Exec. Dir., 7744 E. Visitors View Ct., 99645, P 82,500, M 300, (907) 746-5000, Fax (907) 746-2688, info@alaskavisit.com, www.alaskavisit.com

**Petersburg** · *Petersburg Visitors Info. Center* · Sally Dwyer, Mgr., P.O. Box 649, 99833, P 3,200, (907) 772-4636, (866) 484-4700, Fax (907) 772-2453, visitorinfo@petersburg.org, www.petersburg.org

**Sitka** · *Sitka CVB* · Sandy Lorrigan, Exec. Dir., 303 Lincoln St., Ste. 4, P.O. Box 1226, 99835, P 9,000, M 200, (907) 747-5940, Fax (907) 747-3739, (800) 55-SITKA, scvb@sitka.org, www.sitka.org

**Skagway** · *Skagway CVB* · 245 Broadway, P.O. Box 1029, 99840, P 862, (907) 983-2854, (888) 762-1898, Fax (907) 983-3854, skagwayinfo@gmail.com, www.skagway.com

**Soldotna** · *Kenai Peninsula Tourism Marketing Cncl.* · Shanon Hamrick, Exec. Dir., 35477 Kenai Spur Hwy., Ste. 205, 99669, P 51,000, M 400, (907) 262-5229, (800) 535-3624, Fax (907) 262-5212, info@kenaipeninsula.org, www.kenaipeninsula.org

**Tok** · *Tok's 'Alaska Mainstreet' Visitor Center* · P.O. Box 389, 99780, P 1,405, M 168, (907) 883-5775, info@TokAlaskaInfo.com, www.TokAlaskaInfo.com

**Unalaska** · *Unalaska/Port of Dutch Harbor CVB* · Tammy Peterson, Exec. Dir., P.O. Box 545, 99685, P 4,600, M 64, (907) 581-2612, (877) 581-2612, Fax (907) 581-2613, unalaskacvb@arctic.net, www.unalaska.info

**Valdez** · *Valdez CVB* · David Petersen, Exec. Dir., 104 Chenega, P.O. Box 1603, 99686, P 4,100, M 135, (907) 835-2984, Fax (907) 835-4845, info@valdezalaska.org, www.valdezalaska.org

**White Mountain** · *White Mountain Visitor Info. Center* · % City Hall, P.O. Box 130, 99784, P 194, (907) 638-3411, (907) 638-2230, Fax (907) 638-3421

# Arizona

**Arizona City** · *Sunland Visitor Center* · Cynthia Yates, Dir., P.O. Box 280, 85223, P 35,000, (520) 466-3007, (888) 786-3007, Fax (520) 466-3007, snlndvc@localnet.com, www.sunlandvisitorcenter.org

**Ash Fork** · *Ash Fork Tourism* · Ann McCullough, Dir., 901 W. Rte. 66, P.O. Box 494, 86320, P 900, (928) 637-0204, (928) 637-2245, Fax (928) 637-2442

**Flagstaff** · *Flagstaff Visitor Center* · Heather Ainardi, Dir., 1 E. Rte. 66, 86001, P 62,000, (800) 842-7293, (928) 774-9541, Fax (928) 556-1308, visitorcenter@ci.flagstaff.az.us, www.flagstaffarizona.org

**Florence** · *Pinal County Visitor Center* · Pat Judy, Dir., 330 E. Butte, P.O. Box 967, 85232, P 179,727, (520) 868-4331, (800) 557-4331, Fax (520) 868-1099, visitpinal@pcvc.phxcoxmail.com, www.co.pinal.az.us/visitorcenter

**Glendale** · *Glendale Ofc. Of Tourism & Visitor Center* · Lorraine Pino, Tourism Mgr., 5800 W. Glenn Dr. #140, 85301, P 247,987, (623) 930-4500, Fax (623) 463-2337, tourinfo@visitglendale.com, www.visitglendale.com.

**Lake Havasu City** · *Lake Havasu City CVB* · Char Beltran, Pres., 314 London Bridge Rd., 86403, P 57,000, (928) 453-3444, (800) 242-8278, Fax (928) 453-3344, info@golakehavasu.com, www.golakehavasu.com

**Mesa** · *Mesa CVB* · Robert W. Brinton, Pres./CEO, 120 N. Center, 85201, P 460,000, (480) 827-4700, (800) 283-6372, Fax (480) 827-4704, info@visitmesa.com, www.visitmesa.com.

**Phoenix** · *Greater Phoenix CVB* · J. Steven Moore, Pres./CEO, 400 E. Van Buren #600, 85004, P 3,800,000, (602) 254-6500, (877) 225-5749, Fax (602) 253-4415, www.visitphoenix.com

**Scottsdale** · *Scottsdale CVB* · Rachel Sacco, Pres./CEO, 4343 Scottsdale Rd. #170, Galleria Corporate Center, 85251, P 250,000, (480) 421-1004, (800) 782-1117, Fax (480) 421-9733, visitor information@scottsdalecvb.com, www.scottsdalecvb.com

**Sedona** · *Sedona Chamber Tourism Bur.* · Michelle Conway, Dir. of Tourism, P.O. Box 478, 86339, P 18,000, (928) 204-1123, (928) 282-7722, Fax (928) 204-1064, info@sedonachamber.com, www.visitsedona.com

**Sierra Vista** · *Sierra Vista Visitors Center* · Kay Daggett, 1011 N. Coronado Dr., 85635, P 40,000, (520) 417-6960, (800) 288-3861, Fax (520) 417-4890, info@visitsierravista.com, www.visitsierravista.com.

**Sun City** · *Sun City Visitors Center* · Paul Herrmann, Exec. Dir., 16824 N. 99th Ave., 85351, P 42,000, (623) 977-5000, Fax (623) 977-4224, scvc@suncityaz.org, www.suncityaz.org

**Tempe** · *Tempe CVB* · Ginger Dude, Ofc. Mgr., 51 W. Third St. #105, 85281, P 165,000, (480) 894-8158, (800) 283-6734, Fax (480) 968-8004, info@tempecvb.com, www.tempecvb.com

**Tombstone** · *Tombstone Ofc. of Tourism* · Paula Jean Reed, Chrmn., P.O. Box 248, 85638, P 2,000, (520) 457-3421, (800) 457-3423, Fax (520) 457-3189, oldbirdcage@juno.com, www.tombstoneaz.net

**Tucson** · *Metropolitan Tucson CVB* · Jonathan Walker, Pres., 100 S. Church Ave., 85701, P 1,000,000, M 750, (520) 624-1817, Fax (520) 884-7804, info@visittucson.org, www.visittucson.org

**Yuma** · *Yuma Visitors Bur.* · Robert Ingram, Exec. Dir., 139 S. 4th Ave., 85364, P 120,000, M 300, (928) 783-0071, (800) 293-0071, Fax (928) 783-1897, info@visityuma.com, www.visityuma.com

# Arkansas

**Bentonville** · *Bentonville USA* · Kalene Griffith, Pres., 104 E. Central, 72712, P 33,700, (479) 271-9153, (800) 410-2535, Fax (479) 464-4298, admin@bentonvilleusa.org, www.bentonvilleusa.org

**Fort Smith** · *Fort Smith CVB* · Claude Legris, Exec. Dir., 2 N. B St., 72901, P 80,000, (479) 783-8888, (800) 637-1477, Fax (479) 784-2421, tourism@fortsmith.org, www.fortsmith.org

**Harrison** · *Harrison CVB* · Terry Cook, Exec. Dir., 122 E. Rush, P.O. Box 940, 72602, P 13,000, (870) 741-1789, (888) 283-2163, Fax (870) 741-1159, tcook@harrisonarkansas.org, www.harrisonarkansas.org.

**Hot Springs** · *Hot Springs CVB* · Steve Arrison, CEO, P.O. Box 6000, 71902, P 96,371, (501) 321-2277, (800) 543-2284, Fax (501) 321-2136, hscvb@hotsprings.org, www.hotsprings.org

**Little Rock** · *Little Rock CVB* · Dan O'Byrne, Exec. Dir./CEO, P.O. Box 3232, 72203, P 184,000, (501) 376-4781, (800) 844-4781, Fax (501) 374-2255, lrcvb@littlerock.com, www.littlerock.com

**Pine Bluff** · *Pine Bluff CVB* · Bob Purvis, Exec. Dir., Pine Bluff Conv. Center, One Convention Center Plz., 71601, P 54,000, (870) 536-7600, (800) 536-7660, Fax (870) 850-2105, pbinfo@pinebluff.com, www.pinebluffcvb.org

**Rogers** · *Rogers-Lowell CVB* · Tom Galyon, Dir., 317 W. Walnut, 72756, P 50,000, (479) 636-1240, Fax (479) 636-5485, info@rogerslowell.com, www.rogerslowell.com

# California

**Anaheim** · *Anaheim/Orange County Visitor & Conv. Bur.* · Charles Ahlers, Pres., 800 W. Katella Ave., P.O. Box 4270, 92803, P 2,280,400, M 750, (714) 765-8888, (888) 598-3200, Fax (714) 765-3672, visitorinfo@anaheimoc.org, www.anaheimoc.org

**Bakersfield** · *Bakersfield CVB* · Don I. Cohen, 515 Truxtun Ave., 93301, P 500,000, (661) 852-7282, (866) 425-7353, Fax (661) 325-7074, cvb@visitbakersfield.com, www.visitbakersfield.com

**Berkeley** · *Berkeley CVB* · Barbara Hillman, Exec. Dir., 2015 Center St., 94704, P 105,000, (510) 549-7040, (800) 847-4823, Fax (510) 644-2052, berkeleycvb@mindspring.com, www. visitberkeley.com

**Beverly Hills** · *Beverly Hills Conf. & Visitors Bur.* · Kathy Smits, Dir., 239 S. Beverly Dr., 90212, P 36,000, (310) 248-1015, (800) 345-2210, Fax (310) 248-1020, smits@beverlyhillsbehere.com, www.lovebeverlyhills.org

**Bodega Bay** · *Sonoma Coast Visitor Center* · Brad Evans, Dir., 850 Coast Hwy. 1, P.O. Box 518, 94923, P 1,250, (707) 875-3866, Fax (707) 875-3055, visitorcenter@innatthetides.com, www. bodegabay.com

**Burlingame** · *San Mateo County/Silicon Valley CVB* · Anne LeClair, Pres./CEO, 111 Anza Blvd., Ste. 410, 94010, P 722,762, M 365, (650) 348-7600, Fax (650) 348-7687, (800) 28-VISIT, info@smccvb.com, www.visitsanmateocounty.com

**Carlsbad** · *Carlsbad CVB* · Frankie Laney, Public Rel. Dir., 400 Carlsbad Village Dr., 92008, P 100,000, (760) 434-6093, Fax (760) 434-6056, (800) CARLSBAD, info@visitcarlsbad.com, www.visitcarlsbad.com

**Coronado** · *Coronado Visitors Center* · Susan Enowitz, Exec. Dir., 1100 Orange Ave., 92118, P 26,000, (619) 437-8788, Fax (619) 435-8504, director@coronadohistory.org, www.coronadovisitor center.com

**Costa Mesa** · *Costa Mesa Conf. & Visitor Bur.* · Diane Pritchett, Exec. Dir., P.O. Box 5071, 92628, P 123,955, (714) 435-8530, (866) 918-4749, Fax (714) 435-8522, tourism@southcoastmetro.com, www.travelcostamesa.com

**Davis** · *Yolo County Visitors Bur.* · Diane Parro, Exec. Dir., 105 E St., Ste. 300, 95616, P 185,000, (530) 297-1900, (877) 713-2847, Fax (530) 297-1901, info@yolocvb.org, www.yolocvb.org

**Desert Hot Springs** · *Desert Hot Springs Visitors Hospitality Center* · Eric Pontius, Pres., 67616 Desert View Ave., 92240, P 23,544, (760) 329-7610, (866) 941-7610, info2@deserthotsprings. com, www.deserthotsprings.com

**Escondido** · *San Diego North CVB* · Cami Mattson, Pres./CEO, 360 N. Escondido Blvd., 92025, (760) 745-4741, (800) 848-3336, Fax (760) 745-4796, info@sandiegonorth.com, www.sandiego north.com

**Eureka** · *Humboldt County CVB* · 1034 Second St., 95501, P 128,000, M 400, (707) 443-5097, (800) 346-3482, Fax (707) 443-5115, info@redwoods.info, www.redwoods.info

**Fresno** · *Fresno CVB* · Jeff L. Eben, Pres./CEO, 848 M St., 3rd Flr., 93721, P 500,000, M 365, (559) 445-8300, (800) 788-0836, Fax (559) 445-0122, info@fresnocvb.org, www.fresnocvb.org

**Gilroy** · *Gilroy Visitors Bur.* · Jane Howard, Exec. Dir., 7780 Monterey St., 95020, P 55,000, (408) 842-6436, Fax (408) 842-6438, info@gilroyvisitor.org, www.gilroyvisitor.org

**Hanford** · *Hanford Conv. & Visitor Agency* · Dave Jones, Exec. Dir., 504 W. 7th St., 93230, P 48,000, (559) 582-5024, Fax (559) 582-5730, visithanford@att.net, www.visithanford.com

**Huntington Beach** · *Huntington Beach Mktg. & Visitors Bur.* · Stephen Bone, Pres./CEO, 301 Main St., Ste. 208, 92648, P 200,000, (714) 969-3492, (800) 729-6232, Fax (714) 969-5592, info@surfcityusa.com, www.surfcityusa.com

**Lake Tahoe** · *North Lake Tahoe Resort Assn.* · Andy Chapman, Tourism Dir., P.O. Box 1755, Tahoe City, 96145, P 13,000, M 600, (800) 824-6348, (530) 581-8709, Fax (530) 581-1686, info@ gotahoenorth.com, www.gotahoenorth.com

**Lee Vining** · *Mono Lake Comm. Info. Center* · Erika Obedzinski, Ofc. Dir., Hwy. 395 & Third St., P.O. Box 29, 93541, P 398, (760) 647-6595, Fax (760) 647-6377, info@monolake.org, www. monolake.org

**Lodi** · *Lodi Conf. & Visitors Bur.* · Jasmine Savoie, Exec. Asst., 115 S. School St., Ste. 9, 95240, P 65,000, (209) 365-1195, (800) 798-1810, Fax (209) 365-1191, info@visitlodi.com, www.visitlodi.com

**Long Beach** · *Long Beach Area CVB* · Steven Goodling, Pres./ CEO, One World Trade Center, 3rd Flr., 90831, P 470,000, M 450, (562) 436-3645, (800) 452-7829, Fax (562) 435-5653, info@ longbeachcvb.org, www.visitlongbeach.com

**Los Angeles** · *Los Angeles CVB* · Mark Liberman, Pres., 333 S. Hope St., 18th Flr., 90071, P 18,200,000, M 1,000, (213) 624-7300, (800) 366-6116, Fax (213) 624-9746, www.discoverlosangeles.com

**Lucerne** · *Lake County Visitor Info. Center* · Linda Armstrong, Ofc. Mgr., 6110 E. Hwy. 20, P.O. Box 1025, 95458, P 59,000, (707) 274-5652, (800) 525-3743, Fax (707) 274-5664, info@lakecounty. com, www.lakecounty.com

**Mammoth Lakes** · *Mammoth Lakes Tourism* · Danna Stroud, Dir., 2520 Main St., P.O. Box 48, 93546, P 7,093, (760) 934-2712, Fax (760) 934-7066, (888) GO MAMMOTH, info@visitmammoth. com, www.visitmammoth.com

**Marin County** · *see San Rafael*

**Marina del Rey** · *Marina del Rey CVB* · Tiffani Miller, Op. Mgr., 4701 Admiralty Way, 90292, (310) 305-9545, info@VisitMarina. com, www.VisitMarina.com

**Modesto** · *Modesto CVB* · Jennifer Mullen, Dir., 1150 9th St., Stte. C, 95354, P 246,000, (209) 526-5588, (888) 640-8467, Fax (209) 526-5586, info@visitmodesto.com, www.visitmodesto.com

**Monterey** · *Monterey County CVB* · Steve Wille, Pres./CEO, P.O. Box 1770, 93942, P 386,000, (831) 657-6400, (800) 555-6290, Fax (831) 648-5373, info@mccvb.org, www.seemonterey.com

**Morro Bay** · *Morro Bay Visitors Center* · Peter Candela, CEO, 845 Embarcadero, Ste. D, 93442, P 10,400, (805) 772-4467, (800) 231-0592, Fax (805) 772-6038, baywatch@morrobay.org, www.morrobay.org

**Napa** · *Napa Valley Destination Cncl.* · David Turgeon, COO, 1310 Napa Town Center, 94559, P 133,051, M 4,000, (707) 226-5813, Fax (707) 255-2066, info@legendarynapavalley.com, www.legendarynapavalley.com

**Newport Beach** · *Newport Beach Conf. & Visitors Bur.* · Loretta Walker, Deputy Dir./Ofc. Mgr., 1200 Newport Center Dr., Ste. 120, 92660, P 74,000, (949) 719-6100, Fax (949) 719-6101, (800) 94-COAST, info@visitnewportbeach.com, www.visitnewportbeach.com

**Oakhurst** · *Yosemite Sierra Visitors Bur.* · Dan Cunning, CEO, 41969 Hwy. 41, 93644, P 20,000, M 146, (559) 683-4636, Fax (559) 683-5697, ysvb@yosemitethisyear.com, www.yosemitethisyear.com

**Oceanside** · *California Welcome Center Oceanside* · Leslee Gaul, Dir. of Tourism, 928 N. Coast Hwy., 92054, P 187,000, (760) 721-1101, (800) 350-7873, Fax (760) 722-8336, touristinfo@ oceansidechamber.com, www.visitoceanside.org

**Ontario** · *Ontario CVB* · Bob Brown, Gen. Mgr., 2000 E. Convention Center Way, 91764, P 170,000, (909) 937-3000, (800) 455-5755, Fax (909) 937-3080, info@ontariocvb.com, www.ontariocc.com

**Oxnard** · *Oxnard CVB* · Janet Sederquist, Pres./CEO, 1000 Town Center Dr., Ste. 130, 93036, P 200,000, (805) 385-7545, Fax (805) 385-7571, (800) 2-OXNARD, info@visitoxnard.com, www.visitoxnard.com

**Palm Desert** · *Palm Desert Visitors Center* · Donna Gomez, Mgr., 72-567 Hwy. 111, 92260, P 50,000, (760) 568-1441, (800) 873-2428, Fax (760) 779-5271, vcenter@ci.palm-desert.ca.us, www.palm-desert.org

**Pasadena** · *Pasadena CVB* · Nan Marchand, Exec. Dir., 300 E. Green St., 91101, P 132,000, (626) 795-9311, (800) 307-7977, Fax (626) 795-9656, cvb@pasadenacal.com, www.visitpasadena.com

**Pismo Beach** · *Pismo Beach Conf. & Visitors Bur.* · Suzen Brasile, Exec. Dir., 760 Mattie Rd., 93449, P 8,800, (805) 773-7034, (800) 443-7778, Fax (805) 779-1202, pbcity@pismobeach.org, www.ClassicCalifornia.com

**Pleasanton** · *Tri-Valley CVB* · Amy Blaschka, Exec. Dir., 349 Main St., Ste. 203, 94566, P 190,000, M 350, (925) 846-8910, (888) 874-9253, Fax (925) 846-9502, info@trivalleycvb.com, www.trivalleycvb.com

**Quincy** · *Plumas County Visitor Bur.* · Suzi Brakken, Dir., 550 Crescent St., 95971, P 23,090, (530) 283-6345, (800) 326-2247, Fax (530) 283-5465, pcvb@psln.com, www.plumascounty.org

**Rancho Mirage** · *Palm Springs-Desert Resort Communities CVA* · Jeff Beckelman, Pres./CEO, 70-100 Hwy. 111, 92270, P 300,000, M 900, (760) 770-9000, (800) 967-3767, Fax (760) 770-9001, jbeckelman@palmspringsusa.com, www.palm springsusa.com

**Redding** · *Redding CVB* · Chris Gonzalez, Mgr., 777 Auditorium Dr., 96001, P 90,491, (530) 225-4130, (888) 225-4130, Fax (530) 225-4354, info@visitredding.org, www.visitredding.com

**Redondo Beach** · *Redondo Beach C/C & Visitors Bur.* · Marna Smeltzer, Pres./CEO, 200 N. Pacific Coast Hwy., 90277, P 65,000, (310) 376-6911, (800) 282-0333, Fax (310) 374-7373, info@redondochamber.org, www.redondochamber.org

**Ridgecrest** · *Ridgecrest Area CVB & Film Commission* · Douglas Lueck, Exec. Dir., 139 Balsam St., Ste. 1700, 93555, P 41,000, M 57, (760) 375-8202, (800) 847-4830, Fax (760) 375-9850, www.filmdeserts.com, racvb@filmdeserts.com, www.visitdeserts.com

**Riverside** · *Riverside CVB* · Debbie Megna, Exec. Dir., 3750 University Ave., Ste. 175, 92501, P 300,000, (951) 222-4700, (888) 748-7733, Fax (951) 222-4712, dmegna@riversidecvb.com, www.riversidecvb.com

**Sacramento** · *Sacramento CVB* · Steve Hammond, Pres./CEO, 1608 I St., 95814, P 450,000, M 600, (916) 808-7777, (800) 292-2334, Fax (916) 808-7788, www.discovergold.org, www.sacramentocvb.org

**San Bernardino** · *San Bernardino CVB* · Wayne Austin, Pres./CEO, 1955 Hunts Ln., Ste. 102, 92408, P 204,000, (909) 891-1151, (800) 867-8366, Fax (909) 891-1873, cwc@san-bernardino.org, www.san-bernardino.org

**San Diego** · *San Diego CVB* · Joe Terzi, Pres./CEO, 2215 India St., 92101, P 2,911,468, (619) 236-1212, Fax (619) 696-9371, sdinfo@sandiego.org, www.sandiego.org

**San Francisco** · *San Francisco CVB* · Joe D'Alessandro, Pres./CEO, 201 Third St., Ste. 900, 94103, P 744,230, M 1,800, (415) 974-6900, Fax (415) 227-2602, admin@sanfrancisco.travel, www.onlyinsanfrancisco.com

**San Jose** · *San Jose CVB* · Daniel Fenton, Pres./CEO, 408 Almaden Blvd., 95110, P 1,000,000, (408) 295-9600, Fax (408) 295-3937, (800) SAN JOSE, dfenton@sanjose.org, www.sanjose.org

**San Luis Obispo** · *San Luis Obispo County Visitors & Conf. Bur.* · John Solu, Pres., 811 El Capitan Way, Ste. 200, 93401, P 260,000, (805) 541-8000, (800) 634-1414, Fax (805) 543-9498, info@sanluisobispocounty.com, www.sanluisobispocounty.com

**San Rafael** · *The Marin CVB* · Mark Essman, Pres., 1 Mitchell Blvd., Ste. B, 94903, P 250,000, (415) 925-2060, (866) 925-2060, Fax (415) 925-2063, info@visitmarin.org, www.visitmarin.org

**Santa Barbara** · *Santa Barbara CVB & Film Commission* · Kathy Janega-Dykes, Pres./CEO, 1601 Anacapa St., 93101, P 400,000, M 175, (805) 966-9222, (800) 676-1266, Fax (805) 966-1728, tourism@santabarbaraca.com, www.santabarbaraca.com

**Santa Clara** · *Santa Clara CVB* · Steve VanDorn, Pres., 1850 Warburton Ave., 95050, P 106,000, (408) 244-9660, (800) 272-6822, Fax (408) 244-7830, steve.vandorn@santaclara.org, www.santaclara.org

**Santa Cruz** · *Santa Cruz County Conf. & Visitors Cncl.* · Maggie Ivy, CEO, 1211 Ocean St., 95060, P 255,000, (831) 425-1234, (800) 833-3494, Fax (831) 425-1260, comments@santacruz.org, www.santacruz.org

**Santa Maria** · *Santa Maria Visitors & Conv. Bur.* · Gina Keough, Mgr., 614 S. Broadway, 93454, P 119,000, (805) 925-2403, (800) 331-3779, Fax (805) 928-7559, info@santamaria.com, www.santamaria.com.

**Santa Monica** · *Santa Monica CVB* · Misti Kerns, Pres./CEO, 1920 Main St., Ste. B, 90405, P 84,400, (310) 319-6263, Fax (310) 319-6273, info@santamonica.com, www.santamonica.com

**Santa Rosa** · *Santa Rosa CVB & CA Welcome Center* · Maureen McElroy, Exec. Dir., 9 Fourth St., 95401, P 157,000, (707) 577-8674, (800) 404-7673, Fax (707) 571-5949, info@visitsantarosa.com, www.visitsantarosa.com

**Santa Rosa** · *Sonoma County Tourism Bur.* · Ken Fischang, Pres., 420 Aviation Blvd., Ste. 106, 95403, P 450,000, (707) 522-5800, (800) 576-6662, Fax (707) 539-7252, info@sonomacounty.com, www.sonomacounty.com

**Sherman Oaks** · *San Fernando Valley CVB* · 5121 Van Nuys Blvd., Ste. 200, 91403, P 2,000,000, M 1,000, (818) 377-6388, Fax (818) 379-7077, information@valleyofthestars.org, www.visitvalley ofthestars.org

**Solvang** · *Solvang CVB* · Tracy Farhad, Exec. Dir., 1511 Mission Dr., Ste. A, P.O. Box 70, 93464, P 8,000, (805) 688-6144, (800) 468-6765, Fax (805) 688-8620, info@solvangusa.com, www. solvangusa.com

**Sonora** · *Tuolumne County Visitors Bur.* · Nanci Sikes, Exec. Dir., 542 W. Stockton Rd., P.O. Box 4020, 95370, P 59,500, M 280, (209) 533-4420, (800) 446-1333, Fax (209) 533-0956, tcvb@mlode.com, www.tcvb.com

**South Lake Tahoe** · *see Stateline, NV*

**Temecula** · *Temecula Valley CVB* · Kimberly Adams, Pres./CEO, 26790 Ynez Ct., Ste. B, 92591, P 100,000, (951) 491-6085, (888) 363-2852, Fax (951) 491-6089, info@temeculacvb.com, www. temeculacvb.com

**Vallejo** · *Vallejo CVB* · Mike Browne, Exec. Dir., 289 Mare Island Way, 94590, P 120,000, M 210, (707) 642-3653, (800) 482-5535, Fax (707) 644-2206, vjocvb@visitvallejo.com, www.visitvallejo.com

**Ventura** · *Ventura Visitors & Conv. Bur.* · James Luttjohann, Exec. Dir., 101 S. California St., 93001, P 106,000, (805) 648-2075, (800) 333-2989, Fax (805) 648-2150, tourism@ventura-usa.com, www.ventura-usa.com

**West Hollywood** · *West Hollywood Mktg. & Visitors Bur.* · Bradley Burlingame, Pres., 8687 Melrose Ave., Ste. M38, 90069, P 39,000, (310) 289-2525, (800) 368-6020, Fax (310) 289-2529, info@visitwesthollywood.com, www.visitwesthollywood.com

# Colorado

**Avon** · *Vail Valley Partnership* · Michael Kurz, Pres./CEO, 101 Fawcett Rd.,  Ste. 240, P.O. Box 1130, 81620, P 48,000, (970) 476-1000, (800) 525-3875, Fax (970) 476-6008, info@visitvailvalley.com, www.visitvailvalley.com

**Boulder** · *Boulder CVB* · Mary Ann Mahoney, Exec. Dir., 2440 Pearl St., 80302, P 104,000, (303) 442-2911, (800) 444-0447, Fax (303) 938-2098, visitor@bouldercvb.com, www.bouldercoloradousa.com

**Colorado Springs** · *Colorado Springs CVB* · Mr. Terry Sullivan, Pres./CEO, 515 S. Cascade Ave., 80903, P 587,000, M 700, (719) 635-7506, (800) 368-4748, Fax (719) 635-4968, info@visitcos.com, www.visitcos.com

**Denver** · *VISIT DENVER CVB* · 1555 California St., Ste. 300, 80202, P 2,600,000, (303) 892-1112, Fax (303) 892-1636, www.visitdenver.com

**Empire** · *see Idaho Springs*

**Estes Park** · *Estes Park CVB* · Tom Pickering, Exec. Dir., 500 Big Thompson Ave., P.O. Box 1200, 80517, P 12,000, (970) 577-9900, (800) 443-7837, Fax (970) 577-1677, cvbinfo@estes.org, www.estesparkcvb.com

**Fort Collins** · *Fort Collins CVB* · Jim Clark, Pres./CEO, 19 Old Town Sq., Ste. 137, 80524, P 130,000, M 225, (970) 232-3840, (800) 274-3678, Fax (970) 232-3841, information@ftcollins.com, www.visitftcollins.com

**Grand Junction** · *Grand Junction Visitor & Conv. Bur.* · Debbie Kovalik, Exec. Dir., 740 Horizon Dr., 81506, P 136,000, (970) 244-1480, (800) 962-2547, Fax (970) 243-7393, info@visitgrandjunction.com, www.visitgrandjunction.com

**Greeley** · *Greeley CVB* · Sarah MacQuiddy, Pres., 902 7th Ave., 80631, P 97,000, (970) 352-3567, (800) 449-3866, Fax (970) 352-3572, info@greeleychamber.com, www.greeleychamber.com

**Idaho Springs** · *Tourism Bur. Of Clear Creek County* · 2060 Miner St., P.O. Box 100, 80452, P 9,000, (303) 567-4660, (866) 674-9237, Fax (303) 569-6296, info@clearcreekcounty.org, www.clearcreekcounty.org

**Loveland** · *Loveland Visitor Center* · Vickie Rasmussen, Coord., 5400 Stone Creek Circle, 80538, P 65,000, (970) 667-5728, (800) 258-1278, Fax (970) 667-5211, info@loveland.org, www.loveland.org

**Montrose** · *Montrose Visitors & Conv. Bur.* · Jenni Sopsic, Dir., 1519 E. Main St., 81401, P 18,000, (970) 252-0505, (800) 873-0244, Fax (970) 249-2907, jenni@visitmontrose.net, www.visitmontrose.com

**Silver Plume** · *see Idaho Springs*

**South Fork** · *South Fork Visitors Center* · Traci Gillespie, Ofc. Mgr., 30359 Hwy. 160, 81154, P 750, (719) 873-5512, (800) 571-0881, Fax (719) 873-5693, southfrk@amigo.net, www.southfork.org

**Steamboat Springs** · *Steamboat Springs Chamber Resort Assn./Visitors Center* · Kyleigh DeMicco, Mgr., 125 Anglers Dr. , P.O. Box 774408, 80477, P 10,000, (970) 879-0882, Fax (970) 879-2543, info@steamboatchamber.com, www.steamboatchamber.com

**Telluride** · *Telluride & Mountain Village CVB* · Scott McQuade, CEO, 630 W. Colorado, P.O. Box 1009, 81435, P 3,000, (970) 728-3041, (888) 355-8743, Fax (970) 728-6475, info@visittelluride.com, www.visittelluride.com

# Connecticut

**Hartford** · *Central Reg. Tourism Dist.* · Paul Mayer, Exec. Dir., 31 Pratt St., 4th Flr., 06103, P 1,100,000, (860) 244-8181, (800) 793-4480, Fax (860) 244-8180, paulm@visitctriver.com, www.visitctriver.com

**Hartford** · *Greater Hartford CVB* · H. Scott Phelps, Pres., 31 Pratt St., 4th Flr., 06103, P 822,260, M 220, (860) 728-6789, Fax (860) 293-2365, (800) 446-7811 outside CT, ghcvb@hartfordcvb.org, www.enjoyhartford.com

**Litchfield** · *NW Connecticut CVB* · Janet Sera, Dir., P.O. Box 968, 06759, P 8,000, (860) 567-4506, Fax (860) 567-5214, info@litchfieldhills.com, www.litchfieldhills.com

**New Haven** · *Greater New Haven CVB* · Ginny Kozlowski, Pres./CEO, 169 Orange St., 06510, P 600,000, (203) 777-8550, Fax (203) 782-7755, (800) 332-STAY, www.visitnewhaven.com

**New London** · *Mystic Country CVB* · Donna Simpson, Exec. Dir., 32 Huntington St., 06320, P 300,000, (860) 444-2206, Fax (860) 442-4257, (800) TO ENJOY, info@mysticcountry.com, www.mysticcountry.com

**Norwalk** · *Fairfield County CVB* · Catherine Sidor, Exec. Dir., 297 West Ave., 06850, P 700,000, (203) 853-7770, (800) 866-7925, Fax (203) 853-7775, info@fairfieldcountyctcvb.com, www.visitfairfieldcountyct.com

# Delaware

**Dover** · *Kent County Delaware CVB* · Cynthia Small, Exec. Dir., 435 N. Dupont Hwy., 19901, P 144,000, (302) 734-1736, (800) 233-5368, Fax (302) 734-0167, csmall@visitdover.com, www.visitdover.com

**Wilmington** · *Greater Wilmington CVB* · Sarah Willoughby, Exec. Dir., 100 W. 10th St., Ste. 20, 19801, P 600,000, M 360, (302) 295-2210, (800) 489-6664, Fax (302) 652-4726, info@wilmcvb.org, www.visitwilmingtonde.com

# District of Columbia

**Washington** · *Destination D.C.* · William Hanbury, Pres./CEO, 901 7th St. N.W., 4th Flr., 20001, P 6,000,000, M 1,400, (202) 789-7000, (800) 422-8644, Fax (202) 789-7037, www.washington.org

# Florida

**Bradenton** · *Bradenton Area CVB* · Larry White, Dir., P.O. Box 1000, 34206, P 300,000, (941) 729-9177, Fax (941) 729-1820, (800) 4-MANATEE, info@floridasgulfislands.com, www.floridasgulfislands.com

**Brooksville** · *Hernando County Welcome Center* · Susan Rupe, Dir., 30305 Cortez Blvd., 34602, P 160,000, (352) 754-4405, (800) 601-4580, Fax (352) 754-4406, WelcomeCtr@hernandocounty.us, www.naturallyhernando.org

**Cape Canaveral** · *see Cocoa Village*

**Clearwater** · *St. Petersburg/Clearwater Area CVB* · D.T. Minich, Exec. Dir., 13805 58th St. N., Ste. 2-200, 33760, P 900,000, (727) 464-7200, (877) 352-3224, Fax (727) 464-7222, www.floridas beach.com

**Cocoa Village** · *Florida's Space Coast Ofc. Of Tourism* · Rob Varley, Exec. Dir., 430 Brevard Ave., Ste. 150, 32922, P 543,050, (321) 433-4470, (877) 572-3224, Fax (321) 433-4476, info@ space-coast.com, www.space-coast.com

**Davenport** · *Central Florida Visitors & Conv. Bur.* · Hank Longo, Mgr., 101 Adventure Ct., 33837, P 500,000, (863) 420-2586, (800) 828-7655, Fax (863) 420-2593, www.visitcentralflorida.org

**Daytona Beach** · *Daytona Beach Area CVB* · Sharon Mock, Pres./CEO, 126 E. Orange Ave., 32114, P 65,000, (386) 255-0415, (800) 544-0415, Fax (386) 255-5478, info@daytonabeachcvb.org, www.daytonabeach.com

**Fort Lauderdale** · *Greater Ft. Lauderdale CVB* · Nicki E. Grossman, Pres., 100 E. Broward Blvd., Ste. 200, 33301, P 1,700,000, (954) 765-4466, Fax (954) 765-4467, (800) 22-SUNNY, gflcvb@ broward.org, www.sunny.org

**Fort Myers** · *Lee County Visitors & Conv. Bur.* · Suya Davenport, Exec. Dir., 12800 University Dr., Ste. 550, 33907, P 623,725, (239) 338-3500, (800) 237-6444, Fax (239) 334-1106, vcb@leegov.com, www.fortmyers-sanibel.com

**Fort Pierce** · *St. Lucie County Tourism Dev. Cncl.* · Charlotte Lombard, Tourism Dev. Mgr., 2300 Virginia Ave., 34982, P 271,000, (772) 462-1539, (800) 344-8443, Fax (772) 462-2131, lombardc@ stlucieco.org, www.visitstluciefla.com

**Fort Walton Beach** · *Emerald Coast CVB Inc.* · Darrel Jones, Pres./CEO, 1540 Miracle Strip Pkwy. S.E., P.O. Box 609, 32549, P 181,236, (850) 651-7131, (800) 322-3319, Fax (850) 651-7149, emeraldcoast@co.okaloosa.fl.us, www.destin-fwb.com

**Gainesville** · *Alachua County Visitors & Conv. Bur.* · Roland Loog CDME CMP, Dir., 30 E. University Ave., 32601, P 216,000, (352) 374-5231, (866) 778-5002, Fax (352) 338-3213, info@ visitgainesville.com, www.visitgainesville.com

**Groveland** · *Lake County CVB* · Greg Mihalic, Dir., 20763 U.S. Hwy. 27, 34736, P 269,070, (352) 429-3673, (800) 798-1071, Fax (352) 429-4870, gmihalic@lakecountyfl.gov, www.lakecountyfl.com

**Homosassa** · *Citrus County Visitors & Conv. Bur.* · Marla Chancey, Tourism Dir., 9225 W. Fishbowl Dr., 34448, P 120,000, (352) 628-9305, (800) 587-6667, Fax (352) 628-0703, info@ visitcitrus.com, www.visitcitrus.com

**Jacksonville** · *Visit Jacksonville* · John Reyes, Pres., 550 Water St., Ste. 1000, 32202, P 800,000, M 294, (904) 798-9111, (800) 733-2668, Fax (904) 798-9110, visitorinfo@jaxcvb.com, www.visitjacksonville.com

**Key Largo** · *Florida Keys Visitor Center* · Jackie Harder, Pres., 106000 Overseas Hwy., 33037, P 12,000, M 324, (800) 822-1088, (305) 451-6266, Fax (305) 451-4726, www.fla-keys.com, klchamber@aol.com, www.keylargo.org

**Key West** · *Monroe County Tourist Dev. Cncl.* · Harold Wheeler, Dir., 1201 White St., Ste. 102, P.O. Box 866, 33040, P 78,284, (305) 296-1552, Fax (305) 296-0788, www.fla-keys.com

**Kissimmee** · *Kissimmee CVB* · Tom Lang, Dir., 1925 E. Irlo Bronson Mem. Hwy., 34744, P 190,187, (407) 847-5000, (800) 327-9159, Fax (407) 847-0878, meet@floridakiss.com, www.floridakiss.com

**Lakeland** · *Lakeland CVB* · Jacqueline Johnson, Sr. V.P., 35 Lake Morton Dr., P.O. Box 3607, 33802, P 237,000, (863) 688-8551, Fax (863) 683-7454, info@lakelandchamber.com, www.lakeland chamber.com

**Melbourne** · *Melbourne-Palm Bay & the Beaches CVB* · Chuck Galy, Exec. V.P., 1005 E. Strawbridge Ave., 32901, P 300,000, M 60, (321) 724-5400, (800) 771-9922, Fax (321) 725-2093, chuck@melpb-chamber.org, www.melpb-chamber.org

**Miami** · *Greater Miami CVB* · William D. Talbert III, Pres./CEO, 701 Brickell Ave., Ste. 2700, 33131, P 2,000,000, (305) 539-3000, (800) 933-8448, Fax (305) 539-3125, www.miamiandbeaches.com

**Naples** · *Naples Area Visitors Center* · Michael Reagen, Pres./ CEO, 2390 Tamiami Trail N., Ste. 206, 34103, P 341,000, (239) 262-6141, Fax (239) 262-8374, info@napleschamber.org, www.napleschamber.org

**New Port Richey** · *Pasco County Ofc. of Tourism* · Eric Keaton, Pbl. Comm. Mgr., 7530 Little Rd., Ste. 340, 34654, P 407,800, (727) 847-8990, (800) 842-1873, Fax (727) 847-8168, tourism@ pascocountyfl.net, www.visitpasco.net

**Orlando** · *Orlando/Orange County CVB Inc.* · Gary Sain, Pres./ CEO, 6700 Forum Dr., Ste. 100, 32821, P 1,886,934, (407) 363-5872, (800) 972-3304, Fax (407) 370-5000, info@orlandocvb.com, www.orlandoinfo.com

**Panama City Beach** · *Panama City Beach CVB* · Dan Rowe, Pres./CEO, 17001 Panama City Beach Pkwy., P.O. Box 9473, 32417, P 25,000, (850) 233-6503, (850) 233-5070, Fax (850) 233-5072, (800) PC BEACH, info@visitpanamacitybeach.com, www.visit panamacitybeach.com.

**Pensacola** · *Pensacola Bay Area C/C - Conv. & Visitors Info. Center* · Evon Emerson, 1401 E. Gregory St., 32502, P 385,000, (850) 434-1234, (800) 874-1234, Fax (850) 432-8211, www. visitpensacola.com

**Perry** · *Taylor County Tourism Dev. Cncl.* · Dawn Taylor, Exec. Dir., 428 N. Jefferson St., P.O. Box 892, 32348, P 19,422, (850) 584-5366, (800) 257-8881, Fax (850) 584-8030, taylor chamber@gtcom.net, www.taylorcountychamber.com.

**TOURIST CENTER FOR TAYLOR COUNTY WHICH INCLUDES STEINHATCHEE, PERRY, KEATON BEACH AND ECONFINA.**

**Port Charlotte** · *Charlotte Harbor Visitors Bur.* · Becky Bovell, Dir., 18501 Murdock Cir., Ste. 502, 33948, P 160,454, (941) 743-1900, Fax (941) 743-2245, (888) 4-PUR FLA, www.charlotte harbortravel.com

**Saint Augustine** · *St. Augustine, Ponte Vedra & The Beaches Visitors & Conv. Bur.* · Glenn Hastings, Exec. Dir., 500 San Sabastian View, 32084, P 165,000, (904) 829-1711, (800) 653-2489, Fax (904) 829-6149, ghastings@getaway4florida.com, www.getaway4florida.com

**Saint Petersburg** · *see Clearwater*

**Santa Rosa Beach** · *Walton County Tourist Dev. Cncl.* · Charles Mayers, Exec. Dir., 25777 U.S. 331 S., P.O. Box 1248, 32459, P 43,000, (850) 267-1216, (800) 822-6877, Fax (850) 267-3943, florida@beachesofsouthwalton.com, www.beachesof southwalton.com

**Sarasota** · *Sarasota CVB* · Virginia Haley, Pres., 766 Hudson Ave., Ste. A, 34236, P 315,000, M 370, (941) 955-0991, (800) 522-9799, Fax (941) 955-1929, info@sarasotafl.org, www.sarasotafl.org

**Sebring** · *Highlands County Tourist Dev. Cncl.* · John Scherlacher, Tourism Dir., 1121 U.S. Hwy. 27 S., 33870, P 99,000, (863) 386-1316, (800) 545-6021, Fax (863) 386-1319, info@ visithighlandscounty.com, www.visithighlandscounty.com

**Tallahassee** · *Tallahassee Area CVB* · Sharon Liggett, Pres./CEO, 106 E. Jefferson St., 32301, P 243,300, M 500, (850) 606-2305, (800) 628-2866, Fax (850) 606-2301, vic@visittallahassee.com, www.visittallahassee.com

**Tampa** · *Tampa Bay & Co.* · Paul Catoe, Pres./CEO, 401 E. Jackson St., Ste. 2100, 33602, P 1,140,000, (813) 223-1111, (800) 826-8358, Fax (813) 229-6616, www.visittampabay.com

**Tampa** · *West Tampa Conv. Center* · 3005 W. Columbus Dr., 33607, P 854,000, M 150, (813) 870-0559, (813) 870-3144, Fax (813) 877-8485

**Tampa** · *Ybor City Visitor Info. Center* · Rose Barbie, Mgr., 1600 E. 8th Ave., Ste. B104, 33605, P 800,000, M 450, (813) 241-8838, Fax (813) 242-0398, info@ybor.org, www.ybor.org

**West Palm Beach** · *Palm Beach Tourist Dev. Cncl.* · 1555 Palm Beach Lakes Blvd., Ste. 900, 33401, P 1,200,000, (561) 233-3130, Fax (561) 233-3113, www.palmbeachfl.com

**Ybor City** · *see Tampa-Ybor City Visitor Info. Center*

# Georgia

**Albany** · *Albany CVB* · Lisa Riddle, CVB Dir., 112 N. Front St., 31701, P 170,000, (229) 317-4760, (866) 750-0840, Fax (229) 317-4765, lriddle@albanyga.com, www.visitalbanyga.com.

**Alpharetta** · *Alpharetta CVB* · Janet Rodgers, Pres., 3060 Royal Blvd. S., Ste. 145, 30022, P 50,000, (678) 297-2811, (800) 294-0923, Fax (678) 297-9197, info@awesomealpharetta.com, www.awesomealpharetta.com

**Athens** · *Athens CVB* · Chuck Jones, Dir., 300 N. Thomas St., 30601, P 104,000, (706) 357-4430, (800) 864-4160, Fax (706) 546-8040, cjones@visitathensga.com, www.visitathensga.com

**Atlanta** · *Atlanta CVB* · Spurgeon Richardson, Pres./CEO, 233 Peachtree St. N.E., Ste. 1400, 30303, P 4,000,000, M 1,300, (404) 521-6600, Fax (404) 577-3293, (800) ATLANTA, info@atlanta.net, www.atlanta.net

**Atlanta** · *Cobb County CVB* · Joyce Calandra, CEO, One Galleria Pkwy., Ste. 1A2A, 30339, P 530,000, M 285, (678) 303-2622, (800) 451-3480, Fax (678) 303-2625, cobb@cobbcvb.com, www.cobbcvb.com

**Augusta** · *Augusta CVB* · Barry E. White, Exec. Dir., 1450 Greene St., Ste. 110, P.O. Box 1331, 30903, P 200,000, (706) 823-6600, (800) 726-0243, Fax (706) 823-6609, acvb@augustaga.org, www.augustaga.org

**Brunswick** · *Brunswick-Golden Isles Visitors Bur.* · Bill Tipton, Exec. Dir., 4 Glynn Ave., 31520, P 74,000, (912) 265-0620, (800) 809-1790, Fax (912) 265-0629, cvbservices@bgicvb.com, www.bgicvb.com

**Calhoun** · *Gordon County CVB* · Beth Grubbs, Dir., 300 S. Wall St., 30701, P 51,500, (706) 625-3200, (800) 887-3811, Fax (706) 625-5062, bgrubbs@gordonchamber.org, www.exploregordoncounty.com

**Carrollton** · *Carrollton Area CVB* · Jonathan Dorsey, Exec. Dir., 102 N. Lakeshore Dr., 30117, P 100,000, (770) 214-9746, (800) 292-0871, Fax (770) 830-1765, visit@carrollton-ga.gov, www.visitcarrollton.com

**Cartersville** · *Cartersville-Bartow County CVB* · Ellen Archer, Exec. Dir., 1 Friendship Plaza, Ste. 1, P.O. Box 200397, 30120, P 90,000, (770) 387-1357, (800) 733-2280, cvb@notatlanta.org, www.notatlanta.org

**Clayton** · *Rabun County CVB* · Mary Boland, CVB Dir., 232 Hwy. 441 N., P.O. Box 750, 30525, P 17,500, (706) 782-4812, Fax (706) 782-4810, rabunchamber@gamountains.com, www.gamountains.com

**Columbus** · *Columbus CVB* · Peter Bowden, Pres./CEO, 900 Front Ave., P.O. Box 2768, 31902, P 225,000, (706) 322-1613, (800) 999-1613, Fax (706) 322-0701, ccvb@columbusga.org, www.visitcolumbusga.com

**Covington** · *Covington-Newton County CVB* · Clara Deemer, Dir. of Tourism, 2101 Clark St., P.O. Box 168, 30015, P 90,000, (770) 787-3868, (800) 616-8626, Fax (770) 786-1294, cdeemer@newtonchamber.com, www.newtonchamber.com

**Dalton** · *Dalton CVB* · Margaret Thigpen, Exec. Dir., P.O. Box 6177, 30722, P 87,000, (706) 270-9960, (800) 331-3258, Fax (706) 876-1561, www.visitdaltonga.com, info@visitdaltonga.com, www.daltoncvb.com

**Douglas** · *Douglas Area Welcome Center* · Dorie Bacon, Tourism Coord., 211 S. Gaskin Ave., 31533, P 38,000, (912) 384-4555, (888) 426-3334, Fax (912) 383-6304, tourism@cityofdouglas.com, www.cityofdouglas.org

**Duluth** · *Gwinnett CVB* · Caryn McGarity, Exec. Dir., 6500 Sugarloaf Pkwy., Ste. 200, 30097, P 650,000, (770) 623-3600, (888) 494-6638, Fax (770) 623-1667, info@gcvb.org, www.gcvb.org

**Fort Gaines** · *Clay County Visitors Bur.* · Jean O. Turn, Dir., P.O. Box 275, 39851, P 3,200, (229) 768-2248, Fax (229) 768-2248, www.fortgaines.com

**Gainesville** · *Lake Lanier CVB* · Stacey Dickson, Pres., P.O. Box 2995, 30503, P 175,000, (770) 536-5209, (888) 536-0005, Fax (770) 503-1349, info@lakelaniercvb.com, www.lakelaniercvb.com

**Hazlehurst** · *Hazlehurst-Jeff Davis County Bd. Of Tourism* · 95 E. Jarman St., P.O. Box 546, 31539, P 12,684, (912) 375-4543, Fax (912) 375-7948, www.hazlehurst-jeffdavis.com

**Helen** · *Alpine Helen/White County CVB* · 726 Bruckenstrasse, P.O. Box 730, 30545, P 15,000, (706) 878-3842, (800) 858-8027, Fax (706) 878-4032, info@helenga.org, www.helenga.org

**Jekyll Island** · *Jekyll Island CVB* · Eric Garvey, Dir., 100 James Rd., 31527, P 1,300, (912) 635-4080, (877) 453-5955, Fax (912) 635-4004, egarvey@jekyllisland.com, www.jekyllisland.com

**Jonesboro** · *Clayton County CVB* · Patrick Duncan, Pres., 127 N. Main St., 30236, P 225,000, (678) 610-4242, Fax (678) 610-4087, (800) 662-STAY, pduncan@visitscarlett.com, www.visitscarlett.com.

**Kingsland** · *Kingsland CVB* · Tonya Rosado, Exec. Dir., 1190 E. Boone Ave., P.O. Box 1928, 31548, P 50,000, (912) 729-5999, (800) 433-0225, Fax (912) 729-7258, info@visitkingsland.com, www.visitkingsland.com

**Macon** · *Macon-Bibb County CVB* · Janice W. Marshall, Pres./CEO, 450 Martin Luther King Jr. Blvd., P.O. Box 6354, 31208, P 153,887, (478) 743-3401, (800) 768-3401, Fax (478) 745-2022, maconcvb@maconga.org, www.visitmacon.org

**Madison** · *Madison-Morgan County C/C & CVB* · Marguerite Copelan, Exec. Dir., 115 E. Jefferson St., P.O. Box 826, 30650, P 17,000, (706) 342-4454, (800) 709-7406, Fax (706) 342-4455, marguerite@madisonga.org, www.madisonga.org

**Milledgeville** · *Milledgeville-Baldwin County CVB* · Jane Sowell, Dir., 200 W. Hancock St., P.O. Box 219, 31059, P 50,000, (478) 452-4687, (800) 653-1804, Fax (478) 453-4440, tourism@windstream.net, www.milledgevillecvb.com

**Peachtree City** · *Peachtree City Tourism Assn.* · Lauren Yawn, Exec. Dir., 10 Planterra Way, 30269, P 35,000, (678) 216-0282, (877) 782-4250, Fax (770) 631-2575, info@visitpeachtreecity.com, www.visitpeachtreecity.com

**Perry** · *Perry Area CVB* · Sheila Averett Jones, Exec. Dir., 101 Gen. Courtney Hodges Blvd., P.O. Box 1609, 31069, P 12,000, (478) 988-8000, Fax (478) 988-8005, info@perryga.com, www.perryga.com

**Pine Mountain** · *Pine Mountain Tourism Assn.* · Hank Arnold, Exec. Dir., 101 E. Broad St., P.O. Box 177, 31822, P 1,000, (706) 663-4000, (800) 441-3502, Fax (706) 663-4726, tourism@pine mountain.org, www.pinemountain.org

**Rome** · *Greater Rome CVB* · Lisa Smith, Exec. Dir., 402 Civic Center Dr., 30161, P 94,800, (706) 295-5576, (800) 444-1834, Fax (706) 236-5029, lisa@romegeorgia.org, www.romegeorgia.org

**Roswell** · *Historic Roswell CVB* · Dotty Etris, Exec. Dir., 617 Atlanta St., 30075, P 85,000, (770) 640-3253, (800) 776-7935, Fax (770) 640-3252, info@cvb.roswell.ga.us, www.visitroswellga.com

**Saint Mary's** · *St. Mary's CVB Auth.* · Janet Brinko, Dir., 406 Osborne St., 31558, P 48,000, (912) 882-4000, (800) 868-8687, Fax (912) 882-6246, info@stmaryswelcome.com, www.stmarys welcome.com

**Savannah** · *Savannah Area CVB* · Joseph Marinelli, Pres., 101 E. Bay St., P.O. Box 1628, 31402, P 310,704, (912) 644-6401, Fax (912) 644-6499, (877) SAVANNAH, www.savannahvisit.com

**Statesboro** · *Statesboro CVB* · Jaime Riggs, Exec. Dir., 332 S. Main St., P.O. Box 1516, 30459, P 62,000, (912) 489-1869, (800) 568-3301, Fax (912) 489-2688, scvb@frontiernet.net, www.visitstatesboroga.com

**Thomasville** · *Thomasville CVB* · Katie Brenckle, Tourism Coord., 144 E. Jackson St., P.O. Box 3319, 31799, P 43,000, (229) 228-7977, (866) 577-3600, Fax (229) 228-4188, visitus@rose.net, www. thomasvillega.com

**Thomson** · *Thomson-McDuffie Tourism CVB* · Elizabeth Vance, Exec. Dir., 111 Railroad St., 30824, P 22,140, (706) 597-1000, evance@thomson-mcduffie.net, www.exploremcduffiecounty.com

**Tucker** · *DeKalb CVB* · Jon Manns, Pres./CEO, 1957 Lakeside Pkwy., Ste. 510, 30084, P 700,000, (770) 492-5000, Fax (770) 492-5033, jonm@dcvb.org, www.dcvb.org

**Tybee Island** · *Tybee Island Visitors Info. Center* · Georgeanne Inglis, Mgr., 802 1st St., P.O. Box 491, 31328, P 3,500, (912) 786-5444, (800) 868-2322, Fax (912) 786-5895, vc@tybeevisit.com, www.tybeevisit.com

**Valdosta** · *Valdosta-Lowndes Cty Conf. Center & Tourism Auth.* · Donald Poor, Exec. Dir., 1 Meeting Pl., P.O. Box 1964, 31603, P 106,000, (229) 245-0513, Fax (229) 245-5240, (800) 569-TOUR, dpoor@valdostatourism.com, www.valdostatourism.com

**Vidalia** · *Vidalia Area CVB* · Elizabeth Harvill, Exec. Dir., 100 Vidalia Sweet Onion Dr., Ste. A, 30474, P 15,000, (912) 538-8687, Fax (912) 538-1466, vacvb@bellsouth.net, www.vidaliaarea.com

**Warner Robins** · *Warner Robins CVB* · Marsha Buzzell, Dir., 99 N. 1st St., 31093, P 58,000, (478) 922-5100, Fax (478) 225-2631, cvb@warnerrobinsga.gov, www.warnerrobinsga.gov

**Waycross** · *Waycross Tourism Bur.* · Vickie Leverette, Dir., 315-A Plant Ave., 31501, P 37,000, (912) 283-3744, Fax (912) 283-0121, waycrosstour@accesstc.net, www.swampgeorgia.com

# Hawaii

**Honolulu** · *Hawaii CVB* · John Monahan, Pres./CEO, 2270 Kalakaua Ave., Ste. 801, 96815, P 1,400,000, (808) 923-1811, (800) 464-2924, Fax (808) 924-0290, info@hvcb.org, www. gohawaii.com

**Kaunakakai** · *Moloka'I Visitors Assn.* · Julie Bicoy, Dir., P.O. Box 960, 96748, P 8,100, M 97, (808) 553-3876, (800) 800-6367, Fax (808) 553-5288, mvajulie@gmail.com, www.molokai-hawaii.com

# Idaho

**Boise** · *Boise CVB* · Roberta Patterson, Exec. Dir., 312 S. 9th St., Ste. 100, 83702, P 208,000, (208) 344-7777, (800) 635-5240, Fax (208) 344-6236, receptionist@boisecvb.org, www.boise.org

**Coeur d'Alene** · *Coeur d'Alene Visitors Bur.* · Jonathan Coe, Pres./Gen. Mgr., 105 1st St., 83814, P 43,683, (208) 664-3194, (877) 782-9232, Fax (208) 667-9338, info@coeurdalene.org, www.coeurdalene.org

**Idaho Falls** · *Idaho Falls CVB* · Bob Everhart, Exec. Dir., 630 W. Broadway, P.O. Box 50498, 83405, P 52,000, (208) 523-1010, (866) 365-6943, Fax (208) 523-2255, info@visitidahofalls.com, www.visitidahofalls.com

**Ketchum** · *Sun Valley Ketchum CVB* · Carol Waller, Exec. Dir, 251 Washington Ave., Ste. A, P.O. Box 2420, 83353, P 4,547, (208) 726-3423, (866) 226-8817, info@visitsunvalley.com, www.visitsunvalley.com

**McCall** · *McCall Area Visitors Bur.* · Tamara Sandmeyer, Exec. Dir., 102 N. 3rd St., P.O. Box 350, 83638, P 3,000, (208) 634-7631, (800) 260-5130, Fax (208) 634-7752, info@mccallchamber.org, www.mccallchamber.org

**Pocatello** · *Greater Pocatello CVB* · Rebecca Satter, Exec. Dir., 324 S. Main St., Ste. B, P.O. Box 626, 83204, P 60,000, (208) 235-7659, (877) 922-7659, Fax (208) 233-1527, rsatter@pocatello idaho.com, www.pocatellocvb.com

# Illinois

**Alton** · *Alton Reg.CVB* · Brett Stawar, Pres., 200 Piasa St., 62002, P 100,000, (618) 465-6676, Fax (618) 465-6151, (800) ALTON IL, info@visitalton.com, www.visitalton.com

**Anna** · *Southernmost Illinois Tourism Bur.* · Cindy Cain, Dir., P.O. Box 378, 62906, P 71,500, (618) 833-9928, (800) 248-4373, Fax (618) 833-9924, sitb@ajinternet.net, www.southernmost illinois.com

**Arlington Heights** · *see Prospect Heights*

**Aurora** · *Aurora Area CVB* · Sue Vos, Pres./CEO, 43 W. Galena Blvd., 60506, P 289,708, (630) 897-5581, (800) 477-4369, Fax (630) 897-5589, market@enjoyaurora.com, www.enjoyaurora.com

**Belleville** · *Belleville Illinois Tourism* · Cathleen Lindauer, Dir., 216 E. A St., 62220, P 44,000, (618) 233-6769, (800) 677-9255, Fax (618) 233-2077, clindauer@bellevillechamber.org, www. belleville.net

**Belvidere** · *Northern Illinois Tourism Dev. Ofc.* · Bonnie Heimbach, Exec. Dir., 200 S. State St., 61008, P 3,000,000, (815) 547-3740, Fax (815) 547-3749, nitdo@visitnorthernillinois.com, www.visitnorthernillinois.com.

**Bloomington** · *Bloomington-Normal Area CVB* · Crystal Howard, Dir., 3201 CIRA Dr., Ste. 201, 61704, P 145,000, (800) 433-8226, (309) 665-0033, Fax (309) 661-0743, www.bloomington normalcvb.org

**Carbondale** · *Carbondale Conv. & Tourism Bur.* · Debbie Moore, Exec. Dir., 1185 E. Main St., Ste. 1046, University Mall, 62901, P 49,000, (618) 529-4451, (800) 526-1500, Fax (618) 529-5590, www.cctb.org

**Champaign** · *Champaign County CVB* · Scott Hockman, Exec. Dir., 1817 S. Neil St., Ste. 201, 61820, P 190,000, (217) 351-4133, (800) 369-6151, Fax (217) 359-1809, scotth@champaigncounty. org, www.visitchampaigncounty.org

**Chicago** · *Chicago Ofc. Of Tourism* · Dorothy Coyle, Dir., Chicago Cultural Center, 78 E. Washington St., 4th Flr., 60602, P 2,731,743, (312) 744-2400, Fax (312) 744-2359, (877) CHICAGO, www. explorechicago.org, www.cityofchicago.org/tourism

**Collinsville** · *Gateway Center* · Lisa Smith, Dir. of Sales, One Gateway Dr., 62234, P 24,707, (618) 345-8998, (800) 289-2388, Fax (618) 345-9024, lsmith@gatewaycenter.com, www.gateway center.com

**Danville** · *Danville Area CVB* · Jeanie Cooke, Exec. Dir., 100 W. Main, Ste. 146, 61832, P 83,000, (217) 442-2096, (800) 383-4386, Fax (217) 442-2137, info@danvilleareainfo.com, www.danville areainfo.com

**Decatur** · *Decatur Area CVB* · Denene Wilmeth, Exec. Dir., 202 E. North St., 62523, P 100,000, (217) 423-7000, (800) 331-4479, Fax (217) 423-7455, denene@decaturcvb.com, www.decaturcvb.com

**Du Quoin** · *Du Quoin Tourism Comm.* · Judy Smid, Pres., 20 N. Chestnut St., P.O. Box 1037, 62832, P 6,448, (618) 542-8338, (800) 455-9570, Fax (618) 542-2098, dqmst@comcast.net, www. duquointourism.org

**Elgin** · *Elgin Area CVB* · Kimberly Bless, Pres./CEO, 77 Riverside Dr., 60120, P 285,000, M 100, (847) 695-7540, (800) 217-5362, Fax (847) 695-7668, elgincvb@northernfoxrivervalley.com, www.northernfoxrivervalley.com

**Fairview Heights** · *The Tourism Bur.  Southwestern Illinois* · Jo Kathmann, Pres./CEO, 10950 Lincoln Trail, 62208, P 700,000, (618) 397-1488, (800) 442-1488, Fax (618) 397-1945, info@thetourismbureau.org, www.thetourismbureau.org

**Freeport** · *Freeport/Stephenson County CVB* · Connie Sorn, Exec. Dir., 4596 U.S. Rte. 20 E., 61032, P 48,000, (815) 233-1357, (800) 369-2955, Fax (815) 233-1358, stephcvb@aeroinc.net, www.stephenson-county-il.org

**Galena** · *Galena/Jo Daviess County CVB* · Betsy Eaton, Exec. Dir., 720 Park Ave., 61036, P 22,289, M 300, (815) 777-3557, (877) 464-2536, Fax (815) 777-3566, director@galena.org, www.galena.org

**Galesburg** · *Galesburg Area CVB* · Diane Bruening, Exec. Dir., 2163 E. Main St., P.O. Box 60, 61402, P 33,500, (309) 343-2485, (800) 916-3330, Fax (309) 343-2521, visitors@visitgalesburg.com, www.visitgalesburg.com

**Gurnee** · *Lake County, Illinois CVB* · Maureen Riedy, Pres., 5465 W. Grand Ave., Ste. 100, 60031, P 617,975, M 135, (847) 662-2700, Fax (847) 662-2702, (800) LAKE NOW, tourism@lakecounty.org, www.lakecounty.org

**Jacksonville** · *Jacksonville Area CVB* · Patricia Anderson, Exec. Dir., 310 E. State St., 62650, P 24,000, (217) 243-5678, (800) 593-5678, Fax (217) 243-5862, events@jacksonvilleil.org, www.jacksonvilleil.org

**Joliet** · *Heritage Corridor CVB* · Robert Navarro, CEO, 339 W. Jefferson St., 60435, P 100,000, M 250, (800) 926-2262, Fax (815) 727-2324, info@hccvbil.com, www.heritagecorridorcvb.com

**Kankakee** · *Kankakee County CVB* · Larry Williams, Exec. Dir., 1 Dearborn Sq., Ste. 1, 60901, P 105,000, (815) 935-7390, Fax (815) 935-5169, (800) 74-RIVER, larry@visitkankakeecounty.com, www.visitkankakeecounty.com

**Lake County** · *see Gurnee*

**Lansing** · *Chicago Southland CVB* · Jim Garrett, Pres./CEO, 2304 173rd St., 60438, P 871,138, M 500, (708) 895-8200, (888) 895-8233, Fax (708) 895-8288, info@visitchicagosouthland.com, www.visitchicagosouthland.com

**Lincoln** · *Abraham Lincoln Tourism Bur. of Logan County* · Geoff Ladd, Exec. Dir., 1555 5th St., 62656, P 35,000, (217) 732-8687, Fax (217) 735-9205, info@abe66.com, www.abe66.com

**Lisle** · *Lisle CVB* · Priscilla Tomei, Exec. Dir., 4746 Main St., 60532, P 21,000, (630) 769-1000, (800) 733-9811, Fax (630) 769-1006, lislevisitor@stayinlisle.com, www.stayinlisle.com

**Macomb** · *Macomb Area CVB* · Katherine Walker, Pres., 201 S. Lafayette St., 61455, P 20,000, (309) 833-1315, Fax (309) 833-3575, macvb@macomb.com, www.makeitmacomb.com

**Macomb** · *Western IL Tourism Dev. Ofc.* · Roger Carmack, Exec. Dir., 581 S. Deere Rd., 61455, (309) 837-7460, Fax (309) 833-4754, witdo@visitwesternillinois.info, www.visitwesternillinois.info

**Marion** · *Williamson County CVB* · Shannon Johnson, Exec. Dir., 1602 Sioux Dr., 62959, P 65,000, (618) 997-3690, (800) 433-7399, Fax (618) 997-1874, sjohnson@vistisi.com, www.visitsi.com

**Moline** · *Quad-Cities CVB* · Joe Taylor, Pres./CEO, 1601 River Dr., Ste. 110, 61265, P 400,000, M 400, (309) 747-7800, jtaylor@visitquadcities.com, www.visitquadcities.com

**Mount Vernon** · *Mount Vernon CVB* · Bonnie Jerdon, Dir., 200 Potomac Blvd., P.O. Box 1708, 62864, P 16,300, (618) 242-3151, (800) 252-5464, Fax (618) 242-6849, tourism@mvn.net, www.mtvernon.com.

**Naperville** · *Naperville Dev. Partnership & CVB* · Christine Jeffries, Pres., 212 S. Webster, Ste. 104, 60540, P 140,000, (630) 305-7701, (877) 236-2737, Fax (630) 305-7793, www.naper.org, www.visitnaperville.com

**Oak Brook** · *DuPage CVB* · JoEllen Strittmatter, Exec. Dir., 915 Harger Rd., Ste. 240, 60523, P 904,161, M 300, (630) 575-8070, (800) 232-0502, Fax (630) 575-8078, dcvb@discoverdupagecvb.com, www.discoverdupage.com

**Pekin** · *Pekin Visitors Bur.* · Steve Brown, Exec. Dev. Coord., 111 S. Capitol, 61554, P 33,857, (309) 477-2300, (877) 669-7741, Fax (309) 346-2095, tourism@ci.pekin.il.us, www.pekintourism.com

**Peoria** · *Peoria Area CVB* · Brent Lonteen, Pres./CEO, 456 Fulton St., Ste. 300, 61602, P 344,000, (309) 676-0303, (800) 747-0302, Fax (309) 676-8470, blonteen@peoria.org, www.peoria.org

**Polo** · *Blackhawk Waterways CVB* · Diane Bausman, Exec. Dir., 201 N. Franklin Ave., 61064, P 96,000, (815) 946-2108, (800) 678-2108, Fax (815) 946-2277, www.bwcvb.com

**Pontiac** · *Pontiac Tourism* · Ellie Alexander, Dir., 115 W. Howard St., 61764, P 12,000, (815) 844-5847, (800) 835-2055, Fax (815) 842-3885, tourism@pontiac.org, www.pontiac.org

**Prospect Heights** · *Chicago's North Suburbs CVB* · 8 N. Elmhurst Rd., Ste. 100, 60070, P 17,000, M 40, (847) 577-3666, (800) 955-7259, Fax (847) 577-8306, info@chicagonorthsuburbs.com, www.chicagonorthsuburbs.com

**Quincy** · *Quincy Area CVB* · Holly Cain, Exec. Dir., 532 Gardner Expy., 62301, P 40,300, (217) 214-3700, (800) 978-4748, Fax (217) 214-2721, info@seequincy.com, www.seequincy.com

**Rock Island** · *see Moline*

**Rockford** · *Rockford Area CVB* · Amy Trimble, Interim Dir., 102 N. Main St., 61101, P 400,000, (815) 963-8111, (800) 521-0849, Fax (815) 963-4298, info@gorockford.com, www.gorockford.com

**Rosemont** · *Rosemont CVB* · William Anderson, Gen. Mgr., 9301 W. Bryn Mawr Ave., 60018, P 4,500, (847) 823-2100, Fax (847) 696-9700, rcb@rosemont.com, www.rosemont.com

**Schaumburg** · *Woodfield Chicago Northwest Conv. Bur.* · Fran Bolson, Pres., 1375 E. Woodfield Rd., Ste. 120, 60173, P 640,000, M 300, (847) 490-1010, (800) 847-4849, Fax (847) 490-1212, info@chicagonorthwest.com, www.chicagonorthwest.com

**Shelbyville** · *Shelby County Ofc. of Tourism* · Ms. Freddie Fry, Tourism Dir., 315 E. Main St., 62565, P 20,000, (217) 774-2244, (800) 874-3529, Fax (217) 774-2224, tourism@lakeshelbyville. com, www.lakeshelbyville.com

**Springfield** · *Central IL Tourism Dev. Ofc.* · Heather Wilkins, Exec. Dir., 700 E. Adams St., 62701, (217) 525-7980, (866) 378-7866, Fax (217) 525-8004, citdo@visitcentralillinois.com, www. visitcentralillinois.com

**Springfield** · *Springfield CVB* · Tim Farley, Exec. Dir., 109 N. 7th St., 62701, P 125,000, (217) 789-2360, (800) 545-7300, Fax (217) 544-8711, www.visit-springfieldillinois.com

**St. Charles** · *St. Charles CVB* · Amy Bull, Exec. Dir., 311 N. 2nd St., Ste. 100, 60174, P 33,000, (630) 377-6161, (800) 777-4373, Fax (630) 513-0566, info@visitstcharles.com, www.visitstcharles.com

# Indiana

**Anderson** · *Anderson/Madison County V & CB* · Ralph Day, Exec. Dir., 6335 S. Scatterfield Rd., 46013, P 135,000, (765) 643-5633, (800) 533-6569, Fax (765) 643-9083, info@heartlandspirit. com, www.heartlandspirit.com

**Angola** · *Steuben County Tourism Bur.* · 207 S. Wayne St., 46703, P 33,722, (260) 665-5386, Fax (260) 665-5461, (800) LAKE 101, lakes101@locl.net, www.lakes101.org

**Avon** · *see Danville*

**Bloomington** · *Bloomington/Monroe County CVB* · Mike McAfee, Exec. Dir., 2855 N. Walnut St., 47404, P 110,000, (812) 334-8900, (800) 800-0037, Fax (812) 334-2344, cvb@visitbloomington. com, www.visitbloomington.com

**Carmel** · *Hamilton County CVB* · Brenda Myers, Exec. Dir., 37 E. Main St., 46032, P 261,661, M 195, (317) 848-3181, Fax (317) 848-3191, (800) 776-TOUR, info@hamiltoncountytowns.com, www.hccvb.org

**Columbus** · *Columbus Area Visitors Center* · Cindy Frey, Assoc. Dir., 506 5th St., 47201, P 39,000, (812) 378-2622, (800) 468-6564, Fax (812) 372-7348, visitcol@sbcglobal.net, www.columbus.in.us

**Corydon** · *Harrison County CVB* · Jim Epperson, Dir., 310 N. Elm St., 47112, P 34,500, (812) 738-2138, (888) 738-2137, Fax (812) 738-3609, info@thisisindiana.org, www.thisisindiana.org

**Crawfordsville** · *Montgomery County VCB* · Sharon Kenny, Exec. Dir., 218 E. Pike St., 47933, P 36,000, (765) 362-5200, (800) 866-3973, Fax (765) 362-5215, info@crawfordsville.org, www. crawfordsville.org

**Danville** · *Hendricks County CVB* · Emory Lencke, Exec. Dir., 8 W. Main St., 46122, P 123,476, (317) 718-8750, (800) 321-9666, Fax (317) 718-9913, info@tourhendrickscounty.com, www. tourhendrickscounty.com

**Elkhart** · *Elkhart County CVB* · Diana Lawson, Exec. Dir., 219 Caravan Dr., 46514, P 195,362, (574) 262-8161, (800) 262-8161, Fax (574) 262-3925, ecconv@amishcountry.org, www.amishcountry.org

**Evansville** · *Evansville CVB* · Marilee Fowler, Exec. Dir., 401 S.E. Riverside Dr., 47713, P 170,000, (812) 421-2200, (800) 433-3025, Fax (812) 421-2207, info@evansvillecvb.org, www.evansvillecvb.org

**Fort Wayne** · *Fort Wayne/Allen County CVB* · Daniel R. O'Connell, Pres., 1021 S. Calhoun St., 46802, P 300,000, M 265, (260) 424-3700, (800) 767-7752, Fax (260) 424-3914, visitorinfo@ visitfortwayne.com, www.visitfortwayne.com.

**Greencastle** · *Putnam County/Covered Bridge Country Visitors Bur.* · Karla Lawless, 12 W. Washington St., 46135, P 45,000, (765) 653-8743, (800) 829-4639, Fax (765) 653-0851, cbc@coveredbridgecountry.com, www.coveredbridgecountry.com

**Hammond** · *Lake County CVB* · Speros Batistatos, Pres./CEO, 7770 Corinne Dr., 46323, P 500,000, (219) 989-7770, Fax (219) 989-7777, (800) ALL LAKE, www.lakecountycvb.com

**Huntington** · *Huntington County Visitor & Conv. Bur.* · Rose Meldrum, Exec. Dir., 407 N. Jefferson St., P.O. Box 212, 46750, P 37,521, (260) 359-8687, (800) 848-4282, www.visithuntington.org

**Indianapolis** · *Indianapolis Conv. & Visitors Assn.* · Don Welsh, Pres. & CEO, 37 S. Meridian St., Ste. 410, P.O. Box 7248, 46227, P 865,000, (317) 639-4282, Fax (317) 639-5273, icva@visitindy. com, www.visitindy.com

**Jasper** · *Dubois County Visitors Center* · Kristen Ruhe, Exec. Dir., 2704 Newton St., 47546, P 38,000, (812) 482-9115, (800) 968-4578, Fax (812) 481-2809, info@visitduboiscounty.com, www.visitduboiscounty.com

**Jeffersonville** · *Clark-Floyd County CVB* · James P. Keith, Exec. Dir., 315 Southern Indiana Ave., 47130, P 200,000, (812) 282-6654, (800) 552-3842, Fax (812) 282-1904, tourism@sunnyside oflouisville.org, www.sunnysideoflouisville.org

**Kendallville** · *Noble County, Indiana CVB* · Sarah Thomas, Exec. Dir., 2010 W. North St., P.O. Box 934, 46755, P 9,646, (260) 599-0060, (877) 202-5761, Fax (260) 599-0066, info@visitnoble county.com, www.visitnoblecounty.com

**Knox** · *Starke County Tourism Comm.* · Anthony Manning, Coord., 400 N. Heaton St., 46534, P 25,000, (574) 772-0896, (877) 733-2736, Fax (574) 772-0867, travel@explorestarkecounty.com, www.explorestarkecounty.com

**Kokomo** · *Kokomo/Howard County CVB* · Peggy Hobson, Dir., 1504 N. Reed Rd., 46901, P 82,000, (765) 457-6802, (800) 837-0971, Fax (765) 457-1572, information@visitkokomo.org, www. visitkokomo.org

**Lafayette** · *Lafayette/West Lafayette CVB* · Joann L. Wade, Pres., 301 Frontage Rd., 47905, P 153,875, (765) 447-9999, (800) 872-6648, Fax (765) 447-5062, info@homeofpurdue.com, www.homeofpurdue.com

**Lawrenceburg** · *Dearborn County Conv., Visitor & Tourism Bur.* · Deborah Smith, Dir., 320 Walnut St., 47025, P 50,000, (812) 537-0814, (800) 322-8198, Fax (812) 537-0845, dsmith@ visitsoutheastindiana.com, www.visitsoutheastindiana.com

**Madison** · *Madison Area CVB* · Linda Lytle, Dir., 601 W. 1st St., 47250, P 29,000, (812) 265-2956, (800) 559-2956, Fax (812) 273-3694, info@visitmadison.org, www.visitmadison.org

**Marion** · *Grant County CVB* · Karen Niverson, Exec. V.P., 428 S. Washington, Ste. 261, 46953, P 75,000, (765) 668-5435, (800) 662-9474, Fax (765) 668-5424, info@showmegrantcounty.com, www.showmegrantcounty.com

**Michigan City** · *LaPorte County CVB* · Jack Arnedt, Exec. Dir., 4073 S. Franklin St., 46360, P 120,000, (800) 634-2650, (219) 872-5055, Fax (219) 872-3660, info@laportecountycvb.com, www.visitlaportecountycvb.com

**Mishawaka** · *see South Bend*

**Muncie** · *Muncie Visitors Bur.* · James Mansfield, Exec. Dir., 425 N. High St., 47305, P 70,000, (765) 284-2700, (800) 568-6862, Fax (765) 284-3002, jim@visitmuncie.org, www.visitmuncie.org

**Nashville** • *Brown County CVB* • Jane Ellis, Exec. Dir., 10 N. Van Buren, P.O. Box 840, 47448, P 14,950, (812) 988-7303, (800) 753-3255, Fax (812) 988-1070, info@browncounty.com, www.browncounty.com

**New Castle** • *Henry County CVB* • Susie Thompson, Exec. Dir., 2020 S. Memorial Dr., Ste. I, 47362, P 48,000, (765) 593-0764, (888) 676-4302, Fax (765) 593-0766, info@henrycountyin.org, www.henrycountyin.org

**Plainfield** • *see Danville*

**Plymouth** • *Marshall County CVB* • Mike Woolfington, Exec. Dir., 220 N. Center, P.O. Box 669, 46563, P 38,000, (574) 936-1882, (800) 626-5353, Fax (574) 936-9845, mcw@marshallcounty tourism.org, www.marshallcountytourism.org

**Porter** • *Porter County Conv., Rec & Visitor Comm.* • Lorelei Weimer, Dir., 1420 Munson Rd., 46304, P 150,000, (219) 926-2255, Fax (219) 929-5395, (800) 283-TOUR, info@indianadunes.com, www.indianadunes.com

**Portland** • *Jay County Visitor & Tourism Bur.* • Gyneth Augsburger, Exec. Dir., 118 S. Meridian St., Ste. C, 47371, P 21,500, (260) 726-3366, (877) 726-4481, Fax (260) 726-3372, info@visitjaycounty.com, www.visitjaycounty.com

**Richmond** • *Richmond/Wayne County Conv. & Tourism Bur.* • Mary T. Walker, Exec. Dir., 5701 National Rd. E., 47374, P 71,000, (765) 935-8687, (800) 828-8414, Fax (765) 935-0440, mwalker@visitrichmond.org, www.visitrichmond.org

**Rising Sun** • *Rising Sun/Ohio County CVB* • Sherry Timms, Exec. Dir., 120 N. Walnut St., P.O. Box 112, 47040, P 5,200, (812) 438-4933, (888) 776-4786, Fax (812) 438-4932, stimms@nebvox.net, www.enjoyrisingsun.com

**Rockville** • *Parke County Inc.* • Cathy Harkrider, Exec. Secy., P.O. Box 165, 47872, P 15,000, M 300, (765) 569-5226, Fax (765) 569-3900, pci@ticz.com, www.coveredbridges.com

**Seymour** • *Jackson County Visitor Center* • Tina Stark, Exec. Dir., P.O. Box 607, 47274, P 40,000, (888) 524-1914, Fax (812) 524-1915, jacksoncountyin@verizon.net, www.jacksoncountyin.com

**South Bend** • *South Bend/Mishawaka CVB* • Shari Carroll, Dir., 401 E. Colfax Ave., Ste. 310, P.O. Box 1677, 46634, P 265,000, (574) 232-0231, (800) 519-0577, Fax (574) 289-0358, info@exploresouthbend.org, www.exploresouthbend.org

**Tell City** • *Perry County CVB* • Beverly Minto, Exec. Dir., 601 Main St., Ste. A, P.O. Box 721, 47586, P 20,100, (812) 547-7933, (888) 343-6262, Fax (812) 547-8378, perrycountycvb@psci.net, www.perrycountyindiana.org

**Terre Haute** • *Terre Haute CVB of Vigo County* • David A. Patterson, Exec. Dir., 2155 State Rd. 46, 47803, P 106,829, (812) 234-5555, (800) 366-3043, Fax (812) 234-6750, info@terrehaute.com, www.terrehaute.com

**Vevay** • *Switzerland County Welcome Center* • David Attaway, Exec. Dir., P.O. Box 149, 47043, P 10,000, (812) 427-3237, (800) 435-5688, Fax (812) 427-2184, visitsc@gmail.com, www.vevayin.com

**Vincennes** • *Vincennes/Knox County CVB* • Shyla Beam, Exec. Dir., 779 S. 6th St., 47591, P 40,000, (812) 886-0400, (800) 886-6443, Fax (812) 885-0033, info@vincennescvb.org, www.vincennescvb.org

**Wabash** • *Wabash County CVB* • Trula Cramer, Exec. Dir., 36 E. Market St., P.O. Box 746, 46992, P 35,000, (260) 563-7171, (800) 563-1169, Fax (260) 569-1782, tourism@wabashcountycvb.com, www.wabashcountycvb.com

**Warsaw** • *Kosciusko County CVB* • Mary Kittrell, Dir., 111 Capital Dr., 46582, P 75,667, (574) 269-6090, (800) 800-6090, Fax (574) 269-2405, info@koscvb.org, www.koscvb.org

**Washington** • *Daviess County CVB* • Charles Selby, Exec. Dir., One Train Depot St., P.O. Box 430, 47501, P 28,000, (812) 254-5262, (800) 449-5262, Fax (812) 254-4003, cselby@dcchamber.com, www.daviesscounty.net

**Winchester** • *Randolph County Visitor Info. Center* • Eric Fields, Pres., 112 W. Washington St., 47394, P 27,066, (765) 584-3731, Fax (765) 584-5544, chamber@globalsite.net, www.winchester areachamber.org

# Iowa

**Amana** • *Amana Colonies CVB* • Kristie Wetjen, Exec. Dir., 622 46th Ave., P.O. Box 310, 52203, P 1,500, (319) 622-7622, (800) 579-2294, Fax (319) 622-6395, info@amanacolonies.com, www.amanacolonies.com

**Ames** • *Ames CVB* • Julie Weeks, Dir., 1601 Golden Aspen Dr., Ste. 110, 50010, P 78,000, M 210, (515) 232-4032, (800) 288-7470, Fax (515) 232-6716, info@amescvb.com, www.visitames.com

**Bettendorf** • *see Moline, IL*

**Burlington** • *Greater Burlington CVB* • Beth Nickel, Exec. Dir., 610 N. 4th St., Ste. 200, 52601, P 30,000, (319) 752-6365, Fax (319) 752-6454, (800) 82-RIVER, tourism@growburlington.com, www.visitburlingtoniowa.com.

**Cedar Falls** • *Cedar Falls Tourism & Visitors Bur.* • Kim Burger, Exec. Dir., 6510 Hudson Rd., 50613, P 36,000, (319) 268-4266, (800) 845-1955, Fax (319) 277-9707, visit@cedarfallstourism.org, www.cedarfallstourism.org

**Cedar Rapids** • *Cedar Rapids Area CVB* • Tim Boyle, Pres./CEO, 119 First Ave. S.E, 52401, P 200,000, (319) 398-5009, (800) 735-5557, Fax (319) 398-5089, tim@cedar-rapids.com, www.cedar-rapids.com

**Clear Lake** • *Clear Lake Area CVB* • Nikki Weiss, Tourism Dir., 205 Main Ave., P.O. Box 188, 50428, P 8,200, (641) 357-2159, (800) 285-5338, Fax (641) 357-8141, info@clearlakeiowa.com, www.clearlakeiowa.com.

**Clinton** • *Clinton CVB* • Heather Hilgendorf-Cooley, Dir., 721 S. 2nd St., P.O. Box 1024, 52733, P 27,772, (563) 242-5702, Fax (563) 242-5803, cvb@clintonia.com, www.clintoniowatourism.com

**Coralville** • *Iowa City/Coralville Area CVB* • Josh Schamberger, Exec. Dir./Pres., 900 1st Ave., 52241, P 77,000, M 291, (319) 337-6592, (800) 283-6592, Fax (319) 337-9953, guest@iowacity coralville.org, www.iowacitycoralville.org

**Council Bluffs** • *Council Bluffs CVB* • Bob Mundt, Pres./CEO, 7 N. 6th St., P.O. Box 1565, 51502, P 59,744, (712) 325-1000, (800) 228-6878, Fax (712) 322-5698, cvb@councilbluffsiowa.com, www.councilbluffsiowa.com

**Davenport** • *see Moline, IL*

**Decorah** • *Decorah & Winneshiek County CVB* • 507 W. Water St., 52101, P 8,700, (563) 382-2023, (800) 463-4692, Fax (563) 382-5515, wctc@alpinecom.net

**Des Moines** • *Greater Des Moines CVB* • Greg Edwards, Pres./CEO, 400 Locust, Ste. 265, 50309, P 500,000, M 425, (515) 286-4960, (800) 451-2625, Fax (515) 244-9757, ngood@desmoinescvb.com, www.seedesmoines.com

**Fairfield** • *Fairfield Iowa Conv. & Visitors Center* • Rustin Lippincott, Exec. Dir., 200 N. Main, 52556, P 10,000, (641) 472-2828, Fax (641) 472-7890, rlippincott@travelfairfieldiowa.com, www.travelfairfieldiowa.com

**Fort Madison** • *Fort Madison Area CVB* • Sandy Brown, Exec. Dir., 709 9th St., P.O. Box 425, 52627, P 10,700, (319) 372-5472, (800) 210-TOUR, tourism@visitfortmadison.com, www.visitfort madison.com

**Keokuk** • *Keokuk Area Conv. & Tourism Bur.* • 329 Main St., 52632, P 11,531, (319) 524-5599, (800) 383-1219, info@ keokukiowatourism.org, www.keokukiowatourism.org

**Marshalltown** • *Marshalltown CVB* • Shannon Espenscheid, Dir., 709 S. Center St., P.O. Box 1000, 50158, P 26,009, (641) 753-6645, (800) 697-3155, Fax (641) 752-8373, cvb@marshalltown. org, www.visitmarshalltown.com

**Mason City** • *Mason City CVB* • Sue Armour, Exec. Dir., 25 W. State, Ste. B, 50401, P 30,000, (641) 422-1663, (800) 423-5724, Fax (641) 423-5725, cvb@visitmasoncityiowa.com, www.visit masoncityiowa.com

**Newton** • *Newton CVB* • Linda Bacon, Exec. Dir., 113 First Ave. W., 50208, P 16,000, (641) 792-0299, Fax (641) 791-0879, lindab@pcpartner.net, www.visitnewton.com

**Ottumwa** • *Ottumwa Area CVB* • Kathy Speas, Dir., 102 Church St., P.O. Box 1673, 52501, P 25,000, (641) 684-7000, (800) 564-5274, info@ottumwaiowa.com, www.visitottumwa.com

**Red Oak** • *Western Iowa Tourism Region* • Michele Walker, Exec. Dir., 103 N. Third St., 51566, P 461,879, M 155, (712) 623-4232, (888) 623-4232, Fax (712) 623-9814, witr@traveliowa.org, www. visitwesterniowa.com

**Sioux City** • *Sioux City Conv. & Tourism Bur.* • Aran Rush, Exec. Dir., 801 4th St., P.O. Box 3183, 51102, P 125,000, (712) 279-4800, (800) 593-2228, Fax (712) 279-4900, arush@sioux-city.org, www. siouxcitytourism.com, www.tysoncenter.com

**Walnut** • *Walnut Visitors Center* • Eldon Ranney, Dir., 607 Highland St., P.O. Box 265, 51577, P 897, (712) 784-2100, www.walnutiowa.net

**Waterloo** • *Waterloo CVB* • Aaron Buzza, Exec. Dir., 313 E. 5th St., 50703, P 68,000, (319) 233-8350, (800) 728-8431, Fax (319) 233-2733, susan@travelwaterloo.com, www.travelwaterloo.com

# Kansas

**Abilene** • *Abilene CVB* • Glenda Purkis, Dir., 201 N.W. 2nd, 67410, P 7,000, (785) 263-2231, (800) 569-5915, Fax (785) 263-4125, tourism@abilenecityhall.com, www.abilenekansas.org

**Arkansas City** • *Arkansas City CVB* • Connie Kimsey, Dir., 106 S. Summit, P.O. Box 795, 67005, P 12,000, (620) 442-0236, Fax (620) 441-0048, ac-cvb@arkcitychamber.org, www.arkcity.org

**Atchison** • *Atchison Area Tourism Bur.* • Sally Webb, Tourism Coord., 200 S. 10th St., P.O. Box 126, 66002, P 17,000, (913) 367-2427, Fax (913) 367-2485, tours@atchisonkansas.net, www.atchisonkansas.net

**Colby** • *Colby CVB* • Leilani Thomas, Dir., 350 S. Range #10, 67701, P 8,500, (785) 460-7643, (800) 611-8835, Fax (785) 460-4509, cvb@thomascounty.com, www.colbychamber.com

**Dodge City** • *Dodge City CVB* • Jan Stevens, Dir., 400 W. Wyatt Earp Blvd., P.O. Box 1474, 67801, P 27,000, (620) 225-8186, Fax (620) 225-8268, (800) OLD WEST, cvb@dodgecity.org, www. visitdodgecity.org

**Emporia** • *Emporia CVB* • Betty Senn, Dir., 719 Commercial, 66801, P 27,000, (620) 342-1803, (800) 279-3730, Fax (620) 342-3223, visitors@emporiakschamber.org, www.emporiakschamber.org

**Garden City** • *Finney County Conv. & Tourism Bur.* • Lynn Schoonover, Dir., 1511 E. Fulton Terrace, 67846, P 40,000, (620) 276-3264, (800) 879-9803, Fax (620) 276-3290, ctb@gcnet.com, www.gardencitychamber.net/ctb

**Goodland** • *Sherman County CVB* • Donna Price, Dir., P.O. Box 927, 67735, P 7,400, (785) 890-3515, (888) 824-4222, Fax (785) 890-6980, cvb@goodlandnet.com, www.goodlandnet.com/cvb.

**Hays** • *Hays CVB* • Jana Jordan, Dir., 2700 Vine St., 67601, P 20,000, (785) 628-8202, (800) 569-4505, Fax (785) 628-1471, jjordan@haysusa.com, www.haysusa.net

**Hutchinson** • *Greater Hutchinson CVB* • LeAnn Cox, Dir., 117 N. Walnut, P.O. Box 519, 67504, P 65,000, (620) 662-3391, (800) 691-4282, Fax (620) 662-2168, leannc@hutchchamber.com, www.visithutch.com

**Independence** • *Independence CVB* • Kerrie Manues, Tourism Dir., 322 N. Penn, P.O. Box 386, 67301, P 10,050, (620) 331-1890, (800) 882-3606, Fax (620) 331-1899, tourism@indkschamber.org, www.indkschamber.org

**Kansas City** • *Kansas City Kansas/Wyandotte County CVB* • Bridgette Jobe, Dir., 727 Minnesota Ave., P.O. Box 171517, 66117, P 152,000, (913) 321-5800, (800) 264-1563, Fax (913) 371-3732, info@visitthedot.com, www.visitthedot.com

**Lawrence** • *Lawrence Visitor Center* • Deborah White & Sonia Reetz, Co-Mgrs., 402 N. 2nd, 66044, P 100,000, (785) 865-4499, Fax (785) 865-4488, visinfo@visitlawrence.com, www.visit lawrence.com

**Leavenworth** • *Leavenworth CVB* • Connie Hachenberg, Dir., 518 Shawnee, P.O. Box 44, 66048, P 40,000, (913) 682-4113, (800) 844-4114, Fax (913) 682-8170, connie.cvb@sbcglobal.net, www.lvarea.com/cvb

**Lenexa** • *Lenexa CVB* • Julie Steiner, Dir., 11180 Lackman Rd., 66219, P 48,000, (913) 888-1414, (800) 950-7867, Fax (913) 888-3770, jsteiner@lenexa.org, www.lenexa.org

**Manhattan** • *Manhattan CVB* • Karen Hibbard, Dir., 501 Poyntz Ave., 66502, P 51,707, (785) 776-8829, (800) 759-0134, Fax (785) 776-0679, cvb@manhattan.org, www.manhattancvb.org

**Newton** • *Newton CVB* • Jennifer Mueller, Dir., 500 N. Main, Ste. 101, 67114, P 20,000, (316) 283-2560, (800) 899-0455, Fax (316) 283-8732, jennifer@thenewtonchamber.org, www.thenewton-chamber.org.

**Norton** • *Norton Travel & Tourism* • Karla Reed, Exec. Dir., 104 S. State, P.O. Box 132, 67654, P 2,806, (785) 877-2501, Fax (785) 877-3300, nortoncc@ruraltel.net, www.us36.net/nortonkansas, www.discovernorton.com

**Oberlin** • *Oberlin CVB* • 104 S. Penn, 67749, P 2,100, (785) 475-3441, Fax (785) 475-2128, dcacc@eaglecom.net, www. oberlinks.com

**Olathe** • *Olathe Chamber CVB* • Ashley Holverson, Dir., 18001 W. 106th St., Ste. 160, P.O. Box 98, 66051, P 120,000, (913) 764-1050, (800) 921-5678, Fax (913) 782-4636, cvb@olathe.org, www. olathecvb.org

**Ottawa** • *Franklin County Conv. & Visitors Bur.* • Kristi Lee, Dir., 2011 E. Logan, P.O. Box 203, 66067, P 25,000, (785) 242-1411, Fax (785) 242-2238, director@visitottawakansas.com, www. visitottawakansas.com

**Overland Park** • *Overland Park CVB* • Gerald Cook, Pres., 9001 W. 110th St., Ste. 100, 66210, P 170,000, (913) 491-0123, Fax (913) 491-0015, (800) 262-PARK, jlcook@opcvb.org, www.opcvb.org

**Parsons** · *Labette County CVB* · Jim Zaleski, Tourism Dir., 1715 Corning, 67357, P 11,500, (620) 421-6500, (800) 280-6401, Fax (620) 421-6501, tourism@parsonsks.com, www.parsonschamber.org

**Phillipsburg** · *Phillips County CVB* · Jackie Swatzell, Dir., 270 State St., P.O. Box 326, 67661, P 2,700, (785) 543-2321, Fax (785) 543-0038, cvbcham@ruraltel.net, www.phillipsburgks.us.

**Pittsburg** · *Crawford County CVB* · Craig Hull, Dir., 117 W. 4th St., P.O. Box 1933, 66762, P 38,242, (620) 231-1212, (800) 879-1112, Fax (620) 231-3178, chull@pittsburgareachamber.com, www.visitcrawfordcounty.com

**Russell** · *Russell County CVB* · 445 E. Wichita Ave., P.O. Box 130, 67665, P 4,600, (785) 483-2828, Fax (785) 483-2827, rscocvb@ruraltel.net, www.visitrussellcoks.com

**Sedan** · *Yellow Brick Road Visitors Center* · Nita Jones, Dir., 215 E. Main, 67361, P 1,300, (620) 725-5797, (620) 725-3663, Fax (620) 725-5707, jonesrealtyusa@yahoo.com, sedankansas.com

**Shawnee** · *Shawnee CVB* · Linda Leeper, Pres., 15100 W. 67th St., Ste. 202, 66217, P 58,000, (913) 631-6545, Fax (913) 631-9628, info@shawneekscvb.com, www.shawneekscvb.com

**Topeka** · *Visit Topeka* · Olivia Simmons, Exec. Dir./CEO, 1275 S.W. Topeka Blvd., 66612, P 125,000, (785) 234-1030, (800) 235-1030, Fax (785) 234-8282, info@visittopeka.org, www.visittopeka.org

**Wichita** · *Go Wichita CVB* · John Rolfe, Pres./CEO, 515 S. Main St., Ste. 115, 67202, P 580,000, M 500, (316) 265-2800, (800) 288-9424, Fax (316) 265-0162, www.gowichita.com

**Winfield** · *Winfield Conv. & Tourism* · Sarah Werner, Comm. Events Coord., 123 E. 9th Ave., P.O. Box 640, 67156, P 12,500, (620) 221-2421, (877) 729-7440, Fax (620) 221-2958, tourism@winfieldpartners.org, www.wowwinfield.org

# Kentucky

**Ashland** · *Ashland Area CVB* · Sue G. Dowdy, Exec. Dir., 1509 Winchester Ave., 41101, P 21,000, (606) 329-1007, (800) 377-6249, Fax (606) 329-1056, aacvb@visitashlandky.com, www.visitashlandky.com

**Bardstown** · *Bardstown-Nelson County Visitors Bur.* · One Court Sq., P.O. Box 867, 40004, P 11,000, (502) 348-4877, (800) 638-4877, Fax (502) 349-0804, info@bardstowntourism.com, www.visitbardstown.com

**Benton** · *Marshall County Tourist Comm.* · Randy Newcomb, Exec. Dir., 93 Carroll Rd., 42025, P 30,000, (270) 527-3128, (800) 467-7145, Fax (270) 527-9193, fun@kentuckylake.org, www.kentuckylake.org

**Bowling Green** · *Bowling Green Area CVB* · Vicki Fitch, Exec. Dir., 352 Three Springs Rd., 42104, P 101,000, (270) 782-0800, (800) 326-7465, Fax (270) 842-2104, info@visitbgky.com, www.visitbgky.com

**Campbellsville** · *Taylor County Tourist Comm.* · Marilyn Clarke, Exec. Dir., P.O. Box 4021, 42719, P 23,000, (270) 465-3786, (800) 738-4719, Fax (270) 465-3786, taylorcountytourism@kyol.net, www.campbellsvilleky.com

**Cave City** · *Cave City Tourist & Conv. Center* · Brian Dale, Dir., 502 Mammoth Cave St., 42127, P 2,000, (270) 773-3131, (800) 346-8908, Fax (270) 773-8834, cavecity@scrtc.com, www.cavecity.com

**Covington** · *Northern Kentucky CVB* · Tom Caradonio, Pres./CEO, 50 E. RiverCenter Blvd., Ste. 200, 41011, P 300,000, (859) 261-4677, (800) 447-8489, Fax (859) 261-5135, info@nkycvb.com, www.nkycvb.com

**Danville** · *Danville-Boyle County CVB* · Adam Johnson, Exec. Dir., 105 E. Walnut St., 40422, P 28,000, (859) 236-7794, (800) 755-0076, Fax (859) 236-9134, info@danvillekentucky.com, www.danvillekentucky.com

**Elizabethtown** · *Elizabethtown Tourism & Conv. Bur.* · Sherry Murphy, Exec. Dir., 1030 N. Mulberry St., 42701, P 22,500, (270) 765-2175, (800) 437-0092, Fax (270) 737-6568, www.touretown.com

**Frankfort** · *Frankfort/Franklin County Tourist & Conv. Comm.* · Joy Jeffries, Exec. Dir., 100 Capital Ave., 40601, P 47,000, (502) 875-8687, (800) 960-7200, Fax (502) 227-2604, inquire@visitfrankfort.com, www.visitfrankfort.com

**Georgetown** · *Georgetown-Scott County Tourism Comm.* · John Simpson, Exec. Dir., 399 Outlet Center Dr., P.O. Box 825, 40324, P 42,000, (502) 863-2547, (888) 863-8600, Fax (502) 863-2561, gtown@mis.net, www.georgetownky.com

**Harlan** · *Harlan Tourist & Conv. Comm.* · Kim Collier, Exec. Dir., 201 South Main Street, P.O. Box 489, 40831, P 35,000, (606) 573-4156, Fax (606) 573-9485, htcc@harlanonline.net, www.harlantourism.com

**Harrodsburg** · *Harrodsburg/Mercer County Tour Comm.* · Karen Hackett, Exec. Dir., 488 Price Ave., P.O. Box 283, 40330, P 30,000, (859) 734-2364, Fax (859) 734-9938, tourism@harrodsburgky.com, www.harrodsburgky.com

**Henderson** · *Henderson Tourist Comm.* · Marcia Eblen, Exec. Dir., 101 N. Water St., Ste. B, 42420, P 42,000, (270) 826-3128, Fax (270) 826-0234, info@hendersonky.org, www.hendersonky.org

**Hopkinsville** · *Hopkinsville-Christian County CVB* · Cheryl Cook, Exec. Dir., 2800 Fort Campbell Blvd., 42240, P 70,000, (270) 885-9096, (800) 842-9959, Fax (270) 886-2059, tourism@visithopkinsville.com, www.visithopkinsville.com

**Jamestown** · *see Russell Springs*

**Leitchfield** · *Grayson County Tourist Comm.* · Ilsa Johnson, Exec. Dir., 425 S. Main St., 42754, P 25,600, (270) 259-2735, (888) 624-9951, Fax (270) 230-0615, mail@graysoncountytourism.com, www.graysoncountytourism.com

**Lexington** · *Lexington CVB* · David Lord, Pres., 301 E. Vine St., 40507, P 265,000, (859) 233-1221, (800) 845-3959, Fax (859) 254-4555, www.visitlex.com

**London** · *London/Laurel County Tourist Comm.* · Ken Harvey, Exec. Dir., 140 Faith Assembly Church Rd., 40741, P 56,000, (606) 878-6900, (800) 348-0095, Fax (606) 877-1689, tourism@lltc.net, www.laurelkytourism.com

**Louisville** · *Greater Louisville CVB* · Jim Wood, Pres., 401 W. Main St., Ste 2300, 40202, P 2,000,000, (502) 584-2121, (800) 626-5646, Fax (502) 561-3120, jwood@gotolouisville.com, www.gotolouisville.com

**Mayfield** · *Mayfield Tourism Comm.* · 201 E. College St., 42066, P 37,000, (270) 247-6101, Fax (270) 247-6110, tourism@mayfieldchamber.com, www.mayfieldtourism.com

**Maysville** · *Maysville-Mason County CVB* · Duff Giffen, Exec. Dir., 216 Bridge St., 41056, P 18,000, (606) 564-9419, Fax (606) 564-9416, duff.giffen@maysvilleky.net, www.cityofmaysville.com

**Mount Sterling** · *Mt. Sterling-Montgomery County Tourism Comm.* · 126 W. Main St., 40353, P 24,550, (859) 498-8732, (866) 415-7439, Fax (859) 498-3947, mtourism@mis.net, www.mtsterlingtourism.com

**Murray** · *Murray CVB* · Lindsay Geib, Dir., 201 S. 4th St., P.O. Box 321, 42071, P 15,000, (270) 759-2199, (800) 651-1603, Fax (270) 761-6793, tourism@murray-ky.net, www.tourmurray.com

**Owensboro** · *Owensboro-Daviess County CVB* · Karen Miller, Exec. Dir., 215 E. 2nd St., 42303, P 100,000, (270) 926-1100, (800) 489-1131, Fax (270) 926-1161, info@visitowensboro.com, www.visitowensboro.com

**Paducah** · *Paducah McCracken County CVB* · Mary Hammond, Exec. Dir., 128 Broadway, 42001, P 64,213, (270) 443-8783, Fax (270) 443-0122, (800) PADUCAH, info@paducah.travel, www.paducah.travel

**Paintsville** · *Paintsville Tourism & Conv. Center* · Carol Logsdon, Dir., P.O. Box 809, 41240, P 23,000, (606) 297-1469, (800) 542-5790, Fax (606) 297-1470, tourpvil@foothills.net, www.paintsville.org

**Radcliff** · *Radcliff/Fort Knox Tourism Comm.* · Kelly Barron, Exec. Dir., 562 A1 N. Dixie, P.O. Box 845, 40159, P 22,000, (270) 352-1204, (800) 334-7540, Fax (270) 352-2075, radclifftourism@bbtel.com, www.radclifftourism.org

**Richmond** · *Richmond Tourism & Main St. Dept.* · Lori Murphy, Exec. Dir., 345 Lancaster Ave., 40475, P 30,000, (859) 626-8474, (800) 866-3705, Fax (859) 626-8121, tourism@richmond.ky.us, www.richmondkytourism.com

**Russell Springs** · *Russell County Tourist Comm.* · Renee Bradshaw, Admin. Asst., 650 S. Hwy. 127, P.O. Box 64, 42642, P 17,500, (270) 866-4333, (888) 833-4220, Fax (270) 866-4304, lake@duo-county.com, www.lakecumberlandvacation.com

**Shelbyville** · *Shelbyville/Shelby County Tourist Comm.* · 316 Main St., P.O. Box 622, 40066, P 37,000, (502) 633-6388, (800) 680-6388, Fax (502) 633-7501, tours@shelbyvilleky.com, www.shelbyvilleky.com

**Shepherdsville** · *Shepherdsville-Bullitt County Tourist & Conv. Comm* · Elaine Wilson, Exec. Dir., 395 Paroquet Springs Dr., 40165, P 65,000, (800) 526-2068, Fax (502) 543-4889, (502) 543-TOUR, ewilson@travelbullitt.org, www.travelbullitt.org

**Williamsburg** · *Williamsburg Tourism & Conv. Comm.* · Alvin Sharpe, Dir. of Tourism, P.O. Box 2, 40769, P 5,600, (606) 549-0530, (800) 552-0530, Fax (606) 539-0095, wtour@bellsouth.net, www.williamsburgky.com

**Winchester** · *Winchester-Clark County Tourism Comm.* · Nancy Turner, Dir. of Tourism, 2 S. Maple St., 40391, P 35,056, (859) 744-0556, (800) 298-9105, Fax (859) 744-9229, tourism@tourwinchester.com, www.tourwinchester.com

# Louisiana

**Abbeville** · *Vermilion Parish Tourist Comm.* · P.O. Box 1106, 70511, P 12,000, (337) 898-6600, Fax (337) 893-1807, info@vermilion.org, www.vermilion.org

**Albany** · *Livingston Parish CVB* · Eric Edwards, Dir., 30340 Catholic Hall Rd., P.O. Box 1057, 70711, (225) 567-7899, (888) 317-7899, eric@visitlivingstonparish.com, www.visitlivingstonparish.com

**Alexandria** · *Alexandria/Pineville Area CVB* · Sherry Smith, Exec. Dir., 707 Main St., P.O. Box 1070, 71309, P 54,000, (318) 442-9546, (800) 551-9546, Fax (318) 443-1617, inquire@apacvb.org, www.theheartoflouisiana.com

**Baton Rouge** · *Baton Rouge Area CVB* · Paul Arrigo, Pres./CEO, 730 North Blvd., P.O. Drawer 4149, 70821, P 500,000, (225) 383-1825, Fax (225) 346-1253, (800) LA ROUGE, paul@visitbatonrouge.com, www.visitbatonrouge.com

**Crowley** · *Acadia Parish Tourist, Conv. & Visitors Bur.* · Gwen Hanks, Exec. Dir., 401 Tower Rd., P.O. Box 1342, 70527, P 56,000, (337) 783-2108, Fax (337) 783-2142, aptc@bellsouth.net, www.acadiatourism.org

**Donaldsonville** · *Donaldsonville Tourist Comm.* · Gregory J. Phillips, 318 Mississippi St., P.O. Box 307, 70346, P 9,000, (225) 257-4026, Fax (225) 257-4415, www.tourdonaldsonville.org

**Grand Isle** · *Grand Isle Tourist Comm.* · Josie Cheramie, Pres., 2757 Hwy. 1, P.O. Box 817, 70358, P 1,455, (985) 787-2997, Fax (985) 787-2997, tourism@grand-isle.com, www.grand-isle.com

**Houma** · *Houma Area CVB* · Sharon Alford, Exec. Dir., P.O. Box 2792, 70361, P 140,000, (985) 868-2732, (800) 688-2732, Fax (985) 868-7170, www.houmatravel.com

**Jackson** · *East Feliciana Parish Tourist Comm.* · Audrey Faciane, Exec. Dir., 1752 High St., P.O. Box 667, 70748, P 22,000, (225) 634-7155, Fax (225) 634-7155, tourism1@bellsouth.net, www.felicianatourism.org

**Lafayette** · *Lafayette Conv. & Vistors Center* · Gerald P. Breaux, Exec. Dir., 1400 N.W. Evangeline Thruway, P.O. Box 52066, 70505, P 196,258, (337) 232-3737, (800) 346-1958, Fax (337) 232-0161, gerald@lafayettetravel.com, www.lafayette.travel

**Lake Charles** · *Southwest Louisiana CVB* · Shelley Johnson, Exec. Dir., 1205 N. Lakeshore Dr., P.O. Box 1912, 70602, P 172,200, (337) 436-9588, Fax (337) 494-7952, (800) 456-SWLA, touristinfo@visitlakecharles.org, www.visitlakecharles.org

**Mandeville** · *Louisiana Northshore* · Donna O'Daniels, Exec. Dir., St. Tammany Tourist & Conv. Comm., 68099 Hwy. 59, 70471, P 250,000, (985) 892-0520, (800) 634-9443, Fax (985) 892-1441, mail@louisiananorthshore.com, www.louisiananorthshore.com

**Mansfield** · *DeSoto Parish Tourist Bur.* · Edna Thornton, Dir., 115 N. Washington Ave., P.O. Box 1327, 71052, P 26,000, (318) 872-1177, Fax (318) 871-1875, tourist@bellsouth.net, www.discoverdesoto.com

**Many** · *Sabine Parish Tourist Comm.* · Linda Curtis-Sparks, Tourism Dir., 1601 Texas Hwy., 71449, P 23,500, (318) 256-5880, (800) 358-7802, Fax (318) 256-4137, sptourist@cp-tel.net, www.toledobendlakecountry.com

**Minden** · *Minden Webster Parish Tourist CVB* · Lynn Warnock-Dorsey, Exec. Dir., 110 Sibley Rd., P.O. Box 1528, 71058, P 42,000, (318) 377-4240, (888) 972-7474, Fax (318) 377-4215, lynn@visitwebster.com, www.visitwebster.com

**Morgan City** · *Cajun Coast Visitors & Conv. Bur.* · Carrie Stansbury, Exec. Dir., P.O. Box 2332, 70381, P 60,000, (985) 395-4905, (800) 256-2931, Fax (985) 395-7041, info@cajuncoast.com, www.cajuncoast.com

**Natchitoches** · *Natchitoches Parish Tourist Comm.* · Iris Harper, Exec. Dir., 781 Front St., 71457, P 35,000, (318) 352-8072, (800) 259-1714, Fax (318) 352-2415, est1714@natchitoches.net, www.natchitoches.net

**New Iberia** · *Iberia Parish CVB* · Fran Thibodeaux, Exec. Dir., 2513 Hwy. 14, 70560, P 72,000, (337) 365-1540, (888) 942-3742, Fax (337) 367-3791, info@iberiatravel.com, www.iberiatravel.com

**New Orleans** · *New Orleans Metropolitan CVB* · J. Stephen Perry, Pres./CEO, 2020 St. Charles Ave., 70130, P 675,000, (504) 566-5011, (800) 672-6124, Fax (504) 566-5046, www.neworleanscvb.com, internet@neworleanscvb.com, www.neworleanscvb.com

**Ruston** · *Ruston/Lincoln CVB* · Kyle Edmiston, Pres., 2205 N. Trenton St., P.O. Box 1383, 71270, P 43,000, (318) 255-2031, (800) 392-9032, Fax (318) 255-3481, kedmiston@rustonlincoln.com, www.rustonlincoln.com

**Saint Francisville** · *West Feliciana Parish Tourist Comm.* · Kitty Martin, Dir., P.O. Box 1548, 70775, P 15,000, (225) 635-6769, (800) 789-4221, Fax (225) 635-4626, tourism@stfrancisville.us, www.stfrancisville.us

**Saint Martinville** · *St. Martinville Tourist Info. Center* · Brenda Comeau Trahan, Tourism Dir., 125 S. New Market, P.O. Box 379, 70582, P 8,000, (337) 394-2233, Fax (337) 394-2260, www.acadianmemorial.org, info@acadianmemorial.org, www.stmartinville.org

**Shreveport** · *Shreveport-Bossier Conv. & Tourist Bur.* · Stacy Brown, Pres., 629 Spring, P.O. Box 1761, 71166, P 298,000, (318) 222-9391, (800) 551-8682, Fax (318) 222-0067, info2@sbctb.org, www.shreveport-bossier.org

**Sorrento** · *Ascension Parish Tourist Comm.* · Ramon Gomez, Proj./Events Mgr., 6967 Hwy. 22, 70778, P 120,000, (225) 675-6550, (888) 775-7990, Fax (225) 675-6558, rgomez@eatel.net, www.ascensiontourism.com

**West Monroe** · *Monroe-West Monroe CVB* · Alana Cooper, Exec. Dir., 601 Constitution Dr., P.O. Box 1436, 71294, P 175,000, (318) 387-5691, (800) 843-1872, Fax (318) 324-1752, mwmcvb@monroe-westmonroe.org, www.monroe-westmonroe.org

# Maine

**Bangor** · *Greater Bangor CVB* · Kerrie Tripp, Dir., 40 Harlow St., 04401, P 100,000, M 175, (207) 947-5205, (800) 916-6673, Fax (207) 942-2146, info@visitbangormaine.com, www.visitbangormaine.com

**Portland** · *Greater Portland CVB* · Barbara Whitten, Pres., 94 Commercial St., Ste. 300, 04101, P 230,000, M 475, (207) 772-4994, (207) 772-5800, Fax (207) 874-9043, info@visitportland.com, www.visitportland.com

# Maryland

**Baltimore** · *Baltimore Area CVB* · Cathy Xanthakos, Dir. of Admin., 100 Light St., 12th Flr., 21202, P 786,000, (410) 659-7300, (800) 343-3468, Fax (410) 727-2308, cxanthakos@baltimore.org, www.baltimore.org

**Chester** · *Queen Anne's County Ofc. Of Tourism* · Barbara Siegert, Tourism Mgr., 425 Piney Narrows Rd., 21619, P 45,000, (410) 604-2100, Fax (410) 604-2101, bsiegert@qac.org, www.discoverqueenannes.com

**Denton** · *Caroline Ofc. of Tourism* · Natalie Chabot, Tourism Dir., 15 S. Third St., 21629, P 31,300, (410) 479-0655, Fax (410) 479-5563, info@tourcaroline.com, www.tourcaroline.com

**Easton** · *Talbot County Ofc. of Tourism* · Deborah Dodson, Exec. Dir., 11 S. Harrison St., 21601, P 35,000, (410) 770-8000, Fax (410) 770-8057, ddodson@talbgov.org, www.tourtalbot.org

**Frederick** · *Tourism Cncl. Of Frederick County, Inc.* · John Fieseler, Exec. Dir., 19 E. Church St., 21701, P 221,850, (301) 600-2888, (800) 999-3613, Fax (301) 600-4044, tourism@fredco-md.net, www.fredericktourism.org

**Germantown** · *Montgomery County Visitor Info. Center* · Kelly Groff, Exec. Dir., 12900 Middlebrook Rd., Ste. 1400, 20874, P 873,341, (301) 916-0698, (800) 925-0880, Fax (301) 916-1259, visitmoco@aol.com, www.visitmontgomery.com

**Hagerstown** · *Hagerstown/Washington County CVB* · Thomas Riford, Pres., 16 Public Sq., 21740, P 140,000, M 185, (301) 791-3246, (888) 257-2600, Fax (301) 791-2601, info@maryland memories.org, www.marylandmemories.org

**Ocean City** · *Ocean City CVB* · Michael Noah, Exec. Dir., 4001 Coastal Hwy., 21842, P 10,000, (410) 289-8181, Fax (410) 723-8655, (800) OC OCEAN, mnoah@ococean.com, www.ococean.com

**Rockville** · *Montgomery County Conf. & Visitors Bur. (Admin)* · Kelly Groff, Exec. Dir., 111 Rockville Pike, Ste. 800, 20850, P 873,341, (240) 777-2060, (877) 789-6904, Fax (301) 777-2065, kgroff@visitmontgomery.com, www.visitmontgomery.com

# Massachusetts

**Adams** · *Berkshire Visitors Bur.* · Lauri Klefos, Pres./CEO, 3 Hoosac St., 01220, P 150,000, M 750, (413) 743-4500, (800) 237-5747, Fax (413) 743-4560, bvb@berkshires.org, www.berkshires.org

**Boston** · *Greater Boston CVB* · Patrick Moscaritolo, Pres./CEO, Two Copley Pl. #105, 02116, P 2,000,000, M 1,200, (617) 536-4100, Fax (617) 424-7664, (888) SEE BOSTON, visitus@bostonusa.com, www.bostonusa.com

**New Bedford** · *Southeastern Mass. CVB* · Arthur Motta, Exec. Dir., 70 N. Second St., 02740, P 534,678, M 200, (508) 997-1250, (800) 288-6263, Fax (508) 997-9090, explorer@bristol-county.org, www.bristol-county.org

**Peabody** · *North of Boston CVB* · Julie McConchie, Exec. Dir., 17 Peabody Sq., 01960, P 650,000, M 250, (978) 977-7760, (877) 662-9299, Fax (978) 977-7758, www.escapesnorth.com, info@northofboston.org, www.northofboston.org

**Provincetown** · *Provincetown Tourism Ofc.* · Bob Sanborn, Tourism Dir., Town Hall, 260 Commercial St., 02657, P 3,000, (508) 487-7000, Fax (508) 487-9560, bsanborn@provincetown-ma.gov, www.provincetowntourismoffice.org

**Salem** · *Salem Office of Tourism & Cultural Affairs Inc.* · Kate Fox, Exec. Dir., P.O. Box 630, 01970, P 45,000, M 100, (978) 744-3663, Fax (978) 741-7539, (877) SALEM MA, info@salem.org, www.salem.org

**Somerville** · *Somerville CVB* · Stephen V. Mackey, Pres./CEO, 2 Alpine St., P.O. Box 440343, 02144, P 78,000, (617) 776-4100, info@somervillechamber.org, www.somervillechamber.org

**Springfield** · *Greater Springfield CVB* · Mary Kay Wydra, Pres., 1441 Main St., 01103, P 450,000, M 311, (413) 787-1548, (800) 723-1548, Fax (413) 781-4607, marykay@valleyvisitor.com, www.valleyvisitor.com

**Worcester** · *Central MA/Worcester County CVB* · Donna McCabe, Pres., 30 Elm St., 01609, P 700,000, M 500, (508) 755-7400, (866) 755-7439, Fax (508) 754-2703, www.centralmass.org, dmccabe@worcester.org, www.worcester.org

# Michigan

**Allegan** · *Allegan County Parks, Rec. & Tourism* · 3255 122nd Ave., Ste. 102, 49010, P 105,000, (269) 686-9088, Fax (269) 673-0454, (888) 4-ALLEGAN, parks@allegancounty.org, www.visitallegancounty.com

**Alpena** · *Alpena Area CVB* · Deborah Pardike, Dir., 235 W. Chisholm St., 49707, P 40,000, M 70, (989) 354-4181, Fax (989) 356-3999, (800) 4-ALPENA, info@chartermi.net, www.alpenacvb.com.

**Ann Arbor** · *Ann Arbor CVB* · Mary A. Kerr, Pres., 120 W. Huron St., 48104, P 250,000, M 300, (734) 995-7281, (800) 888-9487, Fax (734) 995-7283, info@annarbor.org, www.visitannarbor.org

**Battle Creek** · *Battle Creek/Calhoun Co. CVB* · Dwight Butt, Pres., 77 E. Michigan Ave., Ste. 100, 49017, P 93,000, (269) 962-2240, (800) 397-2240, Fax (269) 962-6917, info@battlecreek visitors.org, www.battlecreekvisitors.org

**Bay City** · *Bay City CVB* · Shirley Roberts, Exec. Dir., 919 Boutell Pl., Ste. 100, 48708, P 111,000, (989) 893-1222, Fax (989) 893-7016, (888) BAYTOWN, shirley@tourbaycitymi.org, www.tourbaycitymi.org

**Benton Harbor** · *Southwestern Michigan Tourist Cncl.* · Millicent Huminsky, Exec. Dir., 2300 Pipestone Rd., 49022, P 150,000, M 250, (269) 925-6301, Fax (269) 925-7540, info@swmichigan.org, www.swmichigan.org

**Benzonia** · *Benzie County Visitors Bur.* · Mary Carroll, Exec. Dir., 826 Michigan Ave., P.O. Box 204, 49616, P 17,000, (231) 882-5801, (800) 882-5801, Fax (231) 882-9249, director@benzie.org, www.visitbenzie.com.

**Big Rapids** · *Mecosta County Area CVB* · Connie Koepke, Exec. Dir., 246 N. State St., 49307, P 42,391, (231) 796-7640, Fax (231) 796-0832, events@bigrapids.org, www.bigrapids.org

**Cadillac** · *Cadillac Area Visitors Bur.* · Robert Gattin, Exec. Dir., 222 Lake St., 49601, P 11,000, (231) 775-0657, 80022LAKES, Fax (231) 775-1440, (800) 22-LAKES, rgattin@cadillacmichigan.com, www.cadillacmichigan.com

**Calumet** · *Keweenaw CVB* · 56638 Calumet Ave., 49913, P 37,000, M 210, (906) 337-4579, (800) 338-7982, Fax (906) 337-4285, info@keweenaw.info, www.keweenaw.info

**Caro** · *Thumb Area Tourism Cncl.* · Kris McArdle, Mktg. Dir., 157 N. State St., 48723, P 57,500, (810) 569-6856, kris@thumbtourism.org, www.thumbtourism.org

**Charlevoix** · *Charlevoix Area CVB* · 100 Michigan Ave., P.O. Box 388, 49720, P 3,500, (231) 237-0920, (800) 367-8557, Fax (231) 237-0931, info@charlevoixlodging.com, www.charlevoixlodging.com

**Clare** · *Clare County CVB* · P.O. Box 226, 48617, P 28,000, M 50, (989) 386-6400, (800) 233-1359, www.clarecounty.com

**Coldwater** · *Branch County Tourism Bur.* · Debra Yee, Exec. Dir., 20 Division St., 49036, P 43,000, (517) 278-0241, (800) 968-9333, Fax (517) 278-8369, dyee@discover-michigan.com, www.discover-michigan.com

**Detroit** · *Detroit Metro CVB* · Larry Alexander, Pres./CEO, 211 W. Fort St., Ste. 1000, 48226, P 4,500,000, (313) 202-1800, Fax (313) 202-1808, (800) DETROIT, www.visitdetroit.com

**Flint** · *Flint Area CVB* · Gloria DeHart, V.P. of Sales, 502 Church St., 48502, P 431,000, M 285, (810) 232-8900, (877) 354-6864, Fax (810) 232-1515, info@flint.org, www.visitflint.org

**Frankenmuth** · *Frankenmuth CVB* · Jamie Furbush, Pres./CEO, 635 S. Main St., 48734, P 4,800, (989) 652-6106, (800) 386-8696, Fax (989) 652-3841, chamber@frankenmuth.org, www.frankenmuth.org

**Gaylord** · *Gaylord Area Conv. & Tourism Bur.* · 101 W. Main St., 49735, P 23,000, (989) 732-4000, (800) 345-8621, Fax (989) 732-7990, info@gaylordmichigan.net, www.gaylordmichigan.net

**Grand Haven** · *Grand Haven Area CVB* · Marci Cisneros, Exec. Dir., One S. Harbor , 49417, P 187,768, (616) 842-4499, (800) 303-4092, Fax (616) 842-0379, web@visitgrandhaven.com, www.visitgrandhaven.com

**Grand Rapids** · *Grand Rapids/Kent County CVB* · George Helmstead, Exec. V.P., 171 Monroe Ave. N.W., Ste. 700, 49503, P 1,100,000, (616) 459-8287, (800) 678-9859, Fax (616) 459-7291, mailbox@visitgrandrapids.org, www.visitgrandrapids.org

**Grand Rapids** · *West Michigan Tourist Assn.* · Rick Hert, Exec. Dir., 741 Kenmoor Ave., Ste. E, 49546, P 300,000, M 1,000, (616) 245-2217, (800) 442-2084, Fax (616) 954-3924, rick@wmta.org, www.wmta.org

**Grayling** · *Grayling Visitors Bur.* · Ilene Geiss-Wilson, Exec. Dir., P.O. Box 217, 49738, P 13,000, (800) 937-8837, (989) 348-4945, Fax (989) 348-9168, visitor@grayling-mi.com, www.grayling-mi.com

**Holland** · *Holland Area CVB* · Sally Laukitis, Exec. Dir., 76 E. 8th St., 49423, P 110,000, (616) 394-0000, (800) 506-1299, Fax (616) 394-0122, sally@holland.org, www.holland.org

**Howell** · *Livingston County CVB* · 123 E. Washington St., 48843, P 105,000, (517) 548-1795, (800) 686-8474, Fax (517) 546-4115, info@lccvb.org, www.lccvb.org

**Iron Mountain** · *Dickinson Area Partnership* · Lynda Zanon, 600 S. Stephenson Ave., 49801, P 27,400, (906) 774-2002, Fax (906) 774-2004, moreinfo@dickinsonchamber.com, www.dickinsonchamber.com

**Iron Mountain** · *Upper Peninsula Travel & Rec. Assn.* · P.O. Box 400, 49801, P 350,000, M 900, (906) 774-5480, (800) 562-7134, Fax (906) 774-5190, info@uptravel.com, www.uptravel.com

**Ironwood** · *Western U.P. CVB* · P.O. Box 706, 49938, P 35,000, M 125, (906) 932-4850, (800) 522-5657, Fax (906) 932-3455, bigsnow@westernup.info, www.westernup.info

**Kalamazoo** · *Kalamazoo County CVB* · Greg Ayers, Pres., 141 E. Michigan Ave., Ste. 100, 49007, P 287,000, (269) 488-9000, (800) 888-0509, cvbstaff@discoverkalamazoo.com, www.discoverkalamazoo.com

**L'Anse** · *Baraga County CVB* · 755 E. Broad St., 49946, P 8,000, M 100, (906) 524-7444, (800) 743-4908, Fax (906) 524-7454, bctra@up.net, www.baragacountytourism.org

**Lansing** · *Greater Lansing CVB* · W. Lee Hladki, Pres./CEO, 1223 Turner St., Ste. 200, 48906, P 450,000, (517) 487-0077, (888) 252-6746, Fax (517) 487-5151, lhladki@lansing.org, www.lansing.org

**Ludington** · *Ludington Area CVB* · Amy Seng, Exec. Dir., 5300 W. U.S. 10, 49431, P 25,000, M 100, (231) 845-5430, (800) 542-4600, Fax (231) 845-6857, amys@ludington.org, www.destinationludington.org

**Mackinac Island** · *Mackinac Island Tourism Bur.* · 7274 Main St., P.O. Box 451, 49757, P 500, M 240, (906) 847-3783, (800) 454-5227, info@mackinacisland.org, www.mackinacisland.org

**Mackinaw City** · *Mackinaw Area Visitors Bur.* · Diane Klose, Admin. Asst., 10800 W. U.S. 23, 49701, P 900, M 180, (231) 436-5664, (800) 666-0160, Fax (231) 436-5991, info@mackinawcity.com, www.mackinawcity.com

**Marquette** · *Marquette Country CVB* · Pat Black, Exec. Dir., 337 W. Washington St., 49855, P 61,000, (906) 228-7749, (800) 544-4321, Fax (906) 228-3642, mailroom@marquettecountry.org, www.marquettecountry.org

**Midland** · *Midland County CVB* · 300 Rodd St., Ste. 101, 48640, P 80,670, (989) 839-9522, (888) 464-3526, Fax (989) 835-3701, info@midlandcvb.org, www.midlandcvb.org

**Monroe** · *Monroe County Conv. & Tourism Bur.* · 103 W. Front St., 48161, P 145,000, (734) 457-1030, (800) 252-3011, Fax (734) 457-1097, thebureau@monroeinfo.com, www.monroeinfo.com

**Mount Pleasant** · *Mount Pleasant Area CVB* · Chris Rowley, Exec. Dir., 114 E. Broadway, 48858, P 65,000, M 13, (989) 772-4433, (800) 772-4433, Fax (989) 772-2909, visitor@mountpleasantwow.com, www.mountpleasantwow.com.

**Muskegon** · *Muskegon County CVB* · Sam Wendling, Dir., 610 W. Western Ave., 49440, P 170,200, (231) 724-3100, (800) 250-9283, Fax (231) 724-1398, visitmuskegon@co.muskegon.mi.us, www.visitmuskegon.org

**Newberry** · *Newberry Area Tourism Assn.* · P.O. Box 308, 49868, P 8,000, (906) 293-5562, (800) 831-7292, Fax (906) 293-5739, newberry@lighthouse.net, www.newberrychamber.net

**Niles** · *Four Flags Area Cncl. On Tourism* · Melinda Michael, Exec. Dir., P.O. Box 1300, 49120, P 52,000, M 100, (269) 684-7444, Fax (269) 683-3722, info@fourflagsarea.org, www.fourflags area.org

**Oscoda** · *Oscoda CVB* · Amy Ridgway, Pres., P.O. Box 572, 48750, P 7,500, (989) 739-0900, (877) 8-OSCODA, staff@oscoda.com, www.oscoda.com

**Owosso** · *Shiawassee County CVB* · Kimberly Springsdorf, CVB Dir., 215 N. Water St., 48867, P 72,000, (989) 723-1199, Fax (989) 723-8353, cvbshia@shiawassee.org, www.shiawassee.org

**Paradise** · *Paradise Area Tourism Cncl.* · P.O. Box 64, 49768, P 400, (906) 492-3927, info@paradisemi.org, www.paradisemi.org

**Petoskey** · *Petoskey Area Visitors Bur.* · Peter Fitzsimons, Exec. Dir., 401 E. Mitchell St., 49770, P 20,000, (231) 348-2755, (800) 845-2828, Fax (231) 348-1810, info@petoskeyarea.com, www. petoskeyarea.com

**Port Huron** · *Blue Water Area CVB* · 520 Thomas Edison Pkwy., 48060, P 165,000, (810) 987-8687, (800) 852-4242, Fax (810) 987-1441, bluewater@bluewater.org, www.bluewater.org

**Saginaw** · *Saginaw Valley CVB* · Annette Rummel, Pres./CEO, 515 N. Washington Ave., 3rd Flr., 48607, P 210,039, (989) 752-7164, (800) 444-9979, Fax (989) 752-6642, info@visitsaginaw county.com, www.visitsaginawcounty.com

**Saugatuck** · *Saugatuck/Douglas CVB* · Felicia Fairchild, Exec. Dir., P.O. Box 28, 49453, P 3,000, M 134, (269) 857-1701, Fax (269) 857-2319, ffairchild@saugatuck.com, www.saugatuck.com

**Sault Ste. Marie** · *Sault Ste. Marie CVB* · Linda Hoath, Exec. Dir., 536 Ashmun St., 49783, P 15,000, M 33, (906) 632-3366, Fax (906) 632-6161, (800) MI SAULT, info@saultstemarie.com, www. saultstemarie.com

**South Haven** · *South Haven Visitors Bur.* · Lisa Shanley, Exec. Dir., 546 Phoenix St., 49090, P 6,000, M 43, (269) 637-5252, 800SOHAVEN, Fax (269) 637-8710, relax@southhaven.org, www. southhaven.org

**St. Ignace** · *St. Ignace Visitors Bur.* · 6 Spring St., Ste 100, 49781, P 2,700, (906) 643-6950, (800) 338-6660, Fax (906) 643-8067, info@stignace.com, www.stignace.com

**Tawas City** · *Tawas Bay Tourist & Conv. Bur.* · Heidi Dewalt, Secy./Treas., P.O. Box 10, 48764, P 6,000, M 57, (989) 876-6018, (877) TOTAWAS, info@tawas.com, www.tawasbay.com

**Three Rivers** · *River Country Tourism Cncl.* · P.O. Box 214, 49093, P 60,000, M 90, (269) 321-0640, (800) 447-2821, river countryinfo@gmail.com, www.rivercountry.com

**Traverse City** · *Traverse City CVB* · Brad VanDommelen, Pres., 101 W. Grandview Pkwy., 49684, P 18,105, (231) 947-1120, (800) 940-1120, Fax (231) 947-2621, www.visittraversecity.com

**West Branch** · *West Branch Visitors Bur.* · Steven G. Leonard, Exec. Dir., 422 W. Houghton Ave., 48661, P 22,000, M 4, (989) 345-2821, (800) 755-9091, Fax (989) 345-9075, chamber@westbranch. com, www.visitwestbranch.com

**Ypsilanti** · *Ypsilanti Area CVB* · Debbie Locke-Daniel, Exec. Dir., 106 W. Michigan Ave., 48197, P 71,000, (734) 483-4444, (800) 265-9045, Fax (734) 483-0400, dlocke@ypsilanti.org, www. ypsilanti.org

# Minnesota

**Albert Lea** · *Albert Lea CVB* · Susie Petersen, Exec. Dir., 2566 N. Bridge Ave., 56007, P 18,500, (507) 373-2316, (800) 345-8414, Fax (507) 552-1248, cvbdirector@albertlea.org, www.albertlea tourism.org

**Alexandria** · *Alexandria Lakes Area Mktg.* · Coni McKay, Exec. Dir., 206 Broadway, 56308, P 30,000, M 120, (320) 763-3161, (800) 235-9441, Fax (320) 763-6857, info@alexandriamn.org, www.alexandriamn.org

**Austin** · *Austin CVB* · Cheryl Corey, Exec. Dir., 104 11th Ave. N.W., Ste. D, 55912, P 23,000, (507) 437-4563, (800) 444-5713, Fax (507) 433-1052, visitor@austinmn.com, www.austincvb.com

**Baudette** · *Lake of the Woods Tourism* · Denelle Cauble, Exec. Dir., 930 W. Main, P.O. Box 518, 56623, P 4,000, (218) 634-1174, (800) 382-3474, Fax (218) 634-2915, lakwoods@wiktel.com, www.lakeofthewoodsmn.com

**Bemidji** · *Visit Bemidji* · Gayle Quistgard, Exec. Dir., P.O. Box 66, 56619, P 12,076, (218) 759-0164, (800) 458-2223, Fax (218) 759-0810, gayle@visitbemidji.com, www.visitbemidji.com

**Bloomington** · *Bloomington CVB* · 7900 International Dr., Ste. 990, 55425, P 85,000, (952) 858-8500, (800) 346-4289, Fax (952) 858-8854, www.bloomingtonmn.org

**Blue Earth** · *Blue Earth Area CVB* · Shelly Greimann, Dir., 113 S. Nicollet St., 56013, P 4,000, (507) 526-2916, Fax (507) 526-2244, chamber@bevcomm.net, www.blueearthchamber.com

**Burnsville** · *Burnsville CVB* · Amie Burrill, Exec. Dir., 101 W. Burnsville Pkwy., Ste. 150B, 55337, P 62,000, (952) 898-5646, (800) 521-6055, Fax (952) 487-1777, info@burnsvillemn.com, www.burnsvillemn.com

**Caledonia** · *see Harmony*

**Crane Lake** · *Crane Lake Visitors & Tourism Bur.* · 7238 Handberg Rd., 55725, P 150, (218) 993-2901, (800) 362-7405, Fax (218) 993-2902, vacation@visitcranelake.com, www.visit cranelake.com

**Detroit Lakes** · *Detroit Lakes Tourism Bur.* · Cleone Stewart, Tourism Dir., 700 Summit Ave., P.O. Box 348, 56502, P 10,000, (218) 847-9202, (800) 542-3992, Fax (218) 847-9082, cleone@ visitdetroitlakes.com, www.visitdetroitlakes.com

**Duluth** · *Visit Duluth* · Terry Mattson, Pres., 21 W. Superior St., Ste. 100, 55802, P 90,000, M 450, (218) 722-4011, Fax (218) 722-1322, (800) 4-DULUTH, cvb@visitduluth.com, www.visitduluth. com

**Eagan** · *Eagan CVB* · Brent Cory, Exec. Dir., 1501 Central Pkwy., Ste. E, 55121, P 68,000, (651) 675-5546, Fax (651) 675-5545, (866) EAGAN-20, visiteagan@eaganmn.com, www.eaganmn.com

**Fairmont** · *Fairmont CVB* · Stephanie Busiahn, Dir., 323 E. Blue Earth Ave., P.O. Box 976, 56031, P 10,889, (507) 235-8585, (800) 657-3280, Fax (507) 235-8411, director@fairmontcvb.com, www. visitfairmontmn.com

**Faribault** · *Faribault Area Tourism* · Kymn Anderson, Pres., 530 Wilson Ave., P.O. Box 434, 55021, P 28,000, (507) 334-4381, (800) 658-2354, Fax (507) 334-1003, chamber@faribaultmn.org, www.faribaultmn.org

**Grand Rapids** · *Visit Grand Rapids* · Cheri M. Zeppelin, Exec. Dir., 501 S. Pokegama Ave. #3, 55744, P 8,000, (218) 326-9607, (800) 355-9740, Fax (218) 326-8219, cheri@visitgrandrapids.com, www.visitgrandrapids.com

**Harmony** · *Historic Bluff Country/Southeastern Reg. CVB* · Kris Nolte, Exec. Dir., P.O. Box 609, 55939, P M, (800) 428-2030, Fax (507) 886-2934, hbc@harmonytel.net, www.bluffcountry.com

**Hutchinson** · *Hutchinson Area CVB* · Bill Corb, Pres., 2 Main St. S., 55350, P 14,500, (320) 587-5252, (800) 572-6689, Fax (320) 587-4752, info@explorehutchinson.com, www.explorehutchinson.com

**Little Falls** · *Little Falls CVB* · Cathy Van Risseghem, Dir., 606 S.E. First St., 56345, P 8,500, (320) 616-4959, (800) 325-5916, Fax (320) 616-4961, lfcvb@charter.net, www.littlefallsmn.com

**Mankato** · *Greater Mankato CVB* · Anna Thill, Pres., One Civic Center Plz., Ste. 200, 56001, P 42,000, (800) 657-4733, (507) 385-6660, Fax (507) 345-8376, visitors@greatermankato.com, www.greatermankato.com

**Marshall** · *Marshall CVB* · Linda Erb, Exec. Dir., P.O. Box 352-B, 56258, P 12,500, (507) 537-1865, Fax (507) 532-4485, info@visitmarshallmn.com, www.visitmarshallmn.com

**Minneapolis** · *Meet Minneapolis Conv. & Visitors Assn.* · Bill Deef, V.P. Tourism, 250 Marquette Ave. S., Ste. 1300, 55401, P 2,968,000, M 800, (612) 767-8000, (888) 676-6757, Fax (612) 767-8001, www.meetminneapolis.com

**Minneapolis** · *Visit Minneapolis North* · Dave Looby, Exec. Dir., 6200 Shingle Creek Pkwy., Ste. 248, 55430, P 400,000, (763) 566-7722, (800) 541-4364, Fax (763) 566-6526, info@visitminneapolisnorth.com, www.visitminneapolisnorth.com

**Moorhead** · *see Fargo, ND*

**Pipestone** · *Pipestone CVB* · Mick Myers, Exec. Dir., 117 8th Ave. S.E., P.O. Box 8, 56164, P 4,549, (507) 825-3316, (800) 336-6125, Fax (507) 825-3317, pipecham@pipestoneminnesota.com, www.pipestoneminnesota.com.

**Red Wing** · *Red Wing Visitors & Conv. Bur.* · Kathy Silverthorn, Exec. Dir., 420 Levee St., 55066, P 17,000, M 70, (651) 385-5934, (800) 498-3444, Fax (651) 388-3900, visitorscenter@redwing.org, www.redwing.org

**Redwood Falls** · *Redwood Area Tourism* · 200 S. Mill St., 56283, P 5,459, (507) 637-2828, (800) 657-7070, Fax (507) 637-5202, chamber@redwoodfalls.org, www.redwoodfalls.org

**Rochester** · *Rochester CVB* · Brad Jones, Exec. Dir., 30 Civic Center Dr. S.E., Ste. 200, 55904, P 100,000, (507) 288-4331, (800) 634-8277, Fax (507) 288-9144, info@rochestercvb.org, www.visitrochestermn.com

**Saint Cloud** · *Saint Cloud Area CVB* · Julie Lunning, Exec. Dir., 525 Hwy. 10 S., Ste. 1, 56304, P 150,000, (320) 251-4170, (800) 264-2940, Fax (320) 656-0401, julie@granitecountry.com, www.granitecountry.com.

**Saint Paul** · *Saint Paul Conv. & Visitors Auth.* · Karolyn Kirchgesler, Pres./CEO, 175 W. Kellogg Blvd., Ste. 502, 55102, P 267,000, M 400, (651) 265-4900, (800) 627-6101, Fax (651) 265-4999, info@visitsaintpaul.com, www.visitsaintpaul.com

**Shakopee** · *Shakopee CVB* · Carol Schultz, Pres., 1801 E. Cty. Rd. 101, P.O. Box 717, 55379, P 32,000, (952) 445-1660, (800) 574-2150, Fax (952) 445-1669, cschultz@shakopee.org, www.shakopee.org

**Thief River Falls** · *Thief River Falls CVB* · Laura Anderson, Dir., 2042 Hwy. 1 W., P.O Box 176, 56701, P 8,334, (218) 686-9785, Fax (218) 681-3739, trfcvb@mncable.net, www.visittrf.com

**Virginia** · *Iron Range Tourism Bur.* · 403 N. 1st St., 55792, (218) 749-8161, (800) 777-8497, Fax (218) 749-8055, info@ironrange.org, www.ironrange.org

**Wadena** · *Wadena Area CVB* · Shirley Uselman, Dir., 5 Aldrich Ave. S.E., P.O. Box 107, 56482, P 4,292, (218) 632-7704, (877) 631-7704, Fax (218) 632-7705, www.wadena.org

**Willmar** · *Willmar Lakes Area CVB* · Beth Fischer, Exec. Dir., 2104 E. Hwy. 12, 56201, P 20,000, (320) 235-3552, Fax (320) 231-1948, (800) 845-TRIP, info@seeyouinwillmar.com, www.seeyouinwillmar.com

**Winona** · *Visit Winona* · Pat Mutter, Exec. Dir., 160 Johnson St., P.O. Box 1069, 55987, P 27,069, (507) 452-0735, (800) 657-4972, Fax (507) 454-0006, pmutter@visitwinona.com, www.visitwinona.com

**Worthington** · *Worthington Area CVB* · Darlene Macklin, Dir., 1121 Third Ave., 56187, P 11,230, (507) 372-2919, (800) 279-2919, Fax (507) 372-2827, wcofc@frontiernet.net, www.worthingtonmnchamber.com

# Mississippi

**Aberdeen** · *Aberdeen Visitors Bur.* · Deborah Stubblefield, Dir., 204 E. Commerce St., P.O. Box 288, 39730, P 6,500, (662) 369-9440, (800) 634-3538, Fax (662) 369-3436, info@aberdeenms.org, www.aberdeenms.org

**Belzoni** · *Catfish Capital Visitors Center* · Steve Anderson, Exec. Dir., 111 Magnolia St., P.O. Box 145, 39038, P 11,000, (662) 247-4838, (800) 408-4838, Fax (662) 247-4805, catfish@belzonicable.com, www.catfishcapitalonline.com

**Canton** · *Canton CVB* · JoAnn Gordon, Exec. Dir., 147 N. Union St., P.O. Box 53, 39046, P 13,500, (601) 859-1307, (800) 844-3369, Fax (601) 859-0346, canton@cantontourism.com, www.cantontourism.com

**Columbus** · *Columbus CVB* · James Tsismanakis, Exec. Dir., 318 7th St. N., P.O. Box 789, 39703, P 64,000, (662) 329-1191, (800) 327-2686, Fax (662) 329-8969, ccvb@columbus-ms.org, www.columbus-ms.org

**Corinth** · *Corinth Area CVB* · Kristy White, Exec. Dir., 215 N. Filmore St., 38834, P 35,000, (662) 287-8300, (800) 748-9048, Fax (662) 286-0102, tourism@corinth.net, www.corinth.net

**Greenwood** · *Greenwood CVB* · Paige Hunt, Exec. Dir., 111 E. Market St., P.O. Drawer 739, 38935, P 18,000, (662) 453-9197, (800) 748-9064, Fax (662) 453-5526, info@gcvb.com, www.greenwoodms.org

**Grenada** · *Grenada Tourism Comm.* · Walter McCool, Exec. Dir., 95 S.W. Frontage Rd., P.O. Box 1824, 38902, P 23,263, (662) 226-2571, (800) 373-2571, Fax (662) 226-9745, grenadatourism@yahoo.com, www.grenadamississippi.com

**Gulfport** · *Mississippi Gulf Coast CVB* · Richard Forester, Exec. Dir., P.O. Box 6128, 39506, P 335,450, (228) 896-6699, (888) 467-4853, Fax (228) 896-6788, tourism@gulfcoast.org, www.gulfcoast.org

**Hattiesburg** · *Hattiesburg CVB* · Richard Taylor, Dir., 5 Convention Center Plz., 39401, P 65,000, (601) 296-7475, Fax (601) 296-7404, (866) 4-HATTIE, www.visithattie.com

**Jackson** · *Jackson CVB* · Wanda Collier-Wilson, Exec. Dir., 111 Capitol St., Ste. 102, P.O. Box 1450, 39215, P 200,000, (601) 960-1891, (800) 354-7695, Fax (601) 960-1827, wcwilson@visitjackson.com, www.visitjackson.com

**Meridian** · *Meridian/Lauderdale County Tourism Bur.* · Suzy Johnson, Exec. Dir., P.O. Box 5313, 39302, P 75,555, (601) 482-8001, (888) 868-7720, Fax (601) 486-4988, www.visitmeridian.com

**Natchez** • *Natchez CVB* • Connie Taunton, Exec. Dir., 640 S. Canal St., Box C, 39120, P 20,000, (601) 446-6345, (800) 647-6724, Fax (601) 442-0814, info@visitnatchez.org, www.visitnatchez.org

**Oxford** • *Oxford CVB* • Hugh Stump III, Exec. Dir., 102 Ed Terry Blvd., 38655, P 19,000, (662) 234-4680, (800) 758-9177, Fax (662) 232-8680, tourism@oxfordcvb.com, www.oxfordcvb.com

**Ridgeland** • *Ridgeland Tourism Comm.* • Doyle Warrington, Exec. Dir., 1000 Highland Colony Pkwy., Ste. 6006, 39157, P 22,000, (601) 605-5252, (800) 468-6078, Fax (601) 605-5248, info@visitridgeland.com, www.visitridgeland.com

**Starkville** • *Starkville CVB* • Jennifer Glaze, V.P. of Tourism, 200 E. Main St., 39759, P 43,000, (662) 323-3322, (800) 649-8687, Fax (662) 323-5815, info@starkville.org, www.starkville.org

**Tunica** • *Tunica County CVB* • Webster Franklin, Pres./CEO, 13625 Hwy. 61 N., P.O. Box 2739, 38676, P 9,000, (662) 363-3800, Fax (662) 363-1493, (888) 4-TUNICA, tunicams@tunicatravel.com, www.tunicatravel.com

**Tupelo** • *Tupelo CVB* • Linda Butler Johnson, Exec. Dir., 399 E. Main St., P.O. Drawer 47, 38802, P 36,000, (662) 841-6521, (800) 533-0611, Fax (662) 841-6558, visittupelo@tupelo.net, www.tupelo.net

**Vicksburg** • *Vicksburg CVB* • Bill Seratt, Exec. Dir., P.O. Box 110, 39181, P 50,000, (601) 636-9421, (800) 221-3536, Fax (601) 636-9475, dellis@vicksburgcvb.org, www.visitvicksburg.com

**Yazoo City** • *Yazoo County CVB* • Tonja Ray-Smith, Exec. Dir., 332 N. Main St., P.O. Box 186, 39194, P 25,634, (662) 746-1815, (800) 381-0662, Fax (662) 746-1816, tonja.smith@yazoo.org, www.yazoo.org

# Missouri

**Cape Girardeau** • *Cape Girardeau CVB* • Chuck Martin, Exec. Dir., 400 Broadway, Ste. 100, 63701, P 36,000, (573) 335-1631, (800) 777-0068, Fax (573) 334-6702, www.capestorytelling.com, info@visitcape.com, www.visitcape.com

**Carthage** • *Carthage CVB* • Wendi Douglas, Exec. Dir., 402 S. Garrison Ave., 64836, P 13,000, (417) 359-8181, (866) 357-8687, Fax (417) 359-9119, cvb@ecarthage.com, www.visit-carthage.com

**Columbia** • *Columbia CVB* • Lorah Steiner, Dir., 300 S. Providence Rd., 65203, P 90,000, (573) 875-1231, (800) 652-0987, Fax (573) 443-3986, info@gocolumbiamo.com, www.visitcolumbiamo.com

**Independence** • *Independence Tourism Dept.* • Stephanie Roush, Dir., 111 E. Maple, 64050, P 116,000, (816) 325-7111, (800) 748-7323, Fax (816) 325-7932, sroush@indepmo.org, www.visitindependence.com

**Jefferson City** • *Jefferson City CVB* • Steve Picker, Exec. Dir., 100 E. High St., P.O. Box 2227, 65102, P 40,000, (573) 632-2820, Fax (573) 638-4892, info@visitjeffersoncity.com, www.visitjeffersoncity.com

**Joplin** • *Joplin CVB* • Vince Lindstrom, Dir., 602 S. Main St., 64801, P 48,000, (417) 625-4789, (800) 657-2534, Fax (417) 624-7948, cvb@joplinmo.org, www.visitjoplinmo.com

**Kansas City** • *Kansas City Conv. & Vistors Assn.* • Rick Hughes, Pres./CEO, 1100 Main St., Ste. 2200, 64105, P 1,900,000, (816) 221-5242, (800) 767-7700, Fax (816) 691-3805, info@visitkc.com, www.visitkc.com

**Maryland Heights** • *Maryland Heights CVB* • Karen Krispin, Dir., 542 West Port Plz., St. Louis, 63146, P 26,000, (314) 275-9964, Fax (314) 275-9942, (888) MORE2DO, karen@mhcvb.com, www.more2do.org

**Nevada** • *Impact Nevada Tourism* • Glenda Crowder, Tourism Dlr., 225 W. Austin, Ste. 200, 64772, P 20,000, (417) 667-5300, visitors@nevada-mo.com, www.visitnevadamo.com

**Osage Beach** • *Lake of the Ozarks CVB* • Tim Jacobsen, Exec. Dir., P.O. Box 1498, 65065, P 7,000, M 650, (573) 348-1599, (800) 386-5253, Fax (573) 348-2293, info@funlake.com, www.funlake.com

**Saint Charles** • *Greater St. Charles CVB* • David Rosenwasser, Dir./CEO, 230 S. Main St., 63301, P 70,000, (636) 946-7776, (800) 366-2427, Fax (636) 949-3217, gsccvb@historicstcharles.com, www.historicstcharles.com

**Saint Joseph** • *St. Joseph CVB* • Marci Bennett, Exec. Dir., 109 S. 4th, P.O. Box 445, 64502, P 80,000, (816) 233-6688, (800) 785-0360, Fax (816) 233-9120, cvb@stjomo.com, www.stjomo.com

**Saint Louis** • *St. Louis Conv. & Visitors Comm.* • Kathleen Ratcliffe, Pres., 701 Convention Plz., Ste. 300, 63101, P 2,423,200, (314) 421-1023, (800) 916-0092, Fax (314) 421-0039, kratcliffe@explorestlouis.com, www.explorestlouis.com

**Sikeston** • *Sikeston-Miner CVB* • Lynne Williams, Exec. Dir., One Industrial Dr., P.O. Box 1983, 63801, P 20,000, (573) 471-6362, (888) 309-6591, Fax (573) 471-2499, info@visitsikeston-miner.com, www.visitsikeston-miner.com

**Springfield** • *Springfield CVB* • Mr. Tracy Kimberlin, Exec. Dir., 815 E. St. Louis St., Ste. 100, 65806, P 154,000, (417) 881-5300, (800) 678-8767, Fax (417) 881-2231, cvb@springfieldmo.org, www.stayinspringfield.com

**Washington** • *Washington Div. Of Tourism* • 323 W. Main, 63090, P 14,000, (636) 239-2715, Fax (636) 239-1381, (888) 7-WASH MO, tourism@washmo.org, www.washmo.org

# Montana

**Billings** • *Billings CVB* • Joan Kronebusch, Dir., 815 S. 27th St., P.O. Box 31177, 59107, P 130,000, (406) 245-4111, Fax (406) 245-7333, info@billingschamber.com, www.visitbillings.com

# Nebraska

**Beatrice** • *Beatrice/Gage County CVB* • 226 S. 6th St., 68310, P 23,000, (402) 223-2338, Fax (402) 223-2339, infocvb@visitbeatrice.com, www.visitbeatrice.com

**Columbus** • *Columbus/Platte County CVB* • Deb Loseke, Dir., 764 33rd Ave., P.O. Box 515, 68602, P 21,000, (402) 564-2769, Fax (402) 564-2026, dloseke@megavision.com, www.visitcolumbusne.com

**Fairbury** • *Jefferson County Visitors Committee* • Sharon Priefert, Exec. Dir., 518 E St., P.O. Box 274, 68352, P 4,262, (402) 729-3000, Fax (402) 729-3076, jcvc@diodecom.net, www.visitoregontrail.org

**Fremont** • *Fremont & Dodge County CVB* • Leslie Carter, Exec. Dir., P.O. Box 182, 68025, P 35,000, (402) 753-6414, (800) 727-8323, Fax (402) 721-9359, lcarter@fdcvb.org, www.fdcvb.org

**Grand Island** • *Grand Island/Hall County CVB* • Renee Seifert, Exec. Dir., 2424 S. Locust St., Ste. C, 68801, P 51,000, (308) 382-4400, (800) 658-3178, Fax (308) 382-4908, info@visitgrandisland.com, www.visitgrandisland.com

**Hastings** • *Hastings/Adams County CVB* • Kaleena Fong, Exec. Dir., 100 North Shore Dr., P.O. Box 941, 68902, P 24,000, (402) 461-2370, (800) 967-2189, Fax (402) 461-7273, info@visithastingsnebraska.com, www.visithastingsnebraska.com

**Kearney** • *Kearney Visitors Bur.* • Roger Jasnoch, Dir., P.O. Box 607, 68848, P 29,506, (308) 237-3178, (800) 652-9435, Fax (308) 236-9116, rjasnoch@visitkearney.org, www.visitkearney.org

**Lincoln** • *Lincoln CVB* • Jeff Maul, Exec. Dir., 1135 M St., Ste. 300, P.O. Box 83737, 68501, P 250,000, (402) 434-5335, (800) 423-8212, Fax (402) 436-2360, info@lincoln.org, www.lincoln.org

**McCook** • *Red Willow County CVB* • Carol Schlegel, Coord., 107 Norris Ave., P.O. Box 337, 69001, P 11,450, (308) 345-3200, (800) 657-2179, Fax (308) 345-3201, bwchief@qwest.net, www.visitmccook.com

**Norfolk** • *Madison County CVB* • 405 Madison Ave., P.O. Box 386, 68702, P 33,000, (402) 371-2932, (888) 371-2932, Fax (402) 371-0182, mcvb@norfolk.ne.us, www.visitnorfolkne.com

**North Platte** • *North Platte/Lincoln County CVB* • Lisa Burke, Exec. Dir., 219 S. Dewey, P.O. Box 1207, 69103, P 24,000, (308) 532-4729, (800) 955-4528, Fax (308) 532-5914, info@visitnorth platte.com, www.visitnorthplatte.com

**Ogallala** • *Ogallala/Keith County CVB* • Orla Kitt, Tourism & Events Coord., P.O. Box 628, 69153, P 8,877, (308) 284-4066, (800) 658-4390, Fax (308) 284-3126, www.lakemcconaughy.com, info@visitogallala.com, www.visitogallala.com

**Omaha** • *Greater Omaha CVB* • Dana Markel, Exec. Dir., 1001 Farnam, 68102, P 813,170, (402) 444-4660, (866) 937-6624, Fax (402) 444-4511, dmarkel@visitomaha.com, www.visitomaha.com

**South Sioux City** • *South Sioux City CVB* • Donna Goodier, Exec. Dir., 3900 Dakota Ave., Ste. 11, 68776, P 12,000, (402) 494-1307, (866) 494-1307, Fax (402) 494-5010, dgoodier@cableone.net, www.visitsouthsiouxcity.com

**York** • *York County CVB* • Bob Sautter, Dir., 224 W. 6th St., 68467, P 14,500, (402) 362-4575, Fax (402) 362-3344, www.yorkchamber. org, (888) SEE YORK, bobsautter@alltel.net, www.yorkvisitors.org

# Nevada

**Crystal Bay** • *see Incline Village*

**Incline Village** • *Lake Tahoe-Incline Village Crystal Bay Visitor Bur.* • William Hoffman, Exec. Dir., 969 Tahoe Blvd., 89451, P 9,143, (775) 832-1606, Fax (775) 832-1605, (800) GO TAHOE, info@gotahoe.com, www.gotahoenorth.com

**Las Vegas** • *Las Vegas Conv. & Visitors Auth.* • Rossi Ralenkotter, Pres./CEO, 3150 Paradise Rd., 89109, P 1,900,000, (702) 892-0711, (800) 332-5333, Fax (702) 892-2803, www.visitlasvegas.com

**Reno** • *Reno-Sparks Conv. & Visitors Auth.* • Ellen Oppenheim, Pres./CEO, 4001 S. Virginia St., Ste. G, P.O. Box 837, 89504, P 323,670, (775) 827-7600, (800) 443-1482, Fax (775) 827-7666, info@rscva.com, www.visitrenotahoe.com

**Stateline** • *Lake Tahoe Visitors Auth.* • Patrick Kaler, Exec. Dir., 169 Hwy. 50, P.O. Box 5878, 89449, P 30,000, (775) 588-5900, Fax (775) 588-1941, (800) AT TAHOE, info@ltva.org, www. bluelaketahoe.com

**Tonopah** • *Tonopah Conv. Center* • Diane Perchetti, 301 W. Brougher Ave., P.O. Box 408, 89049, P 3,000, (775) 482-3558, Fax (775) 482-3932, www.tonopahnevada.com

# New Jersey

**Atlantic City** • *Atlantic City Conv. & Visitors Auth.* • Jeffrey Vasser, Exec. Dir., 2314 Pacific Ave., 08401, P 380,000, (609) 449-7100, (888) 228-4748, Fax (609) 345-2200, www.atlanticcitynj.com

**Bridgewater** • *Somerset County Bus. Partnership & Visitor Center* • Kimberly Winters, Tourism Coord., 360 Grove St., 08807, P 315,000, (908) 218-4300, Fax (908) 722-7823, www.visitsomerset nj.org, kwinters@scbp.org, www.scbp.org

**Cape May County** • *Cape May County Dept. of Tourism* • Diane Wieland, Dir. of Tourism, 4 Moore Rd., P.O. Box 365, Cape May Courthouse, 08210, P 100,000, (609) 463-6415, (800) 227-2297, Fax (609) 465-4639, tourism@co.cape-may.nj.us, www.thejersey cape.net

**Red Bank** • *Red Bank Visitors Center* • Margaret Mass, Dir., 20 Broad St., P.O. Box 806, 07701, P 12,000, (732) 741-9211, Fax (732) 842-7615, (888) HIPTOWN, www.visit.redbank.com

**Washington** • *Warren County CVB* • Robert Goltz, Pres./CEO, 10 Brass Castle Rd., 07882, P 105,765, M (908) 835-9200, Fax (908) 835-9296, info@visitwarren.com, www.visitwarren.com

# New Mexico

**Albuquerque** • *Albuquerque CVB* • Dale Lockett, Pres./CEO, 20 First Plz. N.W., Ste. 601, P.O. Box 26866, 87125, P 700,000, M 1,000, (505) 842-9918, (800) 733-9918, Fax (505) 247-9101, lockett@itsatrip.org, www.itsatrip.org

**Farmington** • *Farmington CVB* • Debbie Dusenbery, Exec. Dir., 3041 E. Main St., 87402, P 120,000, M 125, (505) 326-7602, (800) 448-1240, Fax (505) 327-0577, fmncvb@earthlink.net, www.farmingtonnm.org

**Gallup** • *Gallup Visitor Info. Center* • Alice Perez, 103 W. Hwy. 66, 87301, P 22,000, (505) 722-2228, (800) 380-4989, Fax (505) 863-2280, alice@thegallupchamber.com

**Las Cruces** • *Las Cruces CVB* • Ken Mompellier, Exec. Dir., 211 N. Water St., 88001, P 85,000, (575) 541-2444, Fax (575) 541-2164, (800) FIESTAS, cvb@lascrucescvb.org, www.lascrucescvb.org.

**Rio Rancho** • *Rio Rancho CVB* • Matt Geishel, CVB Mgr., 3200 Civic Center Cr. N.E., 87144, P 75,000, (505) 891-7258, (888) 746-7262, Fax (505) 892-8328, info@rioranchonm.org, www. rioranchonm.org

**Roswell** • *Roswell Conv. & Civic Center* • Dusty Huckabee, Exec. Dir., 912 N. Main, 88201, P 53,000, (505) 624-6860, Fax (505) 624-6863, www.roswell-nm.gov

**Ruidoso** • *Ruidoso Conv. Center* • Gail Bailey, Dir. of Sales, 111 Sierra Blanca Dr., 88345, P 10,500, (575) 258-5445, Fax (575) 258-5040, www.ruidosoconventioncenter.com

**Santa Fe** • *Santa Fe CVB* • Keith Toler, Exec. Dir., P.O. Box 909, 87504, P 67,000, (505) 955-6200, (800) 777-2489, Fax (505) 955-6222, info@santafe.org, www.santafe.org

**Santa Rosa** • *Santa Rosa Info & Tourism Center* • Richard Delgado, Tourism Dir., 244 S. 4th St., P.O. Box 429, 88435, P 2,640, (575) 472-3763, www.srnm.org , rdelgado@srnm.org, www. santarosanm.org

**Taos** • *Taos Visitors Center* • Michelle Hammer, Supt., 1139 Paseo del Pueblo Sur., 87571, P 31,800, (575) 758-3873, (800) 732-8267, Fax (575) 758-3872, information@taosvisitor.com, www.taosvisitor.com

# New York

**Albany** • *Albany County CVB* • Michele Vennard, Pres./CEO, 25 Quackenbush Sq., 12207, P 300,000, M 300, (518) 434-1217, (800) 258-3582, Fax (518) 434-0887, accvb@albany.org, www. albany.org

**Binghamton** • *Greater Binghamton CVB* • Louis R. Santoni, Sr. V.P. Chamber Svcs., Metrocenter, 49 Court St., P.O. Box 995, 13902, P 200,536, (607) 772-8860, (800) 836-6740, Fax (607) 722-4513, info@visitbinghamton.org, www.visitbinghamton.org

**Buffalo** · *Buffalo/Niagara CVB* · Richard Geiger, Pres./CEO, 617 Main St., Ste. 200, 14203, P 985,000, (716) 852-0511, Fax (716) 852-0131, (800) BUFFALO, info@buffalocvb.org, www.visitbuffaloniagara.com

**Catskill** · *Greene County Tourism Promotion* · Daniela Marino, Dir., Rte. 23B at NYS Thruway, Exit 21, P.O. Box 527, 12414, P 48,195, (518) 943-3223, Fax (518) 943-2296, (800) 355-CATS, tourism@discovergreene.com, www.greenetourism.com

**Chautauqua** · *Chautauqua County Visitors Bur.* · Andrew Nixon, Dir., P.O. Box 1441, 14722, P 141,000, M 325, (716) 357-4569, (800) 242-4569, Fax (716) 357-2284, info@tourchautauqua.com, www.tourchautauqua.com

**Corning** · *Steuben County Conference & Visitors Bur.* · Peggy Coleman, Pres., 1 W. Market St., Ste. 301, 14830, P 98,000, (607) 936-6544, (866) 946-3386, Fax (607) 936-6575, sccvb@corningfingerlakes.com, www.corningfingerlakes.com

**Goshen** · *Orange County Tourism* · Susan H. Cayea, Dir., 124 Main St., 10924, P 375,000, (845) 291-2136, (800) 762-8687, Fax (845) 291-2137, tourism@co.orange.ny.us, www.orangetourism.org

**Hauppauge** · *Long Island CVB* · R. Moke McGowan, Pres., 330 Motor Pkwy., Ste. 203, 11788, P 2,300,000, M 475, (631) 951-3900, (800) 441-4601, Fax (631) 951-3439, www.discoverlongisland.com

**Ithaca** · *Ithaca/Tompkins County CVB* · Fred Bonn, Dir., 904 E. Shore Dr., 14850, P 96,000, (607) 272-1313, (800) 284-8422, Fax (607) 272-7617, info@visitithaca.com, www.visitithaca.com

**Lake Placid** · *Lake Placid-Essex County Visitors Bur.* · James McKenna, Pres./CEO, 49 Parkside Dr., P.O. Box 1570, 12946, P 38,000, M 700, (518) 523-2445, (800) 447-5224, Fax (518) 523-2605, info@lakeplacid.com, www.lakeplacid.com

**Little Valley** · *Cattaraugus County Tourism* · Debra Opserbeck, Tour. Spec., 303 Court St., 14755, P 83,955, (716) 938-2307, (800) 331-0543, Fax (716) 938-2779, visitor@enchantedmountains.info, www.enchantedmountains.info

**Long Island** · *see Hauppauge*

**New York** · *New York City CVB* · George Fertitta, Pres./CEO, 810 7th Ave., 3rd Flr., Visitors Center, 10019, P 11,685,650, (212) 484-1200, Fax (212) 246-6310, www.nycvisit.com

**Plattsburgh** · *Adirondack Coast Visitors & Conv. Bur.* · Michele Powers, Dir. of Tourism, 7061 Rte. 9, P.O. Box 310, 12901, P 200,000, (518) 563-1000, Fax (518) 563-1028, chamber@westelcom.com, www.northcountrychamber.com

**Rochester** · *Greater Rochester Visitors Assn.* · Greg Marshall, V.P., 45 East Ave., Ste. 400, 14604, P 1,000,000, M 450, (585) 279-8300, (800) 677-7282, Fax (585) 232-4822, www.visitrochester.com

**Saratoga Springs** · *Saratoga Conv. & Tourism Bur.* · David Zunker, Pres., 60 Railroad Pl., Ste. 100, 12866, P 27,000, M 375, (518) 584-1531, Fax (518) 584-2969, mail@discoversaratoga.org, www.discoversaratoga.org

**Southampton** · *Hamptons Visitors Cncl.* · P.O. Box 908, 11968, www.hamptonsvisitorscouncil.com

**Syracuse** · *Syracuse CVB* · David Holder, Pres., 572 S. Salina St., 13202, P 460,000, (315) 470-1910, (800) 234-4797, Fax (315) 471-8545, cvb@visitsyracuse.org, www.visitsyracuse.org

**Utica** · *Oneida County CVB* · Kelly Blazosky, Pres., NY State Thruway, Exit 31, P.O. Box 551, 13503, P 253,000, M 123, (315) 724-7221, (800) 426-3132, Fax (315) 724-7335, oneidany@dreamscape.com, www.oneidacountycvb.com

**White Plains** · *Westchester County Ofc. of Tourism* · Kim Sinistore, Dir., 222 Mamaroneck Ave., 10605, P 900,000, (914) 995-8500, (800) 833-9282, Fax (914) 995-8505, tourism@westchestergov.com, www.westchestertourism.com

**Wilmington** · *Whiteface Mountain Reg. Visitors Bur.* · Diane Buckley, Mgr., 5753 NYS Rte. 86, P.O. Box 277, 12997, P 3,000, M 100, (518) 946-2255, Fax (518) 946-2683, (888) WHITEFACE, www.whitefacenewyork.com, info@whitefaceregion.com, www.whitefaceregion.com

# North Carolina

**Albemarle** · *Stanly County CVB* · Chris Lambert, Exec. Dir., 1000 N. 1st St., Ste. 11, P.O. Box 1456, 28002, P 58,100, (704) 986-2583, (800) 650-1476, Fax (704) 986-3685, chris@stanlycvb.com, www.stanlycvb.com

**Alleghany County** · *see Boone*

**Ashe County** · *see Boone*

**Asheboro** · *Randolph County Tourism Dev. Authority* · Tammy O'Kelley, Exec. Dir., 222 Sunset Ave., Ste. 107, 27203, P 138,367, (336) 626-0364, (800) 626-2672, Fax (336) 626-0977, www.visitrandolphcounty.com

**Asheville** · *Asheville CVB* · Mr. Kelly Miller, Exec. Dir./Exec. V.P., 36 Montford Ave., 28801, P 391,000, (828) 258-6102, (828) 258-6101, Fax (828) 254-6054, comments@exploreasheville.com, www.exploreasheville.com

**Avery County** · *see Boone*

**Belmont** · *Gaston County Dept. of Tourism* · Walter Israel, Interim Dir., 620 N. Main St., 28012, P 190,365, (704) 825-4044, (800) 849-9994, Fax (704) 825-4029, walter.israel@co.gaston.nc.us, www.gastontourism.com

**Boone** · *Boone CVB* · Mac Forehand, Dir., 208 Howard St., 28607, P 14,200, (828) 262-3516, (800) 852-9506, Fax (828) 264-6644, info@visitboonenc.com, www.visitboonenc.com

**Boone** · *North Carolina High Country Host* · 1700 Blowing Rock Rd., 28607, P 98,100, M 375, (828) 264-1299, (800) 438-7500, Fax (828) 265-0550, info@highcountryhost.com, www.mountainsofnc.com

**Burlington** · *Burlington/Alamance County CVB* · Robert Cox, V.P., 610 S. Lexington Ave., P.O. Box 519, 27216, P 135,453, (336) 570-1444, (800) 637-3804, Fax (336) 228-1330, info@visitalamance.com, www.visitalamance.com

**Canton** · *see Waynesville*

**Chapel Hill** · *Chapel Hill/Orange County Visitors Bur.* · Laurie Paolicelli, Exec. Dir., 501 W. Franklin St., 27516, P 123,766, (919) 968-2060, (888) 968-2060, Fax (919) 968-2062, info@visitchapelhill.org, www.visitchapelhill.org

**Charlotte** · *Visit Charlotte* · Mike Butts, Exec. Dir., 500 S. College St., Ste. 300, 28202, P 664,342, M 670, (704) 334-2282, (800) 722-1994, Fax (704) 342-3972, mike.butts@visitcharlotte.com, www.visitcharlotte.com

**Cherokee** · *Cherokee Travel & Tourism* · Josie Long, Coord., 498 Tsali Blvd., P.O. Box 460, 28719, P 13,500, (828) 497-9195, (800) 438-1601, Fax (828) 497-2505, travel@nc-cherokee.com, www.cherokee-nc.com

**Columbus** · *Polk County Travel & Tourism* · Melinda Young, Dir., 20 E. Mills St., P.O. Box 308, 28722, P 19,000, (828) 894-2324, (800) 440-7848, Fax (828) 894-6142, visit@firstpeaknc.com, www.firstpeaknc.com

**Cornelius** • *Visit Lake Norman* • Sally Ashworth, Exec. Dir., 19900 W. Catawba Ave., Ste. 102, 28031, P 65,000, (704) 987-3300, (800) 305-2508, Fax (704) 892-5313, info@lakenorman.org, www.visitlakenorman.org

**Davidson** • *see Cornelius*

**Dunn** • *Dunn Area Tourism Auth.* • Brandy Hall, Mktg. Dir., 209 W. Divine St., P.O. Box 310, 28335, P 10,000, (910) 892-3282, Fax (910) 892-4071, www.visitdunn.com, tourism@dunnchamber.com, www.dunntourism.org

**Durham** • *Durham CVB* • Reyn Bowman, Pres./CEO, 101 E. Morgan St., 27701, P 208,816, (919) 687-0288, (800) 446-8604, Fax (919) 683-9555, visitorinfo@durham-cvb.com, www.durham-nc.com

**Edenton** • *Chowan County Tourism Dev. Auth.* • Nancy Nicholls, Tourism Dir., 116 E. King St., P.O. Box 245, 27932, P 15,500, (252) 482-3400, (800) 775-0111, Fax (252) 482-7093, nancy.nicholls@ncmail.net, www.visitedenton.com

**Elizabeth City** • *Elizabeth City/Pasquotank County Tourism & Dev.* • Charlotte Underwood, Dir. of Tourism, 400 S. Water St., Ste. 101, 27909, P 20,000, (252) 335-5330, (866) 324-8948, Fax (252) 335-1733, info@discoverelizabethcity.com, www.discoverelizabethcity.com.

**Fayetteville** • *Fayetteville Area CVB* • John Meroski, Pres./CEO, 245 Person St., 28301, P 302,000, (910) 483-5311, (800) 255-8217, Fax (910) 484-6632, facvb@visitfayettevillenc.com, www.visitfayettevillenc.com

**Greensboro** • *Greensboro Area CVB* • Henri Fourrier, Pres./CEO, 2200 Pinecrost Rd., 27407, P 235,262, (336) 274-2282, (800) 344-2282, Fax (336) 230-1183, hfourrier@visitgreensboronc.com, www.visitgreensboronc.com

**Greenville** • *Greenville-Pitt County CVB* • Debbie Vargas, Exec. Dir./CEO, 303 S.W. Greenville Blvd., P.O. Box 8027, 27835, P 135,000, (252) 329-4200, (800) 537-5564, Fax (252) 329-4205, info@visitgreenvillenc.com, www.visitgreenvillenc.com

**Hendersonville** • *Henderson County Travel & Tourism* • 201 S. Main St., 28792, P 101,000, (828) 693-9708, (800) 828-4244, tourism@historichendersonville.org, www.historichendersonville.org

**Hickory** • *Hickory Metro CVB* • Bebe Leitzh, Pres., 1960-A 13th Ave. Dr. S.E., 28602, P 325,000, (828) 322-1335, (800) 509-2444, Fax (828) 322-8983, bleitzh@hickorymetro.com, www.hickorymetro.com

**High Point** • *High Point CVB* • Charlotte Young, Pres./CEO, 300 S. Main St., P.O. Box 2273, 27261, P 94,739, (336) 884-5255, (800) 720-5255, Fax (336) 884-4352, HPCVB@HighPoint.org, www.HighPoint.org

**Highlands** • *Highlands Visitor Center* • Jan VanHook, Dir., 269 Oak St., P.O. Box 404, 28741, P 3,000, (828) 526-2112, Fax (828) 526-5803, visitor@highlandschamber.org, www.highlandschamber.org

**Huntersville** • *see Cornelius*

**Jacksonville** • *Onslow County Tourism* • Theresa Carter, Mgr., 1099 Gum Branch Rd., 28540, P 154,000, (910) 455-1113, (800) 932-2144, Fax (910) 347-4705, tcarter@jacksonvilleonline.org, www.onslowcountytourism.com

**Kinston** • *Kinston CVB* • Laura Lee Sylvester, Pres., 301 N. Queen St., P.O. Box 157, 28502, P 60,000, (252) 523-2500, (800) 869-0032, Fax (252) 527-1914, llsylvester@kinstonchamber.com, www.visitkinston.com

**Lake Norman** • *see Cornelius*

**Maggie Valley** • *see Waynesville*

**Mitchell County** • *see Boone*

**Morehead City** • *Crystal Coast Tourism Auth.* • Carol Lohr, Exec. Dir., 3409 Arendell St., 28557, P 69,000, (252) 726-8148, (800) 786-6962, Fax (252) 726-0990, brochure@sunnync.com, www.crystalcoastnc.org

**Morganton** • *Burke County Travel & Tourism Comm.* • Rosemary Niewold, Exec. Dir., 102 E. Union St., Courthouse Sq., 28655, P 89,466, (828) 433-6793, (888) 462-2921, Fax (828) 433-6715, rosemary@discoverburkecounty.org, www.discoverburkecounty.org

**New Bern** • *New Bern/Craven County CVB* • Sandra Chamberlin, Dir., 203 S. Front St., P.O. Box 1713, 28563, P 91,436, (252) 637-9400, (800) 437-5767, Fax (252) 637-0250, info@visitnewbern.com, www.visitnewbern.com

**Pinehurst** • *see Southern Pines*

**Raleigh** • *Greater Raleigh CVB* • Dennis Edwards, Pres./CEO, P.O. Box 1879, 27602, P 785,000, (919) 834-5900, (800) 849-8499, Fax (919) 831-2887, visit@visitraleigh.com, www.visitraleigh.com

**Southern Pines** • *CVB of Pinehurst, Southern Pines, Aberdeen Area* • Caleb Miles, Pres./CEO, 10677 Hwy. 15-501, 28387, P 84,000, (910) 692-3330, (800) 346-5362, Fax (910) 692-2493, cvb4golf@ncrrbiz.com, www.homeofgolf.com

**Sparta** • *Alleghany County Welcome Center* • Bob Bamberg, Exec. Dir., 58 S. Main St., P.O. Box 1237, 28675, P 10,900, (336) 372-5473, (800) 372-5473, Fax (336) 372-8251, info@sparta-nc.com, www.sparta-nc.com

**Spruce Pine** • *Mitchell County Visitor Center* • Patti Jensen, Travel/Tourism Dir., P.O. Box 858, 28777, P 15,900, (828) 765-9483, (800) 227-3912, Fax (828) 765-9034, getinfo@mitchell-county.com, www.mitchell-county.com

**Statesville** • *Statesville CVB* • Libba Barrineau, Exec. Dir., 111 Depot Lane, P.O. Box 1109, 28687, P 25,000, (704) 878-3480, (877) 531-1819, Fax (704) 878-3489, info@visitstatesville.org, www.visitstatesville.org

**Thomasville** • *Thomasville Visitors Center* • Mark Scott, Dir., 44 W. Main St., P.O. Box 1512, 27361, P 25,000, (336) 472-4422, (800) 611-9907, mscott@thomasvilletourism.com, www.thomasvilletourism.com

**Watauga County** • *see Boone*

**Waynesville** • *Haywood County Tourism Dev. Auth.* • Lynn Collins, Exec. Dir., 1233 N. Main St., Ste. 1-40, 28786, P 49,650, (828) 452-0152, (800) 334-9036, Fax (828) 452-0153, hctda@smokeymountains.net, www.smokeymountains.net

**Williamston** • *Martin County Tourism Dev. Auth.* • Sarah Katherine Adams, Exec. Dir., 100 E. Church St., P.O. Box 382, 27892, P 25,500, (252) 792-6605, (800) 776-8566, Fax (252) 792-8710, tourism@visitmartincounty.com, www.visitmartincounty.com

**Wilmington** • *Wilmington/Cape Fear Coast CVB* • Kim Hufham, Pres./CEO, 24 N. 3rd St., 28401, P 184,000, (910) 341-4030, (800) 222-4757, Fax (910) 341-4029, visit@capefearcoast.com, www.capefearcoast.com

**Wilson** • *Wilson Visitors Bur.* • Sandra Homes, 4916 E. Hayes Pl., P.O. Box 2882, 27894, P 75,515, (252) 243-8440, (800) 497-7398, Fax (252) 243-7550, info@wilson-nc.com, www.wilson-nc.com

**Winston-Salem** • *Visit Winston-Salem* • Robert McCoy, Pres., 200 Brookstown Ave., 27101, P 227,727, (336) 728-4200, (866) 728-4200, Fax (336) 721-2202, info@visitwinstonsalem.com, www.visitwinstonsalem.com

# North Dakota

**Beulah** · *Beulah CVB* · Steffanie Boeckel, Exec. Dir., 120 Central Ave., P.O. Box 730, 58523, P 3,200, (701) 873-4585, (800) 441-2649, Fax (701) 873-5361, chamber@westriv.com, www.beulahnd.org

**Bismarck** · *Bismarck-Mandan CVB* · Terry Harzinski, Exec. Dir., 1600 Burnt Boat Dr., 58503, P 72,403, M 221, (701) 222-4308, (800) 767-3555, Fax (701) 222-0647, visitnd@discoverbismarck mandan.com, www.bismarckmandancvb.com

**Bottineau** · *Bottineau CVB* · Clint Reinoehl, Coord., 519 Main St., 58318, P 2,500, (701) 228-3849, (800) 735-6932, Fax (701) 228-5130, bcc@utma.com, www.bottineau.com

**Carrington** · *Carrington CVB* · Susan Stoddard, Pres., 871 Main St., P.O. Box 439, 58421, P 2,300, (701) 652-2524, (800) 641-9668, Fax (701) 652-2391, chambergal@daktel.com, www.carringtonnd.com

**Devils Lake** · *Devils Lake Visitors Bur.* · Susan Johnsrud, Tourism Dir., 208 Hwy. 2 W., P.O. Box 879, 58301, P 8,000, (701) 662-4903, (800) 233-8048, Fax (701) 662-2147, tourism@gondtc.com, www.devilslakend.com

**Dickinson** · *Dickinson CVB* · Terri Thiel, Exec. Dir., 72 E. Museum Dr., 58601, P 17,000, (701) 483-4988, (800) 279-7391, Fax (701) 483-9261, cvb@dickinsoncvb.com, www.visitdickinson.com.

**Fargo** · *Fargo-Moorhead CVB* · Cole Carley, Exec. Dir., 2001 44th St. S., 58103, P 175,000, (701) 282-3653, (800) 235-7654, Fax (701) 282-4366, cole@fargomoorhead.org, www.fargomoorhead.org

**Grand Forks** · *Greater Grand Forks CVB* · Julie Rygg, Exec. Dir., 4251 Gateway Dr., 58203, P 59,000, M 100, (701) 746-0444, (800) 866-4566, Fax (701) 746-0775, info@visitgrandforks.com, www.visitgrandforks.com

**Hettinger** · *Dakota Buttes Visitors Cncl.* · Earleen Friez, Secy., P.O. Box 1031, 58639, P 1,350, (701) 567-2531, Fax (701) 567-2690, adamschmbr@ndsupernet.com, www.hettingernd.com

**Jamestown** · *Buffalo City Tourism* · Nina Sneider, Dir., 404 Louis L'Amour Ln., P.O. Box 917, 58402, P 15,500, (701) 251-9145, (800) 222-4766, guestinfo@tourjamestown.com, www.tour jamestown.com

**Jamestown** · *Jamestown Civic Center/CVB* · Pamela Fosse, Dir., 212 3rd Ave. N.E., 58401, P 15,500, (701) 252-4835, Fax (701) 252-8089, director@jamestownciviccenter.com, www.jamestown civiccenter.com

**Minot** · *Minot CVB* · Wendy Howe, Exec. Dir., 1020 S. Broadway, 58701, P 57,000, M 225, (701) 857-8206, (800) 264-2626, Fax (701) 857-8228, info@visitminot.org, www.visitminot.org.

**Rugby** · *Greater Rugby Area CVB* · Dondi Sobolik, Exec. Dir., 224 Hwy. 2 S.W., 58368, P 3,000, (701) 776-5846, Fax (701) 776-6390, rugbychamber@gondtc.com, www.rugbynorthdakota.com

**Williston** · *Williston CVB* · Amy Krueger, Exec. Dir., 212 Airport Rd., 58801, P 15,000, (701) 774-9041, (800) 615-9041, Fax (701) 774-0411, cvbsales@ci.williston.nd.us, www.visitwilliston.com

# Ohio

**Akron** · *Akron/Summit CVB* · Susan Hamo, Pres., 77 E. Mill St., 44308, P 515,000, (330) 374-7560, (800) 245-4254, Fax (330) 374-7626, information@visitakron-summit.org, www.visit akron-summit.org

**Amherst** · *Lorain County Visitors Bur.* · Barb Bickel, Exec. Dir., 8025 Leavitt Rd., 44001, P 285,000, (440) 984-5282, (800) 334-1673, Fax (440) 984-7363, visitors@visitloraincounty.com, www.visitloraincounty.com

**Ashland** · *Ashland Area CVB* · Amy Daubenspeck, Exec. Dir., 10 W. 2nd St., 2nd Flr., 44805, P 52,000, (419) 281-4584, (877) 581-2345, Fax (419) 281-4585, cvb@ashlandoh.com, www.ashlandohio.com

**Austinburg** · *Ashtabula County CVB* · Mark Winchell, Exec. Dir., 1850 Austinburg Rd., 44010, P 104,000, M 420, (440) 275-3202, (800) 337-6746, Fax (440) 275-3210, visitus@visitashtabula county.com, www.visitashtabulacounty.com

**Batavia** · *Clermont County CVB* · June Creager, Exec. Dir., 410 E. Main St., P.O. Box 100, 45103, P 200,000, (513) 732-3600, (800) 796-4282, Fax (513) 732-2244, info@visitclermontohio.com, www.visitclermontohio.com

**Beavercreek** · *Greene County CVB* · Kathleen Young, Exec. Dir., 1221 Meadowbridge Dr., Ste. A, 45434, P 140,000, (937) 429-9100, (800) 733-9109, Fax (937) 429-7726, kyoung@greenecountyohio.org, www.greenecountyohio.org

**Bellefontaine** · *Logan County CVB* · Ed Wallace, Pres./CEO, 100 S. Main St., 43311, P 46,000, (937) 599-5121, Fax (937) 599-2411, (888) LOGAN CO, info@logancountyohio.com, www.logancounty ohio.com

**Bowling Green** · *Bowling Green CVB* · Wendy Stram, Exec. Dir., 119 E. Court St., 43402, P 29,636, (419) 353-9445, (800) 866-0046, Fax (419) 353-9446, info@visitbgohio.org, www.visitbgohio.org

**Cambridge** · *Cambridge/Guernsey County VCB* · Debbie Robinson, Exec. Dir., 627 Wheeling Ave., Ste. 200, 43725, P 40,792, (740) 432-2022, (800) 933-5480, Fax (740) 432-5976, info@ VisitGuernseyCounty.com, www.VisitGuernseyCounty.com

**Canton** · *Canton/Stark County CVB* · John Kiste, Dir., 222 Market Ave. N., 44702, P 379,000, (330) 454-1439, (800) 533-4302, Fax (330) 456-3600, johnk@cantonstarkcvb.com, www.cantonstarkcvb.com

**Chillicothe** · *Ross-Chillicothe CVB* · Kyrsten Vogel, Exec. Dir., 45 E. Main St., P.O. Box 353, 45601, P 75,000, (740) 702-7677, (800) 413-4118, Fax (740) 702-2727, kyrsten@visitchillicotheohio.com, www.visitchillicotheohio.com

**Cincinnati** · *Cincinnati USA CVB* · Dan Lincoln, Pres./CEO, 525 Vine St., Ste. 1500, 45202, P 1,900,000, (513) 621-2142, (800) 543-2613, Fax (513) 621-5020, dlincoln@cincyusa.com, www.cincyusa.com

**Circleville** · *Pickaway County Visitors Bur.* · Charlie Jackson, Exec. Dir., 325 W. Main St., 43113, P 52,000, (740) 474-3636, Fax (740) 477-6800, (888) 770-PICK, cjackson@pickaway.com, www.pickaway.com

**Cleveland** · *Positively Cleveland CVB* · Dennis Roche, Pres., 100 Public Sq., Ste. 100, 44113, P 1,866,519, M 700, (216) 621-4110, (800) 321-1001, Fax (216) 621-5967, cvb@positivelycleveland.com, www.positivelycleveland.com

**Columbus** · *Experience Columbus* · Paul Astleford, Pres./CEO, 277 W. Nationwide Blvd., Ste. 125, 43215, P 1,600,000, M 909, (614) 221-6623, (800) 354-2657, Fax (614) 221-5618, www.experiencecolumbus.com

**Coshocton** · *Coshocton County CVB* · Belinda Williamson, Dir., 401 Main St., P.O. Box 905, 43812, P 36,131, (740) 622-4877, (800) 338-4724, Fax (740) 622-9902, coshcvb@coshocton.com, www.visitcoshocton.com

**Dayton** • *Dayton/Montgomery County CVB* • Jacquelyn Powell, Pres./CEO, 1 Chamber Plaza, Ste. A, 45402, P 780,000, (937) 226-8211, (800) 221-8235, Fax (937) 226-8294, jypowell@daytoncvb.net, www.daytoncvb.com

**Delaware** • *Delaware County CVB* • Debbie Shatzer, Exec. Dir., 44 E. Winter St., 43015, P 156,000, (740) 368-4748, Fax (740) 369-9277, (888) DEL OHIO, info@visitdelohio.com, www.visitdelohio.com

**Findlay** • *Hancock County CVB* • Angela Crist, Exec. Dir./V.P., 123 E. Main Cross St., 45840, P 72,000, (419) 422-3315, (800) 424-3315, Fax (419) 422-9508, info@visitfindlay.com, www.visitfindlay.com

**Fremont** • *Fremont/Sandusky County CVB* • Connie Durdel, Exec. Dir., 712 North St., Ste. 102, 43420, P 62,000, (419) 332-4470, (800) 255-8070, Fax (419) 332-4359, info@sanduskycounty.org, www.sanduskycounty.org

**Hamilton** • *Greater Hamilton CVB* • One High St., 45011, P 61,000, (513) 844-8080, (800) 311-5353, Fax (513) 844-8090, hamiltonohcvb@fuse.net, www.hamilton-cvb.com

**Heath** • *Greater Licking County CVB* • Susan Fryer, Exec. Dir., 455 Hebron Rd., 43056, P 135,800, (740) 345-8224, (800) 589-8224, Fax (740) 345-4403, sfryer@lccvb.com, www.lccvb.com

**Hillsboro** • *Highland County CVB* • Sara Lukens, Dir., 1575 N. High St., Ste 400, P.O. Box 638, 45133, P 41,000, (937) 393-4883, Fax (937) 393-2697, highland.county@dragonbbs.com, www.highlandcounty.com

**Lima** • *Lima/Allen County CVB* • Christine Pleva, Exec. Dir., 144 S. Main St., Ste. 101, 45801, P 110,000, (419) 222-6075, (888) 222-6075, Fax (419) 222-0134, info@lima-allencvb.com, www.lima-allencvb.com

**Mansfield** • *Mansfield/Richland County CVB* • Lee Tasseff, Pres., 124 N. Main St., 44902, P 120,000, (419) 525-1300, (800) 642-8282, Fax (419) 524-7722, visitors@mansfieldtourism.com, www.mansfieldtourism.com

**Marietta** • *Marietta/Washington County CVB* • 121 Putnam St., Ste. 110, 45750, P 62,254, (740) 373-5178, (800) 288-2577, Fax (740) 376-2911, info@mariettaohio.org, www.mariettaohio.org

**Marion** • *Marion Area CVB* • Diane Watson, Exec. Dir., 1713 Marion Mount Gilead Rd., Ste. 110, 43302, P 65,000, (740) 389-9770, (800) 371-6688, Fax (740) 725-9295, info@visitmarionohio.com, www.visitmarionohio.com

**Marysville** • *Union County CVB* • Christy Clark, Dir., 227 E. Fifth St., 43040, P 40,909, (937) 642-6279, (800) 642-0087, Fax (937) 644-0422, cvb@unioncounty.org, www.unioncounty.org

**McConnelsville** • *Morgan County Visitor Center* • 155 E. Main St., P.O. Box 508, 43756, P 14,000, (740) 962-3200, Fax (740) 962-3516, www.morgancounty.org

**Medina** • *Medina County CVB* • Daniel D. Hostetler III, Exec. Dir., 32 Public Sq., P.O. Box 486, 44256, P 151,000, M 220, (330) 722-5502, (800) 860-2943, Fax (330) 723-4713, info@visitmedinacounty.com, www.visitmedinacounty.com

**Mount Vernon** • *Knox County CVB* • Mr. Pat Crow, Dir., 107 S. Main St., 43050, P 55,000, (740) 392-6102, (800) 837-5282, Fax (740) 392-7840, info@visitknoxohio.org, www.VisitKnoxOhio.org

**North Ridgeville** • *North Ridgeville Visitors Bur.* • Ms. Dayle Noll, Pres./CEO, 34845 Lorain Rd., 44039, P 26,000, (440) 327-3737, Fax (440) 327-1474, nrvisbur@nrchamber.com, www.nrchamber.com

**Pomeroy** • *Meigs County Tourism* • Michelle Donovan, Exec. Dir., 238 W. Main St., 45769, P 25,000, (740) 992-2239, Fax (740) 992-7942, (877) MEIGS CO, director@meigscountytourism.com, www.meigscountytourism.com

**Port Clinton** • *Lake Erie Shores & Islands West* • Larry Fletcher, Exec. Dir., 770 S.E. Catawba Rd., 43452, P 40,000, (419) 734-4386, (800) 441-1271, Fax (419) 734-9798, tourism@lake-erie.com, www.shoresandislands.com

**Saint Marys** • *Auglaize & Mercer Counties CVB* • Donna Grube, Exec. Dir., 900 Edgewater Dr., 45885, P 85,000, M 450, (419) 394-1294, (800) 860-4726, Fax (419) 394-1642, seemore@bright.net, www.seemore.org

**Sandusky** • *Lake Erie Shores and Islands* • Joan VanOfferen, Exec. Dir., 4424 Milan, Ste. A, 44870, P 79,000, (419) 625-2984, (800) 255-3743, Fax (419) 625-5009, www.shoresandislands.com

**South Point** • *Greater Lawrence County Area CVB* • Viviane Vallance, Dir., 216 Collins Ave., P.O. Box 488, 45680, P 64,000, (740) 377-4550, (800) 408-1334, Fax (740) 377-2091, vkvallance@zoominternet.net, www.lawrencecountyohio.org

**Springfield** • *Springfield-Clark County CVB* • Kathy McPommell, V.P., 20 S. Limestone St., Ste. 100, 45502, P 168,000, (937) 325-7621, (800) 803-1553, Fax (937) 325-8765, kmcpommell@greaterspringfield.com, www.greaterspringfield.com.

**Tiffin** • *Seneca County CVB* • Malinda Ruble, Dir., 114 S. Washington St., 44883, P 63,000, M 110, (419) 447-5866, Fax (419) 447-6628, (888) SENECA 1, visitor@senecacounty.com, www.senecacounty.com/visitor

**Toledo** • *Greater Toledo CVB* • Steve Miller, Gen. Mgr., 401 Jefferson Ave., 43604, P 300,000, (419) 321-6404, (800) 243-4667, Fax (419) 255-7731, www.dotoledo.org

**Upper Sandusky** • *Wyandot County VCB* • Sara Lou Brown, Exec. Dir., 108 E. Wyandot Ave., Ste. 2, P.O. Box 357, 43351, P 22,000, M 40, (419) 294-3556, (877) 992-6368, Fax (419) 294-3556, wyandotcovb@udata.com, www.visitwyandotcounty.com

**Van Wert** • *Van Wert County CVB* • Larry Lee, Exec. Dir., 136 E. Main St., 45891, P 30,000, (419) 238-9378, (877) 989-2282, Fax (419) 238-4589, info@visitvanwert.org, www.visitvanwert.org

**Washington Court House** • *Fayette County Travel & Tourism* • Roger Blackburn, Exec. Dir., 101 E. East St., 43160, P 32,000, (740) 335-8008, (800) 479-7797, Fax (740) 335-0762, fayettechamber@yahoo.com, www.fayettecountyohio.com

**Waverly** • *Pike County CVB* • Sharon Manson, Exec. Dir., 12455 St., Rte. 104, P.O. Box 134, 45690, P 27,695, (740) 947-9650, Fax (740) 947-7716, piketravel@yahoo.com, www.piketravel.com

**West Union** • *Adams County Travel & Visitors Bur.* • Tom Cross, Exec. Dir., 110 N. Manchester St., 45693, P 27,000, M 52, (937) 544-5454, (877) 232-6764, Fax (937) 544-6957, info@adamscountytravel.org, www.adamscountytravel.org

**Wooster** • *Wayne County CVB* • Martha Starkey, Dir., 428 W. Liberty St., 44691, P 111,564, (330) 264-1800, (800) 362-6474, Fax (330) 264-1141, waynecvb@cs.com, www.waynecountycvb.org

**Zanesville** • *Zanesville-Muskingum CVB* • Tom Poorman, Dir., 205 N. Fifth St., 43701, P 82,000, (740) 455-8282, (800) 743-2303, Fax (740) 454-2963, kashby@zmchamber.com, www.visitzanesville.com

# Oklahoma

**Ardmore** • *Ardmore Tourism Auth.* • Mita Bates, V.P., 410 W. Main, 73401, P 35,000, (580) 223-7765, Fax (580) 223-7825, www.ardmore.org.

**Bartlesville** · *Bartlesville Area CVB* · Maria Swindell Gus, Exec. Dir., 201 S.W. Keeler Ave., P.O. Box 2366, 74005, P 35,000, (918) 336-8708, (800) 364-8708, Fax (918) 337-0216, msgus@bartlesville.com, www.visitbartlesville.com

**Claremore** · *Claremore CVB* · Tanya Andrews, Exec. Dir., 419 W. Will Rogers Blvd., 74017, P 17,500, (918) 341-8688, (877) 341-8688, Fax (918) 342-0663, cvb@claremore.org, www.visitclaremore.org

**Duncan** · *Duncan CVB* · Lois Dawn Jones, Dir., 800 Chisholm Trail Pkwy., P.O. Box 981, 73534, P 25,000, (800) 782-7167, Fax (580) 252-3799, tourism@texhoma.net, www.duncanok.com

**Edmond** · *Edmond CVB* · Cathy Williams-White, Dir., P.O. Box 2970, 73083, P 83,000, (405) 341-4344, Fax (405) 216-7783, cwwhite@visitedmondok.com, www.visitedmondok.com

**El Reno** · *El Reno CVB* · Gene Stroman, Dir., 110 E. Woodson, 73036, P 16,212, (405) 262-8687, (888) 535-7366, Fax (405) 262-4637, info@elreno.org, www.elreno.org

**Guthrie** · *Guthrie CVB* · Mary Coffin, Pres./CEO, 212 W. Oklahoma Ave., P.O. Box 995, 73044, P 10,500, (405) 282-1948, (800) 299-1889, Fax (405) 282-0061, info@guthrieok.com, www.guthrieok.com

**Guymon** · *Guymon Conv. & Tourism Dept.* · Vicki Ayres-McCune, Dir., 802 N.E. 6th St., 73942, P 14,000, (580) 338-5838, Fax (580) 338-1854, cddirector@guymonok.org, www.guymonok.org

**McAlester** · *City of McAlester Tourism Dept.* · Jerry Lynn Wilson, Dir., P.O. Box 578, 74502, P 20,000, (918) 420-3976, Fax (918) 426-0207, tourism@cityofmcalester.com, www.cityofmcalester.com

**Miami** · *Miami CVB* · Amanda Davis, Prog. Exec., 111 N. Main, P.O. Box 760, 74355, P 13,704, (918) 542-4435, Fax (918) 540-1260, info@visitmiamiok.com, www.visitmiamiok.com

**Muskogee** · *Greater Muskogee Area Tourism* · Treasure McKenzie, Tourism Dir., 310 W. Broadway, P.O. Box 797, 74402, P 39,000, (918) 682-2401, (866) 381-6543, Fax (918) 682-2403, tourism@muskogeechamber.org, www.muskogeechamber.org

**Norman** · *Norman CVB* · Stephen Koranda, Exec. Dir., 223 E. Main, 73069, P 107,000, (405) 366-8095, (800) 767-7260, Fax (405) 366-8096, stephen@visitnorman.com, www.visitnorman.com.

**Oklahoma City** · *Oklahoma City CVB* · Mike Carrier, Pres., Div of Greater OKC C/C, 189 W. Sheridan Ave., 73102, P 1,144,400, (405) 297-8912, (800) 225-5652, Fax (405) 297-8888, okccvb@okccvb.org, www.visitokc.com

**Okmulgee** · *Okmulgee Tourism Prog.* · Nolan Crowley, Dir., 112 N. Morton, 74447, P 13,000, (918) 758-1015, Fax (918) 756-6441, okmulgeemainstreet@sbcglobal.net, www.okmulgeeonline.com

**Ponca City** · *Ponca City Tourism Bur.* · Mary Beth Moore, Coord., 420 E. Grand Ave., P.O. Box 1109, 74602, P 26,000, (580) 763-8092, (866) 763-8092, Fax (580) 765-2798, info@poncacitytourism.com, www.poncacitytourism.com

**Shawnee** · *Greater Shawnee Area CVB* · Gordona Rowell, Dir., 131 N. Bell, 74801, P 29,700, (405) 275-9780, (888) 404-9633, Fax (405) 275-9851, info@visitshawnee.com, www.visitshawnee.com

**Stillwater** · *Stillwater CVB* · Cristy Morrison, Exec. Dir., 409 S. Main, P.O. Box 1687, 74076, P 46,383, (405) 743-3697, (800) 991-6717, Fax (405) 372-0765, cristy@visitstillwater.org, www.visitstillwater.org.

**Tahlequah** · *Tahlequah Area C/C Tourism Cncl.* · Kate Kelly, Tourism Dir., 123 E. Delaware St., 74464, P 46,000, M 520, (918) 456-3742, (800) 456-4860, Fax (918) 456-3751, tour@tour tahlequah.com, www.tourtahlequah.com

**Tishomingo** · *Chickasaw Nation CVB* · P.O. Box 363, 73460, (580) 371-2040, (800) 593-3356, Fax (580) 371-9584, www.chickasaw.net

**Tulsa** · *Tulsa CVB* · Suzann Stewart, Sr. V.P., Williams Center Tower II, Two W. Second St. #150, 74103, P 916,079, (918) 585-1201, Fax (918) 592-6244, www.visittulsa.com

# Oregon

**Albany** · *Albany Visitors Assn.* · Jimmie Lucht, Exec. Dir., 250 Broadalbin St. S.W., Ste. 110, P.O. Box 965, 97321, P 43,700, (541) 928-0911, (800) 526-2256, Fax (541) 926-1500, info@albanyvisitors.com, www.albanyvisitors.com.

**Ashland** · *Ashland CVB* · Sandra Slattery, Exec. Dir., 110 E. Main St., P.O. Box 1360, 97520, P 21,000, (541) 482-3486, Fax (541) 482-2350, www.ashlandchamber.com.

**Aurora** · *Aurora Colony Visitors Assn.* · Barbara Johnson, P.O. Box 86, 97002, P 750, M 40, (503) 939-0312, info@auroracolony.com, www.auroracolony.com

**Beaverton** · *Washington County Visitors Assn.* · 11000 S.W. Stratus St., Ste. 170, 97008, P 500,000, M (503) 644-5555, (800) 537-3149, Fax (503) 644-9784, info@wcva.org, www.wcva.org

**Bend** · *Visit Bend* · Laurel Brauns, Welcome Center Mgr., 917 N.W. Harriman St., 97701, P 82,000, (541) 382-8048, (800) 949-6086, Fax (541) 382-8568, info@visitbend.com, www.visitbend.com

**Charleston** · *Charleston Visitor Center* · 91141 Cape Arago Hwy., P.O. Box 5735, 97420, P 5,000, M 40, (541) 888-2311, (541) 888-4875, www.charlestonoregon-merchants.com

**Corvallis** · *Corvallis Tourism* · John Hope-Johnstone, Exec. Dir., 553 N.W. Harrison Blvd., 97330, P 53,200, (541) 757-1544, (800) 334-8118, Fax (541) 753-2664, ccvb@visitcorvallis.com, www.visitcorvallis.com

**Eugene** · *Lane County Oregon Conv. & Visitors Assn.* · Kari Westlund, Pres./CEO, 754 Olive St., P.O. Box 10286, 97440, P 339,740, M 575, (541) 484-5307, (800) 547-5445, Fax (541) 343-6335, info@travellanecounty.org, www.travellanecounty.org

**Gold Beach** · *Gold Beach Visitors Center* · Elizabeth Kuljis, Dir., 94080 Shirley Ln., 97444, P 2,200, (541) 247-7526, (800) 525-2334, Fax (541) 247-0187, visit@goldbeach.org, www.goldbeach.org

**Grants Pass** · *Grants Pass VCB* · Kerrie Walters, Mktg. Coord., 1995 N.W. Vine St., 97526, P 75,500, (541) 476-5510, Fax (541) 476-9574, vcb@visitgrantspass.org, www.visitgrantspass.org

**Klamath Falls** · *Discover Klamath* · Todd Kepple, Exec. Dir., 125 W. Main St., 97601, P 45,000, (541) 882-1501, (800) 445-6728, Fax (541) 884-0219, www.discoverklamath.com

**La Grande** · *Union County Tourism* · Janet Dodson, Exec. Dir., 102 Elm St., 97850, P 25,500, (541) 963-8588, (800) 848-9969, Fax (541) 963-3936, visitlg@eoni.com, www.visitlagrande.com

**Lincoln City** · *Lincoln City Visitor & Conv. Bur.* · Sandy Pfass, Exec. Dir., 801 S.W. Hwy. 101, Ste. 104, 97367, P 7,500, (541) 996-1274, (800) 452-2151, Fax (541) 994-2408, events@lincolncity.org, www.oregoncoast.org

**Medford** · *Medford VCB* · Anne Jenkins, Sr. V.P., 101 E. 8th St., 97501, P 202,310, (541) 779-4847, (800) 469-6307, Fax (541) 776-4808, www.medfordchamber.com, vcb@visitmedford.org, www.visitmedford.org.

**North Bend** · *North Bend Visitor Info. Center* · Barbara Dunham, Mgr., 1380 Sherman Ave. (Hwy. 101), 97459, P 10,000, (541) 756-4613, (800) 472-9176, Fax (541) 756-8527, nbinfo@uci.net, www.northbendcity.org

**Ontario** · *Ontario Visitors & Conv. Bur.* · John Breidenbach, Exec. Dir., 676 S.W. 4th Ave., 97914, P 12,000, (541) 889-8012, (866) 989-8012, Fax (541) 889-8331, ontvcb@fmtc.com, www.ontariochamber.com

**Portland** · *African American Conv. & Tourism-A.C.T.* · Roy Jay, Natl. Pres./CEO, 4300 N.E. Fremont, Ste. 220, P.O. Box 5488, 97228, M 2,310, (503) 229-2326, (800) 909-2882, Fax (503) 698-2896, ACT.NOW@USA.NET, www.blackconventions.com

**Portland** · *Oregon Conv. & Visitor Svcs. Network* · Roy Jay, Pres./CEO, P.O. Box 5488, 97228, P 1,000,000, M 1,000, (503) 244-5794, Fax (503) 293-2094, www.oregoncvb.com

**Portland** · *Travel Portland* · Jeff Miller, Pres./CEO, 1000 S.W. Broadway, Ste. 2300, 97205, P 1,950,000, M 1,100, (503) 275-9750, (800) 962-3700, Fax (503) 275-9774, info@travelportland.com, www.travelportland.com

**Roseburg** · *Roseburg Visitors & Conv. Bur.* · Jean Kurtz, Dir., 410 S.E. Spruce, P.O. Box 1262, 97470, P 21,000, (541) 672-9731, (800) 444-9584, Fax (541) 673-7868, info@visitroseburg.com, www.visitroseburg.com

**Salem** · *Travel Salem* · Angie Morris, CEO, 181 High St., 97301, P 147,000, (503) 581-4325, (800) 874-7012, Fax (503) 581-4540, information@travelsalem.com, www.travelsalem.com

**Seaside** · *Seaside Civic & Conv. Center* · Russell Vandenberg, Gen. Mgr., 415 First Ave., 97138, P 7,000, (503) 738-8585, (800) 394-3303, Fax (503) 738-0198, sales@seasideconvention.com, www.seasideconvention.com

**Seaside** · *Seaside Visitors Bur.* · Mikaela Norval, Dir. of Tourism, 989 Broadway, 97138, P 6,500, (503) 738-3097, (888) 306-2326, Fax (503) 717-8299, visit@seaside-oregon.com, www.seasideor.com

**Winston** · *Winston-Dillard Area Visitors Bur.* · Bernice McClellan, Coord., 30 N.W. Glenhart, P.O. Box 68, 97496, P 10,000, M 125, (541) 679-0118, Fax (541) 679-4270, winstonvic@charter.net, www.winstonoregon.net

# Pennsylvania

**Altoona** · *Allegheny Mountains CVB* · Cheryl Ebersole, Exec. Dir., One Convention Center Dr., 16602, P 54,000, (814) 943-4183, Fax (814) 943-8094, (800) 84-ALTOONA, info@amcvb.com, www.alleghenymountains.com

**Beaver Falls** · *Beaver County Rec. & Tourism Dept.* · Tom King, Dir., Recreation Facility, 121 Bradys Run Rd., 15010, P 186,000, M 110, (724) 891-7030, (800) 342-8192, Fax (724) 891-7085, bctpa@beavercountypa.gov, www.visitbeavercounty.com

**Bedford** · *Bedford County Visitors Bur.* · Dennis Tice, Exec. Dir., 131 S. Juliana St., 15522, P 49,000, M 130, (814) 623-1771, (800) 765-3331, Fax (814) 623-1671, bccvb@bedford.net, www.bedfordcounty.net

**Ben Salem** · *Bucks County Conf. & Visitors Bur.* · Jerry Lepping, Exec. Dir., 3207 Street Rd., 19020, P 600,000, M 500, (215) 639-0300, (800) 836-2825, Fax (215) 642-3277, info@buckscounty.travel, www.buckscounty.travel

**Bloomsburg** · *Columbia-Montour Visitors Bur.* · David Kurecian, Exec. Dir., 121 Papermill Rd., 17815, P 65,000, M 201, (570) 784-8279, (800) 847-4810, Fax (570) 784-1166, itour@cmvb.com, www.itourcolumbiamontour.com

**Bradford** · *Allegheny Natl. Forest Vacation Bur.* · Linda Devlin, Exec. Dir., 80 E. Corydon St., P.O. Box 371, 16701, P 46,500, (800) 473-9370, Fax (814) 368-9370, info@visitanf.com, www.visitanf.com

**Brookville** · *Northwest Penn. Great Outdoors Visitors Bur.* · David Morris, Exec. Dir., 175 Main St., 15825, P 500,000, (814) 849-5197, (800) 348-9393, Fax (814) 849-1969, info@visitpago.com, www.visitpago.com

**Carlisle** · *see Harrisburg*

**Chadds Ford** · *Brandywine Conf. & Visitors Bur.* · Tore Fiore, Exec. Dir., One Beaver Valley Rd., 19317, P 553,000, (610) 565-3679, (800) 343-3983, Fax (610) 361-0459, tfiore@brandywinecvb.org, www.brandywinecountry.org

**Coudersport** · *Potter County Visitors Assn.* · David Brooks, Exec. Dir., P.O. Box 245, 16915, P 18,000, (814) 274-3365, Fax (814) 274-4334, (888) POTTER-2, potter@penn.com, www.visitpottercounty.com

**Danville** · *Columbia-Montour Visitors Bur.* · David Kurecian, Exec. Dir., 316 Mill St., 17821, P 65,000, M 201, (570) 275-8185, Fax (570) 275-1662, itour@cmvb.com, www.itourcolumbiamontour.com

**Erie** · *Visit Erie* · John Oliver, Pres., 208 E. Bayfront Pkwy., Ste. 103, 16507, P 200,000, (814) 454-1000, Fax (814) 459-0241, (800) 524-ERIE, info@visiterie.com, www.visiterie.com

**Gettysburg** · *Gettysburg CVB* · Norris Flowers, Pres., P.O. Box 4117, 17325, P 91,292, M 210, (717) 334-6274, Fax (717) 334-1166, info@gettysburg.travel, www.gettysburg.travel

**Harrisburg** · *Hershey-Harrisburg Reg. Visitors Bur.* · Mary Smith, Pres., 17 S. 2nd St,, 17101, (717) 231-7788, (877) 727-8573, Fax (717) 231-2808, info@hersheyharrisburg.org, www.hersheyharrisburg.org

**Hershey** · *see Harrisburg*

**Hesston** · *Raystown Lake Reg. Visitors Bur.* · Matthew Price, Exec. Dir., RD 1 Box 222A, Seven Points Rd., 16647, P 44,000, M 250, (814) 658-0060, Fax (814) 658-0068, (888) RAYSTOWN, info@raystown.org, www.raystown.org

**Indiana** · *Indiana County Tourist Bur.* · Penny Perman, Exec. Dir., 2334 Oakland Ave., 15701, P 90,000, M 200, (724) 463-7505, (877) 746-3426, Fax (724) 465-3819, info@visitindianacountypa.org, www.visitindianacountypa.org

**Johnstown** · *Greater Johnstown/Cambria County CVB* · Lisa Dailey, Dir., 416 Main St., Ste. 100, 15901, P 150,452, M 275, (814) 536-7993, (800) 237-8590, Fax (814) 539-3370, jstcvb@visitjohnstownpa.com, www.visitjohnstownpa.com

**King of Prussia** · *Valley Forge CVB* · Paul Decker, Pres., 1000 1st Ave., Ste. 101, 19406, P 140,000, (610) 834-1550, (800) 441-3549, Fax (610) 834-0202, info@valleyforge.org, www.valleyforge.org

**Kittanning** · *Armstrong County Tourist Bur.* · Jessica Coil, Tourism Dir., 125 Market St., 16201, P 72,392, M 175, (724) 543-4003, (888) 265-9954, Fax (724) 545-3119, touristbur@co.armstrong.pa.us, www.armstrongcounty.com

**Lancaster** · *Pennsylvania Dutch CVB* · Christopher Barrett, Pres., 501 Greenfield Rd., 17601, P 460,000, M 630, (717) 299-8901, Fax (717) 299-0470, (800) PA DUTCH, info@padutchcountry.com, www.padutchcountry.com

**Lehigh Valley** · *Lehigh Valley CVB* · Michael Stershic, Pres., P.O. Box 20785, 18002, P 600,000, M 490, (610) 882-9200, Fax (610) 882-0343, geninfo@lehighvalleypa.org, www.lehighvalleypa.org

**Lewisburg** · *Susquehanna Valley Visitors Bur.* · Andrew Miller, Exec. Dir., 81 Hafer Rd., 17837, P 37,000, M 250, (570) 524-7234, (800) 525-7320, Fax (570) 524-7282, info@visitcentralpa.org, www.visitcentralpa.org

**Lewistown** • *Juniata River Valley Visitors Bur.* • Jim Tunall, Exec. Dir., Historic Courthouse, One W. Market St., Ste. 103, 17044, P 68,463, (717) 248-6713, (877) 568-9739, Fax (717) 248-6714, jrvvb@juniatarivervalley.org, www.juniatarivervalley.org

**Ligonier** • *Laurel Highlands Visitors Bur.* • Annie Urban, Exec. Dir., 120 E. Main St., Town Hall, 15658, P 856,693, M 511, (724) 238-5661, (800) 333-5661, Fax (724) 238-3673, aurban@laurel highlands.org, www.laurelhighlands.org

**Lock Haven** • *Clinton County Eco. Partnership* • Peter Lopes, Chamber/Tourism Dir., 212 N. Jay St., P.O. Box 506, 17745, P 37,914, M 385, (570) 748-5782, (888) 388-6991, Fax (570) 893-0433, tourism@kcnet.org, www.clintoncountyinfo.com

**Mayfield** • *Lackawanna County CVB* • Tracy Barone, Exec. Dir., 1300 Old Plank Rd., 18433, P 219,000, M 206, (570) 963-6363, Fax (570) 963-6852, (800) 22-WELCOME, info@visitnepa.org, www.visitnepa.org

**Meadville** • *Crawford County CVB* • Juanita Hampton, Exec. Dir., 16709 Conneaut Lake Rd., 16335, P 90,360, (814) 333-1258, (800) 332-2338, Fax (814) 333-9032, welcome@visitcrawford.org, www.visitcrawford.org

**Monroeville** • *CVB of Monroeville, PA* • Sandy Rice, Exec. Dir., #612 Parkvale Bldg., 4220 William Penn Hwy., 15146, P 35,000, (412) 856-7422, (800) 527-8941, Fax (412) 856-6979, sandy@ visitmonroeville.com, www.visitmonroeville.com

**New Castle** • *Lawrence County Tourist Promo. Agency* • JoAnn McBride, Exec. Dir., 229 S. Jefferson St., 16101, P 95,000, M 170, (724) 654-8408, (888) 284-7599, Fax (724) 654-2044, info@ visitlawrencecounty.com, www.visitlawrencecounty.com

**Philadelphia** • *Philadelphia CVB* • Thomas O. Muldoon, Pres., 1700 Market St., Ste. 3000, 19103, (215) 636-3300, Fax (215) 636-3327, info@philadelphiausa.travel, www.philadelphiausa.travel

**Pittsburgh** • *VisitPittsburgh* • Joseph McGrath, Pres./CEO, 425 Sixth Ave., 30th Flr., 15219, P 2,390,000, M 800, (412) 281-0482, (800) 359-0758, Fax (412) 644-5512, info@visitpittsburgh.com, www.visitpittsburgh.com

**Plymouth Meeting** • *see Valley Forge*

**Pottsville** • *Schuylkill County Visitors Bur.* • Mark T. Major, Exec. Dir., 200 E. Arch St., 17901, P 150,000, M 184, (570) 622-7700, (800) 765-7282, Fax (570) 622-8035, tourism@schuylkill. org, www.schuylkill.org

**Reading** • *Greater Reading CVB* • Crystal Seitz, Pres., 201 Washington St., 19602, P 370,000, (610) 375-4085, (800) 443-6610, Fax (610) 375-9606, info@readingberkspa.com, www.readingberkspa.com

**Sharon** • *Mercer County CVB* • Peggy Mazyck, Exec. Dir., 50 N. Water Ave., 16146, P 122,000, M 175, (724) 346-3771, (800) 637-2370, Fax (724) 346-0575, mccvb@mercercountypa.org, www. mercercountypa.org

**State College** • *Central PA CVB* • Betsey Howell, Exec. Dir., 800 E. Park Ave., 16803, P 138,000, M 415, (814) 231-1400, (800) 358-5466, Fax (814) 231-8123, info@centralpacvb.org, www. centralpacvb.org

**Stroudsburg** • *Pocono Mountains Vacation Bur.* • Carl Wilgus, Exec. Dir., 1004 Main St., 18360, P 172,000, M 500, (570) 421-5791, Fax (570) 421-6927, (800) POCONOS, pocomts@poconos.org, www.800poconos.com

**Tunkhannock** • *Endless Mountains Visitors Bur.* • Jean Gasper, Exec. Dir., 4 Werks Plz., 18657, P 145,091, M 250, (570) 836-5431, (800) 769-8999, Fax (570) 836-3927, emvb@epix.net, www. endlessmountains.org

**Warren** • *Warren County Visitors Bur.* • Mike Olewine, Exec. Dir., 22045 Rte. 6, 16365, P 43,876, M 125, (814) 726-1222, (800) 624-7802, Fax (814) 726-7266, info@wcvb.net, www.wcvb.net

**Washington** • *Washington County Tourism Promo. Agency* • J.R. Shaw, Exec. Dir., 273 S. Main St, 15301, P 204,584, M 130, (724) 228-5520, Fax (724) 228-5514, (866) WASH WOW, info@washwow.com, www.visitwashingtoncountypa.com

**Waynesburg** • *Greene County Tourist Promo. Agency* • Jeanie Patton, Exec. Dir., 417 E. Roy Furman Hwy., 15370, P 41,000, M 250, (724) 627-8687, Fax (724) 627-8608, (724) 627-TOUR, tourism@co.greene.pa.us, www.greenecountytourism.org

**Wellsboro** • *Tioga County Visitors Bur.* • Sandra L. Spencer, Exec. Dir., 114 Main St., 16901, P 40,000, (570) 724-0635, Fax (570) 723-1016, (888) TIOGA-28, sspencer@epix.net, www.visit tiogapa.com

**West Chester** • *Chester County Conf. & Visitors Bur.* • Blair Mahoney, Exec. Dir., 17 Wilmont Mews, Ste. 400, 19382, P 475,000, M 460, (610) 719-1730, (800) 566-0109, Fax (610) 719-1736, www.brandywinevalley.com

**Williamsport** • *Lycoming County Visitors Bur.* • Jason Fink, Dir., 210 William St., 17701, P 121,000, (570) 327-7700, (800) 358-9900, Fax (570) 327-7900, visitorinfo@williamsport.org, www. vacationpa.com

**York** • *York County CVB* • Anne Druck, Pres., 155 W. Market St., 17401, P 382,000, (717) 852-9675, (888) 858-9675, Fax (717) 854-5095, info@yorkpa.org, www.yorkpa.org

**Zelienople** • *Butler County Tourism & Conv. Bur.* • Jack Cohen, Exec. Dir., 310 E. Grandview Ave., 16063, P 182,000, (724) 234-4619, (866) 856-8444, Fax (724) 234-4643, visitors@visitbutler county.com, www.visitbutlercounty.com

# Puerto Rico

**San Juan** • *Puerto Rico Conv. Bur.* • Ana Maria Viscasillas, Pres./ CEO, Edificio Ochoa, 500 Tanca #402, 00902, P 4,000,000, M 550, (787) 725-2110, (800) 875-4765, Fax (787) 725-2133, prcbeo@ prcb.org, www.meetpuertorico.com

# Rhode Island

**Newport** • *Newport County CVB* • Evan Smith, Pres./CEO, 23 America's Cup Ave., 02840, P 25,000, (401) 849-8048, (800) 326-6030, Fax (401) 849-0291, info@gonewport.com, www. gonewport.com

**Providence** • *Providence Warwick CVB* • Martha Sheridan, Pres./CEO, 144 Westminster, 2nd Flr., 02903, P 160,000, M 400, (401) 456-0200, Fax (401) 351-2090, information@pwcvb.com, www.pwcvb.com

**Warwick** • *City of Warwick Dept. of Tourism & Culture* • Karen Jedson, Dir., Warwick City Hall, 3275 Post Rd., 02886, P 86,000, (800) 492-7942, Fax (401) 732-7662, karen.jedson@warwickri. com, www.visitwarwickri.com

# South Carolina

**Charleston** • *Charleston Area CVB* • Helen T. Hill, Exec. Dir., 423 King St., 29403, P 583,434, (843) 853-8000, (800) 868-8118, Fax (843) 853-0444, info@charlestoncvb.com, www.charlestoncvb.com

**Columbia** • *Columbia Metropolitan CVB* • Ric Luber, Pres., 1101 Lincoln St., P.O. Box 15, 29202, P 664,229, (803) 545-0000, (800) 264-4884, Fax (803) 545-0013, www.columbiaconvention center.com

**Greenville** • *Greenville CVB* • Chris Stone, Pres., P.O. Box 10527, 29603, P 400,000, M 250, (864) 421-0000, (800) 351-7180, Fax (864) 421-0005, www.greenvillecvb.com

**Greenwood** • *Greenwood Reg. Tourism & Visitors Bur.* • Kelly McWhorter, Exec. Dir., 120 Main St., P.O. Box 40, 29648, P 150,000, (864) 953-2466, (866) 493-8474, Fax (864) 953-2468, info@ visitgreenwoodsc.com, www.visitgreenwoodsc.com

**Hilton Head Island** • *Hilton Head Island-Bluffton CVB* • William G. Miles, Pres./CEO, One Chamber Dr., P.O. Box 5647, 29938, P 42,000, (843) 785-3673, Fax (843) 785-7110, info@ hiltonheadisland.org, www.hiltonheadisland.org.

**Myrtle Beach** • *Myrtle Beach Area CVB* • Dana Lilly, V.P., 1200 N. Oak St., P.O. Box 2115, 29578, P 217,608, (843) 626-7444, (800) 488-8998, Fax (843) 448-3010, info@visitmyrtlebeach.com, www.visitmyrtlebeach.com

**North Myrtle Beach** • *North Myrtle Beach CVB* • Marc Jordan, Pres./CEO, 270 Hwy. 17 N., P.O. Box 349, 29597, P 12,000, (843) 281-2662, Fax (843) 280-2930, info@northmyrtlebeachchamber. com, www.northmyrtlebeachchamber.com

**Rock Hill** • *Rock Hill/York County CVB* • Bennish Brown, Exec. Dir., P.O. Box 11377, 29731, P 170,000, M 75, (803) 329-5200, (800) 866-5200, Fax (803) 329-0145, www.visityorkcounty.com

**Spartanburg** • *Spartanburg CVB* • 298 Magnolia St., 29306, P 261,000, (864) 594-5050, (800) 374-8326, Fax (864) 594-5052, lponder@visitspartanburg.com, www.visitspartanburg.com

# South Dakota

**Aberdeen** • *Aberdeen CVB* • Nancy Krumm, Exec. Dir., 10 Railroad Ave. S.W., P.O. Box 78, 57402, P 24,658, (605) 225-2414, (800) 645-3851, Fax (605) 225-3573, info@visitaberdeensd.com, www.visitaberdeensd.com

**Brookings** • *Brookings Area C/C & CVB* • Al Heuton, Dir., 414 Main Ave., P.O. Box 431, 57006, P 18,703, M 425, (605) 692-6125, (800) 699-6125, Fax (605) 697-8109, chamber@brookings.net, www.brookingssd.com

**Huron** • *Huron CVB* • Peggy Woolridge, Exec. Dir., 1705 Dakota Ave. S., 57350, P 11,500, (605) 352-0000, (800) 487-6673, Fax (605) 352-8321, cvb@huronsd.com, www.huronsd.com

**Mitchell** • *Corn Palace CVB* • Hannah Walters, Dir., 601 N. Main St., P.O. Box 1026, 57301, P 14,558, (605) 996-6223, Fax (605) 996-8273, cvb@cornpalace.com, www.cornpalace.com

**Pierre** • *Pierre CVB* • Laura Schoen Carbonneau, CEO, 800 W. Dakota Ave., P.O. Box 548, 57501, P 16,000, (605) 224-7361, (800) 962-2034, Fax (605) 224-6485, contactchamber@pierre.org, www.pierre.org

**Rapid City** • *Rapid City CVB* • Michelle Lintz, Exec. Dir., P.O. Box 747, 57709, P 68,000, (605) 343-1744, (800) 487-3223, Fax (605) 348-9217, info@visitrapidcity.com, www.visitrapidcity.com

**Sioux Falls** • *Sioux Falls CVB* • Teri Ellis Schmidt, Exec. Dir., 200 N. Phillips Ave., Ste. 102, 57104, P 154,000, (605) 336-1620, (800) 333-2072, Fax (605) 336-6499, sfcvb@siouxfalls.com, www.siouxfallscvb.com

**Watertown** • *Watertown CVB* • Karen D. Witt, Exec. Dir., 1200 33rd St. S.E., P.O. Box 225, 57201, P 20,500, (605) 753-0282, (800) 658-4505, Fax (605) 753-0394, cvb@visitwatertownsd.com, www.visitwatertownsd.com

# Tennessee

**Big Sandy** • *see Paris*

**Bristol** • *see Bristol, VA*

**Chattanooga** • *Chattanooga Area CVB* • Bob Doak, Pres./CEO, 2 Broad St., 37402, P 475,000, M (423) 756-8687, (800) 322-3344, Fax (423) 265-1630, www.chattanoogafun.com

**Clarksville** • *Clarksville-Montgomery County CVB* • Theresa Harrington, Exec. Dir., 25 Jefferson St., Ste. 300, P.O. Box 883, 37041, P 144,602, (931) 647-2331, (800) 530-2487, Fax (931) 645-1574, tourdir@clarksville.tn.us, www.clarksville.tn.us

**Cleveland** • *Cleveland/Bradley CVB* • Melissa Woody, V.P., 225 Keith St. S.W., P.O. Box 2275, 37320, P 95,443, (423) 472-6587, (800) 472-6588, Fax (423) 472-2019, info@clevelandchamber. com, www.visitclevelandtn.com

**Columbia** • *Maury County CVB* • Brenda Pierce, Exec. Dir., 8 Public Sq., 38401, P 70,770, (931) 381-7176, (888) 852-1860, Fax (931) 375-4119, maurycvb@maurycounty-tn.gov, www. antebellum.com

**Cookeville** • *Cookeville-Putnam County CVB* • Laura Canada, CVB Dir., 1 W. First St., 38501, P 68,000, (931) 526-2211, (800) 264-5541, Fax (931) 526-4023, www.cookevillechamber.com, lcanada@cookevillechamber.com, www.mustseecookeville.com

**Crossville** • *Crossville-Cumberland County CVB* • Beth Alexander, Pres./CEO, 34 S. Main St., 38555, P 51,346, (931) 484-8444, (877) 465-3861, Fax (931) 484-7511, thechamber@ crossville.com, www.crossville-chamber.com.

**Franklin** • *Williamson County CVB* • Mark Shore, Exec. Dir., 108 4th Ave. S., Ste. 203, 37064, P 155,000, (615) 791-7554, (866) 253-9207, Fax (615) 550-2707, info@visitwilliamson.com, www.visitwilliamson.com

**Gatlinburg** • *Gatlinburg Dept. of Tourism & Conv. Center* • David Perella, Exec. Dir., 303 Reagan Dr., 37738, P 3,600, (865) 436-2392, (800) 343-1475, Fax (865) 436-3704, www.gatlinburg-tn.com

**Johnson City** • *Johnson City CVB* • Brenda Whitson, Exec. Dir., 603 E. Market St., P.O. Box 180, 37605, P 58,000, (423) 461-8000, Fax (423) 461-8047, whitson@johnsoncitytnchamber.com, www. johnsoncitytnchamber.com

**Kingsport** • *Kingsport CVB* • Jud Teague, Exec. Dir., 151 E. Main St., 37660, P 51,000, (423) 392-8820, (800) 743-5282, Fax (423) 392-8803, kcvb@kcvb.org, www.visitkingsport.com

**Knoxville** • *Knoxville Tourism & Sports Corp.* • Gloria Ray, Pres./CEO, 301 S. Gay St., 37902, P 392,995, (865) 523-7263, (800) 727-8045, Fax (865) 522-3974, www.knoxville.org

**La Vergne** • *Rutherford County CVB* • Mona Herring, V.P., 5093 Murfreesboro Rd., 37086, P 27,255, (615) 893-6565, (800) 716-7560, Fax (615) 890-7600, info@rutherfordchamber.org, www. rutherfordchamber.org

**Lenoir City** • *Loudon County Visitors Bur.* • Mary Bryant, Dir., 1075 Hwy. 321 N., 37771, P 43,000, (865) 986-6822, (888) 568-3662, Fax (865) 988-8959, mbryant@visitloudoncounty.com, www.visitloudoncounty.com

**Memphis** • *Memphis CVB* • Kevin Kane, Pres., 47 Union Ave., 38103, P 1,100,000, (901) 543-5300, (800) 873-6282, Fax (901) 543-5350, kkanemcvb@aol.com, www.memphistravel.com

**Murfreesboro** • *Rutherford County CVB* • Mona Herring, V.P., 501 Memorial Blvd., P.O. Box 864, 37133, P 100,575, (615) 893-6565, (800) 716-7560, Fax (615) 890-7600, info@rutherford chamber.org, www.rutherfordchamber.org.

**Nashville** · *Nashville CVB* · Butch Spyridon, Pres., 1 Nashville Pl., 150 4th Ave. N., Ste. G-250, 37219, P 596,000, (615) 259-4730, (800) 657-6910, Fax (615) 259-4717, nashcvb@visitmusiccity.com, www.visitmusiccity.com

**Oak Ridge** · *Oak Ridge CVB* · Katy Brown, Pres., 102 Robertsville Rd., Ste. C, 37830, P 27,000, (865) 482-7821, (800) 887-3429, Fax (865) 481-3543, info@oakridgevisitor.com, www.oakridgevisitor.com

**Paris** · *Northwest Tennessee Tourism* · P.O. Box 807, 38242, P 235,291, M 100, (731) 593-0171, (866) 698-6386, Fax (731) 644-3051, reelfootlakeoutdoors.com, info@kentuckylaketourism.com, www.kentuckylaketourism.com

**Pigeon Forge** · *City of Pigeon Forge Dept. of Tourism* · Leon Downey, Exec. Dir., 2450 Pkwy., P.O. Box 1390, 37868, P 5,784, M 976, (865) 453-8574, (800) 251-9100, Fax (865) 429-7362, inquire@mypigeonforge.com, www.mypigeonforge.com

**Pulaski** · *Giles County Tourism Found.* · Tim Turner, Coord., 110 N. Second St., 38478, P 29,447, (931) 363-3789, Fax (931) 363-7279, gctourism@gilescountytourism.com, www.gilescounty tourism.com

**Rugby** · *Historic Rugby* · Cheryl Ribbet, Exec. Dir., 5517 Rugby Hwy., P.O. Box 8, 37733, P 85, (423) 628-2441, (888) 214-3400, Fax (423) 628-2266, rugbylegacy@highland.net, www.historic rugby.org.

**Savannah** · *Hardin County CVB* · Rachel Baker, Tourism Dir., 495 Main St., 38372, P 25,000, (731) 925-2364, Fax (731) 925-6987, (800) 552-FUNN, info@tourhardincounty.org, www.tourhardin county.org

**Smyrna** · *Rutherford County CVB* · Mona Herring, V.P., 315 S. Lowry St., 37167, P 38,073, (615) 893-6565, (800) 716-7560, Fax (615) 890-7600, info@rutherfordchamber.org, www.rutherford chamber.org

**Townsend** · *Smoky Mountain CVB* · Herb Handly, Exec. V.P. Tourism, 7906 E. Lamar Alexander Pkwy., 37882, P 4,749, (865) 448-6134, (800) 525-6834, Fax (865) 448-9806, info@smoky mountains.org, www.smokymountains.org

# Texas

**Abilene** · *Abilene CVB* · Nanci M. Liles, Exec. Dir., 1101 N. First, 79601, P 120,000, (325) 676-2556, (800) 727-7704, Fax (325) 676-1630, visitors@abilene.com, www.abilenevisitors.com

**Alvin** · *Alvin CVB* · Julie Siggers, Tourism Dir., 105 W. Willis, 77511, P 48,524, (281) 331-3944, (800) 331-4063, Fax (281) 585-8662, alvincvb@alvintexas.org, www.alvintexas.org

**Amarillo** · *Amarillo Conv. & Visitor Cncl.* · Jerry Holt, V.P., 1000 S. Polk St., 79101, P 190,000, (806) 374-1497, (800) 692-1338, Fax (806) 373-3909, melanie@amarillo-cvb.org, www.visit amarillotx.com

**Archer City** · *Archer City Visitors Center* · Angie Steele, Ofc. Mgr., 101 N. Center, P.O. Box 1070, 76351, P 1,800, (940) 574-2489, Fax (940) 574-2490, host@archercitytx.com, www. archercity.org

**Arlington** · *Arlington CVB* · Jay Burress, Pres./CEO, 1905 E. Randol Mill Rd., 76011, P 370,000, (817) 265-7721, (800) 433-5374, Fax (817) 265-5640, visitinfo@arlington.org, www. arlington.org

**Arlington** · *Arlington CVB* · Mary German, Sr. Dir. Of Client Svcs., 1905 E. Randol Mill Rd., 76011, P 370,000, (817) 461-3888, (800) 342-4305, visitinfo@arlington.org, www.arlington.org

**Austin** · *Austin CVB* · Robert Lander, Pres./CEO, 301 Congress Ave., Ste. 200, 78701, P 998,543, (512) 474-5171, (800) 926-2282, Fax (512) 583-7282, www.austintexas.org

**Bandera** · *Bandera CVB* · Patricia Moore, Exec. Dir., 126 Hwy. 16 S., P.O. Box 171, 78003, P 22,000, (830) 796-3045, (800) 364-3833, Fax (830) 796-4121, director@banderacowboycapital.com, www. banderacowboycapital.com

**Bay City** · *Matagorda County CVB* · Mitch Thames, Pres./CEO, 201 Seventh St., P.O. Box 768, 77404, P 38,000, (979) 245-8333, (800) 806-8333, Fax (979) 245-1622, mitchthames@visitbaycity. org, www.visitmatagorda.com

**Beaumont** · *Beaumont CVB* · Dean Conwell, Dir., 505 Willow St., P.O. Box 3827, 77704, P 115,000, (409) 880-3749, (800) 392-4401, Fax (409) 880-3750, smoye@ci.beaumont.tx.us, www.beaumont cvb.com

**Boerne** · *Boerne CVB* · Larry Wood, Dir., 1407 S. Main, 78006, P 9,300, (830) 249-7277, (888) 842-8080, Fax (830) 249-9626, www.visitboerne.org

**Brady** · *Brady Tourist & Conv. Bur.* · Wendy Ellis, Comm. Dev. Dir., 101 E. 1st St., 76825, P 5,523, (325) 597-3491, (888) 577-5657, Fax (325) 792-9181, info@bradytx.us, www.bradytx.com

**Brazosport** · *Brazosport Conv. & Visitors Cncl.* · Edith Fischer, Dir. of Tourism, 300 Abner Jackson Pkwy., 77566, P 72,000, (979) 285-2501, (888) 477-2505, Fax (979) 285-2505, edithfischer@ sbcglobal.net, www.tourtexas.com/brazosport

**Brenham** · *Brenham/Washington County CVB* · Seneca McAdams, Sales/Mktg. Mgr., 314 S. Austin St., 77833, P 31,000, (979) 836-3695, (888) 273-6426, Fax (979) 836-2540, info@ brenhamtexas.com, www.brenhamtexas.com

**Brownsville** · *Brownsville CVB* · Mariano Ayala, Pres./CEO, 650 FM 802, P.O. Box 4697, 78523, P 176,000, (956) 546-3721, (800) 626-2639, Fax (956) 546-3972, brownsvilleinfo@brownsville.org, www.brownsville.org

**Bryan** · *see College Station*

**College Station** · *Bryan/College Station CVB* · Shannon Overby, Dir., 715 University Dr. E., 77840, P 126,804, (979) 260-9898, (800) 777-8292, Fax (979) 260-9800, www.visitaggieland.com

**Conroe** · *Lake Conroe Area CVB* · Lindsey Hafner, Dir., 505 W. Davis St., 77301, P 53,000, (936) 538-7112, Fax (936) 756-6752, (877) 4-CONROE, info@lakeconroecvb.org, www.lakeconroecvb.org

**Corpus Christi** · *Corpus Christi CVB* · Keith Arnold, Pres./CEO, 101 N. Shoreline Blvd., Ste. 430, 78401, P 281,000, (361) 881-1888, (800) 678-6232, Fax (361) 887-9023, www.visitcorpuschristitx.org

**Dallas** · *Dallas CVB* · Phillip Jones, Pres./CEO, 325 N. St. Paul, Ste. 700, 75201, P 1,189,000, (214) 571-1000, Fax (214) 571-1008, www.visitdallas.com

**Denton** · *Denton CVB* · Kim Phillips, V.P., 414 Pkwy., P.O. Box 1719, 76202, P 110,000, (940) 382-7895, (888) 381-1818, Fax (940) 382-6287, cvb@discoverdenton.com, www.discoverdenton.com.

**Donna** · *Donna Tourist Info. Center* · David De Los Rios, Exec. Dir., 921 Miller Ave., 78537, P 15,000, (956) 464-9640, Fax (956) 464-9686, David_DonnaTC@yahoo.com, www.ci.donna.lib.tx.us

**El Paso** · *El Paso CVB* · William Blaziek, Gen. Mgr., #1 Civic Center Plaza, 79901, P 750,000, (915) 534-0600, Fax (915) 534-0687, www.elpasocvb.com, info@elpasocvb.com, www. visitelpaso.com

**Fort Stockton** · *Fort Stockton CVB* · Crystal Lopez, Dir. of Tourism, 1000 Railroad Ave., P.O. Box 1000, 79735, P 7,846, (432) 336-2264, (877) 336-8525, Fax (432) 336-6114, clopez@ci.fort-stockton.tx.us, www.tourtexas.com/fortstockton.

**Fort Worth** • *Fort Worth CVB* • David DuBois, Pres./CEO, 415 Throckmorton St., 76102, P 670,000, (817) 336-8791, (800) 433-5747, Fax (817) 336-3282, www.fortworth.com

**Fredericksburg** • *Fredericksburg CVB* • Ernest Loeffler, Dir., 302 E. Austin, 78624, P 10,000, (830) 997-6523, (888) 997-3600, Fax (830) 997-8588, www.fredtexlodging.com

**Galveston** • *Galveston Island Visitors Center* • Stacy Gilbert, Dir., 2328 Broadway, 77550, P 65,000, (409) 763-4311, Fax (409) 744-7873, (888) GAL ISLE, www.galveston.com

**Garland** • *Garland CVB* • Lucia Arrant, Mgr., P.O. Box 469002, 75046, P 220,000, (972) 205-2749, (888) 879-0264, Fax (972) 205-3634, larrant@ci.garland.tx.us, www.ci.garland.tx.us

**Georgetown** • *Georgetown CVB* • Cari Miller, Tourism Mgr., 103 W. 7th St., P.O. Box 409, 78627, P 36,000, (512) 930-3545, (800) 436-8696, Fax (512) 930-3697, cvb@georgetowntx.org, www.visitgeorgetown.com

**Granbury** • *Granbury CVB* • Charlie McIlvain CTP, Dir., 116 W. Bridge, 76048, P 7,500, (817) 573-5548, (800) 950-2212, Fax (817) 573-5789, cmcilvain@granburytx.com, www.granburytx.com

**Grand Prairie** • *City of Grand Prairie* • Randy Sisson, Tourism Mgr., 2170 N. Belt Line Rd., 75050, P 160,000, (972) 263-9588, (800) 288-8386, Fax (972) 642-4350, rsisson@gptx.org, www.gptexas.com

**Grapevine** • *Grapevine CVB* • Paul W. McCallum, Exec. Dir., One Liberty Park Plz., 76051, P 49,600, (817) 410-3185, (800) 457-6338, Fax (817) 410-3038, pmccallum@grapevinetexasusa.com, www.grapevinetexasusa.com

**Houston** • *Greater Houston CVB* • Ken Middleton, V.P. of Sales, 901 Bagby, Ste. 100, 77002, P 4,500,000, (713) 437-5200, Fax (713) 227-6336, (800) 4-HOUSTON, www.visithoustontexas.com

**Huntsville** • *Sam Houston Statue & Huntsville Visitor Center* • Kimm Thomas, Mgr., 7600 Hwy. 75 S., P.O. Box 1230, 77342, P 56,000, (936) 291-9726, (800) 289-0389, Fax (936) 291-6636, kthomas@chamber.huntsville.tx.us, www.huntsvilletexas.com.

**Irving** • *Irving CVB* • Maura Gast, CEO, 222 W. Las Colinas Blvd., Ste. 1550, 75039, P 200,000, (972) 252-7476, Fax (972) 257-3153, (800) 2-IRVING, www.irvingtexas.com

**Kemah** • *Kemah Visitors Center* • 604 Bradford, 77565, P 2,330, (281) 334-3181, visitkemah@kemah-tx.com, www.kemah-tx.gov

**Kerrville** • *Kerrville CVB* • Sudie Burditt, Dir., 2108 Sidney Baker, 78028, P 21,000, (830) 792-3535, Fax (830) 792-3230, info@kerrvilletexascvb.com, www.kerrvilletexascvb.com

**Killeen** • *Killeen CVB* • Connie Kuehl, Dir., 3601 South W.S. Young Dr., P.O. Box 1329, 76540, P 120,000, (254) 501-3888, Fax (254) 554-3219, info@killeen-cvb.com, www.killeen-cvb.com

**Kingsville** • *Kingsville CVB* • Carol Ann Anderson, Exec. Dir., 1501 N. Hwy. 77, 78363, P 25,575, (361) 592-8516, (800) 333-5032, Fax (361) 592-3227, cvb@kingsvilletexas.com, www.kingsvilletexas.com

**Laredo** • *Laredo CVB* • Blasita Lopez, Interim Mgr., 501 San Agustin Ave., 78040, P 200,000, (956) 795-2200, (800) 361-3360, Fax (956) 795-2185, lcvb@ci.laredo.tx.us, www.visitlaredo.com

**Longview** • *Longview CVB* • Paul R. Anderson, Sr. V.P., 410 N. Center St., 75601, P 80,000, (903) 753-3281, Fax (903) 758-4791, lcvb@longviewtx.com, www.visitlongviewtexas.com

**Lubbock** • *Lubbock CVB* • Marcy Jarrett, Exec. Dir., 1500 Broadway, 6th Flr., Wells Fargo Center, 79401, P 210,000, (806) 747-5232, (800) 692-4035, Fax (806) 747-1419, marcy@visitlubbock.org, www.visitlubbock.org.

**Lufkin** • *Lufkin CVB* • Jerry Huffman, 1615 S. Chestnut, P.O. Box 1606, 75901, P 34,000, (936) 634-6305, (800) 409-5659, Fax (936) 634-8726, jhuffman@lufkintexas.org, www.visitlufkin.com

**Marshall** • *Marshall Conv. & Visitor Dev.* • Geraldine Mauthe, Dir. of Conv. Svcs., 213 W. Austin St., P.O. Box 1437, 75671, P 25,000, (903) 935-7868, Fax (903) 935-9982, cvb@visitmarshalltexas.org, www.visitmarshalltexas.org

**McAllen** • *McAllen CVB* • Steve Ahlenius, Pres./CEO, 1200 Ash Ave., P.O. Box 790, 78505, P 120,000, (956) 682-2871, (877) MCALLEN, Fax (956) 687-2917, (800) MCALLEN, steve@mcallenchamber.com, www.mcallenchamber.com

**McKinney** • *McKinney CVB* • Diann Bayes, Exec. Dir., 321 N. Central Expy., Ste. 101, 75070, P 120,000, (214) 544-1407, (888) 649-8499, Fax (972) 542-6341, info@visitmckinney.com, www.visitmckinney.com

**Midland** • *Midland CVB* • Rob Cunningham, V.P. Comm. Dev., 109 N. Main , 79701, P 102,000, (432) 683-3381, (800) 624-6435, Fax (432) 682-6435, info@midlandtexas.com, www.midlandtexas.com

**Mineola** • *Mineola CVB* • Lynda Rauscher, Comm. Dev. Dir., 300 Greenville Ave., P.O. Box 179, 75773, P 5,611, (903) 569-6983, Fax (903) 569-0856, (800) MINEOLA, ced@mineola.com, www.mineola.com

**Mineral Wells** • *Mineral Wells Area C/C* • Beth Watson, Exec. Dir., 511 E. Hubbard, P.O. Box 1408, 76068, P 29,000, (940) 325-2557, Fax (940) 328-0850, (800) 252-MWTX, info@mineralwellstx.com, www.mineralwellstx.com

**Nacogdoches** • *Nacogdoches CVB* • Melissa Sanford, Exec. Dir., 200 E. Main, 75961, P 30,000, (936) 564-7351, (888) 653-3788, Fax (936) 462-7688, info@visitnacogdoches.org, www.visitnacogdoches.org.

**New Braunfels** • *New Braunfels CVB* • Judy Young, Dir., 390 S. Seguin Ave., P.O. Box 311417, 78131, P 47,000, (830) 625-2385, (800) 572-2626, Fax (830) 625-7918, nbcc@nbcham.org, www.nbcham.org

**Odessa** • *Odessa CVB* • Linda Sweatt, Dir., 700 N. Grant, Ste. 200, 79761, P 96,948, (432) 333-7871, (800) 780-4678, Fax (432) 333-7858, info@odessacvb.com, www.odessacvb.com.

**Orange** • *Orange CVB* • Darline Zavada, Dir., 803 W. Green Ave., P.O. Box 520, 77631, P 18,643, (409) 883-1011, (800) 528-4906, Fax (409) 988-7321, cvb@orangetx.org, www.orangetexas.org

**Palestine** • *Palestine CVB* • Susan Cottle-Leonard, Dir., 825 Spring St., 75801, P 19,000, (903) 723-3014, (800) 659-3484, Fax (903) 729-6067, palestinecvb@flash.net, www.visitpalestine.com

**Paris** • *Paris Visitor & Conv. Cncl.* • Becky Semple, Dir., 1125 Bonham St., 75460, P 50,016, (903) 784-2501, Fax (903) 784-2503, (800) PARIS TX, visitus@paristexas.com, www.paristexas.com

**Plano** • *Plano CVB* • Mark Thompson, Dir., P.O. Box 860358, 75086, P 250,000, (972) 941-5840, Fax (972) 424-0002, (800) 81-PLANO, www.planocvb.com

**Port Aransas** • *Port Aransas CVB* • Ann B. Vaughan, Exec. Dir., 421 W. Cotter, 78373, P 3,370, (361) 749-5919, (800) 452-6278, Fax (361) 749-4672, info@portaransas.org, www.portaransas.org

**Port Arthur** • *Port Arthur CVB* • Tammy Kotzur, Dir., 3401 Cultural Center Dr., 77642, P 58,000, (409) 985-7822, (800) 235-7822, Fax (409) 985-5584, pacvb@portarthurtexas.com, www.portarthurtexas.com

**Richardson** • *Richardson Conv. & Visitors Bur.* • Geoff Wright, Dir., 411 W. Arapaho Rd., Ste. 105, 75080, P 98,000, (972) 744-4034, (888) 690-7287, Fax (972) 744-5834, cvb@cor.gov, www.richardsontexas.org

**San Angelo** · *San Angelo CVB* · Pamela Miller, V.P. of CVB, 418 W. Avenue B, 76903, P 90,000, (325) 655-4136, Fax (325) 658-1110, chamber@sanangelo.org, www.sanangelo.org

**San Antonio** · *San Antonio CVB* · Scott White, Dir., 203 S. St. Mary's, Ste. 200, 78205, P 1,800,000, (210) 207-6700, (800) 447-3372, Fax (210) 207-6768, www.visitsanantonio.com

**San Marcos** · *San Marcos CVB* · Rebecca Ybarra-Ramirez, Dir., 202 N. CM Allen Pkwy., P.O. Box 2310, 78667, P 50,016, (512) 393-5900, (888) 200-5620, Fax (512) 393-5912, cvb@sanmarcostexas.com, www.toursanmarcos.com.

**Schulenburg** · *Tourist Info. Center* · Mike Stroup, Exec. Dir., 618 N. Main, P.O. Box 65, 78956, P 2,700, (979) 743-4514, (866) 504-5294, Fax (979) 743-9155, info@schulenburgchamber.org, www.schulenburgchamber.org

**Seguin** · *Seguin Area CVB* · Sherry Nefford, Dir., P.O. Box 710, 78156, P 25,090, (830) 379-6382, (800) 580-7322, Fax (830) 379-6971, cvb@seguinchamber.com, www.visitseguin.com

**Sherman** · *Sherman Dept. of Tourism* · April Patterson, Tourism Dir., P.O. Box 2312, 75091, P 40,000, (903) 957-0310, (888) 893-1188, Fax (903) 957-0312, aprilp@ci.sherman.tx.us, www.shermantx.org

**South Padre Island** · *South Padre Island CVB* · Dan Quandt, Exec. Dir., 600 Padre Blvd., 78597, P 2,800, (956) 761-6433, Fax (956) 761-9462, (800) SO PADRE, www.sopadre.com

**Sweetwater** · *Sweetwater CVB* · Jacque McCoy, Exec. Dir., 810 E. Broadway, P.O. Box 1148, 79556, P 11,500, (325) 235-5488, (800) 658-6757, Fax (325) 235-1026, chamber@sweetwatertexas.org, www.sweetwatertexas.org

**Terrell** · *Terrell C/C & CVB* · Sarah Kegerreis, Dir. of Tourism, 1314 W. Moore Ave., 75160, P 18,500, (972) 563-5703, Fax (972) 563-2363, (877) TERRELL, tourism@terrelltexas.com, www.terrelltexas.com

**Tyler** · *Tyler CVB* · Henry M. Bell III, COO, 315 N. Broadway, P.O. Box 390, 75710, P 101,600, (903) 592-1661, Fax (903) 593-2746, hbell@tylertexas.com, www.tylertexas.com.

**Uvalde** · *Uvalde CVB* · Joanne Nelson, Exec. Dir., 300 E. Main St., 78801, P 18,500, (830) 278-4115, Fax (830) 278-3363, joanne@visituvalde.com, www.visituvalde.com

**Van Horn** · *Van Horn CVB* · Brenda Hinojos, Dir., 1801 W. Broadway, P.O. Box 488, 79855, P 2,400, (432) 283-2682, Fax (432) 283-1413, brenda@vanhorncvb.com, www.vanhorntexas.org

**Victoria** · *Victoria CVB* · 3404 N. Ben Wilson, P.O. Box 2488, 77902, P 86,916, (361) 582-4285, (800) 926-5774, Fax (361) 573-5911, info@victoriatexasinfo.com, www.victoriatexasinfo.com.

**Waco** · *Waco CVB* · Elizabeth Taylor, Exec. Dir., 100 Washington Ave., P.O. Box 2570, 76702, P 222,439, (254) 750-5810, (800) 321-9226, Fax (254) 750-5801, lizt@ci.waco.tx.us, www.wacocvb.com

# Utah

**Cedar City** · *Cedar City/Brian Head Tourism & Conv. Bur.* · Maria Twitchell, Exec. Dir., 581 N. Main, 84721, P 22,000, (435) 586-5124, (800) 354-4849, Fax (435) 586-4022, tourism@netutah.com, www.scenicsouthernutah.com.

**Layton** · *Davis Area CVB* · Barbara Riddle, Pres./CEO, 748 W. Heritage Park Blvd., Ste. 201, 84041, P 265,000, (801) 774-8200, (888) 777-9771, Fax (801) 774-8335, info@davisareacvb.com, www.davis.travel

**Logan** · *Cache Valley Visitors Bur.* · Julie Hollist, Dir., 199 N. Main St., 84321, P 47,023, (435) 755-1890, (800) 882-4433, Fax (435) 755-1993, cvinfo@tourcachevalley.com, www.tourcachevalley.com

**Moab** · *Moab Area Travel Cncl.* · Marian DeLay, Exec. Dir., P.O. Box 550, 84532, P 9,000, (435) 259-8825, (800) 635-6622, Fax (435) 259-1376, mdelay@discovermoab.com, www.discovermoab.com

**Monticello** · *Utah's Canyon Country Visitors Bur.* · Charlie DeLorme, Dir., P.O. Box 490, 84535, P 14,200, 4355873235 ext. 4135, (800) 574-4386, Fax (435) 587-2425, www.utahscanyon country.com

**Nephi** · *Juab Travel Cncl.* · Jens Mickelson, Pres., 4 S. Main St., P.O. Box 71, 84648, P 8,000, (435) 623-5203, (800) 748-4361, Fax (435) 623-4609, info@juabtravel.com, www.juabtravel.com

**Ogden** · *Ogden Weber CVB* · Sara Toliver, Pres., 2501 Wall Ave., Ste. 201, 84401, P 86,000, (801) 627-8288, (866) 867-8824, Fax (801) 399-0783, info@ogdencvb.org, www.ogden.travel

**Panguitch** · *Garfield County Ofc. Of Tourism* · K. Bruce Fullmer, Exec. Dir., P.O. Box 200, 84759, P 4,735, (435) 676-1160, (800) 444-6689, Fax (435) 676-8239, travgar@color-country.net, www.brycecanyoncountry.com

**Park City** · *Park City CVB* · Bill Malone, Exec. Dir., 1910 Prospector Ave., P.O. Box 1630, 84060, P 24,500, (435) 649-6100, (800) 453-1360, Fax (435) 649-4132, info@parkcityinfo.com, www.parkcityinfo.com

**Saint George** · *Saint George Area CVB* · Pam Hilton, Mktg. Dir., 1835 Convention Center Dr., Dixie Center, 84790, P 125,000, (435) 634-5747, (800) 869-6635, Fax (435) 628-1619, info@utahstgeorge.com, www.utahstgeorge.com

# Virgin Islands

**Saint Croix** · *Virgin Islands Dept. of Tourism* · Beverly Nicholson-Doty, Commissioner, P.O. Box 224538, Christiansted, 00822, P 60,000, (340) 773-0495, Fax (340) 773-5074, www.usvitourism.vi

**Saint Croix** · *Virgin Islands Dept. of Tourism* · Beverly Nicholson-Doty, Commissioner, 200 Strand St., Custom House, Frederiksted, 00840, P 60,000, (340) 772-0357, Fax (340) 773-5074, www.usvitourism.vi

**Saint Thomas** · *Virgin Islands Dept. of Tourism* · Beverly Nicholson-Doty, Commissioner, P.O. Box 6400, Charlotte Amalie, 00804, P 60,000, (340) 774-8784, (800) 372-8784, Fax (340) 774-4390, www.usvitourism.vi

# Virginia

**Abingdon** · *Abingdon CVB* · Myra Cook, Dir. of Tourism, 335 Cummings St., 24210, P 7,700, (276) 676-2282, (800) 435-3440, Fax (276) 676-3076, acvb@abingdon.com, www.abingdon.com

**Alexandria** · *Alexandria Conv. & Visitors Assn.* · Stephanie Brown, Pres./CEO, 421 King St., Ste. 300, 22314, P 135,000, (703) 838-4200, (800) 388-9119, Fax (703) 838-4683, acva@funside.com, www.funside.com

**Arlington** · *Arlington Conv. & Visitors Svcs.* · Emily Cassell, Mktg. Dir., 1100 N. Glebe Rd., Ste. 1500, 22201, P 189,453, (703) 228-0888, (800) 296-7996, Fax (703) 228-0806, ecassell@arlingtonva.us, www.stayarlington.com

**Ashland** · *Ashland/Hanover Visitors Center* · Donna Baxter, Mgr., 112 N. Railroad Ave, 23005, P 86,320, (804) 752-6766, (800) 897-1479, Fax (804) 752-2380, donnabahvc1@netscape.com, www.town.ashland.va.us

**Bedford** · *Bedford Welcome Center* · Sergei Troubetzkoy CTP, 816 Burks Hill Rd., 24523, P 70,000, (540) 587-5681, Fax (540) 587-5983, sergei@visitbedford.com, www.visitbedford.com

**Blacksburg** · *Blacksburg/Christiansburg Visitors Center* · Shane Adams, Pres./CEO, 103 Professional Park Dr., 24060, P 100,000, (540) 552-2636, 877FORGUID, Fax (540) 552-2639, info@virginianaturally.com, www.virginianaturally.com

**Bluefield** · *Tazewell County Visitor Center* · June Brown, Mgr., 200 Sanders Ln., 24605, P 45,000, (276) 322-1345, (800) 588-9401, Fax (276) 322-3908, tcvc@4seasonswireless.net, www.tazewellcounty.org

**Bristol** · *Bristol CVB* · 20 Volunteer Pkwy., P.O. Box 519, 24203, P 43,000, (423) 989-4850, Fax (423) 989-4867, tourism@bristol chamber.org, www.bristolchamber.org

**Charlottesville** · *Charlottesville-Albemarle CVB* · Kurt Burkhart, Dir., 610 E. Main St., P.O. Box 178, 22902, P 130,000, (434) 293-6789, (877) 386-1103, Fax (434) 295-2176, visitors center@charlottesville.org, www.pursuecharlottesville.com

**Chesapeake** · *Chesapeake Conventions & Tourism* · Kimberly Murden, Dir., 3815 Bainbridge Blvd., 23324, (757) 502-4898, (888) 889-5551, Fax (757) 502-4883, www.visitchesapeake.com

**Fredericksburg** · *Fredericksburg Ofc. Of Tourism & Eco. Dev.* · Karen Hedelt, Interim Dir., 706 Caroline St., 22401, P 21,000, (540) 372-1216, (800) 260-3646, Fax (540) 372-6587, khedelt@fredericksburgva.gov, www.visitfred.com

**Fredericksburg** · *Spotsylvania County Dept. of Tourism* · Rachel Delooze, Mktg. Coord., 10304 Spotsylvania Ave., 22408, P 106,305, (540) 507-7210, (877) 515-6197, Fax (540) 507-7207, rdelooze@spotsylvania.va.us, www.spotsylvania.org

**Hampton** · *Hampton CVB* · Sallie Grant-DiVenuti, Exec. Dir., 1919 Commerce Dr., Ste. 290, 23666, P 138,000, (757) 722-1222, (800) 487-8778, Fax (757) 896-4600, sallie@hamptoncvb.com, www.hamptoncvb.com

**Harrisonburg** · *Harrisonburg Tourism and Visitor Svcs.* · Brenda Black, Tourism Mgr., 212 S. Main St., 22801, P 120,000, M (540) 432-8935, Fax (540) 437-0631, tourism@ ci.harrisonburg.va.us, www.harrisonburgtourism.com

**Hopewell** · *City of Hopewell, Dept. of Tourism* · LuAnn Fortenberry, Dir., 4100 Oaklawn Blvd., 23860, P 23,000, (804) 541-2461, (800) 863-8687, Fax (804) 541-2459, info@hopewellva. gov, www.hopewellva.gov

**Leesburg** · *Loudon Conv. & Vistors Assn.* · Cheryl Kilday, Pres., 112 South St. S.E., Ste. G, 20175, P 268,817, (703) 771-2170, (800) 752-6118, Fax (703) 771-4973, kilday@visitloudon.org, www.visitloudon.org

**Lexington** · *Lexington & the Rockbridge Visitor Center* · Jean Clark, Dir., 106 E. Washington St., 24450, P 34,000, (540) 463-3777, (877) 453-9822, Fax (540) 463-1105, lexington tourismdirector@rockbridge.net, www.lexingtonvirginia.com

**Lorton** · *Fairfax County Visitors Center* · Sue Porter, Dir. of Visitor Svcs., 8180-A Silverbrook Rd., 22079, P 1,000,000, (703) 550-2450, (800) 732-4732, Fax (703) 550-9418, fxva@fxva.com, www.fxva.com

**Lovingston** · *Nelson County Eco. Dev. & Tourism* · Maureen Corum, Dir., 8519 Thomas Nelson Hwy., P.O. Box 636, 22949, P 15,000, (434) 263-7015, (800) 282-8223, Fax (434) 263-6823, info@nelsoncounty.org, www.nelsoncounty.com

**Lynchburg** · *Lynchburg Visitor Info. Center* · Cathy Beeson, Mgr., 216 12th St., 24504, P 243,000, (434) 847-1811, (800) 732-5821, Fax (434) 455-4320, tourism@lynchburgchamber.org, www. discoverlynchburg.org

**Manassas** · *Prince William County/Manassas CVB* · 8609 Sudley Rd., Ste. 105, 20110, P 340,000, (703) 396-7130, (800) 432-1792, Fax (703) 396-7160, info@visitpwc.com, www.visitpwc.com

**McLean** · *Fairfax County Conv. & Visitors Corp.* · 7927 Jones Branch Dr., South Wing 100, 22102, P 1,000,000, (703) 790-0643, Fax (703) 790-5097, fxva@fxva.com, www.fxva.com

**Newport News** · *Newport News Visitor Center* · Janie Tross, Mgr., 13560 Jefferson Ave., 23603, P 185,226, (757) 886-7777, (888) 493-7386, Fax (757) 886-7920, tourism@nngov.com, jtross@nngov.com, www.newport-news.org

**Norfolk** · *Norfolk CVB* · Donna Allen, V.P. Sales, 232 E. Main St., 23510, P 245,000, (757) 664-6620, (800) 368-3097, Fax (757) 622-3663, www.norfolkcvb.com

**Northern Neck** · *see Warsaw-Northern Neck Tourism Cncl.*

**Orange** · *Orange County Dept. of Tourism* · Joe Ward, Dir., 122 E. Main St., P.O. Box 133, 22960, P 29,000, (540) 672-1653, (877) 222-8072, Fax (540) 672-1746, tourorangeco@firstva.com, www. visitocva.com

**Petersburg** · *Petersburg Vistors Center* · Frances Lilly, Supervisor, 425 Cockade Alley, 23803, P 36,000, (804) 733-2400, (800) 368-3595, Fax (804) 861-0883, petgtourism@earthlink.net, www.petersburg-va.org

**Portsmouth** · *Portsmouth CVB* · Lynne Lochen, Dir., 505 Crawford St., Ste. 2, 23704, P 100,000, (757) 393-5327, (800) 757-8782, Fax (757) 393-5327, info@portsva.com, www.portsva.com

**Richmond** · *Richmond Metro CVB* · Jack Berry, Pres., 401 N. 3rd St., 23219, P 1,000,000, (804) 782-2777, (800) 370-9004, Fax (804) 780-2577, www.visit.richmond.com

**Roanoke** · *Roanoke Valley CVB* · David Kjolhede, Exec. Dir., 101 Shenandoah Ave. N.E., 24016, P 288,309, M 180, (540) 342-6025, (800) 635-5535, Fax (540) 342-7119, info@visitroanokeva.com, www.visitroanokeva.com

**Smithfield** · *Smithfield and Isle of Wight CVB* · Judy Winslow, Dir., 335 Main St., 23431, P 40,000, (757) 357-5182, (800) 365-9339, Fax (757) 365-4360, smfdtour@visi.net, www.smithfield-virginia.com

**South Boston** · *Halifax County Tourism Dept.* · Linda Sheppard, Dir., 700 Bruce St., 24592, P 38,000, (434) 572-2543, Fax (434) 517-0021, info@gohalifaxva.com, www.gohalifaxva.com

**Staunton** · *Staunton CVB* · Sheryl Wagner, Dir., 116 W. Beverly St., 3rd Flr., P.O. Box 58, 24402, P 23,500, (540) 332-3865, (800) 342-7982, Fax (540) 851-4005, wagnerss@ci.staunton.va.us, www.visitstaunton.com

**Suffolk** · *Suffolk Div. of Tourism* · Lynette White, Dir. of Tourism, 321 N. Main St., 23434, P 85,000, (757) 923-3880, (866) 733-7835, Fax (757) 923-3882, VisitSuffolk@city.suffolk.va.us., www. suffolk-fun.com

**Virginia Beach** · *Virginia Beach CVB* · James Ricketts, Dir., 2101 Parks Ave., Ste. 500, 23451, P 450,000, (757) 385-4700, (800) 700-7702, Fax (757) 437-4747, vbgov@vbgov.com, www. vbfun.com

**Warrenton** · *Warrenton-Fauquier County Visitor Center* · Becky Crouch, Mgr., 33 N. Calhoun St., 20186, P 65,000, (800) 820-1021, visitorcenter@warrentonva.gov, www.visitfauquier.com

**Warsaw · *Northern Neck Tourism Council*** · Patricia Long, Exec. Dir., P.O. Box 1707, 22572, P 30,000, M 160, (804) 333-1919, (800) 393-6180, Fax (804) 333-5274, nntc@northernneck.org, www.northernneck.org

**Warsaw · *Richmond County Museum & Visitors Center*** · 5874 Richmond Rd., P.O. Box 884, 22572, P 8,000, (804) 333-3607, Fax (804) 333-3408

**West Point · *Virginia's River Country Tourism Cncl.*** · Harla Sherwood, P.O. Box 286, 23149, P 88,000, (800) 527-6360, (804) 758-4917, www.visitrivercountry.org

**Winchester · *Winchester-Frederick Co. CVB*** · Natalie Wills, Exec. Dir., 1400 S. Pleasant Valley Rd., 22601, P 90,000, (540) 542-1326, (877) 871-1326, Fax (540) 450-0099, info@visit winchesterva.com, www.visitwinchesterva.com.

**Woodstock · *Shenandoah County Tourism Cncl.*** · Susie Hill, Dir. of Tourism, 600 N. Main St., Ste. 101, 22664, P 39,000, (540) 459-6220, (888) 367-3960, Fax (540) 459-6228, tourism@shenandoahcountyva.us, www.shenandoahtravel.org

**Wytheville · *Blue Ridge Travel Assn. of VA*** · P.O. Box 1395, 24382, M 100, (800) 446-9670, info@virginiablueridge.org, www.virginiablueridge.org

**Wytheville · *Reg. Visitors Center*** · Rosa Lee Jude, Dir., 975 Tazewell St., 24382, P 28,500, (276) 223-3441, (877) 347-8303, Fax (276) 223-3443, cvb@wytheville.org, www.virginiablueridge.org

**Wytheville · *Wytheville CVB*** · Rosa Lee Jude, Dir., 975 Tazewell St., P.O. Box 533, 24382, P 28,500, (276) 223-3355, (877) 347-8307, Fax (276) 223-3446, cvb@wytheville.org, www.VisitWytheville.com

**Yorktown · *York County Tourism Dev.*** · Kristi Olsen, Tourism Dev. Mgr., P.O. Box 532, 23690, (757) 890-3500, (757) 890-3300, Fax (757) 890-3509, www.yorkcounty.gov/tourism

# Washington

**Clarkston · *Hells Canyon Visitor Bur.*** · Michelle Peters, Pres./CEO, 504 Bridge St., 99403, P 60,000, (509) 758-7489, (877) 774-7248, Fax (509) 751-8767, info@hellscanyonvisitor.com, www.hellscanyonvisitor.com

**Kelso · *see Longview***

**Kennewick · *Tri-Cities VCB*** · Kris Kelley-Watkins, Pres./CEO, 7130 W. Grandridge Blvd., Ste. B, 99336, P 224,000, M 550, (509) 735-8486, (800) 254-5824, Fax (509) 783-9005, info@Visit Tri-Cities.com, www.VisitTri-Cities.com

**Long Beach · *Long Beach Peninsula VB*** · P.O. Box 562, 98631, P 20,300, M 260, (360) 642-2400, (800) 451-2542, Fax (360) 642-3900, ask@funbeach.com, www.funbeach.com

**Longview · *Cowlitz Reg. Conf. Center*** · Mike Moss, Dir., 1900 7th Ave., 98632, P 99,905, (360) 577-3121, Fax (360) 577-6254, www.thecenterofthenorthwest.com

**Packwood · *Destination Packwood*** · Edie Aydelott, Ofc. Mgr., P.O. Box 64, 98361, P 2,000, (360) 494-2223, Fax (360) 494-2216, dpa@lewiscounty.com, www.destinationpackwood.com

**Port Angeles · *Olympic Peninsula Visitors Bur.*** · Diane Schostak, Exec. Dir., 338 W. 1st St., Ste. 104, P.O. Box 670, 98362, P 70,400, (360) 452-8552, (800) 942-4042, info@olympic peninsula.org, www.visitolympicpeninsula.org

**Seattle · *Seattle CVB*** · Tom Norwalk, Pres./CEO, 1 Convention Place, 701 Pike St., Ste. 800, 98101, P 563,000, (206) 461-5800, (866) 732-2695, Fax (206) 461-5855, visitorinfo@visitseattle.org, www.visitseattle.org

**Seattle · *Seattle Southside Visitor Info.*** · Katherine Kertzman, Program Dir., 14220 Interurban Ave. S., Ste. 130, 98168, P 157,830, (206) 575-2489, (877) 885-9452, Fax (206) 575-2529, info@seattlesouthside.com, www.seattlesouthside.com

**Spokane · *Spokane Reg. CVB*** · Harry Sladich, Pres./CEO, 801 W. Riverside, Ste. 301, 99201, P 497,000, M 650, (509) 624-1341, (800) 662-0084, Fax (509) 623-1297, conventions@visitspokane.com, www.visitspokane.com

**Tacoma · *Tacoma Regional CVB*** · Tammy Blount, Pres./CEO, 1119 Pacific Ave., Ste. 500, 98401, P 713,400, M 300, (253) 627-2836, (800) 272-2662, Fax (253) 627-8783, info@traveltacoma.com, www.traveltacoma.com

**Vancouver · *Southwest Washington CVB*** · Kim Bennett, Pres., 101 E. 8th St., Ste. 240, 98660, P 403,000, (360) 750-1553, (877) 600-0800, Fax (360) 750-1933, info@southwestwashington.com, www.southwestwashington.com

**Wenatchee · *Wenatchee Valley CVB*** · Roger Clute, Exec. Dir., 55 S. Wenatchee Ave., Ste. 100, 98801, P 100,000, (509) 663-3723, (800) 572-7753, Fax (509) 663-3983, info@wenatcheevalley.org, www.wenatcheevalley.org

# West Virginia

**Beckley · *Southern West Virginia CVB*** · Doug Maddy, Exec. Dir./CEO, 1406 Harper Rd., 25801, P 225,000, M 400, (304) 252-2244, Fax (304) 252-2252, (800) VISIT WV, travel@visitwv.com, www.visitwv.com

**Bluefield · *Mercer County CVB*** · Beverly Wellman, Exec. Dir., 704 Bland St., P.O. Box 4088, 24701, P 64,980, (304) 325-8438, (800) 221-3206, Fax (304) 324-8483, info@mccvb.com, www.mccvb.com

**Bridgeport · *Greater Bridgeport CVB*** · Cynthia Hunter, Exec. Dir., 164 W. Main St., 26330, P 8,000, (304) 842-7272, (800) 368-4324, Fax (304) 842-1941, info@greater-bridgeport.com, www.greater-bridgeport.com

**Buckhannon · *Buckhannon-Upshur CVB*** · Lori Ulderich Harvey, Exec. Dir., 70 E. Main St., 26201, P 23,000, (304) 472-1651, Fax (304) 472-4620

**Charleston · *Charleston CVB*** · Julie Caldwell, Pres., 200 Civic Center Dr., 25301, P 60,000, (304) 344-5075, (800) 733-5469, Fax (304) 344-1241, info@charlestonwv.com, www.charlestonwv.com

**Elkins · *West Virginia Mountain Highlands Visitors Bur.*** · Bonnie Branciaroli, Exec. Dir., P.O. Box 1456, 26241, P 10,000, M 130, (304) 636-8400, Fax (304) 637-9900, info@mountain highlands.com, www.mountainhighlands.com

**Hinton · *Summers County CVB*** · Londa Justin, Exec. Dir., 206 Temple St., 25951, P 15,000, (304) 466-5420

**Huntington · *Cabell-Huntington CVB*** · Tyson Compton, Exec. Dir., P.O. Box 347, 25701, P 51,000, M 150, (304) 525-7333, (800) 635-6329, Fax (304) 525-7345, info@wvvisit.org, www.wvvisit.org

**Hurricane · *Putnam County CVB*** · Linda Bush, Exec. Dir., #1 Valley Park Dr., 25526, P 53,000, (304) 562-0518, Fax (304) 562-5375, tourism@putnamcounty.org, www.putnamcounty.org/tourism/

**Keyser · *Mineral County CVB*** · Anne Palmer, Exec. Dir., One Grand Central Park, 26726, P 27,234, (304) 788-2513, Fax (304) 788-3887, www.mineralchamber.com

**Lewisburg · *Greenbrier County CVB*** · Kara Dense, Exec. Dir., 540 N. Jefferson St., Box 17, Ste. N, 24901, P 34,693, (304) 645-1000, (800) 833-2068, Fax (304) 647-3001, info@greenbrierwv.com, www.greenbrierwv.com

**Morgantown** · *Greater Morgantown CVB* · Peggy Myers-Smith, Exec. Dir., 68 Donley St., 26501, P 75,000, (304) 292-5081, (800) 458-7373, Fax (304) 291-1354, info@tourmorgantown.com, www.tourmorgantown.com

**Oak Hill** · *New River CVB* · Sharon Cruikshank, Exec. Dir., 310 Oyler Ave., 25901, P 48,655, (304) 465-5617, (800) 927-0263, Fax (304) 465-5618, fayette@wvdsl.net, www.newrivercvb.com

**Parkersburg** · *Greater Parkersburg CVB* · Steven W. Nicely, Pres., 350 7th St., 26101, P 100,000, M 190, (304) 428-1130, (800) 752-4982, Fax (304) 428-8117, info@parkersburgcvb.org, www.greaterparkersburg.com

**South Charleston** · *South Charleston CVB* · Bob T. Anderson Sr., Exec. Dir., 311 D St., P.O. Box 8599, 25303, P 16,000, (304) 746-5552, (800) 238-9488, Fax (304) 746-2970, sochascvb@yahoo.com, www.southcharlestonwv.org

**Summersville** · *Summersville CVB* · Pam Cline, Exec. Dir., 1 Wilderness Rd., P.O. Box 231, 26651, P 2,500, (304) 872-3722, Fax (304) 872-0506, www.summersvillewv.org, pam@summersvillecvb.com, www.summersvillecvb.com

**Weston** · *Lewis County CVB* · Chris Richards, Dir., 499 U.S. Hwy. 33 E., Ste. 102, 26452, P 17,223, (304) 269-7328, (800) 296-7329, Fax (304) 269-3271, tour@stonewallcountry.com, www.stonewallcountry.com

**Wheeling** · *Wheeling CVB* · Frank O'Brien, Exec. Dir., 1401 Main St., 26003, P 36,000, (304) 233-7709, (800) 828-3097, Fax (304) 233-1470, fobrien@wheelingcvb.com, www.wheelingcvb.com

**White Hall** · *CVB of Marion County* · Marianne Moran, Exec. Dir., 2 Mountain Park Dr., P.O. Box 58, 26554, P 57,000, M 107, (304) 368-1123, (800) 834-7365, Fax (304) 333-0155, cvb@marioncvb.com, www.marioncvb.com

# Wisconsin

**Appleton** · *Fox Cities CVB* · Lynn R. Peters, Exec. Dir., 3433 W. College Ave., 54914, P 223,000, (920) 734-3358, Fax (920) 734-1080, tourism@foxcities.org, www.foxcities.org

**Beloit** · *Beloit CVB* · Martha Mitchell, Exec. Dir., 500 Public Ave., 53511, P 37,000, (608) 365-4838, Fax (608) 365-6850, (800) 4-BELOIT, info@visitbeloit.com, www.visitbeloit.com

**Brookfield** · *Brookfield CVB* · Nancy Justman, Exec. Dir., 17100 W. Bluemound Rd., Ste. 203, 53005, P 46,000, (262) 789-0220, (800) 388-1835, Fax (262) 789-0221, nancy@brookfieldcvb.com, www.visitbrookfield.com

**Cedarburg** · *Cedarburg Visitors Center* · Kristine Hage, Exec. Dir., W61 N480 Washington Ave., P.O. Box 104, 53012, P 16,000, (262) 377-9620, (800) 237-2874, Fax (262) 377-6470, info@cedarburg.org, www.cedarburg.org

**Door County** · *see Sturgeon Bay*

**Eau Claire** · *Chippewa Valley CVB* · Linda Adler, Exec. Dir., 3625 Gateway Dr., 54701, P 63,214, M 400, (888) 523-3866, (715) 831-2345, Fax (715) 831-2340, info@chippewavalley.net, www.chippewavalley.net

**Fond du Lac** · *Fond du Lac Area CVB* · Michael Schmal, CEO, 171 S. Pioneer Rd., 54935, P 42,000, (920) 923-3010, (800) 937-9123, Fax (920) 929-6846, visitor@fdl.com, www.fdl.com.

**Green Bay** · *Greater Green Bay CVB* · Brad Toll, Pres., 1901 S. Oneida St., P.O. Box 10596, 54307, P 256,908, (920) 494-9507, (888) 867-3342, Fax (920) 405-1271, visitorinfo@greenbay.com, www.greenbay.com

**Hazelhurst** · *Hazelhurst Info. Center* · Ted Cushing , Chrmn., P.O. Box 67, 54531, P 1,369, M 30, (715) 356-5800, info@hazelhurstwi.com, www.hazelhurstwi.com

**Holmen** · *see Onalaska*

**Janesville** · *Janesville Area CVB* · Christine Rebout, Exec. Dir., 20 S. Main St., Ste. 17, 53545, P 60,000, (608) 757-3171, Fax (608) 754-2115, (800) 48-PARKS, jvlcvb@jvlnet.com, www.janesvillecvb.com

**Kenosha** · *Kenosha Area CVB* · Dennis DuChene, Pres., 812 56th St., 53140, P 150,000, (262) 654-7307, (800) 654-7309, Fax (262) 654-0882, www.kenoshacvb.com

**La Crosse** · *La Crosse Area CVB* · Dave Clements, Exec. Dir., 410 Veterans Memorial Dr., 54601, P 52,000, M 360, (608) 782-2366, (800) 658-9424, Fax (608) 782-4082, info@explorelacrosse.com, www.explorelacrosse.com

**Ladysmith** · *Rusk County Tourism* · Andy Albarado, Dir., 205 W. 9th St. S., 54848, P 15,000, (715) 532-2642, Fax (715) 532-2649, (800) 535-RUSK, www.ruskcounty.org

**Lake Geneva** · *Lake Geneva CVB* · George F. Hennerley, Exec. V.P., 201 Wrigley Dr., 53147, P 7,400, (262) 248-4416, Fax (262) 248-1000, lgcc@lakegenevawi.com, www.lakegenevawi.com

**Madison** · *Greater Madison CVB* · Deb Archer, Pres., 615 E. Washington Ave., 53703, P 220,000, M 550, (608) 255-2537, (800) 373-6376, Fax (608) 258-4950, gmcvb@visitmadison.com, www.visitmadison.com

**Manitowoc** · *Manitowoc Area Visitor & Conv. Bur.* · Kathleen Galas, Pres., 4221 Calumet Ave., P.O. Box 966, 54221, P 35,000, M 150, (920) 683-4388, (800) 627-4896, Fax (920) 683-4876, visitmanitowoc@manitowoc.info, www.manitowoc.info.

**Marshfield** · *Marshfield CVB* · Sharon Kirn, Exec. Dir., 700 S. Central Ave., P.O. Box 868, 54449, P 20,000, (715) 384-4314, (800) 422-4541, Fax (715) 387-8925, sharon@visitmarshfieldwi.com, www.visitmarshfieldwi.com

**Mauston** · *Castle Rock & Petenwell Assn./Juneau County VB* · Barb Baker, Pres., 807 Division St., 53948, P 28,000, M 110, (608) 847-1904, Fax (608) 847-1904, barb@castlerockpetenwell.com, www.castlerockpetenwell.com

**Menomonee Falls** · *Menomonee Falls Visitor Center* · Suzanne Jeskewitz, Exec. Dir., N88 W16621 Appleton Ave., P.O. Box 73, 53052, P 34,600, (262) 251-2430, (800) 801-6565, Fax (262) 251-0969, sue@fallschamber.com, www.menomoneefallschamber.com

**Milwaukee** · *Visit Milwaukee* · Doug Neilson, Pres./CEO, 648 N. Plankinton Ave., Ste. 425, 53203, P 597,000, M 740, (414) 273-3950, (800) 231-0903, Fax (414) 273-5596, www.visitmilwaukee.org

**Oconomowoc** · *Oconomowoc CVB* · 174 E. Wisconsin Ave., P.O. Box 27, 53066, P 13,870, (262) 569-2186, (800) 524-3744, Fax (262) 569-3238, info@oconomowocusa.com, www.oconomowocusa.com

**Onalaska** · *Center for Commerce & Tourism* · Jean Lunde, Dir., 1101 Main St., 54650, P 16,425, (608) 781-9570, (800) 873-1901, Fax (608) 781-9572, info@discoveronalaska.com, www.discoveronalaska.com

**Oshkosh** · *Oshkosh CVB* · Wendy Hielsberg, Exec. Dir., 2401 W. Waukau Ave., 54904, P 63,000, (920) 303-9200, (877) 303-9200, Fax (920) 303-9294, wendy@visitoshkosh.com, www.visitoshkosh.com

**Pewaukee** · *see Waukesha*

**Phillips** · *Price County Tourism Dept.* · Kathy Reinhard, Dir., 126 Cherry St., Rm. 9, 54555, P 15,851, (715) 339-4505, (800) 269-4505, Fax (715) 339-3089, tourism@co.price.wi.us, www.pricecountywi.net

**Rice Lake** · *Rice Lake Tourism Comm.* · 37 S. Main St., 54868, P 10,000, (715) 234-8888, (800) 523-6318, info@ricelaketourism.com, www.ricelaketourism.com

**Rothschild** · *Wausau/Central Wisconsin CVB* · Darien Schaefer, Exec. Dir., 10204 Park Plz., Ste. B, 54474, P 80,000, (715) 355-8788, (888) 948-4748, Fax (715) 359-2306, info@visitwausau.com, www.visitwausau.com

**Stevens Point** · *Stevens Point Area CVB* · Tom Barrett, Exec. Dir., 340 Division St. N., 54481, P 67,692, (715) 344-2556, (800) 236-4636, Fax (715) 344-5818, info@stevenspointarea.com, www.stevenspointarea.com.

**Sturgeon Bay** · *Door County Visitor Bur.* · Jack Moneypenny, Pres./CEO, 1015 Green Bay Rd., P.O. Box 406, 54235, P 29,000, (920) 743-4456, Fax (920) 743-7873, (800) 52-RELAX, info@doorcounty.com, www.doorcounty.com

**Sturtevant** · *Racine County CVB* · Dave Blank, Pres./CEO, 14015 Washington Ave., 53177, P 185,000, (262) 884-6400, (800) 272-2463, Fax (262) 884-6404, dblank@racine.org, www.racine.org

**Superior** · *Superior-Douglas County CVB* · David W. Minor, CEO, 205 Belknap St., 54880, P 45,000, M 450, (715) 394-7716, (800) 942-5313, Fax (715) 394-3810, vacation@superiorchamber.org, www.superiorchamber.org

**Tomah** · *Tomah CVB* · Christopher Hanson, Exec. Dir., 901 Kilbourn Ave., P.O. Box 625, 54660, P 8,000, (608) 372-2166, Fax (608) 372-2167, (800) 94-TOMAH, info@tomahwisconsin.com, www.tomahwisconsin.com

**Waukesha** · *Waukesha & Pewaukee CVB* · Tammy Tritz, Exec. Dir., N14 W23755 Stone Ridge Dr., Ste. 225, 53188, P 77,000, (262) 542-0330, (800) 366-8474, Fax (262) 542-2237, info@visitwaukesha.org, www.visitwaukesha.org

**West Salem** · *see Onalaska*

**Wisconsin Dells** · *Wisconsin Dells Visitor & Conv. Bur.* · P.O. Box 390, 53965, P 3,787, M 650, (608) 254-8088, (800) 223-3557, Fax (608) 254-4293, info@wisdells.com, www.wisdells.com

**Wisconsin Rapids** · *Heart of Wisconsin Bus. & Eco. Alliance* · Connie Loden, Exec. Dir., 1120 Lincoln St., 54494, P 40,000, M 490, (715) 423-1830, Fax (715) 423-1865, info@heartofwi.com, www.heartofwi.com

# Wyoming

**Casper** · *Casper Area CVB* · Aaron McCreight, CEO, 992 N. Poplar St., 82601, P 69,000, (307) 234-5362, (800) 852-1889, Fax (307) 261-9928, visitors@casperwyoming.info, www.casperwyoming.info

**Cheyenne** · *Cheyenne Area CVB* · Darren Rudloff, Pres., One Depot Sq., 121 W. 15th St. #202, 82001, P 83,000, (307) 778-3133, (800) 426-5009, Fax (307) 778-3190, info@cheyenne.org, www.cheyenne.org, www.cheyenne.travel

**Cody** · *Cody Country Visitors & Conv. Cncl.* · Kimberly Jones, Exec. Dir., 836 Sheridan Ave., P.O. Box 2454, 82414, P 25,000, (307) 587-2297, (800) 393-2639, Fax (307) 527-6228, info@codychamber.org, www.codychamber.org

**Evanston** · *Bear River Travel Info. Center & State Park* · Wade Henderson, Supt., 601 Bear River Dr., 82930, P 12,000, (307) 789-6547, (307) 789-6540, Fax (307) 789-2618, www.artsparkshistory.com

**Laramie** · *Albany County Tourism Bd.* · Fred Ockers, Dir., 210 Custer, 82070, P 40,000, (307) 745-4195, (800) 445-5303, Fax (307) 721-2926, director@visitlaramie.org, www.visitlaramie.org

**Rawlins** · *Carbon County Visitors Cncl.* · Lisa Howell, Admin. Asst., 1815 Daley St., P.O. Box 1017, 82301, P 14,000, (307) 324-3020, (800) 228-3547, Fax (307) 324-8440, info@wyomingcarboncounty.com, www.wyomingcarboncounty.com

**Sheridan** · *Sheridan Travel & Tourism* · Penny Becker, Exec. Dir., P.O. Box 7155, 82801, P 25,000, (307) 673-7120, (888) 596-6787, Fax (307) 672-7321, stt@sheridanwyoming.org, www.sheridanwyoming.org,

**C & VB**

# Notes

# Economic Development Organizations

If the area that interests you is not listed in this section, please refer to the **United States Chambers of Commerce** Section. Many chambers double as the Economic Development Council for their area.

## Alabama

### Federal

**U.S. SBA, Alabama Dist. Ofc.** • Tom Todt, Dist. Dir., 801 Tom Martin Dr., Ste. 201, Birmingham, 35211, (205) 290-7101, Fax (205) 290-7404, www.sba.gov/al

### State

**Alabama Dev. Ofc.** • Neal Wade, Dir., 401 Adams Ave., Montgomery, 36130, (334) 242-0400, Fax (334) 353-1300, www.ado.state.al.us

### Communities

**Alexander City** • *Lake Martin Area Eco. Dev. Alliance* • Don McClellan, Dir., 1675 Cherokee Rd., P.O. Box 1105, 35011, P 40,000, (256) 215-4411, dmcclelland@cacc.cc.al.us, lakemartinalliance.com

**Athens** • *Limestone County Eco. Dev. Assn.* • Tom Hill, Pres., 1806 Wilkinson St., P.O. Box 1346, 35612, P 54,164, (256) 232-2386, Fax (256) 233-1034, tomhill@lceda.com, www.lceda.com

**Atmore** • *Escambia County Ind. Dev. Auth.* • Ms. Marshall Rogers, Exec. Dir., 406 S. Trammell St., P.O. Box 1266, 36504, P 35,000, (251) 368-5404, Fax (251) 368-1328, ecidamr@frontier net.net, www.escambiaida.com

**Auburn** • *Auburn EDC* • T. Phillip Dunlap, Dir., City Hall, 144 Tichenor Ave., Ste. 2, 36830, P 47,290, M (334) 501-7270, Fax (334) 501-7298, webecondev@auburnalabama.org, www.auburnalabama.org

**Bessemer** • *City of Bessemer* • Forest Davis, Dir. of Eco. Dev. Dept., 1800 3rd Ave. N., 35020, P 30,000, (205) 424-4060, Fax (205) 426-8374, www.bessemeral.org

**Birmingham** • *City of Birmingham Ofc. of Eco. Dev.* • Tracey Morant Adams, Dir., 710 N. 20th St., 35203, P 265,000, (205) 254-2799, Fax (205) 254-7741, www.birminghamal.gov

**Birmingham** • *Metropolitan Dev. Bd.* • Ted vonCannon, Pres., 500 Beacon Pkwy. W., 35209, P 1,000,000, (205) 942-7284, Fax (205) 942-7319, ted@mdb.org, www.mdb.org

**Brewton** • *Coastal Gateway Eco. Dev. Auth.* • Wiley Blankenship, Pres., 24300 Hwy. 41, 36426, P 77,729, (251) 248-2143, (800) 915-6576, Fax (251) 248-2676, info@cgeda.net, www.cgeda.net

**Cullman** • *Cullman Comm. & Eco. Dev.* • Peggy Smith, Dir., 200 First Ave. N.E., P.O. Box 1009, 35056, P 77,000, (256) 739-1891, Fax (256) 739-6721, cullmaneda@cullmaneda.org, www.cullmaneda.org

**Decatur** • *Morgan County Eco. Dev. Assn.* • Jeremy Nails, Pres./CEO, 300 Market St. N.E., Ste. 2, 35601, P 114,000, M 130, (256) 353-1213, Fax (256) 353-0407, mceda@mceda.org, www.mceda.org

**Decatur** • *North Alabama Ind. Dev. Assn.* • Tate Godfrey, Pres./CEO, 410 Johnston St., Ste. A, P.O. Box 1668, 35602, P 900,000, (256) 353-9450, Fax (256) 353-5982, tgodfrey@naida.com, www.northalabamausa.com

**Double Springs** • *Ind. Dev. Auth. Of Winston County* • Grady Batchelor, Pres., 11 Blake Dr., Ste. 3, 35553, P 25,000, M (205) 269-1780, Fax (205) 269-1780, grady@idawinston.org, www.idawinston.org

**Enterprise** • *Enterprise Coffee Geneva Eco. Dev. Corp.* • Frank Thompson CEcD, Exec. Dir., P.O. Box 310130, 36331, P 50,000, M 70, (334) 393-4769, Fax (334) 393-8127, www.ecgedc.org

**Evergreen** • *Conecuh County Eco. Dev. Auth.* • Daryl Harper, Dir., 100 Depot Sq., 36401, P 14,000, (251) 578-1000, Fax (251) 578-5660

**Florence** • *Shoals Eco. Dev. Auth.* • Forrest Wright CEcD, Pres., 20 Hightower Pl., Ste. 1, P.O. Box 580, 35630, P 143,000, (256) 764-0351, (800) 239-6087, Fax (256) 764-3850, shoalseda@seda-shoals.com, www.seda-shoals.com

**Gadsden** • *Gadsden-Etowah County Ind. Dev. Auth.* • Michael McCain, Exec. Dir., P.O. Box 271, 35902, P 103,059, (256) 543-9423, Fax (256) 547-2351, info@gadsdenida.org, www.gadsdenida.org

**Greenville** • *Butler County Comm. for Eco. Dev.* • Richard McLaney, Exec. Dir., P.O. Box 758, 36037, P 23,000, (334) 371-8400, (800) 743-1210, Fax (334) 371-8402, rmclaney@bcced.com, www.bcced.com

**Huntsville** • *Madison County Comm., Intl. Trade Dev. Center* • Anne Burkett, Dir., Dept. of Planning & Eco. Dev., 100 Northside Sq., 35801, P 280,000, (256) 532-3505, Fax (256) 532-3704, naita@naita.org, www.naita.org

**Lanett** • *Ind. Dev. Auth. of Chambers Co.* • Valerie Gray, Dir., 2102 S. Broad Ave., P.O. Box 269, 36863, P 37,000, (334) 642-1412, Fax (334) 642-6548, vgray@chambersida.com, www.chambersida.com.

**Mobile** • *Mobile Airport Auth.-Brookley Complex* • 1891 9th St., 36615, P 470,000, (251) 438-7334, Fax (251) 694-7667, info@mobairport.com, www.mobairport.com

**Montgomery** • *Alabama Dev. Ofc.* • Neal Wade, Dir., 401 Adams Ave., 36130, (334) 242-0400, Fax (334) 353-1300, www.ado.state.al.us

**Montgomery** • *Montgomery Area Coop. Dev.* • Randall George, Pres., 41 Commerce St., P.O. Box 79, 36101, P 352,000, (334) 834-5200, Fax (334) 265-4745, www.montgomerychamber.com

**Moulton** • *Lawrence County Ind. Dev. Bd.* • Luke Slaton, Exec. Dir., 12001 Alabama Hwy. 157, P.O. Box 367, 35650, P 35,000, (256) 974-0100

**Opelika** • *Opelika EDC* • Alfred F. Cook, Dir., c/o City Hall, 36803, P 25,000, (334) 705-5115, Fax (334) 705-5113

**Pelham** • *Shelby County Eco. & Ind. Dev. Auth.* • James Dedes, Exec. Dir., 1126 County Services Dr., 35124, P 178,182, (205) 620-6640, info@sceida.org, www.sceida.org

**Pell City** • *St. Clair-Blount Eco. Dev. Cncl.* • Edwin Gardner Jr., Exec. Dir., P.O. Box 1999, 35125, P 128,000, (205) 814-1440, chill@stclairedc.com, www.stclairedc.com

**Robertsdale** • *Baldwin County Eco. Dev. Alliance* • Robert Ingram, Pres./CEO, P.O. Box 1340, 36567, P 175,000, (251) 947-2445, Fax (251) 947-4229, ringram@baldwineda.com, www.baldwineda.com

**Russellville** • *Franklin County Dev. Auth.* • Sherri Price, 16109 Hwy. 43, Ste. C, 35653, P 32,000, (256) 332-8726, Fax (256) 332-8728, business@franklineda.com, www.franklineda.com

**Scottsboro** · *Jackson County Eco. Dev. Auth.* · Goodrich Rogers, Pres./CEO, 817 S. Broad St., 35768, P 52,000, (256) 574-1331, (800) 887-1331, Fax (256) 259-0873, jceda@scottsboro.org, www.jacksoncountyeda.org

**Selma** · *Selma & Dallas County Eco. Dev. Auth.* · M. Wayne Vardaman, Exec. Dir., 912 Selma Ave., 36701, P 40,000, (334) 875-8365, (800) 457-3562, Fax (334) 875-8453, vardaman@selmaeda.com, www.selmaalabama.com

**Sylacauga** · *Talladega County Eco. Dev. Auth.* · Calvin Miller, Exec. Dir., P.O. Box 867, 35150, P 81,673, (256) 245-8332, Fax (256) 245-8336, millercalv@tceda.com, www.tceda.com

**Troy** · *Pike County Eco. Dev. Corp.* · Marsha Gaylard, Pres., 100 Industrial Blvd., 36081, P 30,000, (334) 670-2274, Fax (334) 566-2298, mgaylard@troycable.net, www.troy-pike-edc.org

**Tuscaloosa** · *Tuscaloosa County Ind. Dev. Auth.* · P.O. Box 2667, 35403, P 170,000, (205) 349-1414, Fax (205) 349-1416, info@tcida.com, www.tcida.com

**Union Springs** · *Bullock County Dev. Auth.* · Dr. Julian Cope, Admin., 106 E. Conecuh Ave., P.O. Box 87, 36089, P 12,000, (334) 738-5411, Fax (334) 738-5310, bcda@ustconline.net

**Wetumpka** · *Elmore County Eco. Dev. Auth.* · Eric Basinger, Exec. Dir., P.O. Box 117, 36092, P 127,000, (334) 514-5843, Fax (334) 567-1109, eric.basinger@elmoreco.org, www.elmoreeda.com

# Alaska

## Federal

**Eco. Dev. Admin.** · Berney Richert, Eco. Dev. Rep., 550 W. 7th Ave, Ste. 170, Anchorage, 99501, (907) 271-2272, Fax (907) 271-2274, www.doc.gov/eda

**U.S. SBA, Alaska Dist. Ofc.** · Karen Forsland, Dist. Dir., 510 L St., Ste. 310, Anchorage, 99501, (907) 271-4022, Fax (907) 271-4545, www.sba.gov/ak

## State

**Alaska Bus. Dev. Center Inc.** · Gary Selk, Pres., 840 K St., Ste. 202, Anchorage, 99501, (907) 562-0335, Fax (907) 562-6988, abdc@gci.net, www.abdc.org

## Communities

**Anchorage** · *Alaska Ind. Dev. & Export Auth.* · Ted Leonard, Exec. Dir., 813 W. Northern Lights Blvd., 99503, P 700,000, (907) 771-3000, Fax (907) 771-3044, www.aidea.org

**Anchorage** · *Alaska Village Initiative* · Charles Parker, Pres./CEO, 1577 C St., Ste. 304, 99501, P 50,000, M 170, (907) 274-5400, Fax (907) 263-9971, rweaver@akvillage.com, www.akvillage.com

**Anchorage** · *Anchorage Eco. Dev. Corp.* · Bill Popp, Pres./CEO, 900 W. 5th Ave., Ste. 300, 99501, P 260,000, M 170, (907) 258-3700, Fax (907) 258-6646, info@aedcweb.com, www.aedcweb.com

**Anchorage** · *Southwest Alaska Muni. Conf.* · Michael Catsi, Exec. Dir., 3300 Arctic Blvd., Ste. 203, 99503, P 29,078, (907) 562-7380, Fax (907) 562-0438, info@swamc.org, www.swamc.org

**Fairbanks** · *Fairbanks Eco. Dev. Corp.* · Jim Dodson, CEO, 301 Cushman, Ste. 301, 99701, P 89,000, (907) 452-2185, Fax (907) 451-9534, fedc@ak.net, www.investfairbanks.com

**Glennallen** · *Copper Valley Dev. Assn.* · Barbara Challoner, Bus. Mgr., P.O. Box 9, 99588, P 3,086, (907) 822-5001, Fax (907) 822-5009, cvda@cvinternet.net, www.coppervalley.org

**Juneau** · *Juneau Eco. Dev. Cncl.* · Brian Holst, Exec. Dir., 612 W. Willoughby Ave., Ste. A, 99801, P 30,000, (907) 523-2300, Fax (907) 463-3929, info@jedc.org, www.jedc.org

**Kenai** · *Kenai Peninsula Borough Eco. Dev. Dist.* · John Torgerson, Exec. Dir., 14896 Kenai Spur Hwy., Ste. 103A, 99611, P 55,000, (907) 283-3335, Fax (907) 283-3913, info@kpedd.org, www.kpedd.org

**Kotzebue** · *NW Arctic Borough Eco. Dev. Commission* · Jade Hill, Exec. Dir., P.O. Box 1110, 99752, P 7,200, (907) 442-2500, Fax (907) 442-2930, (907) 442-3740, www.nwabor.org

**Palmer** · *Matanuska-Susitna Borough Eco. Dev.* · Dave Hanson, Dir., 350 E. Dahlia, 99645, P 80,000, (907) 745-9508, Dave.Hanson@matsugov.us, www.matsugov.us/business.cfm

**Sitka** · *Sitka Eco. Dev. Assn.* · Garry White, Exec. Dir., 329 Harbor Dr., Ste. 212, 99835, P 8,947, (907) 747-2660, Fax (907) 747-7688, inforequest@sitka.net, www.sitka.net

**Sitka** · *Sitka Eco. Dev. Comm.* · Wells Williams, Planning Dir., 100 Lincoln St., 99835, P 8,947, (907) 747-1824, Fax (907) 747-6138, www.cityofsitka.com

**Skagway** · *Skagway Dev. Corp.* · Trish Simms, 344 7th Ave., P.O. Box 1236, 99840, P 860, (907) 983-3414, skagdev@aptalaska.net, www.skagwaydevelopment.org

**Wrangell** · *Wrangell Eco. Dev. Dept.* · Carol Rushmore, Dir., 205 Brueger St., P.O. Box 531, 99929, P 2,200, (907) 874-2381, Fax (907) 874-3952, ecodev@wrangell.com, www.wrangell.com

# Arizona

## Federal

**U.S. SBA, Arizona Dist. Ofc.** · Robert J. Blaney, Dist. Dir., 2828 N. Central Ave., Ste. 800, Phoenix, 85004, (602) 745-7200, Fax (602) 745-7210, www.sba.gov/az

## State

**Arizona Dept. of Commerce** · Kent Ennis, Interim Dir., 1700 W. Washington, Ste. 600, Phoenix, 85007, (602) 771-1100, Fax (602) 771-1200, www.azcommerce.com

## Communities

**Apache Junction** · *City of Apache Junction Eco. Dev.* · Steve Filipowicz, Eco. Dev. Dir., 300 E. Superstition Blvd., 85219, P 41,000, (480) 474-5064, Fax (480) 474-5110, www.ajcity.net

**Ash Fork** · *Ash Fork Dev. Assn.* · Fayrene Hume, Pres., 518 Louis Ave., P.O. Box 293, 86320, P 2,000, (928) 637-2774, Fax (928) 637-0394

**Avondale** · *Avondale Eco. Dev.* · Dina Mathias, Eco. Dev. Specialist, 11465 W. Civic Center Dr. #210, 85323, P 76,000, (623) 333-1400, Fax (623) 333-0140, dmathias@avondale.org, www.avondale.org

**Benson** · *Southeast AZ Eco. Dev. Group* · George Scott, Exec. Dir., P.O. Box 1312, 85602, P 126,000, (520) 586-2330, saedg@qwestoffice.net, www.saedg.org

**Buckeye** · *Town of Buckeye, Eco. Dev. Dept.* · 1101 E. Ash Ave., 85326, P 33,000, M 37, (623) 349-6150, Fax (623) 349-6099, www.buckeyeaz.gov

**Bullhead City** · *Bullhead Reg. Eco. Dev. Auth.* · Richard Adams, Pres./CEO, 1848 Hwy. 95, Ste. 104, 86442, P 40,720, M 40, (928) 704-6374, Fax (928) 704-6376, bceda@frontiernet.net, www.bullheadeconomicdevelopment.com

**Bullhead City** · *Bullhead Reg. Eco. Dev. Auth.* · 1848 Hwy. 95 Ste. #104, 86442, P 45,000, (928) 704-6374, Fax (928) 704-6376, bceda@frontiernet.net, www.bullheadeconomicdevelopment.com

**Casa Grande** · *Central Arizona Reg. Eco. Dev. Found.* · Barry Albrecht, Exec. Dir., 540 N. Camino Mercado, Ste. 2, 85222, P 74,250, M 150, (520) 836-6868, Fax (520) 836-4898, ceo@caredf.org, www.caredf.org

**Chandler** · *Chandler Eco. Dev. Div.* · Christine Mackay, Dir., P.O. Box 4008, 85224, P 250,000, (480) 782-3030, (888) 663-2489, Fax (480) 782-3040, christine.mackay@chandleraz.gov, www.chandleraz.gov

**Coolidge** · *Growth Management Dept.* · C. Alton Bruce, Eco. Dev. Dir., 131 W. Pinkley Ave., 85228, P 11,000, (520) 723-6075, Fax (520) 723-6079, www.coolidgeaz.com

**Cottonwood** · *Cottonwood Eco. Dev. Cncl.* · Casey Rooney, Dir., 827 N. Main St., 86326, P 76,000, (928) 634-5505, Fax (928) 634-0260, crooney@ci.cottonwood.az.us, www.cottonwoodedc.com

**Douglas** · *Douglas Eco. Cncl.* · Victor Gonzalez, Eco. Dev. Dir., 425 Tenth St., 85607, P 18,000, (520) 417-7310, Fax (520) 364-7507, www.douglasaz.gov

**Eloy** · *Eco. Dev. Group of Eloy* · Gene Wilson, Pres., 628 N. Main St., 85231, P 11,000, (520) 466-1014, (888) 795-3569, Fax (888) 690-2767, info@edgeaz.org, www.edgeaz.org

**Flagstaff** · *City of Flagstaff Comm. Inv.* · 211 W. Aspen Ave., 86001, P 200,000, (928) 779-7632 x7255, Fax (928) 779-7684, ecodev@ci.flagstaff.az.us, www.cityofinnovation.com

**Gilbert** · *Gilbert Eco. Dev. Advisory Bd.* · Dan Henderson CEcD, Bus. Dev. Mgr., 90 E. Civic Center Dr., 85296, P 203,500, (480) 503-6865, Fax (480) 503-6170, dan.henderson@ci.gilbert.az.us, www.ci.gilbert.az.us

**Glendale** · *City of Glendale Eco. Dev. Dept.* · Brian Friedman, Dir., Eco. Dev. Dept., 5850 W. Glendale Ave., 85301, P 242,000, (623) 930-2983, Fax (623) 931-5730, business@glendaleaz.com, www.glendaleaz.com

**Globe** · *Gila County Comm. Dev. Ofc.* · Robert Gould, Dir., 1400 E. Ash, 85501, P 51,000, (928) 425-3231, Fax (928) 425-0829, www.gilacountyaz.gov

**Goodyear** · *Goodyear Eco. Dev. Dept.* · Harry Paxton, Dir., 190 N. Litchfield Rd., 85338, P 44,000, (623) 932-3025, Fax (623) 932-3028, gyecdev@goodyearaz.gov, www.goodyearaz.gov

**Kingman** · *Mohave County Eco. Dev. Div.* · Jonas Peterson, Deputy Dir. of Eco. Dev., P.O. Box 7000, 86402, P 170,000, (928) 753-0723, Fax (928) 753-0776, jonas.peterson@co.mohave.az.us

**Lake Havasu City** · *Partnership for Eco. Dev.* · Gary Kellogg, Pres., 314 London Bridge Rd., 86403, P 51,000, (928) 505-7333, www.lakehavasu.org

**Maricopa** · *Maricopa Eco. Dev. Dept.* · Danielle Casey, Mgr. of Eco. Dev., 45145 W. Madison Ave., P.O. Box 610, 85239, P 20,000, (520) 316-6812, Fax (520) 568-9120, danielle.casey@maricopa-az.gov, www.maricopamatters.com

**Mesa** · *City of Mesa* · William J. Jabjiniak, Eco. Dev. Dir., P.O. Box 1466, 85211, P 456,000, (480) 644-2398, Fax (480) 644-3458, www.cityofmesa.org

**Peoria** · *Peoria Eco. Dev. Dept.* · 8401 W. Monroe St., Rm. 190, 85345, P 146,000, (623) 773-7735, Fax (623) 773-7519, www.peoriaaz.gov

**Phoenix** · *City of Phoenix Comm. & Eco. Dev. Dept.* · Donald Maxwell, Dir., 200 W. Washington, 20th Flr., 85003, P 1,400,000, (602) 262-5040, Fax (602) 495-5097, www.phoenix.gov/econdev/

**Phoenix** · *Greater Phoenix Eco. Cncl.* · Barry G. Broome, Pres./CEO, 2 N. Central Ave., Ste. 2500, 85004, P 3,648,545, (602) 256-7700, (800) 421-4732, Fax (602) 256-7744, info@gpec.org, www.gpec.org

**Prescott** · *City of Prescott, Eco. Dev.* · Jane Bristol, Eco. Dev. Dir., P.O. Box 2059, 86302, P 45,000, (928) 777-1100, Fax (928) 777-1255, citystaff@cityofprescott.net, www.prescotted.com

**Safford** · *Safford Eco. Dev.* · Peter Stasia, Eco. Dev. Dir., 808 S. 8th Ave., P.O. Box 272, 85546, P 10,000, (928) 348-8515, Fax (928) 348-8515, pstasiak@ci.safford.az.us, www.saffordeconomicdevelopment.com

**Sahuarita** · *Sahuarita Eco. Dev.* · Kathy Ward, Eco. Dev. Mgr., 375 W. Sahuarita Center Way, 85629, P 10,000, M (520) 822-8815, kward@ci.sahuarita.az.us, www.ci.sahuarita.az.us

**Saint Johns** · *Eco. Dev. for Apache County* · Dana Overson, Dir., 395 S. First W., 85936, P 69,000, (928) 337-2644, Fax (928) 337-2646, doverson@co.apache.az.us, www.apachecounty.com

**Scottsdale** · *City of Scottsdale, Scottsdale Eco. Vitality Dept.* · Kathy Montalvo, Admin. Asst., 4021 N. 75th St., Ste. 102, 85251, P 220,000, (480) 312-7989, Fax (480) 312-2672, kmontalvo@scottsdaleaz.gov, www.scottsdaleaz.gov

**Sierra Vista** · *Sierra Vista Eco. Dev. Found.* · Bob Shepard, Exec. Dir., P.O. Box 2380, 85636, P 83,000, (520) 458-6948, Fax (520) 458-7453, admin@svedf.org, www.svedf.org

**Superior** · *Eco. Dev. Advisory Bd.* · Melanie Oliver, Town Mgr., 734 Main St., 85273, P 3,200, (520) 689-5752, Fax (520) 689-5822, townmanager@superior-arizona.com, www.superior-arizona.com

**Tempe** · *Tempe C/C Eco. Dev.* · Mary Ann Miller, Pres./CEO, 909 E. Apache Blvd., P.O. Box 28500, 85285, P 165,000, (480) 967-7891, Fax (480) 966-5365, info@tempechamber.org, www.tempechamber.org

**Tolleson** · *Tolleson Eco. Dev.* · Paul Magallanez, Eco. Dev. Dir., 9555 W. Van Buren, 85353, P 5,000, (623) 474-4998, Fax (623) 936-7117, www.tollesonaz.org

**Tucson** · *Tucson Reg. Eco. Opportunities* · Joe Snell, Pres./CEO, 120 N. Stone Ave., Ste. 200, 85701, P 800,000, M 300, (520) 243-1900, Fax (520) 243-1910, info@treoaz.org, www.treoaz.org

**Wickenburg** · *Wickenburg Eco. Dev. Comm* · Gary Edwards, Town Mgr., 155 N. Tegner St., Ste. A, 85390, P 6,077, (928) 684-5451 ext. 522, Fax (602) 506-1580, managersoffice@ci.wickenburg.az.us, www.ci.wickenburg.az.us

**Willcox** · *Willcox Eco. Dev.* · Kathy Smith, Exec. Dir., 1500 N. Circle I Rd., 85643, P 4,000, (520) 384-2272, Fax (520) 384-0293, willcoxchamber@vtc.net, www.willcoxchamber.com

**Winslow** · *City of Winslow Eco. Dev.* · Jim Ferguson, City Mgr., 21 Williamson Ave., 86047, P 9,800, (928) 289-2423, Fax (928) 289-3742, www.ci.winslow.az.us

**Yuma** · *Greater Yuma Eco. Dev. Corp.* · Julie Engel, Pres./CEO, 170 W. 16th St., Ste. 200, 85364, P 196,000, (928) 782-7774, Fax (928) 782-7775, info@greateryuma.org, www.greateryuma.org

# Arkansas

## Federal

**U.S. SBA, Arkansas Dist. Ofc.** · Linda Nelson, Dist. Dir., 2120 Riverfront Dr., Ste. 250, Little Rock, 72202, (501) 324-7379, Fax (501) 324-7394, www.sba.gov/ar

## State

**Arkansas Eco. Dev. Comm.** · Marie Haley, Exec. Dir., One Capitol Mall, Little Rock, 72201, (501) 682-1121, Fax (501) 682-7394, info@arkansasedc.com, www.arkansasedc.com

## Communities

**Arkadelphia** · *Eco. Dev. Corp. of Clark County* · Euodias Goza, Chrmn., P.O. Box 400, 71923, P 11,000, (870) 246-1460, shawnie@arkadelphiaalliance.com

**Benton** · *City of Benton* · Rick Holland, Mayor, 114 S. East St., P.O. Box 607, 72018, P 27,717, (501) 776-5900, Fax (501) 776-5910, www.benton.ar.gov

**Bentonville** · *Bentonville Ind. Dev. Corp.* · Rich Davis, V.P., 200 E. Central Ave., P.O. Box 330, 72712, P 30,000, (479) 273-2841, Fax (479) 273-2180, www.bbvchamber.com

**Booneville** · *Booneville Dev. Corp.* · Vanessa Wyrick, Exec. Dir., 210 E. Main St., P.O. Box 55, 72927, P 4,300, (479) 675-2666, Fax (479) 675-5158, information@booneville.com, www.booneville.com

**Camden** · *Camden Area Ind. Dev. Corp.* · Alan Dean, Pres., 314 Adams S.W., P.O. Box 99, 71711, P 13,000, (870) 836-6426, Fax (870) 836-6400, caidcark@yahoo.com

**Conway** · *Conway Dev. Corp.* · Brad Lacy, Dir. of Eco. Dev., 900 Oak St., 72032, P 120,000, (501) 329-7788, Fax (501) 327-7790, brad@conwayarkansas.org, www.conwayarkansas.org

**Crossett** · *Crossett Eco. Dev. Found.* · Cherub Alford, Grant Writer, 125 Main St., 71635, P (870) 364-8745, Fax (870) 364-2358, mike@cityofcrossett.net, www.considercrossett.net

**El Dorado** · *El Dorado Ind. Dev. Corp.* · Don Wales, Exec. V.P., 111 W. Main, 71730, P 22,000, M 40, (870) 863-6113, Fax (870) 863-6115, www.goeldorado.com

**Fayetteville** · *Fayetteville Eco. Dev. Cncl.* · Steve Rust, Pres./CEO, 21 W. Mountain St., Ste. #301, 72701, P 60,000, (479) 442-8885, Fax (479) 439-0126, kathryn@fayetteville.com, www.fayetteville.com

**Heber Springs** · *Cleburne County Ofc. of Eco. Dev.* · Jim Jackson, Dir., 300 W. Main St., 72543, P 26,000, (501) 362-8402, Fax (501) 362-4605, www.cleburnecountyarkansas.com

**Helena** · *Arkansas Delta Dev./Phillips County Port Auth.* · Martin Chaffin, Exec. Dir., 1201 Hwy. 49 W., P.O. Box 407, 72342, P 28,000, (870) 338-6444, Fax (870) 338-6445, director@helenaharbor.com, www.directorofhelenaharbor.com

**Hope** · *Hempstead County Eco. Dev. Corp.* · Wesley Woodard, Pres., 108 W. 3rd, P.O. Box 971, 71802, P 20,000, (870) 777-8485, Fax (870) 777-5266, hopeusa@sbcglobal.net, www.hopeusa.com

**Hot Springs** · *West Central AR Plan. & Dev. Dist., Inc.* · Dwayne Pratt, Exec. Dir., 835 Central Ave., Ste. 201, P.O. Box 21100, 71903, P 291,449, (501) 525-7577, Fax (501) 525-7677, www.wcapdd.dina.org

**Little Rock** · *Little Rock Port Auth.* · Paul Latture, Exec. Dir., 7500 Lindsey Rd., 72206, P 183,000, (501) 490-1468, Fax (501) 490-1800, platture@comcast.net, www.littlerockport.com

**Magnolia** · *Magnolia Eco. Dev. Corp.* · Steve Keith, Pres., 529 E. Main St., P.O. Box 866, 71754, P 25,000, (870) 234-4352, (800) 206-0889, Fax (870) 234-9291, ea@ccalliance.us, www.medc.cc

**Marion** · *Marion Eco. Dev.* · Kay Brockwell, Dir., 13 Military Rd., 72364, P 10,000, (870) 739-5414, Fax (870) 739-5448, kayb@marionarkansas.org, www.marionarkansas.org

**Monticello** · *Monticello Eco. Dev. Comm.* · Truman Hamilton, Exec. Dir., 211 W. Gaines, P.O. Box 1890, 71657, P 19,000, (870) 367-3076, (888) 909-8019, director@monticelloedc.org, www.monticelloedc.org

**Morrilton** · *Conway County Eco. Dev. Corp.* · John Gibson, Pres., 120 N. Division St., P.O. Box 589, 72110, P 20,300, M 50, (501) 354-2393, Fax (501) 354-8642, macc_ccedc@suddenlinkmail.com, www.morrilton.com

**Paragould** · *Paragould EDC* · Sue McGowan, Dir., 300 W. Court St., P.O. Box 124, 72451, P 24,000, (870) 236-7684, Fax (870) 236-7142, smcgowan@paragould.org, www.paragould.org

**Pine Bluff** · *The Eco. Dev. Alliance of Jefferson County* · Lou Ann Nisbett, Pres./CEO, 510 Main St., P.O. Box 5069, 71611, P 55,085, (870) 535-0110, Fax (870) 535-1643, nisbett@pinebluffchamber.com, www.jeffersoncountyalliance.com

**Russellville** · *Arkansas Valley Alliance for Eco. Dev.* · Jeff Pipkin CEcD, 708 W. Main St., 72801, P 56,000, (479) 858-6555, Fax (479) 858-6496, jpipkin@russellville.org, www.russellville.org

**Wynne** · *Cross County Eco. Dev. Corp.* · Aaron Stewart, Exec. Dir., 1790 N. Falls Blvd., Ste. 2, P.O. Box 234, 72396, P 20,000, (870) 238-9300, Fax (870) 238-7844, info@crosscountychamber.com, www.crosscountychamber.com

# California

## Federal

**U.S. SBA, Fresno Dist. Ofc.** · Carlos Mendoza, Dist. Dir., 2719 N. Air Fresno Dr., Ste. 200, Fresno, 93727, (559) 487-5791, Fax (559) 487-5636, www.sba.gov/ca

**U.S. SBA, Los Angeles Dist. Ofc.** · Alberto Alvarado, Dist. Dir., 330 N. Brand, Ste. 1200, Glendale, 91203, (818) 552-3215, Fax (818) 552-3286, www.sba.gov/ca

**U.S. SBA, San Diego Dist. Ofc.** · Ruben Garcia, Dist. Dir., 550 W. C St., Ste. 550, San Diego, 92101, (619) 557-7250, Fax (619) 557-5894, www.sba.gov/ca

## State

**Sacramento** · Calif Assn. for Local Eco. Dev. Prof. · Wayne Schell, Pres./CEO, 550 Bercut Dr., Ste. G, 95811, (916) 448-8252, Fax (916) 448-3811, wschell@caled.org, www.caled.org

## Communities

**Anaheim** · *City of Anaheim Eco. Dev.* · City Hall East, 200 S. Anaheim Blvd., 1st Flr., 92805, P 328,000, (714) 765-4323, economicdevelopment@anaheim.net, www.anaheim.net

**Apple Valley** · *Apple Valley Eco. Dev.* · Kenneth J. Henderson, Asst. Town Mgr., 14955 Dale Evans Pkwy., 92307, P 75,000, (760) 240-7000, Fax (760) 240-7910, development@applevalley.org, www.applevalley.org

**Arcata** · *Arcata Eco. Dev. Corp.* · Ross Welch, Exec. Dir., 100 Ericson Ct., Ste. #100A, 95521, P 370,000, (707) 822-4616, ross@aedc1.org, www.aedc1.org

**Auburn** · *Placer County Eco. Dev.* · David Snyder, Dir., 175 Fulweiler Ave., 95603, P 317,000, (530) 889-4016, Fax (530) 889-4095, dsnyder@placer.ca.gov, www.placer.ca.gov

**Bakersfield** · *Kern Eco. Dev, Corp.* · Richard Chapman, Pres./CEO, 2700 M St. #200, 93301, P (661) 862-5150, chapmanr@kedc.com, www.kedc.com

**Bakersfield** · *Kern Eco. Dev. Corp.* · Richard Chapman, Pres./CEO, 2700 M St., Ste. 200, 93301, P 774,131, (661) 862-5150, Fax (661) 862-5151, kedc@kedc.com, www.kedc.com

**Belmont** · *San Mateo County Eco. Dev. Assn.* · Dan Cruey, Pres./CEO, 1301 Shoreway Rd., Ste. 150, 94002, P 775,000, M (650) 413-5600, Fax (650) 413-5909, samceda@samceda.org, www..org

**Berkeley** · *Berkeley Eco. Dev.* · 2180 Milvia St., 94704, P 103,000, (510) 981-7530, Fax (510) 981-7099, ecodev@cityofberkeley.info, www.ci.berkeley.ca.us

**Brawley** · *Brawley Eco. Dev. Comm.* · Nicole Nicholas Gilles, CEO, 204 S. Imperial Ave., P.O. Box 218, 92227, P 25,000, (760) 344-3160, Fax (760) 344-7611, www.bedc.ca.gov

**Brea** · *Brea Eco. Dev.* · Eric Nicoll, Dir., 1 Civic Center Circle, Level 2, 92821, P 38,000, (714) 671-4421, Fax (714) 671-4480, ericn@cityofbrea.net, www.ci.brea.ca.us

**Burbank** · *Burbank Eco. Dev.* · Scott McGookin, Mgr., 275 E. Olive Ave., 91510, P 105,000, (818) 238-5180, Fax (818) 238-5174, smcgookin@ci.burbank.ca.us, www.burbankca.org

**Calexico** · *Calexico Redev. Agency* · Ralph Velez, Exec. Dir., 608 Heber Ave., 92231, P 37,652, (760) 768-2177, Fax (760) 357-3831, www.calexico.ca.gov

**California City** · *California City Eco. Dev. Corp.* · James Quiggle, Pres., 8001 California City Blvd., 93505, P 13,500, M 56, (760) 373-2007, Fax (760) 373-1414, californiacityedc@verizon.net, www.californiacityedc.com.

**Camarillo** · *Ventura County Eco. Dev. Assn.* · Darlene Ruz, V.P., 1601 Carmen Dr., Ste. 215, 93010, P 700,500, M 300, (805) 388-3457, Fax (805) 388-9972, info@vceda.org, www.vceda.org

**Carson** · *Carson Eco. Dev.* · Cliff Graves, Mgr., 701 E. Carson St., 90745, P 100,000, (310) 233-4802, (310) 830-7600, cgraves@carson.ca.us, www.ci.carson.ca.us

**Ceres** · *Ceres Eco. Dev.* · Bryan Briggs, Eco. Dev. Mgr., 2720 2nd St., 95307, P (209) 538-5756, Fax (209) 538-5780, bryan.briggs@ci.ceres.ca.us, www.ci.ceres.ca.us

**Chico** · *Tri County EDC* · Marc Nemanic, Dir., 3120 Cohasset Rd., Ste. 5, 95973, P 282,200, (530) 893-8732, Fax (530) 893-0820, www.tricountyedc.org

**Chula Vista** · *South County Eco. Dev. Cncl.* · Cindy Gompper-Graves, Exec. Dir., 1111 Bay Blvd., Ste. E, 91911, P 700,000, (619) 424-5143, Fax (619) 424-5738, info@sandiegosouth.com, www.sandiegosouth.com

**Citrus Heights** · *U.S. SBA, Sacramento Dist. Ofc.* · Jim O'Neal, Dist. Dir., 6501 Sylvan Rd., Ste. 100, 95610, (916) 735-1700, Fax (916) 735-1719, www.sba.gov/ca

**Colton** · *Colton Eco. Dev. Cncl.* · Candace Cassel, Dir., 650 N. La Cadena Dr., 92324, P 52,000, (909) 370-5167, Fax (909) 370-5167, rda@ci.colton.ca.us, www.ci.colton.ca.us

**Colusa** · *Colusa County Eco. Dev. Corp.* · Lynda Reynolds, 2963 Davison Ct., P.O. Box 1077, 95932, P 22,000, (530) 458-3028, lyndareynolds@colusacountyedc.com, www.colusacountyedc.com

**Commerce** · *Comm. Dev. Dept.* · Robert Zarrilli, Dir., 2535 Commerce Way, 90040, P 13,000, (323) 722-4805, Fax (323) 888-6537, www.ci.commerce.ca.us

**Concord** · *Contra Costa Cncl.* · Linda Best, Exec. Dir., 1355 Willow Way, Ste. 253, 94520, P 900,000, (925) 246-1880, Fax (925) 674-1654, info@contracostacouncil.com, www.contracostacouncil.com

**Cypress** · *City of Cypress Comm. Dev.* · Ted Commerdinger, Comm. Dev. Dir., 5275 Orange Ave., P.O. Box 609, 90630, P 47,000, (714) 229-6720, Fax (714) 229-0154, cdd@ci.cypress.ca.us, www.ci.cypress.ca.us

**El Cajon** · *San Diego East County Eco. Dev. Cncl.* · Deanna Weeks, Dir., 1870 Cordell Ct. #202, 92020, P 415,000, (619) 258-3670, Fax (619) 258-3674, www.eastcountyedc.org

**El Centro** · *Imperial County Planning & Eco. Dev.* · Jurg Heuberger, Dir., 801 Main St., 92243, P 144,200, (760) 482-4236, Fax (760) 353-8338, www.imperialcounty.net

**Escondido** · *City of Escondido Eco. Dev. Div.* · Jo Ann Case, Eco. Dev. Mgr., 201 N. Broadway, 92025, P 143,000, (760) 839-4563, Fax (760) 739-7004, www.escondido.org

**Eureka** · *Redwood Region Eco. Dev. Comm.* · 520 E St., 95501, P 127,000, (707) 445-9651, Fax (707) 445-9652, www.rredc.com

**Fairfield** · *Solano EDC* · Mike Ammann, Pres., 360 Campus Ln., Ste. 102, 94534, P 420,000, M 200, (707) 864-1855, Fax (707) 864-6621, mike@solanoedc.org, www.solanoedc.org

**Fontana** · *Fontana Eco. Dev.* · Elisa Grey, Mgr., 8353 Sierra Ave., 92335, P 190,000, (909) 350-6741, Fax (909) 350-6616, www.fontanabusiness.org

**Fortuna** · *Fortuna Bus. Improvement Dist.* · David Reed, Coord., P.O. Box 1000, 95540, P 11,350, (707) 725-9261, Fax (707) 725-0806, info@fortunabusiness.com, www.fortunabusiness.com

**Fountain Valley** · *City of Fountain Valley, Planning Dept.* · Andy Perea, Dir., 10200 Slater Ave., 92708, P 57,000, (714) 593-4400, Fax (714) 593-4525, www.fountainvalley.org

**Fresno** · *Eco. Dev. Corp. serving Fresno County* · Steve Geil, Pres./CEO, 906 N St., Ste. 120, 93716, P 917,515, (559) 476-2500, Fax (559) 233-2156, info@fresnoedc.com, www.fresnoedc.com

**Fullerton** · *City of Fullerton Redevelopment & Eco. Dev.* · Nicole Coats, Project Mgr., 303 W. Commonwealth, 92832, P 133,000, (714) 738-4102, (714) 738-6877, Fax (714) 738-6843, nicolec@ci.fullerton.ca.us, www.cityoffullerton.com

**Garden Grove** · *Garden Grove Eco. Dev.* · Chet Yoshizaki, Dir., 11222 Acacia Pkwy., 92840, P 166,000, (714) 741-5120, business@ci.garden-grove.ca.us, www.ci.garden-grove.ca.us

**Gilroy** · *Gilroy Eco. Dev. Corp.* · Richard Vahner, Pres., 7471 Monterey St., 95020, P 52,000, (408) 847-7611, Fax (408) 842-6010, gilroy@gilroyedc.org, www.gilroyedc.org

**Glendale** · *Glendale Eco. Dev. Svcs.* · Ken Hitts, Mgr., 633 E. Broadway Ste. #201, 91206, P 207,000, (818) 548-3155, Fax (818) 409-7239, khitts@ci.glendale.ca.us, www.ci.glendale.ca.us

**Grass Valley** · *Nevada County Eco. Resource Cncl.* · Gil Mathew, Pres./CEO, 960 McCourtney Rd., Ste. A, 95949, P 95,300, (530) 274-8455, Fax (530) 274-3942, info@ncerc.org, www.ncerc.org

**Hanford** · *Kings County Eco. Dev. Corp.* · John S. Lehn, Pres./CEO, 120 N. Irwin St., 93230, P 144,000, (559) 585-3576, Fax (559) 585-7398, jlehn@co.kings.ca.us, www.kingsedc.org

**Hesperia** · *Hesperia Eco. Dev.* · Steve Lantsberger, Dir., 9700 7th Ave., 92345, P 91,000, (760) 947-1906, Fax (760) 947-1000, www.cityofhesperia.us

**Hollister** · *Eco. Dev. Corp. of San Benito County* · P.O. Box 1265, 95024, P 57,000, (831) 636-1882, Fax (831) 636-1359, edcsbc@hollinet.com

**Huntington Beach** · *Huntington Beach Eco. Dev.* · Stanley Smalewitz, Dir., 2000 Main St., 92648, P 194,000, (714) 536-5582, Fax (714) 375-5087, ssmalewitz@surfcity-hb.org, www.surfcity-hb.org

**Irvine** · *Orange County Bus. Cncl.* · Lucy Dunn, Pres./CEO, 2 Park Plz., Ste. 100, 92614, P 3,000,000, (949) 476-2242, Fax (949) 476-9240, www.ocbc.org

**Irwindale** · *San Gabriel Valley Eco. Partnership* · Cynthia J. Kurtz, Pres./CEO, 4900 Rivergrade Rd., Ste. A310, 91706, P 2,000,000, M 200, (626) 856-3400, Fax (626) 856-5115, www.valleyconnect.com

**EDC**

**Jackson** • *Amador Eco. Dev. Corp.* • Ron Mittelbrunn, Exec. Dir., P.O. Box 1077, 95642, P 36,000, (209) 223-0351, Fax (209) 223-2261, www.amador-edc.org

**Lake Elsinore** • *Lake Elsinore Eco. Dev.* • Cathy Barrozo, GIS Analyst, 130 S. Main St., 92530, P 42,000, (951) 674-3124 x316, Fax (951) 674-2392, cbarrozo@lake-elsinore.org, www.lake-elsinore.org

**Lancaster** • *Greater Antelope Valley Eco. Alliance* • Mel Layne, Pres./CEO, 1028 W. Ave L-12, Ste. 101, 93534, P 450,000, (661) 945-2741, Fax (661) 945-7711, info@aveconomy.org, www.aveconomy.org

**Lemon Grove** • *Lemon Grove Redev. Agency* • Graham Mitchell, City Mgr., 3232 Main St., 91945, P 25,000, (619) 825-3800, Fax (619) 825-3804, www.ci.lemon-grove.ca.us

**Lompoc** • *Lompoc Eco. Dev. Resources* • Kathleen GRiffith, Mgr., 100 Civic Center Plaza, P.O. Box 8001, 93438, P 40,000, (805) 736-1261, Fax (805) 875-8232, www.cityoflompoc.com

**Long Beach** • *Eco. Dev. & Cultural Affairs Bur.* • Robert Swayze, Mgr., Bus. Dev. Center, 110 Pine Ave., Ste. 1100, 90802, P 461,000, (562) 570-3800, Fax (562) 570-3897, www.longbeach.gov

**Los Angeles** • *LA County Eco. Dev. Corp.* • William C. Allen, Pres./CEO, 444 S. Flower St., 34th Flr., 90071, P 10,150,000, (213) 622-4300, Fax (213) 622-7100, www.laedc.org

**Lynwood** • *Eco. Resources Corp.* • Dutch Ross, Pres., 2600 Industry Way, 90262, P 65,000, (310) 537-4610, Fax (310) 762-6211, www.economicresources.org

**Madera** • *Madera County Eco. Dev. Comm.* • Bobby Kahn, Exec. Dir., 2425 W. Cleveland Ave., Ste. 101, 93637, P 135,000, (559) 675-7768, Fax (559) 675-3252, bkahn@maderacountyedc.com, www.maderacountyedc.com

**Martinez** • *City of Martinez Eco. Dev.* • Philip Vince, Mgr., 525 Henrietta St., 94553, P 36,000, (925) 372-3500, Fax (925) 299-5012, www.cityofmartinez.org

**Martinez** • *Contra Costa County Comm. Dev. Agency* • James Kennedy, Dir., 2530 Arnold Dr., Ste. #190, 94553, P 1,100,000, (925) 335-7200, Fax (925) 335-7201, www.ccreach.org

**Merced** • *City of Merced Eco. Dev. Ofc.* • Frank Quintero, Dev. Mgr., 678 W. 18th St., 95340, P 76,000, (209) 385-4788, (800) 723-4788, Fax (209) 723-1780, quinterof@cityofmerced.org, www.cityofmerced.org

**Merced** • *Merced County EDC* • Scott Galbraith, Pres./CEO, 470 W. Main St., Ste. 7, 95340, P 210,000, (209) 723-3889, Fax (209) 723-4450, www.mcedco.com

**Modesto** • *Stanislaus Eco. Dev. & Workforce Alliance* • Bill Bassitt, CEO, P.O. Box 3091, 95353, P 521,497, (209) 567-4985, Fax (209) 567-4944, bassittb@stanalliance.com, www.stanalliance.com

**Montebello** • *Dept. of Comm. Dev.* • Mike Huntley, Dir., 1600 W. Beverly Blvd., 90640, P 70,000, (323) 887-1390, Fax (323) 887-1401, www.cityofmontebello.com

**Moreno Valley** • *Moreno Valley Eco. Dev. Dept.* • Barry Foster, Eco. Dev. Dir., 14177 Frederick St., P.O. Box 88005, 92552, P 180,000, (951) 413-3460, Fax (951) 413-3478, www.moreno-valley.ca.us

**Morgan Hill** • *Morgan Hill Eco. Dev.* • Tammy Brownlow, Project Mgr., 17555 Peak Ave., 95037, P 37,000, (408) 776-7373, Fax (408) 778-7869, tammy.brownlow@morgan-hill.ca.gov, www.morgan-hill.ca.gov

**Needles** • *City of Needles Eco. & Comm. Dev.* • Cindy Semione, Dev. Asst., 817 Third St., 92363, P 6,000, (760) 326-5740, Fax (760) 326-5008, ndlspldr@citlink.net, cityofneedles.com

**Newport Beach** • *Newport Beach Eco. Dev. Div.* • Leigh De Santis, Eco. Dev. Administrator, 3300 Newport Blvd., 92663, P 86,000, (949) 644-3225, (949) 644-3207, Fax (949) 644-3229, ldesantis@city.newport-beach.ca.us, www.city.newport-beach.ca.us

**North Fork** • *North Fork Comm. Dev. Cncl.* • Volney Dunavan, Admin., P.O. Box 1484, 93643, P 3,500, (559) 877-2244, Fax (559) 877-4267, nfcdc@netptc.net, www.northforkcdc.org

**Oakland** • *City of Oakland Comm. & Eco. Dev. Agency* • Gregory Hunter, Deputy Dir. of Redev., 250 Frank H. Ogawa Plz., Ste. 5313, 94612, P 600,000, (510) 238-3015, Fax (510) 238-3691, www.oaklandnet.com

**Oakland** • *Eco. Dev. Alliance for Bus.-EDAB* • Bruce Kern, Dir., 1221 Oak St., Ste. 555, 94612, P 1,498,000, M 600, (510) 272-3874, Fax (510) 272-5007, bkern@edab.org, www.edab.org, www.acgov.org

**Oceanside** • *City of Oceanside Eco. & Comm. Dev.* • Jane McVey, Eco. & Comm. Dev. Dir., 300 N. Coast Hwy., 92054, P 176,644, (760) 435-3352, Fax (760) 722-1057, jmcvey@ci.oceanside.ca.us, www.ci.oceanside.ca.us

**Ontario** • *City of Ontario Redev. Agency* • John P. Andrews, Redev. Dir., 603 N. Euclid, 91762, P 145,000, (909) 395-2005, Fax (909) 395-2290, www.ci.ontario.ca.us

**Oxnard** • *Eco. Dev. Corp. of Oxnard* • Steven L. Kinney, Pres., 400 E. Esplanade Dr., Ste. 301, 93036, P 189,000, (805) 385-7444, (800) 422-6332, Fax (805) 385-7452, steve@edco.us, www.edco.us

**Palm Desert** • *Coachella Valley Eco. Partnership* • Shawnna Trombetta, Dir. of Bus. Dev., 73-710 Fred Waring Dr., Ste. #106, 92260, P 326,000, (760) 340-1575, (888) 318-CVEP, Fax (760) 340-9212, admin@cvep.com, www.cvep.com

**Pasadena** • *City of Pasadena Planning & Dev.* • Richard Bruckner, Dir. of Planning & Dev., 175 N. Garfield, 3rd Flr., 91109, P 140,000, (626) 744-4660, Fax (626) 744-7041, www.cityofpasadena.net

**Pico Rivera** • *Pico Rivera Redevelopment Agency* • Jeff Brauckmann, Admin., 6615 Passons Blvd., P.O. Box 1016, 90660, P 67,000, (562) 801-4379, Fax (562) 801-4765, www.pico-rivera.org

**Placerville** • *El Dorado County Eco. Dev.* • Samuel Driggers, Dir., 330 Fair Ln., 95667, P 177,000, (530) 621-5570, samuel.driggers@edcgov.us, www.edcgov.us

**Quincy** • *Plumas Corp.* • John Sheehan, Exec. Dir., 550 Crescent St., P.O. Box 3880, 95971, P 23,090, (530) 283-3739, Fax (530) 283-5465, plumasco@psln.com, www.plumascounty.org

**Red Bluff** • *Tehama Local Dev. Corp.* • Dexter Wright, Exec. Dir., 1740 Airport Blvd., P.O. Box 1224, 96080, P 65,000, (530) 529-7100, Fax (530) 529-0453, tldc@tehama.net, www.tldc.com

**Redding** • *Eco. Dev. of Shasta County* • Greg O'Sullivan, Pres., 410 Hemsted, Ste. 220, 96002, P 180,000, (530) 224-4920, (800) 207-4278, Fax (530) 224-4921, edc@shastaedc.org, www.shastaedc.org

**Redding** • *Superior Calif. Eco. Dev. Inc.* • Robert Nash, CEO, 499 Hemsted Dr.., Ste. A, 96002, P 250,000, (530) 225-2760, Fax (530) 225-2769, www.scedd.org

**Rialto** • *Rialto Redev. Agency* • Rob Steel, Dir., 131 S, Riverside Ave., 92376, P 97,400, (909) 879-1140, Fax (909) 875-5467, rda@rialtoca.gov, www.ci.rialto.ca.us

**Riverside** • *Inland Empire Eco. Partnership* • Bill Carney, Pres./CEO, 1201 Research Park Dr., Ste. 100, 92507, (951) 779-6700, Fax (951) 779-0675, bcarney@ieep.com, www.ieep.com

**Riverside** · *Riverside County Eco. Dev. Agency* · Robin Zimpser, Asst. CEO, 1325 Spruce St., Ste. #400, P.O. Box 1180, 92502, P 1,946,000, (951) 955-8916, Fax (951) 955-6686, mortiz-sosa@rivcoeda.org, www.rivcoeda.org

**Sacramento** · *Sacramento Area Commerce & Trade Org.* · Barbara A. Hayes, Exec. Dir., 400 Capitol Mall, Ste. 2500, 95814, (916) 441-2144, Fax (916) 441-2312, www.sacto.org

**Sacramento** · *Valley Vision* · Bill Mueller, CEO, 2320 Broadway, 95818, P 457,000, (916) 325-1630, Fax (916) 325-1635, mail@valleyvision.org, www.valleyvision.org

**San Bernardino** · *San Bernardino County Eco. Dev.* · Simone McFarland, Mgr., 215 N. D St. #201, 92415, P 1,970,000, (909) 387-4700, Fax (909) 387-9855

**San Diego** · *San Diego Reg. Eco. Dev. Corp.* · Julie Meier Wright, Pres./CEO, 530 B St., 7th Flr., 92101, P 3,500,000, (619) 234-8484, Fax (619) 234-1935, www.sandiegobusiness.org

**San Diego** · *San Diego Unified Port Dist.* · Charles Wurster, Pres./CEO, 3165 Pacific Hwy., P.O. Box 120488, 92112, (619) 686-6200, (800) 854-2757, Fax (619) 686-6547, www.portofsandiego.org

**San Francisco** · *Mission Eco. Dev. Agency* · Luis Granados, Exec. Dir., 3505 20th St., 94110, P 700,000, (415) 282-3334, Fax (415) 282-3320, lgranados@medasf.org, www.medasf.org

**San Francisco** · *San Francisco Center for Eco. Dev.* · Dennis Conaghan, Exec. Dir., 235 Montgomery St., Flr. 12, 94104, P 740,000, (415) 217-5187, info@sfced.org, www.sfced.org

**San Francisco** · *U.S. SBA, San Francisco Dist. Ofc.* · Mark Quinn, Dist. Dir., 455 Market St., 6th Flr., 94105, (415) 744-6820, www.sba.gov/ca

**San Jose** · *City of San Jose Ofc. Of Eco. Dev.* · Paul Krutko, Dir., 200 E. Santa Clara St., 17th Flr., 95113, P 1,000,000, (408) 535-8181, Fax (408) 292-6719, www.sjeconomy.com

**San Juan Capistrano** · *San Juan Capistrano Eco. Dev.* · Douglas Dumhart, Mgr., 32400 Paseo Adelanto, 92675, P 35,000, (949) 493-1171, (949) 443-6316, Fax (949) 493-1053, ddumhart@sanjuancapistrano.org, www.sanjuancapistrano.org

**San Luis Obispo** · *San Luis Obispo Eco. Dev.* · Claire Clark, Mgr., 990 Palm St., 93401, P 44,000, (805) 781-7164, Fax (805) 781-7109, cclark@slocity.org, www.ci.san-luis-obispo.ca.us

**Santa Ana** · *Southland Eco. Dev. Corp.* · James Davis, Pres., 400 N. Tustin Ave., Ste. 125, 92705, P 4,000,000, (714) 868-0001, Fax (714) 868-0003, www.southlandedc.com

**Santa Ana** · *U.S. SBA, Santa Ana Dist. Ofc.* · Adalberto Quijada, Dist. Dir., 200 W. Santa Ana Blvd., Ste. 700, 92701, (714) 550-7420, Fax (714) 550-0191, www.sba.gov/ca

**Santa Cruz** · *City of Santa Cruz Dept. of Planning & Comm. Dev.* · Ken Thomas, Future Planning, 809 Center St., Rm. 206, 95060, P 54,593, (831) 420-5100, Fax (831) 420-5101, www.ci.santa-cruz.ca.us

**Santa Maria** · *Santa Maria Valley Eco. Dev. Comm.* · Robert P. Hatch, Pres./CEO, 614 S. Broadway, 93454, P 137,000, (805) 925-2403, (888) 768-6274, Fax (805) 928-7559, chmbrchief@aol.com, www.santamariaedc.com

**Santa Monica** · *Santa Monica Eco. Dev. Div.* · Miriam Mack, Mgr., 1901 Main St., Ste. #E, 90405, P 94,000, (310) 458-8906, Fax (310) 391-9996, econdevel.mailbox@smgov.net, www.smgov.net

**Santa Rosa** · *Sonoma County Eco. Dev. Bd.* · Ben Stone, Dir., 401 College Ave., Ste. #D, 95401, P (707) 565-7170, Fax (707) 565-7231, bstone@sonoma-county.org, www.sonoma-county.org

**Seaside** · *City of Seaside Eco. Dev.* · Ray Corpuz, City Mgr., 440 Harcourt Ave., 93955, P 34,000, (831) 899-6700, Fax (831) 899-6227, www.ci.seaside.ca.us

**Shasta Lake** · *City of Shasta Lake* · Fred Castagna, Proj. Mgr., 1650 Stanton Dr., P.O. Box 777, 96019, P 10,000, (530) 275-7400, Fax (530) 275-7414, info@ci.shasta-lake.ca.us, www.ci.shasta-lake.ca.us

**Simi Valley** · *City of Simi Valley* · Brian Gablar, Dir. of Eco. Dev., 2929 Tapo Canyon Rd., 93063, P 125,000, (805) 583-6701, Fax (805) 526-2489, bgabler@simivalley.org, www.simivalley.org

**Sonora** · *Central Sierra Planning Cncl.* · Larry Busby, Exec. Dir., 53 W. Bradford Ave., Ste. 200, 95370, (209) 532-8768, Fax (209) 532-7599, cspc@mlode.com

**Stockton** · *San Joaquin Partnership* · Michael E. Locke, Pres./CEO, 2800 W. March Ln., Ste. #470, 95219, P 664,000, (209) 956-3380, (800) 570-5627, Fax (209) 956-1520, www.sjpnet.org

**Temecula** · *Temecula Eco. Dev.* · 43200 Business Park Dr., 92589, P 101,000, (951) 694-6444, (888) 836-2852, www.cityoftemecula.org

**Thousand Oaks** · *Thousand Oaks Eco. Dev.* · Gary Wartik, Eco. Dev. Mgr., 2100 Thousand Oaks Blvd., 91362, P 125,000, (805) 449-2313, (805) 449-2100, www.toaks.org

**Tulare** · *Tulare County Eco. Dev. Corp.* · Paul Saldana, Pres./CEO, 4500 S. Laspina St., 93274, P 370,000, (559) 688-3388, Fax (559) 688-1406, info@edctulare.com, www.sequoiavalley.com

**Twenty-nine Palms** · *City of Twenty-nine Palms* · Charles LaClaire, Comm. Dev. Dir., 6136 Adobe Rd., 92277, P 27,337, (760) 367-6799, Fax (760) 367-4890, admin@ci.twentynine-palms.ca.us, www.ci.twentynine-palms.ca.us

**Vacaville** · *City of Vacaville* · Michael Palombo, Eco. Dev. Mgr., City Hall, 650 Merchant St., 95688, P 98,000, (707) 449-5114, Fax (707) 449-5149, mpalombo@cityofvacaville.com, www.cityofvacaville.com

**Vallejo** · *City of Vallejo Eco. Dev. Div.* · Susan McCue, Prog. Mgr., 555 Santa Clara St., 94590, P 120,000, (707) 648-4444, Fax (707) 648-4499, econdev@ci.vallejo.ca.us, www.ci.vallejo.ca.us

**Van Nuys** · *Valley Eco. Dev. Center* · Roberto Barragan, Pres., 5121 Van Nuys Blvd., 3rd Flr., 91403, P 213,000, (818) 907-9977, Fax (818) 907-9720, www.vedc.org

**Ventura** · *City of Ventura Eco. Dev.* · 501 Poli St., Rm. 218, P.O. Box 99, 93002, P 104,000, (805) 677-3935, Fax (805) 677-3949, edr@cityofventura.net, www.cityofventura.net

**Victorville** · *Victor Valley Eco. Dev. Dept.* · Keith Metzler, Dir., 14343 Civic Dr., 92392, P 104,000, (760) 955-5032, (760) 955-5000, Fax (760) 269-0080, info@victorvalleyca.com, www.victorvalleyca.com

**Visalia** · *Visalia Eco. Dev. Corp.* · Jim Claybaugh, Exec. Dir., 220 N. Santa Fe, 93292, P 120,000, (559) 773-8332, Fax (559) 734-7479, jim@visaliaedc.com, www.visaliaedc.com

**Vista** · *City of Vista Eco. Dev. Dept.* · 600 Eucalyptus Ave., 92084, P 94,500, (760) 639-6165, Fax (760) 724-3363, edinfo@cityofvista.com, www.cityofvista.com

**Walnut** · *City of Walnut Eco. Dev. Dept.* · Robert M. Wishner, City Mgr., 21201 La Puente Rd., 91789, P 32,000, (909) 595-7543, Fax (909) 595-6095, rwishner@ci.walnut.ca.us, www.ci.walnut.ca.us

**Watsonville** · *Watsonville Eco. Dev.* · Jacqueline Ventura, Admin. Analyst, P.O. Box 50000, 95077, P (831) 768-3095, Fax (831) 763-4114, jventura@ci.watsonville.ca.us, www.ci.watsonville.ca.us

**EDC**

**West Sacramento** · *City of West Sacramento/Eco. Dev.* · Diane Richards, Eco. Dev. Coord., 1110 W. Capital Ave., 95691, P 42,000, (916) 617-4535, Fax (916) 373-5848, dianer@cityof westsacramento.org, www.westsacrda.org

**Westminster** · *Westminster Redevelopment Agency* · Comm. Dev. Dir., 8200 Westminster Blvd., 92683, P 86,000, (714) 898-3311, Fax (714) 373-4684

**Woodland** · *Yolo County Eco. Dev.* · Wes Ervin, Mgr., 625 Court St., 95695, P 185,000, (530) 666-8066, Fax (530) 668-4029, wes.ervin@yolocounty.org, www.yolocounty.org

**Yreka** · *Siskiyou Cty EDC* · Tonya Dowse, Exec. Dir., 1512 S. Oregon St., 96097, P 45,150, (530) 842-1638, Fax (530) 842-2685, scedc@siskiyoucounty.org, www.siskiyoucounty.org

**Yuba City** · *Yuba-Sutter Eco. Dev. Corp.* · Stephen Brammer, COO, 1227 Bridge St., Ste. C, 95991, P 135,200, (530) 751-8555, Fax (530) 751-8515, ysedc@ysedc.org, www.ysedc.org

# Colorado

## Federal

**U.S. SBA, Colorado Dist. Ofc.** · Greg Lopez, Dist. Dir., 721 19th St., Ste. 426, Denver, 80202, (303) 844-2607, Fax (303) 844-6468, www.sba.gov/co

## State

**Colorado Ofc. of Eco. Dev. & Intl. Trade** · Don Elliman, Dir., 1625 Broadway, Ste. 2700, Denver, 80202, (303) 892-3840, Fax (303) 892-3848, don.elliman@state.co.us, www.advance colorado.com

## Communities

**Alamosa** · *San Luis Valley Dev. Resources Group* · Michael D. Wisdom, Exec. Dir., 610 State St., P.O. Box 300, 81101, P 48,506, (719) 589-6099, Fax (719) 589-6299, www.slvdrg.org

**Aurora** · *Aurora Eco. Dev. Cncl.* · Dick Hinson Sr., V.P., 562 Sable Blvd., Ste. 240, 80011, P 300,000, M 135, (303) 340-2101, Fax (303) 340-2111, hinson@auroraedc.com, www.auroraedc.com

**Boulder** · *Boulder Eco. Cncl.* · Frances Draper, Exec. Dir., 2440 Pearl St., 80306, P 103,000, (303) 786-7567, Fax (303) 938-8837, www.boulderbusiness.org

**Brighton** · *Brighton Eco. Dev. Corp.* · Susan Stanton, Exec. Dir., 36 S. Main St., 80601, P 36,000, (303) 655-2155, Fax (303) 655-2153, sstanton@brightonco.gov, www.brightonedc.org

**Broomfield** · *Broomfield Eco. Dev. Corp.* · Donald G. Dunshee, Pres., 2655 W. Midway Blvd., Ste. 370, 80020, P 53,000, M 105, (303) 469-7645, Fax (303) 469-9183, admin@broomfieldbusiness. com, www.broomfieldedc.com

**Canon City** · *Fremont Eco. Dev. Corp.* · Eddie McLish, Eco. Dev. Coord., 402 Valley Rd., 81212, P 47,000, (719) 275-8601, (800) 426-4794, Fax (719) 275-4400, info@fremontedc.org, fremontedc.org

**Castle Rock** · *Castle Rock Eco. Dev. Council* · Judy Woodley, Interim Pres./CEO, 513 Wilcox St., Ste. 230, 80104, P 42,000, M 55, (303) 688-7488, Fax (303) 688-5338, info@credco.org, www. credco.org

**Colorado Springs** · *Colorado Springs Reg. Eco. Dev. Corp.* · Mike Kazmierski, Pres./CEO, 90 S. Cascade Ave., Ste. 1050, 80903, P 654,350, M 300, (719) 471-8183, Fax (719) 471-9733, csedc@ csedc.org, www.coloradosprings.org

**Commerce City** · *City of Commerce City Eco. Dev.* · Brittany Morris, Eco. Dev. Dir., 7887 E. 60th Ave., 80022, P 40,000, (303) 289-3620, Fax (303) 289-3688, commercecityed.com

**Denver** · *Denver Ofc. of Eco. Dev.* · Andre Pettigrew, Exec. Dir., 201 W. Colfax, Dept. 1005, 80202, P 554,000, (720) 913-1999, Fax (720) 913-1802, oed@denvergov.org, www.milehigh.com

**Denver** · *The Downtown Denver Partnership, Inc.* · Tamara Door, Pres./CEO, 511 Sixteenth St., Ste. 200, 80202, P 554,000, (303) 534-6161, Fax (303) 534-2803, info@downtowndenver.com, www.downtowndenver.com

**Durango** · *La Plata Eco. Dev. Action Partnership* · Jack Llewellyn, Exec. Dir., P.O. Box 3874, 81302, P 47,000, (970) 259-1700, Fax (970) 385-7884, jack@durangobusiness.org, www.laplatacountycolorado.org

**Englewood** · *City of Englewood* · Alan White, Dir. of Comm. Dev., 1000 Englewood Pkwy., 80110, P 32,000, (303) 762-2300, Fax (303) 783-6895, commdev@englewoodgov.org, www. englewoodgov.org

**Englewood** · *Southeast Business Partnership* · John Lay, Pres./ CEO, 304 Inverness Way S., Ste. 315, 80112, P 1,371,000, (303) 792-9447, Fax (303) 792-9452, jlay@sebp.org, www.sebp.org

**Fort Collins** · *see Loveland*

**Fort Morgan** · *Morgan County Eco. Dev. Corp.* · Kari Linker, Exec. Dir., 231 Ensign, Ste. B-102, 80701, P 29,308, M 163, (970) 542-3527, (800) 522-4333, Fax (970) 542-3528, mcedc@morgan countyinfo.com, www.morgancountyinfo.com

**Georgetown** · *Clear Creek Eco. Dev. Corp.* · Peggy Stokstad, Pres./CEO, 502 6th St., 2nd Flr., P.O. Box 2030, 80444, P 10,000, (303) 569-2133, Fax (303) 569-3940, info@clearcreekedc.org, www.clearcreekedc.org

**Georgetown** · *Georgetown Promotion Comm.* · Town Hall, 404 6th St., P.O. Box 426, 80444, P 1,000, (303) 569-2555, Fax (303) 569-2705, www.town.georgetown.co.us

**Golden** · *Jefferson Eco. Cncl.* · Preston Gibson, Pres./CEO, 1667 Cole Blvd., Ste. 400, 80401, P 530,000, M 126, (303) 202-2965, Fax (303) 202-2967, info@jeffco.org, www.jeffco.org

**Grand Junction** · *Grand Junction Eco. Partnership* · Ann Driggers, Pres./CEO, 122 N. 6th St., 81501, P 138,000, M 220, (970) 245-4332, (800) 621-6683, Fax (970) 245-4346, gjep@gjep. org, www.gjep.org

**Greeley** · *Upstate Colorado* · Larry Burkhardt, Pres./CEO, 822 7th St., Ste. 550, 80631, P 228,000, M 100, (970) 356-4565, Fax (970) 352-2436, info@upstatecolorado.org, www.upstatecolorado.org

**Holyoke** · *Phillips County Eco. Dev. Corp.* · Nici Bishop, Dir., P.O. Box 424, 80734, P 4,680, M 50, (970) 854-4386, Fax (970) 854-4387, pced@pctelcom.coop, www.phillipscountyco.org

**Julesburg** · *Sedgwick County Eco. Dev. Corp.* · Patricia Stever, Exec. Dir., 100 W. 2nd St., 80737, P 2,700, (970) 474-3504, (800) 226-0069, Fax (970) 474-4008, sced@kci.net, www.sedgwick countyco.com

**La Junta** · *La Junta Eco. Dev.* · Ron Davis, Dir., 1802 Colorado Ave., 81050, P 9,000, (719) 384-6965, Fax (719) 384-6960, ron. davis@ojc.edu, www.lajuntaeconomicdevelopment.net

**Lakewood** · *City of Lakewood* · Rebecca Clark, Dir. of Comm. Planning & Dev., 480 S. Allison Pkwy., Civic Center North, 80226, P 144,000, (303) 987-7730, Fax (303) 987-7090, ed@lakewood. org, www.lakewood-colorado.org

**Littleton** · *Littleton Bus./Ind. Affairs Dept.* · Christian Gibbons, Dir., 2255 W. Berry Ave., 80165, P 42,000, (303) 795-3760, Fax (303) 795-3856, cgibbons@littletongov.org, www.littletongov.org

**Longmont** · *Longmont Area Eco. Cncl.* · John Cody, Pres./CEO, 528 Main St., 80501, P 86,000, (303) 651-0128, Fax (303) 682-5446, laec@longmont.org, www.longmont.org

**Loveland · *Loveland Info. EDC* ·** Dave Elbert, Exec. Dir., 2296 Glen Haven Dr., 80538, (970) 667-0905, Fax (970) 669-4680, delbert38@yahoo.com

**Loveland · *Northern Colorado Eco. Dev. Corp.* ·** Ms. Maury Dobbie, Pres./CEO, 3553 Clydesdale Pkwy., Ste. 230, 80538, P 230,000, M 250, (970) 667-0905, Fax (970) 669-4680, info@ncedc.com, www.ncedc.com

**Montrose · *Montrose Eco. Dev. Corp.* ·** Sandy Head, Pres., 100 Tessitori Ct., Ste. A, 81401, P 38,000, M 160, (970) 249-9438, (800) 270-0211, Fax (970) 249-9459, sandyh@montroseedc.org, www.montroseedc.org

**Northglenn · *City of Northglenn Eco. Dev.* ·** Kristin Sullivan, Eco. Dev. Coord., 11701 Community Center Dr., P.O. Box 330061, 80233, P 37,000, (303) 450-8743, Fax (303) 450-8793, www.northglenn.org

**Pagosa Springs · *Archuleta County Eco. Dev. Assn.* ·** Bart Mitchell, Exec. Dir., P.O. Box 1183, 81147, P 11,000, (970) 731-1443, info@archuletaeconomicdevelopment.org, www.archuletaeconomicdevelopment.org

**Parker · *Parker Eco. Dev. Cncl.* ·** Benjamin Snow, Exec. Dir., 19751 E. Mainstreet, Ste. R-11, 80138, P 42,000, (303) 841-8683, Fax (303) 841-1979, bsnow@parkercolorado.org, www.parkercolorado.org

**Pueblo · *Southern Colo. Eco. Dev. Dist.* ·** Allison Cortner, Exec. Dir., 1104 N. Main St., 81003, P 306,000, (719) 545-8680, Fax (719) 545-9908, allison@scedd.com, www.scedd.com

**Rifle · *Associated Governments of NW Colorado* ·** Aron Diaz, Dir., P.O. Box 351, 81650, P 218,000, (970) 625-1723, Fax (970) 625-1147, www.agnc.org

**Rocky Ford · *Rocky Ford Growth & Progress Inc.* ·** Julie Worley, Exec. Dir., 203 S. Main St., 81067, P 4,286, (719) 254-7414, Fax (719) 254-7416, jworley@ci.rocky-ford.co.us

**San Luis · *Costilla County Eco. Dev. Cncl.* ·** P.O. Box 9, 81152, P 3,500, (719) 672-0999

**Silverthorne · *NW Colorado Cncl. of Govt.* ·** Ashley Wilson, Exec. Dir., 249 Warren Ave., P.O. Box 2308, 80498, (970) 468-0295, (800) 332-3669, Fax (970) 468-1208, www.nwc.cog.co.us

**Stratton · *The Prairie Dev. Corp.* ·** Mrs. Jo Downey, Exec. Dir., 128 Colorado Ave., P.O. Box 202, 80836, P 25,660, (719) 348-5562, (800) 825-0208, Fax (719) 348-5887, www.prairiedevelopment.com

**Thornton · *City of Thornton Dev. Dept.* ·** Jeff Coder, Deputy City Mgr., 9500 Civic Center Dr., 80229, P 117,213, (303) 538-7295, Fax (303) 538-7373, citydevelopment@cityofthornton.net, www.cityofthornton.net

**Trinidad · *Trinidad-Las Animas County Eco. Dev. Inc.* ·** Nancy Lackey, Pres., 134 W. Main St., Ste. 12, 81082, P 16,302, (719) 846-9412, (800) 748-1970, Fax (719) 846-4550, tlac@tlac.net, www.tlac.net

**Wellington · *Wellington Eco. & Bus. Resource Comm.* ·** P.O. Box 1500, 80549, (970) 568-4133, info@wellingtoncolorado chamber.com, www.wellingtoncoloradochamber.com

**Westminster · *Adams County Eco. Dev., Inc.* ·** Bill Becker, Pres./CEO, 12050 Pecos St., Ste. 200, 80234, P 425,000, (303) 450-5106, Fax (303) 252-8230, www.adamscountyed.com

**Westminster · *City of Westminster* ·** Susan Grafton, Eco. Dev. Mgr., 4800 W. 92nd Ave., 80031, P 108,000, (303) 658-2400, Fax (303) 706-3922, sgrafton@cityofwestminster.us, www.cityofwestminster.us

**Wheat Ridge · *City of Wheat Ridge* ·** Ryan Stachelski, Eco. Dev. Mgr., 7500 W. 29th Ave., 80033, P 32,000, (303) 235-2806, Fax (303) 234-5924, rstachelski@ci.wheatridge.co.us, www.ci.wheatridge.co.us

**Yuma · *Yuma County Eco. Dev. Corp.* ·** Pat Duran, Exec. Dir., P.O. Box 244, 80759, P 10,000, (970) 848-3011, Fax (970) 848-3800, ycedc@ConsiderYumaCounty.com, www.ConsiderYumaCounty.com

# Connecticut

## Federal

**U.S. SBA, Connecticut Dist. Ofc. ·** Bernard Sweeney, Dist. Dir., 330 Main St., 2nd Flr., Hartford, 06106, (860) 240-4700, Fax (860) 240-4659, www.sba.gov/ct

## Communities

**Bridgeport · *Ofc. Of Planning & Eco. Dev.* ·** Edward Lavernoich, Deputy Dir., 999 Broad St., 06604, P 135,000, (203) 576-7221, (203) 576-7200, Fax (203) 332-5611, www.ci.bridgeport.ct.us

**Cheshire · *Town of Cheshire Eco. Dev. Comm.* ·** Jerry Sitko, Coord., 84 S. Main St., 06410, P 26,000, (203) 271-6670, Fax (203) 271-6688, jsitko@cheshirect.org, www.cheshirect.org

**Fairfield · *Town of Fairfield Comm. & Eco. Dev.* ·** Mark Barnhart, Dir., 611 Old Post Rd., 06824, P 57,340, (203) 256-3120, Fax (203) 256-3114, www.fairfieldct.org

**Hartford · *Metro Hartford Alliance* ·** John Shemo, V.P. & Dir. of Eco. Dev., 31 Pratt St., 5th Flr., 06103, P 709,000, (860) 525-4451, Fax (860) 293-2592, info@metrohartford.com, www.metrohartford.com

**Monroe · *Monroe Eco. Dev. Comm.* ·** Vinny Mangiacopra, Eco. Dev. Coord., 7 Fan Hill Rd., 06468, P 19,551, (203) 452-5400, Fax (203) 261-6197, www.monroect.org

**New Britain · *New Britain C/C-Eco. Dev.* ·** Bill Carroll, Bus. Dev. Coord., One Court St., 06051, P 72,000, (860) 229-1665, Fax (860) 223-8341, www.newbritainchamber.com

**Old Saybrook · *Eco. Dev. Comm.* ·** Wilma Asch, Exec. Dir., 302 Main St., Town Hall, 06475, P 10,500, (860) 395-3123, Fax (860) 395-3125, wasch@town.old-saybrook.ct.us, www.oldsaybrookct.org

**Waterbury · *Waterbury Dev. Corp.* ·** Leo Frank, CEO, 24 Leavenworth St., 06702, P 140,000, (203) 346-2607, Fax (203) 346-3910, frank@wdconline.org, www.wdconline.org

**Windsor Locks · *Windsor Locks Eco. & Ind. Dev. Comm.* ·** Steven Wawruck Jr., First Selectman, 50 Church St., 06096, P 13,000, (860) 627-1444, Fax (860) 292-1121, selectman@wlocks.com

# Delaware

## State

**Delaware Eco. Dev. Ofc. ·** Alan Levin, Dir., 99 Kings Hwy., Dover, 19901, (302) 739-4271, Fax (302) 739-5749, dedo.delaware.gov

## Communities

**Dover · *Central Delaware Eco. Dev. Cncl.* ·** 435 N. Dupont Hwy., P.O. Box 576, 19901, P 146,000, (302) 678-0892, Fax (302) 678-0189, www.cdedc.org

**Wilmington · *Wilmington Eco. Dev. Corp.* ·** William Abernethy, Dir., 100 W. 10th St., Ste. 706, 19801, P 80,000, (302) 571-9088, Fax (302) 652-5679, www.wedco.org

**Wilmington** · *Wilmington Ofc. Of Eco. Dev.* · Joe DePinto, Dir., 800 N. French St., 3rd Flr., 19801, P 80,000, (302) 576-2120, Fax (302) 571-4326, joedipinto@ci.wilmington.de.us, www.ci.wilmington.de.us

# District of Columbia

## Federal

**Eco. Dev. Admin.** · Herbert C. Hoover Bldg., 14th & Constitution Ave. N.W., Washington, 20230, (202) 482-5081, Fax (202) 273-4781, www.eda.gov

**Ofc. of Natl. Ombudsman** · Martin Gold, Dep. Natl. Ombudsman, 409 3rd St. S.W., MC2120, Washington, 20416, (888) 734-3247, Fax (202) 481-5719, ombudsman@sba.gov, www.sba.gov/ombudsman

## State

**Deputy Mayor's Ofc. For Planning & Eco. Dev.** · Neil Albert, Deputy Mayor, 1350 Pennsylvania Ave. N.W., Ste. 317, Washington, 20004, (202) 727-6365, Fax (202) 727-6703, dmped.eom@dc.gov, dcbiz.dc.gov

## Communities

**Washington** · *Dept. of Housing & Comm. Dev.* · Leila Finucane Edmonds, Dir., 1800 Martin Luther King Jr. Ave. S.E., 20002, (202) 442-7200, Fax (202) 442-8391, www.dhcd.dc.gov

**Washington** · *Greater Washington Bd. of Trade* · John Kane, Pres./CEO, 1725 I St. N.W., Ste. 200, 20006, (202) 857-5900, Fax (202) 223-2648, www.bot.org

# Florida

## Federal

**U.S. SBA, Jacksonville Dist. Ofc.** · Wilfredo Gonzalez, Dist. Dir., 7825 Bay Meadows Way, Ste.100B, Jacksonville, 32256, (904) 443-1900, Fax (904) 443-1980, www.sba.gov/fl

**U.S. SBA, Miami Dist. Ofc.** · Francisco Marrero, Dist. Dir., 100 S. Biscayne Blvd., 7th Flr., Miami, 33131, (305) 536-5521, Fax (305) 536-5058, www.sba.gov/fl

## State

**Enterprise Florida** · John Adams Jr., Pres./CEO, 800 N. Magnolia Ave., Ste. 1100, Orlando, 32803, (407) 956-5600, Fax (407) 956-5599, www.eflorida.com

## Communities

**Apopka** · *Apopka Area Eco. Dev. Cncl.* · Paul Seago, Pres., 180 E. Main St., 32703, P 40,000, (407) 886-1441, Fax (407) 886-1131, pauls@apopkachamber.org, www.apopkachamber.org

**Bartow** · *Central Florida Dev. Cncl.* · Tom Patton, Exec. Dir., 600 N. Broadway Ave., Ste. 300, 33830, P 567,000, (863) 534-4370, Fax (863) 534-0886, tom@cfdc.org, www.cfdc.org

**Bonifay** · *Holmes County Dev. Comm.* · Jim Brook, Exec. Dir., 106 E. Byrd Ave., 32425, P 19,000, (850) 547-4682, Fax (850) 547-4206, hcdc@wfeca.net, www.holmescountyonline.com

**Boynton Beach** · *City of Boynton Beach Eco. Dev.* · Quintus Greene, Dir. of Dev., 100 E. Boynton Beach Blvd., P.O. Box 310, 33425, P 67,000, (561) 742-6372, Fax (561) 742-6357, www.boynton-beach.org

**Bradenton** · *Bradenton Downtown Dev. Auth.* · Karen Kyser, Program Admin., 101 Old Main St., 34205, P 52,000, (941) 932-9440, Fax (941) 932-9552, www.ddabradenton.com

**Bradenton** · *Eco. Dev. Cncl., Manatee C/C* · Nancy A. Engel, Exec. Dir., 222 10th St. W., P.O. Box 321, 34206, P 311,000, M 130, (941) 748-3411, Fax (941) 750-6041, info@ManateeEDC.com, www.manateeEDC.com

**Brooksville** · *Hernando County Ofc. Of Bus. Dev.* · Michael McHugh, Dir., 15800 Flight Path Ave., 34601, P 150,000, (352) 540-6400, Fax (352) 754-5361, www.hernandobusiness.com

**Clearwater** · *City of Clearwater* · William B. Horne, City Mgr., 112 S. Osceola Ave., P.O. Box 4748, 33758, P 110,000, (727) 562-4040, Fax (727) 562-4052, www.myclearwater.com

**Crystal River** · *Citrus County EDC* · Randy Welker, Exec. Dir., 28 N.W. Hwy. 19, 34428, P 130,000, M 70, (352) 795-2000, Fax (352) 795-0009, info@citrusedc.com, www.citrusedc.com

**Daytona Beach** · *County of Volusia Eco. Dev. Dept.* · Phil Ehlinger, Interim Dir., 700 Catalina Dr., Ste. 200, 32114, P 492,984, (386) 248-8048, (800) 554-3801, Fax (386) 238-4761, www.floridabusiness.org

**Fort Lauderdale** · *Broward Alliance* · Joan Goodridge, Exec. V.P., 110 E. Broward Blvd., Ste. 1900, 33301, P 1,000,500, M 800, (954) 524-3113, (800) 741-1420, Fax (954) 524-3167, www.browardalliance.org

**Fort Myers** · *Lee County Ofc. of Eco. Dev.* · James Moore, Exec. Dir., 12800 University Dr., Ste. 300, 33907, P 615,741, (239) 338-3161, (800) 330-3161, Fax (239) 338-3227, edo@leegov.com, www.leecountybusiness.com

**Fort Walton Beach** · *Eco. Dev. Cncl. Of Okaloosa Co.* · Larry Sassano, Pres., P.O. Box 4097, 32549, P 180,291, M 200, (850) 651-7374, Fax (850) 651-7378, info@florida-edc.org, www.florida-edc.org

**Gainesville** · *Gainesville Cncl. For Eco. Outreach* · Brent Christensen, Pres./CEO, 300 E. University Ave., Ste. 100, P.O. Box 2342, 32602, P 240,000, (352) 378-7300, Fax (352) 378-7703, council@gceo.com, www.gceo.com

**Hialeah** · *Hialeah-Dade Dev. Inc.* · Mario Arus, Exec. Dir., 501 Palm Ave., 33010, P 254,000, (305) 884-1219, Fax (305) 884-1740

**Hollywood** · *South FL Reg. Planning Cncl.* · Carolyn Dekle, Exec. Dir., 3440 Hollywood Blvd., Ste. 140, 33021, (954) 985-4416, Fax (954) 985-4417, sfadmin@sfrpc.com, www.sfrpc.com

**Jacksonville** · *Flagler Dev. Group* · Armando Codina, CEO, 10151 Deerwood Park Blvd., Bldg. #100, Ste. 330, 32256, P 1,000,000, (904) 565-4100, Fax (904) 565-4144, www.flaglerdev.com

**Jacksonville** · *Jacksonville Port Auth.* · Roy Schleicher, Sr. Dir. of Mktg. & Trade Dev., 2831 Talleyrand Ave., P.O. Box 3005, 32206, P 1,300,000, (904) 357-3030, Fax (904) 357-3066, info@jaxport.com, www.jaxport.com

**Jacksonville Beach** · *Jacksonville Beach Planning & Dev. Dept.* · Raymond Fisher, Chrmn., 11 N. 3rd St., 32250, P 23,900, (904) 247-6231, Fax (904) 247-6107, planning@jaxbchfl.net, www.jacksonvillebeach.org

**Lake City** · *Columbia County Ind. Dev. Auth.* · Jim Poole, Exec. Dir., 162 S. Marion Ave., 32025, P 66,681, (386) 752-3690, Fax (386) 755-7744, jim@lakecitychamber.com, www.lakecitychamber.com

**Lakeland** · *Lakeland Downtown Dev. Auth.* · Anne B. Furr, Exec. Dir., 228 S. Massachusetts Ave., 33801, P 85,000, (863) 687-8910, Fax (863) 683-2783, anne.furr@lakelandgov.net, www.ldda.org

**Lakeland** · *Lakeland Eco. Dev. Cncl.* · Steven J. Scruggs, Exec. Dir., 210 S. Florida Ave., Ste. 328, 33801, P 93,428, (863) 687-3788, Fax (863) 688-2941, sscruggs@lakelandedc.com, www.lakelandedc.com

**Live Oak** • *Comprehensive Comm. Svcs. Corp.* • Bobbie Lake, Exec. Dir., 511 Goldkist Blvd., 32064, P 12,000, (386) 362-7143, Fax (386) 362-7058

**Live Oak** • *Suwannee County Dev. Auth.* • Dennis Cason, Pres., 816 S. Ohio Ave., P.O. Drawer C, 32064, P 38,500, (386) 362-3071, Fax (386) 362-4758, dcason@suwanneechamber.com, www. suwanneechamber

**Lutz** • *Pasco Eco. Dev. Cncl.* • Mary Jane Stanley CEcD, Pres./CEO, 16506 Pointe Village Dr., Ste. 101, 33558, P 424,355, (813) 926-0827, (800) 607-2726, Fax (813) 926-0829, mjstanley@pascoedc. com, www.pascoedc.com

**Macclenny** • *Baker County Dev. Comm.* • Darryl Register, Exec. Dir., 20 E. Macclenny Ave., 32063, P 25,000, (904) 259-6433, Fax (904) 259-2737, dregister@bakerchamberfl.com, www.baker chamberfl.com

**Mexico Beach** • *Mexico Beach Comm. Dev. Cncl.* • Lynn Marshall, Pres./CEO, P.O. Box 13382, 32410, P 1,300, (850) 648-8196, (888) 723-2546, Fax (850) 648-9403, lynn@mexicobeach. com, www.mexicobeach.com/cdc

**Miami** • *Dade County Ind. Dev. Auth.* • James Wagner Jr., Exec. Dir., 80 S.W. 8th St., Ste. 2801, 33130, P 933,700, (305) 579-0070, Fax (305) 579-0225, info@mdcida.org, www.mdcida.org

**Miami** • *Dept. of Bus. Dev.* • Penelope Townsley, Dir., 111 N.W. 1st St., 19th Flr., 33128, (305) 375-3111, Fax (305) 375-3160, www.miamidade.gov

**Miami** • *Downtown Dev. Auth. of Miami* • Alyce Robertson, Exec. Dir., 200 S. Biscayne Blvd., Ste. 2929, 33131, (305) 579-6675, Fax (305) 371-2423, dda@miamidda.com, www.miamidda.com

**Miami Beach** • *Miami Beach Comm. Dev. Corp.* • Roberto Datorre, Pres., 945 Pennsylvania Ave., 33139, P 350,000, (305) 538-0090, Fax (305) 538-2863, www.miamibeachcdc.org

**Milton** • *City of Milton Planning & Dev. Dept.* • City Hall, P.O. Box 909, 32572, P 7,500, (850) 983-5440, Fax (850) 983-5415, www.ci.milton.fl.us

**Milton** • *Team Santa Rosa Eco. Dev. Cncl.* • Cindy Anderson, Exec. Dir., 6491 Caroline St., Ste. 4, 32570, P 147,000, (850) 623-0174, Fax (850) 623-5932, canderson@teamsantarosa.com, www. teamsantarosa.com

**Naples** • *Eco. Dev. Cncl. Of Collier County* • Tammie Nemecek, Pres./CEO, 3050 N. Horseshoe, Ste. 120, 34104, P 290,000, M 250, (239) 263-8989, (866) 362-7537, Fax (239) 263-6021, edc@ enaplesflorida.com, www.enaplesflorida.com

**Ocala** • *Ocala-Marion County Eco. Dev. Corp.* • Peter Tesch, Pres./CEO, 3003 S.W. College Rd., Ste. 105, 34474, P 271,000, (352) 291-4410, Fax (352) 291-4414, marketing@ocalaedc.org, www.ocalaedc.org

**Orange Park** • *Clay County Dev. Auth.* • Danita Andrews, Dir., 1734 Kingsley Ave., 32073, P 180,000, (904) 264-7373, Fax (904) 269-0363, info@clayedo.com, www.clayedo.com

**Orlando** • *Metro Orlando Eco. Dev. Comm.* • Mike Bobroff, V.P./ COO, 301 E. Pine St., Ste. 900, 32801, P 1,800,023, M 450, (407) 422-7159, Fax (407) 425-6428, info@orlandoedc.com, www. orlandoedc.com

**Palatka** • *Putnam County Dev. Auth.* • Wes Larson, Exec. Dir., 1100 Reid St., P.O. Box 550, 32178, P 72,000, (386) 328-1503, Fax (386) 328-7076, wes@pcccsl.org, www.putnamcountychamber.org

**Palm Coast** • *Enterprise Flagler* • Greg Rawls, Deputy Dir., 20 Airport Rd., Ste. A, 32164, P 92,000, M 935, (386) 586-1224, Fax (386) 586-1226, greg@enterpriseflagler.org, www.enterpriseflagler.org

**Panama City** • *Bay County Eco. Dev. Alliance* • Janet Walermeier, Exec. Dir., 235 W. 5th St., P.O. Box 1850, 32402, P 161,721, (850) 215-3752, Fax (850) 763-6229, janet@bay chamberfl.com, www.baycountyeda.org

**Pensacola** • *Pensacola Area C/C* • Charles Wood, Sr. V.P., Eco. Dev., 117 W. Garden St., P.O. Box 550, 32591, P 305,000, (850) 438-4081, Fax (850) 438-6369, cwood@pensacolachamber.com, www.pensacolachamber.com

**Perry** • *Taylor County Dev. Auth.* • Rick Breer, Exec. Dir., 103 E. Ellis St., P.O. Box 449, 32348, P 19,187, (850) 584-5627, Fax (850) 223-0161, tcda@gtcom.net, www.tcda-fl.org

**Plant City** • *Greater Plant City Eco. Dev. Cncl.* • Marion Smith, Pres., 106 N. Evers St., P.O. Box CC, 33564, P 34,750, (813) 754-1745, (800) 760-2315, Fax (813) 752-8793, info@plantcity.org, www.plantcity.org.

**Pompano Beach** • *Pompano Eco. Group* • Ric Green, Pres./CEO, 2200 E. Atlantic Blvd., 33062, P 101,457, (954) 941-2940, Fax (954) 785-8358, www.pompanobeachchamber.com

**Port Charlotte** • *Charlotte County Eco. Dev. Ofc.* • Don Root, Dir., 18501 Murdock Cir., Ste. 502, 33948, P 154,716, (941) 627-3023, (800) 729-5836, Fax (941) 627-6314, floridaedo@ charlottefl.com, www.floridaedo.com

**Riviera Beach** • *Riviera Beach Comm. Redev. Agency* • Floyd Johnson, Exec. Dir., 2001 Broadway, Ste. 300, 33404, P 35,000, (561) 844-3408, Fax (561) 881-8043, fjohnson@rbcra.org, www. rbcra.org

**Rockledge** • *Eco. Dev. Comm. of Florida's Space Coast* • Lynda Weatherman, Pres./CEO, 597 Haverty Ct., Ste. 100, 32955, P 505,000, (321) 638-2000, (800) 535-0203, Fax (321) 633-4200, info@spacecoastedc.org, www.spacecoastedc.org

**Saint Petersburg** • *Eco. Dev. Dept., City of St. Petersburg* • Dave Goodwin, Dir. of Eco. Dev., One 4th St. N., 9th Flr., P.O. Box 2842, 33731, P 251,151, (727) 893-7100, (800) 874-9026, Fax (727) 892-5465, business@stpete.org, www.stpete.org

**Saint Petersburg** • *St. Petersburg Downtown Partnership* • Dr. Peter Betzer, Pres./CEO, 244 2nd Ave. N., Ste. 201, 33701, P 250,000, (727) 821-5166, Fax (727) 896-6302, peter@ stpetepartnership.org, www.stpetepartnership.org

**Sarasota** • *Eco. Dev. Corp. of Sarasota County* • Kathleen D. Baylis, Pres., 2601 Cattlemen Rd., Ste. 201, 34232, P 375,000, M 465, (941) 309-1200, Fax (941) 309-1209, kbaylis@edc sarasotacounty.com, www.edcsarasotacounty.org

**Sebring** • *Highlands County Eco. Dev. Comm.* • Dan P. Murphy, Exec. Dir., 2113 U.S. 27 S., 33870, P 95,000, M 145, (863) 385-1025, (888) 388-4233, Fax (863) 385-1379, executive@highlands edc.com, www.highlandsedc.com

**Starke** • *Bradford Co. Eco. Dev. Auth.* • Jerome Johns, Chrmn., 100 E. Call St., 32091, P 28,000, (904) 964-5278, Fax (904) 964-2863, pam@ northfloridachamber.com, www.northfloridachamber.com

**Stuart** • *Eco. Cncl. Of Martin County* • Tammy Simoneau, Exec. Dir., 1002 S.E. Monterey Commons Blvd., Ste. 203B, 34996, P 143,000, (772) 288-1225, www.mceconomy.com

**Sunrise** • *City of Sunrise, Ofc. of Eco. Dev.* • Lou Sandora, Dir. of Eco. Dev., 10770 W. Oakland Park Blvd., 33351, P 90,000, (954) 746-3430, Fax (954) 746-3439, www.sunrisefl.gov

**Tampa** • *Greater Tampa C/C - Eco. Dev.* • Bob Rohrlack, Pres./CEO, 615 Channelside Dr., Ste. 108, P.O. Box 420, 33601, P 1,118,988, (813) 228-7777, Fax (813) 223-7899, info@tampa chamber.com, www.tampachamber.com

**EDC**

**Tampa** · *Tampa Bay Partnership* · Stuart Rogel, Pres./CEO, 4300 W. Cypress St., Ste. 250, 33607, P 3,700,000, M 200, (813) 878-2208, Fax (813) 872-9356, srogel@tampabay.org, www.tampabay.org

**Tampa** · *Tampa Port Auth.* · Richard Wainio, Dir., 1101 Channelside Dr., P.O. Box 2192, 33601, (813) 905-7678, Fax (813) 905-5109, www.tampaport.com

**Titusville** · *Space Coast Eco. Dev. Comm.* · Matt Chesnut, Exec. Dir., 2000 S. Washington Ave., Ste. 2, 32780, P 45,000, (321) 269-3221, (800) 749-3224, Fax (321) 567-0051, sedc@titusville.com, www.Nspacecoastedc.org

**West Palm Beach** · *Bus. Dev. Bd. of Palm Beach County Inc.* · Kelly Smallridge, Pres., 310 Evernia St., 33401, P 1,268,548, (561) 835-1008, Fax (561) 835-1160, www.bdb.org

**West Palm Beach** · *West Palm Beach Downtown Dev. Auth.* · Melissa Wohlust, Exec. Dir., 301 Clematis St., Ste. 200, 33401, P 90,000, (561) 833-8873, Fax (561) 833-5870, www.westpalmbeachdda.com

**Winter Haven** · *East Polk Committee of 100* · Jack Barnhart, Exec. Dir., P.O. Box 1420, 33882, P 276,000, M 324, (863) 293-2525, Fax (863) 297-5818, contact@epc100.org, www.epc100.org

# Georgia

## Federal

**U.S. SBA, Georgia Dist. Ofc.** · Terri Denison, Dist. Dir., 233 Peachtree St. N.E., Ste. 1900, Atlanta, 30303, (404) 331-0100, Fax (404) 331-0101, www.sba.gov/ga

## State

**Georgia Dept. of Eco. Dev.** · Heidi Green, Comm., 75 Fifth St. N.W., Ste. 1200, Atlanta, 30308, (404) 962-4000, www.georgia.org

## Communities

**Albany** · *Albany/Dougherty Eco. Dev. Comm.* · 225 W. Broad Ave., 31701, P 96,000, (229) 434-0044, Fax (229) 434-1310, info@choosealbany.com, www.choosealbany.com

**Athens** · *East Athens Dev. Corp.* · Winston Heard, Dir., 410 McKinley Dr., 30601, P 20,000, (706) 208-0048, Fax (706) 208-0015, info@eadcinc.com, www.eadcinc.com

**Atlanta** · *Atlanta Dev.Auth.* · Peggy McCormick, Pres., 86 Pryor St. S.W., Ste. 300, 30303, P 361,000, (404) 880-4100, Fax (404) 880-0863, www.atlantada.com

**Atlanta** · *Fulton County Comm. Dev.* · Michelle Anderson, Eco. Dev. Dept., 141 Pryor St. S.W., Ste. 5001, 30303, P 904,801, (404) 612-3917, Fax (404) 730-8112, www.fultonecd.org

**Blackshear** · *Pierce County Ind. Dev. Auth.* · Jim Waters, Chair, 200 S. Central Ave., P.O. Box 47, 31516, P 17,000, (912) 449-7044, Fax (912) 449-7045, pierceco@accessatc.net, www.pierceco.org

**Brunswick** · *Brunswick & Glynn County Dev. Auth.* · S. Nathan Sparks, Exec. Dir., 4 Glynn Ave., 31520, P 78,000, (912) 265-6629, Fax (912) 265-9460, snathansparks@bwkeda.com, www.georgiasgoldenopportunity.com

**Camilla** · *SW Georgia Reg. Dev. Center* · Dan Bollinger, Dir., 30 W. Broad St., P.O. Box 346, 31730, P 322,000, (229) 522-3552, Fax (229) 522-3558, dbollinger@swgrdc.org, www.swgrdc.org

**Carnesville** · *Franklin County Ind. Bldg. Auth.* · Lyn Allen, Dir. of Eco. Dev., 165 Athens St., P.O. Box 151, 30521, P 22,365, (706) 384-5112, Fax (706) 384-3204, iba@franklin-county.com, www.franklin-county.com

**Carrollton** · *Carroll Tomorrow* · Daniel Jackson, CEO, 200 Northside Dr., 30117, P 107,325, (770) 832-2446, Fax (770) 832-1300, daniel@carroll-ga.org, www.carrolltomorrow.com

**Claxton** · *Claxton-Evans County Ind. Dev. Auth.* · Randy Mayfield, Chrmn., 4 N. Duval St., 30417, P 11,000, (912) 739-1391, Fax (912) 739-3827, info@claxtonevanschamber.com, www.claxtonevanschamber.com

**Clayton** · *Rabun County Eco. Dev. Auth.* · Sean Brady, Exec. Dir., 232 Hwy. 441 N., P.O. Box 761, 30525, P 17,500, (706) 782-4812, Fax (706) 782-4810, sean@gamountains.com, www.gamountains.com

**Cordele** · *Cordele/Crisp Ind. Dev. Cncl.* · Bruce Drennan, Exec. Dir., 202 S. 7th St., P.O. Box 38, 31010, P 23,000, (229) 273-9570, Fax (229) 273-9571, brucedrennan@crispidc.com, www.crispidc.com.

**Cumming** · *Forsyth County Dev.* · Jeff Chance, Dir., 110 E. Main St., 30040, P 110,000, (770) 781-2115, Fax (770) 781-2199, forsythco.com

**Dallas** · *Paulding County Ind. Bldg. Auth.* · C.B. Fair, Chrmn., 455 Jimmy Campbell Pkwy., 30132, P 127,000, (770) 505-7700, Fax (770) 445-3050, www.pauldingcountychamber.org

**Dalton** · *North Georgia CDC Inc.* · Barry Tarter, Exec. Dir., 503 W. Waugh St., 30720, P 209,000, (706) 226-1110, Fax (706) 272-2253, ngcdc@ngcdc.org, www.ngcdc.org

**Darien** · *McIntosh County Dev. Auth.* · David Lyon, Dir., 105 Fort King George Dr., P.O. Box 896, 31305, P 11,500, (912) 437-6659, Fax (912) 437-3505, mcda@darientel.net, www.georgiascoast2success.com

**Dublin** · *Dublin-Laurens County Dev. Auth.* · Cal Wray, V.P., 1200 Bellevue Ave., P.O. Box 818, 31040, P 47,000, (478) 272-5546, Fax (478) 275-0811, cwray@dublinlaurensgeorgia.com

**Eatonton** · *Putnam Dev. Auth.* · Charles Haley, Chair, 305 N. Madison Ave., P.O. Box 4088, 31024, P 18,000, (706) 485-7701, Fax (706) 485-3277, epchamber@eatonton.com, www.eatonton.com

**Fitzgerald** · *Fitzgerald/Ben Hill County Dev. Auth.* · John Flythe, Dir., P.O. Box 218, 31750, P 20,000, (229) 423-9357, Fax (229) 423-1052, jflythe@windstream.net, www.fitzgeraldchamber.org

**Fort Gaines** · *Clay County Eco. Dev. Cncl.* · Ken Penuel, Chrmn., P.O. Box 825, 39851, P 3,500, (229) 768-3238, www.fortgaines.com, www.claycountyga.org

**Fort Oglethorpe** · *see Ringgold*

**Fort Valley** · *Dev. Auth. of Peach County* · Charles Sims, Exec. Dir., 201 Oakland Heights Pkwy., P.O. Box 935, 31030, P 24,000, (478) 825-3826, Fax (478) 825-4187, www.peachcounty.net

**Hazlehurst** · *Joint Dev. Auth. Of Jeff Davis County* · Keith Carter, Exec. Dir., 95 E. Jarman St., P.O. Box 546, 31539, P 12,684, (912) 375-4543, Fax (912) 375-7948, www.hazlehurst-jeffdavis.com

**Hinesville** · *Liberty County Dev. Auth.* · Ronald E. Tolley CEcD, CEO, 425 W. Oglethorpe Hwy., 31313, P 64,000, (912) 368-3356, Fax (912) 368-5585, ron.tolley@lcda.com, www.lcda.com

**Jackson** · *Butts County Ind. Dev. Auth.* · Allan E. White, Exec. Dir., 625 W. Third St., P.O. Box 1085, 30233, P 26,000, (770) 775-4851, Fax (770) 775-3118, buttscoida@bellsouth.net, www.buttscountyida.com

**Jasper** · *Pickens County Dev.* · Larry Toney, Dir. of Eco. Dev., Courthouse Annex, Ste. 204, 52 N. Main St., 30143, P 25,000, (706) 253-8850, pickenscountyga.gov

**Jonesboro** · *Dev. Auth. of Clayton County* · Grant Wainscott, Dir., Jonesboro Historical Courthouse, 121 S. McDonough St., 30236, P 266,814, (770) 477-4591, Fax (678) 479-5385, grant.wainscott@co.clayton.ga.us, www.co.clayton.ga.us

**Macon** · *Middle Georgia Reg. Dev. Center* · Ralph Nix, Exec. Dir., 175 Emery Hwy., Ste. C, 31217, P 440,121, (478) 751-6160, Fax (478) 751-6517, www.mgrdc.org

**Madison** · *Ind. Dev. Comm.* · 115 E. Jefferson St., P.O. Box 826, 30650, P 17,000, (706) 342-4454, (800) 709-7406, Fax (706) 342-4455, www.madisonga.org

**McDonough** · *Henry County Dev. Auth.* · Robert C. White, Exec. Dir., 140 Henry Pkwy., 30253, P 175,000, (770) 288-8000, Fax (770) 288-8008, bwhite@hcda.org, www.hcda.org

**Moultrie** · *Colquitt County Eco. Dev. Corp.* · Darrel Moore, Pres., 116 First Ave. S.E., P.O. Box 487, 31776, P 43,500, (229) 985-2131, Fax (229) 890-2638, moultrie@alltel.net, www.moultriechamber.com

**Rabun County** · *see Clayton*

**Rock Spring** · *NW Georgia Joint Dev. Auth.* · Jeff Mullis, Exec. Dir., 10052 N. Hwy. 27, P.O. Box 220, 30739, P 58,000, (706) 375-5793, (800) 966-8092, Fax (706) 375-5795, www.nwgajda.com

**Rome** · *Coosa Valley Reg. Dev. Center* · William Steiner, Exec. Dir., 1 Jackson Hill Dr., P.O. Box 1798, 30162, P 556,207, (706) 295-6485, Fax (706) 295-6665, wsteiner@cvrdc.org, www.cvrdc.org

**Savannah** · *Savannah Eco. Dev. Auth.* · Lynn Pitts, Sr. V.P., P.O. Box 128, 31402, P 308,000, (912) 447-8450, Fax (912) 447-8455, lpitts@seda.org, www.seda.org

**Springfield** · *Effingham County Ind. Dev. Auth.* · John A. Henry, CEO, 520 W. Third St., P.O. Box 1078, 31329, P 56,000, (912) 754-3301, Fax (912) 754-1236, effingham@effinghamcounty.com, www.effinghamcounty.com

**Statesboro** · *Dev. Auth. of Bulloch County* · Peggy Chapman, Exec. Dir., 102 S. Main St., P.O. Box 303, 30459, P 60,000, (912) 764-6111, Fax (912) 489-3108, peggychapman@statesboro-chamber.org, www.statesboro-chamber.org

**Sylvania** · *Screven County Ind. Dev. Auth.* · Gayle Boykin, Exec. Dir., 101 S. Main St., 30467, P 15,374, (912) 564-7850, Fax (912) 564-0081, www.screvencounty.com

**Sylvester** · *Worth County Eco. Dev. Auth.* · Greg Sellars, Exec. Dir., 204 E. Franklin St., Box 2, 31791, P 22,000, (229) 776-7599, Fax (229) 776-0233, worthcoeda@bellsouth.net, www.worth countyeda.com

**Thomasville** · *Thomasville-Thomas County C/C-Eco. Dev. Div.* · Donald P. Sims, Pres., 401 S. Broad St., P.O. Box 560, 31799, P 45,000, (229) 225-1422, Fax (229) 226-9603, chamber@rose.net, www.thomasvillechamber.com

**Thomson** · *McDuffie County Dev. Auth.* · Mike Carrington, Exec. Dir., 111 Railroad St., 30824, P 22,000, (706) 597-1000, Fax (706) 595-2143, mcarrington@thompson-mcduffie.net, www.thomson-mcduffie.net

**Valdosta** · *Valdosta-Lowndes County Ind. Auth.* · Brad Lofton, Exec. Dir., P.O. Box 1963, 31603, P 98,000, (229) 259-9972, Fax (229) 259-9973, info@industrialauthority.com, www.industrial authority.com

**Vienna** · *Dooly County Eco. Dev. Cncl.* · Robert Jeter, Exec. Dir., 402 Hawkinsville Rd., 31092, P 11,525, (229) 268-4554, Fax (229) 268-4500, doolyedc@sowega.net, www.doolyedc.org

**Villa Rica** · *Downtown Dev. Auth. of Villa Rica* · Barbara Daniell, Mgr., 571 W. Bankhead Hwy., 30180, P 10,200, (678) 785-1000, Fax (770) 459-7003, bdaniell@villarica.org, www.villarica.org

**Warm Springs** · *Meriwether County IDA* · Kip Purvis, Pres., 91 Broad St., P.O. Box 9, 31830, P 22,534, (706) 655-2558, Fax (706) 655-2812, www.meriwetherida.com

**Warner Robins** · *Houston County Dev. Auth.* · Morgan Law, Exec. Dir., 200 Carl Vinson Pkwy., 31088, P 130,000, (478) 923-5470, Fax (478) 923-5472, hcda@houstoncountyga.net, www.houstoncountyga.net

**Waynesboro** · *Dev. Auth. of Burke County* · Jerry C. Long Sr., Exec. Dir., 241 E. Sixth St., 30830, P 23,000, (706) 554-2923, Fax (706) 554-7091, jclong@burkecounty-ga.gov, www.burkecounty-ga.gov

# Hawaii

## Federal

**U.S. SBA, Hawaii Dist. Ofc.** · Karen Sakihama, Acting Dist. Dir., 300 Ala Moana Blvd., Rm. 2-235, Box 50207, Honolulu, 96850, (808) 541-2990, Fax (808) 541-2976, www.sba.gov/hi

## State

**State of Hawaii Dept. of Bus., Eco. Dev. & Tourism** · Ted Liu, Dir., 250 S. Hotel St., Honolulu, 96813, (808) 586-2423, Fax (808) 587-2790, library@dbedt.hawaii.gov, www.hawaii.gov/openforbusiness/

## Communities

**Hilo** · *County of Hawaii, Dept. of Research & Dev.* · Randy Kurohara, Dir., 25 Aupuni St., Rm. 109, 96720, P 162,971, (808) 961-8366, Fax (808) 935-1205, chresdev@co.hawaii.hi.us, www.co.hawaii.hi.us

**Hilo** · *Hawaii Island Eco. Dev. Bd.* · Jacqui Hoover, Exec. Dir., 117 Keawe St., Ste. 107, 96720, P 168,000, (808) 935-2180, Fax (808) 935-2187, www.hiedb.org

**Honolulu** · *City & County of Honolulu* · Mufi Hannemann, Mayor, City Hall, 530 S. King St., Rm. 300, 96813, P 1,000,000, (808) 768-4141, Fax (808) 768-5552, www.honolulu.gov

**Honolulu** · *Eco. Dev. & Tourism of Honolulu* · Theodore Liu, Dir., 250 S. Hotel St., 96813, P 1,285,498, (808) 586-2423, Fax (808) 586-2377, www.hawaii.gov/dbedt

**Honolulu** · *Enterprise Honolulu* · Mike Fitzgerald, Pres./CEO, 737 Bishop St., Ste. 2040, 96813, P 1,276,000, (808) 521-3611, Fax (808) 536-2281, info@enterprisehonolulu.com, www.enterprisehonolulu.com

**Lihue** · *County of Kauai Ofc. of Eco. Dev.* · George Costa, Dir., 4444 Rice St., Ste. 200, 96766, P 62,000, (808) 241-4946, Fax (808) 241-6399, www.kauai.gov

**Lihue** · *Kauai Eco. Dev. Bd.* · Matilda Yoshioka, Pres., 4290 Rice St., 96766, P 63,000, (808) 245-6692, Fax (808) 246-1089, www.kedb.com

**Maui** · *Maui Eco. Dev. Bd.* · Jeanne Skog, Pres./CEO, 1305 N. Holopono St., Ste. 1, Kihei, 96753, P 120,000, (808) 875-2300, Fax (808) 879-0011, info@medb.org, www.medb.org

**Wailuku** · *County of Maui* · Deidre Tegarden, Coord., Ofc. of Eco. Dev., 2200 Main St., Ste. 305, 96793, P 130,000, (808) 270-7710, Fax (808) 270-7995, www.mauicounty.gov

# Idaho

## Federal

**U.S. SBA, Idaho Dist. Ofc.** · Norm Proctor, Dist. Dir., 380 E. Park Center Blvd., Ste. 330, Boise, 83706, (208) 334-1696, Fax (208) 334-9353, www.sba.gov/id

## State

**Idaho Dept. of Comm.** · Don Dietrich, Dir., 700 W. State St., P.O. Box 83720, Boise, 83720, (208) 334-2470, Fax (208) 334-2631, www.commerce.idaho.gov

**EDC**

## Communities

**Boise** · *Boise Valley Eco. Partnership* · Paul Hiller, Exec. Dir., 250 S. 5th St., Ste. 300, P.O. Box 2368, 83701, P 562,932, (208) 472-5229, Fax (208) 472-5201, rwinston@bvep.org, www.bvep.org

**Caldwell** · *Caldwell Eco. Dev. Cncl.* · Steve Fultz, Exec. Dir., P.O. Box 668, 83606, P 44,000, (208) 454-0087, Fax (208) 459-8115, sfultz@caldwellonline.org, www.caldwellonline.org

**Garden City** · *Sage Comm. Resources* · Kathleen Simko, Pres., 125 E. 50th St., 83714, P 415,281, (208) 322-7033, (800) 859-0321, Fax (208) 322-3569, www.sageidaho.com

**Idaho Falls** · *Grow Idaho Falls Inc.* · Linda K. Martin CEcD, CEO, 151 N. Ridge, Ste. A, 83402, P 90,000, (208) 522-2014, (800) 900-2014, Fax (208) 522-3824, linda@growidahofalls.org, www.growidahofalls.org

**Jerome** · *Jerome Eco. & Comm. Dev.* · Ben Marchant, Eco. Dev. Spec., 152 East Ave., 83338, P 18,342, (208) 324-8189, Fax (208) 324-8204, www.ci.jerome.id.us

**Pocatello** · *Bannock Dev. Corp.* · Gynii Gilliam, Exec. Dir., ISU Research & Bus. Park, 1651 Alvin Ricken Dr., 83201, P 70,000, (208) 233-3500, Fax (208) 233-0268, www.bannockdevelopment.org

**Pocatello** · *SE Idaho Cncl. of Govts.* · Kathleen Lewis, Exec. Dir., 214 E. Center, P.O. Box 6079, 83205, P 154,000, (208) 233-4032, Fax (208) 233-4841, kathleen@sicog.org, www.sicog.org

**Rexburg** · *Madison Eco. Dev. Corp.* · Clair D. Boyle, Exec. Dir., 310 N. 2nd E., Ste. 114, 83440, P 28,000, (208) 356-5009, clair@madisoneconomicpartners.org, www.idahobusiness.org

**Twin Falls** · *Region IV Dev. Assn.* · Joe Herring, Exec. Dir., 315 Falls Ave., P.O. Box 5079, 83303, P 180,000, (208) 732-5727, Fax (208) 732-5454, joe@rivda.org, www.rivda.org

**Wallace** · *Silver Valley Eco. Dev. Corp.* · Vince Rinaldi, Exec. Dir., 703 Cedar St., 83873, P 12,827, (208) 752-5511, (800) 523-7889, Fax (208) 556-2351, www.silvervalleyedc.com

**Weiser** · *Washington County Eco. Dev. Comm.* · 309 State St., 83672, P 11,000, (208) 414-0452, info@weiserchamber.com, www.weiserchamber.com

# Illinois

## State

**Dept. of Comm. & Eco. Opportunity** · Warren Ribley, Dir., 620 E. Adams, Springfield, 62701, (217) 785-6276, (800) 226-6632, warren.ribley@illinois.gov, www.enjoyillinois.com

## Communities

**Aledo** · *Mercer Eco. Dev. Partnership* · Jenny Garner, Dir., 2106 S.E. Third St., P.O. Box 267, 61231, P 16,912, (309) 582-7695, Fax (309) 582-7690, www.aledoil.org

**Alexis** · *see Monmouth*

**Aurora** · *Aurora Eco. Dev. Comm.* · Sherman Jenkins, Exec. Dir., 43 W. Galena Blvd., 60506, P 175,000, (630) 897-5500, Fax (630) 897-0469, aedc@aurora-il.org, www.aurora-il.org/aedc

**Berwyn** · *Berwyn Dev. Corp.* · Anthony Griffin, Exec. Dir., 3322 S. Oak Park Ave., 2nd Flr., 60402, P 54,017, M 290, (708) 788-8100, Fax (708) 788-0966, info@berwyn.net, www.berwyn.net

**Biggsville** · *see Monmouth*

**Carbondale** · *Carbondale Bus. Dev. Corp.* · Kevin Baity, Asst. City Mgr. of EDC, 200 S. Illinois Ave., P.O. Box 2047, 62901, P 27,033, (618) 457-3226, kbaity@ci.carbondale.il.us, www.explorecarbondale.com

**Champaign** · *Champaign County Eco. Dev.* · 1817 S. Neil St., Ste. 201, 61820, P 178,591, (217) 351-4133, Fax (217) 359-1809, www.champaigncountyedc.org

**Charleston** · *see Mattoon*

**Chester** · *Randolph County Progress Comm. Inc.* · Edward R. Crow, Exec. Dir., 1 Taylor St., P.O. Box 332, 62233, P 33,900, (618) 826-5000, Fax (618) 826-3750, rndlfedc@egyptian.net, www.randolphco.org

**Chicago** · *Calumet Area Ind. Comm.* · Ted Stalnos, Pres., 1000 E. 111th St., 10th Flr., 60628, P 250,000, M 130, (773) 928-6000, Fax (773) 928-6016, teds@calumetareaindustrial.com, www.calumetareaindustrial.com

**Chicago** · *Mount Greenwood Local Redev. Corp.* · Mary Kiedrow, Exec. Dir., 3333 W. 111 St., Ste. B, 60655, P 18,000, (773) 881-0622, Fax (773) 881-4622, mglrc2000@wowway.com, www.mglrc.com

**Chicago** · *Planning & Dev. Comm. of the City of Chicago* · Chris Raguso, Comm., 121 N. LaSalle, Ste. 1000, 60602, P 3,000,000, (312) 744-9476, Fax (312) 742-9899, www.cityofchicago.org

**Cissna Park** · *Cissna Park Eco. Dev. Bd.* · %Village Hall, 60924, P 1,000, (815) 457-2905

**Clinton** · *Dewitt County Dev. Comm.* · Ken Bjelland, Chrmn., P.O. Box 376, 61727, P 18,000, (217) 935-2126, Fax (217) 935-6840, www.dewittcountyill.com

**Danville** · *Vermilion Advantage-EDC Div.* · Vicki Haugen, Pres., 28 W. North St., 61832, P 85,000, (217) 442-6201, (800) 373-6201, Fax (217) 442-6228, vhaugen@vermilionadvantage.com, www.vermilionadvantage.com

**Decatur** · *Eco. Dev. Corp. of Decatur-Macon County* · Craig Coil, Pres., 101 S. Main St., 62523, P 114,500, (217) 422-9520, Fax (217) 422-9307, ccoil@decaturedc.com, www.decaturedc.com

**Des Plaines** · *Des Plaines Eco. Dev. Comm.* · Mike Conlan, Deputy Dir. of Comm. & Eco. Dev., 1420 Miner St., 60016, P 57,000, (847) 391-5651, Fax (847) 827-2196, www.desplaines.org

**Dixon** · *Lee County Ind. Dev. Assn.* · John R. Thompson, Pres., 101 W. Second St., Ste. 301, 61021, P 35,000, (815) 284-3361, Fax (815) 284-3675, dchamber@essex1.com, www.dixonillinoischamber.com.

**Dolton** · *Village of Dolton Eco. Dev.* · Bert Herzog, Dir., 14014 Park Ave., 60419, P 25,614, (708) 201-3359, Fax (708) 201-3358, www.villageofdolton.com

**Fairfield** · *Fairfield-Wayne County Area Dev. Comm.* · Susan Murphy, Exec. Dir., 121 E. Main St., 62837, P 5,421, (618) 842-4802, Fax (618) 842-4802, adc@fairfieldwireless.net, www.fairfield-il.com

**Flora** · *Flora Ind. Comm.* · Dan Sulsberger, Dir., 131 E. 2nd, P.O. Box 249, 62839, P 5,100, (618) 662-7111, Fax (618) 662-7204, www.florail.us

**Freeport** · *Freeport Area Eco. Dev. Found.* · 27 W. Stephenson St., 61032, P 26,000, (815) 233-1350, Fax (815) 235-4038, www.freeport-il-econ-dev.com

**Gladstone** · *see Monmouth*

**Godfrey** · *River Bend Growth Assn.* · Monica Bristow, Pres., 5800 Godfrey Rd., Alden Hall, 62035, P 100,000, M 650, (618) 467-2280, Fax (618) 466-8289, info@growthassociation.com, www.growthassociation.com

**Granite City** · *Tri-City Reg. Port Dist.* · Robert Wydra, Exec. Dir., 1635 W. 1st St., 62040, P 60,000, (618) 877-8444, (618) 452-3337, Fax (618) 452-3402, bwydra@tricityport.com, www.tricityport.com

**Gulfport** · *see Monmouth*

**Jacksonville** · *Jacksonville Reg. EDC* · Terry Denison, Pres., 221 E. State St., 62650, P 45,000, M 170, (217) 479-4627, Fax (217) 479-4629, terry@jredc.org, www.jredc.org

**Joliet** · *Will County Center for Eco. Dev.* · John E. Greuling, Pres./CEO, 116 N. Chicago St., Ste. 101, 60432, P 690,000, (815) 723-1800, Fax (815) 723-6972, info@willcountyced.com, www.willcountyced.com

**Kankakee** · *Eco. Alliance of Kankakee County* · Michael Van Mill, CEO, 200 E. Ct., Ste. 507, 60901, P 107,000, (815) 935-1177, Fax (815) 935-1181, eda@kankakeecountyeda.com, www.kankakeecountyeda.com

**Kirkwood** · *see Monmouth*

**Lawrenceville** · *Lawrence County Ind. Dev. Cncl.* · Ann Emken, Exec. Dir., 718 11th St., Ste. 2, 62439, P 15,545, M 200, (618) 943-5219, Fax (618) 943-5910, lcidc@lawrencecountyillinois.com, www.lawrencecountyillinois.com

**Libertyville** · *Lake County Partners* · David Young, Pres., 28055 Ashley Cir., Ste. 212, 60048, P 617,000, (847) 247-0137, Fax (847) 247-0423, lcp@lakecountypartners.com, www.lakecountypartners.com

**Lincoln** · *Lincoln & Logan County Dev. Partnership* · Joel Smiley, Exec. Dir., 1555 5th St., 62656, P 31,500, (217) 732-8739, econdev@lincolnlogan.com, www.lincolnlogan.com

**Little York** · *see Monmouth*

**Lockport** · *City of Lockport* · Kimberly Jones, Eco. Dev. Coord., Ofc. of Eco. Dev., 921 S. State St., 60441, P 25,000, M 116, (815) 838-9500, Fax (815) 838-1861, www.lockport.org

**Lomax** · *see Monmouth*

**Loves Park** · *City of Loves Park EDC* · Dan Jacobson, Dir. of Dev., 100 Heart Blvd., City Hall, 61111, P 23,000, (815) 654-5033, Fax (815) 654-5004, www.loves-park.il.us

**Macomb** · *Macomb Area Eco. Dev. Corp* · Kim Pierce, Exec. Dir., 510 N. Pearl St., Ste. 300, 61455, P 21,000, (309) 837-4684, Fax (309) 837-4688, maedco@wiu.edu, www.maedco.org

**Mattoon** · *Coles Together* · Angela Griffin, Pres., 400 Airport Rd., 61938, P 52,000, (217) 258-5627, Fax (217) 235-9492, angela@colestogether.com, www.colestogether.com

**McHenry** · *McHenry County Eco. Dev. Corp.* · Jan Schober, Pres., 5435 Bull Valley Rd., 60050, P 290,000, M 250, (815) 363-0044, Fax (815) 363-0464, info@mcedc.com, www.mcedc.com

**Media** · *see Monmouth*

**Monmouth** · *Western Illinois Eco. Dev. Partnership* · Jolene Willis, Exec. Dir., 88-A Public Sq., Ste. 2, 61462, P 19,000, (309) 734-4253, Fax (309) 734-8811, jwillis@wiedp.org, www.wiedp.org

**Mount Vernon** · *Jefferson County Dev. Corp.* · Mary Ellen Bechtel, Exec. Dir., 200 Potomac Blvd., P.O. Box 523, 62864, P 40,523, (618) 244-3554, Fax (618) 244-7533, mbechtel@jeffcodev.org, www.jeffcodev.org

**Naperville** · *Naperville Dev.Partnership* · Christine Jeffries, Pres., 212 S. Webster St., Ste, 104, 60540, P 140,000, (630) 305-7701, (877) 236-2737, Fax (630) 305-7793, ndp@naper.org, www.visitnaperville.com

**Normal** · *Eco. Dev. Cncl.of the Bloomington-Normal Area* · Marty Vanags, Exec. Dir., 200 W. College Ave., Ste. 402, 61761, P 150,433, (309) 452-8437, mvanags@bnbiz.org, www.bnbiz.org

**Oak Forest** · *City of Oak Forest* · Adam Dotson, Comm. Dev. Dir., 15440 S. Central Ave., City Hall, 60452, P 28,000, (708) 687-4050, Fax (708) 687-1179, www.oak-forest.org

**Oak Lawn** · *Village of Oak Lawn* · Chad Weiler, Dir. of Comm. Dev., 9446 S. Raymond Ave., 60453, P 56,000, (708) 636-4400, Fax (708) 499-7823, www.oaklawn-il.gov

**Oakland** · *see Mattoon*

**Olney** · *Richland County Dev. Corp.* · Brandi Stennett, Exec. Dir., 503 E. Main St., 62450, P 17,000, (618) 392-2305, Fax (618) 392-2405, bstennett@rcdc.com, www.rcdc.com

**Oquawka** · *see Monmouth*

**Orland Park** · *Orland Park Planning/Comm.Dev.* · Robert Sullivan, Dir. of Comm. Dev., 14700 Ravinia Ave., 60462, P 56,876, (708) 403-6115, Fax (708) 403-6215, bsullivan@orland-park.il.us, www.orland-park.il.us

**Ottawa** · *Ottawa Eco. Dev. Task Force* · Boyd Palmer, Chrmn., 633 LaSalle St., Ste. 401, 61350, P 19,000, (815) 433-0084, Fax (815) 433-2405, info@ottawachamberillinois.com, www.ottawachamberillinois.com

**Pana** · *Pana Dept. of Dev.* · Jim Deere, Exec. Dir., 120 E. 3rd St., City Hall, 62557, P 7,100, (217) 562-3109, Fax (217) 562-3823, panail@consolidated.net, www.panaillinois.com, www.panaindustrial.com

**Peoria** · *Eco. Dev. Cncl. for Central IL* · Vickie Clark, COO, 100 S.W. Water St., 61602, P 370,000, (309) 676-7500, Fax (309) 676-7534, info@edc.h-p.org, www.edc.centralillinois.org.

**Pittsfield** · *Pittsfield Eco. Dev. Ofc.* · William McCartney, Dir., 215 N. Monroe, 62363, P 4,614, (217) 285-4484, Fax (217) 285-4485, pittsed@pittsfieldil.org, www.pittsfieldil.org

**Plano** · *Plano Eco. Dev. Corp.* · Rich Healy, 7050 Burroughs Ave., 60545, P 10,000, (630) 552-9119, info@planoedc.org, www.planoedc.org

**Quincy** · *Great River Eco. Dev. Found.* · James Mentesti, Pres., 300 Civic Center Plz., Ste. 256, 62301, P 42,202, (217) 223-4313, Fax (217) 231-2030, gredf@gredf.org, www.gredf.org

**Raritan** · *see Monmouth*

**Riverdale** · *Village of Riverdale Comm. & Eco. Dev.* · Janice Morrissy, Dir., 157 W. 144th St., 60827, P 16,500, (708) 841-2125, Fax (708) 841-7587, jmorrissy@villageofriverdale.org, www.villageofriverdale.org

**Rock Island** · *Quad-City Dev. Group* · Nancy Mulcahey, Pres./CEO, 1830 Second Ave., Ste. 200, 61201, P 360,000, (309) 788-7436, Fax (309) 788-4964, qcdg@quadcities.org, www.quadcities.org

**Rockford** · *Rockford Dept. of Comm. & Eco. Dev.* · Reid Montgomery, Dir., 425 E. State St., 61104, P 150,115, (815) 987-5600, Fax (815) 967-6933, www.rockfordil.gov

**Roseville** · *see Monmouth*

**Springfield** · *Illinois Dept. of Comm. & Eco. Opportunity* · Warren Ribley, Acting Dir., 620 E. Adams, 62701, (217) 782-7500, www.commerce.state.il.us

**Springfield** · *Ofc. Of Planning & Eco. Dev.* · Chuck Rose, Sr. Bus. Projects Mgr., 800 E. Monroe, Ste. 107, 62701, P 111,000, (217) 789-2377, Fax (217) 789-2380, crose@cwlp.com, www.springfield.il.us

**Sterling** · *Greater Sterling Dev. Corp.* · Heather Sotelo, Exec. Dir., 1741 Industrial Dr., 61081, P 16,000, (815) 625-5255, Fax (815) 625-5094, hsotelo@sterlingdevelopment.org, www.sterlingdevelopment.org

**Stronghurst** · *see Monmouth*

**Taylorville** · *Christian County EDC* · Mary Renner, Exec. Dir., 108 W. Market St., 2nd Flr., 62568, P 12,000, (217) 287-2580, Fax (217) 824-6689, www.christiancountyedc.com

**EDC**

**Washington** · *Washington Eco. Dev. Comm.* · Carol Hamilton, 114 Washington Sq., 61571, P 13,500, (309) 444-8909, Fax (309) 444-9225, wcoc@mtco.com, www.washingtoncoc.com.

**Waukegan** · *Waukegan Port Dist.* · Harbor Master, 55 S. Harbor Pl., P.O. Box 620, 60079, (847) 244-3133, Fax (847) 244-1348, www.waukeganport.com

**Wheaton** · *DuPage County Eco. Dev. Dept.* · Tom Cuculich, Dir., 421 N. County Farm Rd., 60187, P 930,000, (630) 407-6700, Fax (630) 407-6702, www.dupageco.org

**Woodridge** · *Village of Woodridge Planning & Dev. Dept.* · Michael Mays, Dir., 5 Plz. Dr., 60517, P 33,253, (630) 719-4711, Fax (630) 719-4906, mmays@vil.woodridge.il.us, www.vil.woodridge.il.us

**Yorkville** · *Yorkville Eco. Dev. Corp.* · Lynn Dubajic, Exec. Dir., 651 Prairie Pointe Dr., Ste. 102, 60560, P 14,000, M 200, (630) 553-0843, Fax (630) 553-0889, dubajic@yedconline.org, www.yedconline.org

**Zion** · *City of Zion Eco. Dev. Corp.* · Delaine Rogers, Eco. Dev. Dir., 2828 Sheridan Rd., 60099, P 22,066, (847) 746-4015, Fax (847) 746-4017, delainer@zion.il.us, www.cityofzion.com

# Indiana

## Federal

**U.S. SBA, Indiana Dist. Ofc.** · Gail Gesell, Dist. Dir., 8500 Keystone Crossing, Ste. 400, Indianapolis, 46240, (317) 226-7272, Fax (317) 226-7259, www.sba.gov/in

## State

**Indiana Eco. Dev. Corp.** · Mitch Roob, Secy. of Comm., One N. Capitol Ave., Ste. 700, Indianapolis, 46204, (317) 232-8992, Fax (317) 233-5123, mroob@iedc.in.gov, www.iedc.in.gov

## Communities

**Anderson** · *Anderson Corp. for Eco. Dev.* · Rob Sparks, Exec. Dir., 205 W. 11th St., 46016, P 133,000, (765) 642-1860, Fax (765) 642-0266, robsparks@cedanderson.com, www.cedanderson.com

**Avon** · *Hendricks County Eco. Dev. Partnership* · Cinda Kelley, Exec. Dir., 5250 E. U.S. Hwy. 36, Ste. 1000-5, 46123, P 104,093, (317) 745-2400, Fax (317) 745-0757, kelley@hcedp.org, www.hcedp.org

**Bedford** · *Lawrence County Eco. Growth Cncl.* · Gene McCracken, Exec. Dir., 1116 16th St., 47421, P 46,413, (812) 275-5123, (812) 275-4493, Fax (812) 279-5998, economic@lawrencecountygrowth.com, www.lawrencecountygrowth.com

**Bloomington** · *Bloomington Eco. Dev. Corp.* · Ron Walker, Pres., 400 W. 7th St., Ste. 101, 47404, P 123,000, (812) 335-7346, Fax (812) 335-7348, rwalker@bedc.bloomington.in.us, www.comparebloomington.org

**Bluffton** · *Wells County Eco. Dev.* · Mike Row, Dir., 211 W. Water St., 46714, P 26,800, (260) 824-0510, Fax (260) 824-5871, mrow@wellsedc.com, www.wellsedc.com

**Bremen** · *Town of Bremen Dept. of Eco. Dev.* · Richard Martin, Dir., 111 S. Center, 46506, P 4,486, (574) 546-2044, Fax (574) 546-5487, townbremenin@mchsi.com, www.bremenin.org

**Clinton** · *Vermillion County Eco. Dev. Cncl.* · William Laubernds, Exec. Dir., 259 Vine St., 47842, P 17,000, (765) 832-3870, Fax (765) 832-3871, susie@vermillioncountyedc.com, www.vermillioncountyedc.com

**Columbus** · *Columbus Eco. Dev. Bd.* · Corey Carr, Exec. Dir., 500 Franklin St., 47201, P 70,000, M 100, (812) 378-7300 ext. 231, Fax (812) 372-6756, www.columbusin.org

**Corydon** · *Harrison County Eco. Dev. Corp.* · Darrell Voelker, Dir., 310 N. Elm St., 47112, P 34,500, (812) 738-2137, Fax (812) 738-6438, dvoelker@hcedcindiana.org, www.hcedcindiana.org

**Crawfordsville** · *Montgomery County Eco. Dev.* · Bill Henderson, Exec. Dir., 309 N. Green St., 47933, P 37,800, (765) 362-6851, Fax (765) 362-6900, info@mcedinc.com, www.mcedinc.com

**Decatur** · *Adams County Eco. Dev. Corp.* · Larry D. Macklin, Exec. Dir., 313 W. Jefferson St., P.O. Box 492, 46733, P 33,625, (260) 724-2588, Fax (260) 724-9735, lmacklin@adamscountyedc.com, www.adamscountyedc.com

**Elkhart** · *North Central Indiana Bus. Assistance Center* · Philip Penn, Pres., 418 S. Main St., P.O. Box 2586, 46515, P 320,000, M 1,200, (574) 293-3209, Fax (574) 294-1859, info@elkhart.org, www.elkhart.org

**Evansville** · *Southwest Indiana EDC* · Greg Wathen, Pres./CEO, 100 N.W. 2nd St., Ste. 208, P.O. Box 20127, 47708, P 300,000, (812) 423-2020, (800) 401-7683, Fax (812) 423-2080, areafacts@southwestindiana.org, www.southwestindiana.org

**Fort Wayne** · *Fort Wayne-Allen County Eco. Dev. Alliance* · 111 W. Wayne St., 46802, P 502,141, (260) 426-5568, Fax (260) 426-0837, email@theallianceonline.com, www.theallianceonline.com

**Fowler** · *Benton County Dev. Corp.* · P.O. Box 511, 47944, P 9,500, (765) 884-1200, Fax (765) 884-3239

**Franklin** · *Johnson County Dev. Corp.* · Cheryl Morphew, Exec. Dir., 2797 N. Morton St., Ste. E, 46131, P 135,951, (317) 736-4300, Fax (317) 736-7220, cmorphew@jcdc.org, www.jcdc.org

**Greencastle** · *Greencastle/Putnam County Dev. Ctr.* · William Dory Jr., Dir., 2 S. Jackson St., 46135, P 38,000, (765) 653-2474, Fax (765) 653-6385, economic_development@greencastle.com, www.greencastleindianaeconomicdevelopment.com

**Greenfield** · *Hancock Eco. Dev. Cncl.* · Dennis Maloy, Dir., One Courthouse Plz., 46140, P 57,000, (317) 477-7241, Fax (317) 477-2353, dmaloy@cedhc.org, www.cedhc.org

**Greenwood** · *see Franklin*

**Hartford City** · *Blackford County Eco. Dev. Corp.* · Rob Cleveland, Exec. Dir., 121 N. High St., P.O. Box 71, 47348, P 14,000, (765) 348-4944, Fax (765) 348-4945, rcleveland@blackfordcoedc.org, www.blackfordcoedc.org

**Huntington** · *Huntington County United Eco. Dev. Corp.* · Mark Whickersham, Exec. Dir., 8 W. Market St., 46750, P 39,293, (260) 356-5688, (888) 356-6660, Fax (260) 358-5692, hcued@onlyinternet.net, www.hcued.com

**Indianapolis** · *Indy Partnership* · Ron Gifford, Pres./CEO, 111 Monument Cir., Ste. 1800, 46204, P 1,882,000, (317) 236-6262, Fax (317) 236-6275, www.indypartnership.com

**Kendallville** · *Eco. Dev. Steering Comm.* · Anita Shepherd, Coord., 122 S. Main St., 46755, P 10,018, (260) 347-1554, (877) 347-1554, Fax (260) 347-1575, info@kendallchamber.com, www.kendallvillechamber.com

**Knox** · *Starke County Dev. Found.* · Charles Weaver, Exec. Dir., 4 N. Main St., 46534, P 25,000, (574) 772-5627, (800) 359-5627, Fax (574) 772-5912, execdir@starkecounty.com, www.starke-county.com

**Kokomo** · *Greater Kokomo Eco. Dev. Alliance* · Jeb Conrad, Pres., 700 E. Firmin St., Ste, 200, 46902, P 85,000, (765) 457-2000, Fax (765) 854-0481, jconrad@khdc.org, www.khdc.org

**Lafayette** · *Greater Lafayette Commerce* · 337 Columbia St., P.O. Box 348, 47902, P 156,169, (765) 742-4044, Fax (765) 742-6276, www.lwldc.org

**Leavenworth** • *Crawford County Eco. Dev. Comm.* • Don DuBois, Exec. Dir., 6225 E. Industrial Ln., Ste. #B, 47137, P 11,076, (812) 739-2248, don@selectcc.com, www.selectcc.com

**Lebanon** • *Boone County Eco. Dev. Corp.* • Dax Norton, Exec. Dir., 218 E. Washington St., 46052, P 52,000, (765) 482-5761, Fax (765) 482-5782, info@booneedc.org, www.booneedc.org

**Liberty** • *Union County Dev. Corp.* • Blanche Stelle, Exec. Dir., 5 W. High St., 47353, P 7,300, (765) 458-5976, Fax (765) 458-5976, ucdc@dslmyway.com, www.ucdc.us.

**Linton** • *Greene County Eco. Dev. Corp.* • Joan Bethell, Exec. Dir., P.O. Box 7, 47441, P 32,573, (812) 847-4500, Fax (812) 847-0936, www.gcedc.us

**Logansport** • *Logansport-Cass County Eco. Dev. Found.* • Judi Barr, Exec. Asst., 311 S. 5th, 46947, P 40,930, M 110, (574) 722-5988, Fax (574) 735-0909, skip@ledf.com, www.ledf.com

**Marion** • *Grant County Eco. Growth Cncl.* • Timothy K. Eckerle, Exec. Dir., 301 S. Adams St., Ste. 109, 46952, P 73,403, (765) 662-0650, (888) 668-3203, Fax (765) 662-8340, www.grantcoin-development.com

**Monticello** • *White County Eco. Dev.* • Connie Neininger, Exex. Dir., 110 N. Main St., P.O. Box 1031, 47960, P 25,267, (574) 583-6557, Fax (574) 583-6230, ledo@whitecountyindiana.us, www.whitecountyin.org

**Mooresville** • *Morgan County Eco. Dev. Corp.* • 4 E. Harrison St., P.O. Box 606, 46158, P 68,656, (317) 831-9544, Fax (317) 831-9548, mcedc@morgancoed.com, www.morgancoed.com

**Mount Comfort** • *see Greenfield*

**New Castle** • *New Castle/Henry County Eco. Dev. Corp.* • 100 S. Main St., Ste. 203, 47362, P 48,000, (765) 521-7402, Fax (765) 521-7404, info@midwestdevelopment.org, www.midwestdevelopment.org

**Newburgh** • *Warrick County Eco. Dev. Dept.* • Larry Taylor, Exec. Dir., 7199 Parker Dr., P.O. Box 875, 47629, P 51,609, (812) 858-3555, Fax (812) 858-3558, bizinfo@warrick-edd.org, www.warrick-edd.org

**North Vernon** • *Jennings County Eco. Dev. Comm.* • Kathy Ertel, Exec. Dir., P.O. Box 15, 47265, P 27,500, (812) 346-2388, Fax (812) 346-7992, kertel@jenningsedc.com, www.jenningsedc.com

**Peru** • *Miami County Eco. Dev. Auth.* • James Tidd, Exec. Dir., 1525 W. Hoosier Blvd., Ste. 201, 46970, P 36,082, (765) 689-0159, (800) 472-0449, Fax (765) 689-0168, info@miamicountyeda.com, www.miamicountyeda.com

**Petersburg** • *Pike County Eco. Dev. Growth Cncl.* • Paul Lake, Exec. Dir., 714 1/2 Main St., P.O. Box 204, 47567, P 13,000, (812) 354-2271, Fax (812) 354-7196, pikegrowth@verizon.net, www.pikecogrowth.org

**Plymouth** • *Plymouth Ind. Dev. Corp.* • Douglas C. Anspach, Exec. Dir., 120 N. Michigan St., 46563, P 10,000, (574) 936-2323, Fax (574) 936-6584, danspach49@yahoo.com, www.plymouthindustrial.com

**Portage** • *Northwest IN Forum, Inc.* • Vincent Galbiati, Pres., 6100 S. Port Rd., 46368, P 787,000, (219) 763-6303, (800) 693-6786, Fax (219) 763-2653, www.nwiforum.org

**Portland** • *Jay County Dev. Corp.* • Bill Bradley, Exec. Dir., 118 S. Meridian St., Ste. B, 47371, P 22,000, (260) 726-9311, Fax (260) 726-4477, bbradley@jaycodev.org, www.jaycountydevelopment.org

**Richmond** • *EDC of Wayne County* • Tim Rogers, Pres./CEO, 500 S. A St., P.O. Box 1919, 47375, P 72,000, (765) 983-4769, (800) 410-GROW, Fax (765) 966-8956, info@edcwc.com, www.edcwc.com

**Rochester** • *Fulton Eco. Dev. Corp.* • Shane Blair, Exec. Dir., 822 Main St., 46975, P 20,600, (574) 223-3326, Fax (574) 224-2329, sblair@fultondevelopment.org, www.fultondevelopment.org

**Rockport** • *Lincolnland Eco. Dev. Corp.* • Tom Utter, Exec. Dir., 2792 N. U.S. Hwy. 23, P.O. Box 276, 47635, P 21,000, (812) 649-2119, Fax (812) 649-2236, lincoln@psci.net, www.ledc.org

**Rushville** • *Rush County Eco. & Comm. Dev. Corp.* • Brad Buening, Exec. Dir., 315 N. Main St., 46173, P 18,016, (765) 938-3232, Fax (765) 932-4191, bbuening@rushecdc.org, www.rushcounty.com/ecdc

**Salem** • *Washington County Eco. Growth Partnership* • Jess Helsel, Pres., 1707 N. Shelby St., Ste. 109, 47167, P 28,000, (812) 883-8803, Fax (812) 883-8739, infoi@wcegp.org, www.wcegp.org

**Seymour** • *Jackson County Ind. Dev. Corp.* • James Plump, Exec. Dir., 301 N. Chestnut St., P.O. Box 783, 47274, P 41,335, (812) 522-4951, Fax (812) 522-1235, jimplump@jcidc.com, www.jcidc.com

**Shelbyville** • *Shelby County Dev. Corp.* • Dan Theobald, Exec. Dir., 16 Public Sq., Ste. A, 46176, P 44,300, (317) 398-8903, Fax (317) 398-8915, d.theobald@shelbydevelopment.com, www.shelbydevelopment.com

**South Bend** • *Project Future* • Patrick M. McMahon, Exec. Dir., 401 E. Colfax Ave., Ste. 305, P.O. Box 1677, 46634, P 265,559, (574) 234-6590, (800) 228-8086, Fax (574) 236-1060, www.projectfuture.org

**Tell City** • *Perry County Dev. Corp.* • 601 Main St., Ste. A, P.O. Box 731, 47586, P 18,843, (812) 547-8377, Fax (812) 547-8378, www.pickperry.com

**Tell City** • *Tell City Eco. Dev. Comm.* • Mary Cardinal, Pres., City Hall Bldg., P.O. Box 515, 47586, P 8,000, (812) 547-5511, Fax (812) 547-5111

**Terre Haute** • *Terre Haute Eco. Dev. Corp.* • 630 Wabash Ave., Ste. 101, 47807, P 105,000, (812) 234-2524, Fax (812) 232-6054, info@terrehauteedc.com, www.terrehauteedc.com

**Tipton** • *Tipton County Eco. Dev. Corp.* • 136 E. Jefferson St., 46072, P 16,577, (765) 675-7417, (800) 461-4907, Fax (765) 675-8917, www.tiptonedc.com

**Vincennes** • *Knox County Dev. Corp.* • 1101 N. 3rd St., P.O. Box 701, 47591, P 41,838, (812) 886-6993, Fax (812) 886-0888, info@kcdc.com, www.kcdc.com

**Walkerton** • *Walkerton Area Eco. Dev. Corp.* • Phillip Buckmaster, Exec. Dir., 612 Roosevelt Rd., 46574, P 2,274, (574) 586-7766, Fax (574) 586-2248, waedc@walkerton.org, www.walkerton.org

**Warsaw** • *Kosciusko Dev. Inc.* • Joy McCarthy-Sessing CEcD, Pres., 313 S. Buffalo St., 46580, P 76,115, (574) 267-6311, (800) 776-6311, Fax (574) 267-7762, jmccarthy-sessing@kdi-in.com, www.kdi-in.com.

**Zanesville** • *see Lebanon*

# Iowa

## Federal

**U.S. SBA, Cedar Rapids Dist. Ofc.** • Dennis Larkin, Branch Mgr., 2750 1st Ave. N.E., Ste. 350, Cedar Rapids, 52402, (319) 362-6405, Fax (319) 362-7861, www.sba.gov/ia

**U.S. SBA, Des Moines Dist. Ofc.** • Joseph Folsom, Dist. Dir., 210 Walnut St., Rm. 749, Des Moines, 50309, (515) 284-4422, Fax (515) 284-4572, www.sba.gov/ia

EDC

## State

**Iowa Dept. of Eco. Dev.** • Mike Tramontina, Dir., 200 E. Grand Ave., Des Moines, 50309, (515) 242-4700, Fax (515) 242-4809, info@iowalifechanging.com, www.iowalifechanging.com

## Communities

**Ackley** • *Ackley Eco. Dev. Comm.* • Michael Nuss, Eco. Dev. Dir., City Hall, 208 State St., 50601, P 1,809, (641) 847-2214, Fax (641) 847-3204, ackley@mchsi.com, www.ackleyiowa.net

**Albia** • *Albia Ind. Dev. Corp.* • Dave Johnson, Pres., Bates Bldg., 1 Benton Ave. W., 52531, P 8,016, (641) 932-7233, Fax (641) 932-3044, aidc@iowatelecom.net, www.albiaindustrial.com

**Algona** • *Palo Alto County EDC* • Maureen Elbert, Exec. Dir., 106 S. Dodge St., Ste. 210, 50511, P 27,310, (515) 295-7979, Fax (515) 295-8873, info@paloaltoiowa.com, www.paloaltoiowa.com

**Altoona** • *Eastern Polk Reg. Dev. Inc.* • Don Coates, Exec. Dir., 119 Second St. S.E., Ste. B, 50009, P 30,000, (515) 957-0088, Fax (515) 957-0089, eprd@iowa-property.com, www.iowa-property.com

**Ames** • *Ames Eco. Dev. Comm.* • Dan Culhane, Pres./CEO, 1601 Golden Aspen Dr., Ste. 110, 50010, P 52,300, M 130, (515) 232-2310, Fax (515) 232-6716, dan@ameschamber.com, www.amesedc.com

**Ankeny** • *Ankeny Eco. Dev. Corp.* • Don Zuck, Exec. Dir., 210 S. Ankeny Blvd., P.O. Box 488, 50021, P 39,000, M 60, (515) 964-0747, Fax (515) 964-0487, www.ankenyedc.com

**Arnolds Park** • *Iowa Great Lakes Ind. Dev. Bd.* • Tom Kuhlman, Exec. Dir., 243 W. Broadway, P.O. Box 9, 51331, P 16,424, (712) 332-2107, Fax (712) 332-7714, tom@okobojichamber.com, www.vacationokoboji.com

**Atlantic** • *Southwest Iowa Planning Cncl.* • M.J. Broomfield, Exec. Dir., 1501 S.W. 7th St., 50022, P 182,531, (712) 243-4196, (866) 279-4720, Fax (712) 243-3458, swipco@swipco.org, www.swipco.org

**Audubon** • *Audubon County Eco. Dev. Corp.* • 800 Market St., 50025, P 6,870, M 100, (712) 563-2742, Fax (712) 563-2537, aced@iowatelecom.net, www.auduboncounty.com

**Avoca** • *Western Iowa Dev. Assn.* • Lori Holste, Exec. Dir., 1911 N. LaVista Height Rd., Ste. 102, P.O. Box 579, 51521, P 11,000, (712) 343-6368, Fax (712) 343-2136, lori@wida.org, www.wida.org

**Bedford** • *Bedford Area Dev. Center* • Deann Hensley, Exec. Dir., 601 Madison, 50833, P 1,600, (712) 523-3637, Fax (712) 523-3384, bedfordareadc@frontiernet.net, www.bedford-iowa.com

**Belle Plaine** • *Belle Plaine Comm. Dev. Corp.* • Jon Dayton, Exec. Dir., 826 12th St., 52208, P 2,878, M 140, (319) 434-6481, Fax (319) 434-6026, BPCDC@netins.net, www.belleplaine communitydevelopment.com

**Belmond** • *BIDCO Ind. Dev.* • Dee Schrodt, Secy., 327 E. Main St., Ste. 100, 50421, P 2,600, M 60, (641) 444-3937, Fax (641) 444-3944, bacoc@frontiernet.net, www.belmond.com

**Bettendorf** • *Bettendorf Dev. Corp.* • Steve VanDyke, Dir., 1609 State St., 52722, P 31,275, M 25, (563) 344-4060, Fax (563) 344-4012, svandyke@bettendorf.org, www.bettendorf.org

**Bloomfield** • *Davis County Dev. Corp.* • John Schroeder, Exec. Dir., 111 S. Washington St., P.O. Box 159, 52537, P 8,513, (641) 664-2300, www.daviscounty.org

**Bondurant** • *see Altoona*

**Boone** • *Boone's Future Inc.* • Robert Fisher, Exec. Dir., 903 Story St., 50036, P 12,805, M 70, (515) 432-7868, Fax (515) 432-3343, boonechamber@iowatelecom.net, www.booneiowa.com

**Burlington** • *Greater Burlington Partnership* • Dennis Hinkle, Pres., 610 N. 4th St., Ste. 200, 52601, P 30,000, (319) 752-6365, (800) 827-4837, Fax (319) 752-6454, dhinkle@growburlington.com, www.growburlington.com

**Carroll** • *Carroll Area Dev. Corp.* • Jim Gossett, Exec. Dir., 407 W. 5th St., P.O. Box 307, 51401, P 21,421, M 40, (712) 792-4383, Fax (712) 792-4384, chamber@carrolliowa.com, www.carrollareadev.com

**Cascade** • *Cascade Eco. Dev. Corp.* • Fred Kremer, Pres., P.O. Box 695, 52033, P 1,958, (563) 852-7214, Fax (563) 852-7554, www.cityofcascade.org

**Cedar Falls** • *Cedar Falls Dept. of Dev. Svcs.* • Bob Seymour, Comm. Svcs. Mgr., 220 Clay St., 50613, P 36,145, (319) 273-8606, Fax (319) 273-8610, bob.seymour@cedarfalls.com, www.50613.com

**Cedar Rapids** • *Priority One, Eco. Dev. Cedar Rapids C/C* • Mark Seckman, Pres., 424 First Ave. N.E., 52401, P 195,000, (319) 730-1420, Fax (319) 398-5228, mseckman@cedarrapids.org, www.priority1.com

**Centerville** • *Appanoose Eco. Dev. Corp.* • Keith Sherman, Pres., 307 N. 13th St., P.O. Box 370, 52544, P 14,000, M 300, (641) 856-3388, Fax (641) 856-6046, aedc@appanoosecounty.org, www.appanoosecounty.org

**Chariton** • *Lucas County Dev. Corp.* • Ruth Comer, Exec. Dir., 104 N. Grand, P.O. Box 735, 50049, P 10,000, (641) 774-4059, Fax (641) 774-2801, ccdc@iowatelecom.net, www.charitonchamber.com

**Charles City** • *Charles City Area Dev. Corp.* • Timothy S. Fox CEcD, Exec. Dir., 401 N. Main St., 50616, P 20,000, M 100, (641) 228-3020, (800) 640-2936, Fax (641) 228-4744, ccadc@charles cityia.com, www.charlescityia.com

**Cherokee** • *Cherokee Area Eco. Dev. Corp.* • Mark Buschkamp, Exec. Dir., 418 W. Cedar St., Ste. B, 51012, P 5,035, (712) 225-5739, Fax (712) 225-1991, markcaedc@evertek.net, www.cherokeeia.com

**Clinton** • *Clinton Reg. Dev. Corp.* • Steven Ames, Pres., 721 S. 2nd St., 52732, P 110,000, M 150, (563) 242-4536, Fax (563) 242-4554, sames@clintondevelopment.com, www.clintondevelopment.com

**Columbus Junction** • *Columbus Comm. Club* • Kirsten Shellabarger, Pres., 232 2nd St., 52738, P 1,900, M 50, (319) 728-7971, Fax (319) 728-7502, www.columbusjunctioniowa.org

**Conrad** • *Conrad Chamber-Main Street* • Darla Ubben, Prog. Dir., 204 E. Center St., P.O. Box 414, 50621, P 1,054, (641) 366-2108, Fax (641) 366-2109, cmspd@heartofiowa.net, www.conrad.govoffice.com

**Coon Rapids** • *Coon Rapids Dev. Group* • Doug Carpenter, Pres., P.O. Box 226, 50058, P 1,310, M 115, (712) 999-2734, (712) 999-2225, crdg@crmu.net, www.coonrapidsiowa.com

**Corning** • *Adams Comm. Eco. Dev. Corp.* • Beth Waddle, Exec. Dir., 710 Davis Ave., 50841, P 1,800, (641) 322-5229, Fax (641) 322-4387, acedc@frontiernet.net, www.adamscountyiowa.com

**Council Bluffs** • *City of Council Bluffs Comm. Dev. Dept.* • Donald Gross, Dir., 209 Pearl St., 51503, P 58,000, (712) 328-4629, Fax (712) 328-4915, community@councilbluffs-ia.gov, www.communitydev.councilbluffs-ia.gov

**Cresco** • *Howard County Eco. Dev.* • Ken Paxton, Eco. Dev. Dir., 101 Second Ave. S.W., P.O. Box 403, 52136, P 9,932, (563) 547-3434, Fax (563) 547-2056, kpaxton@howard-county.com, www.howard-county.com

**Des Moines** • *City of Des Moines - Ofc. of Eco. Dev.* • Rick Clark, City Mgr., City Hall, 400 Robert D. Ray Dr., 50309, P 200,000, (515) 283-4004, Fax (515) 237-1667, www.dmgov.org

**Des Moines** · *Iowa Area Dev. Group* · Rand M. Fisher, Pres., 2700 Westown Pkwy., Ste. 425, 50266, P 540,000, (515) 223-4817, Fax (515) 223-5719, rfisher@iadg.com, www.iadg.com

**DeWitt** · *DeWitt Dev. Co.* · Tami Petsche, Exec. Dir., 1010 6th Ave., 52742, P 5,149, (563) 659-8508, Fax (563) 659-9450, ccd. ceo@dewitt.org, www.dewittdevelopmentcompany.com

**Dubuque** · *Greater Dubuque Dev. Corp.* · Rick Dickinson, Exec. Dir./COO, 300 Main St., Ste. 120, 52001, P 91,000, (563) 557-9049, Fax (563) 557-1059, www.greaterdubuque.org

**Dysart** · *Dysart Dev. Corp.* · Dwayne Luze, Pres., P.O. Box 223, 52224, P 1,303, (319) 476-2332, www.dysartiowa.com

**Eddyville** · *Eddyville Bus. Center* · Ron Richards, Pres., P.O. Box 585, 52553, P 1,500, (641) 969-4952, Fax (641) 969-5528

**Eldora** · *City of Eldora Eco. Dev.* · Deb Crosser, Exec. Dir., 1442 Washington St., 50627, P 3,035, (641) 939-3241, Fax (641) 939-7555, www.eldoraiowa.com

**Elkader** · *Main Street Elkader/Econ. Dev.* · Roger Thomas, Dir., 207 N. Main St., P.O. Box 125, 52043, P 1,500, (563) 245-2770, Fax (563) 245-1033, mse@alpinecom.net, www.elkader-iowa.com

**Fairfield** · *Fairfield Eco. Dev. Assn.* · Brent M. Willett, Exec. Dir., 204 W. Broadway, 52556, P 15,500, M 75, (641) 472-3436, Fax (641) 472-6510, bwillett@fairfieldiowa.com, www.fairfieldiowa.com

**Forest City** · *Forest City Dev. Inc.* · David Kingland, Pres., 145 E. K St., 50436, P 4,500, M 45, (641) 585-5560, Fax (641) 585-2687, www.forestcityia.com

**Fort Dodge** · *The Dev. Corp. of Fort Dodge & Webster County* · John Kramer, Pres., 822 Central Ave., Ste. 406, 50501, P 44,000, (515) 955-7788, Fax (515) 955-5421, john@wcfddevelopment. com, www.wcfddevelopment.com

**Fredericksburg** · *Fredericksburg Comm. Dev. Corp.* · Cindy Lantow, Eco. Dev. Dir., 151 W. Main, P.O. Box 318, 50630, P 984, (563) 237-5725, www.fredericksburgiowa.com

**Garner** · *Garner Area Comm. Betterment Assn.* · Howard Parrott, Secy./Treas., 265 E. Lyon St., 50438, P 2,922, M 105, (641) 923-2739, hmparrot@ncn.net, www.garneriowa.org

**Gladbrook** · *Gladbrook Dev. Corp.* · Denny Gienger, Treas., P.O. Box 309, 50635, P 1,100, (641) 473-3056, Fax (641) 473-3056

**Greenfield** · *Greenfield Main Street Dev. Corp.* · Ginny Kuhfus, Dir., 201 S. First St., P.O. Box 61, 50849, P 2,195, (641) 743-8444, Fax (641) 743-8205, grfld_cc_ms_dev@iowatelecom.net, www. greenfieldiowa.com

**Grinnell** · *Poweshiek Area Dev.* · Bill Menner, Exec. Dir., 927 4th Ave., 50112, P 9,100, (641) 236-1626, Fax (641) 236-2626, bill@ powi80.com, www.powi80.com

**Hampton** · *Franklin County Dev. Assn.* · Karen Mitchell, Eco. Dev. Dir., 5 First St. S.W., 50441, P 11,800, (641) 456-5668, Fax (641) 456-5660, fcda_director@mchsi.com, www.franklincoun-tyiowa.com

**Harlan** · *Shelby County DevelopSource* · David Yamada, Dir. Mktg./Eco. Dev., 1006 6th St., 51537, P 13,000, (712) 755-3569, Fax (712) 733-8921, dyamada@harlannet.com, www. DevelopSource.com

**Hartley** · *Hartley Eco. Dev. Corp.* · Brian Pals, City Admin., 11 S. Central Ave., 51346, P 1,733, (712) 928-2240, Fax (712) 928-2878, www.hartleyiowa.com

**Hull** · *Hull Ind. Dev. Corp.* · Les VanRoekel, City Admin., City Hall, P.O. Box 816, 51239, P 1,960, (712) 439-1521, Fax (712) 439-2512, www.cityofhull.org

**Ida Grove** · *Ida Grove Eco. Dev. Corp.* · Clay Miller, Pres., 501 Second St., P.O. Box 111, 51445, P 2,350, (712) 364-3393, Fax (712) 364-3293, www.idagrovechamber.com

**Independence** · *Buchanan County Eco. Dev. Comm.* · Greg Halverson, Dir., P.O. Box 109, 50644, P 21,000, (319) 334-7497, Fax (319) 334-5982, director@growbuchanan.com, www. growbuchanan.com

**Independence** · *Independence Enterprises, Inc.* · Steve Ohl, Pres., 115 First St. E., 50644, P 6,500, (319) 334-4329, (319) 334-7497, Fax (319) 334-6335, steveohl@indytel.com

**Indianola** · *Warren County Eco. Dev. Corp.* · Tiffany Coleman, Exec. Dir., 515 N. Jefferson Way, Ste. C, 50125, P 43,062, (515) 961-1067, Fax (515) 961-1156, wcedc@mchsi.com, www.wcedc.com

**Inwood** · *Inwood Dev. Corp.* · Carol VanderKolk, City Clerk, P.O. Box 298, 51240, P 875, (712) 753-4833, Fax (712) 753-2538, cityofinwood@hotmail.com, www.inwoodiowa.com

**Iowa City** · *Iowa City Area Dev. Group* · Joseph Raso, Pres., 325 E. Washington St., Ste. 101, 52240, P 125,000, (319) 354-3939, Fax (319) 338-9958, jraso@iowacityarea.com, www.iowacity areadevelopment.com

**Iowa Falls** · *Iowa Falls Area Dev. Corp.* · Thomas Deimerly, Exec. Dir., 520 Rocksylvania Ave., 50126, P 5,200, M 45, (641) 648-5604, Fax (641) 648-3702, ifadc@iafalls.com, www.iowafallsdevelop ment.com

**Jefferson** · *Greene County Dev. Corp.* · Rick Morain, Exec. Dir., 220 N. Chestnut St., 50129, P 10,120, (515) 386-8255, Fax (515) 386-2156, commerce@jeffersoniowa.com, www.greenecounty iowadevelopment.org

**Johnston** · *Iowa Bus. Growth Co.* · Dan Robeson, Exec. V.P., 5409 N.W. 88th St., Ste. 100, 50131, (515) 223-4511, Fax (515) 223-5017, www.iowabusinessgrowth.com

**Knoxville** · *Knoxville C/C Eco. Dev.* · Roxanne Johnson, Exec. Dir., 309 E. Main St., 50138, P 8,270, (641) 828-7555, Fax (641) 828-7978, www.knoxville-iowa.com

**Lake Mills** · *Winn-Worth BETCO* · Teresa Nicholson, Exec. Dir., 203A N. 1st Ave. W., P.O. Box 93, 50450, P 19,000, (641) 592-0800, Fax (641) 592-0801, wwb@wctatel.net, www.win-worthbetco.com

**LeMars** · *LeMars Bus. Initiative Corp.* · Neal Adler, Exec. Dir., 50 Central Ave. S.E., 51031, P 9,500, (712) 546-8821, Fax (712) 546-7218, lemarschamber@frontiernet.net, www.lemarsiowa.com

**Lenox** · *Lenox Dev. Corp.* · Gary Zabel, Dir., P.O. Box 92, 50851, P 1,400, (641) 333-2255, (641) 333-4272, www.lenoxia.com

**Logan** · *Harrison County Dev. Corp.* · Renea Anderson, Exec. Dir., 109 N. 4th Ave., Ste. 2, 51546, P 15,666, M 100, (712) 644-3081, Fax (712) 644-3107, hcdc@iowatelecom.net, www. hcdconline.com

**Lorimor** · *Lorimor Comm. Dev. Corp.* · F. Dennis Orwan, Pres., P.O. Box 63, 50149, P 427, (641) 763-2334, feorwan@grm.net, www.lorimor.org

**Manchester** · *Delaware County Eco. Dev. Comm.* · Donna Boss, Exec. Dir., 200 E. Main St., 52057, P 18,404, (563) 927-3325, Fax (563) 927-2958, www.delawarecountyia.com

**Mapleton** · *Maple Valley Dev. Inc.* · Marsha Craig, Pres., P.O. Box 164, 51034, P 1,300, M 84, (712) 881-1351, (712) 882-1343, www.mapleton.com

**Marcus** · *Marcus for Progress* · Angie Cowan, Dir., 222 N. Main St., 51035, P 1,200, (712) 376-2680, marcus@midlands.net, www. marcusiowa.com

EDC

**Marengo** · *Marengo Ind. Dev. Corp.* · Virgil Head, Pres., P.O. Box 168, 52301, P 2,535, (319) 642-5511, Fax (319) 642-1111, marengoiowa.com

**Marshalltown** · *Marshall Eco. Dev. Impact Comm.* · Joel Akason, Pres., 709 S. Center St., P.O. Box 1000, 50158, P 39,311, (641) 753-6645, (800) 725-5301, Fax (641) 752-8373, akason@marshalltown.org, www.marshalltownworks.com

**Mason City** · *North Iowa Corridor Eco. Dev. Corp.* · Gregg Gillman, Exec. Dir., 25 W. State St., Ste. B, 50401, P 8,200, M 125, (641) 423-0315, (800) 944-1708, info@northiowacorridor.com, www.northiowacorridor.com

**Mitchellville** · *see Altoona*

**Monticello** · *Monticello Dev. Corp.* · Bob Goodyear, P.O. Box 191, 52310, P 3,607, (319) 480-0171, Fax (319) 465-4611, www.ci.monticello.ia.us

**Moravia** · *Moravia Dev. Corp.* · Delores Burkland, P.O. Box 174, 52571, P 713, (641) 724-3660

**Mount Ayr** · *Ringgold County Dev. Corp.* · Sandy Lamb, Coord., 117 S. Fillmore, 50854, P 5,400, (641) 464-3704, Fax (641) 464-3704, rdevco@iowatelecom.net

**Nevada** · *Nevada Eco. Dev. Cncl.* · LaVon Schiltz, Exec. Dir., 516 K Ave., P.O. Box 157, 50201, P 7,000, (515) 382-1430, Fax (515) 382-1460, nedc@iowatelecom.net, www.nevadaec.com

**New Hampton** · *New Hampton Eco. Dev.* · Bob Soukup, Dir. of Eco. Dev., 112 E. Spring St., P.O. Box 435, 50659, P 4,000, (641) 394-2437, Fax (641) 394-4514, info@newhamptonia.com, www.newhamptonia.com

**Oakland** · *Golden Hills Resource Conservation & Dev.* · Shirley Frederiksen, Coord., 712 S. Hwy. 6, P.O. Box 189, 51560, P 200,000, (712) 482-3029, Fax (712) 482-5590, www.goldenhillsrcd.org

**Osceola** · *Clarke County Dev. Corp.* · William Trickey, Exec. Dir., P.O. Box 426, 50213, P 4,659, M 100, (641) 342-2944, Fax (641) 342-6353, info@clarkecountyiowa.com, www.clarkecountyiowa.com

**Ottumwa** · *Ottumwa Eco. Dev. Corp.* · Roger Jones, Exec. Dir., 217 E. Main St., P.O. Box 1288, 52501, P 35,000, M 200, (641) 682-3465, (800) 479-0828, Fax (641) 682-3466, inforequest@ottumwadevelopment.org, www.ottumwadevelopment.org

**Panora** · *Panora Reg. Ind. Dev. Enterprise [PRIDE]* · Orville Terry, Pres., P.O. Box 187, 50216, P 3,000, (641) 755-3124, panora.org

**Pleasant Hill** · *see Altoona*

**Red Oak** · *Red Oak Ind. Found* · George Maher, Exec. Dir., 307 E. Reed St., 51566, P 6,000, M 79, (712) 623-2261, Fax (712) 623-4822, roif@redoakiowa.com, www.redoakiowa.com

**Remsen** · *Remsen Dev. Corp.* · Chris Feller, Pres., P.O. Box 613, 51050, P 1,762, (712) 786-2136, www.remseniowa.net

**Rock Valley** · *Rock Valley Dev. Corp.* · James Vandervelde, Dev. Dir., 1507 Main St., 51247, P 3,000, (712) 476-2576, (712) 470-2137, Fax (712) 476-1074, jvv@cityofrockvalley.com, www.cityofrockvalley.com

**Rockwell City** · *Calhoun County Eco. Dev. Corp.* · Pamela Meeder, Dir., P.O. Box 47, 50579, P 11,000, (712) 297-5601, Fax (712) 297-5481, ccedc@iowatelecom.net, www.calhoundev.com

**Roland** · *Roland Dev. Corp.* · Marc Soderstrum, V.P., P.O. Box 288, 50236, P 1,324, (515) 388-4861, Fax (515) 388-5595, cityhall@cityofroland.org, www.cityofroland.org

**Rolfe** · *Rolfe Dev. Comm.* · 319 Garfield St., 50581, P 675, (712) 848-3124, Fax (712) 848-3128, www.rolfeiowa.com

**Sac City** · *Sac Eco. & Tourism Dev.* · Shirley Phillips, Exec. Dir., 615 W. Main St., 50583, P 12,000, M 70, (712) 662-7383, Fax (712) 662-7399, shirley@saccountyiowa.com, www.saccountyiowa.com

**Saint Ansgar** · *St. Ansgar Eco. Dev. Corp.* · Newlin Jensen, Pres., P.O. Box 244, 50472, P 1,100, (641) 713-4501, (641) 713-4325, www.stansgar.org

**Shenandoah** · *Shenandoah Chamber & Ind. Org.* · Gregg Connell, Exec. Dir., 100 Maple St., 51601, P 6,000, M 300, (712) 246-3455, Fax (712) 246-3456, gconnell@simplyshenandoah.com, www.shenandoahiowa.net

**Sigourney** · *Sigourney Area Dev. Corp.* · 112 E. Washington, 52591, P 2,200, (641) 622-2288, Fax (641) 622-2396, sadc@sigourney.com, www.sigourney.com

**Sioux Center** · *Sioux Center Land Dev.* · 335 1st Ave. N.W., 51250, P 6,000, (712) 722-0761, Fax (712) 722-0760, citysc@siouxcenter.org, www.siouxcenter.org

**Sioux City** · *Siouxland Eco. Dev. Corp.* · Ken Beekley, Dir., 1106 4th St., Ste. 201, 51102, P 190,000, (712) 279-6430, Fax (712) 224-2510, www.siouxlandedc.com

**Sioux City** · *The Siouxland Initiative* · Debi Durham, Pres., 101 Pierce St., 51101, P 143,000, (712) 255-7903, Fax (712) 258-7578, www.siouxlandchamber.com

**Spencer** · *Spencer Industries Found.* · Kathy Everet, Pres., 122 W. 5th St., P.O. Box 7937, 51301, P 18,000, (712) 262-5680, Fax (712) 262-5747, www.spenceriowachamber.org

**Strawberry Point** · *Strawberry Point Eco. Dev. Center* · 105 W. Mission, P.O. Box 85, 52076, P 1,500, (563) 933-4417, Fax (563) 933-4417, econdev@strawberrypt.com, www.strawberrypt.com

**Stuart** · *Midwest Partnership Dev. Corp.* · Jason White, Exec. Dir., 615 S. Division, P.O. Box 537, 50250, P 30,000, M 157, (515) 523-1262, Fax (515) 523-1397, info@midwestpartnership.com, www.midwestpartnership.com

**Stuart** · *Stuart Dev. Corp.* · Everett Shepherd, Pres., 212 S. Division, 50250, P 2,600, M 110, (515) 523-2102, (515) 523-2721, www.stuartiowa.com

**Sumner** · *Sumner's Future Inc.* · Bill Nauholz, P.O. Box 207, 50674, P 2,300, (563) 578-5470, Fax (563) 578-5853

**Tama** · *Tama Ind. Dev. Corp.* · Christopher Bearden, Mayor, 305 Siegel St., 52339, P 2,800, (641) 484-3822, tamacity@iowatele com.net, www.tamacity.govoffice2.com

**Tipton** · *Cedar County Eco. Dev. Comm.* · Stephen Lacina, Exec. Dir., 218 W. 5th St., 52772, P 18,187, M 60, (563) 886-3761, (800) 737-5576, info@cedarcountyia.org, www.cedarcountyia.org

**Urbandale** · *City of Urbandale Comm. Dev.* · Paul Dekker, Dir., 3600 86th St., 50322, P 35,732, (515) 278-3935, Fax (515) 278-3927, pdekker@urbandale.org, www.urbandale.org

**Victor** · *Victor Comm. Dev. Assn.* · Dr. Leonard Seda, Pres., 617 Main St., P.O. Box F, 52347, P 1,000, (319) 647-3240, Fax (319) 647-2727, lseda@netins.net

**Wapello** · *Wapello Dev. Corp.* · Roger Huddle, Secy., P.O. Box 226, 52653, P 2,050, (319) 523-4221, Fax (319) 523-5603

**Washington** · *Washington Eco. Dev. Group* · Ed Raber, Exec. Dir., 205 W. Main St., 52353, P 25,000, (319) 653-3942, Fax (319) 653-5805, wedg@iowatelecom.net, washingtoniowa.org

**Waterloo** · *Black Hawk Eco. Dev., Inc.* · 304 South St., P.O. Box 330, 50704, P 128,012, (319) 235-2960, Fax (319) 235-9171, bhedc@aol.com, www.bhed.org

**Waterloo** · *Greater Cedar Valley Alliance* · Linda Laylin, Dir. Bus. Svcs., 10 W. Fourth St., Ste. 310, 50701, P 164,593, (319) 232-1156, (800) 369-0513, Fax (319) 232-1829, info@cedar valleyalliance.com, www.cedarvalleyalliance.com

**Waukon** · *Allamakee County Eco. Dev.* · Rachelle Howe, Exec. Dir., 101 W. Main St., 52172, P 14,068, (563) 568-2624, (800) 824-1424, Fax (563) 568-6990, aced@mchsi.com, www. allamakeecounty.com

**Waverly** · *Waverly Eco. Dev. Dept.* · Jason Passmore, Econ. Dev. Dir., 200 1st St. N.E., P.O. Box 616, 50677, P 9,000, (319) 352-9210, Fax (319) 352-5772, jason@ci.waverly.ia.us, www.waverlyia.com

**Webster City** · *Webster City Area Assn. of Bus. & Ind.* · Gary Sandholm, EDC Dir., 628 2nd St., P.O. Box 310, 50595, P 8,176, M 215, (515) 832-2564, Fax (515) 832-5130, info@webstercity-iowa.com, www.webstercity-iowa.com

**West Des Moines** · *West Des Moines Dev. Svcs.* · City of West Des Moines, P.O. Box 65320, 50265, P 54,459, (515) 222-3620, Fax (515) 273-0602, www.wdm-ia.com

**West Union** · *Fayette County Eco. Dev. Comm.* · Robin Bostrom, Exec. Dir., 101 N. Vine St., 52175, P 2,500, (563) 422-5073, Fax (563) 422-6322, fced@alpinecom.net, www.fayettecountyia.com

**Wilton** · *Wilton Dev. Corp.* · Jackie Barten, P.O. Box 443, 52778, P 2,900, M 40, (563) 732-5002, www.wiltoniowa.org

# Kansas

## Federal

**U.S. SBA, Kansas Dist. Ofc.** · Wayne Bell, District Dir., 271 W. 3rd St. N., Ste. 2500, Wichita, 67202, (316) 269-6616, Fax (316) 269-6499, www.sba.gov/ks

## State

**Kansas Dept. of Commerce** · Steve Kelly, Bus. Dev., 1000 S.W. Jackson St., Ste. 100, Topeka, 66612, (785) 296-3481, Fax (785) 296-5055, skelly@kansascommerce.com, www.kansascommerce.com

## Communities

**Abilene** · *Abilene Eco. Dev. Cncl.* · James Holland, Comm. Dev. Dir., 419 N. Broadway, P.O. Box 519, 67410, P 6,835, (785) 263-2550, Fax (785) 263-2552, citydevelop@abilenecityhall.com, www.abilenecityhall.com

**Atchison** · *Atchison Eco. Dev. Cncl.* · 515 Kansas Ave., 66002, P 17,000, (913) 367-5500, Fax (913) 367-3654, www.atchison kansas.net

**Burlington** · *Coffey County Eco. Dev.* · Jon Hotaling, Dir., 110 S. 6th St., 66839, P 10,000, (620) 364-8780, Fax (620) 364-2045, jhotaling@coffeycountyks.org, www.coffeycountyks.org.

**Clay Center** · *Clay County Eco. Dev. Group* · Jami Williams, Exec. Dir., 517 Court, 67432, P 9,200, (785) 632-5974, jami@claycounty kansas.org, www.claycountykansas.org

**Colby** · *Thomas County Eco. Dev. Alliance* · Rick Patrick, Exec. Dir., 350 S. Range, Ste. 12, 67701, P 8,258, (785) 460-4511, Fax (785) 460-4509, ecodev@thomascounty.com, www.thomas county.com

**Columbus** · *Columbus Eco. Dev. Corp.* · Jim Dahmen, Chrmn., 224 S. Kansas, 66725, P 3,500, (620) 429-3132, (620) 429-1492, Fax (620) 429-1704, coltelco@columbus-ks.com, www.columbus-ks.com

**Concordia** · *CloudCorp* · Kirk G. Lowell, Exec. Dir., 606 Washington St., P.O. Box 456, 66901, P 5,714, (785) 243-2010, Fax (785) 243-2014, kirk.lowell@cloudcorp.net

**Council Grove** · *Greater Morris County Dev. Corp.* · C. Kay Hutchinson, Exec. Secy., P.O. Box 276, 66846, P 6,200, M 80, (620) 767-7355, Fax (620) 767-2270, kayhutch@tctelco.net, www. councilgrovedevelopment.com.

**Derby** · *City of Derby* · Kathleen Sexton, City Mgr., 611 Mulberry Rd., Ste. 300, 67037, P 22,000, (316) 788-3081, Fax (316) 788-6067, kathysexton@derbyweb.com, www.derbyweb.com

**Dodge City** · *Dodge City/Ford County Dev. Corp.* · Joann Knight, Exec. Dir., 311 W. Spruce St., P.O. Box 818, 67801, P 33,000, M 60, (620) 227-9501, Fax (620) 338-8734, jknight@dodgedev. org, www.dodgedev.org

**El Dorado** · *Butler County Eco. Dev.* · David Alfaro, Dir., 121 S. Gordy, 67042, P 62,000, (316) 322-4242, (800) 794-6907, Fax (316) 322-4245, bced@bucoks.com, www.bucoks.com

**Emporia** · *Reg. Dev. Assn. of East Central Kansas* · Kent Heermann CEcD, Pres., 719 Commercial, P.O. Box 703, 66801, P 26,760, (620) 342-1600, Fax (620) 342-3223, kheermann@ emporiakschamber.org, www.emporia.com/econdev

**Garden City** · *Finney County Eco. Dev. Corp.* · Eric Depperschmidt, Pres., 1509 E. Fulton Terrace, 67846, P 40,000, (620) 271-0388, Fax (620) 271-0588, fcedc@ficoedc.com, www.ficoedc.com

**Goodland** · *Sherman County Eco. Dev. Cncl.* · Helen Dobbs, 104 E. 10th St., P.O. Box 614, 67735, P 6,300, (785) 890-3743, Fax (785) 890-3744, shermancoecdev@goodlandnet.com, www. gogoodlandks.com

**Hays** · *Ellis County Coalition for Eco. Dev.* · Mike Michaelis, Exec. Dir., 2700 Vine St., 67601, P 27,000, (785) 628-3102, Fax (785) 628-1471, mike@haysamerica.net, www.haysamerica.net

**Hiawatha** · *Hiawatha Found. for Eco. Dev.* · Steve Smith, Pres., 720 Oregon St., 66434, P 3,500, M 14, (785) 742-2254, Fax (785) 742-7747, sheila@heartland-realty.com, www.cityofhiawatha.org

**Hill City** · *NW Kansas Planning & Dev. Comm.* · Randall Hrabe, Exec. Dir., 319 N. Pomeroy, P.O. Box 248, 67642, P 106,625, (785) 421-2151, Fax (785) 421-3496, nwkpdc@ruraltel.net

**Hillsboro** · *Hillsboro Dev. Corp.* · Clint Seibel, Exec. Dir., 116 E. Grand, 67063, P 3,000, (620) 947-3458, Fax (620) 947-2585, cseibel@cityofhillsboro.net

**Horton** · *Horton Ind. Dev. Corp.* · 205 E. 8th St., 66439, P 1,900, (785) 486-2681, cityofhorton@hortonkansas.net

**Hugoton** · *Stevens County Eco. Dev. Bd.* · Neal R. Gillespie, Dir., 630 S. Main, 67951, P 5,463, (620) 544-4440, Fax (620) 544-4610, ecodevo@pld.com, www.hugotonchamber.com

**Hutchinson** · *Reno County Eco. Dev. Cncl.* · Dave Kerr, Pres., 117 N. Walnut, P.O. Box 519, 67504, P 65,000, (620) 662-3391, Fax (620) 662-2168, davek@hutchchamber.com, www.hutchecodevo.com

**Independence** · *Montgomery County Action Cncl.* · Brad Eilts, Dir., P.O. Box 588, 67301, P 40,000, (620) 331-3830, Fax (620) 331-3834, eilts@actioncouncil.com, www.actioncouncil.com

**Jewell** · *Jewell County Comm. Dev.* · Martha Matthews, Coord., 606 Broadway St., 66949, P 4,000, (785) 428-3634

**Junction City** · *Junction City/Geary County EDC* · Jeffrey Black, Dir., 701 N. Jefferson, Ste. B104, P.O. Box 1876, 66441, (785) 762-1976, Fax (785) 210-1976, www.jcgced.com

**Kansas City** · *Dept. of Dev.* · LaVert Murray, Dir., 701 N. 7th St., Ste. 421, 66101, P 145,000, (913) 573-5730, Fax (913) 573-5745, www.wycokck.org

**Kingman** · *Kingman County Eco. Dev.* · Jane Wallace, Exec. Dir., 324 N. Main, 67068, P 8,679, (620) 532-3694, www.kingmanks.com

**EDC**

**Kinsley** · *Edwards County Eco. Dev. Corp.* · Lynette Miller, Exec. Dir., 200 E. 6th, P.O. Box 161, 67547, P 3,500, (877) 464-3929, Fax (620) 659-3304, ecedc@sbcglobal.net, www.edwardscounty.org

**Larned** · *Pawnee County Eco. Dev. Comm.* · 502 Broadway, 67550, P 7,600, (620) 285-6916, (800) 747-6919, Fax (620) 285-6917, larnedcofc@gbta.net, www.larnedks.org

**Leavenworth** · *Leavenworth County Dev. Corp.* · Steve Jack, Exec. Dir., 1294 Eisenhower Rd., 66048, P 72,500, M 85, (913) 727-6111, Fax (913) 727-5515, mail@lvcountyed.org, www.lvcountyed.org

**Lenexa** · *Lenexa Eco. Dev. Cncl.* · Blake Schreck, Pres., 11180 Lackman Rd., 66219, P 48,000, M 80, (913) 888-1414, Fax (913) 888-3770, staff@lenexa.org, www.lenexa.org

**Liberal** · *Liberal/Seward County Joint Eco. Dev. Cncl.* · P.O. Box 2199, 67905, P 23,000, (620) 626-2255, Fax (620) 626-0589, ecodevo@cityofliberal.com, www.cityofliberal.com

**Lincoln** · *Lincoln Co. Eco. Dev. Found.* · 216 E. Lincoln Ave., 67455, P 3,400, (785) 524-8954, Fax (785) 524-5206

**McPherson** · *McPherson Ind. Dev. Co.* · Marvin Peters, Exec. Dir., P.O. Box 1008, 67460, P 14,000, (620) 245-2521, Fax (620) 245-2529, marvinp@mcpbpu.com, www.mcphersonks.org

**Minneapolis** · *Minneapolis Dev. Corp.* · Barry Hodges, City Admin., 218 N. Rock St., 67467, P 2,042, M 75, (785) 392-2176, cityminne@nckcn.com, www.minneapolisks.org

**Mound City** · *Linn County Eco. Dev.* · Dennis Arnold, Dir., 306 Main St., P.O. Box 25, 66056, P 9,800, (913) 795-2274, Fax (913) 795-2016, darnold@linncountyks.com, www.linncountyks.com

**Newton** · *Harvey County Eco. Dev. Cncl.* · Mickey Fornaro-Dean, Exec. Dir., 500 N. Main St., Ste. 109, P.O. Box 82, 67114, P 34,000, (316) 283-6033, Fax (316) 283-8732, info@harveycoedc.org, www.harveycoedc.org

**Norton** · *Norton City/County Eco. Dev.* · Diane Becker, Ex. Dir., 113 N. Norton Ave., Ste. B, 67654, P 5,900, (785) 874-4816, Fax (785) 874-4817, nortoneda@ruraltel.net, www.norton.com

**Olathe** · *Olathe Chamber EDC* · Tim McKee, Exec. V.P., 18001 W. 106th St., Ste. 160, P.O. Box 98, 66051, P 120,000, M 100, (913) 764-1050, (800) 921-5678, Fax (913) 782-4636, edc@olathe.org, www.olathe.org

**Osborne** · *Osborne Dept. of Eco. Dev.* · 130 N. First St., 67473, P 1,500, (785) 346-2670, (866) 346-2670, Fax (785) 346-2522, osborneed@ruraltel.net, www.discoverosborne.com

**Ottawa** · *Ottawa/Franklin County Eco. Dev.* · Thomas R. Weigand, Secy./Treas., 109 E. 2nd, P.O. Box 580, 66067, P 27,000, M 72, (785) 242-1000, Fax (785) 242-4792, chambertw@ottawa kansas.org, www.ottawakansas.org

**Overland Park** · *Overland Park Eco. Dev. Cncl.* · Tracey Osborne CCE, Pres., 9001 W. 110th St., Ste. 150, 66210, P 162,000, M 70, (913) 491-3600, Fax (913) 491-0393, info@opedc.org, www.opedc.org

**Pittsburg** · *City of Pittsburg Eco. Dev. Corp.* · Mark Turnbull, Dir., 201 W. 4th St., P.O. Box 688, 66762, P 19,000, (620) 231-4100, Fax (620) 231-0964, mark.turnbull@pittks.org, www.pittks.org

**Russell** · *Russell County EDC* · Cindy Wallace, Exec. Dir., 445 E. Wichita Ave., 67665, P 4,600, (785) 483-4000, Fax (785) 483-2827, rced@russellks.org, www.russellcoks.org

**Sabetha** · *Sabetha Ind. Dev. Corp.* · Doug Allen, City Admin., 805 Main St., P.O. Box 187, 66534, P 2,583, (785) 284-2158, Fax (785) 284-2112, www.skyways.org/towns/sabetha

**Shawnee** · *Shawnee Eco. Dev. Cncl.* · Jim Martin, Exec. Dir., 15100 W. 67th St., Ste. 202, 66217, P 60,000, M 60, (913) 631-6545, Fax (913) 631-9628, jmartin@shawnee-edc.com, www.shawnee-edc.com

**Stockton** · *Rooks County Eco. Dev. Comm.* · Roger Hrabe, Dir., 115 N. Walnut, 67669, P 5,300, (785) 425-6881, (800) 496-9930, Fax same, rooksed@ruraltel.net, www.rookscounty.net

**Topeka** · *City of Topeka Housing & Neighborhood Dev.* · Randy Speaker, Dir., 620 S.E. Madison, 1st Flr., 66607, P 123,000, (785) 368-3711, Fax (785) 368-2546, www.topeka.org

**Tribune** · *Greeley County Comm. Dev.* · Christy Hopkins, Dir., P.O. Box 656, 67879, P 1,350, (620) 376-2548, greeleyc@fairpoint. net, www.greeleycounty.org

**WaKeeney** · *Trego County Eco. Dev.* · Charlene Neish, Dir., 216 N. Main, P.O. Box 355, 67672, P 3,100, (785) 743-5785, Fax (785) 743-5530, tregocoed@ruraltel.net, www.tregocountyks.com

**Wamego** · *Pottawatomie County Eco. Dev. Corp.* · Robert L. Cole, Dir., 1004 Lincoln, P.O. Box 288, 66547, P 18,700, (785) 456-9776, Fax (785) 456-9775, bobcole@ecodevo.com, www. ecodevo.com

**Wellington** · *Sumner County Eco. Dev.* · Janis Hellard, Dir., P.O. Box 279, 67152, P 26,000, (620) 326-8779, Fax (620) 326-6544, scedc@co.sumner.ks.us, www.gosumner.com

**Wichita** · *South Central KS Eco. Dev. Dist. Inc.* · Bill Bolin, Exec. Dir., 209 E. William, Ste. 300, 67202, P 685,000, (316) 262-7035, Fax (316) 262-7062, www.sckedd.org

**Winfield** · *Cowley County Eco. Dev. Partnership* · Heidi Hill, Dir., P.O. Box 832, 67156, P 37,000, (620) 221-9951, Fax (620) 221-7782, www.cowleyfirst.com

# Kentucky

## Federal

**SBA SCORE Louisville** · Federal Bldg, Rm. 188, 600 M.L. King Jr. Pl., Louisville, 40202, (502) 582-5976, Fax (502) 582-5819, www.score-louisville.org

## State

**Kentucky Cabinet for Eco. Dev.** · Larry Hayes, Interim Secy., Old Capital Annex, 300 W. Broadway, Frankfort, 40601, (502) 564-7140, Fax (502) 564-3256, econdev@ky.gov, www.think kentucky.com

## Communities

**Ashland** · *City of Ashland Eco. Dev. Dept.* · Chris Pullem, Dir., P.O. Box 1839, 41105, P 22,000, (606) 327-2005, Fax (606) 326-0787, www.ashlandky.org

**Calhoun** · *McLean County Ind. Found.* · Charles Mann Jr., Pres., 297 Main St., P.O. Box 303, 42327, P 10,000, M 25, (270) 273-9760, Fax (270) 273-9760, chamfond@owensboro.net

**Carrollton** · *Carroll County Comm. Dev. Corp.* · Joan Moore, Exec. Dir., 511 Highland Ave., P.O. Box 334, 41008, P 10,000, (502) 732-7035, Fax (502) 732-7028, development@carrollcountyky. com, www.carrollcountyky.com

**Corbin** · *Corbin Eco. Dev. Agency* · Bruce Carpenter, Exec. Dir., 101 N. Depot St., 40701, P 25,000, (606) 528-6390, Fax (606) 523-6538, becarpenter@corbinky.org, www.corbinky.org

**Covington** · *Northern KY Tri-ED* · Dan Tobergte, Pres., 300 Buttermilk Pike, Ste. 332, P.O. Box 17246, 41017, P 300,000, (859) 344-0040, (888) 874-3365, Fax (859) 344-8130, www.northern kentuckyusa.com

**Danville** · *Boyle County Ind. Found.* · Jody Lassiter, Pres./CEO, 304 S. 4th St., 40422, P 28,000, (859) 236-0636, Fax (859) 236-3197, info@betterindanville.com, www.betterindanville.com

**Edmonton** · *Edmonton-Metcalfe County Ind. Dev. Auth.* · Barry Gilley, Chrmn., P.O. Box 380, 42129, P 10,000, (270) 432-7190, Fax (270) 432-7199

**Florence** · *Northern KY Area Dev. Dist.* · John Mays, Exec. Dir., 22 Spiral Dr., 41042, P 370,000, (859) 283-1885, Fax (859) 283-8178, www.nkadd.org

**Franklin** · *Franklin/Simpson Ind. Auth.* · Dennis Griffin, Dir., 201 S. Main St., P.O. Box 876, 42135, P 18,000, (270) 586-4477, Fax (270) 586-3685, fsindustry@aol.com, www.f-sindustry.com

**Fulton** · *Fulton County Eco. Dev. Partnership* · P.O. Box 1413, 42041, P 7,500, (270) 472-2125, Fax (270) 472-1944, www.westkyeconomic.com

**Greensburg** · *Green County Ind. Found.* · Judy Weatherholt, Pres., 110 W. Court St., 42743, P 11,400, (270) 932-4298, Fax (270) 932-7778, judyweatherholt@greensburgonline.com, www.greensburgonline.com

**Greenville** · *Muhlenberg Eco. Enterprises* · Barbara Williams, Dir. Asst., P.O. Box 636, 42345, P 32,000, (270) 338-4102, Fax (270) 338-4106, BarbaraU.Williams@ky.gov

**Harrodsburg** · *Harrodsburg-Mercer County Ind. Dev. Auth.* · Drew Dennis, Exec. Dir., 488 Price Ave., 40330, P 22,000, (859) 734-0063, www.mercerkybusiness.com

**Hartford** · *Ohio County Ind. Found.* · Hayward Spinks, Pres., P.O. Box 3, 42347, P 23,000, (270) 298-3551, Fax (270) 298-3331, industry@ohiocounty.com, www.ohiocountyindustrialfoundation.com

**Hazard** · *Kentucky River Area Dev. Dist.* · Paul Hall, Exec. Dir., 917 Perry Park Rd., 41701, P 122,000, (606) 436-3158, Fax (606) 436-2144, www.kradd.org

**Henderson** · *Henderson-Henderson County Ind. Found.* · CB West, Pres., 201 N. Main, 42420, P 46,000, (270) 826-9531, Fax (270) 827-4461, www.hendersonky.com

**Henderson** · *Northwest Kentucky Forward* · Kevin Sheilley, Pres./CEO, P.O. Box 674, 42419, P 46,000, (270) 826-7505, Fax (270) 827-2969, kevin@northwestky.com, www.northwestky.com

**Hopkinsville** · *Hopkinsville-Christian County Eco. Dev. Cncl.* · Lee Conrad, Interim Dir., 2800 Fort Campbell Blvd., 42240, P 72,300, (270) 885-1499, Fax (270) 886-2059, info@hopkinsvilleindustry.com, www.hopkinsvilleindustry.com

**Hopkinsville** · *Pennyrile Area Dev. Dist.* · Dan Bozarth, Exec. Dir., 300 Hammond Dr., 42240, P 206,000, (270) 886-9484, (800) 928-7233, Fax (270) 886-3211, www.peadd.org

**Irvine** · *Estill County Dev. Alliance* · Joe Crawford, Exec. Dir., P.O. Box 421, 40336, P 16,000, M 40, (606) 723-2450, info@estillcountyky.net, www.estillcountyky.net

**Kevil** · *Ballard County Eco. & Ind. Dev.* · Terry Simmons, Pres./CEO, 101 Liberty Dr., Ste. 4, 42053, P 9,000, (270) 744-3232, Fax (270) 744-3308, bceidb@brtc.net

**Lebanon** · *Marion County Eco. Dev.* · Tom Lund, Exec. Dir., 223 N. Spaulding Ave., Ste. 300, 40033, P 19,212, (270) 692-6002, (877) 692-6002, Fax (270) 692-0510, tlund@marioncountyky.com, www.marioncountyky.com

**Lexington** · *Bluegrass Area Dev. Dist.* · Lenny Stoltz II, Exec. Dir., 699 Perimeter Dr., 40517, P 600,000, (859) 269-8021, Fax (859) 269-7917, lharris@bgadd.org, www.bgadd.org

**Lexington** · *Lexington-Fayette Urban County Govt.* · Anthony Wright, Dir., Mayor's Ofc. of Eco. Dev., 200 E. Main St., 40507, P 268,080, (859) 258-3131, Fax (859) 258-3194, www.lexingtonky.gov

**London** · *Cumberland Valley Area Dev. Dist.* · Mike Patrick, Exec. Dir., P.O. Box 1740, 40743, P 240,000, (606) 864-7391, Fax (606) 878-7361, mpatrick@cvadd.org, www.cvadd.org

**London** · *Laurel County Ind. Dev. Auth.* · Charles Pennington, Exec. Dir., 4598 Old Whitley Rd., 40744, P 56,000, (606) 864-8115, Fax (606) 878-7107, llcida2@windstream.net

**Louisville** · *Eco. Dev. Dept. of Louisville Metro Gov.* · C. Bruce Taughber, Dir., 444 S. 5th St., Ste. 600, 40202, P 1,000,000, (502) 574-4140, Fax (502) 574-4143, bruce.taughber@louisvilleky.gov, www.louisvilleky.gov

**Louisville** · *Louisville & Jefferson County Riverport Auth.* · Larry McFall, Pres., 6900 Riverport Dr., P.O. Box 58010, 40268, P 300,000, (502) 935-6024, Fax (502) 935-6050, www.jeffersonriverport.com

**Madisonville** · *Madisonville/Hopkins County Eco. Dev. Corp.* · 755 Industrial Rd., 42431, P 60,000, (270) 821-1939, (800) 821-1939, Fax (270) 821-1945, www.kymtec.org

**Mayfield** · *Graves Growth Alliance* · 201 E. College, 42066, P 35,300, (270) 247-0626, Fax (270) 247-6781, mgldc@bellsouth.net, www.mayfield-graves.com

**Maysville** · *Buffalo Trace Area Dev. Dist.* · Amy Kennedy, Exec. Dir., 201 Govt. St., Ste. 300, P.O. Box 460, 41056, P 55,229, (606) 564-6894, Fax (606) 564-0955, akennedy@btadd.com, www.btadd.com

**Middlesboro** · *Bell County Ind. Found.* · Nioma Lawson, Dir., N. 20th St., P.O. Box 788, 40965, P 30,060, (606) 248-1075, Fax (606) 248-8851, chamber@bellcountychamber.com, www.bellcountychamber.com

**Morganfield** · *Union County First* · Kim Humphrey, Exec. Dir., P.O. Box 374, 42437, P 16,000, M 123, (270) 389-9600, Fax (270) 389-0944, www.ucfirst.org

**Mount Sterling** · *Mt. Sterling-Montgomery County Ind. Auth.* · Sandy Romenesko, Exec. Dir., 126 W. Main St., 40353, P 24,500, (859) 498-5400, Fax (859) 498-3947, sandy@mtsterlingchamber.com, www.mtsterlingchamber.com.

**Owensboro** · *Greater Owensboro Eco. Dev. Corp.* · 200 E. 3rd St., Ste. 200, P.O. Box 782, 42302, P 92,000, (270) 926-4339, Fax (270) 926-2178, www.owensboro.com

**Owensboro** · *Green River Area Dev. Dist.* · Mr. Jiten Shah, Exec. Dir., 3860 U.S. Hwy. 60 W., 42301, P 200,000, (270) 926-4433, Fax (270) 684-0714, www.gradd.com

**Paducah** · *Greater Paducah Eco. Dev. Cncl.* · Wayne Sterling, Pres./CEO, 401 Ky Ave., P.O. Box 1155, 42002, P 65,514, M 125, (270) 575-6633, Fax (270) 575-6648, wsterling@gpedc.com, www.gpedc.com

**Prestonsburg** · *Big Sandy Area Dev. Dist.* · Sandy Runyon, Exec. Dir., 110 Resource Ct., 41653, P 160,532, (606) 886-2374, Fax (606) 886-3382, sandy.runyon@bigsandy.org, www.bigsandy.org

**Richmond** · *Richmond Ind. Dev. Corp.* · James H. Howard, Exec. Dir., P.O. Box 250, 40476, P 30,000, (859) 623-1000, Fax (859) 625-1050, ridc@richmond.ky.us, www.richmond-industrial.org

**Shelbyville** · *Shelby County Ind. & Dev. Found.* · Bobby Hudson, Pres., 316 Main St., P.O. Box 335, 40066, P 35,000, (502) 633-5068, Fax (502) 633-7501, www.shelbycountyindustrialfoundation.com

**Somerset** · *Center for Rural Dev.* · Lonnie Lawson, Exec. Dir., 2292 S. Hwy. 27, Ste. 300, 42501, P 500,000, (606) 677-6000, Fax (606) 677-6010, www.centertech.com

**Versailles** · *Woodford County Eco. Dev. Auth.* · Michael Duckworth, Pres., 141 N. Main St., P.O. Box 1509, 40383, P 23,208, (859) 879-5829, (859) 873-5122, Fax (859) 873-4576, woodford@woodfordchamber-ky.com, www.woodfordchamber-ky.com

**EDC**

**Williamsburg** · *Williamsburg Eco. Dev.* · Alvin Sharpe, Coord., P.O. Box 2, 40769, P 5,033, (606) 549-0530, Fax (606) 539-0095, www.williamsburgky.com

**Winchester** · *Winchester-Clark County Ind. Dev. Auth.* · C. Todd Denham, Dir. of Eco. Dev., 2 S. Maple St., 40391, P 35,000, (859) 744-5627, Fax (859) 744-9229, todd@winchesterindustry.com, www.winchesterindustry.com

# Louisiana

## Federal

**U.S. SBA, Louisiana Dist. Ofc.** · Michael Ricks, Dist. Dir., 365 Canal St., Ste. 2820, New Orleans, 70130, (504) 589-2744, Fax (504) 589-2339, www.sba.gov/la

## State

**Louisiana Dept. of Eco. Dev.** · Stephen Moret, Secy., 1051 N. 3rd St., Baton Rouge, 70802, (225) 342-5388, Fax (225) 342-9095, www.ledlouisiana.com

## Communities

**Alexandria** · *Kisatchie-Delta Reg. Plan & Dev. Dist.* · 3516 Parliament Ct., 71303, P 312,026, (318) 487-5454, Fax (318) 487-5451, kdelta@kricket.net, www.kdelta.org

**Bastrop** · *Morehouse Eco. Dev. Corp.* · Kay King, Pres./CEO, Capital One Bank Bldg., 101 Franklin St., Ste. A, 71220, P 30,000, (318) 283-4000, Fax (318) 283-0651, medc@morehouseedc.org, www.morehouseedc.org

**Baton Rouge** · *Capital Region Planning Comm.* · Don Neisler, Exec. Dir., 333 N. 19th St., P.O. Box 3355, 70821, (225) 383-5203, Fax (225) 383-3804, www.crpc-la.org

**Baton Rouge** · *Cncl. For a Better Louisiana* · William Hines, Chrmn., P.O. Box 4308, 70821, (225) 344-2225, Fax (225) 338-9470, info@cabl.org, www.cabl.org

**Bogalusa** · *Washington Eco. Dev. Found. Inc.* · Kenneth Smith, Pres., P.O. Box 668, 70427, P 45,000, (985) 735-7565, Fax (985) 730-2500, widf@bellsouth.net, www.wedf.com

**Denham Springs** · *Livingston Eco. Dev. Cncl. Inc.* · 1810 S. Range Ave., 70726, P 130,000, (225) 665-5223, Fax (225) 665-8171, ledc@demco.org, www.ledc.net

**Hammond** · *Tangipahoa Eco. Dev. Found.* · Bob Basford, Exec. Dir., 1514 Martens Dr., 70401, P 105,000, (985) 549-3170, Fax (985) 549-2127, www.tedf.org

**Jonesboro** · *Jackson Eco. Dev. Corp.* · Frank Johnson, P.O. Box 610, 71251, P 3,900, (318) 259-2385, Fax (318) 259-4177

**Lafayette** · *Lafayette Eco. Dev. Auth.* · Gregg Gothreaux, Pres./CEO, 211 E. Devalcourt St., 70506, P 190,000, (337) 593-1400, Fax (337) 234-3009, information@lafayette.org, www.lafayette.org

**Lake Charles** · *Southwest Louisiana Eco. Dev. Alliance* · George Swift, Pres./CEO, 120 W. Pujo St., P.O. Box 3110, 70602, P 287,001, M 1,000, (337) 433-3632, Fax (337) 436-3727, mail@allianceswla.org, www.allianceswla.org

**Mandeville** · *St. Tammany Eco. Dev. Found.* · Brenda Reine-Bertus, Exec. Dir., 21489 Koop Dr., Ste. 7, 70471, P 230,000, (985) 809-7874, (888) 868-3830, Fax (985) 809-7596, stedfinfo@stedf.org, www.stedf.org

**Minden** · *South Webster Ind. Dist.* · 110 Sibley Rd., 71058, P 28,000, (318) 377-4240, Fax (318) 377-4215, www.minden chamber.com

**Monroe** · *North Delta Reg. Planning & Dev. Dist.* · David Creed, Exec. Dir., 1913 Stubbs Ave., 71201, (318) 387-2572, Fax (318) 387-9054, david@northdelta.org

**Monroe** · *North Louisiana Eco. Dev. Corp.* · Mr. Pat Regan, Pres., 1900 N. 18th St., Ste. 440, 71201, P 149,500, (318) 387-0787, Fax (318) 387-8529, pregan@nledc.org, www.nledc.org

**New Iberia** · *Iberia Ind. Dev. Found.* · Mike Tarantino, Exec. Dir., 101 Burke St., 70560, P 73,000, (337) 367-0834, (888) 879-9669, Fax (337) 367-7421, info@iberiabiz.org, www.iberiabiz.org

**New Orleans** · *Greater New Orleans Inc.* · Michael Hecht, Pres./CEO, 365 Canal St., Ste. 2300, 70130, P 1,151,000, M 150, (504) 527-6900, Fax (504) 527-6970, www.gnoinc.org

**New Orleans** · *Reg. Planning Comm.* · Walter Brooks, Exec. Dir., 1340 Poydras St., Ste. 2100, 70112, (504) 568-6611, Fax (504) 568-6643, rpc@norpc.org, www.norpc.org

**Oakdale** · *Ind. Dev. Bd. of Elizabeth-Oakdale Inc.* · Andrew Hayes, Mayor, P.O. Box 728, 71463, P 8,137, (318) 335-1111

**Opelousas** · *Greater Opelousas Eco. & Ind. Dev. Cncl.* · Gerard Perron, Exec. Dir., 132 E. Landry St., P.O. Box 340, 70571, P 87,000, (337) 948-1391, Fax (337) 407-2283, sleidd@bellsouth.net, www.sleidd.com

**Ruston** · *Ruston-Lincoln Ind. Dev. Corp.* · Scott C. Terry, Exec. Dir., 2111 N. Trenton St., P.O. Box 1383, 71272, P 43,000, (318) 232-7984, (800) 392-9032, Fax (318) 255-3481, sterry@ruston lincoln.org, www.rustonlincoln.org

**Saint Francisville** · *West Feliciana Comm. Dev. Found.* · Steve Jones, CEO, 5934 Commerce St., P.O. Box 3044, 70775, P 15,111, M 200, (225) 635-6767, Fax (225) 635-6885, wfcdf@stfrancisville.org, www.stfrancisville.org

**Shreveport** · *Northwest Louisiana Eco. Dev. Found.* · Kurt Foreman, Pres., 400 Edwards St., 71101, P 390,000, (318) 677-2536, (800) 448-5432, Fax (318) 677-2548, edinquiry@nledf.org, www.nledf.org

**Shreveport** · *The Coord. & Dev. Corp.* · Gray Stothart, V.P., 5210 Hollywood Ave., P.O. Box 37005, 71133, P 378,000, (318) 632-2022, Fax (318) 632-2099, stothart@shreve.net, www.cdconline.org

**Springhill** · *North Webster Parish Ind. Park* · Mitch Stubblefield, Mgr., P.O. Box 176, 71075, P 12,000, (318) 539-5058, Fax (318) 994-2753, websterboard@centurytel.net, www.nwpid.com

**Tallulah** · *Madison Eco. Dev. Found.* · Thomas Joe Williams, Coord., % LA Technical College, P.O. Drawer 1740, 71284, P 14,000, (318) 574-4820, (800) 215-3905, Fax (318) 574-1868, sccox@ltc.edu

**Vidalia** · *Vidalia Eco. Dev.* · Hyram Copeland, Mayor, P.O. Box 2010, 71373, P 6,500, (318) 336-5206, Fax (318) 336-6253, www.seevidalia.com

**Winnsboro** · *Franklin Eco. Dev. Found.* · Kayla France-Knight, Exec. Dir., 3830 Front St., P.O. Box 69, 71295, P 23,000, (318) 435-3781, Fax (318) 435-5398, kaylafrance@bellsouth.net

# Maine

## Federal

**U.S. SBA, Maine Dist. Ofc.** · Maurice Dube, Dist. Dir., 68 Sewall St., Augusta, 04330, (207) 622-8551, Fax (207) 622-8277, www.sba.gov/me

## State

**Maine Dept. of Eco. & Comm. Dev.** · John Richardson, Commissioner, 59 State House Station, Augusta, 04333, (207) 624-9800, Fax (207) 287-2861, biz.growth@maine.gov, www.econdevmaine.com

## Communities

**Auburn** • *Auburn Comm. Eco. Dev.* • Roland Miller, Dir., 60 Court St., 04210, P 23,203, (207) 333-6600, Fax (207) 333-6621, www.auburnmaine.org

**Augusta** • *Augusta Bd. Of Trade* • C. Wayne Mitchell, Exec. Dir., 330 Civic Center Dr., Ste. 2, P.O. Box 2346, 04338, P 75,000, (207) 622-9100, Fax (207) 622-9111

**Bangor** • *Eastern Maine Dev. Corp.* • 40 Harlow St., 04401, P 90,000, (207) 942-6389, (800) 339-6389, Fax (207) 942-3548, info@emdc.org, www.emdc.org

**Belfast** • *City of Belfast* • Joseph Slocum, City Mgr., 131 Church St., City Hall, 04915, P 6,500, (207) 338-3370, Fax (207) 338-2419, www.cityofbelfast.org

**Berwick** • *Town of Berwick* • Keith Trefethen, Town Mgr., 11 Sullivan Sq., P.O. Box 696, 03901, P 6,500, (207) 698-1101, Fax (207) 698-5181, www.berwickmaine.org

**Brewer** • *Ofc. Of Eco. Dev.* • Darcy Main-Boyington, Dir. of Eco. Dev., 80 N. Main St., 04412, P 9,100, (207) 989-7500, Fax (207) 989-8425, www.brewerme.org

**Farmington** • *Greater Franklin Dev. Corp.* • Alison Hagerstrom, Exec. Dir., 107 Church St., P.O. Box 107, 04938, P 30,000, (207) 778-5887, Fax (207) 778-3442, info@greaterfranklin.com, www.greaterfranklin.com

**Fort Kent** • *Ofc. Of Planning & Eco. Dev.* • John Bannen, Eco. Dev. Dir., 416 W. Main St., 04743, P 4,300, (207) 834-3507, Fax (207) 834-3126, www.fortkent.org

**Gardiner** • *Gardiner Eco. Dev. Dept.* • Jason Simcock, Dir., City of Gardiner, 6 Church St., 04345, P 6,746, (207) 582-6888, Fax (207) 582-6895, econdv@gardinermaine.com, www.gardiner-maine.com

**Gorham** • *Gorham Eco. Dev. Corp.* • Thomas Ellsworth, Pres., 286 New Portland Rd., 04038, P 15,000, (207) 854-5077, Fax (207) 856-1300, gedc@gwi.net, www.gorhammeusa.org

**Greenville** • *Ofc. Of Eco. Dev.-Town of Greenville* • John Simko, Town Mgr., 7 Minden St., P.O. Box 1109, 04441, P 1,800, (207) 695-2421, Fax (207) 695-4611, www.greenvilleme.com

**Houlton** • *Houlton Comm. Dev.* • Douglas Hazlett, Town Mgr., 21 Water St., 04730, P 6,400, (207) 532-7113, Fax (207) 532-1304, www.houlton-maine.com

**Jay** • *Town of Jay* • Ruth Marden, Town Mgr., 340 Main St., 04239, P 4,985, (207) 897-6785, Fax (207) 897-9420, www.jay-maine.org

**Lewiston** • *Lewiston-Auburn Eco. Growth Cncl.* • Lucien B. Gosselin, Pres., 415 Lisbon St., P.O. Box 1188, 04243, P 60,000, (207) 784-0161, Fax (207) 786-4412, laegc@economicgrowth.org, www.economicgrowth.org

**Limestone** • *Limestone Dev. Found. Inc.* • Lisa Anderson, Secy., 93 Main St., 04750, P 2,400, (207) 325-4025, Fax (207) 325-3330, chamber@limestonemaine.org, www.limestonemaine.org

**Limestone** • *Loring Dev. Auth.* • Carl Flora, Pres./CEO, 154 Development Dr., Ste. F, 04750, P 1,458, (207) 328-7005, Fax (207) 328-6811, lda@loring.org, www.loring.org

**Lubec** • *Lubec Eco. & Comm. Dev. Ofc.* • 40 School St., 04652, P 1,650, (207) 733-2342, Fax (207) 733-4737

**Old Town** • *Old Town Ind. Dev. Comm.* • Peggy Daigle, City Mgr., 150 Brunswick St., 04468, P 8,100, (207) 827-3965, Fax (207) 827-3966, www.old-town.org

**Portland** • *Planning & Dev. Dept., City of Portland* • Penny Littell, Dir., 389 Congress St., 4th Flr., 04101, P 64,300, (207) 874-8683, www.portlandmaine.gov

**Skowhegan** • *Town of Skowhegan-Eco./Comm. Dev.* • Jeff Hewett, Dir., 225 Water St., 04976, P 9,000, (207) 474-6905, (207) 474-6900, Fax (207) 474-9413, skowecon@skowhegan.org, www.skowhegan.org

**Waterville** • *City of Waterville Eco. Dev.* • Michael Roy, City Mgr., 1 Common St., 04901, P 15,000, (207) 680-4204, Fax (207) 680-4207, mroy@waterville-me.gov, www.waterville-me.gov

**Winslow** • *Town of Winslow EDA* • Michael Heavener, Town Mgr., 114 Benton Ave., 04901, P 8,000, (207) 872-2776, Fax (207) 872-1999, www.winslowmaine.org

# Maryland

## Federal

**U.S. SBA, Maryland Dist. Ofc.** • Stephen Umberger, Dist. Dir., 10 S. Howard St., Baltimore, 21201, (410) 962-6195, Fax (410) 962-1805, www.sba.gov/md

## State

**Maryland Ofc. Of Intl. Trade & Investment** • Linda Goray, 401 E. Pratt St., Baltimore, 21202, (410) 767-0685, Fax (410) 333-4302, lgoray@choosemaryland.org, www.choosemaryland.org

## Communities

**Annapolis** • *Anne Arundel Eco. Dev. Corp.* • Robert Hannon, Pres./CEO, 2660 Riva Rd., Ste. 200, 21401, P 517,000, (410) 222-7410, Fax (410) 222-7415, www.aaedc.org

**Baltimore** • *City of Baltimore Dev. Corp.* • M.J. Brodie, Pres., 36 S. Charles St., Ste. 1600, 21201, P 750,000, (410) 837-9305, Fax (410) 837-6363, www.baltimoredevelopment.com

**Baltimore** • *Dept. of Bus. & Eco. Dev.* • Christian Johansson, Secy., 217 E. Redwood St., 23rd Flr., 21202, (410) 767-6300, Fax (410) 333-8628, cjohansson@choosemaryland.org, www.choosemaryland.org

**Bel Air** • *Harford County Ofc. of Eco. Dev.* • James Richardson, Dir., 220 S. Main St., 21014, P 257,000, (410) 638-3059, (888) 495-SITE, Fax (410) 879-8043, www.harfordbusiness.work

**Cambridge** • *Dorchester County Eco. Dev. Ofc.* • 5263 Bucktown Rd., 21613, P 31,600, (410) 228-0155, Fax (410) 228-9518

**Chestertown** • *Kent County Eco. Dev.* • Jack Steinmetz, Dir., 400 High St., 21620, P 19,197, (410) 778-7434, Fax (410) 778-0810, jsteinmetz@kentgov.org, www.kentcounty.com

**Cumberland** • *Allegany County Dept. of Eco. Dev.* • Matthew Diaz, Dir., 701 Kelly Rd., Ste. 400, 21502, P 73,500, (301) 777-5967, (800) 555-4080, Fax (301) 777-2194, www.alleganyworks.org

**Federalsburg** • *Federalsburg Eco. Dev. Comm.* • Frank M. Adams, Pres., 319 Bloomingdale Ave., 21632, P 2,800, (410) 754-9945, Fax (410) 754-5341, fmadams@comcast.net

**Frederick** • *Frederick County Ofc. of Eco. Dev.* • Laurie Boyer, Exec. Dir., 5340 Spectrum Dr., Ste. A, 21703, P 227,000, (301) 600-1058, (800) 248-2296, Fax (301) 600-2340, jwbrown@fredco-md.net, www.discoverfrederickmd.com

**Hagerstown** • *Hagerstown-Washington County Eco. Dev. Comm.* • Timothy Troxell CEcD, Exec. Dir., 100 W. Washington St., Rm. 103, 21740, P 144,000, (240) 313-2280, Fax (240) 313-2281, ttroxell@hagerstownedc.org, www.hagerstownedc.org

**Indian Head** • *Indian Head Eco. Dev. Comm.* • Randy L. Albright, 4195 Indian Head Hwy., 20640, P 3,422, (301) 743-5511, Fax (301) 743-9008, www.townofindianhead.org

**Largo** • *Prince George's County Eco. Dev. Corp.* • Holman Kwasi, Pres./CEO, 1100 Mercantile Ln., 20774, P 850,000, (301) 583-4650, Fax (301) 772-8540, www.pgcedc.com

**Oakland** • *Garrett County Eco. Dev. Dept.* • Jim Hinebaugh, Exec. Dir., 203 S. Fourth St., Ste. 208, 21550, P 30,000, (301) 334-1921, Fax (301) 334-1985, www.gcedonline.com

**Prince Frederick** • *Calvert County Dept. of Eco. Dev.* • Linda Vassallo, Dir., 175 Main St., 20678, P 85,000, (410) 535-4583, (800) 331-9771, Fax (410) 535-4585, info@ecalvert.com, www.ecalvert.com

**Princess Anne** • *Somerset County Eco. Dev. Comm.* • 11916 Somerset Ave., Rm. 202, 21853, P 25,000, (410) 651-0500, Fax (410) 651-3836, edc@co.somerset.md.us, www.somersetcountyedc.org

**Rockville** • *Montgomery County Dept. of Eco. Dev.* • Steve Silverman, Dir., 111 Rockville Pike, Ste. 800, 20850, P 950,000, (240) 777-2000, Fax (240) 777-2001, www.montgomerycountymd.gov/ded

**Salisbury** • *Salisbury-Wicomico Eco. Dev. Inc.* • One Plaza East, Ste. 501, P.O. Box 4700, 21803, P 89,000, (410) 749-1251, (800) 521-7933, Fax (410) 749-1252, www.swed.org

**Takoma Park** • *Takoma Park Housing & Comm. Dev.* • Sara Anne Daines, Dir. of Eco. & Comm. Dev., 7500 Maple Ave., 20912, P 18,000, (301) 891-7119, Fax (301) 270-4568, www.takomaparkmd.gov

**Towson** • *Baltimore County Dept. of Eco. Dev.* • David Iannucci, Exec. Dir., 400 Washington Ave., 21204, P 785,600, (410) 887-8000, Fax (410) 887-8017, diannucci@baltimorecountymd.gov, www.baltimorecountymd.gov/business

**Westminster** • *Carroll County Ofc. of Eco. Dev.* • Lawrence Twele, Dir., 225 N. Center St., Ste. 101, 21157, P 171,000, (410) 386-2070, Fax (410) 876-8471, www.carrollbiz.org

# Massachusetts

## Federal

**U.S. SBA, Massachusetts Dist. Ofc.** • Robert Nelson, Dist. Dir., 10 Causeway St., Rm. 265, Boston, 02222, (617) 565-5590, Fax (617) 565-5598, www.sba.gov/ma

## Communities

**Chicopee** • *Eco. Dev. Cncl. Of Western Mass.* • Allan Blair, Pres., 255 Padgette St., , Ste. 1, 01022, P 600,000, (413) 593-6421, Fax (413) 593-5126, www.WesternMassedc.com

**Easthampton** • *Eco. Dev. Comm.* • Stuart Beckley, City Planner, 50 Payson Ave., 01027, P 16,000, (413) 529-1406, (413) 529-1460, Fax (413) 529-1433, stuartb@easthampton.org, www.easthampton.org

**Fitchburg** • *Fitchburg Eco. Dev. Div.* • Dave Streb, Exec. Dir., 718 Main St., 01420, P 41,000, (978) 345-1018, Fax (978) 345-0161, dstreb@ci.fitchburg.ma.gov, www.discoverfitchburg.com

**Holyoke** • *Holyoke Ofc. of Planning & Dev.* • Kathleen Anderson, Dir., One Court Plaza, 01040, P 40,115, (413) 322-5655, Fax (413) 534-2299, www.holyoke.org

**Lynn** • *Eco. Dev. & Ind. Corp. of Lynn* • James Cowdell, Dir., Lynn City Hall, Rm. 307, 01901, P 90,000, (781) 581-9399, Fax (781) 581-9731, www.edic-lynn.org

**Orange** • *Orange EDIC* • Ann Marie Holmgren, Chair, ℅ Town Hall, 6 Prospect St., 01364, P 7,500, (978) 544-1100, Fax (978) 544-1101, commdev@townoforange.org, www.townoforange.org

**Plymouth** • *Plymouth County Dev. Cncl.* • Paul Kripps, Exec. Dir., 170 Water St., 02360, P 456,000, M 300, (508) 747-0100, Fax (508) 747-3118, info@seeplymouth.com, www.seeplymouth.com

**Springfield** • *see Chicopee*

**Winchendon** • *Winchendon Planning & Dev. Ofc.* • James Kreidler, Town Mgr., 109 Front St., 01475, P 9,000, (978) 297-0085, (978) 297-3308, Fax (978) 297-5411, www.townofwinchendon.com

# Michigan

## Federal

**U.S. SBA, Michigan Dist. Ofc.** • Richard Temkin, Dist. Dir., 477 Michigan Ave., Rm. 515, Detroit, 48226, (313) 226-6075, Fax (313) 226-4769, www.sba.gov/mi

## State

**Dept. of Energy, Labor & Eco. Growth** • Stanley Pruss, Dir., P.O. Box 30004, Lansing, 48909, (517) 373-1820, Fax (517) 373-2129, www.michigan.gov/dleg

## Communities

**Adrian** • *Lenawee Eco. Dev. Corp.* • James Gartin, Pres./CEO, 5285 W. U.S. 223, Ste. A, 49221, P 100,000, M 450, (517) 265-5141, Fax (517) 263-6065, cjackson@theledc.org, www.onelenawee.com

**Allendale** • *Ottawa County Eco. Dev. Ofc.* • Kenneth J. Rizzio, Exec. Dir., 6676 Lake Michigan Dr., P.O. Box 539, 49401, P 238,314, (616) 892-4120, Fax (616) 895-6670, krizzio@altelco.net, www.ocedo.org

**Alpena** • *Target Alpena Eco. Dev. Corp.* • Lee Shirey, Dir., 235 W. Chisolm, P.O. Box 65, 49707, P 32,700, (989) 354-2666, Fax (989) 356-3999, targetalpena@chartermi.net, www.targetalpena.com

**Ann Arbor** • *Ann Arbor Spark* • Michael Finney, Pres./CEO, 201 S. Division St., Ste. 430, 48104, P 313,000, (734) 761-9317, Fax (734) 761-9062, info@annarborusa.org, www.annarborusa.org

**Bad Axe** • *Huron County EDC* • Carl Osentoski, Exec. Dir., 250 E. Huron Ave., Rm. 303, 48413, P 36,000, (989) 269-6431, (800) 35-THUMB, Fax (989) 269-8209, info@huroncounty.com, www.huroncounty.com

**Battle Creek** • *Battle Creek Unlimited Inc.* • 4950 W. Dickman Rd., Ste. A1, 49037, P 56,000, (269) 962-7526, Fax (269) 962-8096, www.bcunlimited.org

**Bay City** • *Bay County Growth Alliance* • 721 Washington Ave., Ste. 504, 48708, P 110,000, (989) 893-5596, Fax (989) 893-8420

**Bay City** • *Bay Future Inc.* • Frederick Hollister, Pres./CEO, 721 Washington Ave., Ste. 309, 48708, P 111,000, (989) 892-1400, Fax (989) 892-1402

**Big Rapids** • *Mecosta County Dev. Corp.* • William Mrdeza, Exec. Dir., 246 N. State St., 49307, P 40,000, (231) 592-3403, Fax (231) 592-4085, www.mecostaedc.com

**Boyne City** • *Northern Lakes Eco. Alliance* • Andy Hayes, Pres., P.O. Box 8, 49712, P 70,000, (231) 582-6482, Fax (231) 582-3213, info@northernlakes.net, www.northernlakes.net

**Coloma** • *North Berrien Comm. Dev.* • Chana Kniebes, Comm. Dev. Coord., 209 N. Paw Paw St., P.O. Box 1028, 49038, P 15,000, (269) 468-4430, Fax (269) 468-7088, info@coloma-watervliet.org, www.coloma-watervliet.org

**Detroit** • *Detroit Eco. Growth Corp.* • George Jackson Jr., Pres., 500 Griswold, Ste. 2200, 48226, P 2,000,000, (313) 963-2940, Fax (313) 963-8839, www.degc.org

**Detroit** • *Detroit Reg. Eco. Partnership* • John Carroll, Sr. V.P., One Woodward Ave., Ste. 1900, P.O. Box 33840, 48232, P 5,200,000, (313) 964-4000, Fax (313) 964-0183, www.detroitchamber.com

**Detroit** · *Wayne County Eco. Dev.* · Turkia Awada Mullin, Dir., Wayne County Bldg., 3rd Flr., 600 Randolph St., 48226, P 2,100,000, (313) 224-0410, Fax (313) 224-8458, www.waynecounty.com

**Eastpointe** · *City of Eastpointe* · Steve Horstman, Dir., 23200 Gratiot, 48021, P 35,000, (586) 445-5016, Fax (586) 445-5191, stevehorstman@hotmail.com, www.ci.eastpointe.mi.us

**Escanaba** · *Central Upper Peninsula Plan. & Dev. Reg. Comm.* · Lloyd R. Matthes, Exec. Dir., 2415 14th Ave. S., 49829, P 180,000, (906) 786-9234, Fax (906) 786-4442, cuppad@chartermi.net, www.cuppad.org

**Flint** · *Genesee County Metro Planning Comm.* · Julie Hinterman, Dir., 1101 Beach St., Rm. 223, 48502, P 436,141, (810) 257-3010, Fax (810) 257-3185, gcmpc@co.genesee.mi.us, www.gcmpc.org

**Gaylord** · *Northeast Michigan Cncl. Of Governments* · Diane Rekowski, Exec. Dir., 121 E. Mitchell, P.O. Box 457, 49734, P 141,199, (989) 732-3551, Fax (989) 732-5578, ppapendic@nemcog.org, www.nemcog.org

**Grand Rapids** · *Eco. Dev. Found.* · Sandra Bloem, Dir., 1345 Monroe Ave. N.W., Ste. 132, 49505, P 600,000, (616) 459-4825, Fax (616) 458-5736, info@growmichigan.com, www.growmichigan.com

**Grand Rapids** · *The Right Place Inc.* · Birgit Klohs, Pres., 161 Ottawa Ave. N.W., Ste. 400, 49503, P 1,302,000, (616) 771-0325, Fax (616) 771-0555, info@rightplace.org, www.rightplace.org

**Grand Rapids** · *West MI Reg. Planning Comm.* · Dave Bee, Dir., 820 Monroe N.W., Ste. 214, 49503, P 1,100,000, (616) 774-8400, Fax (616) 774-0808, dbee@wmrpc.org, www.wmrpc.org

**Hillsdale** · *Hillsdale County Ind. Dev. Comm.* · Howard Turner, Exec. Dir., 23 Care Dr., 49242, P 48,000, M 200, (517) 437-3200, Fax (517) 437-3735, info@hillsdaleedp.org, www.hillsdaleedp.org

**Howell** · *Eco. Dev. Cncl. of Livingston County* · Fred Dillingham, Dir., 1240 Packard Dr., Ste. 101, 48843, P 129,080, (517) 546-0822, Fax (517) 546-4084, info@livingstonedc.com, www.livingstonedc.com

**Ionia** · *Ionia Downtown Dev. Auth.* · Jason Eppler, City Mgr., 114 N. Kidd, P.O. Box 496, 48846, P 10,569, (616) 527-4170, Fax (616) 527-0810, www.ci.ionia.mi.us

**Iron Mountain** · *Dickinson Area Partnership* · 600 S. Stephenson Ave., 49801, P 27,400, (906) 774-2002, Fax (906) 774-2004, dchamber@dickinsonchamber.com, www.dickinsonchamber.com

**Ironwood** · *Downtown Ironwood Dev. Auth.* · Dan Petersen, Dir. of Comm. Dev., 213 S. Marquette St., 49938, P 6,300, (906) 932-5050, Fax (906) 932-5745, petersend@cityofironwood.org, www.cityofironwood.org

**Ithaca** · *Greater Gratiot Dev. Inc.* · Donald C. Schurr, Pres., 136 S. Main, 48847, P 43,000, (989) 875-2083, Fax (989) 875-2990, donschurr@gratiot.org, www.gratiot.org

**Jackson** · *Enterprise Group of Jackson Inc.* · Scott Fleming, Pres./CEO, 1 Jackson Sq., Ste. 1100, P.O. Box 80, 49204, P 162,000, (517) 788-4455, Fax (517) 782-0061, sfleming@enterprisegroup.org, www.enterprisegroup.org

**Kalamazoo** · *City of Kalamazoo Eco. Dev. & Bus. Assistance* · Jerome Kisscorni, Dir., 445 W. Michigan Ave., Ste. 101, 49007, P 77,145, (269) 337-8082, Fax (269) 337-8429, cokeconomicdevelopment@kalamazoocity.org, www.kalamazoocity.org

**Kalamazoo** · *Southwest Michigan First* · Ron Kitchens, CEO, P.O. Box 50827, 49005, P 241,000, (269) 553-9588, Fax (269) 553-6897, www.southwestmichiganfirst.com

**Kincheloe** · *Eco. Dev. Corp. of Chippewa County* · Kathy Noel, Pres., 5019 W. Airport Dr., 49788, P 35,000, (906) 495-5631, Fax (906) 495-5714, ccedc@sault.com

**Lansing** · *Michigan Eco. Dev. Corp.* · 300 N. Washington Sq., 48913, (517) 373-9808, www.michiganadvantage.org

**Ludington** · *Mason County Growth Alliance* · Julie Van Dyke, Pres./CEO, 5300 W. U.S. 10, 49431, P 28,000, (231) 845-6646, Fax (231) 845-6857, jvandyke@masoncountygrowth.com, www.masoncountygrowth.com

**Marlette** · *Thumb Area-Michigan Works* · Marvin Pichla, Exec. Dir., 3270 Wilson, 48453, P 225,000, (989) 635-3561, Fax (989) 635-2230, www.thumbworks.org

**Marquette** · *Lake Superior Comm. Partnership-Marquette Area C/C* · Amy Clickner, Exec. Dir., 501 S. Front St., 49855, P 64,000, (906) 226-9658, (888) 578-6489, Fax (906) 226-2099, lscp@marquette.org, www.marquette.org

**Mason** · *Ingham County Eco. Dev. Corp.* · Susan Pigg, Eco. Dev. Coord., 121 E. Maple St., 48854, P 275,000, (517) 676-7285, Fax (517) 676-7358, spigg@ingham.org, www.ingham.org

**Midland** · *Midland Tomorrow* · 300 Rodd St., Ste. 201, 48640, P 83,400, (989) 839-0340, Fax (989) 839-7372, info@midlandtomorrow.org, www.midlandtomorrow.org

**Monroe** · *Monroe County Ind. Dev. Corp.* · William P. Morris, Pres., 102 E. Front St., P.O. Box 926, 48161, P 136,000, (734) 241-8081, Fax (734) 241-0813, mail@monroecountyidc.com, www.monroecountyidc.com

**Mount Clemens** · *Macomb County Area Dev. Ofc.* · Robert Tess, Program Mgr., 1 S. Main, 7th Flr., 48043, P 830,000, (586) 469-5285, Fax (586) 469-6787, planning@macombcountymi.gov, www.macombcountymi.gov

**Mount Pleasant** · *Middle MI Dev. Corp.* · George Dunn, Pres., 111 S. University, 48858, P 98,000, (989) 772-2858, Fax (989) 773-2115, info@mmdc.org, www.mmdc.org

**Muskegon** · *Muskegon Area First* · Ed Garner, Pres., 380 W. Western, Ste. 202, 49440, P 172,000, (231) 722-3751, Fax (231) 728-7251, info@muskegon.org, www.muskegonareafirst.org

**Newberry** · *Eco. Dev. Corp. of Luce County* · Carmen McLaren, 407 W. Harrie St., 49868, P 7,024, (906) 293-5982, Fax (906) 293-2904, mclaren@up.net

**Niles** · *Southwestern Michigan Eco. Growth Alliance Inc.* · Sharon J. Witt, Exec. Dir., 1950 Industrial Dr., 49120, P 60,000, M 200, (269) 683-1833, Fax (269) 683-7515, switt@michigan-business.info, www.michigan-business.info

**Novi** · *Novi Comm. Dev. Dept.* · Barbara McBeth, Deputy Dir., 45175 W. Ten Mile Rd., 48375, P 53,677, (248) 347-0475, Fax (248) 735-5600, www.cityofnovi.org

**Port Huron** · *Eco. Dev. Alliance of St. Clair County* · Doug Alexander, Exec. Dir., 735 Erie St., Ste. 250, 48060, P 164,000, (810) 982-9511, Fax (810) 982-9531, www.edascc.com

**Saginaw** · *Saginaw Future Inc.* · JoAnn Crary CEcD, Pres., 515 N. Washington, 3rd Flr., 48607, P 210,000, (989) 754-8222, Fax (989) 754-1715, info@saginawfuture.com, www.saginawfuture.com

**Saline** · *Eco. Dev. Corp.* · Lee Bourgoin, Dir., 100 N. Harris, 48176, P 27,000, (734) 429-4907, www.cityofsaline.org

**Sault Ste. Marie** · *EDC of Sault Ste. Marie* · James F. Hendricks, Exec. Dir., 1301 W. Easterday Ave., 49783, P 15,000, (906) 635-9131, Fax (906) 635-1999, jhendricks@saultedc.com, www.saultedc.com

**EDC**

**Southgate** · *Downriver Comm. Conf.-Eco. Dev. Dept.* · Paula Boase, Eco. Dev. Dir., 15100 Northline Rd., Ste. 135, 48195, P 500,000, (734) 362-3477, Fax (734) 281-6661, paula.boase@dccwf.org, www.dccwf.org

**St. Joseph** · *Berrien County Comm. Dev. Dept.* · Dan Fette, Exec. Dir., 701 Main St., 49085, P 162,453, (269) 983-7111, Fax (269) 982-8611, jarent@berriencounty.org, www.berriencounty.org

**Tawas City** · *Tawas Area Ind. Dev. Corp.* · 402 E. Lake St., P.O. Box 608, 48764, P 6,000, (989) 362-8643, (800) 55-TAWAS, Fax (989) 362-7880, www.tawas.com

**Tecumseh** · *City of Tecumseh Eco. Dev. Dept.* · Paula Holtz, Dir., 112 S. Ottawa St., 49286, P 8,500, (517) 424-6003, pholtz@tecumseh.mi.us, www.tecumseh.mi.us

**Traverse City** · *Traverse Bay Eco. Dev. Corp.* · Tino Breithaupt, Sr. V.P., 202 E. Grandview Pkwy., 49684, P 156,305, (231) 995-7105, Fax (231) 946-2565, tbedc@tcchamber.org, www.tcchamber.org/tbedc

**Waterford** · *Oakland County Planning & Eco. Dev. Dept.* · Dan Hunter, Mgr., 2100 Pontiac Lake Rd., Bldg. 41W, 48328, (248) 858-0720, Fax (248) 975-9555, www.oakgov.com/peds

**Wayne** · *Dept. of Planning & Dev. for the City of Wayne* · Peter McInerney, Comm. Dev. Dir., 3355 S. Wayne Rd., 48184, P 19,051, (734) 722-2002, Fax (734) 722-5052, commdev@ci.wayne.mi.us, www.ci.wayne.mi.us

**West Branch** · *Ogemaw County EDC/MSUE* · Kathy Adair, Pres., 205 S. Eighth St., 48661, P 21,645, (989) 345-0692, Fax (989) 345-1284, www.growogemaw.com

# Minnesota

## Federal

**U.S. SBA, Minnesota Dist. Ofc.** · Edward Daum, Dist. Dir., 100 N. 6th St., Ste. 210-C, Minneapolis, 55403, (612) 370-2324, Fax (612) 370-2303, www.sba.gov/mn

## State

**Dept. of Employment & Eco. Dev.** · Dan McElroy, Comm., 1st Natl. Bank Bldg., 332 Minnesota St., Ste. E200, Saint Paul, 55101, (651) 259-7114, Fax (651) 284-0088, www.deed.state.mn.us

## Communities

**Ada** · *Ada Eco. Dev. Auth.* · 404 W. Main, 56510, P 1,600, (218) 784-5520, Fax (218) 784-2711, www.ci.ada.mn.us

**Alexandria** · *Alexandria Area Eco. Dev. Comm.* · Jason Murray, Exec. Dir., 610 Fillmore St., Ste. 1, 56308, P 33,368, (320) 763-4545, Fax (320) 763-4457, aaedc@rea-alp.com, www.alexmn.org

**Anoka** · *Anoka Eco. Dev. Comm.* · Robert Kirchner, Dir., 2015 1st Ave. N., 55303, P 18,000, (763) 576-2720, Fax (763) 576-2727, www.ci.anoka.mn.us

**Austin** · *Dev. Corp. of Austin* · John Garry, Exec. Dir., 329 N. Main St., Ste. 106L, 55912, P 23,000, (507) 433-9495, (507) 433-9496, Fax (507) 433-9470, austindca@austindca.org, www.spamtownusa.com

**Barnum** · *Build Barnum Ind. Dev.* · Jim Benson, Chrmn., 3743 Main St., 55707, P 585, (218) 389-3224, (218) 389-6814, Fax (218) 389-3235, www.buildbarnum.com

**Bemidji** · *Headwaters Reg. Dev. Comm.* · Cliff Tweedale, Exec. Dir., P.O. Box 906, 56619, P (218) 444-4732, Fax (218) 444-4722, www.hrdc.org

**Blue Earth** · *Blue Earth EDA* · Kathy Bailey, City Admin., 125 W. 6th St., P.O. Box 38, 56013, P 3,621, (507) 526-7336, Fax (507) 526-7352, kb@becity.org, www.becity.org

**Brainerd** · *Brainerd Lakes Area Dev. Corp.* · Sheila Haverkamp, Exec. Dir., 124 N. Sixth St., 56401, P 60,000, M 140, (218) 828-0096, (888) 32-BLADC, Fax (218) 829-8199, info@bladc.org, wwwbladc.org

**Brooklyn Park** · *Eco. Dev. Auth.* · Robert J. Schreier, Exec. Dir., 5200 85th Ave. N., 55443, P 73,000, (763) 493-8059, Fax (763) 493-8391, bpedahp@brooklynpark.org, www.brooklynpark.org

**Champlin** · *City of Champlin Comm. Dev. Dept.* · John Cox, Dev. Dir., 11955 Champlin Dr., 55316, P 23,900, (763) 421-8100, Fax (763) 421-5256, www.ci.champlin.mn.us

**Chaska** · *City of Chaska Comm. Dev. Dept.* · Bart Fischer, Eco. Dev. Coord., 1 City Hall Plaza, 55318, P 20,000, (952) 448-2851, Fax (952) 448-9300, www.chaskamn.com

**Coon Rapids** · *City of Coon Rapids Comm. Dev.* · Marc Nevinski, Comm. Dev. Dir., 11155 Robinson Dr., 55433, P 63,000, (763) 767-6430, Fax (763) 767-6573, www.coonrapidsmn.gov

**Cottage Grove** · *Cottage Grove Eco. Dev. Auth.* · Ryan Schroeder, City Admin., 7516 80th St. S., 55016, P 34,000, (651) 458-2822, Fax (651) 458-2897, info@cottage-grove.org, www.cottage-grove.org

**Detroit Lakes** · *Becher-Lakes Industrial Dev. Corp.* · Larry Remmen, Exec. Dir., 1025 Roosevelt Ave., 56502, P 30,000, (218) 847-5658, Fax (218) 847-8969, lremmen@lakesnet.net

**Detroit Lakes** · *Becker County Eco. Dev.* · John Thomsen, Dir., 712 Minnesota Ave., P.O. Box 1617, 56502, P 30,000, (218) 846-7330, Fax (218) 846-7329, www.co.becker.mn.us

**Detroit Lakes** · *Comm. Dev. Of Detroit Lakes* · Larry Remmen, Dir., 1025 Roosevelt Ave., P.O. Box 647, 56502, P 10,000, (218) 847-5658, Fax (218) 847-8969, lremmen@lakesnet.net, www.ci.detroitlakes.mn.us

**Detroit Lakes** · *Detroit Lakes Dev. Auth.* · Larry Remmen, P.O. Box 647, 56502, P 8,300, (218) 847-5658, Fax (218) 847-8969, lremmen@lakesnet.net, www.ci.detroit-lakes.mn.us

**Detroit Lakes** · *Midwest Minnesota Comm. Dev. Corp.* · Arlen Kangas, Pres., 119 Graystone Plz., Ste. 100, P.O. Box 623, 56502, P 7,500, (218) 847-3191, Fax (218) 844-6345, info@mmcdc.com, www.mmcdc.com

**Duluth** · *Ofc. Of Plan. & Dev.* · Cindy Petkac, City Hall, Rm. 402, 411 W. 1st St., 55802, P 87,000, (218) 730-5580, Fax (218) 730-5904

**Fairmont** · *Fairmont Eco. Dev. Auth.* · Michael Humpal, Asst. City Admin., 100 Downtown Plaza, P.O. Box 751, 56031, P 12,000, (507) 238-9461, Fax (507) 238-9469, ecodevo@fairmont.org, www.fairmont.org

**Fridley** · *City of Fridley Comm. Dev.* · Scott Hickok, Comm. Dev. Dir., 6431 University Ave. N.E., 55432, P 29,000, (763) 572-3590, Fax (763) 571-1287, www.ci.fridley.mn.us

**Grand Marais** · *Cook County/Grand Marais Joint Eco. Dev. Auth.* · Matt Geretschlaeger, Dir., P.O. Box 597, 55604, P 4,700, (218) 387-3067, Fax (218) 387-3018, edamatt@boreal.org

**Grand Rapids** · *Itasca EDC* · Diane Weber, Interim Pres., 12 N.W. 3rd St., 55744, P 43,000, (218) 326-9411, Fax (218) 327-2242, info@itascadv.org, www.itascadv.org

**Granite Falls** · *Granite Falls Eco. Dev. Auth.* · Dennis VanHoff, Exec. Dir., 641 Prentice St., 56241, P 3,081, (320) 564-2255, eda@granitefalls.com, www.granitefalls.com

**Hibbing** · *Hibbing Bus. Dev. Corp.* · 1515 E. 25th St., P.O. Box 783, 55746, P 17,050, (218) 262-6703, Fax (218) 262-7399

**International Falls** · *Koochiching Eco. Dev. Auth.* · Paul Nevanen, Dir., 405 3rd St., 56649, P 15,500, (218) 283-8585, Fax (218) 283-4688, keda@northwinds.net, www.businessupnorth.com

**Jackson** · *Jackson Eco. Dev. Corp.* · 80 W. Ashley St., 56143, P 3,501, (507) 847-4423, edc@cityofjacksonmn.com, www.jacksonmn.com

**Lake City** · *Lake City Eco. Dev. Auth.* · Erin Sparks, Eco. Dev. Dir., 205 W. Center St., 55041, P 5,350, (651) 345-6808, Fax (351) 345-3208, esparks@ci.lake-city.mn.us, www.ci.lake-city.mn.us.

**Le Center** · *Le Center Area Eco. Dev. Auth.* · Don Hayden, Exec. Dir., 10 W. Tyrone St., P.O. Box 54, 56057, P 2,200, (507) 357-6737, Fax (507) 357-6888, donlc@frontiernet.net

**Luverne** · *Luverne Eco. Dev. Auth.* · Jill Wolf, Eco. Dev. Dir., 305 E. Luverne St., P.O. Box 659, 56156, P 4,600, (507) 449-5033, Fax (507) 449-5034, jwolf@cityofluverne.org, www.cityofluverne.org

**Mankato** · *Greater Mankato Growth* · Jonathan Zierdt, Pres./ CEO, 1961 Premier Dr., Ste. 100, 56001, P 50,000, M 750, (507) 385-6640, (800) 697-0652, Fax (507) 345-4451, info@greater mankato.com, www.greatermankato.com

**Minneapolis** · *Minneapolis Comm. Planning & Eco. Dev.* · Mike Christenson, Dir., 105 5th Ave. S., Ste. 1200, Crown Roller Mill, 55401, P 360,000, (612) 673-5095, Fax (612) 673-5100, www.ci.minneapolis.mn.us/cped

**Montevideo** · *Montevideo Eco. Dev. Auth.* · 103 Canton Ave., P.O. Box 517, 56265, P 5,482, (320) 269-6575, Fax (320) 269-9340, eda@montevideomn.org, www.montevideomn.net

**Monticello** · *City of Monticello Eco. Dev.* · 505 Walnut St., Ste. 1, 55362, P 10,000, (763) 271-3208, Fax (763) 295-4404, www. ci.monticello.mn.us

**Morris** · *Stevens County Eco. Imp. Comm.* · Michael Haynes, Exec. Dir., 507 Atlantic Ave., 56267, P 10,634, (320) 585-2609, Fax (320) 585-4814, www.sceic.org

**Ortonville** · *Ortonville Eco. Dev. Auth.* · Vicki Oakes, Secy., 315 Madison Ave., 56278, P 2,000, (320) 839-3428, Fax (320) 839-2613, eda@ortonville.net, www.ortonville.net

**Osakis** · *Osakis Eco. Dev. Auth.* · Angela Jacobson, Admin., P.O. Box 486, 56360, P 1,615, (320) 859-2150, Fax (320) 859-3978, cityhall@cityofosakis.com, www.cityofosakis.com

**Pipestone** · *Pipestone Eco. Dev. Auth.* · Jeff Jones, City Admin., 119 2nd Ave. S.W., 56164, P 4,400, (507) 825-3324, Fax (507) 825-5353, dnelson@cityofpipestone.com, www.progressive pipestone.com

**Red Lake Falls** · *Red Lake Falls Comm. Dev. Corp.* · Allen Bertilrud, Pres., P.O. Box 207, 56750, P 1,590, (218) 253-2143, Fax (218) 253-2141

**Redwood Falls** · *Redwood Area Dev. Corp.* · Julie Rath, Eco. Dev. Spec., 200 S. Mill St., P.O. Box 481, 56283, P 17,000, M (507) 637-4004, Fax (507) 637-4082, julie@redwoodfalls.org, www.radc.org

**Rochester** · *Rochester Area Eco. Dev.* · Gary Smith, Pres., 220 S. Broadway, Ste. 100, 55904, P 100,000, (507) 288-0208, Fax (507) 282-8960, www.raedi.com

**Saint Charles** · *St. Charles Eco. Dev. Auth.* · 830 Whitewater Ave., 55972, P 3,600, (507) 932-3020, Fax (507) 932-5301, www. stcharlesmn.org

**Saint Cloud** · *St. Cloud Area Eco. Dev. Partnership* · Tom Moore, Pres., P.O. Box 1091, 56302, P 150,000, (320) 656-3815, Fax (320) 251-0081, info@scapartnership.com, www.scapartnership.com

**Saint Paul** · *City of St. Paul* · Dept. of Plan. & Eco. Dev., 25 W. 4th, 1300 City Hall Annex, 55102, P 272,243, (651) 266-6565, Fax (651) 228-3261

**Saint Paul** · *Saint Paul Port Auth.* · Louis Jambois, Pres., 345 St. Peter St., Ste. 1900, 55102, (651) 224-5686, (800) 328-8417, Fax (651) 223-5198, info@sppa.com, www.sppa.com

**Saint Peter** · *Dept. of Comm. Dev.* · Russ Wille, Dir., 227 S. Front St., 56082, P 10,401, (507) 934-0661, Fax (507) 934-4917, russw@saintpetermn.gov, www.saintpeteradvantage.com

**Slayton** · *Southwest Reg. Dev. Comm.* · Jay Trusty, Exec. Dir., 2401 Broadway Ave., Ste. 1, 56172, P 130,000, (507) 836-8549, (507) 836-8547, Fax (507) 836-8866, execdir@swrdc.org, www. swrdc.org

**Spicer** · *Spicer Eco. Dev. Auth.* · P.O. Box 431, 56288, P 1,183, (320) 796-5562, Fax (320) 796-2044, spicer06@tds.net, www. spicermn.com

**St. Paul** · *Grand Ave. Bus. Assoc.* · Ben Johnson, Pres., 867 Grand Ave., 55105, P (651) 699-0029, Fax (651) 699-7775, www.grandave.com

**Vadnais Heights** · *Vadnais Heights Eco. Dev. Corp.* · Keith Warner, Exec. Dir., 800 E. County Rd. E, 55127, P 13,500, (651) 204-6000, www.cityvadnaisheights.com

**Virginia** · *Virginia Eco. Dev. Auth.* · John Tourville, Op. Dir., 327 1st St. S., City Hall, 55792, P 8,953, (218) 748-7535, Fax (218) 749-3580, veda@virginiamn.us, www.virginia-mn.com

**White Bear Lake** · *White Bear Lake Area Comm. Dev. Dept.* · Jim Robinson, Comm. Dev. Dir., 4701 Hwy. 61, 55110, P 25,000, (651) 429-8562, Fax (651) 429-8503, www.whitebearlake.org

**Willmar** · *Mid-Minnesota Dev. Comm.* · Donn Winckler, Exec. Dir., 333 6th St. S.W., Ste. 2, 56201, P 116,000, (320) 235-8504, Fax (320) 235-4329, mmrdc@mmrdc.org, www.mmrdc.org

**Worthington** · *Worthington Reg. Eco. Dev. Corp.* · Glen Thuringer, Mgr., 1121 Third Ave., 56187, P 12,000, (507) 372-5515, Fax (507) 372-7165, wredc@frontiernet.net, www.wgtn.net

# Mississippi

## Federal

**U.S. SBA, Mississippi Dist. Ofc.** · Janita R. Stewart, Dist. Dir., 210 E. Capital St., Ste. 900, Jackson, 39201, (601) 965-4378, Fax (601) 965-5629, www.sba.gov/ms

## State

**Mississippi Dev. Auth.** · Gray Swoope, Exec. Dir., 501 N. West St., P.O. Box 849, Jackson, 39205, (601) 359-3449, Fax (601) 359-2832, www.mississippi.org

## Communities

**Belzoni** · *Belzoni-Humphreys Dev. Found.* · Steve Anderson, Exec. Dir., 111 Magnolia St., P.O. Box 145, 39038, P 11,000, M 60, (662) 247-4838, Fax (662) 247-4805, catfish@belzonicable.com, www.belzonims.com

**Booneville** · *Prentiss County Dev. Assn.* · W. Gerald Williams, Exec. Dir., 402 W. Parker Dr., P.O. Box 672, 38829, P 25,556, (662) 728-3505, Fax (662) 728-0086, gwilliams@goprentiss.com, www. goprentiss.com

**Brandon** · *Rankin First Eco. Dev. Auth.* · Tom Troxler, Exec. Dir., 101 Service Dr., P.O. Box 129, 39043, P 128,000, (601) 825-2268, Fax (601) 825-1977, ttroxler@rankinfirst.com, www.rankinfirst.com

**Brookhaven** · *Lincoln County Ind. Dev. Found.* · Cliff Brumfield, Exec. V.P., 230 S. Whitworth Ave., P.O. Box 978, 39602, P 33,166, (601) 833-1411, (800) 613-4667, Fax (601) 833-1412, chb@brookhavenchamber.com, www.brookhavenchamber.com

EDC

**Cleveland** · *Cleveland-Bolivar County Ind. Dev. Found.* · Judson Thigpen III, Exec. Dir., 600 Third St., P.O. Box 490, 38732, P 42,000, (662) 843-2712, (800) 295-7473, Fax (662) 843-2718, judson@clevelandmschamber.com, www.clevelandmschamber.com

**Columbus** · *Columbus-Lowndes Dev. Link* · Joe Max Higgins Jr., CEO, 1102 Main St., P.O. Box 1328, 39703, P 63,000, (662) 328-8369, (800) 748-8882, Fax (662) 327-3417, info@cldlink.org, www.cldlink.org

**Corinth** · *The Alliance* · Gary Chandler, Pres., 810 Tate St., P.O. Box 1089, 38835, P 35,000, M 360, (662) 287-5269, (877) 347-0545, Fax (662) 287-5260, alliance@corinth.ms, www.corinth.ms

**DeKalb** · *Kemper County Eco. Dev. Auth.* · Brian Henson, Exec. Dir., 14062 Hwy. 16 W., 39328, P 12,000, (601) 743-2754, Fax (601) 743-2760, kceda@bellsouth.net, www.kempercounty.com

**Fulton** · *Itawamba County Dev. Cncl.* · Greg Deakle, Exec. Dir., 107 W. Wiygul St., P.O. Box 577, 38843, P 22,000, M 320, (662) 862-4571, (800) 371-8642, Fax (662) 862-5637, icdc@itawamba.com, www.itawamba.com

**Greenwood** · *Greenwood LeFlore/Carroll Eco. Dev. Found.* · Angela Curry, Exec. Dir., 402 Hwy. 82 Bypass, P.O. Box 26, 38935, P 60,000, M 150, (662) 453-5321, (800) 844-SITE, Fax (662) 453-8003, angcur@bellsouth.net, www.glcedf.com

**Gulfport** · *Harrison Co. Dev. Comm.* · Larry Barnett, Exec. Dir., 12292 Interplex Pkwy., 39503, (228) 896-5020, Fax (228) 896-6020, hcdc@mscoast.org, www.mscoast.org

**Gulfport** · *Southern Miss. Plan. & Dev. Dist.* · Leslie Newcomb, Exec. Dir., 9229 Hwy. 49, 39503, P 731,620, (228) 868-2311, (800) 444-8014, Fax (228) 868-2550, www.smpdd.com

**Hattiesburg** · *Area Dev. Partnership* · Angie Godwin, Pres., One Convention Center Plaza, 39401, P 128,171, M 1,000, (601) 296-7500, (800) 238-HATT, Fax (601) 296-7505, adp@theadp.com, www.theadp.com

**Hernando** · *DeSoto Cncl.* · Jim Flanagan, Pres./CEO, 316 W. Commerce St., 38632, P 144,000, M 600, (662) 429-4414, Fax (662) 429-0952, jflanagan@desotocounty.com, www.desotocounty.com

**Houston** · *Chickasaw Dev. Found.* · Joyce East, Exec. Dir., 635 Starkville Rd., P.O. Box 505, 38851, P 19,000, (662) 456-2321, Fax (662) 456-2595, jeastcdf@bellsouth.net, www.cdfhoustonms.org

**Kosciusko** · *Kosciusko-Attala Dev. Corp.* · Steve Zea, Pres., 124 N. Jackson, 39090, P 20,000, (662) 289-2981, Fax (662) 289-2986, info@kadcorp.org, www.kadcorp.org

**Laurel** · *Eco. Dev. Auth. of Jones County* · Wm. M. 'Mitch' Stennett, Pres., 153 Base Dr., Ste. 3, P.O. Box 527, 39441, P 64,958, M 450, (601) 649-3031, Fax (601) 428-2047, www.jonescounty.com, info@edajones.com, www.edajones.com

**Louisville** · *Winston County Eco. Dev. Dist.* · Gerald Mills, Dir., P.O. Box 551, 39339, P 20,160, (662) 773-8719, Fax (662) 773-8909, gmills@winstoncounty.com, www.winstoncounty.com

**McComb** · *Pike County Eco. Dev. Dist.* · J. Britt Herrin, Exec. Dir., 112 N. Railroad Blvd., P.O. Box 83, 39648, P 38,000, (601) 684-2291, (800) 399-4404, Fax (601) 684-4899, pcedd@pikeinfo.com, www.pikeinfo.com

**Meridian** · *East Mississippi Bus. Dev. Corp.* · Wade Jones, Pres., 1901 Front St., Ste. A, P.O. Box 790, 39302, P 78,000, M 600, (601) 693-1306, Fax (601) 693-5638, info@embdc.org, www.embdc.org

**Monticello** · *Lawrence County Comm. Dev. Assn.* · Bob Smira, Pres./CEO, 517 Broad St. E., P.O. Box 996, 39654, P 13,000, (601) 587-3007, Fax (601) 587-0765, info@lawrencecounty.org, www.lawrencecounty.org

**Natchez** · *Natchez-Adams County Dev. Auth.* · Jefferson Rowell, Exec. Dir., 211 Main, Ste. B, P.O. Box 700, 39121, P 34,350, (601) 445-0288, (800) 7-NATCHEZ, Fax (601) 445-0234, jrowelleda@natchezadams.com, www.natchezadams.com

**New Albany** · *Union County Dev. Assn.* · Stephen Surles, Exec. Dir., P.O. Box 125, 38652, P 25,362, M 200, (662) 534-4354, (888) 534-8232, Fax (662) 538-4107, info@ucda-newalbany.com, www.ucda-newalbany.com

**Oxford** · *Oxford-Lafayette Eco. Dev.* · Max D. Hipp CID, Pres., 299 W. Jackson Ave. W., P.O. Box 108, 38655, P 40,000, (662) 234-4651, (800) 880-6967, Fax (662) 234-4655, max@oxfordms.com, www.oxfordms.com

**Pascagoula** · *Jackson County Eco. Dev. Found.* · George Freeland, Exec. Dir., 3033 Pascagoula St., P.O. Drawer 1558, 39568, P 133,000, (228) 769-6263, (800) 362-0103, Fax (228) 762-8431, www.jcedf.org

**Pascagoula** · *Jackson County Port Auth.* · Mark McAndrews, Port Dir., 3033 Pascagoula St., P.O. Box 70, 39568, P 119,000, (228) 762-4041, Fax (228) 762-7476, www.portofpascagoula.com

**Philadelphia** · *Ind. Dev. Auth. of Neshoba County* · David Vowell, Exec. Dir., 256 W. Beacon St., P.O. Box 330, 39350, P 29,000, (601) 656-1000, (877) 752-2643, Fax (601) 656-1066, dvowell@bellsouth.net, www.neshoba.org

**Picayune** · *Partners for Pearl River County* · Ron Fine, Dir., P.O. Box 278, 39466, P 70,000, (601) 749-4919, Fax (601) 749-4250, www.partners.ms

**Purvis** · *Lamar County Eco. Dev. Dist.* · Lasheba Boren, Ofc. Admin., P.O. Box 598, 39475, P 52,000, (601) 794-1011, Fax (601) 794-1025, information@lamarcounty.com, www.lamarcounty.com

**Ridgeland** · *Madison County Eco. Dev. Auth.* · Tim Corsey, Exec. Dir., 623 Highland Colony Pkwy., 39157, P 80,000, (601) 605-0368, (800) 896-5087, Fax (601) 605-8662, tim@madisoncountyeda.com, www.madisoncountyeda.com

**Ripley** · *Tippah County Dev. Found.* · Duane Bullard, Pres./CEO, 212 E. Jefferson St., 38663, P 22,600, M 200, (662) 837-3353, Fax (662) 837-3006, tcdf@dixie-net.com, www.tippahcounty.ripley.ms

**Senatobia** · *Tate County Eco. Dev. Found.* · J.E. Mortimer, Exec. Dir., 135 N. Front St., 38668, P 27,000, (662) 562-8715, Fax (662) 562-5786, jemortimer@cityofsenatobia.com, www.tate-county.com

**Starkville** · *Oktibbeha County Eco. Dev. Auth.* · Jon Maynard, Pres./CEO, 200 E. Main St., 39759, P 42,970, (662) 323-3322, Fax (662) 323-5815, www.starkville.org

**Tupelo** · *Comm. Dev. Found.* · David Rumbarger, Pres./CEO, 300 W. Main St., P.O. Box A, 38802, P 34,211, M 1,425, (662) 842-4521, (800) 523-3463, Fax (662) 841-0693, info@cdfms.org, www.cdfms.org

**Vicksburg** · *Vicksburg-Warren County Eco. Dev. Found.* · Wayne Mansfield, Exec. Dir., P.O. Box 820363, 39182, P 50,000, M 160, (601) 631-0555, Fax (601) 631-6953, www.vicksburgedf.org

**Waynesboro** · *Wayne County EDC* · Larry Harvey, Dir., 610 Azalea Dr., 39367, P 20,000, (601) 735-6056, Fax (601) 735-6246, www.waynesboroinfo.com

**West Point** · *North Miss. Ind. Dev. Assn.* · Joseph Geddie, Exec. Dir., P.O. Box 718, 39773, (662) 494-4633, Fax (662) 494-3231, www.nmida.com

**West Point** · *West Point/Clay County Comm. Growth Alliance* · Amber Smith, Comm. Dev. Dir., 510 E. Broad St., 39773, P 21,000, M 100, (662) 494-5121, Fax (662) 494-6396, www.westpointms.org

**Winona • *Eco. Dev. Partnership* •** Sue Stidham, Exec. Dir., P.O. Box 248, 38967, P 5,705, M 242, (662) 283-4828, Fax (662) 283-5986, mcedp@duckwood.net, www.mcedp.ms

**Yazoo City • *Greater Yazoo Growth & Dev. Found.* •** Henry Cote, Pres., 212 E. Broadway, P.O. Box 172, 39194, P 28,000, (662) 746-1273, Fax (662) 746-7238, ccyazoo@bellsouth.net, www.yazoochamber.org

# Missouri

## Federal

**U.S. SBA, Kansas City Dist. Ofc. •** Gary Cook, Dist. Dir., 1000 Walnut St., Ste. 500, Kansas City, 64106, (816) 426-4840, Fax (816) 426-4848, www.sba.gov/mo

**U.S. SBA, St. Louis Dist. Ofc. •** Dennis Melton, Dist. Dir., 200 N. Broadway, Ste. 1500, Saint Louis, 63102, (314) 539-6600, Fax (314) 539-3785, www.sba.gov/mo

## State

**State of Missouri Dept. of Eco. Dev. •** Linda Martinez, Dir., 301 W. High St., P.O. Box 1157, Jefferson City, 65102, (573) 751-4962, Fax (573) 526-7700, ecodev@ded.mo.gov, www.ded.mo.gov

## Communities

**Belton • *Belton Corp. for Eco. Dev. [BCED]* •** Art Ruiz, Exec. Dir., 7926 E. 171st, Ste. 104, P.O. Box 525, 64012, P 25,000, (816) 331-4449, Fax (816) 322-2826, bced@beltonbced.com, www.beltonbced.com

**Branson • *City of Branson Eco. Dev.* •** 110 W. Maddux, 65616, P 6,500, (417) 337-8589, (417) 337-8548, Fax (417) 334-6095, www.bransonmo.gov

**Cape Girardeau • *Cape Girardeau Area C of C/Eco. Dev.* •** John E. Mehner, Pres./CEO, 1267 N. Mount Auburn Rd., 63701, P 75,000, (573) 335-3312, Fax (573) 335-4686, info@capechamber.com, www.capechamber.com

**Chillicothe • *Chillicothe Ind. Dev. Corp.* •** Fred Simmer, Pres., 514 Washington, P.O. Box 1022, 64601, P 9,500, (660) 646-4071, Fax (660) 646-5571, cdc@chillicothemo.com, www.chillicothemo.com

**Clayton • *City of Clayton, Eco. Dev. Div.* •** Catherine Powers, Dir. of Planning & Dev., 10 N. Bemiston, 63105, P 15,926, (314) 290-8453, Fax (314) 863-0296, cpowers@ci.clayton.mo.us, www.ci.clayton.mo.us

**Clinton • *City of Clinton Eco. Dev. Dept.* •** Christy Maggi, City Admin., 105 E. Ohio, 64735, P 10,000, (660) 885-6121, Fax (660) 885-2023, cmaggi@cityofclintonmo.com, www.clintonmo.com

**Columbia • *Reg. Eco. Dev. Inc.* •** Bernard K. Andrews CEcD, Exec. V.P., 302 Campusview Dr., Ste. 208, P.O. Box 6015, 65205, P 146,626, (573) 442-8303, Fax (573) 443-8834, bka@go columbiamo.com, www.columbiaredi.com

**Ferguson • *City of Ferguson Eco. Dev. Dept.* •** Sam Anselm, City Mgr. Asst., 110 Church St., 63135, P 22,290, (314) 521-7721, Fax (314) 524-5173, sanselm@fergusoncity.com, www.fergusoncity.com

**Fulton • *Fulton Area Dev. Corp.* •** Bruce Hackmann, Pres./CEO, 2625 Fairway Dr., Ste. A, 65251, P 42,000, (573) 642-4841, (877) 642-5964, Fax (573) 642-5964, www.fadc.org

**Grandview • *Grandview Area Eco. Dev. Cncl.* •** Kim Curtis, Exec. Dir., 12500 S. 71 Hwy., Ste. 100, 64030, P 25,500, M 56, (816) 761-6505, Fax (816) 763-8460, ksc@grandview.org, www.grandview.org

**Hannibal • *Northeast Missouri Eco. Dev. Cncl.* •** George Walley, Exec. Dir., 201 N. Third, Ste. 220, 63401, P 40,000, (573) 221-1033, Fax (573) 221-1084, gwalley@nemodev.org, www.nemodev.org

**Harrisonville • *City of Harrisonville Comm. Dev. Dept.* •** Rick DeLuca, Comm. Dev. Dir., 300 E. Pearl St., P.O. Box 367, 64701, P 9,400, (816) 380-8900, Fax (816) 380-8910, developmentdir@ci.harrisonville.mo.us, www.ci.harrisonville.mo.us

**Independence • *Independence Cncl. for Eco. Dev.* •** Tom Lesnak, Pres., 210 W. Truman Rd., 64050, P 114,345, (816) 252-5777, Fax (816) 254-1641, tlesnak@iced.org, www.independencemo.biz

**Joplin • *Joplin Bus. & Ind. Dev. Corp.* •** Rob O'Brian, Pres., 320 E. 4th St., 64801, P 169,031, (417) 624-4150, Fax (417) 624-4303, robrian@joplincc.com, www.joplincc.com

**Kansas City • *Clay County Eco. Dev. Cncl.* •** Jim Hampton, Exec. Dir., 110 N.W. Barry Rd., Ste. 210, 64155, P 180,000, M 700, (816) 468-4989, Fax (816) 468-7778, info@clayedc.com, www.clayedc.com

**Kansas City • *Kansas City Area Dev. Cncl.* •** Robert J. Marcusse, Pres./CEO, 911 Main St., Commerce Tower, Ste. #2600, 64105, P 2,000,000, (816) 221-2121, (888) 99-KCADC, Fax (816) 842-2865, kcadc@thinkKC.com, www.thinkKC.com

**Kansas City • *Platte County Eco. Dev. Cncl. Inc.* •** Burdette Fullerton, Exec. Dir., 11724 N.W. Plaza Cir., Ste. 400, 64153, P 85,000, M 650, (816) 270-2119, Fax (816) 270-2135, pfullerton@plattecountyedc.com, www.plattecountyedc.com

**Kearney • *Kearney Area Dev. Cncl.* •** Jim Eldridge, Secy., 100 E. Washington, P.O. Box 291, 64060, P 7,000, (816) 628-3343, jeldridge@ci.kearney.mo.us, www.kearneyadc.com

**Lamar • *Barton County Comm. Dev. Corp.* •** John Gulick, Eco. Dev. Dir., 102 W. 10th St., 64759, P 12,600, (417) 682-3595, Fax (417) 682-9566, nancy@bartoncounty.com, www.bartoncounty.com

**Lebanon • *Lebanon Ind. Dev. Auth.* •** Laina Starnes, City Clerk, 400 S. Madison, P.O. Box 111, 65536, P 13,000, (417) 532-2156, Fax (417) 532-8388, www.lebanonmissouri.org

**Lee's Summit • *Lee's Summit Eco. Dev. Cncl.* •** James A. Devine, Pres./CEO, 218 S.E. Main St., P.O. Box 710, 64063, P 90,000, (816) 525-6617, Fax (816) 524-8851, www.leessummit.org

**Mexico • *City of Mexico Dept. of Eco. Dev.* •** Russell Runge, Dir., 300 N. Coal, 65265, P 11,390, (573) 581-2100, Fax (573) 581-2305, www.mexicomissouri.net

**Moberly • *Moberly Area Eco. Dev. Corp.* •** Corey Mehaffy, Pres., P.O. Box 549, 65270, P 25,000, (660) 263-8811, Fax (660) 263-8883, cmehaffy@moberly-edc.com, www.moberly-edc.com

**Nevada • *Eco. Dev. of City of Nevada* •** Ron Clow, Dir., 110 S. Ash, 64772, P 20,000, (417) 448-2700, Fax (417) 448-2707, rclow@nevadamo.org, www.nevadamo.org

**Perryville • *Perry County Eco. Dev. Auth.* •** Larry Tucker CEcD, Exec. Dir., 112 W., Ste. Maries St., P.O. Box 109, 63775, P 18,132, (573) 547-1097, Fax (573) 547-7327, perryida@perrycountymo.org, www.perrycountymo.org

**Saint Charles • *St. Charles County Eco. Dev. Center* •** Gregory Prestemon, Pres./Exec. Dir., 5988 Mid Rivers Mall Dr., 63304, P 311,000, (636) 441-6880, Fax (636) 441-6881, www.edcscc.com

**Saint Louis • *St. Louis County Eco. Cncl.* •** Denny Coleman, Pres./CEO, 121 S. Meramec, Ste. 900, 63105, P 1,000,000, (314) 615-7663, Fax (314) 615-7666, www.slcec.com

**Sikeston • *Sikeston Dept. of Eco. Dev.* •** Ed Dust, Dir., 128 N. New Madrid St., 63801, P 17,000, (573) 471-2780, (800) 494-6476, Fax (573) 471-7564, www.sikeston.org

**EDC**

**Springfield** · *Dept. of Planning & Dev.* · Ralph Rognstad, Dir., 840 Boonville Ave., 65802, P 156,228, (417) 864-1031, Fax (417) 864-1030, www.springfieldmo.gov

**Springfield** · *Springfield Bus. & Dev. Corp.* · Greg Williams, Sr. V.P., 202 S. John Q. Hammons Pkwy., P.O. Box 1687, 65801, P 407,092, (417) 862-5567, Fax (417) 862-1611, greg@spring fieldchamber.com, www.business4springfield.com

**Washington** · *City of Washington Eco. Dev. Dept.* · Richard Oldenburg, Dir., 405 Jefferson St., 63090, P 15,000, (636) 390-1004, (636) 667-9310, Fax (636) 239-8945, roldenburg@ ci.washington.mo.us, www.ci.washington.mo.us

**Wright City** · *Wright City Eco. Dev. Dept.* · Karen Girondo, Eco. Developer, P.O. Box 436, 63390, P 3,100, (636) 745-3101, Fax (636) 745-3119, econdevelop@wrightcity.org, www.wrightcity.org

# Montana

## Federal

**U.S. SBA, Montana Dist. Ofc.** · Michelle Johnston, Dist. Dir., 10 W. 15th St., Ste. 1100, Helena, 59626, (406) 441-1081, Fax (406) 441-1090, www.sba.gov/mt

**Colstrip** · *Southeastern Montana Dev. Corp./Small Bus. Dev.* · Jim Atchison, Exec. Dir., 6200 Main St., P.O. Box 1935, 59323, P 30,000, (406) 748-2990, Fax (406) 748-2990, www.semdc.org

**Havre** · *Bear Paw Dev. Corp.* · Paul Tuss, Exec. Dir., 48 2nd Ave., Ste. 202, P.O. Box 170, 59501, P 36,411, (406) 265-9226, Fax (406) 265-5602, www.bearpaw.org

**Kalispell** · *Montana West Eco. Dev.* · Lyle Phillips, CEO, 314 Main St., 59901, P 81,000, (406) 257-7711, (888) 870-5440, Fax (406) 257-7772, lyle@dobusinessinmontana.com, www. dobusinessinmontana.com

**Saint Ignatius** · *Mission Valley Old Town Dev. Corp.* · Stuart Morton, Pres., P.O. Box 400, 59865, P 2,500, (406) 745-2190

## Nebraska

### Federal

**US SBA, Nebraska Dist. Ofc.** · Leon Milobar, Dist. Dir., 10675 Bedford Ave., Ste. 100, Omaha, 68134, (402) 221-4691, Fax (402) 221-3680, www.sba.gov/ne

### State

**Nebraska Dept. of Eco. Dev.** · Richard Baier, Dir., 301 Centennial Mall S., P.O. Box 94666, Lincoln, 68509, (402) 471-3111, Fax (402) 471-3778, richard.baier@nebraska.gov, www.neded.org

### Communities

**Alliance** · *Box Butte Dev. Corp.* · John Olafson, Exec. Dir., 204 E. 3rd, 69301, P 11,374, M 82, (308) 762-1800, Fax (308) 762-4268, info@boxbuttedevelopment.com, www.boxbuttedevelopment.com

**Atkinson** · *Atkinson Dev. Corp.* · Mike Butterfield, Pres., P.O. Box 129, 68713, P 1,244, (402) 925-2801, www.atkinsonne.com

**Bassett** · *Bassett Area Dev.* · Donald Coash, Pres., P.O. Box 145, 68714, P 800, (402) 684-2711, www.bassettnebr.com

**Beatrice** · *Gage County Eco. Dev.* · Terri Dageford, Dir., 5109 W. Scott Rd., Ste. 411, 68310, P 24,000, (402) 223-6650, Fax (402) 223-6651, terri@gced.us, www.gced.us

**Bloomfield** · *Bloomfield Eco. Dev.* · Jason Hefner, Pres., P.O. Box 687, 68718, P 900, (402) 373-2557, (402) 373-2272, www. ci.bloomfield.ne.us

**Cambridge** · *Cambridge Eco. Dev Bd.* · Andela Taylor, Dir., 722 Patterson St., P.O Box Q, 69022, P 1,041, (308) 697-3711, Fax (308) 697-3253, edcity@swnebr.net, www.cambridgene.org

**Central City** · *Merrick County Dev. Corp.* · Clayton Erickson, Mayor, City Hall, P.O. Box 418, 68826, P 9,000, (308) 946-3806, Fax (308) 946-3334

**Chadron** · *Nebraska Northwest Dev. Corp.* · Brenda Johnson, Exec. Dir., 706 W. 3rd St., 69337, P (308) 432-4023, Fax (308) 432-6740, bjnndc@bbc.net, www.nndc.chadron-nebraska.com

**Clay Center** · *Clay Center Comm. Found.* · Linda Redline, Pres., 416 W. South St., P.O. Box 185, 68933, P 867, (402) 762-3356, www.ci.clay-center.ne.us

**Cozad** · *Dawson Area Dev.* · Jennifer Wolf, Exec. Dir., 209 W. 8th St., P.O. Box 106, 69130, P 25,000, (308) 784-3902, Fax (308) 784-3941, jwdad@cozadtel.net

**Curtis** · *Medicine Valley Eco. Dev. Corp.* · P.O. Box 437, 69025, P 800, (308) 367-4122, Fax (308) 367-4125, www.medicinevalleyedc.com

**Falls City** · *Falls City Eco. Dev.* · Becki Cromer, Exec. Dir., 3424 N. Hwy. 73, P.O. Box 574, 68355, P 5,000, (402) 245-2105, Fax (402) 245-2106, info@fallscityedge.com, www.fallscityedge.com

**Fremont** · *Greater Fremont Dev. Cncl.* · Kevin Wilkins, Exec. Dir., 400 E. Military Ave., P.O. Box 182, 68025, P 25,174, (402) 753-8126, Fax (402) 727-2667, gfdc@freemontne.org, www.gfdc.net

**Geneva** · *Fillmore County Dev. Corp.* · Patt Lentfer, Exec. Dir., 1032 G St., 68361, P 7,000, M 80, (402) 759-4910, Fax (402) 759-4455, fillcodevco@windstream.net, www.fillmorecounty development.org

**Gothenburg** · *Gothenburg Comm. Dev. Ofc.* · Anne Anderson, Exec. Dir., 1021 Lake Ave., P.O. Box 263, 69138, P 3,619, (308) 537-3505, Fax (308) 537-2541, annea@gothenburgdelivers.com, www. gothenburgdelivers.com

**Grand Island** · *Grand Island Area Eco. Dev. Corp.* · Marlan Ferguson, Pres., 308 N. Locust St., Ste. 400, P.O. Box 1151, 68802, P 53,000, M 270, (308) 381-7500, (800) 658-4283, Fax (308) 398-7205, giaedc@grandisland.org, www.grandisland.org

**Hartington** · *Hartington Ind. Dev. Corp.* · Chris Miller, Pres., 107 W. State St., P.O. Box 427, 68739, P 1,640, (402) 254-6353, Fax (402) 254-6391, www.ci.hartington.ne.us

**Hastings** · *Hastings Eco. Dev. Corp.* · Mr. Dee Haussler, Exec. Dir., 301 S. Burlington, P.O. Box 1104, 68902, P 25,437, (402) 461-8406, Fax (402) 461-4400, dhaussler@hastingsedc.com, www. hastingsedc.com

**Holdrege** · *Phelps County Dev. Corp.* · Monica Boyken, Exec. Dir., 502 E. Ave., Ste. 201, P.O. Box 522, 68949, P 9,747, M 50, (308) 995-4148, Fax (308) 995-4158, monica@justtheplace nebraska.com, www.justtheplacenebraska.com

**Kearney** · *Buffalo County Eco. Dev. Cncl.* · Jonathan Krebs, Exec. Dir., P.O. Box 607, 68848, P 42,000, (308) 237-9346, Fax (308) 234-2764, www.ci.kearney.ne.us

**Kimball** · *City of Kimball Eco. Dev. Assn.* · Kent Worker, Eco. Dev. Dir., 223 S. Chestnut, 69145, P 4,900, (308) 235-3639, (888) 274-6004, Fax (308) 235-2971, econdev@megavision.com, www. ci.kimball.ne.us

**Lincoln** · *USDA Rural Dev.* · Brenda Darnell, Interim State Dir., Rm. 308, Fed. Bldg., 100 Centennial Mall N., 68508, (402) 437-5551, Fax (402) 437-5408, www.rurdev.usda.gov/ne

**McCook** · *McCook Eco. Dev.* · Rex Nelson, Exec. Dir., 301 Norris Ave., Ste. 200, P.O. Box 626, 69001, P 8,000, (308) 345-1200, (800) 658-4213, Fax (308) 345-2152, medc@mccookne.org, www.mccookne.org

**Nebraska City** · *River Country Eco. Dev. Corp.* · Stephanie Shrader, Exec. Dir., 806 First Ave., 68410, P 7,200, (402) 873-4293, Fax (402) 873-4578, rcedc@windstream.net, www.rivercountryedc.org

**Norfolk** · *Northeast Nebraska Eco. Dev. Dist.* · Tom Higginbotham, Exec. Dir., 111 S. 1st, 68701, P 220,000, (402) 379-1150, Fax (402) 379-9207, thomash@nenedd.org, www.nenedd.org

**North Platte** · *Dev. Corp. of North Platte* · 502 S. Dewey, 69101, P 23,878, (308) 532-1850, (800) 927-7514, Fax (308) 532-8258, devco@grownnorthplatte.org, www.grownnorthplatte.org

**Oakland** · *Oakland Comm. Dev. Corp.* · Jeff Troupe, Pres., 218 N. Oakland Ave., 68045, P 1,400, (402) 685-5706, Fax (402) 685-5706, www.ci.oakland.ne.us

**Ogallala** · *Keith County Area Dev.* · Marion Kroeker, Dir., P.O. Box 418, 69153, P 8,850, M 60, (308) 284-4066, Fax (308) 284-3126, marion@visitogallala.com, www.kcad.org

**Ogallala** · *West Central Neb. Dev. Dist.* · 201 E. 2nd St., Ste. C, P.O. Box 599, 69153, P 103,000, (308) 284-6077, Fax (308) 284-6070, www.west-central-nebraska.com

**Omaha** · *Greater Omaha Eco. Dev. Partnership* · Rod Moseman, V.P. of Eco. Dev., 1301 Harney St., 68102, P 804,000, (402) 346-5905, Fax (402) 346-7050, rmoseman@selectgreateromaha.com, www.selectgreateromaha.com

**Omaha** · *Sarpy County Eco. Dev. Corp.* · Toby Churchill, Exec. Dir., 1301 Harney St., 68102, P 125,000, M 60, (402) 346-5000, Fax (402) 346-7050, tchurchill@omahachamber.org, www.omahachamber.org

**Ord** · *Valley County Eco. Dev. Bd.* · Caleb Pollard, Dir., 1514 K St., 68862, P 4,600, (308) 728-7875, Fax (308) 728-7691, valleycountyed@frontiernet.net, www.ordnebraska.com

**Plattsmouth** · *Plattsmouth Ind. Dev. Corp.* · George Miller, Pres., 136 N. 5th St., 68048, P 6,996, (402) 296-2522, Fax (402) 296-3228, info@plattsmouth.org, www.plattsmouth.org

**Randolph** · *Randolph Comm. Club* · P.O. Box 624, 68771, P 960, M 100, (402) 337-1234, www.ci.randolph.ne.us

**Scottsbluff** · *Twin Cities Dev. Assn., Inc.* · Rawnda Pierce, Exec. Dir., 2620 College Park, 69361, P 35,000, M 150, (308) 635-6710, (877) 635-6710, Fax (308) 635-6704, twincitiesinfo@wncc.net, www.tcdne.org

**Sidney** · *Sidney/Cheyenne County Eco. Dev.* · Gary Person, City Mgr., 1115 13th Ave., P.O. Box 79, 69162, P 15,960, (308) 254-4444, Fax (308) 254-3164, garyperson@cityofsidney.org, www.cityofsidney.org

**Wahoo** · *Wahoo Area Eco. Dev.* · Doug Watts, Exec. Dir., 640 N. Broadway, 68066, P 4,045, M 350, (402) 443-4001, Fax (402) 443-3077, watts@wahoo.ne.us, www.wahoo.ne.us

**Wayne** · *Wayne Area Chamber & Eco. Dev.* · David Simonsen, Exec. Dir., 108 W. 3rd St., 68787, P 6,000, (402) 375-2240, (866) 929-6363, Fax (402) 375-2246, dsimonsen@waedi.org, www.wayneworks.org

**West Point** · *West Point Dev. Corp.* · Glen Prinz, Secy./Treas., P.O. Box 265, 68788, P 3,600, (402) 372-2495, www.ci.westpoint.ne.us

**York** · *York County Dev. Corp.* · 224 W. 6th, 68467, P 14,500, M 125, (402) 362-3333, (888) 733-9675, Fax (402) 362-3344, info@yorkdevco.com, www.comegrowwithyork.org

# Nevada

## Federal

**U.S. SBA, Nevada Dist. Ofc.** · John E. Scott II, Dist. Dir., 400 S. 4th St., Ste. 250, Las Vegas, 89101, (702) 388-6611, Fax (702) 388-6469, www.sba.gov/nv

## State

**Comm. On Eco. Dev./State of Nevada** · Michael Skaggs, Exec. Dir., 108 E. Proctor St., Carson City, 89701, P 50,000, (775) 687-4325, Fax (775) 687-4450, mskaggs@bizopp.state.nv.us, www.expand2nevada.com

**Nevada Dev. Auth.** · A. Somer Hollingsworth, Pres./CEO, 6700 Via Austi Pkwy., Ste. B, Las Vegas, 89119, (702) 791-0000, (888) 466-8293, Fax (702) 796-6483, info@nevadadevelopment.org, www.nevadadevelopment.org

## Communities

**Carson City** · *Northern Nevada Dev. Auth.* · Rob Hooper, Exec. Dir., 704 W. Nye Ln., Ste. 201, 89703, P 150,000, M 400, (775) 883-4413, Fax (775) 883-0494, rhooper@nnda.org, www.nnda.org

**Elko** · *Elko County Eco. Divers. Auth.* · Elaine Barkdull-Spencer, Exec. Dir., 723 Railroad St., 89801, P 46,000, (775) 738-2100, (866) 937-3356, Fax (775) 738-7978, elaine@eceda.com, www.eceda.com

**Ely** · *White Pine County Eco. Divers. Cncl.* · Karen Rajala, Coord., 957 Campton, 89301, P 9,542, (775) 289-3065, Fax (775) 289-8860, wpcedc@mwpower.net, www.elynevada.net

**Fallon** · *Churchill Eco. Dev. Auth.* · Eric Grimes, Exec. Dir., 90 N. Main St., P.O. Box 1236, 89407, P 30,000, (775) 423-8587, Fax (775) 423-1759, ceda@ceda-nv.org, www.ceda-nv.org

**Henderson** · *Henderson Dev. Assoc.* · Alice Martz, CEO, 590 S. Boulder Hwy., 89015, P 262,000, (702) 565-8951, Fax (702) 565-3115, info@hendersonchamber.com, www.hendersonchamber.com

**Las Vegas** · *City of Las Vegas, Ofc. Of Bus. Dev.* · Bill Arent, Interim Dir., 400 Stewart Ave., 89101, P 2,000,000, (702) 229-6551, Fax (702) 385-3128, www.lasvegasnevada.gov

**Las Vegas** · *Southern Nevada Certified Dev. Co.* · Thomas Gutherie, Pres./CEO, 2770 S. Maryland Pkwy., Ste. 212, 89109, P 1,500,000, (702) 732-3998, Fax (702) 738-2705, sncdc@ad.com

**North Las Vegas** · *City of North Las Vegas Planning & Zoning* · Frank Fiori, Dir., 2240 Civic Center Dr., 89030, P 190,000, (702) 633-1537, Fax (702) 649-6091, www.cityofnorthlasvegas.com

**Reno** · *Eco. Dev. Auth. of Western Nevada* · Chuck Alvey, CEO/Pres., 201 W. Liberty St., Ste. 200, 89501, P 330,000, (775) 829-3700, (800) 256-9761, Fax (775) 829-3710, info@edawn.org, www.edawn.org

# New Hampshire

## Federal

**U.S. SBA, New Hampshire Dist. Ofc.** · Witmer Jones, Dist. Dir., 55 Pleasant St., Ste. 3101, Concord, 03301, (603) 225-1400, Fax (603) 225-1409, www.sba.gov/nh

## State

**Bus. Resource Center** · Roy Duddy, Dir., 172 Pembroke Rd., P.O. Box 1856, Concord, 03302, (603) 271-2591, Fax (603) 271-6784, info@nheconomy.com, www.nheconomy.com

## Communities

**Berlin** · *Bus. Enterprise Dev. Corp.* · William J. Andreas, Exec. Dir., P.O. Box 628, 03570, P 110,000, (603) 752-3319, Fax (603) 752-4421, www.bedco.org

**Concord** · *Capital Reg. Dev. Cncl.* · 91 N. State St., P.O. Box 664, 03302, P 200,000, (603) 228-1872, Fax (603) 226-3588, www.crdc-nh.com

**Concord** · *City of Concord Bus. Dev. Div.* · City Hall, 41 Green St., 03301, P 43,000, (603) 225-8595, Fax (603) 228-2701, businessdevelopment@onconcord.com, www.onconcord.com

**Dover** · *City of Dover* · Beth Thompson, Eco. Dev. Dir., 288 Central Ave., 03820, P 28,000, (603) 516-6043, Fax (603) 516-6049, b.thompson@ci.dover.nh.us, www.ci.dover.nh.us

**Exeter** · *Exeter Dev. Comm.* · Sylvia von Aulock, Town Planner, 10 Front St., 03833, P 14,500, (603) 778-0591, Fax (603) 772-4709, www.town.exeter.nh.us

**Keene** · *Monadnock Eco. Dev. Corp.* · John G. Dugan, Pres./ CEO, 39 Central Sq., Ste. 201, 03431, P 70,000, (603) 352-4939, Fax (603) 357-4917, info@monadnock-development.org, www. monadnock-development.org

**Manchester** · *Manchester Eco. Dev. Ofc.* · Jay Minkarah, Dir., 1 City Hall Plaza, 03101, P 109,000, (603) 624-6505, Fax (603) 624-6308, econdev@ManchesterNH.gov, www.yourmanchesternh.com

**Peterborough** · *see Keene*

**Portsmouth** · *Granite State Dev. Corp.* · Alan Abraham, Pres., One Cate St., 3rd Flr., P.O. Box 1491, 03802, P 1,200,000, (603) 436-0009, Fax (603) 436-5547, www.granitestatedev.com

**Rochester** · *City of Rochester* · Kenneth Ortmann, Planning & Dev. Dir., 31 Wakefield St., 03867, P 30,000, (603) 335-1338, Fax (603) 335-7585, kenn.ortmann@rochesternh.net, www.rochesternh.net

**Wilton** · *Wilton Main Street Assoc.* · Sarah Sadowski, Program Dir., P.O. Box 310, 03086, P 1,250, (603) 654-3020, wmsa@tds.net, www.mainstreet.wilton.nh.us

# New Jersey

## Federal

**Fed. Bus. Center** · Tony Rispoli, 300 Raritan Center Pkwy., P.O. Box 7815, Edison, 08818, (732) 225-2200, Fax (732) 225-0812, www.federalbusinesscenters.com

## State

**New Jersey Eco. Dev. Auth.** · Caren S. Franzini, CEO, 36 W. State St., P.O. Box 990, Trenton, 08625, (609) 292-1800, njeda@njeda.com, www.njeda.com

## Communities

**Absecon** · *Eco. Dev. Comm. of City Cncl.* · Lynn Caterson, Council Pres., 500 Mill Rd., Absecon Municipal Complex, 08201, P 7,800, (609) 641-0663, Fax (609) 645-5098, www.absecon-newjersey.org

**Asbury Park** · *Asbury Park Ofc. of Eco. Dev.* · Tom Gilmore, Dir. of Commerce, 1 Municipal Plaza, 07712, P 18,000, (732) 502-5749, Fax (732) 775-1483, www.cityofasburypark.com

**Atlantic City** · *Atlantic City Div. of Planning* · William Crane, Dir., City Hall, Rm. 506, 1301 Bacharach Blvd., 08401, P 40,517, (609) 347-5404, (609) 347-5300, Fax (609) 347-5345, bcrane@cityofatlanticcity.org, www.cityofatlanticcity.org

**Atlantic City** · *Metropolitan Bus. & Citizens Assoc.* · Mr. Gary Hill, Pres., 1616 Pacific Ave., 6th Flr., 08401, P 253,000, (609) 348-1903, Fax (609) 344-5244, comments@acmetbiz.com, www.mbcanj.com

**Bayonne** · *Bayonne Eco. Dev. Corp.* · Michael O'Connor, Exec. Dir., 630 Ave. C, Rm. 10, 07002, P 65,000, (201) 339-0052, Fax (201) 339-0744, bayonne.edc@verizon.net, www.bayonnenj.org

**Bayville** · *Berkeley Twp. Ind. Comm.* · Berkeley Municipal Bldg., P.O. Box B, 08721, P 41,946, (732) 244-7400, Fax (732) 244-3428, www.twp.berkeley.nj.us

**Bridgeport** · *Pureland Ind. Complex* · Charles J. Walters, V.P., P.O. Box 585, 08014, P 7,000, (856) 467-2333, Fax (856) 467-5552, www.purelandindustrialcomplex.com

**Bridgeton** · *City of Bridgeton Dept. of Dev. & Planning* · John Barry III, Dir., 50 E. Broad St., 08302, P 19,000, (856) 451-3407, Fax (856) 455-7421, barryj@cityofbridgeton.com, www.cityof bridgeton.com

**Bridgeton** · *Cumberland County Ofc. Of Planning & Eco. Dev.* · Robert Brewer, Exec. Dir., 790 E. Commerce St., 08302, P 147,000, (856) 453-2177, Fax (856) 453-9138, www.co.cumberland.nj.us

**Bridgeton** · *Cumberland Dev. Corp.* · Anthony M. Stanzione, Exec. Dir., P.O. Box 1021, 08302, P 147,000, (856) 451-4200, Fax (856) 453-9795, cdc@cdcnj.com, www.cdcnj.com

**Bridgewater** · *Somerset County Bus. Partnership* · Thomas Sharpe, Pres./CEO, 360 Grove St. at Rte. 22 E., 08807, P 315,000, M 610, (908) 218-4300, Fax (908) 722-7823, info@somerset businesspartnership.com, www.scbp.org

**Buena Vista** · *Buena Vista Eco. Dev. Advisory Bd.* · Chuck Chiarello, Mayor, 890 Harding Hwy., 08310, P 7,600, (856) 697-2100, Fax (856) 697-8651, www.buenavistatownship.org

**Camden** · *Camden Redev. Agency* · Carrie Turner, Exec. Dir., City Hall, 520 Market St., Ste. 1300, 08101, P 87,000, (856) 757-7600, Fax (856) 964-2262, crainfo@ci.camden.nj.us, www.camden redevelopment.com

**Camden** · *South Jersey Port Corp.* · Joseph A. Balzano, Exec. Dir./CEO, 2nd & Beckett St., 08101, (856) 757-4969, Fax (856) 757-4903, www.southjerseyport.com

**Cape May Court House** · *Ofc. Of Eco. Resources & Capital Planning* · #4 Moore Rd., 08210, P 102,000, (609) 465-6875, Fax (609) 463-1269, www.capemaycountygov.net

**Cherry Hill** · *Cherry Hill Twp. Community Dev.* · 820 Mercer St., 08002, P 70,000, (856) 665-6500, Fax (856) 488-7893, www. cherryhill-nj.com

**Clifton** · *Clifton Eco. Dev.* · Harry Swanson, Eco. Dev. Dir., City Hall, 900 Clifton Ave., 07013, P 81,000, (973) 470-5200, Fax (973) 773-7470, www.cliftonnj.org

**Columbia** · *Knowlton Twp. Eco. Dev.* · Municipal Bldg., 628 Rte. 94, 07832, P 3,000, M 45, (908) 496-4816, Fax (908) 496-8144, deputyclerk@knowlton-nj.com, www.knowlton-nj.com

**Deptford** · *Deptford Twp. Bus. Advisory Comm.* · Charles Kirschner, Chrmn., 1011 Cooper St., 08096, P 27,000, (856) 845-5300, Fax (856) 848-8227, www.deptford-nj.org

**East Orange** · *East Orange Dept. of Eco. Dev.* · Norma Mackey, Eco. Dev. Mgr., 44 City Hall Plaza, Lower Level, 07019, P 78,000, (973) 266-5404, Fax (973) 674-2180, norma@ci.east-orange.nj.us, www.eastorange-nj.org

**Edgewater Park** · *Edgewater Park Eco. Dev. Comm.* · 400 Delanco Rd., 08010, P 7,800, (609) 877-2050, Fax (609) 877-2308, www.edgewaterpark-nj.com

**Edison** · *New Jersey Alliance for Action* · Philip K. Beachem, Pres., P.O. Box 6438, 08818, M 600, (732) 225-1180, Fax (732) 225-4694, www.allianceforaction.com

**Egg Harbor City** • *Egg Harbor City Ind. Park* • Rick Dovey, Chrmn., 500 London Ave., 08215, P 4,500, (609) 965-5264, Fax (609) 965-0715, www.eggharborcity.org

**Elizabeth** • *Elizabeth Dev. Co.* • Daniel Devanney, Exec. Dir., 288 N. Broad St., P.O. Box 512, 07207, P 120,000, (908) 289-0262, Fax (908) 558-1142, www.edcnj.org

**Elizabeth** • *Planning & Comm. Dev.* • Oscar Ocasio, Dir. of Planning, City Hall, 50 Winfield Scott Plaza, 07201, P 120,000, (908) 820-4160, Fax (908) 820-3776, www.elizabethnj.org

**Florence** • *Florence Twp. Eco. Dev. Cncl.* • Municipal Complex, 711 Broad St., 08518, P 10,746, (609) 499-2525, Fax (609) 499-1186, www.florence-nj.com

**Forked River** • *Lacey Twp. Dept. of Comm. Dev.* • John Curtin, Dir., 818 W. Lacey Rd., Municipal Bldg., 08731, P 25,346, (609) 693-1100, Fax (609) 693-8466, www.laceytownship.org

**Freehold** • *Monmouth County Dept. of Eco. Dev. & Tourism* • 31 E. Main St., 07728, P 645,000, (732) 431-7470, Fax (732) 294-5930, www.visitmonmouth.com

**Galloway** • *Galloway Twp. Eco. Dev. Advisory Comm.* • 300 E. Jimmy Leeds Rd., 08205, P 38,207, (609) 652-3700, Fax (609) 652-1967, www.aclink.org/galloway

**Hamilton** • *Twp. of Hamilton Dept. of Tech. & Eco. Dev.* • Michael Angarone, Dir. of Tech., 2090 Greenwood Ave., P.O. Box 00150, 08650, P 90,000, (609) 890-3519, Fax (609) 890-3876, mangarone@hamiltonnj.com, www.hamiltonnj.com

**Hillsborough** • *Hillsborough Twp. Eco. & Bus. Dev. Comm.* • Gene Strupinsky, Bus. Advocate, 379 S. Branch Rd., 08844, P 36,600, (908) 369-4313, Fax (908) 369-6034, ebdc@hillsborough-nj.org, www.hillsborough-nj.org

**Jersey City** • *Jersey City Eco. Dev. Corp.* • Eugene Nelson, CEO, 30 Montgomery St., Rm. 820, 07302, P 240,000, (201) 333-7797, Fax (201) 333-9323, www.jcedc.org

**Kearny** • *Kearny Enterprise Zone/Dev. Corp.* • Town Hall Annex, 402 Kearny Ave., 07032, P 40,513, (201) 955-7400, Fax (201) 998-5171, www.kearnynjuez.org

**Lakewood** • *Lakewood Dev. Corp.* • Russell K. Corby, Exec. Dir., 231 3rd St., 08701, P 60,000, (732) 364-2500, Fax (732) 901-3647, www.twp.lakewood.nj.us

**Long Branch** • *Long Branch Dept. of Eco. Dev.* • Jacob Jones, Dir., 344 Broadway, 07740, P 32,350, (732) 923-2043, Fax (732) 263-0218, www.longbranch.org

**Manalapan** • *Manalapan Twp. Eco. Dev. Comm.* • Tara Lovrich, Admin., 120 Rte. 522, Municipal Complex, 07726, P 33,000, (732) 446-3200, Fax (732) 446-9615, www.twp.manalapan.nj.us

**Mays Landing** • *Hamilton Twp. Ind. Comm.* • Robert Ravell, Chrmn., 6101 13th St., 08330, P 23,000, (609) 625-0368, Fax (609) 909-1348, www.hamiltonbusinesspark.com

**Mickleton** • *East Greenwich Twp. Enterprise Comm.* • James Watson, Dir., 159 Democrat Rd., 08056, P 5,430, (856) 423-0654, Fax (856) 224-0296, www.eastgreenwichnj.com

**Millville** • *Millville Eco. Dev.* • Donald Ayres, Dir., City Hall, 12 S. High St., P.O. Box 609, 08332, P 26,000, (856) 825-7000, Fax (856) 825-3236, www.millville.nj.gov

**Monmouth Junction** • *South Brunswick Twp. Ind. & Commerce Comm.* • Dan Frankel, Chrmn., Planning Dept., P.O. Box 190, 08852, P 41,000, (732) 329-4000, Fax (732) 274-2084, www.sbtnj.net

**Monroe Twp.** • *Monroe Twp. Eco. Dev. Comm.* • Michael C. Konowicz, Chrmn., 1 Municipal Complex, 08831, P 35,000, (732) 521-4400, Fax (732) 521-5659, www.monroetwp.com

**Moorestown** • *Moorestown Dept. of Comm. Dev.* • Thomas Ford, Dir., 2 Executive Dr., Ste. 10B, 08057, P 19,000, (856) 235-0912, Fax (856) 914-3081, www.moorestown.nj.us

**Morristown** • *Morris County Eco. Dev. Corp.* • Maggie Peters, Exec. Dir., 30 Schuyler Pl., P.O. Box 900, 07963, P 490,593, (973) 539-8270, Fax (973) 326-9025, mpeters@co.morris.nj.us, www.morriscountyedc.org

**Mount Holly** • *Burlington County Eco. Dev. & Reg. Planning* • Mark Remsa, Dir., 50 Rancocas Rd., P.O. Box 6000, 08060, P 423,394, (609) 265-5055, Fax (609) 265-5006, www.co.burlington.nj.us

**New Brunswick** • *Middlesex County Ofc. Of Eco. Dev.* • Carl Spataro, Dir., JFK Square, P.O. Box 871, 08901, P 786,971, (732) 745-3433, Fax (732) 745-5911, carl.spataro@co.middlesex.nj.us, www.co.middlesex.nj.us

**New Brunswick** • *New Brunswick Dev. Corp.* • Christopher Paladino, Pres., 120 Albany St., 7th Flr., 08901, P 49,000, (732) 249-2220, Fax (732) 249-4671, www.devco.org

**Newark** • *Eco. Dev. Corp. Essex County* • Deborah Collins, Exec. Dir., 465 Martin Luther King Blvd., Rm. 49, 07102, P 798,000, (973) 621-4457, (973) 621-5420, Fax (973) 621-2545

**Northfield** • *Atlantic County Ofc. of Policy, Planning & Eco. Dev.* • Joseph Maher, Dept. Head, Dolphin Ave. & New Rd., P.O. Box 719, 08225, P 271,015, (609) 645-5898, Fax (609) 645-5836, www.aclink.org

**Old Bridge** • *Old Bridge Eco. Dev. Corp.* • 1 Old Bridge Plaza, 08857, P 64,000, (732) 721-5600, Fax (732) 607-7957, www.oldbridge.com

**Paramus** • *Commerce & Ind. Assn. Of N. J.* • John Galandak, Pres., S. 61 Paramus Rd., 07652, P 1,000,000, M 1,500, (201) 368-2100, Fax (201) 368-3438, info@cianj.org, www.cianj.org

**Paterson** • *City of Paterson Dept. of Comm. Dev.* • Gary Melchiano, Dir. of Eco. Dev., 125 Ellison St., 2nd Flr., 07505, P 139,000, (973) 321-1212, Fax (973) 321-1202, www.cityofpaterson.com

**Perth Amboy** • *Ofc. Of Eco. & Comm. Dev.* • 1 Olive St., 2nd Flr., 08861, P 47,303, (732) 826-1690, Fax (732) 442-9274, www.ci.perthamboy.nj.us

**Piscataway** • *Piscataway Ind. Adv. Comm.* • Jim Perry, Chrmn., 455 Hoes Ln., 08854, P 59,000, (732) 562-2300, Fax (732) 743-2500, www.piscatawaynj.org

**Plainfield** • *Plainfield Ofc. of Eco. Dev.* • 515 Watchung Ave., City Hall, 2nd Flr., 07060, P 48,000, (908) 753-3699, Fax (908) 753-3070, www.plainfield.com

**Rahway** • *Rahway Center Partnership* • Ray Mikell, Exec. Dir., 67 Lewis St., 2nd Flr., P.O. Box 1711, 07065, P 25,000, (732) 396-3545, Fax (732) 396-3693, rmikell9@aol.com

**Rutherford** • *Rutherford Eco. Dev. Comm.* • 176 Park Ave., 07070, P 18,000, (201) 460-3001, Fax (201) 460-3003, www.rutherford-nj.com

**South Orange** • *Organization Dev. Network* • Dr. Peter F. Norlin, 71 Valley St. #301, 07079, P M, 4,200, (973) 763-7337, Fax (973) 763-7488, www.odnetworking.org

**Totowa** • *Passaic County Dept. of Eco. Dev.* • Deborah Hoffman, Dir., 930 Riverview Dr., Ste. 250, 07512, P 499,060, (973) 569-4720, Fax (973) 569-4725, ecodev@passaiccountynj.org, www.passaiccountynj.org

**Trenton** • *Div. of Eco. Dev.* • City of Trenton, 319 E. State St., 08608, P 85,403, (609) 989-3509, Fax (609) 989-4243, www.trentonnj.org

EDC

**Trenton** • *Mercer County Ofc. of Eco. Opportunity* • Mercer County Admin. Bldg., 640 S. Broad St., 08650, P 350,000, (609) 989-6555, Fax (609) 695-4943, charlesh@mercercounty.org, www.mercercounty.org

**Union** • *Union County Eco. Dev. Corp. (UCEDC)* • Thomas Brown, Pres., Liberty Hall Center, 1085 Morris Ave., 07083, P 540,000, (908) 527-1166, Fax (908) 527-1207, www.ucedc.com

**Union City** • *Union City Comm. Dev.* • Kennedy Ng, Dir., 3715 Palisade Ave., 07087, P 65,000, (201) 348-2764, Fax (201) 348-9069

**Vineland** • *Vineland Eco. Dev.* • City Hall, 640 E. Wood St., 4th Flr., 08360, P 59,248, (856) 794-4000, Fax (856) 794-6199, economic development@vinelandcity.org, www.vinelandbusiness.com

**Voorhees** • *Voorhees Twp. Eco. Dev.* • Michael Marchitto Jr., Dir., 620 Berlin Rd., 08043, P 30,000, (856) 216-0473, Fax (856) 428-2514, edc@voorheesnj.com, www.voorheesnj.com

**Washington** • *Warren County Eco. Dev. Corp/* • Robert Goltz, Pres./CEO, 10 Brass Castle Rd., 07882, P 105,765, (908) 835-9200, Fax (908) 835-9296, info@warrencountychamber.org, www.warrencountychamber.org

**Wayne** • *Wayne Twp. Ind. & Eco. Dev. Comm.* • John Szabo, Exec. Dir., 475 Valley Rd., 07470, P 54,069, (973) 694-1800, Fax (973) 694-8136, www.waynetownship.com

**West Milford** • *West Milford Planning Dept.* • 1480 Union Valley Rd., 07480, P 27,000, (973) 728-2796, Fax (973) 728-2843, planning@westmilford.org, www.westmilford.org

**West Orange** • *Downtown West Orange Alliance* • Denise Esposito, Exec. Dir., 66 Main St., 07052, P 46,000, (973) 325-4109, Fax (973) 325-6359, downtown@westorange.org, www.downtownwestorange.org

**Westfield** • *Downtown Westfield Corp.* • Shery Cronin, Exec. Dir., 105 Elm St., 07090, P 30,000, (908) 789-9444, Fax (908) 789-7550, s.cronin@westfieldtoday.com, www.westfieldtoday.com

**Woodbridge** • *Woodbridge Eco. Dev. Corp.* • 90 Woodbridge Center Dr., 2nd Flr., 07095, P 100,000, (732) 602-6029

**Woodbury** • *Gloucester County Bus. & Eco. Dev.* • Lisa Morina, Dir., CC Budd Blvd., Rte. 45, 08096, P 260,000, (856) 384-6930, Fax (856) 384-6938, www.co.gloucester.nj.us

# New Mexico

## State

**State of New Mexico Eco. Dev. Dept.** • Fred Mondragon, Cabinet Secy., 1100 St. Francis Dr., Ste. 1060, Santa Fe, 87505, (505) 827-0300, Fax (505) 827-0328, edd.info@state.nm.us, www.gonm.biz

## Communities

**Albuquerque** • *Albuquerque Eco. Dev. Inc.* • Gary Tonjes, Pres., 851 University Blvd. S.E., Ste. 203, 87106, P 801,000, M 411, (505) 246-6200, (800) 451-2933, Fax (505) 246-6219, info@abq.org, www.abq.org

**Belen** • *Belen Eco. Dev. Corp.* • Claudette Riley, Exec. Dir., 100 S. Main St., 87002, P 7,100, (505) 459-6159, Fax (505) 864-8408, belenedc@belenedc.org, www.belenedc.org

**Carlsbad** • *Carlsbad Dept. of Dev.* • 107 W. Mermod, P.O. Box 1090, 88221, P 25,600, (575) 887-6562, (800) 658-2709, Fax (575) 885-0818, cdod@developcarlsbad.org, www.developcarlsbad.org

**Farmington** • *San Juan Eco. Dev. Service* • Margaret McDaniel, Dir., 5101 College Blvd., 87402, P 126,208, (505) 566-3720, (800) 854-5053, Fax (505) 566-3698, sjeds@sanjuaneds.com, www.sanjuaneds.com.

**Gallup** • *NW New Mexico Cncl. of Governments* • Patty Lundstrom, Exec. Dir., 409 S. 2nd, 87301, P 176,000, (505) 722-4327, Fax (505) 722-9211

**Grants** • *Cibola Communities Eco. Dev. Found.* • Star Gonzales, Exec. Dir., P.O. Box 277, 87020, P 10,000, (505) 287-4802, (800) 748-2142, Fax (505) 287-8224, www.discovergrants.org

**Hobbs** • *Eco. Dev. Corp. of Lea County* • Bethe Cunningham, Pres./CEO, 200 E. Broadway, Ste. A201, P.O. Box 1376, 88241, P 55,000, (575) 397-2039, Fax (575) 392-2300, www.edclc.org

**Las Cruces** • *MVEDA* • Steve Vierck, Pres., 505 S. Main, Ste. 134, P.O. Box 1299, 88004, P 189,000, (505) 525-2852, (800) 523-6833, Fax (505) 523-5707, info@mveda.com, www.mveda.com, www.southwest-advantage.com

**Los Alamos** • *Los Alamos Commerce Dev. Corp.* • Kevin Holsapple, Exec. Dir., 190 Central Park Sq., P.O. Box 1206, 87544, P 18,000, (505) 662-0001, Fax (505) 662-0099, lacdc@losalamos.org, www.losalamos.org/lacdc

**Portales** • *Roosevelt County Comm. Dev.* • Don Thomas, V.P. of Comm. Dev., 100 S. Ave. A, 88130, P 18,500, M (505) 356-8541, (800) 635-8036, Fax (505) 356-8542, chamber@portales.com, www.portales.com

**Raton** • *Raton Eco. Dev. Cncl.* • 100 Clayton Rd., P.O. Box 1211, 87740, P 7,282, (505) 445-3689, (800) 638-6161, Fax (505) 445-3680, ratonchamber@bacavalley.com, www.raton.info

**Rio Rancho** • *AMREP Southwest* • Jimmy Wall Jr., V.P., 333 Rio Rancho Blvd. N.E., 87124, P 62,000, (505) 892-9200, Fax (505) 896-9180, www.amrepsw.com

**Rio Rancho** • *Rio Rancho Eco. Dev. Corp.* • Noreen Scott, Pres./Exec. Dir., 1201 Rio Rancho Blvd., Ste. C, 87124, P 70,000, (505) 891-4305, (800) 544-8373, Fax (505) 891-4297, info@rredc.org, www.rredc.org

**Roswell** • *Chaves County Dev. Found.* • Bob Donnell, Exec. Dir., 131 W. Second St., P.O. Box 849, 88202, P 61,382, (505) 622-1975, Fax (505) 624-6870, rdonnell@chavescounty.net, www.chavescounty.net

**Santa Fe** • *Santa Fe Eco. Dev., Inc.* • Catherine Zacher, Pres., 624 Agua Fria St., P.O. Box 8184, 87504, P 130,000, (505) 984-2842, Fax (505) 989-8614, sfedi@sfedi.org, www.sfedi.org

**Silver City** • *Silver City-Grant County Eco. Dev. Corp.* • John Rossfeld, Pres., 1203 N. Hudson St., P.O. Box 2672, 88061, P 32,000, (505) 534-1045, Fax (505) 538-6391, ralph@silvercitybusiness.com, www.silvercity-business.com

**Tucumcari** • *Greater Tucumcari Eco. Dev. Corp.* • Patrick Vanderpool, Exec. Dir., 1500 W. Tucumcari Blvd., P.O. Box 1392, 88401, P 6,000, M 48, (575) 461-4079, Fax (575) 461-1838, www.tucumcari.biz

# New York

## Federal

**U.S. SBA, Syracuse Dist. Ofc.** • Bernard Paprocki, Dist. Dir., 401 S. Salina St., 5th Flr., Syracuse, 13202, (315) 471-9393, Fax (315) 471-9288, www.sba.gov/ny/syracuse

## State

**Empire State Dev.** • Marisa Lago, Co-Chrmn., 30 S. Pearl St., Albany, 12245, (518) 292-5100, www.empire.state.ny.us

## Communities

**Albany** • *Center for Eco. Growth Inc.* • 63 State St., 12207, P 1,157,000, (518) 465-8975, Fax (518) 465-6681, www.ceg.org

**Albany** • *NYS Eco. Dev. Cncl.* • Brian McMahon, Exec. Dir., 111 Washington Ave., 6th Flr., 12210, P 18,000,000, (518) 426-4058, Fax (518) 426-4059, www.nysedc.org

**Amsterdam** • *City of Amsterdam IDA* • Frank Valiante, Exec. Dir., 61 Church St., 12010, P 19,800, (518) 842-5011, Fax (518) 843-2862, www.amsterdamida.com

**Auburn** • *City of Auburn Ofc. of Plan. & Eco. Dev.* • Jennifer Haines, Memorial City Hall, 24 South St., 13021, P 28,574, (315) 255-4115, Fax (315) 253-0282, www.ci.auburn.ny.us

**Babylon** • *Babylon Ind. Dev. Agency* • Robert Stricoff, CEO, 47 W. Main, Ste. 3, 11702, P 227,000, (631) 587-3679, Fax (631) 587-3675, www.babylonida.org

**Batavia** • *Genessee County Eco. Dev. Center* • Steven G. Hyde, Pres./CEO, 1 Mill St., 14020, P 59,000, (585) 343-4866, Fax (585) 343-0848, gcedc@gcedc.com, www.gcedc.com

**Bath** • *Steuben County Ind. Dev. Agency* • James P. Sherron, Exec. Dir., 7234 Rte. 54, P.O. Box 393, 14810, P 100,000, (607) 776-3316, Fax (607) 776-5039, www.steubencountyida.com

**Belmont** • *Allegany County Ofc. of Dev.* • Crossroad Commerce Conf. Center, 6087 State Rte. 19 N., 14813, P 49,000, (585) 268-7472, Fax (585) 268-7473, development@alleganyco.com, www.alleganyco.com

**Belmont** • *Friendship Empire Zone* • Wendall Brown, Dir., 6087 State Rte. 19N., Ste. 170, 14813, P 2,500, (585) 268-9095, Fax (585) 268-5085, wbrown@accordcorp.org, www.friendshipedz.com

**Bethpage** • *Greater NY Dev. Co./Long Island Dev. Corp.* • Roslyn D. Goldmacher, Pres./CEO, 45 Seaman Ave., 11714, P 2,700,000, (516) 433-5000, (866) 433-5432, Fax (516) 433-5046, biz-loans@gnydc.org, www.lidc.org

**Binghamton** • *Broome County Ind. Dev. Agency* • Richard D'Attilio, Exec. Dir., 44 Hawley St., 5th Flr., P.O. Box 1510, 13902, P 201,533, (607) 584-9000, Fax (607) 584-9009, info@bcida.com, www.bcida.com

**Binghamton** • *Empire State Dev.-Southern Tier* • Kevin McLaughlin, Reg. Dir., 44 Hawley St., Ste. 1508, State Office Bldg., 13901, (607) 721-8605, Fax (607) 721-8613, www.empire.state.ny.us

**Binghamton** • *NYS Trade Adjust. Asst. Ctr.* • Louis G. McKeage, Dir., 81 State St., Ste. 4, 13901, (607) 771-0875, Fax (607) 724-2404, www.nystaac.org

**Buffalo** • *Buffalo Niagara Enterprise* • 665 Main St., Ste. 200, 14203, P 1,292,000, (716) 842-1330, (800) 916-9073, Fax (716) 842-1724, info@buffaloniagara.org, www.buffaloniagara.org

**Buffalo** • *Empire State Dev.-Western NY Region* • Christina Orsi, Reg. Dir., 95 Perry St., Ste. 500, 14203, (716) 846-8260, Fax (716) 856-1744, www.empire.state.ny.us

**Buffalo** • *Erie County Ofc. of Eco. Dev.* • Edward A. Rath County Ofc. Bldg., 95 Franklin St., 10th Flr., 14202, P 952,000, (716) 858-8390, Fax (716) 858-7248, www.erie.gov

**Canandaigua** • *Ontario County Eco. Dev.* • Michael J. Manikowski, Exec. Dir., 20 Ontario St., Ste. 106-B, 14424, P 100,000, (585) 396-4460, Fax (585) 396-4594, golfbag@co.ontario.ny.us, www.ontariocountydev.org

**Canastota** • *Madison County Ind. Dev. Agency* • Kipp Hicks, Exec. Dir., 3215 Seneca Tpk., 13032, P 70,000, (315) 697-9817, Fax (315) 697-8169, director@madisoncountyida.com, www.madisoncountyida.com

**Canton** • *St. Lawrence County Ofc. of Eco. Dev.* • Raymond H. Fountain, Dir., 80 State Hwy. 310, Ste. 8, 13617, P 111,973, (315) 379-9806, Fax (315) 386-2573, slcida@northnet.org, www.slcida.com

**Carmel** • *Putnam County Eco. Dev. Corp.* • Kevin Bailey, Pres., 34 Gleneida Ave., 10512, (845) 228-8066, Fax (845) 225-0311, www.putnamedc.org

**Champlain** • *Town of Champlain IDA* • Robert Casey, Chrmn., P.O. Box 3144, 12919, P 6,700, (518) 298-8160, Fax (518) 298-8896

**Corning** • *Three Rivers Dev. Inc.* • John E. Benjamin, Pres., 114 Pine St., Ste. 201, 14830, P 30,000, (607) 962-4693, Fax (607) 936-9132, www.threeriversdevelopment.com

**Coxsackie** • *Greene County Ind. Dev. Agency* • Alexander Mathes, Exec. Dir., 270 Mansion St., 12051, (518) 731-5500, Fax (518) 731-5520, www.greeneida.com

**Dutchess** • *see New Windsor*

**Elmira** • *Chemung County Ind. Dev. Agency* • George Miner, Dir., 400 E. Church St., 14901, P 90,000, (607) 733-6513, Fax (607) 734-2698, gminer@steg.com, www.steg.com

**Endwell** • *Local Dev. Corp. for Town of Union* • Joseph Moody, Eco. Dev. Dir., 3111 E. Main St., 13760, P 60,000, (607) 786-2945, Fax (607) 786-2321, jmoody@townofunion.com, www.townofunion.com

**Farmingville** • *Town of Brookhaven Supv. Ofc./Eco. Dev.* • Rick Kruse, Dir., 1 Independence Hill, 11738, P 470,000, (631) 451-6563, Fax (631) 451-6925, www.brookhaven.org

**Fonda** • *Montgomery County Eco. Dev. & Planning* • Kenneth Rose, Dir., Bus. Dev. Center, 9 Park St., P.O. Box 1500, 12068, P 51,000, (518) 853-8334, Fax (518) 853-8336, krose@co.montgomery.ny.us, www.co.montgomery.ny.us

**Fort Edward** • *Washington County Local Dev. Corp.* • County Municipal Center, 383 Broadway, 12828, P 61,042, (518) 746-2292, Fax (518) 746-2293, mgalough@co.washington.ny.us, www.wcldc.org

**Garden City** • *Nassau County Ind. Dev. Agency* • Joseph Gioino, Exec. Dir., 1100 Franklin Ave., Ste. 300, 11530, P 1,338,000, (516) 571-4160, Fax (516) 571-4161, www.nassauida.org

**Geneseo** • *Livingston County Eco. Dev. Dept.* • Patrick J. Rountree, Dir., 6 Court St., Rm. 306, 14454, P 65,000, (585) 243-7124, Fax (585) 243-7126, build-here@co.livingston.ny.us, www.build-here.com

**Goshen** • *Orange County Partnership* • Maureen Halahan, Pres./CEO, 40 Matthews St., Ste. 108, 10924, (845) 294-2323, Fax (845) 294-8023, info@ocpartnership.org, www.ocpartnership.org

**Hauppauge** • *Empire State Dev.-Long Island Reg.* • Andrea Lohness, Reg. Dir., 150 Motor Pkwy., Ste. 311, 11788, (631) 435-0717, Fax (631) 435-3399, alohness@empire.state.ny.us, www.nylovesbiz.com

**Hauppauge** • *Suffolk County Dept. of Eco. Dev.* • 100 Veterans Memorial Hwy., P.O. Box 6100, 11788, P 1,419,369, (631) 853-4800, Fax (631) 853-4888, www.suffolkcountyny.gov

**Hempstead** • *Incorporated Village of Hempstead Comm. Dev Agency* • Claude Gooding, Commissioner, 50 Clinton St., Ste. 504, 11550, P 50,000, (516) 485-5737, Fax (516) 485-1667, www.hempsteadeda.org

**Hempstead** • *Planning & Eco. Dev. Agency of Hempstead* • 200 N. Franklin Ave., 11550, P 780,000, (516) 538-7100, Fax (516) 538-4264, www.townofhempstead.org

**Herkimer** • *Herkimer County Ind. Dev. Agency* • Mark Feane, Exec. Dir., 320 N. Prospect St., P.O. Box 390, 13350, P 67,000, (315) 867-1373, Fax (315) 867-1515, ida@herkimercounty.org, www.herkimercountyida.com

**EDC**

**Hornell** · *Hornell Ind. Dev. Agency* · James W. Griffin, Exec. Dir., 40 Main St., 14843, P 11,000, (607) 324-0310, Fax (607) 324-3776, griff@hornellny.com, www.hornellny.com

**Hudson** · *Columbia County Planning Dept.* · Timothy Stalker, Chrmn., 401 State St., 12534, P 63,094, (518) 828-3375, Fax (518) 828-2825, www.columbiacountyny.com

**Islip** · *Town of Islip Eco. Dev. Div.* · William Mannix, Dir., 40 Nassau Ave., 11751, P 300,000, (631) 224-5512, Fax (631) 224-5532, www.isliptown.org

**Ithaca** · *Tompkins County Area Dev., Inc.* · 200 E. Buffalo St., Ste. 102A, 14850, P 100,000, (607) 273-0005, Fax (607) 273-8964, info@tcad.org, www.tcad.org

**Jamestown** · *County of Chautauqua Ind. Dev. Agency* · William Daly, Admin. Dir., 200 Harrison St., 14701, P 141,000, (716) 661-8900, Fax (716) 664-4515, ccida@ccida.com, www.chautauquacounty.biz

**Johnstown** · *Fulton County Eco. Dev. Corp.* · Jeff Bray, Exec. V.P., 110 Decker Dr., Ste. 110, 12095, P 55,073, (518) 773-8700, Fax (518) 773-8701, www.sites4u.org

**Johnstown** · *Fulton County Ind. Dev. Agency* · James Mraz, Exec. Dir., Fulton County Planning Dept., 1 E. Montgomery St., 12095, P 55,073, (518) 736-5660, Fax (518) 762-4597, www.fultoncountyny.gov

**Kingston** · *Ulster County Dev. Corp.* · 5 Development Ct., 12401, P 178,000, (845) 338-8840, Fax (845) 338-0409, www.ulsterny.com

**Little Valley** · *Cattaraugus County Dept. of Eco. Dev. & Tourism* · Thomas Livak, Dir., 303 Court St., 14755, P 83,955, (716) 938-2313, (800) 331-0543, Fax (716) 938-2779, tmlivak@cattco.org, www.cattco.org

**Lockport** · *Lockport IDA* · Alan Hamilton, Chrmn., Town Hall, 6560 Dysinger Rd., 14094, P 21,000, (716) 439-9535, Fax (716) 439-9715, town-lkptida@elockport.com, www.lockportida.com

**Lyons** · *Wayne County Ind. Dev. Agency* · Peg Churchill, Exec. Dir., 16 William St., 14489, P 95,000, (315) 946-5917, Fax (315) 946-5918, wedcny@co.wayne.ny.us, www.wedcny.org

**Malone** · *County of Franklin Ind. Dev. Agency* · Brad Jackson, Exec. Dir., 10 Elm St., Ste. 2, 12953, P 51,134, (518) 483-9472, Fax (518) 483-2900, www.franklinida.org

**Mohawk** · *Mohawk Valley Eco. Dev. Dist.* · Gregory A Eisenhut, Exec. Dir., 26 W. Main St., P.O. Box 69, 13407, P 450,000, (315) 866-4671, Fax (315) 866-9862, mvedd@twcny.rr.com

**Monticello** · *Partnership for Eco. Dev. for Sullivan County* · 198 Bridgeville Rd., 12701, (845) 794-1110, Fax (845) 794-2324, www.scpartnership.com

**New Windsor** · *Empire State Dev.-Mid-Hudson Reg. Ofc.* · Michael Oates, Interim Dir., 33 Airport Center Dr., Ste. 201, 12553, (845) 567-4882, Fax (845) 567-6085, www.empire.state.ny.us

**New Windsor** · *Hudson Valley Eco. Dev. Corp.* · Anthony Campagiorni, Pres./CEO, 555 Hudson Valley Ave., Ste. 106, 12553, (845) 220-2244, Fax (845) 220-2247, www.hvedc.com

**New York** · *Empire State Dev.-NYC* · Marisa Lago, 633 3rd Ave., 37th Flr., 10017, (212) 803-2200, Fax (212) 803-3715, www.empire.state.ny.us

**New York** · *New York City Eco. Dev. Corp.* · 110 Williams St., 4th Flr., 10038, (212) 619-5000, Fax (212) 312-3913, www.nycedc.com

**Newburgh** · *Hudson Valley Reg. Cncl.* · 1662 Rte. 300, 12550, P 1,000,000, (845) 564-4075, hvrc@hvi.net, www.hvregional council.org

**Oneonta** · *Otsego County Eco. Dev. Dept.* · Carolyn Lewis, Eco. Dev. Dir., 242 Main St., 13820, P 61,000, (607) 432-8871, Fax (607) 432-5117, lewisc@otsegocounty.com, www.otsego economicdevelopment.com

**Ontario** · *Town of Onatario Ofc. of Eco. Dev.* · William Riddell, Dir., 6551 Knickerbocker Rd., 14519, P 10,000, (315) 524-5908, Fax (315) 524-7465, riddell@ontariotown.org, www.ontariotown.org

**Orange** · *see New Windsor*

**Oswego** · *Operation Oswego County* · L. Michael Treadwell, Exec. Dir., 44 W. Bridge St., 13126, P 121,785, (315) 343-1545, Fax (315) 343-1546, ooc@oswegocounty.org, www.oswegocounty.org

**Owego** · *Tioga County Ind. Dev. Agency* · Aaron Gowan, Chrmn., 56 Main St., 13827, P 50,000, (607) 687-8255, Fax (607) 687-1435, www.developtioga.com

**Pearl River** · *Rockland Eco. Dev. Corp.* · Eric Dranoff, Chair, Two Blue Hill Plaza, P.O. Box 1575, 10965, P 293,626, (845) 735-0205, Fax (845) 735-5736, www.redc.org

**Penn Yan** · *Yates County IDA* · Steve Griffin, CEO, One Keuka Business Park, 14527, P 24,600, (315) 536-7328, Fax (315) 536-2389, info@yatesida.com, www.yatesida.com

**Plattsburgh** · *The Development Corp.* · Mrs. A. Kurtz, Pres., 61 Area Development Dr., 12901, P 80,000, (518) 563-3100, (888) 699-6757, Fax (518) 562-2232, www.thedevelopcorp.com

**Poughkeepsie** · *Dutchess County Eco. Dev. Corp.* · John MacEnroe, Pres./CEO, 3 Neptune Rd., 12601, P 280,000, (845) 463-5410, Fax (845) 463-5401, dcedc@dcedc.com, www.thinkdutchess.com

**Putnam** · *see New Windsor*

**Rochester** · *County of Monroe Ind. Dev. Agency* · Judy Seil, Exec. Dir., City Place, Ste. 8100, 50 W. Main St., 14614, P 720,000, (585) 753-2000, Fax (585) 753-2028, www.monroecounty.gov

**Rochester** · *Empire State Dev.-Finger Lakes* · Kevin Hurley, Acting Reg. Dir., 400 Andrews St., Ste. 710, 14604, (585) 325-1944, Fax (585) 325-6505, www.empire.state.ny.us

**Rockland** · *see New Windsor*

**Rome** · *Mohawk Valley Edge* · Steven DiMeo, Pres., 153 Brooks Rd., 13441, P 300,000, (315) 338-0393, Fax (315) 338-5694, sjdimeo@mvedge.org, www.mvedge.org

**Salamanca** · *Salamanca Ind. Dev. Agency* · Matt Bull, Proj. Mgr, 225 Wildwood Ave., Ste. 9, 14779, P 6,800, (716) 945-3230, Fax (716) 945-8289, www.salmun.com

**Saranac Lake** · *Adirondack Eco. Dev. Corp.* · 67 Main St., Ste. 200, P.O. Box 1088, 12983, P 150,000, (518) 891-5523, (888) 243-2332, Fax (518) 891-9820, www.aedconline.com

**Saratoga Springs** · *Saratoga Eco. Dev. Corp.* · Dennis Brobston, Pres., 28 Clinton St., 12866, P 196,200, M 350, (518) 587-0945, Fax (518) 587-5855, dbrobston@saratogaedc.com, saratogaedc.com

**Sullivan** · *see New Windsor*

**Syracuse** · *Empire State Dev.* · 620 Erie Blvd. W., Ste. 112, 13204, (315) 425-9110, Fax (315) 425-7156, www.empire.state.ny.us

**Syracuse** · *Onondaga County IDA* · 421 Montgomery St., 14th Flr., 13202, P 486,000, (315) 435-3770, (877) 797-8222, Fax (315) 435-3669, www.syracusecentral.com

**Ulster** · *see New Windsor*

**Utica** · *Empire State Dev.-Mohawk Valley Reg. Ofc.* · Kenneth M. Tompkins, Reg. Dir., 207 Genesee St., Rm. 1604, 13501, (315) 793-2366, Fax (315) 793-2705, www.empire.state.ny.us

**Watkins Glen** · *Schuyler County IDA/Scoped, Inc.* · Kevin Murphy, Chrmn., 2 N. Franklin St., 14891, P 19,500, (607) 535-4341, Fax (607) 535-7221, scoped@scoped.biz, www.scoped.biz

**West Amherst** · *Amherst Ind. Dev. Agency* · James Allen, Exec. Dir., 4287 Main St., 14226, P 115,000, (716) 688-9000, Fax (716) 688-0205, www.amherstida.com

**Westchester** · *see New Windsor*

**White Plains** · *Westchester County Ofc. of Eco. Dev.* · Salvatore Carrera, Dir., 148 Martine Ave., Rm. 903, 10601, (914) 995-2926, Fax (914) 995-3044, www.westchestergov.com/economic

**Yonkers** · *Yonkers Ofc. of Eco. Dev.* · Louis Kirven, Dir., City Hall, 40 S. Broadway, Ste. 416, 10701, P 200,000, (914) 377-6797, Fax (914) 377-6003, Louis.Kirven@YonkersNY.Gov, www.yonkersny.gov

# North Carolina

## Federal

**U.S. SBA, North Carolina Dist. Ofc.** · Lee Cornelison, Dist. Dir., 6302 Fairview Rd., Ste. 300, Charlotte, 28210, (704) 344-6563, Fax (704) 344-6769, www.sba.gov/nc

## State

**North Carolina Dept. of Comm.** · Cindy Messer, Mgr., 3 General Aviation Dr., Fletcher, 28732, (828) 654-9852, Fax (828) 654-9859, cmesser@nccommerce.com, www.nccommerce.com

**North Carolina Dept. of Commerce** · Eugene Byrd, Bus. Dev. Mgr., 301 N. Wilmington, 4301 Mail Service Center, Raleigh, 27699, (919) 733-4151, www.nccommerce.com

## Communities

**Albemarle** · *Stanly County Econ. Dev. Comm.* · 1000 N. 1st St., Ste. 11, 28001, P 60,166, (704) 986-3682, Fax (704) 986-3685, edc@co.stanly.nc.us, www.stanlyedc.org

**Asheboro** · *Randolph County Eco. Dev. Corp.* · Bonnie Renfro, Pres., 919 S. Cox St., Ste. B-2, P.O. Box 2001, 27204, P 135,000, (336) 626-2233, Fax (336) 626-0777, brenfro@rcedc.com, www.rcedc.com

**Asheville** · *Asheville Area C/C-Eco. Dev. Dept.* · Ray Denny, V.P. Eco. Dev., 36 Montford Ave., P.O. Box 1010, 28802, P 224,000, M 2,000, (828) 258-6117, Fax (828) 251-0926, rdenny@asheville chamber.org, www.ashevillechamber.org

**Beech Mountain** · *see Boone*

**Black Mountain** · *see Asheville*

**Blowing Rock** · *see Boone*

**Boone** · *North Carolina Dept. of Commerce* · Joe Holbrook, Sr. Eco. Dev., 206 Southgate Dr., 28607, (828) 262-1345, Fax (828) 262-1495, jholbrook@nccommerce.com, www.investnc.com

**Boone** · *Watauga County Eco. Dev. Comm.* · Joe Furman, Dir., P.O. Box 404, 28607, P 43,117, (828) 264-3082, Fax (828) 265-8080, www.wataugaedc.org

**Brevard** · *Transylvania County Eco. Dev.* · Mark Burrows, Dir., P.O. Box 1578, 28712, P 29,334, (828) 884-3205, Fax (828) 884-3275, mark.burrows@transylvaniacounty.org, econdev.transylvaniacounty.org

**Canton** · *see Waynesville*

**Clyde** · *see Waynesville*

**Danbury** · *Stokes County Eco. Dev.* · Bryan Steen, Dir., 1014 Main St., P.O. Box 20, 27016, P 47,000, (336) 593-2496, Fax (336) 593-2346, questions@stokescounty.org, www.stokescounty.org

**Dobson** · *Surry County Eco. Dev. Partnership Inc.* · Jan Critz, V.P., 118 Hamby Rd., Ste. 146, P.O. Box 1282, 27017, P 73,028, M 150, (336) 401-9900, Fax (336) 401-9901, surryedp@surry.net, www.surryedp.com

**Edenton** · *Edenton-Chowan Eco. Dev.* · Richard Bunch, Exec. Dir., 116 E. King St., P.O. Box 245, 27932, P 16,000, (252) 482-3400, Fax (252) 482-7093, richard.bunch@ncmail.net, www.visitedenton.com

**Edenton** · *Northeastern NC Reg. Eco. Dev. Comm.* · Vann Rogerson, Pres./CEO, 119 W. Water St., 27932, P 340,000, (252) 482-4333, Fax (252) 482-3366, info@ncnortheast.com, www.ncnortheast.com

**Elizabeth City** · *Albemarle Eco. Dev. Comm.* · Wayne Harris, Dir., 405 E. Main St, Ste. 4, P.O. Box 70, 27907, P 40,000, (252) 338-0169, Fax (252) 338-0160, info@discoverec.com, www.discoverec.com

**Elizabethtown** · *Bladen County Eco. Dev. Comm.* · 218A Aviation Pkwy., 28337, P 32,400, (910) 645-2292, Fax (910) 645-2293, edc@bladenco.org, www.bladeninfo.org

**Farmville** · *Farmville Dev. Partnership* · Jan Greene, Admin. Asst., P.O. Box 150, 27828, P 4,500, (252) 753-4670, Fax (252) 753-7313, www.farmville-nc.com

**Forest City** · *Rutherford County Eco. Dev. Comm.* · Tom Johnson, Exec. Dir., 142 E. Main St., Ste. 100, 28043, P 63,570, (828) 248-1716, Fax (828) 248-1771, tjohnson@rutherfordncedc.com, www.rutherfordncedc.com

**Gastonia** · *Gaston County Eco. Dev. Comm.* · Donny Hicks CEcD, Exec. Dir., P.O. Box 2339, 28053, P 195,000, (704) 825-4046, Fax (704) 825-4066, edc@gaston.org, www.gaston.org

**Goldsboro** · *Wayne County Dev. Alliance* · Joanna Thompson, Pres., P.O. Box 1280, 27533, P 114,000, (919) 731-7700, Fax (919) 580-9147, www.waynealliance.org

**Greensboro** · *Greensboro Eco. Dev. Alliance* · Dan Lynch, Pres., 342 N. Elm St., 27401, P 245,000, (336) 387-8302, Fax (336) 510-0295, greensboroeda@greensboro.org, www.greensboroeda.com

**Greenville** · *Pitt County Dev. Comm.* · Wanda Yuhas, Exec. Dir., 111 S. Washington, P.O. Box 837, 27835, P 155,000, (252) 758-1989, Fax (252) 758-0128, pittedc@co.pitt.nc.us, www.locateincarolina.com

**Hazelwood** · *see Waynesville*

**Henderson** · *Vance County EDC* · 1775 Graham Ave., Ste. 105, P.O. Box 2017, 27536, P 44,000, (252) 492-2094, Fax (252) 492-4428, www.vancecountyedc.com

**Hickory** · *Catawba County Eco. Dev. Corp.* · Scott L. Millar, Pres., 1960 13th Ave. Dr. S.E., P.O. Box 3388, 28603, P 148,913, (828) 267-1564, Fax (828) 267-1884, smillar@catawbacountync.gov, www.catawbaedc.org

**High Point** · *High Point Eco. Dev. Corp.* · Mr. Loren Hill, Pres., 211 S. Hamilton St., P.O. Box 230, 27261, P 92,489, (336) 883-3116, Fax (336) 883-3057, loren.hill@highpointnc.gov, www.high-point.net/edc/

**Hillsborough** · *Orange County Eco. Dev. Comm.* · 110 E. King St., P.O. Box 1177, 27278, P 122,000, (919) 245-2325, Fax (919) 644-3008, www.co.orange.nc.us/ecodev

**Jacksonville** · *Onslow County Eco. Dev.* · Jim Reichardt, Dir. of Eco. Dev., 1099 Gum Branch Rd., 28540, P 160,000, (910) 347-3141, Fax (910) 347-2842, jreichardt@jacksonvilleline.org, www.onslowedc.com

**Jefferson** · *Ashe County Eco. Dev. Comm.* · Dr. Patricia Mitchell, Dir. of Eco. Dev., 150 Government Cir., Ste. 2500, 28640, P 25,274, (336) 846-5502, Fax (336) 846-5516, pmitchell@ashencedc.com, www.ashencedc.com

**EDC**

**Kenansville** • *Duplin County EDC* • Cynthia Potter, Admin. Secy., P.O. Box 929, 28349, P 50,000, (910) 296-2180, Fax (910) 296-2184, info@duplinedc.com, www.duplinedc.com

**Kinston** • *Lenoir County Eco. Dev. Dept.* • D. Mark Pope, Exec. Dir., 301 N. Queen St., P.O. Box 897, 28502, P 60,000, (252) 527-1963, Fax (252) 527-1914, mpope@lenoiredc.com, www.lenoiredc.com

**Lenoir** • *Caldwell County Eco. Dev. Comm.* • Alan Wood, Sr. Dev. Mgr., 1909 Hickory Blvd., P.O. Box 2888, 28645, P 77,000, (828) 728-0768, Fax (828) 726-8926, info@caldwelledc.org, www.caldwelledc.org

**Lexington** • *Davidson County Eco. Dev.* • Steve Googe, Exec. Dir., P.O. Box 1287, 27293, P 164,000, (336) 243-1900, Fax (336) 243-3027, slgooge@davidsoncountyedc.com, www.co.davidson.nc.us/dcedc

**Lincolnton** • *Lincoln Eco. Dev. Assn.* • Barry Matherly, Exec. Dir., 502 E. Main St., P.O. Box 2050, 28093, P 63,780, M 130, (704) 732-1511, Fax (704) 736-8451, leda@lincolneda.org, www.lincolneda.org

**Marion** • *McDowell Eco. Dev. Assn.* • Charles Abernathy, Exec. Dir., 25 S. Garden St., P.O. Box 1289, 28752, P 43,000, (828) 652-9391, Fax (828) 652-8775, medainc@verizon.net, www.mcdowelleda.org

**Mocksville** • *Davie County Eco. Dev. Comm.* • Terry Bralley, Pres., 135 S. Salisbury St., 27028, P 36,000, (336) 751-5513, (336) 751-2714, Fax (336) 751-7408, www.co.davie.nc.us, terry.bralley@daviecounty.com, www.daviecounty.com

**Monroe** • *Union County Partnership for Progress* • Maurice Ewing CEcD, Pres./CEO, P.O. Box 1789, 28111, P 160,000, (704) 283-0640, info@unioncpp.com, www.unioncpp.com

**Morehead City** • *Carteret County Eco. Dev. Cncl.* • Dave Inscoe, Exec. Dir., 3615 Arendell St., 28557, P 64,000, M 300, (252) 222-6120, Fax (252) 222-6124, edc@carteret.edu, www.carteretedc.com

**New Bern** • *Craven County EDC* • James T. Davis III, Exec. Dir., 100 Industrial Dr., 28562, P 93,000, (252) 633-5300, Fax (252) 633-3253, cravenedc@cconnect.net, www.cravenedc.com

**North Wilkesboro** • *Wilkes Eco. Dev. Corp.* • Donald Alexander, Exec. Dir., 717 Main St., P.O. Box 727, 28659, P 65,000, (336) 838-1501, Fax (336) 838-1693, dalexander@wilkesedc.com, www.wilkesedc.com

**Oxford** • *Granville Eco. Dev. Comm.* • C. Leon Turner, Exec. Dir., 310 Williamsboro St., P.O. Box 26, 27565, P 53,346, (919) 693-5911, Fax (919) 693-1952, gedcoffice@nc.rr.com, www.granvillecounty.com

**Pinehurst** • *Moore County Partners in Progress* • Ray Ogden, Exec. Dir., P.O. Box 5885, 28374, P 82,292, M 35, (910) 246-0311, Fax (910) 246-0312, econdev@moorebusiness.org, www.moorebusiness.org

**Roanoke Rapids** • *Halifax Dev. Comm.* • Cathy A. Scott, Exec. Dir., P.O. Box 246, 27870, P 57,500, (252) 519-2630, Fax (252) 519-2632, cathyscott@halifaxdevelopment.com, www.halifaxdevelopment.com

**Rocky Mount** • *Carolinas Gateway Partnership* • John Gessaman, Pres./CEO, 427 Falls Rd., 27804, P 143,000, (252) 442-0114, Fax (252) 442-7315, cgp@econdev.org, www.econdev.org

**Salisbury** • *Salisbury-Rowan Eco. Dev. Comm.* • Robert Van Geons, Exec. Dir., 204 E. Innes St., 28144, P 130,000, (704) 637-5526, Fax (704) 637-0173, robert@rowanedc.com, www.rowanedc.com

**Sparta** • *Alleghany County Eco. Dev. Corp.* • Don Adams, County Mgr., 348 S. Main St., P.O. Box 366, 28675, P 10,874, (336) 372-4179, Fax (336) 372-5969, manageralc@skybest.com, www.alleghanycounty-nc.gov

**Spruce Pine** • *Mitchell County Eco. Dev. Comm.* • Jack Dobson, Dir., 167 Locust Ave., 28777, P 15,900, (828) 766-6009, Fax (828) 765-9655, edc@mitchell-county.com

**Statesville** • *Greater Statesville Dev. Corp.* • C. Michael Smith, Dir., 115 E. Front St., 28677, P 70,000, (704) 871-0062, Fax (704) 871-0223, info@greaterstatesville.org, www.greaterstatesville.org

**Troy** • *Montgomery Eco. Dev. Corp.* • Judy Stevens, Exec. Dir., 444 N. Main St., P.O. Box 637, 27371, P 27,000, (910) 572-2575, Fax (910) 572-5193, judy@montgomery-county.com, www.montgomery-county.com

**Wadesboro** • *Anson County Eco. Dev. Dept.* • Misty Harris, Dir. of Eco. Dev., P.O. Box 339, 28170, P 25,500, (704) 694-9513, Fax (704) 694-3138, mharris@co.anson.nc.us, www.ansonedc.org

**Warrenton** • *Warren County Eco. Dev. Comm.* • Dir., 130 N. Main St., P.O. Box 804, 27589, P 20,000, (252) 257-3114, Fax (252) 257-2277, edc@warrencountync.org, www.warrencountync.org

**Washington** • *Beaufort County Eco. Dev. Comm.* • Tom Thompson, Exec. Dir., 705 Page Rd., 27889, P 4,550, (252) 946-3970, Fax (252) 946-0849, info@beaufortedc.com, www.beaufortedc.com

**Waynesville** • *Haywood County Eco. Dev. Comm.* • Mark Clasby, Exec. Dir., 144 Industrial Park Dr., 28786, P 57,097, (828) 456-3737, Fax (828) 452-1352, edc@haywoodnc.net, www.haywoodedc.org

**Weaverville** • *see Asheville*

**Williamston** • *Martin County Eco. Dev. Corp.* • James D. Ward, Exec. Dir., 415 East Blvd., 27892, P 25,078, (252) 792-2044, Fax (252) 792-0993, info@martincountyedc.com, www.martincountyedc.com

**Wilson** • *Wilson Eco. Dev. Cncl.* • Jennifer Lantz, Exec. Dir., 126 W. Nash St., P.O. Box 728, 27894, P 79,000, (252) 237-1115, (800) 241-4920, Fax (252) 237-1116, jlantz@wilsonedc.com, www.wilsonedc.com

**Winston-Salem** • *Winston-Salem Bus Inc.* • Robert E. Leak Jr. CID CEcD, Pres., 1080 W. 4th St., 27101, P 317,643, (336) 723-8955, Fax (336) 716-1069, rleak@wsbusinessinc.com, www.wsbusinessinc.com

**Winton** • *Hertford Co. Eco. Dev. Comm.* • William S. Early, Dir., P.O. Box 429, 27986, P 22,601, (252) 358-7801, Fax (252) 358-7806, bill.early@ncmail.net, www.hertfordcounty.com

**Youngsville** • *Franklin County Eco. Dev. Comm.* • Ronnie Goswick, Dir., 112-D Wheaton Dr., 27596, P 56,000, (919) 554-1863, Fax (919) 554-1781, rgoswick@franklincountync.us, www.franklinedc.com

# North Dakota

## Federal

**U.S. SBA, North Dakota Dist. Ofc.** • James Stai, Dist. Dir., 657 2nd Ave. N., Rm. 218, P.O. Box 3086, Fargo, 58108, (701) 239-5131, Fax (701) 239-5645, north.dakota@sba.gov, www.sba.gov/nd

## State

**North Dakota Econ. Dev. & Finance** • Paul Lucy, Dir., P.O. Box 2057, Bismarck, 58502, (701) 328-5300, Fax (701) 328-5320, plucy@nd.gov, www.growingnd.com

## Communities

**Bismarck** • *Bismarck-Mandan Dev. Assn.* • Russell Staiger, Pres./CEO, 400 E. Broadway Ave., Ste. 417, P.O. Box 2615, 58502, P 95,000, (701) 222-5530, (888) 222-5497, Fax (701) 222-3843, rstaiger@bmda.org, www.bmda.org

**Bottineau** • *Bottineau County Eco.Dev. Corp.* • Diane Olson, EDC Dir., 519 Main St., 58318, P 2,400, M 100, (701) 228-3922, Fax (701) 228-5130, edc@utma.com, www.bottineau.com.

**Carrington** • *Carrington Comm. Dev. Corp.* • Robin Anderson, Pres., 871 Main, P.O. Box 439, 58421, P 2,300, (701) 652-2524, (800) 641-9668, Fax (701) 652-2391, chambergal@daktel.com, www.cgtn-nd.com, www.carringtonnd.com

**Cooperstown** • *Cooperstown/Griggs County Eco. Dev. Corp.* • Becky Meidinger, Dev. Spec., P.O. Box 553, 58425, P 2,500, (701) 797-3712, Fax (701) 797-3713, cooperedc@invisimax.com, ww.growingcooperstown.com

**Devils Lake** • *FORWARD Devils Lake Dev. Corp.* • Chris Schilken, Exec. Dir., P.O. Box 879, 58301, P 7,000, (701) 662-4933, Fax (701) 662-2147, forwarddl@gondtc.com, www.forwarddl.com

**Dickinson** • *Roosevelt-Custer Cncl. For Dev.* • Rod Landblom, Dir., 300 13th Ave., Ste. 3, 58601, P 38,365, (701) 483-1241, Fax (701) 483-1243, info@rooseveltcuster.com

**Fargo** • *Greater Fargo Moorhead Eco. Dev. Corp.* • Brian Walters, Pres., 51 Broadway, Ste. 500, 58102, P 188,000, (701) 364-1900, Fax (701) 293-7819, info@fmedc.com, www.fmedc.com

**Fargo** • *Lake Agassie Reg. Cncl.* • Irvin Rustad, Exec. Dir., 417 Main Ave., 58103, P 150,000, (701) 239-5373, Fax (701) 235-6706, www.lakeagassie.com

**Grand Forks** • *Grand Forks Reg. Eco. Dev. Corp.* • Klaus Thiessen, Pres./CEO, 600 Demers Ave., Ste. 501, 58201, P 100,000, (701) 746-2720, Fax (701) 746-2725, judiths@grandforks.org, www.grandforks.org

**Harvey** • *Harvey Area Eco. Dev. Inc.* • Kim Moon, Dir., 120 8th St. W., 58341, P 1,998, (701) 324-2000, Fax (701) 324-2674, kim@harveynd.com, www.harveynd.com

**Hazen** • *Hazen Comm.Dev.* • Duke Rosendahl, Exec. Dir., 146 Main St. E., P.O. Box 717, 58545, P 2,457, (701) 748-6886, Fax (701) 748-2559, hcd@westriv.com, www.hazennd.org

**Hettinger** • *Adams County Dev. Corp.* • Ed Gold, Exec. Dir., 120 S. Main, P.O. Box 1323, 58639, P 2,554, (701) 567-2531, Fax (701) 567-2690, adamscdc@ndsupernet.com, www.hettingernd.com

**Hillsboro** • *Hillsboro Eco. Dev. Corp.* • Mike Bitz, P.O. Box 502, 58045, P 1,700, (701) 636-2338, (701) 636-4620, www.hillsborond.com

**Kulm** • *Kulm Comm. Dev. Corp.* • Jerry Johnson, Pres., P.O. Box 223, 58456, P 450, (701) 647-2448

**Linton** • *Linton Ind. Dev. Corp.* • Sharon Jangula, Coord., P.O. Box 433, 58552, P 1,321, (701) 254-4267, Fax (701) 254-4223, lidcbek@bektel.com, www.lintonnd.org

**Mayville** • *Traill County Eco. Dev.* • Melissa Hennen, Exec. Dir., 330 3rd St. N.E., Ste, 1856, 58257, P 8,700, (701) 788-4746, tcedc@polarcomm.com, www.tcedc.com

**Minnewaukan** • *Minnewaukan Area Dev. Corp.* • P.O. Box 98, 58351, P 300, (701) 473-5436

**Minot** • *Minot Area Dev. Corp.* • 1020 20th Ave. S.W., 58701, P 52,000, M 265, (701) 852-1075, Fax (701) 857-8234, madc@minotusa.com, www.minotusa.com

**Oakes** • *Oakes Enhancement Inc.* • Gary Schnell, Pres., P.O. Box 365, 58474, P 2,000, (701) 742-3508, Fax (701) 742-3139, oakesnd@drtel.net, www.oakesnd.com

**Rugby** • *Rugby Eco. Dev. Corp.* • P.O. Box 136, 58368, P 3,000, (701) 776-7655, Fax (701) 776-5281, www.rugbynorthdakota.com

**Underwood** • *Underwood Area Eco. Dev. Corp.* • Becky Bowlen, Exec. Dir., P.O. Box 368, 58576, P 1,000, (701) 442-5481, Fax (701) 442-5482, becky@underwoodnd.net, www.underwoodnd.net

**Valley City** • *Valley City-Barnes County Dev. Corp.* • Jennifer Feist, Dir. of Dev., 250 W. Main St., P.O. Box 724, 58072, P 6,900, (701) 845-1891, Fax (701) 845-1892, vdg@hellovalley.com, www.hellovalley.com

**Wahpeton** • *City of Wahpeton Eco. Dev. Dept.* • Jane Priebe CEcD, Dir., 1900 4th St. N., 58075, P 8,567, (701) 642-8559, (888) 850-9544, Fax (701) 642-1428, info@wahpeton.com, www.wahpeton.com

**Washburn** • *Washburn Area Eco. Dev. Assn.* • P.O. Box 608, 58577, P 1,389, (701) 462-3801, Fax (701) 462-8598, www.washburnnd.com

**Williston** • *Tri-County Reg. Dev. Cncl.* • Everette Enno, Exec. Dir., 22 E. Broadway, 2nd Flr., P.O. Box 697, 58802, P 32,863, (701) 577-1358, Fax (701) 577-1363

**Williston** • *Williston Eco. Dev.* • Thomas Rolfstad, Exec. Dir., 22 E. Broadway, P.O. Box 1306, 58802, P 14,000, (701) 577-8110, Fax (701) 577-8880, tomr@ci.williston.nd.us, www.willistonnd.com

# Ohio

## Federal

**U.S. SBA, Cleveland Dist. Ofc.** • Gilbert Goldberg, Dist. Dir., 1350 Euclid Ave., Ste. 211, Cleveland, 44115, (216) 522-4180, Fax (216) 522-2038, www.sba.gov/oh

**U.S. SBA, Columbus Dist. Ofc.** • Thomas Mueller, Dist. Dir., 401 N. Front St., Ste. 200, Columbus, 43215, (614) 469-6860, Fax (614) 469-2391, www.sba.gov/oh

## State

**State of Ohio Strategic Investment Div.** • Steve Schoeny, Dir., 77 S. High St., 29th Flr., P.O. Box 1001, Columbus, 43215, (614) 466-8737, Fax (614) 644-1789, steven.schoeny@development.ohio.gov, www.connectohio.com

## Communities

**Alliance** • *Greater Alliance Dev. Corp.* • Thomas Pukys, Mgr., 2490 W. State St., 44601, P 50,000, M 52, (330) 823-0700, Fax (330) 823-2660, aadf@allianceadf.com

**Ashland** • *Mohican Area Growth Found. Inc.* • Evan Scurti, Dir., 206 Claremont Ave., 44805, P 2,893, (419) 289-3200, Fax (419) 289-3233, www.mohicanareagrowthfoundation.com

**Ashtabula** • *see Jefferson*

**Athens** • *Athens County Eco. Dev. Cncl.* • Todd Shelton, Interim Dir., 340 W. State St., Ste. 26, 45701, P 64,000, (740) 597-1420, Fax (740) 597-1548, todd@businessremixed.com, www.businessremixed.com

**Bellefontaine** • *Logan County Comm. Improvement Corp.* • Ed Wallace, Pres., 100 S. Main St., 43311, P 46,000, (937) 599-5121, Fax (937) 599-2411, ewallace@logancountyohio.com, www.logancountyohio.com

**Brook Park** • *City of Brook Park Dev. Dept.* • Michelle Boczek, Eco. Dev. Commissioner, 6161 Engle Rd., 44142, P 22,000, (216) 433-1300, Fax (216) 433-1511, www.cityofbrookpark.com

**Bryan** · *Williams County Eco. Dev. Corp. [WEDCO]* · Diamond Zimmerman, Coord., 228 S. Main St., 43506, P 39,188, M 100, (419) 636-8727, Fax (419) 636-5589, economic@wedco.info, www.wedco.info

**Cambridge** · *Cambridge-Guernsey County Comm. Improvement Corp.* · Norman Blanchard, Dir., 806 Cochran Ave., 43725, P 40,792, (740) 432-1881, Fax (740) 432-1990, cgccic@verizon.net, www.cgccic.org

**Cambridge** · *Ohio Mid-Eastern Govts. Assn.* · Greg DiDonato, Exec. Dir., 326 Highland Ave., P.O. Box 130, 43725, P 592,776, (740) 439-4471, Fax (740) 439-7783, director@omegadistrict.org, www.omegadistrict.org

**Canton** · *Stark Dev. Bd.* · Stephen L. Paquette, Pres., 116 Cleveland Ave. N.W., Ste. 600, 44702, P 360,000, (330) 453-5900, Fax (330) 453-1793, www.starkcoohio.com

**Chillicothe** · *Eco. Dev. Alliance of Southern Ohio* · Christopher M. Manegold CEcD, CEO, 45 E. Main St., 45601, P 75,000, (740) 772-5100, (877) 70-EDASO, Fax (740) 702-2727, cmanegold@edaso.org, www.edaso.org

**Chillicothe** · *Ross County Comm. Improvement Corp.* · 45 E. Main St., 45601, P 74,000, (740) 702-2720, Fax (740) 702-2727, www.chillicotheohio.com

**Cincinnati** · *Dept. of Comm. Dev.* · Michael Cervay, Dir., 805 Central Ave., Ste. 700, 45202, P 400,000, (513) 352-3950, Fax (513) 352-6257, communitydevelopment@cincinnati-oh.gov, www.cincinnati-oh.gov

**Cincinnati** · *Hamilton County Dev. Co.* · David K. Main, Pres., 1776 Mentor Ave., Ste. 100, 45212, P 800,000, (513) 631-8292, Fax (513) 631-4887, maind@hcdc.com, www.hcdc.com

**Cleveland** · *City of Cleveland Dept. of Eco. Dev.* · Tracey A. Nichols, Dir., 601 Lakeside Ave., Rm. 210, 44114, P 500,000, (216) 664-2406, Fax (216) 664-3681, www.city.cleveland.oh.us

**Columbus** · *Mid-Ohio Reg. Planning Comm.* · 111 Liberty St., Ste. 100, 43215, (614) 228-2663, Fax (614) 228-1904, www.morpc.org

**Conneaut** · *see Jefferson*

**Dayton** · *City of Dayton, Ofc. Of Eco. Dev.* · Shelley Dickstein, Dir., 101 W. 3rd St., City Mgr. Ofc., 45402, P 166,000, (937) 333-3600, Fax (937) 333-4298, shelley.dickstein@cityofdayton.org, www.cityofdayton.org

**Dayton** · *CityWide Dev. Corp.* · Steve Budd, Pres., 8 N. Main St., 45402, (937) 226-0457, Fax (937) 222-7035, www.citywidedev.com

**Dayton** · *Dayton Area C/C Eco. Dev. Div.* · Chris Kershner, V.P., One Chamber Plaza, 45402, P 970,000, (937) 226-1444, Fax (937) 226-8254, www.daytonchamber.org

**Elyria** · *Lorain County Comm. Dev.* · Rebecca Jones, Interim Dir., 226 Middle Ave., 44035, P 284,664, (440) 328-2326, Fax (440) 328-2349, rajones@loraincounty.us, www.loraincounty.us

**Euclid** · *Dept. of Comm. Svc. & Eco. Dev.* · Frank Pietravoia, Dir., 585 E. 222nd St., 44123, P 52,717, (216) 289-8158, Fax (216) 289-8366, www.cityofeuclid.com

**Fairfield** · *Fairfield Dev. Svcs.* · Timothy Bachman, Dir., 5350 Pleasant Ave., 45014, P 41,000, (513) 867-5345, Fax (513) 867-5324, development@fairfield-city.org, www.fairfield-city.org

**Findlay** · *Greater Findlay Inc.* · Ray De Winkle, Pres./CEO, 123 E. Main Cross St., 45840, P 72,000, (419) 422-3313, Fax (419) 422-9508, rdewinkle@greaterfindlayinc.com, www.greaterfindlayinc.com

**Forest Park** · *City of Forest Park Eco. Dev.* · Paul Brehm, Dir., 1201 W. Kemper Rd., 45240, P 20,000, (513) 595-5207, Fax (513) 595-5285, www.forestpark.org

**Fostoria** · *Fostoria Eco. Dev. Corp.* · Joan M. Reinhard, Exec. Dir., 121 N. Main St., 44830, P 15,000, (419) 435-7789, Fax (419) 435-0936, fostoriaed@aol.com, www.fostoriaed.org

**Fremont** · *Sandusky County Eco. Dev. Corp.* · Kay E. Reiter, Exec. Dir., 2511 Countryside Dr., 43420, P 62,000, (419) 332-2882, Fax (419) 332-3347, director@sanduskycountyedc.org, www.sanduskycountyedc.org

**Galion** · *Galion Ind. Dev.* · Joe Kleinknecht, Dir., 106 Harding Way E., 44833, P 11,341, (419) 468-7737

**Geneva** · *see Jefferson*

**Hamilton** · *Butler County Dept. of Eco. Dev.* · Michael Juengling, Dir., 130 High St., 45011, P 351,276, (513) 887-3413, Fax (513) 785-5723, www.butlercounty.biz

**Jefferson** · *Growth Partnership for Ashtabula County* · Joseph Mayernick, Exec. Dir, 17 N. Market St., 44047, P 120,000, (440) 576-9126, (800) 487-4769, Fax (440) 576-5003, joe@ashtabulagrowth.com, www.ashtabulagrowth.com

**Lima** · *Allen Eco. Dev. Group* · Marcel Wagner, Pres./CEO, 144 S. Main, Ste. 200, 45801, P 108,493, (419) 222-7706, (877) 222-7706, Fax (419) 222-7916, info@aedg.org, www.aedg.org

**Lorain** · *Comm. Dev. Dept.-City of Lorain* · Sanford A. Prudoff, Dir., 200 W. Erie Ave., 5th Flr., 44052, P 68,652, (440) 204-2020, Fax (440) 204-2080, www.cityoflorain.org

**Mansfield** · *Comm. Dev. Dept.* · Cynthia Baker, Mgr., 30 N. Diamond St., 8th Flr., 44902, P 54,000, (419) 755-9795, www.ci.mansfield.oh.us

**Mansfield** · *Richland Eco. Dev. Corp.* · Mike Greene, Pres., 24 W. Third St., 44902, P 130,650, (419) 522-7332, Fax (419) 522-7356, mikeg@redec.org, www.redec.org

**Marion** · *Marion CAN DO Inc.* · 205 W. Center St., 43302, P 66,310, (740) 387-2267, (800) 841-7302, Fax (740) 387-5522, www.marioncando.com

**Marysville** · *Union County Eco. Dev.* · Eric S. Phillips, CEO/Dir., 227 E. Fifth St., 43040, P 40,909, (937) 642-6279, (800) 642-0087, Fax (937) 644-0422, chamber@unioncounty.org, www.whereprideresides.org

**Massillon** · *Massillon Dev. Found.* · Bob Sanderson, Exec. Dir., 137 LincolnWay E., 44646, P 33,000, M 60, (330) 833-3146, Fax (330) 833-8944, info@massillonohchamber.com, www.massillonohchamber.com

**Mentor** · *City of Mentor Comm. Dev.* · Ronald Traub, Dir., 8500 Civic Center Blvd., 44060, P 51,000, (440) 974-5740, Fax (440) 205-3605, traub@cityofmentor.com, www.cityofmentor.com

**Mount Vernon** · *Area Dev. Found.* · Steve Waers, Pres., 110 E. High St., 43050, P 54,500, (740) 393-3806, (888) 411-4233, Fax (740) 397-5762, steve@knoxadf.com, www.knoxadf.com

**Napoleon** · *Henry County Comm. Improvement Corp.* · Ralph Lanse, Exec. Dir., 104 E. Washington, Ste. 301, 43545, P 29,000, (419) 592-4637, Fax (419) 599-9865, cic@bright.net, www.hencoed.com

**New London** · *New London Comm. Improvement Corp.* · 115 E. Main St., 44851, P 3,000, M 65, (419) 929-4091, Fax (419) 929-0738, www.newlondonohio.com

**New Philadelphia** · *Comm. Improvement Corp. of Tuscarawas County* · Gary D. Little, Exec. Dir., 330 University Dr. N.E., 44663, P 90,000, (330) 308-7524, Fax (330) 308-7552, garylittle@tusccic.com, www.tusccic.com

**Norwood** · *City of Norwood Dev. Dept.* · Richard Dettmer, Dir., 4645 Montgomery Rd., 45212, P 21,000, (513) 458-4596, www.norwood-ohio.com

**Oak Harbor** · *Ottawa County Comm. Improvement Corp.* · Jamie Beier Grant, Dir., 8043 W. State Rte. 163, Ste. 100, 43449, P 40,500, (419) 898-6242, (866) 734-6789, Fax (419) 898-6244, jbgrant@ocic.biz, www.ocic.biz

**Orrville** · *Orrville Area Dev. Found.* · Jenni Reusser, Pres., 132 S. Main St., 44667, P 8,500, (330) 682-8881, Fax (330) 682-8383, jenni@orrvillechamber.com, www.orrvillechamber.com

**Painesville** · *Lake County Port Auth.* · John Loftus, Exec. Dir., One Victoria Pl., Ste. 265A, 44077, P 232,892, (440) 357-2290, Fax (440) 357-2296, jloftus@lcedc.org, www.lcedc.org

**Piqua** · *City of Piqua Eco. Dev.* · 201 W. Water, 45356, P 21,004, (937) 778-8198, Fax (937) 778-0809, info@piquaoh.org, www.piquaoh.org

**Pomeroy** · *Meigs County EDC* · Perry Varnadoe, Dev. Dir., 238 W. Main St., 45769, P 25,000, (740) 992-3034, Fax (740) 992-7942, director@meigscountyohio.com, www.meigscountyohio.com

**Portsmouth** · *Southern Ohio Growth Partnership* · Robert Huff, Pres./CEO, 342 2nd St., P.O. Box 509, 45662, P 79,195, (740) 353-7647, (800) 648-2574, Fax (740) 353-5824, www.portsmouth.org

**Reno** · Buckeye Hills-Hocking Valley Reg. Dev. Dist. · Misty Casto, Exec. Dir., P.O. Box 520, 45773, P 255,000, (740) 374-9436, Fax (740) 374-8038, info@buckeyehills.org, www.buckeyehills.org

**Saint Clairsville** · *Dept. of Dev. of Belmont County* · Sue Douglass, Exec. Dev. Dir., 117 E. Main St., 43950, P 60,000, (740) 695-9678, Fax (740) 695-1536, contactus@aplacetogrowyour business.com, www.aplacetogrowyourbusiness.com

**Saint Mary's** · *City of St. Mary's Eco. Dev.* · Todd Fleagle, Mgr. Ind. Dev., 101 E. Spring St., 45885, P 8,342, (419) 394-3303 x116, Fax (419) 394-2452, stmarys@cityofstmarys.net, www.cityofstmarys.net

**Sandusky** · *Erie County Eco. Dev. Corp.* · Ron Parthemore, Interim Exec. Dir., 247 Columbus Ave., Ste. 126, 44870, P 80,000, (419) 627-7791, Fax (419) 627-7595, www.eriecountyedc.org

**Sidney** · *West Ohio Dev. Cncl.* · Mike Dodds, Dir., 101 S. Ohio Ave., 2nd Flr., 45365, P 48,000, (937) 498-9554, Fax (937) 498-2472, mdodds@westohiodevelopment.com, www.westohio development.com

**South Point** · *Lawrence Eco. Dev. Corp.* · Dr. Bill Dingus, Exec. Dir., 216 Collins Ave., P.O. Box 488, 45680, P 64,000, (740) 377-4550, Fax (740) 377-2091, dingus@ohio.edu, www.lawrencecountyohio.org

**Springfield** · *Comm. Improvement Corp. of Springfied & Clark County* · Michael McDorman, Pres., 20 S. Limestone St., Ste. 100, 45502, P 168,000, (937) 325-7621, (800) 803-1553, Fax (937) 325-8765, mmcdorman@greaterspringfield.com, www.greaterspringfield.com

**Steubenville** · *Progress Alliance* · Ed Looman, Exec. Dir., 630 Market St., P.O. Box 187, 43952, P 73,894, M 47, (740) 283-2476, Fax (740) 283-2607, elooman@progressalliance.com, www.progressalliance.com

**Struthers** · *CASTLO Comm. Improvement Corp.* · William D. DeCicco, Exec. Dir., 100 S. Bridge St., 44471, P 36,513, (330) 750-1363, Fax (330) 750-1364, wdd@castlo.com, www.castlo.com

**Tiffin** · *Seneca Ind. & Eco. Dev. Corp.* · Richard Focht Jr., Pres./CEO, 62 S. Washington St., 44883, P 55,000, (419) 447-4141, Fax (419) 447-5141, siedc@bpsom.com, www.siedc.com

**Toledo** · *Reg. Growth Partnership* · Steve Weathers, Pres./CEO, 300 Madison Ave., Ste. 270, 43604, P 618,000, (419) 252-2700, Fax (419) 252-2724, www.rgp.org

**Troy** · *Troy Dev. Cncl.* · Charles Cochran, Pres., 405 S.W. Public Sq., Ste. 330, 45373, P 32,000, (937) 339-7809, Fax (937) 339-4944, tdc@troyohiochamber.com, www.troyohiochamber.com

**Urbana** · *Champaign County Eco. Dev.* · Michael Morris, Eco. Dev. Officer, 113 Miami St., 43078, P 38,900, (937) 653-5764, (877) 873-5764, Fax (937) 652-1599, mmorris@co.champaign.oh.us, www.champaignohio.biz

**Van Wert** · *Van Wert County Eco. Dev.* · Nancy Bowen, Dir., 515 E. Main St., 45891, P 30,000, (419) 238-2999, Fax (419) 238-1397, www.vanwertcounty-edg.com

**Warren** · *Youngstown/Warren Reg. C/C* · Walter M. Good, V.P. Eco. Dev., 197 W. Market St., 7th Flr., 44481, P 600,000, M 3,000, (330) 392-6140 ext. 22, Fax (330) 746-0330, regionalchamber@regionalchamber.com, www.regionalchamber.com

**Wauseon** · *Fulton County Eco. Dev.* · Lisa Arend, Dir., 152 S. Fulton St., Ste. 280, 43567, P 42,084, M 22, (419) 337-9215, Fax (419) 337-9285, www.fultoncountyoh.com

**Xenia** · *Xenia Dept. of Comm. Dev.* · Mary Crockett, Dir., 101 N. Detroit St., 45385, P 24,164, (937) 376-7286, Fax (937) 372-8151, mcrockett@ci.xenia.oh.us, www.ci.xenia.oh.us

**Xenia** · *Xenia Eco. Growth Corp.* · Steve Brodsky, Exec. Dir., 181 W. Main St., 45385, P 24,164, (937) 372-6389, (800) GO-XENIA, Fax (937) 372-3509, xegc@xegc.org, www.xegc.org

**Youngstown** · *City of Youngstown Eco. Dev.* · T. Sharon Woodberry, Dev. Dir., 20 W. Federal, Ste. M8, 44503, P 83,000, (330) 744-1708, Fax (330) 744-1951, www.ytowndevelopment.com

**Youngstown** · *Mahoning Valley Eco. Dev. Corp.* · Donald L. French, Exec. Dir., 4319 Belmont Ave., 44505, P 600,000, (330) 759-3668, (330) 369-6026, Fax (330) 759-3686, www.mvedc.com

**Zanesville** · *Zanesville-Muskingum County Port Auth.* · Jerry Nolder, Exec. Dir., 205 N. 5th St., 43701, P 83,388, (740) 455-0742, (800) 988-4388, Fax (740) 452-9703, jerry.nolder@zmcport.com, www.zmcport.com

# Oklahoma

## Federal

**U.S. SBA, Oklahoma Dist. Ofc.** · Dorothy Overal, Dist. Dir., 301 N.W. 6th, Ste. 116, Oklahoma City, 73102, (405) 609-8000, Fax (405) 609-8990, www.sba.gov/ok

## State

**Oklahoma Dept. of Commerce** · Natalie Shirley, Secy. of Commerce, 900 N. Stiles Ave., Oklahoma City, 73126, (405) 815-6552, Fax (405) 815-5199, www.okcommerce.gov

**Oklahoma Industries Auth.** · Paul B. Strasbaugh, Gen. Mgr., 123 Park Ave., Oklahoma City, 73102, (405) 232-9921, Fax (405) 235-5112

## Communities

**Altus** · *Altus/Southwest Area Eco. Dev. Corp.* · 220 E. Commerce, 73521, P 23,000, (580) 481-2287, Fax (580) 481-2203, mayor@cityofaltus.org, www.cityofaltus.org

**Ardmore** · *Ardmore Dev. Auth.* · 410 W. Main, P.O. Box 1585, 73402, P 35,000, (580) 223-6162, Fax (580) 223-7825, bthorsten berg@ardmore.org, www.ardmoredevelopment.com

**Atoka** · *Atoka County Ind. Auth.* · 315 E. A St., P.O. Box 900, 74525, P 14,000, (580) 889-3341, Fax (580) 889-7584, www.atoka city.org

**Bartlesville** • *Bartlesville Dev. Corp.* • Justin McLaughlin, Dir. of Bus. Dev., P.O. Box 2366, 74005, P 35,000, (918) 336-8708, Fax (918) 337-0216, jmclaughlin@bartlesville.com, www.bartlesville.com

**Blackwell** • *Blackwell Ind. Auth.* • Shane Frye, Exec. Dir., 120 S. Main, P.O. Box 150, 74631, P 7,500, (580) 363-2934, Fax (580) 363-1704, info.bia@blackwellchamber.com, www.blackwell industrialauthority.com

**Buffalo** • *Buffalo Eco. Dev.* • James Leonard, Dir., P.O. Box 439, 73834, P 1,200, (580) 735-2521, www.buffalooklahoma.org

**Claremore** • *Claremore Ind. & Eco. Dev. Auth.* • Tim Hight, Exec. Dir, 2000 University Dr., Ste. 2, 74017, P 20,000, (918) 341-4755, Fax (918) 343-7532, thight@claremoredevelopment.com, www.claremoredevelopment.com

**Duncan** • *Duncan Area Eco. Dev. Found.* • Lyle Roggow, Pres., 2124 N. Hwy. 81, 73533, P 43,000, (580) 255-9675, (888) 254-9675, Fax (580) 255-2647, info@ok-duncan.com, www.ok-duncan.com

**Durant** • *Durant Ind. Auth.* • Tommy Kramer, Exec. Dir., 215 N. 4th Ave., 74701, P 15,000, (580) 924-4570, Fax (580) 924-0348, tkramer@durant.org, www.ok-durant.org

**Grove** • *Grove Ind. Dev. Auth.* • 104 W. Third, 74344, P 6,000, (918) 786-6107, Fax (918) 786-8939, www.cityofgrove.com

**Guthrie** • *Logan County Eco. Dev. Cncl.* • Kay Wade, Dir., 212 W. Oklahoma, P.O. Box 995, 73044, P 29,000, (405) 282-0060, (405) 282-1947, Fax (405) 282-0061, www.logancountyedc.com

**Idabel** • *Idabel Ind. Dev. Auth.* • Walt Frey, Chrmn., 7 S.W. Texas St., 74745, P 8,000, (580) 286-3305, Fax (580) 286-6708, iida@idabelok.net

**Lawton** • *Lawton Ind. Found.* • Dana Davis, Pres./CEO, 629 S.W. C Ave., Ste. A, P.O. Box 1376, 73502, P 112,000, (580) 355-3541, (800) 872-4540, Fax (580) 357-3642, ddavis@lawtonfortsill chamber.com, www.lawtonok.org

**Miami** • *Miami Area Eco. Dev. Svc.* • Judee Snodderly, Exec. Dir., 2 N. Main, Ste. 601, 74354, P 35,000, (918) 542-8405, Fax (918) 542-7751, maeds@miami-ok.org, www.miami-ok.org

**Midwest City** • *MWC Comm. & Eco. Dev.* • David Burnett CEcD, Dir. of Dev., 5905 Trosper Rd., P.O. Box 10980, 73140, P 55,000, (405) 733-3801, Fax (405) 733-5633, david.burnett@midwest cityok.com, www.midwestcityok.com

**Muskogee** • *Muskogee Dev. Corp.* • Leisha Haworth, Exec. Dir., 216 W. Okmulgee, 74401, P 40,800, (918) 683-2816, Fax (918) 683-2110, jwooten@muskogeedevelopment.org, www.muskogeedevelopment.org

**Norman** • *Norman Eco. Dev. Coalition* • Don Wood, Exec. Dir., 710 Asp Ave., Ste. 100, 73069, P 103,101, (405) 573-1900, Fax (405) 573-1999, nedc@nedcok.com, www.nedcok.com

**Oklahoma City** • *Oklahoma City Eco. Dev. Found.* • 123 Park Ave., 73102, P 538,000, (405) 297-8900, Fax (405) 297-8908, rroberts@okcchamber.com, www.okcchamber.com

**Tulsa** • *Eco. Dev. Div., Tulsa Metro C/C* • Rusty Linker, New Bus. Dev. Dir., Two W. 2nd St., Ste. 150, 74103, P 810,000, (918) 560-0233, (918) 585-1201, Fax (918) 585-8386, rustylinker@tulsachamber.com, www.tulsachamber.com

**Wewoka** • *Eco. Dev. City of Wewoka* • Tara Morgan, Exec. Dir., P.O. Box 719, 74884, P 3,500, (405) 257-5485, Fax (405) 257-2662, wewokachamber@sbcglobal.net

# Oregon

## Federal

**U.S. SBA, Oregon Dist. Ofc.** • Harry DeWolf, Dist. Dir., 601 S.W. 2nd Ave., Ste. 950, Portland, 97204, (503) 326-2682, Fax (503) 326-2808, www.sba.gov/or

## State

**Oregon Eco. & Comm. Dev. Dept.** • TimMcCabe, Dir., 775 Summer St. N.E., Ste. 200, Salem, 97301, (503) 986-0123, Fax (503) 581-5115, oedd.info@state.or.us, econ.oregon.gov

## Communities

**Albany** • *Albany-Millersburg Eco. Dev. Corp.* • John Pascone, Pres., 435 W. First Ave., P.O. Box 548, 97321, P 45,000, (541) 926-1519, Fax (541) 926-7064, pasconj@peak.org, www.albany-millersburg.com

**Albany** • *Cascade West Eco. Dev.* • Cynthia Solie, Dir., 1400 Queen Ave. S.E., Ste. 205A, 97322, P 209,400, (541) 967-8551, Fax (541) 967-4651, www.ocwcog.org

**Baker City** • *Baker City/County Comm. Dev.* • Jennifer Watkins, Dir., P.O. Box 650, 97814, P 10,500, (541) 523-6541, Fax (541) 524-2024, www.bakercity.com

**Bend** • *Eco. Dev. For Central Oregon* • Roger Lee, Exec. Dir., 109 N.W. Greenwood Ave., Ste. 102, 97701, P 185,230, M 320, (541) 388-3236, Fax (541) 388-6705, info@edcoinfo.com, www.edcoinfo.com

**Dallas** • *Dallas Eco. Dev. Comm.* • Jerry Wyatt, City Mgr., 187 S.E. Court St., 97338, P 15,000, (503) 623-2338, Fax (503) 623-2339, www.ci.dallas.or.us

**Enterprise** • *Northeast Oregon Eco. Dev. Dist.* • Lisa Dawson, Exec. Dir., 101 N.E. First St., Ste. 100, 97828, P 45,000, (541) 426-3598, Fax (541) 426-9058, lisadawson@neoedd.org, www.neoedd.org

**Eugene** • *Lane Cncl. of Govts.* • Steve Dignam, Eco. Dev. Coord., 859 Willamette St., Ste. 500, 97401, P 334,000, (541) 682-4283, Fax (541) 682-4099, susanl.muir@ci.eugene.or.us, www.lcog.org

**Eugene** • *Lane Metro Partnership* • Jack Roberts, Exec. Dir., 1401 Willamette, 2nd Flr., P.O. Box 10398, 97440, P 334,000, (541) 686-2741, Fax (541) 686-2325, business@lanemetro.com, www.lanemetro.com

**Eugene** • *Planning & Dev. Dept.* • Susan Muir, Exec. Dir., 99 W. 10th Ave., 97401, P 145,000, (541) 682-6077, Fax (541) 682-8335, susan.l.muir@ci.eugene.or.us, www.eugene-or.gov

**Hillsboro** • *Hillsboro Downtown Bus. Assn.* • Kay Mattson, Downtown Bus. Mgr., 232 N.E. Lincoln St., Ste. J, P.O. Box 611, 97123, P 88,000, (503) 844-6685, (503) 648-7817, Fax (503) 844-6215, info@hillsborodowntown.org, www.hillsboro downtown.org

**Hillsboro** • *Washington County Ofc. of Comm. Dev.* • Peggy Linden, Prog. Mgr., 328 W. Main, Ste. 100, 97123, P 357,000, (503) 846-8814, Fax (503) 846-2882, www.co.washington.or.us

**Jackson County** • *Southern Oregon Reg. Eco. Dev. Inc. [SOREDI]* • Colleen Padilla, Bus. Dev. Mgr., 673 Market St., Medford, 97504, P 280,000, (541) 773-8946, (800) 805-8740, Fax (541) 779-0953, colleen@soredi.org, www.soredi.org

**Josephine County** • *Southern Oregon Reg. Eco. Dev. Inc. [SOREDI]* • Colleen Padilla, Bus. Dev. Mgr., 673 Market St., Medford, 97504, P 280,000, (541) 773-8946, (800) 805-8740, Fax (541) 779-0953, colleen@soredi.org, www.soredi.org

**Klamath Falls** • *Klamath County Eco. Dev. Assn.* • L.H. 'Trey' Senn, Exec. Dir., 706 Main St., 3rd Flr., P.O. Box 1777, 97601, P 67,000, (541) 882-9600, Fax (541) 882-7648, trey@fireserve.net, www.sobusi.com

**Klamath Falls** • *Small Bus. Dev. Center* • Jamie Albert, Dir., OR Inst. of Tech., 3201 Campus Dr., Boivin Hall 119, 97601, P 56,000, (541) 885-1760, Fax (541) 885-1761, sbdc@oit.edu, www.bizcenter.org

**La Grande** • *Union County Eco. Dev. Corp.* • Mike Sanford, Exec. Dir., P.O. Box 1208, 97850, P 25,110, M 50, (541) 963-0926, Fax (541) 963-0689, ucedc@eoni.com, www.ucedc.org

**McMinnville** • *Yamhill County Dept. of Plan. & Dev.* • Michael Brandt, Dir., 525 N.E. 4th St., 97128, P 89,200, (503) 434-7516, Fax (503) 434-7544, www.co.yamhill.or.us/plan

**Moro** • *County Eco. Dev. Office* • Georgia Macnab, Planning Dir., 110 Main St., Ste. 2, P.O. Box 381, 97039, P 1,900, (541) 565-3601, Fax (541) 565-3078, georgiamac@embarqmail.com, www.co.sherman.or.us

**North Bend** • *Bus. Center* • Debbie Thompson, Secy., 2455 Maple Leaf, 97459, P 62,000, (541) 756-6778, Fax (541) 756-5404, bec@portofcoosbay.com, www.portofcoosbay.com

**Ontario** • *Malheur County Eco. Dev.* • Jim Jensen, Dir., 316 N.E. Goodfellow St., Ste. 2, 97914, P 32,000, (541) 881-0327, Fax (541) 881-0329, ecodev.malheurco.org

**Oregon City** • *Clackamas County Bus. & Eco. Dev. Team* • Gary Barth, Deputy Dir. Bus. & Comm. Svc., 150 Beaver Creek Rd., 97045, P 370,000, (503) 742-4329, Fax (503) 742-4349, garybar@co.clackamas.or.us, www.co.clackamas.or.us/business

**Portland** • *Portland Dev. Comm.* • Bruce Warner, Exec. Dir., 222 N.W. 5th Ave., 97209, P 2,050,650, (503) 823-3200, Fax (503) 823-3368, www.pdc.us

**Redmond** • *City of Redmond Comm. Dev.* • Heather Richards, Interim Dir., 716 S.W. Evergreen Ave., 97756, P 21,109, (541) 923-7721, Fax (541) 548-0706, www.ci.redmond.or.us

**Redmond** • *Redmond Eco. Dev.* • Jon Stark, Mgr., 446 S.W. 7th St., Ste. #B, 97756, P 25,445, (541) 923-5223, Fax (541) 923-6442, redap@redap.org, www.redap.org

**Roseburg** • *CCD Bus. Dev.* • Wayne Luzier, Exec. Dir., 744 S.E. Rose St., 97470, P 200,000, (541) 672-6728, Fax (541) 672-7011, www.ccdbusiness.com

**Salem** • *Strategic Eco. Dev. Corp.-SEDCOR* • Ray Burstedt, Pres., 745 Commercial St. N.E., 97301, P 388,000, (503) 588-6225, Fax (503) 588-6240, rburstedt@sedcor.com, www.sedcor.com

**Springfield** • *City of Springfield Eco. Dev. Div.* • John Tamulonis, Comm. Dev. Mgr., 225 5th St., 97477, P 57,500, (541) 726-3656, (541) 726-3700, Fax (541) 726-2363, jtamulonis@ci.springfield.or.us, www.ci.springfield.or.us

**Sweet Home** • *Sweet Home Eco. Dev. Group* • Ron Moore, Pres., P.O. Box 430, 97386, P 8,300, (541) 367-3061, www.sweethomeoregon.org

**The Dalles** • *Mid-Columbia Eco. Dev. Dist.* • Amanda Remington, Exec. Dir., 515 E. 2nd St., 97058, P 77,000, (541) 296-2266, Fax (541) 296-3283, mcedd@mcedd.org, www.mcedd.org

**Tillamook** • *Eco. Dev. Cncl. of Tillamook County* • Marshall Doak, Exec. Dir., 1906-A 3rd St., 97141, P 24,800, (503) 842-2236, Fax (503) 842-9368, info@edctc.com, www.edctc.com

**Umatilla** • *Port of Umatilla* • Mr. Kim Puzey, Gen. Mgr., P.O. Box 879, 97882, P 62,000, (541) 922-3224, Fax (541) 922-5609, www.portofumatilla.com

**Winston** • *Winston Area Dev. Comm.* • Anita Cox, Chrmn., 30 N.W. Glenhart, P.O. Box 68, 97496, P 10,000, M 10, (541) 679-0118, Fax (541) 679-4270, winstonvic@charter.net, www.winstonoregon.net

# Pennsylvania

## Federal

**U.S. SBA, Philadelphia Dist. Ofc.** • David Dickson, Dist. Dir., 1150 First Ave., Ste. 1001, Philadelphia, 19406, (610) 382-3062, www.sba.gov/pa

**U.S. SBA, Pittsburgh Dist. Ofc.** • Carl Knoblock, Dist. Dir., 411 7th Ave., Ste. 1450, Pittsburgh, 15219, (412) 395-6560, Fax (412) 395-6560, www.sba.gov/pa

## Communities

**Altoona** • *Altoona Blair County Dev. Corp.* • Martin J. Marasco, Pres./CEO, 3900 Industrial Park Dr., 16602, P 137,000, (814) 944-6113, Fax (814) 946-0157, www.abcdcorp.org

**Bedford** • *Bedford County Dev. Assn.* • Bette Slayton, Pres., 1 Corporate Dr., Ste. 101, 15522, P 49,984, (814) 623-4816, (800) 634-8610, Fax (814) 623-6455, www.bcda.org

**Berwick** • *Berwick Ind. Dev. Assn.* • Stephen Phillips, Exec. Dir., 107 S. Market St., Ste. 5, 18603, P 12,000, (570) 752-3612, Fax (570) 752-2334, bida@pa.metrocast.net, www.bida.com

**Bethlehem** • *Lehigh Valley Eco. Dev. Corp.* • Phil Mitman, Pres./CEO, 2158 Ave. C, Ste. 200, 18017, P 600,000, (610) 266-6775, Fax (610) 266-7623, lvedc@lehighvalley.org, www.lehighvalley.org

**Bethlehem** • *Lehigh Valley Ind. Park Inc.* • Kerry Wrobel, Pres., 1720 Spillman Dr., Ste. 150, 18015, P 600,000, (610) 866-4600, Fax (610) 867-9154, www.lvip.org

**Bloomsburg** • *Columbia Alliance for Eco. Growth/Ind. Dev. Auth.* • Edward G. Edwards, Pres., 238 Market St., 17815, P 63,000, (570) 784-2522, Fax (570) 784-2661, chamber@columbiamontourchamber.com, www.columbiamontourchamber.com

**Brackenridge** • *Allegheny Valley Dev. Corp.* • Laurie Singer, Pres., 1030 Broadview Blvd., Ste. 1, 15014, P 50,000, (724) 224-5858, Fax (724) 224-3442

**Brookville** • *Jefferson County Dept. of Dev.* • Craig Coon, Dir. of Comm. & Eco. Dev., Jefferson Pl., 155 Main St., 2nd Flr., 15825, P 46,083, (814) 849-1603, Fax (814) 849-5049, www.jeffersoncountypa.com

**Butler** • *Comm. Dev. Corp. of Butler County* • Diane Mintus Sheets, Exec. Dir., 112 Woody Dr., 16001, P 176,000, (724) 283-1961, (800) 283-0021, Fax (724) 283-3599, commdev@nauticom.net, www.butlercountycdc.com

**Carbondale** • *Carbondale Comm. Dev.* • Nancy Perri, 10 Enterprise Dr., 18407, P 9,804, (570) 282-1255, Fax (570) 282-1426, nperri@echoes.net

**Chambersburg** • *Franklin County Area Dev. Corp.* • L. Michael Ross, Pres., 1900 Wayne Rd., 17202, P 133,000, (717) 263-8282, Fax (717) 263-0662, info@fcadc.com, www.fcadc.com

**Clearfield** • *Clearfield County Eco. Dev. Corp.* • Rob Swales, Exec. Dir., 250 Technology Dr., Ste. 1, 16830, P 82,000, (814) 768-7838, (877) 768-7838, Fax (814) 768-7338, info@clearlyahead.com, www.clearlyahead.com

**Donora** • *Middle Mononghela Ind. Dev. Assn.* • LueAnn Pawlick, Exec. Dir., P.O. Box 491, 15033, P 45,000, (724) 379-5600, Fax (724) 379-9308, lpawlick@mmida.com, mmida.com

**Doylestown** • *Bucks County Eco. Dev. Corp.* • Dr.Kathleen Dominick, Exec. Dir., 2 E. Court St., 18901, P 625,000, (215) 348-9031, Fax (215) 348-8829, rfc@bcedc.com, www.bcedc.com

**East Norriton** • *Montgomery County Ind. Dev. Corp.* • Mr. Carmen Italia Jr., Pres., 420 W. Germantown Pike, 19403, P 750,097, (610) 272-5000, Fax (610) 272-6235, www.mcidc.com

**Easton** • *Easton Redevelopment Auth.* • 1 S. 3rd St., 18042, P 26,000, (610) 250-6721, Fax (610) 250-6607, www.easton-pa.gov

**Erie** • *Greater Erie Ind. Dev. Corp.* • K. Smith, Pres./CEO, 5240 Knowledge Pkwy., 16510, P 276,000, (814) 899-6022, Fax (814) 899-0250, www.connectforsuccess.org

**Exton** • *Chester County Eco. Dev. Cncl.* • Gary Smith, Pres./CEO, 737 Constitution Dr., 19341, P 376,000, (610) 458-5700, Fax (610) 458-7770, www.cceconomicdevelopment.com

**Greensburg** • *Eco. Growth Connection of Westmoreland* • John A. Skiavo, CEO, 40 N. Penn Ave., Ste. 510, 15601, P 375,000, (724) 830-3604, Fax (724) 850-3974, www.economicgrowthconnection.com

**Greenville** • *Greenville Area Eco. Dev. Corp.* • James Lowry, Dir., 12 N. Diamond St., 16125, P 18,000, (724) 588-1161, Fax (724) 588-9881, www.gaedc.org

**Grove City** • *79-80 Interstate Dev. Corp.* • Leann Smith, V.P., 119 S. Broad St., 16127, P 16,000, M 53, (724) 458-6410, Fax (724) 458-6841, info@79-80idc.com, www.79-80idc.com

**Harrisburg** • *Capital Region Eco. Dev. Corp.* • David Black, Pres./CEO, 3211 N. Front St., Ste. 201, 17110, P 550,000, (717) 232-4099, Fax (717) 232-5184, www.harrisburgregionalchamber.org

**Harrisburg** • *Dauphin County Ofc. of Eco. Dev.* • 112 Market, 7th Flr., P.O. Box 1295, 17108, P 257,000, (717) 780-6250, Fax (717) 257-1513, drobinson@dauphinc.org, www.dauphincounty.org

**Harrisburg** • *Pennsylvania Dept. of Comm. & Eco. Dev.* • George Cornelius, Acting Secy., 400 North St., 4th Flr., 17120, (717) 787-3003, Fax (717) 787-6866, www.newpa.com

**Hazleton** • *CAN DO, Inc. [Ind. Dev. Corp.]* • 1 S. Church St., Ste. 200, 18201, P 25,000, (570) 455-1508, Fax (570) 454-7787, cando@hazletoncando.com, www.hazletoncando.com

**Huntingdon** • *Huntingdon County Bus. & Ind.* • Steve Sliver, Pres., 419 14th St., 16652, P 45,000, M 200, (814) 643-4322, Fax (814) 506-1282, staff@hcbi.com, www.hcbi.com

**Indiana** • *Indiana County Center for Eco. Op.* • Dana P. Henry, Pres., 1019 Philadelphia St., 15701, P 90,000, (724) 465-2662, Fax (724) 465-3706, info@indpacoc.org, www.indianacountyceo.com

**Jim Thorpe** • *Carbon County Bur. of Eco. Dev.* • Dawn Ferrante, Dir., P.O. Box 291, 18229, P 59,000, (570) 325-2810, Fax (570) 325-8924, www.carbonecon.com

**Johnstown** • *Johnstown Ind. Dev. Corp.* • Linda Thomson, Pres., 245 Market St., Ste. 200, 15901, P 200,000, (814) 535-8675, Fax (814) 535-8677, www.jari.com

**Kittanning** • *Armstrong County IDC* • Armsdale Admin. Bldg., 124 Armsdale Rd, Ste 205, 16201, P 72,392, (724) 548-1500, Fax (724) 545-7050, idc@co.armstrong.pa.us, www.armstrongidc.org

**Lancaster** • *Eco. Dev. Co. of Lancaster County* • David Nikoloff, Pres., 100 S. Queen St., P.O. Box 1558, 17608, P 482,000, (717) 397-4046, Fax (717) 293-3159, edc@edclancaster.com, www.edclancaster.com

**Lebanon** • *Lebanon Valley Eco. Dev. Corp.* • Charles Blankenship, Pres., 445 Schaeffer Rd., P.O. Box 52, 17042, P 120,000, (717) 274-3180, Fax (717) 274-1367, cblankenship@lvedc.org, www.lvedc.org

**Lewisburg** • *Union County Ind. Dev. Corp.* • Michael Adams, Pres., 155 N. 15th St., 17837, P 36,176, (570) 524-3852, Fax (570) 524-0261, madams@unionco.org, www.unioncoidc.org

**Lewistown** • *Mifflin County Ind. Dev. Corp.* • Robert P. Postal, Pres., 6395 S.R. 103 N., 17044, P 46,400, (717) 242-0393, Fax (717) 242-1842, www.mcidc.org

**Lock Haven** • *Clinton County Eco. Partnership* • Michael K. Flanagan, Pres./CEO, 212 N. Jay St., P.O. Box 506, 17745, P 37,000, M 385, (570) 748-5782, Fax (570) 893-0433, flanagan@kcnet.org, www.clintoncountyinfo.com

**McKeesport** • *McKeesport Ind. Dev.* • Dennis Pittman, Admin., 502 5th Ave., 15132, P 24,040, (412) 675-5020 ext. 601, Fax (412) 675-5049

**Meadville** • *Redev. Auth. Of the City of Meadville* • Andy Walker, Exec. Dir., 984 Water St., 16335, P 13,600, (814) 337-8200, Fax (814) 337-7257, www.redevelopmeadville.com

**Media** • *Delaware County Eco. Dev. Oversight Bd.* • J. Patrick Killian, Dir., 200 E. State St., Ste. 205, 19063, P 570,000, (610) 566-2225, Fax (610) 566-7337, www.delcopa.org

**Mercer** • *Penn-Northwest Dev. Corp.* • Larry D. Reichard, Exec. Dir., 749 Greenville Rd., Ste. 100, 16137, P 122,000, M 80, (724) 662-3705, Fax (724) 662-0283, lreichard@penn-northwest.com, www.penn-northwest.com

**Milford** • *Pike County Ind. Dev. Corp.* • 209 E. Harford St., 18337, P 58,000, (570) 296-7332, Fax (570) 296-2852, vp@pidco.com, www.pidco.com

**Natrona Heights** • *see Brackenridge*

**New Castle** • *Lawrence County Eco. Dev. Corp.* • 100 E. Reynolds St., Ste. 100, 16101, P 95,000, (724) 658-1488, Fax (724) 658-0313, nitch@lawrencecounty.com, www.lawrencecounty.com

**Norristown** • *Montgomery County Dept. of Eco. & Workforce Dev.* • Jerry Birkelbach, Exec. Dir., 1430 Dekalb St., 5th Flr., P.O. Box 311, 19404, P 706,000, (610) 278-5950, Fax (610) 278-5944, www.montcopa.org

**North Cambria** • *Northern Cambria Comm. Dev. Corp.* • Matthew Barczak, Pres., 4200 Crawford Ave., Ste. 200, 15714, P 40,000, (814) 948-4444, Fax (814) 948-4449

**Oil City** • *NW Pennsylvania Reg. Planning & Dev. Comm.* • 395 Seneca St., P.O. Box 1127, 16301, (814) 677-4800, Fax (814) 677-7663, www.nwcommission.org

**Oil City** • *Oil Region Alliance of Bus. & Ind.* • 206 Seneca St., 4th Flr., P.O. Box 128, 16301, P 56,000, (814) 677-3152, Fax (814) 677-5206, www.oilregion.org

**Philadelphia** • *Delaware Valley Reg. Planning Comm.* • Barry Seymour, Exec. Dir., 190 N. Independence Mall West, 19106, P 5,000,000, (215) 592-1800, Fax (215) 592-9125, www.dvrpc.org

**Philadelphia** • *Philadelphia Ind. Dev. Corp.* • 1500 Market St., 2600 Centre Sq. W., 19102, P 1,700,000, (215) 496-8020, Fax (215) 977-9618, www.pidc-pa.org

**Philipsburg** • *Moshannon Valley Eco. Dev. Partnership* • Jeff Mitchell, Pres., 200 Shady Ln., 16866, P 34,000, M 170, (814) 342-2260, Fax (814) 342-2878, www.mvedp.org

**Pittsburgh** • *Allegheny County Dept. of Eco. Dev.* • Dennis Davin, Dir., 425 Sixth Ave., Ste. 800, 15219, P 1,200,000, (412) 350-1000, Fax (412) 642-2217, www.county.allegheny.pa.us

**Pittsburgh** • *Reg. Ind. Dev. Corp. of Southwestern PA* • Donald F. Smith Jr., Pres., 425 6th Ave., Ste. 500, 15219, P 2,100,000, (412) 471-3939, Fax (412) 471-1740, dsmith@ridcswpa.com, www.ridc.org

**Pittston** • *Northeastern Pennsylvania Alliance* • Jeffrey Box, Pres./CEO, 1151 Oak St., 18640, (570) 655-5581, Fax (570) 654-5137, www.nepa-alliance.org

**Pottsville** • *Schuylkill EDC* • Frank J. Zukas, Pres., 91 S. Progress Ave., 17901, P 151,000, (570) 622-1943, Fax (570) 622-2903, www.sed-co.com

**Quakertown** • *Nockamixon-Bucks Ind. & Comm. Dev. Auth.* • Stephen Shelly, Solicitor, 525 W. Broad St., 18951, P 200,000, (215) 538-1400, Fax (215) 538-9033

**Reading** • *Greater Berks Dev. Fund* • Debra Millman, Dir. of Bus. Dev., P.O. Box 8621, 19603, P 375,000, (610) 376-6739, Fax (610) 478-9553, greaterberks@readingpa.com, www.readingpa.com

**Saint Mary's** • *St. Mary's Area Eco. Dev. Corp.* • Raymond Klaiber Jr., Exec. Dir., 111 Erie Ave., 15857, P 14,500, (814) 834-2125, Fax (814) 834-2126, stmarysedc@alltel.net

**Scranton** • *Lackawanna County Ind. Dev. Auth.* • Mary Ellen Clark, Secy., 200 Adams Ave., 5th Flr., 18503, P 212,455, (570) 963-6862, Fax (570) 342-4088

**Shamokin** • *Shamokin Area Ind. Corp.* • Edward Twiggar, Pres., 415 E. Sunbury St., 17872, P 25,000, (570) 648-1541, Fax (570) 988-4436

**Shippensburg** • *Shippensburg Area Dev. Corp.* • Brad Everly, Pres., 53 W. King St., 17257, P 30,000, (717) 532-5509, Fax (717) 532-7501, www.shippensburg.org

**Somerset** • *Somerset County Eco. Dev. Cncl.* • Jeffrey Silka, Exec. Dir., 125 N. Center Ave., P.O. Box 48, 15501, P 82,000, (814) 445-9655, Fax (814) 443-4610, contact@scedc.net, www.scedc.net

**State College** • *Chamber of Bus. & Ind. Of Centre County* • John F. Coleman Jr., Pres./CEO, 200 Innovation Blvd., Ste. 150, 16803, P 124,000, M 1,000, (814) 234-1829, Fax (814) 234-5869, cbicc@cbicc.org, www.cbicc.org

**Sunbury** • *Northumberland County Ind. Dev. Auth.* • James E. King, Dir., 399 S. Fifth St., 17801, P 95,000, M 112, (570) 988-4279, Fax (570) 988-4436, jking@norrycopa.net, www.centralpachamber.com

**Titusville** • *Titusville Ind. Fund* • P.O. Box 425, 16354, P 6,000, (814) 827-3668, Fax (814) 827-2696, www.tcda.org

**Tobyhanna** • *Pocono Mountains Eco. Dev.* • Chuck Leonard, Exec. Dir., 300 Community Dr., Ste. D, 18466, P 163,000, (570) 839-1992, (877) 736-7700, Fax (570) 839-6681, cleonard@pmedc.com, www.pmedc.com

**Uniontown** • *Fay-Penn Eco. Dev. Cncl.* • 2 W. Main St., Ste. 407, 15401, P 148,644, (724) 437-7913, Fax (724) 437-7315, www.faypenn.org

**Washington** • *Redev. Auth. of the County of Washington* • William McGowen, Exec. Dir., 100 W. Beau St., 15301, P 209,000, (724) 228-6875, Fax (724) 228-6829, redevelopment@racw.net, www.racw.net

**Waynesburg** • *Greene County Ind. Dev. Auth.* • Ms. Robbie Matesic, Acting Dir., 49 S. Washington St., 15370, P 40,000, (724) 627-9259, Fax (724) 627-6569, rmatesic@co.greene.pa.us, www.greenecountyida.org

**Wilkes-Barre** • *Greater Wilkes-Barre Chamber's Ind. Fund* • Todd Vonderheid, Pres./CEO, Two Public Square, P.O. Box 5340, 18710, P 353,000, (570) 823-2101, Fax (570) 822-5951, wbcofc@wilkes-barre.org, www.wilkes-barre.org

**Wilkes-Barre** • *Greater Wilkes-Barre Dev. Corp.* • Todd Vonderheid, Pres./CEO, Two Public Square, P.O. Box 5340, 18710, P 353,000, (570) 823-2101, Fax (570) 822-5951, wbcofc@wilkes-barre.org, www.wilkes-barre.org

**Wilkes-Barre** • *Luzerne County Ofc. Of Comm. Dev.* • Andrew Reilly, Dir., 54 W. Union St., 18702, P 328,000, (570) 824-7214, Fax (570) 829-2910, www.luzernecounty.org

**York** • *York County Eco. Dev. Corp.* • Darrell Auterson, Pres., 144 Roosevelt Ave., Ste. 100, 17401, P 416,322, (717) 846-8879, Fax (717) 843-8837, ycedc@ycedc.org, www.ycedc.org

# Puerto Rico

## Communities

**San Juan** • *Puerto Rico Ind. Dev. Co.* • Javier Morales, Exec. Dir., GPO Box 362350, 00936, P 3,920,000, (787) 758-4747, Fax (787) 764-1415, www.pridco.com

# Rhode Island

## Federal

**U.S. SBA, Rhode Island Dist. Ofc.** • Mark Hayward, Dist. Dir., 380 Westminster St., Rm. 511, Providence, 02903, (401) 528-4561, Fax (401) 528-4539, www.sba.gov/ri

## State

**Rhode Island Eco. Dev. Corp.** • Saul Kaplan, Exec. Dir., 315 Iron Horse Way, Ste. 101, Providence, 02908, (401) 278-9100, Fax (401) 273-8270, www.riedc.com

## Communities

**Bristol** • *Bristol Eco. Dev. Comm.* • Diane Williamson, Dir. of Comm. Dev., 10 Court St., 02809, P 24,000, (401) 253-7000, Fax (401) 253-1570, www.onlinebristol.com

**Cranston** • *City of Cranston-Dept. of Eco. Dev.* • Lawrence DiBoni, Dir., City Hall, 869 Park Ave., 02910, P 81,000, (401) 780-3166, Fax (401) 780-3179, www.cranstonri.com

**Cumberland** • *Eco. Dev. Found. of Rhode Island* • Scott A. Gibbs, Pres., 1300 Highland Corp. Dr., Ste. 202, 02864, P 250,000, (401) 658-1050, Fax (401) 658-1064, sgibbs@edf-ri.com, www.edf-ri.com

**Cumberland** • *New England Eco. Dev. Svcs. Inc.* • Scott A. Gibbs, Pres., 1300 Highland Corp. Dr., Ste. 202, 02864, P 250,000, (401) 658-0665, Fax (401) 658-0630, sgibbs@needsinc.com, www.needsinc.com

**East Providence** • *East Providence Eco. Dev. Comm.* • Jeanne Boyle, Dir. of Planning, 145 Taunton Ave., City Hall, 02914, P 48,600, (401) 435-7500, Fax (401) 435-7611, www.eastprovidenceri.com

**Lincoln** • *Lincoln Town Planning Dept.* • T. Joseph Almond, Town Admin., 100 Old River Rd., P.O. Box 100, 02865, P 21,000, (401) 333-1100, Fax (401) 333-3648, www.lincolnri.org

**Pawtucket** • *Dept. of Plan & Redevelopment - City of Pawtucket* • Michael D. Cassidy, Dir., 175 Main St., 02860, P 72,958, (401) 724-5200, Fax (401) 726-6237

**Warwick** • *City of Warwick Dept. of Eco. Dev.* • Warwick City Hall, 3275 Post Rd., 02886, P 86,000, (401) 738-2000

**West Warwick** • *West Warwick Planning Board* • Robert Malavich, Town Planner, 1170 Main St., 02893, P 30,000, (401) 827-9026, Fax (401) 822-9252, www.westwarwickri.org

**Westerly** • *Westerly Town* • Marilyn Shellman, Town Planner, 45 Broad St., 02891, P 22,695, (401) 348-2549, Fax (401) 348-2513, www.westerly.govoffice.com

EDC

# South Carolina

## Federal

**South Carolina Dept. of Commerce** · Joe Taylor Jr., Secy. of Commerce, 1201 Main St., Ste.1600, Columbia, 29201, (803) 737-0400, Fax (803) 737-0418, www.sccommerce.com

## Communities

**Abbeville** · *Abbeville County Dev. Bd.* · Steve Bowles, Dev. Svcs. Dir., P.O. Box 533, 29620, P 26,000, (864) 366-2181, Fax (864) 366-9266, acdb@wctel.net, www.discoverabbeville.com

**Aiken** · *Eco. Dev. Partnership* · Fred Humes, Dir., P.O. Box 1708, 29802, P 170,000, (803) 641-3300, Fax (803) 641-3369, fhumes@edpsc.org, www.edpsc.org

**Allendale** · *Allendale County Dev. Bd.* · Sue Myrick, Cncl. Clerk, P.O. Box 190, 29810, P 11,200, (803) 584-4611, Fax (803) 584-7042, www.allendalecounty.com

**Anderson** · *Anderson County Eco. Dev.* · Heather Jones, Dir., 126 N. McDuffie St., 29621, P 187,000, (864) 260-4386, Fax (864) 260-4369, hjones@andersoncountysc.org, www.advance2anderson.com

**Bamberg** · *Bamberg County Dev. Bd.* · Booker Patrick, Finance Dir., P.O. Box 149, 29003, P 16,991, (803) 245-5191, Fax (803) 245-3027, www.bambergcountydevelopmentboard.com

**Barnwell** · *Barnwell County Eco. Dev. Comm.* · Marshall Martin, Exec. Dir., P.O. Box 898, 29812, P 25,000, (803) 259-1263, Fax (803) 259-0030, bcedc1@bellsouth.net, www.discoverbarnwellcounty.com

**Beaufort** · *Lowcountry Eco. Network* · Kim Statler, Exec. Dir., 917 Bay St., Ste. 207, 29902, P 120,937, (843) 379-3955, Fax (843) 379-3954, www.lowcountrynet.org

**Bennettsville** · *Marlboro County Eco. Dev. Partnership* · Butch Mills, Exec. Dir., 214 E. Market St., 29512, P 28,813, (843) 479-5626, Fax (843) 479-2663, butchmills@marlborocountysc.org, www.marlborocountysc.org

**Bishopville** · *Lee County Eco. Dev. Alliance* · Jeff Burgess, Exec. Dir., 102 E. Council St., P.O. Box 481, 29010, P 20,090, (803) 484-9832, Fax (803) 484-4373, info@leecountysc.com, www.leecountysc.com

**Camden** · *Kershaw County Eco. Dev. Bd.* · Nelson Lindsey, Exec. Dir., 700 W. Dekalb St., P.O. Box 763, 29020, P 52,647, (803) 425-7685, Fax (803) 425-7687, econ.develop@kershaw.sc.gov, www.kershawcountysc.org

**Cheraw** · *see Chesterfield*

**Chesterfield** · *Chesterfield County Eco. Dev. Bd.* · Cherry McCoy, Exec. Dir., P.O. Box 192, 29709, P 43,000, (843) 623-6500, Fax (843) 623-3167, cherryatcc@shtc.net, www.chesterfieldcountysc.org

**Columbia** · *Central SC Alliance* · G. Michael Briggs, Pres./CEO, 1201 Main St., Ste. 100, 29201, P 986,276, (803) 733-1131, (866) 278-9098, Fax (803) 733-1125, info@centralsc.org, www.centralsc.org

**Columbia** · *Palmetto Eco. Dev. Corp.* · Ralph U. Thomas, Pres., 1201 Main St., Ste. 1710, 29201, P 800,000, (803) 254-9211, Fax (803) 771-0233, mail@scpowerteam.com, www.scpowerteam.com

**Conway** · *Myrtle Beach Reg. Eco. Dev. Corp.* · Hugh Owens, Pres./CEO, 2431 Hwy. 501 E., 29526, P 175,000, M 100, (843) 347-4604, Fax (843) 347-2292, info@myrtlebeachdevelopment.com, www.myrtlebeachdevelopment.com

**Dillon** · *Dillon County Dev. Bd.* · Dave Bailey, Exec. Dir., P.O. Drawer 911, 29536, P 32,000, (843) 774-1402, Fax (843) 841-3872, dilloncountydb@bellsouth.net, www.dilloncounty.org

**Fort Mill** · *York County Eco. Dev. Bd.* · Mark Farris, Dir., 1830 Second Baxter Crossing, 29708, P 190,097, (803) 802-4300, Fax (803) 802-4299, mark.farris@yorkcountygov.com, www.ycedb.com

**Fountain Inn** · *Fountain Inn Eco. Dev.* · Van Board, Eco. Dev. Dir., 315 N. Main, 29644, P 6,000, (864) 409-1050, van.board@fountaininn.org, www.fountaininn.org

**Gaffney** · *Cherokee County Eco. Dev. Bd.* · Jim Cook III, Exec. Dir., 101 Campus Dr., 29341, P 53,000, (864) 206-2804, Fax (864) 206-2801, cookj@sccsc.edu, www.cherokeecounty-sc.org

**Georgetown** · *Georgetown County Eco. Dev.* · Wayne Gregory, Dir. of Eco. Dev., 716 Prince St., 29440, P 60,000, (843) 545-3161, Fax (843) 545-3259, info@seegeorgetown.com, www.seegeorgetown.com

**Greenwood** · *Greenwood Partnership Alliance* · Mark H. Warner, CEO, 109 Court Ave. W., 29646, P 67,000, (864) 388-1250, Fax (864) 388-1253, mwarner@partnershipalliance.com, www.partnershipalliance.com

**Hampton** · *Hampton County Eco. Dev. Comm.* · Sandy Fowler, Exec. Dir., P.O. Box 672, 29924, P 21,386, (803) 943-7521, Fax (803) 943-7538, www.hamptoncountyedc.com

**Kingstree** · *Williamsburg County Dev. Bd.* · Frank Hilton McGill Jr., Exec. Dir., P.O. Box 1132, 29556, P 37,217, (843) 382-9393, Fax (843) 382-5353, hmcgill@ftc-i.net, www.williamsburgcountydevelopment.com

**Lancaster** · *Lancaster County Eco. Dev. Corp.* · Allen Keith Tunnell, Pres., 210 W. Gay St., P.O. Box 973, 29721, P 67,000, (803) 285-9471, Fax (803) 285-9472, keith.tunnell@lancastersc-edc.com, www.lancasterscworks.com

**Manning** · *Clarendon County Dev. Bd.* · John Truluck, Exec. Dir., P.O. Box 670, 29102, P 32,000, (803) 435-8813, (800) 729-0973, Fax (803) 435-4925, jtruluck@sc.rr.com, www.clarendoncountyusa.com

**Marion** · *Marion County Eco. Dev. Comm.* · Rodney Berry, Exec. Dir., P.O. Box 840, 29571, P 35,000, (843) 423-8235, Fax (843) 423-8233, rberry@marionsc.org, www.marioncountysc.com

**McCall** · *see Bennettsville*

**McCormick** · *McCormick County Dev. Bd.* · George Woodsby, Eco. Dev. Dir., 362 Airport Rd., 29835, P 10,000, (864) 852-2231, Fax (864) 852-2783, mccormickco@wctel.net, www.mccormickcountysc.gov

**Moncks Corner** · *Berkeley County Eco. Dev. Dept.* · Gene Butler, Eco. Dev. Dir., P.O. Box 6122, 29461, P 160,000, (843) 719-4096, Fax (843) 719-4381, gbutler@co.berkeley.sc.us, www.berkeleycountysc.gov

**North Charleston** · *Charleston Reg. Dev. Alliance* · David Ginn, Pres./CEO, Trident Research Center, 5300 International Blvd., Ste. 103-A, 29418, P 550,000, (843) 767-9300, Fax (843) 760-4535, alliance@crda.org, www.crda.org

**Orangeburg** · *Orangeburg County Dev. Comm.* · C. Gregory Robinson, Exec. Dir., P.O. Box 1303, 29116, P 91,582, (803) 536-3333, Fax (803) 534-1165, grobinson@ocdc.com, www.ocdc.com

**Pageland** · *see Chesterfield*

**Pickens** · *Eco. Dev. Alliance-Pickens County* · A. Ray Farley II CEcD, Exec. Dir., P.O. Box 279, 29671, P 110,757, (864) 898-1500, Fax (864) 898-1550, rfarley@alliancepickens.com, www.alliancepickens.com

**Rock Hill · *Rock Hill Eco. Dev. Corp.* ·** Rick Norwood, Mktg. Mgr., 155 Johnston St., P.O. Box 11706, 29731, P 61,200, (803) 329-7090, Fax (803) 329-7007, rnorwood@ci.rock-hill.sc.us, www.rockhillusa.com

**Saint Matthews · *Calhoun County Dev. Comm.* ·** Courthouse Annex, Rm. 114, 29135, P 15,185, (803) 655-5650, Fax (803) 655-6110, calhounchamber@sc.rr.com, www.calhouncountychamber.org

**Spartanburg · *Spartanburg Dev. Assn.* ·** 1004 S. Pine St., 29302, P 250,000, (864) 585-1007, Fax (864) 573-6534, info@thesda.org, www.thesda.org

**Summerville · *Dorchester County Eco. Dev. Dept.* ·** Jon Baggett, Dir., 402 N. Main St., Ste. C, 29483, P 119,000, (843) 875-9109, Fax (843) 821-9994, info@dorchesterforbusiness.com, www.dorchesterforbusiness.com

**Sumter · *Sumter Dev. Bd.* ·** Jay Schwedler, Pres., 32 E. Calhoun St., 29150, P 112,000, (803) 418-0700, Fax (803) 775-0915, www.sumteredge.com

**Union · *Union County Dev. Bd.* ·** Andrena Powell-Baker, Dir., 207 S. Herndon St., 29379, P 30,000, (864) 319-1097, Fax (864) 319-1099, www.unioncountydevelopment.com

**Walhalla · *Oconee County Eco. Dev. Comm.* ·** James Alexander, Dir., 502 E. Main St., 29691, P 70,840, (864) 638-4210, Fax (864) 638-4209, jalexander@oconeesc.com, www.oconeesc.com

# South Dakota

## Federal

**U.S. SBA, South Dakota Dist. Ofc. ·** John L. Brown II, Dist. Dir., 2329 N. Career Ave., Ste. 105, Sioux Falls, 57107, (605) 330-4243, Fax (605) 330-4215, www.sba.gov/sd

## State

**Dept. of Tourism & State Dev. ·** Richard Benda, Cabinet Secy., 711 E. Wells Ave., Pierre, 57501, (605) 773-3301, Fax (605) 773-3256, www.tsd.sd.gov

## Communities

**Aberdeen · *Aberdeen Dev. Corp.* ·** James C. Barringer, Exec. V.P., 416 Production St. N., 57401, P 25,000, (605) 229-5335, Fax (605) 229-6839, jimbarringer@midco.net, www.adcsd.com

**Aberdeen · *NE Cncl. of Govt.* ·** Eric Senger, Exec. Dir., 2201 6th Ave. S.E., P.O. Box 1985, 57402, (605) 626-2595, Fax (605) 626-2975

**Belle Fourche · *Belle Fourche Dev. Corp.* ·** Teresa Schanzenbach, Exec. Dir., 415 5th Ave., 57717, P 5,000, M 50, (605) 892-2676, (888) 345-5859, Fax (605) 892-4633, director@bellefourchechamber.org, www.bellefourchechamber.org

**Beresford · *Beresford Ind. Dev.* ·** Jerry Zeimetz, City Mgr., 101 N. 3rd, 57004, P 2,100, (605) 763-2008

**Brandon · *Brandon Dev. Found. Inc.* ·** Joel Jorgenson, Dir., 304 Main Ave., P.O. Box 95, 57005, P 7,000, (605) 582-6515, Fax (605) 582-6831, www.brandonsd.com

**Britton · *Britton Dev. Corp.* ·** Tom Farber, Pres., P.O. Box 413, 57430, P 4,000, (605) 448-5150, Fax (605) 448-2810, www.brittonchamber.com

**Centerville · *Centerville Dev. Corp.* ·** Bill Hansen, Eco. Dev. Coord., 2201 State St., 57014, P 1,000, (605) 563-2019, www.centervillesd.org

**Chamberlain · *Lake Francis Case Dev.* ·** April Reis, Exec. Dir., 115 W. Lawler Ave., 57325, P 2,432, (605) 234-4419, Fax (605) 234-4418, lfcdc@midstatesd.net, www.dakotadevelopment.com

**Dakota Dunes · *Dakota Dunes Dev. Co.* ·** Dennis Melstad, Pres., 335 Sioux Point Rd., Ste. 100, 57049, P 2,627, (605) 232-5990, Fax (605) 232-5925, www.dakotadunes.com

**Dell Rapids · *Dell Rapids Dev. Corp.* ·** Lee Burggraff, Pres., 503 W. 4th, 57022, P 3,200, (605) 428-3909, www.dellrapids.net

**Estelline · *Estelline Area Eco. Dev. Corp.* ·** Ed Ebbers, Secy., P.O. Box 278, 57234, P 700, M 130, (605) 873-2241

**Faith · *Faith Country Dev. Corp.* ·** Randy Thomas, Pres., P.O. Box 341, 57626, P 500, (605) 967-2242, (605) 967-2001

**Gregory · *Gregory Bus. & Ind. Dev.* ·** Ron Kyburz, Pres., %City of Gregory, P.O. Box 436, 57533, P 1,350, (605) 835-8270, www.cityofgregory.com

**Hayti · *Hamlin County Ind. Dev. Comm.* ·** Dick Wagner, Chrmn., P.O. Box 237, 57241, P 5,540, (605) 783-3201, Fax (605) 783-3201

**Herreid · *Herreid Eco. Dev. Corp.* ·** Dean Schwartz, Pres., 110 S. Main, P.O. Box 275, 57632, P 500, (605) 437-2294, Fax (605) 437-2278, www.herreidsd.com

**Howard · *Howard Industries* ·** Dave Callies, Secy., P.O. Box 187, 57349, P 900, (605) 772-4561, Fax (605) 772-5492, www.howardsd.com

**Huron · *Greater Huron Dev. Corp.* ·** Jim Borszich, Exec. Dir., 1705 Dakota Ave. S., 57350, P 11,987, M 210, (605) 352-0363, (800) 487-6673, Fax (605) 352-8321, ghdc@huronsd.com, www.huronsd.com

**McLaughlin · *McLaughlin Eco. Dev.* ·** Arnold Schott, Mayor, P.O. Box 169, 57642, P 775, (605) 823-4428, Fax (605) 823-4429

**Mitchell · *Mitchell Area Dev. Corp.* ·** Bryan Hisel, Exec. Dir., 601 N. Main, P.O. Box 1087, 57301, P 18,741, M 210, (605) 996-1140, Fax (605) 996-8273, bhiselmadc@santel.net, www.mitchellsd.org

**Pierre · *Pierre Eco. Dev. Corp.* ·** Jim Protexter, Exec. Dir., 800 W. Dakota, P.O. Box 548, 57501, P 14,000, (605) 224-6610, (800) 962-2034, Fax (605) 224-6485, www.pedco.biz

**Rapid City · *Rapid City Area Eco. Dev. Partnership* ·** 525 University Loop, Ste. 101, 57701, P 119,000, (605) 343-1880, Fax (605) 343-1916, info@rapiddevelopment.com, www.rapiddevelopment.com

**Redfield · *Redfield Dev. Corp.* ·** Corwy Baloun, Pres., 626 Main, 57469, P 2,800, (605) 472-4551, Fax (605) 472-4553, www.redfield-sd.com

**Sioux Falls · *Sioux Falls Dev. Found.* ·** Slater R. Barr, Pres., 200 N. Phillips Ave., Ste. 101, P.O. Box 907, 57101, P 217,500, M 360, (605) 339-0103, Fax (605) 339-0055, slater@siouxfalls.com, www.siouxfallsdevelopment.com

**Spearfish · *Spearfish Eco. Dev. Corp.* ·** Bryan Walker, Eco. Dev. Dir., 106 W. Kansas, P.O. Box 550, 57783, P 13,000, (605) 642-3832, spearfishdevelopment@rushmore.com, www.spearfishdevelopment.com

**Sturgis · *Black Hills Comm. Eco. Dev. Inc.* ·** Jim Doolittle, Exec. Dir., 2885 Dickson Dr., P.O. Box 218, 57785, P 100,000, (605) 347-5837, Fax (605) 347-5223

**Sturgis · *Sturgis Eco. Dev. Corp.* ·** Nort Johnson, Pres., 2885 Dickson Dr., P.O. Box 218, 57785, P 6,500, (605) 347-4906, Fax (605) 347-5223

**Tripp · *Tripp Dev. Corp.* ·** Bob Just, Bd. Member, P.O. Box 105, 57376, P 750, (605) 935-6661

**Tyndall · *Tyndall Dev. Co.* ·** Ron Wagner, Pres., P.O. Box 454, 57066, P 1,239, (888) 877-5035, Fax (605) 589-4109

**Wakonda · *Wakonda Dev. Corp.* ·** Ron Peterson, Treas., 29714 455th Ave., 57073, P 400, (605) 263-3526

**EDC**

**Watertown** · *Focus Watertown* · Craig Atkins, Pres., P.O. Box 332, 57201, P 21,000, M (605) 884-0340, (888) 898-6767, Fax (605) 882-0199, info@focuswatertown.com, www.focuswatertown.com

**Webster** · *Webster Area Dev. Corp.* · Jeff Grobe, Eco. Dev. Coord., P.O. Box 6, 57274, P 1,950, (605) 345-3159, (605) 345-3639, Fax (605) 345-3509, www.webstersd.com

**Wessington Springs** · *Wessington Springs Area Dev. Corp.* · Laura Kieser, Coord., 101 Wallace Ave. S., P.O. Box 132, 57382, P 1,011, M 100, (605) 539-1929, Fax (605) 539-0249, wsprings@venturecomm.net, www.wessingtonsprings.com

**Wilmot** · *Wilmot Comm. Dev. Corp.* · Jeffrey Jurgens, Pres., P.O. Box 160, 57279, P 550, (605) 938-4661

**Winner** · *South Central Dev. Corp.* · Brad Schramm, Exec. Dir., 201 Monroe, P.O. Box 624, 57580, P 3,400, (605) 842-1551, develop@winnersd.org, www.winnersd.org

**Yankton** · *Yankton Ofc. Of Eco. Dev.* · Mike Dellinger, Exec. Dir., 803 E. Fourth St., P.O. Box 588, 57078, P 20,000, M 100, (605) 665-9011, (888) 926-5866, Fax (605) 665-7501, mdellinger@yanktonsd.com, www.yanktonedc.com

# Tennessee

## Federal

**U.S. SBA, Tennessee Dist. Ofc.** · W. Clint Smith, Dist. Dir., 50 Vantage Way, Ste. 201, Nashville, 37228, (615) 736-5881, Fax (615) 736-7232, www.sba.gov/tn

## State

**Tennessee Eco. Dev. Dept.** · Matt Kisber, Comm., 312 Rosa L. Parks Ave., 11th Flr., Nashville, 37243, (615) 741-1888, Fax (615) 741-7306, matt.kisber@state.tn.us, www.state.tn.us/ecd

## Communities

**Athens** · *McMinn County Eco. Dev. Auth.* · Jack Hammontree, Exec. V.P., P.O. Box 767, 37371, P 50,270, M 110, (423) 745-1506, Fax (423) 745-1507, jack@mcminncoeda.org, www.mcminncoeda.org

**Chattanooga** · *Chattanooga Area C/C-Eco. Dev. Dept.* · Trevor Hamilton, V.P. Eco. Dev., 811 Broad St., Ste. 100, 37402, P 492,047, (423) 756-2121, Fax (423) 267-7242, info@chattanoogachamber.com, www.chattanoogachamber.com

**Dayton** · *Rhea Eco. & Tourism Cncl.* · Raymond Walker, Exec. Dir., 107 Main St., 37321, P 29,400, (423) 775-6171, Fax (423) 570-0105, director@rheacountyetc.com, www.rheacountyetc.com

**Gallatin** · *City of Gallatin Eco. Dev. Agency* · Clay Walker, Exec. Dir., 132 W. Main St., Rm. 210, P.O. Box 773, 37066, P 25,000, (615) 451-5940, Fax (615) 451-5941, edainfo@gallatin-tn.gov, www.gallatintn-eda.com

**Hendersonville** · *Eco/Community Dev. Comm. of City of Hendersonville* · Don Long, Dir., 101 Maple Dr. N., 37075, P 42,000, (615) 264-5329, (615) 822-1000, Fax (615) 264-5327, www.gohendersonvilletn.com

**Jackson** · *West Tennessee Ind. Assn.* · Michael M. Philpot, Exec. Dir., 26 Conrad Dr., 38305, (731) 668-4300, (800) 336-2036, Fax (731) 668-7554, westtn@wtia.org, www.wtia.org

**Jasper** · *Marion County Partnership for Eco. Dev.* · Howell Moss, Chrmn., 302 Betsy Pack Dr., 37347, P 27,776, (423) 942-5103, Fax (423) 942-0098, marioncoc@bellsouth.net, www.marioncountychamber.com

**Johnson City** · *Johnson City/Jonesborough/Washington County EDB* · P.C. Snapp, Exec. Dir., 603 E. Market St., Ste. 200, 37601, P 110,000, (423) 975-2380, Fax (423) 975-2385, pcsnapp@jcedb.org, www.jcedb.org

**La Vergne** · *see Murfreesboro*

**Lebanon** · *Wilson County Joint Eco. & Comm. Dev. Bd.* · G.C. Hixson, Exec. Dir., 115 Castle Heights Ave. N., Ste. 102, 37087, P 104,000, (615) 443-1210, Fax (615) 443-0277, info@doingbiz.org, www.doingbiz.org

**Lewisburg** · *Lewisburg Ind. Dev. Bd.* · Terry Wallace, Dir., P.O. Box 1968, 37091, P 10,422, (931) 359-1544, Fax (931) 359-7055, twallace@cityoflew.com, www.lewisburgtn.com

**Loudon** · *Loudon County Eco. Dev. Agency* · Doyle Arp, Chrmn., 274 Blair Bend Dr., 37774, P 37,086, (865) 458-8889, Fax (865) 458-3792, iceda@loudoncountyeda.org, www.loudoncountyeda.org

**Manchester** · *Ind. Bd. Of Coffee County* · Ted Hackney, Exec. Dir., 1329 McArthur, Ste. 4, 37355, P 50,869, (931) 723-5120, Fax (931) 723-5121, ib@coffeetn.com, www.coffeetn.com

**Maryville** · *Eco. Dev. Bd. Of Blount County* · Bryan Daniels CEcD, Exec. V.P., 201 S. Washington St., 37804, P 120,000, (865) 983-7715, Fax (865) 984-1386, info@blountindustry.com, www.blountindustry.com

**Memphis** · *Mid-South Minority Bus. Cncl.* · Luke Yancy III, Pres./CEO, 158 Madison Ave., Ste. 300, 38103, P M, 500, (901) 525-6512, Fax (901) 525-5204, lyancy@mmbc-memphis.org, www.mmbc-memphis.org.

**Mount Juliet** · *see Lebanon*

**Murfreesboro** · *Rutherford County C/C* · Holly S. Weber, V.P. of Eco. Dev., 501 Memorial Blvd., P.O. Box 864, 37133, P 223,000, (615) 869-0345, Fax (615) 278-2013, info@rutherfordchamber.org, www.rutherfordchamber.org

**Newport** · *Newport/Cocke County Eco. Dev. Comm.* · Eddie Lennon, Exec. Dir., 433 Prospect Ave., 37821, P 33,565, (423) 623-3008, Fax (423) 625-1846, eddielennon@bellsouth.net, www.edcncc.com

**Pigeon Forge** · *Pigeon Forge Comm. Dev.* · David Taylor, Dir., 225 Pine Mountain Rd., P.O. Box 1350, 37868, P 5,913, M 704, (865) 429-7474, Fax (865) 429-7322, inquire@cityofpigeonforge.com, www.cityofpigeonforge.com

**Pulaski** · *Pulaski-Giles County Eco. Dev. Comm.* · Dan Speer, Exec. Dir., 203 S. First St., 38478, P 29,269, M (931) 363-9138, Fax (931) 424-4460, dan@gilescountyedc.com, www.gilescountyedc.com

**Savannah** · *Savannah Ind. Dev. Corp.* · Steve Bunnell, CEO, 495 Main St., 38372, P 27,000, (731) 925-8181, Fax (731) 925-6987, info@tourhardincounty.org, www.tourhardincounty.org

**Sevierville** · *Sevier County Eco. Dev. Cncl.* · Allen Newton, Exec. Dir., P.O. Box 4066, 37864, P 81,000, (865) 428-2212, Fax (865) 453-2312, www.scedc.com

**Smyrna** · *see Murfreesboro*

**Union City** · *Obion County Joint EDC* · Jim Cooper, Dir., 214 E. Church St., 38261, P 33,000, (731) 885-0211, Fax (731) 885-7155, jcooper@obioncounty.org, www.obioncounty.org

**Vonore** · *Tellico Reservoir Dev. Agency* · Ron Hammontree, Exec. Dir., 59 Excellence Way., 37885, P 15,000, (865) 673-8599, (800) 562-8732, Fax (423) 884-6869, trda@tds.net, www.tellico.com

**Watertown** · *see Lebanon*

**Waverly** · *Humphreys County Eco. Dev. Cncl.* · John Hedge, Exec. Dir., 301 N. Church St., P.O. Box 218, 37185, P 18,000, (931) 296-5199, Fax (931) 296-2135, humpco_edc@waverly.net

# Texas

## Federal

**U.S. SBA, El Paso Dist. Ofc.** • Phillip Silva, Dist. Dir., 211 N. Florence, Ste. 201, El Paso, 79901, (915) 834-4600, Fax (915) 834-4689, www.sba.gov/tx

**U.S. SBA, Dallas/Fort Worth Dist. Ofc.** • Herbert Austin, Dist. Dir., 4300 Amon Carter Blvd., Ste. 114, Fort Worth, 76155, (817) 684-5500, Fax (817) 684-5516, www.sba.gov/tx

**U.S. SBA, Lower Rio Grande Valley Dist. Ofc.** • Kimberly Jones, Dist. Dir., 222 E. Van Buren Ave., Ste. 500, Harlingen, 78550, (956) 427-8533, Fax (956) 427-8537, www.sba.gov/tx

**U.S. SBA, Houston Dist. Ofc.** • Manuel Gonzalez, Dist. Dir., 8701 S. Gessner Dr., Ste. 1200, Houston, 77074, (713) 773-6500, Fax (713) 773-6550, www.sba.gov/tx

**US SBA, Lubbock Dist. Ofc.** • Herbert Johnston, Dist. Dir., 1205 Texas Ave., Rm. 408, Lubbock, 79401, (806) 472-7462, Fax (806) 472-7487, www.sba.gov/tx

**U.S. SBA, San Antonio Dist. Ofc.** • Dorothy Overal, Acting Reg. Admin., 17319 San Pedro Ave., Ste. 200, San Antonio, 78232, (210) 403-5900, Fax (210) 403-5936, www.sba.gov/tx

## Communities

**Abilene** • *Abilene Ind. Found.* • Bill Ehrie, Pres., 174 Cypress St., Ste. 300, P.O. Box 2281, 79604, P 125,000, (325) 673-7349, Fax (325) 673-9193, www.developabilene.com

**Alice** • *Alice-Jim Wells County EDC* • Dean Kruckenberg, Dir., 612 E. Main St., P.O. Box 1609, 78333, P 40,017, (361) 664-3454, Fax (361) 664-2291, deank@alicetx.org, www.alicetx.org

**Angleton** • *Eco. Dev. Alliance for Brazoria County* • Robert Worley, Pres./CEO, 201 E. Myrtle, Ste. 139, 77515, P 300,000, M 105, (979) 848-0560, (800) 759-1822, Fax (979) 848-0403, info@eda-bc.com, www.eda-bc.com.

**Aransas County** • *see Corpus Christi*

**Bay City** • *Matagorda County Eco. Dev. Corp.* • Owen Bludau, Exec. Dir., 2200 7th St., Ste. 304, 77414, P 39,000, (979) 245-8913, Fax (979) 245-5661, obludau@co.matagorda.tx.us, www.mcedc.net

**Baytown** • *Baytown West Chambers County Eco. Dev. Found.* • Michael Shields, Exec. Dir., 1300 Rollingbrook, Ste. 401, 77521, P 72,000, (281) 420-2961, Fax (281) 422-7682, baytownedf@baytownedf.org, www.baytownedf.org

**Bedford** • *Hurst-Euless-Bedford Eco. Dev. Found.* • Mary Martin Frazior, Dir., 2109 Martin Dr., P.O. Box 969, 76095, P 136,000, (817) 540-1053, Fax (817) 267-5111, maryfrazior@heb.org, www.heb.org

**Bee County** • *see Corpus Christi*

**Bellville** • *Bellville EDC* • 13 E. Main St., P.O. Box 670, 77418, P 4,000, (979) 865-0660, Fax (979) 865-9760, bedc@sbcglobal.net, www.bellville.com

**Belton** • *Belton Eco. Dev. Corp.* • Tommy Baker, Exec. Dir., P.O. Box 1388, 76513, P 18,000, (254) 770-2270, Fax (254) 770-2279, www.beltonedc.org

**Belton** • *Dev. Dist. of Central Texas* • Beth Correa, Coord., P.O. Box 729, 76513, (254) 770-2200, Fax (254) 770-2360, www.ddoct.org

**Brady** • *McCulloch County Ind. Found.* • Wendy Ellis, Pres., 101 E. 1st, 76825, P 8,000, (325) 597-3491, Fax (325) 792-9181, www.bradytx.com

**Brazoria County** • *see Angleton*

**Breckenridge** • *Breckenridge Eco. Dev.* • Virgil Moore, Exec. Dir., 100 E. Elm St., P.O. Box 1466, 76424, P 10,000, (254) 559-6228, Fax (254) 559-7104, vmoore@breckenridgetexas.com, www.breckenridgetexas.com

**Brenham** • *Eco. Dev. Found. Of Brenham* • Page Michel, Pres./CEO, 314 S. Austin St., 77833, P 14,000, (979) 836-8927, Fax (979) 836-3563, edf@brenhamtexas.com, www.brenhamtexas.com/economic

**Brownsville** • *Brownsville Eco. Dev. Cncl.* • Jason Hilts, Pres., 301 Mexico Blvd., Ste. F1, 78520, P 172,000, M 200, (956) 541-1183, (800) 552-5352, Fax (956) 546-3938, info@bedc.com, www.bedc.com

**Bryan** • *see College Station*

**Caldwell** • *Burleson County Ind. Found.* • Sal Zaccagnino, Pres., 301 N. Main, 77836, P 18,000, (979) 567-7979, Fax (979) 567-0818, www.burlesoncountytx.com

**Canadian** • *Canadian EDC* • Tamera Julian, Dir., 119 N. 2nd, 79014, P 2,500, (806) 323-5397, Fax (806) 323-9243, canadiantx@sbcglobal.net, www.canadiantx.com

**Carrollton** • *Carrollton Eco. Dev.* • Brad Mink, Dir., P.O. Box 110535, 75011, P 121,000, (972) 466-3391, Fax (972) 466-4882, econdev@cityofcarrollton.com, www.cityofcarrollton.com

**Carthage** • *Panola County Dev. Found.* • Ms. Tommie Ritter Smith, Secy., 300 W. Panola St., 75633, P 25,000, M 60, (903) 693-6634, Fax (903) 693-8578, chamber@carthagetexas.com, www.carthagetexas.com.

**Childress** • *Childress Eco. Dev. Corp.* • 1902 Ave. G N.W., P.O. Box 10, 79201, P 6,700, (940) 937-8629, Fax (940) 937-2520, cedc1@sbcglobal.net, www.childresstexas.com

**Clarendon** • *Clarendon-Donley County Eco. Dev. Corp.* • Linda Smith, City Secy., P.O. Box 1089, 79226, P 2,000, (806) 874-3438

**Cleveland** • *Cleveland Eco. Dev. Corp.* • Philip Cook, City Mgr., 907 E. Houston St., 77327, P 7,605, (281) 592-2667, Fax (281) 592-6624, pcook@citycleveland.net, www.clevelandtexas.com

**College Station** • *Research Valley Partnership* • Todd McDaniel, Pres./CEO, 1500 Research Pkwy., Ste. 270, 77845, P 150,000, (979) 260-1755, (800) 449-4012, Fax (979) 260-5252, tmcdaniel@researchvalley.org, www.researchvalley.org

**Comanche** • *Comanche Eco. Dev. Corp.* • P.O. Box 144, 76442, P 4,638, (325) 356-2032

**Conroe** • *Greater Conroe Eco. Dev. Cncl.* • Tom Stinson CEcD, Dir., 505 W. Davis St., P.O. Box 2347, 77305, P 45,879, (936) 538-7102, Fax (936) 756-6162, www.gcedc.org

**Coppell** • *City of Coppell Planning Dept.* • Gary Sieb, Dir. of Planning, 255 Parkway Blvd., 75019, P 39,500, (972) 304-3678, Fax (972) 304-7092, gsieb@ci.coppell.tx.us, www.ci.coppell.tx.us

**Corpus Christi** • *Coastal Bend Cncl. of Govts.* • John Buckner, Exec. Dir., 2910 Leopard, P.O. Box 9909, 78469, P 551,000, (361) 883-5743, Fax (361) 883-5749, www.cbcog98.org

**Corpus Christi** • *Corpus Christi Reg. Eco. Dev. Corp.* • Roland Mower, Pres./CEO, 1 Shoreline Plaza, 800 N. Shoreline, Ste. 1300S, 78401, P 319,260, (361) 882-7448, Fax (361) 882-9930, rcmower@ccredc.com, www.ccredc.com

**Crockett** • *Crockett Eco. & Ind. Dev. Corp.* • 1100 Edmiston Dr., P.O. Box 307, 75835, P 7,100, (936) 546-5636, Fax (936) 544-4355, suzanne@crockett.org, www.crockett.org

**Crowell** • *Crowell Ind. Dev.* • Stacy Henry, Pres., P.O. Box 848, 79227, P 1,200, (940) 684-1531

**Crystal City** • *Crystal City Eco. Dev.* • 101 E. Dimmit, P.O. Drawer 706, 78839, P 9,000, (830) 374-2900, Fax (830) 374-2123

**Dallas** • *City of Dallas Dept. of Eco. Dev.* • Karl Zavitkovsky, Dir., City Hall, 1500 Marilla, Rm. 5C South, 75201, P 1,300,000, (214) 670-1685, Fax (214) 670-0158, www.dallas-ecodev.org

**Dallas** • *Greater Dallas Chamber Eco. Dev. Group* • Mike Rosa, V.P., 700 N. Pearl, Ste. 1200, 75201, P 5,000,000, (214) 746-6735, Fax (214) 746-6669, www.dallaschamber.org

**Del Rio** • *Del Rio Area Dev. Found.* • Frank Larson, Pres., 1915 Veteran's Blvd., 78840, P 45,000, (830) 775-3551, Fax (830) 774-1813, info@drchamber.com, www.drchamber.com

**DFW Airport** • *North Texas Comm.* • Dan S. Petty, Pres., P.O. Box 610246, 75261, P 4,600,000, (972) 621-0400, Fax (972) 929-0916, ntc@ntc-dfw.org, www.ntc-dfw.org

**Dumas** • *Dumas Eco. Dev. Corp.* • Mike M. Running, Exec. Dir., 1015 N. Maddox, P.O. Box 595, 79029, P 16,000, (806) 934-3332, (877) 934-3332, Fax (806) 934-0180, running@dumasedc.org, www.dumasedc.org.

**Eagle Pass** • *Maverick County Dev. Corp.* • Judith Canales, Exec. Dir., P.O. Box 3693, 78853, P 47,297, (830) 773-6166, (800) 970-MCDC, Fax (830) 773-6287, info@eaglepassmcdc.com, www.eaglepassmcdc.com

**Early** • *Early Eco. Dev. Corp. Small Bus. Incubator* • Wanda Furgason, CDC, 104 E. Industrial Dr., 76802, P 2,588, (325) 649-9300, Fax (325) 643-4746, wanda@earlytx.com, www.earlychamber.com

**Edinburg** • *Cncl. For South Texas Eco. Progress* • 2540 W. Trenton Rd., P.O. Box 60, 78539, P 2,700,000, (956) 682-6371, (800) 682-6371, Fax (956) 971-3319, www.costep.org

**Edna** • *Jackson County Ind. Found.* • Patrick Brzozowski, Pres., P.O. Box 429, 77957, P 14,500, M 85, (361) 782-5229, Fax (361) 782-5310, jccc@ykc.com, www.jacksoncountytx.com

**El Paso** • *El Paso Reg. Eco. Dev.* • Bob Cook, Pres., 201 E. Main St., Ste. 1711, 79901, P 2,600,000, (915) 534-0523, Fax (915) 534-0516, bcook@elpasoredco.org, www.elpasoredco.org

**Euless** • *see Bedford*

**Farmers Branch** • *Farmers Branch Eco. Dev.* • John Land, Dir., 13000 William Dodson Pkwy., 75234, P 27,000, (972) 919-2512, Fax (972) 247-4836, john.land@farmersbranch.info, www.farmersbranch.info

**Flower Mound** • *Town of Flower Mound Eco. Dev.* • Melissa Glasgow, Dir. of Eco. Dev., 2121 Cross Timbers Rd., 75028, P 62,884, (972) 874-6044, Fax (972) 874-6451, melissa.glasgow@flower-mound.com, www.flower-mound.com/econdev

**Friona** • *Friona Eco. Dev. Corp.* • Bill Stovell, Pres., 621 Main, 79035, P 3,800, (806) 250-3491, Fax (806) 250-2348, fedc@wtrt.net, www.frionachamber.com

**Garland** • *Garland Eco. Dev. Partnership* • Paul Mayer, CEO, 520 N. Glenbrook Dr., 75040, P 240,876, (972) 272-7551, Fax (972) 276-9261, paul.mayer@garlandchamber.com, www.garlandchamber.com

**George West** • *Live Oak County Comm. Dev. Corp.* • P.O. Box 19, 78022, P 12,309, (361) 786-4330, www.georgewest.org/edc.htm

**Georgetown** • *City of Georgetown Eco. Dev. Dept.* • Mark Thomas, Dir., 614 Main St., P.O. Box 409, 78627, P 45,000, (512) 930-8475, Fax (512) 930-8445, ed@georgetowntx.org, www.investgeorgetown.org

**Giddings** • *Giddings Eco. Dev. Corp.* • Joyce Bise, Dir., 118 E. Richmond St., 78942, P 5,400, (979) 540-2721, Fax (979) 542-0950, www.giddingsedc.com

**Gladewater** • *Gladewater Eco. Dev. Corp.* • Lon Welton, Exec. Dir., 213 N. Main, P.O. Box 1445, 75647, P 6,087, (903) 845-5441, Fax (903) 845-1282, gedco@suddenlinkmail.com, www.gladewateredc.com

**Gonzales** • *Gonzales Area Dev. Corp.* • Ross Hendershot Jr., Pres., P.O. Box 904, 78629, P 18,500, (830) 672-6532, Fax (830) 672-6533, www.gonzalestexas.com

**Gorman** • *Gorman Eco. Dev. Corp.* • Cliffa Vaughn, Dir., 118 Kent, P.O. Box 236, 76454, P 1,236, (254) 734-3933, Fax (254) 734-2270, gedc@cctc.net

**Graham** • *Graham Eco. Dev. Cncl.* • Neal Blanton, Exec. Dir., 458 Oak St., P.O. Box 1465, 76450, P 9,000, (940) 549-6006, Fax (940) 549-5030, nblanton@grahamtexas.net, www.cityofgrahamtexas.com

**Grand Prairie** • *Grand Prairie Eco. Dev. Dept.* • Bob O'Neal, Eco. Dev. Dir., P.O. Box 534045, 75053, P 160,000, (972) 237-8160, Fax (972) 237-8161, boneal@gptx.org, www.gptx.org

**Groesbeck** • *Groesbeck Eco. Dev. Corp.* • Sharon Barnes, Exec. Dir., 401 W. Navasota, 76642, P 4,300, (254) 729-5375, Fax (254) 729-8155, srbarnes@glade.net, www.groesbeckedc.com

**Henderson** • *Henderson Eco. Dev. Corp.* • Sue Henderson, Gen. Mgr., 400 W. Main St., 75652, P 12,000, (903) 657-6551, Fax (903) 655-1296, hedco@hendersontx.us, www.hendersontx.us

**Houston** • *Bay Area Houston Eco. Partnership* • Bob Mitchell, Pres., 2525 Bay Area Blvd., Ste. 640, 77058, P 422,000, (281) 486-5535, Fax (281) 486-5068, info@bayareahouston.com, www.bayareahouston.com

**Houston** • *Greater Houston Partnership* • Maria Velasquez, Mgr. of Intl. Bus. Programs, Eco. Dev. Div., 1200 Smith St., Ste. 700, 77002, P 5,087,127, M 2,500, (713) 844-3636, Fax (713) 844-0236, mvelasquez@houston.org, www.houston.org

**Huntsville** • *Huntsville Eco. Dev. Council* • William Baine, City Mgr., 1212 Ave. M, 77340, P 38,500, (936) 291-5400, Fax (936) 291-5409, bbaine@huntsvilletx.gov, www.huntsvilletx.gov

**Hurst** • *see Bedford*

**Jacksonville** • *Jacksonville Dev. Corp.* • Darrell Prcin, Pres., 526 E. Commerce, P.O. Box 1604, 75766, P 15,000, (903) 586-2217, (800) 376-2217, Fax (903) 586-6944, mandy@jacksonvilletexas.com, www.jacksonvilleedc.com

**Jasper** • *Jasper Eco. Dev. Corp.* • Kari Ellis, Exec. Dir., 246 E. Milam, 75951, P 8,500, (409) 383-6120, Fax (409) 383-6122, info@jasperedc.com, www.jasperedc.com

**Jim Wells County** • *see Corpus Christi*

**Keller** • *Eco. Dev., City of Keller* • 1100 Bear Creek Pkwy., P.O. Box 770, 76244, P 37,000, (817) 743-4020, Fax (817) 743-4190, communitydevelopment@cityofkeller.com, www.cityofkeller.com

**Kemah** • *Kemah Comm. Dev. Corp.* • Dr. Glenda Johnson, Pres., 1401 Hwy. 146, 77565, P 2,330, (281) 334-1611, Fax (281) 334-6583, selam@kemah-tx.com, www.kemah-tx.gov

**Kerrville** • *Kerr Eco. Dev. Found.* • Guy Overby, Pres., 1700 Sidney Baker St., Ste. 200, 78028, P 50,000, (830) 896-1157, Fax (830) 896-1175, information@kerredf.org, www.kerredf.org

**Killeen** • *Killeen Eco. Dev.* • John Crutchfield, Pres., One Santa Fe Plz., P.O. Box 548, 76540, P 112,000, (254) 526-9551, Fax (254) 526-6090, jcrutchfield@gkcc.com, www.gkcc.com

**Kingsville** • *Kingsville Eco. Dev. Cncl.* • Dick Messbarger, Exec. Dir., 635 E. King St., P.O. Box 5032, 78364, P 26,331, (361) 592-6438, Fax (361) 592-0866, edc@kingsville.org, www.kingsvilleedc.org

**Kleberg County** • *see Corpus Christi*

**Lago Vista** · *Lago Vista Eco. Dev. Found.* · P.O. Box 4727, 78645, (512) 934-4134, (512) 267-1155, Fax (512) 267-2338, www.lagovistatexas.org

**Laredo** · *Laredo Dev. Found.* · Roger Creery, Exec. Dir., 616 Leal, P.O. Box 2682, 78044, P 224,695, (956) 722-0563, Fax (956) 722-6247, www.ldfonline.org

**Live Oak County** · *see Corpus Christi*

**Longview** · *Longview Eco. Dev. Corp.* · John Stroud, Exec. Dir., 410 N. Center St., 75601, P 60,000, (903) 753-7878, (800) 952-2613, Fax (903) 753-3646, stroud@longviewusa.com, www.longviewusa.com

**Lubbock** · *Lubbock Eco. Dev. Alliance* · Gary Lawrence, CEO, 1500 Broadway, 6th Flr., 79401, P 261,227, (806) 749-4500, Fax (806) 749-4501, gary.lawrence@lubbockeda.org, www.lubbockeda.org

**Madisonville** · *Madison County Eco. Dev. Corp.* · Rick Barrilleaux CEcD, EDFP, Exec. Dir., 113 W. Trinity St., P.O. Box 1392, 77864, P 14,000, (936) 349-0163, Fax (936) 348-2212, mcedc@madisoncountyedc.com, www.madisoncountyedc.com

**McAllen** · *Lower Rio Grande Valley Dev. Cncl.* · Kenneth N. Jones, Exec. Dir., 311 N. 15th St., 78501, P 1,036,636, (956) 682-3481, Fax (956) 631-4670, www.lrgvdc.org

**McAllen** · *McAllen Eco. Dev. Corp.* · Keith Patridge, Pres./CEO, 6401 S. 33rd St., 78503, P 470,000, (956) 682-2875, Fax (956) 682-3077, www.medc.org

**McKinney** · *McKinney Eco. Dev. Corp.* · David Pitstick, Pres./CEO, 321 N. Central Expy., Ste. 200, 75070, P 120,000, (972) 562-5430, (800) 839-6259, Fax (972) 562-1222, info@mckinneyedc.com, www.mckinneyedc.com

**Midland** · *Midland C/C-Eco. Dev. Div.* · Mike Hatley, V.P. of Eco. Dev., 109 N. Main St., 2nd Flr., 79701, P 121,300, (432) 686-3579, (800) 624-6435, Fax (432) 687-8214, krobbins@midlandtxedc.com, www.midlandtxedc.com

**Mineola** · *Mineola Dev. Inc.* · Mercy Rushing, Dev. Dir., 300 Greenville Hwy., P.O. Box 179, 75773, P 5,611, (903) 569-6983, (800) MINEOLA, Fax (903) 569-0856, mlrushing@mineola.com, www.mineola.com

**Monahans** · *Monahans Eco. Dev. Corp.* · Morse Haynes, Eco. Dev. Dir., 303 S. Allen, P.O. Box 61, 79756, P 7,500, (432) 943-2062, Fax (432) 943-2062, monahansedc@monahans.org, www.monahans.org

**Mount Pleasant** · *Mount Pleasant Ind. Found.* · Charles L. Smith, Exec. Dir., 1604 N. Jefferson, 75455, P 28,118, (903) 572-6602, Fax (903) 572-0613, charleslsmith@mpcity.org, www.mpedc.org

**New Braunfels** · *New Braunfels EDC* · Rusty Brockman, Dir. of EDC, 390 S. Seguin Ave., P.O. Box 311417, 78131, P 50,000, (830) 625-2385, (866) 927-0905, Fax (830) 625-7918

**Nueces County** · *see Corpus Christi*

**Odessa** · *Odessa Ind. Dev. Corp.* · Gary Vest, Dir., 700 N. Grant, Ste. 200, P.O. Box 3626, 79760, P 95,000, (877) 363-3772, Fax (432) 333-7858, info@odessaecodev.com, www.odessatex.com

**Pearland** · *Pearland Eco. Dev. Corp.* · Fred Welch, 3519 Liberty Dr., 77581, P 80,000, (281) 652-1627, (800) 240-3684, mail@pearlandedc.com, www.pearlandedc.com

**Plainview** · *Plainview/Hale County Ind. Found.* · David W. Evans, Exec. Dir., 1906 W. 5th, 79072, P 32,000, (806) 293-8536, Fax (806) 293-9554, phcif@nts-online.net, www.phcif.org

**Plano** · *Plano Eco. Dev. Bd.* · Sally Bane, Exec. Dir., 5601 Granite Pkwy., Ste. 310, 75024, P 253,000, (972) 208-8300, Fax (972) 208-8305, sallyb@plano.gov, www.planotexas.org

**Port Neches** · *Port Neches Eco. Dev. Corp.* · Amy Guidroz, Exec. Dir., 1110 Port Neches Ave., P.O. Box 445, 77651, P 15,000, (409) 727-6776, Fax (409) 727-6799, director@pnedc.com

**Post** · *Post Eco. Dev. Corp.* · Giles Dalby, Chrmn. of Bd., 228 E. Main, 79356, P 4,200, (806) 495-2818, Fax (806) 495-2376

**Quanah** · *Quanah Eco. Dev. Corp.* · Eugene Johnson, Exec. Dir., 305 S. Main St., 79252, P 2,950, (940) 663-2690, qedc@speednet.com, www.quanahnet.com/quanaheconomicdevelopment

**Quitman** · *Wood County Ind. Comm.* · Gary McKinley, Exec. Dir., Wood County Airport Terminal Bldg., P.O. Box 578, 75783, P 41,776, (903) 768-2402, (888) 506-3458, Fax (903) 768-2403, woodcic@peoplescom.net, www.woodcountytx.com

**Richardson** · *Richardson Eco. Dev. Partnership* · John Jacobs, Sr. V.P., 411 Belle Grove Dr., 75080, P 97,467, (972) 792-2800, Fax (972) 792-2825, john@telecomcorridor.com, www.telecomcorridor.com

**Robstown** · *Robstown Area Dev. Comm.* · Ken Faughn, Exec. Dir., 1150 E. Main Ave., P.O. Box 111, 78380, P 14,000, (361) 387-3933, Fax (361) 387-7280, radc@verizon.net, www.robstownadc.com

**Rockwall** · *Rockwall Eco. Dev. Corp.* · Sheri Franza, Pres./CEO, 697 E. I-30, P.O. Box 968, 75087, P 30,000, (972) 772-0025, Fax (972) 771-8828, sfranza@rockwalledc.com, www.rockwalledc.com

**Rosenberg** · *Rosenberg Dev. Corp.* · Matt Fielder, Eco. Dev. Dir., P.O. Box 32, 77471, P 28,000, (832) 595-3330, Fax (832) 595-3311, mattf@ci.rosenberg.tx.us, www.ci.rosenberg.tx.us

**San Antonio** · *San Antonio Eco. Dev. Found.* · Mario Hernandez, Pres., 602 E. Commerce St., P.O. Box 1628, 78296, P 1,200,000, (210) 226-1394, Fax (210) 223-3386, edf@sanantonioedf.com, www.sanantonioedf.com

**Seminole** · *Seminole Eco. Dev. Corp.* · Donna Johnson, Exec. Dir., P.O. Box 816, 79360, P 6,505, (432) 758-8804, Fax (432) 758-2349, director@mywdo.com, www.seminoleedc.org

**South Padre Island** · *Eco. Dev. Corp.* · Darla Lapeyre, Exec. V.P., 600 Padre Blvd., 78597, P 2,500, (956) 761-4522, Fax (956) 761-4523, spiedc@aol.com, www.townspi.com

**Southlake** · *City of Southlake Ofc. of Eco. Dev.* · Greg Last, Dir., 1400 Main St., Ste. 300, 76092, P 25,700, (817) 748-8039, Fax (817) 748-8040, econdev@ci.southlake.tx.us, www.cityofsouthlake.com

**Stamford** · *Dev. Corp. of Stamford* · Fareed Hassen, Dir., P.O. Box 669, 79553, P 3,600, (325) 773-2495, Fax (325) 773-2851

**Sudan** · *Sudan Eco. Dev. Corp.* · Greg Lance, Pres., P.O. Box 59, 79371, P 1,039, (806) 227-2112, sudancityhall@yahoo.com

**Sulphur Springs** · *Sulphur Springs/Hopkins County Eco. Dev. Corp.* · Roger Feagly, Exec. Dir., 1200 Enterprise, 75482, P 35,000, (903) 439-0101, Fax (903) 439-6396, www.ss-edc.com

**Sweetwater** · *Sweetwater Enterprise for Eco. Dev.* · Ken Becker, Exec. Dir., P.O. Box 785, 79556, P 15,000, (325) 235-0555, (877) 301-SEED, Fax (325) 235-1026, ken@sweetwatertexas.net, www.sweetwatertexas.net

**Temple** · *Temple Eco. Dev. Corp.* · Lee Peterson, Pres., 1 S. 1st St., 76501, P 60,000, (254) 773-8332, Fax (254) 773-8856, info@choosetemple.com, www.choosetemple.com

**Terrell** · *Terrell Eco. Dev. Corp.* · Danny Booth, Admin., P.O. Box 97, 75160, P 18,500, (972) 524-5704, Fax (972) 563-2363, danny@terrelltexas.com, www.terrelltexas.com

**Weatherford** · *Weatherford Eco. Dev. Auth.* · Dennis Clayton CEcD, Exec. Dir., 1320 Santa Fe Dr., Ste. 200, 76086, P 24,000, (817) 594-9429, (817) 596-0400, Fax (817) 594-4786, dclayton@weatherfordtx.gov, www.ci.weatherford.tx.us

**White Settlement** · *City of White Settlement* · Jim Ryan, Eco. Dev. Dir., Eco. Dev. Dept., 214 Meadow Park Dr., 76108, P 16,000, (817) 246-4971, Fax (817) 367-0885, jryan@wstx.us, www.wstx.us

**Whitesboro** · *Whitesboro Eco. Dev. Corp.* · Janis Crawley, Dir., 111 W. Main, P.O. Box 340, 76273, P 4,400, (903) 564-6105, Fax (903) 564-3311, edc@whitesborotexas.com, www.whitesboro texas.com

**Wichita Falls** · *Wichita Falls Bd. of Comm. & Ind.* · Kevin Pearson, V.P. of Eco. Dev., 900 8th St., Ste. 218, P.O. Box 1860, 76307, P 104,000, (940) 723-2741, Fax (940) 723-8773, wfbci@wf.net, www.wichitafallscommerce.com

**Wills Point** · *Wills Point EDC* · Lettie Clark, Exec. Dir., 36549 Hwy. 64, Ste. 104, P.O. Box 217, 75169, P 4,000, (903) 873-3381, Fax (903) 873-3081, WPEDC@sbcglobal.net, www.cityofwillspoint.com

**Yoakum** · *Yoakum Eco. Dev. Corp.* · Patrick J. Kennedy, Dir., 808 U.S. Hwy. 77A S., P.O. Box 738, 77995, P 5,731, (361) 293-6321, Fax (361) 293-3318, ccook@cityofyoakum.org, www.yoakumusa.com

# Utah

## Federal

**U.S. SBA, Utah Dist. Ofc.** · Stan Nakano, Dir., 125 S. State St., Rm. 2227, Salt Lake City, 84138, (801) 524-3223, Fax (801) 524-4410, www.sba.gov/ut

## State

**Eco. Dev. Corp. of Utah** · Jeffrey Edwards, Pres./CEO, 201 S. Main St., Ste. 2150, Salt Lake City, 84111, M 200, (801) 328-8824, Fax (801) 531-1460, jedwards@edcutah.org, www.edcutah.org

**Labor Comm. Of Utah** · Sherrie Hayashi, Comm., 160 E. 300 S., Ste. 300, P.O. Box 146610, Salt Lake City, 84114, (801) 530-6800, Fax (801) 530-6390, laborcomm@utah.gov, www.laborcommission.utah.gov

## Communities

**Cedar City** · *Cedar City/Iron County Eco. Dev.* · Brennan Wood, Exec. Dir., 10 N. Main St., 84720, P 41,000, (435) 586-2770, Fax (435) 586-2949, www.cedarcity.org

**Fillmore** · *Fillmore City Redev. Agency* · Marlene Cummings, City Recorder, 75 W. Center St., 84631, P 2,300, (435) 743-5233, Fax (435) 743-5195, www.fillmorecity.org

**Logan** · *Cache Eco. Dev.* · Sandra Emile, Pres., 160 N. Main St., 84321, P 105,000, (435) 752-2161, Fax (435) 753-5825, semile@cachechamber.com, www.cachechamber.com

**Moab** · *Moab Area Eco. Dev. Ofc.* · Ken Davey, Specialist, 217 E. Center, 84532, P 8,500, (435) 259-5121, Fax (435) 259-4951, ken@moabcity.org, www.moabcity.org

**Nephi** · *Juab Comm. Eco. Dev. Agency* · Byron Woodland, Dir., 160 N. Main, 84648, P 8,500, (435) 623-3400, Fax (435) 623-4609, byronw@co.juab.ut.us, www.co.juab.ut.us

**Ogden** · *Ogden City Comm. & Eco. Dev.* · Dave Harmer, Dir., 2549 Washington Blvd., Ste. 420, 84401, P 70,000, (801) 629-8910, Fax (801) 629-8993, www.ogdencity.com

**Ogden** · *Weber County Comm.* · Craig Zogmaister, Chrmn., 2380 Washington Blvd., Ste. 360, 84401, P 196,533, (801) 399-8401, Fax (801) 399-8305, www.co.weber.ut.us

**Ogden** · *Weber Eco. Dev. Corp.* · Ron Kusina, Exec. Dir., 2484 Washington Blvd., Ste. 400, 84401, P 213,000, (801) 621-8300, Fax (801) 392-7609, ronk@echamber.cc, www.webergrowth.com

**Orem** · *Comm. For Eco. Dev. In Orem* · Brad Whittaker, Exec. Dir., 777 S. State St., 84058, P 91,000, (801) 226-1521, Fax (801) 226-2678, info@cedo.org, www.cedo.org

**Panguitch** · *Garfield Eco. Dev.* · Justin Fischer, Planner, P.O. Box 77, 84759, P 4,600, (435) 676-8826, Fax (435) 676-8239

**Price** · *Carbon County Eco. Dev.* · Delynn Fielding, Dir., 120 E. Main St., 84501, P 23,000, (435) 636-3295, Fax (435) 636-3210, www.carbon-county.com

**Provo** · *also see Orem*

**Provo** · *Provo City Dept. of Eco. Dev.* · Leland Gamette, Dir., 86 N. University Ave., Ste. 240, 84601, P 116,000, (801) 852-6161, Fax (801) 375-1469, dholmes@provo.utah.gov, www.provo.org

**Tooele** · *Tooele County Eco. Dev.* · Nicole Cline, AICP, 47 S. Main, 84074, P 54,375, (435) 843-3160, Fax (435) 843-3427, ncline@co.tooele.ut.us, www.tooeleeconomicdevelopment.com

# Vermont

## Federal

**U.S. SBA, Vermont Dist. Ofc.** · Darcy Carter, Dist. Dir., 87 State St., Rm. 205, P.O. Box 605, Montpelier, 05601, (802) 828-4422, Fax (802) 828-4485, www.sba.gov/vt

## Communities

**Bennington** · *Bennington County Ind. Corp.* · Peter Odierna, Exec. Dir., 215 South St., P.O. Box 923, 05201, P 35,000, (802) 442-8975, Fax (802) 447-1101, peter@bcic.org, www.bcic.org

**Burlington** · *Greater Burlington Industrial Corp. (GBIC)* · Frank Cioffi, Pres., 60 Main St., P.O. Box 786, 05402, P 146,000, (802) 862-5726, Fax (802) 860-1899, frank@vermont.org, www.gbicvt.org

**Middlebury** · *Addison County Eco. Dev. Corp.* · Robin Scheu, Exec. Dir., 1590 Rte. 7 S., Ste. 2, 05753, P 30,000, (802) 388-7953, Fax (802) 388-0119, info@addisoncountyedc.org, www.addisoncountyedc.org

**Montpelier** · *Central Vermont Eco. Dev. Corp.* · Susan Matthews, Exec. V.P., 1 National Life Dr., P.O. Box 1439, 05601, P 62,000, M 120, (802) 223-4654, (888) 769-2957, Fax (802) 223-4655, cvedc@sover.net, www.central-vt.com/cvedc

**Morrisville** · *Lamoille Eco. Dev. Corp.* · Arthur Sandborn, Exec. Dir., P.O. Box 455, 05661, P 25,000, (802) 888-5640, Fax (802) 888-7612, art@lamoilleeconomy.org, www.lamoilleeconomy.org

**Rutland** · *Rutland Eco. Dev. Corp.* · James B. Stewart, Exec. Dir., 112 Quality Ln., 05701, P 62,265, (802) 773-9147, Fax (802) 773-8009, info@rutlandeconomy.com, www.rutlandeconomy.com

**Saint Albans** · *Franklin County Ind. Dev. Corp.* · Timothy Smith, Exec. Dir., 2 N. Main, P.O. Box 1099, 05478, P 46,000, (802) 524-2194, Fax (802) 524-6793, info@fcidc.com, www.fcidc.com

**Saint Johnsbury** · *Northeastern Vermont Dev. Assn.* · Steven Patterson, Exec. Dir., 36 Eastern Ave., P.O. Box 630, 05819, P 62,438, (802) 748-5181, Fax (802) 748-1223, spatterson@nvda.net, www.nvda.net

**Springfield** · *Springfield Reg. Dev. Corp.* · Bob Flint, Exec. Dir., 14 Clinton St., Ste. 7, 05156, P 26,000, (802) 885-3061, Fax (802) 885-3027, info@springfielddevelopment.org, www.springfielddevelopment.org

**White River Junction** · *Green Mountain Eco. Dev. Corp.* · Joan Goldstein, Exec. Dir., P.O. Box 246, 05001, P 55,000, M 75, (802) 295-3710, Fax (802) 295-3779, jgoldstein@gmedc.com, www.gmedc.com

**Windsor** · *Connecticut River Dev. Corp.* · Winthrop Townsend, Chrmn., 28 River St., P.O. Box 88, 05089, P 45,000, (802) 674-9202, WinTownsend@yahoo.com

# Virgin Islands

## Communities

**St. Croix** · *Virgin Islands Eco. Dev. Auth.* · Percival Clouden, CEO, #116 King St. Frederiksted, 00840, P 1,200,000, (340) 773-6499, www.usvieda.org

**St. Thomas** · *Virgin Islands Eco. Dev. Auth.* · Percival Clouden, CEO, 1050 Norre Gade, Ste. #5, P.O. Box 305038, 00803, P 1,200,000, (340) 714-1700, www.usvieda.org

# Virginia

## Federal

**U.S. SBA, Richmond Dist. Ofc.** · Ronald Bew, Dist. Dir., The Federal Bldg., 400 N. 8th St., Ste. 1150, Richmond, 23219, (804) 771-2400, Fax (804) 771-2764, www.sba.gov/va

## State

**Virginia Eco. Dev. Partnership** · Jeffrey Anderson, Exec. Dir., 901 E. Byrd St., P.O. Box 798, Richmond, 23218, (804) 545-5600, Fax (804) 545-5611, www.yesvirginia.org

## Communities

**Alexandria** · *Alexandria Eco. Dev. Partnership* · Stuart Litvin CEcD, Pres./CEO, 1729 King St., Ste. 410, 22314, P 140,000, (703) 739-3820, Fax (703) 739-1384, info@alexecon.org, www.alexecon.org

**Alleghany** · *see Covington*

**Arlington** · *Arlington County Eco. Dev. Div.* · Terry Holzheimer, Dir., 1100 N. Glebe Rd., Ste. 1500, 22201, P 185,500, (703) 228-0808, Fax (703) 228-0805, www.arlingtonvirginiausa.com

**Charles City** · *Charles City Dept. of Dev.* · Christina Green, Dir., P.O. Box 66, 23030, P 6,926, (804) 652-4707, Fax (804) 829-5819, www.co.charles-city.va.us

**Charlottesville** · *City of Charlottesville Eco. Dev. Dept.* · Aubrey Watts Jr., Dir., P.O. Box 911, 22902, P 45,000, (434) 970-3110, Fax (434) 970-3299, www.charlottesville.org

**Chatham** · *Pittsylvania County Eco. Dev.* · P.O. Box 1122, 24531, P 61,745, (434) 432-7710, Fax (434) 432-7714, www.pittgov.org

**Chesapeake** · *see Norfolk*

**Chesterfield** · *Chesterfield County Eco. Dev.* · E. Wilson Davis Jr., Dir., 9401 Courthouse Rd., Ste. B, P.O. Box 760, 23832, P 300,000, (804) 318-8550, Fax (804) 796-3638, www.chester-fieldbusiness.com

**Christiansburg** · *Montgomery Reg. Eco. Dev. Commission* · 755 Roanoke St., Ste. 2H, 24073, P 88,454, (540) 382-5732, Fax (540) 381-6888, www.yesmontgomery.va.org

**Culpeper** · *Culpeper County Eco. Dev. Ofc.* · Carl Sachs, Dir., 233 E. Davis St., 22701, P 45,000, (540) 727-3410, (800) 793-0631, Fax (540) 727-3448, csachs@culpepercounty.gov, www.culpepercounty.gov

**Culpeper** · *Foreign Trade Zone 185* · Jim Charapich, Pres./CEO, 109 S. Commerce St., 22701, P 45,372, (540) 825-8628, Fax (540) 825-1449, jcharapich@culpepervachamber.com, www.culpepervachamber.com

**Danville** · *City of Danville* · Jeremy Stratton, Eco. Dev. Dir., 427 Patton St., P.O. Box 3300, 24543, P 48,411, (434) 793-1753, Fax (434) 797-9606, econdev@discoverdanville.com, www.discoverdanville.com

**Emporia** · *Emporia-Greensville Ind. Dev. Corp.* · Jack W. Davenport, Exec. Dir., 425-H S. Main St., 23847, P 16,000, (434) 634-9400, Fax (434) 634-0511, www.emporiagreensvilleidc.com

**Fairfax County** · *Fairfax County Eco. Dev. Auth.* · Gerald L. Gordon, Pres./CEO, 8300 Boone Blvd., Ste. 450, Vienna, 22182, P 1,606,529, (703) 790-0600, Fax (703) 893-1269, ggordon@fceda.org, www.fairfaxcountyeda.org

**Falls Church** · *City of Falls Church Ofc. of Eco. Dev.* · Rick Goff, Exec. Dir., 300 Park Ave., 22046, P 10,000, (703) 248-5491, Fax (703) 248-5103, econdev@fallschurchva.gov, www.fallschurchva.gov

**Fincastle** · *Botetourt County Eco. Dev.* · One W. Main St., Box 1, 24090, P 32,000, (540) 473-8239, Fax (540) 473-8207, www.botetourt.org

**Fredericksburg** · *Fredericksburg Ofc. Of Tourism & Eco. Dev.* · Karen Hedelt, Dir., 706 Caroline St., 22401, P 22,000, (540) 372-1216, Fax (540) 372-6587, khedelt@fredericksburgva.gov, www.visitfred.com

**Fredericksburg** · *Spotsylvania County Dept. of Eco. Dev.* · Russell Seymour, Dir., 10304 Spotsylvania Ave., Ste. 440, 22408, P 119,000, (540) 507-7210, Fax (540) 507-7207, www.spotsylvania.org

**Front Royal** · *Eco. Dev. Auth. of Front Royal & Warren County* · Jennifer McDonald, Exec. Dir., 400 D Kendrick Ln., P.O. Box 445, 22630, P 30,000, (540) 635-2182, Fax (540) 635-1853, www.wceda.com

**Galax** · *City of Galax Eco. Dev.* · Keith Holland, City Mgr., 111 E. Grayson St., 24333, P 6,837, (276) 236-5773, Fax (276) 236-2889, www.ingalax.net

**Gate City** · *Scott County Eco. Dev. Auth.* · Penny Horton, Secy., 180 W. Jackson St., 24251, P 23,403, (276) 386-2525, Fax (276) 386-6158, scotteda@mounet.com, www.scottcountyva.org

**Gloucester** · *Dept. of Eco. Dev.* · Douglas Meredith, Dir., 6467 Main St., P.O. Box 915, 23061, P 34,700, (804) 693-1415, Fax (804) 693-6004, dmeredit@gloucesterva.info, www.gloucesterva.info

**Henrico** · *Eco. Dev. Auth. Of Henrico County* · Gary McLaren, Exec. Dir., 4300 E. Parham Rd., 23228, P 281,000, (804) 501-7654, Fax (804) 501-7890, www.henrico.com

**Hopewell** · *City of Hopewell Dept. of Dev.* · Tevya Williams, City Planner, 300 N. Main St., 23860, P 23,101, (804) 541-2220, Fax (804) 541-2318, twilliams@hopewellva.gov, www.hopewellva.gov

**Lawrenceville** · *Brunswick County Ind. Dev. Auth.* · Joan Moore, Exec. Dir., P.O. Box 48, 23868, P 18,000, (434) 848-0248, Fax (434) 848-0202, www.bcida.org

**Leesburg** · *Loudoun County Dept. of Eco. Dev.* · Larry Rosenstrauch, Dir., 1 Harrison St. S.E., MSC #63, 20175, P 500,000, (703) 777-0426, Fax (703) 771-5363, good4biz@loudoun.gov, www.biz.loudoun.gov

**Lexington** · *The Rockbridge Partnership* · Michael B. Webb, Exec. Dir., 6 S. Randolph St., 24450, P 35,000, (540) 463-7346, Fax (540) 463-7348, trp@rockbridge.net, www.rockbridgepartnership.org

**Lynchburg** · *Lynchburg Ofc. of Eco. Dev.* · Marjette L. Glass, Dir., 828 Main St., 10th Flr., 24504, P 65,400, (434) 455-4493, (434) 455-4490, Fax (434) 847-2067, marjette.glass@lynchburgva.gov, www.lynchburgva.gov

EDC

**Manassas** · *Prince William County Dept. of Eco. Dev.* · Martin Briley, Exec. Dir., 10530 Linden Lake Plz., Ste. 105, 20109, P 320,000, (703) 792-5500, Fax (703) 792-5502, econdev@pwcgov.org, www.pwcecondev.org

**Mechanicsville** · *Hanover County Dept. of Eco. Dev.* · Marc Weiss, Dir., 9097 Atlee Station Rd., Ste. 304, 23116, P 100,000, (804) 365-6464, (800) 936-6168, Fax (804) 365-6463, www.hanovercounty.biz

**Newport News** · *Peninsula Cncl. For Workforce Dev.* · Matthew James, Pres./CEO, 11820 Fountain Way, 23606, P 460,000, (757) 826-3327, Fax (757) 826-6706, www.pcfwd.org

**Norfolk** · *Hampton Roads Eco. Dev. Alliance* · Darryl Gosnell, Pres., 500 E. Main St., Ste. 1300, 23510, P 1,670,000, (757) 627-2315, Fax (757) 623-3081, www.hreda.com

**Portsmouth** · *also see Norfolk*

**Portsmouth** · *Portsmouth Dept. of Eco. Dev.* · Steven Lynch, Dir., 200 High St., Ste. 200, 23704, P 100,565, (757) 393-8804, (800) 848-5690, Fax (757) 393-8293, www.portsmouthvaed.com

**Prince George** · *Prince George County* · John Kines, County Admin., 6602 Courts Dr., P.O. Box 68, 23875, P 36,900, (804) 722-8600, Fax (804) 732-3604, jkines@princegeorgeva.org, www.princegeorgeva.org

**Radford** · *New River Valley Eco. Dev. Alliance* · Aric Bopp, Exec. Dir., 6226 University Park Dr., Ste. 2200, 24141, P 165,000, (540) 267-0007, Fax (540) 267-0013, info@nrvalliance.org, www.nrvalliance.org

**Richmond** · *Dept. of Eco. Dev., City of Richmond* · Carthan F. Currin III, Dir., 501 E. Franklin St., Ste. 800, 23219, P 200,000, (804) 646-5633, Fax (804) 646-6793, econdev@richmondgov.com

**Richmond** · *Greater Richmond Partnership* · Gregory H. Wingfield, Pres./CEO, 901 E. Byrd St., Ste. 801, West Tower, 23219, P 1,000,000, M 275, (804) 643-3227, (800) 229-6332, Fax (804) 343-7167, ghw@grpva.com, www.grpva.com

**Roanoke** · *Dept. of Eco. Dev., City of Roanoke* · 117 Church Ave. S.W., 24011, P 95,000, (540) 853-2715, Fax (540) 853-1213, www.roanokeva.gov

**South Boston** · *Ind. Dev. Auth. of Halifax County* · Mike Sexton, Exec. Dir., 515 Broad St., P.O. Box 1281, 24592, P 38,000, (434) 572-1734, Fax (434) 572-1762, meades@halifaxvirginia.com, www.halifaxvirginia.com

**Staunton** · *Staunton Dept. of Eco. Dev.* · William Hamilton, Dir., 116 W. Beverley St., P.O. Box 58, 24402, P 25,000, (540) 332-3869, Fax (540) 851-4008, www.staunton.va.us

**Suffolk** · *also see Norfolk*

**Suffolk** · *City of Suffolk Eco. Dev.* · Cindy Cave, Dir., 127 E. Washington St., Ste. 200, 23434, P 76,586, (757) 514-4040, Fax (757) 923-3628, www.suffolk.va.us

**Virginia Beach** · *Virginia Beach Dept. of Eco. Dev.* · Warren D. Harris, Dir., 222 Central Park Ave., Ste. 1000, 23462, P 440,000, (757) 385-6464, Fax (757) 499-9894, www.yesvirginiabeach.com

**Warm Springs** · *Bath County Ind. Dev. Auth.* · Joe Tuning, Chrmn., P.O. Box 309, 24484, P 4,826, (540) 839-7221, Fax (540) 839-7222, www.bathcountyva.org

**Winchester** · *Winchester-Frederick County Eco. Dev. Comm.* · Patrick Barker, Exec. Dir., 45 E. Boscawen St., 22601, P 100,000, (540) 665-0973, Fax (540) 722-0604, info@winva.com, www.winva.com

**Woodstock** · *Shenandoah County Eco. Dev.* · Susie Hill, Dir. of Eco. Dev., 600 N. Main St., Ste. 101, 22664, P 39,000, (540) 459-6220, Fax (540) 459-6228, shill@shenandoahcountyva.us, www.shenandoah-ed.org

**Wytheville** · *Joint Ind. Dev. Auth. of Wythe County* · Alan Hawthorne, Exec. Dir., 190 S. First St., P.O. Box 569, 24382, P 28,421, (276) 223-3370, Fax (276) 223-3427, jointida@wytheville.org, www.wytheIDA.org

# Washington

## Federal

**U.S. SBA, Washington Dist. Ofc.** · Nancy Porzio, Dist. Dir., 2401 4th Ave., Ste. 450, Seattle, 98121, (206) 553-7310, Fax (206) 553-0194, www.sba.gov/wa

## State

**State Dept. of Comm., Trade & Eco. Dev.** · Rogers Weed, Dir., 128 10th Ave. S.W., P.O. Box 42525, Olympia, 98504, (360) 725-4000, Fax (360) 586-8440, www.cted.wa.gov

## Communities

**Aberdeen** · *Grays Harbor Eco. Dev. Cncl.* · Michael Tracy, Pres., 506 Duffy St., 98520, P 70,500, (360) 532-7888, Fax (360) 532-7922, www.ghedc.com

**Bainbridge Island** · *see Bremerton*

**Bellingham** · *Bellingham Whatcom Eco. Dev. Cncl.* · Nancy Jordan, Exec. Dir., 115 Unity St., Ste. 101, P.O. Box 2803, 98227, P 170,000, (360) 676-4255, (800) 810-4255, Fax (360) 647-9413, bwedc@bwedc.org, www.bwedc.org

**Bremerton** · *Kitsap Eco. Dev. Alliance* · William Stewart, Dir., 4312 Kitsap Way, Ste. 103, 98312, P 240,000, M 50, (360) 377-9499, (877) 465-4872, Fax (360) 479-4653, info@kitsapeda.org, www.kitsapeda.org

**Cathlamet** · *Lower Columbia Eco. Dev. Cncl.* · David Goodroe, Exec. Dir., P.O. Box 243, 98612, P 4,000, (360) 795-3996, Fax (360) 795-3944, lcedc@cni.net, www.lowercolumbiaedc.org

**Chehalis** · *Lewis County Eco. Dev. Cncl.* · Dick Larman, Exec. Dir., 1611 N. National Ave., P.O. Box 916, 98532, P 67,000, (360) 748-0114, Fax (360) 748-1238, lewisedc@localaccess.com, www.lewisedc.com

**Clarkston** · *Palouse Eco. Dev. Cncl.* · 845 Port Way, 99403, P 69,800, (509) 751-9144, Fax (509) 758-1309, www.palouse.org

**College Place** · *see Walla Walla*

**Colville** · *Tri-County Eco. Dev. Dist.* · 347 W. 2nd, Ste. A, 99114, P 40,700, (509) 684-4571, Fax (509) 684-4788, admin@teddonline.com, www.teddonline.com

**Coupeville** · *Island County Eco. Dev. Cncl.* · Sharon Hart, Exec. Dir., 180 N.W. Coveland, P.O. Box 279, 98239, P 77,200, M 120, (360) 678-6889, Fax (360) 678-2976, icedc@whidbey.net, www.islandcountyedc.com

**Everett** · *Eco. Dev. Cncl. of Snohomish County* · Deborah Knutsen, Pres., 728 134th St. S.W., Ste. 128, 98204, P 593,500, M 200, (425) 743-4567, Fax (425) 745-5563, www.snoedc.org

**Ferry County** · *see Colville*

**Garfield** · *Whitman Rural Dev. Corp.* · Maureen Byrne, Secy., P.O. Box 454, 99130, P 610, M 15, (509) 635-1604

**Longview** · *Cowlitz Eco. Dev. Cncl.* · Ted Sprague, Pres., 1452 Hudson, Ste. 208, P.O. Box 1278, 98632, P 94,000, (360) 423-9921, Fax (360) 423-1923, www.cowlitzedc.com

**Moses Lake** · *Big Bend Eco. Dev. Cncl.* · Michael Buchanan, Exec. Dir., 410 W. Third Ave., Ste. E, 98837, P 95,000, (509) 764-8591, Fax (509) 764-8591, bigbendedc@moseslake-wa.com

**Mount Vernon** · *Eco. Dev. Assn. of Skagit County* · Don Wick, Exec. Dir., 204 W. Montgomery, P.O. Box 40, 98273, P 122,000, M 512, (360) 336-6114, Fax (360) 336-6116, don@skagit.org, www.skagit.org

**Pend Orielle County** · *see Colville*

**Port Angeles** · *Clallam County EDC* · Linda Rotmark, Exec. Dir., P.O. Box 1085, 98362, P 67,000, (360) 457-7793, Fax (360) 452-9618, lrotmark@clallam.org, www.clallam.org

**Port Orchard** · *see Bremerton*

**Poulsbo** · *see Bremerton*

**Prescott** · *see Walla Walla*

**Prosser** · *Prosser Eco. Dev. Assn.* · Deb Heintz, Exec. Dir., 1230 Bennett Ave., 99350, P 12,000, (509) 786-3600, Fax (509) 786-2399, info@prosser.org, www.prosser.org

**Raymond** · *Pacific County Eco. Dev. Cncl.* · Cathy Russ, Exec. Dir., 530 Commercial St., 98577, P 21,800, M 160, (360) 875-9330, Fax (360) 875-9305, www.pacificedc.org

**Seattle** · *Enterprise Seattle* · Tom Flavin, CEO, 1301 Fifth Ave., Ste. 2500, 98101, P (206) 389-8650, Fax (206) 389-8651, info@enterpriseseattle.org, www.enterpriseseattle.org

**Silverdale** · *see Bremerton*

**Stevens County** · *see Colville*

**Stevenson** · *Skamania County Eco. Dev. Cncl.* · Peggy Bryan, Exec. Dir., P.O. Box 436, 98648, P 10,024, (509) 427-5110, Fax (509) 427-5122, scedc@skamania-edc.org, www.skamania-edc.org

**Tacoma** · *Eco. Dev. Bd. For Tacoma-Pierce County* · Bruce Kendall, Pres./CEO, P.O. Box 1555, 98401, P 733,700, (253) 383-4726, Fax (253) 383-4676, info@edbtpc.org, www.gopierce.org

**Tacoma** · *Pierce County Dept. of Comm. Svcs.* · Tom Hilyard, Dir., 3602 Pacific Ave., 98418, P 725,000, (253) 798-7205, Fax (253) 798-6604, thilyar@co.pierce.wa.us, www.co.pierce.wa.us

**Vancouver** · *Columbia River Eco. Dev. Cncl.* · 805 Broadway, Ste. 412, 98660, P 392,000, M 160, (360) 694-5006, Fax (360) 694-9927, info@credc.org, www.credc.org

**Waitsburg** · *see Walla Walla*

**Walla Walla** · *Port of Walla Walla* · Paul Gerola, Eco. Dev. Dir., 310 A St., 99362, P 54,000, (509) 525-3100, Fax (509) 525-3101, www.portwallawalla.com

**Winslow** · *see Bremerton*

**Yakima** · *Yakima County Dev. Assn.* · David McFadden, Pres., 10 N. 9th St., P.O. Box 1387, 98907, P 225,000, (509) 575-1140, Fax (509) 575-1508, newvision@ycda.com, www.ycda.com

# West Virginia

## Federal

**U.S. SBA, West Virginia Dist. Ofc.** · Judy McCauley, Dist. Dir., 320 W. Pike St., Ste. 330, Clarksburg, 26301, (304) 623-5631, Fax (304) 623-0023, wvinfo@sba.gov, www.sba.gov/wv

## State

**West Virginia Eco. Dev. Auth.** · David Warner, Exec. Dir., Northgate Bus. Park, 160 Association Dr., Charleston, 25311, (304) 558-3650, Fax (304) 558-0206, www.wveda.org

## Communities

**Beckley** · *4-C Eco. Dev. Auth.* · Judy Radford, Exec. Dir., 116 N. Heber St., Ste. B, 25801, P 188,685, (304) 254-8115, Fax (304) 254-8112, 4ceda@4ceda.org, www.4ceda.org

**Berkeley Springs** · *Morgan County Eco. Dev. Auth.* · William Clark, Exec. Dir., 35 N. Mercer, P.O. Box 86, 25411, P 14,943, (304) 258-8546, Fax (304) 258-7305, www.morgancounty.com/eda

**Buckhannon** · *Upshur County Dev. Auth.* · Stephen Foster, Exec. Dir., 1 Edmiston Way, P.O. Box 109, 26201, P 23,404, (304) 472-1757, Fax (304) 472-4998, info@upshurda.com, www.upshurda.com

**Charleston** · *West Virginia Dev. Ofc.* · Steven Spence, Dir. of Intl. Div., State Capitol Complex, Bldg. 6, Rm. 553, 25305, (304) 558-2234, Fax (304) 558-1189, www.wvdo.org

**Clarksburg** · *Harrison County Dev. Auth.* · Judy Gonzales, Ofc. Admin., P.O. Box 2443, 26302, P 69,088, (304) 623-3596, Fax (304) 623-3598, hcda@westvirginia.com, www.hcdawv.com

**Elkins** · *Randolph County Dev. Auth.* · Mark Doak, Pres., 10 11th St., 26241, P 29,000, (304) 637-0803, Fax (304) 637-4902, www.rcdawv.org

**Fairmont** · *Marion Reg. Dev. Corp.* · Sharon Shaffer, Exec. Dir., 110 Adams St., Ste. 201, P.O. Box 1465, 26555, P 57,000, (304) 333-6732, Fax (304) 333-6735, director@marionrdc.com, www.dobizinmarion.com

**Grafton** · *Taylor County Dev. Auth.* · Bob Gorey, Dir., 214 W. Main St., Rm. 100, 26354, P 16,089, (304) 265-3938, Fax (304) 265-5450, bobgorey@yahoo.com

**Keyser** · *Mineral County Dev. Auth.* · Mona Ridder, Exec. Dir., One Grand Central Bus. Center, Ste. 3011, 26726, P 27,700, (304) 788-2233, Fax (304) 788-2998, info@wv-mcda.com, www.wv-mcda.com

**Marshall** · *see Wheeling*

**Martinsburg** · *Berkeley County Dev. Auth.* · Stephen L. Christian, Exec. Dir., 300 Foxcroft Ave., Ste. 201, P.O. Box 2448, 25401, P 89,000, (304) 267-4144, Fax (304) 267-2283, www.developmentauthority.com

**Maxwelton** · *Greenbrier Valley EDC* · Richard Ellard, Exec. Dir., P.O. Box 33, 24957, P 35,000, (304) 497-4300, Fax (304) 497-4330, info@gvedc.com, www.gvedc.com

**Moorefield** · *Hardy County Rural Dev. Auth.* · Mallie J. Combs, Exec. Dir., P.O. Box 209, 26836, P 13,000, (304) 530-6287, (304) 530-3047, Fax (304) 530-6995, hardyrda@hardynet.com, wvweb.com/www/hardy_county.html

**New Martinsville** · *Greater New Martinsville Dev. Corp.* · Don Riggenbach, Pres., P.O. Box 271, 26155, P 18,000, (304) 455-3825, Fax (304) 455-3637, chamber@wetzelcountychamber.com, www.wetzelcountychamber.com

**Ohio** · *see Wheeling*

**Petersburg** · *Grant County Dev. Auth.* · Bill Ross, Dir., 114 N. Grove St., 26847, P 12,000, (304) 257-2168, Fax (304) 257-5454, www.grantcowv.com

**Point Pleasant** · *Mason County Dev. Auth.* · Charles Humphreys, Exec. Dir., 305 Main St., 25550, P 26,000, (304) 675-1497, Fax (304) 675-1601, mcda@masoncounty.org, www.masoncounty.org

**Princeton** · *Mercer County Eco. Dev. Auth.* · Janet E. Bailey, Exec. Dir., 1500 W. Main St., 24740, P 62,980, (304) 487-2896, Fax (304) 487-5616, mercercounty@citlink.net, www.mercercoeda.com

**Ripley** · *Jackson County Dev. Auth.* · Mark Whitley, Exec. Dir., 104 Miller Dr., 25271, P 38,000, (304) 372-1151, Fax (304) 372-1153, info@jcda.org, www.jcda.org

**EDC**

**Spencer** · *Roane County Eco. Dev. Auth.* · Mark Whitley, Eco. Dev. Dir., P.O. Box 1, 25276, P 15,446, M 80, (304) 927-5189, Fax (304) 927-5953, director@roanecountyeda.org, www.roanecountyeda.org

**Summersville** · *Nicholas County Comm.* · Spurgeon Hinkle, Pres., 700 Main St., Ste. 1, 26651, P 26,500, (304) 872-7830, Fax (304) 872-9602, ncc_pattyneff@yahoo.com, www.nicholascountywv.org

**Webster Springs** · *Webster County Eco. Dev. Auth.* · 139 Baker St., 26288, P 10,000, (304) 847-2145, Fax (304) 847-5198, wcda@websterwv.com, www.websterwv.com

**Wheeling** · *Reg. Eco. Dev. Partnership* · Don Rigby, Exec. Dir., P.O. Box 1029, 26003, P 160,000, (304) 232-7722, Fax (304) 232-7727, tmarking@redp.org, www.redp.org

**Whitehall** · *Region VI Plan. & Dev. Cncl.* · James Hall, Exec. Dir., 34 Mountain Park Dr., 26554, P 253,304, (304) 366-5693, Fax (304) 367-0804, regionvi@regionvi.com, www.regionvi.com

# Wisconsin

## State

**Forward Wisconsin** · 201 W. Washington Ave., Ste. 500, Madison, 53703, (608) 261-2500, Fax (608) 261-2518, www.forwardwi.com

**Wisconsin Dept. of Commerce** · Dick Leinenkugel, Secy. of Commerce, P.O. Box 7970, Madison, 53707, (608) 266-7088, Fax (608) 266-3447, dick.leinenkugel@wisconsin.gov, www.commerce.wi.gov

## Communities

**Algoma** · *Community Dev. Comm.* · Bruce Charles, Chrmn., 416 Fremont St., 54201, P 3,370, (920) 487-5203, Fax (920) 487-3499, algoma@algomacity.org, www.algomacity.org

**Almena** · *Impact Seven Inc.* · William Bay, Pres., 147 Lake Almena Dr., 54805, (715) 357-3334, Fax (715) 357-6233, impact@impactseven.org, www.impactseven.org

**Antigo** · *Langlade County Eco. Dev. Comm.* · Christine Berry, Asst. Dir., 837 Clermont St., 54409, P 20,000, (715) 627-6384, cberry@co.langlade.wi.us, www.langladecounty.org

**Ashland** · *Ashland Area Dev. Corp.* · Dale Kupczyk, Exec. Dir., 422 3rd St. W., Ste. 101, 54806, P 16,000, (715) 682-8344, Fax (715) 682-8415, info@ashlandareadevelopment.org, www.ashlandareadevelopment.org

**Athens** · *Athens Area Dev. Corp.* · Randy Decker, Pres., P.O. Box A, 54411, P 1,102, (715) 257-7531, www.athenswis.com

**Baraboo** · *Baraboo Eco. Dev. Comm.* · Ed Geick, City Admin., 135 4th St., 53913, P 11,710, (608) 355-2715, Fax (608) 355-2719, egeick@cityofbaraboo.com, www.cityofbaraboo.com

**Baraboo** · *Sauk County Dev. Corp.* · Karna O. Hanna, Exec. Dir., 522 South Blvd., P.O. Box 33, 53913, P 60,054, (608) 355-2084, Fax (608) 355-2083, scdc@baraboo.com, www.scdc.com

**Beaver Dam** · *Beaver Dam Area Dev. Corp.* · Trent Campbell, Exec. V.P., 203 Corporate Dr., P.O. Box 492, 53916, P 21,000, (920) 887-4661, bdadc@charter.net

**Beloit** · *Beloit Dept. of Eco. Dev.* · Andrew Janke, Eco. Dev. Dir., 100 State St., City Hall, 53511, P 37,110, (608) 364-6610, Fax (608) 364-6756, jankea@ci.beloit.wi.us, www.ci.beloit.wi.us

**Berlin** · *Berlin Comm. Dev. Corp.* · 108 N. Capron, P.O. Box 272, 54923, P 5,400, (920) 361-5403, Fax (920) 361-5405, www.1berlin.com

**Boscobel** · *City of Boscobel Eco. Dev.* · Arlie Harris, City Admin., 1006 Wisconsin Ave., 53805, P 3,308, (608) 375-4400, Fax (608) 375-4750, cityhall@boscobelwisconsin.com, www.boscobelwisconsin.com

**Cashton** · *Cashton Dev. Corp.* · Scot Wall, Pres., 723 Main St., P.O. Box 70, 54619, P 1,000, M 10, (608) 654-5121, Fax (608) 654-5297

**Chippewa Falls** · *Chippewa County Eco. Dev. Corp.* · Charlie Walker CEcD, Pres./CEO, 770 Scheidler Rd., Ste. 3, 54729, P 65,000, (715) 723-7150, Fax (715) 723-7140, ccedc@chippewa-wi.com, www.chippewa-wi.com.

**Clear Lake** · *Clear Lake Ind. Dev. Corp.* · Al Banink, Clerk/Treas., 350 4th Ave., P.O. Box 48, 54005, P 1,085, (715) 263-2157, Fax (715) 263-2666, vilofcl@cltcomm.net, www.clearlakewi.com

**Cottage Grove** · *Cottage Grove Eco. Dev. Corp.* · Ken Dahl, Eco. Coord., 624 Crawford Dr., 53527, P 10,000, (608) 575-3879, kdahl@netscape.com, www.cottagegroveonline.com

**Cuba City** · *Cuba City Comm. Dev. Corp.* · Richard Brown, 108 N. Main St., 53807, P 2,100, (608) 744-2152, Fax (608) 744-2151, cubacity@pcii.net, www.cubacitywi.com

**Delafield** · *Delafield Plan Comm.* · Ed McAleer, Chair, City Hall, 500 Genesee St., 53018, P 6,876, (262) 646-6220, Fax (262) 646-6223, www.cityofdelafield.com

**Delavan** · *Delavan Dev. Corp.* · Joe Salitros, City Admin., 123 S. Second St., P.O. Box 465, 53115, P 8,128, (262) 728-5585, Fax (262) 728-4566, www.ci.delavan.wi.us

**Dodgeville** · *Eco. Dev. Comm.* · James C. McCaulley, Mayor, 100 E. Fountain St., City Hall, 53533, P 4,568, (608) 930-5228, Fax (608) 930-3520, info@dodgeville.com

**Eau Claire** · *City of Eau Claire Comm. Dev.* · Michael Schatz, Eco. Dev. Admin., 203 S. Farwell St., P.O. Box 5148, 54702, P 63,000, (715) 839-4914, Fax (715) 839-4939, mike.schatz@eauclairewi.gov, www.eauclairedevelopment.com

**Eau Claire** · *Eau Claire Area Eco. Dev. Corp.* · Brian Doudna, Exec. Dir., 101 N. Farwell St., P.O. Box 1108, 54702, P 100,000, (715) 834-0070, (800) 944-2449, Fax (715) 834-1956, ec.info@eauclaire-wi.com, www.eauclaire-wi.com

**Edgerton** · *Eco. Dev. Corp. of Edgerton* · Ramona Flanigan, City Admin., 12 Albion St., 53534, P 5,000, (608) 884-3341, Fax (608) 884-8892, rflanigan@charter.net, www.cityofedgerton.com

**Elkhorn** · *Elkhorn Dev. Co.* · Sam Tapson, City Admin., 9 S. Broad St., P.O. Box 920, 53121, P 8,526, (262) 723-2219, Fax (262) 741-5131, www.cityofelkhorn.org

**Fennimore** · *Fennimore Ind. & Eco. Dev. Corp.* · Linda Parrish, Exec. Dir., 850 Lincoln Ave., 53809, P 2,500, (608) 822-3599, (800) 822-1131, Fax (608) 822-4354, promo@fennimore.com, fennimore.com

**Fennimore** · *Grant County Eco. Dev. Corp.* · Ron Brisbois, Exec. Dir., 1800 Bronson Blvd., 53809, P 49,597, (608) 822-3501, Fax (608) 822-6019, gcedc@grantcounty.org, www.grantcounty.org

**Florence** · *Florence County Eco. Dev. Comm.* · Wendy Gehlhoff, Dir., P.O. Box 88, 54121, P 5,000, (715) 528-3294, Fax (715) 528-5071, info@florencewisconsin.com, www.florencewisconsin.com

**Fond du Lac** · *Fond du Lac County Eco. Dev. Corp.* · Brenda Hicks Sorensen, Pres., 140 N. Main St., P.O. Box 1303, 54936, P 101,000, (920) 929-2928, Fax (920) 929-7126, info@fcedc.com, www.fcedc.com

**Fort Atkinson** · *Fort Atkinson Ind. Dev. Corp.* · Sheldon Mielke, Pres., 244 N. Main St., 53538, P 12,000, M 40, (920) 563-3210, Fax (920) 563-8946, idc@fortchamber.com, www.fortchamber.com/businessdevelopment

**Francis Creek** · *Francis Creek Comm. Dev. Corp.* · Joseph W. Debilzen, Treas., P.O. Box 357, 54214, P 620, (920) 683-5710, www.franciscreek.org

**Friendship** · *Adams County Rural & Ind. Dev. Comm.* · P.O. Box 236, 53934, P 20,000, (608) 339-6945, Fax (608) 339-0052, economicdevelopment@adamscountywi.com, www.adams countywi.com

**Germantown** · *Germantown Planning* · Jeff Retzlaff, Planner, P.O. Box 337, 53022, P 19,400, (262) 250-4735, www.village. germantown.wi.us

**Grantsburg** · *Grantsburg Ind. Dev. Corp.* · Gary Nelson, Pres., P.O. Box 365, 54840, P 1,400, M 90, (715) 463-2405, info@grants burgidc.com, www.grantsburgwi.com

**Green Bay** · *Advance Bus. Dev. Center* · Fred Monique, V.P. Eco. Dev., 2701 Larsen Rd., 54303, P 240,404, (920) 496-9010, Fax (920) 496-6009, monique@titletown.org, www.advancegreenbay.org

**Hartford** · *City of Hartford Eco. Dev. Dept.* · Gary Koppelberger, Coord., 109 N. Main St., 53027, P 13,550, (262) 673-8202, Fax (262) 673-8218, www.ci.hartford.wi.us

**Hurley** · *Iron County Dev. Zone Cncl.* · Mr. Kelly Klein, Coord., 100 Cary Rd., P.O. Box 97, 54534, P 6,500, (715) 561-2922, Fax (715) 561-3103, jenni@ironcountywi.com, www.ironcountywi.com

**Janesville** · *City of Janesville Eco. Dev. Agency* · Douglas Venable, Dir., 18 N. Jackson St., P.O. Box 5005, 53547, P 60,000, (608) 755-3181, Fax (608) 755-3196, venabled@ci.janesville. wi.us, www.ci.janesville.wi.us

**Janesville** · *Forward Janesville Inc.* · John Beckord, Pres., 14 S. Jackson St., 53548, P 60,000, M 600, (608) 757-3160, Fax (608) 757-3170, forward@forwardjanesville.com, www. forwardjanesville.com

**Juneau** · *Juneau Comm. Dev. Auth.* · Bob Buhr, CDA, 150 Miller St., P.O. Box 163, 53039, P 2,498, (920) 386-4800, Fax (920) 386-4802, bbuhr@cityofjuneau.net, www.juneaueconomic development.com

**Kenosha** · *Kenosha Area Bus. Alliance* · Todd Battle, Pres., 600 52nd St., Ste. 120, 53140, P 156,082, (262) 605-1100, Fax (262) 605-1111, info@kaba.org, www.kaba.org

**Kiel** · *Kiel Ind. Dev. Corp.* · John Laun, Secy., 627 Fremont St., P.O. Box 156, 53042, P 3,500, (920) 894-3488, Fax (920) 894-2150, www.kielwi.org

**La Crosse** · *La Crosse Area Dev. Corp.* · James P. Hill, Exec. Dir., 712 Main St., 54601, P 126,838, M 100, (608) 784-5488, (888) 208-0698, Fax (608) 784-5408, ladco@centurytel.net, www. ladcoweb.org

**Ladysmith** · *Ladysmith Comm. Ind. Dev. Corp.* · Al Christianson, City Admin., 120 W. Miner Ave., P.O. Box 431, 54848, P 4,000, (715) 532-2600, Fax (715) 532-2620

**Lancaster** · *Lancaster Eco. Dev. Comm.* · Scot Simpson, City Admin., 206 S. Madison St., 53813, P 4,100, (608) 723-4246, Fax (608) 723-4789, www.lancasterwisconsin.com

**Manitowoc** · *EDC of Manitowoc County* · Kenneth Stubbe, Exec. Dir., 1515 Memorial Dr., P.O. Box 813, 54221, P 81,500, (920) 482-0540, Fax (920) 684-1915, info@edcmc.org, www.edcmc.org

**Manitowoc** · *Manitowoc Ind. Dev. Corp.* · David Less, City Planner, 900 Quay St., 54220, P 35,000, (920) 686-6930, Fax (920) 686-6939, dless@manitowoc.org, www.manitowoc.org

**Marinette** · *Marinette Area Eco. Dev. Corp.* · Mary D. Johns, Exec. Dir., 601 Marinette Ave., 54143, P 21,000, (715) 735-6681, Fax (715) 735-6682, chamber@centurytel.net, www.mandm chamber.com

**Marion** · *Marion Eco. Dev. Corp.* · Tom Pamperin, Secy./Treas., P.O. Box 496, 54950, P 1,250, (715) 754-2535, tpamperin@ premiercommunity.com, www.marion.govoffice2.com

**Marshfield** · *Marshfield Area C/C & Ind.* · Scott Larson, Exec. Dir., 700 S. Central Ave., P.O. Box 868, 54449, P 20,000, (715) 384-3454, Fax (715) 387-8925, info@marshfieldchamber.com, www. marshfieldchamber.com

**Mauston** · *Greater Mauston Area Dev. Corp.* · Barb Martin, Exec. Dir., 103 Division St., 53948, P 28,000, (608) 847-7483, Fax (608) 847-5814, gmadc@mwt.net, www.mauston.com

**Medford** · *Medford Area Dev. Found.* · Mark Hoffman, Pres., 104 E. Perkins St., P.O. Box 172, 54451, P 4,324, (715) 748-4729, www.medfordwis.com

**Menomonie** · *Dunn County Eco. Dev. Corp.* · Robert J. Bossany, Pres., 401 Technology Dr. E., Ste. 400, 54751, P 40,315, (715) 232-4009, Fax (715) 232-4034, info@dunnedc.com, www.dunnedc.com

**Milwaukee** · *Metro Milwaukee Assn. of Commerce* · Timothy Sheehy, Pres., 756 N. Milwaukee St., 53202, P 1,500,000, M 2,000, (414) 287-4100, Fax (414) 271-7753, www.mmac.org

**Monticello** · *Monticello Ind. Dev. Corp.* · Dennis Thoman, Pres., P.O. Box 72, 53570, P 1,207, (608) 938-4610, (608) 938-4383, www.monticello-wi.com

**Neenah** · *Future Neenah Inc.* · 135 W. Wisconsin Ave., P.O. Box 896, 54957, P 25,000, (920) 722-1920, Fax (920) 722-6585, www. neenah.org

**Neillsville** · *Neillsville Dept. of Eco. Dev.* · Diane Murphy, Mayor, 118 W. 5th St., City Hall, 54456, P 2,731, (715) 743-2105, Fax (715) 743-2727, neills@tds.net, www.neillsville-wi.com

**New Glarus** · *New Glarus Comm. Dev. Auth.* · Nicholas Owen, Village Admin., P.O. Box 399, 53574, P 2,107, (608) 527-2510, Fax (608) 527-2062, www.newglarusvillage.com

**New Holstein** · *New Holstein Ind. Dev. Corp.* · Lee Watson, Dir., 2110 Washington St., 53061, P 3,335, (920) 898-5766, Fax (920) 898-5879, lwatson@tcei.com, www.ci.new-holstein.wi.us

**New London** · *New London Eco. Dev.* · Kent Hager, City Admin., 215 N. Shawano St., 54961, P 7,187, (920) 982-8500, Fax (920) 982-8665, www.newlondonwi.org

**New London** · *Waupaca County Eco. Dev. Corp.* · David Thiel, Exec. Dir., N. 3512 Dawn Dr., 54961, P 50,000, (920) 982-1582, Fax (920) 982-9047, wcedc@charter.net, www.wcedc.org

**New Richmond** · *Eco. Dev. Comm.* · Jerry Brown, Eco. Dev. Dir., 156 E. 1st St., 54017, P 7,858, (715) 246-4718, Fax (715) 246-7129, jerrybrown@frontiernet.net, www.ci.new-richmond.wi.us

**Oak Creek** · *Oak Creek Dept. of Comm. Dev.* · Doug Seymour, Dir., 8640 S. Howell Ave., 53154, P 32,000, (414) 768-6526, Fax (414) 768-9587, dseymour@oakcreekwi.org, www.oakcreekwi.org

**Oconomowoc** · *Oconomowoc Bur. of Eco. Dev.* · Robert Duffy, Dir., 174 E. Wisconsin Ave., P.O. Box 27, 53066, P 14,000, (262) 569-2185, (800) 524-3744, Fax (262) 569-3238, info@oconomowocusa. com, www.oconomowocusa.com

**Omro** · *Omro Area Dev. Corp.* · Steve Volkert, Dir., 130 W. Larrabee St., 54963, P 3,500, (920) 685-7005, Fax (920) 685-0384, omromarketing@charterinternet.net, www.omro-wi.com

**Park Falls** · *Park Falls Area Ind. Dev. Corp.* · 1224 S. 4th Ave., 54552, P 3,000, (715) 744-4700, pfacdc@pctcnet.net, www. pfacdc.org

**Pewaukee** · *Waukesha County Eco. Dev. Corp.* · Bill Mitchell, Exec. Dir., 892 Main St., Ste. D, 53072, P 34,000, (262) 695-7900, Fax (262) 695-7902, www.understandingbusiness.org

**EDC**

**Phillips** · *Phillips Ind. Dev. Corp.* · Dennis Mathison, V.P., 174 N. Avon, 54555, P 1,500, (715) 339-2230, Fax (715) 339-4975

**Platteville** · *Platteville Area Ind. Dev. Corp.* · George Krueger, Exec. Dir., 52 Means Dr., Ste. 104, 53818, P 10,000, (608) 348-3050, Fax (608) 348-3426, plattevilleindustry@centurytel.net, www.plattevilleindustry.com

**Prairie du Chien** · *Prairie du Chien Ind. Dev. Corp.* · Dick Mergen, Pres., P.O. Box 247, 53821, P 20,000, (608) 326-8187, Fax (608) 326-8187, www.prairieduchien.org

**Prentice** · *Prentice Ind. Dev. Corp.* · Dale Heikkinen, Pres., 605 Spruce St., 54556, P 640, M 25, (715) 428-2124, Fax (715) 428-2120, daleh@pctcnet.net, www.vil.prentice.wi.gov

**Reedsburg** · *Reedsburg Ind. Dev. Comm.* · Don Lichte, Chrmn., P.O. Box 490, 53959, P 9,028, (608) 524-6404, Fax (608) 524-8458, www.reedsburgwi.gov

**Rhinelander** · *Oneida County Eco. Dev. Corp.* · Jim Kumbera, Exec. Dir., 3375 Airport Rd., P.O. Box 682, 54501, P 33,853, (715) 369-9110, (715) 356-5590, Fax (715) 369-5758, ocedc@newnorth.net, www.ocedc.org

**Rice Lake** · *Red Cedar Dev. Corp.* · Bruce Markgren, Pres., P.O. Box 526, 54868, P 8,312, (715) 234-7008, www.cityofricelake.com

**Richland Center** · *Richland County Eco. Dev. Corp.* · Ronda Fostering, Exec. Dir., 140 Sextonville Rd., P.O. Box 49, 53581, P 18,500, (608) 647-4310, Fax (608) 647-6118, RCEDC@mwt.net, www.richlandcounty.com

**Shawano** · *Shawano County Eco. Progress Inc.* · Stephen Sengstock, Exec. Dir., 1263 S. Main, P.O. Box 35, 54166, P 41,000, (715) 526-5839, Fax (715) 526-2125, scepi@frontiernet.net, www.shawanoecondev.org

**Sheboygan** · *Sheboygan Dev. Corp.* · 712 Riverfront Dr., Ste. 101, 53081, P 113,000, (920) 457-9491, Fax (920) 457-6269

**Shullsburg** · *Shullsburg Comm. Dev. Corp.* · Cheryl Fink, Pres., P.O. Box 3, 53586, P 1,247, M 25, (608) 965-4579, (608) 965-4424, cdc@mhtc.net, www.shullsburgwisconsin.org

**Siren** · *Burnett County Dev. Assn.* · Michael Kornmann, Advisor, 7410 County Rd. K, Ste. 129, 54872, P 16,000, M 12, (715) 349-2979, www.burnettcounty.com

**Soldiers Grove** · *Soldiers Grove Comm. Dev.* · Tammy Kepler, Clerk/Treas., P.O. Box 121, 54655, P 640, (608) 624-3264, Fax (608) 624-5209, sgrove@mwt.net, www.soldiersgrove.com

**Sparta** · *City of Sparta Eco. Dev.* · Ken Witt, City Admin., 201 W. Oak St., 54656, P 9,000, (608) 269-4340, (608) 269-7212, www.spartawisconsin.org

**Sturgeon Bay** · *Door County Eco. Dev. Corp.* · William Chaudoir, Exec. Dir., 185 E. Walnut St., 54235, P 26,000, M 120, (920) 743-3113, Fax (920) 743-3811, bill@doorcountybusiness.com, www.doorcountybusiness.com

**Sturtevant** · *Racine County Eco. Dev. Corp.* · Gordon Kacala, Exec. Dir., 2320 Renaissance Blvd., 53177, P 185,000, (262) 898-7400, gkacala@racinecountyedc.org, www.racinecountyedc.org

**Superior** · *The Dev. Assn. Inc.* · Andrew Lisak, Exec. Dir., 1401 Tower Ave., Ste. 302, 54880, P 71,400, M 160, (715) 392-4749, Fax (715) 392-6131, lisaka@developmentassociation.com, www.developmentassociation.com

**Thorp** · *Thorp Area Dev. Corp.* · P.O. Box 175, 54771, P 1,657, (715) 669-5628, www.cityofthorp.com

**Tomah** · *Forward Tomah Dev. Inc.* · Christopher Hanson, Exec. Dir., P.O. Box 625, 54660, P 8,100, (608) 372-2166, (800) 94-TOMAH, Fax (608) 372-2167, info@tomahwisconsin.com, www.tomahwisconsin.com

**Viroqua** · *Viroqua Dev. Assn.* · Jeff Gohlke, Ind. Coord., 202 N. Main St., 54665, P 4,417, (608) 637-7154, Fax (608) 637-3108, cityadmin@mwt.net, www.viroqua-wisconsin.com

**Waupun** · *Waupun Ind. Dev. Corp.* · Gary Rogers, City Admin., 201 E. Main St., 53963, P 11,000, (920) 324-7919, Fax (920) 324-7939, www.cityofwaupun.org

**Wausau** · *MCDEVCO* · Roger A. Luce, Exec. Dir., P.O. Box 6190, 54402, P 127,280, (715) 845-6231, Fax (715) 845-6235, info@wausauchamber.com, www.wausauchamber.com

**Wauwatosa** · *Wauwatosa Eco. Dev. Corp.* · Gloria Stearns, Exec. Dir., 1414 Underwood Ave., Ste. 402, 53213, P 47,271, (414) 259-9915, Fax (414) 259-9920, wedc@wedc.net, www.wedc.net

**West Allis** · *City of West Allis Dev. Dept.* · John F. Stibal, Dir. of Dev., 7525 W. Greenfield Ave., 53214, P 60,410, (414) 302-8460, Fax (414) 302-8401, www.ci.west-allis.wi.us

**West Bend** · *West Bend Eco. Dev. Corp.* · Dan Anhalt, 400 University Dr., c/o UW-Washington County, 53095, P 30,000, M 40, (262) 335-5218, Fax (262) 338-1771, info@wbachamber.org, www.wbachamber.org

**Winneconne** · *Winneconne Dev. Corp.* · Steve McNeil, Village Admin., 30 S. 1st St., P.O. Box 488, 54986, P 2,500, (920) 582-4381, Fax (920) 582-0660, smcneil@winneconnewi.gov, www.winneconnewi.gov

**Wisconsin Rapids** · *Heart of Wisconsin Bus. & Eco. Alliance* · Connie Loden, Exec. Dir., 1120 Lincoln St., 54494, P 40,000, (715) 423-1830, Fax (715) 423-1865, info@heartofwi.com, www.heartofwi.com

# Wyoming

## Federal

**U.S. SBA, Wyoming Dist. Ofc.** · Steven Despain, Dist. Dir., 100 E. B St., Rm. 4001, Casper, 82601, P (307) 261-6500, Fax (307) 261-6535, www.sba.gov/wy

## Communities

**Casper** · *Casper Area Eco. Dev. Alliance* · Robert Barnes CEcD, Pres./CEO, 300 S. Wolcott, Ste. 300, 82601, P 70,000, (307) 577-7011, (800) 634-5012, Fax (307) 577-7014, info@caeda.net, www.casperworks.biz

**Cheyenne** · *Cheyenne Leads* · Randy Bruns, CEO, 121 W. 15th St., Ste. 304, 82001, P 80,000, (307) 638-6000, Fax (307) 638-7728, leads@cheyenneleads.org, www.cheyenneleads.org

**Cody** · *Cody Retention, Expansion & Education* · Garrett Growney, Chair, 836 Sheridan Ave., 82414, P 9,000, (307) 587-2639, Fax (307) 527-6228, admin@codychamber.org, www.codychamber.org

**Diamondville** · *So. Lincoln County Eco. Dev. Corp.* · Gigi Henkel, Dir., P.O. Box 495, 83116, P 3,500, M 25, (307) 877-9781, Fax (307) 877-6709, slcedc@gmail.com, www.diamondvillewyo.com

**Evanston** · *City of Evanston Eco. Dev.* · Jim Davis, Clerk, City Hall, 1200 Main St., 82930, P 13,000, (307) 783-6300, Fax (307) 783-6390, www.evanstonwy.org

**Evanston** · *Uinta County Eco. Dev. Comm.* · Dell Atkinson, Dir., 225 9th St., 82930, P 21,000, (307) 783-0378, Fax (307) 783-0379, deatkinson@uintacounty.com, www.uintacounty.com

**Gillette** · *Campbell County Eco. Dev. Corp.* · Phillipe M. Chino, Exec. Dir., 201 W. Lakeway Rd., Ste. 1004, P.O. Box 3948, 82717, P 36,000, M 85, (307) 686-2603, (800) 376-0848, Fax (307) 686-7268, ccedc@ccedc.net, www.gillettewyoming.com

**Gillette** • *North East Wyoming Eco. Dev. Coalition* • Linda Harris, Exec. Dir., P.O. Box 4369, 82717, P 53,000, (307) 686-3672, Fax (307) 686-3673, linda@newedc.com, www.newedc.com

**Glendo** • *Glendo Eco. Dev. Assn.* • Brenda Hagen, Town Clerk, 204 S. Yellowstone, P.O. Box 396, 82213, P 250, (307) 735-4242, Fax (307) 735-4422, townofglendo@yahoo.com, www.glendowy.govoffice2.com

**Laramie** • *Laramie Eco. Dev. Corp.* • Karen Gibbons, Pres., 313 S. 2nd St., Ste. B, P.O. Box 1250, 82073, P 29,000, M 165, (307) 742-2212, Fax (307) 742-8200, ledc@laramiewy.org, www.laramiewy.org

**Rawlins** • *Carbon County Eco. Dev. Corp.* • 215 W. Buffalo St., Ste. .304, 82301, P 16,000, (307) 324-3836, Fax (307) 324-3820, info@ccwyed.net, www.ccwyed.net

**Riverton** • *Riverton Mfg. Works* • Phillip Christopherson, 213 W. Main St., Ste. C, 82501, P 10,000, (307) 856-0952, www.manufacturing-works.com

**Rock Springs** • *Sweetwater Eco. Dev. Assn.* • Michelle Hostetler, Dir., 1400 Dewar Dr., Ste. 205A, 82901, P 40,000, M 70, (307) 352-6874, mhostetler@wyoming.com, www.sweda.net

**Sheridan** • *Forward Sheridan* • John N. Thurow, Op. Mgr., 203 S. Main St., Ste. 2003, 82801, P 27,111, M 67, (307) 673-8004, Fax (307) 673-8006, info@forwardsheridan.com, www.forwardsheridan.com

**Torrington** • *Goshen County Eco. Dev. Corp.* • Lisa Johnson, Exec. Dir., 117 W. 22nd Ave., P.O. Box 580, 82240, P 13,000, M 90, (307) 532-5162, Fax (307) 532-7641, progress@goshenwyo.com, www.goshenwyo.com

**Wheatland** • *Wheatland Area Dev. Corp.* • 1560 Johnston St, P.O. Box 988, 82201, P 3,500, (307) 322-4232, Fax (307) 322-1629, wadco@wyomingwireless.com, www.wadco.org

**Worland** • *Washakie Dev. Assn.* • LeAnn Baker, Exec. Dir., 107 S. 7th St., P.O. Box 228, 82401, P 8,500, M 85, (307) 347-8900, wda@rtconnect.net, www.washakiedevelopment.com

**EDC**

# Notes

# The Canadian Chamber of Commerce

## Head Office

360 Albert Street, Suite 420 • Ottawa, Ontario K1R 7X7

Telephone: (613) 238-4000 • FAX: (613) 238-7643

Email: info@chamber.ca • Website: www.chamber.ca

## Toronto Office

55 University Ave., Suite 901 • Toronto, Ontario M5J 2H7

Telephone: (416) 868-6415 • FAX: (416) 868-0189

## Montreal Office

1155 University Street, Suite 709 • Montreal, Quebec H3B 3A7

Telephone: (514) 866-4334 • FAX: (514) 866-7296

## Senior Officers

**Chair of the Board (September 2008–September 2009)**
Roger Thomas, Exec. V.P., North America of Nexen Inc.

**President & Chief Executive Officer**
Honourable Perrin Beatty (c/o Head Office)

**Senior Vice President, Policy**
Shirley-Ann George (c/o Head Office)

**Executive Vice President, Communications and Services**
Michel Barsalou (c/o Head Office)

**Vice President and Chief Financial Officer**
Adéle Laronde, CA (c/o Head Office)

**Senior Vice President, Corporate Relations**
Michael P. Nixon (c/o Toronto Office)

# Canadian Chambers of Commerce

## Alberta

**Alberta Chambers of Commerce** • Ken Kobly, Pres./CEO, 10025-102A Ave., Ste. 1808, Edmonton, T5J 2Z2, P 3,000,000, M 22,000, (780) 425-4180, Fax (780) 429-1061, info@abchamber.ca, www.abchamber.ca

**Airdrie** • *Airdrie C/C* • Mike Brandrick, Pres., 212 Main St. N.E., Box 3661, T4B 2B8, P 30,000, M 350, (403) 948-4412, Fax (403) 948-3141, info@airdriechamber.ab.ca, www.airdriechamber.ab.ca

**Alix** • *Alix C/C* • Clarence Verveda, P.O. Box 145, T0C 0B0, P 825, M 15, (403) 747-2405, Fax (403) 747-2414

**Athabasca** • *Athabasca Dist. C/C* • Joan Veenstra, Secy., P.O. Box 3074, T9S 2B9, P 10,500, M 130, chamber@athabascachamber.ca, www.athabascachamber.ca

**Barrhead** • *Barrhead & Dist. C/C* • Darren Strawson, Pres., P.O. Box 4524, T7N 1A4, P 10,000, M 109, (780) 674-4600, www.barrheadchamber.ca

**Beaverlodge** • *Beaverlodge & Dist. C/C* • Herb Smith, Pres., P.O. Box 303, T0H 0C0, P 2,900, M 65, (780) 354-8785, Fax (780) 354-2101

**Berwyn** • *Berwyn & Dist. C/C* • Linda Johnson, Pres., P.O. Box 250, T0H 0E0, P 606, M 15, (780) 338-3922, vberwyn@wispernet.ca, www.berwyn.govoffice.com

**Blairmore** • *Crowsnest Pass C/C* • Kathy Mountfort, 12707 20th Ave., P.O. Box 706, T0K 0E0, P 5,500, M 130, (403) 562-7108, (888) 562-7108, Fax (403) 562-7493, cnpchamber@shaw.ca, www.crowsnest-pass.com

**Boyle** • *Boyle & Dist. C/C* • Monica Hill, Pres., P.O. Box 496, T0A 0M0, P 850, M 25, (780) 689-6766, www.villageofboyle.com

**Breton** • *Breton & Dist. C/C* • Glory Tornack, Pres., P.O. Box 364, T0C 0P0, P 2,000, M 25, (780) 696-2557, Fax (780) 696-2557

**Brooks** • *Brooks & Dist. C/C* • Kim Buckingham, Mgr., #4-403 2nd Ave. W., P.O. Box 400, T1R 1B4, P 25,000, M 290, (403) 362-7641, Fax (403) 362-6893, manager@brookschamber.ab.ca, www.brookschamber.ab.ca

**Calgary** • *Calgary C/C* • Heather Douglas, Pres./CEO, 100 6th Ave. S.W., T2P 0P5, P 1,000,000, M 3,700, (403) 750-0400, Fax (403) 266-3413, chinfo@calgarychamber.com, www.calgarychamber.com

**Camrose** • *Camrose C/C* • Sharon Anderson, Exec. Dir., 5402 - 48 Ave., T4V 0J7, P 16,500, M 380, (780) 672-4217, Fax (780) 672-1059, camcham@telusplanet.net, www.camrosechamber.ca

**Canmore** • *Tourism Canmore* • John Samms, Exec. Dir., 907 7th Ave., P.O. Box 8608, T1W 2V3, P 17,000, M 200, (403) 678-1295, (866) 226-6673, Fax (403) 678-1296, info@tourismcanmore.com, www.tourismcanmore.com

**Cardston** • *Cardston & Dist. C/C* • Zenith Gaynor, Pres., P.O. Box 1212, T0K 0K0, P 3,500, M 46, (403) 653-2798, info@cardstonchamber.com, www.cardstonchamber.com

**Coaldale** • *Coaldale and Dist. C/C* • Michele McCann, Exec. Dir., P.O. Box 1117, T1M 1M9, P 6,000, M 150, (403) 345-2358, Fax (403) 345-2339, info@coaldalechamber.com, www.coaldale-chamber.com

**Cochrane** • *Cochrane & Dist. C/C* • Gerri Polis, Mgr., 205 1st St. E., Bay 5, T4C 1X6, P 17,000, M 305, (403) 932-0320, Fax (403) 932-6824, c.business@cochranechamber.ca, www.cochranechamber.ca

**Cold Lake** • *Cold Lake Reg. C/C* • Sherri Bohme, Exec. Dir., 4910- 50th Ave., Bay 109, P.O. Box 454, T9M 1P1, P 12,540, M 350, (780) 594-4747, Fax (780) 594-3711, clrcc@incentre.net, coldlakechamber.ca

**Consort** • *Consort & Dist. C/C* • Charlene Robichaud, Pres., P.O. Box 335, T0C 1B0, P 2,300, M 40, (403) 577-7907, psdahl@xplorenet.com, charlene.robichaud@rbc.com, www.village.consort.ab.ca

**Devon** • *Devon & Dist. C/C* • Wade Kosiorek, Ofc. Mgr., 35 Athabasca Ave., T9G 1G5, P 6,300, M 65, (780) 987-5177, Fax (780) 987-5135, devoncc@telus.net

**Didsbury** • *Didsbury & District C/C* • Tammy Brooks, Ofc. Mgr., P.O. Box 981, T0M 0W0, P 4,500, M 80, (403) 335-3265, Fax (403) 335-3265, info@didsburychamber.ca, www.didsburychamber.ca

**Drayton Valley** • *Drayton Valley & Dist. C/C* • Tara Petersen, Admin., P.O. Box 5318, T7A 1R5, P 6,800, M 150, (780) 542-7578, Fax (780) 542-9211, chambrdv@telusplanet.net, www.dvchamber.com

**Drumheller** • *Drumheller & Dist. C/C* • Heather Bitz, Gen. Mgr., 60 - 1 Ave. W., Box 999, T0J 0Y0, P 7,800, M 210, (403) 823-8100, Fax (403) 823-4469, info@drumhellerchamber.com, www.drumhellerchamber.com.

**Edmonton** · *Edmonton C of C/World Trade Centre* · Martin D. Salloum, Pres./CEO, 600 World Trade Centre, 9990 Jasper Ave., T5J 1P7, P 1,034,945, M 3,800, (780) 426-4620, Fax (780) 424-7946, info@edmontonchamber.com, www.edmontonchamber.com

**Edson** · *Edson & Dist. C/C* · Nicole Bethge, Pres., 5433 - 3rd Ave., T7E 1L5, P 8,600, M 300, (780) 723-4918, Fax (780) 723-5545, manager@edsonchamber.com, www.edsonchamber.com.

**Elk Point** · *Elk Point C/C* · Sandy Smith, Pres., Box 639, T0A 1A0, P 1,500, M 58, (780) 724-2966, (780) 724-3810, www.elkpoint.ca

**Evansburg** · *Evansburg & Entwistle C/C* · Sarah Leteta, Mgr., P.O. Box 598, T0E 0T0, P 2,000, M 80, (780) 727-4035, Fax (780) 727-4035, info@partnersonthepembina.com, www.partnerson thepembina.com

**Fairview** · *Fairview & Dist. C/C* · P.O. Box 1034, T0H 1L0, P 3,500, M 120, (780) 835-5999, Fax (780) 835-4033, fairviewchamber@ telus.net, www.fairviewchamber.com

**Falher** · *Falher C/C* · Greg Radstaak, P.O. Box 814, T0H 1M0, P 5,000, M 60, (780) 837-2364, www.falherchamber.com

**Falher** · *Smoky River Reg. Eco. Dev. Bd.* · David Kane, Eco. Dev. Officer, P.O. Box 210, T0H 1M0, P 5,000, (780) 837-2364, Fax (780) 837-2453, dkane@mdsmokyriver.com, www.smokyriverregion.com

**Foremost** · *Foremost & Dist. C/C* · P.O. Box 272, T0K 0X0, P 500, M 50, (403) 867-3077, Fax (403) 867-2700, cofc4mst@ la.shockware.com, www.foremostalberta.com

**Fort Macleod** · *Fort Macleod & Dist. C/C* · Emily McTighe, Pres., P.O. Box 1959, T0L 0Z0, P 3,200, M 83, (403) 553-3391, (877) 622-5366, Fax (403) 553-2426, www.fortmacleod.com

**Fort McMurray** · *Fort McMurray C/C* · Diane Slater, Exec. Dir., 9612 Franklin Ave., Unit 304, T9H 2J9, P 74,000, M 700, (780) 743-3100, Fax (780) 790-9757, fmcoc@telus.net, www.fort mcmurraychamber.ca

**Fort McMurray** · *Fort McMurray Tourism Assn.* · Denise Barrow, Ofc. Mgr., 400 Sakitawaw Trl., T9H 4Z3, P 80,000, M 150, (780) 791-4336, (800) 565-3947, Fax (780) 790-9509, info@ fortmcmurraytourism.com, www.fortmcmurraytourism.com

**Fort Saskatchewan** · *Fort Saskatchewan C/C* · 10030 - 99 Ave., P.O. Box 3072, T8L 2T1, P 16,000, M 301, (780) 998-4355, Fax (780) 998-1515, chamber@fortsaskchamber.com, www. fortsaskchamber.com

**Grande Cache** · *Grande Cache C/C* · Richard Thompson, Pres., P.O. Box 1342, T0E 0Y0, P 4,500, M 60, (780) 827-1217, (888) 827-3790, Fax (780) 827-5351, www.grandecache.ca

**Grande Prairie** · *Grande Prairie C/C* · Dan Pearcy, CEO, #217-11330 106th St., T8V 7X9, P 50,000, M 1,100, (780) 532-5340, Fax (780) 532-2926, info@gpchamber.com, www.gpchamber.com

**Grimshaw** · *Grimshaw & Dist. C/C* · Jason Doris, Pres., P.O. Box 919, T0H 1W0, P 2,500, M 67, info@grimshawchamber.com, www. grimshawchamber.com

**High Level** · *High Level & Dist. C/C* · Silvia Kennedy, Pres., 10803 96th St., T0H 1Z0, P 4,500, M 166, (780) 926-2470, Fax (780) 926-4017, hlchambr@incentre.net, www.highlevelchamber.com

**High River** · *High River & Dist. C/C* · Lynette McCracken, Mgr., P.O. Box 5244, T1V 1M4, P 12,000, M 190, (403) 652-3336, Fax (403) 652-7660, hrdcc@telus.net, www.highriverchamber.com

**Hinton** · *Hinton & Dist. C/C* · Lori Phillips, Exec. Dir., 309 Gregg Ave., T7V 2A7, P 10,000, M 140, (780) 865-2777, (877) 446-8666, Fax (780) 865-1062, hintoncc@telus.net, www.hintonchamber.com

**Jasper** · *Jasper Tourism & Commerce* · Helen Kelleher-Empey, Gen. Mgr., 409 Patrica St., P.O. Box 98, T0E 1E0, P 5,000, M 300, (780) 852-3858, Fax (780) 852-4932, info@jaspercanadianrockies. com, www.jaspercanadianrockies.com

**Killam** · *Killam & Dist. C/C* · Dan Fee, Pres., P.O. Box 189, T0B 2L0, P 1,100, M 35, (780) 385-3977, (780) 385-3034, www.town. killam.ab.ca

**Lacombe** · *Lacombe & Dist. C/C* · Anna Boruck, Pres., 6005-50 Ave., T4L 1K7, P 11,000, M 275, (403) 782-4300, Fax (403) 782-4302, info@lacombechamber.ca, www.lacombechamber.ca

**Leduc** · *Leduc & Dist. C/C* · Iris Yanish, Mgr., 6420-50 St., T9E 7K9, P 20,000, M 550, (780) 986-5454, Fax (780) 986-8108, info@ leduc-chamber.com, www.leduc-chamber.com

**Lethbridge** · *Lethbridge C/C* · Jody Nilsson, Gen. Mgr., 529-6th St. S., Ste. 200, T1J 2E1, P 82,000, M 650, (403) 327-1586, Fax (403) 327-1001, office@lethbridgechamber.com, www.lethbridgechamber.com.

**Lloydminster** · *Lloydminster C/C* · Pat Tenney, Exec. Dir., 4419 - 52nd Ave., T9V 0Y8, P 25,000, M 520, (780) 875-9013, Fax (780) 875-0755, lloydchamber@lloydminsterchamber.com, www. lloydminsterchamber.com

**Marwayne** · *Marwayne & Dist. C/C* · Sharon Kneen, Pres., P.O. Box 183, T0B 2X0, P 569, M 25, (780) 847-3962, marwayne@ hmsinet.ca, www.village.marwayne.ab.ca

**McLennan** · *McLennan C/C* · Jill Moses, Pres., P.O. Box 90, T0H 2L0, P 900, M 33, (780) 324-3894, www.townofmclennan.com

**Millet** · *Millet & Dist. C/C* · 5120 50th St., T0C 1Z0, P 2,000, M 30, (780) 387-4554

**Nanton** · *Nanton C/C* · Jason Calvert, Interim Dir., P.O. Box 711, T0L 1R0, P 2,000, M 75, (403) 336-2000, (403) 646-2029, president@nantonchamber.com, www.nantonchamber.com

**Okotoks** · *Okotoks Dist. C/C* · Susan Klein, Exec. Asst., P.O. Box 1053, T1S 1B1, P 17,000, M 250, (403) 938-2848, Fax (403) 938-6649, okotokschamber@telus.net, www.okotokschamber.ca

**Onoway** · *Onoway & Dist. C/C* · Marinus Landsman, P.O. Box 723, T0E 1V0, P 2,800, M 20, (780) 967-6892, www.onoway.com

**Oyen** · *Oyen & Dist. C/C* · Kari Kuzmiski, Pres., P.O. Box 718, T0J 2J0, P 1,500, M 50, (403) 664-0406, oyenecho@telusplanet.net

**Peace River** · *Peace River C/C* · Don Ames, Gen. Mgr., 9309 100 St., P.O. Box 6599, T8S 1S4, P 6,687, M 207, (780) 624-4166, Fax (780) 624-4663, www.peaceriverchamber.com

**Picture Butte** · *Picture Butte & Dist. C/C* · Andrew Noel, Pres., 120 4th St. N., P.O. Box 540, T0K 1V0, P 1,501, M 80, (403) 732-4302, (403) 732-4555, chamber@picturebutte.ca, www. picturebutte.ca

**Pincher Creek** · *Pincher Creek & Dist. Chamber of Eco. Dev.* · Kim Buckingham, P.O. Box 2287, T0K 1W0, P 7,000, M 150, (403) 627-5199, Fax (403) 627-5850, info@pincher-creek.com, www. pincher-creek.com

**Ponoka** · *Ponoka & Dist. C/C* · Darren Galan, Pres., 4612 50th St., Ste. 3, P.O. Box 4188, T4J 1R6, P 6,500, M 200, (403) 783-3888, Fax (403) 783-3888, chamber@ponoka.org, www.ponokachamber.org

**Provost** · *Provost & Dist. C/C* · Anne Fraser, Secy./Treas., P.O. Box 637, T0B 3S0, P 2,045, M 77, (780) 753-6288, Fax (780) 753-6060

**Red Deer** · *Red Deer C/C* · Tim Creedon, Exec. Dir., 3017 Gaetz Ave., T4N 5Y6, P 82,971, M 890, (403) 347-4491, Fax (403) 343-6188, rdchamber@reddeerchamber.com, www.reddeerchamber.com

**Redwater** · *Redwater & Dist. C/C* · Myron Buryn, Treas., P.O. Box 322, T0A 2W0, P 2,400, M 40, (780) 942-3635

**Rimbey** · *Rimbey C/C* · Mary Rose Barr, Pres., 5025 50th Ave., Box 87, T0C 2J0, P 2,300, M 80, (403) 843-4000, rimbeychamber@rimbey.com, www.rimbey.com

**Rocky Mountain House** · *Rocky Mountain House & Dist. C/C* · 5406 - 48th St., Box 1374, T4T 1B1, P 7,200, M 355, (403) 845-5450, Fax (403) 845-7764, rmhcofc@rockychamber.org, www.rockychamber.org

**Saint Albert** · *Saint Albert C/C* · Lynda Moffet, Exec. Dir., 71 St. Albert Rd., T8N 6L5, P 58,400, M 600, (780) 458-2833, Fax (780) 458-6515, chamber@stalbertchamber.com, www.stalbertchamber.com

**Saint Paul** · *St. Paul & Dist. C/C* · Doug Lamb, Pres., P.O. Box 887, T0A 3A0, P 5,500, M 150, (780) 645-5820, (780) 645-4481, admin@stpaulchamber.ca, www.stpaulchamber.ca

**Sedgewick** · *Sedgewick C/C* · Sue Freadrich, Secy./Treas., T0B 4C0, P 891, M 50, (780) 384-2278, (780) 384-3504, www.sedgewickca.com

**Sexsmith** · *Sexsmith C/C* · Freda King, Pres., P.O. Box 146, T0H 3C0, P 2,300, M 46, (780) 568-4663, chmbrtos@telusplanet.net, www.sexsmith.ca

**Sherwood Park** · *Sherwood Park & Dist. C/C* · Marty Shigehiro, Pres., 100 Ordze Ave., T8B 1M6, P 82,000, M 875, (780) 464-0801, Fax (780) 449-3581, admin@sherwoodparkchamber.com, www.sherwoodparkchamber.com

**Smoky Lake** · *Smoky Lake & Dist. C/C* · Wayne Taylor, Pres., P.O. Box 635, T0A 3C0, P 4,500, M 50, (780) 656-3842, Fax (780) 451-3321, wayne@ethicaladvisor.com, www.smokylakeregion.ca

**Spruce Grove** · *Spruce Grove & Dist. C/C* · Brenda Johnson, Exec. Dir., 99 Campsite Rd., Box 4210, T7X 3B4, P 23,000, M 500, (780) 962-2561, Fax (780) 962-4417, info@sprucegrovechamber.com, www.sprucegrovechamber.com

**Stettler** · *Stettler Reg. Bd. of Trade & Comm. Dev.* · Keith Ryder, Exec. Dir., 6606 50th Ave., T0C 2L2, P 5,700, M 200, (403) 742-3181, (877) 742-9499, Fax (403) 742-3123, info@stettlerboardoftrade.com, www.stettlerboardoftrade.com

**Stony Plain** · *Stony Plain & Dist. C/C* · LeAnn Whaling, 4815 - 44 Ave., T7Z 1V5, P 13,500, M 545, (780) 963-4545, Fax (780) 963-4542, office@stonyplainchamber.ca, www.stonyplainchamber.ca

**Swan Hills** · *Swan Hills C/C* · Rita Krawiec, Pres., P.O. Box 149, T0G 2C0, P 1,800, M 50, (780) 333-2209, (780) 333-4477, www.townofswanhills.com

**Sylvan Lake** · *Sylvan Lake C/C* · Laurie Breeze, Exec. Dir., P.O. Box 9119, T4S 1S6, P 12,500, M 150, (403) 887-3048, Fax (403) 887-3048, info@sylvanlakechamber.com, www.sylvanlakechamber.com

**Taber** · *Taber & Dist. C/C* · Louie Tams, Pres., 4702 - 50 St., T1G 2B6, P 7,671, M 260, (403) 223-2265, Fax (403) 223-2291, tdcofc@telusplanet.net, www.taberchamber.com

**Thorhild** · *Thorhild C/C* · Michelle Boychuk, P.O. Box 384, T0A 3J0, P 3,000, M 40, (780) 398-2292, (780) 398-3550, thorhildchamber@telus.net, www.thorhild.com

**Vegreville** · *Vegreville & Dist. C/C* · Elaine Kucher, Gen. Mgr., 5009 50th Ave., P.O. Box 877, T9C 1R9, P 5,400, M 160, (780) 632-2771, Fax (780) 632-6958, vegchamb@telus.net, www.vegrevillechamber.com

**Vermilion** · *Vermilion & Dist. C/C* · 4924 - 50th St., T9X 0A1, P 4,435, M 110, (780) 853-6593, Fax (780) 853-1740, vermcofc@telusplanet.net, www.vermilionchamber.ca

**Vulcan** · *Vulcan & Dist. C/C* · Trish Standing, Pres., P.O. Box 385, T0L 2B0, P 1,850, M 70, (403) 485-4105, www.vulcanchamber.com

**Westlock** · *Westlock & Dist. C/C* · Lesa Muller-Schmaus, P.O. Box 5917, T7P 2P7, P 5,200, M 78, (780) 349-2903, info@westlock.ca, www.westlock.ca

**Wetaskiwin** · *Wetaskiwin & Dist. C/C* · Brandi La Bonte, Exec. Dir., 4910 55-A St., T9A 2R7, P 12,000, M 232, (780) 352-8003, Fax (780) 352-6226, info@wetaskiwinchamber.ca, www.wetaskiwinchamber.ca

**Whitecourt** · *Whitecourt & District C/C* · 3002 33rd St., P.O. Box 1011, T7S 1N9, P 9,200, M 250, (780) 778-5363, Fax (780) 778-2351, manager@whitecourtchamber.com, www.whitecourtchamber.com

# British Columbia

**British Columbia C/C** · John Winter, Pres., 1201-750 W. Pender St., Vancouver, V6C 2T8, (604) 683-0700, Fax (604) 683-0416, bccc@bcchamber.org, www.bcchamber.org

**100 Mile House** · *South Cariboo C/C* · Howard McMillon, Mgr., P.O. Box 2312, V0K 2E0, P 20,000, M 150, (250) 395-6124, Fax (250) 395-8974, manager@sochamber.ca, www.scaribochamber.org

**Abbotsford** · *Abbotsford C/C* · 32900 S. Fraser Way, Unit 207, V2S 5A1, P 135,000, M 750, (604) 859-9651, Fax (604) 850-6880, acoc@telus.net, www.abbotsfordchamber.com

**Armstrong** · *Armstrong-Spallumcheen C/C* · Patti Noonan, Mgr., P.O. Box 118, V0E 1B0, P 9,600, M 201, (250) 546-8155, Fax (250) 546-8868, armstrong_chamber@telus.net, www.aschamber.com

**Bamfield** · *Bamfield C/C* · John Mass, Pres., P.O. Box 3500, V0R 1B0, P 365, M 40, (250) 728-3006, info@bamfieldchamber.com, www.bamfieldchamber.com

**Barriere** · *Barriere & Dist. C/C* · Lorne Richardson, Mgr., P.O. Box 1190, V0E 1E0, P 3,500, M 55, (250) 672-9221, info@barrieredistrict.com, www.barrieredistrict.com

**Bowen Island** · *Bowen Island C/C* · Tim Rhodes, Pres., P.O. Box 199, V0N 1G0, P 3,500, M 125, (604) 947-9024, Fax (604) 947-0633, info@bowenisland.org, www.bowenisland.org

**Burnaby** · *Burnaby Bd. Of Trade* · Darlene Gering, Pres./CEO, 4555 Kingsway, Unit 201, V5H 4T8, P 150,000, M 850, (604) 412-0100, Fax (604) 412-0102, admin@burnabyboardoftrade.com, www.burnabyboardoftrade.com

**Burns Lake** · *Burns Lake & Dist. C/C* · Kelly Friesen, Mgr., P.O. Box 339, V0J 1E0, P 13,000, M 100, (250) 692-3773, Fax (250) 692-3493, bldcoc@telus.net, www.bldchamber.ca

**Cache Creek** · *Cache Creek C/C* · Ben Roy, Secy., P.O. Box 460, V0K 1H0, P 1,100, M 30, (250) 457-7661, (250) 457-9566

**Campbell River** · *Campbell River & Dist. C/C* · Colleen Evans, Exec. Dir., P.O. Box 400, V9W 5B6, P 30,000, M 500, (250) 287-4636, Fax (250) 286-6490, chamber@campbellriverchamber.ca, www.campbellriverchamber.ca

**Castlegar** · *Castlegar & Dist. C/C* · Pam McLeod, Exec. Dir., 1995 6th Ave., V1N 4B7, P 18,000, M 250, (250) 365-6313, (877) 365-6313, Fax (250) 365-5778, audrey.chamber@shawbiz.ca, www.castlegar.com

**Celista** · *North Shuswap C/C* · Jeff Tarry, Pres., P.O. Box 101, V0E 1L0, P 3,800, M 100, (250) 955-2113, Fax (250) 955-2113, requests@northshuswapbc.com, www.northshuswapbc.com

**Chase** · *Chase & Dist. C/C* · James Gjaltema, Ofc. Mgr., P.O. Box 592, V0E 1M0, P 15,000, M 100, (250) 679-8432, Fax (250) 679-3120, admin@chasechamber.com, www.chasechamber.com

**Chemainus** · *Chemainus & Dist. C/C & Visitor Center* · Ingrid Rennblad, Mgr., P.O. Box 575, V0R 1K0, P 4,500, M 125, (250) 246-3944, Fax (250) 246-3251, ccoc@islandnet.com, www.chemainus.bc.ca

**Chetwynd** · *Chetwynd & Dist. C/C* · Helene Weightman, Mgr., P.O. Box 870, V0C 1J0, P 7,000, M 90, (250) 788-3345, Fax (250) 788-3655, manager@chetwyndchamber.ca, www.pris.bc.ca

**Chilliwack** · *Chilliwack C/C* · Sue Attrill, CEO, 45966 Yale Rd., Unit 16, V2P 2M3, P 80,000, M 515, (604) 793-4323, Fax (604) 793-4303, sue@chilliwackchamber.com, www.chilliwackchamber.com

**Christina Lake** · *Christina Lake C/C* · Sheldon Weigel, Pres., Hwy. 3 & Kimura Rd., V0H 1E2, P 1,500, M 54, (250) 447-6161, Fax same, chamber@christinalake.com, www.christinalake.com

**Clearwater** · *Clearwater & Dist. C/C* · Bill Cairns, Mgr., Box 1988, V0E 1N0, P 5,000, M 100, (250) 674-2646, Fax (250) 674-3693, info@clearwaterbcchamber.com, www.clearwaterbc-chamber.com

**Cloverdale** · *Cloverdale Dist. C/C* · Bill Reid, Interim Exec. Dir., 17685 56A Ave., Unit 201, V3S 1G4, P 40,000, M 300, (604) 574-9802, Fax (604) 574-9122, clovcham@axion.net, www.cloverdale.bc.ca

**Coquitlam** · *Tri-Cities C/C* · Suzette McFaul, CEO, 1209 Pinetree Way, V3B 7Y3, P 200,000, M 830, (604) 464-2716, Fax (604) 464-6796, info@tricitieschamber.com, www.tricitieschamber.com

**Courtenay** · *Comox Valley C/C & Visitor Center* · Dianne Hawkins, Exec. Dir., 2040 Cliffe Ave., V9N 2L3, P 65,000, M 675, (250) 334-3234, (888) 357-4471, Fax (250) 334-4908, admin@comoxvalleychamber.com, www.comoxvalleychamber.com

**Cranbrook** · *Cranbrook C/C* · Karin Penner, Mgr., P.O. Box 84, V1C 4H6, P 22,000, M 450, (250) 426-5914, (800) 222-6174, Fax (250) 426-3873, cbkchamber@cyberlink.bc.ca, www.cranbrookchamber.com

**Crawford Bay** · *Kootenay Lake C/C* · Andre Laporte, Exec. Dir., P.O. Box 120, V0B 1E0, P 1,600, M 60, (250) 227-9315, info@kootenaylake.bc.ca, www.kootenaylake.bc.ca

**Creston** · *Creston C/C* · Mimika Coleman, Mgr., P.O. Box 268, V0B 1G0, P 15,000, M 200, (250) 428-4342, Fax (250) 428-9411, crestonchamber@kootenay.com, www.crestonchamber.com

**Cumberland** · *Cumberland C/C & Visitors Center* · Mary Kornelsen, Mgr., P.O. Box 250, V0R 1S0, P 3,000, M 70, (250) 336-8313, Fax (250) 336-2455, cumbcham@shaw.ca, www.cumberlandbc.org

**Dawson Creek** · *Dawson Creek & Dist. C/C* · Stefanie Oestreich, Mgr., 10201 10th St., V1G 3T5, P 12,500, M 300, (250) 782-4868, Fax (250) 782-2371, info@dawsoncreekchamber.ca, www.dawsoncreekchamber.ca

**Delta** · *Delta C/C* · Peter Roaf, Exec. Dir., 6201 60th Ave., V4K 4E2, P 100,000, M 400, (604) 946-4232, Fax (604) 946-5285, ed@deltachamber.com, www.deltachamber.com

**Duncan** · *Duncan-Cowichan C/C* · Cathy Mailhot, Mgr., 381 Trans-Canada Hwy., V9L 3R5, P 80,000, M 340, (250) 748-1111, Fax (250) 746-8222, chamber@duncancc.bc.ca, www.duncancc.bc.ca

**Elkford** · *Elkford C/C* · Melody Anderson, Mgr., P.O. Box 220, V0B 1H0, P 2,800, M 70, (250) 865-4614, (877) 355-9453, Fax (250) 865-2442, info@tourismelkford.ca, www.tourismelkford.ca

**Enderby** · *Enderby & Dist. C/C* · Tate Bengtson, Exec. Dir., P.O. Box 1000, V0E 1V0, P 7,000, M 125, (250) 838-6727, Fax (250) 838-0123, enderbychamber@sunwave.net, www.enderbychamber.com

**Esquimalt** · *Esquimalt C/C* · Sandy Rozon, 1153 Esquimalt Rd., P.O. Box 36019, V9A 7J5, P 16,151, (250) 704-2525, Fax (250) 380-6932, info@esquimaltchamber.com, www.esquimaltchamber.com

**Falkland** · *Falkland & Dist. C/C* · Margaret Dalamore, Mgr., P.O. Box 92, V0E 1W0, P 800, M 10, falklandchamber@yahoo.ca, www.falklandbc.ca

**Fernie** · *Fernie C/C* · Lynn Flokstra, Mgr., 102 Commerce Rd., V0B 1M5, P 4,900, M 310, (250) 423-6868, Fax (250) 423-3811, office@ferniechamber.com, www.ferniechamber.com

**Fort Langley** · *see Langley*

**Fort Nelson** · *Fort Nelson & District C/C* · Val Lefebvre, Exec. Dir., P.O. Box 196, V0C 1R0, P 5,000, M 200, (250) 774-2956, Fax (250) 774-2958, info@fortnelsonchamber.com, www.fortnelsonchamber.com

**Fort St. James** · *Fort St. James C/C* · Mindy Thompson, Mgr., P.O. Box 1164, V0J 1P0, P 5,000, M 110, (250) 996-7023, Fax (250) 996-7047, fsjameschamb@fsjames.com, www.fortstjameschamber.com

**Fort St. John** · *Fort St. John & Dist. C/C* · Annette Oake, Mgr., 9325 100 St., Unit 202, V1J 4N4, P 18,000, M 400, (250) 785-6037, Fax (250) 785-6050, fsjchamber@awink.com, www.fsjchamber.com

**Gabriola Island** · *Gabriola C/C* · Carol Ramsay, Mgr., P.O. Box 249, V0R 1X0, P 4,500, M 83, (250) 247-9332, Fax (250) 247-9332, giccmanager@shaw.ca, www.gabriolaisland.org

**Galiano Island** · *Galiano Island C/C* · Carolyn Jerome, Pres., P.O. Box 73, V0N 1P0, (250) 539-2233, info@galianoisland.com, www.galianoisland.com

**Gibsons** · *Gibsons & Dist. C/C* · Lisa Houle, Exec. Dir., P.O. Box 1190, V0N 1V0, P 25,000, M 240, (604) 886-2325, Fax (604) 886-2379, gibsonsbcchamber@telus.net, www.gibsonsbc.ca/chamber

**Golden** · *Kicking Horse Country C/C* · Ruth Kowalski, Exec. Dir., P.O. Box 1320, V0A 1H0, P 8,800, M 221, (250) 344-7125, Fax (250) 344-6688, info@goldenchamber.bc.ca, www.goldenchamber.bc.ca

**Grand Forks** · *Chamber of Commerce of City of Grand Forks* · Cher Wyers, Mgr., P.O. Box 1086, V0H 1H0, P 4,235, M 145, (250) 442-2833, (866) 442-2833, Fax (250) 442-5688, gfchamber@sunshinecable.com, www.grandforkschamber.com

**Greenwood** · *Greenwood Bd. Of Trade* · Al Warren, Pres., P.O. Box 430, V0H 1J0, P 900, M 30, (250) 445-6323, Fax (250) 445-6166, gbtic@direect.ca, www.greenwoodcity.com

**Harrison Hot Springs** · *Harrison Agassiz C/C* · Robert Reyerse, Pres., P.O. Box 429, V0M 1K0, P 7,500, M 70, (604) 796-3664, Fax (604) 796-3694, infoserve@harrison.ca, www.harrison.ca

**Hope** · *Hope & Dist. C/C* · Karen Scalise, Ofc. Mgr., P.O. Box 588, V0X 1L0, P 10,000, M 100, (604) 869-3111, Fax (604) 869-8208, info@hopechamber.bc.ca, www.hopechamber.bc.ca

**Houston** · *Houston & Dist. C/C* · Maureen Czirfusz, Mgr., P.O. Box 396, V0J 1Z0, P 3,500, M 93, (250) 845-7640, Fax (250) 845-3682, hchamber@telus.net, www.houstonchamber.ca

**Inveremere** · *Columbia Valley C/C* · Al Miller, Pres., P.O. Box 1019, V0A 1K0, P 10,000, M 275, (250) 342-2844, Fax (250) 342-3261, info@cvchamber.ca, www.cvchamber.ca

**Kamloops** · *Kamloops C/C* · Deb McClelland, Exec. Dir., 1290 W. Trans-Canada Hwy., V2C 6R3, P 84,000, M 750, (250) 372-7722, (800) 662-1994, Fax (250) 828-9500, mail@kamloopschamber.bc.ca, www.kamloopschamber.bc.ca

**Kaslo** · *Kaslo & Dist. C/C* · P.O. Box 329, V0G 1M0, P 1,036, M 55, (250) 353-7323, info@kaslochamber.com, www.kaslochamber.com

**Kelowna** · *Kelowna C/C* · Weldon LeBlanc, CEO, 544 Harvey Ave., V1Y 6C9, P 100,400, M 1,670, (250) 861-3627, Fax (250) 861-3624, info@kelownachamber.org, www.kelownachamber.org

**Keremeos** · *Similkameen Country C/C* · Gary Yuzik, Pres., 427 7th Ave., P.O. Box 490, V0X 1N0, P 5,000, M 126, (250) 499-5225, Fax (250) 499-5225, siminfo@nethop.net, www.similkameen country.org

**Kimberley** · *Kimberley & Dist. C/C & Visitors Center* · Sioban Staplin, Exec. Dir., 270 Kimberley Ave., V1A 3N3, P 7,000, M 200, (250) 427-3666, (866) 913-3666, Fax (250) 427-5378, info@ kimberleychamber.ca, www.kimberleychamber.com

**Kitimat** · *Kitimat C/C* · Lorie Johnson, Mgr., P.O. Box 214, V8C 2G7, P 10,500, M 190, (250) 632-6294, (800) 664-6554, Fax (250) 632-4685, kitimatchamber@telus.net, www.visitkitimat.com

**Ladysmith** · *Ladysmith C/C & Visitor Info. Center* · Brian Bancroft, Pres., 132C Roberts St., P.O. Box 598, V9G 1A4, P 7,200, M 210, (250) 245-2112, Fax (250) 245-2124, info@ladysmithcofc. com, www.ladysmithcofc.com

**Lake Country** · *Lake Country C/C & Visitors Center* · Linda Wilson, Mgr., 9522 Main St., Unit 40, V4V 2L9, P 10,000, M 211, (250) 766-5670, (888) 766-5670, Fax (250) 766-0170, admin@ lakecountrychamber.com, www.lakecountrychamber.com

**Lake Cowichan** · *Cowichan Lake Dist. C/C* · Katherine Worsley, Coord., P.O. Box 824, V0R 2G0, P 6,953, M 107, (250) 749-3244, Fax (250) 749-0187, lcchamber@shaw.ca, www.cowichanlake.ca

**Langley** · *Greater Langley C/C* · Lynn Whitehouse, Exec. Dir., 5761 Glover Rd., Unit 1, V3A 8M8, P 125,000, M 1,100, (604) 530-6656, Fax (604) 530-7066, info@langleychamber.com, www. langleychamber.com

**Likely** · *Likely & Dist. C/C* · P.O. Box 29, V0L 1N0, P 350, M 45, (250) 790-2458, chamber@likely-bc.ca, www.likely-bc.ca

**Lillooet** · *Lillooet & Dist. C/C* · Bruce Jaffary, Pres., P.O. Box 650, V0K 1V0, P 2,800, M 50, (250) 256-4364, Fax (250) 256-4314, deverell@telus.net, www.lillooetchamberofcommerce.com

**Lumby** · *Lumby & Dist. C/C* · Stephanie Sexsmith, Mgr., P.O. Box 534, V0E 2G0, P 5,800, M 100, (250) 547-2300, Fax (250) 547-2390, lumbychamber@shaw.ca, www.monasheetourism.com

**Lytton** · *Lytton & Dist. C/C* · Peggy Chute, Exec. Dir., P.O. Box 460, V0K 1Z0, P 3,000, M 70, (250) 455-2523, Fax (250) 455-6669, lyttoncofc@telus.net, www.lytton.ca

**Mackenzie** · *Mackenzie C/C* · Kelly McEachnie, Mgr., P.O. Box 880, V0J 2C0, P 5,300, M 75, (250) 997-5459, Fax (250) 997-6117, mackcoc@mackbc.com, www.mackenziechamber.ca

**Madeira Park** · *Pender Harbour & Egmont C/C* · Kerry Milligan, Mgr., P.O. Box 265, V0N 2H0, P 2,500, M 125, (604) 883-2561, (877) 873-6337, Fax (604) 883-2561, chamber@penderharbour.ca, www.penderharbour.ca

**Maple Ridge** · *Maple Ridge-Pitt Meadows C/C* · Dean Barbour, Exec. Dir., 22238 Lougheed Hwy., V2X 2T2, P 90,000, M 600, (604) 463-3366, Fax (604) 463-3201, admin@ridgemeadowschamber. com, www.ridgemeadowschamber.com

**Mayne Island** · *Mayne Island Comm. C/C* · Peter Sara, Chrmn., P.O. Box 2, V0N 2J0, P 900, M 50, (250) 539-5034, info@mayne islandchamber.ca, www.mayneislandchamber.ca

**McBride** · *McBride & Dist. C/C* · Danielle Alan, Exec. Dir., P.O. Box 2, V0J 2E0, P 2,500, M 65, (250) 569-3366, come2mcbride@ telus.net, www.mcbridebc.info

**Mill Bay** · *South Cowichan C/C* · Rosalie Power, Mgr., 2720 Mill Bay Rd., Unit 368, V0R 2P1, P 15,000, M 155, (250) 743-3566, Fax (250) 743-5332, southcowichanchamber@shaw.ca, www. southcowichanchamber.org

**Mission** · *Mission Reg. C/C* · Sue Jackson, Mgr., 34033 Lougheed Hwy., V2V 5X8, P 37,500, M 390, (604) 826-6914, (877) 826-6914, Fax (604) 826-5916, manager@missionchamber.bc.ca, www. missionchamber.bc.ca

**Nakusp** · *Nakusp & Dist. C/C & Visitor Center* · Marilyn Rivers, Mgr., P.O. Box 387, V0G 1R0, P 1,700, M 150, (250) 265-4234, Fax (250) 265-3808, chamber@nakusparrowlakes.com, www. nakusparrowlakes.com

**Nanaimo** · *Greater Nanaimo C/C* · S.D. (Lee) Mason, Exec. Dir., 2133 Bowen Rd., V9S 1H8, P 130,000, M 875, (250) 756-1191, Fax (250) 756-1584, info@nanaimochamber.bc.ca, www.nanaimo chamber.bc.ca

**Nelson** · *Nelson & Dist. C/C & Visitors Center* · Tom Thomson, Exeec. Dir., 225 Hall St., V1L 5X4, P 9,700, M 480, (250) 352-3433, (877) 663-5706, Fax (250) 352-6355, info@discovernelson.com, www.discovernelson.com

**New Denver** · *Slocan Dist. C/C* · Jeff Bustard, Pres., P.O. Box 448, V0G 1S0, P 2,000, M 50, (250) 358-2228, (250) 358-2719, chamber@slocanlake.com, www.slocanlake.com

**New Westminster** · *New Westminster C/C* · David Brennan, Exec. Dir., 601 Queens Ave., V3M 1L1, P 58,000, M 340, (604) 521-7781, Fax (604) 521-0057, nwcc@newwestchamber.com, www. newwestchamber.com

**North Vancouver** · *North Vancouver C/C* · Naomi Yamamoto, Pres., 102-124 W. 1st St., V7M 3N3, P 130,000, M 900, (604) 987-4488, Fax (604) 987-8272, info@nvchamber.ca, www.nvchamber.ca

**Okanagan Falls** · *see Oliver*

**Oliver** · *South Okanagan C/C* · Bonnie Dancey, CEO, P.O. Box 460, V0H 1T0, P 15,000, M 390, (250) 498-6321, (866) 498-6321, Fax (250) 498-3156, info@oliverchamber.bc.ca, www.oliverchamber.bc.ca

**Osoyoos** · *see Oliver*

**Parksville** · *Parksville & Dist. C/C* · Mike Bourcier, Exec. Dir., P.O. Box 99, V9P 2G3, P 39,000, M 457, (250) 248-3613, Fax (250) 248-5210, info@chamber.parksville.bc.ca, www.chamber. parksville.bc.ca

**Peachland** · *Peachland C/C* · Darlene Hartford, Mgr., 5812 Beach Ave., V0H 1X7, P 4,880, M 100, (250) 767-2455, Fax (250) 767-2420, peachlandchamber@shawcable.com, www.peachland chamber.bc.ca

**Pemberton** · *Pemberton & Dist. C/C* · Shirley Henry, Mgr., P.O. Box 370, V0N 2L0, P 7,000, M 172, (604) 894-6477, Fax (604) 894-5571, info@pembertonchamber.com, www.pembertonchamber.com

**Pender Island** · *Pender Island C/C* · P.O. Box 123, V0N 2M0, P 2,500, M 100, (250) 629-3988, travel@penderislandchamber. com, www.penderislandchamber.com

**Penticton** · *Penticton & Wine Country C/C* · Lorraine Renyard, Mgr., 553 Railway St., V2A 8S3, P 35,000, M 700, (250) 492-4103, Fax (250) 492-6119, chamber@penticton.org, www.penticton.org

**Pitt Meadows** · *see Maple Ridge*

**Port Alberni** · *Alberni Valley C/C* · Mike Carter, Exec. Dir., 2533 Port Alberni Hwy., V9Y 8P2, P 20,000, M 300, (250) 724-6535, Fax (250) 724-6560, avcoc@alberni.net, www.avcoc.com

**Port Hardy** · *Port Hardy & Dist. C/C* · Yana Hrdy, Mgr., P.O. Box 249, V0N 2P0, P 4,500, M 200, (250) 949-6500, Fax (250) 949-6653, phcc@cablerocket.com, www.ph-chamber.bc.ca

**Port McNeill** · *Port McNeill & Dist. C/C* · Cheryl Jorgenson, Mgr., P.O. Box 129, V0N 2R0, P 3,100, M 100, (250) 956-3131, Fax (250) 956-3132, pmccc@island.net, www.portmcneill.net

**Port Renfrew** · *Port Renfrew C/C* · Tim Cash, Exec. Dir., General Delivery, V0S 1K0, P 300, M 40, (250) 647-0160, Fax (250) 647-0160, lynne@bobfassl.com, www.portrenfrewcommunity.com

**Powell River** · *Powell River C/C* · Kim Miller, Mgr., 6807 Wharf St., V8A 1T9, P 23,000, M 250, (604) 485-6080, office@powellriverchamber.com, www.powellriverchamber.com

**Prince George** · *Prince George C/C* · Sherry Sethen, Exec. Dir., 890 Vancouver St., V2L 3P5, P 81,000, M 920, (250) 562-2454, Fax (250) 562-6510, chamber@pgchamber.bc.ca, www.pgchamber.bc.ca

**Prince Rupert** · *Prince Rupert & Dist. C/C* · Lynne Graham, Exec. Dir., 215 Cow Bay Rd., Unit 100, V8J 1A2, P 13,500, M 245, (250) 624-2296, Fax (250) 624-6105, manager@princerupertchamber.ca, www.princerupertchamber.ca

**Princeton** · *Princeton & Dist. C/C & Visitors Center* · Lori Thomas, Mgr., P.O. Box 540, V0X 1W0, P 5,000, M 100, (250) 295-3103, Fax (250) 295-3255, chamber@nethop.net, www.princeton.ca

**Qualicum Beach** · *Qualicum Beach C/C* · Judi Ainsworth, Gen. Mgr., 124 W. 2nd Ave., P.O. Box 59, V9K 1S7, P 8,502, M 275, (250) 752-0960, Fax (250) 752-2923, chamber@qualicum.bc.ca, www.qualicum.bc.ca

**Quathiaski Cove** · *Discovery Islands C/C* · Lynden McMartin, Pres., P.O. Box 190, V0P 1N0, P 3,800, M 93, (866) 285-2724, chamber@discoveryislands.ca, www.discoveryislands.ca/chamber

**Quesnel** · *Quesnel & Dist. C/C* · Coralee Oakes, Mgr., 679-B Hwy. 97 S., V2J 4C7, P 25,000, M 220, (250) 747-0125, Fax (250) 747-0126, qchamber@quesnelbc.com, www.quesnelchamber.com

**Radium** · *Radium Hot Springs C/C* · Kent Kebe, Mgr., 7556 Main St. E., P.O. Box 225, V0A 1M0, P 800, M 120, (250) 347-9331, Fax (250) 347-9127, info@radiumhotsprings.com, www.radiumhotsprings.com

**Revelstoke** · *Revelstoke C/C* · John Dewitt, Exec. Dir., P.O. Box 490, V0E 2S0, P 8,800, M 254, (250) 837-5345, Fax (250) 837-4223, revelstokechamber@telus.net, www.seerevelstoke.com

**Richmond** · *Richmond C/C* · Craig Jones, Exec. Dir., Ste. 101, South Tower, 5811 Cooney Rd., V6X 3M1, P 181,203, M 1,200, (604) 278-2822, Fax (604) 278-2972, cjones@richmondchamber.ca, www.richmondchamber.ca

**Rossland** · *Rossland C/C* · Maritza Reilly, Mgr., P.O. Box 1385, V0G 1Y0, P 3,800, M 188, (250) 362-5666, Fax (250) 362-5399, commerce@rossland.com, www.rossland.com

**Saanich Peninsula** · *see Sidney*

**Salmo** · *Salmo & Dist. C/C* · Heather Street, Mgr., P.O. Box 400, V0G 1Z0, P 3,300, M 30, (250) 357-2596, Fax same, salmoch@telus.net, www.salmo.net

**Salmon Arm** · *Salmon Arm & Dist. C/C* · Corryn Garyston, Gen. Mgr., 20 Hudson Ave. N.E., Unit 101, P.O. Box 999, V1E 4P2, P 17,000, M 395, (250) 832-6247, (877) 725-6667, Fax (250) 832-8382, admin@sachamber.bc.ca, www.sachamber.bc.ca

**Salt Spring Island** · *Salt Spring Island C/C* · Laura Moore, Exec. Dir., 121 Lower Ganges Rd., V8K 2T1, P 10,000, M 350, (250) 537-4223, Fax (250) 537-4276, chamber@ssisland.com, www.saltspringtourism.com

**Seton** · *Shalalth Dist. C/C* · Dennis DeYagher, Pres., P.O. Box 2067, V0N 3B0, P 800, M 20, (250) 259-8268, snor@uniserve.com

**Sechelt** · *Sechelt & Dist. C/C* · Colleen Clark, Exec. Dir., P.O. Box 360, V0N 3A0, P 8,500, M 350, (604) 885-0662, (877) 633-2963, Fax (604) 885-0691, secheltchamber@dccnet.com, www.secheltchamber.bc.ca

**Sicamous** · *Sicamous & Dist. C/C* · Doreen Favel, Exec. Dir., P.O. Box 346, V0E 2V0, P 3,166, M 200, (250) 836-3313, Fax (250) 836-4368, sicamouschamber@cablelan.net, www.sicamouschamber.bc.ca

**Sidney** · *Saanich Peninsula C/C* · Eileen Leddy, Exec. Dir., 201-2453 Beacon Ave., P.O. Box 2014, V8L 3S3, P 45,000, M 400, (250) 656-3616, Fax (250) 656-7111, info@peninsulachamber.ca, www.peninsulachamber.ca.

**Smithers** · *Smithers Dist. C/C* · Heather Gallagher, Mgr., P.O. Box 2379, V0J 2N0, P 5,217, M 200, (250) 847-5072, (800) 542-6673, Fax (250) 847-3337, chamber@smitherschamber.com, www.smitherschamber.com

**Sooke** · *Sooke Harbour C/C* · John Zaremba, Mgr., 2070 Phillips Rd., P.O. Box 18, V9Z 0E4, P 11,000, M 176, (250) 642-6112, info@sookeharbourchamber.com, www.sookeharbourchamber.com

**Sorrento** · *South Shuswap C/C* · Nancy Kyle, Ofc. Mgr., P.O. Box 7, V0E 2W0, P 8,000, M 100, (250) 675-3515, Fax (250) 675-3516, sorrentochamber@telus.net, www.southshuswapchamberofcommerce.org

**Sparwood** · *Sparwood & Dist. C/C* · Paul Wortley, Mgr., P.O. Box 1448, V0B 2G0, P 4,211, M 110, (250) 425-2423, Fax (250) 425-7130, manager@sparwoodchamber.bc.ca, www.sparwoodchamber.bc.ca

**Squamish** · *Squamish C/C* · Victoria Rigdon, Mgr., 38551 Loggers Ln., Ste. 102, V8B 0H2, P 16,000, M 500, (604) 815-4991, Fax (604) 815-4998, kenny@squamishchamber.com, www.squamishchamber.ca

**Stewart** · *Stewart-Hyder Intl. C/C* · Gwen McKay, Mgr., P.O. Box 306, V0T 1W0, P 500, M 60, (250) 636-9224, (888) 366-5999, Fax (250) 636-2199, info@stewart-hyder.com, www.stewart-hyder.com

**Summerland** · *Summerland Chamber of Eco. Dev. & Tourism* · Sharon Lusch, Mgr., 15600 Hwy. 97, P.O. Box 130, V0H 1Z0, P 12,000, M 750, (250) 494-2686, Fax (250) 494-4039, sharon.lusch@shawbiz.ca, www.summerlandchamber.bc.ca

**Surrey** · *Surrey Bd. Of Trade* · Anita Huberman, CEO, 101-14439 104th Ave., V3R 1M1, P 460,000, M 1,300, (604) 581-7130, Fax (604) 588-7549, info@businessinsurrey.com, www.businessinsurrey.com

**Surrey** · *White Rock & South Surrey C/C* · Doug Hart, Exec. Dir., #101 2430 King George Hwy., V4P 1H5, P 90,000, M 800, (604) 536-6844, Fax (604) 536-4994, info@whiterockchamber.com, www.whiterockchamber.com

**Tahsis** · *Tahsis C/C* · Corinne Dahling, Pres., P.O. Box 278, V0P 1X0, P 600, M 20, (250) 934-6425, Fax (250) 934-6667, info@tahsischamberofcommerce.com, www.tahsischamberofcommerce.com

**Terrace** · *Terrace & Dist. C/C* · Stacy Mann, Exec. Dir., 4511 Keith Ave., V8G 1K1, P 18,000, M 350, (250) 635-2063, Fax (250) 635-2573, terracechamber@telus.net, www.terracechamber.com

**Tofino** · *Tofino-Long Beach C/C* · Michael Tilitzky, Mgr., P.O. Box 249, V0R 2Z0, P 1,600, M 250, (250) 725-2530, Fax (250) 725-3296, info@tourismtofino.com, www.tourismtofino.com

**Trail** · *Trail & Dist. C/C* · Naomi McKimmie, Exec. Dir., 200-1199 Bay Ave., V1R 4A4, P 19,000, M 240, (250) 368-3144, Fax (250) 368-6427, tcoc@netidea.com, www.trailchamber.bc.ca

**Ucluelet** · *Ucluelet C/C* · Marny Saunders, Gen. Mgr., P.O. Box 428, V0R 3A0, P 1,800, M 140, (250) 726-2766, Fax (250) 726-4611, marny@uc, www.ucmuchamber.ca

**Vananda** · *Texada Island C/C* · Elayne Boloten, Secy., P.O. Box 249, V0N 3K0, P 1,200, M 95, (604) 486-7457, Fax (604) 486-6703, www.texada.org

**Vancouver** • *Kitsilano C/C* • Terry Clark, Exec. Dir., 2628 Granville St., Unit 207, V6H 4B4, P 75,000, M 395, (604) 731-4454, (877) 312-1898, Fax (604) 681-4545, www.kitsilanochamber.com

**Vancouver** • *Tourism Vancouver-Tourist Info. Centre* • Rick Antonson, Pres./CEO, Plaza Level, 200 Burrard St., V6C 3L6, P 2,200,000, M 1,200, (604) 683-2000, Fax (604) 682-6839, info@tourismvancouver.com, www.tourismvancouver.com

**Vancouver** • *Vancouver Bd. Of Trade* • Darcy Rezac, Mgr. Dir., 400 - 999 Canada Pl., V6C 3E1, P 2,200,000, M 5,700, (604) 681-2111, Fax (604) 681-0437, contactus@boardoftrade.com, www.boardoftrade.com

**Vanderhoof** • *Vanderhoof & Dist. C/C* • Erin Siemens, Mgr., P.O. Box 126, V0J 3A0, P 4,500, M 170, (250) 567-2124, (800) 752-4094, Fax (250) 567-3316, info@hwy16.com, www.vanderhoof chamber.com

**Vernon** • *Greater Vernon C/C* • Val Trevis, Mgr., 701 Hwy. 97 S., V1B 3W4, P 50,000, M 710, (250) 545-0771, Fax (250) 545-3114, info@vernonchamber.ca, www.vernonchamber.ca

**Victoria** • *Greater Victoria C/C* • Bruce Carter, CEO, 100-852 Fort St., V8W 1H8, P 350,000, M 1,550, (250) 383-7191, Fax (250) 385-3552, chamber@gvcc.org, www.victoriachamber.ca.

**Victoria** • *WestShore C/C* • Chris Ricketts, Pres., 2830 Aldwynd Rd., V9B 3S7, P 50,000, M 400, (250) 478-1130, Fax (250) 478-1584, chamber@westshore.bc.ca, www.westshore.bc.ca

**Wells** • *Wells & Dist. C/C* • Wanda Johnstone, Mgr., P.O. Box 123, V0K 2R0, P 250, M 50, (250) 994-3223, Fax (250) 994-3331, vic@wellsbc.com, www.wellsbc.com

**West Vancouver** • *West Vancouver C/C* • Leagh Gabriel, Exec. Dir., 1846 Marine Dr., V7V 1J6, P 43,000, M 300, (604) 926-6614, Fax (604) 925-7220, admin@westvanchamber.com, www.westvanchamber.com

**Westbank** • *Westbank & Dist. C/C* • Leah Thordarson, Mgr., 2375 Pamela Rd., Unit 4, V4T 2H9, P 40,000, M 450, (250) 768-3378, (866) 768-3378, Fax (250) 768-3465, chamber@westbankcham ber.com, www.westbankchamber.com

**Whistler** • *Whistler C/C* • Fiona Famulak, Mgr., 4230 Gateway Dr., Unit 201, V0N 1B4, P 10,000, M 830, (604) 932-5922, Fax (604) 932-3755, chamber@whistlerchamber.com, www.whistlerchamber.com

**Williams Lake** • *Williams Lake & Dist. C/C* • Claudia Blair, Exec. Dir., P.O. Box 4878, V2G 2V8, P 12,000, M 300, (250) 392-5025, Fax (250) 392-4214, visitors@telus.net, www.williamslakechamber.com

# Manitoba

**Manitoba C/C** • Graham S. Starmer, Pres., 227 Portage Ave., Winnipeg, R3B 2A6, P 1,200,000, M 10,000, (204) 948-0100, Fax (204) 948-0110, mbchamber@mbchamber.mb.ca, www.mbchamber.mb.ca

**Altona** • *Altona & Dist. C/C* • Vic Loewen, Pres., P.O. Box 329, R0G 0B0, P 3,900, M 150, (204) 324-8793, Fax (204) 324-1314, chamber@shopaltona.com, www.shopaltona.com

**Arborg** • *Arborg & Dist. C/C* • Mr. Lorne Floyd, Pres., P.O. Box 415, R0C 0A0, P 6,000, M 50, (204) 376-2878, lnlfloyd@mts.net

**Ashern** • *Ashern & Dist. C/C* • Glenn Nordenbos, Pres., Box 582, R0C 0E0, P 1,350, M 80, (204) 768-2346, Fax (204) 768-2088, info@ashern.ca, www.ashern.ca

**Beausejour** • *Beausejour & Dist. C/C* • Doug Germaine, Pres., Box 224, R0E 0C0, P 8,000, M 85, (204) 268-3502, Fax (204) 268-3502, chamber@mybeausejour.com, www.mybeausejour.com/cham

**Birtle** • *Birtle & Dist. C/C* • Pres., P.O. Box 278, R0M 0C0, P 750, M 30, (204) 842-3460, www.town.birtle.mb.ca

**Boissevain** • *Boissevain & Dist. C/C* • Donna Fraser, Pres., P.O. Box 547, R0K 0E0, P 2,000, M 50, (204) 534-6040, Fax (204) 534-6042, rhonda.coupland@gov.mb.ca, www.boissevain.ca

**Brandon** • *Brandon C/C* • Nathan Peto, Gen. Mgr., 1043 Rosser Ave., R7A 0L5, P 43,000, M 951, (204) 571-5340, Fax (204) 571-5347, info@brandonchamber.ca, www.brandonchamber.ca

**Carberry** • *Carberry & Dist. C/C* • Betty Buurma, Pres., Box 101, R0K 0H0, P 3,000, M 50, (204) 834-2700, Fax (204) 834-2842, carberrysigns@mts.net, www.townofcarberry.ca

**Carman** • *Carman & Comm. C/C* • Heidi Sandulak, Pres., Box 249, R0G 0J0, P 2,880, M 124, (204) 750-3050, ccchamber@gmail.com, www.townofcarman.com

**Churchill** • *Churchill C/C* • Rose Preteau, Pres., Box 176, R0B 0E0, P 900, M 50, (204) 675-2022, Fax (204) 675-2021, churchillchamber@mts.net, www.churchill.ca

**Crystal City** • *Crystal City & Dist. C/C* • Doug Treble, Box 56, R0K 0N0, P 750, M 36, (204) 873-2427, Fax (204) 873-2656, chamberofcommerce@crystalcitymb.ca, www.crystalcitymb.ca

**Cypress River** • *Cypress River C/C* • Jim Cassels, Pres., P.O. Box 261, R0K 0P0, P 200, M 22, (204) 743-2119, Fax (204) 743-2339, www.cypressriver.ca

**Dauphin** • *Dauphin & District C/C* • Lisa Fee, Coord., 100 Main St. S., R7N 1K3, P 10,000, M 187, (204) 622-3140, Fax (204) 622-3141, lisa@dauphinchamber.ca, www.dauphinchamber.ca

**Deloraine** • *Deloraine & Dist. C/C* • Ms. Sigrid DeKezel, Pres., P.O. Box 748, R0M 0M0, P 1,500, M 50, (204) 747-2940, Fax (204) 747-2940, www.deloraine.org

**Elkhorn** • *Elkhorn C/C* • Sharlean Bickerton, Pres., Box 141, R0M 0N0, P 490, M 20, (204) 845-2073, (204) 845-2388, alearis@mts.net, www.elkhorn.mb.ca

**Eriksdale** • *Eriksdale & Dist. C/C* • Randy Mason, Pres., P.O. Box 434, R0C 0W0, P 900, M 55, (204) 739-2078, (204) 739-2140, rufus1@highspeedcrow.ca, www.eriksdale.com

**Falcon Beach** • *Falcon West Hawk C/C* • Theresa Young, Pres., Box 187, R0E 0N0, P 400, M 54, (204) 349-2294, info@chamber-southwhiteshell.ca, www.chamber-southwhiteshell.ca

**Fisher Branch** • *Fisher Branch C/C* • John Plett, Pres., Box 566, R0C 0Z0, P 500, M 36, (204) 372-6253, Fax (204) 372-8545, testocki@mts.net

**Flin Flon** • *Flin Flon & Dist. C/C* • Idelette Badenhorst, Secy./Mgr., 235-35 Main St., R8A 1J7, P 9,000, M 100, (204) 687-4518, Fax (204) 687-4456, flinflonchamber@mts.net, www.cityofflinflon.com/chamber

**Gilam** • *Gilam C/C* • John Cullen, Pres., P.O. Box 366, R0B 0L0, P , M , (204) 652-5135, Fax (204) 652-5155, jcullen@hydro.mb.ca

**Glenboro** • *Glenboro Comm. Dev. Corp.* • Christine Tanasichuk, Dev. Officer, Box 296, R0K 0X0, P 1,500, M 200, (204) 827-2575, Fax (204) 827-2575, gcdc@glenboro.com, www.glenboro.com

**Grandview** • *Grandview & Dist. C/C* • Brad Kempf, P.O. Box 28, R0L 0Y0, P 1,000, M 35, (204) 546-5250, grandviewchamberofcommerce@hotmail.com, www.grandviewmanitoba.net

**Grunthal** • *Grunthal & Dist. C/C* • Leonard Hiebert, Pres., P.O. Box 678, R0A 0R0, P 3,000, M 50, (204) 434-6750, Fax (204) 434-9353, jwk6@mts.net

**Hamiota** • *Hamiota C/C* • Wayne Mathison, Pres., P.O. Box 403, R0M 0T0, P 1,000, M 45, (204) 764-2487, (204) 764-3050, Fax (204) 764-3055, midwestrec@hamiota.com, www.hamiota.com

**Hartney** • *Hartney & Dist. C/C* • Carol Thomas, Pres., P.O. Box 224, R0M 0X0, P 450, M 40, (204) 858-2089, Fax (204) 858-2089, slwevans@mts.net

**Headingley** • *Headingley Reg. C/C* • Jill Ruth, Pres., 5353 Portage Ave., R4H 1J9, P , M , (204) 889-3132, Fax (204) 831-0816, dwhitermofheadingley@mts.net, www.rmofheadingley.ca

**Killarney** • *Killarney & Dist. C/C* • Ms. Lee Bartley, Pres., Box 809, R0K 1G0, P 3,500, M 100, (204) 523-4202, Fax (204) 523-4202, killarney chamberofcommerce@hotmail.com, www.killarneymanitoba.com

**La Salle** • *La Salle & Dist. C/C* • Donna Bell, Pres., P.O. Box 608, R0G 1B0, P 3,000, M 39, (204) 736-4555

**Lac Du Bonnet** • *Lac Du Bonnet & Dist. C/C* • Donna Tschetter, Pres., P.O. Box 598, R0E 1A0, P 3,350, M 125, (204) 345-8194, kimbuhay@mts.net, www.lacdubonnetchamber.com

**Landmark** • *Landmark & Area C/C* • Brian Ryall, Pres., P.O. Box 469, R0A 0X0, P , M , (204) 355-4035, Fax (204) 355-4800, office@landmarkonline.ca

**Macgregor** • *MacGregor & Dist. C/C* • Keith McFall, Pres., P.O. Box 685, R0H 0R0, P 3,024, M 45, (204) 685-2945, (204) 685-2033, edbraak@mts.net, www.macgregorchamber.com

**Melita** • *Melita & Dist. C/C* • Murray Cameron, Pres., P.O. Box 666, R0M 1L0, P 1,200, M 71, (204) 522-3285, Fax (204) 522-3536, gvanbese@mts.net, www.melitamb.ca

**Minnedosa** • *Minnedosa & Dist. C/C* • Don Farr, Pres., Box 857, R0J 1E0, P 5,000, M 103, (204) 867-2951, Fax (204) 867-3641, chamber@minnedosa.com, www.minnedosa.com/chamber

**Morden** • *Morden & Dist. C/C* • Cheryl Link, Mgr., 311 N. Railway St., R6M 1S9, P 7,000, M 235, (204) 822-5630, Fax (204) 822-2041, chamber@mordenmb.com, www.mordenchamber.com

**Morris** • *Morris & Dist. C/C* • Peggy Penner, Pres., P.O. Box 98, R0G 1K0, P 1,650, M 75, (204) 746-2223, Fax (204) 746-8963, fehrscle@mts.net, www.town.morris.mb.ca

**Neepawa** • *Neepawa & Dist. C/C* • Michelle Gerrard, Pres., Box 726, R0J 1H0, P 3,500, M 170, (204) 476-5292, Fax (204) 476-5231, neepawachamber@mts.net, www.neepawachamber.mb.ca

**Niverville** • *Niverville C/C* • Debbie Pearason, Pres., P.O. Box 157, R0A 1E0, P 2,600, M 80, (204) 388-4294, Fax (204) 388-6731, chamber@niverville.com, www.niverville.com

**Notre Dame** • *Notre Dame C/C* • Lise Deleurme, Pres., P.O. Box 107, R0G 1M0, P 619, M 60, (204) 248-2073, Fax (204) 248-2847, deleurme@mts.net, www.notre-dame-de-lourdes.ca

**Oak Lake** • *Oak Lake C/C* • Greg Vincent, Pres., P.O. Box 23, R0M 1P0, P , M , (204) 855-3287, Fax (204) 855-3287, gvincent@mts.net

**Oakville** • *Oakville & Dist. C/C* • Warren Bracken, Pres., P.O. Box 263, R0H 0Y0, P 600, M 50, (204) 267-2792, (204) 267-2112, Fax (204) 267-7015, bingram@mts.net

**Pilot Mound** • *Pilot Mound & Dist. C/C* • Carolanne Bayne, Pres., P.O. Box 356, R0G 1P0, P 1,000, M 50, (204) 825-2432, Fax (204) 825-2438, chamberofcommerce@pilotmound.com

**Pinawa** • *Pinawa C/C* • Marsha Sheppard, P.O. Box 544, R0E 1L0, P , M , (204) 753-2747, Fax (204) 753-8478, chamber@granite.mb.ca, www.pinawachamber.com

**Plum Coulee** • *Plum Coulee & Dist. C/C* • Moira Porte, Pres., Box 392, R0G 1R0, P 800, M 32, (204) 829-3615, Fax (204) 325-4132, brewstr@mts.net, www.plumcoulee.com

**Portage la Prairie** • *Portage la Prairie & Dist. C/C* • Michele Redmond, Exec. Dir., 11-2nd St. N.E., R1N 1R8, P 18,000, M 275, (204) 857-7778, Fax (204) 857-4095, info@portagechamber.com, www.portagechamber.com

**Rivers** • *Rivers & Dist. C/C* • Jean Young, Secy./Treas., P.O. Box 795, R0K 1X0, P 1,100, M 50, (204) 328-7316, Fax (204) 328-4460, mbeever@mts.net

**Riverton** • *Riverton & Dist. C/C* • Bernice Danielson, Pres., P.O. Box 238, R0C 2R0, P 560, M 60, (204) 378-2855, rivertoncoop@mts.net, www.rivertoncanada.com

**Roblin** • *Roblin & Dist. C/C* • Gerald Stuart, Pres., P.O. Box 160, R0L 1P0, P 1,800, M 85, (204) 937-3194, (204) 937-2176, Fax (204) 937-3817, rdcoc@mts.net, www.roblinmanitoba.com

**Rosenort** • *Rosenort & Dist. C/C* • Alvin Rempel, Pres., P.O. Box 222, R0G 1W0, P , M , (204) 746-4217, Fax (204) 746-8878, alvdia@mts.net, www.rosenortchamber.blogspot.com

**Rossburn** • *Rossburn & Dist. C/C* • Valerie White, Secy., P.O. Box 579, R0J 1V0, P 500, M 30, (204) 859-2409, (204) 859-3334, Fax (204) 859-2134, wheatland@mts.net, www.town.rossburn.mb.ca

**Russell** • *Russell & Dist. C/C* • Mark Keating, Pres., P.O. Box 579, R0J 1W0, P 2,000, M 100, (204) 773-2456, Fax (204) 773-3525, chamber@russellmb.com, www.russellmb.com

**Saint-Boniface** • *Saint-Boniface C/C* • Mr. Alain Laurencelle, Pres., boulevard Provencher, bureau 212, CP 204, R2H 3B4, P 100,000, M 150, (204) 235-1406, Fax (204) 233-1017, info@ccfsb.mb.ca, www.ccfsb.mb.ca

**Selkirk** • *Selkirk & Dist. C/C* • Beverley Clagg, Ofc. Mgr., 200 Eaton Ave., R1A 0W6, P 25,000, M 130, (204) 482-7176, Fax (204) 482-5448, sadcoc@mts.net, info@selkirkanddistrictchamber.ca, www.selkirkanddistrictchamber.ca

**Shoal Lake** • *Shoal Lake C/C Inc.* • Norm Sims, Pres., P.O. Box 547, R0J 1Z0, P 1,150, M 70, (204) 759-3343, Fax (204) 759-2740, cyrilp@mts.net, www.shoallake.ca

**Somerset** • *Somerset & Dist. C/C* • Audrey Bessette, Mgr., P.O. Box 64, R0G 2L0, P 650, M 55, (204) 744-2170, somcdc@mts.net

**Souris** • *Souris & Glenwood C/C* • Colleen Robbins, Pres., P.O. Box 795, R0K 2C0, P 1,653, M 85, (204) 483-2070

**Sprague** • *Piney & Dist. C/C* • Dennis Konchak, Pres., P.O. Box 50, R0A 1Z0, P , M , (204) 437-2259, Fax (204) 437-2561, dwk@wiband.ca

**Ste. Rose du Lac** • *Ste. Rose & Dist. C/C* • Trefor Gates, Pres., P.O. Box 688, R0L 1S0, P 1,050, M 50, (204) 447-2196, Fax (204) 447-2692, storestarter@yahoo.ca, www.town.sterosedulac.mb.ca

**Steinbach** • *Steinbach C/C* • Paul Neustuedter, Pres., P.O. Box 1795, R5G 1N4, P 11,066, M 264, (204) 326-9566, Fax (204) 346-3638, stbcofc@mts.net, www.steinbachchamberofcommerce.com

**Stonewall** • *Stonewall & Dist. C/C* • Deborah Jensen, Pres., Box 762, R0C 2Z0, P 5,000, M 76, (204) 467-8377, (204) 467-7125, info@stonewallchamber.com, www.stonewallchamber.com

**St-Pierre-Jolys** • *St. Pierre C/C* • Marcel Mulaire & Wilma Arnold, Co-Pres., Box 71, R0A 1V0, P 1,000, M 75, (204) 433-7123, Fax (204) 433-3015, marcel@delowater.ca, www.stpierrejolys.com

**Swan River** • *Swan River C/C* • Colleen Immerkar, Exec. Asst., P.O. Box 1540, R0L 1Z0, P 4,500, M 165, (204) 734-3102, Fax (204) 734-4342, srcc@svcn.mb.ca

**Teulon** • *Teulon & Dist. C/C* • Michael Ledarney, Pres., P.O. Box 139, R0C 1H0, P 5,000, M 40, (204) 886-3555, Fax (204) 886-3232, president@teulon.ca, www.teulon.ca

**The Pas** • *The Pas & Dist. C/C* • Alan Gibb, Pres., Box 996, R9A 1L1, P 12,800, M 170, (204) 623-7256, Fax (204) 623-2589, tpinfo@mts.net, www.thepaschamber.com

**Thompson** • *Thompson C/C* • Keith MacDonald, Pres., P.O. Box 363, R8N 1N2, P 15,000, M 185, (204) 677-4155, Fax (204) 677-3434, commerce@mts.net, www.thompsonchamber.mb.ca

**Treherne** • *Treherne & Dist. C/C* • Keith Sparling, Pres., P.O. Box 344, R0G 2V0, P , M , (204) 723-2774, Fax (204) 723-2665, ksparling@inethome.ca, www.treherne.ca

**Virden** • *Virden & Dist. C/C* • Geraldine Fowler, Ofc. Mgr., Box 899, R0M 2C0, P 3,500, M 110, (204) 748-3955, Fax (204) 748-3955, virdencc@mts.net, www.virden.ca

**Waskada** • *Waskada & Dist. C/C* • Margie Hannah, Pres., P.O. Box 239, R0M 2E0, P 150, M 15, (204) 673-2656, (204) 673-2522, Fax (204) 673-2535, waskada@shurgro.com, www.waskada.ca

**Winkler** • *Winkler C/C* • Brenda Storey, Exec. Dir., 185 Main St., R6W 1B4, P 9,000, M 280, (204) 325-9758, Fax (204) 325-8290, chamber@winkleronline.com, www.winklerchamber.com

**Winnipeg** • *Aboriginal C/C* • Wilf Lavallee, Pres., 203-350 Portage Ave., R3C 0C3, P , M , (204) 237-9359, Fax (204) 947-0145, info@aboriginalchamber.ca, www.aboriginalchamber.ca

**Winnipeg** • *Winnipeg C/C* • Dave Angus, Pres./CEO, 100 - 259 Portage Ave., R3B 2A9, P 700,000, M 1,800, (204) 944-8484, Fax (204) 944-8492, info@winnipeg-chamber.com, www.winnipeg-chamber.com

**Zhoda** • *Pansy & Dist. C/C* • Michael Narth, P.O. Box 87, R0A 2P0, P 750, M 12, (204) 425-3530, Fax (204) 425-3048

# New Brunswick

**New Brunswick C/C** • Peter Lindfield, Pres., 1 Canada Rd., Edmundston, E3V 1T6, (506) 737-1866, Fax (506) 737-1862, info@nb.aibn.com

**Baie Ste-Anne** • *Baie Ste-Anne C/C* • Seraphie Martin, 346 CH Riviere du Portage, E9A 1G8, P 2,000, (506) 228-4837

**Bathurst** • *Greater Bathurst C/C* • Donna Landry, Gen. Mgr., 725 College St., CEI Bldg., E2A 4B9, P 50,000, M 311, (506) 548-8498, Fax (506) 548-2200, bathcham@nbnet.nb.ca, www.bathurst chamber.ca

**Bouctouche** • *Bouctouche C/C* • 59 Erving Blvd., Ste. 301, E4S 3K6, P 3,000, M 95, (506) 743-2411, Fax (506) 743-8991, chambouc@nb.aibn.com, www.bouctouche.ca

**Campbellton** • *Campbellton Reg. C/C* • Greg Davis, Pres., 18 Water St., P.O. Box 234, E3N 3G4, P 7,000, M 215, (506) 759-7856, Fax (506) 759-7557, crcc@nbnet.nb.ca, www.campbellton regionalchamber.ca

**Caraquet** • *La Chambre de Commerce de Caraquet* • Reginald Boudreau, Pres., 220 boul. St-Pierre W., P.O. Box 5570, E1W 1B8, P 4,200, M 200, (506) 727-2931, Fax (506) 727-3191, chambre@nb.aira.com, www.chambregrandcaraquet.com

**Centreville** • *Centreville C/C* • Kathleen Simonson, Secy., 836 Central St., E7K 2E7, P 550, M 45, (506) 276-3674, www.village ofcentreville.ca

**Edmundston** • *Edmundston Reg. C/C* • Mrs. Amelie Jarret, Gen. Mgr., 1 Canada Rd., E3V 1T6, P 18,000, M 350, (506) 737-1866, Fax (506) 737-1862, info@ccedmundston.com, www.ccedmundston.com

**Florenceville** • *Florenceville C/C* • Robert McNutt, P.O. Box 601, E7L 1Y7, P 862, M 43, (506) 392-0900, (506) 392-5249, www.florencevillenb.ca

**Fredericton** • *Enterprise Fredericton* • Doug Motty, Exec. Dir., 570 Queen St., Ste. 102, E3B 6Z6, P 125,000, (506) 444-4686, Fax (506) 444-4649, www.enterprisefredericton.ca

**Fredericton** • *Fredericton C/C* • Anthony Knight, CEO, 270 Rookwood Ave., P.O. Box 275, E3B 4Y9, P 46,000, M 860, (506) 458-8006, Fax (506) 451-1119, fchamber@frederictonchamber.ca, www.frederictonchamber.ca

**Grand Bay - Westfield** • *River Valley C/C* • Cindy Price, Mgtg. Mgr., P.O. Box 3123, E5K 4V4, P 12,000, M 87, (506) 657-6369, Fax (506) 657-6361, www.rvchamberofcommerce.com

**Grand' Digue** • *Cocagne & Notre Dame C/C* • Mr. Gilles Allain, Pres., 27 Michel Rd., E4R 4V9, P 9,000, M 45, (506) 532-8956, Fax (506) 576-6073, gallain@mobility.blackberry.net

**Grand Falls** • *Grand Falls Dist. C/C* • Melanie Ouellette-Toner, Gen. Dir., 81 Burgess St., Ste. 300, E3Y 1C6, P 10,000, M 180, (506) 473-1905, Fax (506) 475-7755, gfcocgs@nbnet.nb.ca, www.grandfalls.com

**Grand Manan** • *Grand Manan C/C* • Joan Gallant, Secy./Treas., 101 Green St., E5G 3B7, P 2,800, M 100, (506) 662-3442, info@grandmanannb.com, www.grandmanannb.com

**Hampton** • *Hampton Area C/C* • Gail Kilpatrick, Secy., 27 Centennial Rd., Unit 6, E5N 6N3, P 5,000, M 82, (506) 832-2559, Fax (506) 832-2807, hacc@nbnet.nb.ca, www.hamptonareachamber.org

**Miramichi** • *Greater Miramichi C/C* • Veronique Arsenault, Exec. Dir., P.O. Box 342, E1N 3A7, P 18,000, M 200, (506) 622-5522, Fax (506) 622-5959, mirchamber@nb.aibn.com, www.miramichi chamber.com

**Moncton** • *Greater Moncton C/C* • Valerie Roy, CEO, 910 Main St., Ste. 100, E1C 1G6, P 120,000, M 800, (506) 857-2883, Fax (506) 857-9209, www.gmcc.nb.ca

**Oromocto** • *Oromocto and Area C/C* • Lloyd Chambers, Pres., P.O. Box 20124, E2V 2R6, P 25,000, M 100, (506) 446-6043, Fax (506) 446-6925, oromoctochamber@nb.aibn.com, www.oromocto chamber.nb.ca

**Richibucto** • *Kent-Centre C/C* • Richard Thebeau, Pres., 9235 Main St., Ste. 1, E4W 4B4, P 1,409, M 32, (506) 523-7870, Fax (506) 523-7850, kccc@richibucto.org, www.richibucto.org

**Rogersville** • *Rogersville C/C* • Ivan Bourque, Pres., 11033 Principal St., E4Y 2L7, P 3,000, M 84, (506) 775-2728, www.rogersville.info

**Sackville** • *Greater Sackville C/C* • 87-8 Main St., E4L 4A9, P 5,600, M 120, (506) 364-8911, Fax (506) 364-8082, gscc@eastlink.ca, www.sackvillechamber.ca

**Saint Andrews** • *St. Andrews C/C* • Julie Crichton, Exec. Dir., 46 Reed Ave., E5B 1A1, P 1,900, M 110, (506) 529-3555, Fax (506) 529-8095, stachamb@nbnet.nb.ca, www.standrewsbythesea.ca

**Saint Francois** • *Saint Francois C/C* • Camille Landry, Pres., P.O. Box 378, E7A 1G4, P 1,575, M 225, (506) 992-6050, Fax (506) 992-6067

**Saint John** • *Saint John Bd. Of Trade* • Imelda Gilman, Pres., 40 rue King St., P.O. Box 6037, E2L 4R5, P 120,000, M 650, (506) 634-8111, Fax (506) 632-2008, info@sjboardoftrade.com, www.sjboardoftrade.com

**Saint-Simon** • *Saint-Simon C/C* • 403 S. le Boutheller St., E8P 1Z6, P 800, M 30, (506) 727-2467

**Shippagan** • *Shippagan C/C* • Donald Hachey, 227 Blvd. JD Gauthier, E8S 1N2, P 3,000, M 129, (506) 336-3993, Fax (506) 336-3993, chambredecommercedeshippagan@nb.aibn.com, www.ville.shippagan.com

**St. Stephen** • *St. Stephen Area C/C* • 73 Milltown Blvd., Ste. 112, E3L 1G5, P 5,000, M 150, (506) 466-7703, Fax (506) 466-7753, info@town.ststephen.nb.ca, www.town.ststephen.nb.ca

**Sussex** · *Sussex and Dist. C/C* · Phil Sellars, Pres., 66 Broad St., Ste. 2, P.O. Box 5152, E4E 5L2, P 20,000, M 125, (506) 433-1845, Fax (506) 433-1886, sdcc@nb.aibn.com, www.sdccinc.org

**Woodstock** · *Greater Woodstock C/C* · Lynn Rose, Pres., 220 King St., Unit 2, E7M 1Z8, P 5,000, M 135, (506) 325-9049, Fax (506) 328-4683, woodstockchamberofcommerce@nb.aibn.com

# Newfoundland

**Newfoundland & Labrador C/C** · Paul Brocklehurst, P.O. Box 352, Gander, A1V 1W7, P 516,900, M 2,700, (709) 651-6522, Fax (709) 256-5808, execdirector@nlchamber.ca, www.nlchamber.ca

**Bonavista** · *Bonavista Area C/C* · Neal Tucker, Pres., P.O. Box 280, A0C 1B0, P 6,500, M 55, Fax (709) 468-2495, info@bacc.ca, www.bacc.ca

**Carbonear** · *Baccalieu Trail Bd. of Trade* · Bob White, College of the North Atlantic, A1Y 1A7, P 9,000, M 174, (709) 596-4555, Fax (709) 596-4565, staff@baccalieutrail.ca, www.baccalieutrail.ca

**Clarenville** · *Clarenville Area C/C* · Terri-Lynn Davis, Ofc. Mgr., 292A Memorial Dr., A5A 1P1, P 5,270, M 122, (709) 466-5800, Fax (709) 466-5803, info@clarenvilleareachamber.net, www.clarenvilleareachamber.net

**Corner Brook** · *Greater Corner Brook Bd. of Trade* · 11 Confederation Dr., P.O. Box 475, A2H 6E6, P 25,000, M 280, (709) 634-5831, Fax (709) 639-9710, sherry@gcbbt.com, www.gcbbt.com

**Deer Lake** · *Deer Lake C/C* · Tammy Harding, Exec. Dir., 9A Church St., A8A 1C9, P 4,900, M 167, (709) 635-3260, Fax (709) 635-5857, info@deerlakechamber.com, www.deerlakechamber.com

**Gander** · *Gander & Area C/C* · Hazel Bishop, Exec. Dir., 109 Trans-Canada Hwy., A1V 1P6, P 40,000, M 282, (709) 256-7110, Fax (709) 256-4080, ganderchamber@ganderchamber.nf.ca, www.ganderchamber.nf.ca

**Grand Falls-Windsor** · *Exploits Reg. C/C* · Sean Cooper, Exec. Dir., P.O. Box 272, A2A 2J7, P 35,000, M 200, (709) 489-7512, Fax (709) 489-7532, info@exploitschamber.com, www.exploitschamber.com

**Happy Valley** · *Labrador North C/C* · Sterling Payton, Pres., P.O. Box 460, A0P 1E0, P 8,500, M 150, (709) 896-8787, Fax (709) 896-8039, admin@chamberlabrador.com, www.chamberlabrador.com

**Kelligrews** · *Conception Bay Area C/C* · Glenda Noseworthy, Admin., 702 Conception Bay Hwy., Ste. 3, A1X 3A5, P 25,000, M 200, (709) 834-5670, Fax (709) 834-5760, info@cbachamber.com, www.cbachamber.com

**Labrador City** · *Labrador West C/C* · Patsy Ralph, Bus. Mgr., P.O. Box 273, A2V 2K5, P 12,000, M 87, (709) 944-3723, Fax (709) 944-4699, lwc@crrstv.net, www.labradorwestchamber.ca

**Lewisporte** · *Lewisporte & Area C/C* · Philip Patey, Pres., P.O. Box 953, A0G 3A0, P 4,000, M 88, (709) 535-2500, Fax (709) 535-2482, lacc@easlewisporte.ca, www.lewisporteareachamberofcommerce.ca

**Mount Pearl** · *Mount Pearl C/C* · Barry Furlong, Pres., 253 Commonwealth Ave., A1N 4L3, P 26,000, M 190, (709) 364-8513, (709) 364-2130, Fax (709) 364-8500, info@mountpearlchamber.com, www.mountpearlchamber.com

**Placentia** · *Argentia Area C/C* · Mr. Chris Newhook, Exec. Dir., P.O. Box 109, A0B 2Y0, P 51,000, M 73, (709) 227-0003, Fax (709) 227-0016, www.argentiachamber.org

**Port-Aux-Basques** · *Port-Aux-Basques & Area C/C* · William Bailey, Pres., P.O. Box 1389, A0M 1C0, P 10,000, M 100, (709) 695-3688, Fax (709) 695-7925, pabchamber@thezone.net, www.pabchamber.com

**Saint John's** · *St. John's Bd. of Trade* · Bruce Templeton, Chair, P.O. Box 5127, A1C 5V5, P 180,000, M 800, (709) 726-2961, Fax (709) 726-2003, info@bot.nf.ca, www.bot.nf.ca

**Springdale** · *Springdale C/C* · Glen Seabright, Pres., P.O. Box 37, A0J 1T0, P 3,100, M 30, (709) 673-3837, Fax (709) 673-3897

**St. Anthony** · *St. Anthony & Area C/C* · P.O. Box 650, A0K 4S0, P 10,000, M 75, (709) 454-6667, stanthonyandareachamber@yahoo.ca

**Stephenville** · *Bay St. George C/C* · 35 Carolina Ave., A2N 3P4, P 8,000, M 100, (709) 643-5854, Fax (709) 643-6398, bsgcoc@wec-center.nl.ca, www.bsgcc.org

# Northwest Territories

**Northwest Territories C/C** · John Curan, Exec. Dir., 4910-50th Ave., Box 13, Yellowknife, X1A 3S5, P 42,000, M 850, (867) 920-9505, Fax (867) 873-4174, admin@nwtchamber.com, www.nwtchamber.com

**Fort Simpson** · *Fort Simpson C/C* · Kirby Groat, P.O. Box 240, X0E 0N0, P 1,300, M 50, (867) 695-2253, kwgroat@northwestel.net

**Fort Smith** · *Fort Smith C/C* · Bernie Minute, P.O. Box 121, X0E 0P0, P 2,600, M 65, (867) 872-8400, (867) 872-3473

**Hay River** · *Hay River C/C* · Stephanie Fisher, Exec. Asst., 10K Gagnier St., X0E 1G1, P 3,700, M 120, (867) 874-2565, Fax (867) 874-3631, info@hayriverchamber.com, www.hayriverchamber.com

**Norman Wells** · *Norman Wells & Dist. C/C* · P.O. Box 400, X0E 0V0, P 700, M 50, (867) 587-6609, www.normanwells.com

**Yellowknife** · *Yellowknife C/C* · Ellie Sasseville, Exec. Dir., 4910-50th Ave., Box 21, X1A 3S5, P 50,000, M 500, (867) 920-4944, Fax (867) 920-4640, generalmanager@ykchamber.com, www.ykchamber.com

# Nova Scotia

**Nova Scotia Chambers of Commerce** · Tim Tucker, Exec. Dir., 605 Prince St., P.O. Box 54, Truro, B2N 5B6, P 934,000, M 50, (902) 895-6329, Fax (902) 897-6641, tim@nschamber.ca, www.nschamber.ca

**Annapolis** · *Annapolis & Dist. Bd. Of Trade* · Tina Halliday, Admin., P.O. Box 2, B0S 1A0, P 7,000, M 98, (902) 532-5454, (902) 526-0944, info@tradeannapolis.com, www.tradeannapolis.com

**Antigonish** · *Antigonish C/C* · Phil Hughes, Pres., 21-B James St. Plz., B2G 1R6, P 18,836, M 185, (902) 863-6308, Fax (902) 863-2656, contact@antigonishchamber.com, www.antigonishchamber.com

**Berwick** · *Berwick & Dist. Bd. Of Trade* · Terry Gayle, Pres., P.O. Box 664, B0P 1E0, P 2,500, M 85, (902) 538-8068

**Bridgewater** · *Bridgewater & Area C/C* · Ann O'Connell, Exec. Dir., 220 North St., B4V 2V6, P 20,000, M 170, (902) 543-4263, Fax (902) 543-1156, bacc@eastlink.ca, www.bridgewaterchamber.com

**Chester** · *Chester Municipal C/C* · Angela Jessome, Exec. Dir., 4171 Hwy., RR 2, Ste. 13, B0J 1J0, P 10,000, M 200, (902) 275-4709, Fax (902) 275-4709, admin@chesterareans.com, www.chesterareans.com

**Dartmouth** • *Halifax C/C* • Valerie Payn, Pres./CEO, 656 Windmill Rd., Ste. 200, B3B 1B8, P 300,000, M 2,000, (902) 468-7111, Fax (902) 468-7333, info@halifaxchamber.com, www.halifaxchamber.com

**Digby** • *Digby & Area Bd. Of Trade* • Kristy Herron-Bishop, Pres., P.O. Box 641, B0V 1A0, P 10,000, M 50, (902) 834-2204, (902) 245-8879, kristy@ns.sympatico.ca, www.tartannet.ns.ca/~dabot

**Kentville** • *Atlantic Provinces C/C* • Bill Denyar, Pres./CEO, 325 Main St., P.O. Box 832, B4N 4H8, P 2,300,000, M 15,000, (902) 678-6284, Fax (902) 678-7420, janice@apcc.ca, www.apcc.ca

**Kentville** • *Eastern Kings C/C* • Judy Rafuse, Exec. Dir., P.O. Box 314, B4N 3X1, P 40,000, M 380, (902) 678-4634, Fax (902) 678-5448, executivedirector@ekcc.ca, www.ekcc.ca

**Lantz** • *East Hants & Dist. C/C* • Tanya-Eisnor Whynot, Ofc. Mgr., P.O. Box 1053, B2S 3G7, P 15,000, M 165, (902) 883-1010, Fax (902) 883-7862, info@ehcc.ca, www.ehcc.ca

**Liverpool** • *South Queens C/C* • David Noel, Dir., P.O. Box 1378, B0K 1K0, P 12,500, M 30, (902) 354-4163, Fax (902) 354-2354, secretary@southqueenschamber.com, www.southqueenschamber.com

**Lunenburg** • *Lunenburg Bd. Of Trade* • Andria Wicker, P.O. Box 1300, B0J 2C0, P 2,600, M 200, (902) 634-3170, lbt@ns.aliantzinc.ca, www.lunenburgns.com

**New Glasgow** • *Pictou County C/C* • Faus Johnson, Exec. Dir., 980 E. River Rd., B2H 3S8, P 47,500, M 230, (902) 755-3463, Fax (902) 755-2848, info@pictouchamber.com, www.pictouchamber.com.

**Parrsboro** • *Parrsboro C/C & Bd. of Trade* • Frank Hartman, Pres., P.O. Box 297, B0M 1S0, P 1,650, M 75, (902) 254-2892, admin@parrsborodistrictboardoftrade.com, www.parrsboro districtboardoftrade.com

**Pictou County** • *see New Glasgow*

**Port Hawkesbury** • *Strait Area C/C* • Shannon McDougal, Exec. Dir., 4 MacIntosh Ave., Unit 2, B9A 3K5, P 35,000, M 187, (902) 625-1588, Fax (902) 625-5985, straitareacoc@ns.sympatico.ca, www.straitchamber.ca

**Riverport** • *Riverport Dist. Bd. Of Trade* • Matt Durnford, Pres., P.O. Box 28, B0J 2W0, P 1,000, M 30, (902) 766-4104, Fax (902) 766-4104, www.riverport.org

**Springhill** • *Springhill C/C* • Anne Newman, Pres., P.O. Box 1030, B0M 1X0, P 4,000, M 60, (902) 597-8462, (902) 763-3011, amcentre@eastlink.ca

**Sydney** • *Sydney and Area C/C* • Michael MacSween, Exec. Dir., P.O. Box 131, B1P 1G9, P 100,000, M 590, (902) 564-6453, Fax (902) 539-7487, info@sydneyareachamber.ca, www.sydney areachamber.ca

**Tatamagouche** • *North Shore Comm. Dev. Assn.* • Linda Byers, Chair, 225 Main St., P.O. Box 152, B0K 1V0, P 1,000, M 15, (902) 657-3811, Fax (902) 657-2619, www.tatamagouchetoday.com

**Truro** • *Truro & Dist. C/C* • Tim Tucker, Exec. Dir., 605 Prince St., P.O. Box 54, B2N 5B6, P 46,000, M 403, (902) 895-6328, Fax (902) 897-6641, tim@trurochamber.com, www.trurochamber.com

**Windsor** • *West Hants C/C* • Gordon Winston, Pres., P.O. Box 2188, B0N 2T0, P 19,000, M 70, (902) 798-5106, info@whcc.ca, www.whcc.ca

**Yarmouth** • *Yarmouth Area C/C* • Jim Greig, Exec. Dir., P.O. Box 532, B5A 4B4, P 28,000, M 192, (902) 742-3074, Fax (902) 749-1383, info@yarmouthchamberofcommerce.com, www.yarmouthchamberofcommerce.com

# Nunavut

**Baker Lake** • *Baker Lake C/C & EDC* • P.O. Box 149, X0C 0A0, P 1,700, (867) 793-2874, Fax (867) 793-2509

**Iqaluit** • *Baffin Reg. C/C* • Hal Timer, Exec. Dir., Box 59, Bldg. 607, X0A 0H0, P 15,000, M 120, (867) 979-4654, (867) 979-4656, Fax (867) 979-2929, execdir@baffinchamber.ca, www.baffinchamber.ca

**Rankin Inlet** • *Kivalliq C/C* • Ellie Cansfield, Pres., P.O. Box 146, X0C 0G0, P 7,500, M 150, (867) 645-2817, Fax (867) 645-2483, krmanson@artic.ca

# Ontario

**Ontario C/C** • Len Crispino, Pres./CEO, 180 Dundas St. W., Ste. 505, Toronto, M5G 1Z8, P 10,000,000, M 65,000, (416) 482-5222, Fax (416) 482-5879, info@occ.on.ca, www.occ.on.ca

**Alliston** • *Alliston & Dist. C/C* • Michael Keith, Pres., 519 Victoria St. E., P.O. Box 32, L9R 1T9, P 25,000, M 330, (705) 435-7921, Fax (705) 435-0289, info@adcc.ca, www.adcc.ca

**Amherstburg** • *Amherstburg C/C* • Susie White, Ofc. Admin., 268 Dalhousie St., P.O. Box 101, N9V 2Z3, P 20,000, M 130, (519) 736-2001, Fax (519) 736-9721, acoc@mnsi.net, www.amherst burgchamberofcommerce.ca

**Apsley** • *see Lakefield*

**Aurora** • *Aurora C/C* • Carla Adams, Exec. Dir., 6-14845 Yonge St., Ste. 321, L4G 6H8, P 49,000, M 785, (905) 727-7262, Fax (905) 841-6217, info@aurorachamber.on.ca, www.aurorachamber.on.ca

**Bancroft** • *Bancroft & Dist. C/C* • Kimberly Crawford, Gen. Mgr., 17 Snow Rd., Ste. 1, Box 539, K0L 1C0, P 16,000, M 350, (613) 332-1513, (888) 443-9999, Fax (613) 332-2119, chamber@commerce.bancroft.on.ca, www.bancroftdistrict.com

**Barrie** • *Greater Barrie C/C* • Sybil Goruk, Exec. Dir., 97 Toronto St., L4N 1V1, P 125,000, M 1,200, (705) 721-5000, Fax (705) 726-0973, chadmin@barriechamber.com, www.barriechamber.com

**Belleville** • *Belleville & Dist. C/C* • Angela Genereaux, Gen. Mgr., 5 Moira St. E., P.O. Box 726, K8N 5B3, P 46,000, M 600, (613) 962-4597, (888) 852-9992, Fax (613) 962-3911, info@belleville chamber.ca, www.bellevillechamber.ca

**Blenheim** • *Blenheim & Dist. C/C* • Betty Russell, Secy., P.O. Box 1353, N0P 1A0, P 5,500, M 60, (519) 676-8090

**Blind River** • *Blind River C/C* • Edward Ritchie, Pres., P.O. Box 998, P0R 1B0, P 3,600, M 87, (705) 356-2555, Fax (705) 356-3911, chamber@blindriver.com, www.brchamber.ca

**Bobcaygeon** • *Bobcaygeon C/C* • Ruth Ann Wilson, Ofc. Mgr., 21 Canal St. E., P.O. Box 388, K0M 1A0, P 2,000, M 222, (705) 738-2202, (800) 318-6173, Fax (705) 738-1534, chamber@bobcaygeon.org, www.bobcaygeon.org

**Bolton** • *Caledon C/C* • Kelly Darnley, Exec. Dir., P.O. Box 626, L7E 5T5, P 58,000, M 400, (905) 857-7393, (888) 599-9967, Fax (905) 857-7405, info@caledonchamber.com, www.caledonchamber.com

**Bracebridge** • *Bracebridge C/C* • 1 Manitoba St., 2nd Flr., P1L 1S4, P 14,000, M 400, (705) 645-5231, Fax (705) 645-7592, chamber@bracebridgechamber.com, www.bracebridgechamber.com

**Brampton** • *Brampton Bd. Of Trade* • Gary Collins, CEO, 33 Queen St. W., 2nd Flr., L6Y 1L9, P 400,000, M 1,100, (905) 451-1122, Fax (905) 450-0295, admin@bramptonbot.com, www.bramptonbot.com

**Brantford** · *Brantford Brant C/C* · Charlene Nicholson, CEO, 77 Charlotte St., N3T 2W8, P 100,000, M 800, (519) 753-2617, Fax (519) 753-0921, chamber@brcc.ca, www.brantfordbrantchamber.com

**Brockville** · *Brockville & Dist. C/C* · Diana Dodge-Phillips, Exec. Dir., 3 Market St. W., Ste. 1, K6V 7L2, P 22,000, M 560, (613) 342-6553, Fax (613) 342-6849, info@brockvillechamber.com, www.brockvillechamber.com

**Buckhorn** · *see Lakefield*

**Burleigh Falls** · *see Lakefield*

**Burlington** · *Burlington C/C* · Keith Hoey, Pres., 414 Locust St., Ste. 201, L7S 1T7, P 155,000, M 1,057, (905) 639-0174, Fax (905) 333-3956, info@burlingtonchamber.com, www.burlingtonchamber.com

**Caledonia** · *Caledonia Reg. C/C* · Barbara Martindale, Exec. Dir., 1 Grand Trunk Ln., P.O. Box 2035, N3W 2G6, P 9,000, M 236, (905) 765-0377, Fax (905) 765-6730, crcc@mountaincable.net, www.caledonia-ontario.com

**Cambridge** · *Cambridge C/C* · Greg Durocher, Pres., 750 Hespeler Rd., N3H 5L8, P 118,000, M 1,900, (519) 622-2221, Fax (519) 622-0177, admin@cambridgechamber.com, www.cambridgechamber.com

**Campbellford** · *Trent Hills C/C* · Nancy Allanson, Exec. Dir., 51 Grand Rd., P.O. Box 376, K0L 1L0, P 12,000, M 250, (705) 653-1551, Fax (705) 653-1629, info@trenthillschamber.ca, www.trenthillschamber.ca

**Carleton Place** · *Carleton Place & Dist. C/C* · Cindy Hobbs, Mgr., 175 Bridge St., K7C 2V8, P 9,800, M 184, (613) 257-1976, Fax (613) 257-8170, manager@cpchamber.com, www.cpchamber.com

**Chatham** · *Chatham-Kent C/C* · Gail Antaya, Pres./CEO, 54 Fourth St., N7M 2G2, P 44,000, M 500, (519) 352-7540, Fax (519) 352-8741, info@chatham-kentchamber.ca, www.chatham-kentchamber.ca

**Cobourg** · *Northumberland Central C/C* · Northumberland Mall, 1111 Elgin St. W., K9A 5H7, P 18,000, M 425, (905) 372-5831, Fax (905) 372-2411, info@cobourgchamber.com, www.cobourgchamber.com

**Collingwood** · *Collingwood C/C* · Trish Irwin, Gen. Mgr., 25 Second St., L9Y 1E4, P 17,000, M 525, (705) 445-0221, info@collingwoodchamber.com, www.collingwoodchamber.com

**Concord** · *see Vaughan*

**Cornwall** · *Cornwall & Area C/C* · Lezlie Strasser, Exec. Mgr., 113 2nd St. E., Ste. 100, K6H 1Y5, P 46,000, M 650, (613) 933-4004, Fax (613) 933-8466, strasser@cornwallchamber.com, www.cornwallchamber.com

**Dryden** · *Dryden Dist. C/C & Tourism Center* · 284 Government St., P8N 2P3, P 35,000, M 250, (807) 223-2622, (800) 667-0935, Fax (807) 223-2626, chamber@maildrytel.net, www.drydenchamber.ca

**Dunnville** · *Dunnville C/C* · Sandy Passmore, Pres., 231 Chestnut St., P.O. Box 124, N1A 2X1, P 12,000, M 100, (905) 774-3183, Fax (905) 774-9281, chamberofcommerce@mountaincable.net, www.dunnvillechamberofcommerce.ca

**Durham** · *West Grey C/C* · Greta Kennedy, Secy./Treas., P.O. Box 800, N0G 1R0, P 2,500, M 50, (519) 369-5750, Fax (519) 369-5750, info@westgreychamber.ca, www.westgreychamber.ca

**Dutton** · *Dutton & Dunwich C/C* · Jim Corneil, Pres., P.O. Box 547, N0L 1J0, P 3,000, M 77, (519) 762-6060, Fax (519) 762-0934, www.ddchamber.ca

**Elliot Lake** · *Elliot Lake & Dist. C/C* · Todd Stencill, Gen. Mgr., 255 Hwy. 108 N., P.O. Box 81, P5A 2J6, P 12,500, M 130, (705) 848-3974, Fax (705) 848-7121, elchamber@onlink.net, www.elliotlakechamber.com

**Englehart** · *Englehart & Dist. C/C* · Stacey Borgford, Pres., P.O. Box 171, P0J 1H0, P 1,800, M 55, (705) 544-2244

**Fenelon Falls** · *Fenelon Falls & Dist. C/C* · 15 Oak St., K0M 1N0, P 2,000, M 120, (705) 887-3409, Fax (705) 887-6912, info@fenelonfallschamber.com, www.fenelonfallschamber.com

**Fergus** · *Centre Wellington C/C* · Roberta Scarrow, Gen. Mgr., 400 Tower St. S., N1M 2P7, P 28,000, M 350, (519) 843-5140, (877) 242-6353, Fax (519) 787-0983, chamber@cwchamber.ca, www.cwchamber.ca

**Fort Erie** · *Greater Fort Erie C/C* · Karen Audet, Op. Mgr., 660 Garrison Rd., Unit 1, L2A 6E2, P 32,000, M 315, (905) 871-3803, Fax (905) 871-1561, info@greaterforteriechamber.com, www.greaterforteriechamber.com

**Fort Frances** · *Fort Frances C/C* · Dawn Booth, Mgr., 474 Scott St., P9A 1H2, P 8,000, M 175, (807) 274-5773, (800) 820-FORT, Fax (807) 274-8706, thefort@fortfranceschamber.com, www.fortfranceschamber.com

**Georgetown** · *Halton Hills C/C* · Sue Walker, Gen. Mgr., 328 Guelph St., L7G 4B5, P 53,000, M 520, (905) 877-7119, Fax (905) 877-5117, sue@haltonhillschamber.on.ca, www.haltonhillschamber.on.ca

**Gloucester** · *Eastern Ottawa C/C* · David Brault, Pres., 310-2183 Ogilvie Rd., K1J 1C8, P 100,000, M 160, (613) 745-3578, Fax (613) 745-8575, info@easternottawa.com, www.easternottawa.com

**Grand Bend** · *Grand Bend & Area C/C* · Christine Bregman, Ofc. Mgr., 1-81 Crescent, P.O. Box 248, N0M 1T0, P 40,000, M 200, (519) 238-2001, (888) 338-2001, Fax (519) 238-5201, info@grandbendtourism.com, www.grandbendtourism.com

**Grimsby** · *Grimsby & Dist. C/C* · Jinny Day, Exec. Dir., 424 S. Service Rd., L3M 4E8, P 22,000, M 237, (905) 945-8319, Fax (905) 945-1615, info@grimsbychamber.com, grimsbychamber.com

**Guelph** · *Guelph C/C* · Lloyd Longfield, Pres./CAO, 485 Silvercreek Pkwy. N., Unit 15, N1H 7K5, P 115,000, M 813, (519) 822-8081, Fax (519) 822-8451, chamber@guelphchamber.com, www.guelphchamber.com

**Hagersville** · *Hagersville & Dist. C/C* · Brenda Marshfelter, Pres., P.O. Box 1090, N0A 1H0, P 2,600, M 70, (905) 768-3384

**Haliburton Highlands** · *Haliburton Highlands C/C* · Nick Lawrence, Pres., P.O. Box 147, Minden, K0M 2K0, P 18,000, M 360, (705) 286-1760, (877) 811-6111, Fax (705) 286-6016, admin@hhchamber.on.ca, www.hhchamber.on.ca

**Hamilton** · *Hamilton C/C* · John Dolbec, CEO, 555 Bay St. N., L8L 1H1, P 510,000, M 2,000, (905) 522-1151, Fax (905) 522-1154, hdcc@hamiltonchamber.on.ca, www.hamiltonchamber.on.ca.

**Hastings** · *see Campbellford*

**Hawkesbury** · *Hawkesbury C/C* · Richard Denis, Pres., 2 John St., Box 36, K6A 2R4, P 10,000, M 225, (613) 632-8066, Fax (613) 632-3324, info@hcoc.ca, www.hcoc.ca

**Hearst** · *C/C of Hearst, Mattice-Val Cote* · Ghislain Jacques, Pres., P.O. Box 987, P0L 1N0, P 6,000, M 110, (705) 372-2838, Fax (705) 372-2840, tourisme@hearst.ca, www.hearstcoc.com

**Huntsville** · *Huntsville/Lake of Bays C/C* · Kelly Haywood, Gen. Mgr., 8 West St. N., P1H 2B6, P 20,466, M 621, (705) 789-4771, Fax (705) 789-6191, chamber@huntsvillelakeofbays.on.ca, www.huntsvillelakeofbays.on.ca

**Ingersoll** · *Ingersoll Dist. C/C* · Ann Campbell, Gen. Mgr., 132 Thames St. S., N5C 2T4, P 15,000, M 205, (519) 485-7333, Fax (519) 485-6606, anncampbell@ingersollchamber.com, www.ingersollchamber.com

**Ingleside** · *South Stormont C/C* · Lesley O'Gorman, Pres., P.O. Box 489, K0C 1M0, P 1,800, M 62, (613) 537-4427, Fax (613) 537-9439, info@sscc.on.ca, sscc.on.ca

**Innisfil** · *Greater Innisfil C/C* · Claudia Carmona, Ofc. Admin., 7896 Young St., L9S 1L5, P 34,000, M 190, (705) 431-4199, Fax (705) 431-6628, info@innisfilchamber.com, www.innisfilchamber.com

**Iroquois Falls** · *Iroquois Falls & Dist. C/C* · Rose-Marie Purdy-Peever/Carol Fortier, 727 Synagogue Ave., P.O. Box 840, P0K 1G0, P 5,700, M 50, (705) 232-4656, Fax (705) 232-4656, ifchamber@hotmail.com, www.iroquoisfallschamber.com

**Kemptville** · *North Grenville C/C* · Wendy Chapman, Exec. Dir., 5 Clothier St. E., P.O. Box 1047, K0G 1J0, P 15,000, M 225, (613) 258-4838, Fax (613) 258-3801, info@northgrenvillechamber.com, www.northgrenvillechamber.com

**Kenora** · *Kenora & Dist. C/C* · Laurene Manson-Sillery, Chamber Mgr., 205 Second St. S., P.O. Box 471, P9N 3X5, P 22,000, M 225, (807) 467-4646, Fax (807) 468-3056, kenorachamber@kmts.ca, www.kenorachamber.com

**Keswick** · *Georgina C/C* · Christina Thomas, Gen. Mgr., 22937 Woodbine Ave., RR 2, L4P 3E9, P 45,000, M 278, (905) 476-7870, Fax (905) 476-6700, admin@georginachamber.com, www.georginachamber.com

**Kincardine** · *Kincardine & Dist. C/C* · Jackie Pawlikowski, Ofc. Mgr., 721A Queen St., 3rd Flr., P.O. Box 115, N2Z 2Y6, P 12,000, M 125, (519) 396-9333, Fax (519) 396-5529, kincardine.cofc@bmts.com, www.kincardinechamber.com

**King City** · *King Twp. C/C* · 2075 King Rd., L7B 1A1, P 5,000, M 200, (905) 833-5321, Fax (905) 833-2300, online@king.ca, www.township.king.on.ca

**Kingston** · *Greater Kingston C/C* · Bob Scott, Gen. Mgr., 67 Brock St., K7L 1R8, P 140,000, M 875, (613) 548-4453, (888) 855-4555, Fax (613) 548-4743, info@kingstonchamber.on.ca, www.kingstonchamber.on.ca

**Kirkland Lake** · *Kirkland Lake Dist. C/C* · Rosemary Kmyta, Ofc. Coord., 400 Government Rd. W., P.O. Box 966, P2N 3L1, P 9,000, M 125, (705) 567-5444, Fax (705) 567-1666, klcofc@ntl.sympatico.ca, www.kirklandlakechamber.com

**Kitchener** · *Greater Kitchener Waterloo C/C* · Joan Fisk, Pres./CEO, 80 Queen St. N., P.O. Box 2367, N2H 6L4, P 300,000, M 1,900, (519) 576-5000, (888) 672-4760, Fax (519) 742-4760, admin@greaterkwchamber.com, www.greaterkwchamber.com

**Kleinburg** · *see Vaughan*

**Lakefield** · *Kawartha Lakes C/C, Eastern Region* · Sherry Boyce-Found, Gen. Mgr., 12 Queen St., P.O. Box 537, K0L 2H0, P 15,000, M 340, (705) 652-6963, (888) 565-8888, Fax (705) 652-9140, info@kawarthachamber.ca, www.kawarthachamber.ca

**Leamington** · *Leamington & Dist. C/C* · Mrs. Chris Chopchik, Gen. Mgr., 21 Talbot St. E., P.O. Box 321, N8H 3W3, P 35,000, M 400, (519) 326-2721, (800) 250-3336, Fax (519) 326-3204, christinec@leamingtonchamber.com, www.leamingtonchamber.com

**Lindsay** · *Lindsay & Dist. C/C* · Gayle Jones, Gen. Mgr., 4 Victoria Ave. N., K9V 4E5, P 21,000, M 618, (705) 324-2393, Fax (705) 324-2473, info@lindsaychamber.com, www.lindsaychamber.com

**Listowel** · *North Perth C/C* · Tami Chauvin, Gen. Mgr., 580 Main St. W., N4W 1A8, P 14,000, M 14, (519) 291-1551, Fax (519) 291-4151, tami@npchamber.com, www.npchamber.com

**London** · *London C/C* · Gerry Macartney, Gen. Mgr./COO, 101-244 Pall Mall St., N6A 5P6, P 331,000, M 1,000, (519) 432-7551, Fax (519) 432-8063, info@londonchamber.com, www.londonchamber.com

**Manotick** · *Rideau C/C* · P.O. Box 247, K4M 1A3, M 60, (613) 692-6262, info@rideauchamber.com, www.rideauchamber.com

**Maple** · *see Vaughan*

**Markdale** · *Markdale C/C* · P.O. Box 177, N0C 1H0, P 1,400, M 90, (519) 986-4612, (888) 986-4612, Fax (519) 986-4612, markdalechamber@cablerocket.com, www.village.markdale.on.ca

**Markham** · *Markham Bd. Of Trade* · Richard Cunningham, Pres./CEO, 80F Centurian Dr.. Ste. 206, L3R 8C1, P 265,000, M 1,050, (905) 474-0730, Fax (905) 474-0685, info@markhamboard.com, www.markhamboard.com

**Merrickville** · *Merrickville & Dist. C/C* · Hugh MacLennan, 317 Brock St. W., K0G 1N0, P 2,500, M 150, (613) 269-2229, Fax same, info@merrickville.com, www.realmerrickville.ca

**Midland** · *Southern Georgian Bay C/C* · Denise Hayes, Bus. Mgr., 208 King St., L4R 3L9, P 43,000, M 485, (705) 526-7884, Fax (705) 526-1744, info@sgbchamber.ca, www.southerngeorgianbay.on.ca

**Milton** · *Milton C/C* · Sandy Martin, Exec. Dir., 251 Main St. E., Ste. 104, L9T 1P1, P 75,000, M 756, (905) 878-0581, Fax (905) 878-4972, info@miltonchamber.ca, www.miltonchamber.ca.

**Mindemoya** · *Manitoulin Island C/C* · Claude Proulx, Pres., P.O. Box 307, P0P 1S0, P 13,000, M 150, (705) 377-7501, office@manitoulinchamber.com, www.manitoulinchamber.com

**Mississauga** · *Mississauga Bd. Of Trade* · Sheldon Leiba, Pres./CEO, 77 City Center Dr., Ste. 701, L5B 1M5, P 650,000, M 1,500, (905) 273-6151, Fax (905) 273-4937, info@mbot.com, www.mbot.com

**Morrisburg** · *South Dundas C/C* · Barb Scott, Pres., P.O. Box 288, K0C 1X0, P 10,000, M 140, (613) 543-3443, Fax (613) 652-4120, info@southdundaschamber.com, www.southdundaschamber.com

**Mount Forest** · *Mount Forest & Dist. C/C* · Crystal Seifreid, Ofc. Mgr., 514 Main St. N., N0G 2L2, P 5,000, M 130, (519) 323-4480, Fax (519) 323-1557, mfchamber@wightman.ca, www.mountforest.ca

**New Hamburg** · *New Hamburg Bd. Of Trade* · Paul Knowles, Pres., 121 Huron St., N3A 1K1, P 6,500, M 95, (519) 662-6628, nhbot@golden.net, www.newhamburg.ca

**Newmarket** · *Newmarket C/C* · Debra Scott, Pres./CEO, 470 Davis Dr., L3Y 2P3, P 75,000, M 650, (905) 898-5900, Fax (905) 853-7271, info@newmarketchamber.ca, www.newmarketchamber.ca

**Newmarket** · *York Region Tourism* · 17250 Yonge St., L3Y 6Z1, P 866,000, (905) 883-3442, (888) 448-0000, Fax (905) 895-3482, tourism@york.ca, www.yorktourism.com

**Niagara Falls** · *The Chamber of Commerce at Niagara Falls Canada C/C* · Carolyn A. Bones, Pres., 4056 Dorchester Rd., L2E 6M9, P 82,000, M 770, (905) 374-3666, Fax (905) 374-2972, info@niagarafallschamber.com, www.niagarafallschamber.com

**Niagara-on-the-Lake** · *Niagara-on-the-Lake C/C & Visitors Bur.* · Janice Thomson, Exec. Dir., 26 Queen St., P.O. Box 1043, L0S 1J0, P 13,000, M 500, (905) 468-1950, Fax (905) 468-4930, admin@niagaraonthelake.com, www.niagaraonthelake.com

**Nipigon** · *Nipigon C/C* · Judi Bernard, Pres., 22 Third St., P.O. Box 760, P0T 2J0, P 2,000, M 45, (807) 887-0740, Fax (807) 887-0741, nipigonchamber@vianet.ca, www.nipigon.net

**North Bay** · *North Bay & Dist. C/C* · Patti Carr, Exec. Dir., 1375 Seymour St., P.O. Box 747, P1B 8J8, P 56,000, M 875, (705) 472-8480, (888) 249-8998, Fax (705) 472-8027, nbcc@northbaychamber.com, www.northbaychamber.com

**Norwich** · *Norwich Twp. C/C* · Andrew Malcolm, Pres., 41 Main St. W., N0J 1P0, P 10,000, M 75, (519) 424-5000, president@norwichchamberofcommerce.ca, www.norwichchamberofcommerce.ca

**Oakville** • *Oakville C/C* • John Sawyer, Exec. Dir., 2521 Wyecroft Rd., L6L 6P8, P 150,000, M 1,000, (905) 845-6613, Fax (905) 845-6475, info@oakvillechamber.com, www.oakvillechamber.com.

**Orangeville** • *Greater Dufferin Area C/C* • Lucy Kristan, P.O. Box 101, L9W 2Z5, P 52,000, M 435, (519) 941-0490, Fax (519) 941-0492, info@gdacc.ca, www.gdacc.ca

**Oshawa** • *Greater Oshawa C/C* • Bob Malcolmson, Gen. Mgr./CEO, 44 Richmond St. W., Ste. 100, L1G 1C7, P 150,000, M 880, (905) 728-1683, (905) 725-4523, Fax (905) 432-1259, info@oshawachamber.com, www.oshawachamber.com

**Ottawa** • *Ottawa C/C* • Erin Kelly, Exec. Dir., 1701 Woodward Dr., Ste. LL-20, K2C 0R4, P 1,000,000, M 900, (613) 236-3631, Fax (613) 236-7498, info@ottawachamber.ca, www.ottawachamber.ca

**Owen Sound** • *Owen Sound & Dist. C/C* • Bert Loopstra, Mgr., 704 6th St. E., P.O. Box 1028, N4K 6K6, P 24,800, M 510, (519) 376-6261, Fax (519) 376-5647, osdcc@bmts.com, www.oschamber.com

**Parry Sound** • *Parry Sound Area C/C* • 70 Church St., P2A 1Y9, P 6,500, M 360, (705) 746-4213, (800) 461-4261, Fax (705) 746-6537, info@parrysoundchamber.ca, www.parrysoundchamber.ca

**Pembroke** • *Upper Ottawa Valley C/C* • Lorraine MacKenzie, Mgr., 611 TV Tower Rd., P.O. Box 1010, K8A 6Y6, P 30,000, M 300, (613) 732-1492, Fax (613) 732-5793, manager@upperottawavalleychamber.com, www.upperottawavalleychamber.com

**Perth** • *Perth & Dist. C/C* • Madeline Bouvier & Carol Quattroccho, Co-Mgr., 34 Herriott St., K7H 1T2, P 17,000, M 370, (613) 267-3200, (888) 319-3204, welcome@perthchamber.com, www.perthchamber.com

**Peterborough** • *Greater Peterborough C/C* • Stuart Harrison, Gen. Mgr., 175 George St. N., K9J 3G6, P 81,084, M 1,050, (705) 748-9771, (877) 640-4037, Fax (705) 743-2331, info@peterboroughchamber.ca, www.peterboroughchamber.ca

**Picton** • *Prince Edward County C/C* • Jan Demille, Ofc. Mgr., 116 Main St., K0K 2T0, P 24,000, M 320, (613) 476-2421, (800) 640-4717, Fax (613) 476-7461, pec@reach.net, www.pecchamber.com

**Pointe au Baril** • *Pointe au Baril C/C* • Lillian White, Mgr., P.O. Box 67, P0G 1K0, P 400, M 60, (705) 366-2331, Fax (705) 366-2331, info@pointeaubarilchamber.com, www.pointeaubarilchamber.com

**Port Colborne** • *Port Colborne-Wainfleet C/C* • Edith Wagner, Ofc. Mgr., 76 Main St. W., L3K 3V2, P 25,060, M 192, (905) 834-9765, Fax (905) 834-1542, office@pcwchamber.com, www.pcwchamber.com

**Port Dover** • *Port Dover Bd. of Trade* • Paul Morris, Pres., P.O. Box 239, N0A 1N0, P 6,000, M 250, (519) 583-1314, Fax (519) 583-3275, info@portdover.ca, www.portdover.ca

**Port Elgin** • *Saugeen Shores C/C* • Joanne Robbins, Gen. Mgr., 559 Goderich St., N0H 2C4, P 12,000, M 405, (519) 832-2332, (800) 387-3456, Fax (519) 389-3725, chamberinfo@saugeenshores.ca, www.saugeenshores.ca

**Port Hope** • *Port Hope & Dist. C/C* • Wendy Giroux, Mgr., 58 Queen St., L1A 3Z9, P 17,000, M 320, (905) 885-5519, Fax (905) 885-1142, thechamber@porthope.ca, www.porthopechamber.com

**Port Perry** • *Scugog C/C* • Tony Janssen, Pres., 181 Perry St., P.O. Box 1282, L9L 1A7, P 22,000, M 180, (905) 985-4971, (800) 416-2057, Fax (905) 985-7698, info@scugogchamber.ca, www.scugogchamber.ca

**Port Rowan** • *Long Point Country C/C* • Cindy Vanderstar, P.O. Box 357, N0E 1M0, P 4,000, M 80, (519) 586-8577, info@portrowan-longpoint.org, www.portrowan-longpoint.org

**Prescott** • *Prescott & Dist. C/C* • Debbie Lawless, Secy., P.O. Box 2000, K0E 1T0, P 4,200, M 140, (613) 925-2171, (613) 925-3480, www.prescottanddistrictchamber.com

**Red Lake** • *Red Lake Dist. C/C* • Kiera Andersen, Pres., P.O. Box 430, P0V 2M0, P 6,000, M 65, (807) 727-3722, Fax (807) 727-3285, chamber@gored-lake.com, www.red-lake.com

**Renfrew** • *Renfrew & Area C/C* • Kevin Bossy, Pres., 161 Raglan St. S., K7V 1R2, P 8,500, M 155, (613) 432-7015, Fax (613) 432-8645, info@renfrewareachamber.ca, www.renfrewareachamber.ca

**Richmond Hill** • *Richmond Hill C/C* • Leslie Walker, CEO, 376 Church St. S., L4C 9V8, P 181,000, M 600, (905) 884-1961, Fax (905) 884-1962, info@rhcoc.com, www.rhcoc.com.

**Ridgetown** • *Ridgetown & Dist. C/C* • P.O. Box 522, N0P 2C0, P 3,450, M 90, (519) 359-6597, ridgetownchamber@sympatico.ca, www.ridgetown.com

**Sarnia** • *Sarnia/Lambton C/C* • Garry McDonald, Pres., 556 N. Christina St., N7T 5W6, P 130,000, M 975, (519) 336-2400, Fax (519) 336-2085, info@sarnialambtonchamber.com, www.sarnialambtonchamber.com

**Sauble Beach** • *Sauble Beach C/C* • Jessika Husak, Pres., General Delivery, N0H 2G0, P 3,500, M 110, (519) 422-1262, (519) 422-1051, info@saublebeach.com, www.saublebeach.com

**Sault Ste. Marie** • *Sault Ste. Marie C/C* • Shelley Barich, Gen. Mgr., 334 Bay St., P6A 1X1, P , M , (705) 949-7152, Fax (705) 759-8166, info@ssmcoc.com, www.ssmcoc.com.

**Scarborough** • *see Toronto*

**Selwyn** • *see Lakefield*

**Simcoe** • *Simcoe & Dist. C/C* • Yvonne Di Pietro, Gen. Mgr., Chamber Plaza, 95 Queensway W., N3Y 2M8, P 48,000, M 350, (519) 426-5867, Fax (519) 428-7718, chamber@simcoechamber.on.ca, www.simcoechamber.on.ca.

**Sioux Lookout** • *Sioux Lookout C/C* • Anne Reid, Exec. Asst., #11 First Ave., P.O. Box 577, P8T 1A8, P 5,500, M 150, (807) 737-1937, Fax (807) 737-1778, chamber@siouxlookout.com, www.siouxlookout.com

**Smiths Falls** • *Smiths Falls & Dist. C/C* • 77 Beckwith St. N., K7A 2B8, P 9,100, M 300, (613) 283-1334, (800) 257-1334, Fax (613) 283-4764, sfchamber@smithsfalls.ca, www.smithsfalls.ca/sfchamber

**Smithville** • *West Lincoln C/C* • P.O. Box 555, L0R 2A0, P 12,000, M 150, (905) 957-1606, Fax (905) 957-4628

**St. Catharines** • *St. Catharines-Thorold C/C* • Walter Sendzik, Exec. Dir., One St. Paul St., P.O. Box 940, L2R 6Z4, P 150,000, M 1,100, (905) 684-2361, Fax (905) 684-2100, info@sctchamber.com, www.sctchamber.com.

**St. Thomas** • *St. Thomas & Dist. C/C* • R.W. Hammersley, Pres./CEO, 555 Talbot St., N5P 1C5, P 68,000, M 750, (519) 631-1981, Fax (519) 631-0466, mail@stthomaschamber.on.ca, www.stthomaschamber.on.ca.

**Stoney Creek** • *Stoney Creek C/C* • Dave Cage, Exec. Dir., 21 Mountain Ave. S., L8G 2V5, P 58,000, M 425, (905) 664-4000, Fax (905) 664-7228, sccc@bellnet.ca, www.chamberstoneycreek.com

**Stony Lake** • *see Lakefield*

**Stratford** • *Stratford & Dist. C/C* • Garry Lobsinger, Gen. Mgr., 55 Lorne Ave. E., N5A 6S4, P 30,000, M 400, (519) 273-5250, Fax (519) 273-2229, info@stratfordchamber.com, www.stratfordchamber.com

**Sturgeon Falls** • *West Nipissing C/C* • Renee Beauparlant, Pres., 200 Main St. Unit B, P.O. Box 4592, P2B 1P2, P 14,000, M 80, (705) 753-5672, cofcwn@vianet.ca

**Sudbury** • *Greater Sudbury C/C* • Debbi M. Nicholson, Pres./CEO, 40 Elm St., Ste. 1, P3C 1S8, P 160,000, M 1,007, (705) 673-7133, Fax (705) 673-2944, cofc@sudburychamber.ca, www.sudbury chamber.ca

**Tavistock** • *Tavistock C/C* • Andrew Raymer, Pres., P.O. Box 670, N0B 2R0, P 2,500, M 50, (519) 655-2700

**Thornhill** • *see Vaughan*

**Thorold** • *see St. Catharines*

**Thunder Bay** • *North of Superior Tourism Assn.* • Bruce Fallen, Exec. Dir., 920 Tungsten St., Ste. 206A, P7B 5Z6, P 200,000, M 300, (807) 346-1130, (800) 265-3951, Fax (807) 346-1135, info@nosta. on.ca, www.northofsuperior.org

**Thunder Bay** • *Thunder Bay C/C* • Mary Long-Irwin, Pres., 200 S. Syndicate Ave., Ste. 102, P7E 1C9, P 120,000, M 1,300, (807) 624-2626, Fax (807) 622-7752, chamber@tb-chamber.on.ca, www. tb-chamber.on.ca

**Tilbury** • *Tilbury & Dist. C/C* • Exec. Dir., P.O. Box 1299, N0P 2L0, P 4,300, M 120, (519) 682-3040, Fax (519) 682-3123

**Tillsonburg** • *Tillsonburg Dist. C/C* • Suzanne Renken, Gen. Mgr., 2 Library Ln., P.O. Box 113, N4G 4H3, P 15,000, M 130, (519) 983-6085, Fax (519) 842-2941, srenken@ody.ca, www.tillsonburg.ca

**Timmins** • *Timmins C/C* • Keitha Robson, Mgr., P.O. Box 985, P4N 7H6, P 45,000, M 610, (705) 360-1900, Fax (705) 360-1193, info@ timminschamber.on.ca, www.timminschamber.on.ca

**Tobermory** • *Tobermory C/C* • Brenda Haythorne, Coord., P.O. Box 250, N0H 2R0, P 1,000, M 85, (519) 596-2452, Fax (519) 596-2452, chamber@tobermory.org, www.tobermory.org

**Toronto** • *Toronto Bd. Of Trade* • Carol Wilding, Pres./CEO, P.O. Box 60, 1 First Canadian Pl., M5X 1C1, P 4,262,199, M 10,000, (416) 366-6811, Fax (416) 366-2483, rrichardson@bot.com, www.bot.com

**Tottenham** • *Tottenham Dist. C/C* • Jill Jones, Gen. Mgr., 4 Mill St. E., P.O. Box 922, L0G 1W0, P 10,000, M 150, (905) 936-4100, (888) 258-4727, Fax (905) 936-4664, tottenhamchamberof commerce@bellnet.ca, www.tottenhamchamber.on.ca

**Trenton** • *Quinte West C/C* • Suzanne Andrews, Mgr., 97 Front St., K8V 4N6, P 43,000, M 350, (613) 392-7635, (800) 930-3255, Fax (613) 392-8400, info@quintewestchamber.on.ca, www. quintewestchamber.on.ca

**Uxbridge** • *Uxbridge Twp. C/C* • Randy Lowewen, Mgr., 2 Campbell Dr., Ste. 810, L9P 0A3, P 18,500, M 112, (905) 852-7683, Fax (905) 852-1352, randy@uxcc.ca, www.uxcc.ca

**Vaughan** • *Vaughan C/C* • Deborah Bonk, CEO, 160 Applewood Crescent, Ste. 32, L4K 4H2, P 255,000, M 976, (905) 761-1366, Fax (905) 761-1918, info@vaughanchamber.ca, www.vaughan chamber.ca

**Walkerton** • *Walkerton & Dist. C/C* • Tracey Cassidy, Mgr., 4 Park St., P.O. Box 1344, N0G 2V0, P 10,000, M 230, (519) 881-3413, (888) 820-9291, Fax (519) 881-4009, chamberinfo@wightman.ca

**Wasaga Beach** • *Wasaga Beach C/C* • Trudie McCrea, Ofc. Mgr., 550 River Rd. W., P.O. Box 394, L9Z 1A4, P 16,000, M 250, (705) 429-2247, (866) 292-7242, Fax (705) 429-1407, info@wasagainfo. com, www.wasagainfo.com

**Waterdown** • *Flamborough C/C* • Arend Kersten, Exec. Dir., P.O. Box 1030, L0R 2H0, P 39,000, M 250, (905) 689-7650, Fax (905) 689-1313, admin@flamboroughchamber.ca, www.flamborough chamber.ca

**Waterloo** • *see Kitchener*

**Wawa** • *Wawa Tourist Info. Center* • P.O. Box 500, P0S 1K0, P 3,600, (705) 856-2244, Fax (705) 856-2120, info@wawa.cc, www.wawa.cc

**Welland** • *Welland/Pelham C/C* • Dolores Fabiano, Exec. Dir., 32 E. Main St., L3B 3W3, P 49,000, M 450, (905) 732-7515, Fax (905) 732-7175, chamber@iaw.on.ca, www.wellandpelhamchamber.com

**Westport** • *Westport & Rideau Lakes C/C* • Colin Horsfal, Pres., 1 Spring St., P.O. Box 157, K0G 1X0, P 2,500, M 110, (613) 273-2929, Fax same, wrlcc@rideau.net, www.westportrideaulakes.on.ca

**Whitby** • *Whitby C/C* • Margot Weir, CEO, 128 Brock St. S., L1N 4J8, P 120,000, M 1,000, (905) 668-4506, Fax (905) 668-1894, info@whitbychamber.org, www.whitbychamber.org

**Windsor** • *Windsor-Essex Reg. C/C* • Linda E. Smith, Pres., 2575 Ouellette Pl., N8X 1L9, P 323,000, M 1,300, (519) 966-3696, Fax (519) 966-0603, info@windsorchamber.org, windsorchamber.org

**Woodbridge** • *see Vaughan*

**Woodstock** • *Woodstock Dist. C/C* • Martha Dennis, Gen. Mgr., 425 Dundas St., Ste. 3, N4S 1B8, P 35,000, M 360, (519) 539-9411, Fax (519) 456-1611, info@woodstockchamber.on.ca, www. woodstockchamber.on.ca

**Young's Point** • *see Lakefield*

# Prince Edward

**Alberton** • *West Prince C/C* • John Lane, Chair, 455 Main St., P.O. Box 220, C0B 1B0, P 1,100, M 50, (902) 853-4555, Fax (902) 853-3298, resourceswest.pe.ca

**Charlottetown** • *Greater Charlottetown Area C/C* • Kathy Hambly, Exec. Dir., 127 Kent St., P.O. Box 67, C1A 7K2, P 42,691, M 850, (902) 628-2000, Fax (902) 368-3570, chamber@charlotte townchamber.com, www.charlottetownchamber.com

**Crapaud** • *South Shore C/C* • Cathie Thomas, Admin., P.O. Box 127, C0A 1J0, P 50,000, M 100, (902) 437-2510, www.southshore chamber.pe.ca

**Kensington** • *Kensington and Area C/C* • Glenna Lohnes, Mgr., P.O. Box 234, C0B 1M0, P 6,000, M 100, (902) 836-3209, kacc@pei. aibn.com, www.kensingtonchamber.com

**Lower Montague** • *Eastern Kings & Queens C/C* • Mary Elliot, 11 Sunset Ln., C0A 1R0, P 137,000, M 1,300, (902) 838-4791, (800) 274-3825, Fax (902) 836-4427, eichamber@yahoo.com

**Summerside** • *Greater Summerside C/C* • John J. MacDonald, Gen. Mgr., 263 Harbour Dr., Ste. 10, C1N 5P1, P 17,000, M 325, (902) 436-9651, Fax (902) 436-8320, info@chamber.summerside. ca, www.chamber.summerside.ca

# Quebec

**Federation des chambres de commerce du Quebec** • Margeurite Saubat, 555 Rene-Levesque Blvd. W., 19th Flr., Montreal, H2Z 1B1, P 6,000,000, M 54,000, (514) 844-9571, Fax (514) 844-0226, www.fccq.ca.

**Alma** • *Chambre de Commerce Lac-Sainte-Jean-Est* • 625, rue Bergeron ouest, G8B 1V3, (418) 662-2734, Fax (418) 669-2220

**Amos** • *Chambre de Commerce D'Amos-Region* • Martin Veilleux, Dir. Gen., C.P. 93, J9T 3A5, (819) 732-8100, Fax (819) 732-8101, ccar@ccar.qc.ca, www.ccar.qc.ca

**Baie-Comeau** • *Chambre de Commerce de Manicouagan* • Danielle Goyette Vaugeois, Exec. Dir., 67 LaSalle Place, Local #302, G4Z 1K1, (418) 296-2010, Fax (418) 296-5397, info@ccmanic. qc.ca, www.ccmanic.qc.ca

**Becancour** • *Chambre de Commerce de Becancour* • 1045 ave. Nicolas Perrot, G9H 3B7, M 302, (819) 294-6010, Fax (819) 294-6020, info@ccibecancour.ca, www.ccibecancour.ca

**Beloeil** • *Vallee du Richelieu C/C* • Johanne Trudeau, Secy., 220, rue Brebeuf, bureau 102, J3G 5P3, (450) 464-3733, Fax (450) 446-4163, chambre@ccvr.qc.ca, www.ccvr.qc.ca

**Coaticook** • *Chambre de Commerce de la Region de Coaticook* • Marco Des Marais, Dir. Gen., 150, rue Child, J1A 2B3, P 9,000, M 250, (819) 849-4733, Fax (819) 849-6828, ccirc@abacom.com, www.ccircoaticook.ca

**Drummondville** • *Chambre de Commerce de Drummond* • Alain Cote, 234 Saint Marcel St., C.P. 188, J2B 6V7, P 80,000, M 1,100, (819) 477-7822, Fax (819) 477-2823, info@ccid.qc.ca, www.ccid.qc.ca

**East-Angus** • *Chambre de Commerce de East Angus et Region* • 288 Maple Ave., J0B 1R0, P 4,000, M 100, (819) 832-4950, Fax (819) 832-2719, ccea@bellnet.ca

**Ferme-Neuve** • *Chambre de Commerce de Ferme Nueve* • Diane Bissonnette, Dir., 125 12th rue, J0W 1C0, (819) 587-3882, Fax (819) 587-2444

**Ile d'Orleans** • *Chambre de Commerce de L'Ile D'Orleans* • Mary Langolis, Dir., 490, Cote du Pont, St-Pierre, G0A 4E0, P 8,000, M 220, (418) 828-0880, Fax (418) 828-2335, www.cciledorleans.com

**Joliette** • *Chambre de Commerce du Grand Joliette* • Yvan Beausejour, Pres., 500, boul Dollar, J6E 4M4, (450) 759-6363, Fax (450) 759-5012, info@ccgj.qc.ca, www.ccgj.qc.ca

**Jonquiere** • *Chambre de Commerce de Jonquiere* • 2240 rue Montpetit, C.P. 211, G7X 6A3, (418) 695-1362

**La Baie** • *Chambre de Commerce & D'Ind. De Ville de la Baie* • 285 Boul. Grande Baie Nord, G7B 3K4, (418) 544-8961, Fax (418) 544-4358

**Lachenaie** • *Chambre de Commerce de Terrebonne/lache-naie* • Robert Lalancette, Dir. Gen., 1025, montee Masson, bureau 301, J6W 5H9, (450) 471-8779, Fax (450) 471-5610, info@ccterrebonne.qc.ca, www.ccterrebonne.qc.ca

**L'Assomption** • *Chambre de Commerce de L'Assomption* • 375 rue st-Pierre, C.P. 3027, J5W 4M9, (450) 589-2405, Fax (450) 589-9213, www.cclassomption.qc.ca

**Laval** • *Chambre de Commerce et D'Industrie de Laval* • 1555, boul. Chomedey, bureau 200, H7V 3Z1, P 286,000, M 2,300, (450) 682-5255, Fax (450) 682-5735, info@ccilaval.qc.ca, www.ccilaval.qc.ca

**Levis** • *Chambre de Commerce de Levis* • Michel Pare, Pres., 4950, boul. de la Rive-Sud, bureau 206, G6V 4Z6, (418) 837-3411, Fax (418) 837-8497, cclevis@cclevis.ca, www.cclevis.ca

**Longueuil** • *Chambre de Commerce et D'Industrie de la Rive-Sud* • Yvon Rudolphe, Pres., 85, rue Saint-Charles Ouest, bureau 101, J4H 1C5, P 400,000, M 1,700, (450) 463-2121, Fax (450) 463-1858, info@ccirs.qc.ca, www.ccirs.qc.ca

**Louiseville** • *Chambre de Commerce Mrc de Maskinonge* • Marc Plante, Gen. Mgr., 255, boul St-Laurent ouest #101, J5V 1K2, P 35,000, M 200, (819) 228-8582, Fax (819) 228-8989, ccmm@cgocable.ca

**Maniwaki** • *Chambre de Commerce et d'Industrie de Maniwaki* • 171, rue Principale Sud, J9E 1Z8, P 5,500, M 200, (819) 449-6627, Fax (819) 449-7667, valerie@ccimki.ca, www.ccimki.ca

**Mascouche** • *Chambre de Commerce de Mascouche* • Robert Filion, Dir. Gen., 2822A, chemin Ste-Marie, Ste. 240, J7K 1N4, P 35,000, M 225, (450) 966-1536, Fax (450) 966-1531, info@ccmascouche.com, www.ccmascouche.com

**Mirabel** • *Chambre de Commerce de Mirabel* • Yves Legault, Pres., 13665, boul. du Cure-Labelle, Ste. 208, J7J 1L2, (450) 433-1944, Fax (450) 433-5168, info@ccmirabel.com, www.ccmirabel.com

**Montreal** • *Board of Trade of Metropolitan Montreal* • Isabelle Hudon, Pres./CEO, 380 St. Antoine St. W. #6000, H2Y 3X7, P 3,000,000, M 7,000, (514) 871-4000, Fax (514) 871-1255, info@ccmm.qc.ca, www.btmm.qc.ca

**Nicolet** • *Chambre de Commerce de Nicolet* • 30, rue Notre-Dame, J3T 1G1, (819) 293-4537, Fax (819) 293-6092, chambre@chambre-cnicolet.org, www.chambre-cnicolet.org

**Normandin** • *Chambre de Commerce du Secteur de Normandin* • Denise Paquet, Dir. Gen., 1048, rue St-Cyrille, G8M 4R9, (418) 274-7206, Fax (418) 274-7171, ccnormandin@hotmail.com

**Pointe-Calumet** • *Chambre de Commerce du Lac Des Deux-Montagnes* • 190, 41st Avenue, Ste. 400, J0N 1G2, (450) 472-7535, Fax (450) 472-0229

**Pointe-Claire** • *West Island of Montreal C/C* • Andree Belanger, Dir. Gen., 207, Place Frontenac, H9R 4Z7, P 350,000, M 1,000, (514) 697-4228, Fax (514) 697-2562, info@ccoim.ca, www.wimcc.ca

**Quebec** • *Chambre de Commerce de Quebec* • Daniel Denis, Pres., 17, rue St-Louis, G1R 3Y8, M 4,000, (418) 692-3853, Fax (418) 694-2286, info@ccquebec.ca, www.ccquebec.ca

**Rimouski** • *Chambre de Commerce de Rimouski-Neigette* • Louis Olivier Carre, Pres., 125, rue de l'Eveche Ouest #101, CP 1296, G5L 8M2, M 350, (418) 722-4494, Fax (418) 722-8402, ccriki@ccrimouski.com, www.ccrimouski.com

**Roberval** • *Chambre de Commerce de Roberval* • Pascal Gagnon, Dir. Gen., C.P. 115, G8H 2N4, P 11,000, M 200, (418) 275-3504, Fax (418) 275-0851, info@ccisr.qc.ca, www.ccisr.qc.ca

**Rouyn-Noranda** • *Chambre de Commerce du Rouyn-Noranda Regional* • Julie Bouchard, Exec. V.P., 225 Blvd. Rideau, C.P. 634, J9X 5Y6, P 40,000, M 1,100, (819) 797-2000, Fax (819) 762-3091, julie.bouchard@ccirn.qc.ca, www.ccirn.qc.ca

**Saint-Jean-de-Matha** • *Chambre de Commerce St-Jean-de-Matha* • Regis Morissette, Pres., 1159 route Louis-Cyr, J0K 2S0, P 3,030, M 52, (450) 886-0599, Fax (450) 886-3123, info@chambrematha.com, www.chambrematha.com

**Saint-Martin-de-Beauce** • *Chambre de Commerce de St-Martin de Beauce* • Serge Thibault, Pres., C.P. 2022, G0M 1B0, P 2,500, M 44, (418) 382-5549, Fax (418) 382-5512, chambre@st-martin.qc.ca, www.st-martin.qc.ca

**Salaberry-de-Valleyfield** • *Chambre de Comm. Reg. de Salaberry-de-Valleyfield* • 100, rue Ste-Cecile, bureau 400, J6T 1M1, (450) 373-8789, Fax (450) 373-8642, info@ccrsv.com, www.ccrsv.com

**Sept Iles** • *Chambre de Commerce de Sept-Iles* • Ginette Lehoux, Gen. Mgr., 700, Boul Laure, bureau 204, G4R 1Y1, P 25,000, M 400, (418) 968-3488, Fax (418) 968-3432, ccsi@globetrotter.net

**Sept-Iles** • *Corporation Touristique de Sept-Iles, Inc.* • Mylene Barbeau, Gen. Mgr., 1401 Blvd. Laure, G4R 4K1, P 29,000, (418) 962-1238, Fax (418) 968-0022, www.ville.septiles.qc.ca

**Sorel** • *Chambre de Commerce Sorel-Tracy Metropolitan* • Rachel Doyon, Gen. Dir., 67 George St., J3P 1C2, (450) 742-0018, Fax (450) 742-7442, ccstm@ccstm.qc.ca, www.ccstm.qc.ca

**St-Donat** • *Tourist Info. Office of St-Donat* • Sophie Charpentier, Dir., 536, rue Principale, J0T 2C0, P 4,300, M , (819) 424-2833, (888) 783-6628, Fax (819) 424-3809, tourisme@saint-donat.com, www.saint-donat.com

**Ste-Agathe-des-Monts** • *Sainte-Agathe-des-Monts C/C* • Daniel Des Jardins, Gen. Mgr., 24, rue St-Paul-Est, C.P. 323, J8C 3C6, P 10,000, M 340, (819) 326-3731, (888) 326-0457, Fax (819) 326-3936, info@sainte-agathe.org, www.sainte-agathe.org

**Ste-Justine** • *Chambre de Commerce de Ste-Justine* • Patrice Pouliot, Pres., 167, Rte. 204, G0R 1Y0, (418) 383-5397, Fax (418) 383-5398, sjustine@sogetel.net, www.stejustine.net

**St-Gabriel-de-Brandon** • *Chambre de Commerce de Brandon* • 151 St. Gabriel, C.P. 778, J0K 2N0, (450) 835-2105, Fax same

**St-Georges** • *Chambre de Commerce de St-Georges* • Brigitte Busque, Pres., 8585, boul Lacroix, bureau 310, G5Y 5L6, (418) 228-7879, Fax (418) 228-8074, www.ccstgeorges.com

**St-Jerome** • *Chambre de Commerce St-Jerome* • Jocelyne Legare, Dir. Gen., 309, rue De Villemure, J7Z 5J5, (450) 431-4339, Fax (450) 431-1677, chambre@ccisj.qc.ca, www.ccisj.qc.ca

**St-Laurent** • *Chambre de Commerce de St-Laurent* • Robert Petit, Gen. Mgr., 935 Decarie, Ste. 204, H4L 3M3, M 840, (514) 333-5222, Fax (514) 333-0937, info@ccstl.qc.ca, www.ccstl.qc.ca

**St-Raymond** • *Chambre de Commerce de St-Raymond* • 100, rue St-Jacques Bureau 1, G3L 3Y1, P 9,000, (418) 337-4049, Fax (418) 337-8017

**Temiscaming** • *Chambre de Commerce de Temiscaming-Kipawa* • 15 Humphrey St., C.P. 442, J0Z 3R0, (819) 627-6160, (819) 627-1846, www.temiscaming.net

**Trois-Rivieres** • *Chambre de Commerce et D'Industries* • Jean-Claude Gendron, Coordonnateur, 168 Bonaventure, P.O. Box 1045, G9A 5K4, P 126,000, M 850, (819) 375-9628, Fax (819) 375-9083, info@ccdtr.com, www.ccdtr.com

**Trois-Rivieres** • *Ofc de Tourisme et des Congres de Trois Rivieres* • 1457, rue Notre Dame center, G9A 4X4, P 125,000, M 150, (819) 375-1122, Fax (819) 375-0022, info@tourismetrois-rivieres.com, www.v3r.net

**Val d'Or** • *Chambre de Commerce de Val d'Or* • Marc Bertrand, Pres., 400, 3rd Ave., J9P 1R9, (819) 825-3703, Fax (819) 825-8599, ccvd@cablevision.qc.ca, www.ccvc.qcc.a

**Weedon** • *Chambre de Commerce de la Region de Weedon* • David Gauthier, Pres., 280 9th Ave., J0B 3J0, (819) 877-5124, Fax (819) 877-1111, chambrede.commerce@qc.aira.com, www.ccweedon.com

# Saskatchewan

**Saskatchewan C/C** • Dale Lemke, Pres., 1630 - 1920 Broad St., Regina, S4P 3V2, P 1,000,000, M 1,500, (306) 352-2671, Fax (306) 781-7084, info@saskchamber.com, www.saskchamber.com

**Aylsham** • *Aylsham & Dist. Bd. of Trade* • Marlene Britton, Secy., P.O. Box 185, S0E 0C0, P 350, M 30, (306) 862-4849, (306) 862-4506, mgbritton@sasktel.net

**Big River** • *Big River & Dist. C/C* • Clarice Hunter, Treas., P.O. Box 763, S0J 0E0, P 800, M 50, (306) 469-4888, Fax (306) 469-4475, www.bigriver.ca

**Broadview** • *Broadview C/C* • Doris Norbeck, Pres., P.O. Box 508, S0G 0K0, P 650, M 32, (306) 696-2533

**Coronach** • *Coronach Comm. C/C* • Jackie Marshall, Pres., P.O. Box 577, S0H 0Z0, P 950, M 26, (306) 267-2077, Fax (306) 267-2047, marshalljackie@hotmail.com

**Cut Knife** • *Cut Knife C/C* • Gwenn Kaye, Pres., P.O. Box 504, S0M 0N0, P 560, M 35, (306) 398-2277

**Eastend** • *Eastend C/C* • Bonnie Gleim, Pres., P.O. Box 534, S0N 0T0, P 650, M 45, (306) 295-3663, (306) 295-3322, www.dinocountry.com

**Esterhazy** • *Esterhazy & Dist. C/C* • P.O. Box 778, S0A 0X0, P 2,800, M 45, (306) 745-5405, Fax (306) 745-6797, esterhazy.ed@sasktel.net

**Estevan** • *Estevan & Dist. Bd. of Tourism, Trade & Commerce* • 1133 4th St., Unit 303, S4A 0W6, P 10,700, M 300, (306) 634-2828, Fax (306) 634-6729, estevanchamber@sasktel.net, www.estevanchamber.ca

**Foam Lake** • *Foam Lake C/C* • Mr. Darcy McLean, P.O. Box 238, S0A 1A0, P 1,300, M 50, (306) 272-3328, www.foamlake.com

**Fort Qu'Appelle** • *Fort Qu'Appelle & Dist. C/C* • P.O. Box 1273, S0G 1S0, P 10,000, M 120, (306) 332-5717, Fax (306) 332-1287, ps.dunk@sasktel.net, www.fortquappelle.com

**Fox Valley** • *Fox Valley C/C* • Delia Hughes, Secy., Railway Box 72, S0N 0V0, P 350, M 45, (306) 666-2139

**Herbert** • *Herbert & Dist. C/C* • Connie Redekop, Pres., Box 190, S0H 2A0, P 840, M 25, (306) 784-2422, (306) 784-2510

**Humboldt** • *Humboldt & Dist. C/C* • Donna Lynn Dyok, Exec. Dir., Hwy. 5 E., Box 1440, S0K 2A0, P 5,700, M 160, (306) 682-4990, Fax (306) 682-5203, humboldtchamber@sasktel.net, www.humboldtchamber.ca

**Kenaston** • *Kenaston & Dist. C/C* • ML Whittles, Pres., P.O. Box 386, S0G 2N0, P 320, M 28, (306) 252-2236, www.kenaston.sasktelwebsite.net

**Kerrobert** • *Kerrobert C/C* • P.O. Box 408, S0L 1R0, P 1,111, M 45, (306) 834-2361, kerrobert@sasktel.net, www.kerrobert.com

**La Ronge** • *La Ronge & Dist. C/C* • Bill Hogan, Pres., P.O. Box 1046, S0J 1L0, P 6,800, M 100, (306) 425-2612

**Langenburg** • *Langenburg C/C* • P.O. Box 610, S0A 2A0, P 1,200, M 55, (306) 743-2231, Fax (306) 743-2873

**Maple Creek** • *Maple Creek C/C* • P.O. Box 1776, S0N 1N0, P 2,609, M 35, (306) 622-3133

**Meadow Lake** • *Meadow Lake & Dist. C/C* • P.O. Box 1168, S9X 1Y8, P 6,000, M 120, (306) 236-4447, Fax (306) 236-4487, mltouristinfo@sasktel.net, www.nwreda.ca

**Melfort** • *Melfort & Dist. C/C* • Lori Fettes, Mgr., P.O. Box 2002, S0E 1A0, P 7,000, M 145, (306) 752-4636, Fax (306) 752-9505, melfortchamber@sasktel.net, www.melfortchamber.com

**Melville** • *Melville & Dist. C/C* • 420 Main St., P.O. Box 429, S0A 2P0, P 4,700, M 62, (306) 728-4177, Fax (306) 728-5911, melvillechamber@sasktel.net, www.melvillechamber.com

**Moose Jaw** • *Moose Jaw C/C* • Brian Martynook, Exec. Dir., 88 Saskatchewan St. E., S6H 0V4, P 35,000, M 490, (306) 692-6414, Fax (306) 694-6463, chamber@mjchamber.com, www.mjchamber.com

**Moosomin** • *Moosomin C/C* • Kevin Weedmark, Pres., P.O. Box 819, S0G 3N0, P 2,300, M 100, (306) 435-2445, Fax (306) 435-2540, world_spectator@sasktel.net

**Nipawin** • *Nipawin & Dist. C/C* • Cindy Murphy, Exec. Dir., P.O. Box 177, S0E 1E0, P 5,000, M 195, (306) 862-5252, Fax (306) 862-5350, nipawin.chamber@sasktel.net, www.nipawinchamber.ca

**Norquay** • *Norquay & Dist. C/C* • P.O. Box 457, S0A 2V0, P 600, M 35, (306) 594-2324, Fax (306) 594-2028, dwaynedahl@sasktel.net, www.townofnorquay.ca

**North Battleford** • *Battlefords C/C* • Linda Machniak, Exec. Dir., P.O. Box 1000, S9A 3E6, P 60,000, M 353, (306) 445-6226, Fax (306) 445-6633, b.chamber@sasktel.net, www.battlefordschamber.com.

Canadian C/C

**Outlook** · *Outlook & Dist. C/C* · Ken Fehr, P.O. Box 431, S0L 2N0, P 2,500, M 55, (306) 867-2083, Fax (306) 867-2084, www.town. outlook.sk.ca/chamber.htm

**Prince Albert** · *Prince Albert & Dist. C/C* · Lyn Brown, CEO, 3700 2nd Ave. W., S6W 1A2, P 45,000, M 520, (306) 764-6222, Fax (306) 922-4727, pachamber@sasktel.net, www.princealbert chamber.com

**Redvers** · *Redvers C/C* · P.O. Box 249, S0C 2H0, P 917, M 47, (306) 452-3155, Fax (306) 452-3155, rrace@sasktel.net, www. townofredvers.ca

**Regina** · *Regina C/C* · John Hopkins, CEO, 2145 Albert St., S4P 2V1, P 199,974, M 1,088, (306) 757-4658, Fax (306) 757-4668, info@reginachamber.com, www.reginachamber.com

**Saint Walburg** · *St. Walburg C/C* · Susan Hamm, Secy., P.O. Box 501, S0M 2T0, P 800, M 45, (306) 248-3223, townofstwalburg@ sasktel.net, www.stwalburg.com

**Saskatoon** · *Greater Saskatoon C/C* · Kent Smith-Windsor, Exec. Dir., 104-202 4th Ave. N., S7K 0K1, P 215,000, M 1,600, (306) 244-2151, Fax (306) 244-8366, chamber@eboardoftrade.com, www. eboardoftrade.com.

**Shaunavon** · *Shaunavon C/C* · Joan Gregoire, Pres., P.O. Box 1048, S0N 2M0, P 1,800, M 70, (306) 297-2412, shaunavon chamber@hotmail.com, www.shaunavon.com

**Spiritwood** · *Spiritwood & Dist. C/C* · Wayne Reed, P.O. Box 267, S0J 2M0, P 900, M 116, (306) 883-2267, Fax (306) 883-2136, town.of.spiritwood@sasktel.net, www.townofspiritwood.ca

**Swift Current** · *Swift Current C/C* · Jennifer Lyster, Interim Dir., 885 6th Ave. N.E., S9H 2M9, P 16,800, M 425, (306) 773-7268, Fax (306) 773-5686, info@swiftcurrentchamber.ca, www.swift currentchamber.ca.

**Tisdale** · *Tisdale & Dist. C/C* · 918 93rd Ave. W., P.O. Box 219, S0E 1T0, P 8,000, M 110, (306) 873-4257, Fax (306) 873-4241, tisdalechamber@sasktel.net, www.townoftisdale.com

**Turtleford** · *Turtleford C/C* · Guy Patenaude, Pres., P.O. Box 580, S0M 2Y0, P 480, M 20, (306) 845-2081

**Watrous** · *Watrous & Dist. C/C* · Kristie Pilling, Treas., P.O. Box 906, S0K 4T0, P 1,808, M 60, (306) 946-3369, www.town ofwatrous.com

**Watson** · *Watson & Dist. C/C* · Debbie Schwartz, Treas., P.O. Box 686, S0K 4V0, P 800, M 50, (306) 287-3224, (306) 287-3636

**Weyburn** · *Weyburn C/C* · Jeff Richards, Mgr., 11 Third St. N.E., S4H 0W5, P 10,000, M 140, (306) 842-4738, Fax (306) 842-0520, manager@weyburnchamber.com, www.weyburnchamber.com

**Wynyard** · *Wynyard & Dist. C/C* · Nancy Pitzel, V.P., P.O, Box 508, S0A 4T0, P 2,000, M 75, (306) 554-2224, Fax (306) 554-3226

**Yorkton** · *Good Spirit Reda Eco. Dev. Inc..* · Phil DeVos, Gen. Mgr., 23D Smith St. W., S3N 0H9, P 17,000, (306) 783-7332, Fax (306) 783-0165, office@goodspiritreda.net, www.goodspiritreda.net

**Yorkton** · *Yorkton C/C* · Juanita Polegi, Exec. Dir., P.O. Box 1051, S3N 2X3, P 20,000, M 450, (306) 783-4368, Fax (306) 786-6978, office@chamber.yorkton.sk.ca, www.chamber.yorkton.sk.ca

# Yukon

**Yukon C/C** · J.D. Austin, Pres./CEO, 307 Jarvis St., Ste. 101, Whitehorse, Y1A 2H3, P 30,000, M 130, (867) 667-2000, Fax (867) 667-2001, ycc@yukonchamber.com, www.yukonchamber.com

**Dawson City** · *Dawson City C/C* · Cheryl Thompson, P.O. Box 1006, Y0B 1G0, P 2,000, M 135, (867) 993-5274, Fax (867) 993-6817, dccc@dawson.net, www.dawson.net

**Whitehorse** · *Whitehorse C/C* · Rick Karp, Pres., 101 - 302 Steele St., Y1A 2C5, P 24,000, M 350, (867) 667-7545, Fax (867) 667-4507, business@whitehorsechamber.ca, www.whitehorse chamber.ca

# American Chambers of Commerce Abroad

American Chambers of Commerce Abroad are voluntary associations of American enterprises and individuals doing business in a particular country, as well as firms and individuals of that country who operate in the U.S.

Along with pursuing trade policy initiatives, AmChams make available publications and services and sponsor a variety of business development programs. The AmChams represent the concerns and interests of the business community at the highest levels of government and business in trade policy development.

AmChams also:

- Develop mutually prosperous and amicable economic, social and commercial relations between U.S. businesses and service industries, and those of the host country.

- Represent members' views on policy and regulatory matters to both U.S. and host country governments, and interpret the point of view of other countries to the American business public.

- Promote local economic and social contributions for the benefit of host countries.

## Albania

**Tirana** · *American Chamber of Commerce in Albania* · Floreta Luli-Faber, Exec. Dir., Rr. Deshmoret e 4 Shkurtit, Sky Tower, Kati II, Ap 3, M 200, 355-42-259779, Fax 355-42-235350, info@amcham.com.al, www.amcham.com.al

## Argentina

**Buenos Aires** · *American Chamber of Commerce in Argentina* · Alejandro Diaz, CEO, Viamonte 1133, Piso 8, 1053, M 600, 5411-4371-4500, Fax 5411-4371-8400, amcham@amchamar.com.ar, www.amchamar.com.ar

## Armenia

**Yerevan** · *American Chamber of Commerce in Armenia* · Elen Ghazarian, Exec. Dir., Marriott Armenia Hotel Rm. 313, 1 Amiryan Street, 374-10-599187, Fax 374-10-599256, amcham@arminco.com, www.amcham.am

## Asia

**Philippines** · *Asia-Pacific Cncl. Of American Chambers of Comm* · Kristin E. Paulson, Chrmn., % Marsman Drysdale Group, Penthouse, 8767 Paseo de Roxas, Makati City, 1200, 632-89-30000, Fax 632-89-30999, www.apcac.org

## Australia

**Sydney, NSW** · *American Chamber of Commerce in Australia* · Charles Blunt, CEO, 88 Cumberland St. #4, 2000, M 700, 812-92-411907, Fax 612-92-515220, ceo@amcham.com.au, www.amcham.com.au

## Austria

**Vienna** · *American Chamber of Commerce in Austria* · Dr. Patricia A. Helletzgruber, Exec. Dir., Porzellangasse 35, A-1090, M 500, 431-31-95751, Fax 431-31-95151, office@amcham.at, www.amcham.or.at

## Bahrain

**Manama** · *American Chamber of Commerce Bahrain* · Lynn Thorvilson, V.P. of Programs, P.O. Box 20451, 973-17-580516, Fax 973-17-580035, info@amcham-bahrain.org, www.amcham-bahrain.org

## Bangladesh

**Dhaka** · *American Chamber of Commerce in Bangladesh* · A. Garfur, Exec. Dir., Room No. 319, Dhaka Sheraton Hotel, 880-28-330001, Fax 880-29-349217, amcham@amchambd.org, www.amchambd.org

## Belgium

**Brussels** · *American Chamber of Commerce in Belgium* · Scott Beardsley, Pres., Rue du commerce 39-41, Handelsstraat, B-1000, M 875, 322-51-36770, Fax 322-51-33590, gchamber@amcham.be, www.amcham.be

## Bolivia

**La Paz** · *American Chamber of Commerce of Bolivia* · Anna Maria Galindo, Gen. Mgr., Avenida 6 de Agosto N 2455, Edificio Belisario Salinas y Pedro Salazar, M 140, 591-22-443939, Fax 591-22-443972, amchambo@entelnet.bo, www.amchambolivia.com

## Brazil

**Rio de Janeiro** · *American Chamber of Commerce for Brazil-Rio de Janiero* · Ricardo de Albuquerque Mayer, Exec. Dir., Praca Pio X, 15, 5th Flr., 20040-020, M 600, 55-21-32139206, Fax 55-21-22230438, vanessabarros@amchamrio.com, www.amchamrio.com.br

**Sao Paulo, S.P.** · *American Chamber of Commerce for Brazil-Sao Paulo* · Gabriel Rico, CEO, Chacara Santo Antonio, Rua da Paz, no. 1431, 04713-001, M 2,700, 55-11-51803618, Fax 55-11-51803719, amhost@amcham.com.br, www.amcham.com.br

# Bulgaria

**Sofia** · *American Chamber of Commerce in Bulgaria* · Valentin Georgiev, Exec. Dir., Business Park Sofia, Mladost 4 area, Bldg. 2, Flr. 6, 1766, M 200, 359-29-742743, Fax 359-29-742741, amcham@amcham.bg, www.amcham.bg.

# Cambodia

**Phnom Penh** · *American Cambodian Bus. Cncl.* · Bretton G. Sciaroni, Chrmn., No. 56 Samdech Sothearos Blvd, Khan Daun Penh, 855-23-210225, Fax 855-23-213089

# Canada

**Peterborough** · *American Chamber of Commerce in Canada* · Robert Bathgate, Pres./CEO, 650 Parkhill Road W., PH # 3, Ontario, K9J 6N6, 416-77-78512, Fax info@amchamcanada.ca, www. amchamcanada.ca

# Chile

**Santiago** · *Chilean-American Chamber of Commerce* · Jaime Bazan, CEO, Av. Pdte. Kennedy 5735, Of. 201, Piso 2, Torre Poniente, Las Condes, M 1,200, 562-29-09700, Fax 562-21-20515, amcham@amchamchile.cl, www.amchamchile.cl

# China

**Beijing** · *American Chamber of Commerce PRC Beijing* · John Watkins, Chrmn., China Resources Bldg. #1903, 8 Jianguomenbei, 100005, M 600, 86-10-85190800, Fax 86-10-85191910, amcham@ amcham-china.org.cn, www.amcham-china.org.cn

**Guangzhou** · *American Chamber of Commerce in South China* · Harley Seyedin, Pres., M-1603 Guangdong Intl. Hotel, 339 Huanshi Dong Rd. East, 510098, M 300, 86-20-83351476, Fax 86-20-83321642, amcham@amcham-southchina.org, www. amcham-southchina.org

**Shanghai** · *American Chamber of Commerce in Shanghai* · J. Norwell Coquillard, Chrmn., Shanghai Centre #568, 1376 Nanjing Rd. W., 200040, M 1,900, 86-21-62797119, Fax 86-21-62797643, info@amcham-shanghai.org, www.amcham-shanghai.org

# Colombia

**Bogota** · *Colombian-American Chamber of Commerce* · Miguel Gomez Martinez, Exec. Dir., Calle 98 #22-64 Ofc. 1209, PO Box 8008, M 400, 571-62-37088, Fax 571-62-16838, direct@ amchamcolombia.com.co, www.amchamcolombia.com.co

# Costa Rica

**San Jose** · *Costa Rican-American Chamber of Commerce* · Lynda Solar Hartley, Gen. Mgr., Apdo. Postal 4946, 1000, M 400, 506-22-202200, Fax 506-22-202300, chamber@amcham.co.cr, www.amcham.co.cr

# Cote d'Ivoire

**Abidjan** · *American Chamber of Commerce Cote d'Ivoire* · Riviera Attoban, BP 2282, 6, 225-22-426866, Fax 225-22-423064, amchamci@amchamci.org, amchamci.org

# Croatia

**Zagreb** · *American Chamber of Commerce in Croatia* · Damir Vucic, Exec. Dir., Radnicka 47, 10000, 385-14-836777, Fax 385-14-836776, info@amcham.hr, www.amcham.hr

# Cyprus

**Nicosia** · *Cyprus-American Bus. Assn.* · P.O. Box 21455, CY-1509, 357-22-889830, Fax 357-22-668630, cyaba@cyaba.com. cy, www.cyaba.com.cy

# Czech Republic

**Prague** · *American Chamber of Commerce in the Czech Republic* · Weston Stacey, Exec. Dir., Dusni 10, CZ-11000, M 350, 420-2-22329430, Fax 420-2-22329433, amcham@amcham.cz, www.amcham.cz

# Denmark

**Copenhagen** · *American Chamber of Commerce in Denmark* · Stephen Brugger, Exec. Dir., Christians Brygge 26, DK-1559, 453-39-32932, Fax 453-31-30517, mail@amcham.dk, www.amcham.dk

# Dominican Republic

**Santo Domingo** · *American Chamber of Commerce of the Dominican Republic* · William Malamud, Exec. V.P., Avenida Sarasota No. 20, Torre Empresearial 6to. Piso, M 3,000, 809-38-10777, Fax 809-38-10286, wmalamud@amcham.org.do, www. amcham.org.do

# Ecuador

**Guayaquil** · *Ecuadorian-American Chamber of Commerce-Guayaquil* · Jorge Farah, Exec. Dir., Ave. Francisco de Orellana y Alberto Borges, Edificio Centrum, Piso 6, Oficina 5, M 500, 593-42-693470, Fax 593-42-693465, director@amchamecuador.org, www. amchamecuador.org

**Quito** · *Ecuadorian-American Chamber of Commerce-Quito* · Bernardo Traversari, Exec. Dir., Edif. Multicentro 4P, La Nina y Avda. 6 de Diciembre, M 800, 593-22-507450, Fax 593-22-504571, info@ecamcham.com, www.ecamcham.com

# Egypt

**Cairo** · *American Chamber of Commerce in Egypt* · Hisham Fahmy, Exec. Dir., 33 Soliman Abaza St., Dokki-Giza, 12311, M 600, 202-33-381050, Fax 202-33-381060, infocenter@amcham.org.eg, www.amcham.org.eg

# El Salvador

**San Salvador** · *American Chamber of Commerce of El Salvador* · Carmen Aida Munoz, Exec. Dir., World Trade Center Torre II Local 308, 89 Avendia Norte, Colonia Escalon, M 397, 503-22-639494, Fax 503-22-639393, contact@amchamsal.com, www.amchamsal.com

# European Union

**Brussels, Belgium** · *American Chamber of Commerce to the European Union* · Susan Danger, Exec. Dir., Ave. des Arts/Kunstlaan 53, Box 5, 1000, 322-51-36892, Fax 322-51-37928, sdanger@amcham.be, www.eucommittee.be

# Finland

**Helsinki** · *American Chamber of Commerce in Finland* · Kristiina Helenius, Mgr. Dir., Annankatu 32, 7th Flr., 100, 358-451335028, Fax 358-96-75387, kristiina.helenius@amcham.fi, www.amcham.fi

# France

**Paris** · *American Chamber of Commerce in France* · Oliver Griffith, Mgr. Dir., 156 boulevard Haussmann, F-75008, M 500, 331-56-434561, Fax 331-56-434560, amchamfrance@amcham-france.org, www.amchamfrance.org

# Georgia

**Tbilisi** · *American Chamber of Commerce in Georgia* · Amy Denman, Exec. Dir., 1 Nutsubidze St., 177, M 80, 995-32-251437, Fax 995-32-250495, adenman@amcham.ge, www.amcham.ge

# Germany

**Frankfurt** · *American Chamber of Commerce in Germany* · Dierk Muller, Gen. Mgr., Borsenplatz 7-11, D-60313, M 3,000, 496-99-291040, Fax 49-69-92910411, info@amcham.de, www.amcham.de

# Ghana

**Cantonments-Accra** · *American Chamber of Commerce in Ghana* · Victoria Cooper-Enchia, Pres., P.O. Box CT 2869, M 70, 233-21-247562, Fax 233-21-780919, info@amchamghana.org, www.amchamghana.org

# Greece

**Athens** · *American-Hellenic Chamber of Commerce* · Exec. Dir., 109-111 Messoghion Ave., Politia Business Center, GR-115 26, M 1,000, 30-210-699-3559, Fax 30-210-698-5687, info@amcham.gr, www.amcham.gr

# Guatemala

**Guatamala City** · *American Chamber of Commerce in Guatemala* · Carolina Castellanos, Exec. Dir., 5a ave. 5-55 zona 14, Torre I, Europlaza, Nivel 5, 1014, M 450, 502-23-333899, Fax 502-23-683536, trade@amchamguate.com, www.amchamguate.com

# Haiti

**Delmas** · *American Chamber of Commerce & Ind. in Haiti* · Marline Lamothe, CEO, P.O. Box 13486, 509-51-13024, marline lamothe@yahoo.com, www.amchamhaiti.org

# Honduras

**Tegucigalpa** · *Honduran-American Chamber of Commerce* · Reyna Patricia Lopez, Exec. Dir., Apdo. Postal 1838, M 540, 504-23-27043, Fax 504-23-22031, plopez@amchamhonduras.org, www.amchamhonduras.org

# Hong Kong (China)

**Hong Kong** · *American Chamber of Commerce in Hong Kong* · Steve De Krey, Chrmn., 1904 Bank of America Tower, 12 Harcourt Rd., Central, M 2,000, 852-25-306900, Fax 852-28-101289, amcham@amcham.org.hk, www.amcham.org.hk

# Hungary

**Budapest** · *American Chamber of Commerce in Hungary* · Peter David, Exec. Dir., Szent Istvan ter 11., H-1051, M 570, 361-26-69880, Fax 361-26-69888, info@amcham.hu, www.amcham.hu

# India

**New Delhi** · *American Chamber of Commerce in India* · Ajay Singha, Exec. Dir., PHD House, 4th Flr., 4/2, Siri Institutional Area, August Kranti Marg, 110016, M 261, 91-11-26109471, Fax 91-11-26109106, amcham@amchamindia.com, www.amchamindia.com

# Indonesia

**Jakarta** · *American Chamber of Commerce in Indonesia* · Mark Smith, Dir., World Trade Centre 11th Flr., Jl. Jend Sudirman Kav 29-31, 12920, M 430, 622-15-262860, Fax 622-15-262861, director@amcham.or.id, www.amcham.or.id

# Iraq

**Baghdad** · *American Chamber of Commerce in Iraq* · Timothy Mills, Pres., #316 Ishtar Sheraton Hotel & Towers, 964-790-1351894, events@amchamiraq.com, www.amchamiraq.com

# Ireland

**Dublin** · *American Chamber of Commerce of Ireland* · Joanne Richardson, CEO, 6 Wilton Pl., 2, M 340, 353-16-616201, Fax 353-16-616217, info@amcham.ie, www.amcham.ie

# Israel

**Tel Aviv** · *Israel-America Chamber of Commerce* · Tamar Guy, Exec. Dir., 35 Shaul Hamelech Blvd., PO Box 33174, IL-61333, M 700, 972-36-952341, Fax 972-36-951272, amcham@amcham.co.il, www.amcham.co.il

# Italy

**Milano** · *American Chamber of Commerce in Italy* · Simone Crolla, Via Cantu 1, I-20123, M 1,000, 390-28-690661, Fax 390-28-057737, amcham@amcham.it, www.amcham.it

# Ivory Coast

*See Cote d'Ivoire*

**U.S. C/C Abroad**

# Jamaica

**Kingston** · *American Chamber of Commerce of Jamaica* · Becky Stockhausen, CEO, 81 Knutsford Blvd., Rm. 127, 5, M 189, 876-92-97866, Fax 876-92-98597, amcham@cwjamaica.com, www.amchamjamaica.org

# Japan

**Okinawa** · *American Chamber of Commerce in Okinawa* · Justin Wentworth, Exec. Dir., 1-10-27 Oyama, Ste. 2A, 901-2223, M 115, 819-88-985401, Fax 819-88-985411, admin@accokinawa. org, www.accokinawa.org

**Tokyo** · *American Chamber of Commerce in Japan* · Samuel Kidder, Exec. Dir., Masonic 39, MT Bldg. 10F, 2-4-5 Azabudai, Minato-ku, 106-0041, M 3,028, 813-34-335381, Fax 813-34-368454, info@accj.or.jp, www.accj.or.jp

# Jordan

**Amman** · *American Chamber of Commerce in Jordan* · Abeer Al-Refai, CEO, PO Box 840817, 11184, M 340, 962-65-651860, Fax 962-65-651862, inquiries@amcham.jo, www.amcham.jo

# Kenya

**Nairobi** · *American Chamber of Commerce of Kenya* · P. O. Box 9746-00100, 254-02-6750721, Fax 254-02-3750448, info@ acck.org, www.acck.org

# Korea

**Seoul** · *American Chamber of Commerce in Korea* · David Ruch, Chrmn., #4501, Korea Trade Center, 159-1, Samsung-dong, Kangnam-ku, 135-729, M 2,100, 822-56-42040, Fax 822-56-42050, info@amchamkorea.org, www.amchamkorea.org

# Kosovo

**Prishtina** · *American Chamber of Commerce in Kosovo* · Mimoza Kusari-Lila, Exec. Dir., Gustav Majer #6, 10000, 381-38-246012, Fax 381-38-248012, info@amchamksv.org, www. amchamksv.org

# Kuwait

**Safat** · *American Business Council of Kuwait* · Muna Al Fuzai, Exec. Dir., P.O. Box 29992, 13159, 965-93-37142, Fax muna@ abckw.org, www.abckw.org

# Kyrgyz Republic

**Bishkek** · *American Chamber of Commerce in the Kyrgyz Republic* · Ainura Cholponkulova, Exec. Dir., 191 Sovetskaya, Ofc. #123, 720011, 996-312-680907, Fax 996-312-681172, www. amcham.kg

# Latvia

**Riga** · *American Chamber of Commerce in Latvia* · Liga Bertulsone, Exec. Dir., Torna 4 IIA-301, LV-1050, M 110, 371-72-12204, Fax 371-72-12204, amcham@amcham.lv, www.amcham.lv

# Lebanon

**Beruit** · *American Lebanese Chamber of Commerce* · Salim Zeenni, Pres., P.O. Box 175093, M 200, 961-19-85330, Fax 961-19-85331, info@amcham.org.lb, www.amcham.org.lb

# Lithuania

**Vilnius** · *American Chamber of Commerce in Lithuania* · Aiste Andziuleviciute, Exec. Dir., Lukiskiu 5, Rm. 204, LT-01108, M 72, 370-52-611181, Fax 370-52-126128, acc@iti.lt, www.acc.lt

# Luxembourg

**Luxembourg** · *American Chamber of Commerce in Luxembourg* · Margot Parra, Mktg. Dir., 6 rue Antoine de St-Exupery, BP 542, L-1432, M 118, 35-24-31756, Fax 352-26-094704, info@amcham.lu, www. amcham.lu

# Macedonia

**Skopje** · *American Chamber of Commerce in Macedonia* · Michelle Osmanli, Exec. Dir., Mitropolit T. Gologanov 42, Flr. 3, 1000, 389-23-216714, Fax 389-23-135441, Sharon@amcham.com. mk, amcham.com.mk

# Malaysia

**Kuala Lumpur** · *American Malaysian Chamber of Commerce* · Valerie McDonough, Exec. Dir., 22 Jalan Imbi, AMODA Bldg., 11.03-11.05 Level 11, 55100, M 350, 603-21-482407, Fax 603-21-428540, info@amcham.com.my, www.amcham.com.my

# Mexico

**Mexico, DF** · *American Chamber of Commerce of Mexico, A.C.* · Guillermo Wolf, Dir., Lucerna 78, Col. Juarez, 6600, M 2,500, 52-55-51413820, Fax 52-55-51413836, amchammx@amcham. com.mx, www.amcham.com.mx

# Netherlands

**Amsterdam** · *American Chamber of Commerce in the Netherlands* · Riette Blacquiere, Exec. Dir., WTC D-tower, 6th Floor, Schiphol Blvd. 171, NL-1118 BG, M 1,000, 312-07-951848, Fax 312-07-951850, office@amcham.nl, www.amcham.nl

# New Zealand

**Auckland** · *American Chamber of Commerce in New Zealand* · Mike Hearn, Exec. Dir., P.O. Box 106002, 1001, M 300, 649-30-99140, Fax 649-30-91090, amcham@amcham.co.nz, www. amcham.co.nz

# Nicaragua

**Managua** · *American Chamber of Commerce of Nicaragua* · Avil Ramirez, Exec. Dir., Apdo. Postal 2720, M 160, 505-26-73099, Fax 505-26-73098, publicrelations@amcham.org.ni, www. amcham.org.ni

# Norway

**Oslo** · *American Chamber of Commerce in Norway* · Jason Turflinger, Mgr. Dir., Lille Grensen 5, N-0159, M 150, 472-24-15010, Fax 472-24-15011, amcham@amcham.no, www.amcham.no

# Pakistan

**Karachi** · *American Business Council of Pakistan* · Amer Mirza, Exec. Dir., GPO Box 1322, 74400, 922-15-676436, Fax 922-15-660135, abcpak@cyber.net.pk, www.abcpk.org.pk

# Panama

**Panama** · *American Chamber of Commerce & Ind. of Panama* · David Hunt, Exec. Dir., Apdo. 0843-00152, M 385, 507-30-13881, Fax 507-30-13882, amcham@panamcham.com, www.panamcham.com

# Paraguay

**Asuncion** · *Paraguayan-American Chamber of Commerce* · Gerald McCulloch, Exec. Dir., 25 de mayo #2090 and Mayor Bullo, M 375, 595-21-221926, Fax 595-21-222265, pamcham@pamcham.com.py, www.pamcham.com.py

# Peru

**Lima** · *American Chamber of Commerce of Peru* · Aldo Defilippi, Exec. Dir., Av. Victor Andres Belaunde 157, San Isidro, 27, M 450, 511-24-14317, Fax 511-24-10709, info@amcham.org.pe, www.amcham.org.pe

# Philippines

**Manila** · *American Chamber of Commerce of the Philippines* · Robert W. Sears, Exec. V.P., 2nd Flr., Corinthian Plaza Bldg., Paseo De Roxas, Makati City, 1229, M 651, 632-81-87911, Fax 632-81-13081, amchamrp@mozcom.com, www.amchamphilippines.com

# Poland

**Warsaw** · *American Chamber of Commerce in Poland* · Dorothy Dabrowska, Exec. Dir., Warsaw Financial Center, ul. Emilii Plater 53, PL-00-113, M 300, 482-25-205999, Fax 482-25-205998, office@amcham.com.pl, www.amcham.com.pl

# Portugal

**Lisbon** · *American Chamber of Commerce in Portugal* · Graca Didier, Exec. Dir., Rua D. Estefania 155, 5 Esq, P-1000-154, M 650, 351-213-572561, Fax 351-213-572580

# Romania

**Bucharest** · *American Chamber of Commerce in Romania* · Anca Harasim, Exec. Dir., 11 Ion Cimpineanu Str. Sector 1, Union International Center, RO-010031, M 120, 402-13-124834, Fax 402-13-124851, harasim@amcham.ro, www.amcham.ro

# Russia

**Moscow** · *American Chamber of Commerce in Russia* · Andrew Somers, Pres., Dolgorukovskaya ul. 7, 14th Flr., Sadovaya Plaza, RU-127006, M 750, 749-59-612141, Fax 749-59-612142, info@amcham.ru, www.amcham.ru

# Saudi Arabia

**Al-Khobar** · *American Business Association, Eastern Province* · David Cantrell, Pres., P.O. Box 3672, 31952, M 470, 966-38-825288, Fax 966-38-825288, abaep@abaksa.org, www.abaksa.org

**Jeddah** · *American Businessmen of Jeddah* · Michelle Abboud, Ofc. Mgr., % Intercontinental Jeddah, P.O. Box 8483, 21482, M 250, 966-26-634784, Fax 966-26-522284

# Serbia & Montenegro

**Belgrade** · *American Chamber of Commerce in Serbia & Montenegro* · Bojana Ristic, Exec. Dir., Vlajkoviceva 30/III/10, 11000, 381-11-3345961, Fax 381-11-3247771, info@amcham.yu, www.amcham.yu

# Singapore

**Singapore** · *American Chamber of Commerce in Singapore* · Dom LaVigne, Exec. Dir., 1 Scotts Rd., #23-03/04 Shaw Centre, 228208, M 2,500, 656-23-50077, Fax 656-73-25917, info@amcham.org.sg, www.amcham.org.sg

# Slovak Republic

**Bratislava** · *American Chamber of Commerce in the Slovak Republic* · Jake Slegers, Exec. Dir., Hotel Crowne Plaza, Hodzovo nam. 2, 82206, M 250, 421-2-54640534, Fax 421-2-59340556, office@amcham.sk, www.amcham.sk

# Slovenia

**Ljubljana** · *American Chamber of Commerce in Slovenia* · Janez Moder, Exec. Dir., Por Hribom 55, SLO-1000, M 75, 386-15-816285, Fax 386-15-816287, office@amcham.si, www.amcham.si

# South Africa

**Houghton, Johannesburg** · *American Chamber of Commerce in South Africa* · Carol O'Brien, Exec. Dir., P.O. Box 1132, 2041, M 190, 7880265, Fax 8801632, admin@amcham.co.za, amcham.co.za

# Spain

**Barcelona** · *American Chamber of Commerce in Spain* · Glynis Andrews, Exec. Dir., Tuset 8, Entlo. 3a, E-08006, M 600, 349-34-159963, Fax 349-34-151198, info@amchamspain.com, www.amchamspain.com

# Sri Lanka

**Colombo** · *American Chamber of Commerce in Sri Lanka* · Chullante Jayasuriya, Exec. Dir., 1st Flr., Ofc. Bldg. South Wing, Colombo Hilton Hotel, Lotus Rd., 1, M 400, 941-12-336073, Fax 941-12-336072, info@amcham.lk, www.amcham.lk

U.S. C/C Abroad

# Sweden

**Stockholm** · *American Chamber of Commerce in Sweden* · Berit Salheim, Mgr. Dir., PO Box 16050, S-10321, 468-50-612610, Fax 468-50-612613, amcham@chamber.se, www.amchamswe.se

# Switzerland

**Zurich** · *Swiss-American Chamber of Commerce* · Martin Naville, CEO, Talacker 41, CH-8001, M 2,300, 414-34-437201, Fax 414-34-972270, info@amcham.ch, www.amcham.ch

# Taiwan, ROC

**Taipei** · *American Chamber of Commerce in Taipei* · Andrea Wu, Pres., Minsheng E. Road, Sec. 3, #129, Suite 706, 10596, M 980, 886-2-27188226, Fax 886-2-27188182, amcham@amcham.com.tw, www.amcham.com.tw

# Thailand

**Bangkok** · *American Chamber of Commerce in Thailand* · Judy Benn, Exec. Dir., 93/1 Diethelm Tower A, 7th Flr., Wireless Rd., Lumpini, Pathumwan, 10330, M 600, 660-22-541041, Fax 660-22-511605, service@amchamthailand.com, www.amchamthailand.com

# Trinidad & Tobago

**Port of Spain** · *American Chamber of Commerce of Trinidad & Tobago* · Desiree Gobin-Seecharan, Exec. Dir., 62A Maraval Rd., M 290, 868-62-24466, Fax 868-62-89428, inbox@amchamtt.com, www.amchamtt.com

# Turkey

**Istanbul** · *Turkish-American Bus. Assn.* · Senem Artun, Financial & Admin. Mgr., Buyukdere Caddesi #18, Tankaya apt. Kat. 7 20 Sisli, TR-34360, M 650, 90-212-2910916, Fax 90-212-2910645, senemartun@amcham.org, www.amcham.org.

# Ukraine

**Kyiv** · *American Chamber of Commerce in Ukraine* · Jorge Zukoski, Pres., 42/44 Shovkovychna Street, LL1 Flr., 1601, M 569, 380-44-490-5800, Fax 380-44-490-5801, chamber@chamber.ua, www.amcham.kiev.ua

# United Arab Emirates

**Dubai** · *American Bus. Cncl. Of Dubai & the Northern Emirates* · Cara Nazari, Exec. Dir., P.O. Box 9281, M 540, 971-43-407566, Fax 971-43-407565, admin@abcdubai.com, www.abcdubai.com

# United Kingdom

**London** · *BritishAmerican Business* · Peter Hunt, Mgr., 75 Brook St., W1K 4AD, M 1,400, 44-20-72909888, Fax 44-20-74919172, ukinfo@babinc.org, www.babinc.org

# Uruguay

**Montevideo** · *Chamber of Commerce Uruguay-USA* · Magdalena Aonzo, Mgr., Plaza de Independencia 831, Ofc. 209, Edif. Plaza Mayor, 11000, M 150, 598-29-089186, Fax 598-29-089187, info@ccuruguayusa.com, www.ccuruguayusa.com

# Uzbekistan

**Tashkent** · *American Chamber of Commerce in Uzbekistan* · Tatyana Bystrushkina, Exec. Dir., 2 Afrosiab St., 41 Buyuk Turon St. 3rd Flr., 100031, M 86, 998-71-140-0877, Fax 998-71-140-0977, office@amcham.uz, www.amcham.uz

# Venezuela

**Caracas** · *Venezuelan-American Chamber of Commerce & Ind.* · Carlos Tejera, Gen. Mgr., Torre Credival, Piso 10, 2da Av. de Campo Alegre, 1010-A, 58-212-2630833, Fax 58-212-2631829, venam@venamcham.org, www.venamcham.org

# Vietnam

**Hanoi** · *American Chamber of Commerce-Hanoi* · Adam Sitkoff, Exec. Dir., Hilton Opera Hanoi, 1 Le Thanh Tong Street, M 300, 844-93-42790, Fax 844-93-42787, info@amchamhanoi.com, www.amchamhanoi.com

**Ho Chi Minh City** · *American Chamber of Commerce in Vietnam* · Herb Cochran, Exec. Dir., 76 Le Lai St. Dist. 1, New World Hotel, Rm. 323, M 450, 848-82-43562, Fax 848-82-43572, amcham@hcm.vnn.vn, www.amchamvietnam.com

# Foreign Tourist Information Bureaus

If the country you are interested in is not listed, please refer to **Foreign Embassies in the United States**.

## Algeria

**Algerian Natl. Ofc. of Tourism** • 02 Rue Ismail Kerrar, Blvd. Ché Guevara, Algiers, 16000, 213-21-713060, Fax 213-21-713059, ont@ont-dz.org, www.ont-dz.org

## Antigua & Barbuda

**Ministry of Tourism** • P.O. Box 363, Saint Johns, 268-46-20480, Fax 268-46-22836, www.antigua.gov.ag

**Antigua & Barbuda Dept. of Tourism** • 610 Fifth Ave., Ste. 311, New York, NY, 10020, 212-54-14117, (888) 268-4227, Fax (646) 215-6008, info@antigua-barbuda.org, www.antigua-barbuda.org

## Aruba

**Aruba Tourism Auth.** • 1000 Harbor Blvd, Weehawken, NJ, 07087, 201-33-00800, 800-86-27822, Fax 201-55-84767, ata.pr@aruba.com, www.aruba.com

## Australia

**Tourism Australia** • 2121 Ave. of the Stars, Los Angeles, CA, 90067, (310) 695-3200, (800) 333-0262, Fax 310-69-53201, www.australia.com

## Austria

**Austrian Natl. Tourist Ofc.** • P.O. Box 1142, New York, NY, 10108-1142, (212) 944-6880, Fax (212) 730-4568, travel@austria.info, www.austria.info/us

## Bahamas

**Bahamas Tourist Ofc.** • 1200 S. Pine Island Rd., Ste. 750, Plantation, FL, 33324, (954) 236-9292, Fax (954) 236-9282, www.bahamas.com

**Bahamas Tourist Ofc.** • 150 E. 52nd St., 28th Flr. N, New York, NY, 10022, (212) 758-2777, Fax (212) 753-6531, www.bahamas.com

**Bahamas Tourist Ofc.** • 8770 W. Bryn Mawr Ave., Ste. 1300, Chicago, IL, 60631, (773) 867-8377, (800) 224-3681, Fax (773) 867-2910, www.bahamas.com

**Bahamas Tourist Ofc.** • 11400 W. Olympic Blvd., Ste. 200, Los Angeles, CA, 90064, (310) 312-9544, Fax (310) 312-9545, www.bahamas.com

## Barbados

**Barbados Tourism Auth.** • Harbour Rd., P.O. Box 242, Bridgetown, 246-42-72623, Fax 246-42-64080, btainfo@barbados.org, www.barbados.org

**Barbados Tourism Auth.** • 800 Second Ave., 2nd Flr., New York, NY, 10017, (212) 986-6516, (800) 221-9831, Fax (212) 573-9850, www.visitbarbados.org

## Belgium

**Tourist Info. Ofc.** • Grote Markt 13, Antwerp, 2000, 323-23-20103, Fax 323-23-11937, toerisme@antwerpen.be, www.dma.be

**Belgian Tourist Ofc.** • 220 E. 42nd St., Ste. 3402, New York, NY, 10017, (212) 758-8130, Fax (212) 355-7675, info@visitbelgium.com, www.visitbelgium.com

**Brussels Intl. Tourism** • Hotel de Ville-Grand-Place, Brussels, 1000, 322-51-38940, Fax 322-51-38320, tourism@brusselsinternational.be, www.brusselsinternational.be

## Belize

**Belize Tourist Bd.** • P.O. Box 325, Belize City, 501-22-31913, info@travelbelize.org, www.travelbelize.org

**Belize Tourism Ind. Assn.** • 10 N. Park St., P.O. Box 62, Belize City, M 500, 501-22-71144, Fax 501-22-78710, director@btia.org, www.btia.org

## Bermuda

**Bermuda Dept. of Tourism** • 310 Madison Ave., Ste. 201, New York, NY, 10017, (212) 818-9800, Fax (212) 983-5289, www.bermudatourism.com

## Botswana

**Botswana Tourism Bd.** • Private Bag 0047, Gaborone, 267-39-53024, Fax 267-39-08675, board@botswanatourism.co.bw, www.botswanatourism.co.bw

## British Virgin Islands

**British Virgin Islands Tourist Bd.** • Tropical Aisle Bldg, PO Box 376, Road Town, Tortola, 284-49-43514, Fax 284-49-46179, info@bviccha.org, www.bviccha.org

## Burkina Faso

**Ministry of Tourism** • P.O. Box 7007, Ouagadougou, 22-63-30963, Fax 22-63-30964, www.culture.gov.bf

## Canada

**Tourism Canada** • 1055 Dunsmuir St., Ste. 1400, P.O. Box 49230, Vancouver, British Columbia, V7X 1L2, 604-63-88300, Fax 604-63-88425, www.travelcanada.ca

**Travel Manitoba** • 155 Carlton St., 7th Flr., Winnipeg, Manitoba, R3C 3H8, 204-92-77838, 800-66-50040, Fax 204-92-77828, www.travelmanitoba.com

**Tourism Saskatchewan** • 1922 Park St., Regina, Saskatchewan, S4N 7M4, 306-78-79600, 877-23-72273, Fax 306-78-70715, www.sasktourism.com

**Tourism Whistler** • 4010 Whistler Way, Whistler, British Columbia, V0N 1B4, 604-93-23928, 888-86-92777, Fax 604-93-27231, www.tourismwhistler.com

**Tourism British Columbia** • #300-1803 Douglas St., Victoria, British Columbia, V8W 9W5, 250-35-66363, 800-43-55622, Fax 250-35-68246, www.tourismbc.com

**Northwest Territories Arctic Tourism** • P.O. Box 610, Yellowknife, Northwest Territories, X1A 2N5, M 200, 867-87-35007, 800-66-10788, Fax 867-87-34059, www.explorenwt.com

**Nunavut Tourism** • P.O. Box 1450, Iqaluit, X0A 0H0, 867-97-96551, Fax 867-97-91261, info@nunavuttourism.com, www.nunavuttourism.com

**Klondike Visitors Assn.** • P.O. Box 389C, Dawson City, Yukon Territory, Y0B 1G0, M 250, 867-99-35575, Fax 867-99-36415, kva@dawson.net, www.dawsoncity.ca

**Dept. of Tourism, Culture & Rec.** • P.O. Box 8700, St. Johns, Newfoundland, A1B 4J6, 709-72-90659, 800-56-36353, info@gov.nl.ca, www.gov.nl.ca

**Tourism Prince Edward Island** • P.O. Box 2000, Charlottetown, Prince Edward, C1A 7N8, 800-46-34734, Fax 902-36-85277, www.gentleisland.com

**Tourism New Brunswick** • P.O. Box 12345, Campbellton, New Brunswick, E3N 3T6, 800-56-10123, Fax 506-78-92044, www.tourismnewbrunswick.ca

**Tourism Quebec** • 1255 Peel St., Montreal, Quebec, H3B 4V4, 514-86-41610, Fax 514-86-43838, info@tourisme.gouv.qc.ca, www.bonjourquebec.com

**Tourism Toronto** • 207 Queen's Way West, Box 126, Toronto, Ontario, M5J 1A7, M 190, 416-20-32600, Fax 416-20-36753, toronto@torcvb.com, www.torontotourism.com

# Cape Verde

**Promex Centro Promocao Du Turismo** • Box 89/C, Praia, 23-86-22621, Fax 23-86-22657, www.virtualcapeverde.net

# Caribbean

**Caribbean Organization for Tourism** • 80 Broad St., 32nd Flr., New York, NY, 10004, (212) 635-9530, Fax (212) 635-9511, www.caribbeantravel.com

# Chile

**Natl. Tourism Bd. Of Chile** • Eliodoro Yanez 2473, Santiago, 562-78-56609, Fax 562-78-56874, www.visit-chile.org

# China

**China Natl. Tourist Ofc.** • 317 Lexington Ave., Ste. 912, New York, NY, 10017, (212) 760-8218, (800) 670-2228, Fax (212) 760-8809, info@cnto.org, www.cnto.org

# Colombia

**Ministry of Eco. Dev.** • Viceminister of Tourism, Calle 28 No. 13A-15 piso 18, Bogota, 571-28-39558, Fax 571-28-11181, www.colombiaemb.org

# Costa Rica

**Costa Rica Tourist Bd.** • P.O. Box 777-1000, San Jose, 1000, 506-29-95800, Fax 506-22-00243, info@visitcostarica.com, www.visitcostarica.com

# Croatia

**Croation National Tourist Ofc.** • P.O. Box 251, Zagreb, 385-14-699333, Fax 385-14-557827, info@htz.hr, www.croatia.hr

# Cyprus

**Cyprus Tourism Organization** • P.O. Box 24535, Nicosia, 1390, 357-22-691100, Fax 35-73-31644, www.visitcyprus.org.cy

**Cyprus Trade Centre** • 13 E. 40th St., New York, New York, 10016, 212-21-39100, Fax 212-21-32918, www.cyprustradeny.org

# Czech Republic

**TATRA Travel Bur. Inc.** • 45 Main St., Ste. 840, Brooklyn, NY, 11201, (212) 486-0533, Fax (212) 486-1456, info@tatratravel.com, www.czechtourism.com

# Denmark

**Euro Tourist** • P.O. Box 1139, Aalborg, 9100, 459-81-13400, Fax 459-81-13944, mail@eurotourist.dk, eurotourist.dk

# Dominican Republic

**Dominican Republic Tourism Bd.** • 136 E. 57th St., Ste. 803, New York, NY, 10022, (212) 588-1012, (888) 374-6361, Fax (212) 588-1015, drtourismboardny@verizon.net, www.godominicanrepublic.com

**Secretary of State of Turismo** • Av. Mexico esq. Av. 30 Margo, Santo Domingo, 809-22-14660, Fax 809-68-23806, www.dominicana.com.do

# Egypt

**Egyptian Tourist Auth.** • 630 Fifth Ave., Ste. 2305, New York, NY, 10111, (212) 332-2570, (877) 773-4978, Fax (212) 956-6439, www.egypt.travel

# Eritrea

**Ministry of Tourism** • PO Box 1010, Asmara, 291-11-26997, Fax 291-11-26949, ona12@eol.com.er

# Fiji

**Fiji Visitors Bur.** • 5777 W. Century Blvd., Ste. 220, Los Angeles, CA, 90045, (310) 568-1616, Fax (310) 670-2318, infodesk@bulafiji-americas.com, www.fijime.com

**Fiji Visitors Bur.** • P.O. Box 9217, Nadi, 679-67-22433, Fax 679-67-20141, marketing@bulafiji.com, www.bulafiji.com

# Finland

*See Scandinavia*

# France

**French Government Tourist Ofc.** • 825 3rd Ave., 29th Flr., New York, NY, 10022, (212) 838-7800, Fax (212) 838-7855, www.franceguide.com/us

# The Gambia

**Dept. of State for Tourism & Culture** • The Quadrangle, Banjul, 22-02-27593, Fax 22-02-27753, www.visitthegambia.gm

# Germany, Federal Rep. of

**German Natl. Tourist Ofc.** • 122 E. 42nd St., Ste. 2000, New York, NY, 10168-0072, (212) 661-7200, Fax (212) 661-7174, germanyinfo@d-z-t.com, www.cometogermany.com

# Greece

**Greek Natl. Tourism Organization** • 645 Fifth Ave., 9th Flr., New York, NY, 10022, (212) 421-5777, Fax (212) 826-6940, info@ greektourism.com, www.greektourism.com

# Grenada

**Grenada Bd. Of Tourism** • 305 Madison Ave., Ste. 2145, New York, NY, 10165, (212) 687-9554, (800) 927-9554, Fax (212) 682-4748, noel@rfcp.com, www.grenadagrenadines.com

# Honduras

**Honduras Institute of Tourism** • P.O. Box 3261, Tegucigalpa, FM, 504-22-22124, Fax 504-22-26621, tourisminfo@iht.hn, www. letsgohonduras.com

# Hong Kong, China

**Hong Kong Tourism Bd.** • 10940 Wilshire Blvd., Ste. 2050, Los Angeles, CA, 90024, (310) 208-4582, Fax (310) 208-1869, www. discoverhongkong.com/usa

# Hungary

**Ministry of Eco. Affairs & Tourism** • Vigado u. 6, Budapest, 1051, 361-23-54537, Fax 361-23-54436, www.gm.hu

**Hungarian Natl. Tourist Bd.** • 350 5th Ave., Ste. 7107, New York, NY, 10118, (212) 695-1221, Fax (212) 695-0809, info@ gotohungary.com, www.gotohungary.com

# Iceland

*See Scandinavia*

# India

**Government of India Tourist Ofc.** • 1270 Ave. of the Americas, Ste. 1808, New York, NY, 10020, (212) 586-4901, Fax (212) 582-3274, www.incredibleindia.org

# Ireland

**Tourism Ireland** • 345 Park Ave., 17th Flr., New York, NY, 10154, (212) 418-0800, Fax (212) 371-9052, www.discoverireland.com

**Irish Tourist Bd.** • Baggot St. Bridge, Dublin, 2, 353-16-024000, Fax 353-16-024100, www.ireland.travel.ie

# Israel

**Israel Ministry of Tourism** • 800 Second Ave., 16th Flr., New York, NY, 10017, (212) 499-5644, Fax (212) 499-5645, info@ goisrael.com, www.goisrael.com

**Israel Government Tourist Ofc.** • 6380 Wilshire Blvd., Ste. 1700, Los Angeles, CA, 90048, (323) 658-7463, Fax (323) 658-6543, www.goisrael.com

# Italy

**Italian Government Tourist Bd.** • 630 Fifth Ave., Ste. 1565, New York, NY, 10111, (212) 245-5618, Fax (212) 586-9249, www. italiantourism.com

**Italian Government Tourist Bd.** • 12400 Wilshire Blvd., Ste. 550, Los Angeles, CA, 90025, (310) 820-4498, Fax (310) 820-6357, www.italiantourism.com

# Japan

**Japan Natl. Tourist Organization** • 1 Rockefeller Plaza, Ste. 1250, New York, NY, 10020, (212) 757-5640, Fax (212) 307-6754, www.japantravelinfo.com

**Japan Natl. Tourist Organization** • 515 S. Figueroa St., Ste. 1470, Los Angeles, CA, 90071, (213) 623-1952, Fax (213) 623-6301, www.japantravelinfo.com

**Japan Travel Bur. Intl. Inc.** • 1 Rockefeller Plaza, Ste. 1250, New York, NY, 10020, (212) 757-5640, Fax (212) 307-6754, www. japantravelinfo.com

# Jordan

**Jordan Info. Bur.** • 3504 International Dr., Washington, DC, 20008, (202) 265-1606, Fax (202) 667-0777, www.na.visitjordan.com

# Korea, Republic of

**Korea Tourism Organization** • Two Executive Dr., Ste. 750, Fort Lee, NJ, 07024, (201) 585-0909, (800) 868-7567, Fax (201) 585-9041, ny@kntoamerica.com, tour2korea.com

# Latvia

**Latvia Tours** • Kralyku Street 8, Riga, LV 1050, 371-70-85001, Fax 371-78-20020, hq@latviatours.lv, latviatours.lv

# Lesotho

**Ministry of Tourism, Culture & Environment** • P.O. Box 52, Maseru, 100, 9266-22-311054, Fax 9266-22-310194, ps@ tourism.gov.ls

# Luxembourg

**Luxembourg Bd. Of Eco. Dev.** • 17 Beekman Pl., New York, NY, 10022, (212) 888-6664, Fax (212) 888-6116, www.luxembourg newyork.com

**Luxembourg Natl. Tourist Ofc.** • P.O. Box 1001, Luxembourg, 1010, 352-42-828220, Fax 352-42-828230, info@ont.lu, www. visitluxembourg.lu

# Madagascar

**Ministry of Commerce & Tourism** • P.O. Box 454, Ambohidahy, Antananarivo, 26-12-27292, Fax 26-12-31280

# Malawi

**Malawi Ministry of Tourism** • P/Bag 326, Lilongwe, 265-17-75499, Fax 265-17-70650, tourism@malawi.net

# Malaysia

**Malaysia Tourism Promotion Bd.** • P.O. Box 10328, Kuala Lumpur, 50480, 603-26-935188, Fax 603-26-935884, tourism@tourism.gov.my, tourism.gov.my

**Malaysia Tourism Promotion Bd.** • 818 W. 7th St., Ste. 970, Los Angeles, CA, 90017, (213) 689-9702, (800) 336-6842, Fax (213) 689-1530, malaysiainfo@aol.com, www.tourismmalaysiausa.com

**Tourism Malaysia** • 120 E. 56th St., Ste. 810, New York, NY, 10022, (212) 754-1113, Fax (212) 754-1116, mtpb@aol.com, www.tourismmalaysia.gov.my

**Malawi Ministry of Tourism** • P/Bag 326, Lilongwe, 265-17-75499, Fax 265-17-70650, tourism@malawi.net

# Mexico

**Mexico Tourism Bd.** • 400 Madison Ave., Ste. 11C, New York, NY, 10017, (212) 308-2110, Fax (212) 308-9060, newyork@visitmexico.com, www.visitmexico.com

**Mexico Tourism Bd.** • 225 N. Michigan Ave., Ste. 1850, Chicago, IL, 60601, (312) 228-0517, Fax (312) 228-0515, chicago@visitmexico.com, www.visitmexico.com

**Mexico Tourism Bd.** • 1880 Century Park E., Ste. 511, Los Angeles, CA, 90067, (310) 282-9112, Fax (213) 282-9116, losangeles@visitmexico.com, www.visitmexico.com

**Consejo de Promocian Turistico de Mexico** • 4507 San Jacinto, Ste. 308, Houston, TX, 77004, (713) 772-2581, Fax (713) 772-6058, www.visitmexico.com

# Micronesia

**Federated States of Micronesia** • 3049 Ualena St., Ste. 910, Honolulu, HI, 96819, (808) 836-4775, Fax (808) 836-6896, fsmcghnl@aol.com, www.fsmembassy.org/honolu~/.htm

# Morocco

**Moroccan National Tourist Ofc.** • 7208 Sand Lake Rd., Ste. 204, Orlando, FL, 32819, (407) 264-0133, Fax (407) 264-0134, www.visitmorocco.com

# Myanmar

**Myanmar Travels & Tours** • 77-91 Sule Pagoda Rd., Yangon, 1, 950-12-83997, Fax 950-12-54417, mtt.mht@mptmail.net.mm

# Namibia

**Namibia Tourism Bd.** • Private Bag 13244, Windhoek, 2646-12-909004, Fax 264-61-254848, info@namibiatourism.com.na, www.namibiatourism.com

# Nepal

**Ministry of Tourism** • Singh Durbar, Kathmandu, 977-12-25870, Fax 977-12-27758, www.welcomenepal.com

# Netherlands

**Netherlands Bd. Of Tourism** • 355 Lexington Ave., 19th Flr., New York, NY, 10017, (917) 720-1285, (888) 464-6552, Fax (212) 370-9507, information@holland.com, www.holland.com

# Netherlands Antilles

**Curacao Tourist Bd.** • 1 Gateway Center, Ste. 2600, Newark, NJ, 07102, (973) 353-6200, (800) 328-7222, Fax (973) 353-6201, www.curacao.com

# New Zealand

**Tourism New Zealand** • P.O. Box 95, Wellington, 644-91-75400, Fax 644-91-53817, www.purenz.com

# Nigeria

**Nigerian Tourism Dev. Corp.** • PMB 167, Abuja, 2340-95-230418, Fax 2340-95-230962

# Norway

*See Scandinavia*

# Pakistan

**Pakistan Tourism Dev. Corp.** • P.O. Box 1465, Islamabad, 44000, 925-19-219705, Fax 925-19-219729, www.tourism.gov.pk

# Papau New Guinea

**Tourism Promotion Auth. of Papau New Guinea** • P.O. Box 1291, Port Moresby, 121, 675-32-00211, Fax 675-32-01629, www.paradiselive.org.pg

# Paraguay

**Direccion de Turismo de Paraguay** • Arq. Hugo Cataldo, Dir., Palma 468, Asuncion, 595-21-441530, Fax 595-21-491230

# Philippines

**Philippine Conv. & Visitors Corp.** • P.O. Box EA-459, Manila, 1004, 632-52-59318, Fax 632-52-16165, pcvcnet@dotpcvc.gov.ph, www.dotpcvc.gov.ph

**Philippine Dept. of Tourism** • 556 Fifth Ave., 1M, New York, NY, 10036, (212) 575-7915, www.wowphilippines.com.ph

**Philippine Dept. of Tourism** • 30 N. Michigan Ave., Ste. 913, Chicago, IL, 60602, (312) 782-2475, Fax (312) 782-2476, www.wowphilippines.com.ph

# Poland

**ORBIS Travel Co. Ltd.** • 2 Annopd Str., Warsaw, 03-236, 482-25-190412, Fax 482-25-190433

**Polish Natl. Tourist Ofc.** • 5 Marine View Plaza, Hoboken, NJ, 07030, (201) 420-9910, Fax (201) 584-9153, www.poland.travel

# Portugal

**Portuguese Trade Comm. & Tourism Ofc.** • 590 Fifth Ave., 4th Flr., New York, NY, 10036, (212) 354-4610, (800) 767-8842, Fax (212) 575-4737, www.portugalglobal.pt

# Russian Federation

**Russian Natl. Tourist Ofc.** • 224 W. 30th St., Ste. 701, New York, NY, 10001, (646) 473-2233, (877) 221-7120, Fax (646) 473-2205, info@russia-travel.com, www.russia-travel.com

# Saint Kitts & Nevis

**St. Kitts Tourism Auth.** • Pelican Mall, PO Box 132, Basseterre, 869-46-54040, 877-53-31555, Fax 869-46-58794, info@stkitts tourism.kn, www.stkitts-tourism.com

**St. Kitts & Nevis Tourist Bd.** • 414 E. 75th St., 5th Flr., New York, NY, 10021, (212) 535-1234, (800) 582-6208, Fax (212) 734-6511, info@stkittstourism.kn, www.stkitts-tourism.com

# Saint Lucia

**St. Lucia Tourist Bd.** • P.O. Box 221, Castries, 758-45-24094, 800-45-63984, Fax 758-45-31121, slutour@candw.lc, www.stlucia.org

**St. Lucia Tourist Bd.** • 800 Second Ave., Ste. 910, New York, NY, 10017, (800) 456-3984, Fax (212) 867-2795, www.stlucia.org

# Saint Vincent & The Grenadines

**St. Vincent & the Grenadines Tourist Ofc.** • 801 Second Ave., 21st Flr., New York, NY, 10017, (212) 687-4981, Fax (212) 949-5946, svgtony@aol.com, www.svgtourism.com

# Samoa

**Samoa Tourism Auth.** • P.O. Box 2272, Apia, 6-85-63103, Fax 6-85-20886, info@visitsamoa.ws, www.visitsamoa.ws

# Scandinavia

**Scandinavian Tourist Bd.** • 655 Third Ave., New York, NY, 10017, (212) 885-9700, Fax (212) 885-9710, info@goscandinavia.com, www.goscandinavia.com

# Scotland

**Greater Glasgow & Clyde Valley Tourist Bd.** • 11 George Sq., Glasgow, G2 10Y, M 800, 4414-15-664029, Fax 4414-12-489541, conventions@seeglasgow.com, www.seeglasgow.com

**Perthshire Tourist Bd.** • Lower City Mills, West Mill St., Perth, PH1 5QP, 4417-38-627958, Fax 4417-38-630416, info@ptb.ossian.net, www.perthshire.co.uk

# Serbia

**Natl. Tourism Organization of Serbia** • Decansak 8A, Belgrade, 11000, 3811-13-232586, Fax 3811-13-221068, ntos@yubc.net, www.serbia-tourism.org

# Singapore

**Singapore Tourist Promotion Bd.** • 5670 Wilshire Blvd., Ste. 1550, Los Angeles, CA, 90036, (323) 677-0808, www.visitsingapore.com

**Singapore Tourism Bd.** • 1156 Ave. of the Americas, Ste. 702, New York, NY, 10036, (212) 302-4861, Fax (212) 302-4801, www.visitsingapore.com

# Slovenia

**Slovenian Tourist Bd.** • Dunajska 156, Ljubljana, 1000, 386-15-891840, Fax 11386-15-891841, info@slovenia.info, www.slovenia-tourism.si

# South Africa

**South African Tourism Bd.** • 500 Fifth Ave., Ste. 2040, New York, NY, 10110, (212) 730-2929, (800) 593-1318, Fax (212) 764-1980, www.southafrica.net

# Spain

**Tourist Ofc. Of Spain** • 8383 Wilshire Blvd., Ste. 956, Beverly Hills, CA, 90211, (323) 658-7188, Fax (323) 658-1061, www.okspain.org

**Tourist Ofc. of Spain** • 845 N. Michigan Ave., Ste. 915-E, Chicago, IL, 60611, (312) 642-1992, Fax (312) 642-9817, www.spain.info

**Tourist Ofc. of Spain** • 1395 Brickell Ave., Ste. 1130, Miami, FL, 33131, (305) 358-1992, Fax (305) 358-8223, www.spain.info

**Tourist Ofc. Of Spain** • 666 Fifth Ave., 35th Flr., New York, NY, 10103, (212) 265-8822, Fax (212) 265-8864, oetny@tourspain.us, www.spain.info

# Sri Lanka

**Sri Lanka Tourist Bd.** • Mo 80, Galle Road, Colombo, 3, 94-14-37059, Fax 94-14-37953, tourinfo@sri.lanka.net, srilankatourism.org

**Tourist Info. Section** • Embassy of Sri Lanka, 2148 Wyoming Ave. N.W., Washington, DC, 20008, (202) 483-4025, Fax (202) 232-7181, slembassy@slembassyusa.org, www.slembassy usa.org

# Suriname

**Suriname Tourism Found.** • P.O. Box 656, Paramaribo, 59-74-10357, Fax 59-74-77786, stsur@sr.net, www.sr.net/users/stsur

# Sweden

*See Scandinavia*

Foreign Tour Info

# Switzerland

**Switzerland Tourism** • 608 Fifth Ave., Ste. 202, New York, NY, 10020, (212) 757-5944, (877) 784-8037, Fax 212-26-26116, www.myswitzerland.com

# Tahiti

**Tahiti Tourism Bd.** • 300 Continental Blvd., Ste. 160, El Segundo, CA, 90245, (310) 414-8484, (800) 365-4949, Fax (310) 414-8490, info@tahiti-tourisme.com, www.tahiti-tourisme.com

# Taiwan

**Taiwan Visitors Assn.** • One E. 42nd St., 9th Flr., New York, NY, 10017, (212) 867-1632, Fax (212) 867-1635, www.go2taiwan.net

**Taiwan Visitors Assn.** • 555 Montgomery St., Ste. 505, San Francisco, CA, 94111, (415) 989-8677, Fax (415) 989-7242, www.go2taiwan.net

# Tanzania

**Tanzania Tourist Bd.** • P.O. Box 2485, Dar es Salaam, 2552-22-111244, Fax 2552-22-116420, www.tanzaniatouristboard.com

# Thailand

**Tourism Auth. of Thailand** • 611 N. Larchmont Blvd., 1st Flr., Los Angeles, CA, 90004, (323) 461-9814, Fax (323) 461-9834, tatla@ix.netcom.com, www.tourismthailand.org

**Tourism Auth. of Thailand** • 61 Broadway, Ste. 2810, New York, NY, 10006, (212) 432-0433, Fax (212) 269-2588, info@tatny.com, www.tourismthailand.org

**Tourism Auth. of Thailand** • 202 Ratchadaphisek Rd., Bangkok, 10310, 662-69-41222, Fax 662-69-41400, www.tourismthailand.org

# Trinidad & Tobago

**Trinidad & Tobago Tourism & Ind. Dev. Co.** • P.O. Box 222, Port of Spain, 868-62-36022, Fax 868-62-57548, tourism-info@tidco.co.tt, www.visittnt.com

# Tunisia

**Tunisian Tourist Ofc.** • 1, Av. Mohamed V, Tunis, 1000RP, 216-13-41077, Fax 216-13-50997, info@tourismtunisia.com, ww.tourismtunisia.com

# Turkey

**Turkish Tourist Ofc.** • 2525 Massachusetts Ave. N.W., Washington, DC, 20008, (202) 612-6800, (877) 367-8875, Fax (202) 319-7446, dc@tourismturkey.org, www.tourismturkey.org

# United Kingdom

*Also see Ireland, Scotland & Wales*

**Visit Britain** • Thames Tower, Black's Rd., London, W6 9EL, 4420-88-469000, Fax 4420-85-630302, industry.relations@visitbritain.org, www.visitbritain.com/ukindustry

**Isle of Man Dept. of Tourism** • St Andrew's House Douglas, Douglas, IM1 2PX, 4416-24-686801, Fax 4416-24-686800, tourism@gov.im, www.gov.im/tourism

**Visit Britain** • 551 Fifth Ave., Ste. 701, New York, NY, 10176, (212) 986-2266, (800) 462-2748, travelinfo@visitbritain.org, www.visitbritain.org

# Venezuela

**Venezuelan Tourism Assn.** • P.O. Box 3010, Sausalito, CA, 94966, M 350, (415) 331-0100, www.venezuelanadventures.com

# Wales

**Wales Tourist Bd.** • Brunel House, 2 Fitzalan Rd., Cardiff, CF24 0UY, 4429-20-499909, Fax 4429-20-485031, info@tourism.wales.gov.uk, www.visitwales.com

# Zambia

**Zambia Natl. Tourist Bd.** • P.O. Box 30017, Lusaka, 10101, M 267, 26-12-29087, Fax 260-12-25174, zntb@zamnet.zm, www.zambiatourism.com

# Foreign and Ethnic Chambers of Commerce in the United States

## Africa

**Africa-Texas Chamber of Commerce & Industries** • Prof. C. Achebe, Pres., Greenway Park, 2455 N.E. Loop 410, Ste. 237, San Antonio, TX, 78217, M 22, (210) 590-4100, (800) 881-3298, Fax (210) 824-9004, africa-txchamber@usa.com, www.africa texaschamber.com

**African Chamber of Commerce-Dallas/Ft. Worth Metro** • P.O. Box 421231, Dallas, TX, 75342, M 550, (214) 421-6155, Fax (214) 291-7195, www.africanchamberdfw.org

## Angola

**U.S.-Angola Chamber of Commerce** • 1100 17th St. N.W., Ste. 1100A, Washington, DC, 20036, M 90, (202) 857-0789, Fax (202) 223-0540, mdacruz@us-angola.org, www.us-angola.org

## Argentina

**Argentine-American Chamber of Commerce** • 630 Fifth Ave., 25th Flr., New York, NY, 10111, M 100, (212) 698-2238, Fax (212) 698-2239, info@argentinechamber.org, www.argentine chamber.org

## Australia

**Australian Consulate General** • 150 E. 42nd, , 34th Flr., New York, NY, 10017, (212) 351-6500, Fax (212) 351-6501, www. australianyc.org

## Austria

**Austrian Trade Comm.** • 11601 Wilshire Blvd., Ste. 2420, Los Angeles, CA, 90025, (310) 477-9988, Fax (310) 477-1643, losangeles@austriantrade.org, www.austriantrade.org

**Austrian Trade Comm. In New York** • 120 W. 45th St., 9th Flr., New York, NY, 10036, (212) 421-5250, Fax (212) 421-5251, www.austriantrade.org

**U.S.-Austrian Chamber of Commerce** • 165 W. 46th St., Ste. 1112, New York, NY, 10036, M 140, (212) 819-0117, Fax (212) 819-0345, memberservices@usatchamber.com, www.usatchamber.com

## Azerbaijan

**U.S.-Azerbaijan Chamber of Commerce** • 1212 Potomac St. N.W., Washington, DC, 20007, M 60, (202) 333-8702, Fax (202) 333-8703, chamber@usacc.org, www.usacc.org

## Barbados

**Barbados Investment & Dev. Corp.** • 800 2nd Ave., New York, NY, 10017, (212) 867-6420, Fax (212) 682-5496, bidc@bidc.org, www.bidc.org

## Belgium

**Belgian-American Chamber of Commerce in the U.S.** • c/o Consulate General of Belgium, 1065 Ave. of the Americas, 22nd Flr., New York, NY, 10036, M 115, (212) 340-6271, Fax (212) 340-6270, info@belcham.org, www.belcham.org

## Brazil

**Brazil-U.S. Business Cncl.** • 1615 H St. NW, Washington, DC, 20062, M 7, (202) 463-5485, Fax (202) 463-3126, host@brazil council.org, www.brazilcouncil.org5

**Brazilian-American Chamber of Commerce Inc.** • 509 Madison Ave., Ste. 304, New York, NY, 10022, M 500, (212) 751-4691, Fax (212) 751-7692, info@brazilcham.com, www. brazilcham.com

**Brazilian-American Chamber of Commerce of Florida** • P.O. Box 310038, Miami, FL, 33231, M 300, (305) 579-9030, Fax (305) 579-9756, info@brazilchamber.org, www.brazilchamber.org

## Chile

**North American-Chilean Chamber** • 30 Vesey St., Ste. 506, New York, NY, 10007 , M 110, (212) 233-7776, Fax (212) 233-7779

## China

**U.S.-China Chamber of Commerce** • Siva Yam, Pres., 55 W. Monroe St., Ste. 630, Chicago, IL, 60603, M 300, (312) 368-9911, Fax (312) 368-9922, info@usccc.org, www.usccc.org

**U.S. Rep Office, China Chamber of Intl. Commerce** • 2001 Jefferson Davis Hwy., Ste. 608, Arlington, VA, 22202, (703) 412-9889, Fax (703) 412-5889, www.ccpit.org

## Colombia

**Colombian-American Chamber of Commerce** • 2355 St. Salzedo, Ste. 316, Coral Gables, FL, 33134, M 230, (305) 446-2542, Fax (305) 446-2038

**Colombian Government Trade Bur.** • 608 Brickell Key Dr., Ste. 801, Miami, FL, 33131, (305) 374-3144, Fax (305) 372-9365, www.proexport.com.co

## Cyprus

**Cyprus-U.S. Chamber of Commerce** • 55 Paramus Rd., Paramus, NJ, 07652, M 150, (201) 444-5609, Fax (201) 444-0445, cyprususchamber@aol.com, www.cyprususchamber.com

## Denmark

**Danish American Chamber of Commerce** • 885 Second Ave., 18th Flr., New York, NY, 10017, M 250, (212) 705-4945, Fax (212) 754-1904, info@daccny.com, www.daccny.com

# Ecuador

**Ecuadorian-American Chamber of Commerce** • 3403 N.W. 82nd Ave., Ste. 310, Miami, FL, 33122, (305) 539-0010, Fax (305) 591-0868, ecuacham@bellsouth.net, www.ecuachamber.com

# Europe

**European-American Business Cncl.** • 919 18th St. N.W., Ste. 220, Washington, DC, 20006, M 55, (202) 828-9104, Fax (202) 828-9106, katie@eabc.org , www.eabc.org

# Finland

**Finnish American Chamber of Commerce** • 866 U.N. Plaza, Ste. 250, New York, NY, 10017, (212) 821-0225, Fax (212) 750-4418, faccnyc@verizon.net, www.facc-ny.com

**Finnish American Chamber of Commerce-Pacific Coast** • P.O. Box 3058, Tustin, CA, 92781, (949) 637-2537, services@faccpacific.com, www.faccpacific.com

# France

**French-American Chamber of Commerce** • 122 E. 42nd St., Ste. 2015, New York, NY, 10168, (212) 867-0123, Fax (212) 867-9050, info@faccnyc.org, www.faccnyc.org, M 500

**French-American Chamber of Commerce** • 10390 Santa Monica Blvd., Ste. 130, Los Angeles, CA, 90025, M 300, (323) 651-4741, Fax (323) 651-2547, info@frenchchamberla.org, www.frenchchamberla.org

# Germany

**German-American Chamber of Commerce** • 75 Broad St., 21st Flr., New York, NY, 10004, M 900, (212) 974-8830, Fax (212) 974-8867, info@gaccny.com, www.gaccny.com

**German-American Chamber of Commerce** • 1600 JFK Blvd., 4 Penn Center, Ste. 200, Philadelphia, PA, 19103, M 250, (215) 665-1585, Fax (215) 665-0375, admin@gaccphiladelphia.com, www.gaccphiladelphia.com

**German-American Chamber of the Midwest** • 401 N. Michigan Ave., Ste. 3330, Chicago, IL, 60611, M 650, (312) 644-2662, Fax (312) 644-0738, info@gaccom.org, www.gaccom.org

**German-American Chamber of the Southern U.S.** • 530 Means St., Ste. 120, Atlanta, GA, 30318, M 400, (404) 586-6800, Fax (404) 586-6820, info@gaccsouth.com, www.gaccsouth.com

# Greece

**Hellenic-American Chamber of Commerce** • 780 Third Ave., 16th Flr., New York, NY, 10017, (212) 629-6380, Fax (212) 564-9281, hellenicchamber-nyc@att.net, www.hellenicamerican.cc

# Haiti

**Haitian-American Chamber of Commerce** • 11767 S. Dixie Hwy., Ste. 275, Miami , FL, 33156, (305) 733-9066, info@haitian americanchamber.com, www.haitianamericanchamber.com

**Haitian Chamber of Commerce** • Pres., P.O. Box 1052, New York, NY, 10150, M 987, (917) 613-9912, haitiancommerce@gmail.com

# Hungary

**Hungarian-American Chamber of Commerce** • 205 Deanza Blvd., PMB 157, San Mateo, CA, 94402-3989, (650) 573-7351

# Iceland

**Icelandic-American Chamber of Commerce** • 800 Third Ave., 36th Flr., New York, NY, 10022, M 300, (646) 282-9360, Fax (646) 282-9369, www.iceland.org

# Indonesia

**American-Indonesian Chamber of Commerce** • 317 Madison Ave., Ste. 1619, New York, NY, 10017, (212) 687-4505, Fax (212) 687-5844, wayne@aiccusa.org, www.aiccusa.org

# Ireland

**Ireland Chamber of Commerce in the U.S.** • 556 Central Ave., New Providence, NJ, 07974, M 500, (908) 286-1300, Fax (908) 286-1200, info@iccusa.org, www.iccusa.org

# Israel

**American-Israel Chamber of Commerce-Chicago** • 500 Lake Cook Rd., Ste. 350, Deerfield, IL, 60015, (847) 597-7070, Fax (847) 597-7067, info@americaisrael.org, www.americaisrael.org

**American-Israel Chamber of Commerce, SE Region** • 1150 Lake Hearn Dr., Ste. 130, Atlanta, GA, 30342, M 560, (404) 843-9426, Fax (404) 843-1416, aiccse@aiccse.org, www.aiccse.org

**Ohio-Israel Chamber of Commerce** • P.O. Box 39007, Cleveland, OH, 44139, (216) 965-4474, Fax (440) 248-4888, OHisraelchamber@ameritech.net, www.ohioisraelchamber.com

# Italy

**Italy American Chamber of Commerce** • 730 Fifth Ave., Ste. 600, New York, NY, 10019, M 300, (212) 459-0044, Fax (212) 459-0090, info@italchamber.org, www.italchamber.org

**Italian American Chamber of Commerce of Chicago** • 500 N. Michigan Ave., Ste. 506, Chicago, IL, 60611, M 200, (312) 553-9137, Fax (312) 553-9142, info@italianchamber.us, www.italianchamber.us

**Italy-American Chamber of Commerce West** • 10350 Santa Monica Blvd., Ste. 210, Los Angeles, CA, 90025, M 100, (310) 557-3017, Fax (310) 557-1217, info@iaccw.net, www.iaccw.net

# Japan

**Japan Bus. Assn. of Houston** • 12651 Briar Forest Dr., Ste. 105, Houston, TX, 77077, (281) 493-1512, Fax (281) 531-6730, jbahou@airmail.net, www.jbahouston.org

**Japan Bus. Assn. of Southern California** • 1411 W. 190th St., Ste. 270, Gardena, CA, 90248, (310) 515-9522, Fax (310) 515-9722, jba@jba.org, www.jba.org

**Japanese Chamber of Commerce & Ind. of New York** • 145 W. 57th St., 6th Flr., New York, NY, 1001, M 3509, (212) 246-8001, Fax (212) 246-8002, info@jcciny.org, www.jcciny.org

**Japanese Chamber of Commerce-Southern California** • 244 San Pedro St., Ste. 504, Los Angeles, CA, 90012, M 250, (213) 626-3067, Fax (213) 626-3070, office@jccsc.com, www.jccsc.com

# Korea, Republic of

**Korean American Chamber of Commerce of LA** • 3435 Wilshire Blvd., Ste. 2450, Los Angeles, CA, 90010, M 1,000, (213) 480-1115, Fax (213) 480-7521, www.koreanchamberla.com

**Korea Chamber of Commerce and Ind. in the USA** • 460 Park Ave., Ste. 410, New York, NY, 10022, M 350, (212) 644-0140, Fax (212) 644-9106, webmaster@kocham.org, www.kocham.org

# Latin America

**Cncl. of the Americas** • 680 Park Ave., New York, NY, 10065, M 5,000, (212) 628-3200, Fax (212) 517-6247, www.councilof theamericas.org

**Intercontinental C/C** • 8541 S. Redwood Rd., West Jordan, UT, 84084, (801) 601-1149, Fax (801) 601-1150, renetta@icccbiz.org, www.icccbiz.org

**Latin American Chamber of Commerce** • 3512 W. Fullerton, Chicago, IL, 60647, M 200, (773) 252-5211, Fax (773) 252-7065, www.latinamericanchamberofcommerce.com

**Latin Chamber of Commerce of USA** • 735 N.W. 22nd Ave., Miami, FL, 33125, M 2,000, (305) 642-3870, Fax (305) 642-0653, info@camacol.org, www.camacol.org

# Luxembourg

**Luxembourg American Chamber of Commerce** • 17 Beekman Pl., New York, NY, 10022, M 100, (212) 888-6701, Fax (212) 935-5896, info@luxembourgbusiness.org, www. luxembourgbusiness.org

**Luxembourg Bd. of Eco. Dev.** • One Sansome St., Ste. 830, San Francisco, CA, 94104, (415) 788-0816, Fax (415) 788-0985, sanfrancisco.cg@mae.etat.lu, www.luxembourgsf.com

# Malaysia

**Malaysian Trade Comm.** • 313 E. 43rd St., 3rd Flr., New York, NY, 10017, (212) 682-0232, Fax (212) 983-1987, newyork@ matrade.gov.my, www.matrade.gov.my

# Mexico

**Mexican Intl. Chamber of Commerce & Ind.** • 555 Saturn Blvd., Ste. B163, San Diego, CA, 92154, M 1,000, (619) 463-9426, mexicotradecenter@yahoo.com, www.mexchamber.com

**U.S.-Mexico Chamber of Commerce** • 901 Main St, 43rd Flr., Dallas, TX, 75202, M 1,500, (214) 747-1996, Fax (214) 747-1994, swusmx@netzero.net, www.usmcoc.org

# Middle East

**Arab American Chamber of Commerce** • 1050 17th St. N.W., Ste. 600, Washington, DC, 20036, (202) 347-5800, Fax (202) 521-4050, aacc@arabchamber.org, www.arabchamber.org

**National U.S.-Arab Chamber of Commerce** • 420 Lexington Ave., Ste. 2034, New York, NY, 10170, M 425, (212) 986-8024, Fax (212) 986-0216, ghage@nusacc.org, www.nusacc.org

**National U.S.-Arab Chamber of Commerce** • 1023 15th St. N.W., Ste. 400, Washington, DC, 20005, M 300, (202) 289-5920, Fax (202) 289-5938, info@nusacc.org, www.nusacc.org

**National U.S.-Arab Chamber of Commerce in LA** • 8921 S. Sepulveda Blvd., Ste. 206, Los Angeles, CA, 90045, M 250, (310) 646-1499, Fax (310) 646-2462, info@nusacc.org, www.nusacc.org

# Norway

**Norwegian-American Chamber of Commerce** • 655 Third Ave., Ste. 1810, New York, NY, 10017, M 125, (212) 421-1655, www.naccusa.org

# Peru

**Peruvian American Chamber of Commerce** • 12973 S.W. 112th St., Ste. 174, Miami, FL, 33186, M 200, (786) 393-0512, www.peruvianchamber.org

# Philippines

**Philippine American Chamber of Greater Chicago** • 3413 N. Milwaukee Ave., Chicago, IL, 60641, M 100, (773) 545-4330, Fax (773) 334-5994, www.philamchamberchicago.org

# Portugal

**Portuguese American Chamber of Commerce of New Jersey** • Hilda T. Pinheiro, Exec. Dir., 51-55 Prospect, Newark, NJ, 07105, M 200, (973) 491-5200, Fax (973) 589-0979, chamber@ paccnj.org, www.paccnj.org

# Puerto Rico

**Puerto Rican Chamber of Commerce** • 3550 Biscayne Blvd., Ste. 306, Miami, FL, 33137, M 250, (305) 571-8006, Fax (305) 571-8007, ldr@puertoricanchamber.com, www.puertorican chamber.com

# Russia

**Russian-American Chamber of Commerce** • 970 Sidney Marcus Blvd., Ste. 1504, Atlanta, GA, 30324, M 200, (404) 202-7713, alla@russianamericanchamber.com , www.russian americanchamber.com

# Saint Lucia

**St. Lucia Natl. Dev. Corp.** • 800 2nd Ave., Ste. 400J, New York, NY, 10017, (212) 867-2952, Fax (212) 370-7867, www.stluciandc.com

# Saudi Arabia

**Royal Embassy of Saudi Arabia, Commercial Ofc.** • 601 New Hampshire Ave. N.W., Washington, DC, 20037, (202) 337-4088, Fax (202) 342-0271, saco@resa.org, www.saudicommercial office.com

# Singapore

**Intl. Enterprise Singapore** • 55 E. 59th St., Ste. 21A, New York, NY, 10022-1122, (212) 421-2207, Fax (212) 888-2897, newyork@ iesingapore.gov.sg, www.iesingapore.com

Foreign C/C in U.S.

# Spain

**Spain-U.S. Chamber of Commerce** • 350 5th Ave., Ste. 2600, New York, NY, 10118, M 450, (212) 967-2170, Fax (212) 564-1415, info@spainuscc.org, www.spainuscc.org

**Spain-U.S. Chamber of Commerce in Florida** • 1221 Brickell Ave., Ste. 1540, Miami, FL, 33131, M 400, (305) 358-5988, Fax (305) 358-6844, www.spain-uschamber.com

# Sweden

**Swedish-American Chamber of Commerce** • 570 Lexington Ave., 20th Flr., New York, NY, 10022, M 300, (212) 838-5530, Fax (212) 755-7953, info@saccny.org, www.saccny.org

**Swedish-American Chamber of Commerce** • 452 Tehami St., San Francisco, CA, 94103, M 70, (415) 781-4188, Fax (415) 781-4189, info@sacc-sf.org, www.sacc-usa.org/sf

# Switzerland

**Swiss American Chamber of Commerce** • New York Chapter, 500 Fifth Ave., Ste. 1800, New York, NY, 10110, (212) 246-7789, Fax (212) 246-1366, newyork@amcham.ch, www.amcham.ch

**Swiss American Chamber of Commerce** • P.O. Box 26007, San Francisco, CA, 94126, M 75, (415) 433-6679, swissamerican chamber@hotmail.com, www.amcham.ch

# Thailand

**Thai Trade Center** • 61 Broadway, Ste. 2810, New York, NY, 10006, (212) 482-0077, Fax (212) 482-1177, info@thaitradeny. com, www.thaitradeusa.com

# United Kingdom

**British American Bus. Cncl.** • 703 Market St., Ste. 1314, San Francisco, CA, 94103, M 245, (415) 296-8645, Fax (415) 296-9649, info@babcsf.org, www.babcsf.org

**British American Bus. Cncl.** • 11766 Wilshire Blvd., Ste. 1230, Los Angeles, CA, 90025, M 503, (310) 312-1962, Fax (310) 312-1914, info@babcla.org, www.babcla.org

**British American Bus. Cncl.–Orange County** • 25422 Trabuco Rd., Ste. 105-266, Lake Forest, CA, 92630 M 160, (949) 472-2221, Fax (949) 472-2215, info@babcoc.org, www.babcoc.org

**British American Bus. Inc.** • 52 Vanderbilt Ave., 20th Flr., New York, NY, 10017, M 470, (212) 661-4060, nyinfo@babinc.org, www.babinc.org

# Uzbekistan

**American-Uzbekistan Chamber of Commerce** • 1800 Massachusetts Ave., Washington, DC, 20036, M 75, (202) 973-5967, aucconline@gmail.com, www.aucconline.com

# Venezuela

**Venezuelan-American Chamber of Commerce** • 1850 Coral Way, Coral Gables, FL, 33145, M 300, (786) 953-6372, Fax (786) 953-5326, info@venezuelanchamber.org, www.venezuelan chamber.org

# Foreign Chambers of Commerce

## Albania

**Tirana** · *Chamber of Commerce & Ind. of Tirana* · Rr. Kavajes No. 6, M 2,000, 355-42-230284, Fax 355-42-227997, sekretaria@cci.al, www.cci.al

## Algeria

**Alger** · *Algerian Chamber of Commerce & Ind.* · BP 100 1er Nov., 16003, 213-21-967777, Fax 213-21-967070, infos@caci.dz, www.caci.dz

## Antigua & Barbuda

**Saint John's** · *Antigua & Barbuda Chamber of Commerce & Ind.* · P.O. Box 774, M 175, 268-46-20743, Fax 268-46-24575, chamcom@candw.ag

## Argentina

**Buenos Aires** · *Argentina Chamber of Commerce* · Av. L.N. Alem 36, 1003, M 3,150, 5411-43-318051, Fax 5411-43-319972, comext@cac.com.ar, www.cac.com.ar

**Buenos Aires** · *Argentine Chamber of Exporters* · Av. Roque Saenz Pena 740, Piso 1, 1035, M 500, 5411-43-94482, Fax same, contacto@cera.org.ar, www.cera.org.ar

**Buenos Aires** · *Camara Argentina de Comercio Electronico* · Calle 25 de Mayo 611 Piso 2, 1005, M 204, 5411-59-177435, contacto@cace.org.ar, www.cace.org.ar

**Cordoba** · *Central Region Chamber of Commerce* · Rosario de Santa Fe, 231 Piso 4, 5000, M 200, 5435-14-214804, Fax 5435-14-243869

## Aruba

**Oranjestad** · *Aruba Chamber of Commerce & Ind.* · Lorraine de Souza, Dir., P.O. Box 140, M 10,000, 297-58-21120, Fax 297-58-83200, secretariat@arubachamber.com, www.arubachamber.com

## Australia

**Albany, WA** · *Albany Chamber of Commerce & Ind.* · 63 Grey Street East, 6330, M 430, 618-98-422577, Fax 618-98-423040, ceo@albanycci.org.au, www.albanycci.org.au

**Brisbane, QLD** · *Queensland Chamber of Commerce and Ind.* · 375 Wickham Terrace, 4000, M 3,000, 617-38-422244, Fax 617-38-323195, info@cciq.com.au, www.cciq.com.au

**Cairns, QLD** · *Cairns Chamber of Commerce* · P.O. Box 2336, 4870, M 800, 617-40-311838, Fax 617-40-311838, info@cairnschamber.com.au, www.cairnschamber.com.au

**Darwin, NT** · *Northern Territory Chamber of Commerce & Ind.* · GPO Box 1825, 801, M 1,400, 618-89-828100, Fax 618-89-811405, darwin@chambernt.com.au, www.chambernt.com.au

**Deakin West, ACT** · *ACT & Region Chamber of Commerce & Ind.* · P.O. Box 192, Canberra, 2600, M 900, 612-62-835200, Fax 612-62-822436, chamber@actchamber.com.au, www.actchamber.com.au

**East Perth, WA** · *Chamber of Commerce & Ind. of Western Australia* · 180 Hay St., PO Box 6209, 6892, M 5,000, 618-93-657555, Fax 618-93-657550, info@cciwa.com, www.cciwa.com

**Hobart, TAS** · *Tasmanian Chamber of Commerce & Ind.* · GPO Box 793, 7001, M 2,500, 613-62-363600, Fax 613-62-311278, admin@tcci.com.au, www.tcci.com.au

**Queen Victoria Terr ACT** · *Australian Chamber of Commerce & Ind.* · P.O. Box E14, 2600, 616-27-32311, Fax 616-27-33196,

**Sydney, NSW** · *State Chamber of Commerce (New South Wales)* · GPO Box 4280, 2000, M 30,000, 612-93-508100, Fax 612-93-508199, nick.davy@thechamber.com.au, www.thechamber.com.au

**Unley, SA** · *South Australian Employers' Chamber of Commerce* · 136 Greenhill Rd., 5061, M 3,200, 618-83-000000, Fax 618-83-000001, enquiries@business-sa.com, www.business-sa.com

## Austria

**Feldkirch** · *Wirtschaftskammer Vorarlberg* · Wichnergasse 9, A-6800, 435-52-23050, Fax 435-52-230514, office@wkvlbg.at, wko.at/vlbg

**Graz** · *Economic Chamber of Styria* · P.O. Box 1038, A-8021, M 45,000, 43-31-66010, Fax 433-16-601361, office@wkstmk.at, wko.at/stmk

**Innsbruck** · *Tyrolean Chamber of Commerce* · Meinhardstrasse 14, A-6020, 4-35-90905, Fax 4359-09-051467, offfice@wktirol.at, wko.at/tirol

**Vienna** · *International Congress Vienna* · Bˆrsegasse 9/8, A-1010, 4315-32-100014, Fax 4315-32-100030, office@icon-vienna.net, www.icon-vienna.net

**Vienna** · *Vienna Chamber of Commerce & Ind.* · Stubenring 8-10, A-1010, 4-31-51450, Fax 431-51-37787, office@wkwien.at, wko.at/wien

## Bahamas

**Grand Bahama** · *Grand Bahama Chamber of Commerce* · PO Box F-40808, Freeport, M 240, 242-35-28329, Fax 242-35-23280, gbchamber@batelnet.bs, www.gbchamber.com

**Nassau** · *Bahamas Chamber of Commerce* · Dionisio D. Aguilar, Pres., Shirley St. & Collins Ave., P.O. Box N-665, M 348, 242-32-22145, Fax 242-32-24649, www.thebahamaschamber.com

## Bahrain

**Manama** · *Bahrain Chamber of Commerce & Ind.* · P.O. Box 248, M 7,000, 973-17-576666, Fax 973-17-576600, bcci@bcci.bh, www.bcci.bh

## Bangladesh

**Chittagong** · *Chittagong Chamber of Commerce & Ind.* · Chamber House, 38, Agrabad C/A, 4100, M 5,000, 880-31-713366, Fax 880-31-710183, ccci@globalctg.net, www.chittagongchamber.com

**Dhaka** · *Federation of Bangladesh Chambers of Comm. & Ind.* · 60, Motijheel C/A, M 1,700, 880-29-560102, Fax 880-27-176030, fbcci@bol-online.com, www.fbcci-bd.org

**Khulna** • *Khulna Chamber of Commerce & Ind.* • Chamber Mansion 5, KDA C/A, PO Box 26, M 1,984, 880-41-721695, Fax 880-41-725365, kcci@bttb.net.bd, www.khulnachamber.com

# Barbados

**Bridgetown** • *Barbados Chamber of Commerce & Ind.* • P.O. Box 189, M 207, 246-42-62056, Fax 246-42-92907, bdscham@ caribsurf.com, www.bdscham.com

**Bridgetown** • *Barbados Investment & Dev. Corp.* • PO Box 1250, M 508, 246-42-75350, Fax 246-42-67802, bidc@bidc.org, www.bidc.com

# Belgium

**Antwerp** • *Chamber of Commerce & Ind. of Antwerp* • Markgravestraat 12, 2000, M 3,000, 323-23-22219, Fax 323-23-36442, info.aw@voka.be, www.voka.be

**Brussels** • *Federation of Chambers of Commerce & Ind.* • Avenue Louise 500, B-1050322-20-90550, Fax 322-20-90568, fedcci@cci.be, www.cci.be

**Kortrijk** • *Chamber of Commerce West Flanders* • Casinoplein, Box 10, 8500, M 4,300, 325-62-35051, Fax 325-62-18564, info@ kukwul.voka.de, www.kukwul.voka.de

# Belize

**Belize City** • *Belize Chamber of Commerce & Ind.* • 63 Regent St., P.O. Box 291, M 300, 501-22-73148, Fax 501-22-74984, bcci@ btl.net, www.belize.org

# Bermuda

**Hamilton** • *Bermuda Chamber of Commerce* • Diane Gordon, P.O. Box HM 655, HM CX, M 750, 441-29-54201, Fax 441-29-25779, dgordon@bcc.bm, www.bermudacommerce.com

# Bolivia

**La Paz** • *Chamber of Commerce of Bolivia* • P.O. Box 7, M 1,500, 591-23-78606, Fax 591-23-91004, cnc@boliviacomercio.org.bo, www.boliviacomercio.org.bo

**Santa Cruz** • *Chamber of Commerce & Ind. of Santa Cruz* • Av. Las Americas, Ste. 7, Casilla 180, M 1,500, 591-33-334555, Fax 591-33-342353, cainco@cainco.org.bo, cainco.org.bo

# Bosnia & Herzegovina

**Tuzla** • *Chamber of Eco. of Federation of Bosnia and Hercegovina* • Mitra T. Uce 118, B1H-75000, 387-75-281600, Fax 387-75-281601, novosped@bih.net.ba

# Brazil

**Rio de Janeiro** • *National Confederaton of Ind.* • Av. General Justo, 307, 20021-130, 552-13-804920, Fax 552-13-804920, sgr@ cnc.com.br, www.cnc.com.br

**Sao Paulo** • *Federation of Industries of Sao Paulo* • Paulista Avenue 1313, 01311-923, M 9,500, 551-12-536433, Fax 551-12-531972, cin@cin.org.br, www.cin.org.br

# Bulgaria

**Sofia** • *Bulgaria-Azerbaijan Chamber of Commerce & Ind.* • 42B, Rodopski Izvor str.,, 1680, M 500, 359-29-582701, office@ bg-az.com, www.bg-az.com

**Sofia** • *Bulgarian Chamber of Commerce & Ind.* • 9 Iskar Str., 1058, 359-28-117400, Fax 359-29-873209, bcci@bcci.bg, www.bcci.bg

# Burkina Faso

**Ouagadougou** • *Chamber of Commerce & Ind.* • P.O. Box 502, 226-50-306114, Fax 226-50-306116, www.ccia.bf

# Cameroon

**Douala** • *Chamber of Commerce, Ind. & Mines of Cameroon* • B.P. 4011, 237-34-29881, Fax 237-34-25596, cride-g77@camnet.cm

# Cape Verde

**Mindelo SV** • *Camara de Comercio, Industria y Servicos* • CP 728, M 450, 238-23-28495, Fax 238-23-28496

# Cayman Islands

**Grand Cayman** • *Cayman Islands Chamber of Commerce & Better Bus.* • Wil Pineau, CEO, 2nd Flr., Macdonald Square Bldg., P.O. Box 1000 GT, M 629, 345-94-98090, Fax 345-94-90220, info@ caymanchamber.ky, www.caymanchamber.ky

# Chile

**Valdivia** • *Camara de Comercio e Ind. De Valdivia* • Picarte St. 461 - of. 21, M 55, 566-32-13288, Fax 566-32-13288

# China

**Beijing** • *China Cncl. for the Promotion of Intl. Trade* • 1 Fuxingmenwai St., 100860, 8610-68-013344, Fax 8610-68-011370, www.ccpit.org

**Chengdu** • *China Cncl. for the Promotion of Intl. Trade* • 11th Flr., Guo Ji Shang Hui Hui Guan, No. 36 Shu Xing Xi Jie, 610036, M 2,800, 8628-61-963022, Fax 8628-61-963098, yiyang189@ yahoo.com.cn, www.ccpit-sichuan.org

**Quingdao** • *China Chamber of Intl. Commerce* • Yan'an 3 Rd., Rm. 1005, 266071, M 300, 8653-23-897505, Fax 8653-23-897507, qdccpit@public.qd.sd.cn

# Colombia

**Buenaventura** • *Camara de Comercio de Buenaventura* • Calle 1 No. 1A-88, M 4,500, 572-24-24508, Fax 572-24-34202, presidencia@ccbun.org, www.ccbun.org

**Cartagena** • *Camara de Comercio de Cartagena* • Santa Teresa St. No 32-41, 2117, M 15,000, 575-65-01110, Fax 575-65-01126, camaradecomercio@cccartagena.org.co, www.cccartagena.org.co

**Medellin** • *Medellin Chamber of Commerce* • Av. Oriental 52-82, M 4,156, 574-51-38244, Fax 574-51-37757, rroldany@ camaramed.org.co, www.camaramed.org.co

# Costa Rica

**San Jose** • *Chamber of Commerce of Costa Rica* • P.O. Box 1114, 1000, M 1,200, 506-22-10005, Fax 506-25-69680, camara@camara-comercio.com, www.camara-comercio.com

# Cote d'Ivoire

**Abidjan** • *Chambre de Commerce et d'Industrie* • BP 1399, 1, M 156, 225-20-331600, Fax 225-20-323942, contact@cci-ci.org, www.cci-ci.org

# Croatia

**Zagreb** • *Croatian Chamber of Eco.* • Rooseveltov trg 2, P.O. Box 630, 10000, M 60,000, 385-14-561555, Fax 385-14-828380, hgk@hgk.hr, www.hgk.hr

# Cuba

**Havana** • *Chamber of Commerce of the Republic of Cuba* • 21 No. 661 esq.A, Vedado, PO Box 370, 10 400, M 610, 53-75-51321, Fax 53-73-33042, correo@camara.com.cu, www.camaracuba.cu

# Cyprus

**Limassol** • *Famagusta Chamber of Commerce & Ind.* • Iacovos Hadjivarnavas, Secy./Dir., P.O. Box 53124, 3300, M 600, 357-25-370165, Fax 357-25-370291, chamberf@cytanet.com.cy, www.fcci.org.cy

**Nicosia** • *Cyprus Chamber of Commerce & Ind.* • P.O. Box 21455, 1509, M 8,000, 357-26-69500, Fax 357-26-69048, chamber@ccci.org.cy, www.ccci.org.cy

# Denmark

**Copenhagen** • *Danish Chamber of Commerce* • Boersen, 1217, 453-37-46000, Fax 453-37-46080, info@danskerhverv.dk, www.danskerhverv.dk

# Dominican Republic

**Santo Domingo** • *Santo Domingo Chamber of Commerce* • P.O. Box 815, M 1,255, 809-68-22688, Fax 809-68-52228, camara.sto.dgo@codetel.net.do, www.ccpsd.org.do

# Ecuador

**Guayaquil** • *Guayaquil Chamber of Commerce* • Av. Francisco de Orellana y V.H Sicouret, Edif. Las Camaras P.3, M 9,000, 593-42-682771, Fax 593-42-682725, www.lacamara.org

**Quito** • *Camara de Industriales de Pichincha* • P.O. Box 17-01-2438, M 1,000, 593-22-452500, Fax 593-22-448118, camara@camindustriales.org.ec, www.camindustriales.org.ec

# Egypt

**Cairo** • *Cairo Chamber of Commerce* • 4 Midan El Falaki, 202-35-58261, Fax 202-35-63603, www.cairochamber.org.eg

**Cairo** • *Federation of Egyptian Chambers of Commerce* • 4 El Falaki Sq., 202-35-51813, Fax 202-35-57940

# El Salvador

**San Salvador** • *Camara De Comercio E Industria De El Salvador* • P.O. Box 1640, M 1,900, 503-22-313000, Fax 503-22-714461, camara@camarasal.com, www.camarasal.com

# Estonia

**Tallinn** • *Estonian Chamber of Commerce* • Toom-Kooli 17, 10130, M 3,000, 372-60-40060, Fax 372-60-40061, koda@koda.ee, www.koda.ee

# Finland

**Helsinki** • *Central Chamber of Commerce of Finland* • P.O. Box 1000, 101, 3589-42-426200, Fax 358-96-50303, keskuskauppakamari@chamber.fi, www.chamber.fi

**Jyvaskyla** • *Central Finland Chamber of Commerce* • Sepankatu 4, 40100, M 360, 358-14-652400, Fax 358-14-652411, anja.raisanen@chamber.fi, www.centralfinlandchamber.fi

**Kuopio** • *Kuopio Chamber of Commerce* • Kasarmikatu 2, 70110, M 800, 3581-72-663800, Fax 3581-72-823304, www.kuopiochamber.fi

**Lahti** • *Hame Chamber of Commerce* • Ruahankatu 10, 15110, M 800, 358-38-216000, Fax 358-38-216050, info@hamechamber.fi, www.hamechamber.fi

**Tampere** • *Tampere Chamber of Commerce* • Kehrasaari B, 33200, M 1,150, 358-32-300555, Fax 358-32-300550, www.tampere.chamber.fi

**Turku** • *Turku Chamber of Commerce* • Puolalankatu 1, 20100, M 1,400, 358-22-743400, Fax 358-22-743440, kauppakamari@turku.chamber.fi, www.turku.chamber.fi

# France

**Marseille** • *Chamber of Commerce & Ind. of Marseille Provence* • 35, rue Sainte-Victoire, 13292, 331-91-138655, Fax 331-91-138501, www.marseille-provence.cci.fr

**Paris** • *Chamber of Commerce & Ind. of France* • Avenue d'Iena 45, F-75769, 331-40-693700, Fax 331-47-206128, service.courrier@acfci.cci.fr, www.acfci.cci.fr

**Paris** • *Chamber de Commerce et D'Industrie de Paris* • 27 Av. Friedland, 75382, M 30,000, 331-05-657069, Fax 331-55-657070, www.ccip.fr

# Gambia

**Banjul** • *Gambia Chamber of Commerce & Ind.* • P.O. Box 333, M 275, 22-02-27765, Fax 22-02-29671, gcci@qanet.com, www.gambiachamber.gm

# Germany, Federal Rep. of

**Berlin** • *Deutscher Industrie und Handelstag* • Breite Strasse 29, 10178, 493-02-03080, Fax 4930-20-3081000, diht@berlin.dihk.de, www.diht.de

**Bremen** • *Bremen Chamber of Commerce* • PO Box 105107, 28051, 4942-13-637240, Fax 4942-13-637246, www.handelskammer-bremen.de

Foreign C/C

**Dusseldorf** · *Dusseldorf Chamber of Ind. & Commerce* · Ernst-Schneider-Platz 1, 40212, 4921-13-557220, Fax 4921-13-557400, ihkdus@duesseldorf.ihk.de, www.duesseldorf.ihk.de

**Hannover** · *Hannover Chamber of Ind. & Commerce* · Schiffgraben 49, 30175, 4951-13-107200, Fax 4951-13-107456, info@hannover.ihk.de, www.hannover.ihk.de

# Ghana

**Accra** · *Assn. of Ghana Industries* · P. O. Box AN - 8624, M 1,500, 233-21-779023, Fax 233-21-773143, agi@agighana.org, www.agighana.org

**Accra** · *Ghana Natl. Chamber of Commerce* · P.O. Box 2325, M 2,000, 2330-00-000000, Fax 233-21-255202, info@ghanachamber.org, www.ghanachamber.org

**Takoradi** · *Sekondi-Takoradi Reg. Chamber of Commerce* · P.O. Box 45, M 150, 233-31-22385, Fax 233-31-23588, takoradi@ghanachamber.org, www.ghanachamber.org

# Greece

**Athens** · *Union of Hellenic Chambers of Commerce* · 7 Academias St., 10671, 301-36-32702, Fax 301-36-22320, info@acci.gr, www.acci.gr

**Crete** · *Heraklion Chamber of Commerce & Ind.* · 9, Koroneou Str., P.O. Box 1154, Heraklion, 71110, M 12,000, 308-12-29013, Fax 308-12-22914, root@ebeh.gr, www.ebeh.gr

**Patras** · *Patras Chamber of Commerce & Ind.* · 58 Michalakopoulou St., 26110, 306-12-77779, Fax 306-12-76519, www.patrascc.gr

**Piraeus** · *Piraeus Chamber of Commerce & Ind.* · PO Box 185-31, 18531, M 12,000, 3021-04-177241, Fax 3021-04-178680, evep@pcci.gr, www.pcci.gr

**Thessaloniki** · *Thessaloniki Chamber of Commerce & Ind.* · 29 Tsimiski Str., 54624, M 21,000, 3023-10-370100, Fax 3023-10-370114, root@ebeth.gr, www.ebeth.gr

# Grenada

**Saint George's** · *Grenada Chamber of Ind. & Commerce* · P.O. Box 129, M 180, 473-44-02937, Fax 473-44-06621, info@grenadachamber.org, www.grenadachamber.org

# Guam

**Hagatna** · *Guam Chamber of Commerce* · Reina A. Leddy, Pres., 173 Aspinall Ave., Ste. 101, Ada Plaza Center Bldg., 96910, M 320, 671-47-26311, Fax 671-47-26202, gchamber@guamchamber.com.gu, www.guamchamber.com.gu

# Guatemala

**Guatemala City** · *Camara de Comercio de Guatemala* · 10a. Calle 3-80, zona 1, 1001, M 5,500, 502-23-268840, Fax 502-22-291897, info@camaradecomercio.org.gt, www.negociosenguatemala.com

**Guatemala City** · *Camara de Industria de Guatemala* · Ruta 6, 9-21 zona 4, nivel 12 Edificio, 214, M 1,475, 502-23-809000, Fax 502-23-341090, info@industriaguate.com, www.industriaguate.com

# Guyana

**Georgetown** · *Georgetown Chamber of Commerce & Ind.* · 156 Waterloo Street, M 85, 592-22-63519, Fax 592-22-63519, info@georgetownchamberofcommerce.org, georgetownchamberofcommerce.org

# Honduras

**Tegucigalpa** · *Tegucigalpa Chamber of Commerce & Ind.* · P.O. Box 3444, M 1,700, 50-43-28110, Fax 50-43-12049

# Hong Kong (China)

**Hong Kong** · *Hong Kong General Chamber of Commerce* · 22/F United Centre, 95 Queensway, M 4,150, 852-25-299229, Fax 852-25-279843, chamber@chamber.org.hk, www.chamber.org.hk

**Hong Kong** · *Hong Kong Trade Dev. Cncl.* · 38th Flr., Ofc. Tower, Convention Plaza, 1 Harbour Rd., Wanchai, 852-25-844333, Fax 852-28-240249, hktdc@tdc.org.hk

# Hungary

**Budapest** · *Budapest Chamber of Commerce & Ind.* · Kristina Krt 99, 1016, 361-48-82111, Fax 361-48-82119, www.bkik.hu

**Budapest** · *Hungarian Chamber of Commerce* · Kossuth ter. 6-8, 1055, 361-47-45141, Fax 361-47-45149, intdept@mkik.hu, www.mkik.hu

**Zalaegerszeg** · *Chamber of Commerce of Zala County* · PO Box 211, 8900, M 18,800, 369-25-50514, Fax 369-25-50525, zmkik@zmkik.hu, www.zmkik.hu

# Iceland

**Reykjavik** · *Iceland Chamber of Commerce* · Kringlan 7, 103, M 397, 354-51-07100, Fax 354-56-86564, info@chamber.is, www.vi.is

# India

**Mubai** · *Bombay Industries Assn.* · Sahakar Bhavan, Kurla Indl estate, LBS Marg Ghatkopar, 400086, 912-28-386637, Fax 912-28-386829, info@biaindia.org, www.biaindia.org

**Mumbai** · *Indo-American Chamber of Commerce* · 1-C Vulcan Insurance Bldg., Churchgate, 400 020, M 2,800, 912-22-821413, Fax 912-22-046141, ho@iaccindia.com, www.iaccindia.com

**New Delhi** · *Federation of Indian Chambers of Commerce & Ind.* · Federation House, Tansen Marg, 110 001, M 500, 112-37-38760, Fax 911-13-320714, ficci@ficci.com, www.ficci.com

# Iran

**Tehran** · *Iran Chamber of Commerce, Industries & Mines* · 254 Taleghani Ave., P.O. Box 15875-4671, 15814, 9821-88-8846031, Fax 9821-88-825111, info@iccim.ir, www.iccim.ir

# Ireland

**Cork** · *Cork Chamber of Commerce* · Conor Healy, CEO, Fitzgerald House, Summerhill North, M 900, 3532-14-509044, Fax 3532-14-508568, info@corkchamber.ie, www.corkchamber.ie

**Drogheda** · *Drogheda & Dist. Chamber of Commerce* · Patricia Rooney, Pres., Chamber Bldgs., 10 Dublin Rd., M 180, 3534-19-833544, Fax 3534-19-841609, president@droghedachamber.com, www.droghedachamber.com

**Dublin** · *Chambers Ireland* · 17 Merrion Sq., 2, M 10,000, 353-14-004300, Fax 353-16-612811, info@chambers.ie, www.chambers.ie

**Dublin** · *Dublin Chamber of Commerce* · PJ Timmins, CEO, 7 Clare St., 2, M 2,500, 353-16-130800, Fax 353-16-766043, info@dubchamber.ie, www.dubchamber.ie

**Galway** · *Galway Chamber of Commerce & Ind.* · Commerce House, Merchants Rd., M 450, 353-91-563536, Fax 353-91-561963, info@galwaychamber.com, www.galwaychamber.com

**Limerick** · *Chamber of Commerce of Limerick* · 96 O'Connell St., M 700, 353-61-415180, Fax 353-61-415785, info@limerickchamber.ie, www.limerickchamber.ie

**Sligo** · *Sligo Chamber of Commerce* · 16 Quay Street, M 370, 353-71-61274, Fax 353-71-60912, info@sligochamber.ie, www.sligochamber.ie

**Waterford** · *Waterford Chamber of Commerce* · 2 George's St., P , M 600, 353-51-872639, Fax 353-51-876002, info@waterfordchamber.ie, www.waterfordchamber.ie

**Wexford** · *Wexford Chamber of Ind. & Commerce* · The Ballast Office, Crescent Quay, M 220, 353-53-22226, Fax 353-53-24170, info@wexfordchamber.ie, www.wexchamber.ie

# Ireland, Northern

**Londonderry** · *Londonderry Chamber of Commerce* · Bishop Street, 1 St. Columb's Ct., BT48 6PT, 287-12-62379, Fax 287-12-86789, info@londonderrychamber.co.uk, www.londonderrychamber.co.uk

# Israel

**Haifa** · *Chamber of Commerce & Ind. of Haifa and North* · 53 Haatzmaut Rd., P.O. Box 33176, 31331, M 600, 972-48-626364, Fax 972-48-645428, main@haifachamber.org.il, www.haifachamber.com

**Jerusalem** · *Jerusalem Chamber of Commerce* · P.O. Box 2083, 91020, M 250, 972-26-254333, Fax 972-26-254335

**Tel Aviv** · *Federation of Israeli Chambers of Commerce* · 84 Hahashmonaim St., P.O. Box 20027, 67132, M 5,000, 972-35-631020, Fax 972-35-619027, chamber@chamber.org.il, www.chamber.org.il

# Italy

**Alessandria** · *Alessandria Chamber of Commerce* · via San Lorenzo 21, 15100, 39-13-13131, Fax 391-31-43186, camera.commercio@al.camcom.it, www.al.camcom.it

**Bologna** · *Camera di Commercio, Ind, Art, E Ag di Bologna* · Piazza Affari, Piazza Costituzione 8, 40128, 395-16-093111, Fax 395-16-093451, www.bo.camcom.it

**Genova** · *Genova Chamber of Commerce* · via Garibaldi 4, 16124, 39-10-27041, Fax 391-02-704300, camera.genova@ge.camcom.it, www.ge.camcom.it

**Milano** · *Milano Chamber of Commerce* · via Meravigli 9/B, 20123, 3-92-85151, Fax 392-85-154232, urp@mi.camcom.it, www.mi.camcom.it

**Rome** · *Chamber of Commerce & Ind. of Italy* · Piazza Sallustio 21, I-00187, 3-96-47041, Fax 396-47-44741, unioncamere@unioncamere.it

**Rome** · *Rome Chamber of Commerce* · v. de Burro 147, 186, 39-65-20821, Fax 396-67-90547

**Trieste** · *Trieste Chamber of Commerce* · Piazza Della Borsa 14, 34121, M 19,000, 39-40-67011, Fax 394-06-701321, promo@ts.camcom.it, www.ts.camcom.it

# Ivory Coast

*See Cote d'Ivoire*

# Jamaica

**Kingston** · *Jamaica Chamber of Commerce* · 39 Hope Rd., P.O. Box 172, 10, M 780, 876-92-20150, Fax 876-92-49056, info@jamaicachamber.org.jm, www.jamaicachamber.org.jm

# Japan

**Hiroshima** · *Hiroshima Chamber of Commerce* · 44 Matomachi 5-chome, Naka-ku, 730-8510, 818-22-226610, Fax 818-22-220108

**Hokkaido** · *Sapporo Chamber of Commerce & Ind.* · Kita-1 Nishi-2, Chuo-ku, Sapporo, 060-8610, M 25,000, 811-12-311122, Fax 811-12-311078, kokusaj@sapporo-cci.or.jp, www.sapporo-cci.or.jp

**Kawasaki** · *Kawasaki Chamber of Commerce & Ind.* · 11-2, Ekimaehoncho, Kawasaki-ku, 210-0007, M 13,000, 814-42-114111, Fax 814-42-114118, kokusai@kawasaki-cci.or.jp, www.kawasaki-cci.or.jp

**Kobe** · *Kobe Chamber of Commerce & Ind.* · 1 Minatojima-Nakamachi, 6-chome, Chuo-ku, 650-8543, 817-83-035806, Fax 817-83-062348, info@kobe-cci.or.jp, www2.kobe-cci.or.jp

**Osaka** · *Osaka Chamber of Commerce & Ind.* · 2-8 Hommachi-Bashi, Chuo-ku, 540-0029, 816-69-446400, Fax 816-69-446293, intl@osaka.cci.or.jp, www.osaka.cci.or.jp

**Tokyo** · *Japan Chamber of Commerce & Ind.* · 3-2-2 Marunouchi, Chiyoda-ku, 100-0005, M 520, 813-32-837851, Fax 813-32-166497, info@jcci.or.jp, www.jcci.or.jp

# Jordan

**Amman** · *Jordan Chamber of Commerce* · P.O. Box 7029, 11118, 962-65-665492, Fax 962-65-685997, info@jocc.org.jo, www.jocc.org.jo

**Amman** · *Amman Chamber of Commerce* · Shaker Bin Zaid St., P.O. Box 287, 11118, 962-65-666151, Fax 962-65-666155, info@ammanchamber.org.jo, www.ammanchamber.org

# Kazakhstan

**Almaty** · *Chamber of Commerce & Ind. of Kazakhstan* · P.O. Box 1966, 47300, M 500, 831-72-323833, Fax 831-72-323833, akmcci@dan.kz, www.chamber.kz

# Kenya

**Nairobi** · *Kenya Natl. Chamber of Commerce & Ind.* · P.O. Box 47024, 100, M 15,000, 254-22-20867, Fax 254-23-34293

**Foreign C/C**

# Korea, Republic of

**Busan** · *Busan Chamber of Commerce & Ind.* · 853-1, Bumchun-Dong, Busanjin-Ku, 614-721, M 6,000, 825-19-907086, Fax 825-19-907099, youme@pcci.or.kr, www.pcci.or.kr

**Seoul** · *Korea Chamber of Commerce & Ind.* · CPO Box 25, M 71, 822-31-63566, Fax 822-75-79475, trade@kccioa.kcci.or.kr, www.kcci.or.kr

# Kuwait

**Kuwait City** · *Kuwait Chamber of Commerce & Ind.* · P.O. Box 775 Safat, Kuwait, 13008, M 30,000, 965-18-05580, Fax 965-22-433858, kcci@kcci.org.kw, www.kuwaitchamber.org.kw

# Kyrgyzstan

**Bishkek** · *Chamber of Commerce of the Kyrgyz Republic* · 107 Kievskaya str., 720001, M 349, 9963-12-210565, Fax 9963-12-210575

# Latvia

**Riga** · *Latvian Chamber of Commerce & Ind.* · Valdemara str. 35, 1010, M 778, 371-67-201102, info@chamber.lv, www.chamber.lv

# Lebanon

**Beirut** · *Chamber of Commerce & Ind. of Beirut & Mt. Lebanon* · P.O. Box 11-1801, M 20,000, 961-14-85461, info@ccib.org.lb, www.ccib.org.lb

# Lithuania

**Kaunas** · *Kaunas Reg. Chamber of Commerce, Ind. & Crafts* · P.O. Box 2111, LT-3000, M 300, 370-37-229212, Fax 370-72-08330, chamber@chamber.lt, www.chamber.lt

**Panevezys** · *Panevezys Reg. Chamber of Commerce, Ind. & Crafts* · Respublikos g. 34, 35173, M 300, 370-45-463687, Fax 370-45-462227, panevezys@chambers.lt, www.ccic.lt

**Siauliai** · *Siauliai Reg. Chamber of Commerce, Ind. & Crafts* · Vilniaus str. 88, LT-76285, M 180, 370-41-523224, Fax 370-41-523903, siauliai@chambers.lt, www.rumai.lt

**Vilnius** · *Assn. of Lithuanian Chambers of Commerce & Ind.* · J. Tumo-Vaizganto str. 9/1-63A, 2001, M 1,600, 370-52-612102, Fax 370-52-612112, info@chambers.lt, www.chambers.lt

# Luxembourg

**Luxembourg-City** · *Grand Duchy of Luxembourg Chamber of Commerce* · 7, rue Alcide Gasperi, L-2981, M 35,000, 352-42-39391, Fax 35-24-38326, chamcom@cc.lu, www.cc.lu

# Madagascar

**Antananarivo** · *Chamber of Commerce & Ind. Antananarivo* · 20, rue Henry Razanatseheno Antaninarenina, 101, M 60, 2612-02-2220211, contact@cci-tana.org, www.cci-tana.org

# Malawi

**Blantyre** · *Malawi Confederation of Chambers of Commerce & Ind.* · P.O. Box 258, M 400, 265-18-71988, Fax 265-18-71147, mcci@mccci.org, www.mccci.org

# Malaysia

**Kuala Lumpur** · *Malaysian Intl. Chamber of Commerce & Ind.* · P.O. Box 12921, 50792, M 1,100, 603-62-017708, Fax 603-62-107705, radha@micci.com, www.micci.com

# Malta

**Valletta** · *Malta Chamber of Commerce* · Exchange Buildings, Republic Street, VLT05, M 826, 356-21-233873, Fax 356-21-245223, admin@maltachamber.org.mt, www.chamber.org.mt

# Marshall Islands

**Majuro, MH** · *Majuro Chamber of Commerce* · P.O. Box 1226, 96960, M 50, 692-62-53250, Fax 692-62-53505, commerce@ntamar.net, www.marshallislandschamber.net

# Mauritius

**Port-Louis** · *Mauritius Chamber of Commerce & Ind.* · 3 Royal St., M 400, 230-20-83301, Fax 230-20-80076, mcci@intnet.mu, www.mcci.org

# Mexico

**Cozumel** · *Cozumel Chamber of Commerce* · 20 Av. sur No. 916, Quintana Roo, 77600, M 1,800, 529-87-20583, Fax 529-87-25014,

**Delegacion Cuauhtemoc** · *Mexico City Chamber of Commerce* · Paseo de la Reforma, Ste. 42, Col. Centro, Mexico DF, 6048, 5255-36-852269, Fax same, sos@ccmexico.com.mx, www.camaradecomercio.com.mx

**Fresnillo** · *Fresnillo Chamber of Commerce* · America, Ste. 1, A.P. 18, Zacatecas, 99000, M 400, 524-93-21082, Fax 524-93-23578, canacofr@server.uaf.mx,

**Merida** · *Merida Chamber of Commerce* · Av Itzaes, Ste. 273 x39, Yucatan, 97070, M 700, 529-92-53033, Fax 529-92-55933, canameri@prodigy.net.mx

**Puebla** · *Puebla Chamber of Commerce* · Ave. Reforma, Ste. 2704, 7 Piso, Puebla, 72140, M 3,021, 5222-22-480800, Fax 5222-22-310655, canacq@axtel.net, www.canacopuebla.org.mx

**Saltillo** · *Saltillo Chamber of Commerce* · Av. Universidad, Ste. 514, Coahuila, 25260, M 2,300, 528-41-55611, Fax 528-41-52903, conasalt@mcsa.net.mx

**Tijuana** · *Tijuana Chamber of Commerce* · Xavier Villaurritia 1271 Zona Rio, Baja California Norte, 22320, M 8,000, 5270-00-000000, Fax 5270-00-000000, web@canacotijuana.com, www.canacotijuana.com

**Victoria** · *Victoria Chamber of Commerce* · Juarez 14 y 15, Ste. 324, A.P. 113, Tamaulipas, 87000, M 1,400, 521-31-20031, Fax 521-31-20031, canvitam@tamps1.telmex.net.mx

**Zapopan** · *National Chamber of Commerce of Guadalajara* · Av. Vallarta, Ste. 4095, Jalisco, 45000, M 12,000, 523-12-29020, Fax 523-12-17950, comexca@vianet.com.mx

**La Paz** · *La Paz Chamber of Commerce* · Mexico 1970 E/Bravo y Allende, Baja California Sur, 23040, 526-12-122751, correo@canacolapaz.com, www.canacolapaz.com

# Micronesia

**Colonia** · *Yap State Div. of Commerce & Industries* · PO Box 36, Yap State, 96943, M 50, 691-35-02182, Fax 691-35-02571, yapci@mail.fm, fsminvest.fm/yap

**Tofol** · *Kosrae State Chamber of Commerce* · P.O. Box 600, Kosrae State, 96944, M 17, 691-37-03044, Fax 691-37-02066, kosraeci@mail.fm, fsminvest.fm/kosrae

**Weno** · *Chuuk State Chamber of Commerce* · Larry Bruton, Pres., P.O. Box 700, Truk Islands, Chuuk State, 96942, M 27, 691-33-02318, Fax 691-33-02314, fsminvest.fm/chuuk

# Moldova

**Chisinau** · *Chamber of Commerce & Ind. of the Rep. of Moldova* · 151 Stefan cel Mare Av, 2004, M 1,200, 373-22-21552, Fax 373-22-41453, 151 Stefan cel Mare Av, www.chamber.md

# Mongolia

**Ulaanbaatar** · *Ulaanbaatar Chamber of Commerce* · P.O. Box 254, 210136, M 400, 976-13-29910, Fax 976-13-11385, ubcc@magicnet.mn

# Mozambique

**Maputo** · *Mozambique Chamber of Commerce* · P.O. Box 1836, M 200, 258-14-91970, Fax 258-14-90428, cacomo@teledata.mz, www.teledata.mz/cacomo/index.htm

# Namibia

**Windhoek** · *Namibia National Chamber of Commerce & Ind.* · P.O. Box 9355, M 900, 264-61-228809, Fax 264-61-228009, www.ncci.org.na

# Nepal

**Kathmandu** · *Federation of Nepalese Chambers of Commerce & Ind.* · P.O. Box 269, M 595, 977-14-262218, Fax 977-14-262007, fncci@mos.com.np, www.fncci.org

# Netherlands, The

**Amsterdam** · *Chamber of Commerce & Ind. For Amsterdam* · PO Box 2852, 1000 CW, 312-05-314000, Fax 312-05-314799, post@amsterdam.kvk.nl, www.amsterdam.kvk.nl

**Arnhem** · *Chamber of Commerce & Ind. for Central Gelderland* · P.O. Box 9292, 6800 GA, 312-63-538888, Fax 312-63-538999, www.kvk.nl

**Eindhoven** · *Kamer van Koophandel Oost-Brabant* · P.O. Box 735, 5600 AS, 314-02-323911, Fax 314-02-449505, info@eindhoven.kvk.nl, www.eindhoven.kvk.nl

**Gouda** · *Central Holland Chamber of Commerce & Ind.* · P.O. Box 57, 2803 PA, M 15,000, 311-82-569111, Fax 311-82-571050, info@gouda.kvk.nl, www.kvk.nl

**Hilversum** · *Chamber of Commerce & Ind. for Gooi- & Eemland* · P.O. Box 378, 1200 AJ, M 50,000, 313-56-721212, Fax 313-56-234931, info@gooi-eemland.kvk.nl, www.gooi-eemland.kvk.nl

**Leeuwarden** · *Kamer van Koophandel Friesland* · P.O. Box 699, 8901 BL, 315-82-954321, Fax 315-82-128460, info@leeuwarden.kvk.nl, www.leeuwarden.kvk.nl

**Lelystad** · *Flevoland Reg. Chamber of Commerce* · P.O. Box 123, 8200 AC, M 25,000, 313-20-286286, Fax 313-20-222543, www.flevoland.kuk.nl

**The Hague** · *Chamber of Commerce & Ind. The Hague* · P.O. Box 29718, 2502 LS, 317-03-287100, Fax 317-03-247738, www.denhaag.kuk.nl

**Tilburg** · *Midden-Brabant Chamber of Commerce and Ind.* · P.O. Box 90154, 5000 LG, M 30,000, 311-35-944122, Fax 311-34-686215, info@tilburg.kvk.nl, www.tilburg.kvk.nl

**Woerden** · *Chamber of Commerce of the Netherlands* · Watermolenlaan 1, 3447, 313-48-426911, Fax 313-48-424368, post@vvk.kvk.nl

**Zwolle** · *Northern Overyssel Chamber of Commerce* · P.O. Box 630, 8000 AP, M 16,000, 313-84-553800, Fax 313-84-537424

# Netherlands-Antilles

**Willemstad** · *Curacao Chamber of Commerce* · John H. Jacobs, Exec. Dir., Kaya Junior Salas 1, P.O. Box 10, Curacao, M 15,782, 599-94-613918, Fax 599-94-615652, businessinfo@curacao-chamber.an, www.curacao-chamber.an

# New Zealand

**Auckland** · *Auckland Reg. Chamber of Commerce & Ind.* · 100 Mayoral Drive, P.O. Box 47, 1140, M 8,000, 649-30-96100, Fax 649-30-90081, auckland@chamber.co.nz, www.aucklandchamber.co.nz

**Dunedin** · *Otago Chamber of Commerce & Ind.* · John Christie, CEO, P.O. Box 5713, 9031, M 1,100, 643-47-90181, Fax 643-47-70341, office@otagochamber.co.nz, www.otagochamber.co.nz

**Hamilton** · *Waikato Chamber of Commerce & Ind.* · P.O. Box 1122, M 560, 647-83-95895, Fax 647-83-94581, admin@waikato-chamber.co.nz, www.waikatochamber.co.nz

**Lower Hutt** · *Hutt Valley Chamber of Commerce & Ind.* · David Kiddey, P.O. Box 30653, 5040, M 350, 644-93-99821, Fax 644-93-99824, info@hutt-chamber.org.nz, www.hutt-chamber.org.nz

**Rotorua** · *Rotorua Chamber of Commerce* · 1209 Hinemaru St., P.O. Box 385, 3040, M 430, 647-34-98365, Fax 647-34-91388, info@rotchamber.co.nz, www.rotchamber.co.nz

**Tauranga** · *Chamber of Commerce Tauranga Region* · P.O. Box 414, 3140, M 850, 647-57-79823, Fax 647-57-70364, chamber@tauranga.org.nz, www.tauranga.org.nz

**Wellington** · *New Zealand Chambers of Commerce & Ind.* · P.O. Box 1590, 6001, 644-47-22725, Fax 644-41-71767, www.newzealandchambers.co.nz

**Wellington** · *Wellington Reg. Chamber of Commerce* · P.O. Box 1590, M 1,150, 644-91-46500, Fax 644-91-46424, Info@wellingtonchamber.co.nz, www.wgtn-chamber.co.nz

**Whangarei** · *Northland Chamber of Commerce* · P.O. Box 1703, M 320, 649-43-84771, Fax 649-43-84770, info@northchamber.co.nz, www.northchamber.co.nz

Foreign C/C

# Niger

**Niamey** · *Chamber of Commerce, Ag. & Ind.* · P.O. Box 209, M 170, 22-77-32210, Fax 22-77-36668, cham209n@intnet.ne

# Nigeria

**Lagos** · *Nigerian Assn. of Chamber of Comm, Ind. Mines & Ag.* · P.M.B. 12816, M 156, 2340-17-612099, Fax 2340-14-964737, contact@naccima.com, www.naccima.com

**Lagos** · *The Lagos Chamber of Commerce & Ind.* · P.O. Box 109, 234-77-46617, Fax 234-27-01009, info@lagoschamber.com, www. lagoschamber.com

# Norway

**Kristiansand** · *Kristiansand Chamber of Commerce* · Rdhusgt. 6, Postboks 269, 4663, 473-80-24370, Fax 473-81-23979, post@ kristiansand-chamber.no, www.kristiansand-chamber.no

**Oslo** · *Assn. of Norwegian Chambers of Commerce* · Herman Thrap-Meyer, CEO, P.O. Box 2900, Solli, 230, 472-25-41755, Fax 472-25-61700, h.thrap-meyer@hsh-org.no, www.chamber.no

**Oslo** · *Oslo Chamber of Commerce* · P.O. Box 2874 Solli, 230, M 250, 472-21-29400, Fax 472-21-29401, mail@chamber.no, www.chamber.no

**Stavanger** · *Stavanger Chamber of Commerce* · P.O. Box 182, N-4001, M 3,500, 475-15-10880, Fax 475-15-10881, post@ stavanger-chamber.no

**Trondheim** · *Mid Norway Chamber of Commerce & Ind.* · P.O. Box 778, 7408, M 800, 477-38-83110, Fax 477-38-83111, firmapost@trondheim-chamber.no, www.trondheim-chamber.no

# Oman

**Ruwi** · *Oman Chamber of Commerce & Ind.* · P.O. Box 1400, 112, 968-24-707674, Fax 968-24-708497, occi@chamberoman. com, www.chamberoman.com

# Pakistan

**Faisalabad** · *Faisalabad Chamber of Commerce & Ind.* · East Canal Road, Canal Park, 38000, M 2,500, 924-19-230265, Fax 924-19-230270, info@fcci.com.pk, www.fcci.com.pk

**Gujranwala** · *Gujranwala Chamber of Commerce & Ind.* · Aiwan-e-Tijarat Rd., Trust Plaza, 52250, M 3,500, 925-53-256701, Fax 925-53-254440, info@gcci.org.pk, gcci.org.pk

**Karachi** · *Federation of Pakistan Chambers of Commerce* · P.O. Box 13875, 75600, M 167, 922-15-873691, Fax 922-15-874332, info@fpcci.com.pk, www.fpcci.com.pk

**Karachi** · *Overseas Investors Chamber of Commerce & Ind.* · P.O. Box 4833, 74000, M 164, 922-12-410814, Fax 922-12-427315, info@oicci.org, www.oicci.org

**Lahore** · *Lahore Chamber of Commerce & Ind.* · 11-Shahrah-e-Aiwan-e-Tijarat, 54000, M 8,000, 92400-00-000000, Fax 924-26-368854, www.lcci.org.pk

**Rawalpindi** · *Rawalpindi Chamber of Commerce & Ind.* · P.O. Box 323, 46000, M 2,000, 925-15-584397, Fax 925-15-586849, rcci@bestnet.pk, www.rcci.org.pk

**Sialkot** · *Sialkot Chamber of Commerce & Ind.* · P.O. Box 1870, 51310, M 6,000, 925-24-261881, Fax 925-24-268835, scci@skt. comsats.net.pk, www.scci.com.pk

# Panama

**Panama** · *Camara de Comercio, Industrias & Ag de Panama* · P.O. Box 74, 1, M 1,300, 507-20-73442, Fax 507-20-73421, arbitraje@ panacamara.org, www.panacamara.com

# Papua New Guinea

**Port Moresby** · *Papua New Guinea Chamber of Commerce & Ind.* · P.O. Box 1621, 121, 675-32-13057, Fax 675-32-10566, pngcci@global.net.pg, www.pngcci.org.pg

# Peru

**Cusco** · *Camara de Comercio, Industrias de Cusco* · Manco Inca N. 206, Wancha, M 300, 511-46-33434, Fax 511-46-33434, camcusco@camaralima.org.pe, www.camaralima.org.pe

# Portugal

**Azores Islands** · *Chamber of Commerce & Ind. of the Azores* · Rua Ernesto do Canto, 13, Ponta Delgada, 9500, M 680, 351-96-22427, Fax 351-96-24268

**Lega Da Palmeria** · *Ind. Assoc. of Portuense* · P.O. Box 1092, 4450-617, M 2,000, 3512-29-981500, Fax 3512-29-956039, aludgero@aep.mailpac.pt, www.aeportugal.pt

**Lisboa** · *Chamber of Commerce & Ind. of Portugal* · Rua Portas de Santo Antao 89, P-1194, 351-13-224050, Fax 351-13-224051, port.chamber.ci@mail.telepac.pt

**Lisbon** · *Investment, Trade & Tourism of Portugal* · Av. 5 de Outubro 101, 1050, 3512-17-909500, Fax 3512-17-938028, www.icep.pt

**Porto** · *Chamber of Commerce and Ind. of Porto* · Palacio da Bolsa, Rua Ferreira Borges, 4050-253, M 700, 3512-23-399000, Fax 3512-23-399090, correio@cciporto.pt, www.cciporto.com

# Qatar

**Doha** · *Qatar Chamber of Commerce & Ind.* · P.O. Box 402, M 2,600, 974-45-59111, Fax 974-46-61693, info@qcci.com, www.qcci.or

# Romania

**Bacau** · *Chamber of Commerce, Ind. & Ag. Bacau* · Str. Libertatii No 1, 600052, M 500, 402-34-570010, Fax 402-34-571070, www. cciabc.ro

**Bucharest** · *Chamber of Commerce of Romania & Bucharest Muni.* · 2 Octavian Goga Blvd., Sector 3, 79502, 4021-31-9011418, ccir@ccir.ro, www.ccir.ro

# Russian Federation

**Moscow** · *Chamber of Commerce & Ind. of the Russian Fed.* · 6 Ilyinka Str., 109012, M 9,430, 749-56-200009, Fax 749-56-200360, tpprf@tpprf.ru, eng.tpprf.ru

# Rwanda, Republic of

**Kigali** · *Chamber of Commerce & Ind. of Rwanda* · P.O. Box 319, 2-50-83538, Fax 2-50-83532, frsp@rwanda1.com

# Saint Kitts & Nevis

**Basseterre** · *St. Kitts & Nevis Chamber of Ind. & Commerce* · P.O. Box 332, M 140, 809-46-52980, Fax 809-46-54490, skn chamber@caribsurf.com, www.stkittsnevischamber.org

# Saint Lucia

**Castries** · *St. Lucia Chamber of Commerce, Ind. & Ag.* · Exec. Dir., P.O. Box 482, M 139, 758-45-23165, Fax 758-45-36907, info@ stluciachamber.org, www.stluciachamber.org

# Samoa

**Apia** · *Dept. of Trade, Commerce & Ind.* · P.O. Box 862, 98682, 6-85-20471, Fax 6-85-21646

**Apia** · *Samoa Chamber of Commerce* · P.O. Box 2014, M 135, 6-85-31090, Fax 6-85-31089

# Saudi Arabia

**Dammam** · *Chamber of Commerce & Ind., Eastern Province* · P.O. Box 719, 31421, M 13,000, 966-38-571111, Fax 966-38-570607, info@chamber.org.sa, www.chamber.org.sa

**Dammam** · *Federation of GCC Chambers of Commerce & Ind.* · P.O. Box 2198, 31541, 966-38-265943, Fax 966-38-266794, fgccc@ fgccc.org, www.fgccc.org

**Riyadh** · *Cncl. of Saudi Chambers of Commerce & Ind.* · P.O. Box 16683, 11474, M 97, 966-14-053200, Fax 966-14-024747, council@saudichambers.org.sa, www.saudichambers.org.sa

**Riyadh** · *Riyadh Chamber of Commerce & Ind.* · P.O. Box 596, 11421, 966-14-040044, Fax 966-14-021103, www.riyadh chamber.com

# Scotland

**Glasgow** · *Glasgow Chamber of Commerce* · 30 George Sq., G2 1EQ, M 2,000, 4414-12-042121, Fax 4414-12-212336, chamber@ glasgowchamber.org, www.glasgowchamber.org

# Senegal

**Dakar** · *Chamber of Commerce and Ind.* · P.O. Box 118, 22-12-38213, Fax 22-12-39363

# Serbia

**Belgrade** · *Chamber of Eco. of Serbia* · Resavska st. 12-15, P.O. Box 959, 11000, 3811-13-240611, Fax 3811-13-239009

**Belgrade** · *Belgrade Chamber of Commerce and Ind.* · Kneza Milosa 12, 11000, M 40,000, 3811-12-641355, Fax 3811-12-642029, mmj@kombeg.org.rs, www.kombeg.org.rs

# Singapore

**Singapore** · *Singapore Intl. Chamber of Commerce* · 6 Raffles Quay, Ste. 10-01, 48580, M 815, 656-50-00988, Fax 656-22-42785, general@singnet.com.sg, www.sicc.com.sg

# Slovak Republic

**Bratislava** · *Slovak Chamber of Commerce & Ind.* · Gorkeho 9, 81603, 4217-54-433291, Fax 4217-54-131159, sopkurad@sopk. sk, www.scci.sk

# Slovenia

**Ljubljana** · *Chamber of Commerce & Ind. of Slovenia* · Dimiceva 13, 1000, 386-15-898000, Fax 386-15-898100, info link@gzs.si, www.gzs.si/eng

# South Africa

**Cape Town** · *Cape Town Reg. Chamber of Commerce* · P.O. Box 205, 8001, M 4,500, 272-14-024300, Fax 272-14-024302, info@ capechamber.co.za, www.capetownchamber.com

**East London** · *Border-Kei Chamber of Bus.* · P.O. Box 11179, Southernwood, 5213, M 800, 274-37-438438, Fax 274-37-432249, info@bkcob.co.za, www.bkcob.co.za

**Johannesburg** · *Johannesburg Chamber of Commerce and Ind.* · Private Bag 34, Auckland Park, 2006, M 4,000, 271-17-265300, Fax 271-14-822000, info@vericom.co.za, www.jcci.co.za

**Johannesburg** · *South African Chamber of Bus.* · P.O. Box 44164, Linden, 2104, M 47,000, 271-13-589711, Fax 271-13-589774, www.sacob.co.za

**KwaZulu-Natal** · *Durban Chamber of Commerce & Ind.* · P.O. Box 1506, Durban, 4000, M 4,300, 273-13-351000, Fax 273-13-321288, chamber@durbanchamber.co.za, www.durbanchamber.co.za

**Vereeniging** · *Vereeniging Chamber of Commerce & Ind.* · P.O. Box 4522, 1930, M 200, 271-64-552148, Fax 271-64-554485, emp@cyberserv.co.za

# Spain

**Barcelona** · *Spain Chamber of Commerce* · Avda. Diagonal 452-454, 8006, 343-41-69300, Fax 343-41-69301

**Bilbao** · *Chamber of Commerce and Ind. of Bilbao* · Gran Vla 13, 48001, M 65,000, 349-44-706500, Fax 349-44-220061 atencionaclientes@camarabilbao.com, www.camarabilbao.com

**Cordoba** · *Chamber of Commerce of Cordoba* · Perez de Castro 1, 14003, 349-57-296199, Fax 349-57-202106, info@camara cordoba.com, www.camaracordoba.com

**Madrid** · *Madrid Chamber of Commerce and Ind.* · C/ Ribera del Loira, 56-58, 28042, M 35,000, 341-53-83500, Fax 341-53-83677, www.camaramadrid.es

**Valencia** · *Valencia Chamber of Commerce & Ind.* · Poeta Querol 15, 46002, M 60, 346-35-11301, Fax 346-35-16349, www.camarav.es

# Sri Lanka

**Colombo** · *Ceylon Chamber of Commerce* · 50, Navam Mawatha, 2, M 516, 941-12-421745, Fax 941-12-449352, info@ chamber.lk, www.chamber.lk

# Sudan

**Khartoum** · *Union of Sudanese Chambers of Commerce* · P.O. Box 81, 11123, M 5,000, 249-11-781886, Fax 249-11-780748

**Foreign C/C**

# Suriname

**Paramaribo** · *Chamber of Commerce & Ind.* · P.O. Box 149, 59-74-74536, Fax 59-74-74779, chamber@sr.net, www.suriname directory.biz

# Swaziland

**Mbabane** · *Swaziland Chamber of Commerce & Ind.* · P.O. Box 72, M 500, 268-40-40768, Fax 268-40-90051, fsecc@business-swaziland.com, www.business-swaziland.com

# Sweden

**Gavle** · *Chamber of Commerce of Central Sweden* · P.O. Box 296, SE-80104, M 465, 462-66-62080, Fax 462-66-62099, chamber@mhk.cci.se, www.mhk.cci.se

**Gothenburg** · *Western Sweden Chamber of Commerce* · Massans Gata 18, P.O. Box 5253, S-402 25, M 3,000, 463-18-35900, Fax 463-18-35936

**Jonkoping** · *Jonkoping Chamber of Commerce* · Elmiavagen 11, 554 54, M 400, 463-63-01430, Fax 463-61-29579, info@jonkoping.cci.se, www.jonkoping.cci.se

**Karlstad** · *Wermland Chamber of Commerce* · S. Kyrkogatan 6, 65224, M 1,150, 465-42-21480, Fax 465-42-21490, info@handels kammarenvarmland.se, www.handelskammarenvarmland.se

**Lulea** · *Norrbotten Chamber of Commerce* · Storgatan 9, 97238, M 400, 469-20-12210, Fax 469-20-94857, info@north.cci.se, www.north.cci.se

**Malmo** · *Chamber of Commerce of Southern Sweden* · Skeppsbron 2, 21120, M 2,700, 464-06-902400, Fax 464-06-902490, info@handelskammaren.com, www.handelskammaren.com

**Orebro** · *Chamber of Commerce Malardalen* · Box 8044, 70008, M 350, 461-91-66160, Fax 461-96-117750, info@handelskammarenmalardalen.se, www.handelskammaren malardalen.se

**Skelleftea** · *Vesterbotten Chamber of Commerce* · Expolaris Center, 93178, M 320, 469-10-37800, Fax 469-10-37877, info@ac.cci.se, www.ac.cci.se

**Stockholm** · *Stockholm Chamber of Commerce* · Box 16050, 10321, M 2,500, 468-55-510000, Fax 468-56-631600, info@chamber.se, www.chamber.se

# Switzerland

**Geneva** · *Geneva Chamber of Commerce & Ind.* · PO Box 5039, 1211, M 1,500, 412-28-199111, Fax 412-28-199100, ccig@cci.ch, www.ccig.ch

**Zurich** · *Swiss Business Federation* · Hegibachstrasse 47, CH-8032, 411-42-13535, Fax 411-42-13434, info@economie suisse.ch, www.economiesuisse.ch

# Syria

**Aleppo** · *Aleppo Chamber of Commerce* · P.O. Box 1261, M 20,000, 9632-12-238236, Fax 9632-12-213493, alepchmb@mail.sy, www.aleppochamber.com

**Damascus** · *Damascus Chamber of Commerce* · P.O. Box 1040, M 11,000, 9631-12-211339, Fax 9631-12-225874, dcc@net.sy, www.dcc-sy.com

**Damascus** · *Federation of Syrian Chambers of Commerce* · Mousa Bin Nosair St., P.O. Box 5909, M 210, 9631-13-311504, Fax 9631-13-331127, syr-trade@mail.sy, www.fedcommsyr.org

# Taiwan

**Taipei** · *World Taiwanese Chambers of Commerce* · 7G06, No 5, Hsin-Yi Road Sec 5, 110, M 40,000, 8862-87-881466, Fax 8862-87-881533, wtccmail@ms67.hinet.net, www.tccseattle.org

# Tanzania

**Arusha** · *Arusha Chamber of Commerce, Ag. & Ind.* · P.O. Box 551, M 80, 255-25-03722

# Thailand

**Bangkok** · *Bd. of Trade of Thailand* · 150 Rajbopit Rd., 10200, M 75, 662-22-10555, Fax 662-22-53995

**Bangkok** · *The Thai Chamber of Commerce* · 150 Rajbopit Rd., 10200, M 2,000, 660-26-221860, Fax 660-22-253372, tcc@thaiechamber.com, www.thaiechamber.com

# Tonga, South Pacific

**Nuku'alofa** · *Tonga Chamber of Commerce & Ind.* · P.O. Box 1704, M 106, 6-76-25168, Fax 6-76-26039, admin@tongachamber.org, www.tongachamber.org

# Trinidad & Tobago

**Port of Spain** · *Trinidad & Tobago Chamber of Ind. & Commerce* · Joan Ferreira, CEO, P.O. Box 499, M 532, 868-63-76966, Fax 868-63-77425, chamber@chamber.org.tt, www.chamber.org.tt

**San Fernando** · *South Trinidad Chamber of Ind. & Commerce* · P.O. Box 80, M 198, 868-65-25613, Fax 868-65-34983, execoffice@stcic.org, www.stcic.org

# Turkey

**Ankara** · *Ankara Chamber of Commerce* · Soputori, 6530, 9031-22-857850, Fax 9031-22-863446, www.ato.acc.org.tr

**Ankara** · *Union of Chambers, Ind. & Commodity Exchanges* · Ataturk Bulvari No. 149, Bakanliklar, 6582, M 293, 9031-24-138000, Fax 9031-24-183268, info@tobb.org.tr, www.tobb.org.tr

**Izmir** · *Izmir Chamber of Commerce* · Ataturk cad. No:126 Pasaport, 35210, 9023-24-449292, Fax 9023-24-462251, info@izto.org.tr, www.izto.org.tr

# Uganda

**Kampala** · *Uganda Natl. Chamber of Commerce & Ind.* · P.O. Box 3809, M 6,000, 2546-14-503024, Fax 2546-14-230310, info@chamberuganda.com, www.chamberuganda.com

# Ukraine

**Ivano-Frankivsk** · *Ivano-Frankivsk Chamber of Commerce and Ind.* · 9, Rozumovskogo str., 76014, M 137, 3803-42-523347, Fax same, office@cci.if.ukrtel.net

**Sumy** · *Sumy Chamber of Commerce & Ind.* · 7a. Chervonogvardijska Str., 40030, M 144, 3805-42-600390, Fax 3805-42-210041, chamber@cci.sumy.ua, www.cci.sumy.ua

# United Arab Emirates

**Abu Dhabi** · *Federation of UAE Chambers of Commerce & Ind.* · H.E. Abdulla Sultan Abdulla, Secy. Gen., P.O. Box 3014, 971-26-214144, Fax 971-26-339210, info@fcciuae.ae, www.fcciuae.com

**Abu Dhabi** · *Abu Dhabi Chamber of Commerce & Ind.* · P.O. Box 662, M 40,787, 971-26-214000, Fax 971-26-215867, services@adcci.gov.ae, www.abudhabichamber.ae

**Ajman** · *Ajman Chamber of Commerce & Ind.* · P.O. Box 662, 971-67-422177, Fax 971-67-471666, info@ajcci.gov.ae, www.ajcci.gov.ae

**Dubai** · *Dubai Chamber of Commerce & Ind.* · P.O. Box 1457, M 30,000, 971-42-280000, Fax 971-42-028888, customercare@dubaichamber.ae, www.dubaichamber.ae

**Sharjah** · *Sharjah Chamber of Commerce & Ind.* · P.O. Box 580, M 32,000, 971-65-116600, Fax 971-65-681119, scci@sharjah.gov.ae, www.sharjah.gov.ae

# United Kingdom

**Birmingham** · *Birmingham Chamber of Ind. & Commerce* · 75 Harborne Rd., B15 3DH, M 3,500, 4412-14-546171, Fax 4412-14-558670, info@birmingham-chamber.com, www.birmingham-chamber.com

**Bristol** · *Bristol Chamber of Commerce & Ind.* · 16 Clifton Park, BS8 3BY, M 2,300, 4411-79-737373, Fax 4411-79-745365, enquiries@bcci.westec.co.uk

**London** · *London Chamber of Commerce & Ind.* · 33 Queen St., EC4R 1AP, M 3,000, 4420-72-484444, Fax 4420-74-890391, lc@londonchamber.co.uk, www.londonchamber.co.uk

**London** · *Intl. Chamber of Commerce-United Kingdom* · 12 Grosvenor Pl., SW1X 7HH, M 350, 4420-78-389363, Fax 4420-72-355447, annopara@iccorg.co.uk, www.iccuk.net

**Manchester** · *Greater Manchester Chamber of Commerce & Ind.* · Churchgate House, 56 Oxford St., M60 7HJ, M 2,950, 4416-12-363210, Fax 4416-12-364160, info@gmchamber.co.uk, www.mcci.co.uk

**Staffordshire** · *North Staffordshire Chamber of Commerce & Ind.* · Commerce House, Festival Park, Stoke-on-Trent, ST1 5BE, M 1,100, 4417-82-202222, Fax 4417-82-202448, membership@nscci.co.uk, www.nscci.co.uk

# Uruguay

**Montevideo** · *Camara Nacional de Comercio* · Misiones 1400, 11000, M 1,000, 598-29-61277, Fax 598-29-61243

# Wales

**Cardiff** · *Cardiff Chamber of Commerce, Trade & Ind.* · St Davids House E., Wood St., CF101ES, M 1,500, 4402-92-0348280, Fax 4402-92-0377653, www.cardiffchamber.co.uk

# Yugoslavia

**Belgrade** · *Yugoslav Chamber of Commerce & Ind.* · Terazije 23, 11000, 3841-13-248400, Fax 3811-13-248754, info@pkj.co.yu, www.pkj.co.yu

# Zambia

**Kitwe** · *Kitwe & Dist. Chamber of Commerce & Ind.* · 8 Kantanta Street, Engineers House, 10101, M 128, 260-22-25345, Fax 260-22-25345, info@kitwechamber.com, kitwechamber.com

**Lusaka** · *Zambia Assn. of Chambers of Commerce & Ind.* · P.O. Box 30844, 10101, M 400, 260-12-53020, Fax 260-12-52483, zacci@zamnet.zm, www.zacci.org.zm

**Ndola** · *Ndola & District Chamber of Commerce & Ind.* · P.O. Box 240241, P 500,000, M 90, 260-26-19296, Fax 260-26-19297, shyams@zamnet.zm

# Zimbabwe

**Harare** · *Zimbabwe Natl. Chamber of Commerce* · P.O. Box 1934, 263-47-49737, Fax 263-47-50375, linda@zncc.co.zw, www.zncc.co.zw

**Harare** · *Confederation of Zimbabwe Industries* · P.O. Box 3794, M 720, 263-42-51490, Fax 263-42-52424, czi@zarnet.sc.zw

Foreign C/C

# Notes

# U.S. Congress

## The One Hundred and Eleventh Congress
## First Session

**U.S. Capitol Switchboard**       **(202) 224-3121**

### Addressing Correspondence

*To a Senator:*
The Honorable (full name)
United States Senate
Washington, DC 20510

Dear Senator (last name):

*To a Representative:*
The Honorable (full name)
United States House of Representatives
Washington, DC 20515

Dear Representative (last name):

### Key Websites

White House       http://www.whitehouse.gov

Senate Home Page    http://www.senate.gov

House Home Page     http://www.house.gov

## Alabama

**State Capitol** • Montgomery, AL 36130 (334) 242-7100
**Governor** • Robert Riley (R) 2010
**Senate** • Richard C. Shelby (R) 2011, Jeff Sessions (R) 2015
**Representatives** • Jo Bonner (R), Bobby Bright (D), Mike Rogers (R), Robert Aderholt (R), Parker Griffith (D), Spencer Bachus (R), Artur Davis (D)

## Alaska

**State Capitol** • Juneau, AK 99811-0001 (907) 465-3500
**Governor** • Sarah Palin (R) 2010
**Senate** • Lisa Murkowski (R) 2011, Mark Begich (D) 2015
**Representative** • Don Young (R)

## Arizona

**State Capitol** • Phoenix, AZ 85007 (602) 542-4331
**Governor** • Jan Brewer (R) 2010
**Senate** • John McCain (R) 2011, Jon L. Kyl (R) 2013
**Representatives** • Ann Kirkpatrick (D), Trent Franks (R), John Shadegg (R), Ed Pastor (D), Harry Mitchell (D), Jeff Flake (R), Raul Grijalva (D), Gabrielle Giffords (D)

## Arkansas

**State Capitol** • Little Rock, AR 72201 (501) 682-2345
**Governor** • Mike Beebe (D) 2010
**Senate** • Mark Pryor (D) 2009, Blanche Lincoln (D) 2011
**Representatives** • Marion Berry (D), Vic Snyder (D), John Boozman (R), Mike Ross (D)

## California

**State Capitol** • Sacramento, CA 95814 (916) 445-2841
**Governor** • Arnold Schwarzenegger (R) 2010
**Senate** • Dianne Feinstein (D), 2013 Barbara Boxer (D) 2011
**Representatives** • Mike Thompson (D), Wally Herger (R), Daniel E. Lungren (R), Tom McClintock (R), Doris Matsui (D), Lynn Woolsey (D), George Miller (D), Nancy Pelosi (D), Barbara Lee (D), Ellen Tauscher (D), Jerry McNerney (D), Jackie Speier (D), Pete Stark (D), Anna Eshoo (D), Michael Honda (D), Zoe Lofgren (D), Sam Farr (D), Dennis Cardoza (D), George Radanovich (R), Jim Costa (D), Devin Nunes (R), Kevin McCarthy (R), Lois Capps (D), Elton Gallegly (R), Howard McKeon (R), David Dreier (R), Brad Sherman (D), Howard Berman (D), Adam Schiff (D), Henry Waxman (D), Xavier Becerra (D), Vacant, Diane Watson (D), Lucille Roybal-Allard (D), Maxine Waters (D), Jane Harman (D), Laura Richardson (D), Grace Napolitano (D), Linda Sanchez (D), Ed Royce (R), Jerry Lewis (R), Gary Miller (R), Joe Baca (D), Ken Calvert (R), Mary Bono (R), Dana Rohrabacher (R), Loretta Sanchez (D), John Campbell (R), Darrell Issa (R), Brian Bilbray (R), Bob Filner (D), Duncan Hunter (R), Susan Davis (D)

## Colorado

**State Capitol** • Denver, CO 80203 (303) 866-2471
**Governor** • Bill Ritter (D) 2010
**Senate** • Michael Bennet (D) 2011, Mark Udall (D) 2015
**Representatives** • Diana DeGette (D), Jared Polis (D), John Salazar (D), Betsy Markey (D), Doug Lamborn (R), Mike Coffman (R), Ed Perlmutter (D)

## Connecticut

**State Capitol** • Hartford, CT 06106 (860) 566-4840
**Governor** • M. Jodi Rell (R) 2010
**Senate** • Christopher J. Dodd (D) 2011, Joseph I. Lieberman (ID) 2013
**Representatives** • John Larson (D), Joe Courtney (D), Rosa DeLauro (D), James Himes (D), Christopher Murphy (D)

## Delaware

**State Capitol** • Dover, DE 19901 (302) 739-4101
**Governor** • Jack Markell (D) 2012
**Senate** • Edward E. Kaufman (D) 2015, Thomas Carper (D) 2013
**Representative** • Michael N. Castle (R)

# District of Columbia

**District Building** • Washington, D.C. 20002 (202) 727-1000

**Representative** • Eleanor Holmes Norton (D)

# Florida

**State Capitol** • Tallahassee, FL 32399 (850) 488-2272

**Governor** • Charlie Crist (R) 2010

**Senate** • Bill Nelson (D) 2013, Mel Martinez (R) 2011

**Representatives** • Jeff Miller (R), Allen Boyd (D), Corrine Brown (D), Ander Crenshaw (R), Ginny Brown-Waite (R), Cliff Stearns (R), John Mica (R), Alan Grayson (D), Gus Bilirakis (R), C.W. Bill Young (R), Kathy Castor (D), Adam Putnam (R), Vern Buchanan (R), Connie Mack (R), Bill Posey (R), Tom Rooney (R), Kendrick Meek (D), Ileana Ros-Lehtinen (R), Robert Wexler (D), Debbie Wasserman Schultz (D), Lincoln Diaz-Balart (R), Ron Klein (D), Alcee Hastings (D), Suzanne M. Kosmas (D), Mario Diaz-Balart (R)

# Georgia

**State Capitol** • Atlanta, GA 30334 (404) 656-1776

**Governor** • Sonny Perdue (R) 2010

**Senate** • Johnny Isakson (R) 2011, Saxby Chambliss (R) 2015

**Representatives** • Jack Kingston (R), Sanford Bishop Jr. (D), Lynn Westmoreland (R), Henry Johnson Jr. (D), John Lewis (D), Tom Price (R), John Linder (R), Jim Marshall (D), Nathan Deal (R), Paul Broun (R), Phil Gingrey (R), John Barrow (D), David Scott (D)

# Hawaii

**State Capitol** • Honolulu, HI 96801 (808) 586-0013

**Governor** • Linda Lingle (R) 2010

**Senate** • Daniel K. Inouye (D) 2011, Daniel K. Akaka (D) 2013

**Representatives** • Neil Abercrombie (D), Mazie Hirono (D)

# Idaho

**State Capitol** • Boise, ID 83720 (208) 334-2100

**Governor** • C.L. Otter (R) 2010

**Senate** • James E. Risch (R) 2015, Michael Crapo (R) 2011

**Representatives** • Walt Minnick (D), Mike Simpson (R)

# Illinois

**State Capitol** • Springfield, IL 62706 (217) 782-6830

**Governor** • Pat Quinn (D) 2010

**Senate** • Richard Durbin (D) 2015, Roland Burris (D) 2011

**Representatives** • Bobby Rush (D), Jesse Jackson Jr. (D), Daniel Lipinski (D), Luis Gutierrez (D), Vacant, Peter Roskam (R), Danny Davis (D), Melissa L. Bean (D), Janice Schakowsky (D), Mark Steven Kirk (R), Deborah Halvorson (D), Jerry Costello (D), Judy Biggert (R), Bill Foster (D), Timothy Johnson (R), Donald Manzullo (R), Phil Hare (D), Aaron Schock (R), John Shimkus (R)

# Indiana

**State Capitol** • Indianapolis, IN 46204 (317) 232-4567

**Governor** • Mitch Daniels (R) 2012

**Senate** • Richard G. Lugar (R) 2013, Evan Bayh (D) 2011

**Representatives** • Peter J. Visclosky (D), Joe Donnelly (D), Mark Souder (R), Steve Buyer (R), Dan Burton (R), Mike Pence (R), Andre Carson (D), Brad Ellsworth (D), Baron Hill (D)

# Iowa

**State Capitol** • Des Moines, IA 50319 (515) 281-5211

**Governor** • Chet Culver (D) 2010

**Senate** • Charles E. Grassley (R) 2011, Tom Harkin (D) 2015

**Representatives** • Bruce Braley (D), David Loebsack (D), Leonard Boswell (D), Tom Latham (R), Steve King (R)

# Kansas

**State Capitol** • Topeka, KS 66612 (785) 296-3232

**Governor** • Kathleen Sebelius (D) 2010

**Senate** • Sam Brownback (R) 2011, Pat Roberts (R) 2015

**Representatives** • Jerry Moran (R), Lynn Jenkins (R), Dennis Moore (D), Todd Tiahrt (R)

# Kentucky

**State Capitol** • Frankfort, KY 40601 (502) 564-2611

**Governor** • Steven Beshear (D) 2011

**Senate** • Jim Bunning (R) 2011, Mitch McConnell (R) 2015

**Representatives** • Edward Whitfield (R), Brett S. Guthrie (R), John Yarmuth (D), Geoff Davis (R), Harold Rogers (R), Ben Chandler (D)

# Louisiana

**State Capitol** • Baton Rouge, LA 70804 (225) 342-7015

**Governor** • Bobby Jindal (R) 2012

**Senate** • Mary Landrieu (D) 2015 David Vitter (R) 2011

**Representatives** • Steve Scalise (R), Joseph Cao (R), Charlie Melancon (D), Jim McCrery (R), Rodney Alexander (R), William Cassidy (R), Charles Boustany Jr. (R)

# Maine

**State Capitol** • Augusta, ME 04333 (207) 287-3531

**Governor** • John Baldacci (D) 2010

**Senate** • Susan Collins (R) 2015, Olympia Snowe (R) 2013

**Representatives** • Chellie Pingree (D), Michael Michaud (D)

# Maryland

**State Capitol** • Annapolis, MD 21401 (410) 974-3901

**Governor** • Martin O'Malley (D) 2010

**Senate** • Benjamin Cardin (D) 2013, Barbara A. Mikulski (D) 2011

**Representatives** • Frank M. Kratovil (D), C.A. Dutch Ruppersberger (D), John Sarbanes (D), Donna F. Edwards (D), Steny Hoyer (D), Roscoe Bartlett (R), Elijah Cummings (D), Chris Van Hollen (D)

# Massachusetts

**State House** • Boston, MA 02133 (617) 725-4000

**Governor** • Deval Patrick (D) 2010

**Senate** • Edward M. Kennedy (D) 2013, John Kerry (D) 2015

**Representatives** • John Olver (D), Richard Neal (D), James McGovern (D), Barney Frank (D), Niki Tsongas (D), John Tierney (D), Edward Markey (D), Michael Capuano (D), Stephen Lynch (D), William Delahunt (D)

# Michigan

**State Capitol** • Lansing, MI 48909 (517) 373-3400

**Governor** • Jennifer Granholm (D) 2010

**Senate** • Carl Levin (D) 2015, Debbie Stabenow (D) 2013

**Representatives** • Bart Stupak (D), Peter Hoekstra (R), Vernon Ehlers (R), Dave Camp (R), Dale Kildee (D), Fred Upton (R), Mark Schauer (D), Mike Rogers (R), Gary Peters (D), Candice Miller (R), Thaddeus McCotter (R), Sander Levin (D), Carolyn Kilpatrick (D), John Conyers Jr. (D), John Dingell (D)

# Minnesota

**State Capitol** • Saint Paul, MN 55155 (651) 296-3391

**Governor** • Tim Pawlenty (R) 2010

**Senate** • Norm Coleman (R) 2009, Amy Klobuchar (D) 2013

**Representatives** • Timothy Walz (D), John Kline (R), Erik Paulsen (R), Betty McCollum (D), Keith Ellison (D), Michele Bachmann (R), Collin Peterson (D), James L. Oberstar (D)

# Mississippi

**State Capitol** • Jackson, MS 39205 (601) 359-3100

**Governor** • Haley Barbour (R) 2012

**Senate** • Thad Cochran (R) 2015, Roger Wicker (R) 2013

**Representatives** • Travis Childers (D), Bennie Thompson (D), Gregg Harper (R), Gene Taylor (D)

# Missouri

**State Capitol** • Jefferson City, MO 65102 (573) 751-3222

**Governor** • Jay Nixon (D) 2012

**Senate** • Christopher S. Bond (R) 2011, Claire McCaskill (D) 2013

**Representatives** • William Clay (D), W. Todd Akin (R), Russ Carnahan (D), Ike Skelton (D), Emanuel Cleaver (D), Sam Graves (R), Roy Blunt (R), JoAnn Emerson (R), Blaine Luetkemeyer (R)

# Montana

**State Capitol** • Helena, MT 59620 (406) 444-3111

**Governor** • Brian Schweitzer (D) 2012

**Senate** • Max Baucus (D) 2015, Jon Tester (D) 2013

**Representative** • Dennis Rehberg (R)

# Nebraska

**State Capitol** • Lincoln, NE 68509 (402) 471-2244

**Governor** • Dave Heineman (R) 2010

**Senate** • Mike Johanns (R) 2015, Ben Nelson (D) 2013

**Representatives** • Jeff Fortenberry (R), Lee Terry (R), Adrian Smith (R)

# Nevada

**State Capitol** • Carson City, NV 89701 (775) 684-5670

**Governor** • Jim Gibbons (R) 2010

**Senate** • John Ensign (R) 2013 Harry Reid (D) 2011

**Representatives** • Shelley Berkley (D), Dean Heller (R), Dina Titus (D)

# New Hampshire

**State Capitol** • Concord, NH 03301 (603) 271-2121

**Governor** • John Lynch (D) 2010

**Senate** • Jeanne Shaheen (R) 2015 Judd Gregg (R) 2011

**Representatives** • Carol Shea-Porter (D), Paul Hodes (D)

# New Jersey

**State Capitol** • Trenton, NJ 08625 (609) 292-6000

**Governor** • Jon Corzine (D) 2010

**Senate** • Frank Lautenberg (D) 2015 Robert Menendez (D) 2013

**Representatives** • Robert Andrews (D), Frank LoBiondo (R), John Adler (D), Christopher Smith (R), Scott Garrett (R), Frank Pallone Jr. (D), Leonard Lance (R), William Pascrell Jr. (D), Steven Rothman (D), Donald Payne (D), Rodney Frelinghuysen (R), Rush Holt (D), Albio Sires (D)

# New Mexico

**State Capitol** • Santa Fe, NM 87501 (505) 476-2200

**Governor** • Bill Richardson (D) 2010

**Senate** • Jeff Bingaman (D) 2013, Tom Udall (D) 2015

**Representatives** • Martin T. Heinrich (D), Harry Teague (D), Ben R. Lujan (D)

# New York

**State Capitol** • Albany, NY 12224 (518) 474-7516

**Governor** • David Paterson (D) 2010

**Senate** • Charles Schumer (D) 2011, Vacant

**Representatives** • Timothy Bishop (D), Steve Israel (D), Peter King (R), Carolyn McCarthy (D), Gary Ackerman (D), Gregory Meeks (D), Joseph Crowley (D), Jerrold Nadler (D), Anthony Weiner (D), Edolphus Towns (D), Yvette Clarke (D), Nydia Velazquez (D), Michael E. McMahon (D), Carolyn Maloney (D), Charles Rangel (D), Jose Serrano (D), Eliot Engel (D), Nita Lowey (D), John Hall (D), Vacant, Paul D. Tonko (D), Maurice Hinchey (D), John McHugh (R), Michael Arcuri (D), Daniel B. Maffei (D), Christopher J. Lee (R), Brian Higgins (D), Louise McIntosh Slaughter (D), Eric J.J. Massa (D)

U.S. Congress

# North Carolina

**State Capitol** • Raleigh, NC 27603 (919) 733-5811

**Governor** • Beverly Perdue (D) 2012

**Senate** • Richard Burr (R) 2011, Kay R. Hagan (D) 2015

**Representatives** • G.K. Butterfield (D), Bob Etheridge (D), Walter Jones (R), David Price (D), Virginia Foxx (R), Howard Coble (R), Mike McIntyre (D), Larry Kissell (D), Sue Wilkins Myrick (R), Patrick T. McHenry (R), Heath Shuler (D), Mel Watt (D), Brad Miller (D)

# North Dakota

**State Capitol** • Bismarck, ND 58505 (701) 328-2200

**Governor** • John Hoeven (R) 2012

**Senate** • Kent Conrad (D) 2013, Byron Dorgan (D) 2011

**Representative** • Earl Pomeroy (D)

# Ohio

**State Capitol** • Columbus, OH 43266 (614) 466-3555

**Governor** • Ted Strickland (D) 2010

**Senate** • Sherrod Brown (D) 2013, George Voinovich (R) 2011

**Representatives** • Steve Driehaus (D), Jean Schmidt (R), Michael Turner (R), Jim Jordan (R), Robert Latta (R), Charles Wilson (D), Steve Austria (R), John Boehner (R), Marcy Kaptur (D), Dennis Kucinich (D), Marcia L. Fudge (D), Patrick Tiberi (R), Betty Sutton (D), Steven LaTourette (R), Mary Jo Kilroy (D), John A. Boccieri (D), Timothy Ryan (D), Zachary Space (D)

# Oklahoma

**State Capitol** • Oklahoma City, OK 73105 (405) 521-2342

**Governor** • Brad Henry (D) 2010

**Senate** • James Inhofe (R) 2015, Tom Coburn (R) 2011

**Representatives** • John Sullivan (R), Dan Boren (D), Frank Lucas (R), Tom Cole (R), Mary Fallin (R)

# Oregon

**State Capitol** • Salem, OR 97310 (503) 378-3111

**Governor** • Ted Kulongoski (D) 2010

**Senate** • Jeff Merkley (D) 2015, Ron Wyden (D) 2011

**Representatives** • David Wu (D), Greg Walden (R), Earl Blumenauer (D), Peter A. DeFazio (D), Kurt Schrader (D)

# Pennsylvania

**State Capitol** • Harrisburg, PA 17120 (717) 787-2500

**Governor** • Edward Rendell (D) 2010

**Senate** • Arlen Specter (R) 2011, Robert Casey Jr. (D) 2013

**Representatives** • Robert Brady (D), Chaka Fattah (D), Kathy Dahlkemper (D), Jason Altmire (D), Glen Thompson (R), Jim Gerlach (R), Joe Sestak (D), Patrick Murphy (D), Bill Shuster (R), Christopher Carney (D), Paul Kanjorski (D), John Murtha (D), Allyson Schwartz (D), Michael Doyle (D), Charles W. Dent (R), Joseph Pitts (R), Tim Holden (D), Tim Murphy (R), Todd Russell Platts (R)

# Rhode Island

**State Capitol** • Providence, RI 02903 (401) 222-2080

**Governor** • Don Carcieri (R) 2010

**Senate** • Sheldon Whitehouse (D) 2013, Jack Reed (D) 2015

**Representatives** • Patrick Kennedy (D), James Langevin (D)

# South Carolina

**State Capitol** • Columbia, SC 29211 (803) 734-2100

**Governor** • Mark Sanford (R) 2010

**Senate** • Jim DeMint (R) 2011, Lindsey Graham (R) 2015

**Representatives** • Henry E. Brown Jr. (R), Joe Wilson (R), J. Gresham Barrett (R), Bob Inglis (R), John Spratt Jr. (D), James Clyburn (D)

# South Dakota

**State Capitol** • Pierre, SD 57501 (605) 773-3212

**Governor** • Mike Rounds (R) 2010

**Senate** • John Thune (R) 2011, Tim Johnson (D) 2015

**Representative** • Stephanie Herseth Sandlin (D)

# Tennessee

**State Capitol** • Nashville, TN 37423 (615) 741-2001

**Governor** • Phil Bredesen (D) 2010

**Senate** • Lamar Alexander (R), 2015 Bob Corker (R) 2013

**Representatives** • Phil Roe (R), John J. Duncan Jr. (R), Zach Wamp (R), Lincoln Davis (D), Jim Cooper (D), Bart Gordon (D), Marsha Blackburn (R), John Tannner (D), Steve Cohen (D)

# Texas

**State Capitol** • Austin, TX 78711 (512) 463-2000

**Governor** • Rick Perry (R) 2010

**Senate** • Kay Bailey Hutchison (R), 2013 John Cornyn (R) 2015

**Representatives** • Louie Gohmert (R), Ted Poe (R), Sam Johnson (R), Ralph Hall (R), Jeb Hensarling (R), Joe Barton (R), John Abney Culberson (R), Kevin Brady (R), Al Green (D), Michael McCaul (R), K. Michael Conaway (R), Kay Granger (R), Mac Thornberry (R), Ron Paul (R), Ruben Hinojosa (D), Silvestre Reyes (D), Chet Edwards (D), Sheila Jackson-Lee (D), Randy Neugebauer (R), Charles Gonzalez (D), Lamar Smith (R), Pete Olson (R), Ciro Rodriguez (D), Kenny Marchant (R), Lloyd Doggett (D), Michael Burgess (R), Solomon Ortiz (D), Henry Cuellar (D), Gene Green (D), Eddie Bernice Johnson (D), John Carter (R), Pete Sessions (R)

# Utah

**State Capitol** • Salt Lake City, UT 84114 (801) 538-1000

**Governor** • Jon Huntsman Jr. (R) 2012

**Senate** • Robert Bennett (R) 2011, Orrin G. Hatch (R) 2013

**Representatives** • Rob Bishop (R), Jim Matheson (D), Jason Chaffetz (R)

# Vermont

**State Capitol** • Montpelier, VT 05609 (802) 828-3333

**Governor** • James Douglas (R) 2010

**Senate** • Patrick J. Leahy (D) 2011, Bernard Sanders (I) 2013

**Representative** • Peter Welch (D)

# Virginia

**State Capitol** • Richmond, VA 23219 (804) 786-2211

**Governor** • Tim Kaine (D) 2009

**Senate** • Jim Webb (D) 2013, Mark R. Warner (D) 2015

**Representatives** • Robert Wittman (R), Glen Nye III (D), Robert Scott (D), J. Randy Forbes (R), Tom Perriello (D), Robert Goodlatte (R), Eric Cantor (R), James P. Moran (D), Rick Boucher (D), Frank Wolf (R), Gerald E. Connolly (D)

# Washington

**State Capitol** • Olympia, WA 98504 (360) 902-4111

**Governor** • Christie Gregoire (D) 2012

**Senate** • Maria Cantwell (D) 2013, Patty Murray (D) 2011

**Representatives** • Jay Inslee (D), Rick Larsen (D), Brian Baird (D), Doc Hastings (R), Cathy McMorris Rogers (R), Norman Dicks (D), Jim McDermott (D), David Reichert (R), Adam Smith (D)

# West Virginia

**State Capitol** • Charleston, WV 25305 (304) 558-2000

**Governor** • Joe Manchin III (D) 2012

**Senate** • Robert C. Byrd (D) 2013, John D. Rockefeller IV (D) 2015

**Representatives** • Alan B. Mollohan (D), Shelley Moore Capito (R), Nick J. Rahall II (D)

# Wisconsin

**State Capitol** • Madison, WI 53707 (608) 266-1212

**Governor** • Jim Doyle (D) 2010

**Senate** • Russell Feingold (D) 2011, Herbert Kohl (D) 2013

**Representatives** • Paul Ryan (R), Tammy Baldwin (D), Ronald Kind (D), Gwen Moore (D), F. James Sensenbrenner Jr. (R), Thomas Petri (R), David Obey (D), Steve Kagen (D)

# Wyoming

**State Capitol** • Cheyenne, WY 82002 (307) 777-7434

**Governor** • Dave Freudenthal (D) 2010

**Senate** • Michael Enzi (R) 2015, John Barrasso (R) 2013

**Representative** • Cynthia M. Lummis (R)

# Notes

# Foreign Embassies in the United States

## Afghanistan

**Embassy of Afghanistan** • His Excellency Said Tayed Jawad, 2341 Wyoming Ave. N.W., Washington, DC, 20008, (202) 483-6410, Fax (202) 483-6488, info@embassyofafghanistan.org, www.embassyofafghanistan.org

## African Republic, Central

**Embassy of Central African Republic** • His Excellency Emmanuel Touaboy, 1618 22nd St. N.W., Washington, DC, 20008, (202) 483-7800, Fax (202) 332-9893

## Albania

**Embassy of the Republic of Albania** • His Excellency Aleksander Sallabanda, 2100 S St. N.W., Washington, DC, 20008, (202) 223-4942, Fax (202) 628-7342, www.embassyofalbania.org

## Algeria

**Embassy of the People's Democratic Rep. of Algeria** • His Excellency Abdallah Baali, 2118 Kalorama Rd. N.W., Washington, DC, 20008, (202) 265-2800, Fax (202) 667-2174, mail@algeria-us.org, www.algeria-us.org

## Andorra

**Embassy of Andorra** • Two United Nations Plaza, 27th Flr., New York, NY, 10017, (212) 750-8064, Fax (212) 750-6630, andorra@un.int

## Angola

**Embassy of the Republic of Angola** • Her Excellency Josefina Pitra Diakite, 2108 16th St. N.W., Washington, DC, 20009, (202) 785-1156, Fax (202) 785-1258, angola@angola.org, www.angola.org

## Antigua & Barbuda

**Embassy of Antigua & Barbuda** • Her Excellency Deborah Mae Lovell, 3216 New Mexico Ave. N.W., Washington, DC, 20016, (202) 362-5122, Fax (202) 362-5225, embantbar@aol.com

## Arab Emirates

*See United Arab Emirates*

## Argentina

**Embassy of the Argentine Republic** • His Excellency D. Hector Marcos Timerman, 1600 New Hampshire Ave. N.W., Washington, DC, 20009, (202) 238-6400, Fax (202) 332-3171, www.embassyofargentina.us

## Armenia

**Embassy of the Republic of Armenia** • His Excellency Tatoul Markarian, 2225 R St. N.W., Washington, DC, 20008, (202) 319-1976, Fax (202) 319-2982, www.armeniaemb.org

## Australia

**Embassy of Australia** • His Excellency Dennis James Richardson, 1601 Massachusetts Ave. N.W., Washington, DC, 20036, (202) 797-3000, Fax (202) 797-3168, www.austemb.org

## Austria

**Embassy of Austria** • Dr. Andreas Riecken, 3524 International Ct. N.W., Washington, DC, 20008, (202) 895-6700, Fax (202) 895-6750, www.austria.org

## Azerbaijan

**Embassy of the Republic of Azerbaijan** • His Excellency Yashar Aliyev, 2741 34th St. N.W., Washington, DC, 20008, (202) 337-3500, Fax (202) 337-5911, azerbaijan@azembassy.com, www.azembassy.com

## Bahamas

**Embassy of the Commonwealth of the Bahamas** • His Excellency Cornelius Alvin Smith, 2220 Massachusetts Ave. N.W, Washington, DC, 20008, (202) 319-2660, Fax (202) 319-2668, bahemb@aol.com

## Bahrain

**Embassy of the Kingdom of Bahrain** • Her Excellency Houda Ezra Ebrahim Nonoo, 3502 International Dr. N.W., Washington, DC, 20008, (202) 342-0741, Fax (202) 362-2192, www.bahrainembassy.org

## Bangladesh

**Embassy of the People's Republic of Bangladesh** • His Excellency M. Humayun Kabir, 3502 International Dr. N.W., Washington, DC, 20008, (202) 244-0183, Fax (202) 244-5366, www.bangladoot.org

## Barbados

**Embassy of Barbados** • His Excellency John Ernest Beale, 2144 Wyoming Ave. N.W., Washington, DC, 20008, (202) 939-9200, Fax (202) 332-7467, washington@foreign.gov.bb

## Belarus

**Embassy of the Republic of Belarus** • His Excellency Mikhail Khvostov, 1619 New Hampshire Ave. N.W., Washington, DC, 20009, (202) 986-1604, Fax (202) 986-1805, usa@belarusembassy.org, www.belarusembassy.org

# Belgium

**Embassy of Belgium** • His Excellency Jan Matthysen, 3330 Garfield St. N.W., Washington, DC, 20008, (202) 333-6900, Fax (202) 333-3079, washington@diplobel.org, www.diplobel.org/usa

# Belize

**Embassy of Belize** • His Excellency Nestor E. Mendez, 2535 Massachusetts Ave N.W., Washington, DC, 20008, (202) 332-9636, Fax (202) 332-6888, www.embassyofbelize.org

# Benin

**Embassy of the Republic of Benin** • His Excellency Segbe Cyrille Oguin, 2124 Kalorama Rd. N.W., Washington, DC, 20008, (202) 232-6656, Fax (202) 265-1996, www.beninembassyus.org

# Bolivia

**Embassy of the Republic of Bolivia** • Her Excellency Erika Angela Duenas Loayza, 3014 Massachusetts Ave. N.W., Washington, DC, 20008, (202) 483-4410, Fax (202) 328-3712, www.bolivia-usa.org

# Bosnia & Herzegovina

**Embassy of Bosnia & Herzegovina** • His Excellency Mitar Kujundzic, 2109 E St. N.W., Washington, DC, 20037, (202) 337-1500, Fax (202) 337-1502, www.bhembassy.org

# Botswana

**Embassy of the Republic of Botswana** • His Excellency Lapologang Caesar Lekoa, 1531-1533 New Hampshire Ave. N.W., Washington, DC, 20036, (202) 244-4990, Fax (202) 244-4164, www.botswanaembassy.org

# Brazil

**Brazilian Embassy** • His Excellency Antonio de Aguiar Patriota, 3006 Massachusetts Ave. N.W., Washington, DC, 20008, (202) 238-2700, Fax (202) 238-2827, www.brasilemb.org

# Brunei

**Embassy of the State of Brunei Darussalam** • 3520 International Ct. N.W., Washington, DC, 20008, (202) 237-1838, Fax (202) 885-0560, info@bruneiembassy.org, www.brunei embassy.org

# Bulgaria

**Embassy of the Republic of Bulgaria** • His Excellency Latchezar Petkov, 1621 22nd St. N.W., Washington, DC, 20008, (202) 387-0174, Fax (202) 234-7973, office@bulgaria-embassy. org, www.bulgaria-embassy.org

# Burkina Faso

**Embassy of Burkina Faso** • His Excellency Paramanga Ernest Yonli, 2340 Massachusetts Ave. N.W., Washington, DC, 20008, (202) 332-5577, Fax (202) 667-1882, www.burkinaembassy-usa.org

# Burundi

**Embassy of the Republic of Burundi** • His Excellency Celestin Niyongabo, 2233 Wisconsin Ave. N.W., Ste. 212, Washington, DC, 20007, (202) 342-2574, Fax (202) 342-2578, www.burundi embassy-usa.org

# Cambodia

**Royal Embassy of Cambodia** • His Excellency Heng Hem, 4530 16th St. N.W., Washington, DC, 20011, (202) 726-7742, Fax (202) 726-8381, cambodia@embassy.org, www.embassyofcambodia.org

# Cameroon

**Embassy of the Republic of Cameroon** • His Excellency Joseph Foe-Atangana, 2349 Massachusetts Ave. N.W., Washington, DC, 20008, (202) 265-8790, Fax (202) 387-3826, www.ambacam-usa.org

# Canada

**Embassy of Canada** • His Excellency Michael H. Wilson, 501 Pennsylvania Ave. N.W., Washington, DC, 20001, (202) 682-1740, Fax (202) 682-7726, www.canadianembassy.org

# Cape Verde

**Embassy of the Republic of Cape Verde** • Her Excellency Maria de Fatima da Veiga, 3415 Massachusetts Ave. N.W., Washington, DC, 20007, (202) 965-6820, Fax (202) 965-1207, www.capeverdeusaembassy.org

# Chad

**Embassy of the Republic of Chad** • His Excellency Bechir Mahamoud Adam, 2002 R St. N.W., Washington, DC, 20009, (202) 462-4009, Fax (202) 265-1937

# Chile

**Embassy of Chile** • His Excellency Mariano Fernandez, 1732 Massachusetts Ave. N.W., Washington, DC, 20036, (202) 785-1746, Fax (202) 887-5579, www.chile-usa.org

# China

**Embassy of the People's Republic of China** • His Excellency Wen Zhong Zhou, 2300 Connecticut Ave. N.W., Washington, DC, 20008, (202) 328-2500, Fax (202) 328-2582, www.china-embassy.org

# Colombia

**Embassy of Colombia** • Her Excellency Maria Carolina Barco Isakson, 2118 Leroy Pl. N.W., Washington, DC, 20008, (202) 387-8338, Fax (202) 232-8643, www.colombiaemb.org

# Comoros

**Embassy of the Union of Comoros** • His Excellency Mohamed Toihiri, 866 United Nations Plz., Ste. 418, New York, NY, 10017, (212) 750-1637, Fax (212) 750-1657, www.comoros.un.int

# Congo, Democratic Rep. of

**Embassy of the Democratic Republic of Congo** • Her Excellency Faida Mitifu, 1726 M St. N.W., Ste. 601, Washington, DC, 20036, (202) 234-7690, Fax (202) 234-2609

# Congo, Republic of

**Embassy of the Republic of the Congo** • His Excellency Serge Mombouli, 4891 Colorado Ave. N.W., Washington, DC, 20011, (202) 726-5500, Fax (202) 726-1860, info@embassyofcongo.org, www.embassyofcongo.org

# Costa Rica

**Embassy of Costa Rica** • His Excellency F. Tomas Duenas, 2114 S St. N.W., Washington, DC, 20008, (202) 234-2945, Fax (202) 265-4795, consulate@costarica-embassy.org, www.costarica-embassy.org

# Cote d'Ivoire

**Embassy of the Republic of Cote d'Ivoire** • His Excellency Yao Charles Koffi, 2424 Massachusetts Ave. N.W., Washington, DC, 20008, (202) 797-0300, Fax (202) 462-9444

# Croatia

**Embassy of the Republic of Croatia** • Her Excellency , Kolinda Grabar-Kitarovic, 2343 Massachusetts Ave. N.W., Washington, DC, 20008, (202) 588-5899, Fax (202) 588-8936, www.croatiaemb.org

# Cuba

*No Diplomatic Relations*

# Cyprus

**Embassy of the Republic of Cyprus** • His Excellency Andreas S. Kakouris, 2211 R St. N.W., Washington, DC, 20008, (202) 462-5772, Fax (202) 483-6710, info@cyprusembassy.net, www.cyprusembassy.net

# Czech Republic

**Embassy of the Czech Republic** • His Excellency Petr Kolar, 3900 Spring of Freedom St. N.W., Washington, DC, 20008, (202) 274-9100, Fax (202) 966-8540, washington@embassy.mzv.cz, www.mzv.cz

# Denmark

**Royal Danish Embassy** • His Excellency Friis Arne Petersen, 3200 Whitehaven St. N.W., Washington, DC, 20008, (202) 234-4300, Fax (202) 328-1470, wasamb@um.dk, www.ambwashington.um.dk

# Djibouti

**Embassy of the Republic of Djibouti** • His Excellency Roble Olhaye, 1156 15th St. N.W., Ste. 515, Washington, DC, 20005, (202) 331-0270, Fax (202) 331-0302

# Dominica

**Embassy of the Commonwealth of Dominica** • 3216 New Mexico Ave. N.W., Washington, DC, 20016, (202) 364-6781, Fax (202) 364-6791, embdomdc@aol.com

# Dominican Republic

**Embassy of the Dominican Republic** • His Excellency Flavio Dario Espinal, 1715 22nd St. N.W., Washington, DC, 20008, (202) 332-6280, Fax (202) 265-8057, embassy@us.serex.gov.do , www.domrep.org

# East Timor

**Embassy of the Democratic Republic of Timor Leste** • 4201 Connecticut Ave. N.W., Ste. 504, Washington, DC, 20008, (202) 966-3202, Fax (202) 966-3205

# Ecuador

**Embassy of Ecuador** • His Excellency Luis Benigno Gallegos Chiriboga, 2535 15th St. N.W., Washington, DC, 20009, (202) 234-7200, Fax (202) 667-3482, embassy@ecuador.org, www.ecuador.org

# Egypt

**Embassy of the Arab Republic of Egypt** • His Excellency , Sameh Hassan Shoukry, 3521 International Ct. N.W., Washington, DC, 20008, (202) 895-5400, Fax (202) 244-4319, embassy@egyptembassy.net, www.egyptembassy.net

# El Salvador

**Embassy of El Salvador** • His Excellency Rene A. Leon, 1400 16th St. N.W., Ste. 100, Washington, DC, 20036, (202) 265-9671, Fax (202) 232-3763, correo@elsalvador.org, www.elsalvador.org

# Equatorial Guinea

**Embassy of the Republic of Equatorial Guinea** • Her Excellency Purificacion Angue Ondo, 2020 16th St. N.W., Washington, DC, 20009, (202) 518-5700, Fax (202) 518-5252, info@equatorialguinea.org, www.equatorialguinea.org

# Eritrea

**Embassy of the State of Eritrea** • His Excellency Ghirmai Ghebremariam, 1708 New Hampshire Ave. N.W., Washington, DC, 20009, (202) 319-1991, Fax (202) 319-1304, embassyeritrea@embassyeritrea.org, www.embassyeritrea.org

# Estonia

**Embassy of Estonia** • His Excellency Vaino Reinart, 2131 Massachusetts Ave. N.W., Washington, DC, 20008, (202) 588-0101, Fax (202) 588-0108, info@estemb.org, www.estemb.org

# Ethiopia

**Embassy of Ethiopia** • His Excellency Dr. Samuel Assefa Lemma, 3506 International Dr. N.W., Washington, DC, 20008, (202) 364-1200, Fax (202) 686-9551, www.ethiopianembassy.org

# European Union

**Delegation of the European Comm.** • His Excellency John Bruton, 2300 M St. N.W., Washington, DC, 20037, (202) 862-9500, Fax (202) 429-1766, www.eurunion.org

# Fiji

**Embassy of the Republic of the Fiji Islands** • 2000 M St. N.W., Ste. 710, Washington, DC, 20036, (202) 466-8320, Fax (202) 466-8325, fijiemb@earthlink.net, www.fijiembassydc.com

# Finland

**Embassy of Finland** • His Excellency Pekka Lintu, 3301 Massachusetts Ave. N.W., Washington, DC, 20008, (202) 298-5800, Fax (202) 298-6030, info@finland.org, www.finland.org

# France

**Embassy of France** • His Excellency Pierre Nicolas Vimont, 4101 Reservoir Rd. N.W., Washington, DC, 20007, (202) 944-6000, Fax (202) 944-6166, www.info-france-usa.org

# Gabon

**Embassy of the Gabonese Republic** • His Excellency Carlos Victor Boungou, 2034 20th St. N.W., Ste. 200, Washington, DC, 20009, (202) 797-1000, Fax (202) 332-0668, info@gabonembassy. net, www.gabonembassy.net

# Gambia, The

**Embassy of the Gambia** • 1424 K St. N.W., Ste. 600 , Washington, DC, 20005, (202) 785-1379, Fax (202) 785-1430, www.gambiaembassy.us

# Georgia

**Embassy of the Republic of Georgia** • His Excellency Batu Kutelia , 2209 Massachusetts Ave. N.W., Washington, DC, 20008, (202) 387-2390, Fax (202) 387-0864, embgeorgiausa@yahoo.com, www.georgiaemb.org

# Germany, Federal Rep. of

**Embassy of the Federal Republic of Germany** • His Excellency Dr. Klaus Scharioth, 4645 Reservoir Rd. N.W., Washington, DC, 20007, (202) 298-4000, Fax (202) 298-4249, german-embassy-us@germany.info, www.germany.info

# Ghana

**Embassy of Ghana** • 3512 International Dr. N.W., Washington, DC, 20008, (202) 686-4520, Fax (202) 686-4527, info@ghana embassy.org, www.ghanaembassy.org

# Great Britain

*See United Kingdom*

# Greece

**Embassy of Greece** • His Excellency Alexandros P. Mallias, 2217 Massachusetts Ave. N.W., Washington, DC, 20008, (202) 939-1300, Fax (202) 939-1324, www.mfa.gr

# Grenada

**Embassy of Grenada** • His Excellency Denis G. Antoine, 1701 New Hampshire Ave. N.W., Washington, DC, 20009, (202) 265-2561, Fax (202) 265-2468, www.grenadaembassyusa.org

# Guatemala

**Embassy of Guatemala** • His Excellency Francisco Villagran de Leon, 2220 R St. N.W., Washington, DC, 20008, (202) 745-4952, Fax (202) 745-1908, info@guatemala-embassy.org, www. guatemala-embassy.org

# Guinea

**Embassy of the Republic of Guinea** • His Excellency Mory Karamoko Kaba, 2112 Leroy Pl. N.W., Washington, DC, 20008, (202) 986-4300, Fax (202) 986-3800, embaguinea@aol.com, www.guineaembassy.com

# Guinea-Bissau

*No Information Available*

# Guyana

**Embassy of Guyana** • His Excellency Bayney Karran, 2490 Tracy Pl. N.W., Washington, DC, 20008, (202) 265-6900, Fax (202) 232-1297, guyanaembassy@hotmail.com, www.guyana.org

# Haiti

**Embassy of the Republic of Haiti** • His Excellency Raymond Alcide Joseph, 2311 Massachusetts Ave. N.W., Washington, DC, 20008, (202) 332-4090, Fax (202) 745-7215, embassy@haiti.org, www.haiti.org

# Holy See

**Apostolic Nunciature** • His Excellency Pietro Sambi, 3339 Massachusetts Ave. N.W., Washington, DC, 20008, (202) 333-7121, Fax (202) 337-4036, www.holyseemission.org

# Honduras

**Embassy of Honduras** • His Excellency Roberto Flores Bermudez, 3007 Tilden St. N.W., Ste. 4-M, Washington, DC, 20008, (202) 966-2604, Fax (202) 966-9751, embhondu@aol.com, www. hondurasemb.org

# Hungary

**Embassy of the Republic of Hungary** • His Excellency Ferenc Somogyi, 3910 Shoemaker St. N.W., Washington, DC, 20008, (202) 362-6730, Fax (202) 966-8135, www.huembwas.org

# Iceland

**Embassy of Iceland** • His Excellency Hjalmar Hannesson, 1156 15th St. N.W., Ste. 1200, Washington, DC, 20005, (202) 265-6653, Fax (202) 265-6656, www.iceland.org

# India

**Embassy of India** • His Excellency Renendra Sen, 2107 Massachusetts Ave. N.W., Washington, DC, 20008, (202) 939-7000, Fax (202) 483-3972, www.indianembassy.org

# Indonesia

**Embassy of the Republic of Indonesia** • His Excellency Sudjadnan Parnohadiningrat, 2020 Massachusetts Ave. N.W., Washington, DC, 20036, (202) 775-5200, Fax (202) 775-5365, www.embassyofindonesia.org

# Iran

*No Diplomatic Relations*

# Iraq

**Embassy of the Republic of Iraq** • His Excellency Samir Shakir Mahmood Sumaida'ie, 3421 Massachusetts Ave. N.W., Washington, DC, 20007, (202) 742-1600, Fax (202) 462-5066, www.iraqiembassy.org

# Ireland

**Embassy of Ireland** • His Excellency Michael Collins, 2234 Massachusetts Ave. N.W., Washington, DC, 20008, (202) 462-3939, Fax (202) 232-5993, www.irelandemb.org

# Israel

**Embassy of Israel** • His Excellency Sallai Moshe Meridor, 3514 International Dr. N.W., Washington, DC, 20008, (202) 364-5500, Fax (202) 364-5607, www.israelemb.org

# Italy

**Embassy of Italy** • His Excellency Giovanni Castellaneta, 3000 Whitehaven St. N.W., Washington, DC, 20008, (202) 612-4400, Fax (202) 518-2151, www.ambwashingtondc.esteri.it

# Ivory Coast

*See Cote d'Ivoire*

# Jamaica

**Embassy of Jamaica** • His Excellency Anthony Johnson, 1520 New Hampshire Ave. N.W., Washington, DC, 20036, (202) 452-0660, Fax (202) 452-0081, dcm@jamaicaembassy.org, www.embassyofjamaica.org

# Japan

**Embassy of Japan** • His Excellency Ichiro Fujisaki, 2520 Massachusetts Ave. N.W., Washington, DC, 20008, (202) 238-6700, Fax (202) 328-2187, www.embjapan.org

# Jordan

**Embassy of the Hashemite Kingdom of Jordan** • His Royal Highness Prince Zeid Raad Zeid al Hussein, 3504 International Dr. N.W., Washington, DC, 20008, (202) 966-2664, Fax (202) 966-3110, www.jordanembassyus.org

# Kazakhstan

**Embassy of the Republic of Kazakhstan** • His Excellency Erlan A. Idrissov, 1401 16th St. N.W., Washington, DC, 20036, (202) 232-5488, Fax (202) 232-5845, www.kazakhembus.com

# Kenya

**Embassy of the Republic of Kenya** • His Excellency Peter N.R.O. Ogego, 2249 R St. N.W., Washington, DC, 20008, (202) 387-6101, Fax (202) 462-3829, www.kenyaembassy.com

# Korea

**Embassy of Korea** • His Excellency Han Duk-soo, 2450 Massachusetts Ave. N.W., Washington, DC, 20008, (202) 939-5600, Fax (202) 387-0250, www.koreaembassyusa.org

# Kuwait

**Embassy of the State of Kuwait** • His Excellency Salem Abdullah Al Jaber Al-Sabah, 2940 Tilden St. N.W., Washington, DC, 20008, (202) 966-0702, Fax (202) 966-0517

# Kyrgyzstan

**Embassy of the Kyrgyz Republic** • Her Excellency Zamira Beksultanovna Sydykova, 2360 Massachusetts Ave. N.W., Washington, DC, 20008, (202) 338-5141, Fax (202) 338-5139, www.kyrgyzembassy.org

# Laos

**Embassy of the Lao People's Democratic Republic** • His Excellency Phiane Philakone, 2222 S St. N.W., Washington, DC, 20008, (202) 332-6416, Fax (202) 332-4923, www.laoembassy.com

# Latvia

**Embassy of Latvia** • His Excellency Andrejs Pildegovics, 2306 Massachusetts Ave. N.W., Washington, DC, 20008, (202) 328-2840, Fax (202) 328-2860, www.latvia-usa.org

# Lebanon

**Embassy of Lebanon** • His Excellency Antoine Chedid, 2560 28th St. N.W., Washington, DC, 20008, (202) 939-6300, Fax (202) 939-6324, info@lebanonembassyus.org, www.lebanonembassyus.org

# Lesotho

**Embassy of the Kingdom of Lesotho** • His Excellency David Mohlomi Rantekoa, 2511 Massachusetts Ave. N.W., Washington, DC, 20008, (202) 797-5533, Fax (202) 234-6815, lesothoembassy@ verizon.net, www.lesothoemb-usa.gov.ls

# Liberia

**Embassy of the Republic of Liberia** • His Excellency M. Nathaniel Barnes , 5201 16th St. N.W., Washington, DC, 20011, (202) 723-0437, Fax (202) 723-0436, www.embassyofliberia.org

# Liechtenstein

**Embassy of the Principality of Liechtenstein** • Her Excellency Claudia Fritsche, 2900 K St. N.W., Ste. 602B, Washington, DC, 20006, (202) 331-0590, Fax (202) 331-3221, tamara.brunhart@was.rep.llv.li, www.liechtenstein.li

# Lithuania

**Embassy of the Republic of Lithuania** • His Excellency Audrius Bruzga, 2622 16th St. N.W., Washington, DC, 20007, (202) 234-5860, Fax (202) 328-0466, www.ltembassyus.org

# Luxembourg

**Embassy of the Grand Duchy of Luxembourg** • His Excellency Jean-Paul Senninger, 2200 Massachusetts Ave. N.W., Washington, DC, 20008, (202) 265-4171, Fax (202) 328-8270, www.luxembourgusa.org

# Macedonia

**Embassy of the Republic of Macedonia** • His Excellency Zoran Jolevski, 2129 Wyoming Ave. N.W., Washington, DC, 20008, (202) 667-0501, Fax (202) 667-2131, usoffice@macedonian embassy.org, www.macedonianembassy.org

# Madagascar

**Embassy of the Republic of Madagascar** • His Excellency Jocelyn Bertin Radifera, 2374 Massachusetts Ave. N.W., Washington, DC, 20008, (202) 265-5525, Fax (202) 265-3034, malagasy@embassy.org

# Malawi

**Embassy of Malawi** • Her Excellency Hawa Olga Ndilowe, 1029 Vermont Ave. N.W., Ste. 1000, Washington, DC, 20005, (202) 721-0270, Fax (202) 721-0288, www.malawidc.com

# Malaysia

**Embassy of Malaysia** • 3516 International Ct. N.W., Washington, DC, 20008, (202) 572-9700, Fax (202) 572-9882

# Maldives

**Embassy of the Republic of Maldives** • 800 2nd Ave., Ste. 400E, New York, NY, 10017, (212) 599-6195, Fax (212) 661-6405, info@maldivesembassy.us, www.maldivesembassy.us

# Mali

**Embassy of the Republic of Mali** • His Excellency Abdoulaye Diop, 2130 R St. N.W., Washington, DC, 20008, (202) 332-2249, Fax (202) 332-6603, info@maliembassy.us, www.maliembassy.us

# Malta

**Embassy of Malta** • His Excellency Mark Anthony Miceli Farrugia, 2017 Connecticut Ave. N.W., Washington, DC, 20008, (202) 462-3611, Fax (202) 387-5470, www.magnet.mt

# Marshall Islands

**Embassy of the Republic of the Marshall Islands** • 2433 Massachusetts Ave. N.W., 1st Flr., Washington, DC, 20008, (202) 234-5414, Fax (202) 232-3236, info@rmiembassyus.org, www. rmiembassyus.org

# Mauritania

**Embassy of the Islamic Republic of Mauritania** • His Excellency Ibrahima Dia, 2129 Leroy Pl. N.W., Washington, DC, 20008, (202) 232-5700, Fax (202) 319-2623, info@mauritania embassy.us, mauritaniaembassy.us

# Mauritius

**Embassy of Republic of Mauritius** • His Excellency Keerteecoomar Ruhee, 4301 Connecticut Ave. N.W., Ste. 441, Washington, DC, 20008, (202) 244-1491, Fax (202) 966-0983, mauritius.embassy@verizon.net

# Mexico

**Embassy of Mexico** • His Excellency Arturo Sarukhan Casamitjana, 1911 Pennsylvania Ave. N.W., Washington, DC, 20006, (202) 728-1600, Fax (202) 728-1698, www.embassyofmexico.org

# Micronesia

**Embassy of the Federated States of Micronesia** • His Excellency , Yosiwo P. George, 1725 N St. N.W., Washington, DC, 20036, (202) 223-4383, Fax (202) 223-4391, www.fsmembassydc.org

# Moldova

**Embassy of the Republic of Moldova** • His Excellency Nicolae Chirtoaca, 2101 S St. N.W., Washington, DC, 20008, (202) 667-1130, Fax (202) 667-1204, www.embassyrm.org

# Monaco

**Embassy of Monaco** • His Excellency Gilles Alexandre Noghes, 3400 International Dr. N.W., Ste. 2K-100, Washington, DC, 20008, (202) 234-1530, Fax (202) 234-1530, embassy@monaco-usa.org, monaco-usa.org

# Mongolia

**Embassy of Mongolia** • His Excellency Khasbazaryn Bekhbat, 2833 M St. N.W., Washington, DC, 20007, (202) 333-7117, Fax (202) 298-9227, www.mongolianembassy.us

# Montenegro

**Embassy of the Republic of Montenegro** • His Excellency Miodrag Vlahovic, 1610 New Hampshire Ave. N.W., Washington, DC, 20009, P, 64,000, (202) 234-6108, Fax (202) 234-6109

# Morocco

**Embassy of the Kingdom of Morocco** • His Excellency Aziz Mekouar, 1601 21st St. N.W., Washington, DC, 20009, (202) 462-7980, Fax (202) 462-7643

# Mozambique

**Embassy of the Republic of Mozambique** • His Excellency Armando Alexandre Panguene, 1525 New Hampshire Ave. N.W., Washington, DC, 20036, (202) 293-7146, Fax (202) 835-0245, embamoc@aol.com, www.embamoc-usa.org

# Myanmar

**Embassy of the Union of Myanmar** • His Excellency Myint Lwin, 2300 S St. N.W., Washington, DC, 20008, (202) 332-3344, Fax (202) 332-4351, info@mewashingtondc.com, www.mewashingtondc.com

# Namibia

**Embassy of the Republic of Namibia** • His Excellency Patrick Nandago, 1605 New Hampshire Ave. N.W., Washington, DC, 20009, (202) 986-0540, Fax (202) 986-0443, www.namibianembassyusa.org

# Nauru

**Embassy of the Republic of Nauru** • Her Excellency Marlene Inemwin Moses, 800 Second Ave., New York, NY, 10017, (212) 937-0074, Fax (212) 937-0079

# Nepal

**Embassy of Nepal** • 2131 Leroy Pl. N.W., Washington, DC, 20008, (202) 667-4550, Fax (202) 667-5534, info@nepalembassyusa.org, www.nepalembassyusa.org

# Netherlands

**Royal Netherlands Embassy** • Her Excellency Renee Jones-Bos, 4200 Linnean Ave. N.W., Washington, DC, 20008, (202) 244-5300, Fax (202) 362-3430, www.netherlands-embassy.org

# New Guinea

*See Papua New Guinea*

# New Zealand

**Embassy of New Zealand** • His Excellency Roy Neil Ferguson, 37 Observatory Cir. N.W., Washington, DC, 20008, (202) 328-4800, Fax (202) 667-5227, www.nzembassy.com

# Nicaragua

**Embassy of the Republic of Nicaragua** • 1627 New Hampshire Ave. N.W., Washington, DC, 20009, (202) 939-6570, Fax (202) 939-6545

# Niger

**Embassy of the Republic of Niger** • Her Excellency Aminata Maiga Djibrilla, 2204 R St. N.W., Washington, DC, 20008, (202) 483-4224, Fax (202) 483-3169, www.nigerembassyusa.org

# Nigeria

**Embassy of the Federal Republic of Nigeria** • 3519 International Ct. N.W., Washington, DC, 20008, (202) 986-8400, Fax (202) 362-6541, www.nigeriaembassyusa.org

# Northern Ireland

*See United Kingdom*

# Norway

**Royal Norwegian Embassy** • His Excellency Wegger Christian Strommen, 2720 34th St. N.W., Washington, DC, 20008, (202) 333-6000, Fax (202) 337-0870, www.norway.org

# Oman

**Embassy of the Sultanate of Oman** • Her Excellency Hunaina Sultan Ahmed Al Mughairy, 2535 Belmont Rd. N.W., Washington, DC, 20008, (202) 387-1980, Fax (202) 745-4933

# Pakistan

**Embassy of Pakistan** • His Excellency Husain Haqqani , 3517 International Ct. N.W., Washington, DC, 20008, (202) 243-6500, Fax (202) 686-1544, info@embassyofpakistanusa.org, www.pakistan-embassy.org

# Palau

**Embassy of the Republic of Palau** • His Excellency Hersey Kyota, 1701 Pennsylvania Ave. N.W., Ste. 300, Washington, DC, 20006, (202) 452-6814, Fax (202) 452-6281, imfp@palauembassy.com, www.palauembassy.com

# Panama

**Embassy of the Republic of Panama** • His Excellency Federico Humbert Arias, 2862 McGill Terrace N.W., Washington, DC, 20007, (202) 483-1407, Fax (202) 483-8413, info@embassyofpanama.org, www.embassyofpanama.org

# Papua New Guinea

**Embassy of Papua New Guinea** • His Excellency Evan Jeremy Paki, 1779 Massachusetts Ave. N.W., Ste. 805, Washington, DC, 20036, (202) 745-3680, Fax (202) 745-3679, www.pngembassy.org

# Paraguay

**Embassy of Paraguay** • His Excellency James Spalding Hellmers, 2400 Massachusetts Ave. N.W., Washington, DC, 20008, (202) 483-6960, Fax (202) 234-4508, secretaria@embaparusa.gov.py, www.embaparusa.gov.py

# Peru

**Embassy of Peru** • His Excellency Felipe Ortiz de Zevallos Madueno, 1700 Massachusetts Ave. N.W., Washington, DC, 20036, (202) 833-9860, Fax (202) 659-8124, www.peruvianembassy.us

# Philippines

**Embassy of the Republic of the Philippines** • His Excellency Willy Calaud Gaa, 1600 Massachusetts Ave. N.W., Washington, DC, 20036, (202) 467-9300, Fax (202) 328-7614, info@philippineembassy-usa.org, www.philippineembassy-usa.org

# Poland

**Embassy of the Republic of Poland** • His Excellency , Robert Kupiecki, 2640 16th St. N.W., Washington, DC, 20009, (202) 234-3800, Fax (202) 328-6271, www.polandembassy.org

# Portugal

**Embassy of Portugal** • His Excellency Joao de Vallera, 2012 Massachusetts Ave. N.W., Washington, DC, 20036, (202) 328-8610, Fax (202) 462-3726, www.portugal.org

# Qatar

**Embassy of the State of Qatar** • His Excellency Ali Bin Fahad Al-Hajri, 2555 M St. N.W., Washington, DC, 20037, (202) 274-1600, Fax (202) 237-0061, info@qatarembassy.net, www.qatarembassy.net

# Romania

**Embassy of Romania** • His Excellency Adrian Cosmin Vierita, 1607 23rd St. N.W., Washington, DC, 20008, (202) 332-4846, Fax (202) 232-4748, office@roembus.org, www.roembus.org

# Russian Federation

**Embassy of the Russian Federation** • His Excellency Sergey I. Kislyak, 2650 Wisconsin Ave. N.W., Washington, DC, 20007, (202) 298-5700, Fax (202) 298-5735, www.russianembassy.org

# Rwanda

**Embassy of Republic of Rwanda** • His Excellency James Kimonyo, 1714 New Hampshire Ave. N.W., Washington, DC, 20009, (202) 232-2882, Fax (202) 232-4544, www.rwandemb.org/rwanda/

# Saint Kitts & Nevis

**Embassy of Saint Kitts & Nevis** • His Excellency Dr. Izben Cordinal Williams, 3216 New Mexico Ave. N.W., Washington, DC, 20016, (202) 686-2636, Fax (202) 686-5740, www.embassy.gov.kn

# Saint Lucia

**Embassy of Saint Lucia** • 3216 New Mexico Ave. N.W., Washington, DC, 20016, (202) 364-6792, Fax (202) 364-6723

# Saint Vincent & The Grenadines

**Embassy of Saint Vincent & the Grenadines** • Her Excellency La Celia Prince, 3216 New Mexico Ave. N.W., Washington, DC, 20016, (202) 364-6730, Fax (202) 364-6736, mail@embsvg.com, www.embsvg.com

# Samoa

**Embassy of the Independent State of Samoa** • His Excellency Ali'loaiga Feturi Elisaia, 800 Second Ave., 4th Flr., New York, NY, 10017, (212) 599-6196, Fax (212) 599-0797

# San Marino

**Embassy of the Republic of San Marino** • His Excellency Paolo Rondelli, 2650 Virginia Ave. N.W., Washington, DC, 20037, (202) 250-1535

# Sao Tome & Principe

**Embassy of Sao Tome & Principe** • His Excellency Ovidio Pequeno, 1211 Connecticut Ave. N.W., Ste. 300, Washington, DC, 20036, (202) 775-2075, Fax (202) 775-2077

# Saudi Arabia

**Royal Embassy of Saudi Arabia** • His Excellency Adel A.M. Al-Jubeir, 601 New Hampshire Ave. N.W., Washington, DC, 20037, (202) 342-3800, Fax (202) 944-3113, info@saudiembassy.net, www.saudiembassy.net

# Senegal

**Embassy of the Republic of Senegal** • His Excellency Dr. Amadou Lamine Ba, 2112 Wyoming Ave. N.W., Washington, DC, 20008, (202) 234-0540, Fax (202) 332-6315

# Serbia

**Embassy of Serbia** • His Excellency Ivan Vujacic, 2134 Kalorama Rd. N.W., Washington, DC, 20008, (202) 332-0333, Fax (202) 332-3933, www.serbiaembusa.org

# Seychelles

**Embassy of the Republic of Seychelles** • His Excellency Ronald Jean Jumeau, 800 Second Ave., Ste. 400C, New York, NY, 10017, (212) 972-1785, Fax (212) 972-1786

# Sierra Leone

**Embassy of Sierra Leone** • His Excellency Bockari K. Stevens , 1701 19th St. N.W., Washington, DC, 20009, (202) 939-9261, Fax (202) 483-1793, info@embassyofsierraleone.net, www.embassyofsierraleone.org

# Singapore

**Embassy of the Republic of Singapore** • Her Excellency Chan Heng Chee, 3501 International Pl. N.W., Washington, DC, 20008, (202) 537-3100, Fax (202) 537-0876, www.mfa.gov.sg/washington

# Slovak Republic

**Embassy of the Slovak Republic** • His Excellency Peter Burian, 3523 International Ct. N.W., Washington, DC, 20008, (202) 237-1054, Fax (202) 237-6438, www.slovakembassy-us.org

# Slovenia

**Embassy of the Republic of Slovenia** • 2410 California St. N.W., Washington, DC, 20008, (202) 386-6610, Fax (202) 386-6633

# Solomon Islands

**Embassy of the Solomon Islands** • His Excellency Collin Beck, 800 Second Ave., Ste. 400L, New York, NY, 10017, (212) 599-6192, Fax (212) 661-8925

# Somalia

*Embassy ceased operations May 8, 1991*

# South Africa

**Embassy of the Republic of South Africa** • His Excellency Welile Augustine Witness Nhlapo, 3051 Massachusetts Ave. N.W., Washington, DC, 20008, (202) 232-4400, Fax (202) 265-1607, info@saembassy.org, www.saembassy.org

# Spain

**Embassy of Spain** • His Excellency Jorge Dezcallar de Mazarredo, 2375 Pennsylvania Ave. N.W., Washington, DC, 20037, (202) 452-0100, Fax (202) 833-5670, emb.washington@maec.es, www.spainemb.org

# Sri Lanka

**Embassy of Democratic Socialist Rep. of Sri Lanka** • His Excellency Jaliya Wickramasuriya, 2148 Wyoming Ave. N.W., Washington, DC, 20008, (202) 483-4025, Fax (202) 232-7181, www.slembassyusa.org

# Sudan

**Embassy of the Republic of the Sudan** • His Excellency Akec Khoc, 2210 Massachusetts Ave. N.W., Washington, DC, 20008, (202) 338-8565, Fax (202) 667-2406, www.sudanembassy.org

# Suriname

**Embassy of the Republic of Suriname** • His Excellency Jacques Ruben Constantijn Kross, 4301 Connecticut Ave. N.W., Ste. 460, Washington, DC, 20008, (202) 244-7488, Fax (202) 244-5878, www.surinameembassy.org

# Swaziland

**Embassy of the Kingdom of Swaziland** • His Excellency Ephraim Mandlenkosi M. Hlophe, 1712 New Hampshire Ave. N.W., Washington, DC, 20009, (202) 234-5002, Fax (202) 234-8254

# Sweden

**Embassy of Sweden** • His Excellency Sven Jonas Hafstroem, 2900 K St. N.W., Washington, DC, 20007, (202) 467-2600, Fax (202) 467-2699, www.swedenabroad.com

# Switzerland

**Embassy of Switzerland** • His Excellency Urs Johann Ziswiler, 2900 Cathedral Ave. N.W., Washington, DC, 20008, (202) 745-7900, Fax (202) 387-2564, www.swissemb.org

# Syria

**Embassy of the Syrian Arab Republic** • His Excellency Dr. Imad Moustapha, 2215 Wyoming Ave. N.W., Washington, DC, 20008, (202) 232-6313, Fax (202) 234-9548, info@syrembassy.net, www.syrianembassy.us

# Tajikistan

**Embassy of the Republic of Tajikistan** • His Excellency Abdujabbor Shirinov, 1005 New Hampshire Ave. N.W., Washington, DC, 20037, (202) 223-6090, Fax (202) 223-6091, www.tjus.org

# Tanzania

**Embassy of the United Republic of Tanzania** • His Excellency Ombeni Yohana Sefue, 2139 R St. N.W., Washington, DC, 20008, (202) 939-6125, Fax (202) 797-7408, balozi@tanzania embassy-us.org, www.tanzaniaembassy-us.org

# Thailand

**Embassy of Thailand** • 1024 Wisconsin Ave. N.W., Washington, DC, 20007, (202) 944-3600, Fax (202) 944-3611, info@thaiembdc.org, www.thaiembdc.org

# Togo

**Embassy of the Republic of Togo** • 2208 Massachusetts Ave. N.W., Washington, DC, 20008, (202) 234-4212, Fax (202) 232-3190

# Tonga

**Embassy of the Kingdom of Tonga** • Her Excellency Fekitamoeloa Tupoupai Utoikamanu, 250 E. 51st St., New York, NY, 10022, (917) 369-1025, Fax (917) 369-1024

# Trinidad & Tobago

**Embassy of the Republic of Trinidad & Tobago** • Her Excellency Glenda Morean Phillip, 1708 Massachusetts Ave. N.W., Washington, DC, 20036, (202) 467-6490, Fax (202) 785-3130, www.ttembassy.org

# Tunisia

**Embassy of Tunisia** • 1515 Massachusetts Ave. N.W., Washington, DC, 20005, (202) 862-1850, Fax (202) 862-1858

# Turkey

**Embassy of the Republic of Turkey** • His Excellency Nabi Sensoy, 2525 Massachusetts Ave. N.W., Washington, DC, 20008, (202) 612-6700, Fax (202) 612-6744, www.turkishembassy.org

# Turkmenistan

**Embassy of Turkmenistan** • His Excellency Meret Bairamovich Orazov, 2207 Massachusetts Ave. N.W., Washington, DC, 20008, (202) 588-1500, Fax (202) 588-0697, www.turkmenistanembassy.org

# Uganda

**Embassy of the Republic of Uganda** • His Excellency Perezi Karukubiro Kamunanwire, 5911 16th St. N.W., Washington, DC, 20011, (202) 726-7100, Fax (202) 726-1727, ugembassy@aol.com, www.ugandaembassy.com

# Ukraine

**Embassy of Ukraine** • His Excellency Oleh Shamshur, 3350 M St. N.W., Washington, DC, 20007, (202) 349-2920, Fax (202) 333-0817, www.ukraineinfo.us

# United Arab Emirates

**Embassy of the United Arab Emirates** • His Excellency Yousef Al Otaiba, 3522 International Ct. N.W., Washington, DC, 20008, (202) 243-2400, Fax (202) 243-2432, info@uae-embassy.org, www.uae-embassy.org

# United Kingdom

**British Embassy** • His Excellency Sir Nigel Elton Sheinwald, 3100 Massachusetts Ave. N.W., Washington, DC, 20008, (202) 588-6500, Fax (202) 588-7870, www.britainusa.com

# Uruguay

**Embassy of Uruguay** • His Excellency Carlos Alberto Gianelli, 1913 I St. N.W., Washington, DC, 20006, (202) 331-1313, Fax (202) 331-8142, uruwashi@uruwashi.org, www.uruwashi.org

# Uzbekistan

**Embassy of the Republic of Uzbekistan** • His Excellency Abdulaziz Kamilov, 1746 Massachusetts Ave. N.W., Washington, DC, 20036, (202) 877-5300, Fax embassy@uzbekistan.org, www.uzbekistan.org

# Venezuela

**Embassy of the Bolivarian Republic of Venezuela** • 1099 30th St. N.W., Washington, DC, 20007, (202) 342-2214, Fax (202) 342-6820, despacho@embavenez-us.org, www.embavenez-us.org

# Vietnam

**Embassy of Vietnam** • His Excellency Le Cong Phung, 1233 20th St. N.W., Ste. 400, Washington, DC, 20036, (202) 861-0737, Fax (202) 861-0917

# Yemen

**Embassy of the Republic of Yemen** • His Excellency Abdulwahab Al Hajjri, 2319 Wyoming Ave., Washington, DC, 20008, (202) 965-4760, Fax (202) 337-2017, information@yemenembassy.org, www.yemenembassy.org

# Yugoslavia

*See Serbia*

# Zambia

**Embassy of the Republic of Zambia** • Her Excellency Dr. Inonge Mbikusita Lewanika, 2419 Massachusetts Ave. N.W., Washington, DC, 20008, (202) 265-9717, Fax (202) 332-0826, www.zambiaembassy.org

# Zimbabwe

**Embassy of the Republic of Zimbabwe** • His Excellency Dr. Machivenyika T. Mapuranga, 1608 New Hampshire Ave. N.W., Washington, DC, 20009, (202) 332-7100, Fax (202) 483-9326, info@zimbabwe-embassy.us, www.zimbabqw-embassy.us

# United States Embassies

## Accepted Forms for Addressing Mail

### Posts with APO/FPO Numbers

*APO/FPO Address:*
Name
Organization
PSC of Unit number, Box number
APO AE 09080 or APO AA 34038 or APO AP 96337

*International Address:*
Name of Person/Section
American Embassy
P.O. Box (use street address only when P.O. Box is not supplied)
Manama, Bahrain

### Posts without APO/FPO Numbers

*Diplomatic Pouch Address:*
Name of Person/Section
Name of Post
Department of State
Washington, DC 20521-four digit add-in

*International Address:*
Name of Person/Section
American Embassy
Jubilaeumstrasse 93
3005 Bern, Switzerland

**Note:** Do not combine any of the above forms (e.g. international plus APO/FPO addresses). This will only result in confusion and possible delays in delivery.

To eliminate delays, it is important to address your correspondence to a section or position, rather than an officer by name.

**Sections:**
Commercial Office
Economic/Commercial Office
Financial Attaches
Political Office
Labor Office
Consular Office
Administrative Office
Regional Security Office
Scientific Attaches
Agricultural Office
Public Affairs Office
Cultural Affairs Office
Export/Import Office

# Afghanistan

**Kabul** • Great Masoud Road; APO AE 09806, Tel 937-00-108001, Fax 937-00-108564, kabul.usembassy.gov, vacant

# Albania

**Tirana** • Rruga Elbasanit 103, Dept. of State, 9510 Tirana Pl., Dulles, VA 20189, Tel 355-42-247285, Fax 355-42-232222, tirana.usembassy.gov, Ambassador John Withers II

# Algeria

**Algiers** • 5 Chemin Cheikh Bachir Ibrahimi, El-Biar, 16030, Tel 2137-70-082000, Fax 213-21-607335, algiers.usembassy.gov, Ambassador David Pearce

# Angola

**Luanda** • Rua Houari Boumedienne #32, Tel 2442-22-641000, Fax 2442-22-641232, luanda.usembassy.gov, Ambassador Dan W. Mozena

# Antigua & Barbuda

*The post closed June 30, 1994*

# Argentina

**Buenos Aires** • Avenida Colombia 4300, Unit 4334, APO AA 34034,, Tel 5411-57-774533, Fax 5411-57-774240, argentina.usembassy.gov, Ambassador Earl A. Wayne

# Armenia

**Yerevan** • 1 American Ave., Tel 374-14-64700, Fax 374-14-64742, yerevan.usembassy.gov, Ambassador Marie L. Yovanovitch

# Australia

**Canberra** • Moonah Pl., Yarralumla, A.C.T. 2600, PSC 277 APO AP 96549,, Tel 612-62-145600, Fax 612-62-145970, canberra.usembassy.gov, Ambassador Dan Clune

# Austria

**Vienna** • Boltzmanngasse 16, 1090, Tel 43-13-13390, Fax 431-31-00682, vienna.usembassy.gov, Ambassador Scott F. Kilner

# Azerbaijan

**Baku** • Azadliq Prospect 83, 1007, Tel 9941-24-980335, Fax 9941-24-656671, azerbaijan.usembassy.gov, Ambassador Anne E. Derse

# Bahamas

**Nassau** • P.O. Box N-8197, Tel 242-32-21181, Fax 242-32-87838, nassau.usembassy.gov, Ambassador Timothy Zuniga Brown

# Bahrain

**Manama** • Bldg. 797, Rd. 3119, Block 331, Zing, Tel 973-17-242700, Fax 973-17-270547, manama.usembassy.gov, Ambassador Adam J. Ereli

# Bangladesh

**Dhaka** • Diplomatic Enclave, Madani Ave., Baridhara, Tel 880-28-855500, Fax 880-28-823744, dhaka.usembassy.gov, Ambassador James F. Moriarty

# Barbados

**Bridgetown** • Wildey Bus Park, Wildey, St. Michael BB 14006, FPO AA 34055, Tel 246-22-74000, Fax 246-43-10179, bridgetown.usembassy.gov, Interim Ambassador Dr. Brent Hardt

# Belarus

**Minsk** • 46 Starovilenskaya Str. 220002, PSC 78 Box B Minsk, APO AE 09723, Tel 375172101283, Fax 3751-72-347853, belarus.usembassy.gov, Ambassador Jonathan Moore

# Belgium

**Brussels** • 27 Blvd du Regent, 1000, PSC 82 Box 002, APO AE 09710, Tel 322-50-82111, Fax 322-51-12725, brussels.usembassy.gov, Ambassador Wayne J. Bush

# Belize

**Belmopan** • Floral Park Rd., Unit 7401, APO AA 34025, Tel 501-82-24011, Fax 501-82-24012, belize.usembassy.gov, Ambassador vacant

# Benin

**Cotonou** • Rue Caporal Bernard Anani, B.P. 2012, Tel 229-21-300650, Fax 229-21-300384, cotonou.usembassy.gov, Ambassador Gayleatha B. Brown

# Bermuda

**Hamilton** • 16 Middle Rd., Devonshire DV 03, Tel 441-29-51342, Fax 441-29-51592, Consul General Gregory W. Slayton

# Bolivia

**La Paz** • Ave. Arce #2780, APO AA 34032, Tel 591-22-168000, Fax 591-22-168111, bolivia.usembassy.gov, Ambassador Krishna Urs

# Bosnia-Herzegovina

**Sarajevo** • Alipasina 43, 71000, Tel 387-33-445700, Fax 387-33-659722, sarajevo.usembassy.gov, Ambassador Charles English

# Botswana

**Gaborone** • P.O. Box 90, Tel 267-39-53982, Fax 267-39-56947, botswana.usembassy.gov, Ambassador Stephen J. Nolan

# Brazil

**Brasilia** • SES Avenida das Nacoes 801, Lote 3, 70403-900, Unit 3500, APO AA 34030, Tel 5561-33-127000, Fax 5561-33-127676, brasilia.usembassy.gov, Ambassador Clifford Sobel

# Brunei

**Bandar Seri Begawan** • Third Floor-Teck Guan Plaza, Jalan Sultan, Unit 4280 Box 40, FPO AP 96507, Tel 673-22-29670, Fax 673-22-25293, bandar.usembassy.gov, Ambassador Emil Skodon

# Bulgaria

**Sofia** • 16 Kozyak St., 1407, Tel 359-29-375100, Fax 359-29-375320, bulgaria.usembassy.gov, Ambassador Nancy McEldowney

# Burkina Faso

**Ouagadougou** • 622 Avenue Raoul Follereau,Koulouba Sector 4, Tel 226-50-306723, Fax 226-50-312368, ouagadougou.usembassy.gov, Ambassador Samuel C. Laeuchli

# Burma

**Rangoon** • 110 University Ave., Box B, APO AP 96546, Tel 95-15-36509, Fax 95-16-50480, rangoon.usembassy.gov, Ambassador Larry M. Dinger

# Burundi

**Bujumbura** • Avenue des Etas-Unis; B.P. 1720, Tel 257-22-207000, Fax 257-22-222926, burundi.usembassy.gov, Ambassador Patricia Moller

# Cambodia

**Phnom Penh** • #1 St. 96, Unit 8166, Box P, APO AP 96546, Tel 855-23-728000, Fax 855-23-728600, cambodia.usembassy.gov, Ambassador Carol A. Rodley

# Cameroon

**Yaounde** • 6.050 ave Rosa Parks, BP 817, Tel 237-22-201500, yaounde.usembassy.gov, Ambassador Janet E. Garvey

# Canada

**Ottawa, Ontario** • 490 Sussex Dr., K1N 1G8, P.O. Box 866, Ogdensburg, NY 13669, Tel 613-68-85335, Fax 613-68-83082, ottawa.usembassy.gov, Ambassador David Wilkins

# Cape Verde, Republic of

**Praia** • Rua Abilio Macedo No. 6 Plateau, Tel 238-26-08900, Fax 238-26-11355, praia.usembassy.gov, Ambassador Marianne M. Myles

# Central African Republic

**Bangui** • Avenue David Dacko, P.O. Box 924, Tel 236-21-610200, Fax 236-21-614494, bangui.usembassy.gov, Ambassador Frederick B. Cook

# Chad

**N'Djamena** • Ave. Felix Eboue, B.P. 413, Tel 235-25-16211, Fax 235-25-15654, ndjamena.usembassy.gov, Ambassador Louis Nigro

# Chile

**Santiago** • Av. Andres Bello 2800, APO AA 34033, Tel 562-33-03000, Fax 562-33-03710, santiago.usembassy.gov, Ambassador Paul Simons

# China

**Beijing** • No. 55 An Jia Lou Lu 100600, PSC 461, Box 50, FPO AP 96521, Tel 8610-85-313000, Fax 8610-85-314200, beijing.usembassy.gov, Ambassador Clark T. Randt. Jr.

# Colombia

**Bogota** • Cra. 45 No. 24B-27, APO AA 34038, Tel 571-31-50811, Fax 571-31-52197, bogota.usembassy.gov, Ambassador William Brownfield

# Congo, Democratic Republic of

**Kinshasa** • 310 Ave. des Aviateurs, Kin-Gombe, APO AE 09828, Tel 2438-15-560151, Fax 2438-15-560175, kinshasa.usembassy.gov, Ambassador William J. Garvelink

# Congo, Republic of the

**Brazzaville** • BDEAC Building 4th Floor, APO AE 09828, Tel 24-28-11481, brazzaville.usembassy.gov, Ambassador Allan W. Eastham

# Costa Rica

**San Jose** • Pavas, San Jose, Unit 2501, APO AA 34020, Tel 506-25-192000, Fax 506-25-192305, sanjose.usembassy.gov, Ambassador Peter Cianchette

# Cote D'Ivoire

**Abidjan** • Riviera Golf, 01 BP 1712, Tel 225-22-494000, Fax 225-22-494323, abidjan.usembassy.gov, Ambassador Wanda Nesbitt

# Croatia

**Zagreb** • Thomasa Jeffersona 2, Tel 385-16-612200, Fax 385-16-612373, zagreb.usembassy.gov, Ambassador Robert A. Bradtke

# Cuba

**Havana** • (USINT) Swiss Embassy, Calzada entre L & M, Vedado, Tel 537-83-33551, Fax 537-83-32095, havana.usint.gov,

# Cyprus

**Nicosia** • Metochiou and Ploutarchou Sts., PSC 815, FPO AE 09836, Tel 357-22-393939, Fax 357-22-780944, nicosia.usembassy.gov, Ambassador Frank Urbancic

# Czech Republic

**Prague** • Trziste 15, 11801 Prague 1, Unit 5630 Box 1000, APO AE 09727, Tel 4202-57-022000, Fax 4202-57-022809, prague.usembassy.gov, Ambassador Richard W. Graber

# Denmark

**Copenhagen** • Dag Hammarskjolds Alle 24, 2100, PSC 73, APO AE 09716,, Tel 453-34-17100, Fax 453-54-30223, denmark.usembassy.gov, Charge d'Affaires Terence McCulley

# Djibouti, Republic of

**Djibouti** • Plateau du Serpent, Blvd. Marechal Joffre, B.P. 185, Tel 25-33-53995, Fax 25-33-53940, djibouti.usembassy.gov, Ambassador James Swan

# Dominican Republic

**Santo Domingo** • Corner of Calle Cesar Nicolas Penson & Calle Leopoldo Navarro, Unit 5500, APO AA 34041-5500, Tel 809-22-12171, Fax 809-68-67437, santodomingo.usembassy.gov, Ambassador Roland W. Bullen

# East Timor

**Dili** • Av. de Portugal, Pantai Kelapa, Unit 8129 Box D, APO AP 96520, Tel 670-33-24684, Fax 670-33-13206, Ambassador Hans G Klemm

# Ecuador

**Quito** • Ave. Avigiras E12-170 y Ave. Eloy Alfaro, APO AA 34039, Tel 593-23-985000, spanish.ecuador.usembassy.gov, Ambassador Heather Hodges

# Egypt

**Cairo** • (North Gate) 8, Kamal El-Din Salah St., Garden City, Unit 64900, APO AE 09839-4900, Tel 202-27-973300, Fax 202-27-973200, cairo.usembassy.gov, Ambassador Francis J. Ricciardone

# El Salvador

**San Salvador** • Blvd. Santa Elena, Antiguo Cuscatlan, Unit 3116, APO AA 34023, Tel 503-25-012999, Fax 503-25-012150, sansalvador.usembassy.gov, Charge d'Affaires Robert Blau

# Equatorial Guinea

**Malabo** • Carretera de Aeropuerto, KM-3 El Paraiso, Apt. 95, Tel 24-00-98895, Fax 24-00-98894, malabo.usembassy.gov, Ambassador Donald C. Johnson

# Eritrea

**Asmara** • 179 Alaa St., P.O. Box 211, Tel 291-11-20004, Fax 291-11-27584, eritrea.usembassy.gov, Ambassador Ronald K. McMullen

# Estonia

**Tallin** • Kentmanni 20, 15099, PSC 78 Box T, APO AE 09723, Tel 372-66-88100, Fax 372-66-88265, estonia.usembassy.gov, Charge d'Affaires Karen B. Decker

# Ethiopia

**Addis Ababa** • Entoto St., P.O. Box 1014, Tel 2511-15-174000, Fax 2511-15-174001, ethiopia.usembassy.gov, Ambassador Donald Yamamoto

# Fiji

**Suva** • 31 Loftus St., Tel 679-33-14466, Fax 679-33-02267, suva.usembassy.gov, Ambassador C. Steven McGann

# Finland

**Helsinki** • Itainen Puistotie 14B, 00140, PSC 78, Box H, APO AE 09723, Tel 358-96-16250, Fax 3589-61-625135, finland.usembassy.gov, Charge d'Affaires Michael A. Butler

# France

**Paris** • 2 Avenue Gabriel, 75382 Paris Cedex 08, PSC 116, APO AE 09777-5000, Tel 331-43-122222, Fax 331-42-669783, france.usembassy.gov, Charge d'Affaires Mark A. Pekala

# Gabon

**Libreville** • Blvd. Du Bord de Mer, B.P. 4000, Tel 24-17-62003, Fax 24-17-45507, libreville.usembassy.gov, Ambassador Eunice Reddick

# The Gambia

**Banjul** • Fajara, Kairaba Ave., Tel 220-43-92856, Fax 220-43-92475, banjul.usembassy.gov, Ambassador Barry L. Wells

# Georgia

**Tbilsi** • 11 George Balanchine St. 0131, Unit 7060, APO AE 09742, Tel 995-32-277000, Fax 995-32-532310, georgia.usembassy.gov, Ambassador John Tefft

# Germany, Federal Republic of

**Berlin** • Pariser Platz 2 4-5, 10017, PSC 120, Box 1000, APO AE 09265, Tel 49-30-83050, germany.usembassy.gov, Charge d'Affaires John M. Koenig

# Ghana

**Accra** • No. 24 4th Circular Rd Cantonments, Tel 233-21-741150, Fax 233-21-741692, ghana.usembassy.gov, Ambassador Donald G. Teitelbaum

# Greece

**Athens** • 91 Vasillissis Sophias Ave., 10160, PSC 108 Box 11 APO AE 09842, Tel 3021-07-212951, athens.usembassy.gov, Ambassador Daniel Speckhard

# Grenada

**St. George's** • Lance Aux Epines, Tel 473-44-41173, Fax 473-44-44820, Ambassador Mary M. Ourisman

# Guatemala

**Guatemala City** • 7-01 Reforma, Zone 10, APO AA 34024, Tel 502-23-264000, Fax 502-23-264654, guatemala.usembassy.gov, Ambassador Stephen G. McFarland

# Guinea

**Conakry** • Transversale No. 2, Ratoma, P.O. Box 603, Tel 224-65-104000, Fax 224-65-104297, conakry.usembassy.gov, Charge d'Affaires Elizabeth Raspolic

# Guinea-Bissau

**Bissau** • PO Box 297 Bissau Codex, Tel 24-52-52282, Fax 24-52-22273, dakar.usembassy.gov,

# Guyana

**Georgetown** • 100 Young and Duke Sts., Tel 592-22-54900, Fax 592-22-58497, georgetown.usembassy.gov, Ambassador John M. Jones

# Haiti

**Port-Au-Prince** • Tabarre 41, Tel 509-22-98000, Fax 509-22-98028, haiti.usembassy.gov, Ambassador Janet Ann Sanderson

# The Holy See

**Vatican City** • Via delle Terme Deciane 26, Rome 00153, PSC 59, Box 66, APO AE 09624, Tel 3906-46-743428, Fax 390-65-758346, vatican.usembassy.gov, Charge d'Affaires Julieta Valls Noyes

# Honduras

**Tegucigalpa** • Avenida La Paz, Postal 3453, Tel 504-23-69320, Fax 504-23-69037, honduras.usembassy.gov, Ambassador Hugo Llorens

# Hong Kong

**Hong Kong** • 26 Garden Rd., PSC 461, Box 1, FPO AP 96521, Tel 852-25-239011, Fax 852-28-451598, hongkong.usconsulate.gov, Consul General Joseph R. Donovan

# Hungary

**Budapest** • 1054 Szabadsag Ter 12, Unit 5270 Box 40, APO AE 09731, Tel 361-47-54400, Fax 361-47-54764, hungary.usembassy. gov, Charge d'Affaires Jeffrey Levine

# Iceland

**Reykjavik** • Laufasvegur 21, Tel 354-56-29100, Fax 354-56-29118, iceland.usembassy.gov, Ambassador Carol van Voorst

# India

**New Delhi** • Shanti Path, Chanakaya Puri 110021, Tel 9111-24-198000, Fax 9111-24-190017, newdelhi.usembassy.gov, Charge d'Affaires Peter Burleigh

# Indonesia

**Jakarta** • Jl Merdeka Selatan 4-5, 10110, Box 8129, FPO AP 96520, Tel 6221-34-359000, Fax 6221-34-359922, jakarta. usembassy.gov, Ambassador Cameron Hume

# Iraq

**Baghdad** • APO AE 09316, Tel iraq.usembassy.gov, Ambassador Christopher R. Hill

# Ireland

**Dublin** • 41 Elgin Rd., Ballsbridge, Tel 353-16-688777, Fax 353-16-689946, dublin.usembassy.gov, Ambassador Daniel Rooney

# Ireland, Northern

**Belfast** • (CG) Danesfort House, 223 Stranmillis Rd., BT95GR, Unit 8400, Box 40, APO AE 09498-4040, Tel 4428-90-386100, Fax 4428-90-681301, usembassy.org.uk/nireland, Consul General Susan M. Elliott

# Israel

**Tel Aviv** • 71 Hayarkon St., APO AE 09830, Tel 972-35-197575, Fax 972-35-173227, telaviv.usembassy.gov, Ambassador James B. Cunningham

# Israel

**Rome** • Via Vittorio Veneto 121-00187, PSC 59, Box 100, APO AE 09624, Tel 39-06-46741, Fax 3906-46-742244, rome.usembassy. gov, Charge d'Affaires Elizabeth L. Dibble

# Jamaica

**Kingston** • 142 Old Hope Rd., Tel 876-70-26000, Fax 876-70-26001, kingston.usembassy.gov, Ambassador vacant

# Japan

**Tokyo** • 10-5, Akasaka 1-chome, Minato-ku 107-8420, Unit 45004, Box 258, APO AP 96337-5004, Tel 813-32-245000, Fax 813-35-051862, tokyo.usembassy.gov, Interim Charge d'Affaires James P. Zumwalt

# Jordan

**Amman** • P.O. Box 354, Amman 11118,, APO AE 09892, Tel 962-65-906000, Fax 962-65-920121, amman.usembassy.gov, Ambassador Robert Stephen Beecroft

# Kazakstan

**Astana** • 23-22 S. No.3, Ak Bulak 4 010010, Tel 771-72-702100, Fax 771-72-340890, www.usembassy.kz., Ambassador Richard E. Hoagland

# Kenya

**Nairobi** • United Nations Ave., P.O. Box 606 00621, APO AE 09831-4100, Tel 2542-03-636000, Fax 2542-03-633410, nairobi. usembassy.gov, Ambassador Michael E. Ranneberger

# Korea

**Seoul** • 32 Sejongno, Jongno-gu, Seoul 110-710, Unit 15550, APO AP 96205-5550, Tel 822-39-74114, Fax 822-73-88845, seoul. usembassy.gov, Ambassador Kathleen Stephens

# Kuwait

**Kuwait** • P.O. Box 77, Safat 13001, PSC 1280, Unit 69000 APO AE 09880-9000, Tel 965-22-591001, Fax 965-25-380282, kuwait. usembassy.gov, Ambassador Deborah K. Jones

# Kyrgyz Republic

**Bishkek** • 171 Prospekt Mira, 720016, Tel 9963-12-551241, Fax 9963-12-551264, kyrgyz.usembassy.gov, Ambassador Tatiana C. Gfoeller

# Laos

**Vientiane** • Rue Bartolonie; B.P. 114, Unit 8165, Box V, APO AP 96546, Tel 856-21-267000, Fax 856-21-267190, laos.usembassy. gov, Ambassador Ravic R. Huso

# Latvia

**Riga** • Raina Boulevard 7, LV-1510, PSC 78, Box R, APO AE 09723, Tel 371-67-036200, Fax 371-67-820047, riga.usembassy.gov, Ambassador Bruce Rogers

# Lebanon

**Beirut** • Antelias, P.O. Box 70-840, Tel 961-45-42600, Fax 961-45-44136, beirut.usembassy.gov, Ambassador Michele J. Sison

# Lesotho

**Maseru** • 254 Kingsway Ave., 100, P.O. Box 333, Tel 266-22-312666, Fax 266-22-310116, maseru.usembassy.gov, Ambassador Robert Nolan

# Liberia

**Monrovia** • 111 United Nations Dr., P.O. Box 98, Tel 231-77-054826, Fax 231-77-010370, monrovia.usembassy.gov, Ambassador Linda Thomas-Greenfield

# Lithuania

**Vilnius** • Akmenu 6, LT-03106, PSC 78, Box V, APO AE 09723, Tel 370-52-665500, Fax 370-52-665510, vilnius.usembassy.gov, Ambassador John A. Cloud

# Luxembourg

**Luxembourg** • 22 Blvd. Emmanuel-Servais, 2535, Unit 1410, APO AE 09126-1410, Tel 35-24-60123, Fax 35-24-61401, luxembourg.usembassy.gov, Ambassador Ann L. Wagner

# Macedonia, Republic of

**Skopje** • str. Samoilova Nr. 21, Unit 7120, Box 1000 APO AE 09737, Tel 389-23-102000, Fax 389-23-102499, macedonia.usembassy.gov, Ambassador Philip T. Reeker

# Madagascar

**Antananarivo** • 14-16 Rue Rainitovo, Antsahavola 101 B.O., Tel 2612-02-221257, Fax 2612-02-234539, antananarivo.state.gov, Ambassador R. Niels Marquardt

# Malawi

**Lilongwe** • 16 Jomo, Kenyatta Rd., P.O. Box 30016, Tel 265-17-73166, Fax 265-17-70471, lilongwe.usembassy.gov, Ambassador Peter Bodde

# Malaysia

**Kuala Lumpur** • 376 Jalan Tun Razak, 50400, APO AP 96535-8152, Tel 603-21-685000, Fax 603-21-422207, malaysia.usembassy.gov, Ambassador James R. Keith

# Mali

**Bamako** • ACI 2000, Rue 243, Porte 297, Tel 223-20-702300, Fax 223-20-702479, mali.usembassy.gov, Ambassador Gillian Milovanovic

# Malta

**Valletta** • 3 St. Anne's St., Floriana, P.O. Box 535, CMR 01, Tel 356-25-614000, Fax 356-21-243229, malta.usembassy.gov, Charge d'Affaires Jason Davis

# Marshall Islands, Republic of

**Majuro** • PO Box 1379, 96960, Dept. of State, 4380 Majuro Pl, Washington, DC 20521-4380, Tel 692-24-74011, Fax 692-24-74012, majuro.usembassy.gov, Ambassador Clyde Bishop

# Mauritania

**Nouakchott** • 228 Rue Abdallaye, 42-100, B.P. 222, Tel 222-52-52660, Fax 222-52-51592, mauritania.usembassy.gov, Ambassador Mark M. Boulware

# Mauritius

**Port Louis** • Rogers House 4th Flr., P.O. Box 544, Tel 230-20-24400, Fax 230-20-89534, mauritius.usembassy.gov, Charge d'Affaires Virginia M. Blaser

# Mexico

**Mexico City, D.F.** • Paseo de la Reforma 305, 06500 Mexico DF, P.O. Box 9000, Brownsville, TX 78520-0900, Tel 5255-50-802000, Fax 5255-55-119980, mexico.usembassy.gov, Ambassador Antonio Garza Jr.

# Micronesia

**Kolonia** • PO Box 1286, Pohnpei, Federated States of Micronesia 96941, Tel 691-32-02187, Fax 691-32-02186, kolonia.usembassy.gov, Ambassador Miriam Hughes

# Moldova

**Chisinau** • Strada Alexei Mateevici #103, 2009, Tel 373-22-408300, Fax 373-22-233044, moldova.usembassy.gov, Ambassador Asif J. Chaudhry

# Mongolia

**Ulaanbaatar** • Micro District 11, Big Ring Rd, CPO 1021, PSC 461, Box 300, FPO AP 96521-0002, Tel 976-11-329095, Fax 976-13-20776, mongolia.usembassy.gov, Ambassador Mark C. Minton

# Montenegro

**Podgorica** • Ljubljanska bb, 81000, Tel 382-81-225417, Fax 382-81-241358, podgorica.usembassy.gov, Ambassador Roderick W. Moore

# Morocco

**Rabat** • 2 Ave. Mohamed El Fassi, PSC 74, APO AE 09718, Tel 212-37-762265, Fax 212-37-769639, rabat.usembassy.gov, Charge d'Affaires Robert P. Jackson

# Mozambique

**Maputo** • Avenida Kaunda 193, P.O. Box 783, Tel 258-21-492797, Fax 258-21-490114, maputo.usembassy.gov, Ambassador vacant

# Namibia

**Windhoek** • 14 Lossen Str., PB12029, Tel 2646-12-958500, Fax 2646-12-958603, windhoek.usembassy.gov, Ambassador G. Dennise Mathieu

# Nepal

**Kathmandu** • Maharajgunj, Tel 977-14-007200, Fax 977-14-007272, nepal.usembassy.gov, Ambassador Nancy J. Powell

# Netherlands

**The Hague** • Lange Voorhout 102, 2514 EJ, PSC 71, APO AE 09715, Tel 317-03-102209, Fax 317-03-614688, thehague.usembassy.gov, Charge d'Affaires Michael Gallagher

# Netherlands Antilles

**Curacao** • J.B. Gorsiraweg #1, Tel 599-94-613066, Fax 599-94-616489, curacao.usconsulate.gov, Consul General Timothy J. Dunn

# New Zealand

**Wellington** • 29 Fitzherbert Ter., Thorndon, PSC 467, Box 1, APO AP 96531-1034, Tel 644-46-26000, Fax 644-49-90490, newzealand.usembassy.gov, Charge d'Affaires Dr. David Keegan

# Nicaragua

**Managua** • Carretera Sur. KM 5.5, APO AA 34021, Tel 505-22-527100, Fax 505-22-527304, nicaragua.usembassy.gov, Ambassador Robert Callahan

# Niger

**Niamey** • Rue Des Ambassades, B.P. 11201, Tel 227-20-733169, Fax 227-20-735560, niamey.usembassy.gov, Ambassador Bernadette Mary Allen

# Nigeria

**Abuja** • Plot 1075, Diplomatic Drive, Central District, Tel 234-94-614000, Fax 234-94-614171, nigeria.usembassy.gov, Ambassador Robin R. Sanders

# Norway

**Oslo** • Henrik Ibsens gate 48, 0244, PSC 69, Box 1000, APO AE 09707, Tel 472-13-08540, Fax 472-25-62751, norway.usembassy.gov, Ambassador Ben Whitney

# Oman

**Muscat** • P.O. Box 202, P.C. 115, Madinat Al Sultan Qaboos, Tel 968-24-643400, Fax 968-24-699771, oman.usembassy.gov, Ambassador Gary Grappo

# Pakistan

**Islamabad** • Diplomatic Enclave, Ramna 5, Unit 62200, APO AE 09812-2200, Tel 925-12-080000, Fax 925-12-276427, islamabad.usembassy.gov, Ambassador Anne W. Patterson

# Palau

**Koror** • PO Box 6028, PW 96940, Tel 680-58-72920, Fax 680-58-72911, palau.usembassy.gov, Charge d'Affaires Mr. Bezner

# Panama

**Panama** • Edificio 783, Avenida Demetrio Basilio Lakas,, Unit 0945 APO AA 34002, Tel 507-20-77000, Fax 507-31-75568, panama.usembassy.gov, Ambassador Barbara J. Stephenson

# Papua New Guinea

**Port Moresby** • Douglas St., P.O. Box 1492, APO AP 96553, Tel 675-32-11455, Fax 675-32-00637, portmoresby.usembassy.gov, Charge d'Affaires Tom Weinz

# Paraguay

**Asuncion** • 1776 Mariscal Lopez Ave., Casilla Postal 402, Unit 4711, APO AA 34036, Tel 595-21-21371, Fax 595-21-213728, paraguay.usembassy.gov, Ambassador Liliana Ayalde

# Peru

**Lima** • Avenida La Encalada Cdra 17-Surco, APO AA 34031-5000, Tel 511-43-43000, Fax 511-61-82397, lima.usembassy.gov, Ambassador P. Michael McKinley

# Philippines

**Manila** • 1201 Roxas Rd.., PSC 500, APO AP 96515-1000, Tel 632-30-12000, Fax 632-30-12017, manila.usembassy.gov, Ambassador Kristie A. Kenney

# Poland

**Warsaw** • Aleje Ujazdowskie 29/31 540, Unit 5010, APO AE 09730, Tel 482-25-042000, Fax 482-25-042226, poland.usembassy.gov, Ambassador Victor Ashe

# Portugal

**Lisbon** • Av Forcas Armadas 1600-081, PSC 83, APO AE 09726, Tel 3512-17-273300, Fax 3512-17-269109, portugal.usembassy.gov, Ambassador Thomas F. Stephenson

# Qatar

**Doha** • 22 February St., Al-Lu qta Dist., Box 520, APO AE 09898, Tel 974-48-84101, Fax 974-48-84176, qatar.usembassy.gov, Ambassador Joseph Evan LeBaron

# Romania

**Bucharest** • Tudor Arghezi 7-9, District 2, 020942, Dept. of State, 5260 Bucharest Pl, Washington, DC 20521-5260, Tel 402-12-003300, Fax 402-12-003442, bucharest.usembassy.gov, Charge d'Affaires Jeri Guthrie-Corn

Embassies, U.S.

# Russia

**Moscow** • Bolshoy Devyatinskiy Pereulok No. 8, 121099, PSC 77, APO AE 09721, Tel 749-57-285000, Fax 749-57-285090, moscow. usembassy.gov, Ambassador John Beyrle

# Rwanda

**Kigali** • 2657 Ave. de la Gendarmerie, Tel 25-05-96400, Fax 25-05-96591, rwanda.usembassy.gov, Ambassador Stuart Symington

# Samoa

**Apia** • 5th Floor, ACB House, Metafele, PSC 467, Box 1, APO AP 96531-1034, Tel 6-85-21631, Fax 6-85-22030, samoa.usembassy. gov, Charge d'Affaires Robin L. Yeager

# Saudi Arabia

**Riyadh** • Diplomatic Quarter, Unit 61307, APO AE 09803-1307, Tel 966-14-883800, Fax 966-14-887360, riyadh.usembassy.gov, Charge d'Affaires David H. Rundell

# Scotland

**Edinburgh** • (CG) 3 Regent Ter. EH7 5BW, PSC 801, Box E, FPO AE 09498-4040, Tel 4413-15-568315, Fax 4413-15-576023, london. usembassy.gov/scotland., Consul General Lisa Vickers

# Senegal

**Dakar** • B.P. 49, Avenue Jean XXIII, Tel 2213-38-292100, Fax 2213-38-222991, dakar.usembassy.gov, Ambassador Marcia S. Bernicat

# Serbia

**Belgrade** • Kneza Milosa 50, 11000, Tel 3811-13-619344, Fax 3811-13-618230, belgrade.usembassy.gov, Ambassador Cameron Munter

# Sierra Leone

**Freetown** • Southridge-Hill Station, Tel 232-22-515000, Fax 232-22-515225, freetown.usembassy.gov, Ambassador June C. Perry

# Singapore

**Singapore** • 27 Napier Rd., 258508, PSC Box 470, FPO AP 96507-0001, Tel 656-47-69100, Fax 656-47-69340, singapore.usembassy. gov, Ambassador vacant

# Slovak Republic

**Bratislava** • P.O. Box 309, 814-99, Unit 5840, APO AE 09736, Tel 4212-54-433338, Fax 4212-54-418861, slovakia.usembassy.gov, Charge d'Affaires Keith A. Eddins

# Slovenia

**Ljubljana** • Preservova 31, 1000, Unit 7140, APO AE 09739, Tel 386-12-005500, Fax 386-12-005555, ljubljana.usembassy.gov, Charge d'Affaires Bradley Freden

# South Africa

**Pretoria** • 877 Pretorius St, Arcadia, Tel 271-24-314000, Fax 271-23-422299, southafrica.usembassy.gov, Charge d'Affaires Helen LaLime

# Spain

**Madrid** • Serrano 75, 28006, PSC 61, APO AE 09642, Tel 349-15-872200, Fax 349-15-872303, madrid.usembassy.gov, Charge d'Affaires Arnold Chacon

# Sri Lanka

**Colombo** • 210 Galle Rd., Colombo 3, Tel 941-12-498500, Fax 941-12-437345, colombo.usembassy.gov, Ambassador Robert O. Blake, Jr.

# Sudan

**Khartoum** • Ali Abdel Latif St., Unit 64105, P.O. Box 699, Tel 2491-87-016000, Fax 2491-83-774137, sudan.usembassy.gov, Charge d'Affaires Alberto Fernandez

# Suriname

**Paramaribo** • Dr. Sophie Redmondstraat 129, Tel 59-74-72900, Fax 59-74-10972, suriname.usembassy.gov, Ambassador Lisa Bobbie Schreiber Hughes

# Swaziland

**Mbabane** • 7th Fl. Central Bank Bldg., Warner St., P.O. Box 199, Tel 268-40-46441, Fax 268-40-45959, swaziland.usembassy.gov, Ambassador Maurice S. Parker

# Sweden

**Stockholm** • Dag Hammarskjolds Vag 31, SE-115 89, Unit 5750, APO AE 09744, Tel 468-78-35300, Fax 468-66-11964, stockholm. usembassy.gov, Charge d'Affaires Robert Silverman

# Switzerland

**Bern** • Sulgeneckstrasse 19, CH-3007, Tel 413-13-577011, Fax 413-13-577344, bern.usembassy.gov, Charge d'Affaires Leigh Carter

# Syria

**Damascus** • Al Mansour St. No. 2, P.O. Box 29, Unit 70200 Box D, APO AE 09892, Tel 96311-33-914444, Fax 96311-33-913999, damascus.usembassy.gov, Charge d'Affaires Maura Connelly

# Taiwan

**Taipei** • American Institute in Taiwan, #7 Lane 134, Xinyi Road, Section 3, 10659, Tel 8862-21-622000, Fax 8862-21-622251, ait.org.tw

# Tajikistan

**Dushanbe** • 109-A Ismoili Somoni Ave., 734019, Tel 9923-72-292000, Fax 9923-72-292050, dushanbe.usembassy.gov, Ambassador Tracey Jacobson

# Tanzania

**Dar Es Salaam** • 686 Old Bagamoyo Rd., P.O. Box 9123, Tel 2552-22-668460, Fax 2552-22-668421, tanzania.usembassy.gov, Charge d'Affaires Larry Andr

# Thailand

**Bangkok** • 120/122 Wireless Rd., 10330, APO AP 96546, Tel 662-20-54000, Fax 662-20-54306, bangkok.usembassy.gov, Ambassador Eric John

# Togo

**Lome** • 4332 Boulevard Gnassingbe Eyadema, BP 852, Tel 228-26-15470, Fax 228-26-15501, togo.usembassy.gov, Ambassador Patricia Hawkins

# Trinidad & Tobago

**Port-Of-Spain** • 15 Queen's Park West, P.O. Box 752, Tel 868-62-26371, Fax 868-82-25905, trinidad.usembassy.gov, Charge d'Affaires Len Kusnitz

# Tunisia

**Tunis** • Les Berges du Lac 1053, Unit 6360 APO AE 09734, Tel 216-71-107000, Fax 216-71-963263, tunis.usembassy.gov, Ambassador Robert Godec

# Turkey

**Ankara** • 110 Ataturk Bulvari, PSC 93, Box 5000, APO AE 09823, Tel 9031-24-555555, Fax 9031-24-670019, ankara.usembassy.gov, Ambassador James F. Jeffrey

# Turkmenistan

**Ashgabat** • 9 1984 St., Tel 993-12-350045, Fax 993-12-392614, turkmenistan.usembassy.gov, Ambassador Richard M. Miles

# Uganda

**Kampala** • 1577 Ggaba Rd., P.O. Box 7007, Tel 2564-14-259791, Fax 2564-14-259794, kampala.usembassy.gov, Ambassador Steven A. Browning

# Ukraine

**Kyiv** • 4 Hlybochtska, Tel 3804-44-904000, Fax 3804-44-904085, kyiv.usembassy.gov, Ambassador William Taylor

# United Arab Emirates

**Abu Dhabi** • Al-Sudan St., P.O. Box 4009, Unit 6010, APO AE 09825, Tel 971-24-142200, Fax 971-24-142575, uae.usembassy.gov, Ambassador Richard G. Olson

# United Kingdom

**London, England** • 24 Grosvenor Sq., W1A 1AE, Unit 8400, FPO AE 09498-4040, Tel 4420-74-999000, Fax 4420-76-299124, london.usembassy.gov, Charge d'Affaires Richard LeBaron

# United States

**U.S. Mission to the United Nations** • 140 E. 45th St., New York, NY 10017, Tel 212-41-54000, Fax 212-41-54443, usunnew york.usmission.gov, Ambassador Zalmay Khalilzad

# Uruguay

**Montevideo** • Lauro Muller 1776, APO AA 34035, Tel 598-24-187777, Fax 598-24-188611, montevideo.usembassy.gov, Charge d'Affaires Robin Matthewman

# Uzbekistan

**Tashkent** • 82 Chilanzarskaya, Tel 9987-11-205450, Fax 9987-11-206335, www.usembassy.uz., Ambassador Richard B. Norland

# Venezuela

**Caracas** • Calle F con Calle Suapure, Colinas de Valle Arriba, APO AA 34037, Tel 5821-29-756411, Fax 5821-29-078106, venezuela. usembassy.gov, Charge d'Affaires John Caufield

# Vietnam

**Hanoi** • 7 Lang Ha St., Dong Da Dist, PSC 461, Box 400, FPO AP 96521-0002, Tel 844-38-505000, Fax 844-38-505010, vietnam. usembassy.gov, Ambassador Michael W. Michalak

# Yemen

**Sanaa** • Sa'Awan St., P.O. Box 22347, Tel 967-17-552000, Fax 967-13-03182, yemen.usembassy.gov, Ambassador Stephen Seche

# Zambia

**Lusaka** • Corner of Independence and United Nations Aves., P.O. Box 31617, Tel 2602-11-250955, Fax 2602-11-252225, zambia. usembassy.gov, Ambassador Donald E. Booth

# Zimbabwe

**Harare** • 172 Herbert Chitepo Ave., P.O. Box 3340, Tel 263-42-50593, Fax 263-47-96488, harare.usembassy.gov, Ambassador James McGee

Embassies, U.S.

# Notes

# Notes

# Notes

# Yellow Pages Directory

## 2009 Directory of Services and Products

## Advertising

### All Seasons Communications

Erin Proctor • 5455 34 Miles Rd. • Romeo, MI 48065 • (586) 752-6381 • Fax (586) 752-6539 • eproctor@allseasons communications.com • www.allseasons communications.com

### City Magnet

P.O. Box 529 • Sunrise Beach, MO 65079 • (573) 374-6200

### David Advertising Inc.

526 Superior Ave. E., Ste. 300 • Cleveland, OH 44114 • (216) 687-1818

### Digicolor Advertising & Design

Brent Haynes • RR 3, Box 347, Mayhew Rd. • New Cumberland, WV 26047 • (304) 564-5213

### Dolphin Consulting & Design

Kathy Meadows • 222 Walnut St. • Ravenswood, WV 26164 • (304) 942-2282 • kmmeadows@mail.casinternet.net

### Eventive Marketing

David Saalfrank • 200 Varick St. • New York, NY 10014 • (212) 463-9700 • davids@eventivemarketing.com • www.eventivemarketing.com

### Fox Pro Media

Greg Fox • 5801 River Rd. • New Orleans, LA 70123 • (800) 841-9532 • info@fox promedia.com • www.foxpromedia.com

### New Atlas dot Com Inc.

Jerry Wright • 304 N. Meridian Ave., Ste. G • Oklahoma City, OK 73107 • (405) 942-8527 • (866) 942-8527 • Fax (405) 943-5750 • maps@newatlas.com • www.newatlas.com • *See our ad on page 7*

### Signs Manufacturing Corp.

Bill Watson • 4610 Mint Way • Dallas, TX (214) 339-2227 • (800) 333-7137 • Fax (214) 339-9987 • www.signsmanu facturing.com

## Arts & Entertainment

### Buddy Lee Attractions Inc.

38 Music Sq., Ste. 300 • Nashville, TN 37203 • (615) 244-4336 • www.buddy leeattractions.com

### Entertainment Publications

1414 E. Maple Rd. • Troy, MI 48083 • (248) 404-1000 • www.entertainment.com

### Event Productions & Management

9139 Barney Broxson Rd. • Milton, FL 32583 • (850) 983-9519 • stageforrent@ aol.com • www.stageforrent.com

## Legion Fireworks Co.

Frank M. Coluccio • 10 Legion Ln. •
Wappingen Falls, NY 12590 • (914)
831-8328 • frank@legionfireworks.com •
www.legionfireworks.com

## Melrose Pyrotechnics

P.O. Box 302 • Kingsburg, IN 46345 •
(219) 393-5522 • (800) 771-7976 •
www.melrosepyro.com

## Loveland High Plains Art Council

125 E. 7th St. • P.O. Box 7006 • Loveland,
CO 80537 • (970) 663-2940 • Fax (970)
669-7390 • lhpac@sculptureinthepark.org •
www.sculptureinthepark.org

## Banners/Signs

## Design Decorators Inc.

Joan Krieger • 3076 Jasper St. • Philadelphia, PA 19134 • (215) 634-8300

## Display Sales

10925 Nesbitt Ave. S. • Bloomington,
MN 55437 • (952) 885-0100 • (800)
328-6195 • Fax (952) 885-0099 • sales@
displaysales.com • www.displaysales.com

## Four Seasons Banner Co.

Carolyn Foster • 831 Railroad St., Ste. 1 •
Port Orange, FL 32129 • (386) 760-6851 •
(800) 741-6852 • Fax (386) 788-4315 •
fsb831408@aol.com • www.fourseasons
banner.com

## GP Designs Inc.

Rick Dillon • 318 E. 12th St. • Marion,
IN 46953 • (800) 888-3833 • sales@gp
designs.biz • www.gpdesigns.biz

## Main Street Designs Inc.

Kristi Downs • 7101 143rd Ave. N.W., Ste.
F • Ramsey, MN 55303 • (763) 506-0860 •
(800) 755-3039 • information@mainstreet
designs.com • www.mainstreetdesigns.com

## Signs and Signs

P.O. Box 859 • Mayfield, KY • 42066 •
(207) 247-7219 • signsandsigns@bell
south.net

## Buildings, Steel

## Rockford Steel Buildings

6800 E. Hampden Ave. • Denver, CO
80224 • (303) 758-4141 • (800) 964-
8335 • www.scg-grp.com

## Sunward Consolidated Group

6800 E. Hampden Ave. • Denver, CO 80224 • (303) 758-4141 • (800) 964-8335 • www.scg-grp.com

## WedgCor Steel Buildings

6800 E. Hampden Ave. • Denver, CO 80224 • (303) 758-4141 • (800) 964-8335 • www.scg-grp.com

## Business Services

### Constant Training

Joe Constance • 1987 E. M-28 • Marquette, MI • 49855 • (906) 249-5555 • (800) 816-7919 • Fax (906) 249-5555 • joe@constanttraining.com • www.constanttraining.com

### Corporate Investigations Inc.

2275 Swallow Hill Rd., Ste. 500 • Pittsburgh, PA 15220 • (412) 429-2400 • (800) 600-0244 • Fax (412) 429-2410 • www.ciilink.com

### Dolphin Consulting & Design

Kathy Meadows • 222 Walnut St. • Ravenswood, WV 26164 • (304) 942-2282 • kmmeadows@mail.casinternet.net

### HR On Call

Dick Clark • 821 W. Louise Ave. • Morristown, TN 37813 • 423-327-5270 • dick clark@hroncall.com • www.hroncall.com

## Chamber Awards

### Chamber Awards

5953 River Bend Dr. • Benbrook, TX 76132 • (817) 735-0090 • (800) 964-6308 • chamberawards@cfjmfg.com • www.chamberawards.com

### Coates Designers

Alan Coates • P.O. Box 1273 • Franklin, TN 28744 • (828) 349-9700 • (800) 428-8899 • alan@coatesplaques.com • www.coatesplaques.com

### The Pin Center

2408 Las Verdes St. • Las Vegas, NV 89102 • (702) 227-6200

### Todd-Brandt Inc.

P.O. Box 1944 • Bonita Springs, FL 34133 • (239) 947-0085 • www.todd-brandt.com

## Chamber Supplies

### Leland Co. Ltd.

Alan Hudson • 827 Rte. 44 • P.O. Box 219 • Brownsville, VT 05037 • (802) 484-7723 • www.lelandcompany.com

## Christmas Decorations

### All American Christmas Co.

Steve Broyles • 384 Broyles St. • P.O. Box 208 • Sparta, TN 38583 • (931) 836-1212 • Fax (931) 836-2002 • info@aachristmas.com • www.aachristmas.com

**4**

## American Christmas Inc.

1135 Bronx River Ave. • Bronx, NY
10472 • (718) 402-9700 • Fax (718) 402-
9704 • magic@americanxmas.com • www.
americanxmas.com

## Dixie Decorations

355 Industrial Park • P.O. Box 81 •
Montevallo, AL 35115 • (205) 665-1225 •
(800) 423-4260 • Fax (205) 665-1263 •
dixiedecorations@bellsouth.net • www.
dixiedecorations.com

## Computer Software– Membership Management

## Chamber Data Systems Inc.

JoAnn McDonough • 15221 Berry Trl.,
Ste. 507 • Dallas, TX 75248 • (972) 233-
1299 • cdsi@chamberdata.com • www.
chamberdata.com

## ChamberMaster

Doug Hennum • 14391 Edgewood Dr. •
Baxter, MN 56425 • (218) 825-9200 •
(800) 825-9171 • Fax (360) 350-4787 •
info@chambermaster.com • www.
chambermaster.com

## ChamberWare

24328 Highlander Rd. • West Hills, CA
91307 • (818) 999-0700 • info@chamber
ware.com • www.chamberware.com

## Decals

## Leland Co. Ltd.

Alan Hudson • 827 Rte. 44 • P.O. Box
219 • Brownsville, VT 05037 • (802) 484-
7723 • www.lelandcompany.com

## Displays–Outdoors

## Dixie Decorations

355 Industrial Park • P.O. Box 81 •
Montevallo, AL 35115 • (205) 665-1225 •
(800) 423-4260 • Fax (205) 665-1263 •
dixiedecorations@bellsouth.net • www.
dixiedecorations.com

## Liberty Flags & Specialty Co.

P.O. Box 398 • Reedsburg, WI 53959 •
(608) 524-2834 • www.americasflag.com

## Directory Publishers

## Community Matters Inc.

Layne Mullin • 4113 Honor Dr. • Frisco,
TX 75034 • (972) 370-1778 • (800)
380-2450 • Fax (972) 370-1766 •
info@communitymattersinc.com •
www.communitymattersinc.com •
*See our ad on page 8*

## Morning Star Publishing House

Curtis Courtney • 159 Dickerson Ln. •
Elgin, TX 78621 • (512) 281-2981 • (800)
369-9377 • morningstarph@juno.com •
*See our ad on page 9*

## Village Profile

Joe Nugara • 33 N. Geneva St. • Elgin, IL 60120 • (800) 600-0134 • jcn@village profilemail.com • www.villageprofile.com

## Exhibit Displays & Graphics

### EXPOGO!

Doug Hilburn • 1502 N. 23rd St. • Wilmington, NC 28405 • (910) 452-3976 • (800) 891-1869 • Fax (910) 452-2090 • info@expogo.com • www.expogo.com

### Kwik-Fold Displays

Dennis Dunda • 64 Laurel Ave. • Binghamton, NY 13905 • (607) 722-4377 • displays@kwikfold.com • www.kwikfold.com

### Midwest Trade Show Displays

1600 W. 26th St. • Marion, IN 46953 • (765) 662-9645

### Plaid Dog Studios

Dave or Claudette Phelps • 970-412-7893 • Fax 970-461-5904 • www.plaiddogstudios.com • claudette@plaiddogstudios.com

## Fund Raising

### America's Favorite Fundraising Products Co.

Richard Bramen • P.O. Box 782 • Grandview, MO 64030 • (816) 761-8700 • Fax (816) 761-2931 • amerfav@live.com • www.americas-favorite.com

### Convergent Nonprofit Solutions

221 N. Hogan St., Ste. 333 • Jacksonville, FL 32202 • (904) 651-3210 • www.convergentnonprofit.com

### Fremont Dev. Group

Gerald Bartels • 6065 Roswell Rd., Ste. 930 • Atlanta, GA 30328 • (404) 459-0401 • Fax (404) 459-0403 • jbartels@fremontdevelopment.com • www.fremontdevelopment.com

### Funding Solutions

Tom Mucks • 11804 Onion Hollow Run • Austin, TX 78739 • (512) 917-9946 • (800) 603-5148 • tpmucks@funsol.com • www.funsol.com

## Integrity Fundraising

Rick Kiernan • 2221 Peachtree Rd., Ste. 624D • Atlanta, GA • 30309 • (919) 270-2137 • (866) 459-2379 • rick@integrity fundraising.net • www.integrityfund raising.net

## Stellar Fundraising Executives Inc.

Jerry Hinson • 438 Osceola Ave. • Jacksonville Beach, FL 32250 • (888) 897-4667 • Fax (904) 270-0189 • info@stellarfund raising.com • www.stellarfundraising.com

## Graphic Design

## Becky Hawley Design LLC

5105 Edgewood Ct. • Loveland, CO 80538 • (970) 797-0450 • becky@becky designs.com • www.beckydesigns.com

## Digicolor Advertising & Design

Brent Haynes • RR 3, Box 347, Mayhew Rd. • New Cumberland, WV 26047 • (304) 564-5213

## Guide Publishers

## Chamber Publishing

Russ Jones • 7 Lynde St. • Salem, MA 01907 • (978) 741-3344 • (800) 734-7573 • Fax (978) 741-3377 • russ.jones4@ verizon.net • www.chamberpublishing group.com

## City Directory Inc.

Jan Ersland • P.O. Box 265 • Belmond, IA 50421 • (641) 444-4468 • (641) 444-5150 • cdi@kalnet.com

## Great Lakes Publishing Inc.

212 Kent St. • P.O. Box 499 • Portland, MI 48875 • (517) 647-4444 • (800) 647-8909 • Fax (517) 647-4101 • info@great lakespub.com • www.greatlakespub.com

## Media Ventures Inc.

Tracy Persson • 200 Connecticut Ave., Ste.
D • Norwalk, CT 06854 • (203) 852-
6570 • Fax (203) 852-6571 • tpersson@
mediaventuresinc.com • www.media
venturesinc.com

## Morning Star Publishing House

Curtis Courtney • 159 Dickerson Ln. •
Elgin, TX 78621 • (512) 281-2981 • (800)
369-9377 • morningstarph@juno.com •
*See our ad on page 9*

## Village Profile

Joe Nugara • 33 N. Geneva St. • Elgin, IL
60120 • (800) 600-0134 • jcn@village
profilemail.com • www.villageprofile.com

## Health Insurance

## Chamber Choice

7000 Stonewood Dr.. Ste. 251 • Westford,
PA • 15090 • (800) 377-3539 • www.
chamberchoice.com

## Health Services Administrators

135 Wood Rd. • Braintree, MA • 02184 •
(781) 848-4950 • www.hsabrokers.com

## Map Publishers/ Cartography

## Chamber Publishing

Russ Jones • 7 Lynde St. • Salem, MA
01907 • (978) 741-3344 • (800) 734-7573 •
Fax (978) 741-3377 • russ.jones4@verizon.
net • www.chamberpublishinggroup.com

## Commerce Quest Cartographics Inc.

Thomas Lubrecht • 133 N. Main St. •
Walton, KY 41094 • (859) 282-1462 •
commercequest@insightbb.online.com

## Community Matters Inc.

Layne Mullin • 4113 Honor Dr. • Frisco,
TX 75034 • (972) 370-1778 • (800)
380-2450 • Fax (972) 370-1766 • info@
communitymattersinc.com • www.
communitymattersinc.com • *See our
ad on page 8*

## Keith Map Services Inc.

60 Schillinger Rd. N. • Mobile, AL 36608 •
(251) 633-5588 • (800) 342-6277 • www.
keithmaps.com

## Liberty Marketing

Tony Bliss • 204 N. West St. • Arlington, TX 76011 • (817) 860-3110 • Fax (817) 860-7113 • Tony.Bliss@libertymapads.com • www.libertymapads.com

## Map Sales & Services

1100 Lebanon Rd. • Nashville, TN 37210 • (615) 242-3388 • mapsas@mapagents.com • www.mapagents.com

## Media Ventures Inc.

Tracy Persson • 200 Connecticut Ave., Ste. D • Norwalk, CT 06854 • (203) 852-6570 • Fax (203) 852-6571 • tpersson@mediaventuresinc.com • www.mediaventuresinc.com

## Morning Star Publishing House

Curtis Courtney • 159 Dickerson Ln. • Elgin, TX 78621 • (512) 281-2981 • (800) 369-9377 • morningstarph@juno.com

## National Map Marketing

2510 Nicollet Ave. S. • Minneapolis, MN • 55404 • (763) 541-0026 • (800) 872-5166 • Fax (612) 872-1855 • www.nationalmap.com

## New Atlas dot Com Inc.

Jerry Wright • 304 N. Meridian Ave., Ste. G • Oklahoma City, OK 73107 • (405) 942-8527 • (866) 942-8527 • Fax (405) 943-5750 • maps@newatlas.com • www.newatlas.com • *See our ad on page 7*

## Village Profile

Joe Nugara • 33 N. Geneva St. • Elgin, IL
60120 • (800) 600-0134 • jcn@village
profilemail.com • www.villageprofile.com

## Marketing–Direct

## Creative Marketing

703 N. Llano St. • Fredericksburg, TX •
78624 • (830) 997-8515 • creative@ktc.com

## Kennickell Print & Communications

Al Kennickell • 1700 E. President St/ •
Savannah, GA 31404 • (912) 233-4532 •
(800) 673-6455 • Fax (912) 232-1360 •
sales@kennickell.com • www.kennickell.com

## Market Segments Inc.

700 Rte. 46 E. • Fairfield, NJ 07004 •
(973) 808-7722

## Marketing–Online

## CGI Communications

Amy Curran • 130 E. Main, 8th Flr. •
Rochester, NY 14604 • (800) 398-3029 •
Fax (585) 427-0075 • info@cgicom
munications.com • www.cgicommuni
cations.com

## Membership Development

## Chamber Development Services

Joan Testa • 2009 Stonecourt Dr. • Bedford, TX 76021 • (817) 247-9677 • joan@
chamberdevelopment.com • www.chamber
development.com

## First Community Development

6045 Atlantic Blvd. • Norcross, GA 30071 •
(770) 448-7171 • Fax (770) 448-7513 •
sdorough@fcdusa.com • www.fcdusa.com

## Sales Development Associations

Patrick Hoey • 167 Auburn St. • Auburn, MA
01501 • (508) 832-3300 • phoey9@aol.com

## Motivational Speakers

### Event Learning

Neil T. Newcomb • 506 Hillside Dr. • Marquette, MI 49855 • (906) 225-1759 • (800) 450-0048 • nnewcomb@eventlearning.com • www.eventlearning.com

### Speakers Unlimited

P.O. Box 27225 • Columbus, OH 43227 • (614) 864-3703 • mike@speakersunlimited.com • www.speakersunlimited.com

## Outdoor Drama

### FLW Outdoors

Ron Lappin • 30 Gamble Ln. • Benton, KY • 42025 • (270) 252-1588 • info@flwoutdoors.com • www.flwoutdoors.com

## Plaques

### Coates Designers

Alan Coates • P.O. Box 1273 • Franklin, TN 28744 • (828) 349-9700 • (800) 428-8899 • alan@coatesplaques.com • www.coatesplaques.com

## Publishers

### Alpha Omega Publications

804 N. 2nd Ave. E. • Rock Rapids, IA 51246 • (800) 682-7391 • tdwilson@aop.com • www.aophomeschooling.com

### Atlantic Publication Group

Richard Barry • P.O. Box 30007 • Charlestown, SC 29417 • (843) 747-0025 • Fax (843) 744-0816 • richard@atlanticpublicationgrp.com • www.atlanticpublicationgrp.com

### Atlantic West Publishers Inc.

Ed Burzminski • 525 S. Douglas St., Ste. 270 • El Segundo, CA 90245 • (800) 814-7289

### Cherbo Publishing

Jack Cherbo • 5535 Balboa Blvd., Ste. 108 • Encino, CA 91316 • (818) 783-0040 • Fax (818) 783-0044 • jcherbo@cherbopub.com • www.cherbopub.com

## CommunityLink

**A division of Craig Williams Creative Inc.**
4742 Holts Prairie Rd. • P.O. Box 306 • Pinckneyville, IL 62274-0306 • (618) 357-8653 • (800) 455-5600 • www.communitylink.com

## Community Mapping

Sheldon Cohen • 872 Massachusetts Ave., Ste. 1-6 • Cambridge, MA 02139 • (617) 492-5551

## Harbor House Publishers

Candi Wynn • 221 Water St. • Boyne City, MI 49712 • (231) 582-2814 • www.harborhouse.com

## Heron Publishing

4432 Commercial Way • Spring Hill, FL 34606 • (352) 596-0209 • (800) 785-1800 • www.heronfla.com

## Latitude 3 Media Group

P.O. Box 380665 • Birmingham, AL 35238 • (205) 949-1600 • (866) 222-3722 • Fax (205) 949-1601 • www.latitude3.com

## Loyalty Publishing Inc.

1227 W. Glen Ave., Ste. A • Peoria, IL 61614 • (309) 692-3978

## Magnum Publications

Lawson McLeod • P.O. Box 3500 • West Columbia, SC 29171 • (803) 739-6900 • marketing@magnuminternational.com • www.magnuminternational.com

## Med Info Communications

P.O. Box 210325 • Columbia, SC 29221 • (803) 319-4109 • www.medinfocommunications.com

## Morgan Wynn Publishing

Floyd Allen • P.O. Box 83986 • Phoenix, AZ 85071 • (602) 843-5170 • floyd@morganwynnpublishing.com • www.morganwynnpublishing.com

## Morning Star Publishing House

Curtis Courtney • 159 Dickerson Ln. • Elgin, TX 78621 • (512) 281-2981 • (800) 369-9377 • morningstarph@juno.com • *See our ad on page 9*

## Spotlight Publications

Matt Carrelli • 530 W. 9th St. • Newport, KY 41071 • (866) 621-9255 • Fax (866) 621-9255 • mcarrelli@spotlight-publications.com • www.spotlight-publications.com • *See our ad on page 10*

## T.G. Privette Publishing

Tom Privette • 507 Lebanon Church Rd. • Mebane, NC 27302 • (949) 619-3610 • www.tgprivettepublishing.com

## Target Marketing

Philip Hageman • 541 Buttermilk Pike, Ste. 100 • Crescent Springs, KY 41017 • (800) 933-3909 • phageman@chambermapproject.com • www.chambermapproject.com

## The Chamber Executive Network Newsletter

Richard Hakes • P.O. Box 603 • Storm Lake, IA 50588 • (712) 732-7718 • hakesd@iw.net • www.bestchambers.com

## World Book Publishing

233 N. Michigan Ave., 20th Flr. • Chicago, IL 60661 • (312) 729-5800 • www.worldbook.com

## Printing

## Hulett Printing Inc

Dwane Berens • 2040 W. Sinto Ave. • Spokane, WA 99201 • (509) 326-1611

## Johnson Printing

Laurie Hedger • 1880 S. 57th Ct. • Boulder, CO • 80301 • (303) 443-1576 • (800) 824-5505 • Fax (303) 998-7590 • www.jpcolorado.com

## Seasonal Decorations–Exterior

## Brandano Displays Inc.

John Brandano • 2000 Banks Rd., Ste, 212 • Margate, FL 33063 • (954) 956-7266 • (800) 777-6903 • information@brandano.com • www.brandano.com

## Display Sales

10925 Nesbitt Ave. S. • Bloomington, MN 55437 • (952) 885-0100 • (800) 328-6195 • Fax (952) 885-0099 • sales@displaysales.com • www.displaysales.com

# Dixie Decorations

355 Industrial Park • P.O. Box 81 • Montevallo, AL 35115 • (205) 665-1225 • (800) 423-4260 • Fax (205) 665-1263 • dixiedecorations@bellsouth.net • www.dixiedecorations.com

# GP Designs Inc.

Rick Dillon • 318 E. 12th St. • Marion, IN 46953 • (800) 888-3833 • sales@gpdesigns.biz • www.gpdesigns.biz

## Tourism & Business Development

# Development Counsellors Intl.

Ted M. Levine • 215 Park Ave. S., 10th Flr. • New York, NY 10003 • (212) 725-0707 • Fax (212) 725-2254 • ted.levine@dc-intl.com • www.aboutdci.com

# Estes Park Convention & Visitors Bureau

Tom Pickering • 500 Big Thompson Ave. • P.O. Box 1200 • Estes Park, CO 80517 • (970) 577-9900 • (800) 443-7837 • Fax (970) 577-1677 • cvbinfo@estes.org • www.estesparkcvb.com

# Henderson Chamber of Commerce

Alice Martz • 590 S. Boulder Hwy. • Henderson, NV 89015 • (702) 565-8951 • Fax (702) 565-3115 • info@hendersonchamber.com • www.hendersonchamber.com

## Round Top Chamber of Commerce

Laurie Fisbeck • P.O. Box 216 • Round Top, TX 78954 • (979) 249-4042 • Fax (979) 249-2085 • info@roundtop.org • www.roundtop.org

## Travel

### Chamber Discoveries

1300 E. Shaw, Ste. 127 • Fresno, CA 93710 • (559) 244-6600 • www.chamber discoveries.com

### Fun Time Tours

2315 Old Philadelphia Pike • P.O. Box 10395 • Lancaster, PA 17605 • (717) 394-2821 • www.funtimesunshine.com

## Global Link Travel

Robert Baker • 542 Main St. • Bennington, VT 05201 • (802) 442-8400

## Visitor Information Displays

### Profile Display

Steve Souder • P.O. Box 23780 • Charlotte, NC • 28227 • (888) 877-6345 • Fax (704) 545-8743 • www.profilemediagroup.com

## Website Design

### Ads R Us

4600 S.W. 9th St. • Des Moines, IA • 50315 • (515) 287-6633 • (800) 607-0494

### All Seasons Communications

Erin Proctor • 5455 34 Miles Rd. • Romeo, MI • 48065 • (586) 752-6381 • Fax (586) 752-6539 • eproctor@allseasons communications.com • www.allseasons communications.com

### ChamberMaster

Doug Hennum • 14391 Edgewood Dr. • Baxter, MN • 56425 • (218) 825-9200 • (800) 825-9171 • Fax (360) 350-4787 • info@chambermaster.com • www.chamber master.com

# Notes